CONTRACTS IN CONTEXT
From Transaction to Litigation

ASPEN CASEBOOK SERIES

CONTRACTS IN CONTEXT
From Transaction to Litigation

NADELLE GROSSMAN
Associate Professor of Law
Marquette University Law School

ERIC ZACKS
Associate Professor of Law
Wayne State University Law School

 Wolters Kluwer

Published by Wolters Kluwer in New York.

Wolters Kluwer Legal & Regulatory U.S. serves customers worldwide with CCH, Aspen Publishers, and Kluwer Law International products. (www.WKLegaledu.com)

To contact Customer Service, e-mail customer.service@wolterskluwer.com, call 1-800-234-1660, fax 1-800-901-9075, or mail correspondence to:

    Wolters Kluwer
    Attn: Order Department
    PO Box 990
    Frederick, MD 21705

Printed in the United States of America.

1 2 3 4 5 6 7 8 9 0

ISBN 978-1-4548-7703-5

Library of Congress Cataloging-in-Publication Data

Names: Grossman, Nadelle, author. | Zacks, Eric A., author.
Title: Contracts in context : from transaction to litigation / Nadelle
   Grossman, Associate Professor of Law, Marquette University Law School;
   Eric Zacks, Associate Professor of Law, Wayne State University Law School.
Description: New York : Wolters Kluwer, 2019. |
   Includes bibliographical references and index.
Identifiers: LCCN 2018061425
Subjects: LCSH: Contracts–United States. | LCGFT: Casebooks (Law)
Classification: LCC KF801.A7.G76 2019 | DDC 346.7302/2–dc23
LC record available at https://lccn.loc.gov/2018061425

About Wolters Kluwer Legal & Regulatory U.S.

Wolters Kluwer Legal & Regulatory U.S. delivers expert content and solutions in the areas of law, corporate compliance, health compliance, reimbursement, and legal education. Its practical solutions help customers successfully navigate the demands of a changing environment to drive their daily activities, enhance decision quality and inspire confident outcomes.

Serving customers worldwide, its legal and regulatory portfolio includes products under the Aspen Publishers, CCH Incorporated, Kluwer Law International, ftwilliam.com and MediRegs names. They are regarded as exceptional and trusted resources for general legal and practice-specific knowledge, compliance and risk management, dynamic workflow solutions, and expert commentary.

To Brendan, Harlowe, Jake and Nate,
for supporting me through this project.

N.G.

To Renée, for everything.

E.Z.

SUMMARY OF CONTENTS

CONTENTS

A. OVERVIEW

You are undoubtedly already familiar with the concept of a contract. After all, you have probably created a Facebook or Twitter account and agreed to the terms of use. Those terms of use likely constitute contracts. In addition, you have probably signed a written document labeled "contract" with your cell phone company. That written document also sets out the terms of a contract, meaning the promises that you and the phone company each have agreed to make. Even your order of a menu item when dining out might constitute a contract with the restaurant.

While you might identify those arrangements as contracts, you might not have thought about what makes them contracts. In short, what makes them contracts is that they set out promises that, if breached, would be enforced by a court. In other words, a contract only exists where a party makes a promise, and only where the other party could receive a remedy in court if the first party failed to perform that promise.

Yet not every promise that appears at first blush to be a contract is enforceable. For example, what if your cell phone company locked the front door and would not let you escape unless you signed the cell phone "contract." Would you be bound to pay your cell phone company then? Your gut probably is telling you that you should not be bound by the contract in that circumstance due to the threat to your safety that caused you to agree. And your gut would be right.

This book will provide you with knowledge and skills so that you can analyze whether these and other arrangements are contracts that a court will enforce. In addition, this book goes beyond the law to also teach you typical contracting practices, as well as typical contract structure and terms. By studying these practices, structures, and terms, you will learn how lawyers help clients use contracts to achieve their goals. This book will also help you develop skills such as problem identification and solving as well as client counseling—skills that are essential to lawyers advising clients on contracts.

This book uses problems as well as a simulation to help you develop this knowledge and these skills. Through these problems and simulation, you will engage in a hands-on, active learning experience. Through tasks such as reviewing draft contracts and suggesting provisions, you will be able to apply the knowledge and skills taught in this book to typical situations encountered in practice. Moreover, you will have the opportunity to think through some of the ethical dilemmas you might face as a lawyer representing a client on a contract, and how you might solve those dilemmas in accordance with your professional responsibilities.

It is our hope that this material will give you a strong foundation in contract law and practice that you can use to help advance your future clients' goals.

B. DESIGN AND CONTENT CHOICES OF THIS TEXTBOOK

This section explains the more important design and content choices we made in writing this book. We include this discussion because many of these features are unique and are not "typical" for a 1L textbook on Contracts. As such, we felt we should explain these design and content choices up front, so you understand the bases for our decisions. We hope this material will convince you as to the wisdom of our choices.

We also include this material to help set your expectations for what this book will do—and not do. We believe that it is important to set these expectations up front, so you can better understand our goals as you proceed through this material.

1. Includes Extensive Problems and a Simulation

One of the unique aspects of our book is the extent of the practice problems it contains. We include problems after each case to test your understanding of the law from the case, the court's holding and reasoning from the case, and your ability to analyze a new situation using that law. We also include a large number of problems outside of cases, after we discuss substantive aspects of contract law and practice. In addition, we include a simulation with questions in an Appendix to the book. A simulation is a scenario that presents evolving facts modeled on a real-life situation. It then places you in the role of lawyer and asks you to perform certain tasks for your simulated client.

We include extensive problems and a simulation for many reasons.

First, we believe that students can obtain a higher mastery of the skills of legal analysis and reasoning—core lawyering skills—by actually performing those skills. Here, the problems and the simulation introduce facts and pose specific questions designed to help you practice these skills.

Second, one of the key attributes of a good lawyer is her ability to solve problems. Legal problems are not solved by simply knowing the law. Instead, legal problems are solved by a lawyer who, when presented with all of the facts, identifies her client's interests and helps her client further that interest in compliance with law. A lawyer simply cannot develop this problem-solving skill without practicing it. The simulation and problems presented in this book are designed to provide many opportunities for you to practice these problem-solving skills.

As you perform these problem-solving tasks, you will see that a complete solution to a problem often does not come from contracts and contract law alone. Instead, you will learn that problem-solving requires that a lawyer keep her eyes open for solutions in other areas of the law, as well as outside the law. Moreover, a lawyer must always utilize her own common sense, all to help the client protect its interests. This result-oriented perspective is most effectively practiced through the kind of problem-solving activities we include in this book.

Third, through the simulation and other practice problems included in this book, you will begin to see the types of ethical and moral dilemmas that a lawyer faces. You can then begin to think about how to resolve those dilemmas in the safety of a classroom, where you are free from the risks of lawyer discipline or malpractice claims. In addition, our practice problems will allow you to begin to develop your professional identities as you perform tasks customarily assigned to attorneys.

Fourth, the simulation and practice problems are designed to give you a sense for the types of tasks lawyers perform every day. Those tasks might include, for example, drafting a provision of a contract or advising your client as to whether a contract adequately protects its interests. Similarly, with respect to a contract dispute, a client may seek advice about settlement and negotiation strategy (and whether or not to settle) in addition to the litigation attorney's task of pursuing or defending a contract claim. Through these experiences, you will see that what you do for your client has a real impact on your client's success. Moreover, performing these tasks will make you a more active participant in the learning process.

Keep in mind that the facts of the simulation evolve as your client makes decisions based on your prior advice. Thus, where the book discusses contract formation, the corresponding sections of the simulation present facts and problems relating to contract formation. Later, as the book discusses the terms of the contract, the corresponding sections of the simulation presents facts and problems focusing on the terms of the contract. In addition to allowing us to explore contractual concepts as they unfold in the book, those changes make the simulation more realistic. Thus, they will give you some sense for how a transaction develops in real life and how your relationship with your client evolves with the transaction.

2. Reviews Typical Contract Structure and Terms

Any lawyer who deals with contracts must be familiar with the typical structure of a contract. She is also expected to be familiar with some terms that are common among contracts. That is because, as you will learn in Chapter 2, contract law is largely private law. In other words, parties create the terms they would like to govern their business relationship, and courts will enforce those terms so long as they meet the mandatory (i.e., required) aspects of contract law.

With this in mind, this textbook devotes an entire chapter—Chapter 3—to the study of the typical contract structure and terms. Moreover, this textbook presents sample contract language throughout, often showing how parties customize their contracts in light of the law studied in a particular section.

We include this material on contract structure and terms to help ready you for practice. In fact, even before then, many of you will participate in internships, clinics, and practicums throughout your law school careers. In those positions, as well as in practice, you will often be asked to review a contract. In some cases, you might be asked to draft or comment on a contract. In all of these cases, it would be difficult to undertake the task without having a basic understanding of the contract's design or a familiarity with some of the terms you can expect to see in that contract. That familiarity will allow you to begin to see how lawyers can use contract structure and terms to help clients achieve their goals.

In addition, being familiar with the typical design and content of contracts can enhance your comprehension of the legal doctrines that arise in the dispute context. The opposite is true as well—you will better understand the reason for contractual provisions if you understand the legal basis for, or limit on, that provision. For example, as you will see in Chapter 3, when drafting a contract, parties often include a nonbinding background section called recitals that sets out the parties' purpose for entering into the contract. They do that for a number of reasons, including to help third parties and courts interpret the contract. Thus, as you will see in Chapter 12, courts commonly look to recitals to determine the parties' intent, where it is not clear from the parties' respective obligations. Such a purpose provision could also impact the court's decision whether a supervening event, such as the passage of a new law, should excuse one of the parties from its obligations under that contract.

However, as a word of caution, this book is not designed to make you an expert on contract structure or terms. You will need to undertake many other experiences—both in law school and in practice—to achieve that status. But it is designed to lay a foundation for that expertise.

3. Presents Role of Transactional Attorneys

As the discussion above explained, this textbook not only presents material about contract law, but also explains how contracts can actually be used to achieve clients' goals. The "transactional" perspective, as noted in the book's title, captures this notion—that contracts are used to achieve clients' goals in a transaction. Moreover, it captures the notion that lawyers—called transactional lawyers—represent those clients in helping them enter into and perform those transactions.

By considering contracts and contract law from the transactional perspective, this textbook will enable you to learn how contracts are used to protect clients' interests, how clients obtain information about their contractual counterparties through due diligence, and how lawyers facilitate the negotiation and drafting of contracts, among other typical contract lawyering tasks. It will also present you with some of the ethical dilemmas transactional lawyers face and give you the opportunity to consider how to resolve those dilemmas. Through this material, this textbook will help you begin to develop your professional identity.

4. Explanatory Text Presents Material

While this textbook presents some legal principles through cases, it presents a significant amount of content through explanatory text. This contrasts with the typical Contracts textbook's approach, which is to present nearly all of the law through cases.

We present contract law through explanatory text because we believe it is a practical and efficient way to present the law. A study of cases simply cannot provide the breadth of law that an explanatory presentation can, for the law presented in each case is limited to the specific legal doctrine or doctrines at issue in that case.

Nevertheless, a lawyer must be able to read a case and distill the law from that case. Therefore, this book includes many cases to allow you to develop these skills. However, we believe there are diminishing returns on having students repeat this skill throughout a Contracts course. Thus, we focus much more of our book on the solving of legal problems using the law rather than on the distillation of law from cases.

Moreover, presenting the law of contracts only through cases potentially gives the impression that all contracts end up in litigation. Nothing could be further from the truth. In fact, only a tiny fraction of contracts end up in litigation. To negate this false impression, we believe it is important for you to study contracts and contract law by seeing how both can be used to achieve parties' goals, in addition to seeing some of the instances of failed contracts in litigation.

In addition, because of this book's transactional perspective, some material is most effectively presented through explanatory text rather than cases. For example, the material on contract structure and terms is presented to demonstrate how contracts can be used to help the client achieve its goals. While the law provides some limits on structure and terms, so long as those limits are met, the parties can agree on an endless number of terms. Indeed, apart from the baseline limits imposed on parties under the law, parties are free to contract however they wish. For that reason, it would be odd to present that material by only considering contract terms that have been litigated.

Despite these benefits of a textual description of the law, we must caution the reader up front that contract laws are often complex and nuanced, making them tricky to describe through explanatory text. However, that challenge also exists for courts, which have to describe those same laws in their decisions. At least with explanatory text, we can omit the nuances in the law that are either aberrational or of limited applicability. To the extent that you need to know those nuances or specific rules, you can certainly research them.

5. Presents Law from Different States

While this design feature is not unlike other textbooks, we do want to close with a brief discussion of which states' laws this book covers.

Like most 1L contracts textbooks, this textbook does not rely solely on the law of one state. Rather, this textbook incorporates contract law from different states. It takes this approach for many reasons. First, looking at the laws in different states allows us to look at generally applicable rules without focusing on the specific state from which that rule came. Second, looking at different states' laws allows you to make a judgment about the wisdom of differing approaches to the law. Third, seeing a variety of approaches to the same legal principle will reveal the diversity that exists in contract law. That revelation should make it clear why you always need to research the law of the applicable jurisdiction, given the variation in states' laws. Finally, looking at the law in many jurisdictions gives us a much broader and richer pool of law from which to draw. That, in turn, allows us to select the law that serves as the most effective teaching tool.

Because this book presents much material in an expository manner, without case headings indicating the jurisdiction of the case, there is a risk that the reader will see the law discussed textually as if that law is universal. We want to caution the reader against drawing this conclusion. In most instances, we describe the law as it is in effect in a majority of jurisdictions. However, sometimes we explain the minority approach to the law, where the courts are trending toward that minority approach. We also sometimes contrast the majority and minority approaches.

We present the material in this way to achieve our goal of helping you learn the structure of contract law, the policies served by contract law, and the typical approach to specific contract law doctrines. However, it is not intended to be used as a resource for the law of any particular jurisdiction. Thus, you will *always* have to research the law that is applicable in your jurisdiction when an issue of contract law arises.

C. OVERVIEW OF BOOK ORGANIZATION

This book's organization generally tracks the life cycle of a contract, from formation to performance to (in some cases) dispute. However, it begins in Part I with some background on what contracts are and why they are used (Chapter 1), how contract law is structured and which contract law governs a particular contract (Chapter 2), and how contracts are typically structured and the types of terms they typically contain (Chapter 3).

Then, Part II delves into contract formation. First, Chapter 4 walks through mutual assent, explaining why and how parties fulfill that requirement of contract formation. The next two chapters also address mutual assent, each focusing on specialized rules that apply in different situations. In particular, Chapter 5 speaks to mutual assent to sale-of-goods transactions in light of the specialized rules that apply to those contracts, while Chapter 6 focuses on mutual assent for contracts that are formed electronically. Chapter 7 then discusses the other requirement of contract formation: consideration. Chapter 8 discusses specialized rules on mutual assent and consideration that apply to option contracts.

Part III, which is comprised of three chapters, also addresses contract formation, but it is geared toward the role of the lawyer in that process. Namely, Chapter 9 discusses the role of the lawyer as transactional advisor. Next, Chapter 10 explores pre-contract formation activities that parties often undertake, usually with the help of lawyers, to prepare to enter a contract, while Chapter 11 discusses the role of the lawyer in negotiating and drafting a contract. That material also discusses the role of the client in those situations, as a basis to better understand the role of the lawyer.

The next part of the book—Part IV—covers the performance of a contract. Chapter 12 first explains how a lawyer helps a client perform a contract. As that chapter explains, the terms of a contract are not merely the expressed terms, but also terms implied by law. That chapter also explains how parties modify a contract to change its terms. Chapter 13 then explores what happens when the parties attach different meanings to one another's words or conduct in creating a contract or to one of the contract terms: in other words, where there is an ambiguity. That chapter explains how a court resolves each of these situations. Chapter 14 also discusses contract terms and performance, but it does so in the context of a sale-of-goods transaction, to which specialized rules apply. Chapter 15 then discusses what evidence a court will exclude at trial to prove the existence of a contract where the parties have prepared a final writing reflecting that contract.

Part V of the book contemplates what happens when one of the parties has failed to perform an obligation under that contract. In that situation, the disappointed party sues, and the parties invoke one or more of the doctrines in Part V.

Chapter 16 reviews the various excuses a party might have to its performance. From an act of God to the other party's material breach, these doctrines excuse a party from performing even though its behavior otherwise appears to be a breach. Chapters 17 through 21 then discuss defenses to enforcement that arise out of public policy concerns that are viewed as superseding the policies underlying contract enforcement.

Chapter 17, after introducing the concept of a defense to enforcement, discusses the defense known as the Statute of Frauds, which is a defense tied to the satisfaction of required formalities. Next, Chapter 18 discusses the defense of incapacity, which is a defense based on the age or mental condition of the party seeking "out" of its contractual obligation. Chapter 19 then discusses the defenses of duress and undue influence, both of which involve some defect in the process of contract formation involving some amount of excessive pressure that induces the other party to assent to the contract. Chapter 20, which discusses the defense of misrepresentation, also focuses on a defect in the process of contract formation, focusing on the information provided (or not provided) to a party to induce it to enter into the contract. Finally, Chapter 21 discusses the defenses of unconscionability and public policy, both of which, to some extent, look to the terms of the contract.

Sometimes a party in litigation is not successful in her claim of breach. Typically, that party will argue other causes of action as well—that is, the party will allege not only that the other party breached an agreed-upon term of a contract, but that there is another basis to recover apart from a breach of contract. Part VI, composed of two chapters, explores the most commonly argued alternative theories of recovery. The first one, discussed in Chapter 22, is known as promissory estoppel. The second, discussed in Chapter 23, is restitution. These chapters will also explain how those theories might exist even where no bargained-for contract is alleged to exist.

Part VII assumes a party has breached a contractual obligation, as no excuse or defense to enforcement has justified that party in not performing that obligation. It then explores what remedy or remedies the injured party might receive. Chapter 24 first discusses the purposes for remedies, as well as what types of remedies a court may award. As that discussion explains, courts typically award monetary damages for breach. Chapter 25 then explores limits on the recovery of those damages. Next, Chapter 26 reviews two alternative remedies to damages: specific performance and agreed remedies, while Chapter 27 lays out types of damages that are disallowable.

Part VIII contains only one chapter—Chapter 29. That chapter discusses rights, duties, and responsibilities of "third parties," a term that refers to people who are not parties to a contract.

D. OVERVIEW DIAGRAM

The following is a flowchart that shows a contract's life cycle, which, again, generally tracks this book's organization. You can use this flowchart not only to see visually the logic of this book's organization, but also to see how each topic relates to each other topic covered in this course. As you can see, each topic is interrelated with each other topic, all converging around the issue of whether a court will enforce a promise.[1] This contrasts with other courses such as torts and criminal law, where you study the elements of multiple torts and crimes during the course. In this course, with the exception of restitution, your entire study is devoted to determining whether a court will enforce a party's promise and award the other party a remedy for breach.

This flowchart will be expanded at each new part of the book, to show how the material from that part of the book fits in. That should help you to see how each doctrine you study relates to the material you already studied, so that you can start to synthesize the course as you progress through it.

---

1. The only exception to this is restitution, which need not involve a promise. But restitution *can* involve a promise. Moreover, restitution sometimes protects a party in a situation resembling a bargain relationship. These are the likely reasons why Contracts textbooks cover restitution, and why we continue that practice.

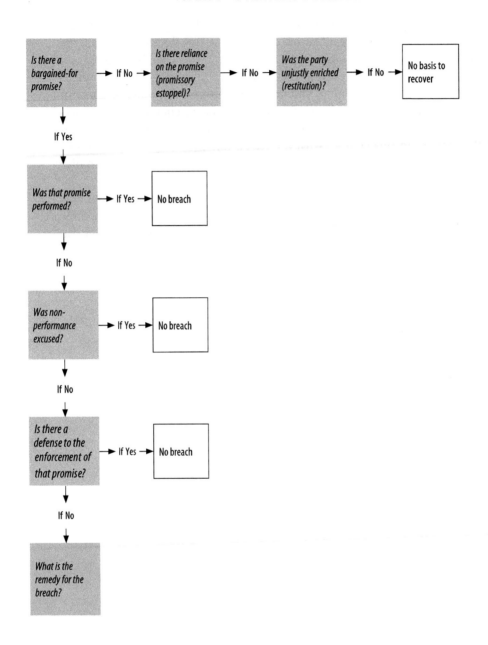

ACKNOWLEDGMENTS

I want to thank all of my research assistants who have performed valuable research, editing, and other assistance for this project, including Adam Barraza, Erik Gustafson, Kelsey McCarthy, Sheldon Oppermann, Katie Pegelow, Henry Russo and David Webb, with special gratitude to Adam Barraza, who worked on this book as if it were his own. I would also like to thank my academic cheerleader Kali Murray for her wisdom and encouragement throughout the project. I would like to thank Marquette University Law School, and especially Dean Joseph Kearney, for supporting me over the course of this book project.

—*Nadelle*

I would like to express my gratitude to my research assistants, Alex Krasuski, John Meads, Linda Mifsud, Charles Roarty, and Kaitlyn York, for their diligence while working on this casebook. I am also appreciative of the support I have received from Wayne State University Law School not only while I was working on this project but throughout my academic career; and in this respect I am particularly indebted to my colleagues Jon Weinberg and Vince Wellman. I have been blessed by, and am grateful for, the love, patience, and support of my wife Renée and children Asher, Micah, and Leah. I also wanted to thank my parents for their encouragement, example, and love.

—*Eric*

We would like to thank Rick Mixter for seeing the value in this book's approach and paving the way for this book's publication. In addition, we would like to thank Sarah Hains for her tireless editorial work on this book. We are grateful to reviewers who reviewed and provided useful feedback on our book. Finally, we would like to thank all of the authors whose articles we include in the book for letting us include passages from your written works—they all help enrich the material.

—*Nadelle and Eric*

CONTRACTS IN CONTEXT
From Transaction to Litigation

INTRODUCTION TO CONTRACT LAW AND PRACTICE

Part I of this textbook is largely introductory. That is, it introduces you to what a contract is (Chapter 1) as well as explains the design of and policies underlying contract law (Chapter 2). As you will learn from Chapter 2, one of contract law's main policy objectives is to give effect to the agreed-upon terms of the contracting parties. Hence, it is important to have a sense for what terms parties often agree on, to better understand the law that supports, and at times does not support, the enforcement of those terms. Chapter 3 will provide that background, examining the typical parts of a contract and explaining how parties use contracts to obtain benefits they seek while protecting them from risks that might undermine those benefits.

CHAPTER 1

What Is a Contract?
Why Is It Used?

A. DEFINITION OF CONTRACT

A **contract** is a promise or set of promises that is enforceable by a court. Where a promise is enforceable, that means a court will award a remedy if that promise is broken, or breached. Here, the term **promise** has a specific legal meaning: it refers to a person's statement or other manifestation (i.e., demonstration) of his or her intent to either perform an act, refrain from performing an act, or give up a legal right in the future. It must justify the person to whom the promise is made—the **promisee**—in believing that the person making the promise—the **promisor**—is committed to performing the promise.

Because the concept of "promise" in contract law refers to a promise to perform or refrain from performing an act or to give up a legal right, promises as to mental state are not enforceable under contract law. For example, a promise to love your sibling for as long as you live is not the kind of promise that contract law enforces. As a policy matter, you might ask yourself whether this is the kind of promise that the law should enforce. On the one hand, enforcement of this type of promise would make you more thoughtful before uttering a promise to love in the future. On the other hand, enforcement of this kind of promise might prevent you from expressing your emotions, concerned that those expressions could be enforced. And such enforcement could bring to the legal realm a quality best left to the emotional realm.

Contract law also does not generally enforce promises over which a person retains absolute discretion to perform. This type of promise is referred to as an **illusory promise** because, while it might look like a promise, it is only an illusion. Because the promisor retains discretion to perform, the promisee is not justified to think that the promisor is committed to doing or not doing the promised act.

For example, suppose your brother buys a beach house. Your brother tells you, "I promise that you can use my beach house whenever you want, if I wish." Here, since your brother is retaining absolute discretion to decide whether or not to let you use his beach house, he is not making a promise to which you are justified in thinking he is committed. As such, this is not a promise for purposes of contract law.

A promise is also illusory if a party can decide to stop performing on his promise at any time. Thus, a promise to provide accounting services for five years is illusory if the accountant can decide to stop providing those services at any time. However, if the accountant is required to provide notice of termination a certain period of time before termination, that notice period may take the promise out of the realm of being illusory.

Along these same lines, a promise to agree to contractual terms (to be determined) in the future—often referred to as an agreement to agree—is generally not the kind of promise a court will enforce. That is because the party is not setting out what it is promising to do in the future. Only once the parties agree on the content of the obligations, or where the party agrees to restrict its discretion in how the open terms are to be determined, might there be a contract.

The following diagram depicts this definition of a contract—that is, that some promises are enforceable by courts and constitute contracts, while others are not.

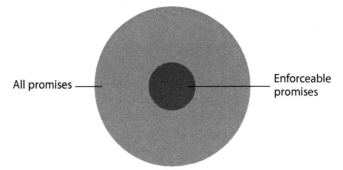

As this diagram shows, promises that are enforceable by courts are a subset of all promises.

Again, contract law provides the "rules of the game" for making and enforcing contracts. Among other things, it tells us what types of promises are enforceable as contracts, what defenses are available to people who make otherwise valid contractual promises, how to interpret the terms of contractual promises, and what remedies are available if someone breaches a contract.

PRACTICE PROBLEM 1-1

As a threshold matter, you should begin to consider what factors help determine whether a promise should be enforceable. In each of the factual scenarios below, consider whether the promise is in fact a promise and, if so, whether the promise should be enforceable as a contract. Do not worry that you have not yet studied contract law, and therefore, cannot use that knowledge to inform your answers. Instead, rely on your "gut" sense of whether these arrangements *should* be enforceable and then consider the possible reasons supporting or underlying your answer.

1. An uncle is concerned about his 15-year-old nephew's behavior, so he tells him the following: "If you refrain from gambling, smoking, drinking, and cursing until you are 21, I will pay you $10,000." The nephew refrains from such behavior until the age of 21.

2. The most valuable player of a professional basketball team decides to leave the team for a team located in a warmer climate. The owner of the star's original team publishes the following letter in the city's main newspaper:

> Dear Citizens,
>   I am very disappointed in the actions of our star player, but rest assured, our disappointment will not last long. I guarantee that we will win a championship before he does.
> Signed,
> Disappointed Owner

The next year, the basketball star's new team wins the championship.

3. Your college roommate calls you up and asks if you want to meet for coffee. You agree to meet her at 9:00 A.M. the next morning, but you are unable to meet her because you overslept. Would your answer change if your college roommate was flying across the country for your meeting?

Later chapters will delve into what remedies a court awards when it enforces a promise. But for now, keep in mind that the most common remedy a court awards due to a breach of a contractual promise is monetary damages.

People often refer to the papers that they sign—leases with landlords, loan applications with credit card companies, and even online purchase orders with merchants like Amazon—as contracts. However, technically speaking, those papers are merely documentations of their contracts. In other words, the papers themselves are not the contract. Rather, the substance of the promises those papers contain, assuming those promises are the kind a court will enforce, constitutes the contract. However, consistent with this commonplace use, this book will sometimes refer to the document that reflects the terms of a contract as the contract.

B. WHY PEOPLE CONTRACT

As you will learn in subsequent chapters, an effective lawyer must go beyond merely understanding *what* a contract is. An effective lawyer must also understand *why* her client is entering into—or has entered into—a contract. That is because in representing a client, especially in connection with the formation of a contract, the lawyer's job is to advance the client's goals. A lawyer simply cannot help a client achieve its goals through a contract if the lawyer does not know or understand those goals.

Even when representing a client in a contract dispute, a lawyer must understand why the client entered into that contract in the first place. That knowledge directs the **litigator**—a term used to refer to a lawyer who represents a client in litigation—in what interests to protect in litigation.

While no one could possibly catalog every reason a person enters into a contract, there are several reasons that commonly motivate people to enter into contracts. First, one of the key reasons people enter contracts is to plan for the future. That is because the future is unknown and thus risky. People seek to protect themselves from the unknown and risky future by obtaining enforceable promises from other parties about what those other parties will do or not do in the future for the party seeking protection. While the other party may ultimately breach and not perform a promise it made for the future, there are remedies—such as money damages—that the aggrieved party can obtain if the other party does breach.

This is likely the reason why you would want to enter into a lease contract with a landlord for an apartment you intend to live in. Without a contract specifying how long you have the right to live in that apartment, you would face the risk that the landlord could kick you out with little notice. Yet that would be extremely inconvenient to you, especially if you were asked to move out in the middle of law school exams.

People also enter contracts to obtain something that they want from another party—such as property or a service. The person who wants that property or service must typically pay for it. A contract facilitates this type of economic exchange by setting out its terms. Again, if one of the parties does not fulfill its promise under that contract, then the aggrieved party can seek a remedy from a court. Your entry into an apartment lease agreement could certainly be explained by this reason as well. That contract would give you the right to live in an apartment for an agreed-upon time—which is something you would value given that you need somewhere to sleep, eat, and store your items. Surely you would value the apartment over the money you would agree to pay for it or you would not have entered into the lease in the first place.

The view that contracts make both parties better off has been challenged, at least when applied to consumer contracts. **Consumer contracts** are those contracts entered into between consumers who consume products and services and merchants, who are in the business of supplying those goods and services. Often, they provide the terms of sale of a good or service from the merchant to the consumer. Some critics argue that consumers do not actually know how to value the costs to them of the obligations they take on in those contracts. For example, do you know the cost of having to comply with the terms of your online agreement with Apple for their iTunes service? Without knowing those terms, it is difficult, if not impossible, to determine whether that contract is worthwhile to you. On the other hand, consumers continue to enter into such agreements on a regular basis—presumably they do so because these contracts provide those consumers with benefits (and burden them with obligations) that are acceptable to them.

Sometimes parties enter contracts for strategic reasons. This is particularly true for businesses, which enter into contracts to further their future business plans. For example, businesses often buy out their competitors through purchase agreements. By buying out a competitor, a business can both grow and avoid having to compete with the former competitor.

Sometimes parties enter contracts to establish long-term relationships. That is, while contracts set out legal obligations that a court will enforce, parties often view them as tools to establish a long-term relationship with another party. This would be true, for example, with a long-term supply agreement, where a supplier of a product hopes to supply that product to the party in need of that product for some time. Here, the personal connections established through the process of negotiating and then performing that contract can be as important, if not more important, than the specific terms of the contract.

This "relational" role of contracting sometimes runs counter to the planning purpose for contracting. The following excerpt from an article by Professor Stewart Macaulay explains why this might be so with some relationships:

> "Not only are contract and contract law not needed in many situations, their use may have, or may be thought to have, undesirable consequences. Detailed negotiated contracts can get in the way of creating good exchange relationships between business units. If one side insists on a detailed plan, there will be delay while letters are exchanged as the parties try to agree on what should happen if a remote and unlikely contingency occurs.
>
> In some cases they may not be able to agree at all on such matters and as a result a sale may be lost to the seller and the buyer may have to search elsewhere for an acceptable supplier. Many businessmen would react by thinking that had no one raised the series of remote and unlikely contingencies all this wasted effort could have been avoided. Even where agreement can be reached at the negotiation stage, carefully planned arrangements may create undesirable exchange relationships between business units. Some businessmen object that in such a carefully worked out relationship one gets performance only to the letter of the contract. Such planning indicates a lack of trust and blunts the demands of friendship, turning a cooperative venture into an antagonistic horse trade. Yet the greater danger perceived by some businessmen is that one would have to perform his side of the bargain to its letter and thus lose what is called "flexibility." Businessmen may welcome a measure of vagueness in the obligations they assume so that they may negotiate matters in light of the actual circumstances."[1]

Finally, parties enter contracts as a way to equalize informational and control imbalances between them. That is, often one party (a principal) retains a third party (an agent) to act on the principal's behalf. For example, employers

---

1. *See* Stewart Macaulay, *Non-Contractual Relations in Business: A Preliminary Study*, 28 Am. Soc. Rev. 55, 64 (1963).

(principals) hire employees (agents) to work on the employers' behalf. Employers and employees, however, have different interests as well as information and control imbalances. How can the employer protect itself so that the employee will perform the assigned tasks effectively? The employer will probably be unable to monitor the employee's performance all of the time, even if a manager is assigned, as having to constantly monitor an employee undermines the very benefits of hiring an employee to perform assigned tasks. Even if the employer detects that the employee is not performing as desired, what are the employer's remedies? The following excerpt more fully describes this purpose for contracting:

> Contracts exist in part to detect and constrain opportunistic actions of one of the contractual promisors (an economic agent of the other with respect to a particular promised task). Contracts are distinct from other creations of economic agency relationships because the contract provides a legally enforceable remedy to the promissee [sic] (the principal) if the promisor's obligations specified in the contract (i.e., the agent's tasks) are not fulfilled. As a result, the contract can provide the principal with the ability to alleviate the information and control disparities that ordinarily exist. The contract can be seen as an attempt, however imperfect, to address the information and control asymmetries between two parties based on known or contemplated differences in personal interests.[2]

Keep in mind that there are other reasons why parties enter into contracts as well. The above discussion highlights some of the more common reasons, but people, given their special circumstances, often have unique reasons for entering into contracts.

Moreover, parties often have multiple reasons for entering into contracts. Although one might be a primary reason, all of the reasons together might justify a person's entry into the contract.

PRACTICE PROBLEM 1-2

1. Think about the interactions you had with others over the past two weeks. Which of those interactions might constitute contracts? Why did you enter into those arrangements? Was it to plan for the future? To obtain something of value? To establish a relationship with the counterparty? For another reason?

2. What benefits might you receive from entering into a contract to lease an apartment? What benefits would a landlord receive by entering into a contract to lease an apartment to you?

---

2. Eric Zacks, *The Moral Hazard of Contract Drafting*, 42 Fla. St. U. L. Rev. 991, 1002-03 (2015).

3. What information asymmetries exist between you and a landlord *before* you enter into a lease for an apartment? In other words, what does the landlord know that you do not? What do you know that the landlord does not?

4. What information and control asymmetries exist *once the lease contract has been signed* and each party begins to perform?

5. How does the below form lease agreement reduce these asymmetries? What else could you or the landlord do (both before and after the contract is executed) to reduce these asymmetries?

STATE OF INDIANA
RESIDENTIAL LEASE

THIS AGREEMENT is made and entered into by and between

TENANT(S) _____

and LANDLORD
Name:_____

Address:_____

In consideration of the promises and obligations specified in this Lease, the Landlord and Tenant agree as follows:

I. DESCRIPTION OF LEASED PREMISES

Tenant agrees to lease from Landlord and Landlord agrees to lease to Tenant a certain residential unit known as unit number_____(Premises) with a common address of _____.

II. TERM OF LEASE

This Lease shall be effective for a period of one (1) year commencing on _____, and will end ____, unless otherwise specified within this Lease. This agreement is only for the stated term and is NOT automatically renewable. Landlord and Tenant must agree in writing if tenancy is to continue.

III. RENT

Rent amount $_____ per _____ due on or before the _____ day of each _____, Rent checks shall be made payable to Landlord and mailed directly to Landlord. **ALL TENANTS, IF MORE THAN ONE, SHALL BE JOINTLY AND SEVERALLY LIABLE FOR THE FULL AMOUNT OF ALL PAYMENTS DUE UNDER THIS AGREEMENT.**

IV. SECURITY DEPOSIT

Upon execution of this agreement, Tenant agrees to pay a security deposit in the amount of $_____ to be held by _____.

V. GENERAL USE BY TENANT

The Premises shall be used by Tenant only for the purpose of a personal residence for Tenant and his/her spouse and dependent family members and for no other purpose.

VI. TENANT'S BASIC RESPONSIBILITIES

Tenant shall be responsible to follow the basic guidelines set forth within this Lease, while residing within the Premises and agrees and promises, as follows:

A. To maintain the Premises and surrounding grounds in a neat and orderly fashion and in compliance with all policies and procedures set forth within this Lease.
B. To follow all policies and procedures of Landlord.
C. To NOT allow any Guests or invites to reside on the Premises without prior written consent of Landlord.
D. To be responsible for the behavior of his/her family members residing within the Premises, as well as guests visiting the Premises.
E. To NOT permit in or about the Premise any pets unless specifically authorized by Landlord in writing.
F. To NOT make excessive noise or engage in activities which unduly disturb neighbors or other tenants in the building in which the Premises are located.
G. To be responsible, at Tenant's expense, for all routine maintenance of the Premises and keep the Premises in as good repair as on the first day of the lease term, normal wear and tear excepted.
H. Upon the end of the terms, to vacate the premises and immediately deliver the keys, garage door openers, parking permits, etc., and the Tenant's forwarding address to the Landlord.

VII. ACCESS TO THE PREMISES

Landlord reserves the right to access the Premises, at reasonable times with at least 12 hours advance notice, by a designated representative for purposes including but not limited to: Annual inspections; periodic inspections; inspections at the time of vacating the Premises; and repairs and replacements. Landlord may enter without advance notice with consent of the Tenant for emergency situations.

VIII. LOSS OR DAMAGE TO RESIDENCE

Notwithstanding any provision in this Lease to the contrary, if the Premises are destroyed or damaged through no fault of Tenant, to such an extent as will make the Premises untenable, Tenant may move out unless Landlord promptly proceeds to repair and rebuild. Tenant may move out if the repair work causes undue hardship. If Tenant remains: rent abates to the extent Tenant is denied normal full use of the Premises until they are restored. If the Premises are damaged to a degree which does not render them untenable, Landlord shall repair them as soon as possible.

IX. HOLD HARMLESS

Tenant agrees to hold Landlord harmless for any claims of damages to persons or property and any other costs or expenses relating to or arising from any accident or occurrence due directly to Tenant's use and occupancy of the Premises which is not due to the fault of Landlord.

X. ASSIGNMENT AND SUBLETTING

Tenant shall not assign this Lease, sublet the Premises or any part thereof, or permit the use or occupancy of any part of the Premises by anyone other than Tenant, his/her spouse, and dependent family members.

XI. TENANT IMPROVEMENTS

Tenant may NOT personalize the Premises, at Tenant's expense, with paint, wallpaper, carpet or other decorative items, without prior written request to Landlord. All fixtures and improvements of a permanent nature are to be left intact when Tenant leaves the Premises. Any improvements by Tenant of a temporary nature may be removed and the original item replaced at the time of vacating the Premises.

XII. ILLEGAL ACTIVITY

No activity considered to be illegal shall be performed within the Premises.

XIII. MODIFICATION OF LEASE

This Lease may not be amended, assigned, modified or supplemented without the written signatures of all parties to this Lease.

XIV. MISCELLANEOUS PROVISIONS

No waiver of any condition or covenant of this Lease or failure to exercise a remedy by either Landlord or Tenant shall be considered to imply or constitute a further waiver by such party of the same or any other condition, covenant or remedy.

XV. NOTICE

All notices required to be given under this Lease will be made in writing and will be sent by registered or certified mail to the parties as follows:

Landlord/Agency:

Tenant:

IN WITNESS to their agreement, the persons signing this Lease execute it for the Landlord and Tenant:

TENANT   LANDLORD

_____   _____

Date:_____   Date:_____

C. CONTRACT POLICY

This section discusses the various policies supported by contract law. The term **policy** refers to the rationale for a legal rule, or a set of legal rules. Knowing the policies served by legal rules is important for many reasons. For one, a lawyer must know the purpose of a rule to be an effective advocate for the client in litigation. That is because a litigator must know a rule's purpose to be able to establish how that purpose is furthered by the lawyer's argued application of the rule. Moreover, courts can change common law rules by overruling precedent. Or they can interpret ambiguous rules. One of the most effective ways a litigator can convince a court that such a change is needed is to demonstrate how the rule actually undermines the policy it is intended to serve. Transactional lawyers, too, must be aware of the policies behind rules so that they can anticipate how a court might react to contract terms, contract language, and their clients' behavior.

To begin our policy discussion, contracts are often described as private law. That is because the parties to a contract are free to agree on whatever contractual terms they wish, and a court will generally enforce those agreed-upon terms. That is because there is a strong policy in contract law of giving effect to the terms of the parties' bargain. Here, the policy is often described as **the policy of freedom of contract**. This policy supports giving effect to the agreed-upon terms of parties' bargained-for contract.

Moreover, where a party breaches a promise it made in a contract, courts enforce the promise against the breaching party. If the terms of a contract are enforced in one situation, parties to other contracts may rest assured that if there is a breach under their contracts, so, too, will they be enforced. In that way, enforcement of each individual contract serves **a policy of predictability and reliance**.

Enforcing the agreed-upon contract terms also tends to support **the policy of efficiency**. The term "efficiency" refers to the most effective use of resources to accomplish a desired outcome with the fewest transaction costs. Here, it is often thought that parties are best able to determine the value of their own resources, and to determine when it is in their best interest to trade those resources for something else of value via a contract and how to do so. In other words, each party in a contract is willing to give up something because what he will receive in exchange is more valuable to him. By enforcing those contracts as privately agreed on, contract law supports this exchange of resources, thereby promoting efficiency.

To better see the rationale for these policies, suppose that Julia Newman owns and manages East Side Apartment Complex. Julia has leased an apartment to Michelle Moore for one year. Suppose also that Julia terminated Michelle's lease before the end of the one-year term. In this situation, a court would enforce Julia's promise to lease the apartment to Michelle for the year. The court would therefore award Michelle a remedy, possibly by ordering Julia to pay any excess in rent that Michelle has to pay to a different landlord for the rest of the lease term.

A court would enforce the term of this contract because that is what the parties agreed on—thus the court would be implementing *the policy of freedom of contract*. Moreover, the court would enforce this lease term because it would want Michelle to get the benefit she bargained for—and planned for. Thus, Michelle and other similarly situated future tenants could rely on the legal system to ensure that landlords performed on their promises, supporting *the policy of predictability and reliance*. And, this enforcement would promote the exchange of resources that the parties had decided up front was economically beneficial—Michelle exchanging money (monthly rent) for Julia's promise to lease her an apartment. Michelle valued Julia's tenancy more than the promised monthly rent, and vice versa. By enforcing Julia's promise, the court would be promoting the *policy of efficiency*. Thus, a court's enforcement of the landlord's promise would support all three of the policies mentioned above.

However, a court does not enforce a contract, or a contractual term, that violates a policy that it sees as more important than the policies mentioned above. In the area of contract law, sometimes **the policy of fairness** preempts the policies of freedom of contract, predictability/reliance, and efficiency. These competing policies often give rise to specific defenses to enforcement of a contract.

For example, suppose in entering into the lease with Julia, Michelle lied about her monthly income. In fact, she did not have the income that she represented to Julia that she had and shortchanged the last two monthly rent payments because she did not have enough money to pay. In this situation, while Julia had promised to let Michelle lease the apartment, it would be unfair to force Julia to pay any excess rent Michelle incurs in leasing an alternate location when Michelle lied about her ability to pay rent, and in fact failed to pay the amount of monthly rent she promised to pay. Thus, a court would likely not enforce Julia's promise against her.

Keep in mind that the policies discussed above are not the only policies that explain or justify contract law. There are others, too, that underlie contract law. However, they are the policies that most often are cited when justifying the existence of either contract law as a general proposition or specific contractual rules.

You will want to consider what policy is served by every rule of contract law you encounter. In each instance, you will only truly understand the law if you understand the policy rationale for that law. To better understand this concept, consider judicial decisions as being forward-looking in that they will affect future contracting behavior (because other parties will rely on the judicial decision), and not just backward-looking and focused on the case at hand. This often can help you argue to a court that your client's preferred application of the law better serves the policy concerns of contract law. Moreover, if you argue for a change in law, you will either need to explain why the law does not further its intended policy or explain how some other policy dictates a different rule.

Also, keep in mind that contracts and contract law do not operate in a vacuum. Contract terms and parties' contracting behavior might also be governed by other legal schemes as well. And sometimes, those competing legal schemes will dictate that a contract or contract term not be enforced despite contract laws' policies in favor of enforcement.

For example, while a partnership agreement is a contract governed by contract law, that contract is also governed by partnership law.[3] Suppose two partners agree in their partnership agreement that one partner will not be liable to the other in conducting partnership business, even for that partner's willful misconduct. Contract law's policies of freedom of contract and predictability would support giving effect to this contract term. However, under partnership law, a partner cannot be immune from liability for that partner's own willful misconduct.[4] Thus, in this example, partnership law policies would supersede contract law policies, and if this term were challenged, a court would not enforce it.

PRACTICE PROBLEM 1-3

What policies are served by the following rules of contract law?

1. If the parties to a contract agree that, before they will be bound to a contract, they both must sign a mutually acceptable formal writing, then (subject

---

3. A partnership is an association of two or more people to carry on a business for profit. *See* Revised Unif. P'ship Act § 102(11) (last amended 2013) (1997).
4. Revised Unif. P'ship Act § 105(c)(8) (last amended 2013) (1997).

to some exceptions ignored here) they will both need to sign that formal writing to be bound to that contract.

2. A person who is adjudged mentally incompetent can avoid a contract she has otherwise validly entered into.

3. While Tony contracted to sell his car to Bernice for $1,000, Tony later decided that he wanted to keep his car. If Bernice sued, a court would enforce Tony's promise.

The *Duffner* case, set out below, demonstrates a court's analysis of how to determine whether to enforce a particular contract based on policy concerns. In particular, it shows how a court balances the contract law policies discussed above against competing policies, such as the undesirability of restraining trade. But before we delve into that case—the first case in this textbook—we review some basics on how to read a case. As you will see, we have also included notes in the margin of the *Duffner* case to help you identify the parts of a case.

1. How to Read a Case

When you first are presented with a case, you will want to identify the basic information about the case—that is, (1) the names of the *parties* to the lawsuit, (2) the *court* deciding the case, (3) which *state's law* applies, and (4) the *procedural history*—meaning how the lower courts ruled on the lawsuit. You can garner much of this information—at least the names of the parties to the dispute and the court deciding the case—just from the heading of the opinion. Usually the court deciding the dispute will describe the holding of the lower court or courts in the beginning of its opinion, though sometimes it only sets out the lower court's or courts' holdings later in the opinion.

At the next level of review, you will want to identify what *issue or issues* the court is deciding. Here, a court does not consider any issue it wants—an issue must be properly raised on appeal by one of the parties. Sometimes, a party asks an appellate court to review the lower court's statement of law on that issue. An appellate court reviews the law applicable to an issue before the court *de novo*, meaning anew. Thus, an appellate court does not defer to the lower court's statement of law. However, if a party is asking an appellate court to review the lower court's findings of fact, the appellate court gives those findings deference. Thus, an appellate court typically only overturns a lower court's findings of fact where those findings are clearly erroneous.

Keep in mind that appellate courts are not fact-gathering courts; only trial courts gather facts through pre-trial and trial proceedings. As such, sometimes appellate courts present facts in a way to support their holding, and not in a complete or balanced fashion. Moreover, sometimes appellate opinions fail to give the full contextual background for an issue. Where that occurs in the cases we include in this book and where we feel more information is needed to fully understand the relevant issue, we have included supplemental information in the notes after the case. However, you will always want to keep in mind these limitations of appellate opinions when you read the facts they set out.

At the next level of review, you will want to (1) identify what *law* the court is applying to the issue or issues on appeal, (2) the court's *holding* on that issue or those issues—in other words, its decision, and (3) the court's *reasoning* for its holding—in other words, *why* the court is holding as it is. As you identify the applicable law, be careful to not think of "law" in too narrow of a sense. As we explain in Chapter 2, contract law comes primarily from previous judicial decisions, so a court's statements of law might come from other cases. And those precedents might stand for many propositions, all of which constitute the law.

Finally, at the end of each case, the court will issue its *judgment.* In its judgment, the court will explain its decision as to the rights of each party. For example, if the court is ordering a party to take any action such as pay damages, the court does so in its judgment. This is also where the court says whether it is affirming the lower court's holding or reversing that holding.

We sometimes include concurring and dissenting opinions as well. A *concurring opinion* is an opinion written by a judge who agrees with the majority's holding, but not its reasoning. A *dissenting opinion* is an opinion written by a judge who disagrees even with the majority's holding. When you see a concurring or dissenting opinion, you will want to focus on the differences between that opinion and the majority opinion. If you agree with one of those opinions more than the other, you will want to reflect on *why* you do.

Be active and think critically as you read through a court's decision, especially its statement of law, holding, and reasoning. That is, always ask yourself these types of reflection questions:

1. Is the court's statement of law consistent with other courts' statements of law? If not, how do they differ and why do they differ? Is the law of the earlier decided case binding on the later court? If so, how does the later court reconcile that difference?
2. Does the court's holding further contract law's traditional policies of predictability and reliance, freedom of contract, and efficiency? If not, does the court's holding instead further some other policy such as fairness?
3. Is it likely that events occurring at the time the court decided the case outside of the context of the specific dispute affected the court's holding? If so, how?

To help you become an active learner, and to help you organize your thoughts, after each case, we include comprehension and thought questions. Those questions are included to ensure you understand the key points from the case. They are also designed to help you think critically about the case. You may want to write out your answers to these questions, to practice forming statements of law and synthesizing written legal analysis.

We also include hypothetical variations after each case. Those variations ask you to think beyond the case, to how variations on the facts or law might affect the outcome of the case. You will certainly want to write out your analysis on those questions, as that process will help you remember your analysis. Practicing writing out your answer will also help you prepare for a Contracts essay exam or bar exam.

Moreover, these questions and hypothetical variations will help prepare you to think like a lawyer. After all, a layperson could read many of the included cases and understand the statements of fact and law as well as the court's holding and reasoning. But what will distinguish you from a nonlawyer will be your ability to solve the client's next problem using your knowledge of contract law, contract law design and terms, and contract law policies coupled with your skills of legal reasoning and problem identification—skills you will hone through the comprehension and thought questions and hypothetical variations.

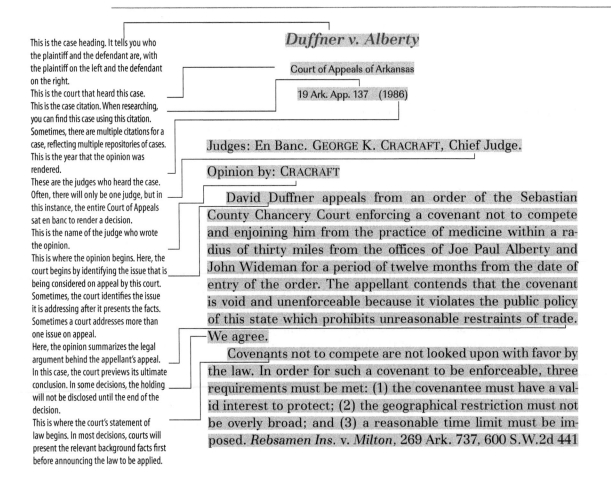

This is the case heading. It tells you who the plaintiff and the defendant are, with the plaintiff on the left and the defendant on the right.
This is the court that heard this case.
This is the case citation. When researching, you can find this case using this citation. Sometimes, there are multiple citations for a case, reflecting multiple repositories of cases.
This is the year that the opinion was rendered.
These are the judges who heard the case. Often, there will only be one judge, but in this instance, the entire Court of Appeals sat en banc to render a decision.
This is the name of the judge who wrote the opinion.
This is where the opinion begins. Here, the court begins by identifying the issue that is being considered on appeal by this court. Sometimes, the court identifies the issue it is addressing after it presents the facts. Sometimes a court addresses more than one issue on appeal.
Here, the opinion summarizes the legal argument behind the appellant's appeal. In this case, the court previews its ultimate conclusion. In some decisions, the holding will not be disclosed until the end of the decision.
This is where the court's statement of law begins. In most decisions, courts will present the relevant background facts first before announcing the law to be applied.

Duffner v. Alberty

Court of Appeals of Arkansas

19 Ark. App. 137   (1986)

Judges: En Banc. GEORGE K. CRACRAFT, Chief Judge.

Opinion by: CRACRAFT

David Duffner appeals from an order of the Sebastian County Chancery Court enforcing a covenant not to compete and enjoining him from the practice of medicine within a radius of thirty miles from the offices of Joe Paul Alberty and John Wideman for a period of twelve months from the date of entry of the order. The appellant contends that the covenant is void and unenforceable because it violates the public policy of this state which prohibits unreasonable restraints of trade. We agree.

Covenants not to compete are not looked upon with favor by the law. In order for such a covenant to be enforceable, three requirements must be met: (1) the covenantee must have a valid interest to protect; (2) the geographical restriction must not be overly broad; and (3) a reasonable time limit must be imposed. *Rebsamen Ins.* v. *Milton*, 269 Ark. 737, 600 S.W.2d 441

(Ark. App. 1980). It is not argued that the geographic restriction was overbroad or that the time limitation was unreasonable. Appellant contends only that there was not a sufficient interference with appellees' business interests to warrant enforcement of the covenant. It is clear that such covenants will not be enforced unless a covenantee had a legitimate interest to be protected by such an agreement and that the law will not enforce a contract merely to prohibit ordinary competition. *Import Motors, Inc.* v. *Luker*, 268 Ark. 1045, 599 S.W.2d 398 (1980). The test of reasonableness of contracts in restraint of trade is that the restraint imposed upon one party must not be greater than is reasonably necessary for the protection of the other, and not so great as to injure a public interest.

The court identifies the specific legal test to be utilized in this case.

Contracts in partial restraint of trade, where ancillary to a sale of a business or profession with its goodwill, are valid to the extent reasonably necessary to the purchaser's protection, and are looked upon with greater favor than such an agreement ancillary to an employer-employee or professional association relationship. *Madison Bank & Trust* v. *First National Bank of Huntsville*, 276 Ark. 405, 635 S.W.2d 268 (1982); *Marshall* v. *Irby*, 203 Ark. 795, 158 S.W.2d 693 (1942); *Easley* v. *Sky, Inc.*, 15 Ark. App. 64, 689 S.W.2d 356 (1985). Where the covenant grows out of an employment or other associational relationship, the courts have found an interest sufficient to warrant enforcement of the covenant only in those cases where the covenantee provided special training, or made available trade secrets, confidential business information or customer lists, and then only if it is found that the associate was able to use information so obtained to gain an unfair competitive advantage. *See Orkin Exterminating Co., Inc.* v. *Weaver*, 257 Ark. 926, 521 S.W.2d 69 (1975); *Rector-Phillips-Morse, Inc.* v. *Vroman*, 253 Ark. 750, 489 S.W.2d 1 (1973); *All-State Supply, Inc.* v. *Fisher*, 252 Ark. 963, 483 S.W.2d 210 (1972); *Girard* v. *Rebsamen Ins. Co.*, 14 Ark. App. 154, 685 S.W.2d 526 (1985). The validity of these covenants depends upon the facts and circumstances of each particular case. *Evans Laboratories, Inc.* v. *Melder*, 262 Ark. 868, 562 S.W.2d 62 (1978).

Throughout its opinion, the court states the source of law — in this case, common law decisions made by prior courts — that will be used to help decide the case.

Here, Dr. Joe Paul Alberty and Dr. John Wideman were orthopedic surgeons who had been engaged in the practice of their profession in Fort Smith, Arkansas, as partners for many years. Appellant completed his residency training in orthopedic surgery in June of 1984, at a clinic in Temple, Texas, and afterwards determined to locate in Fort Smith and associate himself with the appellees. The terms and conditions of appellant's association

The next part of the discussion is the court's recitation of certain facts.

with the appellees' practice was reduced to a letter agreement. It is not questioned that all of those involved were fully aware of the document's provisions. Under the terms of the agreement the appellees agreed to pay all general expenses and certain specific expenses listed in the agreement were to be paid by the physician who incurred them. Each physician was assigned a private office and paid rent to the Alberty-Wideman partnership. Certain portions of the office and the medical equipment owned by the partnership were to be used in common and the practice would be organized as an association of individual professional associations, but appellant would initially practice as a sole proprietorship. Call schedules would be shared equally. At the end of one year the appellant would arrange financing to buy his share of the equity in the furniture and equipment and would have an option to purchase an interest in the condominium offices. The agreement contained a covenant that should the appellant desire to leave the group he would not practice within a radius of thirty miles of the offices of the appellees for a period of one year from the date of termination. It was agreed that the appellant would be furnished rent and overhead at no expense for the first three months, at one-third the normal rate during the fourth month, and two-thirds that rate in the fifth month. Appellant would begin paying his equal share beginning with the sixth month. There was no agreement to share income or new patients with the appellant and individual billings were made and collected for services rendered by each physician. Appellant practiced with appellees under this arrangement until late in the spring of 1985, when he joined another orthopedic clinic which conducted its practice in the same building in which the appellees' offices were located.

During the twelve-month period following the commencement of the association, the appellant treated 1207 patients and it was undisputed that during the first nine months of that association his personal receipts were in excess of $300,000.00. After leaving the association with appellees, the appellant requested of them the files on twenty-eight patients, which he testified had been treated by him while the association continued and were receiving follow-up medical attention only. The chancellor specifically found that during the continuance of the agreement the appellant "had access to the confidential patient files of the plaintiffs, had use of plaintiffs' office furniture and equipment, and utilized for his own benefit the good professional reputation and goodwill of the plaintiffs." The chancellor found the restrictive covenant to be reasonable and that the appellees had a valid and enforceable right to protect their substantial investment in their medical practice, and to protect their established medical clientele. An injunction was entered restraining the appellant from engaging in the practice of medicine within a radius of thirty miles from appellees' offices for a period of twelve months commencing on the date of the decree.

Although contracts between individuals ought not to be entered into lightly, all other considerations must give way where matters of public policy are involved. From our review of all the facts and circumstances, we are of the opinion that the contract provision prohibiting appellant from practicing medicine within thirty miles of the City of Fort Smith constitutes an undue interference with the interests of the public right of availability of the orthopedic surgeon it prefers to use and that the covenant's enforcement would result in an unreasonable restraint of trade.

The court in this instance provides its holding (which differed from the lower court's) with respect to the application of the legal test to the facts in this case.

Here the contract did not relate to the sale of a business and its goodwill. The appellees' goodwill remained with them. The benefits which the appellant obtained from the reputation and goodwill of his former associates would be no greater than that of an employee in any other established business. It is only in those instances where goodwill has, for valid consideration, been transferred that the purchaser has a legitimate pecuniary interest in protecting against its being drained by competition from the seller.

The following paragraphs contain the court's reasoning — that is, the reasons for its holding.

Nor were any trade secrets, formulas, methods, or devices which gave appellant an advantage over the appellees involved here. At the time he joined the association he had received his training and skills elsewhere and brought them with him. There is nothing in the record to indicate that he learned any trade secret or surgical procedures from the appellees which were not readily available to other orthopedic surgeons. To the contrary, the record reflects that while in the association he performed some orthopedic surgical procedures which the appellees did not perform.

Although the chancellor found that the appellant had access to appellees' confidential patient files, there was no evidence that he attempted to memorize them or use information from those files to entice any of their former patients to become patients of his new association. Although there was evidence that he obtained the files on twenty-eight persons from the appellees, it was explained that these were not new patients but those who were receiving follow-up medical attention after having undergone surgery by the appellant during his association with the appellees. Other than those twenty-eight persons receiving post-operative care, he testified that he had not seen more than two of appellees' former patients.

We cannot conclude from the evidence that appellant maintained a personal relationship or acquaintance with appellees' patients or that their "stock of patients" was appropriated by the appellant when he left their offices. There was also evidence that appellees' income increased after appellant left the association. We conclude that the enforcement of this covenant would do no more than prohibit ordinary competition. Reversed.

This is the court's judgment—that the decision of the lower court is reversed.

Understanding the Case:

1. *Public Policy:*   You may think, after reading *Duffner*, that contracts are often not enforced for public policy reasons. This is not the situation. Judges rarely do not enforce a party's contractual promise based on public policy concerns. Presumably, judges are reluctant to announce, as a matter of law, that certain promises offend policy interests and that such offended interests supersede the desire of the parties to have their contractual promises enforced.

2. *Burden of Proof:*   It is important in each case to focus on which party bears the burden of proof with respect to the issue at hand. In the *Duffner* case, Alberty and Wideman attempted to enforce the non-compete covenant against Duffner. Alberty and Wideman therefore had the burden of demonstrating that a valid contract existed (which we will study in future material). Duffner, on the other hand, was not contesting that he had entered into the contract. Instead, he was arguing an affirmative defense, namely, that the contract was not enforceable because of public policy reasons. Typically, the party asserting the defense bears the burden of proving each element of the defense. However, because non-compete covenants "are not looked upon with favor by the law," the test for validity required satisfaction by Alberty and Wideman of the three-factor test discussed in the opinion.

3. *Appeal:*   As discussed before the case, an appeals court is typically constrained to correcting incorrect application of the law. In other words, an appeals court will not consider new evidence. It can decide, however, that the lower court did not focus on the "right" facts or did not arrive at the "right" legal conclusion based on those facts. In the *Duffner* case, that is precisely what happened: while relying on the same set of facts presented to the lower court, the appeals court determined that the non-compete covenant was not reasonable.

Comprehension and Thought Questions:

1. Why do you think covenants not to compete are "not looked upon with favor by the law"?

2. Sometimes, covenants not to compete are enforceable contracts. Why was the covenant in this instance not enforceable?

3. Why do you think courts use the three-factor test identified above with respect to the enforceability of covenants not to compete? What policies or interests does that test serve?

4. The court could have concluded that the covenant not to compete was enforceable, as did the chancellor in the lower court opinion. What facts do you think support such a conclusion?

Hypothetical Variations:

1. Imagine that Alberty and Wideman had purchased all of Greg's (another doctor) ownership interests in the medical practice for $1 million, and that the sales agreement included a promise by Greg not to compete with the medical practice in the state for one year. Do you think that covenant would have been enforceable? Make the arguments for and against enforceability based on the law discussed in the case.

2. Imagine that Greg did not have any ownership interests in the medical practice, but that Alberty and Wideman nevertheless agreed to pay Greg $250,000 as "severance pay" upon the termination of his employment with them. In exchange, Greg promised not to compete with the medical practice in the state for one year. Do you think the covenant would have been enforceable? Make the arguments for and against enforceability based on the law discussed in the case.

3. Imagine that Greg's employment was terminated because it was discovered that he had copied patient contact information onto a personal computer. Do you think Greg's original covenant not to compete (which mirrored Duffner's) would have been enforceable? Make the arguments for and against enforceability based on the law discussed in the case.

You have now completed your review of the first case. You may be wondering what you are supposed "to do" with the *Duffner* case now that you have understood it and how it might be useful to you later, whether on exams or in practice. There are a number of misconceptions about these questions among first-year law students, so it makes sense to clarify the role of cases upfront.

a. Cases help you learn the "law"

Whether on the exam or in practice, you will need to know the law—the legal rules and their purposes and policies, and the factors and elements that make up those rules, including the specific standards and tests they provide. Cases generally discuss what the law is and how it should be applied in a particular situation. You will need to develop an understanding of each factor or element of the law and what each factor or element means. You cannot answer the question "Was a contract formed?" if you do not know what is legally required to form a contract. Accordingly, we can use the cases to help identify what those legal requirements are. In *Duffner*, for example, we learn what the law in Arkansas is with respect to the enforceability of non-compete covenants.

b. Learning legal analysis: cases as useful examples of law applied to particular facts

Knowing what happened in a case and the law from a case is not enough. More important, you must learn how to engage in legal analysis. On exams and in practice, you will be expected to analyze how the law should be applied in a particular, and often novel, situation. As mentioned above, you will obviously need to know what the law is in order to be able to see how it applies in a particular situation, but cases also can provide some guidance as to how and why the law should be applied in particular factual situations.

So how do you do this? In the Hypothetical Variations above, you were asked to assess the enforceability of covenants not to compete in differing contexts. In order to answer those questions, presumably you would have needed to understand what the legal test for enforceability was in Arkansas and to be able to identify each part of the test. The hypotheticals, however, contained facts that were different from those contained in *Duffner*. Next you were asked to determine whether the difference in facts suggests different outcomes based on the same legal tests. In other words, did those hypothetical variations alter outcome-determinative facts? In deciding that, you had to assess whether the sale of Greg's interests in the medical practice (Question 1), payment of severance (Question 2), or bad behavior by Greg (Question 3) would or should lead to the law being applied differently than in *Duffner*. Moreover, you had to be able to justify your answer and identify the counterarguments and why those were not compelling.

For example, you may have concluded that Greg's bad behavior (copying the patient information onto a personal computer) suggests that the covenant not to compete should be enforceable against him. But, how do you know? You need to be able to point out similarities and distinctions between the present case and previous cases elucidating the law and explain why those similarities or distinctions justify your conclusion. Why does it matter if Greg behaved badly? How is that different from Duffner's behavior? How is the law and its policies or rationale served (or not served) by enforcing the covenant in Greg's situation but not Duffner's?

Each time you consider how the law should apply in a particular situation, you need to ask yourself and be able to explain: How do you know? How do you know that Greg's covenant not to compete is enforceable? What facts are you relying on, and why? Often, you will be able to answer these questions by relying on previous cases where similar (or different) facts were present and particular legal conclusions were reached.

As part of your legal analysis, you need to be able to identify and assess the counterarguments to your legal conclusion. The same facts you rely on (such as Greg's bad behavior) may actually suggest a different legal conclusion where those new facts are outcome-determinative. Again, by looking to previous cases with similar or different facts (such as *Duffner*), you will be able to tease out what these counterarguments might be and determine how to justify them.

In other words, for legal analysis purposes, cases simply are not important in and of themselves. Contracts and other first year courses are not courses of history, and the cases are not designed to be learned as such. They instead are useful as tools: as examples of legal analysis, as examples of how the law was applied by a particular court to a particular factual situation, and as examples of enunciation of legal rules and policies. These examples then can be used to assess what "could" or "should" be the legal result in the novel factual situation you are now facing.

Now that you understand why we included *Duffner* as well as the Hypothetical Variations, you might want to revisit those Hypothetical Variations. As you do, ask yourself: What variable or fact changed? What does that suggest about how the law will be applied in the hypothetical, and how do you know? Does your conclusion undermine or further contract law policies generally?

Once you understand the law and how it might be applied to a new situation, you can then use these lessons to protect your client when (1) drafting and negotiating contracts and (2) litigating disputes over contracts.

Now that you have studied Contracts basics, read through and answer the questions that follow the Simulation Problem for Chapter 1, which is located in Appendix A.

CHAPTER 2

Structure and Role of Contract Law

A. CONSTRUCT OF CONTRACT LAW

As Chapter 1 explained, public policy sometimes warrants not giving effect to the parties' contractual promises. That happens where specific legal doctrines give way to other policy concerns, such as fairness. For example, a court will generally not enforce a contract induced by fraud. That is because a court would view the fraud by one party as tainting the process of contract formation. Other contract law rules invalidate specific contractual provisions because they are substantively unfair. In either case, these rules are *mandatory* because the parties cannot eliminate them by private agreement. These mandatory rules are presented in Chapters 17-21.

While mandatory rules cannot be eliminated by private agreement, they can often be tailored to an extent by the parties. In particular, the parties can spell out standards by which to determine if the rules have been satisfied or include contractual terms to demonstrate that the parties do not need the protection of mandatory contract law doctrines. In that way, many of these rules differ from the mandatory rules you are studying in criminal law, which cannot be modified by agreement.

One example of a mandatory rule is **mutual assent**. As Chapter 4 will discuss, to form a contract as a bargain, the parties must mutually assent to it—that is, manifest, or demonstrate to one another, their intent to be bound by the bargain. Parties cannot eliminate this legal requirement by private agreement, which makes it mandatory. However, the parties can agree on the standard to be used to determine what amounts to mutual assent.

For example, assume Michelle Chen wants to lease an apartment from Julia Newman. In this situation, Julia can specify that to show Michelle's assent to the lease, Michelle must sign a copy of the written documentation reflecting the terms of the lease and deliver that to Julia no later than 5:00 P.M. that day. If Michelle complies, she will have manifested her assent to Julia. If not, Michelle will show she does not intend to be bound. In this way, while contract law requires both parties to manifest their assent to create a contract through a bargain, Julia is able to spell out what conduct she is looking for from Michelle to show her assent.

Finally, many contract rules are not mandatory. Instead, they constitute gap-fillers to the parties' bargain. Such gap-fillers apply by default, which means they apply where the parties have not otherwise agreed between themselves to a different standard. Where the parties have agreed on a different contractual standard, these default gap-fillers do not apply at all, and the agreed-upon standard applies.

As an example of a default gap-filler, suppose that at the end of her lease term, Michelle requests her full $500 deposit back from Julia. However, Julia only refunds Michelle $300 of her deposit. In her cover note with the returned deposit, Julia says that she withheld $200 from Michelle's returned deposit because Michelle had underpaid her last month's rent by $200. Thus, this represented an amount Michelle owed Julia.

Here, assuming the lease was silent on what deductions Julia could make from the deposit, one must look to see if the law supplies a gap-filler that permits Julia to make this deduction. In fact, state landlord-tenant statutes often permit landlords to withhold from a tenant's deposit amounts the tenant failed to pay in rent.[1] Thus, while the lease itself did not permit Julia to withhold this amount, the state default rule on deposits did.

It is not unusual for Michelle's lease with Julia to not have listed out every deduction Julia could make from Michelle's deposit. In fact, no contract can address every term that is relevant to a contractual relationship, as it is impossible to predict the future and what scenarios may come to pass as the parties perform under the contract. While Michelle's lease with Julia could have addressed deductions from the deposit, because it did not, the default term applies.

As you read this book, you will want to consider whether a given rule is mandatory or default. You will also want to consider the rationale for your answer. Thinking through this construct will not only help you understand contract law better, but also help you identify the areas where you can help your client tailor the terms of a contract to create value.

The following diagram depicts the determinants of the parties' bargain.

---

1. *See, e.g.,* Wis. Stat. Ann. § 704.28 (2014) (providing that "When a landlord returns a security deposit to a tenant after the tenant vacates the premises, the landlord may withhold from the full amount of the security deposit only amounts reasonably necessary to pay for . . . (b) Unpaid rent for which the tenant is legally responsible").

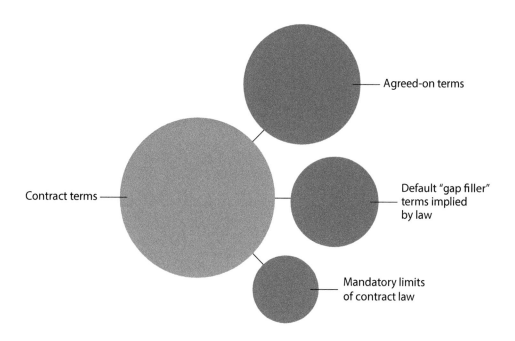

Contract terms

Agreed-on terms

Default "gap filler" terms implied by law

Mandatory limits of contract law

PRACTICE PROBLEM 2-1

In *McDonald v. Mianecki*, 398 A.2d 1283 (1979), Joseph Mianecki, a builder, agreed to build a home for the McDonalds for $44,500. During construction and once they moved in, the McDonalds noticed that there were problems with the water in the home—it stained fixtures and everything else it came in contact with, had a bad odor and taste, and "when left standing the water fizzled like 'Alka-Seltzer.'" Eventually, it even failed to meet New Jersey state standards of potability. Despite several requests, Mianecki failed to fix the problem. Thus, the McDonalds sued.

While the construction contract did not include an express promise from Mianecki to make the home habitable, the New Jersey Supreme Court implied such a promise, called a warranty. Specifically, the court found that a builder of a home "impliedly warrant[s] that a house which they construct will be of reasonable workmanship and habitability." The court justified this warranty, which it called an implied warranty of habitability, on many grounds, including (1) that it reflects the expectations of the parties (for a buyer, the purchase of a new home is often the most important transaction they will enter into) and (2) that the parties are not in an equal bargaining position (the average buyer lacks the skills and expertise to make an adequate inspection, and most defects are undetectable even to the most observant layperson). Therefore, the purchaser relies heavily on the expertise of the builder.

The court stated that it was not addressing whether the builder could expressly disclaim this warranty. However, subsequent to the case, the New Jersey legislature passed a statute saying that any such waivers would violate public policy.

1. Since the New Jersey legislature passed the statute, is the implied warranty of habitability mandatory or default? How do you know?

2. What policies are served by the implied warranty of habitability?

3. Assume New Jersey does not preclude builders from disclaiming the implied warranty of habitability, as is true in some states. Would your answer to either Question 1 or Question 2 change? Why or why not?

B. CONTRACT LAW IS STATE LAW

By and large, contracts are private law. That means the parties to a contract can agree on any terms they wish, and the law will uphold those terms. However, contract law contains many mandatory rules that regulate how contracts are formed and when a party's failure to perform amounts to a breach. Contract law also contains some default rules, which apply absent the parties' agreement to the contrary. But before you study what those rules are, first you need to understand the sources of contract law.

By and large contract law is a matter of state law. That means states create the laws that regulate contracts. Consequently, there are 50 sets of contract laws in the United States.

One of the major benefits to having such variety is that it allows states to choose those rules they believe are most beneficial. Once a state adopts a specific rule of contract law, other states can observe whether that rule is beneficial and if so, adopt it too. In this way, the law can evolve positively toward more effective legal rules.

On the other hand, there are downsides to such variation. Importantly, commercial parties use contracts to set out the terms of a commercial exchange. With so many different laws out there, parties have to expend time, energy, and money becoming informed of the law that applies to their transaction and to contract with respect to the law of that state. The resources it takes to become informed are even higher if one considers that which law applies might not always be clear.

This lack of certainty as to which state's law applies and what the law is in that state has understandably led to efforts to make the law from state to state more uniform, especially in the area of commercial transactions. Those efforts are discussed in Section D of this chapter. Moreover, parties can try to provide for more certainty by including a choice-of-law provision. This is discussed below in Section C.

Despite the variety among state contractual rules, states share many common core contractual principles and concepts. That is because all U.S. contract law has shared roots in the English common law. Those common principles and concepts allow an attorney in one state to understand the broad framework and contract law concepts in other states, even if the lawyer does not know the specific rules in that other state.

While contract law is governed by state law, you should be aware that some contract law is a matter of federal law. For example, agreements to arbitrate contract disputes are governed by a federal law known as the Federal Arbitration Act (FAA).[2] Where federal law such as the FAA addresses a matter of contract law, that federal law takes priority over any contradictory state law. Thus, the FAA preempts any contradictory state laws on arbitration of contract disputes. However, state contract law can and often does still play a role even in these preempted areas. Importantly, under the FAA, state contract law still determines whether parties formed a contract containing an arbitration clause, and whether the contract containing the arbitration clause is enforceable.

In addition, international law governs some contracts. For example, the United Nations Convention on Contracts for the International Sale of Goods (CISG), governs some international sales contracts. Specifically, the CISG is a treaty that applies to contracts for the sale of goods—meaning tangible, personal property—between parties with places of business in different countries that have adopted the treaty. Because the United States has adopted this treaty, it applies to contracts for the sale of goods between parties in the United States and parties in other CISG-adopting countries.

C. CHOICE OF LAW

By default—meaning, unless the parties have agreed otherwise—the law that governs a contract is the law of the state with the most significant relationship to the transaction and the parties covered by the contract. Courts usually determine this by looking at (1) where the transaction was negotiated, (2) where the parties were when they entered into the contract, (3) where any property is located that is the subject of the contract, (4) where the parties will be when they perform the contract, and (5) where the parties reside, if they are natural persons, or where the parties are headquartered or organized, if they are businesses. In other words, there are many factors that courts consider in determining which law governs a contract, making the choice somewhat unpredictable from the contracting parties' perspectives.

---

2. Arbitration Act, 43 Stat. 883, Pub. L. No. 68-401 (1925).

However, consistent with the idea that parties can choose the terms of their contract under the policy of freedom of contract, parties can choose which state's laws they want to govern their contract. The selected state's laws then govern all matters on which the parties contract.

Parties choose which state's laws govern their contract so there is predictability as to which state's laws will govern. And by selecting a given state's laws to apply, the parties can choose to apply the state's laws that they feel will best protect their interests under the contract.

This freedom is especially important given that a dispute under a contract can be brought in virtually any state's court. In other words, just because a contract is governed by a state's laws does not mean disputes under that contract must be litigated in that state.[3]

However, not every choice-of-law provision will be respected by every court. In fact, in many states, courts will not give effect to the parties' contractual choice of law where there is not a substantial relationship between the chosen state and the parties or transaction and there is no other reasonable basis for the parties' choice of law. On the other hand, some states extend the reach of their contract laws by deeming there to be a substantial relationship where a contract involves more than a threshold amount, so long as the courts in that state have jurisdiction over the contract parties. For example, Delaware deems there to be a substantial relationship to the state if the contract involves $100,000 or more and the parties are subject to the jurisdiction of the Delaware courts and can be served with process there.[4]

Moreover, in many states, a court will not give effect to the parties' contractual choice of law where doing so would violate a fundamental policy in that state, or the choice would violate a statute of that state enacted to protect that state's citizens.

To see how these doctrines work in practice, consider a situation where an employee who resides in California works remotely for a technology company incorporated and headquartered in Texas. The parties enter into an employment agreement remotely from their home bases. Suppose in the course of his employment, the employee will gain access to confidential information about the employer's technology and clients. The employer is worried that if and when the employee leaves the company, he will use its technology or confidential client information to compete with the company. To stem this concern, the employer includes a "non-compete" in the employee's employment agreement. As you saw in Chapter 1, a **non-compete** is essentially a promise by an employee to not work for a competitor of the employer for an agreed-upon period of time after his employment terminates and within an agreed-upon geographic

---

3. Parties can, however, agree on which forum will hear their dispute.

4. *See* Del. Code Ann. tit. 6, § 2708 (1993). Some states also have separate venue thresholds that may be higher.

region. Through the non-compete, the employer can ensure that the employee does not use the employer's confidential information to benefit a competitor post-employment to the detriment of the company that developed this technology and information.

Courts in California do not enforce non-competes by employees,[5] while courts in Texas do, assuming they meet a reasonableness test.[6]

Here, if the parties do not specify a governing law in the employment agreement, there is a chance that California law will apply. That is because the employee lives and works in California, entered the employment agreement from California, and performs his side of the bargain in California. However, because California law holds that non-competes by employees are not enforceable, applying California law to the contract would undermine the benefits of the non-compete to the employer. Courts in Texas, in contrast, might enforce this non-compete.

To address this uncertainty and protect the benefits it bargained for, the employer would want to specify that Texas law governs the employment agreement. The following is a typical choice-of-law provision that the employer could include in this contract:

> Texas law governs all matters arising under or relating to this Contract.

But what if the employee sues the company in California seeking to have the non-compete declared invalid? Will a California court enforce the non-compete since it is governed by Texas law—a state that upholds such non-competes? Or will the court invalidate this non-compete because it would not be valid under California law?

Here, there is clearly a substantial relationship between Texas and this transaction. Not only is the employer incorporated and headquartered in Texas, but the employer signed and performed the employment agreement in Texas. Thus, there appears to be a substantial relationship between Texas and the parties and transaction. Consequently, a court in California would likely not hold the non-compete as invalid because of a lack of relationship to Texas.

However, a court in California might still invalidate the non-compete on the grounds that it violates a fundamental policy of California of protecting the right of California's residents to work where they choose. It also hinders competition by limiting the ability of California companies to hire the employee for a time after his employment ends. And a California court would undoubtedly find that California has a materially greater interest in protecting the free mobility of labor and competition of California companies than does Texas.

---

5. *See, e.g.,* Silguero v. Creteguard, Inc., 187 Cal. App. 4th 60, 70 (2010) (citing Cal. Bus. Prof. Code § 16600).

6. *See, e.g.,* Alex Sheshunoff Mgmt. Servs., L.P. v. Johnson, 209 S.W.3d 644, 648 (Tex. 2006) (citing Tex. Bus. & Com. Code § 15.50).

As such, a court in California would likely determine that the non-compete is invalid.

In sum, parties to a contract can choose the state whose laws they wish to apply to their contract so long as that choice bears a reasonable relationship to the parties and the transaction. And they would want to do so to achieve more certainty for the enforcement of their contract. However, notwithstanding a choice-of-law provision, a court still might not apply the selected law to give effect to a fundamental policy of that state. As such, parties cannot ever be absolutely certain which state's laws will apply. As a lawyer, you would want to flag this risk for your client before they enter into a contract with a provision that might not be enforceable in a state with an interest in the transaction.

The following case shows how a court evaluates the enforceability of the parties' choice-of-law provision. As you read this case, ask yourself if the court applies the tests described above on choice-of-law, or if it applies a different test.

Swanson v. The Image Bank, Inc.
Supreme Court of Arizona
206 Ariz. 264 (2003)

JONES, Chief Justice.

Appellants, The Image Bank, Inc. and Swanstock, Inc. (collectively "TIB"), sought review of the court of appeals' decision affirming the trial court's grant of partial summary judgment in favor of Appellee, Mary Virginia Swanson ("Swanson"). The judgment awarded treble damages under Arizona Revised Statutes ("A.R.S.") § 23–355 (1995) for bad faith breach of an employment contract. We granted review to determine whether the contract's express choice-of-law provision assigning Texas substantive law to govern any controversy arising out of the contract precludes recovery of a statutory claim for treble damages under A.R.S. § 23–355. After full review, we hold that the contractual choice of Texas law governs the remedies available to Swanson for breach of the contract and we reverse the treble damage award. Jurisdiction is established under Article 6, Section 5(3) of the Arizona Constitution and A.R.S. § 12–120.24 (2003).

FACTS

From 1991 to 1997, Swanson owned Swanstock, Inc., an Arizona corporation that represented owners of fine art photography. She resided permanently in Arizona and operated Swanstock, Inc. from this state. The Image Bank, Inc. is a New York corporation with its home office in Texas. In June 1997, The Image Bank purchased Swanstock, Inc. and retained Swanson to operate the company as its president, creative director, and chief executive officer pursuant to a negotiated employment contract. The contract contained provisions regarding compensation to be received upon termination and the application of Texas law as the law under which the contract should be governed and construed. Each party was represented by counsel during the contract negotiations.

TIB terminated Swanson in July 1999 "other than for cause" but refused to make the severance payments required by the contract. Swanson filed suit, followed by a motion for partial summary judgment, alleging breach of the employment contract and claiming TIB violated A.R.S. § 23–352 (1995) which provides that "[n]o employer may withhold or divert any portion of an employee's wages. . . ." In addition to damages at law for the breach, Swanson sought treble damages pursuant to A.R.S. § 23–355.[7] The trial court determined that TIB breached the employment contract with Swanson and awarded Swanson $150,000 in severance pay. Notwithstanding the parties' express agreement that Texas law should control, the trial court trebled the damages under § 23–355, finding that the statute set forth a "fundamental public policy" of Arizona and, as such, should supersede the choice-of-law provision in the contract.

TIB appealed on two grounds. First, the company contended Swanson was not entitled to receive severance pay because she failed to perform her duties and therefore anticipatorily repudiated the contract. The court of appeals disagreed and applied Texas law to this issue, concluding that Swanson's actions did not constitute an anticipatory breach. This court declined review of that issue.

Second, TIB asserted the treble damage award under § 23–355 was improper and based its argument on the choice-of-law provision requiring the application of Texas law to the contract. The court of appeals, again disagreeing with TIB, applied Restatement (Second) of Conflict of Laws § 187 (1971) (hereafter "Restatement") and upheld the treble damage award on the theory that Arizona law does not permit prospective contractual waiver of claims under § 23–355 in the case of unreasonable, bad-faith withholding of wages. The choice-of-law provision was held to be invalid as a violation of a "fundamental policy" of Arizona under both subsections (1) and (2) of Restatement § 187.

DISCUSSION

Arizona courts apply the Restatement to determine the applicable law in a contract action. If a contract includes a specific choice-of-law provision, we must determine whether that choice is "valid and effective" under Restatement § 187. Choice-of-law issues are questions of law, which we decide *de novo*.

---

7. [1] A.R.S. § 23–355 reads: "If an employer . . . shall fail to pay wages due any employee, such employee may recover in a civil action against an employer or former employer an amount which is treble the amount of the unpaid wages."

A. Applicability of the Restatement

The choice-of-law provision in the employment contract reads:

> This Agreement shall be governed by and construed in accordance with the internal laws of the State of Texas, *without regard to the principles of conflicts [sic] of laws.*

(Emphasis added.) TIB claims this provision forecloses the application of conflict of laws principles set forth in the Restatement because the parties, by including the last phrase, expressed their unequivocal intent that Texas law control the relationship. TIB argues the court of appeals improperly overrode that intent by engaging in a § 187 analysis. TIB further contends that absent fraud or overreaching, parties are always free to preclude a § 187 analysis by choosing the state whose law will govern their relationship and the available remedies. These arguments are not sound and we do not adopt them.

When more than one state has a relationship to or an interest in a contract, courts apply a conflicts analysis to determine which state's law should govern. However, neither a statute nor a rule of law permitting parties to choose the applicable law confers unfettered freedom to contract at will on this point. Consistent with this principle, Restatement § 187, comment g reads:

> Fulfillment of the parties' expectations is not the only value in contract law; regard must also be had for state interests and for state regulation. The chosen law should not be applied without regard for the interests of the state which would be the state of the applicable law with respect to the particular issue involved in the absence of an effective choice by the parties.

Section 187 provides a mechanism by which to balance the interests of both the parties and the states. Therefore, when parties include an express choice-of-law provision in a contract, we will perform a § 187 analysis to ascertain the appropriate balance between the parties' circumstances and the states' interests. By so doing, we determine as a matter of law whether the provision is valid and thus whether it should govern the parties' contractual rights and duties.

B. Restatement § 187 Analysis

Restatement § 187 outlines the test used to decide whether the parties' chosen law will govern:

> (1) The law of the state chosen by the parties to govern their contractual rights and duties will be applied if the particular issue is one which the parties could have resolved by an explicit provision in their agreement directed to that issue.
> (2) The law of the state chosen by the parties to govern their contractual rights and duties will be applied, even if the particular issue is one which the

parties could not have resolved by an explicit provision in their agreement directed to that issue, unless either

(a) the chosen state has no substantial relationship to the parties or the transaction and there is no other reasonable basis for the parties' choice, or

(b) application of the law of the chosen state would be contrary to a fundamental policy of a state which has a materially greater interest than the chosen state in the determination of the particular issue and which, under the rule of § 188, would be the state of the applicable law in the absence of an effective choice of law by the parties.

In deciding whether the parties' choice will govern, we first determine whether the disputed issue is one which the parties could have resolved by an explicit provision in their agreement. As identified by the court of appeals, "[t]he 'particular issue' here is whether parties may contractually waive any statutory right or claim to treble damages under § 23–355." *Swanson,* 202 Ariz. at 234, ¶ 25, 43 P.3d at 182. The parties agree, as do we, that Arizona law applies to this threshold issue. *See* Restatement § 187 cmt. c (the question whether the parties could have resolved a particular issue by explicit agreement directed to that issue is a question to be determined by the local law of the state selected by application of the rule set forth in Restatement § 188).[8]

The court of appeals held that Arizona law does not allow parties to an employment contract to preclude such recovery. The court did so on the basis that Arizona law prohibits waiver of the remedy in light of the underlying purposes and goals of Arizona's wage statutes and the legislative objectives sought to be achieved. By implication, the court held that unless waiver is expressly permitted by the statute, it is necessarily prohibited. Our analysis, however, leads to

---

8. [3] Restatement § 188 provides as follows:

(1) The rights and duties of the parties with respect to an issue in contract are determined by the local law of the state which, with respect to that issue, has the most significant relationship to the transaction and the parties under the principles stated in § 6.

(2) In the absence of an effective choice of law by the parties (see § 187), the contacts to be taken into account in applying the principles of § 6 to determine the law applicable to an issue include:

(a) the place of contracting,

(b) the place of negotiation of the contract,

(c) the place of performance,

(d) the location of the subject matter of the contract, and

(e) the domicile, residence, nationality, place of incorporation and place of business of the parties.

These contacts are to be evaluated according to their relative importance with respect to the particular issue.

(3) If the place of negotiating the contract and the place of performance are in the same state, the local law of this state will usually be applied, except as otherwise provided in §§ 189–199 and 203.

the conclusion that the court of appeals erred in its interpretation of Arizona law and the proper application of Restatement § 187.

First, we do not find support for the court's implicit holding that an Arizona statute must expressly permit parties to resolve an issue in order to satisfy Restatement § 187(1). We do not interpret § 187(1) so narrowly. Section 187(1) places few limitations on parties' right to contract. Examples of issues that parties may not determine by explicit agreement include questions involving capacity, formalities, and validity. Thus, parties cannot vest themselves with capacity to contract by so stating in an agreement, nor can they dispense with the formal legal elements of a valid contract. Generally speaking, however, parties do have the power to determine the terms of their contractual engagements. We find this to be particularly true in this case where parties of relatively equal bargaining power, both represented by counsel, selected the law of the state to govern their contract.

Second, the plain language of § 23–355 neither expressly nor impliedly prohibits modification or waiver of a statutory remedy. Typically, when the Arizona Legislature intends to preclude employers and employees from avoiding statutory rights or remedies with an express contractual provision, the statute either prohibits waiver or voids contractual provisions that limit an employee's rights or an employer's liabilities. Section 23–355 includes no language of prohibition and gives no indication that the legislature intended to preclude the parties' right as a matter of contract to resolve by express language the damages available upon breach of an employment contract.

Further, we note that under the plain language of the statute, the award of treble damages for the bad-faith withholding of wages is discretionary with the court. When the court, by express direction of the legislature, is given discretion to reject treble damages, it follows that parties to a contract, at least arguably, may likewise exercise discretion to choose a jurisdiction that does not provide for them.

In light of the above, we hold that Arizona statutory law does not preclude parties from agreeing by express contractual provision in a negotiated contract to surrender the right to a statutory remedy under § 23–355. Because they may do so by express provision, it follows, under the law, that they may do so by adopting the law of another state.

We further hold that the court of appeals erred by collapsing the analysis of subsections (1) and (2)(b) of Restatement § 187 by engaging in a discussion of state policy. Therefore, because the disputed issue in the instant case is one that the parties were able to resolve pursuant to the express language of § 187(1), we need not address the question whether application of the law of Texas, the state chosen by the contracting parties, would violate a fundamental policy of Arizona.

DISPOSITION

We hold that parties experienced in business, represented by counsel, and having relatively equal bargaining strength, may, by express provision in a negotiated contract, surrender the statutory remedy under A.R.S. § 23–355. We therefore validate and give effect to the parties' choice of Texas law to govern this controversy. Accordingly, that portion of the court of appeals' opinion addressing the treble damage award is vacated and the matter is remanded to the superior court for further proceedings consistent with this opinion.

. . .

Understanding the Case:

1. *Treble Damages:*   Treble damages are damages that are three times the amount of otherwise recoverable compensation damages. Thus, in this case, the lower court awarded Swanson $450,000, or three times the $150,000 contractual severance amount TIB owed Swanson, due to TIB's failure to pay her that severance. Treble damages both encourage people to bring their claims—here, employees such as Swanson who have been deprived of contractually promised compensation—and also deter undesirable conduct—here, an employer's withholding of legally owed compensation.

Comprehension and Thought Questions:

1. Which state's laws did the employment agreement specify as governing?
2. Will an Arizona court always uphold the parties' choice of law? If not, in what circumstances will an Arizona court not uphold such a choice? What policies does such a rule support?
3. Did the court uphold the parties' choice of law in this case? Why or why not?
4. Did the court respect the language in the parties' contract that stated that their choice of law applied "without regard to the principles of conflicts [sic] of laws"?
5. Do you think most laypeople understand the consequences of picking a state's laws to govern a contract?

Hypothetical Variations:

1. What if Swanson lived and worked in Arizona, but TIB, who drafted the employment agreement, selected Texas law to govern to avoid having to pay treble damages in the circumstance addressed in this case?
2. What if A.R.S. § 23-355 required a court to award the employee treble damages?

PRACTICE PROBLEM 2-2

Harley Shaw was just accepted to law school at the Des Moines School of Law. Before starting school, Harley visited Des Moines to find somewhere to live. After touring several apartments, he decided he liked The Mirage Apartments best. So he met with the leasing officer, Bernice Angel, about leasing an apartment at The Mirage Apartments. While Bernice was located in Des Moines, The Mirage Apartments were owned by a company called Mirage Corp., which is headquartered in Spokane, Washington.

At Harley's request, Bernice e-mailed a copy of Mirage Corp.'s standard lease to Harley. That lease contained the following provision:

> If either party must bring legal action to enforce any provision of this lease, the prevailing party shall be entitled to recover its attorneys' fees and costs from the other party.

The draft lease did not identify a governing law.

1. Assuming Harley ends up leasing an apartment at The Mirage Apartments, which state's law would likely govern the lease? Iowa

2. Should the parties pick which state's laws will govern the lease? Why or why not? maybe- avoid dispute

3. If the parties decide to insert a governing law provision into the lease, which state's laws should they pick to govern the lease—Iowa's or Washington's? For your reference, the state laws on attorneys' fee provisions in leases are set out below.

4. If we assume that Washington law governs this lease, does that mean that if Harley has to sue Mirage Corp. under the lease for any reason, he must do so in a Washington court?

5. What if the parties select Washington law to govern, and Mirage Corp. ends up suing Harley in Iowa (assuming there is personal jurisdiction over him there) for past due rent? Will Harley successfully be able to argue that the choice of law violates a fundamental policy in Iowa?

Iowa § 562A.11
1. A rental agreement shall not provide that the tenant or landlord:
    a. Agrees to waive or to forego rights or remedies under this chapter provided that this restriction shall not apply to rental agreements covering single family residences on land assessed as agricultural land and located in an unincorporated area;
    b. Authorizes a person to confess judgment on a claim arising out of the rental agreement;
    c. Agrees to pay the other party's attorney fees; or
    d. Agrees to the exculpation or limitation of any liability of the other party arising under law or to indemnify the other party for that liability or the costs connected therewith.

[handwritten margin note: → mandatory; can't contract out of it]

2. A provision prohibited by subsection 1 included in a rental agreement is unenforceable. If a landlord willfully uses a rental agreement containing provisions known by the landlord to be prohibited, a tenant may recover actual damages sustained by the tenant and not more than three months' periodic rent and reasonable attorney fees.

Washington Rev. Code § 4.84.330

In any action on a contract or lease . . . where such contract or lease specifically provides that attorneys' fees and costs, which are incurred to enforce the provisions of such contract or lease, shall be awarded to one of the parties, the prevailing party, whether he or she is the party specified in the contract or lease or not, shall be entitled to reasonable attorneys' fees in addition to costs and necessary disbursements.

Attorneys' fees provided for by this section shall not be subject to waiver by the parties to any contract or lease . . . . Any provision in any such contract or lease which provides for a waiver of attorneys' fees is void.

As used in this section "prevailing party" means the party in whose favor final judgment is rendered.

D. GOVERNING LAW

1. Common Law

Now that you know that contract law is primarily state law and how to determine which state's laws govern a contract, you must next determine what the law is in that state.

Contract law is largely a matter of common law. The term **common law** refers to the accumulation of judicial decisions in a particular jurisdiction.

Common law develops as follows: where there is a dispute between two or more parties to a contract that cannot be resolved by the parties themselves, either of those parties can seek to have a court resolve that dispute. Eventually a trial court issues a decision in that case in the form of a judicial opinion. That opinion contains the court's holding as well as the court's reasoning. Those opinions create common law in that jurisdiction on the matters decided by the court in those cases.

If one of the parties to a dispute is not satisfied with the trial court's decision—either with the facts as found by the court, with its statement of law, or with how the court applied the law to the facts—it can appeal that decision or any aspect of that decision to the next highest court. An **appeal** is essentially a request that the court next up the ladder in the judicial hierarchy review the trial court's decision. In terms of the standard of review, an appellate court will review the trial court's statement of law *de novo*—meaning, anew, without deferring to the trial court's statement of law. However, an appellate court reviews a trial court's findings of fact only to determine if they are clearly erroneous. The reason appellate courts apply this deferential standard to trial courts' findings of fact is because appellate courts do not conduct independent fact-finding; only the trial courts do. Thus, appellate courts largely defer to trial courts' findings of fact.

If an appellate court agrees to hear an appeal, then it, too, issues a decision on the matter appealed. This decision, too, creates common law in that jurisdiction.

If the appellate court disagrees with the trial court—either on its statement of law or findings of fact—the appellate court can overrule the trial court's decision, or the relevant part of that decision. That is because higher courts' decisions take precedence over lower courts' decisions.

But what is to prevent a judge from deciding a case based on that judge's whim? After all, if a judge decided a case based on his or her whim, or what he or she had for breakfast that day, there would be little consistency in decision-making. That, in turn, would lead to unpredictability and uncertainty in our system of justice.

It is the doctrine of **stare decisis** that provides the essential stability and predictability to our common law system. Under that doctrine—which, literally translated, means "to stand by that which is decided"—a court must follow the law from prior decisions of the deciding court or of higher-ranking appellate courts. Thus, cases serve as **precedents** for future cases—that is, authoritative statements of law for future decisions. That is true not only for contracts cases, but for all cases decided by courts. Consequently, if a later case involves essentially the same dispute as a previous case being decided by the same court or a higher-ranking court, the court must follow the precedent set by the prior case.

Despite the general need to follow precedents in a common law system such as ours, sometimes courts overrule existing law. This is done where either a rule of law proves to be unwise or impractical, or social norms change, necessitating a different rule to reflect those changing norms.

Also, if a legislature passes a statute that conflicts with or is otherwise inconsistent with common law, courts must stop following that common law and must instead follow the statute. That is because in the hierarchy of law, statutes take precedence over the common law. As you will see in Section D.3 below, there are in fact some instances where state legislatures have passed statutes on matters affecting contract law. Thus, those statutes take priority over any inconsistent common law.

The following is a diagrammatic representation of the relationship between the common law and statutory law:

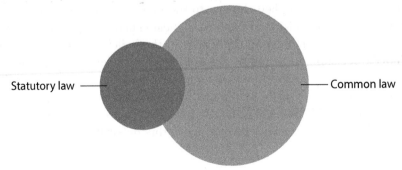

Statutory law ——   —— Common law

As this diagram shows, where the common law and statutory law overlap—that is, address the same topic of contract law—the statute takes priority over the common law. Otherwise the common law applies. This diagram further shows, through the comparative sizes of the circles, that the common law of contracts is more extensive than the statutory law of contracts.

Finally, keep in mind that each case has its own set of facts. And those facts play a central role in a court's decision. In fact, changing one outcome-determinative fact could change the outcome of a case. Moreover, how the facts are portrayed to a judge can affect the outcome of a case. For this reason, it is important to always think about the factual context in a given case, and how either a change in a fact, or even a change in how a fact could have been presented by a lawyer, might lead to a different outcome.

2. Classic Common Law vs. Modern Common Law

The fact that contracts are largely governed by the common law raises the question how that common law developed, and what goals it served. This discussion will briefly review the historical development of the common law of contracts in the United States. In so doing, it will explore the guiding principles that were followed in deciding those classic cases. This discussion will also explore more modern principles that guide contract law judicial decisions. However, do not think that the classic cases, and the guiding principles that animated them, are no longer relevant. As you will see from this discussion and throughout the book, many of those classic principles remain quite relevant and underlie many doctrines courts continue to apply today.

Contract law in the United States largely developed in the nineteenth century. As the U.S. economy grew during the Industrial Revolution, there was a need for a mechanism to enforce promises for future performance. Courts developed contract law to respond to that need.

During that period, courts tended to defer to the parties' expression of the contract and enforced the terms of the contract agreed upon by the parties. That deference and freedom of contract led to economic certainty, as parties could be assured that the court would enforce the terms of their economic exchange. Such certainty was largely provided through doctrines such as "**caveat emptor,**" which means let the buyer beware. In other words, courts did not police the fairness of the bargain or the bargaining process absent egregiously bad conduct by the counterparty. If a buyer or another contractual party wanted a specific protection under a contract, such as an assurance about the quality of the product it was buying under the contract, it had to negotiate for that protection.

That era of certainty and of freedom of contract is often referred to as the **classic period** in contract law. However, the classic period is not confined to the nineteenth century. In fact, many doctrines in contract law continue to represent the classic approach to contract law, setting out clear, bright-line rules that favor enforcing the parties' bargain. You will thus see that many of the laws included in this book are classic in nature, and that some courts continue to strongly favor classic laws.

However, by the late nineteenth and early twentieth century, there was a sense that the common law was out of touch with reality. That is, judges were no longer viewed as bringing about a just result by simply enforcing the bargain as struck by parties, for that ignored the fairness of the bargain and the bargaining process. Legislators stepped into the arena and began to provide statutory protections for relationships often governed by contract. For example, starting in the late 1800s, state legislatures began passing consumer protection statutes designed to protect consumers from unethical and exploitive activity by merchants.

Courts, too, responded to the perceived deficiencies in the classical common law. They responded by creating doctrines to police the fairness of the bargain, and weaknesses in the bargaining parties or process. Courts also created alternative doctrines for promissory recovery where the bargain theory did not provide a remedy, yet fairness suggested that a party should recover on a promise.

This era of policing the bargain and protecting commercial parties is known as the **modern period** in contract law. Moreover, laws that are designed to police the bargain, bargaining parties, and bargaining processes are referred to as taking the modern approach to the law.

You will identify many of the doctrines discussed in this book as modern in nature. For example, you will see the modern theory at work when you study many of the "defenses" in Chapters 17-21, as well as promissory estoppel as an alternative theory of recovery in Chapter 22. However, keep in mind that the modern theory of contracts did not only give rise to these specific legal doctrines. You will see that many classical contract law rules, too, have tinges of the modern theory. That is especially the case where this book relies on the Restatement, for the Restatement has taken a decidedly modern view of contracts and contract law.

3. Statutory Law and Uniform Laws

There are some aspects of contract law that are not common law but rather statutory in nature. Statutes are laws passed by the legislature. Of course Congress, too, can pass statutes on matters of contract law. The Federal Arbitration Act, discussed above, is one example of Congress passing a statute affecting contracts.

When a legislature passes a statute on a particular matter of contract law, that statute takes priority over any inconsistent state common law. However, the common law still applies where that statute is silent on a particular topic. Moreover, the common law can develop to clarify any ambiguities in that statute. Thus, the common law remains an important part of contract law even where there is a relevant statute.

One example of a state contract law statute is a **statute of frauds**. As you will see in Chapter 17, a state's statute of frauds is a statute that requires certain contracts to be in writing and signed by the party against whom the contract is being enforced. These requirements exist to decrease the likelihood that someone will defraud the court by lying as to the existence of an important contract. Where a statute of frauds exists, it takes priority over any inconsistent common law. However, statutes of frauds do not address every issue involving the writing or signature requirements. For example, often statutes of frauds do not specify whether multiple writings can together satisfy the statute of frauds, nor do they specify whether a typed signature at the bottom of an e-mail satisfies the signature requirement. The common law fills those gaps and might specify, for example, that multiple writings can together satisfy the statute of frauds and that a party meets the signature requirement by typing its name at the bottom of an e-mail.

Importantly, every state has a statute that governs contracts for sales of goods. The term **goods** refers to tangible personal property such as tables and mouse pads. It does not, however, cover real estate or service contracts.

Except Louisiana, every state's statute governing sales of goods is based on Article 2 of the **Uniform Commercial Code** (UCC). The UCC is a set of uniform acts issued by the Uniform Law Commission (ULC, also known as the NCCUSL) together with the American Law Institute (ALI).[9] Both of those organizations seek to reduce uncertainty in the law stemming from the lack of uniformity among states in areas where uniformity is seen as desirable. To become the law in a state, the legislature of a state must adopt a statute based on one of these uniform acts.

The promulgators' goal for the UCC was to achieve uniformity in states' laws on commercial transactions. The reason for uniformity in the area of commercial transactions is to remove the uncertainty as to what law applies to those transactions. They have also sought to simplify and clarify contractual terms through standardizing those terms. The use of standardized terms reduces transaction costs, as parties do not have to negotiate or document those terms for them to apply. Together, a single set of predictable legal standards across all states and standardized contractual terms can facilitate interstate commercial transactions, thereby increasing interstate commerce and bolstering the economy.

In addition to Article 2 on sales of goods, the UCC contains Article 2A on leases; Article 3 on negotiable instruments; Article 4 on bank deposits; Article 4A on funds transfers; Article 5 on letters of credit; Article 6 on bulk transfers;

---

9. *Uniform Commercial Code UCC*, ali.org, http://www.ali.org/publications/show/uniform-commercial-code (last visited Sept. 22, 2018).

Article 7 on warehouse receipts, bills of lading, and other documents of title; and Article 9 on secured transactions. Article 1 sets out general provisions of the UCC such as definitions and rules of interpretation. It applies to all other articles of the UCC, including Article 2.

The reach of the UCC—especially Article 2—is actually broader than the code itself suggests. That is because, in addition to governing transactions that fall within its scope, the UCC often serves as a source of guidance for states even in transactions that do not fall within its scope. So, for example, while Article 2 does not apply to transactions in real estate, courts deciding disputes between parties to a real estate contract often look to Article 2 to help resolve that dispute. As such, the UCC even shapes transactions governed by the common law.

Professor Karl Llewellyn was the principal drafter of the original version of Article 2, which was first published in the 1950s. His goal was to bring the law on transactions for goods in line with business practice so that it reflected the expectation of parties engaged in these transactions. One of the primary ways Llewellyn achieved this was through Article 2's standardized default terms—that is, he wrote those standard default terms to reflect actual business practices. Today, Article 2 continues to set out standard default contractual terms that reflect customary business practices.

Despite the seeming uniformity in this area of law, states can—and often do—make changes to the versions of these uniform acts their legislatures adopt. Some of those changes are made at the time the state adopts one of these uniform acts. Some changes are made through amendments to the statute after its initial adoption. Either way, the consequence is that each state has its own state-specific variations of Article 2. That means in advising a client on contract law governed by Article 2, you would still need to research that state's version of Article 2.

On the other hand, most of Article 2 simply sets out default gap-filler terms rather than mandatory terms. Parties are free to include in their contracts terms different than those default gap-filler terms. In fact, sophisticated commercial parties, in dealing with one another, often do contract around those default terms.

This book considers some of the more salient sections of Article 2, to make sure you are familiar with the scope of the statute and how it operates. The book also includes some material on Article 2 to allow you to begin working with a statute in a field that is primarily regulated by the common law. This is an important skill to develop not only for the field of contracts, but for other legal fields as well.

4. Restatement (Second) of Contracts

As mentioned above, the creation of the UCC was largely due to the efforts of the ALI together with the ULC. The ALI has pursued other projects, too, to address the historic lack of certainty and uniformity in the area of contracts. Namely, in 1932, the ALI created a summary of contract law called the Restatement of Contracts. The ALI adopted an updated version of this restatement in 1981. This updated version is called the Restatement (Second) of Contracts.

The design of each of these restatements is to set out black-letter rules. Each rule is followed by commentary explaining the rule. The commentary also includes illustrations of how the rule applies to different scenarios. Many of those illustrations are based on actual cases.

The primary difference between the first Restatement of Contracts and the Restatement (Second) of Contracts is that the first Restatement of Contracts sought to achieve predictability and uniformity, sometimes at the expense of flexibility. It did that by providing rules using clear, rigid standards. However, by the time the ALI adopted the Restatement (Second) of Contracts, it realized the need for more generalized, flexible rules. Thus, the rule summaries in the Restatement (Second) of Contracts are broader and give more discretion to courts.

The Restatement (Second) of Contracts is not law, as it is not a statute. It also is not a uniform act that states can adopt by enacting a law based on it, like the UCC. Again, it is designed to merely summarize the law of contracts.

Interestingly, the Restatement (Second) of Contracts does not always reflect the law as it exists in a majority of states. Rather, it reflects what the drafters view as the "best" law. In some cases, the "best" law is not the law in a majority of states, but rather the law as it is hoped to exist. Even so, judges often look to the Restatement (Second) of Contracts for guidance in resolving open questions of contract law. In that way, the Restatement (Second) of Contracts serves as a useful authority for judges when developing common law through their decisions. And to the extent it sets out aspirational standards, it also helps drive states toward adopting those standards.

The Restatement (Second) of Contracts is not the only law restatement that exists. In fact, the ALI has issued restatements in many other areas of law as well, including torts,[10] property,[11] agency,[12] and restitution.[13] Because the Restatement (Second) of Contracts is the restatement that modern courts look to in deciding matters of contract law, this book refers to that restatement simply as the Restatement. Where this book refers either to the first Restatement of Contract, or to any other restatement of law, it specifies what other restatement is being referred to.

---

10. Restatement (Second) of Torts (1965).
11. Restatement (Third) of Prop.: Mortgs. (1997).
12. Restatement (Third) of Agency (2006).
13. Restatement of Restitution (1937).

PRACTICE PROBLEM 2-3

Imagine you are a judicial clerk for Sam Stone, a justice on the Iowa Supreme Court. Justice Stone, along with the other members of the Iowa Supreme Court, just heard oral arguments from counsel to Butch Builder and Harry Homeowner on the implied warranty of habitability. Specifically, Builder's counsel argued that while Iowa common law creates an implied warranty of habitability for a builder who builds a home for a homeowner, the law should allow a builder to expressly disclaim this implied warranty. Homeowner's counsel, on the other hand, argued that the law should not allow the builder to disclaim this implied warranty in any circumstance, as it would allow the stronger party (the builder) to remove a key protection for the weaker party (the homeowner) in a context where a homeowner has no expertise and no control.

Justice Stone asks you to research whether any Iowa court has ruled on this question before. He also asks you to research approaches taken by courts in other states to this question. Finally, he asks you to see if there is anything in Iowa's version of Article 2 of the Uniform Commercial Code on implied warranties relating to the sale of goods that could be used to support an outcome in this case.

Before you conduct this research (and for purposes of this question, DO NOT perform this research!), first answer the following questions:

1. What if a lower Iowa court ruled on this question in a similar case five years ago and expressly allowed such a disclaimer? Would the Iowa Supreme Court be bound by that holding? *probably*

2. Assume that the Iowa Supreme Court was faced with a similar question 50 years ago. At that time, the court allowed the builder to expressly disclaim the implied warranty. However, Justice Stone wants to hold now that a builder can no longer disclaim the implied warranty. Is it possible for the court to reverse itself on this matter? If so, should it? What are some reasons for and against this action? *yes+yes ; see H.O's counsel argument*

3. What if you find that the Supreme Courts of a handful of other states have upheld such disclaimers? Would the Iowa Supreme Court be bound by those holdings? *no- only persuasive*

4. What if Iowa's version of Article 2 of the UCC allows for the disclaimer of a similar waiver in the context of the sale of a good? How will that likely impact the Iowa Supreme Court's decision in this case? *persuasive, but a home is diff from a good*

5. If the Iowa Supreme Court ends up holding that such disclaimers are *per se* void and not enforceable, would such a rule seem more in line with the classic perspective of contract law or the modern view of contract law? *MODERN*

E. RELATIONSHIP OF CONTRACT LAW TO OTHER AREAS OF LAW

The existence of a 1L course devoted to contracts might give you the impression that contracts exists as a separate field of practice. But that is not the case. In fact, even the largest U.S. law firms, whose attorneys have some of the most specialized practices, do not have separate practice groups called contracts. This is because while knowing contract law is often necessary for a lawyer in helping the client achieve its goals, it is not sufficient. Rather, contracts are merely one tool attorneys in virtually all practice areas use to help their clients achieve their goals. As such, attorneys in many fields of practice need to know contract law.

For example, real estate lawyers help their clients buy, manage, develop, finance, sell, and otherwise deal in real estate. Real estate lawyers need to know contract law, as contracts are the primary tool through which clients effectuate those transactions. However, real estate lawyers must also be able to advise their clients on the specific real property laws applicable to these transactions. Moreover, real estate lawyers would be expected to know the terms customarily included in the relevant real estate contracts.

Similarly, many tax lawyers advise their clients on the tax implications of planned transactions. Tax lawyers need to know contract law to understand not only the structure of the transaction that the contract sets out, but also how to protect the client's interests in that transaction through the contract. Yet that knowledge would clearly not be adequate for the tax lawyer. Instead, tax lawyers must also know the tax consequences of the structure of the transaction as laid out in the contract and how to minimize those consequences in compliance with tax law.

Even lawyers who represent defendants in tort actions need to know contract law, to be able to draft enforceable settlement agreements. And if the tort involves fraud or some other wrongdoing arising out of a contractual relationship, the lawyer would have an even greater need to understand contract law, to be able to mount an effective defense. But again, that knowledge would not be sufficient, as the tort lawyer would also need to understand the relevant tort law, as well as litigation procedure.

In sum, knowing contract law is important in almost all legal practice areas; however, it is not sufficient for competently representing clients. Thus, as you take future law school classes, you will want to think about how you can employ the knowledge from your Contracts course to solve problems raised in those classes.

Now that you have studied the structure and role of contract law, read through and answer the questions that follow the Simulation Problem for Chapter 2, which is located in Appendix A.

CHAPTER 3

Parts of a Contract and Contract Terms

This chapter explains the typical structure and terms of written contracts. We include this material because it is essential for you to understand, beyond the law, how the business needs of your clients are served by the structure and content of each contract. It also is important for you to understand how parties can use contract structure and terms to satisfy the legal requirements for contract formation discussed in the forthcoming chapters. Finally, this chapter will allow you to see how parties can use contract terms to customize how mandatory aspects of contract law apply to them, as well as how they can use contract terms to modify default rules.

Another one of our primary goals in this chapter is to familiarize you with the "big picture" of what the typical contract contains. That way, you can start to understand the rationale for contract terms now, in the safety of a classroom environment, instead of when you are in practice and "thrown into the deep end" of a transaction involving many different contracts.

We should note at the outset that although there is no single contractual structure, and the content of each contract varies with the transaction, the same issues appear time and time again in written contracts. Thus, this chapter explores the typical organizational structure of a contract. In doing so, it also considers many terms and provisions that are common in contracts.[1]

Appendices B and C at the end of this casebook set out two complete sample contracts: a purchase agreement (Appendix B) and an employment agreement (Appendix C). As you complete each subsection of this chapter, you will want to examine the relevant section of each of these sample contracts to determine

---

1. The word "term" refers to the substance of the parties' agreement on discrete aspects of their contractual relationship. The word "provision" refers to the textual depiction of that term in the written contract.

whether you can identify where the relevant section appears, whether you can determine why it was drafted the way it was, and whether you have any concerns with the drafted provisions based on the reading. Moreover, you will want to consider *why* each party would or would not want to include the provision you are examining. We have included Practice Problems tied to these sample contracts as well, to help walk you through these tasks. By performing these tasks, you will begin to understand how to draft and structure contracts.

A. FACTORS IN DETERMINING STRUCTURE AND CONTENT OF CONTRACT

1. Purpose

The content and structure of a contract are driven primarily, if not exclusively, by the functions of the contract. Therefore, when preparing a contract, an attorney needs to understand first and foremost what the client's purpose of the contract is. In other words, the lawyer needs to understand why the client needs the contract. As discussed in Chapter 1, a contract often serves many purposes, including helping the parties plan for the future and forcing the parties to share information and to build trust as they start a relationship. Recall, though, the basic definition of a contract: a promise that, if broken, allows the aggrieved party to obtain a remedy. This means that the contract should contain the promises and terms that your client deems important and wants to be able to rely on. The existence of a legal remedy should deter the other party from breaching any contractual promises and also provide an avenue for redress for your client in the event that the other party breaks a promise.

2. Legal Requirements

To properly form a contract, the written document reflecting that contract needs to satisfy a number of legal requirements. Those requirements will be explored in detail in later chapters. In Section B, we will refer briefly to the different legal requirements that each part of a written contract is designed to satisfy so that you will understand the doctrines and their relationship with the written contract better as you encounter them later in the book.

3. Protect Expected Transaction Value for the Client

Typically, the different terms of a contract exist to protect the value of the transaction to the client. That means a term typically is included to ensure that your client receives exactly what it sought from the transaction. For example, if your client is entering a contract for landscaping services with a landscaping company, what does your client expect to receive from this transaction? The most obvious answer is, of course, landscaping services. But what does that mean? What type and quality of landscaping services? How often will the services be rendered? Who is responsible for performing the services? What happens if your client is not satisfied with the services or if the company fails to provide them? This list could go on and on, but for now we can say that contractual terms are designed to address the risks, both known and unknown, associated with entering into any promissory relationship, to ensure the client gets what it bargained for. Since we cannot physically control other parties and whether they perform as desired, we attempt to legally control them by entering into a relationship (the contract) that provides the aggrieved party with a remedy if the other party does not perform as desired.

Identifying what is appropriate to include in a contract will require you to develop what experienced transactional attorneys call good "business sense," or the ability to identify the realistic risks and relevant issues that need to be addressed in the contract. This skill takes time to develop and is one of those frustrating growing pains that all attorneys must endure. You can start now, though. When examining a prospective contractual relationship, instead of thinking about contract doctrine, you should start by thinking about what your client wants, and what can go wrong in the relationship. In the landscaping services relationship above, there are many things that could go wrong. If you can identify what they are, then you will have a pretty good list of issues that should be addressed in the contract. The different provisions discussed in Section B below provide different, often overlapping, avenues to address those issues.

PRACTICE PROBLEM 3-1

Imagine that you are a solo practitioner and are engaged to represent your first client, AmeriCo Inc. AmeriCo is contemplating entering into a contract with an office equipment leasing company, Kary Services, Inc. Your client's CEO and owner, Tracey Foster, informs you that Kary Services will provide certain office equipment to AmeriCo on a temporary basis. This apparently will represent a significant cost savings to AmericCo. Tracey asks you to begin preparing a draft of an agreement between AmeriCo and Kary Services.

1. What questions do you have for Tracey before you start preparing the agreement? *Cost?, how long?, what equipment?, maintenance? flexibility*

2. As you begin to think about what the contract should include, what can "go wrong" in the relationship between AmeriCo and Kary?

→ equip malfunction & they don't fix
→ overcharge
→ cancel rental when she still needs it

B. SPECIFIC PARTS OF THE CONTRACT AND TYPICAL CONTENT

1. Beginning Sections of the Written Contract

a. Title

Most written contracts will contain a title at the top of the first page of the agreement. For example, a lease for real property often will have the words "Lease Agreement" at the top of the first page. A separate title at the top, however, is not required to form a contract or for written contracts in particular. Instead, **titles** help inform the reader, whether the counterparty, a third party or an adjudicator, about the basic subject matter of the agreement. Again, because titles are not required, an agreement may cover many different topics, regardless of what the title is or whether there is a title to the agreement at all.

b. Preamble

The **preamble** is the opening sentence or phrase in the agreement, and it generally sets forth the title of the agreement, the parties' names, and the date of the agreement. The sample below contains a typical preamble.

EMPLOYMENT AGREEMENT

> This Employment Agreement ("Agreement"), is entered into on this 16th day of March, 2019, between Sunnyside DayCare, LLC, a Delaware limited liability company ("Employer"), and Jeff Rison ("Employee").

From the preamble, we understand that the two named parties have entered into an employment agreement on March 16, 2018.

There are a couple of issues to consider with the preamble. First, identifying the proper contract parties in the preamble is extremely important and one of the minefields for newer attorneys. Identifying the proper parties means, for example, identifying if any of the parties is a business organization and, if so, identifying the correct business organization that is a party. This might be especially tricky if there are multiple business organizations that are affiliated through common ownership. Moreover, if one of the parties is a business organization, you need to make sure the right person has signed the contract on behalf of that organization. Chapter 9 will help you analyze that question.

You need to know and specify the parties in the contract because individuals and business organizations (such as corporations and limited liability companies) are generally treated as distinct for purposes of contract liability. This means that you need to be very careful about which individual or entity is supposed to be "on the hook" (in other words, contractually bound) for both your client and the counterparty to the contract.

For example, imagine that a plumbing company has contracted with a home-owner to fix some water pipes. If an individual plumber signs the contract instead of the plumbing company, then the homeowner will be able to sue the plumber individually (and not the plumbing company) if the plumber fails to perform any of the obligations in the agreement. If the plumber does not have a lot of assets but the plumbing company does, this could be a bad result for the homeowner, who might not be able to collect if the plumber does not perform the promised obligations. The opposite may be true if the plumbing company is a party but has scant assets.

Another issue to consider is the date of the agreement. By default, the date of the agreement is the effective date, or trigger date, for when the parties' performance obligations become due. This may not be desirable in all instanc-es. For example, if you were signing a contract for waste removal services but did not need the services for a few months, then while the agreement would bear the date it was entered into, you would want the contract to specify that the agreement is not effective until the date on which services are to be first rendered. This is often addressed either in the preamble or in the deal terms provisions, which are discussed below.

Many written contracts take the form of a letter agreement (such as the employment agreement in Appendix C). While those agreement formats might not contain a traditional preamble, they still need to specify the parties to the agreement and the effective date, if different from the date the parties sign. Can you identify the parties and the effective date to the employment agreement in Appendix C?

c. Defined terms

Typically, the preamble is followed by a section of the contract creating defined terms. A **defined term** is a term that has a specific meaning every time it is used within the Agreement. It is created by capitalizing the first letter in the term and then describing what that term means for purposes of the agreement, much as a dictionary sets out the definitions of words. Although a contract might have a separate section listing out many defined terms, contracts often also create defined terms in a substantive section of the contract. The pream-ble to the Employment Agreement set out above takes this approach. In it, "Employee" has been defined as "Jeff Rison." By putting "Employee" in quo-tation marks, we know it is a defined term. Usually where defined terms are created in a substantive part of the contract, they are placed in parentheses following the concept that they define (in this instance, Jeff Rison). By creating this defined term, we understand what Employee means each time it is used throughout the agreement. Thus, the agreement does not have to repeat Jeff Rison's full name throughout the agreement whenever it refers to him.

Defined terms serve many purposes. For one, they help simplify contracts because they eliminate the need to reproduce lengthy or complicated definitions each time a concept is referred to in the agreement. For example, a contract may discuss what the purchase price for particular goods is in multiple places in the agreement. For example, the purchase price will be discussed in reference to when it is to be paid, what happens if the purchase price is not paid on time, who is responsible for paying the purchase price, and so on. What if the purchase price is based on a complicated formula that fluctuates based on the amount of goods purchased each month? By defining "Purchase Price" once (based on that formula), then the parties can simply use that defined term throughout the contract without having to reinsert the full formula every time.

Where a written contract has a separate section setting out defined terms, it is important to read each defined term carefully. The most important details of the agreement often are contained within the definitions.

Each time you encounter a capitalized term within an agreement, you should figure out what that term means by searching for its definition. You should never assume that the capitalization is irrelevant or that everyone knows what a capitalized term means when it is used.

PRACTICE PROBLEM 3-2

Realizing that Kary Services will insist on using its own "form" of equipment lease agreement, you do not draft an equipment lease agreement. Eventually, Kary Services' attorney sends over a draft that contains the following introductory section:

Equipment Lease Agreement

This Equipment Lease Agreement ("Agreement"), dated July _____, 2019, is between AmeriCo Inc. ("AmeriCo"), Tracey Foster, the owner of AmeriCo ("Owner"), and Kary Services, LLC, a Delaware limited liability company and subsidiary of Kary Services, Inc. ("Kary"). *proper party!*

1. Explain to your client any concerns you have based on the preamble.
2. What changes might you propose to the preamble? *don't make Tracey party*

d. Recitals

Many, though not all, written contracts contain **recitals**, which are explanatory sentences below the preamble that explain the reasons for the contract as well as a basic explanation of what the contract is intended to accomplish. They can be short or long and can be labeled "Recitals" or "Background" or even have no title at all. Some attorneys believe that more extensive recitals are particularly important for complicated contracts that might end up in litigation because the recitals can help simplify for the adjudicator what was ultimately supposed to happen in the overall transaction. Conversely, in a simple contract, recitals may be very short or even eliminated. The simple recitals from an employment agreement are below.

RECITALS

This Agreement sets out the terms on which Employer has agreed to hire Employee.

If there was more background relevant to this contract, then the recitals would be more involved. For example, imagine that the agreement was instead a consulting and non-compete agreement pursuant to which Jeff Rison was agreeing to provide services to Sunnyside following Sunnyside's purchase of Jeff's day-care business. Jeff was also agreeing to not compete with Sunnyside for three years after the sale. In that instance, the recitals might be used to describe the larger transaction and to provide a full context for this contract, which might be particularly important with respect to the enforceability of Jeff's promise not to compete.

Because recitals are typically only providing background information regarding the contract and are often viewed as nonbinding, they should not contain important or detailed performance obligations unless those obligations are repeated in the body of the agreement. Alternatively, some attorneys specifically incorporate recitals into the agreement as being binding provisions, with a short statement to that effect.

e. The parties' agreement

After the recitals, most written contracts contain words that indicate that the parties agree to all of the provisions that follow in the agreement. A sample from the professional services agreement appears below.

Therefore, the parties agree as follows:

The "Therefore" is based on the reasons for entering into the contract provided by the recitals. If recitals are omitted, it is common to provide a more basic "The parties agree as follows:".

These words help manifest the parties' intentions to be bound by the written agreement. That intention is further supported by the preamble and the signature block. Accordingly, this helps satisfy the contract law requirements of mutual assent and consideration discussed in Chapters 4-8.

2. Principal Promises and Deal Terms

a. Deal promises

After the beginning provisions described above, most contracts contain the substantive deal terms of the transactions. The **deal terms** define the basic promises of the parties. In other words, who is supposed to pay, and who is supposed to render services or otherwise perform the main bargained-for task? When your client talks about needing a contract, these are the types of provisions they generally have in mind.

This provision describes what each party is promising to do in the contract. It addresses:

1. What the basic promises of each party are;
2. How the promises are to be performed, including in terms of quality, standards of performance, logistical and other requirements; and
3. When each side has to perform.

In a basic services agreement, one party is promising to perform services and the other party is promising to pay for the services. Before an attorney drafts the key promises, however, he or she needs to speak with the client. Through that conversation, the lawyer can figure out what the "deal" is, meaning what the client expects the obligations of each party to be, which typically will be addressed by asking about 1-3 above.

This is where a lawyer can start to use his or her business sense. For example, consider the employment agreement between Sunnyside DayCare, LLC and Jeff Rison mentioned above. If you are representing Jeff, you probably would want to ask Jeff what services Jeff will be providing; to whom will he report at the company; how much Jeff will be paid for the services; and how often he will be paid. Once you have a better idea of the deal terms, then you are ready to prepare or review the key performance provisions. As you prepare the written agreement, if you need to confirm certain information with the client or have questions, you can include a note in brackets to discuss that information and any questions with the client (or send an e-mail enumerating all of the open issues). This bracketed language and the brackets themselves will be taken out later, when you send the draft to the other party's attorney. If it is in brackets, it means that it has not been finalized yet or needs to be confirmed. Of course, other attorneys may use different systems to keep track of the open issues that need to be addressed before sending a contract draft to the counterparty's attorney.

Below is a sample provision containing the contractual deal provisions proposed by Sunnyside and the bracketed questions for Jeff Rison that his attorney had for Jeff after reviewing the contract. It is important to note that the questions below can be generated without much knowledge of the transaction. The attorney instead just tried to think about the relevant issues involved with having the lawyer's client, Jeff Rison, provide consulting services. In other words, you need to think about how to ensure your client receives the benefits or value he is seeking under the agreement.

1. Services

During the term of your employment, you shall act as the Company's general manager. You shall have the power, authority, duties, and responsibilities as are reasonably necessary for the position. [SHOULD THERE BE ANY LIMITS

ON THE GENERAL MANAGER'S AUTHORITY (SUCH AS ENTERING INTO TRANSACTIONS BEYOND A CERTAIN DOLLAR THRESHOLD)?] The Company shall have the authority to expand or limit your power, authority, duties, and responsibilities, and to override your actions. You shall devote your best efforts and full business time and attention exclusively to the business and affairs of the Company. [CONFIRM THIS WILL BE A FULLTIME POSITION] During the term of your employment, you will report directly to the President. [CONFIRM]

As you can see from the above example, the attorney reviewing the contract did not assume that any of the provisions were final as written. Instead, he or she recognized the need for client input and tried to highlight those areas that the client should focus on.

It is important to take your time when preparing or reviewing the key deal terms. These provisions will vary widely depending on the type of transaction. For example, some contracts involve only a single performance, such as a sale of a particular asset (such as the crane in the Crane Purchase Agreement in Appendix B). In such an instance, the deal terms would address the seller's obligation to deliver the particular asset and the buyer's obligation to pay the purchase price for the particular asset.

PRACTICE PROBLEM 3-3

1. Your client, AmeriCo, informs you that it expects to pay $500 per month for each high-speed high-volume color printer it leases from Kary Services. Kary also will be obligated to maintain the printers. Draft the performance provisions for the contract between AmeriCo and Kary Services. Include any draft notes or questions for your client in brackets.

2. Imagine that you were asked to represent Jeff Rison in connection with his employment agreement with Sunnyside. Identify the deal and performance provisions of the Employment Agreement attached as Appendix C. What questions do you have for Jeff after reviewing those sections?

b. Term and termination

Many written contracts typically have a section concerning the term of the contract. The **term** of a contract addresses the length of time during which the parties are obligated to perform their promises under the contract, including the key performance obligations described above. A contract's term should be discussed with the client. Does your client want the contract to be in place for a long time or a short time? This is not a question that the attorney can necessarily answer without client input. If the client feels that the contract secures important future benefits that she wants to be able to rely on for many years, then obviously a longer term for the contract would be appropriate. On the other hand, the client may want a shorter term for the contract when dealing with a new or unknown supplier.

Many contracts contemplate a continuing relationship between the parties. In those contracts, the parties have ongoing or recurring promises that need to be performed over a long term. Other contracts are based on a single performance to be performed at a particular time, such as a contract for goods to be sold and delivered at a particular place and time. In that scenario, once that single performance has taken place, the term of the agreement will be over and the parties may have very little to do with one another (unless, for example, the performance was defective).

Many contracts also contain provisions that address shortening or extending the term of the contract. A provision that permits one party to shorten the contract's term is known as a **termination provision**. It is typical for a client to want to be able to terminate the contract early if the other party does not perform as required under the contract. Sometimes, though, a client may want the ability to terminate the contract even if the other party had performed its obligations as required.

For example, consider the employment agreement between Jeff Rison and Sunnyside above. Jeff might prefer an employment agreement that contains an explicit term, such as three years. If Jeff's employment is for a term, Jeff would likely negotiate to have Sunnyside pay Jeff severance compensation if Jeff is terminated before the end of the term without "Cause." That means if Sunnyside terminates Jeff's employment before the end of year three without having "Cause" to do so, then it would have a duty to pay Jeff the agreed-upon severance. In contrast, if Sunnyside terminates Jeff's employment when "Cause" existed, then likely it would not owe Jeff this severance. Because much rides on what constitutes "Cause," this defined term would be heavily negotiated by the parties.

On the other hand, Sunnyside may prefer (like many employers) to employ their employees on an at-will basis, meaning that Sunnyside could terminate Jeff's employment at any time and for any or no reason without liability. In the United States, virtually all states have a default rule that employment is at-will. Thus, if an employment agreement does not specify a term or specific undertaking to be performed by the employee, the employee is deemed to be employed at-will.

Whether a party should be able to terminate a contract early depends largely on the parties, their relationship, and the larger context. For example, where one party has spent a lot of time or effort to create a relationship or has committed a lot of resources based on the presumed existence of the contract in the future, the contract would likely make it difficult to terminate early. For example, if a manufacturer is going to have to spend a lot of money to buy special equipment to supply a product to a particular customer, the manufacturer would not want the customer to be able to terminate the contract very easily.

Otherwise, the manufacturer could be left in a situation where the customer never purchases enough finished products to justify the manufacturer's purchase of the special equipment.

The following is a sample term and termination provision:

6. Termination

a. This Agreement begins on the date first written above and terminates on the one-year anniversary of that date; except that this Agreement's term will be extended for additional one-year periods unless one party provides written notice of its intention not to extend the term of this Agreement at least thirty days before the end of the then-current term.

   b. Either party may terminate all or part of this Agreement should the other party breach this Agreement, including any of its representations and warranties, but only if the aggrieved party has provided written notice of the breach to the breaching party, and the breaching party has not cured such breach within five days from the date of such notice.

As you can see, the provision provides for the basic term of one year. It also provides for the ability of a party to terminate early if the other party has breached so long as the other party received notice of the occurrence of the breach and not cured the breach within a certain amount of time following its receipt of notice.

In addition, the above provision also provides for automatic renewal of one-year terms unless one party elects otherwise. This provision is known as an "evergreen" provision because, like the evergreen, it renews every year. Assuming that the relationship has gone well, and that neither party wants to exit the relationship, the term will automatically be extended at the end of each year for an additional year unless one party provides written notice to the other to the contrary.

As you can tell from this discussion, term and termination provisions need to be carefully tailored to fit the client's expectations regarding the duration of the other party's obligations, both in the ordinary course of the relationship where neither party has breached as well as following a breach of the agreement by the other party. Thus, a lawyer would want to consider, as discussed above, whether the client needs the assurance of a longer term or a shorter term, whether the client needs the right to "get out" of the contract early, or whether the client needs the option to extend the term if desired.

Termination provisions also often address the effect of termination on other obligations under the agreement. That is because termination does not mean all of the parties' obligations are terminated. For example, what if Jeff had provided ten days of service to Sunnyside DayCare before Jeff decided to terminate the agreement? In that instance, while Jeff has terminated his services, the agreement should not provide that the contract completely terminates at that time—if it did, Sunnyside could not sue Jeff to enforce the contract against him, as there would be no contract to enforce! Moreover, even if Jeff performs employment services for the full three years, while his employment term would end at that time, the employment contract would undoubtedly provide that some aspects of Jeff's employment agreement will survive the end of Jeff's employment term. For example, the agreement might provide that at the end of Jeff's employment term, Sunnyside has to pay Jeff for all services he performed before the end of the term. It might also contain a promise by Jeff not to compete with Sunnyside for a period of time after his employment term ends. In other words, while lawyers and business people often refer to the termination of a contract (by which they mean the termination of the primary performance obligations under the contract), often many obligations survive beyond the date of a contract's termination. Attorneys help advise clients regarding which obligations should survive termination and prepare and negotiate the written contract accordingly.

c. Conditions

Sometimes a party might not want to agree unconditionally to perform the promises stated in the written contract. Instead, the party might want to include **conditions**, which are requirements that must be satisfied in order to trigger a particular party's obligations under the contract. These are most common in significant financial transactions, such as substantial purchase or borrowing transactions. Examples of conditions to a purchase agreement for a crane are below.

Article 6
Buyer's Conditions

The Buyer is obligated to consummate the transactions that this Agreement contemplates only if each of the following conditions has been satisfied or waived on or before the Closing Date:

(1) The Seller's representations and warranties in this Agreement must have been true in all material respects when made, and must be true in all material respects as of the Closing Date, with the same force and effect as though made on and as of the Closing Date.

(2) The Seller must have performed all of the covenants required to be performed by Seller as of the Closing Date.

(3) All consents required for Seller to transfer title to the Crane to Buyer must have been received.

If a condition is not satisfied, then as a matter of law, the party protected by the condition is not required to perform under the contract. Sometimes a contract's termination provision provides that the non-occurrence of a condition gives a party a right to terminate the contract. Thus, the non-occurrence of a condition might not only free a party from having to perform obligations under a contract, but also give that party a right to terminate the contract.

For example, when you sign a purchase agreement to purchase a home, the agreement might include a condition stating that you must be satisfied with an inspection of the house. If you are not satisfied with the inspection, then you will be excused from performing under the contract. That means, you would not have a duty to pay the purchase price for the house. Similarly, banks often include in their loan agreements many conditions that need to be satisfied before they are obligated to lend money, such as the requirement for the borrower to deliver to the bank updated financial statements and executed transaction documents (such as a promissory note). If the borrower does not deliver these documents to the lender, the lender does not have a duty to lend money.

It is important when drafting conditions to include provisions that address the effect of a condition not being satisfied if the effect is more than simply relieving a party of an obligation. For example, if a buyer of a home is not satisfied with the home inspection, then a condition to the buyer's duty to buy the home has not been satisfied, and as a matter of law, the buyer does not have a duty to buy the house. But if the buyer also wants its deposit back, then the purchase agreement must specify that the seller has an obligation to return the buyer's deposit, for that consequence does not automatically follow from the non-satisfaction of a condition.

Contracts for an express term or undertaking (without a closing) typically do not require conditions in order for each party to be obligated under the key deal terms. For example, a contract for plumbing services usually will not contain conditions stating what requirements need to be met before the plumbing company will render its services. Instead, the contractual obligations (the promise to render services and promise to pay) will become immediately effective.

PRACTICE PROBLEM 3-4

Your commercial client wants to lend $1,000,000 to another business. What are some <u>conditions</u> that you might want to include in the loan agreement?

---

3. Representations and Warranties

Representations and warranties are important contractual tools commonly used to help ensure each party to a contract receives the "benefits" for which the party bargained. They do that by allocating risk between the contract parties as to the accuracy of certain facts. Representations and warranties also help each party obtain information from the other, all to ensure that each party gets the benefits it expects under the contract.

For this section, imagine that two parties have entered into an agreement regarding the sale of a crane used in construction. The sample Crane Purchase

Agreement below includes representations and warranties of the selling party in Article 2 and of the buying party in Article 3.

Article 2
Seller's Representations and Warranties

The Seller represents and warrants to Buyer as follows:

3.1 **Corporate Organization and Existence.** The Seller is a corporation duly incorporated, validly existing, and in good standing under the laws of Delaware.

3.2 **Due Authorization.** The Seller has all requisite corporate power and authority necessary to enter into and perform this Agreement.

3.3 **Enforceability.** This Agreement constitutes a binding obligation of Seller, enforceable against Seller in accordance with its terms.

3.4 **Ownership of Crane.** The Seller owns the Crane free of all Liens.

3.5 **Condition of Crane.** The Crane is in good condition, except for ordinary wear and tear.

Article 3 Buyer's
Representations and Warranties

The Buyer represents and warrants to Seller as follows:

4.1 **Corporate Organization and Existence.** The Buyer is a corporation duly incorporated, validly existing, and in good standing under the laws of Delaware.

4.2 **Authority.** The Buyer has all requisite corporate power and authority necessary to enter into and perform this Agreement.

4.3 **Enforceability.** This Agreement constitutes a binding obligation of Buyer, enforceable against Buyer in accordance with its terms.

a. What is a representation?

Contracts like the Crane Purchase Agreement often set out a party's representations together with its warranties in one section of the contract. While that structure might suggest that representations and warranties are the same thing, in fact a representation is slightly different than a warranty.

A **representation** is an *assertion*—or statement—of a fact made as of a specific point in time to induce reliance. In other words, a representation is a statement that one party to a contract makes to induce the other party or parties to either enter into the contract or to perform the deal terms in the contract. Thus, in Article 3 of the Crane Purchase Agreement, Seller is representing to Buyer, among other things, that it owns the Crane, and that the Crane is in good condition, except for ordinary wear and tear. Seller is making these statements to induce Buyer to enter into the contract and to pay for the Crane when the time comes for Buyer to pay. From Buyer's perspective, Buyer cares about whether Seller owns the Crane and about its condition. If Seller did not own the Crane, it would not be able to sell it, or, if Seller did purport to sell the Crane, Buyer would be running the risk that the true owner would assert a claim of ownership over the Crane later. Moreover, if the Crane were not in good condition (subject to ordinary wear and tear), then Buyer would likely have wanted to pay less for it, as the Crane would be worth less to Buyer.

b. What is a warranty?

A **warranty**, in contrast, is a party's *promise* that a given fact is true as of a stated time. Thus, in Article 3 of the Crane Purchase Agreement, Seller is promising that it owns the Crane and that the Crane is in good condition, subject to ordinary wear and tear. By virtue of stating that a party "represents and warrants" as to a fact, both a representation and warranty is made about that same fact.

A contract often includes both representations and warranties because they provide different remedies. That is, as you will learn in Chapter 18, where a party makes a misrepresentation—in other words, one of a party's representations made in a contract is untrue—the aggrieved party can, if the other elements of a misrepresentation claim are met, rescind the contract. That means the party can essentially get out of the contract. In contrast, where a party breaches a warranty, the breaching party owes damages to the other party due to the injury arising from that breach. By virtue of including factual statements as both representations and warranties, a party thus preserves for itself the ability to select which remedy it desires if a fact stated in the contract later turns out not to be true.

c. "Typical" representations and warranties

You will note that the representations and warranties in Sections 3.1 through 3.3 of the Crane Purchase Agreement mirror those in Sections 4.1 through 4.3—the only difference is that they switch the parties making the representations and warranties. These representations and warranties are fairly standard in contracts made by businesses. The representations and warranties in Sections 3.1 and 4.1 give the other party assurances that the party is actually a validly existing legal entity. If it were not, its contracts might not be valid. The representations and warranties in Sections 3.2 and 4.2 give the other party comfort about the authority of the business organization to enter into the contract, as well as authority of the person signing the contract on behalf of that entity. That is important because, as we will see in Chapter 9, a person must have authority to bind a business organization. Similarly, the representation and warranty in Sections 3.3 and 4.3 give the receiving party comfort about the enforceability of its contract rights and remedies against the other party. Thus, that party assures the other that none of the defenses discussed later in this book applies.

There are other representations and warranties that are also typically included in business contracts, such as the condition of the goods or services being purchased. As with the deal terms, you need to figure out what is important to your client and what risks your client might face to be able to craft the representations and warranties in a way that ensures your client benefits from the transaction in the way it expects.

PRACTICE PROBLEM 3-5

Review the Crane Purchase Agreement in Appendix B. Imagine that you represent Buyer. What are some additional topics or issues you think might need to be covered in Seller's representations and warranties?

d. How representations and warranties are used

Now that you understand what representations and warranties are, it is important to understand how they are used in contracts.

i. Risk allocation

You might ask why Seller does not simply tell Buyer to do Buyer's own investigation and confirm all of the facts that Buyer is seeking to include in a representation or warranty. For example, why should Seller make a representation or warranty that the Crane is in good condition when Buyer can simply inspect the Crane? The answer to this question has to do with the risk allocation function that representations and warranties serve in a contract.

Representations and warranties help allocate risk in several ways. Representations and warranties allocate risk by making a party responsible if a fact included in its representations and warranties is not true. For example, in the case of the Crane Purchase Agreement, if after buying the Crane, Buyer discovers that the Crane is in poor condition and is not usable, Buyer would allege that Seller made a misrepresentation and breached a warranty that was included in the contract regarding the condition of the Crane. If the Buyer sought to rescind the contract, it would pursue its misrepresentation claim. If, on the other hand, the Buyer sought monetary damages, it would pursue its breach of warranty claim. If it were successful, Buyer would be entitled to receive damages, likely the difference in value between the condition of the Crane as warranted (i.e., in good condition) and the actual condition of the Crane (i.e., poor condition). Accordingly, Seller would bear the risk of loss in the event that the fact stated in its representation and warranty (the "good" condition of the Crane) is not true because Buyer would have various remedies available to it if it turned out the Crane was not in good condition. Without this representation and warranty, Buyer may have been left without a remedy once it discovered the Crane's poor condition after purchasing it.

In addition to these common law remedies, attorneys commonly expressly condition their clients' performance on the truth of the counterparty's representations and warranties. If any of those representations and warranties is not true, then the client would be excused from performance by the express terms of the written contract.

ii. Confirming due diligence

Representations and warranties serve another function, too: they provide information to the other party about the facts represented and warranted. For example, when Seller represents and warrants that the Crane is in good condition, that statement provides valuable information to Buyer about the condition of the Crane.

Representations and warranties provide an incentive for the party providing that representation and warranty to verify the accuracy of the represented and warranted fact. For example, let's assume that Buyer inspected the Crane and determined that, as far as Buyer could tell, the Crane was in good operating condition. It still is possible that Buyer is wrong, and, moreover, it is possible that Seller either knows Buyer is wrong or is in a better position to determine whether Buyer is wrong (because Seller is the current owner and operator of the Crane). By asking Seller to make a representation and warranty about the Crane's condition, Buyer can gain the advantage of Seller's superior knowledge as to the Crane's condition.

Because of the possible consequences of making a misrepresentation or breaching a warranty, once Seller has been asked (and has agreed) to make a representation and warranty, Seller and its counsel should discuss each of the representations and warranties to determine whether it is true. Accordingly, if you were representing Seller, you would want to ask Seller if the Crane is in fact in good operating condition. This question might be preceded by a discussion along the lines of this section explaining the implications of making a representation and warranty.

iii. Modifying representations and warranties

Parties often qualify representations and warranties. Qualifying a representation and warranty means adding a standard to reduce the strength of the representation and warranty. Doing so reduces the due diligence burdens as well as lowers the risk of liability for the party making the representation and warranty. For example, if Seller's representation and warranty states that the Crane is in good operating condition "in all material respects," then even if Seller is unaware of any problems with the operating condition, Seller will only be liable for those problems that are significant enough to make the representation and warranty untrue. Seller also presumably will only be responsible for disclosing those defects that cause the representation not to be true. Thus, the qualifier "in all material respects" lowered the risk to Seller.

Similarly, parties may qualify their representations and warranties with "knowledge." For example, Seller could represent that "to Seller's knowledge, the Crane is in good operating condition." By adding knowledge as a qualifier, Seller will only be liable if the Crane is not in good operating condition and Seller knew about it. Of course, Buyer may resist the inclusion of any knowledge qualifiers because they place the risk of the unknown on Buyer. Buyer may want Seller to be liable for any problems with the Crane's operating condition, even if Seller did not know about them.

It is important to remember that there is not a "right" or "wrong" way to allocate risk through representations and warranties. Instead, attorneys try to find a formulation of representations and warranties that allocate risk in a manner satisfactory to both parties. You are trying to protect your client with the most favorable formulation of the representations and warranties, just as the opposing attorney is trying to protect her client.

PRACTICE PROBLEM 3-6

Assume you once again represent Buyer under the Crane Purchase Agreement set out in Appendix B. As you know, Seller is making the following representation and warranty about the Crane:

> The Crane is in good condition, except for ordinary wear and tear.

What concerns might you or your client have about the representation and warranty as drafted? How might you modify the representation and warranty to address those concerns?

4. Covenants

A **covenant** sets out a party's promises as to what it will do or not do in the future. Thus, covenants capture the very essence of a contract, as they reflect the parties' promises for the future. In this way, covenants provide value to a party in a transaction. They give the party to whom the covenant is made the right to enforce the duty set out in that covenant if it is not performed as specified.

Depending on the type of transaction, a written contract may contain an entire section devoted to covenants for certain purposes. In fact, the section of a contract setting out the parties' principal promises discussed above is largely composed of covenants, setting out the parties' basic promises in the contract. However, covenants appear elsewhere, too. In fact, most written contracts have covenants sprinkled throughout the entire text.

For this section, we will continue to use the example of an agreement regarding the sale of a crane used in construction. The following are the pre-closing covenants from the Crane Purchase Agreement set out in Appendix B. That means these covenants apply in the gap period between the time the parties sign the contract and closing, which is the time the sale of the crane actually occurs and the buyer pays the purchase price.

Article 5
Seller's Pre-Closing Covenants

Beginning on the date of this Agreement to the Closing Date, Seller shall perform as follows:

4.1 **Maintain Crane.** The Seller shall maintain the Crane in good condition, ordinary wear and tear excepted.

4.2 **Not Sell or Encumber Crane.** The Seller shall not sell, grant a lien on, or otherwise encumber, the Crane.

. . .

Article 8
Post-Closing Covenants

The parties shall perform as follows following the Closing:

8.1 **Taxes.** Each party shall pay half of any state or local sales or transfer taxes payable with respect the transfer of the Crane from Seller to Buyer under this Agreement.

8.2 **Confidential.** Neither party will disclose the terms of this Agreement to any person unless required by law or court order.

a. Use of covenants

As discussed above, covenants set out the parties' promises for the future. These promises, as with other terms, are designed to make sure that the promisee receives the benefits she bargained for. **Affirmative covenants** are covenants that require some overt act by the promisor, or promises to "do something." **Negative covenants** are covenants that require the promisor to refrain from doing particular acts, or promises "*not* to do something."

Examples of affirmative and negative covenants appear in Article 5 of the Crane Purchase Agreement excerpted above. First, you need to consider why these covenants exist. In the Crane Purchase Agreement, Buyer presumably wants to know that the Crane will be in good condition when Buyer buys it and that Buyer will be able to own the Crane without anyone else having any claims on it.

To address the first concern, Section 5.1 contains a specific affirmative covenant by Seller to maintain the Crane in the ordinary course of business. To address the second concern, and also to increase the likelihood that the sale will occur, Section 5.2 contains a specific covenant by Seller not to sell the Crane to someone else or to encumber the Crane. If Seller does not perform either of these covenants as required, Seller has breached.

If a covenant is breached—meaning, not performed as promised—then the aggrieved party can sue the other on the basis of that breach. The aggrieved party could then obtain a remedy for that breach. In addition, in a contract with a closing, if the contract includes as a condition to closing that that the other party must have performed its covenants, then upon a breach, the aggrieved party may "walk" from the transaction and not close. Of course, as you saw from the above discussion of conditions, the ability to walk away would be addressed in a separate section within the written agreement.

b. Time periods

When developing covenants, it is important to think about the time period during which they will apply. Many covenants, such as the promise to perform the bargained-for services, may apply during the entire term of the contract. Other covenants, like promises to keep certain information confidential, may apply during the term of the contract and for some specified period of time after the contract has been terminated. In other types of transactions, such as sale transactions, certain types of covenants may be necessary only during the time between the date on which the contract is signed and the date on which the property is sold (the closing date).

In sale transactions, the purchase takes place sometime after the contract is signed. Attorneys typically think about the world of covenants for such transactions in terms of two time periods, the pre-closing period and the post-closing period. The *pre-closing period* is the period of time between the signing of the agreement and closing. The *post-closing period* is the period of time after title to the purchased asset has transferred to the buyer on the closing date. The following diagram captures these two time periods along the spectrum of contractual performance:

Contract timeline—contract with closing

Parties bound but key obligations not due yet—pre-closing covenants apply	Any post-closing and surviving obligations due (e.g., confidentiality)
Parties sign the contract—reps/warranties made	CLOSING: Key obligations due (once conditions satisfied or waived)

For the pre-closing period, the buyer will want to insert covenants to obligate the selling party to act in a way to maintain the value of the purchased asset and otherwise facilitate the transaction. As discussed above, Buyer in the Crane Purchase Agreement presumably wants to know that that Crane will be in good condition when Buyer purchases it, even if the closing will not occur for several months. Accordingly, Section 5.1 contains a covenant by Seller to maintain the Crane in good condition pending Closing. This covenant is designed to obligate Seller not to neglect the Crane by failing to make routine repairs. If Seller fails to perform this obligation, Buyer is entitled to a remedy. Again, this covenant is linked to a condition that permits Buyer not to consummate the sale if Seller fails to comply with its covenants. Seller may also be liable to Buyer for damages for breaching that covenant. This is a pre-closing covenant because it would not be appropriate for Seller to continue to be obligated to maintain the Crane after the closing (i.e., once Buyer is the owner of the Crane).

As indicated above, other covenants, such as the covenant to perform promised services in accordance with a particular standard, may continue throughout the term of the contract.

Moreover, as is discussed above under termination, sometimes covenants survive termination of the contractual relationship. For example, in Article 8 of the Crane Purchase Agreement above, the covenants regarding sharing payment of any sales taxes and confidentiality begin at closing and extend beyond the term of the contract. If these covenants only applied prior to the closing, then each party could claim that it had not agreed to share any tax bill with respect to the sale that happened after the closing. Experienced attorneys consider how the relationship between the parties will change as time passes and draft the contract's covenants accordingly.

Similarly, some covenants survive the termination of services under a contract for a term. For example, as you saw in *Duffner*, sometimes employment contracts contain negative covenants obligating the employee not to compete with the employer and not to solicit customers and employees for some period of time after the termination of employment. That type of covenant survives—and, in fact, only starts to apply—once the employment term ends. Thus, the following diagram captures the typical time period for covenants in the contract for a term:

Contract timeline—term contract

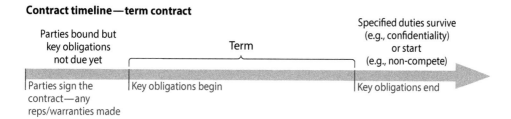

c. Developing covenants

It is important to remember that it is the attorney's job to figure out what the client wants from the transaction and then to determine how to prevent the other party's conduct from lessening the certainty that the deal will occur or lowering the value of the transaction to the client. You may have noticed, for example, that the covenants in Article 4 could be incomplete. Despite the covenants, Seller could still fail to deliver the Crane in the condition desired by Buyer. The following is a short list of possible pre-closing behavior by Seller that could be problematic from Buyer's perspective:

1. Seller using the Crane too much (or even using it at all);
2. Seller failing to maintain insurance on the Crane;
3. Seller not permitting Buyer to inspect the Crane prior to the sale; and
4. Seller negotiating or agreeing with another party to sell the Crane.

As with representations and warranties, covenants allocate risk between the parties. Covenants shift the risk of certain future behavior (such as the disclosure of the terms of the Crane Purchase Agreement) or future events (such as the Crane not being maintained) to the party making the covenant. When considering covenants, you should think about what issues your client might be concerned with and then discuss those issues with her. It is only with client input that an attorney can draft appropriate covenants tailored to client's needs.

As with representations and warranties, there is not a "correct" way to allocate risk through covenants. Instead, attorneys try to work out covenants that are acceptable to both parties. You are trying to protect your client through the various covenants, just as the opposing attorney is trying to protect her client.

PRACTICE PROBLEM 3-7

1. Once again, assume you represent the buyer of a Crane. Your client plans to purchase the Crane one month from the date the parties enter into the contract to give your client time to have the Crane inspected and to arrange for a bank loan. What are some pre-closing covenants that you might negotiate for in the purchase agreement beyond those set out in Article 5 of the Crane Purchase Agreement in Appendix B?

2. Imagine that you are representing Jeff again in connection with his employment agreement with Sunnyside as described in Appendix C. What covenants is Jeff being asked to make in the employment agreement? Which ones do you think you should flag for discussion with Jeff?

d. Qualifying covenants

The language chosen for covenants is obviously important. A client generally is only going to get the benefit of the chosen language in the contract, so the covenant language must be appropriate, specific, and comprehensive. On the other hand, it is important to realize that there often is a happy middle ground that delivers what each party can reasonably accept without insisting on strict covenants. For example, in the scenario of the Crane Purchase Agreement, what if Section 5.1 required Seller to maintain the Crane "in the condition consistent with Seller's past practices"? That standard may not be sufficient for Buyer if Seller's past practices had been not to do anything to maintain the Crane. In that instance, the covenant might not provide much protection for Buyer.

On the other hand, if the covenant required Seller to maintain the Crane "in accordance with best industry practices," then Seller may be uncomfortable. What are "best industry practices"? That might seem to be too extreme or too ambiguous of a standard. Once again, you need to bear in mind the remedies for a breach of a covenant. Seller's breach of the covenant to maintain the Crane in accordance with best industry practices would permit Buyer to sue, but it also might permit Buyer to refuse to purchase the Crane. Seller's counsel will want to avoid language that makes it too easy for Seller to commit an immaterial breach and that will nevertheless permit Buyer to walk from the transaction.

In such an instance, the parties might agree to language somewhere between the two positions, such as a covenant to maintain the Crane "in good condition, ordinary wear and tear excepted." This standard might appear reasonable enough to each party to address Buyer's concerns about Seller appropriately maintaining the Crane as well as Seller's concerns about promising a level of maintenance that is inappropriate or debatable.

As with representations and warranties, a lawyer needs to consider what exceptions are appropriate for particular covenants. For example, what if Section 8.2 required each party to keep the terms of the Agreement confidential, without any exceptions? That language would cause a party to breach even if the government audited Buyer and required Buyer to disclose the terms of the Agreement. It seems inappropriate for Seller to be able to sue for a breach of the covenant in that instance. That is why the parties agreed that the covenant should be to keep the terms confidential "except as required by law or court order."

You will develop a familiarity with typical covenant exceptions and qualifications as you acquire more experience with contracts. By now, though, you are hopefully already developing an appreciation for reading each provision of the contract carefully and considering its purpose, language, and limits.

PRACTICE PROBLEM 3-8

Assume you drafted the Crane Purchase Agreement set out in Appendix B and sent it to Seller and its counsel. Upon receiving that draft, Seller's counsel called you concerned because the Crane's boom has started to rust. What changes, if any, do you propose making to the Crane Purchase Agreement to address this concern? As you consider what changes to make, be prepared to discuss with your client why you need to include a covenant in the Crane Purchase Agreement about the Crane's condition despite the fact that there is also a representation and warranty in the agreement about the Crane's condition.

5. Miscellaneous

In addition to the substantive terms discussed above, contracts often include numerous "rules of the game" type provisions. Those provisions help the parties as well as third parties (such as courts) give effect to the other substantive provisions of the agreement. Often these provisions appear near the end of the contract in a "catch-all" section labeled "Miscellaneous." However, junior attorneys would be well advised to pay close attention to these provisions, as often there are important issues hiding among the seemingly innocuous "boilerplate." This section addresses a few of the important provisions often found near the end of a contract.

a. Governing law

It is important for the written contract to indicate what jurisdiction's law will govern the contract. A sample provision is below.

> All questions concerning the construction, validity and interpretation of this letter agreement and the exhibits to this letter agreement will be governed by and construed in accordance with the domestic laws of the State of Pennsylvania, without giving effect to any choice of law or conflict of law provision or rule (whether of the State of Pennsylvania or any other jurisdiction) that would cause the application of the laws of any jurisdiction other than the State of Pennsylvania.

As discussed in Chapter 2, you should consider what governing law is appropriate given who your client is, where your client is located, and where performance under the contract will take place. As you also saw in Chapter 2, sometimes these "choice of law" provisions will not be respected, depending on which court hears the lawsuit and the type of contract or contract provision at issue.

b. Venue/personal jurisdiction

Another common provision is a venue and personal jurisdiction provision. A sample provision is below.

> Any disputes arising out of or seeking to enforce this Agreement will be subject to the exclusive jurisdiction to the state and federal courts located in Oakland County, Pennsylvania, and claims with respect to this Agreement may not be brought in any other venue or forum. Each party irrevocably consents to the jurisdiction of the state and federal courts located in Oakland County, Pennsylvania.

Venue provisions allow the parties to designate particular courts to hear any disputes arising with respect to the agreement. You will want to know where your client can sue or be sued. Parties are often reluctant to agree to an unfavorable venue, such as courts located in another state where only the counterparty is located. If the parties cannot agree on a venue, parties can either specify multiple venues or delete the venue provision completely and avoid agreeing up front which court(s) can hear a dispute between the parties.

The provision that includes a consent to personal jurisdiction is intended to prevent claims by one of the parties that a court (perhaps a court in a state with which the party has little contact) lacks jurisdiction over that party. For example, if you were representing a Michigan resident and the contract provided for Michigan courts as the exclusive venue, you would not want your client to be unable to bring the lawsuit against the Wisconsin counterparty just because the counterparty had never had any business operations in, or connections with, Michigan. Keep in mind that you will learn about venue in your Civil Procedure class. Our goal here is to simply explain how a contract can spell out which court hears a dispute between contracting parties.

c. Expenses

Sometimes parties include a provision that requires the losing party in any lawsuit concerning the contract to pay the other party's attorneys' fees. These provisions often also provide that each party will otherwise be responsible for all of its own fees and expenses associated with entering into the contract. You will learn about limits on these types of provisions in Chapter 27.

d. Non-assignment

By default, contract rights are freely **assignable**. That means a new party can essentially stand in the shoes of a party to receive the benefits promised under the contract. So, for example, if your client's office lease agreement is silent on assignment, that means your client can assign its rights under the lease. Therefore, your client can find someone new to take its place under the lease and use the leased office space.

However, as you may know from experience, typically landlords do not like that outcome. The same is true for other contracting parties. Parties to a contract often have done an investigation of the other party to the contract and accordingly do not want to be forced to have a contractual relationship with an unknown party. Therefore, contracts often include a provision that restricts the other party's ability to assign its rights. Those provisions often also prevent the other party from delegating its duties under a contract. Under such a provision, not only would your client not be able to assign its rights under the lease mentioned above, but it also could not delegate its duties, meaning, largely, its duty to pay rent.

Sometimes contracts contain blanket prohibitions on assignment of rights and delegation of duties, and sometimes they preclude these actions without the other party's consent. A sample provision is below.

> Neither party may assign any of its rights or delegate any performance under this Agreement without the other party's consent. Any purported assignment or delegation in violation of this provision is void.

Keep in mind that sometimes there are exceptions to the prohibition on assignment. For example, a contract might permit the assignment of rights and delegation of duties to a company that is the purchaser of, or successor to, the original contracting company.

Chapter 29 discusses the concepts of assignment and delegation, as well as limits on the enforceability of non-assignment and non-delegation clauses.

e. Integration clause

After spending so much time preparing a written contract, parties often want to be able to rely exclusively on the provisions and promises contained in the contract. An example of an **integration clause** is below.

> This Agreement reflects the final, exclusive agreement between the parties on the matters contained in this Agreement. All earlier and contemporaneous negotiations and agreements between the parties concerning the matters addressed in this Agreement are expressly merged into and superseded by this Agreement.

This clause is intended to make it clear that neither party can rely on any prior agreements concerning the contract matter other than those set forth in the current written agreement. Otherwise, there can be disagreements about whether other or different promises were actually made between the parties. Chapter 15, which covers the parole evidence rule, will explore in detail whether and when such a clause precludes a party from introducing evidence of prior agreements that either conflict with or supplement the written agreement.

6. End of Contract

Written contracts typically require that each party sign at the end of the contract. Some contracts, however, have additional pieces or parts that follow the signatures.

a. Signature block

The signature block is the space provided at the end for the parties to sign. Contracts usually include a concluding sentence right before the signature blocks reiterating the parties' intention to agree to the written contract. As discussed in the section above regarding the preamble, the parties named in the signature blocks are the parties against whom the contract can be enforced. Accordingly, you should be very careful when considering which person or entity should be specified in the contract. Again, the parties named in the preamble should be the same as those named in the signature block.

A sample signature block is below.

> The parties below execute and deliver this Employment Agreement as of the date first set forth above.
>
> Company: Sunnyside DayCare, LLC   Employee: Jeff Rison
>
> By: _____   _____
>
> Name: Patricia Mead   Name: Jeff Rison
>
> Title: President

Note that Jeff Rison is signing this agreement individually, while Patricia Mead is signing the agreement on behalf of Sunnyside DayCare, LLC—this is what the "By:" line means. Sunnyside DayCare, LLC is signing the agreement "by" Patricia Mead signing on its behalf in her capacity (her "Title") as its president.

Accordingly, Patricia is not signing this agreement individually and typically would not have personal liability under the contract for Sunnyside DayCare's failure to perform under the agreement.

As you will see in Chapter 4, one of the elements for contract formation is mutual assent. If both named parties actually sign the contract (in the signature block, in the example above) and deliver their signatures to the other party, then presumably the parties have satisfied the requirement of mutual assent.

b. Disclosure schedules and exhibits

A party may need to prepare schedules of exceptions to the representations and warranties to make the representations and warranties true. For example, a representation and warranty may state "Except as set forth on Schedule 3.10, Seller has not been subject to any audits for the past two years." The Seller's counsel would need to prepare Schedule 3.10 and list any audits during the past two years. By disclosing the required information, the representation and warranty becomes true (because if all of the audits are disclosed on the schedule, then Seller has not been subject to any audit other than those on the schedule), and Seller avoids making a misrepresentation. If such disclosure schedules are prepared, they typically follow the signature blocks.

Exhibits also follow the parties' signature blocks. **Exhibits** are usually the forms of instruments, certificates, or other agreements to be delivered in the future. For example, Section 2.4(a)(ii) of the Crane Purchase Agreement set out in Appendix B calls for a bill of sale to be attached as Exhibit A. Exhibit A, then, would contain a "form" bill of sale to be delivered at the closing to convey title to the Crane. Until the bill of sale is separately signed, when the purchase price is actually paid, it is not an operative document. The form of the bill of sale, however, does constitute part of the agreement.

C. PREPARING THE WRITTEN CONTRACT

At this point you may be wondering how attorneys have the time to draft from scratch written contracts that are appropriately tailored to the current transaction. The short answer is that attorneys do not start from scratch each time, as that would be too time-intensive and too expensive for the client, who is typically paying the drafting attorney by the hour. Instead, attorneys rely on what is known colloquially as "precedent," or agreements for similar transactions that have been used in the past. Chapter 11 will explore the use of precedents and provide other guidance in how to draft a contract.

Now that you have studied the parts of a contract and contract terms, please read through and answer the questions that follow the Simulation Problem for Chapter 3, which is located in Appendix A.

PART II

CONTRACT FORMATION

As you know from Part I, typically parties create contracts as bargains. Part II walks through the elements required to form that type of contract. In particular, Chapter 4 explains the first element of a bargained-for contract—mutual assent. Chapter 5 also discusses mutual assent, but in the specific context where a contract is formed through online contracting. Chapter 6, too, discusses mutual assent, but for a contract that involves the sale of a good, which is governed by Article 2 of the Uniform Commercial Code. Chapter 7 then discusses the second element of bargained-for contract—consideration. Finally, Chapter 8 discusses the specialized application of the rules on mutual assent and consideration in the context of an option contract.

The following diagram shows where the topics covered in Part II fit into the larger scheme of this course.

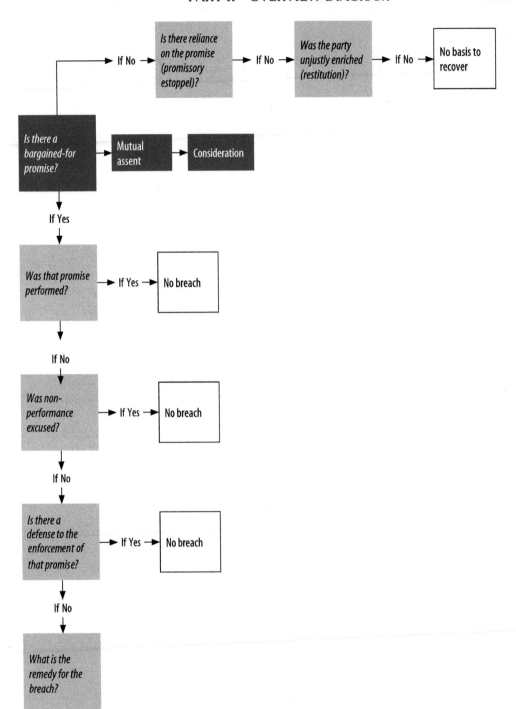

CHAPTER 4

Mutual Assent to an Exchange

Recall from Chapter 1 that a contract is a promise or set of promises that a court will enforce. For this purpose, a promise is a person's statement or other manifestation of his or her intent to perform or refrain from performing an act in the future. To be a promise for purposes of contract law, that statement or manifestation must justify the promisee in believing that the promisor is *committed* to performing that act or refraining from performing that act.

But what type of promises are enforceable? The main type of promise that a court will enforce is a promise made through a bargain. The concept of bargain does not mean an especially low price, like a bargain price for jeans. Rather, in the context of contract law, the term **bargain** refers to a promise given by the promisor specifically to induce something of legal value in exchange. More specifically, the party making the promise—the promisor—is bargaining for either a return promise or performance. So, for example, a promise by a steel manufacturer to supply steel to a contractor in exchange for the contractor's promise to pay for that steel is an example of a bargain, as each party has made a promise to induce something of legal value in exchange from the other party.

To take another example more directly relevant to you: you likely entered into a bargained-for contract when you bought your cell phone. In the transaction, your cell phone company promised to provide you with cellular phone service. It did so in exchange for your return promise to pay them an agreed-upon monthly rate. This arrangement, too, amounts to a bargain, as each party made a promise to induce the other party to give something in exchange—in this case, a return promise.

Whether a court will enforce your and the cell phone company's promises made in this bargain should one party not perform is a separate question that requires a study of types of bargains courts enforce, as well as reasons courts do not enforce bargained-for contracts. However, step one in the analysis is to determine whether a promise is even of the type a court will enforce. Here, since each party made a promise to induce a return promise, we have a bargain, and each promise is potentially the type that courts enforce as a contract.

Examples of other common types of bargains include apartment lease agreements, student loan agreements, car purchase (or lease) agreements, airline ticket purchase agreements, clothing purchase agreements, and restaurant food purchase agreements. In each of these instances, the parties bargained for an exchange of promises.

PRACTICE PROBLEM 4-1

Consider whether the following arrangements are bargains based on your initial exposure to the concept of bargain: *[handwritten: gift, nothing given in exchange]*

1. Your friend Joe, who is a 2L, gives you his Contracts outline. *[handwritten: → gift nothing given in exchange]*

2. Your friend Joe gives you his Contracts outline and rubs his thumb and fingers together in a gesture that suggests he wants money. *[handwritten: → no? no agreement]*

3. Your friend Joe promises to give you his Contracts outline. *[handwritten: nothing in exchange]*

4. Your friend Joe promises to give you his Contracts outline if he decides he is willing to share a copy. *[handwritten: illusory promise: not really giving anything]*

3. Your friend Joe promises to give you his Contracts outline. When he does, you give him $10 to thank him for doing so. *[handwritten: NO]*

4. Your friend Joe promises to give you his Contracts outline if you print it out. *[handwritten: if = condition = not a bargain, condition of the gift, not doing anything for Joe]*

5. Your friend Joe promises to give you his Contracts outline if you print it out for him. *[handwritten: more of a give/get = yes]*

6. Your friend Joe promises to give you his Contracts outline if you pay him $10 for it. *[handwritten: yes → classic]*

7. Your friend Joe promises to give you his Contracts outline if you let him borrow your bike for a week. *[handwritten: yes]*

[handwritten margin note: gift promise, a gift promise]

Keep in mind that not all agreements are bargains. Parties may agree, but not intend for there to be any legal consequence from that. For example, you might agree with your classmate that Contracts is an excellent class. However, you and your classmate are not seeking any sort of exchange. Thus, you have not created a bargain, though you have an agreement. Thus, only some types of agreements are bargains—those agreements contemplating an exchange. This broad nature of agreements is reflected on the below diagram.

Moreover, not all bargains are enforceable contracts. One example is where a bargain involves two parties trading performances. In that circumstance, neither party is providing a promise. Therefore, no contract is created. Similarly, not all bargained-for contracts are enforced. An example is a contract to kill someone for money. While there is a bargained-for contract between the parties here, a court would not enforce either promise for public policy reasons. Future chapters will explore types of bargained-for contracts that courts do not enforce. The fact that bargains are a subset of agreements, and that not all bargains amount to enforceable contracts, is reflected on the below diagram.

Finally, not every contract is created through a bargain. As you will learn in Chapter 22, reliance on a promise can also serve as a basis to enforce that promise. In that situation, it is reliance that justifies enforcement, and not the existence of a bargain. The below diagram also captures this with the box outside of the inverse pyramid showing the alternate, non-bargain route to contract.

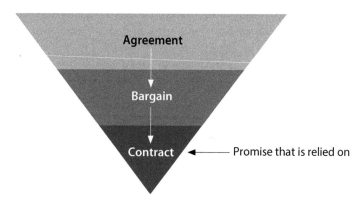

Thus, the primary route to arriving at an enforceable contract is through a bargain. A bargained-for contract exists where (1) the parties manifest their mutual assent to the terms of an exchange; and (2) one party makes a promise to induce either a return promise or performance, and the return promise or performance is actually induced by that initial promise. Here, the return promise or performance bargained for in exchange is called **consideration**.

This chapter, along with the next several chapters, address requirement (1), which is known as *mutual assent*. Chapter 7 addresses requirement (2), consideration.

Keep in mind that an arrangement does not need to be identified as a contract to constitute one. Instead, if an arrangement satisfies the elements of a contract, then it is a contract regardless of what the parties know or think. Thus, it is important for you as a lawyer to understand the elements of a contract so you can advise your client as to whether your client, or a counterparty, is contractually bound where the question arises.

Before we explore the bargained-for-contract element of mutual assent, we should first explore the contexts in which this inquiry comes up. Thus, Section A will explore why and when this type of inquiry might arise. Then, Section B will delve into the requirements of mutual assent.

A. CONTRACT INQUIRY IN TRANSACTIONS AND LITIGATION

For a transactional lawyer, the question of whether your client has entered into a contract is typically relevant in two scenarios. One is where you want to make sure the other party or parties are bound contractually to their promises given to your client. Here, the transactional lawyer needs to make sure the elements of contract are satisfied, which is a foundational requirement for your client to enforce a contract against the counterparty.

For example, if you represent the seller of a business agreeing to sell it for $1 million, you would want to make sure the parties properly created a contract in which the buyer promised to pay the $1 million. That way, if the buyer tried to back out, you would be prepared to counter by explaining why the parties had properly created a contract. As you will discover through the rest of this chapter and the other chapters on mutual assent, through contract language, you have some power to control when and how the parties mutually assent.

The second scenario where a transactional lawyer often needs to analyze whether a contract exists is to ensure that the client is not contractually bound where it does not intend to be. In other words, a lawyer sometimes must ensure that the client cannot be forced to perform a promise to which the client did not intend to be legally bound. In this situation, the transactional lawyer needs to know how a contract is created to ensure that those elements are not satisfied.

For example, sometimes parties to a potential contract write up the agreed-upon terms in a preliminary writing called a **term sheet**. Sometimes both parties sign a copy of that term sheet. While the writing is labeled "term sheet," implying that this is merely a preliminary writing and not a contract, that fact alone does not prevent the term sheet from constituting a contract. That is because the contract inquiry looks at all of the facts and circumstances, not only the title of the written document. Thus, a transactional lawyer must caution the client on what actions to take (and not to take) to ensure that the client does not create a contract through a term sheet or otherwise through its conduct. Chapter 10 discusses term sheets in more detail, including how to prevent a client from being prematurely bound to a term sheet.

Litigators also need to be able to analyze the elements of a contract. Sometimes this question comes up where a client wants to avoid a contractual obligation. In that case, the litigator might need to explain why the elements of contract were not satisfied, thus precluding enforcement of the allegedly breached promise. Or, if the litigator represents a client seeking to enforce a contract against a counterparty, then that litigator would need to be able to demonstrate to the court at the outset how the contract elements were satisfied. There are other reasons, too, for litigators to prove that a contract either existed or did not exist. For example, a litigator might represent a client in arguing that the client was not bound to a contract to avoid application of a mandatory arbitration provision in that contract, which would require that client to arbitrate all disputes arising between the parties. Or a litigator might draft a settlement agreement in connection with pending arbitration. In that situation, the litigator would want to carefully prepare the settlement agreement to ensure that it properly satisfies the contract elements so that, if necessary, it may enforce that contract in the future should the need arise.

B. OBJECTIVE NATURE OF MUTUAL ASSENT

Recall that a contract created through a bargain requires an agreement of the parties. Again, in this context, an agreement "is a manifestation of mutual assent on the part of two or more persons."[1] This section develops this mutual assent element.

First, mutual assent must be **manifested**. That means each party must *show* its mutual assent through its outward manifestations—that is, through its words and acts. If the reasonable interpretation of each party's words and acts indicates assent to a proposed contract, then there is mutual assent. That is true even if the party subjectively did not want to assent to an exchange.

Because this test looks at how a reasonable person would view the other party's outward manifestations rather than their actual subjective intentions, this is an *objective test*.

Traditionally, some courts stated that the test for determining mutual assent is based on whether the parties had a "meeting of the minds"[2] at the same time,

---

1. Restatement (Second) of Contracts § 3 (1981).
2. *See, e.g.,* Mactier's Adm'rs v. Frith, 6 Wend. 102, 139 (N.Y. 1830).

upon the same subject matter, and in the same sense. Even courts today sometimes use this language.[3] However, despite the use of language suggesting that this test is subjective and therefore looks at the parties' actual states of minds, courts generally apply the test objectively.

Under this test, a party can manifest assent even without knowing the terms of a contract. This is often described as a **"duty to read"**[4] because a party is presumed to have read the terms of a contract when she manifests assent, even if she has not actually read the terms. In reality, a party does not have a legal duty to read the proposed terms of a contract, as a legal duty means a party can be liable for failing to perform that duty. But it means she cannot avoid a contractual obligation on the basis that she did not read the terms—at least where she is not misled or misinformed about the content of those terms and the terms are not intentionally kept from her. Chapters 17-21 will discuss these types of defenses to enforcement.

The objective nature of the mutual assent inquiry filters out manifestations that a party knows or has reason to know the other party will not interpret as assent.[5] For example, if a party waves her arms in the air after discussing a proposed bargain, this would not amount to assent where the party seeing the arm wave knew or had reason to know the other party did not intend this wave as assent. This would be true, for example, where the wave was understood to mean "goodbye" at the end of the parties' discussion of the terms of the proposed bargain.

The risk with the objective nature of mutual assent is that a party may be bound to a contract where she did not intend to be bound. This could happen, for example, where a party manifests an intent to be bound but secretly does not want to be bound, such as where she jokingly manifests assent. In this situation, the party would still be bound, as she is held to the reasonable meaning of her manifestation.

The following case, *Lucy v. Zehmer*, is a classic case that demonstrates the objective nature of the mutual assent inquiry.

Lucy v. Zehmer
Supreme Court of Appeals of Virginia
196 Va. 493 (1954)

BUCHANAN, J., delivered the opinion of the court.

. . .

---

3. *See, e.g.*, Mgmt. Computer. Servs., Inc. v. Hawkins, Ash, Baptie & Co., 557 N.W.2d 67, 75 (Wis. 1996).

4. Restatement (Second) of Contracts § 23 cmt. e (1981).

5. Restatement (Second) of Contracts § 19(2) (1981).

The instrument sought to be enforced was written by A. H. Zehmer on December 20, 1952, in these words:

> "We hereby agree to sell to W. O. Lucy the Ferguson Farm complete for $50,000.00, title satisfactory to buyer,"

and signed by the defendants, A. H. Zehmer and Ida S. Zehmer.

. . .

On the night of December 20, 1952, around eight o'clock, [Lucy] took an employee to McKenney, where Zehmer lived and operated a restaurant, filling station and motor court. While there he decided to see Zehmer and again try to buy the Ferguson farm. He entered the restaurant and talked to Mrs. Zehmer until Zehmer came in. He asked Zehmer if he had sold the Ferguson farm. Zehmer replied that he had not. Lucy said, "I bet you wouldn't take $50,000.00 for that place." Zehmer replied, "Yes, I would too; you wouldn't give fifty." Lucy said he would and told Zehmer to write up an agreement to that effect. Zehmer took a restaurant check and wrote on the back of it, "I do hereby agree to sell to W. O. Lucy the Ferguson Farm for $50,000 complete." Lucy told him he had better change it to "We" because Mrs. Zehmer would have to sign it too. Zehmer then tore up what he had written, wrote the agreement quoted above and asked Mrs. Zehmer, who was at the other end of the counter ten or twelve feet away, to sign it. Mrs. Zehmer said she would for $50,000 and signed it. Zehmer brought it back and gave it to Lucy, who offered him $5 which Zehmer refused, saying, "You don't need to give me any money, you got the agreement there signed by both of us."

The discussion leading to the signing of the agreement, said Lucy, lasted thirty or forty minutes, during which Zehmer seemed to doubt that Lucy could raise $50,000. Lucy suggested the provision for having the title examined and Zehmer made the suggestion that he would sell it "complete, everything there," and stated that all he had on the farm was three heifers.

Lucy took a partly filled bottle of whiskey into the restaurant with him . . . and he and [Zehmer] had one or two drinks together. Lucy said that while he felt the drinks he took he was not intoxicated, and from the way Zehmer handled the transaction he did not think he was either.

December 20 was on Saturday. Next day Lucy telephoned to J. C. Lucy and arranged with the latter to take a half interest in the purchase and pay half of the consideration. On Monday he engaged an attorney to examine the title. The attorney reported favorably on December 31 and on January 2 Lucy wrote Zehmer stating that the title was satisfactory, that he was ready to pay the purchase price in cash and asking when Zehmer would be ready to close the deal. Zehmer replied by letter, mailed on January 13, asserting that he had never agreed or intended to sell.

The defendants insist that the evidence was ample to support their contention that the writing sought to be enforced was prepared as a bluff or dare to force Lucy to admit that he did not have $50,000; that the whole matter was a joke; that the writing was not delivered to Lucy and no binding contract was ever made between the parties.

. . .

The appearance of the contract, the fact that it was under discussion for forty minutes or more before it was signed; Lucy's objection to the first draft because it was written in the singular, and he wanted Mrs. Zehmer to sign it also; the rewriting to meet that objection and the signing by Mrs. Zehmer; the discussion of what was to be included in the sale, the provision for the examination of the title, the completeness of the instrument that was executed, the taking possession of it by Lucy with no request or suggestion by either of the defendants that he give it back, are facts which furnish persuasive evidence that the execution of the contract was a serious business transaction rather than a casual, jesting matter as defendants now contend.

. . .

If it be assumed, contrary to what we think the evidence shows, that Zehmer was jesting about selling his farm to Lucy and that the transaction was intended by him to be a joke, nevertheless the evidence shows that Lucy did not so understand it but considered it to be a serious business transaction and the contract to be binding on the Zehmers as well as on himself. The very next day he arranged with his brother to put up half the money and take a half interest in the land. The day after that he employed an attorney to examine the title. The next night, Tuesday, he was back at Zehmer's place and there Zehmer told him for the first time, Lucy said, that he wasn't going to sell and he told Zehmer, "You know you sold that place fair and square." After receiving the report from his attorney that the title was good he wrote to Zehmer that he was ready to close the deal.

Not only did Lucy actually believe, but the evidence shows he was warranted in believing, that the contract represented a serious business transaction and a good faith sale and purchase of the farm.

In the field of contracts, as generally elsewhere, "We must look to the outward expression of a person as manifesting his intention rather than to his secret and unexpressed intention. The law imputes to a person an intention corresponding to the reasonable meaning of his words and acts." *First Nat. Bank v. Roanoke Oil Co.*, 169 Va. 99, 114, 192 S.E. 764, 770.

At no time prior to the execution of the contract had Zehmer indicated to Lucy by word or act that he was not in earnest about selling the farm. They had argued about it and discussed its terms, as Zehmer admitted, for a long time. Lucy testified that if there was any jesting it was about paying $50,000 that night. The contract and the evidence show that he was not expected to pay the money that night. Zehmer said that after the writing was signed he laid it down on the counter in front of Lucy. Lucy said Zehmer handed it to him. In any event there had been what appeared to be a good faith offer and a good faith acceptance, followed by the execution and apparent delivery of a written contract. Both said that Lucy put the writing in his pocket and then offered Zehmer $5 to seal the bargain. Not until then, even under the defendants' evidence, was anything said or done to indicate that the matter was a joke. Both of the Zehmers testified that when Zehmer asked his wife to sign he whispered that it was a joke so Lucy wouldn't hear and that it was not intended that he should hear.

The mental assent of the parties is not requisite for the formation of a contract. If the words or other acts of one of the parties have but one reasonable meaning, his undisclosed intention is immaterial except when an unreasonable meaning which he attaches to his manifestations is known to the other party. . . .

Whether the writing signed by the defendants and now sought to be enforced by the complainants was the result of a serious offer by Lucy and a serious acceptance by the defendants, or was a serious offer by Lucy and an acceptance in secret jest by the defendants, in either event it constituted a binding contract of sale between the parties. . . .

Comprehension and Thought Questions:

1. What conduct did the Zehmers engage in that arguably manifested their assent to a contract with Lucy?

2. What test does the court use to determine whether that conduct amounted to assent by the Zehmers? Is that test consistent or inconsistent with the objective natural of mutual assent? Why?

3. How does the court apply that test?

4. Why does Zehmer whispering to his wife that the transaction was a joke not preclude a finding of mutual assent?

Hypothetical Variations:

1. What if Lucy knew before the Zehmers signed that the Zehmers were joking? would come out diff bc Lucy knew better

2. What if immediately after the Zehmers signed, Mr. Zehmer gave the document to Lucy and said "Here is your contract—not! As we both know, this was a joke"?

3. What if Lucy knew that Mr. Zehmer was drunk to the point of not understanding the consequences of his actions? Same as #1

To see *why* mutual assent is tested objectively, imagine what would happen if the Zehmers had to actually intend to be bound for there to be mutual assent—that is, if mutual assent were a subjective test. If that were the case, while the situation would have looked the same from Lucy's perspective, if the Zehmers were actually joking, they could avoid the contract, and if they were serious, they could not. Yet no one would know the Zehmers' actual intent other than the Zehmers. In other words, a subjective test would undermine much of the certainty associated with the doctrine of mutual assent, as a party could always later claim, upon realizing that it struck a bad deal, that it subjectively did not intend to be bound.

PRACTICE PROBLEM 4-2

This problem will ask you to apply the doctrine of mutual assent to a hypothetical situation. To do this, you need to identify the applicable legal doctrine and break down that doctrine into different elements. Then you will need to assess whether each element has been satisfied. For example, as you hopefully have learned, mutual assent requires that each party manifest its assent to an exchange, and the other party has to be justified in believing such manifestation indicates such party's assent—in other words, that a reasonable person would understand the manifestation as indicating assent.

A law student needs a job, and she notices that the floor of a nearby restaurant is quite dirty. She approaches the manager and says, "I will sweep and mop your floor for $25." The manager says, "I really ought to let you do it," and then walks away. In her mind, the law student believes that the manager agreed to a contract. Does mutual assent exist? To answer this question, you should proceed as follows by examining each element of mutual assent:

1. Did the law student make any manifestations of assent? How do you know? What facts indicate this? Are there any facts that suggest otherwise?

2. If the student did manifest assent, would a reasonable person understand those manifestations as indicating assent to an exchange? How do you know? What characteristics of the manifestation make it reasonable or unreasonable to indicate this? Be sure to consider how characteristics may be interpreted in multiple ways and that there may be multiple characteristics of a manifestation.

3. Did the manager make any manifestations of assent? When? How do you know? What facts indicate this? Are there any facts that suggest otherwise?

4. If the manager did make manifestations of assent, would a reasonable person understand those manifestations as indicating assent to an exchange? How do you know? What facts indicate this? Are there any facts that suggest otherwise? Note that a party may have made multiple manifestations, which individually *or* together may make it reasonable for a party to believe that the other party was manifesting assent to an exchange.

Once you have finished your analysis above, it is necessary for you to draw a conclusion based on the characteristics and facts that suggest mutual assent does or does not exist. You can base this conclusion on an overall assessment of the manifestations as well as your determination that your conclusion better reflects or serves the contract law policies discussed in Chapter 1.

The objective analysis for mutual assent applies to the words and acts of all the parties to the purported contract. Each party to a contract would have to manifest assent to be bound. If only some of the parties to the contract manifest assent and others do not, then only the parties who manifested assent would be bound, assuming under the terms of the contract, less than all of the parties could be bound.

Finally, while the need for mutual assent is a mandatory aspect of contract law, the parties can create their own rules as to what manifestation will amount to assent. This is typically done in significant transactions, where the parties intend to create a formal writing reflecting the terms of the contract. In that circumstance, as we saw in Chapter 3, in the discussion of the signature blocks, typically the lawyer for the party who drafts the writing inserts a provision indicating that assent by a party occurs only once that party signs and delivers a counterpart of that contract to the other party.

The following case demonstrates the objective nature of the mutual assent inquiry in a more modern context of a dispute. It also exemplifies an exception to the objective test. As you read this case, see if you can identify the exception.

Moreno v. Smith
Supreme Court of Georgia
299 Ga. 443 (2016)

BLACKWELL, Justice.

Dolores Moreno is the mother of Gina Moreno, and in 2004, Dolores acquired a residential property in Gwinnett County. Three years later, Dolores gave a one-half interest in the property to Gina as a gift, and around the same time, Dolores and Gina signed a document that purports to be a contract. According to that document, Dolores agreed to sell her remaining one-half interest in the property to Gina, and Gina agreed to pay $75,000 to Dolores in $400 monthly installments. After six more years passed, Gina had made no payments to Dolores, and Dolores filed a lawsuit against Gina for breach of contract and for an equitable accounting as between tenants in common.[6] The trial court granted partial summary judgment to Dolores, concluding that the undisputed evidence showed as a matter of law that Dolores and Gina had entered into a binding and enforceable contract for the purchase and sale of the property. Following a bench trial on the question of a remedy, the trial court

---

6. [1] During the pendency of this lawsuit, Dolores passed away, Michael T. Smith was appointed as the temporary administrator of her estate, and Smith was substituted as the plaintiff. For purposes of this opinion, however, it is unnecessary to distinguish between Dolores and her estate, and for the sake of simplicity, we refer to both as "Dolores."

awarded damages to Dolores for breach of contract. . . . Gina appeals, and we reverse in part, vacate in part, and remand for further proceedings consistent with this opinion.

Gina contends that the trial court erred when it awarded partial summary judgment to Dolores and concluded as a matter of law that Dolores and Gina had entered into a binding and enforceable contract. We agree. Although the document that Dolores and Gina signed purports to be a binding contract, Gina offered evidence that tends to show that no contract was made. Indeed, Gina submitted an affidavit in opposition to the motion for summary judgment in which she said, among other things, that she had signed the document in question at the request of her mother for the sole purpose of enabling Dolores to demonstrate an interest in the property and that she was earning income from it. Gina also said in her affidavit that, as of the time the document was signed, Dolores consistently had made statements to indicate that Gina was not expected to pay anything to Dolores for the property.[7]

"It is well settled that an agreement between two parties will occur only when the minds of the parties meet at the same time, upon the same subject-matter, and in the same sense." *Cox Broadcasting Corp. v. Nat. Collegiate Athletic Assn.*, 250 Ga. 391, 395, 297 S.E.2d 733 (1982). To determine whether the parties had the mutual assent or meeting of the minds that is essential for the formation of a binding and enforceable contract, courts apply an objective theory of intent whereby one party's intention is deemed to be that meaning a reasonable man in the position of the other contracting party would ascribe to the first party's manifestations of assent, or that meaning which the other contracting party knew the first party ascribed to his manifestations of assent.

More specifically, as one prominent commentator has explained,

> in those unusual instances in which one intends that one's assent have no legal consequences[,] [u]nder the objective theory, a court will honor that intention if the other party has reason to know it. And it will honor it if the other party actually knows it. . . . The same result has been reached even though a written agreement is made as a sham, for the purpose of deceiving others, with an oral understanding that it will not be enforced.

E. Allan Farnsworth, Contracts § 3.7, at 122 (2d ed. 1990) (citations and footnote omitted; emphasis in original). "The circumstances surrounding the making of the contract, such as correspondence and discussions, are relevant in deciding if there was a mutual assent to an agreement, and courts are free to consider such extrinsic evidence." *McReynolds v. Krebs*, 290 Ga. 850, 853, 725 S.E.2d 584 (2012) (citation and punctuation omitted). *See also* Farnsworth,

---

7. [5] Gina brought forward other evidence at trial that was consistent with her claim that neither she nor Dolores intended to make a binding and enforceable contract when they signed the document.

supra at 123-124 ("Circumstances, rather than words, may also indicate a party's intention not to be bound. . . . [And] the fact that the parties to an agreement are members of the same family is given weight as showing an intention not to be legally bound." (Citation omitted)). "And where such extrinsic evidence exists and is disputed, the question of whether a party has assented to the contract is generally a matter for the jury." *Fletcher v. C.W. Matthews Contracting Co.*, 322 Ga. App. 751, 754 (1) (a), 746 S.E.2d 230 (2013) (citation and punctuation omitted).

Dolores relies on the parol evidence rule, arguing that where a written contract is facially clear and complete, extrinsic evidence of contractual intent is immaterial and inadmissible to vary the terms of the contract. "Although parol evidence cannot be used to contradict or vary the terms of a valid written agreement, parol evidence may be used to show no valid agreement ever went into existence." *BellSouth Advertising & Pub. Corp. v. McCollum*, 209 Ga. App. 441, 444, 433 S.E.2d 437 (1993) (citations and punctuation omitted). In particular, "the basic rule that a sham contract or a contract that the parties understood was not to be binding may be refuted by parol evidence to show that there was, in fact, no contract, is sensible and widely followed." 6-25 Corbin on Contracts § 25.21 (2016).

Gina brought forward admissible evidence to show that Dolores and Gina did not intend to make a binding and enforceable contract when they signed the document, that the document was a mere sham, and that no binding and enforceable contract existed. And although it is the parties' intent at the time they allegedly entered the contract that matters, the evidence presented by Gina of their discussions at that time is arguably bolstered by other evidence of the circumstances surrounding the purported contract, including the ongoing relationship between the parties as mother and daughter, the undisputed fact that Dolores gifted a one-half interest in the property to Gina, the subsequent failure of Gina to make any monthly payments to Dolores, the failure of Dolores to assert a breach more promptly, and the repeated statements of Dolores that the property belonged to Gina and that Gina did not have to pay her anything. Dolores disputed that evidence and presented her own evidence to show that she and Gina entered into a binding and enforceable contract. But courts are not authorized to weigh disputed evidence and resolve conflicts in the evidence on summary judgment. Accordingly, we conclude that there is a genuine issue of disputed fact about the existence of a binding and enforceable contract in this case, and the trial court erred by granting partial summary judgment to Dolores on her claim for breach of contract.

Because a genuine issue of material fact remains as to whether Gina breached any contract, we not only reverse the grant of partial summary judgment, but we also must reverse the award of damages for breach of contract. . . . For these reasons, therefore, the judgment of the trial court is reversed in part and vacated in part, and the case is remanded for further proceedings consistent with this opinion.

Judgment reversed in part and vacated in part, and case remanded with direction.

All the Justices concur.

Understanding the Case:

1. *Extrinsic Evidence to Determine Parties' Intent:* Dolores argued that the parol evidence rule precluded Gina from introducing evidence of the parties' intent to be bound because the formal written contract the parties signed clearly reflected the parties' intent to be bound and reflected all of the terms of sale. However, the court held that the parol evidence rule does not prevent a party from introducing evidence as to the parties' actual intent to be bound. Thus, Gina was allowed to introduce evidence to show that while the parties signed the written document labeled "Contract," it was a farce, and they did not actually intend to be bound by it. You will study the parol evidence rule in Chapter 15, but in general, that rule precludes a court from considering a contract term that conflicts with or supplements (i.e., adds to) a final written document reflecting all of the terms of a contract.

2. *Motion for Summary Judgment:* In this case, Dolores moved for summary judgment. In that motion, Dolores argued that, based on the pleadings (meaning her complaint and her daughter Gina's answer) and pretrial discovery, even when viewed in a light most favorable to the defendant (Gina), Dolores was entitled to judgment as a matter of law.[8] That is because, as she argued, Gina's evidence of the parties' intent was inadmissible under the parol evidence rule, as discussed above. That means her evidence of the parties' intent (the signed written contract) would be the only evidence to show the parties' intent. However, the Georgia Supreme Court reversed the lower court's grant of summary judgment on that issue, holding that Gina's evidence of the parties' intent was *not* precluded by the parol evidence rule, and could be introduced. The court then remanded the case for a trial on the issue of the parties' intent to be bound.

3. *Ownership of Property as Tenants in Common:* According to Gina's presentation of facts, Dolores conveyed a half-interest in the subject property to Gina as a *gift*. At that time, the parties owned the property as tenants in common—a

---

8. *See, e.g.,* Jefferson v. Waveny Care Center, Inc., 40 A.3d 825, 828 (Conn. Super. Ct. 2010) ("[S]ummary judgment shall be rendered forthwith if the pleadings, affidavits and any other proof submitted show that there is no genuine issue as to any material fact and that the moving party is entitled to judgment as a matter of law. In deciding a motion for summary judgment, the trial court must view the evidence in the light most favorable to the nonmoving party. . . .") (Internal quotation marks omitted.)

real property concept you will study in your Property course. Why, then, did the parties sign a written contract showing that Dolores *sold* the property to Gina? One possible answer is so that Dolores's creditors would think that Dolores was earning income from the property (the $400 monthly installments Gina would owe to pay the purchase price per the formal written contract). Those creditors, in turn, would lend Dolores money secured by that future income.

Comprehension and Thought Questions:

1. What was the test the court used to determine whether Dolores and Gina intended to be bound?

2. Is that test entirely objective (looking only at what a reasonable person would interpret the manifestation to mean), or does it also look at the parties' subjective (i.e., actual) intent? If the latter, how does the court's test for mutual assent factor in the parties' subjective intents in deciding mutual assent?

3. What evidence did Gina introduce to show that she and her mom in fact did not intend to be bound by the signed written document?

4. Whose version of facts did the court believe?

5. Do you agree that the test for mutual assent *should* consider whether one party knew the other party's subjective intention in the circumstances described in *Moreno*? Or should the mutual assent inquiry always be an objective inquiry?

6. Under the court's test, what is to prevent a party to any contract who seeks to avoid contractual obligations from arguing that the parties did not actually intend to be bound?

Hypothetical Variations:

1. What if, on remand, the trial court does not believe Gina's evidence that Gina and Dolores signed the written document as a sham to which the parties did not intend to be bound?

2. What if Gina had made several monthly payments on the $75,000 and subsequently stopped paying—and then, when her mom sued to enforce the contract, Gina argued that the written contract was a sham and that her mom had actually given her a one-half interest in the property as a gift?

3. What if Gina and Dolores were not related?

4. Assume Dolores intended to give a one-half interest in her property to Gina at some point and that she either needed to retain ownership over the entire property, or at least generate income from the property (or any portion of the property) to obtain loans she needed. How could she have achieved that result short of preparing a written document of sale that did not actually reflect her intent? In considering this question, keep in mind that parties can include terms in contracts that become effective in the future.

C. OFFER

Under the classic analysis of mutual assent, parties arrive at mutual assent through a process of offer and acceptance. An **offer** is one party's manifestation of his willingness to enter into a bargain, justifying the offeree in believing that her acceptance will conclude a bargain.[9] The person who makes the offer, the **offeror**, specifies the proposed terms of the bargain in the offer—in other words, what promise or promises he intends to make, and what he seeks in exchange. Consistent with the objective theory of mutual assent, an offer must justify the person (or persons) to whom the offer is made—the **offeree** (or offerees)—in understanding that the offeree's assent to that offer is invited and will conclude the bargain.

Whether a manifestation is an offer depends on the facts and circumstances. For example, when determining whether an oral statement is an offer, a court may examine the tone of voice, the number or type of persons to whom the statement was directed, the completeness of the business terms in the statement, whether the statement covers all possible or necessary terms, previous negotiations between the parties, the location of the parties when the statement was made, and the context of the statement.

If the offeree manifests assent to the offer, then the offeree has accepted the offer. If the offer is not accepted, then there is no bargain. Section D below discusses the concept of acceptance.

Because an offer must confer on the offeree the power to accept, if an offeree knows or has reason to know that the offeror has *not* conferred on him the power to accept, then the offeror has not made an offer. This sometimes occurs where a person acting on behalf of a business organization does not have power to bind the company. For example, if you walked into a Best Buy store and a person with a name badge labeled "salesperson" offered to sell you the company, you clearly would not think the salesperson could sell the company to you. Linking this discussion to Chapter 9, the salesperson would not have authority to enter this type of contract. As such, the salesperson has not made you an offer.

Similarly, there is no offer where an offeror reserves the right for itself to conclude a bargain. For example, where a seller gives a price quote to a prospective buyer, the quote is commonly understood as not conferring on the buyer the power to accept. That is because the seller does not commit itself to a contract upon the buyer's placing of an order, without knowing the quantity of items being ordered or a delivery date. Thus, a price quote is commonly viewed as inviting an offer to purchase. However, if a seller gives a price quote in response to a buyer's request for a quote for, say, 100 printers to be delivered on

---

9. Restatement (Second) of Contracts § 24 (1981).

October 1, then the price quote in this circumstance might be an offer, given that all the essential terms other than price were already specified by the buyer when the seller gave the price quote. This conclusion would be more obvious still if the price quote included language such as "for immediate acceptance," as this language would lead the buyer to reasonably believe that his assent would conclude the bargain.

PRACTICE PROBLEM 4-3

Dale Villanova, a new business law attorney, met with Miranda Foote, the owner of One Vista Plaza, about Dale possibly leasing shared office space at One Vista Plaza for Dale's new legal practice. After touring office space #3 in Suite 22, Dale asked to see a copy of Miranda's lease agreement. In response, Miranda e-mailed a copy of her "standard" lease agreement to Dale. In her e-mail, Miranda wrote "Dale, as requested, here is a standard contract for office space #3 in Suite 22. I hope you become a tenant! I look forward to hearing back from you."

Below is an excerpt of the first five sections from that agreement, along with the signature block. The document Miranda sent also had a section on termination of lease and a section labeled "general," which included governing law.

SHARED OFFICE SPACE LEASE AGREEMENT

This **Shared Office Space Lease Agreement** (this "Agreement"), dated this _____ day of October, 2019, is between Miranda Foote ("Landlord"), and _____ ("Tenant").

The parties agree as follows:

Section 1. Lease. Landlord agrees to lease to Tenant shared office space #3 in Suite 22 at One Vista Plaza in Springfield, Columbia (the "Premises") for two years beginning December 1, 2019 (the "Term"), unless this lease is terminated sooner under Section 6.

Section 2. Excluded Property. Tenant acknowledges and agrees that other tenants occupy shared office spaces #1 and #2 in Suite 22 at One Vista Plaza. As such, Tenant does not have any right to occupy either shared office space #1 or #2. Landlord represents to Tenant that the tenants who occupy shared office spaces #1 and #2 are aware and have agreed that they have no right to occupy office space #3.

Section 3. Use of Premises. Tenant may only use shared office space #3 in Suite 22 for Tenant's business needs. Moreover, Tenant may use all areas identified by Landlord as common areas, to include the waiting area for Suite 22 and public areas in One Vista Plaza. Tenant may not use the Premises for any other purposes.

Section 4. Rent. Tenant shall pay Landlord $1,200 each month during the Term ("Rent"), to be paid in advance no later than the fifth day of each month during the Term.

Section 5. Deposit. In addition to Rent, Tenant shall pay Landlord a deposit of $1,200 no later than the second business day after the date of this Agreement. Landlord shall return this deposit to Tenant no later than 60 days after the end of the Term, which deposit Landlord may reduce by

(a) any amount which Landlord reasonably determines is necessary to return the Premises to the condition it was in at the start of the Term, excluding ordinary wear and tear,

(b) any amount of Rent remaining unpaid, and

(c) any portion of Rent to be payable by Tenant during the remaining Term, if Landlord terminates this Agreement before the end of the Term under Section 6.

If the deposit is reduced under Section 5(c), such reduction is in addition to any other rights and remedies Landlord has upon an early termination of this Agreement.

[portions omitted]

To signify their agreement to this Agreement, the parties have signed and delivered this Agreement as of the date set forth in the preamble.

Landlord:
___//ss Miranda Foote//_____

Tenant:

_____

---

1. Has Miranda made an offer to Dale? Which facts point to the existence of an offer and which point to no offer? Make sure to reference the rule or requirements for an offer when developing your answer. *Yes; signed, definite price*

2. What if Miranda had delivered a copy of the above lease agreement to Dale without having first signed on the Landlord's signature line? Would Miranda have made an offer? *maybe no, maybe yes?*

3. What if in her cover e-mail with the above lease agreement, Miranda informed Dale that she had given a similar lease agreement to two other prospective tenants, and that she would consider to whom to lease once she heard back from the interested prospective tenants? Would Miranda have made an offer in that situation? What if in her cover e-mail to each of the three prospective tenants, Miranda had said that she would lease shared office space #3 in Suite 22 to the <u>first to respond</u>? *→ yes*

4. If you represented Miranda, what advice would you have given her to ensure that she would not be bound by the lease she sent to Dale, assuming that was her intention? *don't sign it, specify in the body of the email that it isn't an offer*

[left margin handwritten notes:] *not illusory b/c has discretion for who; sub clauses, but s/w will cause; certainty of terms = yes; definite P; all of the three → yes; b/c signing; no power like a quote*

[right margin handwritten notes:] *power in his power to accept*

1. Certainty of Terms

Even where a party intends to make an offer, her manifestation often cannot be understood as an offer if the essential terms of the bargain she proposes cannot be determined with reasonable certainty.[10] The term **reasonable certainty** means that a court can tell (1) when a party breaches and (2) how to provide an appropriate remedy for that breach.[11]

While courts vary as to how they decide what terms are "essential," many view a term as essential if it is important to the transaction. To state the rule differently, it is often not reasonable to conclude that a manifestation—even a manifestation that clearly manifests a person's intent to be bound— is an offer where that manifestation does not make it reasonably clear what the central terms of the exchange are.

To help you identify the "essential terms" of a contract, recall from Chapter 3 that usually written contracts set out the parties' principal promises after the definitions section of the contract, where there is a definition section. That section of the written contract is where the parties usually lay out the essential terms. Of course, you can't always just look for the terms there to determine what is essential to the parties, as you might be the person who has to decide what terms are essential and therefore should be placed in that part of the contract! Plus, not all contracts are reflected by writings. Still, thinking about where such essential terms often appear in written contracts might help you identify which terms are essential in a contract versus which terms are not.

To see how these rules work, let us continue with our factual scenario from the above problem. Assume Miranda Foote meets with Dale Villanova to discuss Dale's potential lease of shared office space. During that meeting, Miranda informs Dale that she has two spaces available for lease in One Vista Plaza, both in Suite 22—office spaces #2 and #3. While each has a base rent of $1,200, Miranda indicates that this base rate is adjusted up or down based on the prospective tenant's credit score. Moreover, if the prospective tenant is willing to sign a multi-year lease, that can lower the monthly rent.

[handwritten margin note: i.e., price (an essential term) not determined w/ reasonable certainty]

Here, even if Miranda uses language suggesting that she is committed to leasing one of these spaces to Dale or refers to her communication to Dale as an "offer," Miranda might not have made an offer. That is because, despite Miranda's clear manifestation of her intent to be bound, she has failed to specify the essential terms of the lease. In other words, even if Dale says "I accept," we still don't know what property he is leasing and the monthly rent. It should be obvious that premises and rent are central terms to a lease.[12]

Essential terms are to be distinguished from nonessential, or ancillary terms. **Ancillary terms**, while important to a bargain, are not the parties' main

---

10. Armstrong v. Rohm and Haas Co., 349 F. Supp. 2d 71, 78-79 (D. Mass. 2004).
11. Restatement (Second) of Contracts § 33 (1981).
12. *See, e.g.,* Walker v. Keith, 382 S.W.2d 198, 202 (Ky. 1964).

focus in the bargain. Thus, the parties' failure to agree to ancillary terms will rarely prevent the existence of mutual assent.

For example, in the case of Dale's lease of shared office space from Miranda Foote, we can expect that their lease will address terms ranging from Miranda's duty to keep common areas safe to Dale's duty to allow Miranda access to Dale's space so that she can perform regular maintenance. But these terms are not the heart of the bargain. Again, the essence is the lease of the premises in exchange for the monthly rent. As such, the parties' failure to specify or agree on these types of ancillary terms will rarely prevent the existence of mutual assent (unless, of course, one or both of the parties manifests an intent to not be bound until these terms are agreed on).

You can think about this framework as a sliding scale: the more important the terms are that are not agreed upon by the parties, the less likely it is reasonable for the other party to view a manifestation as an offer, even if the manifestation indicates a commitment. In contrast, the less important the terms are that are not agreed upon by the parties, the less likely it is that such non-agreed-upon terms will prevent a party's manifestation from amounting to assent.

Nevertheless, performance can remove any uncertainty that exists in a bargain's terms. The following is the Restatement's approach to removing uncertainty in this way:

Restatement § 34 Certainty and Choice of Terms; Effect of Performance or Reliance

. . .

(2) Part performance under an agreement may remove uncertainty and establish that a contract enforceable as a bargain has been formed.

. . .

To see how this rule works, suppose Miranda Foote gives Dale the keys to Suite 22 at One Vista Plaza with an invoice for "shared office space #3 in Suite 22" for $1,200 for the first month's rent. Dale pays the invoiced $1,200 without any objection. Moreover, each month Miranda invoices Dale $1,200 and he pays it. Here, Dale's and Miranda's respective performances have given certainty to the essential terms of the leased premises and rent. Specifically, Miranda's act of giving Dale the keys to Suite 22 and invoicing Dale for shared office space #3 and Dale's act of taking those keys and using that shared space identifies the leased space. And Miranda's act of invoicing Dale $1,200 a month, and Dale's act of paying that amount each month, evidences the amount of rent. Consequently, with these terms established, a court would be able to determine whether either party breached one of these terms and award a remedy for such a breach.

Some courts that follow modern contract law do not require that the essential terms be reasonably certain in order to conclude that there is mutual assent, where the parties' manifestations otherwise show an intent to be bound. They apply the mutual assent doctrine flexibly in an attempt to reflect modern

At least a month-to-month lease

business practices. Still, if the parties did not assent to an essential term and such a term cannot be inferred, a court will not find mutual assent.

You will see a modern approach to mutual assent when you study mutual assent under Article 2 of the UCC in Chapter 5. While that chapter focuses on contracts for the sale of goods governed by Article 2, as Chapter 2 noted, oftentimes the UCC influences the law in non-UCC transactions. Thus, courts are often influenced by the UCC's flexible approach to mutual assent even in non-UCC cases.

Remember that these rules on mutual assent apply unless the parties have agreed otherwise. Thus, a party can always manifest an intent to not assent unless and until every single term—no matter how minor—is agreed on. In fact, in significant transactions where both parties are represented by counsel, the parties typically do not intend to be bound until every term that is to be reflected in the final written document has been agreed on. To manifest this intent, a lawyer will usually mark each preliminary version of the formal written document as a "draft." A lawyer will also ensure that any preliminary writing, such as a term sheet, contains language indicating that the client does not intend to be bound unless and until the client has signed a formal writing containing *all* of the terms of the contract. Chapter 10, in the discussion on term sheets, contains an example of this type of language.

In contrast, parties might decide they want to be bound without pinning down with definiteness all essential terms. In this case, a lawyer can help prepare a formal written document reflecting the terms the parties have agreed on, and set out a formula or process for how the open essential term will be determined.[13]

This situation comes up, for example, where a buyer wishes to buy a business, an ownership interest in that business, or an asset that does not have an easily determined fair market value. In these situations, since there is no fair market value (which is understood to mean the price a willing buyer is willing to pay and a willing seller is willing to accept in the open market), the parties often cannot set the price up front. So they instead either specify a formula for determining purchase price or create a process to determine the purchase price. The following is a sample provision setting up a process to determine the fair market value and, in turn, the purchase price of shares of stock of a company.

> The Buyer shall pay the Seller fair market value for the Shares. The parties shall identify an independent appraiser mutually satisfactory to them to determine fair market value of the Shares. The parties shall equally share the costs of the independent appraiser.

---

13. The parties will need to set out a process to determine the open term, and not merely agree to agree on that open term in the future, for courts often do not enforce agreements to agree as to essential terms. You will study this in Chapter 13.

Note that it often takes multiple provisions of a writing to fully lay out contractual terms. For example, while the above contract term creates a duty of the Buyer to pay the purchase price and specifies how to determine the purchase price, it does not specify when the purchase price is payable, and the method of payment. These terms are undoubtedly set out elsewhere in the contract.

The key to drafting a provision that lays out a process to determine an essential term, like the one above, is to make sure the process will not fail. If the process can fail (for example, in the above contract, if the parties cannot mutually agree on an independent appraiser), then the contract should specify the consequences of such failure, such as the termination of the contract.

PRACTICE PROBLEM 4-4

Professor Judd announces during class one day that she is looking for a Contracts student to perform research for her next summer on a topic of contract law. She asks interested students to apply. Ayo Okonjo is one of the five students who applies. She, along with each of the other applicants, meets with Professor Judd to discuss the position. As the professor tells each applicant, the professor has not yet decided on a specific topic for research. But she wants to hire a student who is good at research and writing and interested in contracts.

Professor Judd meets with each student. In each meeting, she tells each student that the student can work for either pay or credit, as the student chooses. If for pay, the student will be paid $15 an hour. If for credit, the student will receive one credit for every 60 hours worked.

After meeting each student, the professor decides to hire Ayo. In her note with the good news, Professor Judd tells Ayo "I am thrilled that you are interested in doing research work for me this summer. After meeting with all applicants, I have decided to hire you, as you have such strong research and writing skills, and have demonstrated a strong interest in contracts. I look forward to hearing back from you to confirm that you would like the position." Ayo immediately responds and indicates that she accepts the position.

Once summer starts, Ayo realizes the position is not what she was expecting. Professor Judd apparently was expecting the research assistant to perform 50 hours of research per week. The two had not discussed hours during the interview, so the high number of hours came as a surprise to Ayo. Moreover, the topic Professor Judd decided to write about was how to format a contract for maximum readability—a topic that Ayo was not interested in.

Ayo is considering whether she really needs to perform this work for Professor Judd. You are a classmate of hers. Be prepared to discuss with her the following questions:

[handwritten margin notes: "yes, uncertain things are errors ancillary up to offer"]

1. Did Professor Judd make an offer to Ayo for Ayo to work for her for the summer? Why or why not? *[handwritten: yes, essential terms clear; may be not if no true exhaust it self]*

2. Assume Professor Judd did not make an offer and that therefore there is no mutual assent. Do you see any other risks to Ayo of not performing the work for Professor Judd? How do you advise Ayo in light of those risks?

3. If Ayo had consulted you before she prepared her response to Professor Judd, how would you have advised her to respond? *[handwritten: → more details/specifics]*

2. Ads as (Not) Offers

Newspaper ads, television ads, internet ads, product catalogues, and other solicitation materials broadcast to the public are commonly not viewed as offers. Instead, they usually are viewed as invitations to make an offer. That is because these types of communications are generally understood to be marketing material, emphasizing the high points of the relevant product or service to the public, rather than containing the specific terms of the proposed bargain. The fact that they are broadcast to large audiences further reinforces the fact that they are not intended to be offers. In other words, based on the content of, or words used in, the communication as well as the number of recipients of the message, it may not be reasonable to believe that the message is a manifestation of willingness to enter into a bargain with everyone who views it, inviting each recipient to accept and conclude the bargain.

However, in some circumstances, a business's advertisement does constitute an offer. Some of the factors courts consider in deciding whether an advertisement is an offer include whether the advertisement is complete and definite enough as to items, prices, and quantities such that there is nothing left to negotiate; and whether there is language of commitment. In sum, a court will consider whether a reasonable person would understand the advertisement as an offer.

The *Chang* case, set out below, demonstrates a court's analysis of whether an advertisement is an offer.

Chang, et al. v. First Colonial Savings Bank
Supreme Court of Virginia
242 Va. 388 (1991)

HASSELL, Justice.

The primary issue that we consider in this appeal is whether a newspaper advertisement constitutes an offer which, when accepted, creates a legally enforceable contract.

The litigants stipulated the relevant facts. Chia T. Chang and Shin S. Chang, who resided in the Richmond area, read the following advertisement which appeared in local newspapers on November 18, 1985. The advertisement states in part:

> You Win 2 ways WITH FIRST COLONIAL'S Savings Certificates
>
> 1 Great Gifts
> 2 & High Interest
>
> . . .
>
> Saving at First Colonial is a very rewarding experience. In appreciation for your business we have Great Gifts for you to enjoy NOW—and when your investment matures you get your entire principal back PLUS GREAT INTEREST.
> Plan B: 3 ½ Year Investment
>
> . . .
>
> Deposit $14,000 and receive two gifts: a Remington Shotgun and GE CB Radio, OR an RCA 20" Color-Trac TV, and $20,136.12 upon maturity in 3 ½ years.
> Substantial penalty for early withdrawal. Allow 4-6 weeks for delivery. Wholesale cost of gifts must be reported on IRS Form 1099. Rates shown are . . . 8¾% for Plan B. All gifts are fully warranted by manufacturer. DEPOSITS INSURED TO 100,000 by FSLIC. Interest can be received monthly by check.

Relying upon this advertisement, the Changs deposited $14,000 with First Colonial Savings Bank on January 3, 1986. They received a color television that day from First Colonial and expected to receive the sum of $20,136.12 upon maturity of the deposit in three and one-half years. First Colonial also gave the Changs a certificate of deposit when they made their deposit.

When the Changs returned to liquidate the certificate of deposit upon its maturity, they were informed that the advertisement contained a typographical error and that they should have deposited $15,000 in order to receive the sum of $20,136.12 upon maturity of the certificate of deposit.

First Colonial did not inform the Changs nor were the Changs made aware that the advertisement contained an error until after the certificate of deposit had matured. First Colonial, however, did display in its lobby pamphlets which contained the correct figures when the Changs made their deposit.

The Changs instituted this proceeding in the general district court seeking to recover $1,312.19, the difference between the $20,136.12 amount in the advertisement and $18,823.93, the amount that First Colonial actually paid to the Changs. The general district court awarded a judgment in favor of the Changs, and First Colonial appealed that judgment to the circuit court. The circuit court held that the advertisement did not constitute an offer but was an invitation to bargain or negotiate and entered a judgment in favor of First Colonial. We awarded the Changs an appeal.

The Changs argue that when members of the public reasonably rely upon a bank advertisement which offers a specific gift and dollar amount upon maturity in return for a deposit of a sum certain, and the bank fails to notify those who made deposits of an error in the advertisement until the certificate of deposit matures, then the specific term of the advertisement constitutes an offer which, when accepted, is a binding and enforceable contract. First Colonial argues, however, that the advertisement did not constitute an offer but rather was an invitation to make an offer because the advertisement was directed to the general public and required no performance on the part of the parties to whom it was directed.

The general rule followed in most states, and which we adopt, is that newspaper advertisements are not offers, but merely invitations to bargain. However, there is a very narrow and limited exception to this rule. "[W]here the offer is clear, definite, and explicit, and leaves nothing open for negotiation, it constitutes an offer, acceptance of which will complete the contract." *Lefkowitz v. Great Minneapolis Surplus Store, Inc.*, 251 Minn. 188, 191, 86 N.W.2d 689, 691 (1957). As Professor Williston observed:

> In any event there can be no doubt that a positive offer may be made even by an advertisement or general notice. . . . The only general test which can be submitted as a guide is an inquiry whether the facts show that some performance was promised in positive terms in return for something requested.

Applying these principles to the facts before us, we hold that the advertisement constituted an offer which was accepted when the Changs deposited their $14,000 with the Bank for a period of three and one-half years. A plain reading of the advertisement demonstrates that First Colonial's offer of the television and $20,136.12 upon maturity in three and one-half years was clear, definite, and explicit and left nothing open for negotiation.[14]

Even though the Bank's advertisement upon which the Changs relied may have contained a mistake caused by a typographical error, under the unique facts and circumstances of this case, the error does not invalidate the offer. First Colonial did not inform the Changs of this typographical error until after it had the use of the Changs' $14,000 for three and one-half years. Additionally, applying the general rule to which there are certain exceptions not applicable here, a unilateral mistake does not void an otherwise legally binding contract.

---

14. [*] First Colonial also argues that a contract did not exist until the Changs offered to deposit the sum of $14,000 with First Colonial and it made a counter offer which was accepted by the Changs. Pursuant to the terms of this purported counter offer, a contract was created and memorialized in the form of the certificate of deposit which was issued by the Bank to the Changs, and that the terms of the certificate of deposit were not breached because such terms set forth an interest rate of 8.75% which the Bank used to determine that it owed the Changs $18,823.93 upon maturity of the certificate of deposit. We reject this argument because of our holding that the advertisement constituted an offer which was accepted by the Changs.

. . .

We also reject First Colonial's argument that the advertisement did not create a contract because there was no meeting of the minds. As we stated in *Gibney & Co. v. Arlington B. Co.*, 112 Va. 117, 70 S.E. 485 (1911):

> The offerer has a right to prescribe in his offer any conditions as to time, place, quantity, mode of acceptance, or other matters, which it may please him to insert in and make a part thereof, and the acceptance to conclude the agreement must in every respect meet and correspond with the offer, neither falling within or going beyond the terms proposed, but exactly meeting them at all points and closing with these just as they stand.

Id. at 120-21, 70 S.E. at 487 (citation omitted). When the Changs tendered their $14,000 to First Colonial for three and one-half years, they complied with all of the conditions in First Colonial's offer. Hence, there was a meeting of the minds and an enforceable contract.

Accordingly, we will reverse the judgment of the circuit court and enter final judgment here in favor of the Changs for $1,312.19 plus interest.

Reversed and final judgment.

Understanding the Case:

1. *Multiple Plaintiffs:* In *Chang*, the plaintiffs were not only the Changs but others like the Changs who deposited money into a bank account with First Colonial Bank. You can tell that there were multiple plaintiffs from the heading, which lists plaintiffs as the Changs "et al."—meaning "and others." Likewise, the court's statement of facts explains that there were multiple plaintiffs who deposited money with the Bank.

2. *Confusion with "Meeting of the Minds":* After analyzing whether there was an offer in *Chang*, the court analyzed whether there had been a "meeting of the minds." However, in its "meeting of the minds" analysis, the court simply analyzed whether the Changs had accepted the Bank's offer. In other words, the court used the phrase "meeting of the minds" to describe the final step in creating mutual assent—acceptance. Some courts use the phrase "meeting of the minds" in this way. Others use the "meeting of the minds" phrase to capture the entire process of mutual assent, picking up both offer and acceptance.[15] However, many courts reject the "meeting of the minds" phrase on the grounds that it implies there must be an actual, *subjective* agreement by the parties' minds to the bargain, which is not consistent with the objective nature of mutual assent.

---

15. *See, e.g.*, Bloomington Partners, LLC v. City of Bloomington, 364 F. Supp. 2d 772, 779 (C.D. Ill. 2005).

Comprehension and Thought Questions:

1. What was the purpose of the court's "offer" inquiry? In other words, *why* was the court analyzing whether the First Colonial Savings Bank made an offer? *no offer = no K*

2. According to the court, what is the general rule on whether ads are offers? What exception does the court identify? Does this exception seem sensible? In other words, what policy or policies does it serve? *seems sensible; fairness; objectivity*

3. Did the court find that the Bank made an offer through its advertisement? *yes*

4. Why didn't the existence of an error in the Bank's advertisement preclude the ad from being an offer? *see 2 reasons given*

5. In contrast, to what extent do you think the court's holding was affected by the fact that the Bank's "mistake" was in the Bank's favor? *Should* that fact affect the court's holding? *Gproaby alot; no - had they given too much, might not induce mean a cliff.*

6. What should the Bank have done to avoid being bound by its advertisement to give two gifts to individuals who deposited $14,000 into an account with the Bank? *inauded some kind of disclaimer, not been so specific; required PM to come in + negotiate*

Hypothetical Variations:

1. What if the Changs had known about the error in the advertisement when they deposited their $14,000? *→ might be cliff y/c mistake not "unilateral"*

2. What if First Colonial Savings Bank's advertisement ended by saying "interested parties must contact one of our customer service representatives for more details"? *→ would have made act ≠ offer b/c no clearity as to essential items (undruts certainty + definiteness)*

As you saw in *Chang*, courts analyze all the facts and circumstances to determine if a manifestation is an offer. That was true even though, in general, ads are not offers. Because mutual assent is a facts-and-circumstances inquiry, you, too, will want to avoid drawing conclusions about certain types of communications either always being—or never being—offers. The same is true for certain types of communications always being or never being acceptances.

3. Offer as Consumer Protection

One factor some courts consider in determining whether a party made an offer is whether the communication is misleading.

For example, in *Izadi vs. Machado (Gus) Ford, Inc.*, a case decided by the Florida District Court of Appeals in 1989,[16] Gus Machado Ford, a Ford

---

16. 550 So. 2d 1135 (Fla. Dist. Ct. App. 1989).

dealership, advertised a "minimum $3,000 trade-in allowance."[17] This trade-in value was displayed prominently at the top of the ad (though infinitesimally fine print below this said it was only for the 1988 Eddie Bauer Aerostar or Turbo T-Bird in stock), followed by a listing of three different Ford vehicles for sale.

For the last car in the list, the 1988 Ford Ranger pickup with full factory equipment, the final price was listed as $3,595. This price reflected the initial price of $7,095, with a $3,000 reduction for "any trade *worth* $3,000,"[18] as well as a $500 factory rebate.

Izadi showed up at the dealer with his clunker of a trade-in and $3,595 in cash. However, Gus Machado Ford informed Izadi that his trade-in was not "worth" $3,000 and would not sell him the Ranger for $3,595. Izadi sued, alleging, among other things, that Gus Machado Ford had made an offer to sell the Ranger for $3,595 plus any trade-in, which Izadi accepted when he showed up with his trade-in and his money.

Gus Machado Ford moved to dismiss Izadi's complaint, arguing that the fine print clearly said that the $3,000 trade-in allowance only applied to trade-ins for purchases of the 1988 Eddie Bauer Aerostar or Turbo T-Bird, and that the calculation of the purchase price for the Ranger said the $3,000 trade-in allowance was only for a trade "worth" $3,000. Because Izadi's trade-in was not "worth" $3,000, he would not get that allowance.

The court refused to dismiss Izadi's complaint. On the contract claim, the court stated that "an allegedly binding offer must be viewed as a whole, with due emphasis placed upon each of what may be inconsistent or conflicting provisions. . . . In this case, that process might well involve disregarding both the superfine print and apparent qualification as to the value of the trade-in, as contradictory to the far more prominent thrust of the advertisement to the effect that $3,000 will be allowed for any trade-in on any Ford."[19] Thus, the court held that the ad could potentially constitute an offer with an unqualified $3,000 trade-in allowance.

Moreover, as a separate basis to find a contract, the court noted that the carefully chosen language and arrangement of the ad were designed to wrongly "make the public believe that it [the $3,000 trade-in allowance] would be honored."[20] The use of this bait-and-switch technique "invokes the applicability of a line of persuasive authority that a binding offer may be implied from the very fact that deliberately misleading advertising intentionally leads the reader to the conclusion that one exists."[21]

---

17. *Id.* at 1136.
18. *Id.* (emphasis added).
19. *Id.* at 1138.
20. *Id.* at 1139.
21. *Id.* at 1140.

Thus, as the *Izadi* case shows, a court can interpret a manifestation as an offer to protect a party from a deceptive business practice. Especially in the case of an advertisement that a merchant uses to bait customers into coming to buy, only to switch out the product or service for something else (higher priced), the equities might compel courts to find an offer.

4. Consumer Protection Acts

The offer inquiry is not the only way—or even the primary way—to protect consumers from unfair and deceptive practices by businesses. There are numerous state and federal laws, rules, and regulations to protect consumers from unfair and deceptive business practices. In fact, in the *Izadi* case, Izadi also alleged that Gus Machado Ford's behavior violated Florida's Deceptive and Unfair Trade Practices Act, and the court likewise did not dismiss that claim.

Consumer protection laws in general seek to prevent deceptive and unfair business practices in many different types of consumer transactions ranging from consumer credit transactions to car purchase and lease transactions. Moreover, many of these statutes authorize not only private enforcement actions, as occurred in *Izadi*, but also governmental enforcement.[22]

For example, many states have enacted a law based on the Uniform Trade Practices and Consumer Protection Law (UTPCPL). This model act was promulgated by the Federal Trade Commission along with the Council of State Governments in 1967 and was amended in 1970s. Though there are several state-specific variations of this act, in one common variation, the act lists out prohibited unfair and deceptive practices.[23] It often also has a catchall that generally prohibits "unfair methods of competition and unfair or deceptive acts or practices."[24] The act then provides for private enforcement in addition to enforcement by the state attorney general.[25] Private enforcement means consumers can enforce the act.

The Michigan Consumer Protection Act is an example of a state statute that is based on the UTPCPL and prohibits numerous misleading contracting practices. The following is an excerpt from Michigan Consumer Protection Act § 445.903:

> 445.903 Unfair, unconscionable, or deceptive methods, acts, or practices in conduct of trade or commerce; rules; applicability of subsection (1)(hh).
>
> Sec. 3. (1) Unfair, unconscionable, or deceptive methods, acts, or practices in the conduct of trade or commerce are unlawful and are defined as follows:

---

22. *See, e.g.*, 15 U.S.C. § 6103 (2012).

23. *See* Tenn. Code Ann. § 47-18-104 (2017).

24. *See* Tenn. Code Ann. § 47-18-104(a) (2017) ("Unfair or deceptive acts or practices affecting the conduct of any trade or commerce constitute unlawful acts or practices and are Class B misdemeanors.").

25. *See* Tenn. Code Ann. §§ 47-18-109, 114 (2017).

(a) Causing a probability of confusion or misunderstanding as to the source, sponsorship, approval, or certification of goods or services.

(b) Using deceptive representations or deceptive designations of geographic origin in connection with goods or services.

(c) Representing that goods or services have sponsorship, approval, characteristics, ingredients, uses, benefits, or quantities that they do not have or that a person has sponsorship, approval, status, affiliation, or connection that he or she does not have.

(d) Representing that goods are new if they are deteriorated, altered, reconditioned, used, or secondhand.

(e) Representing that goods or services are of a particular standard, quality, or grade, or that goods are of a particular style or model, if they are of another.

(f) Disparaging the goods, services, business, or reputation of another by false or misleading representation of fact.

(g) Advertising or representing goods or services with intent not to dispose of those goods or services as advertised or represented.

. . .

This definition actually goes all the way to Subsection (ll)! In other words, the Michigan Consumer Protection Act lists out a total of 38 unfair, unconscionable, or deceptive methods, acts, or practices, all of which are prohibited. And under the statute, both the Michigan attorney general and individuals injured by a violation have the power to enforce Section 3.

Many of these consumer protection acts reverse the historic doctrine of *caveat emptor*, which means "let the buyer beware." Under this doctrine, historically, the only protections consumers received were those protections for which they specifically negotiated in contracts, along with protections under tort law for egregious cases of intentional fraud. However, modern consumer protection acts protect consumers through, among other things, implying warranties about a product's quality or suitability, creating new causes of action, and empowering governmental agencies to enforce consumer protection laws. You will study some of these implied terms in Chapter 14, when you study the terms of sale-of-goods contracts under Article 2 of the UCC.

Congress has also passed numerous laws designed to protect consumers. For example, in 1968, Congress passed the Consumer Credit Protection Act, known as the Truth in Lending Act. This Act requires financial institutions to provide consumers disclosures on consumer credit transactions so that consumers can fully understand the cost of credit and can comparison shop.[26] The Act also gives consumers three days to rescind (i.e., back out of) any consumer financing transaction covered by the Act, to protect consumers from high-pressure tactics.[27]

---

26. *See* 15 U.S.C. § 1601 (2012).
27. *See* 15 U.S.C. § 1635(a) (2012).

Congress also protects consumers through specialized agencies. Importantly, the Federal Trade Commission's Bureau of Consumer Protection enforces consumer protection laws and otherwise protects consumers against unfair, deceptive, or fraudulent practices.[28] It also focuses on industry-wide issues and provides information to federal and state legislatures and agencies in connection with their rulemaking and enforcement efforts.

More recently, in 2010, Congress created the Consumer Financial Protection Bureau (CFPB) to address many consumer concerns revealed during the 2008 financial crisis. The CFPB protects consumers not only by enforcing federal consumer financial laws, but also by ensuring consumers receive enough information about price, risks, and terms of financial transactions so that they can understand the transaction and can comparison shop. The CFPB also educates consumers so consumers can more effectively navigate their financial choices.

There are, of course, other protections of consumers, too. A law school course on Consumer Law would delve into these and other protections in much more detail.

PRACTICE PROBLEM 4-5

Suppose Miranda Foote advertises shared office space for rent at One Vista Plaza in the *Springfield Daily*, a local magazine with a circulation of 2,000. The advertisement appears as follows:

One Vista Plaza is now leasing!
One Vista Plaza includes shared office spaces ideal for new professionals
With lease terms as short as 1 month
Rent as low as $800 a month   } not definite = not an offer
Contact Miranda Foote to get your lease started today

Upon seeing this advertisement, Dale Villanova, a new business law attorney, immediately calls Miranda and tells her that he saw this advertisement and that he would like to lease a shared office space for six months for $800 a month. In response, Miranda tells Dale that he can only get this rate if he agrees to lease the shared office space for a five-year period.

Dale is upset, as he thought the ad indicated that he could rent a space for as short a time period as a month and still pay $800 a month. On the other hand, he knew this was a great deal—in fact, he was not expecting to find a shared office space in Springfield that he could lease under a short-term lease

---

28. Federal Trade Commission, *Bureaus & Offices*, https://www.ftc.gov/about-ftc/bureaus-offices (last visited Sept. 22, 2018).

for less than $1,000 a month. That is why he jumped at this opportunity as soon as he saw it.

Assume Dale decides to press Miranda to lease him shared office space for $800 a month and with a six-month lease term, "per her advertisement." Miranda seeks your advice on the matter. Specifically, she wants to know the following:

1. Has Miranda likely offered to lease shared office space for $800 a month? Why or why not? Be sure to cite relevant law in your answer.
2. How can Miranda change her ad to make it clear that it is not an offer, while at the same time not discouraging interested prospective tenants from contacting her?

Can the clickwrap/misuna ca offer [handwritten margin note]

5. Offer Revocation

Assume an offer is made. Even then, the offeror retains some level of control over that offer. That is because the offeror can, at any time before the offeree accepts the offer, revoke the offer. A **revocation** is a manifestation by an offeror that he no longer intends to be bound by the bargain he proposed in the offer. A revocation removes the power of the offeree to accept the offer.

A revocation is effective when manifested to the offeree. However, it need not be manifested directly to the offeree. That is, a revocation can be manifested *indirectly*, where the offeree obtains reliable information that the offeror has done something inconsistent with an intent to be bound by the offer. On the other hand, mere rumors or unreliable information would not revoke an offer if a reasonable person would not give credit to that information.

To see how these rules work in practice, assume Miranda Foote makes an offer to Dale Villanova to lease shared office space at One Vista Plaza for $1,200 a month. Before Dale has a chance to accept this offer, another party, Sharon Hill, comes along and offers Miranda $1,500 per month for the same space. Miranda agrees to lease the space to Sharon, who is willing to pay more. In this situation, Miranda would want to revoke her offer to Dale by telling Dale that she no longer intends to lease the space to him. Miranda would then enter into a lease with Sharon.

But what if Dale accepts Miranda's offer *before* Miranda communicates a revocation of that offer? Would Miranda's act of accepting Sharon's offer automatically revoke Miranda's offer to Dale? It would not. After all, Dale would not have learned about Miranda's contract with Sharon. Thus, Dale would not have seen any manifestation from Miranda indicating that she no longer intended to be bound to a contract with Dale. As such, Miranda's offer to Dale is still effective, and Dale can still accept it.

Assume that Dale does in fact accept Miranda's offer. Is this state of affairs possible—where Miranda has two contracts to lease the same premises? The short answer is yes. Both Dale and Sharon would have a contract with Miranda to lease the same space. While clearly unadvisable from Miranda's perspective, this situation is absolutely possible. Clearly, though, Miranda is going to fail to perform her promise to either Dale or Sharon. In this situation, the party who does not get the premises can sue Miranda for breach, and potentially receive monetary damages as a remedy. Still, litigation is not inevitable. In this situation, Dale might instead use Miranda's breach as leverage to negotiate a below-market price on some other shared office space Miranda owns. Miranda would agree to this if she thinks it will be cheaper for her to lease that other space at a below-market price than defend herself in a lawsuit and possibly have to pay damages.

Assume, instead, that before accepting Miranda's offer, Dale hears from another tenant in Suite 22 of One Vista Plaza that Miranda has already leased the only open shared office space in Suite 22 to Sharon. In that case, Miranda still has not directly communicated to Dale that she no longer intends to lease the space to Dale. However, Dale learned indirectly, through a communication from a reliable person, of Miranda's actions of leasing to Sharon the very same space Dale intended to lease. Now, Dale would no longer be reasonable to think Miranda still intends to be bound to a contract with him, as he knows Miranda has leased the exact same space to someone else. Thus, that indirect communication revokes Miranda's offer.

While parties can—and often do—modify these default rules on mutual assent, some rules are mandatory in the sense that a court will not enforce a change to them. That is the case with revocation. Namely, while parties can agree on conduct that does (or does not) amount to revocation, they cannot make an offer irrevocable unless the promise to make that offer irrevocable is supported by either consideration or reliance. Where a party's promise to keep an offer open is supported by consideration from the offeree, that creates an **option contract**, and the offer thereby becomes irrevocable for a period of time. Option contracts are discussed in Chapter 8. Where a party's promise to keep an underlying offer open is relied on by the offeree, that promise may be enforced due to that reliance under the doctrine of promissory estoppel. Promissory estoppel is discussed in Chapter 22. But again, absent these situations, a party is not bound by her promise to not revoke an offer for a set period of time, and despite that promise, the offeror can revoke her offer at any time.

Thus, even if Miranda were to promise Dale that she would not revoke her offer to lease shared office space in One Vista Plaza to Dale for two days, Miranda would still be free to revoke her offer unless her promise was supported by consideration or reliance.

PRACTICE PROBLEM 4-6

SpringfieldSwap is an online Facebook group through which residents of Springfield who elect to be members of the group can buy and sell items and services to other group members. A member of the group sells an item or service by describing the item or service to be provided in a posting. Pursuant to the rules of the group, which are available to all members on the Facebook site, anyone who is interested in buying the item or obtaining the listed service must indicate in a comment below the posting that she is "interested." If a person indicates she is "interested," she must contact the seller within 24 hours from the date of posting "interested" to make arrangement for pick-up of the item or service. If she does not, then the seller can move on to the next person who commented that she was "interested." On the other hand, if a person is no longer interested in an item or services within those 24 hours and before she has made arrangements to pick up the good or made arrangements for the services to be provided, she can post a comment below her prior comment indicating she "passes" on that item or service. In that situation, again, the seller moves onto the next person who indicated she was "interested." A failure of a person who posted "interested" to contact the person who posted the good or service for sale within those 24 hours also constitutes a "pass." Once an item is sold or a service no longer available, the seller must promptly mark the item as "sold" to let all other group members know that the item or service is no longer available.

Harriet Blumenfeld lives in Springfield and is a member of SpringfieldSwap. At 9:00 A.M. on Thursday, August 15, Harriet made the following post on SpringfieldSwap:

> Looking for a babysitter this Saturday? If so, I am available to babysit any time between 5:00 P.M. and 11:00 P.M. I am CPR certified and have extensive experience working with kids of all ages. I can provide references on request. Please message me if interested.

By 9:30 A.M., Harriet had received two comments from people indicating they were "interested" in having her babysit on Saturday night. The first comment was by Ben Zee, posted at 9:28 A.M. Ben needed Harriet to babysit for him so he could attend an important work event. The second person who was "interested" in having Harriet babysit was Veronica Villa, who posted she was "interested" at 9:29 A.M.

At 10:30 A.M., Harriet sent Ben a message through Facebook Messenger asking Ben what hours he wanted Harriet to babysit on Saturday night. Harriet also informed Ben in that message that her hourly rate was $15. Ben saw the message. He was expecting to pay $15 an hour, as that was the typical rate charged in the area. However, Ben did not have time to respond to Harriet's message at all that day.

At 9:00 A.M. on Friday August 16, in searching for her own posting to see who else had responded to it, Harriet came across another posting for babysitting services on Saturday night, by Felix Schat. Harriet noticed that Ben was the first of three people who had indicated he was "interested" in Felix's babysitting services. Ben had posted "interested" in Felix's babysitting services on Thursday at 10:00 A.M. Ben had not indicated below his original comment that he "passed" on those services.

Seeing that other posting without any indication that Ben had passed on the other person's babysitting services, Harriet concluded that Ben had decided to not have her babysit on Saturday night. So, she contacted Veronica and they firmed up plans for Harriet to babysit Veronica's children on Saturday night.

However, Harriet received a message at 5:00 P.M. on Friday August 16 from Ben. Ben was responding to Harriet's message confirming that $15 an hour was fine, and that he wanted Harriet to babysit from 6:00 P.M. to 10:00 P.M. Saturday night. He also gave Harriet his address.

Upon seeing this message, Harriet reached out to you, her lawyer friend, ✗ to ask for your advice. Specifically, Harriet wants your advice on the following:

1. Did either Harriet or Ben make an offer in this situation? If so, who and when? *Harriet ; Ben, both?*

2. If we assume Ben made the offer, was that offer revoked when Ben posted that he was interested in having Felix babysit on Saturday night? *no*

3. If we assume Harriet made the offer, was that offer revoked when Harriet agreed to provide babysitting services to Veronica? *no*

4. What, if anything, should Harriet do next to avoid potential contractual liability?

6. Death of Offeror; Destruction of Offered Property

What happens in the unlikely event Miranda dies after offering Dale a lease of shared office space at One Vista Plaza but before he accepts? By default, an offeror's death terminates an offer. That termination happens even if the offeree does not learn of that death before purportedly accepting. Note that this rule is a vestige of the historic rules of mutual assent and is inconsistent with the objective theory of mutual assent. However, it presumes that the offeror is a necessary party to perform the bargain, and that without the offeror, there is little reason for the bargain to exist.

Where an offeree dies, similarly, no mutual assent can exist. In that case, the offeree is no longer alive to accept the offer.

Therefore, in our scenario, if Miranda were to die after offering Dale a lease of shared office space at One Vista Plaza and before Dale accepts, her death would terminate the offer. That is true even if Dale did not learn of Miranda's death before sending her his purported acceptance.

If, however, Miranda worked for a corporation or other similar type of business organization, her death would not terminate the offer. That is because Miranda would not be the offeror in that case. Rather, the offeror would be the business organization. And the death of an employee or other person involved with a business organization does not usually trigger the termination of the business organization. That is one of the advantages of using a business organization such as a corporation, which by default has a perpetual life—the business continues despite the comings and goings (including death) of employees, directors, and shareholders (the people who "own" the corporation).

Similarly, by default, the destruction of property essential to performing a contract also terminates an offer. So, for example, if One Vista Plaza were destroyed in a fire, Miranda's offer to Dale (before he accepted) would be terminated. That is because the property essential to Miranda's performance of the contract no longer would exist.

Remember, though, that these are only the default rules. Thus, even if Miranda works for a corporation, Miranda could modify the default rule by specifying in the offer that it terminates upon Miranda's death.[29] Miranda might specify this if, for example, she knows that after her death, the corporation she works for would not want to enter into new leases, or would institute new criteria on who could lease premises.

7. Lapse of the Offer

An offeror can specify how long the offeree has to accept the offer. Where an offeror specifies a time period for acceptance, the offer expires at the end of that time period.

Even where an offer does not specify a deadline for acceptance, by default, an offer lapses at the end of a reasonable time.[30] What is reasonable depends on the facts and circumstances. Relevant facts and circumstances might include the contemplated manner of acceptance, the nature (such as size and complexity) of the proposed contract, the course of dealings between the parties, and any usages of trade.

To see how these rules work in practice, once again, consider Dale Villanova's potential lease of shared office space from Miranda Foote. Suppose in

---

29. In practice, though, this type of change to the default rules is not common because it would be unusual for a transaction of significance—one in which the parties are represented by counsel—to depend so significantly on the life of a single person. Plus, there is usually a fairly low risk that an essential person will die in the short period between the making of the offer and its acceptance.

30. Restatement (Second) of Contracts § 41(1) (1981).

her offer to Dale, Miranda says "If you want this shared office space, you must let me know no later than tomorrow at 5:00 P.M." If Dale wants to accept Miranda's offer, he would need to communicate that acceptance to Miranda no later than 5:00 P.M. the following day because Miranda said Dale had to accept by then.

Suppose, however, that Miranda did not mention an expiration date and time in her offer. In that case, her offer would lapse after a reasonable time based on the facts and circumstances. If Miranda and Dale typically respond to one another's correspondences within two days, then their course of performance might suggest that Dale has two days to accept. Dale might argue that it would be reasonable for him to have more than two days, given the significance of his decision whether to be bound to the lease. On the other hand, if Dale knows there is another prospective tenant anxiously waiting to find out whether Dale is going to be leasing the space, then that might cause the offer to lapse sooner.

Keep in mind that even where an offer specifies a time period for acceptance, an offeror can revoke the offer at any time—*even before the end of that time period.* That is because, as discussed above under revocation, the offeror has no legal obligation to keep the offer open. Again, the only exception is where an offer is made firm under an option contract or due to reliance.

PRACTICE PROBLEM 4-7

Continuing with the facts from Practice Problem 4-6, suppose Ben becomes busy with work so he does not respond to Harriet's message to arrange a start time for babysitting until noon on Saturday. At that time, Harriet responds to Ben's message indicating that, as of 10:00 A.M. that day, she committed to babysitting for Veronica that night.

Ben is disappointed, as he is rarely on SpringfieldSwap, and because of his busy schedule, is virtually never the first person to indicate he is "interested" in an item or service he wants. So he responds to Harriet informing her that she violated the rules of SpringfieldSwap by not following through with babysitting and that he is going to report her to the site administrator.

Again, assume Harriet has come to you for advice. Specifically, she wants you to do the following:

1. Explain to her whether she violated any of the rules of SpringfieldSwap by not providing Ben with babysitting services. *no, 24 hrs- lapsed offer*

2. Assuming your answer to the first question is "no," draft for Harriet a response to Ben in which she explains why she did not violate SpringfieldSwap's rules, but that is respectful and diplomatic to avoid escalating the situation with Ben. *use a word like "unfortunately"*

D. ACCEPTANCE

Once it is determined that an offer exists (and has not otherwise been revoked or terminated), then mutual assent occurs when the offeree accepts that offer. Again, **acceptance** is the offeree's manifested assent to the offeror's proposed bargain.[31] It must be unequivocal and unconditional. The fact that acceptance must be unequivocal means that there must not be any doubt as to whether a manifestation is an acceptance. And if a response appears to be an acceptance but is conditioned on some other manifestation by the offeree, then it is not an acceptance.

There are two methods of acceptance that contain different rules, depending on what type of acceptance the offer invites. In one situation, an offer requires or invites acceptance by making a return promise. This type of offer is said to be for a **bilateral contract**. The root "bi" mean two and "lateral" means sides. Thus, two sides are making promises. How those types of contracts are accepted is addressed in the next section—Section D.1.

The other situation involves an offer requiring acceptance only by performance. This type of offer is said to be for a **unilateral contract** because only one side (denoted by the root "uni") is making a promise. The other side is actually performing what the promisor has requested. Section D.2 below discusses how acceptance works in unilateral contracts.

Keep in mind that these categorizations, while useful, can sometimes be misleading. For one, very few contracts are unilateral. Virtually all contracts—especially ones of significance—are bilateral. While some of those contracts have conditions to a party's key obligations, the parties are still bound to perform when those conditions are satisfied. The point here is that having a separate category for unilateral contracts exaggerates their role in contract law. In fact, the unilateral contract category is very small.

Second, a contract may have more than two parties. It is quite common in the business world to have many parties to a contract. You may even be familiar with a **multilateral contract**. For example, if you are married and have together with your spouse borrowed money from a lender to buy a house, most likely you have entered a contract with you and your spouse as borrowers and the bank as lender. This discussion of bilateral contracts is not limited to two contracting parties.

Finally, sometimes it is difficult to categorize a contract as bilateral or unilateral. This can happen with charitable pledges given for naming or other similar rights. Some courts see those as bilateral contracts, where the donor promises to make a donation to the charity in the future and, in exchange, the charity promises to name something after that donor.[32] Other courts see these

---

31. Restatement (Second) of Contracts § 50 (1981).
32. *See* William A. Drennan, *Charitable Naming Rights Transactions: Gifts or Contracts?*, 2016 Mich. St. L. Rev. 1267, 1300-06 (2016).

as unilateral contracts, where the donor promises to make a donation in the future if the charity actually names something after that donor.[33]

In short, while the "bilateral" and "unilateral" categorizations are useful tools to help you determine if there is mutual assent, you should not feel overly tied to these categories if they impair your analysis. For these and other reasons, the Restatement has dropped use of these terms.[34] However, we use these categories because the common law continues to reflect them.

Finally, as you review this material on offer and acceptance, keep in mind that offer and acceptance are analytical tools for finding mutual assent. However, sometimes it is difficult to identify a specific offer or acceptance. That is especially true where the parties are making contemporaneous manifestations, such as through an in-person or telephonic conversation. The good news is that mutual assent can exist even if a precise offer and acceptance cannot be identified and the point of arriving at mutual assent cannot be determined.[35] The fluidity of circumstances should not prevent you from trying to identify when mutual assent exists, especially in circumstances where it matters *when* the parties arrived at mutual assent. However, it should give you comfort knowing that where there is clear mutual assent, you need not worry about identifying who made an offer and who accepted.

1. Bilateral Contract

a. What is a bilateral contract?

In most cases, an offeror proposes an exchange of promises in the offer and is looking for the offeree to say or do something that manifests his assent to the offer, signaling his making of the return promise requested in the offer. Where an offeree manifests assent in this way, by making a manifestation amounting to a return promise, this is referred to as **promissory acceptance**. It means both parties have made promises to one another. Again, this type of contract is often referred to as a bilateral contract.

Our ongoing scenario, of Miranda Foote leasing shared office space to Dale Villanova, presents a case of a bilateral contract. In that scenario, Miranda made an offer to Dale of a lease and was looking for Dale to accept her offer. By accepting, Dale would be making a series of promises set out in the written document, including a promise to pay rent at the times and in the amounts specified in the document. And Miranda would be promising, among other things, to let Dale use shared space #3 for the amount of time specified in the lease.

---

33. *Id.*
34. *See* Restatement (Second) of Contracts § 1 reporter's note, cmt. f (1981).
35. Restatement (Second) of Contracts § 22(2) (1981).

Most contracts are bilateral contracts. You are likely a party to many bilateral contracts yourself. For example, your apartment lease is bilateral: you have promised to pay rent (among other promises) in exchange for your landlord's promise to let you use your apartment (among other promises). Your phone service contract is bilateral: the phone service provider has promised to provide you specified services and in exchange, you have promised to pay the agreed-upon monthly amount. Even your contract with Twitter is a bilateral contract. There, you have (possibly unknowingly?) promised to abide by Twitter's Terms of Service and, in exchange, Twitter has agreed to let you use Twitter's services. (Chapter 6 addresses some special concerns with mutual assent to these types of online agreements.)

Nearly all, if not all, of the contracts a business enters into with other businesses are bilateral contracts. That is because given the size of business-to-business transactions and often their long duration in terms of time for performance, each party seeks a promise from the other party about what it will do in the future, whether it be supplying a service or product.

b. Manner of promissory acceptance

Where an offeror is looking for an offeree to accept by making a return promise, often an offeror will specify in the offer the required manner of that acceptance. Where an offeror specifies the required manner of acceptance, then the offeree must accept through that manner.

For example, in Dale's lease with Miranda, Miranda initially signed the bottom of a document called "Lease Agreement," with all terms filled in, and then sent it to Dale. At the end of the "Lease Agreement" was a blank signature line for Dale to sign. By including that blank line, Miranda was looking for Dale to accept by signing on that line and returning his signed signature page back to Miranda. This is the typical way parties manifest assent to bilateral contracts in commercial transactions. In other words, the offeror looks for the offeree to take two steps to manifest assent: to sign on its signature line and deliver a copy of that signed page back to the offeror. The typical contract set out in Chapter 3 contained this invited method of acceptance.

But suppose that when submitting a copy of the written lease to Dale, Miranda included in her cover note the following: "to accept my offer, call me no later than 9:00 P.M. tonight." Here, Miranda has specified a different manner of promissory acceptance than signing: a phone call by 9:00 P.M. Thus, to accept, Dale can call Miranda by 9:00 P.M. that night.

But *must* Dale accept Miranda's offer by calling? Can he not instead accept by signing the lease document and sending it back to Miranda by e-mail?

To answer this question, consider that while sometimes an offer will specify the manner of acceptance, it does not always require that the offeree accept *only* using that manner. In other words, the offer's specified manner of acceptance is not always exclusive. Whether or not the offer's manner of acceptance is exclusive depends on what is reasonable based on the language of the offer and other relevant facts and circumstances. Those other facts and circumstances might include, for example, the parties' relationship or their course of dealing with one another in other similar transactions. If the offer does not unambiguously specify an exclusive manner of acceptance, then the offeree may accept using any reasonable manner.

What a reasonable manner of acceptance is depends on the facts and circumstances. Reasonableness in this context would take into account things like the typical manner of communication used by the parties, the typical manner of communication for that type of transaction, the level of formality expected for an acceptance in that type and size of transaction, and other manifestations by the offeror as to acceptable manner of acceptance.

So, where Miranda says to Dale "to accept my offer, call me no later than 9:00 P.M. tonight," clearly Dale can accept Miranda's offer by calling her by 9:00 P.M. However, Miranda has not indicated that calling is the *only way* to accept: she has not said "to accept, you *must* call me." Thus, arguably Miranda has not precluded other reasonable manners of acceptance (assuming there have not been any prior interactions of the parties to establish that this is not reasonable.)

Dale would then argue that affixing his signature to the lease and sending it back to Miranda by e-mail is another reasonable manner of acceptance. In support, he would point out that Miranda would still receive his acceptance within the time frame contemplated in Miranda's offer. Plus, a signature at the bottom of the lease would more reflect the formality that typically accompanies leases than an oral acceptance. In fact, Miranda was looking for Dale's signature as his acceptance when she sent him the lease with a space for him to sign. It would strengthen Dale's argument further if the parties' other communications had been by e-mail, showing that Miranda finds this channel of communication acceptable.

Keep in mind that even if an offeror specifies an exclusive manner of promissory acceptance in an offer, she may later manifest that she is willing to modify the exclusive manner of acceptance.

So, for example, if Miranda had said in her offer "to accept, you must call me, and I must hear from you by 9:00 P.M. tonight," she has manifested that a call is the exclusive manner of acceptance (and that the offer will lapse unless she hears from him by then). Yet if Dale e-mailed Miranda his acceptance and Miranda responded by saying "I look forward to having you as a tenant," then clearly Miranda has demonstrated that she is not insisting on a phone call acceptance. In other words, she modified that requirement to allow an acceptance by e-mail. Alternatively, some courts might see Dale's acceptance through an improper manner as a rejection of Miranda's offer, and as a new offer to Miranda (it would actually be a counteroffer, discussed below). Miranda accepts that offer when she says, "I look forward to having you as a tenant."

Before we move on, consider why the default rule for mutual assent is that an offeree can accept using any reasonable manner. Here, contract law supports the policy of giving effect to the parties' manifested intentions. This was described in Chapter 1 as the policy of freedom of contract. The default rule furthers these policies by giving effect to the parties' manifestations regardless of what form they take. By giving effect to the reasonable meaning of their manifestations, the law is also supporting the need for predictability and reliance in contractual dealings.

c. Notice of promissory acceptance

Unless an offer states otherwise, for a promissory acceptance to be effective, an offeror must receive notice of that acceptance. With that notice, the offeror can begin to plan for his performance of his promise.

As mentioned above, in significant transactions, the offeree will accept an offer by signing a writing reflecting the proposed contract, usually labeled "Agreement." The offeree then delivers a copy of that signed writing to the offeror. That delivery notifies the offeror of the offeree's acceptance. That was how Dale manifested his assent to the lease offer from Miranda in our ongoing scenario.

However, even without the offeror receiving notice of the offeree's acceptance, at least under the Restatement, the offeree's acceptance will still be effective if the offeree exercised reasonable diligence in notifying the offeror of his acceptance.[36] In that case, even if the offeror does not actually learn of the offeree's acceptance, the offeree has done everything in his control to notify the offeror of his acceptance. Thus, he is protected in performing on the bargain he has assented to. To avoid this result, an offeror who wants to ensure that it finds out about acceptance would want to specify that an acceptance is effective upon receipt. By altering the default rule in that fashion, a party can eliminate the risk that the offeree will accept and use reasonable diligence to communicate that to the offeror, yet the offeror does not find out about that acceptance.

d. Promissory acceptance and the mailbox rule

The concept that an acceptance becomes effective where an offeree uses reasonable diligence to notify the offeror of that acceptance is also reflected in the mailbox rule. Under the **mailbox rule**, where acceptance by mail is a reasonable manner of acceptance, then unless an offer specifies otherwise, an acceptance delivered by mail is effective when properly dispatched rather than when received by the offeror. Dispatch of a mailed acceptance is generally thought to

---

36. Restatement (Second) of Contracts § 56 (1981).

occur when it is deposited in the mail or otherwise placed out of the possession of the offeree, beginning on a path of conveyance toward the offeror.

However, the mailbox rule only applies where an acceptance has been properly dispatched and the sender takes ordinary precautions to ensure its safe delivery. Where either is not the case, the mailbox rule does not apply unless the offeror nonetheless receives the acceptance within the same time it would have had the acceptance been properly dispatched. Where the acceptance is not properly dispatched and is not received within the time it would have been had it been properly dispatched, acceptance will be effective only when received. Of course, that assumes that the offer has not yet lapsed.

The purpose of the mailbox rule is to protect an offeree who relies on the dispatch of his acceptance in preparing to or beginning to perform a bargain. Where an offeror does not preclude acceptance through the mail or other similar non-simultaneous communication mode, he must live with the consequences of that choice. That means possibly having a bargain without knowing about it until the offeror receives the acceptance.

While the mailbox rule might seem like a relic of a time when parties transacted business by mail, it continues to be relevant in modern day. That is because some courts have applied it to non-simultaneously dispatched acceptances dispatched through mediums such as fax and e-mail.[37]

PRACTICE PROBLEM 4-8

Lola Gomez is a recent law school graduate from New York State School of Law who has been looking for the perfect firm associate position in New York to start her legal career. Lola was thrilled when she received a phone call from Jan Smith, the managing partner of Rover & Glover LLP (which everyone calls RoGlo for short), inviting Lola to interview for an associate position at that firm. Lola was very excited, as RoGlo did exactly the kind of work Lola wanted to do in practice—consumer protection work. As an associate attorney at RoGlo, Lola would be able to learn from some of the best consumer lawyers in the city.

During her interview on Monday, July 15, Lola interviewed with five RoGlo attorneys. Her last interview was with Jan Smith. In that meeting, Jan informed Lola that firm management would be meeting that Friday to discuss all interviewees and would make associate offers the following week. Lola would hear from Jan by phone if she received an offer.

The following Monday, July 22, Jan called Lola. She told Lola the RoGlo attorneys enjoyed meeting with Lola and that RoGlo wanted to make Lola an

---

37. *See, e.g.,* Bazak Int'l Corp. v. Tarrant Apparel Grp., 378 F. Supp. 2d 377, 383 (S.D.N.Y. 2005).

offer to join RoGlo as an associate attorney. The position would not be in the consumer law practice group. The specific practice group Lola would work in was to be determined. Lola would receive the same starting salary the other new associate attorneys received, though Jan did not mention what that was on the call. (Lola knew she could look up the prior year's starting salary information online, and that salaries do not change significantly from year to year.) Jan also said that Lola would be eligible to receive additional bonuses tied to the number of hours worked each year, without specifying how much she would receive for how many hours worked.

Lola expressed her excitement at receiving the offer and told Jan, "This is wonderful news. I am so fortunate to have this opportunity to work at RoGlo." However, she also indicated she was disappointed at not being assigned to the consumer law practice group. She said she was sure she could get over that hurdle and would call Jan the following day to confirm.

Lola did not have time to call Jan back the next day, July 23. However, she did send Jan an e-mail in which she said, "I have thought about it and I know I will be happy working at RoGlo even if I don't work in the consumer law group." Because RoGlo's IT group was doing significant work that week, Lola's e-mail bounced back to her as undelivered. Thus, Jan did not receive it.

However, on Thursday, July 25, Lola unexpectedly received an offer of employment from another law firm she had interviewed with. This firm offered her more base pay than RoGlo. Moreover, she would be working in the consumer law group, as she wanted. Lola accepted this offer on the spot.

Lola then called Jan the morning of Friday, July 26. On that call, she informed Jan, "I apologize for taking so long to get back to you. But I wanted to take my time in thinking about this important decision. I decided I really don't want to work at a firm unless I can work in the consumer law department. So I am going to have to decline your offer."

Jan said she was disappointed, as she thought that Lola had already accepted RoGlo's offer (IT was able to retrieve all undelivered e-mails from the outage).

Lola quickly made an excuse to get off the phone and called you for advice.

1. Advise Lola on whether she and RoGlo likely mutually assented to Lola's employment by RoGlo. In your analysis, consider each manifestation and how it is likely to be characterized in the bargain analysis.

2. Assume the parties did not mutually assent to Lola's employment by RoGlo. Should Lola be concerned with any other consequences as a result of her behavior? What would you have done if you were Lola?

e. Acceptance of a bilateral contract by performance

In some circumstances, it is reasonable to accept an offer either by return promise or by performance. Where this is the case, and the offeree begins to perform, the offeree's performance amounts to promissory acceptance. In other words, even where an offeree chooses to accept by performing her promise, by default, beginning to perform manifests to the offeror the offeree's assent (and promise to complete performance). As such, there is mutual assent to the proposed bargain at that time.

As mentioned above, in most cases of a promissory acceptance, the offeror will learn of the offeree's acceptance when the offeree communicates that acceptance to the offeror, often by delivering to the offeror the offeree's signed copy of the proposed agreement. However, where an offeree accepts by performance, there is a risk that the offeror will not learn of that performance. While the law does not impose a legal duty on the offeree to notify the offeror of his acceptance, by default, his failure to use reasonable diligence to notify the offeror of his acceptance where he has reason to know that the offeror will not otherwise learn of his acceptance *discharges* the offeror. The concept of **discharge** means that the offeror will have no duty to perform on his promise. Thus, an offeree who chooses to accept an offer by performance would be wise to notify an offeror of his performance.

To see this in action, suppose Miranda makes Dale an offer to lease shared office space by sending Dale a written Lease Agreement and asking him to sign and return his signature page to Miranda. Now suppose Section 4 of that written Lease Agreement requires Dale to pay Miranda a deposit of $1,200 no later than the first day of the lease term. Here, suppose that, instead of signing, Dale sends Miranda a check for $1,200 for the deposit. In this case, Dale's act of sending Miranda a check amounts to a beginning of performance of Dale's obligations under the lease. That act would amount to Dale's acceptance and promise to perform Dale's obligations under the Lease Agreement. That is because while Miranda's offer contemplates that the lease will be accepted by signing the Lease Agreement, Miranda has not said that that is the *only* way to accept. And it seems reasonable for Dale to be able to accept by sending Miranda his deposit check, which clearly indicates his assent to the lease. Obviously, Miranda will learn of this performance when she receives the check (assuming Dale properly addresses it to Miranda).

f. Implied contracts

Sometimes mutual assent, rather than being manifested through spoken or written words, is implied through the parties' conduct and relationship with one another. Where this occurs, the resulting contract is said to be an **implied-in-fact contract**. In other words, the existence of the contract is implied from the "facts" of the parties' conduct and relationship rather than from their spoken or written expressions.

Implied-in-fact contracts can arise where one party requests that the other provide property or a service, but no price or other terms are agreed upon. That request is seen as an offer. The request carries with it an implication that the requestor promises to pay market rate for the property or service. And if the party to whom the request is made delivers the requested property or service, or otherwise acts in a way to demonstrate a willingness to satisfy the request, that party is deemed to have accepted the offer.

For example, imagine that Dale decides he would like to lease Suite 22 in One Vista Plaza. Before moving in, Dale requests that Mr. Bubbles' Cleaning Service clean Suite 22. The cleaning crew leaves him a $150 invoice for the service after they are done.

Here, Dale's request amounted to an offer to pay for Mr. Bubbles' cleaning services, even if Dale and Mr. Bubbles did not discuss rate or other terms of the contract. And Mr. Bubbles' acceptance of Dale's offer is implied from its cleaning of Suite 22.

No implied-in-fact contract exists, however, where there is an express contract between the parties on the same subject. So, for example, if in response to Dale's request, Mr. Bubbles quotes him a price of $100 to clean Suite 22, then when Dale orders those cleaning services, the contract (including price) is governed by the quote rather than implied from conduct.[38]

You will want to distinguish implied-in-fact contracts from **implied-in-law contracts**. This section addresses the former—contracts implied from the parties' conduct and relationship. The latter "contracts" are not actually contracts, but recoveries in restitution due to unjust enrichment, which a person may receive where she confers a benefit on a third party in circumstances where it is unjust for the beneficiary to retain and not pay for the benefit. These are called implied-in-law contracts because the law imposes on the beneficiary the obligation to pay for the benefit received. However, there is no contractual duty, as there is no contract between the parties.

To provide a brief comparison of implied-in-fact and implied-in-law contracts, imagine that your car breaks down on a highway, so you park on the side of the highway. Assume you call a tow truck to tow your car to safety. The tow truck driver indeed tows your car off the highway. He then gives you an invoice for $50. Here, because you called the tow truck driver, you requested he provide services. While you did not specify a price, your request carries with it an implication that you will pay the typical rate for a tow. By showing up to tow your car, the tow truck driver manifests his acceptance. Thus, you have created an implied-in-fact contract.

Now imagine that instead of calling a tow truck driver when your car breaks down, you decide to hoof it home. So you leave your car on the side of the highway. A tow truck driver sees it and tows it off the highway to safety. The tow truck driver then sends you an invoice for $50. Here, you never requested that the tow truck driver tow your car to safety. However, he conferred that benefit

---

38. Here, Mr. Bubbles' quote is likely an offer because it is provided in response to your request, and all other essential terms (such as premises to be cleaned) have been established. Note that Dale would want to be sure that the lease permits him to clean Suite 22. As a matter of courtesy, he would want to make sure the other shared office tenants in Suite 22 were fine with this action.

on you and expects to be paid for it given that he is in the business of towing cars for money. Here, if you do not pay, the tow truck driver likely has a claim for restitution because he conferred a benefit on you, and it would not be just for you not to pay for that benefit. Your duty to pay the driver would be called an implied-in-law contract because of that legal duty to pay the driver—but not because you actually created a contract.

Do not worry if this distinction is not entirely clear yet. It should become clearer when you study restitution in Chapter 23.

g. Promissory nonacceptance: other ways to categorize offeree's response

The complexity of human speech and behavior poses a challenge to finding an unequivocal, unconditional acceptance. To take an example, assume Miranda Foote offers Dale Villanova a lease of shared office space for $1,200 a month. In response to this offer, Dale says, "I would like to lease this office space, though I need to run this by my mom before I sign the lease agreement." Has Dale accepted Miranda's offer? Specifically, do Dale's words unequivocally and unconditionally manifest Dale's assent to the proposed terms of the lease? Arguably yes, as Dale's statement, "I would like to lease this shared office space" arguably indicates an intent to be bound to the lease. However, his reference to his desire to "run this by my mom" suggests that his acceptance is conditioned on getting some sort of green light from her. On the other hand, running the lease by his mom may only be a formality and not undermine his assent. In any event, Dale has likely not manifested assent, since his acceptance must be unequivocal and unconditional.

In fact, there are many ways one can characterize a response to an offer that is not an acceptance, based on all the facts and circumstances. The following is a list of possible ways to characterize a response to an offer. Each of these characterizations is discussed below.

Potential ways to characterize response to offer other than acceptance	Sample language
Rejection	"I have decided to lease a different property" or "I do not want to enter this lease"
Counteroffer	"I can't afford to pay $1,200 a month, but would you accept $1,000 a month instead?"
Keep under consideration	"Let me think about it"
Keep under consideration and inquire into different terms	"While I'll have to think about your offer, I'd be ready to accept right now if you would lower the price to $1,200 a month"
Silence	

A **rejection** is a manifestation of an intent to not enter a bargain on the terms of the offer. In other words, it is an unequivocal "no" to the terms of the offer. A rejection terminates an offer. That is because it signals to the offeror that the offeree does not intend to accept the offer. The offeror can then pursue other arrangements for the item or service that was offered. However, a rejection terminates an offer even if the offeror does not take steps in reliance on the rejection.

To see how this works, assume Miranda offers Dale a lease of shared office space. However, Dale decides to lease other shared office space. If Dale tells Miranda he is no longer interested in leasing that space, that response would amount to a rejection of Miranda's offer, as it would clearly manifest to Miranda that Dale does not intend to accept her offer. If, hours later, Dale changes his mind and tries to accept Miranda's offer, it would be too late—Dale already rejected the offer. Either Miranda—or Dale—would have to make a new offer, which the other party would have to accept, to arrive at mutual assent.

A **counteroffer** occurs where an offeree does not accept an offer, but instead proposes a substitute bargain. In this way, the party who used to be the offeree now becomes the offeror. A counteroffer is often referred to as a *conditional acceptance*. That is because in it, the original offeree indicates a willingness to conclude a bargain on the terms of the offer but *conditioned on* the offeror agreeing to the offeree's additional or different terms. In this way, a counteroffer keeps negotiations going.

By default, a counteroffer amounts to a rejection of the offer. That is because the counteroffer is understood to reflect the offeree's intent of only concluding a bargain on the terms of the offer if the offeree's additional or different terms are assented to by the offeror. However, an offeree might manifest an intent to not reject an offer and to keep it under consideration, even when making a counteroffer. The facts-and-circumstances nature of the mutual assent inquiry permits this type of conclusion.

There may even be successive counteroffers. For example, suppose Miranda makes Dale an offer to lease shared office space #3 in Suite 22 for $1,500 a month. If Dale says $1,500 a month is too high but that he would be willing to pay $1,200 a month, then he has made a counteroffer. That is, Dale has proposed substitute terms for the same lease. Yet because he has indicated that he is not willing to lease that space for $1,500 a month, he has rejected Miranda's offer. Dale has conferred the power of acceptance on Miranda with the new, substitute rent amount of $1,200 a month. Here, if Miranda says that $1,200 a month is too low, and that she would not rent the space for less than $1,350 a month, then Miranda has rejected Dale's counteroffer and created a new counteroffer with the substitute price term of $1,350 a month. If Dale accepts this monthly rental amount, then he and Miranda have a bargain. Of course, the process could continue if Dale and Miranda continue haggling over the monthly rent, with each party replacing the other as the new counter-offeror when he or she proposes a new monthly rent, conferring on the other the power to accept.

Under classical common law, courts view any manifestation by an offeree with terms in addition to or different from the offer as a counteroffer, even if the offeree does not clearly reject the terms of the offer in that manifestation. That is because under classical common law, courts require an acceptance to be the mirror image of the offer. This is known as the **mirror image rule**. The mirror image rule led to what is known as the **last shot rule**: that is, the party who circulates the last set of proposed bargain terms before the other party accepts has its terms govern. Thus, whoever happens to make the last counteroffer before the other party starts performing (i.e., the "last shot") has its terms govern the contract.

Recognizing the unfairness of these rules' application, many modern courts do not automatically assume that an offeree's response to an offer that includes additional or different terms is a counteroffer. Instead, modern courts will examine all of the parties' manifestations and conduct to determine their intent. Even those courts will determine that the offeree's manifestation is a counteroffer if it finds that the offeree's assent is conditioned on the offeror assenting to the offeree's additional or different terms. But absent such a clear condition to acceptance, a court might characterize an offeree's response as something other than a counteroffer with a rejection of the offer—such as an inquiry as to different or additional terms, or an acceptance coupled with a request to amend.

Specifically, with an inquiry as to different or additional terms, the offeree simply inquires whether the offeror would be willing to consider other terms but does not indicate that his willingness to conclude a bargain depends on the offeror agreeing to these other terms. Or a court might characterize a response by an offeree that includes additional or different terms as an acceptance accompanied by an offer to amend the bargains' terms. As you will study in Chapter 12, an **amendment** is a change in the agreed-upon terms. A party might accept an offer and immediately propose an amendment where it indicates that it is willing to enter a bargain on the terms proposed in the offer, often because the offeree wants to accept before the offer lapses or is revoked. However, the offeree wants the offeror to change a term, often to make the bargain more suitable for both parties.

Sometimes an offeree indicates that he would like to continue considering the offer. That type of statement does not amount to an acceptance as the offeree has not unequivocally manifested an intent to be bound by the offer. Nor does that manifestation amount to a rejection, as the offeree has also not indicated that he does not intend to be bound by the offer. Here, so long as the offer does not lapse, the offeree can continue to consider it. However, there always remains a risk that the offeror will revoke the offer, as the offeror always retains that right before the offeree accepts unless the offer is firm under an option contract. Thus, an offeree waits to accept an offer at his own risk.

Finally, sometimes an offeree remains silent in the face of an offer. Silence does not typically amount to an acceptance or a rejection. That is because silence is the absence of a manifestation. Thus, it does not indicate any intent of the offeree. That is true even where an offeror indicates in the offer that the offeree may accept by silence. In that event, if the offeree remains silent *with the intent to* not *accept*, he is deemed to not have accepted. To find otherwise would essentially place an onus on an offeree to always respond to offers, even unsolicited ones, or risk being unknowingly bound. However, where an offer invites acceptance by silence and an offeree remains silent *with an intent to accept*, then the offeree's silence does amount to acceptance. While this rule runs counter to the typical objective nature of the mutual assent inquiry given that it focuses on the offeree's subjective intent, the offeror is the person who is creating the uncertainty surrounding the offeree's acceptance. Thus, it is hard for him to complain about the inquiry into the offeree's subjective intent in this situation.

There are other situations, too, where an offeree's silence amounts to acceptance. In one situation, prior dealings might make silence a reasonable manner of assent. In another, where a party makes an offer and the offeree accepts benefits offered with a reasonable opportunity to reject them, even without knowing that the offeror expects payment for them, the offeree's acceptance of the benefits can amount to acceptance of the offer.

Keep in mind that the above list is not exclusive. In other words, there are surely other ways one can characterize a manifestation by an offeree without fitting it into one of the categories discussed above. Importantly, though, that response would not amount to acceptance. Yet acceptance of an offer is necessary to create mutual assent.

The following case demonstrates some of these mutual assent concepts in action.

Ehlen v. Melvin
Supreme Court of North Dakota
823 N.W.2d 780 (2012)

Kapsner, Justice.

Paul Ehlen appeals from a judgment dismissing his action against John M. Melvin and LynnDee Melvin ("Melvins") to enforce a purchase agreement, from a judgment for costs, and from an amended judgment. We affirm, concluding the district court's finding the parties did not mutually consent to the purchase agreement is not clearly erroneous.

I

The Melvins own real property in McIntosh County. In February 2011, Kevin Schmitz contacted the Melvins and informed them Ehlen was interested in purchasing the property. Schmitz was interested in leasing some property for grazing his cattle, and he planned to lease the property from Ehlen if Ehlen purchased it from the Melvins.

On February 16, 2011, Ehlen sent the Melvins a document entitled "Purchase Agreement," offering the Melvins $850,000 for the property. The agreement provided the closing of the sale of the property would occur on or before March 1, 2011, and the total amount for the purchase would be paid on or before the closing date. Ehlen also attached a one-page document entitled "Amendment to Purchase Agreement," which itemized a list of additional terms. Ehlen had signed the documents.

On February 18, 2011, the Melvins reviewed Ehlen's offer with their attorney. The Melvins modified some of the terms on the agreement, including the correct spelling of LynnDee Melvin's name and the legal description of the property. The Melvins also added multiple terms to the purchase agreement and the amendment, including that the property was being sold "as is," that the mineral rights conveyed by them were limited to only those rights they owned, and that the land was subject to a federal wetland easement and an agricultural lease. The parties had not previously negotiated the added terms. The Melvins hand-wrote all of the changes on the documents they received from Ehlen and they initialed each change. The Melvins signed the documents and sent them back to Ehlen.

Ehlen did not contact the Melvins after they sent the documents back to him. On February 24, 2011, Schmitz told the Melvins the deal was off and Ehlen was concerned about some of the modified terms. Schmitz contacted the Melvins later and informed them "the deal was back on." The Melvins did not have any contact with Ehlen. The Melvins contacted the title company on March 1, 2011, and learned Ehlen had not paid the money for the property or initialed the amendments the Melvins made. The Melvins' attorney sent Ehlen a letter dated March 2, 2011, to confirm that the "transaction started and contemplated between [Ehlen] and [the Melvins] is hereby terminated."

Ehlen sued the Melvins to enforce the "Purchase Agreement," alleging it was a binding and enforceable contract. After a court trial, the district court ruled there was no contract, the purchase agreement and the amendment to the purchase agreement constituted an offer to purchase property from the Melvins, the Melvins made a counteroffer in writing, and Ehlen failed to accept the counteroffer. The court ordered the dismissal of Ehlen's claims with prejudice and awarded the Melvins the costs of litigation and attorney fees. A judgment was subsequently entered. The Melvins filed an affidavit for costs and attorney fees and Ehlen objected. The court entered an order awarding the Melvins $2,890.40 in costs but ruled the award of attorney fees in its prior order was in error. A judgment for costs was entered. The court also entered an amended judgment incorporating the changes occurring after the initial judgment.

II

Ehlen argues the district court misapplied the law by mischaracterizing the changes the Melvins made to the purchase agreement as a counteroffer requiring a separate acceptance from Ehlen. Ehlen contends the agreement is a valid and binding contract and the Melvins breached the agreement. Ehlen claims he accepted any counteroffer that was made.

This Court has said the existence of a written contract is not purely a legal question:

> [W]hether an unambiguous written agreement constitutes a valid contract is a question of law for the court. However, we have noted that the determination of mutual consent, although resulting in a legal conclusion, necessarily involves factual questions. Thus, the determination of the existence of a contract is a purely legal question only when mutual consent, and the other requisite elements of a contract, are demonstrated clearly and unambiguously on the face of the written contract.

Jerry Harmon Motors, Inc. v. First Nat. Bank & Trust Co., 472 N.W.2d 748, 752 (N.D. 1991) (citations omitted). When the existence of a contract is not purely a legal question, it is a question of fact and the trier of fact determines whether a contract is intended to be a complete, final, and binding agreement. Findings of fact are reviewed under a clearly erroneous standard. A finding is clearly erroneous when it is induced by an erroneous view of the law, there is no evidence to support it, or based on the entire record, we are left with a definite and firm conviction a mistake has been made. The district court determines credibility issues, and we will not reweigh evidence or reassess credibility, nor do we reexamine findings of fact made upon conflicting evidence (citations omitted).

A party suing for breach of contract has the burden of proving the existence of a contract, breach of the contract, and damages. "A contract requires parties capable of contracting, consent of the parties, a lawful object, and sufficient consideration." *Stout v. Fisher Indus., Inc.*, 1999 ND 218, ¶ 11, 603 N.W.2d 52; see also N.D.C.C. § 9-01-02. Consent must be mutual and it is "not mutual unless the parties all agree upon the same thing in the same sense." N.D.C.C. § 9-03-16. "'The parties' mutual assent is determined by their objective manifestations, not their secret intentions.'" *B.J. Kadrmas*, 2007 ND 12, ¶ 11,

727 N.W.2d 270 (*quoting Lire, Inc. v. Bob's Pizza Inn Restaurants, Inc.*, 541 N.W.2d 432, 434 (N.D. 1995)).

The acceptance of a contract must comply with the terms of the offer. The acceptance of a contract must be absolute and unqualified, and a qualified acceptance is a counter proposal. This Court has said:

> It is also equally well established that any counter proposition or any deviation from the terms of the offer contained in the acceptance is deemed to be in effect a rejection, and not binding as an acceptance on the person making the offer, and no contract is made by such qualified acceptance alone. In other words the minds of the parties must meet as to all the terms of the offer and of the acceptance before a valid contract is entered into. It is not enough that there is a concurrence of minds of the price of the real estate offered to be sold.

(citations omitted).

Greenberg, at 868 (*quoting Beiseker v. Amberson*, 17 N.D. 215, 116 N.W. 94 (1908)). In *Stonewood Hotel Corp., Inc. v. Davis Dev., Inc.*, 447 N.W.2d 286, 290 (N.D. 1989), this Court further said:

> an acceptance must be absolute and unqualified or at least separable from those parts of the acceptance which are not absolute and unqualified. Thus, not every new proposal constitutes a qualified acceptance or counteroffer. An acceptance is not necessarily invalidated by proposing changes or additions. . . . An acceptance which requests a change or addition to the terms of the offer is not thereby invalidated unless the acceptance is made to depend on an assent to the changed or added terms.

(citations omitted).

Here, the "Purchase Agreement" and "Amendment to the Purchase Agreement" the Melvins received was an offer from Ehlen to purchase the property. Although the Melvins signed the agreement, the district court found the Melvins made substantive changes and additions to the agreement and the parties did not agree upon the essential terms. The evidence supports the court's finding. There was evidence the purchase price was the only term in the agreement the Melvins had approved before they received Ehlen's offer. The Melvins added various terms, including that the property was sold "as is," the mineral rights were limited, the property was subject to a federal wetlands easement and an agricultural lease, and the Melvins wanted to remove some equipment from the property. The Melvins made substantive changes to the agreement before signing it and their acceptance was not unqualified. To form a contract, the offer and acceptance must express assent to the same thing. We conclude the evidence supports the court's finding that the parties did not agree to the essential terms of the agreement and the Melvins' modifications to the agreement constituted a counteroffer.

Ehlen contends the Melvins accepted the agreement and it is a binding contract because the agreement stated, "THIS IS A LEGALLY BINDING

CONTRACT BETWEEN BUYERS AND SELLERS." However, the Melvins made material changes and added new terms to the agreement and the parties did not sign the same agreement. The parties must agree on the same thing in the same sense, and the use of the words that a document is "a legally binding contract" does not mean that a contract exists.

Ehlen also argues he accepted any counteroffer the Melvins made. The district court found Ehlen never accepted the Melvins' counteroffer, and the evidence supports the court's finding. "'It is a general rule of law that silence and inaction, or mere silence or failure to reject an offer when it is made, do not constitute an acceptance of the offer.'" *B.J. Kadrmas*, 2007 ND 12, ¶ 13, 727 N.W.2d 270 (quoting 17A Am. Jur. 2d Contracts § 103 (1991)). Ehlen did not sign the modified agreement or initial the changes. There was no evidence he complied with the terms of the agreement. There also was evidence the deal was off because Ehlen was concerned about terms of his offer that were modified by the Melvins. The evidence supports the court's finding that Ehlen did not accept the Melvins' counteroffer.

We conclude the district court's findings of fact are not clearly erroneous and its findings support its conclusions of law.

III

[The court also determined that neither the parol evidence rule nor the statute of frauds prevented the Melvins from proving that their changes amounted to a counteroffer.]

. . .

We conclude the evidence supports the district court's finding that a contract between Ehlen and the Melvins to purchase the Melvins' real property did not exist. We affirm.

GERALD W. VANDE WALLE, C.J., MARY MUEHLEN MARING, DANIEL J. CROTHERS and DALE V. SANDSTROM, JJ., concur.

Understanding the Case:

1. *Typical Real Estate Transaction Documents:* Most states have a "form" real estate purchase agreement. That form contains terms that apply by default, unless modified by the parties, though some of the terms specified in that form purchase agreement are mandatory under state law. The form purchase agreement sometimes provides a space at the end where the parties can modify the default terms. Alternatively, in some states, parties modify defaults by using a form "amendment." That is what occurred in *Ehlen*, where Ehlen originally sent the Melvins not only a signed Purchase Agreement, but also an Amendment to Purchase Agreement. In that circumstance, the amendment was not really functioning as an amendment, which is an

agreed-upon change in terms of an existing contract. Rather, it was a way for Ehlen to change the default terms in the form Purchase Agreement. Thus, the Purchase Agreement together with the Amendment to Purchase Agreement constituted the offer.

2. *Purchase of Property "As Is":* In the case, the Melvins modified Ehlen's "offer" so that they were selling the property "as is." When a party sells property "as is," that generally means that the party sells the property without warranties, which, if you recall from Chapter 3, are promises that a fact is or will be true for an agreed-upon period of time. Thus, a buyer must conduct its own due diligence to ensure that it identifies any risks it is taking with the purchase, as the seller is not standing behind any promises as to the condition of the property. However, buying a property "as is" does not necessarily mean a buyer cannot recover where a seller commits misrepresentation, which, stated generally, is a misstatement of a current or past fact on which a buyer relies in assenting. You will read about misrepresentations in Chapter 20.

3. *Purchase of Property Subject to Title Impairments:* The Melvins modified Ehlen's "offer" so that they were only conveying the mineral rights they owned. And they noted that the property to be conveyed was subject to a federal wetlands easement and an agricultural lease. The Melvins made these changes because they only wanted to transfer to Ehlen those rights that they had in the subject property. The easement and lease are known as impairments to title, as they limit what a person can do with property to which they have title. You will likely learn about easements and leases in your Property class.

Comprehension and Thought Questions:

1. When and how did Ehlen make an offer? *agreement + amendments = offer*

2. What test did the court use to determine whether the Melvins accepted that offer? *whether offer + acceptance express assent to same thing*

3. How did the court apply that test? Specifically, did the Melvins accept Ehlen's offer and if not, why not? *no; substantial changes to essential terms*

4. How did the court know that the Melvins' acceptance of Ehlen's offer was conditioned on Ehlen agreeing to the Melvins' changed terms and, therefore, not an acceptance? *signed + initialed*

5. Why weren't the Melvins bound when they signed the Purchase Agreement in light of the language in the contract that said "THIS IS A LEGALLY BINDING CONTRACT BETWEEN BUYERS AND SELLERS"?

6. Why didn't Ehlen's silence indicate his assent to the Melvins' counteroffer?

7. What was the legal effect, if any, of Schmitz notifying the Melvins that the deal "was off" and then later notifying them that it was "back on"? Should the court have given legal effect to these manifestations?

— maybe notice of rejection

Hypothetical Variations:

1. What if the only changes the Melvins made to the offer they received from Ehlen was to state that the sale of the property was "as is"?

2. What if the only changes the Melvins made to the offer they received from Ehlen was to exclude from the purchase a light fixture in one of the bedrooms worth $100, which was easily replaceable?

3. What if the facts were the same as in the case, but Ehlen had deposited the purchase price with the title company by March 1? *this would likely constitute an acceptance by performance*

2. Unilateral Contract

In contrast to contracts accepted by return promise, in some cases, a party may *only* accept an offer by performing—such as by engaging in the act or refraining from the act sought by the offeror in the offer. While offers seeking a manifestation of assent *only* through performance are much less common, they typically occur with offers of rewards and offers of bonuses or other similar contingent payments. In these situations, a reasonable person would view the offeror as not wanting to be committed to performing on his promise unless and until the offeree performs. Typically, that is because (1) the offeree's performance is uncertain to occur, and (2) the offeror does not want to be bound unless and until the offeree performs the uncertain task.

Moreover, the offeree is not bound unless and until he completes performance with an intent to accept the offer. In other words, even if an offeree starts to perform an act specified in an offer for a unilateral contract with an intent to accept the offer, and before completing performance decides he no longer wants to complete that act, he can abandon performance without creating any contractual liability. Again, that is because he is not contractually bound to complete performance.

Because acceptance only occurs once the offeree completes performance, under classic contract law, an offeror could revoke an offer at any time before the offeree completed performance. While this was seen as unfair to an offeree who almost completed performance only to have the offer revoked right out from under his nose, courts justified it on the basis that offerees, too, are not bound to complete performance even after they have started.[39] Thus, just as an offeror can revoke an offer for a unilateral contract at any time before the offeree completes performance, so, too, can an offeree stop performing the act specified in the offer before completing the act, with no obligation to finish the act.

However, modern courts have realized the inequities of allowing an offeror to revoke an offer where an offeree has started to perform and the offeror, in

---

39. *See, e.g.*, Tetrick v. Sloan, 339 P.2d 613, 616-18 (Cal. Ct. App. 1959) (seller could revoke unilateral contract with broker any time before the broker found a buyer willing to purchase the property on terms satisfactory to seller).

contrast, has done nothing more than make an offer.[40] Thus, now, the general rule is that where an offeree has partly performed the act requested by the offeror, then the offeror's offer becomes irrevocable. The offer remains irrevocable for a reasonable period, sufficient to allow the offeree time to finish performance. Once the offeree completes performance, then the offeror is bound to perform.

The Restatement liberalizes this even further, causing an offer for a unilateral contract to become irrevocable once the offeree "tenders or begins the invited performance or tenders a beginning of it."[41] Thus, under the Restatement, where an offeree *begins* to perform the act requested by the offeror, or tenders (meaning unconditionally presents to the offeror) all or part of the money or property requested by the offeror, the offer thereby becomes irrevocable for a reasonable period of time, to allow the offeree time to complete performance.

Because the offer becomes irrevocable for a period of time due to the offeree's part performance or tender, this arrangement is often described as an option contract. In fact, the Restatement has rejected the unilateral contract concept, instead describing that arrangement as a type of option contract.[42] Viewed in this way, the offeree's part performance or tender effectively amounts to its acceptance of the offeror's implied offer to hold the underlying offer open for as long as is reasonably necessary to allow the offeree to complete performance. The offeree's part performance is seen as consideration for the offeror's offer to hold the underlying offer open.

Keep in mind that *preparing* to perform is not the same thing as *beginning* to perform. For example, assume that a real estate brokerage company instructs a real estate agent in January that the company will pay the agent a 3% commission from home sales that the agent brokers that year. Also assume that the agent prints up business cards and orders glossy calendars to send out to prospective clients that year. Now assume that in late January, before the agent has done any other work, the company informs the agent that it is revoking its offer. Whether that offer is revocable depends on whether the agent has "begun performing." Here, the agent likely has not begun performing, as none of the acts she has taken (printing solicitation material) provides to the real estate brokerage company the performance it was seeking—that is, the brokerage of home sales. On the other hand, if the agent had worked with one or more clients who had bought or sold houses (or were in the process of buying or selling houses) using that agent's brokerage services, then that would amount to a

---

40. *See, e.g.*, Hutchinson v. Dobson-Bainbridge Reality Co., 217 S.W.2d 6, 10-11 (Tenn. Ct. App. 1946) (it would be unjust to allow seller to revoke his unilateral contract with his broker until the offer expired given that the broker had already begun to perform and incurred expenses in the process).

41. Restatement (Second) of Contracts § 45(1) (1981).

42. Restatement (Second) of Contracts § 45 cmt. a (1981).

beginning of the performance requested by the real estate brokerage company. That, in turn, would cause the offeror's offer to be irrevocable.[43]

As a final point: if it is reasonable to accept an offer by return promise, then the offer is not an offer for a unilateral contract. Instead, it is understood as inviting acceptance by either performance or a return promise. Because performance in that context effectively amounts to promissory acceptance, it is discussed in Section D.1 above. Thus, these rules on unilateral contracts only apply to those few offers that require acceptance by performance.

To see how these rules work in practice, suppose you lost your dog Duncan. You are distraught and decide to post posters about your lost dog throughout your neighborhood. The poster appears as follows:

LOST DOG!

Last seen at Main St. and University Ave.

$100 REWARD

If found, please call (123) 456-7890

Here, your poster amounts to an offer. It specifies all details about the proposed exchange—your commitment to pay a $100 reward to the person who finds (and impliedly, returns) Duncan.

To see why this is a unilateral contract, suppose your neighbor Bob sees your poster. He comes over to your house and says he'll look for Duncan. Has Bob accepted your offer?

To answer that question, ask yourself whether someone who sees your poster is reasonable to understand the poster as conferring on them the power to accept by simply expressing a verbal commitment "I accept." Surely not. In fact, you know that no one would reasonably interpret your poster as inviting them to accept by making a return promise, as finding a lost dog is not something anyone has control over. In other words, Bob's response to you is not the kind of manifestation you are looking for, and Bob would be unreasonable to think it was. Moreover, from his perspective, Bob would not want to make this kind of commitment, for if he does not find Duncan—which is entirely possible—he would breach his promise to you.

---

43. For a similar case, see Cook v. Coldwell Banker/Frank Laiben Realty Co., 967 S.W.2d 654 (Mo. Ct. App. 1998).

Rather than a *promise* to find Duncan, you are instead looking for someone—either Bob or someone else—to *actually find* Duncan. That is what you meant in your poster by "if found, please call (123) 456-7890." You are looking for someone to *perform* by finding Duncan, not by promising you that they will find Duncan. When they do find and return Duncan, they have accepted your offer. At that time, you will then be obligated to pay the reward specified in your offer.

That is not to say that you and Bob could not restructure your arrangement so that it constitutes a bilateral contract. You could. Again, since contracts are private law, parties can agree on whatever terms they wish, so long as those terms are enforceable. Here, you could make a promise to pay Bob a reward conditioned on Bob finding Duncan. As you saw in Chapter 3, a **conditional promise** is a promise that only becomes due once a condition is satisfied. Once the condition is satisfied, the promise becomes due. As a refresher, the word *condition* refers to something that is not certain to occur, but that must occur before the obligation arises. Thus here, your promise to pay Bob the reward would only be triggered if and when Bob finds Duncan.

Bob, in turn, could make a promise to *try to* find Duncan. In other words, Bob could commit himself to doing something within his control. This technique—of converting a promise to achieve a certain result (finding the lost dog) to a promise to simply use a level of effort, or to try to achieve that result—is advisable not only with unilateral contracts, but bilateral contracts, too. It is a common response where one party requests that the other achieve a result over which the other party does not have control. Here, though, Bob's making of a promise to try to find Duncan would allow him to perform on his promise even if he does not achieve the result—the location of Duncan.

While we therefore *can* modify the terms of the bargain proposed in the offer so that the parties form a bargain at the outset, *should* we? Does that change reflect the intention of the parties? Here, it likely does not. From your perspective, you do not want to have to make a contract containing a conditional promise to pay a reward with each person who is likely to look for Duncan. And from Bob and other likely searchers' perspectives, it is doubtful they would want to have to use any level of effort to look for Duncan. In other words, while we can modify the terms of the bargain to make it a bilateral contract, this does not reflect the intent of the parties.

Now, back to the scenario where your poster manifests your intent to pay a reward to the person who finds Duncan: suppose that after you post the poster and Bob starts searching for Duncan, you realize how nice it is to not have a loud, crazy dog in your house. So, you decide to take the poster down, manifesting your intent to no longer be bound by your promise of a reward. Subsequently, Bob finds Duncan and calls you to notify you of that fact and to collect his reward. Did you revoke your offer before Bob found Duncan, meaning Bob is out of luck?

Under the classical common law of unilateral contracts, Bob would have been out of luck. That is because under classical common law, an offeree of a unilateral contract had to *complete* performance to accept the offer.[44] Thus, you would have been free to revoke your offer of a reward at any time before Bob completed performance by finding Duncan and calling you.

Perhaps surprisingly, even under modern contract law, Bob did not accept before you revoked your offer. According to your offer, you promised to pay a reward to the person who "found" Duncan. Here, Bob did not find Duncan. While he is *trying* to find Duncan, *he has not found Duncan at all*. Thus, Bob has not performed any part of the task specified in your offer, and you are free to revoke your offer before Bob finds Duncan. While this outcome might seem unfair, there are other doctrines (specifically, promissory estoppel, discussed in Chapter 22), that might protect Bob's interest.

Three final points are worthy of note.

First, there is no specific requirement that an offeror be notified where an offeree accepts by performance. However, as was discussed above, where an offeree can and does accept by performance yet the offeror does not learn of that performance within a reasonable time (and does not indicate that he does not need to receive such notice), then the offeror's duty to perform his promise is discharged. In other words, while there is no legal duty for an offeree of a unilateral contract to communicate his acceptance to the offeror, his failure to do so in circumstances where the offeror will not otherwise learn of that acceptance discharges the offeror, even after the offeree has performed. Thus, an offeree would be wise to notify an offeree of his performance where he performs an act with an intent to accept.

Second, where an offer invites acceptance by performance or by a return promise, the above rules do not apply. Instead, an offeree's beginning of performance or tender of part performance manifests the offeree's assent to the offer, thereby concluding the mutual assent process.

Third, as a word of caution and to reiterate this point from above, do not feel overly compelled to categorize a contract as either bilateral or unilateral. That is because not every contract fits neatly into the bilateral or unilateral category. The key is to determine whether the parties' words and conduct objectively manifest their intent to be bound to a bargain. If so, the mutual assent element of contract has been satisfied.

---

44. *See* Petterson v. Pattberg, 161 N.E. 428, 429-30 (N.Y. 1928).

PRACTICE PROBLEM 4-9

Attaboi Construction Inc. is a small company that manages construction projects in the northeastern part of Florida. Recently, Attaboi's chief financial officer (CFO) retired. So the board of directors of Attaboi decided to work with a "headhunter" to find a new CFO. After meeting with several potential headhunters, Attaboi's board decided to retain headhunter Anne Brooks to conduct the search. The board chair, Theresa Kennedy, then sent Anne the following letter.

Anne Brooks
1000 Main St.
Jacksonville, Florida 32034

September 30, 2019

Dear Ms. Brooks

Attaboi Construction Inc. (the "Company") has decided to retain your services to help the Company identify and hire a new, full-time chief financial officer ("CFO") that meets the qualifications the Company has previously disclosed to you. If and when you are able to identify a suitable CFO for the Company and after the Company and that new CFO have entered into an employment agreement on terms acceptable to the Company, then the Company will pay you a broker's fee equal to one month's salary of the new CFO.

We look forward to working with you.

Sincerely,

Attaboi Construction Inc.

//Theresa Kennedy//

Theresa Kennedy, Board Chair

Anne introduces the Attaboi board to numerous candidates for the CFO position. She even introduces them to Stacey Tompkins, the former CFO of a Fortune 500 company. While the board thinks Stacey would be fantastic, the company cannot afford her salary requirements.

After one month, Anne is not able to identify any other candidates that Attaboi views as suitable and within its budget. So Theresa tells Anne that Attaboi no longer needs her help.

One week later, Stacey contacts Theresa to let her know that Stacey would be interested in the position if she could do it on a part-time basis. She believes that, given the small size of Attaboi, she would be able to manage the position while working 20 hours per week. Consequently, she would be willing to work for a salary that is within Attaboi's budget. A few days later, Attaboi and Stacey enter into an independent contractor agreement for $10,000 per month for Stacey to provide 20 hours of financial consulting services to Attaboi per week.

Anne finds out and sends Attaboi a letter demanding that it pay her a broker's fee of $10,000.

1. Have Attaboi and Anne created a bargain in which Attaboi has agreed to pay Anne this broker's fee? Explain the basis for your answer.   Yes

Now that you have studied mutual assent, read through and answer the questions that follow the Simulation Problem for Chapter 4, which is located in Appendix A.

CHAPTER 5

Mutual Assent Under UCC Article 2

As discussed in Chapter 2, the Uniform Commercial Code (UCC) is a set of uniform acts issued by the Uniform Law Commission (ULC) together with the American Law Institute (ALI). Through the UCC, these organizations have sought to reduce uncertainty in commercial transactions by creating uniformity among states' laws. They have also sought to simplify and clarify contractual terms by standardizing those terms. The use of standardized terms for commercial transactions reduces transaction costs, as parties do not have to negotiate or document those terms for them to apply. Predictable rules across all states and standardized contractual terms facilitate interstate commercial transactions.

This chapter focuses on the article of the UCC that relates to contracts for the sale of goods—Chapter 2. Section A first discusses the types of contracts—sale-of-goods contracts—to which Article 2 of the UCC applies. Then, Section B discusses the UCC's general approach to regulation, while Section C introduces Article 2's general approach. Section D then discusses mutual assent rules under Article 2, and how they apply to sale-of-goods contracts.

A. WHEN DOES ARTICLE 2 OF THE UCC APPLY?

The term "goods" generally refers to tangible, movable property. It does not include real estate or intangible assets like patents and copyrights. And since Article 2 applies to *sale* transactions, it does not apply to lease transactions or transactions granting interests in property through rights other than sales.

As you start out your law practice, some goods you might need to purchase include a computer and printer, a desk, and a chair. You would likely also need to buy supplies such as paper and printer ink. All of these transactions would fall under Article 2, as they would be sale-of-goods transactions.

Sometimes contracts for the sale of goods include a non-sale-of-goods component. These are referred to as mixed-purpose contracts. A mixed-purpose contract can be a mixture of a sale-of-goods and either a non-sale transaction (such as a lease transaction), or a sale transaction, but of non-goods (such as services).

In the case of mixed-purpose contracts, case law in a majority of states holds that Article 2 only applies where the predominant purpose of the contracts is the sale of goods. This test looks to what the primary thrust of the contract is. The test typically looks at the intention of the parties as well as the contractual language, the nature of the seller's business, how much of the contract price is allocated to the sale of goods versus other components or services, and the purpose for which the consumer sought the item. If its primary thrust is to sell a good, then Article 2 applies. If not, then Article 2 does not apply.

One common example of a mixed-purpose contract—one that you may very well enter into at the start of your practice—is the sale of a computer coupled with a service plan for that computer. That mixed-purpose contract covers the sale of the good—your computer—along with the supply of a service—the service plan. Here, the predominant purpose of this contract is clearly the purchase of a computer. The service component is only in support of your purchase of that good. Thus, this contract would be governed by Article 2.

While Section D discusses the difference in mutual assent rules in a contract governed by Article 2 and a contract not governed by Article 2, there are many other differences between contracts governed by Article 2 and contracts not governed by Article 2, apart from the rules on mutual assent. The following case shows one of those differences and reveals a common reason why defendants argue that a contract is *not* governed by Article 2.

Hagman v. Swenson
Supreme Court, Appellate Division, First Department, New York
149 A.D.3d 1 (2017)

ACOSTA, J.P.

Mixed transaction contracts, involving both goods and services, require a determination as to whether the transaction is predominantly one for goods or one for services, for statute of limitations purposes. In this case, the issue is raised in the context of a contract that provides for interior design services, including the procurement of furniture and other items required for achieving the desired design. Interestingly, notwithstanding that interior design services are apparently in much demand in New York, to our knowledge, there are no published opinions on this issue in this state. The action arises from an unpaid bill mostly for furniture and other items. The primary question on appeal is whether plaintiff's breach of contract claim is governed by the four-year statute of limitations set forth in UCC 2-725 for breach of a sale-of-goods contract or the six-year statute of limitations in CPLR 213 for breach of a services contract. We find that the transaction in this case is predominantly one for services, and the sale of goods is merely incidental to the services provided. Accordingly, plaintiff's breach of contract claim is timely.

Plaintiff, an expert in interior and exterior design, alleges that she and defendant Kristen Swenson entered into a contract in June 2007 for interior design services. The contract provided that Ms. Swenson would be liable for payment of plaintiff's creative design services as well as the cost of furniture and other tangible items needed to achieve plaintiff's vision. Plaintiff alleged in the complaint that the predominant feature of the contract was her creative design services, with the furniture and other tangible items being incidental to such services.

Pursuant to the contract, from December 2007 through July 2010, plaintiff renovated and decorated numerous rooms in defendants' home in Tuxedo Park, New York. She also provided landscaping, exterior painting, and other exterior decorating services, which were billed separately. Plaintiff ultimately performed interior design services for three of defendants' houses. Defendants relied on plaintiff's creativity and vision as well as her choice, arrangement, and placement of each tangible item. Ms. Swenson allegedly accepted and approved plaintiff's designs and all furniture and items that plaintiff chose, placed, and arranged at the Tuxedo Park home.

Plaintiff delivered bills to defendants on a regular basis. The bills included "list prices" for the various items. The "list prices" consisted of the price of furniture and other items that plaintiff paid her suppliers, i.e., the "net price," and plaintiff's fee for creative design services. Plaintiff alleges that this fee arrangement is standard in the interior design industry. She billed defendants in the same manner for her work at each of the three houses.

According to plaintiff, defendants paid the bills until June 2009. Thereafter, they made only partial payments, or no payments; their last payment was made on or about March 14, 2010. Plaintiff's final bill for services at the Tuxedo Park home was delivered to defendants in July 2010. As of July 2010, defendants had failed to pay $52,859.04 under the contract.

On or about May 11, 2015, plaintiff served a summons and complaint on defendants alleging breach of contract against Ms. Swenson, and unjust enrichment, quantum meruit, and account stated against both defendants.

Defendants moved to dismiss the complaint based upon documentary evidence, on statute of limitation grounds, and for failure to state a cause of action. Of most relevance here, defendants argued that the contract was predominantly for the sale of goods and was therefore subject to the four-year statute of limitations provided in UCC 2-275. They argue that the undated contract between Ms. Swenson and plaintiff has a provision that states that a design fee of $1,200 will be charged at the start of the job, but that provision had been crossed out. It also states that the products and materials were to be shown to Ms. Swenson, purchased by plaintiff, and "charged at List price," that "[a]ll advice and design suggestions such as construction, cabinetry, painting and using clients [sic] existing items will be charged at $200/hour," and that "[a]ll purchases including Tax and Delivery will be paid in full before delivery."

There is also a handwritten contract signed by plaintiff and Ms. Swenson, dated June 10, 2009, which states:

> "I Kristen Swenson will purchase all furniture and accessories shown in photos or in person by Karolina Hagman through Karolina Hagman and only from Karolina Hagman.
>
> "I will not purchase or get similar or actual furniture or accessories through someone else or from somewhere else as shown to me by Karolina Hagman.
>
> "I will allow Karolina Hagman and team to photograph and to publish or have published photos to her of my house and the inside of the rooms in Tuxedo Park, NY. [capitalization and spelling regularized]"

In opposition, plaintiff acknowledged that the parties agreed to cross out the $1,200 "design fee" and that Ms. Swenson would not need to pay this fee. Plaintiff states that when they signed the contract, she explained to Ms. Swenson that her creative services fee would be "built as mark-ups, into the cost of the goods/materials" charged to defendants. Defendants allegedly understood the fee structure.

Plaintiff asserted in her affidavit that in addition to her interior design fee, which was incorporated into the list prices, she billed defendants a $200/hour consulting fee. This fee was separate, and included specific items, such as construction, cabinetry, and painting. Of the $52,859.04 outstanding, plaintiff claims that only $4,000 (for 20 hours) is for consulting work in connection with the exterior of the home, kitchen layout, and bathroom layout.

From December 2007 to July 2010, plaintiff designed and decorated the Tuxedo Park home, including living rooms, hallways, dining rooms, sitting rooms, most of the five bedrooms, and three servants' rooms. She spent hundreds of hours designing and furnishing the home.

By order entered February 25, 2016, Supreme Court granted defendants' motion to dismiss the complaint. The court reasoned that because the contract discusses "products and materials," and the large majority of the outstanding bills involve goods, the services are "incidental" to the purchase of goods, and the four-year statute of limitations applies, barring the complaint. In addition, the court found that plaintiff failed to state a cause of action against Michael Swenson.

We conclude, to the contrary, that the breach of contract claim is governed by the six-year statute of limitations for breach of services contracts and is thereby timely. Generally, breach of contract actions are governed by CPLR

213(2), which provides for a six-year statute of limitations. However, breaches of sale-of-goods contracts are governed by the four-year statute of limitations set forth in UCC 2-725. In the instant case there is a "mixed" transaction, involving both goods and services, which requires a determination whether the transaction is predominantly one for goods or predominantly one for services.

While New York courts do not appear to have directly confronted whether an interior design contract is one for goods or services, they have addressed analogous situations. For example, in *Schenectady Steel Co.*, 43 A.D.2d at 237, 350 N.Y.S.2d 920, the Third Department held that a contract for the creation of a bridge, which included the furnishing of structural steel, was a contract for services. Similarly, in *Gibraltar Mgt. Co., Inc. v. Grand Entrance Gates, Ltd.*, 46 A.D.3d 747, 748, 848 N.Y.S.2d 684 (2d Dept. 2007), the Second Department held that a contract for construction of new entrances, which included, inter alia, the purchase of gates, was primarily one for services (*cf. Outdoor Scenes v. Grace & Sons, Inc.*, 111 Misc.2d 36, 38, 443 N.Y.S.2d 583 (concluding that a contract for the purchase and implantation of trees was a goods contract, based on the absence of an argument that the trees were "part of an integral scheme and design," which could allege a "service-oriented contract").

Moreover, other jurisdictions that have adopted the predominant purpose test have found interior design contracts to be contracts for services, not goods.

In this case, the contract was primarily for interior design services, and the provision of furniture and accessories was merely incidental. Thus, the six-year statute of limitations applies. This conclusion is supported by the fact that plaintiff is an expert in the field of interior design, and it is clear from the contract that Ms. Swenson hired her for that reason. The contract, which is on plaintiff's interior design company's letterhead, states that plaintiff will provide advice and design suggestions regarding construction, cabinetry, painting, and using the clients' existing items. Plaintiff stated that she designed most of the rooms throughout defendants' Tuxedo Park house, and the contract provides that she will select products and materials, show them to Ms. Swenson, and then purchase them on her behalf. In addition, the contract provides that defendants will be charged "List price," which plaintiff states is understood in the industry to include both the cost of the materials as well as a percentage service fee. Moreover, the contract acknowledges that certain "custom work" will be done by "interior designers work people," and a number of the invoices referenced such "custom made" items. Finally, plaintiff and Ms. Swenson also agreed that plaintiff could use and publish photographs of the items to show off plaintiff's work, which demonstrates that plaintiff's value is attributed to the selection of the various items and putting them together for a particular scheme, not merely to her acting as a retailer.

The motion court improperly focused on the fact that most of the bills at issue listed goods purchased by plaintiff for Ms. Swenson. While the cost of materials greatly exceeds the cost of labor, this factor should not have been the sole consideration; the court should have looked to the nature of the transaction. Plaintiff selected the items purchased, and the contract was primarily for the value that she added. The fact that title to the furniture and items would transfer to defendants is incidental to the purpose of the contract.

Since defendants do not dispute the existence of the interior design contract, or that the contract covers the issues at hand, the quantum meruit and unjust enrichment claims against Ms. Swenson were correctly dismissed as duplicative of the breach of contract claim.

. . .

Accordingly, the order of the Supreme Court, New York County (Eileen A. Rakower, J.), entered February 25, 2016, which granted defendants' motion to dismiss the complaint, should be modified, on the law, to reinstate plaintiff's breach of contract claim, and otherwise affirmed, without costs.

Order, Supreme Court, New York County (Eileen A. Rakower, J.), entered February 25, 2016, modified, on the law, to reinstate plaintiff's breach of contract claim, and otherwise affirmed, without costs.

All concur.

Understanding the Case:

1. *Structure of New York Courts:* There are four judicial departments in New York. Each judicial department has several trial courts, many of which are specialized based on type of case. New York's general trial courts (in other words, not its specialized courts) are called Supreme Courts. In general, if an opinion of one of those general trial courts is appealed, it is appealed to the Appellate Division of the Supreme Court for that department. New York's highest court is called the Court of Appeals. The trial court that initially decided *Hagman* was the Supreme Court, New York County. Since New York County falls within the first judicial department, the defendant's appeal went to the Appellate Division, First Department. Each state structures its judicial system slightly differently. Learning the judicial system for the state where you practice is important to understanding the legal landscape in that state. It can also help you understand the posture of cases you read, in discovering their precedential value.

2. *Statute of Limitations:* A statute of limitations is a law that sets out the maximum time for a party to bring a claim covered by that statute. In general, a cause of action "accrues"—thus triggering the start of the statute of limitations—when the breach occurs.

Comprehension and Thought Questions:

1. What was the consequence in *Hagman* of whether the contract was for services versus goods?

2. What test did the court use to determine if the contract was one for services or goods?

3. Why do you think the trial court focused exclusively on the price of goods versus the price of services in deciding what aspect of the contract predominated?

4. Should a court focus exclusively on the price factor, or should it consider all the facts and circumstances?

5. Do you think the parties knew the difference between the statute of limitations under a service contract versus the statute of limitations under a contract for the sale of goods when they entered into the contract? Should that affect the court's analysis?

Hypothetical Variations:

1. What if Hagman was also a furniture retailer and made profits from furniture sales in addition to making money through charging customers a service fee? *doesn't change terms/purpose of K*

2. What if Swenson had paid the full amounts Hagman had invoiced her for the interior design work, but in May 2015, sued Hagman for breach of contract for defects in the quality of the design work Hagman performed in January 2009 and May 2010? Would either claim be precluded by the statute of limitations? *no*

3. What if the parties acknowledged in the contract that the contract was primarily for the sale of goods? *might be diff; burden of Ks*

PRACTICE PROBLEM 5-1

Ben Bridges just opened his own law firm in which he will provide trust and estates legal services. One of his first orders of business is to acquire access to the library resources he will need to serve his clients. One library resource Ben acquires is a license to the Legal Document Reporter, a service that contains forms that Ben can download and modify in drafting his clients' wills and trusts. The subscription also includes, upon initiation, a three-volume set of books on how to effectively draft wills and trusts. Ben plans to use these books as a resource in preparing the wills and trusts he builds using the Legal Document Reporter.

Ben is invoiced $200 each month for his Legal Document Reporter subscription.

1. Is Bill's contract for the Legal Document Reporter governed by UCC Article 2? *no*

2. Why might it matter whether Bill's contract is governed by Article 2?

└ SOL for breach claims

B. THE UCC'S GENERAL APPROACH

The typical statute with which you are likely familiar enumerates actions that are prohibited. For example, the criminal code of each state sets out the elements of crimes. If someone commits an act that meets each of the elements of the crime specified in the code, he or she is guilty of the crime. Needless to say, citizens covered by that code do not have the choice whether or not to comply with the code.

The UCC is different in that it largely sets out **default terms**—that is, terms that apply to contracts for the sale of goods unless the parties have agreed otherwise. Those default terms thus act as "gap-fillers." That means those terms apply to fill the gaps in the terms of the parties' contract. You will learn about some of those gap-filling terms in Chapter 14, when you study the terms of the contract under Article 2. Other default terms apply to the contracting parties' conduct and create default consequences that attach to that conduct. The rules on mutual assent we discuss in Section D below are the latter type, setting out default rules that govern the mutual assent process.

C. INTRODUCTORY COMMENTS ABOUT ARTICLE 2

We begin our discussion of Article 2 with four introductory comments. These introductory comments relate not only to the discussion in this chapter, but to all discussions throughout the book on Article 2.

First, for some reason students, and even some attorneys, think that Article 2 only applies to contracts for sales of goods *between merchants*. As is discussed in more detail below, a merchant is generally someone who either deals in goods of the kind involved in the contract, or who otherwise is a business professional and, as such, gives off the impression that he or she has knowledge or skills relating to the goods or practices in that transaction. *That is not the case!* Article 2 applies to contracts between merchants as well as contracts between a merchant and a consumer and contracts between two non-merchants, such as a contract for the sale of a bike to a friend. However, some provisions of Article 2 apply differently where one or both parties are merchants. In some areas, the UCC provides greater protections to consumers than to merchants on the basis that merchants can protect themselves. Consumers, on the other hand, have very little to no negotiating leverage or specialized knowledge when entering into contracts with merchants.

Second, Article 2 does not regulate every aspect of a sale-of-goods transaction. In other words, Article 2 is not an exclusive statute regulating those contracts. For example, while Article 2 uses the term offer, it does not define it. Where Article 2 does not address a specific matter, then the common law of contracts applies.[1] As such, the common law rules discussed in Chapter 4 apply to sale-of-goods transactions unless the matter is specifically addressed by Article 2.

Third, in the modern economy, contracts for the sale of goods are rarely formed in face-to-face exchanges. In fact, under modern contracting practices, most sales of goods from a merchant, whether to another merchant or to a consumer, occur electronically. Where consumers purchase goods—especially electronics—in store, often merchants include their contractual terms in the packaging for those goods. While the rules on mutual assent discussed in this chapter generally apply to contracts formed in these ways, a whole body of case law has developed—and continues to develop—as to how those rules apply to nontraditional contract-formation situations. That is true for contracts for the sale of goods and other types of contracts that businesses enter into. Chapter 6 discusses how the traditional rules on mutual assent—both under the common law and under Article 2—apply when the contract is formed in these modern ways.

Finally, sale-of-goods transactions usually occur without the involvement of legal counsel. As you will learn in Chapter 11, while lawyers sometimes help their clients prepare or update their "form" documents for the purchase and sale of goods, those lawyers are not typically involved in the specific transactions entered into using those forms. As such, this chapter does not discuss at any length the role of the transactional lawyer in a client's sale-of-goods transaction. However, keep in mind that there are always exceptions to every rule. In other words, it is possible that you will have a client who will want your legal advice as it enters into a sale-of-goods transaction. Moreover, a lawyer would get involved in a sale-of-goods transaction gone awry, where litigation ensues.

D. UCC RULES GOVERNING MUTUAL ASSENT

If a contract is governed by Article 2, specific rules apply to the formation of that contract. While those rules are not wildly different from the common law rules of mutual assent discussed in Chapter 4, there are some differences.

The following is Article 2's general statement of the rules on mutual assent:

§ 2-204. **Formation in General.**

(1) A contract for sale of goods may be made in any manner sufficient to show agreement, including conduct by both parties which recognizes the existence of such a contract.

(2) An agreement sufficient to constitute a contract for sale may be found even though the moment of its making is undetermined.

---

1. U.C.C. § 1-103(b) (1977).

(3) Even though one or more terms are left open a contract for sale does not fail for indefiniteness if the parties have intended to make a contract and there is a reasonably certain basis for giving an appropriate remedy.

As you may have thought as you read this section, in many respects, this section is consistent with the modern common law principles on mutual assent discussed in Chapter 4. Namely, similar to the modern contract common law rules on mutual assent, Section (1) recognizes any manner of assent by the parties. It expressly contemplates assent through conduct of the parties, similar to the common law rules on implied-in-fact contracts. Next, Section (2), also consistent with the modern contract common law, permits mutual assent to exist even if the exact time of its making cannot be determined. In that case, it is typically the parties' actions that indicate they have mutually assented. Finally, Section (3) reflects the oft-followed common law rule that parties can enter into a contract even if they have not agreed on every term.

However, in other respects, this rule recognizes a broader range of conduct amounting to mutual assent than do the common law rules. Here, in a potential broadening of modern contract common law, the UCC recognizes the existence of mutual assent *even where not all essential terms have been agreed on*, so long as there is a reasonably certain basis for giving an appropriate remedy for breach. For example, even if the parties have not fixed a price for the goods being sold, that does not preclude a finding of mutual assent. In that case, under the default rule in § 2-305, the price is "a reasonable price at the time for delivery."[2] And if the parties have not agreed on delivery time or location, § 2-308 and § 2-309 establish those default terms.

Many of the provisions of the UCC, such as § 2-204, are designed to give legal recognition to the modern commercial practices of parties. In doing so, they often broaden the classic common law rules. And even if the common law on mutual assent in some states is as broad as this or other provisions of the UCC, the UCC is designed to apply uniformly in all states for sale-of-goods transactions. That contrasts with the general common law of contracts, which lacks uniformity and varies from state to state.

1. Offer and Acceptance Under the UCC

While § 2-204(1) recognizes that mutual assent may be made in any manner sufficient to show agreement, Article 2 also recognizes that mutual assent typically occurs through offer and acceptance. The following section of Article 2 sets out specific rules applicable to offers and acceptances for sales of goods.

§ 2-206. Offer and Acceptance in Formation of Contract.

---

2. U.C.C. § 2-305(1) (1999).

(1) Unless otherwise unambiguously indicated by the language or circumstances

    (a) an offer to make a contract shall be construed as inviting acceptance in any manner and by any medium reasonable in the circumstances;

    (b) an order or other offer to buy goods for prompt or current shipment shall be construed as inviting acceptance either by a prompt promise to ship or by the prompt or current shipment of conforming or nonconforming goods, but the shipment of nonconforming goods does not constitute an acceptance if the seller seasonably notifies the buyer that the shipment is offered only as an accommodation to the buyer.

(2) Where the beginning of a requested performance is a reasonable mode of acceptance an offeror who is not notified of acceptance within a reasonable time may treat the offer as having lapsed before acceptance.

This section creates default rules on mutual assent. In each instance, the default rule permits a broad range of conduct to manifest assent, similar to courts that take a modern approach to contract law as seen in the common law. First, under Section (1), by default an offer invites acceptance in any manner and by any medium that is reasonable in the circumstances. This is consistent with contract common law studied in Chapter 4, which also deemed an offer as inviting acceptance in any reasonable manner and by any reasonable medium.

The rest of Section (1) then spells out the default rule for what is reasonable where a party places an order for goods. Specifically, under Subsection (1)(b), by default, a seller may accept by either shipping the ordered goods or by making a promise to ship those goods. If a seller accepts by shipping goods, and those goods are nonconforming—meaning, they do not conform to the buyer's specifications—then the shipment is not acceptance if the seller notifies the buyer that the nonconforming shipment is an accommodation. In other words, a seller can avoid accepting an offer and promptly being in breach of the contract by informing a buyer that the shipment is not an acceptance, but instead is an alternate shipment in an effort to appease the buyer. In that case, the shipment would be a new offer, which a buyer can accept or reject. Thus, under this Section, an imperfect tender does not amount to acceptance.

Of course, as the lead-in to Section (1) says, the parties' language or the circumstances might indicate a contrary intent. Thus, the parties may alter the default rules in that section. But that intent must be "unambiguously indicated" from the parties' language or the circumstances.

To see how this works, imagine that Custom Print is a business that creates customized, printed invitations. Custom Print needs more cream-colored stationary paper. So it submits an order for "5,000 sheets of heavy card-stock, full-sized, cream-colored stationary paper" to its supplier, Paper Supplier Inc. Upon receiving this order, to accept, Paper Supplier could either ship the ordered product, or respond to Custom Print with a confirmation that it will be shipping that paper.

Now suppose that Paper Supplier does not have the paper that Custom Print ordered in stock. Instead, it ships 5,000 sheets of paper that otherwise meet Custom Print's order, but that are off-white instead of cream-colored. Upon receiving that shipment, Custom Print can do one of two things: it can either accept the different product, which means it accepts Paper Supplier's counter-offer, or it can reject that offer by declining to accept the off-white paper. Of course, Custom Print could pursue a third option, which is to accept the accommodated shipment while also seeking other bargaining advantages on a shipment of cream-colored paper when it becomes available. If it did that, it would use its right to return the off-white paper as leverage to obtain that concession.

Section (2) of § 2-206 is also generally consistent with the common law default rule discussed in Chapter 4 in requiring notice of acceptance by performance to be communicated to an offeror. If the offeree's acceptance by performance is not communicated to the offeror in a reasonable time, under Section (2), the offer is treated as having lapsed.

2. Terms of the Bargain: Different Terms in Manifestations

If you recall from Chapter 4, under classic common law, if a purported acceptance contains terms that are different from or additional to the offer, the manifestation is not acceptance. That is because acceptance is not the "mirror image" of the offer. Instead, the acceptance is treated as a counteroffer. While modern courts are more likely to find mutual assent in this situation as they consider the parties' manifested intents, modern courts do not presume that a purported acceptance with different or additional terms is an acceptance.

Article 2 significantly changes this analysis. Under § 2-207(1), a party often *does* accept an offer even if the acceptance contains additional or different terms than the offer. The following is § 2-207:

§ 2-207. Additional Terms in Acceptance or Confirmation.

(1) A definite and seasonable expression of acceptance or a written confirmation which is sent within a reasonable time operates as an acceptance even though it states terms additional to or different from those offered or agreed upon, unless acceptance is expressly made conditional on assent to the additional or different terms.

(2) The additional terms are to be construed as proposals for addition to the contract. Between merchants such terms become part of the contract unless:

(a) the offer expressly limits acceptance to the terms of the offer;

(b) they materially alter it; or

(c) notification of objection to them has already been given or is given within a reasonable time after notice of them is received.

(3) Conduct by both parties which recognizes the existence of a contract is sufficient to establish a contract for sale although the writings of the parties do not otherwise establish a contract. In such case the terms of the particular contract consist of those terms on which the writings of the parties agree,

together with any supplementary terms incorporated under any other provisions of this Act.

Due to § 2-207's complexity, each paragraph is discussed separately.

2-207(1)

Section (1) reflects the default rule discussed above, that a buyer and a seller of goods form a contract even though the offeree's acceptance contains terms that differ from the terms of the offer.[3] This default rule applies "unless acceptance is expressly made conditional on assent to the additional or different terms." In other words, the offeree must clearly indicate that it is "unwilling to proceed with the transaction unless the additional or different terms are included in the contract."[4] Where that occurs, under the common law rules of mutual assent (which have not been displaced by specific language in Article 2), the original offeree makes a counteroffer, thereby becoming the new offeror. The other party must then either accept or reject that counteroffer.

Returning to our example, suppose that when Paper Supplier receives Custom Print's order, it sends a confirmation to Custom Print before it ships the paper. That confirmation states, among other things:

> Paper Supplier is not liable for any damage to or destruction of any paper product it supplies once Paper Supplier places that product with a carrier with instructions to deliver it to the buyer. At that time, the risk of loss associated with the product is placed on the buyer.

Now assume that when the paper is shipped two weeks later, the carrier gets in an accident and the paper is destroyed. Did the parties have a contract? Under the common law mirror image rule, because Paper Supplier's form included an additional term which Custom Print did not agree to, the parties did not have a contract. In contrast, under § 2-207(1), the parties undoubtedly formed a contract despite the fact that Paper Supplier's form included a new term.

It is important to consider *why* § 2-207(1) provides for a default rule of mutual assent even though the acceptance contains different or additional terms. While § 2-207 does not only apply where the transacting parties are businesses with their own "forms," it was drafted with those transactions in mind. That is likely because of these transactions' prevalence and importance to our economy. In transactions between sophisticated commercial parties, often each party has its own "form" that it uses, either to place an order with another

---

3. § 2-207(1) also addresses terms of the contract where the parties have already formed a contract and one party sends a written confirmation of the terms. Because this chapter addresses mutual assent rather than terms of the contract where one exists, it does not address this other situation contemplated by Section (1).

4. Lee R. Russ, Annotation, *What Constitutes Acceptance "Expressly Made Conditional" Converting It to Rejection and Counteroffer Under UCC 2-207(1)*, 22 A.L.R. 4th 939, 948-49 (1983).

commercial party (as the buyer) or when it ships its goods (as the seller). Each of those forms includes "boilerplate" terms—or fine print that each party likely does not even read upon receiving it. Oftentimes, the parties' boilerplate terms do not agree. For example, a business such as Custom Print that is ordering print paper from a commercial printing company such as Paper Supplier might have an order form that provides that the seller of the ordered goods is liable for all damages incurred by the buyer due to its use of the ordered goods, whereas the seller's order confirmation form might cap its liability for such damages at the purchase price for the ordered goods and disclaim liability for all indirect damages. Yet usually the parties' behavior indicates that they intend to be bound despite the differences in the terms of their forms. Here, that would occur where the seller sends the ordered paper.

Under the common law last-shot rule, whichever party supplied its form last before the other party performed would have its terms govern. In our example, if the seller shipped the paper to the buyer after it sent its confirmation, when the buyer paid the invoice, the buyer would be deemed to assent to the seller's terms. Thus, all of the seller's terms would govern.

The UCC drafters recognized the irrationality of the last shot rule. After all, why should the party who last supplied its form before the other party performed have all of its terms govern? Hence, they crafted the UCC rules on mutual assent to reflect the reality of modern commercial practices between merchants and to encourage these commercial transactions.

Of course, the fact that mutual assent exists despite a difference in terms in the offer and acceptance raises the question of what terms govern the transaction.

§ 2-207(2)

Section (2) addresses this question—where there is mutual assent despite the acceptance containing additional (as compared to conflicting) terms. In that circumstance, the additional terms are viewed as proposals for addition to the contract. In other words, while the parties have a contract, by default, the additional terms *do not* automatically become a part of the contract. For the additional terms to become a part of the contract, the counterparty must expressly agree to those terms.

However, if the contract is between merchants, a different rule applies.

First, it is important to understand what a merchant is, given that Section (2) applies differently to transactions between merchants as compared to transactions that are not between merchants. § 2-104 defines a merchant as

> a person who [1] deals in goods of the kind or [2] otherwise by his occupation holds himself out as having knowledge or skill peculiar to the practices or goods involved in the transaction or [3] to whom such knowledge or skill may be attributed by his employment of an agent or broker or [4] other intermediary who by his occupation holds himself out as having such knowledge or skill

In other words, a merchant is someone who either deals in goods of the kind involved in the contract, or who otherwise is a business professional and, as such, gives off the impression that he or she has knowledge or skills relating to the goods or practices in that transaction.[5] Thus, the concept of merchant is transaction-specific. For example, someone who works in sales at a paper supply company is likely a merchant for purposes of paper sales contracts. However, that person would not be a merchant in a transaction to buy lunch for his sales team.

In transactions between merchants, by default under § 2-207, the additional terms *do* become part of the contract except in three circumstances: (1) the offer expressly limits acceptance to its terms, (2) those additional terms materially alter the contract, or (3) notification of objection to those terms has already been given or is given within a reasonable time after notice of the terms is received.

The first exception notes the ability of a party to control the effect of its manifestations. That is, an offeror can prevent the other party's purported acceptance with additional terms from amounting to acceptance by expressly indicating that its offer is conditioned on the offeree's acceptance of the offered terms. This preserves the common law mirror-image rule, but only because the offeror has expressly manifested an intent for that rule to apply. Thus, there will be mutual assent only if the offeree accepts the terms in the offer.

Under the second exception, an additional term does not become part of a contract between merchants if the term materially alters the contract unless the counterparty expressly agrees to that term. The term "material" is not defined in the UCC. However, the comment to § 2-207 gives examples of terms that would materially alter the contract.[6] The examples include a clause negating standard UCC warranties, a clause reserving to the seller the power to cancel upon the buyer's failure to meet an invoice when due, and a clause requiring that complaints be made in a time materially shorter than is customary or reasonable. In each of these examples, the contract "result[s] in surprise or hardship if incorporated without express awareness by the other party."

Note that the examples of material terms given in the comment do not necessarily affect the essential terms of the contract: they do not add to the price, quantity, or delivery terms. That is because even nonessential terms can be material—or an important part of the transaction. In other words, even a nonessential term might be necessary to ensure that a party receives its expected benefits under a contract.

Under the third exception, an additional term does not become a part of the contract between merchants if notice of objection has already been given or is given in a reasonable time. Thus, if a party indicates at the outset that it finds

---

5. U.C.C. § 2-104 cmt. 2 (1999).
6. U.C.C. § 2-207 cmt. 4 (1999).

a specific term or terms objectionable, or upon receiving the other party's purported acceptance indicates that a term or terms are objectionable, then the purported acceptance does not conclude mutual assent. This applies regardless of whether the additional term would be considered material.

You may be wondering why § 2-207 has a dual-structured framework to determine whether additional terms in an acceptance become a part of a contract, one for contracts not between merchants and the other for contracts between merchants. The rationale is because in transactions involving consumers, this framework protects a consumer from a merchant essentially imposing its terms on the consumer without the consumer expressly agreeing to those terms. However, merchants are assumed to have enough leverage, awareness, and relevant knowledge to be able to protect themselves from being bound to terms with which they do not agree.

Returning to our above example, recall that Paper Supplier's confirmation states as follows:

> Paper Supplier is not liable for any damage to or destruction of any paper product it supplies once Paper Supplier places that product with a carrier with instructions to deliver it to the buyer. At that time, the risk of loss associated with the product is placed on the buyer.

We already analyzed above how this new term does not prevent the formation of a contract for this transaction. But the next question is: Is this term part of the parties' contract?

To begin, both Custom Print and Paper Supplier are likely merchants of paper. Paper Supplier deals in goods of the kind covered by the order, as it is a supplier of stationary paper. Custom Print also deals in goods of that kind, as it, in turn, sells such paper to its customers. Moreover, representatives from Custom Print who are responsible for ordering paper are undoubtedly knowledgeable about typical practices involved with ordering paper. Similarly, Paper Supplier's representatives responsible for accepting orders are undoubtedly knowledgeable about typical practices involved with fulfilling paper orders.

As such, Paper Supplier's additional term by default is part of the contract unless one of the exceptions discussed above applies. Here, the first exception does not apply, as Custom Print's order did not expressly state that acceptance could only be on the terms in the order. Under the second exception, we have to evaluate whether Paper Supplier's term is material. Whether it is material may depend on how long it takes to transport the paper (if it takes time, the term is less reasonable), which party could better protect itself from losses in transportation (if Paper Supplier could buy insurance to cover the paper, and select a responsible carrier, it is more likely that it is unfair to shift risk of loss in transportation to Custom Print), and what is customary in this type of transaction. If the term is material, it does not become a part of the contract. If the term is not material, then we evaluate whether it is excluded under the third exception. Under the facts, the third exception would not prevent the addition-al term from being included in the contract, as Custom Print did not give notice before the contract was formed, or even after it received the confirmation, that it objected to that term.

Dealing with Conflicting Terms Under § 2-207

Before we discuss Section (3) of § 2-207, let us pause to consider an oddity of § 2-207.

As you recall, Section (1) of § 2-207 provides that parties may form a con-tract despite there being additional or conflicting terms in the acceptance. Sec-tion (2) then laid out a framework to determine whether the additional terms in the acceptance become part of the contract. However, Section (2) did not discuss what happens to any *conflicting terms* included in the acceptance. While you might be thinking Section (3) addresses that situation, alas, it does not.

What, then, happens to conflicting terms in an expression that amounts to an acceptance under Section (1)? Courts tend to take one of three approaches to this oddity of § 2-207.

One approach is to analyze conflicting terms also under Section (2) above. Courts that do this view the omission of conflicting terms from § 2-207 as a drafting error. Thus, they apply the framework from Section (2) even to conflicting terms.

Another approach is to simply ignore the different terms on the theory that § 2-207 does not provide for them.

A third approach, and the most common, is to resort to the common law rules on the premise that those rules apply to sale-of-goods contracts unless they are displaced by Article 2. Applying the common law, terms included in an acceptance that are different from terms in an offer do not become part of the contract. This approach is known as the "knock-out" rule, since the conflicting terms knock one another out of the contract. These courts then look to Article 2 to see if there is a gap-filler for the knocked-out term. If so, the court fills the gap in the contract with that term.

§ 2-207(3)

Section (3) of § 2-207 addresses the situation where the parties' writings do not meet the test for mutual assent, yet their conduct demonstrates they intend to be bound. That might occur where, for example, a party's purported acceptance is a counteroffer because the party expressly states that its assent is conditioned on the other party assenting to its additional or different terms. Where the other party does not so assent, yet the parties begin to perform, the parties' performances show that they have a contract. In these situations, Sec-tion (3) provides that the terms of the contract are those on which the parties' writings agree, along with any gap-filling terms supplied by Article 2.

The following case exemplifies the liberalized nature of the mutual as-sent inquiry under the UCC as compared to under the common law. It also demonstrates how § 2-207 applies to determine the terms of the bargain where the parties' manifestations differ on terms.

General Steel Corp. v. Collins
Court of Appeals of Kentucky
196 S.W.3d 18 (2006)

COMBS, Chief Judge.

General Steel Corporation ("General Steel") appeals from an order of the Clay Circuit Court denying its motion to compel arbitration under the terms of a commercial contract. The trial court determined that the arbitration clause upon which General Steel relies was not enforceable. We affirm.

On May 21, 2004, Steve Collins, as the authorized representative of Collins Game Room & Restaurant, agreed to purchase a building engineered to specifications and delivered by General Steel, a Colorado corporation. Above the signature line, the written contract provided as follows:

> THIS ORDER IS SUBJECT TO THE TERMS AND CONDITIONS ON THIS PAGE AND ON THE SEPARATE CONDITIONS PAGE WHICH I ACKNOWLEDGE RECEIVING. BUYER HEREBY ACKNOWLEDGES RECEIPT OF A COMPLETED COPY OF THIS AGREEMENT AND AGREES TO ALL OF THE TERMS HEREIN CONTAINED. BUYER'S SIGNATURE REPRESENTS ACCEPTANCE OF GENERAL STEEL CORPORATION'S OFFER AS SET FORTH HEREIN AND CONSTITUTES A BINDING CONTRACT. SELLER APPROVES THE TERMS AND CONDITIONS AS SUBMITTED HEREIN TO BUYER AND DOES NOT AGREE TO ANY ALTERATION OR MODIFICATIONS ADDED OR OTHERWISE SOUGHT BY BUYER. ANY ADDITIONAL PROVISIONS, CHANGES OR MODIFICATIONS TO THIS ORDER SOUGHT BY BUYER SHALL BE VOID AND OF NO EFFECT UNLESS AGREED IN A SEPARATE WRITING SIGNED BY BOTH PARTIES.

Enumerated paragraph 16 of the separate "conditions" page contained a dispute resolution clause requiring arbitration of "[a]ny controversy or claim arising out of or relating to this contract, or the breach thereof," naming Denver, Colorado, as the situs of the arbitration. Collins obliterated the arbitration clause by marking it out entirely.

On December 15, 2004, Donna Collins, d/b/a Collins Game Room & Restaurant (referred to collectively as "Collins"), filed a complaint against General Steel. Collins sought to recover the $24,000.00 deposit made in May toward the purchase of the steel building. General Steel answered and denied that Collins was entitled to a refund of the deposit. It also demanded that the complaint be dismissed and that the matter be referred to arbitration "as set forth within the contract and pursuant to motion filed herein." Following a hearing, the trial court denied the motion. This appeal followed.

General Steel contends that the trial court erred by concluding that there was "no meeting of the minds" with respect to an agreement to arbitrate any dispute arising between the parties. It argues that Collins's obliteration of the arbitration provision of the contract did not affect the enforceability of the clause. It also contends that the trial court lacked jurisdiction to decide the issue. We disagree.

KRS 417.050 reads in pertinent part as follows:

> A written agreement to submit any existing controversy to arbitration or a provision in written contract to submit to arbitration any controversy thereafter arising between the parties is valid, enforceable and irrevocable, save upon such grounds as exist at law for the revocation of any contract.

(Emphasis added.) KRS 417.060 provides:

> (1) On application of a party showing an agreement described in KRS 417.050, and the opposing party's refusal to arbitrate, the court shall order the parties to proceed with arbitration. **If the opposing party denies the existence of the agreement to arbitrate, the court shall proceed summarily to the determination of the issue so raised**. The court shall order arbitration if found for the moving party; otherwise, the application shall be denied. (Emphasis added.)

The emphasized language in KRS 417.060(1) is a savings clause. It reserves for adjudication by a court all issues concerning the existence or validity of the agreement of parties to submit to alternative dispute resolutions.

While "any doubts concerning the scope of arbitrable issues should be resolved in favor of arbitration," *Moses H. Cone Mem'l. Hosp. v. Mercury Constr. Corp.*, 460 U.S. 1, 24-25, 103 S. Ct. 927, 941, 74 L.Ed.2d 765 (1983) (emphasis added), the existence of a valid arbitration agreement as a threshold matter must first be resolved by the court. The court—not an arbitrator—must decide whether the parties have agreed to arbitrate based on rudimentary principles governing contract law. The Clay Circuit Court did not exceed its jurisdiction under KRS 417.050 by refusing to order arbitration in this matter; nor did it err by determining that the parties had not reached a meeting of the minds to arbitrate their disputes.

General Steel contends that the arbitration clause remained binding on the parties despite Collins's clear and deliberate obliteration of the arbitration provision. It argues that sections of the Uniform Commercial Code ("UCC") as adopted by Kentucky apply so as to void Collins's attempt to nullify the provision. We disagree.

KRS 355.2-207 provides, in relevant part, as follows:

> (1) A definite and seasonable expression of acceptance or a written confirmation which is sent within a reasonable time operates as an acceptance even though it states terms additional to or different from those offered or agreed upon, unless acceptance is expressly made conditional on assent to the additional or different terms.

(2) The additional terms are to be construed as proposals for addition to the contract. . . .

(3) Conduct by both parties which recognizes the existence of a contract is sufficient to establish a contract for sale although the writings of the parties do not otherwise establish a contract. In such case the terms of the particular contract consist of those terms on which the writings of the parties agree, **together with any supplementary terms** incorporated under any other provisions of this chapter. (Emphasis added.)

This section of the UCC was intended to alter the "mirror-image" rule of the common law under which the terms of an acceptance were required to be identical to the terms of the offer.

This section of the Code recognizes that in current commercial transactions, the terms of the offer and those of the acceptance will seldom be identical. Rather, under the current "battle of the forms," each party typically has a printed form drafted by his attorney and containing as many terms as could be envisioned to favor that party in his sales transactions. Whereas under common law the disparity between the fine-print terms in the parties' forms would have prevented the consummation of a contract when these forms are exchanged, Section 2-207 recognizes that in many, but not all, cases the parties do not impart such significance to the terms on the printed forms.

A court may conclude that the parties have formed a contract even where the acceptance of the offer contains terms additional to or different from those stated in the offer. As long as the parties demonstrate their mutual assent to the essential terms of an agreement, a written contract is deemed to exist. Under these circumstances, the contract is construed to consist of the essential terms of the offer to which the offeree's response has pledged its agreement.

General Steel's argument depends upon a fundamental misconception of the purpose and effect of KRS 355.2-201. A majority of jurisdictions holds that the conflicting terms between an offer pursuant to KRS 355.2-207 and acceptance are properly subject to the "knockout" rule. Where the terms of the offer and acceptance are clearly at odds, they cancel out one another, and neither becomes a part of the contract. Under KRS 355.2-201(1), the effect of Collins's obliteration of the arbitration clause was to eliminate it from the parties' agreement.[7]

General Steel argues in the alternative that the provisions of the arbitration clause remained binding despite the obliteration because the terms of the contract provided that General Steel would not agree to any alterations or modifications; that the buyer accepted all conditions and terms by his signature; and that any attempt by the buyer to alter or to modify the contract was void. We disagree.

---

7. [4] Section 2-207(2) is inapplicable since it addresses the treatment of additional terms supplied by the offeree rather than different or deleted terms.

Collins clearly and deliberately rejected the arbitration provision contained in the offer. By executing the general terms of the contract, Collins did not waive his right to reject the specific arbitration clause proposed by General Steel. Although this arbitration provision was material to the terms of the parties' agreement, it was not essential to consummation of the contract.

General Steel last contends that "the modification sought by plaintiff herein is a material alteration of the terms of the contract not supported by any consideration." We disagree. Collins has not sought a "modification" of the parties' agreement. As correctly construed by the court pursuant to the provisions of the Uniform Commercial Code, the mutual agreement never included a requirement for arbitration. The trial court did not err by refusing to enforce this term of General Steel's form contract against Collins as Collins never assented to the totality of the form as offered by General Steel.

We affirm the order of the Clay Circuit Court.

ALL CONCUR.

Understanding the Case:

1. *Background Facts:* In this case, the contract at issue was for construction of a steel building to be used by the Collinses in their establishment, the Collins Game Room and Restaurant. Eventually there was a disagreement about what materials were to be supplied by General Steel under the contract.[8] As a result, the Collinses sought to have General Steel return their $24,000 deposit because they decided to not move forward with the contract with General Steel.

2. *Uniform Arbitration Act:* In 1925, Congress passed the Federal Arbitration Act (FAA). The FAA affirms the enforceability of arbitration provisions of contracts. According to Section 2 of the FAA, such provisions are "valid, irrevocable, and enforceable, save upon such grounds as exist at law or in equity for the revocation of any contract."[9] The FAA applies to contracts involving interstate commerce. To the extent a contract relates entirely to commerce within one state, it might instead be governed by a state's equivalent to the FAA. As you saw in *General Steel*, Kentucky indeed has adopted such an equivalent statute. According to KRS 417.050, a "written agreement to submit any existing controversy to arbitration or a provision in written contract to submit to arbitration any controversy thereafter arising between the parties is valid, enforceable and irrevocable, save upon such grounds as exist at law for the revocation of any contract." Chapter 6 discusses arbitration in more detail.

---

8. Brief for Appellant, General Corporation Steel v. Collins, 196 S.W.3d 18 (2006), Civ. Action No. 04-CI-00505.

9. 9 U.S.C. § 2 (2012).

Comprehension and Thought Questions:

1. Were the Collinses challenging the existence of the contract to buy the steel building, or only the inclusion of the arbitration clause in that contract?

2. Why did the Collinses not want to arbitrate their dispute with General Steel?

3. Why did the court address the Collinses' challenge to the arbitration clause instead of leaving that question to the arbitrator or arbitrators?

4. What test does the court use to determine whether the Collinses were bound by the arbitration clause?

5. How does the court apply that test in this case?

6. Why didn't the language above the signature line lead the court to ignore the Collinses' hand deletion of the arbitration provision?

7. Do you think the "knock-out rule" is the best approach to address offers and acceptances with conflicting terms? Or as a policy matter, do you think one of the other approaches discussed before the case is better?

Hypothetical Variations:

1. What if this case involved a contract for the sale of real property that included a steel building on it?

2. What if General Steel had included the following language immediately before the arbitration clause: "General Steel's assent to this contract is conditioned on the Collinses agreeing to all of General Steel's proposed terms, including to the arbitration clause"?

3. What if the court viewed the omission of "different terms" from Section (2) of 2-207 as an unintentional omission and therefore applied that section in resolving this dispute?

PRACTICE PROBLEM 5-2

Returning to our ongoing fact pattern, recall that Custom Print submits an order for 5,000 sheets of heavy card-stock, full-sized, cream-colored stationary paper to its supplier, Paper Supplier. For purposes of this question, assume that the back of Custom Print's order form includes the following term:

> Paper Supplier shall be liable for any damage to or destruction of the product ordered hereunder until that product is tendered to, and received by, Custom Print at its premises noted on the front of this order form.

Once again, when Paper Supplier receives Custom Print's order, it sends a confirmation to Custom Print before it ships the paper. That confirmation states, among other things:

Paper Supplier is not liable for any damage to or destruction of any paper product it supplies once Paper Supplier places that product with a carrier with instructions to deliver it to Custom Print. At that time, the risk of loss associated with the product is placed on Custom Print.

When the paper is shipped two weeks later, the carrier gets in an accident and the paper is destroyed. One week later, Paper Supplier sends Custom Print an invoice for the 5,000 sheets of paper ordered by Custom Print that were destroyed in transit.

Custom Print contacts you to help it determine whether it is liable for pay for that destroyed paper. How do you counsel your client on this matter?

CHAPTER 6

"Forms," Electronic Contracting, Smart Contracts, and Mutual Assent

Chapters 4 and 5 explained how parties typically arrive at mutual assent through the *process* of offer and acceptance. The word "process" is emphasized because the classic rules on mutual assent presume a process whereby one party, an offeror, makes an offer. The offeree then responds, either with an acceptance or some other manifestation, such as a rejection or a counteroffer with proposed substitute terms.

However, the reality is that most contracts nowadays have little to no back-and-forth bargaining. Rather, one party—often a business—supplies its form to the customer and the customer must decide whether or not to accept the offer reflected in that form. Businesses also supply their forms when transacting with other businesses.

Businesses use forms where they repeatedly enter into the same type of transaction with many counterparties who are similarly situated. The use of a form prevents the business from having to negotiate the terms of each contract with each counterparty, saving the business and its counterparty costs associated with negotiating and drafting a contract for each transaction. This is especially true where the transaction is of such a small size that it does not justify these "transaction costs." Moreover, a business favors a form contract so that it does not have to administer its compliance with hundreds, thousands, or even millions of contracts with different terms. By using one form, the business can more easily ensure that it remains in compliance with the terms in all of its contracts.

Form contracts are often referred to as **adhesion contracts**, as well as "take-it-or-leave-it" contracts. That is because often a party with a stronger bargaining position, such as a large merchant, gives its "form" contract to a weaker party, such as a consumer, and insists that the consumer agree to the merchant's terms if the consumer wants to do business with the merchant. Thus, the consumer must essentially stick—or adhere—to the terms proposed in the form. If the consumer does not want to adhere to those terms, her only option is to not do business with the merchant. In other words, she cannot negotiate those terms.

One of the primary concerns with adhesion contracts is that they afford a merchant a chance to include any terms it wishes in the form—including terms that are unfair to the consumers. Empirical evidence suggests that most people do not read the terms of an adhesion contract. For example, in a recent study, Professors Jonathan Obar and Anne Oeldorf-Hirsch created a fake social networking service called NameDrop.[1] They then asked over 500 college students to join NameDrop as a prelaunch evaluation of the service. The fictitious site included online terms pursuant to which, among other things, users agreed to assign their first born to NameDrop and to allow NameDrop to share their private data with government agencies, including the U.S. National Security Agency. One hundred percent of study participants agreed to these terms (in most cases, without reading them), showing that most people ignore online terms, even where those terms are outrageous.

As you know from Chapter 4, the rules on mutual assent generally do not consider the fairness of offered terms. They also generally do not consider whether a person read or understood terms, though the *DeFontes* case presented in Section A below demonstrates how mutual assent rules can provide some protection to consumers from being bound by hidden terms. However, the fairness of terms, and the appearance and process through which parties arrive at mutual assent, do factor into a court's consideration of defenses to enforcement. Importantly, as you will study in Chapter 21, the doctrine of unconscionability can protect consumers and other contractual counterparties from unfair terms as well as from being bound where terms are complex or hidden. Moreover, as you saw in Chapter 4, consumer protection statutes protect consumers from being treated unfairly by sellers.

In the modern economy, businesses use three main contracting processes to create these types of form contracts. One way is through **shrinkwrap**, where terms are included with the product (usually software or computer hardware) purchased by a customer in store. The second way is through **clickwrap**, where an online user clicks a box to indicate agreement with a business's terms. And the third way is through **browsewrap**, where an online user is deemed to have

---

1. Jonathan Obar & Anne Oeldorf-Hirsch, *The Biggest Lie on the Internet: Ignoring the Privacy Policies and Terms of Service Policies of Social Networking Services* (August 24, 2016). TPRC 44: The 44th Research Conference on Communication, Information and Internet Policy 2016, SSRN: https://ssrn.com/abstract=2757465 (last visited Sept. 22, 2018).

agreed to a business's terms by browsing its website. The discussion below considers whether and how customers or, in the case of clickwrap and browse-wrap, users, assent to terms presented in these ways.

This chapter refers to terms based upon their delivery process (e.g., "click-wrap" or "clickwrap terms"), as opposed to referring to various types of con-tracts (e.g., "clickwrap contracts"). It does so because to call these arrange-ments contracts is to presume that these terms have met the requirements to create a contract. However, before we can draw that conclusion, we must con-sider whether and how customers and users assent to terms proposed by busi-nesses through these modern channels. Sections A, B, and C address how par-ties arrive at mutual assent through shrinkwrap, clickwrap, and browsewrap, respectively. Section D presents material designed to help you think critically about these methods of modern contracting. Finally, Section E discusses smart contracts, where contracts are formed automatically, without people involved.

A. SHRINKWRAP TERMS

In the typical shrinkwrap scenario, a customer walks into a store and buys either software or an item of computer hardware. Customers also purchase software or hardware over the phone or online. Often the business that is sell-ing that software or hardware is an intermediary selling the software or hard-ware on behalf of the merchant. Here, it may be easier to think of Best Buy or Amazon selling iPhones. When the customer takes possession of the product, either in store or by delivery, sometimes the outside of the product packaging indicates that terms are included in the packaging with the product. However, the outside of the package frequently does not contain this warning, yet terms are shrinkwrapped in with the product purchased. Thus, the customer can only view the terms once she opens the product's package.

In terms of content, usually the merchant's shrinkwrapped terms provide that by keeping the product past a specified time, such as 30 days—or in the case of software, by installing the software—the customer is deemed to have assented to the merchant's terms. On the other hand, the terms often also specify that the customer can reject the terms or the product by returning the product within that time period.

The problem with this exchange for purposes of analyzing mutual assent is that the customer's assent typically comes in the form of doing nothing except keeping the product. In other words, the customer is deemed to assent unless she manifests that she does not assent by returning the product. This does not comport with the notion that a party must do something other than remain silent to assent. However, as the following case shows, courts often contort traditional mutual assent principles to find that a business's shrinkwrap terms are binding on the customer.

The shrinkwrap terms in the below case, *DeFontes v. Dell, Inc.*, include what is often called a **mandatory arbitration clause**. That type of clause requires the party or parties bound by it to waive their right to litigate disputes in court. Instead, the party or parties bound by the clause must resolve their dispute through binding arbitration.

Arbitration is a private process to resolve disputes out of court, by using a designated arbitrator or arbitrators. Parties often opt to arbitrate disputes because it is thought by some to be quicker and cheaper than litigation. It also allows the parties to select as an arbitrator someone who is an expert in the types of transactions at issue.

Where a contract specifies that arbitration is binding, a party may not challenge the arbitration award in court. Essentially, the parties have contracted away their right to pursue a claim in court for the dispute covered by binding arbitration.

As arbitration is a private process, arbitrators do not follow the rules of civil procedure or other rules that apply to judicial cases. Instead, they follow their own internal procedural rules. For example, applicable arbitration rules include their own procedures for how to initiate an arbitration claim, and how and by when the respondent must file a response.[2]

One commonly selected arbitration forum is the American Arbitration Association (AAA). The AAA has its own rules to govern disputes before it, depending on the nature of the dispute. For example, AAA's Consumer Arbitration Rules govern arbitrations between businesses and consumers where the business has a standardized, nonnegotiable contract with a mandatory arbitration provision.[3]

An arbitrator or arbitrators' award is generally not public. As such, arbitration awards do not create precedent, and are not searchable. That can mean it is harder to discover "repeat offenders," such as parties who repeatedly breach contracts, engage in unfair practices to cause others to enter into contracts, or enforce contracts in bad faith.

In addition, some studies show that consumers fare poorly in arbitration. For example, in a recent study, Professors Horton and Chandrasekher found that arbitration awards favored consumers just 35 percent of the time.[4] Commentators believe that arbitration disfavors consumers in part because businesses are repeat players in arbitration. Thus, arbitrators are reluctant to rule against fee-paying businesses for fear that those firms will take their arbitration

---

2. *See, e.g.*, American Arbitration Association, Commercial Arbitration Rules and Mediation Procedures, amended and effective Oct. 1, 2013, https://adr.org/commercial (last visited Sept. 22, 2018).

3. *See* American Arbitration Association, Consumer Arbitration Rules, amended and effective Sept. 1, 2014, https://adr.org/consumer (last visited Sept. 22, 2018).

4. David Horton & Andrea Cann Chandrasekher, *After the Revolution: An Empirical Study of Consumer Arbitration*, 104 Geo. L.J. 57 (2015).

business elsewhere. However, other studies have found that consumers are not quite as disfavored in arbitration.[5]

In addition to setting out an obligation of the parties to arbitrate their disputes, many arbitration clauses remove the ability of consumers to act as a class. The Supreme Court has upheld such a class-waiver provision,[6] which prevents consumers from joining with other similarly situated consumers to make joint claims against businesses where individual claims are not economically justified. The result is that consumers usually cannot pursue their small individual claims against the large corporate merchant with deep pockets, as they cannot join forces with other similarly situated consumers to obtain a meaningful remedy from the seller. After all, what lawyer would represent an individual consumer in a $20 claim against a large merchant?

For these and other reasons, consumers often do not like to submit their disputes to binding arbitration. They therefore challenge arbitration clauses on one of several grounds, including that the consumer did not assent to the clause. The *DeFontes* case, next, demonstrates this type of challenge.

DeFontes v. Dell, Inc.
Supreme Court of Rhode Island
984 A.2d 1061 (2009)

Chief Justice WILLIAMS (ret), for the Court.

The defendants, Dell, Inc. f/k/a Dell Computer Corp. (Dell), Dell Catalog Sales LP (Dell Catalog), Dell Marketing LP (Dell Marketing), QualxServ, LLC (QualxServ), and BancTec, Inc. (BancTec), collectively (defendants), appeal from a Superior Court order denying their motion to stay proceedings and compel arbitration. This case is the first of two companion cases now before this Court. It arises out of a long-frustrated putative class-action suit brought against the defendants. For the reasons set forth below, we affirm the judgment of the Superior Court.

I

Facts and Travel

This litigation began on May 16, 2003, when Mary E. DeFontes, individually and on behalf of a class of similarly situated persons, brought suit against Dell, alleging that its collection of taxes from them on the purchase of Dell

---

5. *See, e.g.,* Sarah R. Cole & Kristen M. Blankley, *Empirical Research on Consumer Arbitration: What the Data Reveals*, 113 Penn. St. L. Rev. 1051, 1052-53 (2009) (concluding from their study that "the consumer arbitration process provides a more pro-consumer environment for claims adjudication than does the traditional court system").

6. AT&T Mobility LLC v. Concepcion, 563 U.S. 333 (2011).

optional service contracts violated the Deceptive Trade Practices Act, G.L.1956 chapter 13.1 of title 6. Ms. DeFontes asserted that service contracts, such as the option service contract offered by Dell, were not taxable within the State of Rhode Island. Nicholas Long joined the suit as a plaintiff, and an amended complaint was filed on July 16, 2003, that also added Dell subsidiaries Dell Catalog and Dell Marketing, and two service providers, QualxServ and BancTec as defendants.

Dell is an international computer hardware and software corporation. Within the Dell corporate umbrella, Dell Catalog and Dell Marketing primarily are responsible for selling computers via the internet, mail-order catalogs, and other means to individual and business consumers. Dell ships these orders throughout all fifty states from warehouses located in Texas and Tennessee. As part of these purchases, Dell offers consumers an optional service contract for on-site repair of its products, with Dell often acting as an agent for third-party service providers, including BancTec and QualxServ. Parties opting to purchase a service contract are charged a "tax," which is either paid to the State of Rhode Island directly or collected by the third-party service provider and then remitted to the state.

The two initial plaintiffs, Ms. DeFontes and Mr. Long, engaged in slightly different transactions. Ms. DeFontes purchased her computer through Dell Catalog and selected a service contract with BancTec. She paid a total of $950.51, of which $13.51 was characterized as tax on the service contract. Mr. Long purchased his computer through Dell Marketing and opted for a service contract managed by Dell. In total, he paid $3,037.73, out of which $198.73 was designated as tax paid on the service contract. There is no allegation that Dell improperly retained any of the collected tax. Several months after plaintiffs filed their amended complaint, defendants filed a motion to stay proceedings and compel arbitration, citing an arbitration provision within the parties' purported agreements. The defendants argued that the arbitration provision was part of a "Terms and Conditions Agreement," which they contended plaintiffs had accepted by accepting delivery of the goods. Specifically, they averred that plaintiffs had three separate opportunities to review the terms and conditions agreement, to wit, by selecting a hyperlink on the Dell website, by reading the terms that were included in the acknowledgment/invoice that was sent to plaintiffs sometime after they placed their orders, or by reviewing the copy of the terms Dell included in the packaging of its computer products.

The hearing justice issued a written decision on January 29, 2004. He first addressed which state law to apply to the parties' dispute. After determining that the choice-of-law provision included in the terms and conditions agreement, which identified Texas as the controlling jurisdiction, was enforceable, he then analyzed whether the parties had, in fact, agreed to be bound by the terms and conditions agreement. The hearing justice found that although plaintiffs had three opportunities to review the terms, none was sufficient to give rise to a contractual obligation. First, he noted that plaintiffs could have reviewed the terms and conditions agreement had they clicked a hyperlink that appeared on Dell's website. The hearing justice found, however, that this link was "inconspicuously located at the bottom of the webpage" and insufficient to place customers on notice of the terms and conditions. Nevertheless, the hearing justice noted that the terms and conditions agreement also appeared both in the acknowledgment that Dell sent to plaintiffs when they placed their orders and later within the packaging when the computers were delivered.

The hearing justice noted that "courts generally recognize that shrinkwrap agreements, paper agreements enclosed within the packaging of an item, are sufficient to put consumers on inquiry notice of the terms and conditions of a transaction." He also observed, however, that shrinkwrap agreements generally contain an express disclaimer that explains to consumers that they can reject the proposed terms and conditions by returning the product. The crucial test, according to the hearing justice, was "whether a reasonable person would have known that return of the product would serve as rejection of those terms." He looked to the introductory language of the terms and conditions agreement, which he quoted as follows,

> *"PLEASE READ THIS DOCUMENT CAREFULLY! IT CONTAINS VERY IM-PORTANT INFORMATION ABOUT YOUR RIGHTS AND OBLIGATIONS, AS WELL AS LIMITATIONS AND EXCLUSIONS THAT MAY APPLY TO YOU. THIS DOCUMENT CONTAINS A DISPUTE RESOLUTION CLAUSE.*

> "This Agreement contains the terms and conditions that apply to purchases by Home, Home Office, and Small Business customers from the Dell entity named on the invoice ('Dell'). By accepting delivery of the computer systems, related products, and/or services and support, and/or other products described on that invoice. [*sic*] You ('Customer') agrees [*sic*] to be bound by and accepts [*sic*] these terms and conditions * * * These terms and conditions are subject to change without prior written notice at any time, in Dell's sole discretion."

The hearing justice found that this language was insufficient to give a reasonable consumer notice of the method of rejection. He found that defendants' failure to include an express disclaimer meant that they could not prove that plaintiffs "knowingly consent[ed]" to the terms and conditions of the agreement. Accordingly, the hearing justice found that Plaintiffs could not be compelled to enter arbitration.

. . .

An order of final judgment was entered on March 29, 2004, from which defendants timely appealed. Additionally, defendants filed a motion to stay the Superior Court proceedings. That motion was denied and, after defendants appealed that decision, the two matters were consolidated. On June 13, 2005, upon discovery that Ms. DeFontes was an employee of plaintiffs' counsel, plaintiffs filed an assented to motion to substitute a proposed class representative that replaced Ms. DeFontes with Julianne Ricci. After plaintiffs filed a substituted first amended class action complaint, defendants renewed their motion to stay the proceedings and to compel arbitration, which was denied, as was defendants' subsequent motion for entry of final judgment of that order.

II

Discussion

We review the trial court's denial of a motion to compel arbitration *de novo*. The parties acknowledge that because their transactions involved interstate commerce, the Federal Arbitration Act (FAA) is applicable. Congress enacted the FAA to "overrule the judiciary's longstanding refusal to enforce agreements to arbitrate." *Dean Witter Reynolds Inc. v. Byrd,* 470 U.S. 213, 219-20, 105 S. Ct. 1238, 84 L.Ed.2d 158 (1985). It requires enforcement of privately negotiated arbitration agreements "save upon such grounds as exist at law or in equity for the revocation of any contract." 9 U.S.C. § 2. Thus, once a court is "satisfied that the making of the agreement for arbitration or the failure to comply therewith is not an issue" it "shall make an order directing the parties to proceed to arbitration in accordance with the terms of the agreement." 9 U.S.C. § 4.

Yet, the United States Supreme Court has been equally insistent that "arbitration is a matter of contract and a party cannot be required to submit to arbitration any dispute which he has not agreed so to submit." *Howsam v. Dean Witter Reynolds, Inc.,* 537 U.S. 79, 83, 123 S. Ct. 588, 154 L.Ed.2d 491 (2002) (quoting *United Steelworkers of America v. Warrior & Gulf Navigation Co.,* 363 U.S. 574, 582, 80 S. Ct. 1347, 4 L.Ed.2d 1409 (1960)). The determination of whether the parties have formed an agreement to arbitrate is a matter of state contract law. Moreover, a hearing justice's determination of "[w]hether a party has agreed to be bound by arbitration is a question of law subject to this Court's de novo review." *Stanley-Bostitch, Inc. v. Regenerative Environmental Equipment Co.,* 697 A.2d 323, 325 (R.I. 1997) (citing *Providence Teachers' Union v. Providence School Committee,* 433 A.2d 202, 205 (R.I. 1981)).

. . .

We therefore evaluate whether plaintiffs are bound by the terms and conditions agreement by resorting to a careful review of the provisions of the U.C.C. Under U.C.C. § 2-204, contracts for the sale of goods may be formed "in any manner sufficient to show agreement, including conduct by both parties which recognizes the existence of such a contract." Tex. Bus. & Com. Code Ann. § 2.204 (Vernon 1994). The U.C.C. creates the assumption that, unless circumstances unambiguously demonstrate otherwise, the buyer is the offeror and the seller is the offeree. Moreover, U.C.C. § 2-206 provides in relevant part,

> "(a) Unless otherwise unambiguously indicated by the language or circumstances,
>> (1) an offer to make a contract shall be construed as inviting acceptance in any manner and by any medium reasonable in the circumstances;

(2) an order or other offer to buy goods for prompt or current shipment shall be construed as inviting acceptance either by a prompt promise to ship or by the prompt or current shipment of conforming or nonconforming goods * * *." Tex. Bus. & Com. Code Ann. § 2.206 (Vernon 1994).

If contract formation occurred at the moment Dell's sales agents processed the customer's credit card payment and agreed to ship the goods, as plaintiffs argue, then any additional terms would necessarily be treated as "[a]dditional [t]erms in [a]cceptance or [c]onfirmation" under U.C.C. § 2-207 or offers to modify the existing contract under U.C.C. § 2-209. Yet, the modern trend seems to favor placing the power of acceptance in the hands of the buyer after he or she receives goods containing a standard form statement of additional terms and conditions, provided the buyer retains the power to "accept or return" the product.

The eminent Judge Frank Easterbrook has authored what are widely considered to be the two leading cases on so-called "shrinkwrap" agreements. In *ProCD, Inc. v. Zeidenberg,* 86 F.3d 1447, 1452-53 (7th Cir. 1996), the court challenged the traditional understanding of offer and acceptance in consumer transactions by holding that a buyer of software was bound by an agreement that was included within the packaging and later appeared when the buyer first used the software. The court first held that U.C.C. § 2-207 was inapplicable because in cases involving only one form, the "battle-of-the-forms" provision was irrelevant. It then proceeded to evaluate the agreement under U.C.C. § 2-204 and reasoned that "[a] vendor, as master of the offer, may invite acceptance by conduct, and may propose limitations on the kind of conduct that constitutes acceptance. A buyer may accept by performing the acts the vendor proposes to treat as acceptance." *ProCD, Inc.,* 86 F.3d at 1452. In *Hill v. Gateway 2000, Inc.,* 105 F.3d 1147, 1148-49 (7th Cir. 1997), the court expanded its earlier holding in *ProCD* beyond transactions involving software where the consumer is prompted to accept or decline the terms when he first uses the program. It determined that when a merchant delivers a product that includes additional terms and conditions, but expressly provides the consumer the right to either accept those terms or return the product for a refund within a reasonable time, a consumer who retains the goods beyond that period may be bound by the contract. Judge Easterbrook explained,

> "Practical considerations support allowing vendors to enclose the full legal terms with their products. Cashiers cannot be expected to read legal documents to customers before ringing up sales. If the staff at the other end of the phone for direct-sales operations such as Gateway's had to read the four-page statement of terms before taking the buyer's credit card number, the droning voice would anesthetize rather than enlighten many potential buyers. Others would hang up in a rage over the waste of their time. And oral recitation would not avoid customers' assertions (whether true or feigned) that the clerk did not read term X to them, or that they did not remember or understand it." *Id.* at 1149.

The defendants argue that *ProCD* represents the majority view and we have found considerable support for their contention. Moreover, as plaintiffs' counsel has initiated nationwide litigation, a number of sister jurisdictions have decided more or less the precise issue put before us in defendants' favor. For instance, in *Stenzel v. Dell, Inc.*, 870 A.2d 133 (Me. 2005), the Maine Supreme Judicial Court reviewed a similar terms and conditions agreement sent to Dell customers that included the language,

> "By accepting delivery of the computer systems, related products, and/or services and support, and/or other products described on that invoice [, the customer] agrees to be bound by and accepts these terms and conditions. If for any reason Customer is not satisfied with a Dell-branded hardware system, Customer may return the system under the terms and conditions of Dell's Total Satisfaction Return Policy * * *." *Id.* at 140.

The court held that by "accepting delivery of the computers, and then failing to exercise their right to return the computers as provided by the agreement, [the plaintiffs] expressly manifested their assent to be bound by the agreement * * *." *Id.*

Courts have not been universal in embracing the reasoning of *ProCD* and its progeny, however. In *Step-Saver Data Systems, Inc. v. Wyse Technology*, 939 F.2d 91, 98 (3d Cir. 1991), the court determined that when parties exchange the shipment of goods for remuneration the existence of a contract is not in doubt; rather, any dispute relates solely to the nature of its terms. After deciding that U.C.C. § 2-207 applies to situations in which a party sends a confirmatory document that claims to establish additional terms of the contract, the court held that U.C.C. § 2-207 "establishes a legal rule that proceeding with a contract after receiving a writing that purports to define the terms of the parties' contract is not sufficient to establish the party's consent to the terms of the writing to the extent that the terms of the writing either add to, or differ from, the terms detailed in the parties' earlier writings or discussions." *Id.* at 99. The court therefore held that a licensing agreement affixed to the packaging constituted a proposal for additional terms that was not binding unless expressly agreed to by the purchaser.

. . .

After reviewing the case law pertaining to so-called "shrinkwrap" agreements, we are satisfied that the *ProCD* line of cases is better reasoned and more consistent with contemporary consumer transactions. It is simply unreasonable to expect a seller to apprise a consumer of every term and condition at the moment he or she makes a purchase. A modern consumer neither expects nor desires to wade through such minutia, particularly when making a purchase over the phone, where full disclosure of the terms would border on the sadistic. Nor do we believe that, after placing a telephone order for a computer, a reasonable consumer would believe that he or she has entered into a fully consummated agreement. Rather, he or she is aware that with delivery comes a multitude of standard terms attendant to nearly every consumer transaction.

We therefore decline to adopt the minority view, as urged by plaintiffs, that a contract is fully formed when a buyer orders a product and the seller accepts payment and either ships or promises to ship. Instead, formation occurs when the consumer accepts the full terms after receiving a reasonable opportunity to refuse them. Yet in adopting the so-called "layered contracting" theory of formation, we reiterate that the burden falls squarely on the seller to show that the buyer has accepted the seller's terms after delivery. Thus, the crucial question in this case is whether defendants reasonably invited acceptance by making clear in the terms and conditions agreement that (1) by accepting defendants' product the consumer was accepting the terms and conditions contained within and (2) the consumer could reject the terms and conditions by returning the product.

On the first question, defendants notified plaintiffs that "[b]y accepting delivery of the computer systems, related products, and/or services and support, and/or other products described on that invoice[,] You ('Customer') agrees to be bound by and accepts those terms and conditions." This language certainly informed plaintiffs that defendants intended to bind them to heretofore undisclosed terms and conditions, but it did not advise them of the period beyond which they will have indicated their assent to those terms. The defendants argue that the meaning of the term "accepting delivery" is apparent to a reasonable consumer. We are not so sure. "Acceptance of goods" has a technical meaning not easily discernable to the average consumer. A consumer may believe that simply by opening the package he or she has agreed to be bound by the terms and conditions contained therein. Indeed, many of the courts that have enforced so-called "approve-or-return" agreements cite language informing the consumer of a specific period after which he or she will have accepted the terms. The more problematic issue, however, is whether plaintiffs were aware of their power to reject by returning the goods.

Significantly, the agreement sent to Ms. DeFontes, who is no longer a plaintiff in this case, contained additional language advising her of the method of rejection. The introductory provision of the terms and conditions agreement that defendants sent to her stated, "[i]f for any reason Customer is not satisfied with a Dell-branded hardware system, Customer may return the system under the terms and conditions of Dell's Total Satisfaction Return Policy * * *." In doing so, defendants explicitly contrasted acceptance of the terms with rejection of the goods, albeit while retaining some ambiguity whether rejection of defendants' proposed terms could reasonably be construed as dissatisfaction with "Dell-branded hardware." Many of the cases upholding shrinkwrap agreements cite explicit disclaimers advising consumers of their right to reject the terms. Such explicit language is also present in some of the foreign cases in which defendants have prevailed. Although the above language is significantly clearer, the terms and conditions agreement sent to Ms. DeFontes nevertheless made the important connection between acceptance of the terms by accepting delivery and rejection by returning the goods.

That this language is absent in the documents sent to current plaintiffs Mr. Long and Ms. Ricci is troubling and raises the specter that they were unaware of both their power to reject and the method with which to do so. The introductory provision that purportedly bound plaintiffs does not mention either the "Total Satisfaction Return Policy" or the thirty-day period in which a consumer may exercise his or her right to return the product. Rather, this policy is explained, if at all, in a distinct section of the terms and conditions agreement, which confusingly informed plaintiffs that "Dell Branded Hardware systems and parts that are purchased directly from Dell by an end-user Customer may be returned by Customer in accordance with Dell's 'Total Satisfaction Return Policy' in effect on the date of the invoice." Thus, the consumer is left to construe these provisions together and infer that his or her right to reject the terms extends beyond what would commonly be understood as the moment of delivery. This separate provision not only fails to establish a clear relationship between the consumer's acceptance of the terms by retaining the goods and his or her right to reject the terms by returning the product, but it further obscures the matter by forcing the consumer to refer to a separate document if he or she wants to discover the full terms and conditions of the "Total Satisfaction Return Policy." Even if the consumer reviews the total satisfaction return policy, we are not convinced that the policy clearly explains to a reasonable consumer that his or her right to return the product includes rejection of the terms and conditions agreement. We believe the hearing justice rightly concluded that although "Dell does provide a 'total satisfaction policy' whereby a customer may return the computer, this return policy does not mention the customer's ability to return based on their unwillingness to comply with the terms."

In reviewing the language of the terms and conditions agreement it cannot be said that it was reasonably apparent to the plaintiffs that they could reject the terms simply by returning the goods. We believe that too many inferential steps were required of the plaintiffs and too many of the relevant provisions were left ambiguous. We are not persuaded that a reasonably prudent offeree would understand that by keeping the Dell computer he or she was agreeing to be bound by the terms and conditions agreement and retained, for a specified time, the power to reject the terms by returning the product. Because we hold that the hearing justice properly denied the defendants' motion to compel arbitration on the ground that the plaintiffs did not agree to be bound by the terms and conditions agreement, we need not discuss any of the alternative grounds the hearing justice offered for denying the defendants' motion to compel arbitration. We must note, however, that the hearing justice found that the purported agreement "fails to bind Defendants in any genuine way" because it gave the defendants the right to change the terms of the agreement "without prior written notice at any time, in Dell's sole discretion." Although we recognize the existence of a formidable argument that such language rendered the purported agreement illusory, we shall leave the analysis of that argument for another day, in keeping with our general aversion towards reaching issues that prove unnecessary for the disposition of the case at bar.

III

Conclusion

For the reasons set out above, the judgment of the Superior Court is affirmed. The papers of the case are returned to the Superior Court.

Chief Justice SUTTELL and Justice ROBINSON did not participate.

Understanding the Case:

1. *Arbitration clause:* The preamble and arbitration clause at issue in *De-Fontes* are as follows:

> This Agreement contains the terms and conditions that apply to purchases by Home, Home Office, and Small Business customers from the Dell entity named on the invoice ("Dell") that will be provided to you ("Customer") on orders for computer systems and/or related products sold in the United States. You agree to be bound by and accept this agreement as applicable to your purchase of product(s) or services(s) from Dell. By accepting delivery of the computer systems and/or other products described on that invoice, Customer agrees to be bound by and accepts these terms and conditions.
>
> THESE TERMS AND CONDITIONS APPLY (I) UNLESS THE CUSTOMER HAS SIGNED A SEPARATE FORMAL PURCHASE AGREEMENT WITH DELL, IN WHICH CASE THE SEPARATE AGREEMENT SHALL GOVERN; OR (II) UNLESS OTHER DELL STANDARD TERMS APPLY TO THE TRANSACTION.
>
> These terms and conditions are subject to change without prior written notice at any time, in Dell's sole discretion.
>
> . . .
>
> **12 Binding Arbitration.**
> ANY CLAIM, DISPUTE, OR CONTROVERSY (WHETHER IN CONTRACT, TORT, OR OTHERWISE, WHETHER PREEXISTING, PRESENT OR FUTURE, AND INCLUDING STATUTORY, COMMON LAW, INTENTIONAL TORT, AND EQUITABLE CLAIMS) AGAINST DELL, its agents, employees, successors, assigns or affiliates (collectively for purposes of this paragraph, "Dell") arising from or relating to this Agreement, its interpretation, or the breach, termination or validity thereof, the relationships which result from this Agreement (including, to the full extent permitted by applicable law, relationships with third parties who are not signatories to this Agreement), Dell's advertising, or any related purchase SHALL BE RESOLVED EXCLUSIVELY AND FINALLY BY BINDING ARBITRATION ADMINISTERED BY THE NATIONAL ARBITRATION FORUM (NAF) under its Code of Procedure then in effect. . . . The arbitration will be

limited solely to the dispute or controversy between Customer and Dell. Any award of the arbitrator(s) shall be final and binding on each of the parties, and may be entered as a judgment in any court of competent jurisdiction. . . .[7]

2.   *Different Versions of Terms and Conditions:* As the court noted, the terms and conditions Dell gave to DeFontes were different from those given to other plaintiffs, including Long and Ricci. The terms and conditions shrink-wrapped with DeFontes's computer advised DeFontes that "[i]f for any reason Customer is not satisfied with a Dell-branded hardware system, Customer may return the system under the terms and conditions of Dell's Total Satisfaction Return Policy." This language was absent from the terms and conditions given to Long and Ricci. The inclusion of this language makes DeFontes's argument against acceptance significantly weaker. This is likely why, as the court mentions, DeFontes was ultimately removed as a plaintiff from the lawsuit.

Comprehension and Thought Questions:

1.   Why do you think plaintiffs did not want to arbitrate their claims against Dell?

2.   Why did the court focus only on whether the parties mutually assented to Dell's terms presented through shrinkwrap, and not through those terms presented through browsewrap?

3.   What test did the court use to determine whether plaintiffs assented to Dell's shrinkwrapped terms, including its arbitration provision?

4.   Does the court's test comport with the objective theory of acceptance?

5.   Using the court's test, did plaintiffs assent to those terms?

6.   Do you think the "practical considerations" that Judge Easterbrook was referring to in *Hill v. Gateway* justify ignoring the traditional analysis of mutual assent in favor of allowing "vendors to enclose the full legal terms with their products"?

7.   Given that consumers tend not to read terms shrinkwrapped with products, when they do read those terms, do not fully understand them, and cannot negotiate those terms, do you think courts should continue to apply the traditional mutual assent doctrine to shrinkwrapped terms? Alternatively, should contract law let go of the concept of mutual assent for these types of contracts? What alternative tests could courts use?

Hypothetical Variations:

1. What if the language in Dell's terms expressly provided that if the customer was not satisfied with the Dell-branded hardware system, the customer's sole remedy would be to exchange it for a replacement system?

---

7. Defontes v. Dell, 2008 WL 8138516 (R.I.) (Appellate Brief) (2008).

2. What would the outcome of the case likely have been if the court had decided to follow *Step-Saver*?

3. Imagine that a Dell salesperson had informed the plaintiffs, when they were ordering the computers, that the computers would be delivered accompanied by additional terms. Assuming that the court followed *Step-Saver*, what do you think the outcome would have been in this case?

PRACTICE PROBLEM 6-1

Chaim Latts, a tax attorney with his own practice, decided to buy a new computer keyboard for his home office. After doing research, he decided to buy the Pewlitt Hackard (PH) 12479 wireless, ergonomic keyboard with USB port. Chaim bought the keyboard through Amazon for $65. He bought the keyboard by placing it in his Amazon cart and then hitting the button "Buy." In other words, Chaim never saw nor had to agree to any terms before placing his order for the keyboard.

While Amazon fulfilled Chaim's order, the keyboard was sold and shipped directly from PH, as a "third-party seller." In other words, Amazon merely served as an agent for PH in the transaction between PH and Chaim, not as the seller. Indeed, PH charged Chaim's credit card when the keyboard was shipped.

The keyboard arrived two days later in an Amazon box. The keyboard itself was wrapped in plastic, with a booklet wrapped inside with the keyboard marked "Instructions." Since Chaim knows how to use a typical computer keyboard, he set the booklet aside and started to use the keyboard.

They keyboard worked fine at first. However, three weeks after he purchased the keyboard, the keyboard started to make random selections on the screen. While Chaim initially was able to override these random selections by wiggling the mouse, after another two weeks, the mouse could no longer override the keyboard to stop it from making random selections. At one point, the keyboard even deleted a portion of a brief Chaim had spent three hours writing. Given his billable rate of $350 an hour, the keyboard cost Chaim at least $1,050 in billable time.

Angry, Chaim sought to return the item to Amazon. The Amazon representative informed Chaim that since PH had sold Chaim the keyboard as a third-party seller, Chaim had to direct his complaint to PH's customer service department.

Chaim contacted PH customer service department and reported the problem he was having with his keyboard. He then demanded a full refund (explaining that he had no more confidence in PH products) as well as $1,050 to compensate him for the three hours he lost writing the portion of the brief that had been deleted by the keyboard. While the customer service representative who Chaim spoke with was apologetic, he explained that under PH's warranty, PH was only required to repair or replace the defective keyboard. Plus, PH was not liable for any other losses as a result of a defective keyboard, including the time Chaim lost writing the portion of the brief that had been deleted.

Chaim responded that he had never seen or agreed to any warranty or limitation on PH's liability. The representative informed Chaim that he could find those terms in the Instructions wrapped with the keyboard when he opened it. He also told Chaim how to find those terms online, on PH's website.

Since Chaim could not find the booklet that came with the keyboard, he looked up the terms of the booklet online. The following are the relevant provisions from that booklet:

1. *Limited Warranty*. Customer acknowledges that this limited warranty applies to PH keyboard model numbers 12003, 12004, 12444, 12479, 12480 and 12490 in lieu of any express warranties. Under this limited warranty, PH warrants that from the date of purchase of the keyboard by you, as shown on your receipt, and for the subsequent 90 days, conditioned on normal use and maintenance by you, the keyboard will be free of defects for its intended use. All other warranties are hereby disclaimed to the fullest extent permitted by applicable law.

2. *Exclusive Remedy*. If there is a defect in your keyboard during the warranty period as described above, you must provide your receipt from your purchase of the keyboard along with a return of the defective keyboard to PH to the address listed below, at your expense and packaged with the same degree of care with which the keyboard was originally sent to you. If it finds that your keyboard is defective, PH will repair or replace, at its option, your defective keyboard. You understand that the repair or replacement of your defective keyboard is your exclusive remedy for a defective keyboard.

3. *Limitation of Liability*. PH disclaims any liability for any losses suffered by you, including any consequential damages you may suffer, as a result of a defective keyboard.

4. *Customer Agreement*. By opening and using your keyboard, you are deemed to agree to these terms.

After reading those terms, Chaim seeks your advice on the following:

1. Was there a contract between Chaim and PH for the purchase and sale of the keyboard?

2. If so, when was that contract formed? Were PH's above terms included in that contract?

3. If not, what would PH's terms have had to provide in order to bind Chaim and other consumers?

B. CLICKWRAP TERMS

Businesses are increasingly setting out the terms of sale for goods and services online. In the typical scenario, the consumer visits the seller's website and identifies the goods (such as software) or services, or combination thereof, the consumer would like to buy. Before finalizing the order, the seller's website loads a webpage titled "Terms." The consumer must scroll through those terms to reach the box at the end. The box at the end says "I agree." Sometimes, the user must place her initials in a box to indicate her agreement to the terms. The consumer must check the box or place her initials to complete the order or to download the software.

In the case of clickwrap, courts fairly routinely conclude that a contract exists on the terms set out in the "Terms." By presenting the item to be purchased as well as the contractual terms to govern that purchase, the seller is seen as manifesting his or her willingness to enter into a bargain on the order's proposed "Terms." Thus, through these manifestations, the seller is the offeror. Here, the seller confers on the offeree—the consumer—the power to accept by clicking the "I agree" button. And by clicking "I agree" or inserting her initials, the consumer manifests his or her assent.

Once again, you might question whether the consumer has truly assented to the seller's terms by scrolling absentmindedly through them without reading them. In fact, often a consumer does not even have to scroll through terms to accept them.[8] But as discussed above under the *DeFontes* case, the inquiry into mutual assent does not inquire into whether the consumer read or understood the terms proposed in the offer, so long as the consumer is not misled or misinformed about the content of the terms and the terms are not intentionally kept from the consumer.

C. BROWSEWRAP TERMS

The mutual assent analysis using the traditional offer and acceptance framework is even more strained where a business presents terms through browsewrap. In the typical browsewrap scenario, a business's terms are available through a hyperlink on the business's website. However, the terms are not displayed unless the customer clicks on that hyperlink. Sometimes the customer does not even see that link unless the customer scrolls down to the bottom of the page. And even if the customer sees the hyperlink for the terms, often the customer does not need to click on that hyperlink to order whatever product is

---

8. *See* Fteja v. Facebook, Inc., 841 F. Supp. 2d 829, 837-38 (S.D.N.Y. 2012).

being offered on the website. Rather, the terms typically say that the customer is "deemed" to have assented to them by ordering the product.[9]

Browsewrap is used not only where there is a seller/buyer relationship. In fact, it is commonly used in the case of free software. There, usually the software provider's terms and conditions provide that the user is deemed to assent to its terms when the user downloads the software.[10] Browsewrap is also used where a user of a website seeks nothing other than access to the website. YouTube is one example of this type of relationship.[11] In those cases, the business's terms usually provide that the user is deemed to assent to the business's terms by browsing the business's website.

The following case is another example of how courts strain the traditional mutual assent doctrine to fit modern electronic contracting. This case, like *DeFontes*, involves a mandatory arbitration clause. In this case, the court must determine whether plaintiffs assented to that clause, which was presented through browsewrap.

Hines v. Overstock.com, Inc.
District Court, Eastern District of New York
668 F. Supp. 2d 362 (2009)

MEMORANDUM AND ORDER

JOHNSON, Senior District Judge.

Plaintiff Cynthia Hines ("Plaintiff" or "Hines") initiated this purported class action pursuant to the Court's diversity jurisdiction, alleging that defendant Overstock.com, Inc.'s ("Defendant" or "Overstock") decision to impose a "restocking fee" amounted to a breach of contract, fraud, and a violation of New York General Business Law sections 349 and 350. Presently before the Court is Defendant's motion to dismiss or stay for arbitration, or alternatively to transfer venue (the "Motion"). For the reasons set forth below, the Motion is DENIED in its entirety.

BACKGROUND

Overstock is an online, "closeout" retailer. On or about January 8, 2009, Plaintiff purchased an Electrolux Oxygen 3 Ultra Canister vacuum from Overstock's website. After receiving the vacuum, Plaintiff returned it to Defendant and was reimbursed the full amount she had paid for it, minus a $30.00 restocking fee. Plaintiff claims that she had been advised that she could return the vacuum

---

9. Nguyen v. Barnes & Noble Inc., 763 F.3d 1171, 1176 (9th Cir. 2014).
10. Kwan v. Clearwire Corp., No. C09-1392JLR, 2012 WL 32380 (W.D. Wash 2012).
11. https://www.youtube.com/t/terms (last visited Sept. 22, 2018).

without incurring any costs and that Defendant never disclosed that a restocking fee would be charged.

In support of the Motion, Defendant avers that: "All retail purchases from Overstock are conducted through Overstock's Internet website. When an individual accesses the website, he or she accepts Overstock's terms, conditions and policies, which govern all of Overstock's customer purchases." Overstock's "Terms and Conditions" ("Terms and Conditions") state that "Entering this Site will constitute your acceptance of these Terms and Conditions" and include a provision that requires that "any dispute relating in any way to your visit to the Site . . . be submitted to confidential arbitration in Salt Lake City, Utah."

Plaintiff affirms, however, that she "never had any notice that disputes with Overstock.com require mandatory arbitration in Salt Lake City, Utah." Plaintiff affirms that when she accessed Overstock's website to purchase the vacuum, she was never made aware of the Terms and Conditions; specifically, Plaintiff avers that: "Because of this lawsuit, I later learned that if you scroll down to the end of the website page or pages, there is in smaller print placed between 'privacy policy' and Overstock.com's registered trademark, the words 'site user terms and conditions*'. I did not scroll down to the end of the page(s) because it was not necessary to do so, as I was directed each step of the way to click on to a bar to take me to the next step to complete the purchase."

DISCUSSION

I. Request to Stay or Dismiss for Arbitration

The Federal Arbitration Act ("FAA"), 9 U.S.C. § 1 *et seq.*, provides that that "[i]f any suit or proceedings be brought in any of the courts of the United States upon any issue referable to arbitration under an agreement in writing for such arbitration, the court in which such suit is pending, upon being satisfied that the issue involved such suit or proceedings is referable to arbitration under such an agreement, shall on application of one of the parties stay the trial of the action." The caselaw is clear that "[w]hen all of the issues raised in a litigation lie within the scope of an arbitration agreement, courts have the discretion to dismiss the action rather than issue an order directing a stay." *Sea Spray Holdings, Ltd. V. Pali Fin. Group. Inc.*, 269 F.Supp.2d 356, 366 (S.D.N.Y. 2003).

In deciding a motion to stay or dismiss in favor of arbitration, a court must begin by answering two questions: "(1) whether the parties agreed to arbitrate, and if so, (2) whether the scope of that agreement encompasses the asserted claims." *Chelsea Square Textiles, Inc. v. Bombay Dyeing & Mfg. Co.*, 189 F.3d 289, 294 (2d Cir. 1999). With respect to the first question, the FAA provides that a written arbitration agreement "shall be valid, irrevocable, and enforceable, save upon such grounds as exist at law or in equity for the revocation of any contract." 9 U.S.C. § 2. The Court therefore begins by examining whether, as a matter of state law, the underlying arbitration agreement is valid.

In determining which state law controls, the Court applies the choice-of-law rules of the forum state. New York's choice-of-law rules apply a "center of gravity" or "grouping of contacts" approach in contract cases to determine which state has "the most significant relationship to the transaction and the parties," considering "the places of negotiation and performance; the location of the subject matter; and the domicile or place of business of the contracting parties." *Zurich Ins. Co. v. Shearson Lehman Hutton, Inc.*, 84 N.Y.2d 309, 317, 618 N.Y.S.2d 609, 642 N.E.2d 1065 (N.Y. 1994) (internal quotation marks and citation omitted).

In the instant case, the parties have not briefed the choice-of-law issue. The Court concludes, however, that under both New York and Utah law, Defendant has not carried its burden of demonstrating the existence of a valid arbitration agreement because Defendant has shown neither that Plaintiff had notice of the Terms and Conditions, nor that a reasonable user of the website would have.

It is a basic tenet of contract law that in order to be binding, a contract requires a "meeting of the minds" and "a manifestation of mutual assent." The making of contracts over the internet "has not fundamentally changed the principles of contract." *Register.com, Inc. v. Verio, Inc.*, 356 F.3d 393, 403 (2d Cir. 2004). On the internet, the primary means of forming a contract are the so-called "clickwrap" (or "click-through") agreements, in which website users typically click an "I agree" box after being presented with a list of terms and conditions of use, and the "browsewrap" agreements, where website terms and conditions of use are posted on the website typically as a hyperlink at the bottom of the screen. Unlike a clickwrap agreement, a browsewrap agreement "does not require the user to manifest assent to the terms and conditions expressly ... [a] party instead gives his assent simply by using the website." *Southwest Airlines Co. v. BoardFirst, L.L.C.*, No. 06-CV-0891-B, 2007 WL 4823761 at *4 (N.D. Tex. Sept. 12, 2007). In ruling upon the validity of a browsewrap agreement, courts consider primarily "whether a website user has actual or constructive knowledge of a site's terms and conditions prior to using the site." *Id.* at *5; *see also Specht v. Netscape Communications Corp.*, 306 F.3d 17, 20 (2d Cir. 2002) (finding no notice).

In *Specht*, the plaintiffs had downloaded free software from the defendant's website; because they did not scroll down the page, they did not see the notice advising site-users to review and agree to the software license agreement's terms prior to downloading. The Second Circuit held that the plaintiffs were not bound by the license agreement's terms because they "were responding to an offer that did not carry an immediately visible notice of the existence of license terms or require unambiguous manifestation of assent to those terms." *Id.* at 31.

In the instant case, it is clear that Plaintiff had no actual notice of the Terms and Conditions of Use. Defendant has also failed to show that Plaintiff had constructive notice. The Hawkins Affidavit, upon which Defendant relies, conclusory states that by accessing Overstock's website, an individual accepts Overstock's Terms and Conditions—but, crucially, does not explain how a site-user such as Plaintiff is made aware of the Terms and Conditions. Despite Defendant's assertion that "all customers to Overstock's website are *advised* of the company's terms and conditions prior to their entry onto the site," neither the Hawkins Affidavit nor any other evidence submitted by Defendant refute Plaintiff's sworn statement that she was never advised of the Terms and Conditions and could not even see the link to them without scrolling down to the bottom of the screen—an action that was not required to effectuate her purchase. Notably, unlike in other cases where courts have upheld browsewrap agreements, the notice that "Entering this Site will constitute your acceptance of these Terms and Conditions," was only available within the Terms and Conditions. Hines therefore lacked notice of the Terms and Conditions because the website did not prompt her to review the Terms and Conditions and because the link to the Terms and Conditions was not prominently displayed so as to provide reasonable notice of the Terms and Conditions. Very little is required to form a contract nowadays—but this alone does not suffice.

II. Request to Transfer to Utah Pursuant to the Forum Selection Clause

Defendant next argues that the Court should transfer the case pursuant to 28 U.S.C. § 1406(a), claiming that the Eastern District is an improper venue for this action because the mandatory forum selection clause in the Terms and Conditions requires the action to be brought in Utah. This argument fails for similar reasons.

The Second Circuit applies a four part test to determine when to dismiss a case based on a forum selection clause; the first part of this test requires the court to determine "whether the [forum selection] clause was reasonably communicated to the party resisting enforcement." *Phillips v. Audio Active Ltd.,* 494 F.3d 378, 383 (2d Cir. 2007). As with the arbitration clause, Defendant simply asserts that all customers on their website are advised of the Terms and Conditions, which include the forum selection clause. Again, however, Defendant has failed to explain how Plaintiff and its other customers were "advised" of the Terms and Conditions, or to cite a single case that suggests that merely posting such terms on a different part of a website constitutes reasonable communication of a forum selection clause. Defendant has therefore failed to show that venue is improper in this District because of the forum selection clause.

[The court also rejected the defendant's argument that the case should be transferred to Utah based on the *forum non conveniens* doctrine.]

CONCLUSION

For the foregoing reasons, the Defendant's Motion is DENIED in its entirety. The parties are directed to contact Magistrate Judge Mann's Chambers in order to proceed expeditiously with discovery.

Understanding the Case:

1. *Contract Language:* The following is an excerpt of the disputed *Overstock* terms and conditions:

Terms and Conditions

This website—http://www.overstock.com (the "Site") is being made available to you free-of-charge. The terms "you", "your", and "yours" refer to anyone accessing, viewing, browsing, visiting or using the Site. The terms "Overstock.com", "we", "us", and "our" refer to Overstock.com, Inc., its affiliates and subsidiaries. We reserve the right to change the nature of this relationship at any time and to revise these Terms and Conditions from time to time as we see fit. As such, you should check these Terms and Conditions periodically. Changes will not apply to any orders we have already accepted unless the law requires. If you violate any of the terms of these Terms and Conditions you will have your access canceled and you may be permanently banned from accessing, viewing, browsing and using the Site. Your accessing, viewing, browsing and/or using the Site after we post changes to these Terms and Conditions constitutes your acceptance and agreement to those changes, whether or not you actually reviewed them. At the bottom of this page, we will notify you of the date these Terms and Conditions were last updated.

Entering the Site will constitute your acceptance of these Terms and Conditions. If you do not agree to abide by these terms, please do not enter the Site.

DISPUTES

If you access the Site from within the United States or Canada, any dispute relating in any way to your visit to the Site, to these Terms and Conditions, to our Privacy and Security Policy, to our advertising or solicitation practices or to products you purchase through the Site shall be submitted to confidential arbitration in Salt Lake City, Utah, USA, except that, to the extent you have in any manner violated or threatened to violate Overstock.com's intellectual property rights, Overstock.com may seek injunctive or other appropriate relief in any state or federal court in the State of Utah, USA and you consent to exclusive jurisdiction and venue in such courts. Arbitration under this Agreement shall be conducted under the rules then prevailing of the American Arbitration Association. The arbitrator's award shall be binding and may be entered as a judgment in any court of competent jurisdiction. To the fullest extent permitted by applicable law, no arbitration under this Agreement shall be joined to an arbitration involving any other party subject to this Agreement, whether through class arbitration proceedings or otherwise.

2. *Subsequent Disposition:* Following the Eastern District of New York's decision, Overstock appealed to the Second Circuit of the United States Court of Appeals, which affirmed the District Court's holding.[12]

3. *Dual Choice of Law:* Before determining whether Hines had assented to Overstock's terms, the court addressed which state's laws controlled. Consistent with the test presented in Chapter 2, to decide this where a contract has

---

12. Hines v. Overstock.com, Inc., 380 F. App'x 22, 23 (2d Cir. 2010).

not selected a governing law, the court looked at which state had "the most significant relationship to the transaction and the parties." However, because the defendant had not argued this point in its brief, the court applied each of the laws of New York and Utah—the two states' laws that were potentially applicable. In that fashion, regardless of which law actually should apply, the court would reach the same outcome.

Comprehension and Thought Questions:

1. Why do you think Hines did not want to arbitrate her claim against Overstock?

2. What test did the court use to determine whether Hines assented to Overstock's terms, including its arbitration provision?

3. Does the court's test comport with the objective theory of acceptance?

4. Using the court's test, did Hines assent to those terms?

5. Is the court's holding consistent with the common law "duty to read"?

6. Should a consumer's assent to a merchant's browsewrap terms depend on notice to the consumer of those terms rather than on a user's conduct manifesting assent?

Hypothetical Variations:

1. What if the link to Overstock's terms had been displayed at the bottom of the screen when Hines ordered so that Hines did not have to scroll down to see that link when she placed her order?

2. What if Hines actually clicked on the link to Overstock's terms but had not read them?

3. Assume you are Overstock's lawyer after the above lawsuit has been resolved. Overstock asks you to advise it how it can make its terms binding on customers. What changes do you suggest to ensure customers who buy products on Overstock.com are bound by Overstock's terms?

D. DISAPPEARANCE OF MUTUAL ASSENT IN ELECTRONIC CONTRACTING

As you read the material in this chapter, you were undoubtedly struck by how different the modern contracting process is compared to the classic back-and-forth of offer and acceptance. Yet as you also saw, courts apply those classic common rules of mutual assent to these modern contracting processes. Doing so oftentimes requires them to warp what amounts to a manifestation of assent, as well as create special rules on notice of terms.

To help you think critically about the material in this chapter, below is an excerpt from an influential article written by Professor Mark Lemley on the disappearance of mutual assent as a result of electronic contracting. As you read this, consider whether you agree or disagree with Professor Lemley on the disappearance of mutual assent. Several questions designed to help you think through Professor Lemley's ideas follow this article.

Assent by both parties to the terms of a contract has long been the fundamental principle animating contract law. Indeed, it is the concept of assent that gives contracts legitimacy and distinguishes them from private legislation. But in to-day's electronic environment, the requirement of assent has withered away to the point where a majority of courts now reject any requirement that a party take any action at all demonstrating agreement to or even awareness of terms in order to be bound by those terms. The result, as Peggy Radin has put it, is "to move the word consent far from what it used to mean, and far from what it has meant in the political, legal, and social understanding of the institution of contract."

18. Standard Form Contracts

The disintegration of assent results from the confluence of three different elements in the online environment. The first is the ease with which electron-ic contracting permits the imposition of standard form contracts on a large, anonymous mass of users. Anyone can now "contract" with those she encoun-ters online by merely drafting a legal form and seeking whatever assent to that form the courts require. Standard form contracts have been with us for decades, and they can serve useful purposes in reducing transaction costs in mass-market, repeat-play settings. In the online environment, these standard-form agreements take the form of clickwrap licenses—agreements that visitors to a Web site sign electronically by clicking "I agree" to a standard set of terms. Clickwraps put some pressure on the classical notion of assent derived from bargained agreements, because they substitute a blanket, take-it-or-leave-it as-sent for the classical notion that the parties actually thought about and agreed to the terms of the deal.

Offline, such agreements are not all that common, in part because it is too much effort to get consumers to sign the standard forms. While they do exist in many contexts—renting cars is an oft-used example—most consumer trans-actions do not involve any written contract with the vendor at all. Merchants and consumers at grocery stores, restaurants, bookstores, clothing stores, and countless other retail outlets seem perfectly able to enter into contracts without a written agreement specifying their rights and obligations. Nonetheless, many of those same retail outlets impose standard form contracts on their online us-ers, probably because it is easier to get someone to click "I agree" as part of an online transaction than it is to have a clerk obtain a signature on a written form.

Because the user has "signed" the contract by clicking "I agree," every court to consider the issue has held clickwrap licenses enforceable. There is nothing inherently troubling about enforcing clickwrap licenses. Blanket assent to a form contract is still assent, albeit a more attenuated form than the assent that drives contract theory. But the prevalence of such standard form contracts online has arguably conditioned both consumers and courts to expect the retailer to set the terms of the deal in writing, even when there is no similar expectation for parallel transactions offline.

B. Shrinkwrap Licenses

The growing judicial acceptance of shrinkwrap licenses has further under-mined classical notions of assent. These licenses, common in the pre-packaged sale of physical copies of software in the 1980s and 1990s, included a license packaged within the shrinkwrap or loaded on the computer and provided that breaking the shrinkwrap or running the program constituted acceptance of the terms of the contract. At least in the classic shrinkwrap license, the user never clicks or signs an agreement to any such terms. Rather, the theory of the shrink-wrap license is that the user manifests assent to those terms by engaging in a particular course of conduct that the license specifies constitutes acceptance.

So-called "unilateral" contracts accepted by performance, while rare in the of-fline world, are not unheard of. Two things make shrinkwrap licenses different, and more troubling, than traditional unilateral contracts. First, the user does not receive the contract terms until after she has shelled out money for the prod-uct. While some software products have a notice that terms are included inside, others do not, and in any event we do not generally think of necessary terms to an agreement being available only after the consumer has made the decision to purchase. In theory, shrinkwrap licenses solve this problem by permitting the buyer to return the software for a full refund, though that option is sufficiently inconvenient as to be impractical and in any event turns out in practice to be illusory: software vendors and retail stores generally refuse to accept software returned under those conditions. Second, the specified conduct that indicates acceptance is the opening of a package and the loading of software the consumer has already paid for—precisely the conduct one would expect the user to engage in if she had been unaware of the shrinkwrap license. Unlike a typical unilateral contract, in which one party accepts an offer by engaging in conduct that unmis-takably indicates assent—say, painting my house—the conduct used as evidence of a shrinkwrap contract is hardly unambiguous evidence of assent.

Until 1996, every court to consider the validity of a shrinkwrap license held it unenforceable. The tide began to turn with Judge Easterbrook's 1996 opinion upholding a shrinkwrap license in ProCD, Inc. v. Zeidenberg. ProCD held Zeiden-berg bound to terms he first saw when he loaded ProCD's software into his computer, even though he paid for the software before being made aware of the terms. The court's legal reasoning is certainly questionable. Judge Easterbrook relied on U.C.C. section 2-204, which provides that a contract can be formed in any way the parties agree. But arguably he should have treated the additional terms as a proposed modification to the contract Zeidenberg entered into when he handed money to a store clerk in exchange for a box containing software. Un-der U.C.C. section 2-209, such proposed new terms can become part of the con-tract without additional consideration, but not if they make material changes to the contract, as ProCD's terms likely did. ProCD also distinguished U.C.C. sec-tion 2-207, which deals with the situation of standard forms exchanged by the parties. The court reasoned that section 2-207 could not apply unless the parties exchanged at least two forms, an interpretation that finds some support in the language of the section but that leads to the peculiar result that merchant buyers get more protection against a seller's standard form than consumers do. Despite these and other problems, the ProCD opinion has proved influential. While a number of courts since 1996 have continued to reject shrinkwrap licenses, still more courts have followed ProCD and enforced those licenses.

Both the clickwrap and shrinkwrap cases may have conditioned courts to abandon the idea of assent when it comes to browsewraps. Legally, there is a big difference between a unilateral statement of desires and a statement of terms to which the other party has agreed. But once we have expanded agreement to include clicking on a Web site or engaging in conduct that we would expect the buyer to engage in anyway, it seems only a small step to enforce a unilateral statement of terms. As the argument goes, if we refuse to enforce browsewraps, a site owner will simply impose the same restrictions via clickwrap or shrinkwrap. Since no one reads the latter forms of contract anyway, and owners can include whatever terms they want, it seems a sort of formalism to require them to go through the effort of requiring some weak manifestation of assent.

C. Web Sites as Property

The final nail in the online assent coffin is the overlap between contract claims and concepts of property. The fact that almost all of the Internet cases to enforce a browsewrap come up in the property/trespass context inclines courts to take real property rules and apply them to contract law. I don't need agreement to my "no-trespassing" sign in the physical world: I only need to give notice of my desire to enforce the property rights the law has already given me. So perhaps it's not surprising that the courts in this context make the seemingly small jump to concluding the same is true of contract law. If I told you what I wanted you to do (or not to do) with my Web site, and you did something different, you must have breached the agreement that allowed you to come onto the site.

The problem is that the shift from property law to contract law takes the job of defining the Web site owner's rights out of the hands of the law and into the hands of the site owner. Property law may or may not prohibit a particular "intrusion" on a Web site, but it is the law that determines the answer to that question. The reason my "no-trespassing" sign is effective in the real world is not because there is any sort of agreement to abide by it, but because the law already protects my land against intrusion by another. If the sign read "no walking on the road outside my property," no one would think of it as an enforceable agreement. If we make the conceptual leap to assuming that refusing to act in the way the site owner wants is also a breach of contract, it becomes the site owner rather than the law that determines what actions are forbidden. The law then enforces that private decision. One might like or dislike the vesting of such control in a site owner as a matter of policy, but doing so is an abandonment of the notion of assent. It is easier to abandon that notion if we conflate property and contract (call it "protract") in this way.

Mark A. Lemley, *Terms of Use*, 91 Minn. L. Rev. 459 (2006).

Comprehension and Thought Questions:

1. According to Professor Lemley, how have clickwrap and shrinkwrap affected the mutual assent analysis for browsewrap?

2. Do you agree with Professor Lemley that through the enforcement of browsewrap terms, courts are essentially enforcing unilateral statements of terms through which website owners set their own property rights on their website?

3. Do you think courts should skip the traditional mutual assent analysis in the electronic contracting context, to avoid forcing an analysis that does not fit? If so, is there another way to protect the same consumer interests that mutual assent is designed to protect?

PRACTICE PROBLEM 6-2

Jenny Grey decides to purchase an all-in-one desktop computer system. Jenny buys this computer from Computer Source Inc. because Computer Source is offering this "discontinued" product at a discount price of $800—$300 lower than its historic price. Also, Jenny wants to buy this computer from Computer Source because it offers computer support services.

Jenny places this computer in her online cart on Computer Source's webpage. She also places in her online cart a $300 Service Plan for her computer. According to the summary of the plan's terms, which are displayed when Jenny places the plan in her cart, Computer Source protects all covered computer hardware from accidents and defects for three years. If any of that hardware is defective or damaged during those three years, Computer Source will repair or replace it at no charge to the customer. In addition, under that plan, Computer Source will provide 24-hour customer support for three years.

Content with her selections, Jenny hits the "check out" button on Computer Source's webpage. When she hits that button, a new page loads that asks Jenny to check a box saying she has read Computer Source's terms. Jenny checks that box, although she did not read Computer Source's terms. In fact, as Jenny later finds out, those terms were not available on the page with the box that she was required to check—in fact, they were not accessible once a customer started the "check out" process. Instead, the terms were available before the order process was started, through a link at the bottom of Computer Source's webpage. While that link was displayed on the bottom of that page, Jenny did not need to (and did not) click on those terms to proceed to check out or to complete her purchase.

Had Jenny read those terms and conditions, she would have seen that under the Service Plan, Computer Source's repair/replacement obligation is capped at the purchase price for the hardware covered under the plan. That means Computer Source is only obligated to repair or replace Jenny's computer up to a cost of $800. Moreover, those terms include the following language in Sections 17 and 18:

17. Mandatory Arbitration. Any controversy or claim arising out of or relating to this Agreement, or the breach hereof, shall be settled by arbitration administered by the American Arbitration Association in accordance with its Commercial Arbitration Rules and judgment on the award rendered by the arbitrator may be entered in any court having jurisdiction thereof.

Claims shall be heard by a single arbitrator. The place of arbitration shall be Wilmington, Delaware. Hearings will take place pursuant to the standard procedures of the Commercial Arbitration Rules that contemplate in-person hearings. The prevailing party shall be entitled to an award of reasonable attorney fees.

18. <u>Your Acceptance</u>. If Customer does not wish to be bound by these terms and conditions, Customer must return the product(s) and/or service(s) bought from Computer Source within 14 days of Customer's receipt of Customer's order. Otherwise, Customer is deemed to accept these terms.

When Jenny's computer arrives, she notices that it is running slowly. Also, periodically the screen goes blank and the computer reboots itself. Jenny contacts Computer Source's 24-hour service line to try to resolve the problem. Three days, five telephone calls, and one customer support home visit later, Jenny discovers that the computer needs a complete overhaul—a new motherboard, new central processing unit, and new internal hard drive. So she sends it to Computer Source to repair or replace, per the Service Plan. After five days, a representative from Computer Source's service department calls Jenny to tell her that they cannot replace her computer because to do so would exceed their capped coverage of $800. The representative indicates that the cost increased after the model was discontinued, at which point it became much harder to repair or replace defective components.

Jenny expresses outrage and tells the representative that she will return the computer then. The representative tells Jenny that per the terms, it is too late to return the computer.

Jenny decides to contact you to consider her legal rights and remedies. Specifically:

1. Is Jenny bound by Computer Source's terms listed on its website? If so, when was she bound by those terms?

2. Assuming Jenny is bound to Computer Source's terms, what are her options?

E. SMART CONTRACTS

Electronic contracting processes in fact have innovated even beyond browsewrap. More currently, businesses have started to use "smart" contracts by automating their entry into contracts. Thus, an algorithm that translates contract language into code determines when to enter into a contract as well as the contract's terms. That algorithm is stored using blockchain technology. Blockchain technology produces a distributed ledger of transactions that allows many computers to keep an identical record of those transactions. Thus, there is no master copy of those transactions nor a single master computer to manipulate, making the stored record trustworthy.

Smart contracts allow a business to save money and reduce inefficiencies by eliminating transaction costs associated with repeated entry into the same type of contract. They also reduce human error and irrational decision-making as to the terms of the contract, for those functions are automated using a protocol.

To see this, imagine a bank that makes personal loans to customers. Under the classic contractual framework, someone at that bank—likely a loan officer—would review the customer's application and decide whether to approve the customer for the requested loan and if so, how much to lend and at what rate. That loan officer would then prepare all of the loan documents to reflect those terms using the bank's "forms." However, doing so introduced some potential for mistake and suboptimal decision-making by the loan officer. It also required the loan officer's time to review the customer's application and prepare the forms.

With a smart contract, the bank can create an algorithm that will automatically approve a loan application for a customer if certain conditions are met. Those conditions would undoubtedly include information specified in the customer's loan application (which is coded for the computer to read), and a credit score above a minimum number. That approval would result automatically from the information in the customer's application and credit score, coded from language into a computer program. That program would also determine the customer's interest rate and would prepare the relevant loan documents to reflect all of that information. Thus, no person at the bank would need to be involved in the contracting process.

In some transactions, both parties enter into the contract through automation. That might occur, for example, with the automatic ordering and sale of component parts between a supplier and a buyer.

In these smart contracts, you might consider whether a computer algorithm can manifest assent. As you consider that, remember that there was a human behind the algorithm, setting out which parameters would lead to a loan and at what rate.

While automating entry into contracts is important, what many people view as most innovative about smart contracts is that their performance is automated. That means, in turn, that smart contracts cannot be breached, as they contain self-executing codes that ensure that the parties perform.

For example, in the same loan agreement mentioned above, the bank's program might make an auto-withdrawal of funds from the customer's account where that customer has not paid the loan on time. In that way, the bank would not need to sue the customer for breach. In addition, contracts can be self-executing by both parties, such as with stock traders who use algorithms to decide when to sell or buy stock. Chapter 12 will discuss automation in the performance of contracts in more detail.

Now that you have studied electronic contracting, read through and answer the questions that follow the Simulation Problem for Chapter 6, which is located in Appendix A.

CHAPTER 7

Consideration

Recall that a contract exists where (1) the parties have manifested assent to the terms of a bargain, (2) in which one party makes a promise in exchange for either a return promise or performance. So far, we have focused on element (1)—mutual assent. In this chapter, we focus on the second element.

In general, element (2) requires that a party makes a promise *to induce* the making of a return promise or the rendering of a return performance. In other words, where a party makes a promise, that promise is "supported by consideration" where the promise is made *to induce a return promise or performance* and the return promise or performance that is provided *is induced by the promisor's promise*.[1]

The term "consideration" is also used to refer to what is given in such a bargain in exchange for a promise—meaning the return promise or performance. However, implicit in use of the term is the legal conclusion that the return promise or performance satisfies the legal test for consideration. In other words, not everything given in exchange for a promise amounts to consideration—only if it is induced by the promise (and induces the return promise) and meets the other criteria discussed in Section B below does it amount to consideration.

Note that while this description of consideration suggests that a party makes a single promise in any contract, in most cases, each party makes a set of promises. For example, in the sale of a car, the seller would promise not only to sell the car to the buyer at the closing date (which would be the key promise), but also to keep the car safe and maintain the car until closing. In this situation, all of the seller's promises are grouped together and viewed as a single set for purposes of the consideration analysis. Thus, here, the consideration question looks at what induced the seller to make this set of promises, and whether what

---

1. Restatement (Second) of Contracts § 71 (1981).

is given in exchange was in fact induced by the seller's promises. You will want to keep this in mind as you read this chapter, which often explores whether a party's "promise" is supported by consideration. That discussion applies equally where a party makes a set of promises.

You might already be wondering *why* the law only enforces promises that are supported by consideration.[2] Stated differently, why is a promise that lacks consideration unenforceable? Section A explores the rationales for the consideration doctrine. Once you understand the doctrine's background and rationale, you can better understand how the doctrine applies. Section B then explores the specific requirements of the consideration doctrine and explains how to satisfy them, while Section C extends that discussion to formal written contracts. Finally, Section D presents a modern example of litigation involving the consideration doctrine.

A. JUSTIFICATION FOR CONSIDERATION DOCTRINE

To understand the reasons for consideration, we briefly consider the historical underpinnings of the doctrine. The following is a short passage from an article written by Professor Val Ricks on the genesis of the consideration doctrine. You will find several questions following this passage.

> Consideration entered the law 460 years ago as a central element of the common law form of action called assumpsit. Most lawyers have heard some short version of the rise of assumpsit. The common law of the sixteenth century was organized around forms of action. Legal prohibitions on conduct and, conversely, protections of freedom often took the shape of procedural limitations on these forms of action. In the common law system, a wrong could be remedied or a right vindicated only if it fit within a form. But the common law had a general, residual form of action in which wrongs could be alleged and remedied that were not covered by other forms. This general form was called trespass on the case. Judges in the late fifteenth and early sixteenth centuries began enforcing promises generally in a species of trespass on the case called assumpsit. Assumpsit is a past tense form of the Latin verb meaning "to undertake." To promise was to undertake. Breach of a promise or undertaking became known as a trespass.
>
> Plaintiffs' lawyers preferred assumpsit to older, less straightforward forms for enforcing promises, such as covenant and debt. The assumpsit action took a simple approach to promise enforcement by focusing primarily on three questions. First, was a promise made? Second, was the promise worthy of enforcement, i.e. was it the kind of promise that should be actionable? And third, was the promise breached? Jury decisions as to questions one and three were generally allowed to stand. Juries were competent to say whether a promise and breach

---

2. Of course, reliance on a promise may lead to the enforcement of that promise, as discussed in Chapter 22. But such enforcement results from equity, and is not automatic, as with a bargained-for contract.

had occurred. But judges occasionally asserted control over juries by deciding question two as a matter of law.

For largely historical reasons, sixteenth century judges' decisions as to which kinds of promises were actionable usually took the form of giving meaning to the word consideration. The law required this word to be alleged in nearly every plaintiff's assumpsit pleading. Besides promise and breach, the only other concept common to every assumpsit complaint was consideration. This word was therefore the most likely candidate for legal development within the form of action. If a jury found for a plaintiff, then the plaintiff's pleadings relative to promise, consideration, and breach became findings of fact, and judges could then rule on them as a matter of law. Judges turned to construction of this murky word consideration in order to limit the jury's power to remedy breach of promise, in order to say which kinds of promises were actionable and which were not.

Val D. Ricks, *The Sophisticated Doctrine of Consideration*, 9 Geo. Mason L. Rev. 99, 99-102 (2000).

In a later part of his article, Professor Ricks argues that "consideration was not at its inception a hard and fast requirement for recovery in assumpsit or contract."[3] Professor Ricks argues that the consideration doctrine would be useful today if it maintained that flexibility and was not an essential element to enforcing a promise.[4]

Comprehension and Thought Questions:

1. What role should this historical development play in consideration's application in modern contract law?

2. Assuming the consideration doctrine used to be applied flexibly and was not an essential requirement of bargain, should we restore that flexibility today? Why or why not?

3. If we allow courts some flexibility in applying the consideration doctrine, do we need to look to other legal doctrines to restrict courts in deciding which promises to enforce and which to not enforce? Why or why not?

Many courts and commentators who are not as tethered to consideration on the basis of its historical underpinning still favor its use. Specifically, in their view, the consideration doctrine supports society's view as to what types of promises courts *should* enforce. In that way, consideration serves a channeling function, only channeling to the courts promises seen by society as creating economic value. Moreover, proponents argue that the consideration requirement ensures that only those promises that are well thought out are enforced. That is because a person acts more deliberately and less emotionally in respect

---

3. Val D. Ricks, *The Sophisticated Doctrine of Consideration*, 9 Geo. Mason L. Rev. 99, 103 (2000).

4. *Id.* at 141-43.

of a promise made as part of an exchange than a gratuitous promise. In that way, consideration serves a cautionary function. Finally, proponents believe consideration often serves an evidentiary function, as there is usually more evidence of the making of a bargained-for promise than a gratuitous promise.[5]

Yet, many question whether consideration remains relevant today. First, consideration seems to poorly serve the channeling function given that society is generally unfamiliar with the consideration doctrine—without that public awareness, the public would not know which promises they can enforce and which they cannot enforce. Moreover, the fact that, as you will see below, it only takes the proverbial peppercorn to satisfy the exchange requirement calls into question the channeling function. Plus, consideration may not successfully be serving a cautionary function given the little deliberation that parties give to bargains in the modern economy, as you saw in Chapter 6 on electronic contracting. And nothing about the consideration doctrine suggests why a bargained-for promise is better evidenced than a gratuitous promise.

Consistent with the view that consideration is not relevant, evidence shows that a bargain is rarely successfully challenged on the basis of there not being consideration. In the context of commercial dealings in particular, consideration is almost never a contested issue because commercial parties rarely, if ever, give a promise to another party gratuitously without exacting something of legal value in return. In fact, doing so could expose the people who manage that commercial party to liability.[6] That, then, only leaves noncommercial transactions that might run afoul of the consideration doctrine. And again, given the ease with which its requirements are satisfied, consideration tends to not be a stumbling block to enforcement of those promises unless they are clearly gratuitous. And even those promises are sometimes enforced, not because there is a bargain, but as you will study in Chapter 22, because of a party's reliance on the promise.

B. DETERMINING THE EXISTENCE OF CONSIDERATION

While Section A examined the historical underpinnings and justification for the consideration doctrine, this section explores how courts determine whether the consideration requirement is satisfied.

As introduced at the start of this chapter, consideration for a promise exists where that promise is made to induce something in exchange, and what is

---

5. These various functions of consideration were famously explored in Professor Lon Fuller's *Consideration and Form*, 41 Colum. L. Rev. 799 (1941).

6. Most states's business organization laws permit the governing body to make charitable contributions. However, just because such contributions are permitted does not mean actually making them would fulfill the governing body's fiduciary duties to act in the organization's best interests. *See* 1 Treatise on the Law of Corporations § 4:4 (3d).

sought in exchange is given on the basis of the promise. The term consideration also refers to what is actually given in exchange for the promise. That may be a return promise, as with a bilateral contract, or it may be performance, as with a unilateral contract.

It is important to note at the outset that consideration must exist for each set of promises in a bargain. In a bilateral contract, that means that each party's promise or set of promises must be supported by consideration, which means that they must be made to induce the other party's return promise or promises.

1. Promise to Make a Gift or Promise Made Due to Moral Obligation Not Consideration

A promise to make a gift is not enforceable as a bargained-for contract. That is because the promise is not made to induce anything in exchange. Rather, it is made to confer a gratuity on the other party.

Likewise, a promise made solely out of a sense of moral obligation is not consideration. That is because in this case, whatever gave rise to the promisor's sense of moral obligation—often a benefit conferred on him in the past that he felt morally obligated to repay in some way—was not conferred on him to induce him to make a return promise or performance.

To see how these rules work, consider the situation where an 18-year-old daughter promises her parents that she will wash their car. Once the daughter washes her parent's car, they pay her $10. Here, the daughter did not make the promise to her parents to wash their car *to induce them to pay her*. In fact, she had already washed their car when they decided to pay her. Thus, the daughter's promise to wash her parents' car did not induce her parents' payment, and their payment is not consideration.

Suppose instead that the daughter's parents give her $10 and, feeling grateful and morally obligated to return the favor, the daughter promises to wash their car. Here, her parents' act of paying her $10 would not amount to consideration for the daughter's promise to wash their car. That is because her promise to wash her parents' car was not made to induce her parents to pay her $10. In fact, that act had been completed *before* she made her promise.

Sometimes it can be difficult to tell whether a promise or performance was bargained for—meaning sought in exchange for a promise.

For example, suppose Ken Newman is your uncle. You tell Uncle Ken you are looking to lease a two-bedroom apartment in Springfield for a year. Uncle Ken tells you that he will lease you a two-bedroom apartment for a year for free. However, in that same conversation, he tells you that Brit Newman, his son, is having a hard time in his first year of law school. He asks you if you will help Brit with his studies, at least for the rest of his first year. You tell Uncle Ken that of course you will help cousin Brit.

Here, what happens if in a month or two after you start to lease Uncle Ken's apartment, you have a falling out with Uncle Ken and he asks you to vacate the apartment? Do you have a contract with Uncle Ken for that space for a year? This question requires you to determine whether there is consideration to support Uncle Ken's promise to lease that space to you. If this devolved into a legal dispute (which, unfortunately, sometimes happens with family members), you would argue that there is consideration to support Uncle Ken's promise. Namely, you promised Uncle Ken that you would help cousin Brit with his studies for the rest of his 1L year in exchange for Uncle Ken's promise to lease you his two-bedroom apartment. On the other hand, based on the above facts, it does not appear that Uncle Ken was bargaining for your return promise. Rather, you gave Uncle Ken a promise to help cousin Brit *after* Uncle Ken promised to let you occupy his two-bedroom apartment for a year for free. Thus, your promise was made out of a sense of moral obligation, but not to induce Uncle Ken to make his promise to you—something he had already done.

Keep in mind that there might be more than one reason for a promisee to give a return promise or performance. So long as the promisee was *in part* induced by the promisor's promise to give a return promise or performance, and that return promise or performance was sought by the promisor, the consideration element is satisfied.

In our example, suppose Uncle Ken tells you that he will let you use his two-bedroom apartment for a year for free if, in exchange, you help cousin Brit with his first-year law school studies. Also suppose that while there is some value to Uncle Ken of having you help cousin Brit, the value of that assistance is nowhere near $12,000—the market rate of rent for his two-bedroom apartment for a year. Here, it seems Uncle Ken promised you that you could lease that apartment for two reasons—one was to induce you to help cousin Brit and the other was gratuitous. In this example, there would be consideration for Uncle Ken's promise. Just because Uncle Ken was partly motivated by his desire to provide for you—his family member—does not preclude your return promise from constituting consideration.

PRACTICE PROBLEM 7-1

Are the following promises made by you and your friend supported by consideration? Make sure you consider the arguments that will be made by someone disagreeing with your conclusion.

1. You promise to paint your friend's apartment with her because she asked you to help and she is a longtime friend. No

2. You promise to paint your friend's apartment because you secretly hope to be invited over for dinner at her new place. After you paint the apartment, your friend promises to invite you over for dinner. No

3. You promise to paint your friend's apartment with her and in fact do so, and afterwards, your friend promises to pay you $500. no

4. You promise to paint your friend's apartment with her if your friend promises to "buy you a beer" afterwards. Your friend promises to do so. yes

5. You promise to paint your friend's apartment with her if your friend promises to pay you $500. Your friend agrees. yes

2. Not Nominal or Sham

Courts generally do not question the value of what is given in exchange for a promise, even if the proposed consideration seems unfair or one-sided—so long as something is given in exchange for a promise, courts conclude that the promise is supported by consideration. Thus, it is sometimes quipped, even a "mere peppercorn" will satisfy the consideration requirement.

However, if it is questioned in litigation, courts will not conclude that a return promise or performance is consideration for a promise where the purported consideration is clearly nominal or a sham. The word **nominal** means the consideration is of a token value. The word **sham** means the consideration is a deception or trick (regarding the appearance of consideration), and not something actually to be delivered. You may recall this issue arising in *Moreno v. Smith*, discussed in Chapter 4, where the court examined whether the agreement for the daughter to make payments over time to purchase her mother's real property interests was intended to be respected or whether it was a sham (meaning that the parties never actually expected the stated consideration to be paid).

So, for example, if Uncle Ken never intended for you to help cousin Brit study for law school, but simply asked you to make this return promise to make it seem like you were giving something back to Uncle Ken, then your promise back to Uncle Ken would be a sham, given solely to make it seem like there was consideration for Uncle Ken's promise when in fact there was not. It would thus not constitute consideration for Uncle Ken's promise.

If Uncle Ken asked you to give him $1 every month in exchange for his promise to lease you his two-bedroom apartment, your payment would not amount to consideration. That is because what you would be giving in exchange would be nominal—that is, it would be a token amount, clearly not intended to induce Uncle Ken to make his promise to you to lease you the two-bedroom apartment. Similarly, merely including a recital in the written contract that the consideration received was valuable and sufficient generally will not make it so.[7] In other words, you cannot manufacture legal consideration if, from an objective standpoint, the parties were not actually bargaining for the exchange promised (and were instead merely pretending that they were).

---

7. *See, e.g.*, Dougherty v. Salt, 125 N.E. 94, 95 (N.Y. 1919).

PRACTICE PROBLEM 7-2

Your mother tells you that she wants to make sure you receive an extra $10,000 as an inheritance (meaning, property to be transferred to you at her death) in preference to your siblings. To prevent your siblings from getting upset at this, you and your mom sign a piece of paper in which you promise to visit your mom once a year for the rest of her life.

1. Is your mother's promise supported by consideration?
2. What if your mom was cantankerous and visits with her were difficult to tolerate?
3. Would it affect your analysis if your mother had not told you about wanting to make sure you got the extra $10,000 *as an inheritance*?

3. Benefit/Detriment Test

Under classic common law, in analyzing whether a return promise or performance amounts to consideration for a promise, in addition to looking at mutual inducements for a promise, courts used to look for whether that return promise or performance either benefited the promisor or was a legal detriment to the promisee. They conducted the benefit/detriment test because they assumed that a party would not make a promise giving rise to a contract unless it got something back from the other party that either benefitted the promisor or, alternatively, involved the other party suffering a detriment such as by giving up a legal right.

The following is perhaps the most well-known consideration case. As you read it, see if you can identify how the court determined whether consideration existed, including the relevance of the benefit/detriment test.

Hamer v. Sidway
Court of Appeals of New York, Second Division
27 N.E. 256 (N.Y. 1891)

This action was brought upon an alleged contract.

. . . The plaintiff presented a claim to the executor of William E. Story, Sr., for $5,000 and interest from the 6th day of February, 1875. She acquired it through several mesne assignments from William E. Story, 2d. The claim being rejected by the executor, this action was brought.

It appears that William E. Story, Sr., was the uncle of William E. Story, 2d; that at the celebration of the golden wedding of Samuel Story and wife, father and mother of William E. Story, Sr., on the 20th day of March, 1869, in the presence of the family and invited guests, he promised his nephew that if he would refrain from drinking, using tobacco, swearing, and playing cards or billiards for money until he became 21 years of age, he would pay him the sum of $5,000. The nephew assented thereto, and fully performed the conditions inducing the promise. When the nephew arrived at the age of 21 years, and on the 31st day of January, 1875, he wrote to his uncle, informing him that he had performed his part of the agreement, and had thereby become entitled to the sum of $5,000. The uncle received the letter, and a few days later, and on the 6th day of February, he wrote and mailed to his nephew the following letter:

> "Buffalo, Feb. 6, 1875. W. E. Story, Jr.—Dear Nephew: Your letter of the 31st ult. came to hand all right, saying that you had lived up to the promise made to me several years ago. I have no doubt but you have, for which you shall have five thousand dollars, as I promised you. I had the money in the bank the day you was twenty-one years old that I intend for you, and you shall have the money certain. . . . Willie, you are twenty-one, and you have many a thing to learn yet. This money you have earned much easier than I did, besides acquiring good habits at the same time, and you are quite welcome to the money. Hope you will make good use of it. . . .
>
>   Truly yours,
>   W. E. STORY.
>   P. S. You can consider this money on interest."

The nephew received the letter, and thereafter consented that the money should remain with his uncle in accordance with the terms and conditions of the letter. The uncle died on the 29th day of January, 1887, without having paid over to his nephew any portion of the said $5,000 and interest. . . .

The question which provoked the most discussion by counsel on this appeal, and which lies at the foundation of plaintiff's asserted right of recovery, is whether by virtue of a contract defendant's testator, William E. Story, became indebted to his nephew, William E. Story, 2d, on his twenty-first birthday in the sum of $5,000. The trial court found as a fact that "on the 20th day of March, 1869, * * * William E. Story agreed to and with William E. Story, 2d, that if he would refrain from drinking liquor using tobacco, swearing, and playing cards or billiards for money until should become twenty-one years of age, then he, the said William E. Story, would at that time pay him, the said William E. Story, 2d, the sum of $5,000 for such refraining, to which the said William E. Story, 2d, agreed," and that he "in all things fully performed his part of said agreement."

The defendant contends that the contract was without consideration to support it, and therefore invalid. He asserts that the promisee, by refraining from the use of liquor and tobacco, was not harmed, but benefited; that that which he did was best for him to do, independently of his uncle's promise,—and insists that it follows that, unless the promisor was benefited, the contract was without consideration,—a contention which, if well founded, would seem to leave open for controversy in many cases whether that which the promisee did or omitted to do was in fact of such benefit to him as to leave no consideration to support the enforcement of the promisor's agreement. Such a rule could not be tolerated, and is without foundation in the law.

The exchequer chamber in 1875 defined "consideration" as follows: "A valuable consideration, in the sense of the law, may consist either in some right, interest, profit, or benefit accruing to the one party, or some forbearance, detriment, loss, or responsibility given, suffered, or undertaken by the other." Courts "will not ask whether the thing which forms the consideration does in fact benefit the promisee or a third party, or is of any substantial value to anyone. It is enough that something is promised, done, forborne, or suffered by the party to whom the promise is made as consideration for the promise made to him." Anson, Cont. 63. "In general a waiver of any legal right at the request of another party is a sufficient consideration for a promise." Pars. Cont. *444. . . . Pollock in his work on Contracts (page 166,) after citing the definition given by the exchequer chamber, already quoted, [124 N.Y. 546] says: "The second branch of this judicial description is really the most important one. 'Consideration' means not so much that one party is profiting as that the other abandons some legal right in the present, or limits his legal freedom of action in the future, as an inducement for the promise of the first."

Now, applying this rule to the facts before us, the promisee used tobacco, occasionally drank liquor, and he had a legal right to do so. That right he abandoned for a period of years upon the strength of the promise of the testator that for such forbearance he would give him $5,000. We need not speculate on the effort which may have been required to give up the use of those stimulants. It is sufficient that he restricted his lawful freedom of action within certain prescribed limits upon the faith of his uncle's agreement, and now, having fully performed the conditions imposed, it is of no moment whether such performance actually proved a benefit to the promisor, and the court will not inquire into it; but, were it a proper subject of inquiry, we see nothing in this record that would permit a determination that the uncle was not benefited in a legal sense. . . .

The order appealed from should be reversed, and the judgment of the special term affirmed, with costs payable out of the estate. All concur.

Understanding the Case:

1. *Mesne Assignments:* The court states that the plaintiff in this case acquired the note made by William E. Story, Sr. payable to his nephew, William E. Story, 2d, through several "mesne assignments." An assignment of a note occurs where the payee on the note assigns his or her rights under that note (especially the right to receive money from the obligor) to another person. Where that occurs, the assignee (i.e., the person to whom the note is assigned) now is essentially the new payee on the note. The word "mesne," which derives from French and means intermediate or intervening, indicates that there were several assignments before the note reached the hands of the plaintiff.

Comprehension and Thought Questions:

1. Who is the plaintiff in this case?
2. What promise is the plaintiff seeking to enforce in this case?
3. How was the mutual assent element satisfied in this contract?
4. On what basis does the defendant argue that his promise is not enforceable?
5. What test does the court use in determining whether that promise is enforceable?
6. How does the court apply that test in this case?
7. Did it matter that William E. Story, 2d arguably benefited from his performance in applying that test?

Hypothetical Variations:

1. What if instead of giving up his right to use tobacco and alcohol, William E. Story, 2d promised to give up his use of cocaine in exchange for his uncle's promise?
2. What if the uncle attached little value to the promise given by William E. Story, 2d in exchange for the uncle's promise to pay $5,000?
3. What if William E. Story, 2d decided when he turned 16 to stop using tobacco and alcohol, and when he turned 21, his uncle congratulated him on this wonderful achievement and promised to pay his nephew $5,000 for this effort?

Today, while courts often refer to the benefit/detriment test, many do not apply its literal meaning.[8] In other words, they do not search for whether consideration for a promise either benefited the promisor or detrimented the promisee. Rather, so long as what is provided by the promisee in exchange for the promisor's promise is what is sought by the promisor and meets the other requirements in this section, then the court will conclude that there is consideration.

While the consideration analysis under either the bargained-for test or the benefit/detriment test usually does not yield different results, it can at the margin, where it is not clear whether purported consideration either benefits the promisor or detriments the promisee.

To take an example, suppose one of your clients, Jeff Jones, owes Larry Lender $2,000. As is customarily done in this type of circumstance, Jeff signs a promissory note evidencing this $2,000 debt. Eventually Jeff pays this debt in full. Consequently, Jeff does not owe Larry any money. So, Jeff asks Larry to

---

8. Some courts, however, continue to conduct the benefit/detriment test for consideration. *See, e.g.,* Intercon Mfg. v. Centrifugal Casting Machine Co., 875 P.2d 1149, 1152 (Okla. App. 1993). Moreover, some states, such as North Dakota and Oklahoma, have codified the benefit/detriment language. 2 Corbin on Contracts § 5.8 (2018).

mark the promissory note "paid in full" and to return it to Jeff. Larry says he will do these things if Jeff pays Larry $50.

Here, under the benefit/detriment test, Larry's promise to mark the note with "paid in full" and to return it to Jeff might not amount to consideration for Jeff's promise to pay Larry $50. That is because while Larry's promise is bargained for in the sense that it is sought by Jeff, the action arguably does not benefit Jeff or detriment Larry. Here, Jeff does not benefit because there is nothing Larry could do with the promissory note once Jeff paid off the debt it evidences. There are no rights or remedies for Larry to enforce under the note—it simply documents a debt that has been paid in full. Moreover, canceling the note is not a detriment to Larry. Again, Larry is not giving up any rights or remedies by marking the note with "paid in full" and returning it to Jeff. Arguably, the payment is to cover Larry's administrative costs with returning the note, but it is hard to believe such action costs $50. However, this arrangement might satisfy the bargained-for test, since Larry provided exactly the performance Jeff sought to induce by his promise, and was induced to perform on the basis of Jeff's promise.

Keep in mind that courts that use the benefit/detriment test also look at whether a promisor received a benefit or the promisee suffered a detriment *in exchange for* a promise when conducting the consideration analysis. In other words, courts also apply the bargained-for test. The difference is that under the bargained-for test, courts do not require that they find such a benefit or detriment. Rather, they focus their analysis solely on whether the promisor made the promise to induce the return promise or performance by the promisee, and whether the promisee was so induced to provide the return promise or performance. Of course, even in a modern court, the presence of a benefit to a promisee or detriment to a promisor may provide evidence of consideration. The more significant the benefit to be received by the promisor, for example, the more it may suggest that the promise made by the promisor in exchange for the benefit received was supported by consideration.

4. Consideration Versus Condition of Gift

Sometimes it is hard to tell whether what is being given in exchange for a promise is consideration or simply a condition to a gift. That is because sometimes a person receiving a gift must take some action to receive the gift—an action that could be mistaken for consideration.

A famous example offered by the late Professor Williston involves a benevolent man who tells a homeless person that if the homeless person goes around the corner to a clothing shop, he can buy himself a coat on the credit of the man.[9] Is the homeless person's action of going around the corner consideration

---

9. Samuel Williston & Richard A. Lord, A Treatise on the Law of Contracts § 7:18 (4th ed. 1993).

for the benevolent man's promise or simply an action that is a condition to the homeless person's receipt of a gift of a coat?

To determine whether the requested action is consideration or a conditional gift, you must identify whether the promisor had an interest in that action. Was it something that the promisor was bargaining for, to induce his promise? If so, then the requested action is consideration. If not, then it is a condition to a gift, and not consideration for the promisor's promise.

In the above example, the benevolent man was clearly not bargaining for the homeless person to walk around the corner. He had no interest in that action. Rather, that action was simply what the homeless person had to do to receive the man's gift. Thus, the homeless person's action was not consideration for the man's promise.

To take another example, suppose Uncle Ken tells you that if you come to his office and grab the keys to his two-bedroom apartment, you can use that apartment for free for a year. Here, Uncle Ken is clearly not bargaining for you to come to his office. Rather, this action is simply a condition that you must fulfill to receive his gift. As such, there is no consideration for Uncle Ken's promise to you.

The distinction between consideration and a condition to a gift can get especially fuzzy with charitable subscriptions. In those situations, the "donor" promises to give something of value—such as money—to charity. Where the charitable subscription is not made for anything in exchange, the consideration requirement is not met. However, it becomes a harder case where the donor requests or seeks some recognition for her subscription. Where that occurs, the key is to determine whether recognition is the price of the subscription—meaning, is sought by the donor—or if that is irrelevant to the donor. Finally, keep in mind that courts can be less exacting in their test for consideration in these circumstances. That is because of the social benefit provided by charitable subscriptions.

PRACTICE PROBLEM 7-3

Sally Patterson promises to donate $100,000 to the university where she earned her bachelor's degree to create a scholarship fund. At the bottom of the written subscription form Sally signed, she added the following language: "It is understood that the scholarship fund will be publicly known as the 'Sally Patterson Scholarship Fund.'"

1. Is Sally's promise supported by consideration? Yes

2. Assume that the matter were litigated and a court concluded that Sally's promise is not supported by consideration. Assume that you represent the university. How would you advise the university to modify its subscription form with respect to future promised donations?

5. Preexisting Duty Rule

Sometimes a party promises to perform an act she is already legally obligated to perform, in exchange for a new promise from the other party. In that case, the promisor is providing the new promise in exchange for nothing new. Rather, she is simply getting the benefit of the other party's performance, which she already had the legal right to receive. In this case, generally speaking, the new promise is not supported by consideration, as the other party had a preexisting duty to perform. For this reason, this rule is often referred to as the **preexisting duty rule**.

You might ask yourself why a party would ever provide a new promise in exchange for the other party's promise to perform a duty she was already legally obligated to perform. Often this occurs where a promisee places undue pressure on the promisor to provide a new promise. You will see that Chapter 19 describes some defenses that would prevent the enforcement of a promise provided as a result of such undue pressure. Other times, though, a party provides a new promise due to changed circumstances not anticipated by the parties when they entered into the contract. As you will see in Chapter 12 in the discussion on modifications to the contract, courts often enforce such modified promises where the modification is fair and equitable in view of the changed circumstances.

To see the preexisting duty rule in action, suppose your client Dale Villanova has entered into a lease with Miranda Foote to lease shared office space #3 in Suite 22 at One Vista Plaza for $1,200 a month, for a full year. Suppose also that at some point during that year, Miranda demands that Dale pay Miranda an additional $100 per month. Miranda tells Dale that if he does not pay her this extra $100 per month, she will remove his belongings and lease that shared office space to someone else. Here, if he promises to pay an extra $100 per month and later regrets that decision, Dale would argue that his promise to pay Miranda an additional $100 was not supported by consideration. That is because Miranda had a legal duty to lease Dale the shared office space per the lease. She cannot now demand additional consideration from Dale where, in exchange, she is promising to do nothing more than perform her legal duty under the lease. Thus, there is no consideration to support Dale's promise to pay Miranda an additional $100.

Moreover, Dale's promise to pay an additional $100 to Miranda might not be enforceable due to the defense of duress or another defense tied to Miranda's excessive pressure placed on Dale. Those defenses are discussed in Chapter 19.

However, the preexisting duty rule does not prevent enforcement of a promise where the other party's obligations are doubtful or *genuinely* disputed. So, for example, if Miranda asked Dale to pay her an additional $100 because she genuinely believed Dale underpaid his deposit by $100, Dale's promise would be supported by consideration—Miranda's agreeing to not seek to recover the

[handwritten margin note: not giving Dale anything "new"]

shortage in Dale's deposit. On the other hand, if Dale had paid his deposit in full, and Miranda had merely conjured up a pretend dispute to get Dale to agree to pay an additional $100 per month, then again, Dale's promise would not be supported by consideration.

PRACTICE PROBLEM 7-4

A thief decides to steal a painting from a city's art museum. The museum's board of directors posts a reward of $50,000 for the capture of the perpetrator. A city police detective catches the suspect and obtains a confession from him.

1. Is the detective entitled to the reward? *no - pre-existing duty*

2. Would it matter if the crime occurred in a precinct other than the detective's and that the detective did the entire investigation during off-duty hours? *yes*

[handwritten margin notes: unilateral; good Samaritan who turned in painting to museum would be entitled to award; would not be entitled to award]

---

6. Illusory Promises

Finally, remember from Chapter 1 that a promise that is illusory (where the promissor retains the discretion not to perform) is not the kind of promise that contract law enforces. This also applies where a return promise is illusory. Thus, an illusory return promise is not consideration for a promise.

C. DOCUMENTING THE EXISTENCE OF CONSIDERATION

If you recall from Chapter 3, one of the first sections of a written contract lays out the parties' principal promises and deal terms. For example, as Chapter 3 discussed, in a basic service contract, that part of the written contract will lay out the service provider's obligation to provide services, and the obligation of the customer to pay for those services. Thus, that section of the contract documents what consideration each party is giving (usually a set of promises) to induce the counterparty's promises. That is so even though written contracts typically do not refer to what each party is agreeing to provide under the contract as "consideration," and often do not describe the parties' mutual obligations as inducing one another. In other words, no specific language is needed to satisfy the consideration requirement.

In older contracts and even in some modern ones, attorneys also often included, together with the parties' statement of agreement, a recitation about the existence of consideration and/or its sufficiency in an attempt to support a finding of consideration. For example, suppose that your uncle Ken has agreed to lease you an apartment for free for a year. You then prepare a written document acknowledging that consideration exists for Uncle Ken's promise. The language that you might include to that effect appears as follows:[10]

> In consideration of the mutual obligations of the parties set forth herein, the parties agree as follows:

Has the consideration element been satisfied by the acknowledgment of the parties? The short answer is no. The parties themselves cannot conclusively deem consideration to exist (although there are special rules with respect to option contracts, as discussed in Chapter 8).[11] If consideration does not actually exist to support a promise, then as a matter of law, that promise is not enforceable as a bargained-for contract.

Nevertheless, in some jurisdictions, the parties' acknowledgment that consideration exists creates a rebuttable presumption as to the existence of consideration. However, such an acknowledgment does not conclusively establish the existence of consideration. Thus, a court would not enforce a promise, even if the contract in question included the above language, where one of the parties was able to demonstrate that there was in fact no consideration for its promise.

In some contracts, the existence of consideration is not apparent. For example, suppose you start a law firm called Legal Center Inc. You own all of the shares of stock of Legal Center and are the only lawyer who works for Legal Center. You decide that Legal Center needs to upgrade its computer equipment. Since Legal Center does not currently have the money needed for the upgrade, you contact Local Bank N.A. on behalf of Legal Center to obtain a $5,000 loan. Local Bank is willing to make the loan to Legal Center, but only if you personally guarantee the loan. In other words, you personally would be obligated to repay Local Bank from your own personal assets if Legal Center does not have the money (generated from client fees) to repay the loan as and when it is due.

You agree and sign a document labeled Guaranty setting out your obligation. However, it is not apparent from the face of that document why you are personally guaranteeing the obligation of Legal Center. In other words, that document would not lay out the consideration you are receiving by providing a personal Guaranty to Local Bank. Thus, the Guaranty would likely include recitals[12] to explain why you are guaranteeing the loan to Legal Center: because you are the sole owner of Legal Center and you will benefit from the loan being made to Legal Center. By including that language in the recitals, if you were to challenge the Guaranty on the basis of a lack of consideration, Local Bank could easily establish what the consideration was for your promise. Accordingly, although

---

10. You saw similar language in Chapter 3, after the discussion of the recitals of a written contract.

11. Dougherty v. Salt, 125 N.E. 94 (N.Y. 1919).

12. Recall from Chapter 3 that recitals are statements of background facts that immediately follow the preamble in a written agreement.

parties cannot create consideration just by reciting in a writing that it in fact exists, they can set forth their reasons for entering into a transaction (as well as a clear exchange of promises) that will suggest to a court that consideration exists.

PRACTICE PROBLEM 7-5

Jersey Vale is a real estate renovator (also known as a house flipper) who, together with Ric Kuntz, buys old or poorly maintained houses, renovates them, and then resells them at a profit. Jersey and Ric created a corporation called "Jersey Ric's Reno Inc." for purposes of their real estate renovation business.

One year ago, Jersey's wife Rita Stigmeier was diagnosed with kidney cancer. Fortunately, doctors thought her cancer was treatable with surgery coupled with chemotherapy. Since then, Rita has been receiving medical treatment from various medical service providers around Springfield. As a result of these treatments, Rita beat her cancer; however, she also racked up $50,000 in medical bills, including a $30,000 bill owed to Browning Hospital, a for-profit hospital.

Eventually, Rita fell behind on her bill owed to Browning. On October 15, 2019, Browning sent Rita a letter indicating that Browning was going to sue her to collect on that bill unless Rita agreed to a payment plan for her medical bill. The hospital also demanded that Jersey give Browning a security interest in all of his shares of Jersey Ric's Reno. With that security interest, if Rita ever stopped paying Browning the amounts she owed it from her medical treatment, Browning would be able to collect directly out of proceeds generated by Jersey Ric's Reno that were payable to Jersey. Browning demanded that both actions be completed by November 15 or Browning would proceed with its lawsuit against Rita.

Browning attached to its letter a copy of the security agreement it wanted Jersey to enter into to document this transaction. The following is an excerpt of the first part of that agreement:

SECURITY AGREEMENT

This Security Agreement (this "Agreement"), dated as of November 15, 2019, is between Browning Hospital Inc., a Delaware corporation ("Browning"), and Jersey Vale ("Vale").

Now, therefore, in consideration of the mutual agreements set forth herein, the parties agree as follows:

1. Vale hereby grants a security interest in all of the shares of stock he owns in Jersey Ric's Reno Inc. (the "Shares") to secure any amounts owing by Rita Stigmeier to Browning either now or hereafter. The security interest grant-

---

ed herein continues in effect until Rita Stigmeier has repaid Browning all amounts owed to Browning (the term of this security interest, the "Term").

2. Vale agrees to not sell, convey, grant a lien on, or otherwise encumber the Shares during the Term except in favor of Browning pursuant to the terms of this Agreement.

. . .

The parties have executed and delivered this Agreement as of the date set forth in the preamble.

Browning Hospital Inc.:

By: _____
Name:
Title:

_____
Jersey Vale

Browning gave no consideration?

You are one of Browning's in-house counsel. On November 30, you learn of this transaction from Bob Smith, who works in Browning's billing department. At your request, Smith sent you a copy of the above security agreement.

1. Assuming Jersey enters into the above agreement, do you have any concerns about the formation of this contract? If so, do you suggest any changes to the language of the above draft to protect Browning from those risks?

2. Do you have any concerns with the content of the excerpted draft agreement? Are those concerns that you should raise with your client, or are they concerns that Jersey should raise?

D. CONSIDERATION IN ACTION

The following case demonstrates the continued relevance of the consideration doctrine. It also demonstrates how the above requirements are applied in a challenge to a contract on the basis of the lack of consideration.

Pennsy Supply, Inc. v. American Ash Recycling Corp.
Superior Court of Pennsylvania
895 A.2d 595 (2006)

Opinion by Orie MELVIN, J.:

Appellant, Pennsy Supply, Inc. ("Pennsy"), appeals from the grant of preliminary objections in the nature of a demurrer in favor of Appellee, American Ash

Recycling Corp. of Pennsylvania ("American Ash"). We reverse and remand for further proceedings.

The trial court summarized the allegations of the complaint as follows:

> The instant case arises out of a construction project for Northern York High School (Project) owned by Northern York County School District (District) in York County, Pennsylvania. The District entered into a construction contract for the Project with a general contractor, Lobar, Inc. (Lobar). Lobar, in turn, subcontracted the paving of driveways and a parking lot to [Pennsy].
>
> The contract between Lobar and the District included Project Specifications for paving work which required Lobar, through its subcontractor Pennsy, to use certain base aggregates. The Project Specifications permitted substitution of the aggregates with an alternate material known as Treated Ash Aggregate (TAA) or AggRite.
>
> The Project Specifications included a 'notice to bidders' of the availability of AggRite at no cost from [American Ash], a supplier of AggRite. The Project Specifications also included a letter to the Project architect from American Ash confirming the availability of a certain amount of free AggRite on a first come, first served basis.
>
> Pennsy contacted American Ash and informed American Ash that it would require approximately 11,000 tons of AggRite for the Project. Pennsy subsequently picked up the AggRite from American Ash and used it for the paving work, in accordance with the Project Specifications.
>
> Pennsy completed the paving work in December 2001. The pavement ultimately developed extensive cracking in February 2002. The District notified . . . Lobar[] as to the defects and Lobar in turn directed Pennsy to remedy the defective work. Pennsy performed the remedial work during summer 2003 at no cost to the District.
>
> The scope and cost of the remedial work included the removal and appropriate disposal of the AggRite, which is classified as a hazardous waste material by the Pennsylvania Department of Environmental Protection. Pennsy requested American Ash to arrange for the removal and disposal of the AggRite; however, American Ash did not do so. Pennsy provided notice to American Ash of its intention to recover costs.

[handwritten margin note: offer; acceptance]

Trial Court Opinion, 5/27/05, at 1-3 (footnote omitted). Pennsy also alleged that the remedial work cost it $ 251,940.20 to perform and that it expended an additional $ 133,777.48 to dispose of the AggRite it removed.

On November 18, 2004, Pennsy filed a five-count complaint against American Ash alleging breach of contract (Count I); breach of implied warranty of merchantability (Count II); breach of express warranty of merchantability (Count III); breach of warranty of fitness for a particular purpose (Count IV); and promissory estoppel (Count V). American Ash filed demurrers to all five counts. Pennsy responded and also sought leave to amend should any demurrer be sustained. The trial court sustained the demurrers by order and opinion dated May 25, 2005 and dismissed the complaint. This appeal followed.

. . .

"Preliminary objections in the nature of a demurrer test the legal sufficiency of the complaint." *Hospodar v. Schick*, 2005 PA Super 319, 885 A.2d 986, 988 (Pa. Super. 2005).

> When reviewing the dismissal of a complaint based upon preliminary objections in the nature of a demurrer, we treat as true all well-pleaded material, factual averments and all inferences fairly deducible therefrom. Where the preliminary objections will result in the dismissal of the action, the objections may be sustained only in cases that are clear and free from doubt. To be clear and free from doubt that dismissal is appropriate, it must appear with certainty that the law would not permit recovery by the plaintiff upon the facts averred. Any doubt should be resolved by a refusal to sustain the objections. Moreover, we review the trial court's decision for an abuse of discretion or an error of law.

Id. In applying this standard to the instant appeal, we deem it easiest to order our discussion by count.

Count I raises a breach of contract claim. "A cause of action for breach of contract must be established by pleading (1) the existence of a contract, including its essential terms, (2) a breach of a duty imposed by the contract and (3) resultant damages." *Corestates Bank, N.A. v. Cutillo*, 1999 PA Super 14, 723 A.2d 1053, 1058 (Pa. Super. 1999). While not every term of a contract must be stated in complete detail, every element must be specifically pleaded. Clarity is particularly important where an oral contract is alleged.

Instantly, the trial court determined that "any alleged agreement between the parties is unenforceable for lack of consideration." Trial Court Opinion, 5/27/05, at 5. The trial court also stated "the facts as pleaded do not support an inference that disposal costs were part of any bargaining process or that American Ash offered the AggRite with an intent to avoid disposal costs." *Id.* at 7 (emphasis added). Thus, we understand the trial court to have dismissed Count I for two reasons related to the necessary element of consideration: one, the allegations of the Complaint established that Pennsy had received a conditional gift from American Ash, and, two, there were no allegations in the Complaint to show that American Ash's avoidance of disposal costs was part of any bargaining process between the parties.[13]

It is axiomatic that consideration is "an essential element of an enforceable contract." *Stelmack v. Glen Alden Coal Co.*, 339 Pa. 410, 414-415, 14 A.2d 127, 128 (1940). *See also Weavertown Transport Leasing, Inc v. Moran*, 2003

---

13. [3] To the extent the trial court may also be understood to have dismissed Count I for failure to plead a contract with the requisite specificity, see Trial Court Opinion, 5/27/05, at 7-8, we disagree. Paragraphs 9-10, and 16 of the Complaint allege the required elements of a contract claim. Critically, paragraph 10 alleges American Ash was to furnish AggRite "for use on the Project in accordance with the Project Specifications," thereby identifying the oral contract's essential term, later alleged in paragraph 16 to have been breached.

PA Super 385, 834 A.2d 1169, 1172 (Pa. Super. 2003) (stating, "[a] contract is formed when the parties to it (1) reach a mutual understanding, (2) exchange consideration, and (3) delineate the terms of their bargain with sufficient clarity."). "Consideration consists of a benefit to the promisor or a detriment to the promisee." *Weavertown*, 834 A.2d at 1172 (citing *Stelmack*). "Consideration must actually be bargained for as the exchange for the promise." *Stelmack*, 339 Pa. at 414, 14 A.2d at 129.

> It is not enough, however, that the promisee has suffered a legal detriment at the request of the promisor. The detriment incurred must be the 'quid pro quo', or the 'price' of the promise, and the inducement for which it was made. . . . If the promisor merely intends to make a gift to the promisee upon the performance of a condition, the promise is gratuitous and the satisfaction of the condition is not consideration for a contract. The distinction between such a conditional gift and a contract is well illustrated in Williston on Contracts, Rev. Ed., Vol. 1, Section 112, where it is said: 'If a benevolent man says to a tramp,' If you go around the corner to the clothing shop there, you may purchase an overcoat on my credit, 'no reasonable person would understand that the short walk was requested as the consideration for the promise, but that in the event of the tramp going to the shop the promisor would make him a gift.'

Weavertown, 834 A.2d at 1172 (quoting *Stelmack*, 339 Pa. at 414, 14 A.2d at 128-29). Whether a contract is supported by consideration presents a question of law.

The classic formula for the difficult concept of consideration was stated by Justice Oliver Wendell Holmes, Jr. as "the promise must induce the detriment and the detriment must induce the promise." John Edward Murray, Jr., MURRAY ON CONTRACTS § 60 (3d. ed. 1990), at 227 (citing *Wisconsin & Michigan Ry. v. Powers*, 191 U.S. 379, 24 S. Ct. 107, 48 L. Ed. 229 (1903)). As explained by Professor Murray:

> If the promisor made the promise for the purpose of inducing the detriment, the detriment induced the promise. *If, however, the promisor made the promise with no particular interest in the detriment that the promisee had to suffer to take advantage of the promised gift or other benefit, the detriment was incidental or conditional to the promisee's receipt of the benefit.* Even though the promisee suffered a detriment induced by the promise, the purpose of the promisor was not to have the promisee suffer the detriment because she did not seek that detriment in exchange for her promise.

Id. § 60. C, at 230 (emphasis added). This concept is also well summarized in AMERICAN JURISPRUDENCE:

> As to the distinction between consideration and a condition, it is often difficult to determine whether words of condition in a promise indicate a request for consideration or state a mere condition in a gratuitous promise. An aid, though not a conclusive test, in determining which construction of the promise is more

reasonable is an inquiry into *whether the occurrence of the condition would benefit the promisor. If so, it is a fair inference that the occurrence was requested as consideration.* On the other hand, if the occurrence of the condition is no benefit to the promisor but is merely to enable the promisee to receive a gift, the occurrence of the event on which the promise is conditional, though brought about by the promisee in reliance on the promise, is not properly construed as consideration.

17A AM. JUR. 2d § 104 (2004 & 2005 Supp.) (emphasis added).

Upon review, we disagree with the trial court that the allegations of the Complaint show only that American Ash made a conditional gift of the AggRite to Pennsy. In paragraphs 8 and 9 of the Complaint, Pennsy alleged:

> American Ash actively promotes the use of AggRite as a building material to be used in base course of paved structures, and provides the material free of charge, in an effort to have others dispose of the material and thereby avoid incurring the disposal costs itself. . . . American Ash provided the AggRite to Pennsy for use on the Project, which saved American Ash thousands of dollars in disposal costs it otherwise would have incurred.

Accepting these allegations as true and using the Holmesian formula for consideration, it is a fair interpretation of the Complaint that American Ash's promise to supply AggRite free of charge induced Pennsy to assume the detriment of collecting and taking title to the material, and critically, that it was this very detriment, whether assumed by Pennsy or some other successful bidder to the paving subcontract, which induced American Ash to make the promise to provide free AggRite for the project. Paragraphs 8-9 of the Complaint simply belie the notion that American Ash offered AggRite as a conditional gift to the successful bidder on the paving subcontract for which American Ash desired and expected nothing in return.[14]

We turn now to whether consideration is lacking because Pennsy did not allege that American Ash's avoidance of disposal costs was part of any bargaining process between the parties. The Complaint does not allege that the parties discussed or even that Pennsy understood at the time it requested or accepted the AggRite that Pennsy's use of the AggRite would allow American Ash to avoid disposal costs.[15] However, we do not believe such is necessary.

---

14. [4] We understand the contract between Lobar and the District required Lobar to use certain specified base aggregates and permitted the substitution of AggRite for those aggregates. Realistically, however, it is a fair inference from this Complaint that the successful bidder on the paving subcontract could not have used anything other than the free material authorized by Lobar's contract with the District.

15. [5] Pennsy's complaint, by placing the allegation in paragraph 8 that American Ash promotes AggRite and provides it free of charge, before the allegations in paragraphs 9-10 related to formation of the oral contract, is arguably structured to suggest Pennsy did contemplate American Ash's avoidance of disposal costs. We note also that during oral argument on the preliminary objections, Pennsy's counsel represented "it was understood by everybody that this [i.e., avoidance of disposal costs] was what American Ash was getting in return for [providing the AggRite for free]." Transcript of Proceedings, Feb. 1, 2005, at 14-15.

[handwritten margin note: "bargaining not necessary showing consideration"]

The bargain theory of consideration does not actually require that the parties bargain over the terms of the agreement. . . . According to Holmes, an influential advocate of the bargain theory, what is required [for consideration to exist] is that the promise and the consideration be in 'the relation of reciprocal conventional inducement, each for the other.'

E. Allen Farnsworth, FARNSWORTH ON CONTRACTS § 2.6 (1990) (citing O. Holmes, THE COMMON LAW 293-94 (1881)). Here, as explained above, the Complaint alleges facts which, if proven, would show the promise induced the detriment and the detriment induced the promise. This would be consideration. Accordingly, we reverse the dismissal of Count I.

. . .

Understanding the Case:

1. *Procedural Posture:* In this instance, American Ash had argued that the factual allegations in Pennsy's complaint, even if true, did not support a legal conclusion that a contract was formed. Thus, American Ash moved for a demurrer, which is essentially a motion to dismiss the plaintiff's complaint. The trial court granted that demurrer, holding that even if all of the factual allegations contained in Pennsy's complaint were true, those factual allegations would not support a finding of legal liability. The court of appeals reversed. In reversing the trial court's decision, the appeals court was simply overruling the trial court's grant of a demurrer. In other words, that court was not determining that American Ash was liable for a contract breach. Thus, at trial, American Ash could still dispute Pennsy's factual allegations.

2. *UCC and Implied Warranties:* As the court of appeals noted at the start of its opinion, Pennsy sought to recover from American Ash on the basis of (1) breach of contract, (2) breach of implied warranty of merchantability, (3) breach of express warranty of merchantability, (4) breach of warranty of fitness for a particular purpose, and (5) promissory estoppel. You may be wondering why Pennsy was suing American Ash for breach of warranty given that the facts did not identify any warranties communicated by American Ash to Pennsy in connection with the delivery of the AggRite. As you consider this question, remember what this contract was for—AggRite, an aggregate material used for paving. As a tangible, movable item, AggRite falls within the definition of a "good" under UCC Article 2. As such, assuming the contract was for a "sale" (and not merely a gift, as American Ash argued) of the AggRite, then, as you will learn in Chapter 14, the sale contained a number of implied terms, including implied warranties. It is those implied warranties that Pennsy argued were breached in the sale.

Comprehension and Thoughts Questions:

[handwritten margin note: whether the promises were "in fact" bargained for]

1. What test does the court use to determine the existence of consideration?

2. According to the court, why are the concepts of benefit and detriment relevant to the consideration inquiry? *[handwritten: To determine whether one promise "induced" the other]*

[margin: facts alleged in the complaint]

3. What was the benefit arguably enjoyed by American Ash and/or the detriment suffered by Pennsy in this transaction? *Penny paid cost of removal*

4. In applying the court's test, did the court find that Pennsy's complaint adequately pled that American Ash's promise to provide AggRite was supported by consideration? *Yes – removal costs*

5. What facts were important to the court in drawing that conclusion?

6. Should a court require that there be a benefit to a promisor or a detriment to a promisee in determining the existence of consideration for a promisor's promise?

[margin: no blc facts bc means the same]

Hypothetical Variations:

[margin: $100 not really a benefit / that would increase them up to give away the waste]

1. Would the court's decision have changed if Pennsy had signed a piece of paper that described the AggRite as a "gift"? Should it? *yes ; no*

[margin: om maybe? blc this might be "nominal" or "sham"]

2. Would the court's decision have changed if the disposal costs were $100? What about $1,000,000? *no*

3. Imagine that a neighbor offers to provide you with a can of gasoline that she no longer needs for her lawnmower because she is obtaining a lawn service. It turns out you did not need the gasoline, and so, a year later, you seek to dispose of it before it gets too old. The nearest hazardous material disposal center is 100 miles away. Should your neighbor have to pay your transportation costs to dispose of this gas? Is this situation different from Pennsy? Why or why not?

[margin notes below: no / gratuitous promise / gift]

[no]

[you took on downsides of having the gas in exchange for the benefits / not "consideration"]

CHAPTER 8

Special Bargain Rules for Option Contracts

An option contract is a contract to hold an offer open. In other words, an option contract is a contract in which an offeror promises to hold an offer open for acceptance for an agreed-upon period of time (called the option period). That means the offeror may not revoke the offer during the option period. Practically speaking, then, an option gives a party time to decide whether to enter into the underlying contract without having to worry that the offeror will revoke the offer.

As with all contracts, there must be consideration to support the offeror's promise to hold the underlying offer open. Often the consideration for the offeror's promise to keep the offer open during the option period is money, but any type of consideration can support an offeror's promise to hold the underlying offer open under an option contract.

Section A first reviews the typical circumstances in which option contracts are used. It also presents a typical form of option contract. Then, Section B discusses the nuances of the mutual assent rules studied in Chapters 4 and 5 when applied to option contracts. Section C explains some of the nuances of the consideration doctrine when applied to option contracts. Finally, Section D explains how the concepts underlying option contracts have been used to support the creation of irrevocable offers in other contexts, where an express option contract is not contemplated.

A. TYPICAL OPTION CONTRACT SITUATION AND FORM

People enter into option contracts when one party seeks to have an offer held open for a period of time and the other party is willing to do so. They are commonly used in the case of real estate transactions, where a potential buyer wishes to have some time to decide whether or not to purchase the real estate. They are also commonly used by corporations to grant their employees a right to purchase stock, which represents an ownership interest in the corporation. These are referred to as stock options.

To see more clearly why a party would seek an option contract, imagine Dong Lee has just moved to Fresno, California, for his first job as an economics professor. Upon moving to Fresno, Dong immediately looks for somewhere to live. He finds a house at 1313 W. Elm Street that suits him well. The current owner of 1313 W. Elm Street, Eloise Sharp, has listed the house for either rent or sale. The sale price is $150,000 and monthly lease payments are $800. Unfortunately, Dong does not have enough money to buy the house, so Dong can only lease the house. However, he does not want to lose his rent payments if he ultimately decides to buy the house after he has worked and saved up some money. So Dong and Eloise enter into a lease agreement for Dong's current occupancy of the house. The lease agreement includes an option to purchase that gives Dong two years (the lease term) to decide if he wants to buy the house. If he exercises his option, some of his rent payments would count toward the purchase price. After negotiations, the parties agree that half of each of Dong's rent payments would be applied toward the purchase price if Dong exercises his purchase option.

The following is a standard form California lease agreement with option to purchase that the parties would enter into in connection with this transaction.[1]

_____

1. The standard form agreement is available at https://eforms.com/rental/ca/california-residential-lease-with-option-to-purchase-lease-to-own/ (last visited Sept. 25, 2018).

CALIFORNIA RESIDENTIAL LEASE AGREEMENT
-WITH OPTION TO PURCHASE-

THIS AGREEMENT MADE and entered into on this _____ day of _____,
20____ by and between, _____ [name of Lessor],
with a mailing address of _____ City of
_____, in the State of _____ and _____
_____ [name of Lessee], with a mailing address of _____
_____ City of _____, in the State of
_____.

Lessee, hereby leases to Lessee, his/her heirs or assignees, the premises situated in
the City of _____, County of _____, State of
California, legally described as, with the street address of _____
_____ upon the following terms and conditions:

1. **Option to Purchase**: In consideration of the Lessee meeting all obligations as
stated herein under this lease, the Lessor hereby grants the Lessee an option to
purchase under the following terms and conditions:

I.   The option price is terms of purchase will be _____
     dollars ($_____).

II. Lessee understands that time is of the essence in this agreement. The option
     will expire without notice and be of no further effect if not exercised on or
     before the _____ day of _____, 20____

III. Lessee has paid the sum of _____ dollars
     ($_____) as a non-refundable option consideration that will be
     applied toward the purchase price of the property if, and only if, Lessee
     exercises this option to purchase. In the event Lessee fails to exercise the
     option or defaults under any terms of the lease, the option will be void and all
     monies will be retained by Lessor as liquidated damages and not as a penalty.
     The option consideration will be refundable only if 1) a pre-closing home
     inspection by a certified home inspector reveals structural damage in excess
     of four (4)% of the option price of the property (provided, however, that
     lesser damage will be the responsibility of Lessor to correct prior to closing);
     or (2) Lessor fails or is unable to meet any of the obligations set forth in the
     lease option agreement.

IV. _____ percent (____%) of the rent paid pursuant to this lease
     agreement will be applied as additional option consideration to reduce the
     option price if and only if the Lessee exercises this option to purchase,
     provided, however, that no payments made after the 15th of any month for
     which rent is due, or for which payment tendered is returned NSF, shall be
     credited towards a reduction in the option price.

V.   The option shall be exercised by mailing or delivering written notice to the Lessor prior to the expiration of this agreement. Notice, if mailed, shall be by certified mail, postage prepaid, to the Lessor at the address set forth below, and shall be deemed to have been given upon the day shown on the postmark of the envelope in which such notice is mailed.

VI.   This purchase option is not contingent upon Lessee's ability to obtain financing from a lender.

VII.   Personal Property: Said lease shall include the following personal property:

_____

2. **Term**: The term hereof shall commence on this _____ day of _____, 20____ and continue for a period of _____ and ending on the _____ day of _____, 20____.

3. **Rent**: Rent shall be per month, payable in advance, upon the first day of each calendar month to Lessor or his or her authorized agent at the following address:

_____

In the event the rental payment is not received within _____ (___) days after the due date, Lessee agrees to pay a late charge of _____ dollars ($_____) plus interest at _____ percent (___%) per annum on the delinquent amount and will not be applied as an additional consideration towards the option price of the property. Any check tendered in payment of rent that is returned NSF will be subject to a service charge of _____ dollars ($_____) be applied as an additional consideration towards the option price of the property.

4. **Utilities**: Lessee shall be responsible for the payment of all utilities and services except for _____.

5. **Use**: The premises shall be used as a residence and for no other purpose without prior written consent of Lessor.

6. **Maintenance, Repairs or Alterations**: Lessee shall maintain the premises in a clean and sanitary manner including all equipment, appliances, furniture and furnishings therein, and shall surrender the same at termination thereof, in as good condition as received, normal wear and tear excepted. Lessee shall be responsible for damages caused by his/her negligence and that of his/her family, or invitees or guests. Lessee shall maintain any surrounding grounds, including lawns and shrubbery, and keep the same clear of rubbish and weeds, if such grounds are part

of the premises and are exclusively for use of the Lessee. Lessee shall make no alterations to the buildings or improvements on the Premises or construct any building or make any other improvements on the Premises without the prior written consent of Lessor. Any and all alterations, changes, and/or improvements built, constructed or placed on the Premises by Lessee shall, unless otherwise provided by written agreement between Lessor and Lessee, are and will become the property of Lessor and remain on the Premises at the expiration or earlier termination of this Agreement.

7. Entry and Inspection: Lessee shall permit Lessor or Lessor's agents to enter the premises at reasonable times and upon reasonable notice for the purpose of inspecting the premises or for making necessary repairs.

8. Possession: If Lessor is unable to deliver possession of the premises at the commencement hereof, Lessor shall not be liable for any damage caused thereby nor shall this agreement be void or voidable, but Lessee shall not be liable for any rent until possession is delivered. Lessee may terminate this agreement if possession is not delivered within the term hereof.

9. Security/Damage Deposit: The security deposit of _____ dollars ($_____) shall secure the performance of the Lessee's obligations hereunder. Lessor may apply all or portions of said deposit on account of Lessee's obligations hereunder. Upon exercise of the option, Lessor shall credit said deposit towards the purchase price of the property.

10. Deposit Funds: In the event Lessee does not exercise the purchase option, any returnable portion of the security/damage deposit shall be refunded within _____ (___) days from the date possession is delivered to Lessor or his/her authorized agent.

11. Attorney Fees: The prevailing party shall be entitled to all costs incurred in connection with any legal action brought by either party to enforce the terms hereof or relating to the demised premises, including reasonable attorneys' fees.

12. Notices: Any notice which either party may or is required to give may be given by mailing the same, postage prepaid, to Lessee or at such other places as may be designated by the parties from time to time.

13. Heirs, Assigns, Successors: This lease and option shall include and insure to and bind the heirs, executors, administrators, successors, and assigns of the respective parties hereto.

14. Default: If Lessee shall fail to pay rent when due or perform any term hereof after not less than _____ (___) days written notice of such default given in the manner required by law, the Lessor at his/her option may terminate all rights of the Lessee hereunder, unless Lessee, within said time, shall cure such default. If Lessee abandons or vacates the property while in default of payment of rent, Lessor may consider any property left on premises to be abandoned and may dispose of the same in any manner allowed by law. In the event the Lessor reasonably believes that such abandoned property has not value, it may be discarded.

15. Encumbrances: Lessee shall take title to the property subject to: a) Real Estate Taxes not yet due and 2) Covenants, conditions, restrictions, reservations, rights, rights of way, and easements of record, if any.

16. Examination of Title: Lessee shall have _____ (____) days from the date of receipt of title report to examine the title to the property and to report, in writing, any valid objections thereto. Any exceptions to the title which would be disclosed by examination of the records shall be deemed to have been accepted unless reported in writing with said timeframe. If Lessee objects to any exceptions to the title, Lessor shall use all due diligence to remove such exceptions at his/her own expenses within sixty (60) days thereafter. But if such exceptions cannot be removed within the sixty (60) days allowed, all rights and obligations hereunder may, at the election of the Lessee, terminate and end unless he/she elects to purchase the property subject to such exceptions.

17. Evidence of Title: Lessor shall provide evidence of title in the form of a policy of title insurance at Lessor's expense.

18. Bill of Sale: The personal property identified in Section 1, Title VII shall be conveyed by bill of sale.

19. Closing: Closing shall be within ____ days from the exercise of the option unless otherwise extended by other terms of this agreement.

17. GOVERNING LAW AND VENUE. This Option to Purchase Agreement shall be governed, construed and interpreted by, through and under the Laws of the State of California. The parties further agree that the venue for any and all disputes related to this Option to Purchase shall be _____ County, California.

18. MEGAN'S LAW DATABASE DISCLOSURE: Notice: Pursuant to Section 290.46 of the Penal Code, information about specific registered sex offenders is made available to the public via an Internet Web site maintained by the Department of Justice at www.meganslaw.ca.gov. Depending on an offender's criminal history, this information will include either the address at which the offender resides or the community of residence and ZIP Code in which he or she resides. (Neither Seller nor Brokers are required to check this website. If Buyer wants further information, Broker recommends that Buyer obtain information from this website during Buyer's inspection contingency period. Brokers do not have expertise in this area.)

19. Closing Costs: Lessee shall be responsible for all closing costs other than those referenced herein as being the responsibility of the Lessor.

20. Prorations: Tax and insurance escrow account, if any, to be transferred intact to Lessee with no prorations. Interest and other expenses of the property to be prorated as of the date of closing. In witness whereof, the parties hereto have executed this agreement the day and year first above written.

All parties agree to the terms and conditions of this agreement made on the _____ day of _____, 20____.

SELLER/LANDLORD'S SIGNATURE: _____

Print: _____

SELLER/LANDLORD'S SIGNATURE: _____

Print: _____

- -

BUYER/TENANT'S SIGNATURE: _____

Print: _____

BUYER/TENANT'S SIGNATURE: _____

Print: _____

- -

AGENT'S SIGNATURE: _____

Print: _____

- -

WITNESS'S SIGNATURE: _____

Print: _____

PRACTICE PROBLEM 8-1

Assume that Dong Lee and Eloise Sharp enter into a California Residential Lease Agreement with Option to Purchase similar to that set out above for 1313 W. Elm Street. Recall that the sales price for the house is $150,000 and monthly lease payments are $800. The parties have agreed that half of each of Dong's rent payments will be applied toward the purchase price if Dong exercises his purchase option.

1. Where do the parties insert each of the terms that they have negotiated into the above form? *1 — option to purchase*

2. What other terms do they still need to negotiate to complete the above document? *consideration.*

B. MUTUAL ASSENT UNDER OPTION CONTRACTS

The rules of mutual assent you previously studied in Chapters 4-6 apply to option contracts. In other words, there are no special rules that apply to mutual assent where the applicable contract assented to is an option contract.

Those rules of mutual assent also generally apply to the optionee's acceptance of the underlying offer. Thus, as with any other offer, the option contract can specify the manner of accepting the underlying offer. For example, Section 1.V of the above form option contract requires the Lessee to exercise the option by delivering written notice to the Lessor at the Lessor's address indicated in the contract.

However, there are a few variations on the rules of acceptance of the underlying offer in an option contract. First, if acceptance can be by non-simultaneous communication such as mail, then the mailbox rule does not apply. Instead, acceptance is only effective when received. The mailbox rule does not apply by default in this situation because the optionee has the whole negotiated option period to accept the underlying offer. Applying the mailbox rule in that situation would give the optionee extra time he or she did not bargain for.

Second, because an option contract makes the underlying offer firm for the option period, almost nothing that the offeree does during the option period affects the underlying offer. In fact, the offeree could even reject the underlying offer, yet that offer would remain in place during the option period. Thus, in our ongoing example, even if Dong Lee notifies Eloise Sharp that Dong does not intend to exercise his option to purchase 1313 W. Elm Street, at any point during the option period, Dong can reverse course and instead decide to exercise the option.

However, there is an exception to an offeree's ability to accept an offer underlying an option contract even after he has rejected it. That exception occurs where the offeror relies on that rejection by making alternative arrangements for the subject of the underlying offer. In that case, under the doctrine of promissory estoppel discussed in Chapter 22, considerations of fairness might outweigh respecting the terms of the parties' bargain and lead a court to find that the offeree no longer has a right to accept the offer.

C. CONSIDERATION FOR OPTION CONTRACTS

Because option contracts are contracts, there must be consideration to support the offeror's promise to keep the underlying offer open. Section 1.III. in the sample option contract set out above includes a space for the parties to set out the consideration the tenant will pay for the offeror's promise to keep the underlying offer open during the option period.

However, in many states, there are some exceptions to the consideration requirement for option contracts. Often these exceptions are provided by statute. For example, under UCC § 2-205, a signed writing from a merchant that gives the counterparty assurances that the merchant's offer to sell or buy will be held open is irrevocable either for the stated period or, if no period is stated, then for a reasonable period. This is so even if there is no consideration supporting the merchant's promise. The drafters of the UCC eliminated the consideration requirement in this instance because they wanted to give effect to the clear and deliberate intentions of the merchant. Thus, they favored giving effect to those intentions over the policy considerations for consideration discussed in Chapter 7.

The common law in some states also liberalizes the consideration requirements for option contracts. For example, in some jurisdictions, nominal consideration suffices.[2] And in others, a formal seal replaces the need for consideration.[3]

The Restatement takes an approach similar to the UCC. Specifically, Section 87 dispenses with the need for consideration for an option contract so long as the option contract is in writing, signed by the offeror, recites that there is consideration, and proposes an exchange on fair terms within a reasonable period of time.[4]

The following case exemplifies how a court might view a contract where a party retains discretion to perform as an option contract even where it was not identified as such. It also sheds light on the nuances of consideration for an option contract.

---

2. *See, e.g.*, Kowal v. Day, 20 Cal. App. 3d 720, 98 Cal. Rptr. 118 (2d Dist. 1971).
3. *See, e.g.*, Jolles v. Wittenberg, 253 S.E.2d 203 (1979).
4. Restatement (Second) of Contracts § 87 (1981).

Steiner v. Thexton
Supreme Court of California
48 Cal. 4th 411 (2010)

MORENO, J.

. . .

I. FACTUAL AND PROCEDURAL BACKGROUND

In 2003, Steiner, a real estate developer, was interested in purchasing and developing several residences on a 10-acre portion of Thexton's 12.29-acre parcel of land. County approvals for a parcel split and development permits were required. Thexton had previously rejected an offer from a different party for $750,000 because that party wanted Thexton to obtain the required approval and permits. The written agreement between Steiner and Thexton, prepared by Steiner, provided for Thexton to sell the 10-acre parcel for $500,000 by September 2006 if Steiner decided to purchase the property after pursuing, at his own expense, the county approvals and permits. Paragraph 7 of the "Contingencies" section of the agreement provided Steiner was not obliged to do anything and could cancel the transaction at any time at his "absolute and sole discretion. . . ."

After Steiner and Thexton signed the agreement on September 4, 2003, Steiner began pursuing the necessary county approvals and, together with his partial assignee Siddiqui, ultimately spent thousands of dollars. In May and August 2004, Thexton cooperated with Steiner's efforts by signing, among other things, an application to the county planning department for a tentative parcel map. In October 2004, however, Thexton asked the title company to cancel escrow and told Steiner he no longer wanted to sell the property. Steiner nevertheless proceeded with the final hearing of the parcel review committee and apparently obtained approval for a tentative map. Steiner opposed cancelling escrow and filed suit seeking specific performance of the agreement. In his answer, Thexton asserted various defenses, including that the agreement constituted an option unsupported by consideration.

Following a bench trial, the trial court entered judgment in favor of Thexton. It concluded the agreement was unenforceable against Thexton "because it is, in effect, an option that is not supported by any consideration." First, it pointed out that the agreement bound Thexton to sell the property to Steiner for $500,000 for a period of up to three years while Steiner retained "'absolute and sole discretion'" to cancel the transaction. "The unilateral nature of this agreement," the trial court explained, "is the classic feature of an option."

Second, in concluding, "[b]ased on the evidence and the language of the contract itself, . . . that the option was not supported by consideration," the trial court noted no money was paid to Thexton for his grant of the option to purchase the property, nor did he receive any other benefit or thing of value in exchange for the option.[5] The trial court rejected plaintiffs' claim that the agreement obligated them to expeditiously proceed with the parcel split and that their work and expenses constituted sufficient consideration for the option. The trial court reasoned that the adequacy of consideration is measured as of the time a contract is entered into and pointed out the agreement did not bind plaintiffs to do anything; rather, it gave them the power to terminate the transaction at any time. Finally, the trial court rejected plaintiffs' claim that, in the absence of consideration for the option, their efforts merited applying the doctrine of promissory estoppel. The Court of Appeal affirmed for the reasons given by the trial court and we granted review.

II. DISCUSSION

We consider whether the agreement was an option and, if so, whether the option was irrevocable because it was supported by sufficient consideration. We conclude, for the following reasons, that the agreement is an irrevocable option.

A. The Sales Agreement Constitutes an Option

Plaintiffs contend the Court of Appeal erred when it concluded the sales agreement constituted an option. We disagree. We begin by briefly setting forth the established law concerning what constitutes an option.

As this court explained long ago, "When by the terms of an agreement the owner of property binds himself to sell on specified terms, and leaves it discretionary with the other party to the contract whether he will or will not buy, it constitutes simply an optional contract." (*Johnson v. Clark* (1917) 174 Cal. 582, 586, 163 P. 1004.) Thus, an option to purchase property is "a unilateral agreement. The optionor offers to sell the subject property at a specified price or upon specified terms and agrees, in view of the payment received, that he will hold the offer open for the fixed time. Upon the lapse of that time the matter is completely ended and the offer is withdrawn. If the offer be accepted upon the terms and in the time specified, then a bilateral contract arises which may become the subject of a suit to compel specific performance, if performance by either party thereafter be refused." (*Auslen v. Johnson* (1953) 118 Cal. App. 2d 319, 321-322, 257 P.2d 664.)

In the present case, although the agreement was titled "REAL ESTATE PURCHASE CONTRACT," the label is not dispositive. Rather, we look through the agreement's form to its substance. Viewing the substance, we conclude, as did the trial court, that the agreement between Steiner and Thexton contained "the classic feature[s] of an option." First, the agreement obliged Thexton to

---

5. [6] The agreement required Steiner to pay $1,000 into an escrow account, but the trial court concluded the payment did not constitute consideration.

hold open an offer to sell the parcel at a fixed price for three years. Second, Steiner had the power to accept the offer by satisfying or waiving the contingencies and paying the balance of the purchase price; however, because of the escape clause, Steiner was not obligated to do anything. The relevant term provided "It is expressly understood that [Steiner] may, at [his] absolute and sole discretion during this period, elect not to continue in this transaction and this purchase contract will become null and void."

Moreover, it appears that the term's broad and express language permitted Steiner to terminate the agreement even if all contingencies had been satisfied—indeed, Steiner testified at trial that the term gave him the power to terminate the agreement at any time for any reason, including if he had found a better deal. For that reason we reject the notion, advanced by Steiner and various amici curiae, that the agreement should instead be construed as a bilateral contract subject to a contingency. It is true, as amicus curiae California Association of Realtors explains, that a common form of real estate contract binds both parties at the outset (rendering the transaction a bilateral contract) while including a contingency, such as a loan or inspection contingency, that allows one or both parties to withdraw should the contingency fail. However, withdrawal from such a contract is permitted only if the contingency fails. By contrast, the agreement here placed no such constraint on Steiner. Rather, it limited Thexton's ability to withdraw, but explicitly allowed Steiner to terminate at any time for any reason.[6] Even had the agreement obligated Steiner, as he contends, to move expeditiously to remove the contingencies, we would nonetheless conclude that the "absolute and sole" right to withdraw he enjoyed means the agreement is an option.

. . .

In light of the foregoing reasons, we conclude the Court of Appeal correctly construed the so-called "purchase contract" as an option. We next consider whether the option was irrevocable.

B. Sufficient Consideration Rendered the Option Irrevocable

"An option is transformed into a contract of purchase and sale when there is an unconditional, unqualified acceptance by the optionee of the offer in harmony with the terms of the option and within the time span of the option contract. [Citation.]" (*Erich v. Granoff* (1980) 109 Cal. App. 3d 920, 928, 167 Cal. Rptr. 538.) At the time Thexton terminated the agreement, plaintiffs had not unconditionally accepted the offer within the terms of the option. Plaintiffs had not satisfied or waived all of the contingencies and deposited the balance of the purchase price into the escrow account. Therefore, the option never ripened

---

6. [8] Thus, bilateral contracts subject to a contingency, which are widely used in real estate transactions, are not affected by our holding.

into a purchase contract. However, even if an option has not yet ripened into a purchase contract, it may nonetheless be irrevocable for the negotiated period of time if sufficient bargained-for consideration is present.

"[A]n option based on consideration contemplates two separate [contracts], i.e., the option contract itself, which for something of value gives to the optionee the irrevocable right to buy under specified terms and conditions, and the mutually enforceable agreement to buy and sell into which the option ripens after it is exercised. Manifestly, then, an irrevocable option based on consideration is a contract. . . ." (*Torlai v. Lee* (1969) 270 Cal. App. 2d 854, 858, 76 Cal. Rptr. 239.) Conversely, an option without consideration is not binding on either party until exercised; until then, the option "'is simply a continuing offer which may be revoked at any time.' [Citation.]" (*Thomas v. Birch* (1918) 178 Cal. 483, 489, 173 P. 1102.)

Civil Code section 1605 defines consideration as "[a]ny benefit conferred, or agreed to be conferred, upon the promisor, by any other person, to which the promisor is not lawfully entitled, or any prejudice suffered, or agreed to be suffered, by such person, other than such as he is at the time of consent lawfully bound to suffer, as an inducement to the promisor. . . ." Thus, there are two requirements in order to find consideration. The promisee must confer (or agree to confer) a benefit or must suffer (or agree to suffer) prejudice. We emphasize either alone is sufficient to constitute consideration; "it is not necessary to the existence of a good consideration that a benefit should be conferred upon the promisor. It is enough that a 'prejudice be suffered or agreed to be suffered' by the promisee. [Citation.]" (*Bacon v. Grosse* (1913) 165 Cal. 481, 490-491, 132 P. 1027.)

It is not enough, however, to confer a benefit or suffer prejudice for there to be consideration. As we held in *Bard v. Kent, supra*, the second requirement is that the benefit or prejudice "'must actually be bargained for as the exchange for the promise.'" Put another way, the benefit or prejudice must have induced the promisor's promise. . . .

The lower courts concluded no such consideration supported the option. They reasoned no money was paid for the grant of the option nor did the work performed and expenses incurred by plaintiffs in pursuit of a parcel split benefit Thexton. Citing *O'Connell v. Lampe* (1929) 206 Cal. 282, 285, 274 P. 336, and *Drullinger v. Erskine* (1945) 71 Cal. App. 2d 492, 495, 163 P.2d 48, the lower courts explained that the "adequacy of consideration" must be measured at the time an agreement was entered into. The lower courts concluded that, at the time Steiner and Thexton struck their bargain, the promise to seek the parcel split was unenforceable because the escape clause gave plaintiffs the power to terminate the transaction at any time for any reason. Thus, the lower courts held, Steiner's promise was illusory and did not constitute valid consideration. The courts found it immaterial that plaintiffs had begun to perform, because plaintiffs were under no actual obligation to do so. To the contrary, we conclude as a matter of law that plaintiffs' part performance of the bargained-for promise to seek a parcel split created sufficient consideration to render the option irrevocable.

It is true that Steiner's promise to undertake the burden and expense of seeking a parcel split may have been illusory at the time the agreement was entered into, given the language of the escape clause. However, there can be no dispute that plaintiffs subsequently undertook substantial steps toward obtaining the parcel split and incurred significant expenses doing so.[7] Among other things, plaintiffs paid for the required civil engineering and surveying for the parcel and spent a number of months applying to the county planning department for a tentative parcel map, proceeding with the final hearing of the parcel review committee, and obtaining approval of the tentative map. On this record, the only possible conclusion is that Steiner both conferred a bargained-for benefit on Thexton and suffered bargained-for prejudice unaffected by his power to cancel, making up for the initially illusory nature of his promise.

It is undisputed that a parcel split of the 12.29 acres was necessary for Thexton to be able to sell a portion of his land to anyone while still retaining a two-acre parcel for himself to live on. There is also no dispute that Thexton did not want to have to go through the process of obtaining the parcel split himself. Indeed, he had previously rejected an offer of $750,000 for the 10 acres ($250,000 more than Steiner was to pay for the parcel) because that buyer wanted Thexton to obtain the required approval. It is clear then that a critical part of Thexton's willingness to sell was that Steiner would bear the expense, risk, and burden of seeking the parcel split. Indeed, there is evidence that Thexton told Steiner it was important to him that any interested buyer undertake the process of obtaining the parcel split. Thus, both elements of consideration were present. First, the effort to obtain the parcel split clearly conferred a benefit on Thexton and constituted prejudice suffered by plaintiffs.[8] Second, the promise to pursue the split was plainly bargained-for and induced Thexton to grant the option. Accordingly, plaintiffs' part performance cured the illusory nature of their promise.[9]

---

7. [10] Plaintiffs completed 75 to 90 percent of the work needed to obtain the parcel split and county approvals and alleged they collectively spent $60,000 in doing so. We have no occasion to consider whether any act, no matter how small, would be sufficient part performance to make an option irrevocable.

8. [11] As Steiner's counsel acknowledged at oral argument, the outcome might have been different had plaintiffs' efforts been exclusively in their own interest, such as only securing county approvals to develop the 10-acre parcel.

9. [12] Although our conclusion is based upon plaintiffs' part performance of the promise to obtain a parcel split, we also note the agreement required Steiner to deposit $1,000 into escrow, which he did. The trial court concluded the payment did not constitute consideration because Steiner would recover the money if he terminated the agreement; thus, the money did not confer a benefit on Thexton. However, even assuming the trial court's interpretation of the agreement is accurate, it is not clear its ultimate conclusion is correct. As previously discussed, for consideration to exist it is sufficient that a promisee suffers bargained-for prejudice. By placing the money

. . .

In conclusion, we hold plaintiffs' part performance of their bargained-for promise to seek a parcel split cured the initially illusory nature of the promise and thereby constituted sufficient consideration to render the option irrevocable.

III. DISPOSITION

The judgment of the Court of Appeal is reversed and the case is remanded for further proceedings.

Understanding the Case:

1. *Contract Language:*   The following is the relevant language from the Real Estate Purchase Contract in *Steiner*, with relevant language italicized:

Martin A. Steiner and/or Assignee, hereinafter called 'Buyer,' offers to pay to FAS Family Trust, Paul Thexton, hereinafter called 'Seller,' the purchase price of Five Hundred Thousand Dollars ($ 500,000.00) for 10 acres of a 12.29 acre property situated in the County of Sacramento . . . hereinafter called 'Property'. . . .

TERMS OF SALE:

1. Upon the Seller's acceptance escrow shall be opened and $1,000 . . . shall be deposited by Buyer, applicable toward purchase price.

2. During the escrow term, Seller shall allow Buyer an investigation period to determine the financial feasibility of obtaining a parcel split for development of the Property. Buyer shall have no direct financial obligation to Seller during this investigation period as Buyer will be expending sums on various professional services needed to reach the financial feasibility determination. Buyer hereby warranties that all fees shall be paid for said professional services by Buyer and neither the Seller nor the Property will in any way be obligated or indebted for said services. [¶] . . . [¶]

5. Buyer will pay for the required civil engineering and surveying for the entire parcel map. Any agency requirements of Seller's remaining 2.29 acre parcel will be paid by Seller. Any agency requirements for planning, development or entitlement of the 10 acre parcel will be paid by Buyer. [¶] . . . [¶]

10. If any condition herein stated has not been eliminated or satisfied within the time limits and pursuant to the provisions herein, or if, prior to close of

---

in escrow, Steiner gave up use of the money for as much as three years. This arguably constituted prejudice to Steiner even if he ultimately got the money back. In light of our conclusion regarding plaintiffs' part performance, we need not resolve the effect of the escrow payment.

escrow, Seller is unable or unwilling to remove any exceptions to the title objected to, and Buyer is unwilling to take title subject thereto, then this Contract shall at the end of the applicable time period, become null and void. [¶] . . . [¶]

17. Buyer hereby agrees to purchase the above described Property for the price upon the terms and conditions herein expressed. . . . [¶] . . . [¶]

CONTINGENCIES:

The Buyer shall have from date of acceptance until the closing of escrow to satisfy or waive the items listed herein below:

1. Seller is aware that Buyer plans to subdivide, apply for planning entitlements and develop 10 acres from the existing parcel and agrees to cooperate, as needed, with Buyer as Buyer attempts to obtain the necessary permits and authorizations from the various local jurisdictions.

2. Buyer at his sole option and expense will conduct all necessary investigations, engineering, architectural and economic feasibility studies as outlined earlier in this Contract.

3. Both Buyer and Seller understand that Buyer could have substantial investment during this development period.

4. Buyer shall hereby indemnify and hold Seller harmless for any acts, errors or omissions of Buyer or Buyer's agents; and Buyer and Buyer's agent hereby agree that, upon the performance of any test, they will leave the Property in the condition it was in prior to those tests.

5. By acceptance of this offer, the Seller has granted Buyer and/or Buyer's agents, the right to enter upon subject Property for the purpose of conducting said tests and investigations.

6. Buyer shall indemnify and hold Seller harmless for any costs associated with Buyer's investigations. In the event that this contract is terminated prior to the close of escrow, Buyer shall deliver to Seller the originals or copies of all information, reports, tests, [etc.]

7. It is the intent of Buyer that the time period from execution of this contract until the closing of escrow is the time that will be needed in order to be successful in developing this project. *It is expressly understood that the Buyer may, at its absolute and sole discretion during this period, elect not to continue in this transaction and this purchase contract will become null and void.*

CLOSE OF ESCROW:

Upon successful completion of subdividing the 10 acres from the existing parcel, Buyer will pay Seller the balance of the purchase price to escrow and close immediately.

Buyer will move expeditiously with the parcel split. It is anticipated it will take one to three years, due to existing governmental requirements.

Buyer will give quarterly reports to Seller as to progress of the parcel split.

If parcel split is not completed by September 1, 2006 this real estate purchase contract will be cancelled.

2. *Conditional Performance:* As an alternative to his option contract argument, Steiner argued that he and Thexton had entered into a contract for the

underlying transaction—the actual purchase and sale of the ten acres, which purchase was conditioned on certain events happening. You may recall from Chapter 3 that parties can do that—that is, they can obligate themselves to perform contractual obligations *conditioned on* certain events occurring. Until those events occur, there is no duty to perform. However, the occurrence of the events must to some extent be outside of the control of the party who is protected by that condition. Where that party retains complete discretion to perform his obligation, such as in this case, the party is not bound by the underlying contract.

3. *Implied Duty of Good Faith and Fair Dealing:* Steiner argued that he did not retain absolute discretion to decide to purchase the ten-acre property because his discretion was limited by the implied duty of good faith and fair dealing. As you will learn in Chapter 12, this implied duty exists in all contracts, and generally speaking, ensures a party acts without ill motive and reasonably. However, the court rejected this argument, holding that the parties had "contracted around" the implied duty by expressly giving Steiner absolute discretion to decide to buy the parcel.

Comprehension and Thought Questions:

1. What test does the court use to distinguish an option contract from a contract that is binding for the underlying transaction, subject to conditions? *leaves one party discretion to buy while binding seller (unilateral)*

2. How did the court know that Steiner and Thexton had entered into an option contract and not a contract for the sale of the ten-acre lot that was subject to various conditions, including obtaining county approvals and permits? *obliged Thexton to sell, but not Steiner (escape clause)*

3. Do you agree with the court's holding? *no - court still backed out of the contract*

4. Why did the lower court analyze whether there was consideration for Thexton's promise to hold the underlying offer open only at the moment the parties entered into the contract? *b/c need consideration for there to be a K*

5. Why does this court not limit its analysis of the existence of consideration to the moment the parties entered into the option contract? *maybe treated it as an offer with men*

6. Which court's approach do you think better effectuates the parties' intent? How about other policies of contract law?

7. In analyzing considerations, how did the court know that the parcel split was "bargained for" by Thexton? *↳ history of rejecting, wanted someone else to pay expense of this*

Hypothetical Variations:

1. What if, shortly after Steiner and Thexton entered into the Real Estate Purchase Contract, Thexton received a better offer for the ten acres, and he informed Steiner before Steiner undertook any work toward obtaining permits and approvals for a parcel split that the contract was terminated? *no consideration = no K = no obligation*

consideration

2. What if after having spent $20,000 and six months trying to get the necessary county permits and approvals, Steiner decided to not buy the ten-acre parcel. Could Thexton successfully sue Steiner to enforce Steiner's obligation to buy that parcel? *no, option Is only Thexton bound*

3. What if the second sentence in paragraph 7 of the Real Estate Purchase Contract had not been included in the contract, and Thexton declared that the contract was terminated before Steiner had finished the process of obtaining the county permits and approvals?

Could not back out bc would, in that case, just have been a binding purchase agreement subject to conditions

D. OPTION THEORY: UNILATERAL CONTRACTS AND PROMISSORY ESTOPPEL

While option contracts are essentially unmatured bilateral contracts for the underlying transaction—that is, they become binding bilateral contracts for the underlying transaction once the optionee accepts the underlying offer—courts often analogize them to unilateral contracts. They do so for two reasons. One reason is because in an option contract, as you saw in *Steiner*, one of the parties (the optionee/offeree) has discretion to decide whether or not to accept. Similarly, if you recall from Chapter 4, in a unilateral contract, the offeree has discretion to decide whether or not to accept the offer by performing the requested act. Still, despite the discretionary nature of acceptance, the method of acceptance for each is different—that is, an offeree must accept an offer for a unilateral contract through performance, while an offeree of a firm offer must accept in the manner required in the option contract or, if no manner is specified, in a reasonable manner. That usually means acceptance by return promise.

The second reason that courts often analogize between option contracts and unilateral contracts is that in both cases, the offeree must provide some consideration to keep the underlying offer open (i.e., to make an irrevocable or firm offer) for a period of time. In the case of option contracts, the consideration is often (though not always) the payment of a specified sum of money. In the case of unilateral contracts, it is the offeree's start to performance that provides the consideration to keep the offeror's offer firm.

Courts often also analogize to option contracts in the context of promissory estoppel claims. You will study promissory estoppel in Chapter 22. For purposes of this chapter, you should understand that, with promissory estoppel, a court may enforce a promise against a party not because the promise was bargained for, but due to the promisee's reasonable reliance on that promise. Sometimes the relevant promise a court enforces under promissory estoppel is a promise (or set of promises) contained in an offer. In that circumstance, where the promisee reasonably relies on that offer, a court might hold the promisor to its offer for a period of time, to allow the offeree an opportunity to accept, even though the offer is not an option contract of the type described in this chapter. In that circumstance, the offeree's reliance on the offer is enough both to manifest its assent to the "option contract," and to supply consideration for the promisor's promise to keep its offer open.

For example, imagine that DevCo is a general contractor. It is seeking to be picked as the general contractor to build a building for AltoMax. In preparing its bid to become the general contractor for AltoMax's project, DevCo needs to obtain bids from subcontractors to perform specific aspects of the work and from suppliers to supply materials. DevCo will not accept these bids unless and until it knows that it has secured AltoMax's acceptance of DevCo's bid to become the general contractor. In this instance, imagine that BrickCo provides DevCo a bid to supply brick for $200,000. DevCo uses that bid to prepare its own bid to AltoMax, in hopes of getting picked as the general contractor. However, suppose that after DevCo has submitted its bid to AltoMax, BrickCo decides it does not want to supply bricks for the project. Under the classic mutual assent rules, BrickCo could revoke its offer at any time until DevCo accepted it, which DevCo would not yet have done. But if BrickCo revokes its offer while AltoMax is considering bids from general contractors, DevCo would be stuck: It would either have to revoke its bid just because one of its suppliers has decided it does not want to perform or, once it is awarded the project, find an alternate brick supplier, potentially at a higher price.

In this situation, a court very well could find that BrickCo's offer is irrevocable for a period of time to allow DevCo an opportunity to accept that offer once it is awarded the general contractor position. The court would not find that DevCo and BrickCo specifically negotiated an option contract that would make BrickCo's offer firm for a period of time because that in fact did not happen. The court nevertheless may protect DevCo because BrickCo knew that DevCo was going to rely on its subcontractor bid, and DevCo did in fact rely on that bid in making its bid to AltoMax to become the general contractor for the project.[10] In that way, a court would effectively find that BrickCo made a firm offer because it knew DevCo was going to rely on that offer even before accepting it.

PRACTICE PROBLEM 8-2

Jerome Butte is an incoming 1L at the Great Plains Law School located in Wichita, Kansas. The month before school starts, Jerome visits Wichita to find a place to live. After touring many apartment complexes, Jerome decides that he would like to rent an apartment at The Pines, the nicest apartment complex close to campus. He finds The Pines especially attractive because it is running

---

10. For a case holding along these lines, see Drennan v. Star Paving Co., 51 Cal.2d 409 (1958).

a special: if a new tenant refers another new tenant who ends up leasing an apartment at The Pines, the referring tenant gets a free month of rent. Assuming Jerome could find another incoming 1L to rent an apartment at The Pines, then Jerome could afford rent at the Pines. So, on July 15, Jerome calls Virginia Heffernan, the leasing manager of The Pines, to inform her that Jerome would like to lease an apartment. Jerome also indicates on the call that before he signs the lease agreement, he wants to find another incoming 1L whom he can refer as a new tenant. As he tells Virginia, he is confident that he can find another tenant within two days. He then asks Virginia if The Pines will still have an available apartment in two days. Virginia responds that she will make sure she holds an apartment open for Jerome for two days, as she does still have apartments available for rent that she would like to fill.

1. Is The Pines contractually obligated to hold an apartment open for Jerome for two days? *No Consideration*

2. What if Jerome offers to pay The Pines $10 to hold an apartment open for him for two days and Virginia agrees to this, even though both know that Jerome will not actually pay the money? *"Sham" consideration?*

3. What if Jerome pays Virginia $10 to hold an apartment open for him for two days, but the following afternoon, Jerome calls Virginia to tell her that he no longer wants to rent an apartment at The Pines, as he could not find another tenant to refer. However, later that afternoon, Jerome finds another student who wants to rent an apartment at The Pines, so Jerome calls Virginia back to exercise his option and lease an apartment at the Pines. On that call, Virginia informs Jerome that she has already set up appointments to show other prospective tenants the open apartments the following day and she therefore might not be able to rent to Jerome. Is The Pines contractually obligated to lease an apartment to Jerome? *not a real rejection, still has option*

Now that you have studied option contracts, read through and answer the questions that follow the Simulation Problem for Chapter 8, which is located in Appendix A.

PART III

CONTRACT FORMATION PROCESSES

Like Part II, Part III also relates to the contract formation stage. However, while Part II described the legal elements for bargained-for contract formation, this part describes processes and practical steps the lawyer and client take to satisfy those legal elements. It does that by first, in Chapter 9, discussing the various factors a lawyer must consider in deciding whether or not to take on the client representation. Assuming the client has properly retained the lawyer, Chapter 10 then discusses typical pre-contract-formation steps that clients and lawyers often take to prepare the client to contract. Those steps include performing due diligence to obtain information about the contractual counterparty and proposed transaction, and preparing a term sheet to ensure that there is agreement in principle by the parties to the terms of the contract. Assuming those steps do not surface any concerns, then the next step, discussed in Chapter 11, is to negotiate and draft the formal written contract.

CHAPTER 9

Lawyers' Representation of Clients in Contracting

You are likely familiar with what a litigator does. After all, popular television shows often depict the litigator in action, making a dramatic closing argument or asking a witness tough questions on the stand. While popular culture often does not *accurately* depict the litigator in action, it at least has provided you with some narrative about the role and value of an attorney in litigation.

In contrast, you may not be familiar with what a transactional lawyer does. However, working as a transactional lawyer is equally challenging and rewarding. It is, though, quite different from a litigation practice. This chapter will introduce you to this transactional role that many lawyers serve. First, in Section A, it will introduce you to what it means to be a transactional lawyer and describe the functions that transactional lawyers serve. Next, Section B will discuss some of the key factors a transactional lawyer must consider when deciding to represent a new client, or an existing client on a new business transaction, especially where the lawyer may be representing multiple parties in that same transaction. Finally, Section C will explore who the client is where the client is a business organization rather than a natural person. That discussion is important for transactional lawyers, as the lawyer must ensure the right party is bound to the contract. It also explains how a natural person binds a business organization to a contract given that business organizations are legal constructs and cannot act except through the people who act for them.

A. INTRODUCTION TO TRANSACTIONAL LAWYERS

In England, lawyers are divided into two types—solicitors and barristers. Solicitors advise clients on legal matters. If the matter is to be resolved in litigation, then the solicitor retains a barrister to represent the client's interests at trial. Thus, there is specialized training for the barrister in courtroom advocacy.

In the United States, there is no such distinction between attorneys who can provide legal advice to clients and those who can appear before a court. However, there are attorneys who devote much of their practices to interacting with a court on behalf of clients. Those attorneys are called litigators, deriving from the term litigation, which is an action before a court to *enforce* a legal right. In litigation, the client might be either the party initiating the dispute or the party defending itself in the dispute. But either way, the goal is for the lawyer to help the client resolve that dispute in the most efficient and favorable manner possible.

Often litigators specialize in particular fields of law. For example, tax litigators represent clients in connection with tax disputes either at the state or local level. And intellectual property (IP) litigators represent clients in connection with the unauthorized use of IP.

However, despite their frequent portrayal on television shows and in the movies, litigators are not the only type of attorneys. In fact, many attorneys help their clients *obtain* and *transfer* legal rights through contracts. Attorneys who help their clients obtain and transfer legal rights through contracts are called **transactional attorneys**. Specifically, transactional attorneys represent their clients in furthering their goals through business transactions. In other words, the transactional lawyer represents the client in the context of a desired business transaction and not in the context of a dispute.

Contracts are the primary tool used by transactional attorneys to effectuate those business transactions. For example, imagine Great Yums Inc. owns a restaurant in Springfield, Columbia. The owner of Great Yums, Cynthia Holmes, decides to expand Great Yums's business by opening a new location in the suburbs of Springfield. Doing so will require Great Yums to lease a space in the suburbs. It will likely also require Great Yums to have that space retrofitted to ensure that it works for the restaurant. And Great Yums will likely require a loan from a bank to be able to afford these construction costs. Great Yums will largely use contracts to achieve this transaction. In particular, Great Yums will enter into (1) a lease agreement with a landlord for the leased space; (2) a construction agreement for the retrofitting of that space; and (3) a loan agreement to provide for the loan. For all of these contracts, the transactional lawyer will help Great Yums negotiate the terms of the contracts; either draft or review drafts of the contracts to ensure they provide Great Yums with the benefits it is seeking, protect it from potential risks, and reflect customary terms; ensure the transaction complies with law; and help the client perform these contracts.

In fact, some lawyers *only* advise their clients on business transactions, and do not engage in any litigation work at all. Those lawyers represent their clients on all sorts of business transactions, from sales of assets to commercial bank loans. At larger law firms, lawyers often even specialize in different types of transactions. So, for example, some lawyers only work on purchase and sale transactions (these lawyers are often called mergers and acquisitions (M&A) lawyers), while others only work on commercial transactions like bank loans.

Transactional attorneys serve many purposes. They first make sure that the transaction complies with the law. That might mean making sure the transactional promises are legally enforceable (one of the topics of this course) and ensuring that the client obtains the necessary governmental and third-party authorizations to consummate the transaction. Transactional attorneys also seek to protect the value of the transaction to the client. For example, as discussed in Chapter 3, attorneys can draft a contract that contains appropriate representations, warranties, covenants, conditions, and other provisions that will provide a client with relief or remedy if the opposing party does not deliver as promised.

Through their familiarity with various transaction structures and contract terms and conditions, transactional attorneys lower the transaction costs associated with consummating a transaction. Also, the more unfamiliar a client is with a particular type of transaction, the more significant the transaction, and the less sophisticated the client is, the more help or value she may receive from the services of a transactional attorney, who may have represented many clients in that type of transaction. For example, many people probably would not retain the services of an attorney when signing a contract for $300 worth of landscaping services, as the contract value is relatively small, the services fairly straightforward and commonly understood, and the risks low. They should retain a transactional attorney, however, when selling a family business for $1 million since it is probably a once-in-a-lifetime type of transaction with which the client is unfamiliar, in addition to being more consequential in terms of value.

Transactional attorneys also increase the probability that the client will achieve its business goals. They do that by identifying the risks that could undermine the client's realization of benefits from a transaction and help the client manage those risks through contract terms and other avenues. In addition, they help preserve flexibility in case the client wants to pursue future opportunities.

In 1984, Professor Ronald Gilson wrote a very influential article on the benefits transactional lawyers provide to their clients. The following is an excerpt from that article:

> What do business lawyers really do? Embarrassingly enough, at a time when lawyers are criticized with increasing frequency as nonproductive actors in the economy, there seems to be no coherent answer. That is not, of course, to say that answers have not been offered; there are a number of familiar responses that we have all heard or, what is worse, that we have all offered at one time or another without really thinking very hard about them. The problem is that, for surprisingly similar reasons, none of them is very helpful.

Clients have their own, often quite uncharitable, view of what business lawyers do. In an extreme version, business lawyers are perceived as evil sorcerers who use their special skills and professional magic to relieve clients of their possessions. Kurt Vonnegut makes the point in an amusing way. A law student is told by his favorite professor that, to get ahead in the practice of law, "a lawyer should be looking for situations where large amounts of money are about to change hands." Though this advice is hardly different from standard professional suggestions about how to build a practice, the reasons offered for the advice lay bare a quite different view of the business lawyer's function:

> In every big transaction [the professor said], there is a magic moment during which a man has surrendered a treasure, and during which the man who is due to receive it has not yet done so. An alert lawyer will make that moment his own, possessing the treasure for a magic microsecond, taking a little of it, passing it on. If the man who is to receive the treasure is unused to wealth, has an inferiority complex and shapeless feelings of guilt, as most people do, the lawyer can often take as much as half the bundle, and still receive the recipient's blubbering thanks.[1]

Clients frequently advance other more charitable but still negative views of the business lawyer that also should be familiar to most practitioners. Business lawyers are seen at best as a transaction cost, part of a system of wealth redistribution from clients to lawyers; legal fees represent a tax on business transactions to provide an income maintenance program for lawyers. At worst, lawyers are seen as deal killers whose continual raising of obstacles, without commensurate effort at finding solutions, ultimately causes transactions to collapse under their own weight.

Lawyers, to be sure, do not share these harsh evaluations of their role. When my question—what does a business lawyer really do?—is put to business lawyers, the familiar response is that they "protect" their clients, that they get their clients the "best" deal. In the back of their minds is a sense that their clients do not appreciate them, that clients neither perceive nor understand the risks that lawyers raise, and that as a result clients do not recognize that it is in their best interest when lawyers identify the myriad of subtle problems unavoidably present in a typical transaction.

A more balanced view is presented in the academic literature. Here the predominant approach has been functional. The lawyer is presented as a counselor, planner, drafter, negotiator, investigator, lobbyist, scapegoat, champion, and, most strikingly, even as a friend. Certainly this list of functions rings true enough. An experienced practitioner can quickly recall playing each of these roles.

Despite the surface dissimilarity of these characterizations of what a business lawyer does, they do share both an important similarity and a common failure. To be sure, the unfavorable views ascribed to the client reflect the view that business lawyers reduce the value of a transaction, while both the quite favorable view held by business lawyers themselves and the more neutral but still positive view offered in the academic literature assume that business lawyers increase

---

1. [4] K. Vonnegut, God Bless You, Mr. Rosewater 17-18 (1965).

the value of a transaction. But both sides do seem to agree on the appropriate standard by which the performance of business lawyers should be judged: If what a business lawyer does has value, a transaction must be worth more, net of legal fees, as a result of the lawyer's participation. And the common failure of all of these views is not their differing conclusions. Rather, it is the absence of an explanation of the relation between the business lawyer's participation in a transaction and the value of the transaction to the clients. In other words, precisely how do the activities of business lawyers affect transaction value?

Ronald J. Gilson, *Value Creation by Business Lawyers: Legal Skills and Asset Pricing*, 94 Yale L.J. 239, 241-43, 255 (1984).

Comprehension and Thought Questions:

1. Does it really matter what value transactional lawyers bring to a business transaction so long as clients are willing to pay those lawyers for their services? In other words, why do we even need to rationalize the role of the transactional lawyer?

2. Suppose you represent Mom & Pop Shop Inc., a mid-sized convenience store, in selling all of its assets to Big Super, a national supermarket chain. Why do you suppose Mom & Pop Shop retained you to represent it in this transaction? What benefits do you think you will bring Mom & Pop Shop in your representation?

Since Gilson's article, many other commentators have questioned the value of transactional lawyers. For example, Professor Steven Schwarcz conducted a survey of lawyers and clients on what value transactional lawyers provide.[2] He concluded from his study that transactional lawyers provide value by reducing regulatory costs to clients in transactions, such as "by providing expertise in the law and regulations that generally govern the transaction and by understanding the rationale for the contractual provisions in the transaction documents."[3]

To the extent a business transaction calls for knowledge of a specialized area of law—such as tax law or IP law—the transactional lawyer may need to find someone with that expertise to assist on the transaction if the lawyer does not herself have that knowledge. For example, if a client decides to sell all its assets, including IP, then an IP lawyer will need to advise the client on how to transfer its IP. This is a transactional task, as this task involves granting IP rights to a buyer, not resolving a dispute with the third party. Similarly, a tax lawyer—someone with specialized knowledge of the Internal Revenue Code and other tax laws—might be needed to advise the client on which transaction

---

2. Steven L. Schwarcz, *Explaining the Value of Transactional Lawyering*, 12 Stan. J.L. Bus. & Fin. 486 (2007).

3. *Id.* at 501.

structure will minimize taxes to the client. This, too, is a transactional task, for it involves advancing the client's legal rights at the lowest tax cost possible. It does not, however, involve a dispute by or against the client.

Attorneys other than transactional attorneys also work with contracts on behalf of their clients. Litigators, for example, must understand contract law, structure, terms, and practices. That is because a litigator might either represent her client in pursuing a third party for breach of contract or defend her client from such a breach claim. Or if the dispute is not about a contract, the plaintiff and defendant might settle the dispute through a settlement agreement. That settlement agreement is a contract.

Lawyers also enter into contracts to further their own interests. For example, lawyers enter into contracts with their clients setting out the terms of the representation. And they buy supplies, office furniture, and the like through contracts. A lawyer might also lease office space under a lease agreement, which is also a contract.

Thus, lawyers in all areas of practice, and in all types of practices, must be familiar with contract design, content, and law, both to represent their clients and for their own personal needs.

PRACTICE PROBLEM 9-1

Your friend Dana Vollner contacts you right after you graduate law school, but before you are licensed to practice law. Dana asks you what type of lawyer or lawyers you would recommend she contact in connection with her purchase of a beauty salon. To make this purchase happen, she will need to borrow $30,000 from a bank. Finally, Dana wants to make sure this purchase and loan will not create excess tax liabilities for her or her husband. Advise Dana what she should look for when screening lawyers to perform this legal work for her.

B. DECIDING TO REPRESENT A CLIENT ON A TRANSACTION

When either an existing client or a new client approaches a lawyer about performing legal work for that client or prospective client, a lawyer must carefully consider taking on that representation. In other words, a lawyer should not agree to accept any client who walks in the door and should not agree to work on any legal matter an existing client wants the lawyer to work on. Instead, the lawyer must be mindful that she becomes a fiduciary of her clients, charged with protection her clients' best interests. More specifically, the lawyer has a host of professional responsibilities under the Rules of Professional Conduct promulgated by the oversight authority in the state where she is licensed to practice law.[4]

First, a lawyer should be sure she is competent to provide the requested representation. In the case of a potential transaction, that means not only knowing contract law and other applicable laws, but also knowing customary contract structure and terms for that type of transaction, as well as having relevant skills, such as the skills of negotiating and drafting contracts.[5] If a lawyer is not competent on any of these matters, she can either become competent through study, or associate herself with another lawyer who is competent.[6]

So, for example, if a business client requests a transactional lawyer who does not specialize in IP to represent it in connection with a license of IP, that lawyer would likely be competent in the contract formation requirements of the license agreement (a contract), in the structure and many of the terms of that contract, and in the skills of negotiating and drafting that contract. However, unless that lawyer had previously studied or worked with IP licensing, that lawyer would likely not be competent to represent the client in the IP-specific areas of the transaction. Thus, the lawyer would likely want to associate with an IP lawyer to ensure she addresses any IP-specific laws and customary terms in the license.

Second, a lawyer needs to be diligent, by ensuring she has adequate time, energy, and resources to provide for the requested representation.[7] Without time, energy, and resources, a lawyer cannot be adequately prepared or thorough on a transaction, risking a violation of the Rules of Professional Conduct. A lawyer who does not devote adequate time, energy, or resources to a client matter also risks being sued by the client for the tort of malpractice if the lawyer makes a mistake in the representation.[8]

Third, in considering whether to take on a new client, or a new matter for an existing client, you will also want to consider whether the client will be able to pay its legal bills. Here, some clients seeking transactional advice will ask you to take an ownership interest in the business instead of being paid a fee. While you will undoubtedly study this in a course on Professional Responsibility, you should be aware of the risks that come with receiving an ownership

---

4. The oversight authority is usually a state's supreme court.

5. Model Rules of Prof'l Conduct, r. 1.1 (2014). Per the rule, competence requires that a lawyer have the knowledge and skills necessary to address the client's matter.

6. Model Rules of Prof'l Conduct, r. 1.1 cmt. 2 (2014).

7. Model Rules of Prof'l Conduct, r. 1.3 cmt. 1 (2014). To be diligent, a lawyer must commit herself to furthering the client's interests.

8. Restatement (Third) of the Law Governing Lawyers § 52 cmt. c (2000); Restatement (Second) of Torts § 298 (1965). Just because a lawyer has violated the Model Rules of Professional Conduct does not mean she has violated the law. The Model Rules merely set out professional standards of conduct for lawyers. They do not constitute civil or criminal law. However, sometimes where a lawyer engages in conduct that violates the Rules—such as a neglect of the client's matter before the lawyer—that conduct also constitutes a civil wrong, called a tort.

interest in a business client. Namely, it could compromise your independent judgment and drive you to want to consummate the transaction not because that transaction is beneficial to the client, but so that you can get paid.

Importantly, before taking on a representation, a lawyer needs to make sure she does not have a conflict of interest.[9] Broadly speaking, a **conflict of interest** exists where a lawyer either has a personal interest or a duty to an existing or former client that conflicts with the lawyer's duties to a client.[10] For example, a conflict exists where a lawyer represents multiple parties to a transaction, as all those parties have different goals under the transaction, even if they all want the transaction to happen.[11] A lawyer also has a conflict in the situation described above—where she receives an ownership interest in the client in lieu of fees.

A conflict also exists where a lawyer represents an opposing party in an unrelated transaction. This would occur, for example, where a lawyer represents client A in buying a business, where the lawyer also represents client B, a supplier, negotiating a supply agreement with client A. This creates a conflict for the lawyer because while, as a lawyer, she has a fiduciary duty to act in client A's best interest in the purchase transaction, she is working against that very same client's interests in the supply transaction. As an additional difficulty, in this situation, the lawyer would likely have confidential information about client A from representing it in the purchase transaction that the lawyer would risk disclosing during the supply transaction.

In each of these examples, the lawyer's duty to act in the best interest of a client is materially limited by her responsibilities to a current or former client, or due to her own interests. What is limited is the lawyer's ability to consider, recommend, or carry out an appropriate course of action for the client as a result of the lawyer's other responsibilities or interests. For example, in the case of a transaction where a lawyer represents multiple parties, that might mean the lawyer is unable to negotiate as strongly on behalf of all clients as she could have had she only represented one of those clients.

If a lawyer has a conflict, she needs to determine whether that conflict is consentable, meaning a type of conflict to which the client can consent. In general, conflicts are consentable only if the lawyer can still provide competent, diligent representation to the affected client or clients.[12] The following comment to Rule 1.7 of the Model Rules of Professional Conduct attempts to capture some of the factors a lawyer should consider in determining whether she can and should undertake such a joint representation:

---

9. Model Rules of Prof'l Conduct, r. 1.7 (2014).
10. Restatement (Third) of the Law Governing Lawyers § 121 (2000).
11. Restatement (Third) of the Law Governing Lawyers § 130 cmt. a (2000).
12. Model Rules of Prof'l Conduct, r. 1.7(b)(1) (2015).

[28] Whether a conflict is consentable depends on the circumstances. For example, a lawyer may not represent multiple parties to a negotiation whose interests are fundamentally antagonistic to each other, but common representation is permissible where the clients are generally aligned in interest even though there is some difference in interest among them. Thus, a lawyer may seek to establish or adjust a relationship between clients on an amicable and mutually advantageous basis; for example, in helping to organize a business in which two or more clients are entrepreneurs, working out the financial reorganization of an enterprise in which two or more clients have an interest or arranging a property distribution in settlement of an estate. The lawyer seeks to resolve potentially adverse interests by developing the parties' mutual interests. Otherwise, each party might have to obtain separate representation, with the possibility of incurring additional cost, complication or even litigation. Given these and other relevant factors, the clients may prefer that the lawyer act for all of them.

Even if a conflict is consentable, a lawyer needs to think about the consequences of asking a client to consent to a conflict. Sometimes clients do not want to give this consent, as they worry that the lawyer could disclose confidential information about that client to the jointly represented client.[13] Clients also worry about the reverse—that the lawyer will acquire confidential information from the other client that will disqualify the lawyer from representing the consenting client in the future.

Where a lawyer is retained by multiple parties to the same transaction with their consent, she must clearly explain the limitations in her joint representation to all parties. The limitations the lawyer must disclose include her inability to advocate for one party against another, as well as her inability to keep relevant information from one client confidential from another, as she has a duty of candor toward both clients. The lawyer must also explain that if the relationship between any of those prospective clients sours, the lawyer must withdraw from representing all of them.

Finally, in deciding to represent a prospective client, a lawyer should consider the character of the client. Does that potential client seem trustworthy? Does that potential client have a history of complying with the law? Does that potential client, as well as the main principals with whom you will be working, seem like they will respect the lawyer's role as legal advisor? These types of questions can help you determine if the client is someone who will use the lawyer's counsel to skirt the law, or someone whose association might tarnish the lawyer's reputation. These questions can also help a lawyer decide if the client is someone with whom that lawyer will enjoy working.

---

13. Model Rules of Prof'l Conduct, r. 1.7 cmts. 30-31 (2015).

PRACTICE PROBLEM 9-2

Shelly O'Neill is a Michigan real estate lawyer who received her law license in 2005. In her first five years of practice, Shelley represented dozens of clients in acquiring commercial real estate in Michigan. Shelley also advised those clients in raising money to develop those properties.

In 2010, Shelly stopped practicing so that she could stay home with her kids. However, she kept her law license active during this time by paying the annual bar fees and completing the necessary continuing legal education (CLE) hours.

Shelly recently returned to practice. Upon her return, Dan Developer asked Shelly to represent him in connection with his purchase of a new real estate project. Dan is particularly excited because he plans to raise the money he needs to develop the property using crowdfunding, a new method of raising capital from investors that became permissible in Michigan starting in 2014. With crowdfunding, Dan will be able to raise money from third-party investors through an electronic portal, instead of having to personally reach out to each potential investor, as he used to do.

1. Is Shelly competent to represent Dan in this transaction?

2. Assume Frances Bello, a recently retired executive who landed a lot of money in her retirement, contacts Dan through the funding portal and indicates that she would like to become a major investor in Dan's new real estate development project. After additional communications in which Dan explains that you are doing the legal work for him on this transaction, Frances contacts you and asks you if you will represent her in the transaction too. How do you respond?

C. UNDERSTANDING HOW CLIENTS CONTRACT; WHO IS THE CLIENT?

As an attorney, you will undoubtedly work with and for businesses. Businesses typically act through legal entities, such as corporations and partnerships. This section explains how legal entities act, so that you can ensure the counterparty legal entity is bound by a contract. This section will also help you identify who your client is when you are dealing with a business entity. This is important so that you can ensure you adequately protect your client's interests as you discharge your professional responsibilities described above.

1. Natural Person as Contracting Party

Natural persons, such as yourself, often enter into contracts. For example, as a consumer—or someone who enters into contracts to buy (i.e., consume) goods and services for personal reasons—you have likely entered into a contract with Facebook, Twitter, Instagram, and other social media sites when you created your accounts with those sites (recalling the many issues with mutual assent for such contracts discussed in Chapter 6); you have undoubtedly entered into a contract with your cell phone provider; and you entered into a contract with the restaurant from which you last ordered food.

Natural persons also enter into nonconsumer contracts. For example, you might enter into an employment agreement with an employer where you and your employer have agreed on a specific length of employment, salary, and other employment duties and rights. In that case, the contract is not for your purchase of a service that you will "consume"; instead, it is for services you will be providing.

Obviously, when your client is a natural person, you should be clear in the engagement letter with your client that you are representing that individual personally and not representing any other family member or a business entity with which he or she is associated.

2. Organizational Entities as Contracting Parties

Not all contracts are between natural persons. In fact, in most contracts, at least one party, if not both, are artificial persons. The term **artificial person** captures business organizations such as corporations, partnerships, and limited liability companies, as well as other types of legal entities such as trusts.

For example, suppose Neil Voos is the Vice President of Sales at CompuSell Inc. Neil contacts you and asks you to review a sales contract he has prepared in which CompuSell will be selling 50 customized computers to CompuBuy Inc. In this example, your client is CompuSell because you are providing CompuSell with advice. Even though Neil had contacted you, he was not seeking personal advice from you. In fact, Neil will not be entering into the contract for himself—instead, he (or whoever else signs the contract) will be entering into this contract *on behalf of* CompuSell. Thus, CompuSell will be a party, and not Neil nor whoever else at CompuSell signs the written agreement.

It is important to understand when you are representing a business organization rather than a natural person who works for that legal organization so that you know to whom you owe your fiduciary duties as a lawyer. In fact, it may come to pass that one of the natural persons who is your primary contact at your client (such as Neil Voos, the Vice President of Sales) develops a conflict of interest with the business organization you represent. In that situation, it is your duty to ensure that the officer understands that you represent the interests of the organization and not the officer.

It is equally important to understand when a business organization is entering into a contract so that the contract properly reflects that reality, and does not unintentionally bind a natural person who speaks on behalf of that organization. Thus, as you review the draft contract that Neil Voos has prepared, you would want to ensure that Neil himself is not a party to the contract. Instead, only CompuSell is a party. Similarly, you would want to ensure that CompuBuy is contractually bound even though an individual will be signing on behalf of CompuBuy. The next section explains how to ensure that business organizations are bound to contracts in light of the fact that business organizations are legal fictions and cannot act except through people.

a. Authority

Business organizations cannot act except through the people who work for them. As an example, a salesperson from AT&T, Verizon, or another cellular phone company had to sign the document labeled "contract" on behalf of the cellular phone company for you to obtain cellular service from that company.

Agency law governs the power of a person to affect the legal relations of another.[14] A person "affects another's relations" where she binds the other to a contract. In the context of this discussion, therefore, we are exploring how a natural person binds a business organization to a contract.

Most commonly, business organizations enter into contracts through their employees.[15] In this situation, the employee who acts on behalf of the business organization is referred to as the **agent**.[16] The employer on whose behalf the agent acts is known as the **principal**.[17]

While employees commonly bind their principals to contracts, not every employee can bind his employer to every contract. Instead, an employee must have authority to rightfully bind his employer. The word **authority** means the rightful power of an agent to affect his principal's legal relations.[18] So, for example, if Neil Voos, the Vice President of Sales at CompuSell Inc. has authority to enter sales contracts on behalf of his employer, CompuSell, that means Neil has been given the power to bind CompuSell to sales contracts. Thus, when Neil signs a sales contract on behalf of CompuSell, CompuSell will be bound by that contract.

---

14. Restatement (Third) of Agency § 1.01 (2006).

15. Sometimes business organizations act through their nonemployees. We will ignore that situation here, and leave it to a class on Business Organizations to develop that further.

16. Legally, an agent is someone who acts on behalf of another, and is subject to the other's control. This is satisfied by employees because they are subject to the control of their supervisors. Even the President, Chief Executive Officer, or other highest-ranking officer is subject to the control of others, for that person is answerable to the board of directors.

17. In Chapter 1, these same terms were used to describe economic relationships where one party (a principal) has control and informational advantages over another. Those terms have a slightly different meaning in this section, when discussing how business organizations act. This section uses the terms in their legal sense, which is governed by agency law. Restatement (Third) of Agency § 1.01 (2006).

18. Restatement (Third) of Agency § 1.01 (2006).

An employee obtains authority to bind his employer to a contract in several ways. One is where he is granted **express actual authority**. Here, assume Michael Smith, the President of CompuSell, expressly asked Neil to enter into the aforementioned sales contract. In this case, Neil would have express actual authority to enter that contract. The authority is *actual* because it was actually given to Neil by his superior, Michael Smith. It is *express* because Smith expressly said that Neil had this authority.

Often employees are impliedly given authority to bind their employees. An employee has **implied actual authority** where the employee is given express actual authority to do something, but that expression does not specify every action the employee needs to take to perform that act. That express manifestation, though, implies that the employee can take whatever action is necessary or reasonably understood by the agent as being incidental to achieve the action expressly authorized.

So, for example, while Michael Smith expressly authorized Neil to enter the sales contract on behalf of CompuSell, Michael did not expressly authorize Neil to prepare the other documents the sales contract requires CompuSell to deliver. However, preparing those documents is necessary and incidental for this type of transaction. Therefore, preparing those other documents is clearly an action Neil is impliedly authorized to take as well.

Sometimes an employee purports to act on behalf of an employer, but that employee does not actually have authority to bind his employer. For example, suppose that while Neil is the Vice President of Sales and is generally authorized to enter into sales contracts, Michael expressly tells Neil not to enter into a contract with CompuBuy. However, Neil enters into a sales contract with CompuBuy anyway, because CompuBuy offers a price for computers that is simply too good for Neil to pass up.

In this case, Neil lacks authority to enter this contract with CompuBuy—Michael took that actual authority away from Neil when he expressly told Neil not to enter a contract with CompuBuy. However, there are a number of agency law doctrines that might still lead CompuSell to be bound by the contract. One of those doctrines is apparent authority. **Apparent authority** exists where a principal (i.e., the employer) makes a manifestation to a third party that makes that third party reasonably believe that the agent has authority, even if the agent does not actually have authority. In this case, Michael's conferring the title of Vice President of Sales on Neil, and authorizing Neil to present himself as the Vice President of Sales to third parties, might create such an appearance. Consequently, CompuBuy might reasonably believe Neil could bind CompuSell to this contract. If so, CompuSell would indeed be bound.

As this example demonstrates, an employer (like CompuSell) can be bound to a contract through the actions of an employee (like Neil) even where the employee does not have authority. Of course, where that happens, the employee would be liable to his employer for damages due to his exceeding his authority.

In this example, that would mean that Neil could be liable to CompuSell for the costs associated with the undesired contract with CompuBuy.

Finally, even where an employee purports to enter into a contract on behalf of his employer without authority to act, the employer can later ratify that action, retroactively giving authority. Specifically, **ratification** occurs where a principal, with knowledge of all material facts, affirms a contract entered on its behalf. In the above example, if upon becoming informed about the contract with CompuBuy, Michael Smith tells Neil that he did good work entering the contract with CompuBuy, and instructs the shipping department to deliver the purchased computers to CompuBuy, these actions indicate that Michael Smith is affirming CompuSell's desire to be bound to the contract with CompuBuy. That ratification means that Neil's actions are deemed rightful from the start.

If an agent lacks authority or other power to bind a principal (such as through apparent authority or ratification), then the agent cannot manifest assent on behalf of the principal. Thus, lack of authority is one defense to mutual assent. As discussed in Section C below, to avoid this defense, you should verify at the outset that the agent who is manifesting assent on behalf of an organizational counterparty has authority to bind that party.

Note that where an agent with authority acts on behalf of his principal organization, the agent himself is not bound by the resulting contract. Thus, by default, Neil would not be bound by the contract with CompuBuy even though he signs that contract as follows:

In Witness Whereof, the parties have entered into this Agreement as of the date first written above.

CompuSell Inc.
By: //ss// Neil Voos
Name: Neil Voos
Title: Vice President of Sales

CompuBuy Inc.
By:
Name:
Title:

However, if Neil is not careful, he could accidentally bind himself to the contract in addition to, or instead of, CompuSell. He could do that by manifesting his intent to be bound personally. For example, if Neil signed this Agreement without including his title and without indicating above his name that he is signing for CompuSell, he could personally be bound.

Keep in mind that this discussion is merely a summary of some of the agency law principles that are most commonly at issue when contracting with business organizations. However, the discussion is an oversimplification of agency law. For a more complete discussion of agency law, we suggest you take a class on agency law, or a Business Associations course that covers agency law principles.

b. Authority in action

The following case presents the question of authority of a son to bind his mother to a contract. While this case does not involve a business organization as the principal, it raises the same issues that arise where an agent purports to act on behalf of a business organization. As you review the case, consider the various ways in which the son could have been legally authorized to so act.

Koricic v. Beverly Enterprises Nebraska
Supreme Court of Nebraska
278 Neb. 713 (2009)

CONNOLLY, J.

The appellant, Frank Koricic (Frank), lived with his elderly mother, Manda Baker (Manda), and assisted her in her daily affairs. When her health declined, she was admitted to Beverly Hallmark, a nursing home in Omaha, Nebraska. At Manda's admission, Frank signed several documents for her. One of the documents was an optional arbitration agreement.

This appeal presents the issue whether Frank had authority to act as Manda's agent and to enter into the arbitration agreement for her. The district court determined that because Frank had actual authority to enter into the arbitration agreement, the agreement bound her estate. Although we agree that Frank had authority to sign the mandatory paperwork for admission, we conclude that Frank did not have authority to sign the arbitration agreement because it was not a condition of admission. We reverse the district court's order dismissing Frank's complaint.

Born in what is now Croatia in 1912, Manda immigrated to Omaha in 1958. She had a limited ability to read, speak, or understand English. Frank immigrated to Omaha in 1966 and lived with Manda for most of the following 40 years.

As Manda aged, Frank assisted her in managing her affairs. In 1998, when Manda's health started declining, Frank began signing medical authorizations for her. He testified that he signed only medical documents at the hospital and that Manda signed all other documents. Frank stated that he would explain documents to Manda and that if she wanted them signed, she would have Frank sign for her. Frank testified that he never signed anything without discussing it with Manda and that he never signed anything she did not agree with. Frank described their relationship as a collaborative effort, with him serving as Manda's advisor and interpreter. While he might offer advice, he took only the actions Manda directed him to take. Manda was never declared incompetent, and she never granted Frank power of attorney over her affairs.

In November 2005, Frank took Manda to Beverly Hallmark. It is undisputed that Manda was competent when she was admitted to Beverly Hallmark. Frank accompanied Manda during her admission, and after Frank placed her in her room, an employee of Beverly Hallmark took Frank to the office where he signed the paperwork for her admission. Manda was not present when Frank signed the admission papers, and Frank never discussed the content of the admission paperwork with her. Frank claimed that he did not read any of the paperwork and that the employee did not explain any of the documents.

One of the papers Frank signed was a "Resident and Facility Arbitration Agreement" that Beverly Hallmark presented to all residents upon admission. At the top of the agreement, it states that it is not a condition of admission. The agreement provides that "any and all claims, disputes, and controversies . . . arising out of, or in connection with, or relating in any way to the Admission Agreement or any service or health care provided by the Facility to the Resident shall be resolved exclusively by binding arbitration . . . ."

Before Manda died in September 2007, she allegedly sustained injuries and pain and suffering because of Beverly Hallmark's negligence. Frank, as Manda's next of kin and trustee of her estate, filed suit against Beverly Enterprises-Nebraska, Inc., formerly doing business as Beverly Hallmark; Beverly Health and Rehabilitation Services, Inc.; and Beverly Enterprises, Inc. (collectively Beverly Hallmark), alleging negligence, breach of contract, and breach of fiduciary duty. Beverly Hallmark moved to dismiss the case and to compel arbitration under the arbitration agreement. Frank argued that Beverly Hallmark could not enforce the arbitration agreement against Manda's estate because Frank, not Manda, had signed the arbitration agreement.

The district court concluded that the arbitration agreement was valid and enforceable against Manda's estate. Because Manda had authorized Frank to sign medical authorizations for her as early as 1998, the court concluded that Frank had actual authority to sign the arbitration agreement. And because all allegations, if true, would fall under the arbitration agreement, the district court dismissed the case without prejudice to arbitration.

Frank asserts that the trial court erred in determining (1) that Frank had authority as Manda's agent to sign the arbitration agreement for her and (2) that the agreement bound her estate.

Generally, whether an agency relationship exists presents a factual question. The scope of an agent's authority also is a question of fact. In a bench trial of a law action, the trial court's factual findings have the effect of a jury verdict and will not be disturbed on appeal unless clearly wrong.

Because arbitration is purely a matter of contract, we first determine whether an agreement to arbitrate exists under basic contract principles. Here, because Manda did not sign the arbitration agreement, we focus on whether Frank acted as Manda's agent with authority to enter into the arbitration agreement. So we begin with a discussion of agency law. Beverly Hallmark bears the burden of proving Frank's authority and that his acts were within the scope of his authority. Beverly Hallmark claims that Frank, as an agent, had actual authority to bind Manda to the arbitration agreement or, in the alternative, that he had apparent authority.

An "agent" is a person authorized by the principal to act on the principal's behalf and under the principal's control. For an agency relationship to arise, the principal "manifests assent" to the agent that the agent will "act on the principal's behalf and subject to the principal's control."[19] And the agent "manifests assent or otherwise consents so to act."[20] An agency relationship may be implied from the words and conduct of the parties and the circumstances of the case evidencing an intention to create the relationship irrespective of the words or terminology used by the parties to characterize or describe their relationship.

Actual authority is authority that the principal expressly grants to the agent or authority to which the principal consents. A subcategory of actual authority is implied authority, which courts typically use to denote actual authority either to (1) do what is necessary to accomplish the agent's express responsibilities or (2) act in a manner that the agent reasonably believes the principal wishes the agent to act, in light of the principal's objectives and manifestations. When a principal delegates authority to an agent to accomplish a task without specific directions, the grant of authority includes the agent's ability to exercise his or her discretion and make reasonable determinations concerning the details of how the agent will exercise that authority.

Frank signed medical documents for Manda under her instructions for 10 years. Frank and Manda discussed her health care treatment options, and she repeatedly consented to his signing for her. Frank testified that Manda expressly gave him permission to sign medical documents for her but that he never signed for her without her express permission. He testified that "when she was kind of more sick I was signing, you know, all the time in the hospital." Manda never objected to Frank's signing medical documents for her.

The record shows that in November 2005, Frank and Manda went to Beverly Hallmark to admit her to the nursing home. During his deposition, Frank recounted their conversation, stating that Manda understood she was being admitted to the nursing home and that Frank would take care of the necessary admission documents:

> [*Beverly Hallmark's counsel:*] Before you got to the nursing home, had you talked with [Manda] about the fact that you were going to take her there?
>
> [*Frank:*] **Yeah** . . . .

---

19. [7] Restatement (Third) of Agency § 1.01 at 17 (2006).

20. [8] *Id.*

. . .

Q. And she understood that you were going to meet with the office people?

A. **What everybody, whatever was going to be done, she trusts me. And I went over there and done the best I can.**

Q. You talked to her about that before you got there that day?

A. **Right.**

Q. She understood that, you know, whatever needed to be done in the office, you were going to do it for her?

A. **Right.**

Q. You talked about that with her?

A. **Together, again together, we agree together, we do it together.**

Based on Frank's testimony, Manda authorized Frank to sign the paperwork required for her admission to Beverly Hallmark.

But the arbitration agreement is another matter—Beverly Hallmark did not require it as a condition of Manda's admission. The agreement was optional and was not required for Manda to remain at the facility. We agree with the district court's finding that an agency relationship existed between Manda and Frank. We also agree that as Manda's agent, Manda authorized Frank to sign the required admission papers. But we conclude that his actual authority did not extend to signing an arbitration agreement that would waive Manda's right of access to the courts and to trial by jury. The district court's finding that Frank had actual authority to sign the arbitration agreement was clearly erroneous.

Having concluded that Frank's actual authority did not extend to signing the arbitration agreement, we now turn to Beverly Hallmark's contention that Frank had apparent authority to bind Manda to the arbitration agreement. Beverly Hallmark claims that because Manda allowed Frank to leave her room with an employee of Beverly Hallmark to sign the required admission papers, it reasonably believed that Frank had authority to sign the arbitration agreement.

Apparent authority is authority that is conferred when the principal affirmatively, intentionally, or by lack of ordinary care causes third persons to act upon an agent's apparent authority. Apparent authority gives an agent the power to affect the principal's legal relationships with third parties. The power arises from and is limited to the principal's manifestations to those third parties about the relationships. Stated another way, apparent authority for which a principle may be liable exists only when the third party's belief is traceable to the principal's manifestation and cannot be established by the agent's acts, declarations, or conduct. Manifestations include explicit statements the principal makes to a third party or statements made by others concerning an actor's authority that reach the third party and the third party can trace to the principal. For

apparent authority to exist, the principal must act in a way that induces a reasonable third person to believe that another person has authority to act for
him or her. Whether an agent has apparent authority to bind the principal is
a factual question determined from all the circumstances of the transaction.
Whether Beverly Hallmark can trace Frank's alleged authority to sign the arbitration agreement to Manda's actions and whether Beverly Hallmark reasonably relied upon Frank's actions in signing the arbitration agreement present
factual questions.

Here, Manda and Frank discussed her admission before she reached the
facility. Frank left with an employee of Beverly Hallmark to sign the admission
papers while Manda remained in her room. No evidence suggests that (1) Manda knew Frank would be asked to sign an arbitration agreement, (2) Manda
represented to a Beverly Hallmark employee that she authorized Frank to sign
the arbitration agreement, or (3) she later ratified the agreement. And we do
not believe that the Beverly Hallmark employee could reasonably believe that
Frank had authority to sign the arbitration agreement under these circumstances. Beverly Hallmark knew of Manda's limited ability to understand these
documents, or she would not have been asking her son Frank to sign them
for her. Nothing in the record suggests that a reasonable person should have
expected an arbitration agreement to be included with admission documents
for a nursing home. So Beverly Hallmark was not justified in relying solely on
Manda's authorization of Frank to sign admission papers as apparent authority
to bind her to an arbitration agreement. We conclude that these circumstances
preclude Beverly Hallmark from relying on the doctrine of apparent authority.

We reverse the trial court's order to dismiss Frank's complaint and remand
the cause for further proceedings.

Comprehension and Thought Questions:

1. What is the test to determine when someone is someone else's agent?
2. Was Frank Manda's agent? If so, how did Frank become Manda's agent?
3. What is the test to determine whether an agent has actual authority to
bind a principal?
4. Did Frank have authority to enter into the nursing home admissions contract on behalf of Manda? What about the arbitration agreement?
5. What is the test to determine whether an agent has the power to bind a
principal under apparent authority?
6. Why are Frank's statements made in his deposition not sufficient to create apparent authority to sign an arbitration agreement on behalf of Manda?
7. Manda was admitted to the nursing home and stayed there for many
months. Why is her stay not considered ratification of Frank's signing of the
arbitration agreement?

Hypothetical Variations:

1. What if, after Frank signed the arbitration agreement, Frank told Manda that he had signed and Manda never objected to that? *ratification*

2. What if Manda had told the nursing home staff in what appeared to be the only sentence she had memorized in English "Frank can sign all papers on my behalf for my admission"? *Still not clear*

3. What if the arbitration agreement had been a condition to Manda's admission? *binding, Frank had authority*

PRACTICE PROBLEM 9-3

Hoshi Fujita is the Vice President of Sales of Durable Glass Inc., a company that makes specialized, ultra-durable glass for commercial uses. As the Vice President of Sales, it is Hoshi's job to receive all orders placed by customers and decide which of those orders Durable Glass will fill. She then sends a written confirmation for those orders that Durable Glass will fill, showing Durable Glass's agreement to the order. If any order is unusual, Hoshi typically asks the President to approve before she sends a written confirmation.

Recently, Hoshi received a large order from The Garrett Group Inc., an existing customer, who needs glass for its latest hotel project. While this order is large, Durable Glass has received two similarly large orders before. In those instances, Hoshi handled all aspects of the sale. On the other hand, the order calls for Durable Glass to cut the ordered glass in unique shapes. To do so will require Durable Glass to purchase a specialized piece of glass-cutting equipment that costs around $500,000. It is because of the unique shapes of the ordered glass, and the need to buy a specialized piece of equipment to make those cuts, that Hoshi is a little hesitant to send a written confirmation.

Durable Glass's President is currently out of town, and Hoshi is not quite sure what to do. So she calls you, Durable Glass's outside counsel, with the following questions:

1. Does Hoshi have authority to accept The Garrett Group's latest order? *yes*

2. Does Hoshi have authority to purchase the specialized piece of glass-cutting equipment? *implied?*

3. If Hoshi does not have authority to fill The Garrett Group's order or to purchase the specialized piece of glass-cutting equipment, what are the consequences to her, and to Durable Glass, if Hoshi signs these contracts nonetheless? *Not binding unless "apparent authority"*

4. If Hoshi does not currently have authority to fill The Garrett Group's order or to purchase the specialized piece of glass-cutting equipment, how can Hoshi become authorized? *ask - get express authority*

c. Verifying authority

In significant, non-ordinary course transactions, the board of directors (or equivalent top governing body) must approve the transaction to give an agent actual authority to enter into the contract. In those transactions, typically each party insists on verifying the counterparty agent's authority by receiving (1) a certified copy of the board of directors' resolutions in which the board approved the contract and the agent's entry into the contract, as well as (2) representations and warranties within the contract about the authority of the party to enter into the contract and the board of directors' approval of the contract.

Recall back to the transaction described above, where Neil Voos, the Vice President of Sales of CompuSell, is proposing to sell 50 personal computers to CompuBuy. It is unlikely that this transaction is so significant to CompuSell that CompuSell's board of directors would need to approve that transaction. That is because the facts suggest that Neil has been negotiating that transaction on his own, as part of his ordinary duties.

However, assume that CompuSell is getting out of the business of selling personal computers to focus on its business computing segment, and therefore is selling all of its personal computing assets. In that case, CompuSell's board would likely need to approve the transaction, as it would likely be outside of the ordinary course of CompuSell's business.[21] In this example, not only would CompuBuy demand to see CompuSell board's approval of this transaction, but CompuBuy would also demand to receive the protection of representations and warranties about CompuSell's authority to enter into this contract. That way, if any of those representations and warranties were not true, CompuBuy would have a remedy.

The following are sample representations and warranties to this effect. Recall that you previously saw similar representations and warranties in Chapter 3, when you reviewed customary contract terms. These representations and warranties are included in virtually all contracts of significance involving business organizations. As you read them, keep in mind that the preamble to this contract would have already defined CompuSell as the "Seller" and CompuBuy as the "Buyer." Moreover, the preamble would have already defined the contract as this "Agreement." So this excerpt uses these terms without defining them. Following these representations and warranties is a sample certificate through which CompuBuy would verify that CompuSell's board approved the transaction.

Article 3   Seller's Representations and Warranties

The Seller represents and warrants to the Buyer as follows:

(1) The Seller has all corporate power and authority to enter into and perform this Agreement.

(2) The Seller's board of directors has approved of the Seller's entry into and performance of this Agreement, and no other corporate action is necessary

---

21. Corporate law statutes require board or shareholder approval depending on the significance and/or type of transaction.

> for the Seller to enter into and perform its obligations under this Agreement.
>
> (3) This Agreement is a binding obligation of the Seller, enforceable against the Seller in accordance with this Agreement's terms.[22]

Below is the instrument through which CompuBuy would verify that CompuSell's board approved the sale of its personal computer business, and that the board authorized the Vice President of Sales (currently Neil Voos) to sign the relevant documents. This instrument is titled "Secretary's Certificate" because the secretary of a business organization has the job of keeping and verifying corporate records. Thus, in this instrument, the secretary of CompuSell verifies the information CompuBuy has requested.

SECRETARY'S CERTIFICATE

The undersigned, the Secretary of CompuSell Inc., a Columbia corporation (the "Company"), certifies that she is familiar with the facts certified in this certificate and is duly authorized to certify the same, and further certifies, in connection with the Purchase Agreement dated as of August 20, 2019, between the Company and CompuBuy Inc., a Columbia corporation, as follows:

1. Exhibit 1 is a correct and complete copy of the resolutions duly adopted by the Company's Board of Directors; such resolutions have not been altered, amended, or rescinded and remain in full force and effect on the date of this certificate.

2. Since July 1, 2015, each of the below individuals has been the duly elected, qualified, and acting officer of the Company listed next to his respective name, and the following is each such officer's genuine signature:

Name:	Title:	Signature:
Michael Smith	President	_____
Neil Voos	Vice President of Sales	_____

IN WITNESS WHEREOF, the undersigned has executed this certificate as of this 20th day of August, 2019.

_____
Secretary

---

22. Note that this representation and warranty does not address authority—instead, it provides an assurance to the Buyer that each provision of the contract is enforceable against the Seller. However, it is included because it is typically included with the representations and warranties on authority.

Exhibit 1

Resolutions Adopted at a Meeting of the Board of Directors (the "Board") of CompuSell Inc., a Columbia corporation (the "Company") on August 10, 2019

WHEREAS, the Board deems it advisable and in the best interests of the Company to enter into a Purchase Agreement with CompuBuy Inc., a Columbia corporation (the "Buyer"), in the form presented to the Board (the "Agreement"), pursuant to which the Company will sell all of its personal computer assets to the Buyer (the "Transaction").

NOW, THEREFORE, BE IT RESOLVED, that the Board hereby authorizes and approves the Transaction; and be it further

RESOLVED, that the Purchase Agreement be, and hereby is, authorized and approved; and be it further

RESOLVED, that the Company be, and it hereby is, authorized, empowered and directed to enter into and perform its obligations under the Agreement and each document, certificate and instrument required by the Agreement or any other applicable laws in order to consummate the Transaction, including, without limitation, any bill of sale, security agreement, or assignment and assumption agreement (the "Transaction Documents"); and be it further

RESOLVED, that the President and Vice President of Sales of the Company (each, an "Officer") be, and each hereby is, authorized, empowered and directed to execute and deliver the Agreement and each of the Transaction Documents, in the name of and on behalf of the Company, with such terms, conditions, modifications and amendments as the Officer may reasonably determine in her discretion to be necessary or advisable, such determination to be conclusively evidenced by the Officer's execution, acknowledgment and/or delivery of the Agreement and the Transaction Documents; and be it further

RESOLVED, that each Officer be, and hereby is, authorized, empowered and directed on behalf of the Company to (i) finalize, make, enter into, execute, deliver, file and record any and all other documents and instruments, (ii) pay or cause to be paid any and all expenses and fees and disburse such other funds of the Company, and (iii) take any and all such other actions as the Officer may determine in her discretion to be necessary or advisable to effectuate the foregoing resolutions, the taking of any such action to be conclusive evidence of the exercise of such discretionary authority; and be it further

RESOLVED, that any and all actions taken by any officer, director, employee or agent of the Company prior to the date hereof in connection with, and consistent with, the foregoing resolutions, the taking of any such action to be conclusive evidence of the exercise of such authority, are hereby ratified, approved and confirmed in all respects.

As you may have noted, in the resolutions (so named since each action of approval starts with the archaic word "resolved") attached as Exhibit 1 to the Secretary's Certificate, CompuSell's board has authorized two officers to sign the relevant documents—the President and the Vice President of Sales. Typically, boards authorize several officers to sign documents in case one is not available. You will also note that the board has not named Neil Voos or CompuSell's current

President, Michael Smith, in the resolutions adopted by the board approving this transaction. That is because if something happens to Neil or Michael, the board wants whoever else is appointed to serve in their respective office positions to be able to sign the documents without having to redo the board resolutions.

PRACTICE PROBLEM 9-4

Refer back to Practice Problem 9-3. Assume Durable Glass's board of directors needs to approve Durable Glass's purchase of the specialized glass-cutting equipment needed to fill The Garrett Group's order. Hoshi went ahead and prepared the following resolutions for the board of directors to adopt at its upcoming meeting and has asked you to review them before the meeting. Review these resolutions and advise Hoshi whether you have any concerns about these resolutions, including as to their grant of authority to Hoshi to enter into the purchase contract with Incline Manufacturing Inc., the company who will be selling Durable Glass the specialized glass-cutting equipment.

> WHEREAS, the board of directors of Durable Glass Inc. (the "Company") has decided that it is in the Company's best interest for the Company to purchase specialized glass-cutting equipment (the "Equipment") from Incline Manufacturing Inc. (the "Seller") pursuant to a contract to be entered into with the Seller (the "Contract");
>
> NOW, THEREFORE, BE IT HEREBY RESOLVED, that the Company's purchase of the Equipment is hereby approved; and be it further
>
> RESOLVED, that the Contract is hereby approved.

[handwritten marginalia: "doesn't authorize anyone to do anything" and "do what's necessary to effectuate as approval" clause]

d. Which entity is bound?

Oftentimes, businesses operate through numerous affiliated business organizations. So, for example, CompuSell might be a corporate "parent" company that has several subsidiaries, each of which is owned either entirely or in part by the parent company. Companies use subsidiaries for many reasons, including to separate out separate lines of business or assets.

While the purpose of such organizational groups is beyond the scope of this course, for purposes of contracts, it is important to make sure you identify the correct organization or organizations that will be a party to a contract. This is true not only for the counterparty, but also for your client. Thus, if CompuSell housed its entire personal computing sales business within a subsidiary called CompuSell PC Inc., it would be CompuSell PC that would need to be a party to the asset purchase agreement with CompuBuy, and not parent company CompuSell (note that the letters "PC" might be the only difference between these legal companies.). The following is a diagramed representation of the client's organizational structure. It is often useful to create a diagram like this for your client, if they have not already created one, so you can keep the different business organizations straight for contracting and other purposes.

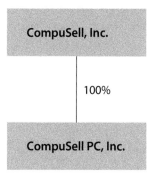

PRACTICE PROBLEM 9-5

Continuing with Practice Problem 9-4, assume that Durable Glass has a subsidiary called Durable Glass Custom Inc. through which Durable Glass conducts all highly customized glass manufacturing projects. Durable Glass created a separate subsidiary for this customized work because it helps Durable Glass separately account for the expenses and revenue of customized project.

Because The Garrett Group's order calls for specialized glass shapes, the order will be accepted by Durable Glass Custom Inc. Moreover, Durable Glass Custom Inc. will be purchasing the specialized glass-cutting equipment from Incline Manufacturing Inc. All of the officers of Durable Glass are the same as for Durable Glass Custom Inc.

The following is the signature page to the contract between Durable Glass Custom and Incline Manufacturing. Do you have any concerns with this signature page?

In Witness Whereof, the parties have executed and delivered this Agreement as of the date first written above.

Durable Glass Inc. & Durable Glass Custom Inc.
By: _____.
Name: Hoshi Fujita,
Title: Vice President

Incline Manufacturing Inc.

By: _____
Name: _____
Title: _____

Now that you have studied the lawyer's role in contracting, read through and answer the questions that follow the Simulation Problem for Chapter 9, which is located in Appendix A.

CHAPTER 10

Pre-Bargain Diligence and Documentation

Although you have already studied the elements for contract formation, the reality is that with negotiated contracts—meaning, contracts that are negotiated by the parties, usually with the assistance of counsel—parties often undertake many steps *before* manifesting assent to a contract. Those steps are designed, first, to help each party figure out if it is even on the same page as the other party as to the essential terms of the potential transaction to be reflected in the contract. Second, those steps are undertaken to find out more information so that the party can better understand the risks it faces in consummating a transaction with the other party.

In significant transactions, the parties may take their first steps during what is called the **term sheet stage**. During that stage, the parties negotiate the important terms of the potential transaction to see if they agree on those terms. If they do, the parties often memorialize the terms they agree on in a writing such as a term sheet. They do this because there is no sense in negotiating all of the terms of a proposed transaction—especially one that is complex and would require significant effort and multiple contracts to document—if the parties can not even agree on the most important terms. There are other reasons, too, for parties to prepare a written term sheet. The term sheet stage is discussed below in Section B.

Another significant pre-formation process is referred to as the **due diligence stage**, and is discussed below in Section C. As you will see, during the due diligence stage, each party obtains information relevant to the potential transaction. Armed with that information, the party can decide whether it wants to enter into a transaction with the other party. If so, the party can use the information it acquires during due diligence to decide how best to protect its interests in the transaction.

Often in connection with the due diligence process, parties enter into a confidentiality agreement. That agreement ensures that each party maintains the confidentiality of information provided to it by the other party during the due diligence process. Those agreements are discussed in Section D.

Keep in mind that there may be other steps parties take pre-contract as well, depending on the party and the potential transaction being explored. For example, often a party retains advisors such as a lawyer, a financial advisor, and an accountant, or any combination thereof, to help it decide whether to pursue a transaction in the first place. This chapter, however, focuses on the pre-contract steps a client takes with the assistance of lawyers. In simple transactions and many consumer transactions, none or very few of these pre-contract steps will be taken.

A. SAMPLE PRE-BARGAIN PROCESS

Before we discuss pre-contract stages in more detail, it is useful to describe the pre-contract formation process for a simulated transaction. This simulation will hopefully give you a narrative of how the parties act as the important business terms are negotiated, and as due diligence is performed. This simulation should also give you a sense for how information gathered during due diligence can impact the business terms.

In this simulated transaction, U.S. Crane Co. ("Crane Co"), a large U.S.-based company that manufactures and sells industrial cranes, is proposing to buy Crane Supply Inc.'s business. Crane Supply Inc. ("Supply") is a company that supplies Crane Co. with certain components Crane Co. uses to manufacture its cranes. For this description and to help you keep the parties straight, Crane Co. is referred to as "Manufacturer" and Supply is referred to as "Supplier."

> At a meeting of the board of directors of Manufacturer, Jack Blane, the President of Manufacturer, recommends that Manufacturer explore a potential acquisition of Supplier. Blane recommends this acquisition because he believes Manufacturer can more cost-effectively manufacture its cranes if it has total control over the manufacturing of the crane components supplied by Supplier. Manufacturer's Chief Financial Officer presents his estimate of how much he believes it will cost Manufacturer to acquire Supplier, as well as his estimate of how much Manufacturer will save by acquiring Supplier. Based on these estimates, the Chief Financial Officer estimates that Supplier is worth somewhere between $12 million and $15 million. At a purchase price of greater than $15 million, the transaction is no longer financially beneficial to Manufacturer. After this presentation and a long discussion, the board of directors of Manufacturer authorizes Blane to explore this acquisition, subject to Manufacturer not paying more than $15 million.

Blane then sets up a meeting with Marie Shaw, the President of Supplier, to discuss a potential acquisition. During that meeting, Blane explains why Manufacturer is interested in buying Supplier. He says based on the information he has about Supplier, Manufacturer would be willing to pay around $10 million for Supplier, assuming no major concerns turn up during Manufacturer's due diligence investigation of Supplier and its business operations. Blane also explains the benefits of the transaction to Supplier: Supplier will have a captive buyer for its crane components, which means Supplier's operations and employees will largely remain intact. In addition, Supplier's owners will be handsomely paid in exchange for their ownership interests in Supplier. Shaw says she will discuss this potential transaction with Supplier's board of directors.

A week later, Supplier's board of directors authorize Shaw to explore a potential sale to Manufacturer, but only if the price is at least $12 million, with a goal of getting $15 million. Shaw then communicates to Blane that Supplier is interested in the transaction, at a price of $15 million. After extensive discussions and the preparation of many estimates of how much Supplier is worth, Shaw and Blane settle on a purchase price of $13 million. This price assumes that no major concerns turn up during due diligence.

Seller Counsel LP, the law firm representing Supplier, then sends to Buyer Counsel LP, Manufacturer's lawyers, a Confidentiality Agreement to make sure the information Supplier will be supplying to Manufacturer during due diligence will be kept in confidence. After brief negotiations, the parties enter into this agreement.

Next, Buyer Counsel LP sends to Seller Counsel LP a due diligence checklist listing out all of the documents Manufacturer wishes to review during due diligence. Supplier works with Seller Counsel LP to collect all of the documents on that checklist, to organize them, and to make them available to Manufacturer and Buyer Counsel LP. Manufacturer's team reviews the due diligence documents as they are provided. In addition, Blane and others at Manufacturer meet with Shaw and other key officers at Supplier to discuss Supplier's financial condition, business operations, business prospects for the future, and other relevant information.

While due diligence is ongoing, Blane and Shaw meet to discuss other important transaction terms. They discuss terms such as when the sale would occur and which Supplier functions and employees positions might no longer be needed after the sale. As they discuss and agree on these important terms, the parties write up those terms in a document that they label "Term Sheet." Once they agree on the important terms, and those terms are reflected in the written term sheet, both parties have their respective legal counsel review the term sheet. Following this review, Blane and Shaw sign the term sheet. Per Buyer Counsel LP's request, the term sheet specifically says that it is not binding, and that neither party will be bound until they enter into a definitive written purchase agreement.

Three weeks later, due diligence is complete. During due diligence, Buyer Counsel LP discovers that Supplier is a defendant in a lawsuit filed by Nuts and Bolts Inc. and is potentially liable to Nuts and Bolts Inc. for up to $1 million.

The lawsuit is expected to be resolved in the next few months. Buyer Counsel LP flags this risk for Blane and Manufacturer's board of directors. Blane negotiates with Shaw to have $1 million of the purchase price held back—meaning, not paid at closing—until this case is resolved. If Supplier is liable to Nuts and Bolts Inc., then the hold-back amount will be used to pay that liability. If not, or if Supplier is not liable for the full $1 million, then any unused portion of the hold-back amount will be paid to Supplier once the lawsuit is resolved. Shaw agrees to this revision to the purchase price.

B. TERM SHEETS

1. What Is a Term Sheet? Sample Term Sheet

Term sheets go by many different names. Sometimes they are called letters of intent when they are structured as letters. Sometimes they are called memorandums of understanding when written as memoranda. Whatever they are called and however they are structured, they lay out the terms of a proposed transaction that the parties feel are important to agree on up front, before formal written documents, many of which are contracts, are prepared.

The following is a sample term sheet. It reflects sample terms for Manufacturer's acquisition of Supplier, per the pre-bargain process described in Section A. Remember that per that narrative, Manufacturer only learned about Supplier's possible $1 million liability stemming from a lawsuit after the parties had agreed on the term sheet. Thus, the below term sheet does not reflect the price adjustment the parties agreed to upon Manufacturer learning of this potential liability. This term, however, would clearly be reflected in the definitive purchase agreement.

ASSET PURCHASE TERM SHEET

The purpose of this term sheet is to set out the terms for the proposed purchase by U.S. Crane Co. ("Manufacturer") of all of the assets of Crane Supply Inc. ("Supplier").

1. <u>Assets to be sold</u>: Manufacturer would buy all of Supplier's assets, free and clear of all liens. The Assets to be sold include all of the following owned or used by Seller in its business:

   a. Furniture and fixtures.
   b. Machinery and equipment.
   c. Inventory and works-in-progress.
   d. Supplies.
   e. Rights under contracts, including under property and equipment leases.
   f. Trademarks, copyrights, patents, and other intangible assets.
   g. Cash and cash equivalents.
   h. Accounts and notes receivable.

---

2. <u>Purchase Price</u>: Manufacturer would pay Supplier $13 million by wire transfer of immediately available funds on the Closing Date.

3. <u>Assumption of Liabilities</u>: Manufacturer would assume Supplier's obligations and liabilities under Suppliers contracts. Manufacturer would not assume any other of Supplier's obligations or liabilities.

4. <u>Closing Date</u>: The transaction described by this term sheet would occur on October 31, 2019.

5. <u>Exclusivity</u>: As long as Supplier and Manufacturer are actively negotiating the terms of an acquisition by Manufacturer of Supplier's assets, and for a period of 60 days thereafter, Supplier shall not negotiate with any third party for the sale of its assets.

6. <u>Term Sheet Not Binding</u>: Other than Section 5 and Section 6, which are binding on the parties, this term sheet does not create legally binding obligations of the parties. Neither party will be legally bound to consummate a transaction of the nature described in this term sheet unless and until both parties sign and deliver a definitive asset purchase agreement reflecting the terms in this term sheet along with other terms and conditions on which the parties agree and which are customary for transactions of the type this term sheet contemplates. Until that time, either party may discontinue or withdraw from negotiations without incurring any legally binding obligations.

U.S. Crane Co.

<u>//Jack Blane//</u>
Jack Blane, President
Date:

Crane Supply Inc.

<u>//Marie Shaw//</u>
Marie Shaw, President
Date:

2. Purposes for Term Sheets

Term sheets serve many purposes. First, term sheets allow parties to determine whether they agree on terms important to the parties before documenting the transaction in formal contracts and other related documents. With complex transactions and legal counsel involved to protect their clients' interests, those documents might take up hundreds of pages. Often a client does not want its lawyers to draft or review those documents without at least knowing it agrees with the counterparty in principle on the important terms. To save time and other resources, parties ensure they agree on the important terms first, by reflecting those agreed-upon terms in a term sheet. If they do, the parties can then task their lawyers with preparing the formal transaction documents. It also helps build trust between the parties as they negotiate the basic terms of the transaction. This relational role of contract negotiation is discussed in more depth in Chapter 11. It was also discussed in Chapter 1 with respect to the reasons parties enter into contracts, though that discussion contemplated a more regular, ongoing business relationship where parties may opt for less specificity in their contract.

In addition, term sheets help parties track their negotiation progress. Where parties negotiate transaction terms, it is often useful for them to list out all the terms on which the parties agree in a single place. By cataloging the terms on which the parties agree, the parties can keep track of their progress, as well as identify the terms they still need to negotiate.

Term sheets may also help set parameters for how the parties will act during final negotiations. For example, as is reflected in Section 5 of the above term sheet, the parties might agree in a term sheet that a seller will not seek a better deal than the one currently offered by the buyer for some agreed-upon period of time. This type of term is known as an "exclusivity" provision because it requires the parties to exclusively deal with one another in pursuing a potential transaction for an agreed-upon period of time. Sometimes the parties set forth confidentiality obligations in term sheets as well, which ensure that the parties' confidential information, or possibly the proposed terms of the transaction, are not disclosed to third parties. As discussed below, these sorts of "rules of negotiations" are usually binding, even if the rest of the term sheet is not. Transactional attorneys help clients sort through which term sheet provisions should be binding and which should not, and ensure that the term sheet reflects that intent.

Term sheets also help the drafter of the formal documents—as well as the people who review those documents—ensure that those documents reflect the terms agreed on by the parties. Thus, it serves as a checklist for the draftsperson and reviewers to use to ensure the final, definitive documents reflect the agreed-upon transaction terms.

While term sheets have great utility, they also have potential downsides. One is that they potentially bind the parties where one of the parties did not intend for that to be the case. That concern is addressed below, in connection with discussion of the *Quake* case. Another concern is that term sheets can take significant time and resources to negotiate—time and resources that could potentially be better spent negotiating the final definitive transaction documents. Finally, term sheets might lead parties to agree on transaction terms too soon, before due diligence is completed and all information about potential risks of the transaction is exposed. In that circumstance, the existence of a term sheet might prevent a party from obtaining protections it would have otherwise bargained for had it not agreed to a term sheet, for fear of being seen as someone who "re-trades" the deal and goes back on his or her word.

PRACTICE PROBLEM 10-1

Jasmine Chen currently works as a finance manager. She was recently approached by Natgo Food Source Inc., a national food distributor, to become Natgo's Chief Financial Officer (CFO). In Jasmine's first few conversations with Bryce Williams, Natgo's President, she learned what her position and duties would be as Natgo's CFO. She was also told that her annual salary would be in the range of between $250,000 and $270,000 and that she would receive other standard benefits that Natgo provides its other officers, such as health insurance and vacation time. Jasmine would also be bound by a non-compete. In that conversation, Jasmine indicated that she would only consider working for Natgo if she received job security for a minimum of two years. Bryce indicated that was acceptable.

In Jasmine's latest conversation with Bryce, Bryce asked Jasmine if she wants Natgo to prepare a term sheet to reflect the proposed terms of Jasmine's employment, or if Natgo should go ahead and ask its lawyer to draft Jasmine's employment agreement. Uncertain how to respond, Jasmine has come to you for your advice. Namely, she wants to know whether or not she should ask Natgo to prepare a term sheet to reflect the proposed terms of her employment before it tasks its lawyer with preparing a draft of Jasmine's employment agreement. In your advice, make sure you explain to Jasmine what a term sheet is and what purposes its serves, in addition to advising Jasmine whether she should have Natgo prepare a term sheet.

3. Binding vs. Nonbinding

As the above discussion explains, term sheets are tools to help parties arrive at agreement on important transaction terms. Their purpose is usually not to serve as the final, definitive document creating enforceable obligations relating to the transaction whose terms are set out in the term sheet.

Occasionally, however, parties intend to be bound by the term sheet to consummate the transaction. Usually where that occurs, the formal documents are seen by the parties as largely perfunctory, serving only to formalize the existing contractual relationship between the parties. In that case, the parties are bound by the term sheet pending preparation of those formal documents, so long as the term sheet meets the requirements of a contract. Thus, in addition to manifesting their assent to the term sheet, the term sheet must set out the parties' respective promises with sufficient clarity that a court could enforce them if breached.

More commonly, parties do not intend the term sheet to bind them to consummate the transaction described in the term sheet, but do intend to be bound by specific provisions of the term sheet. The specific provisions to which they usually intend to be bound are those that set parameters for how the parties will act as they negotiate the remaining terms of the proposed transaction. Common term sheet provisions that set out parameters for how parties will deal with one another, and that parties intend to be binding, include provisions providing for exclusivity in negotiations; provisions obligating the parties to negotiate terms of the final, definitive documents in good faith; provisions obligating a party to provide access to its properties, personnel, and records to the other in furtherance of the other party's due diligence; and provisions obligating the party receiving information and documents to maintain the confidentiality of the information and documents disclosed.

To express the parties' intent to be bound to these specific provisions, usually a term sheet will expressly identify the provisions to which the parties intend to be bound. You can see such language in Section 6 of the above term sheet. There, while the language disclaims an intent to be bound by the term sheet for the underlying transaction, which is the asset sale, it expressly acknowledges that the parties intend to be bound by Section 5 on exclusivity in negotiations.

To be clear, the fact that the parties are bound by a specific provision of the term sheet does not mean they are bound to consummate the underlying transaction. Thus, in the above example, Supplier has a duty to deal exclusively with Manufacturer while the parties are actively negotiating an asset sale, and for 60 days thereafter. That duty does not, however, obligate Supplier to sell its assets to Manufacturer.

Section 6 of the above term sheet also makes this intent clear. Specifically, it states that except for Section 5, to which the parties are bound, "this term sheet does not create legally binding obligations of the parties." Thus, it specifically negates an intent to be bound apart from the single provision on exclusivity in negotiations (and Section 6 itself). Section 6 goes even further, identifying the actions that the parties intend to manifest their assent—signing and delivering a definitive asset purchase agreement.

Sometimes term sheets are not clear as to the parties' intent to be bound. To help guide this analysis, the Restatement lists the following factors to determine whether a term sheet is binding on the parties:

1) the extent to which express agreement has been reached on all the terms to be included,
2) whether the contract is of a type usually put in writing,
3) whether it needs a formal writing for its full expression,
4) whether it has few or many details,
5) whether the amount involved is large or small,
6) whether it is a common or unusual contract,
7) whether a standard form of contract is widely used in similar transactions, and

8) whether either party takes any action in preparation for performance during the negotiations.[1]

As this list suggests, while the label "term sheet" is a factor in deciding the parties' intent to be bound, it is not conclusive of the parties' manifested intent.[2]

The following case demonstrates how a court will resolve an inquiry into the parties' intent to be bound to a preliminary writing that was ambiguous as to the parties' intent in a real-life situation. In this case, Quake Construction, Inc. is the disappointed party—that is, the party who thought there was a contract even though the parties only had a preliminary writing (in this case, a "letter of intent") and contemplated formalizing the terms of the contract in a final writing. As you read this case, try to identify the key arguments Quake makes for this letter of intent to be an offer, as well as American Airlines and Jones Brothers Construction Corporation's argument that the letter of intent was not an offer. Whose arguments did the majority find persuasive? What about the dissent? Whose argument do you find persuasive?

Quake Construction, Inc. v. American Airlines, Inc.
Supreme Court of Illinois
141 Ill.2d 281 (1990)

Justice CALVO delivered the opinion of the court:

Plaintiff, Quake Construction, Inc. (Quake), filed a four-count, third-amended complaint against defendants, American Airlines, Inc. (American), and Jones Brothers Construction Corporation (Jones). In count I, plaintiff sought damages for breach of contract. Plaintiff based counts II, III and IV on detrimental reliance, waiver of condition precedent, and impossibility of contract, respectively. Upon defendants' motion, the circuit court of Cook County dismissed the complaint with prejudice, pursuant to section 2-615 of the Illinois Code of Civil Procedure. On appeal, the Appellate Court, First District, with one justice dissenting, reversed the dismissal of counts I, II and III, affirmed the dismissal of count IV, and remanded the cause to the circuit court. We granted defendants' petition for leave to appeal.

Quake alleged in its complaint the following facts. In February 1985, American hired Jones to prepare bid specifications, accept bids, and award contracts for construction of the expansion of American's facilities at O'Hare International Airport. Quake received an invitation to bid on the employee facilities and automotive maintenance shop project (hereinafter referred to as the project), and in April 1985 submitted its bid to Jones. Jones orally notified Quake that

---

1. Restatement (Second) of Contracts § 27 cmt. c (1981).

2. *See* Teachers Ins. & Annuity Ass'n of Am. v. Tribune Co., 670 F. Supp. 491, 497 (S.D.N.Y. 1987) ("Labels such as 'letter of intent' or 'commitment letter' are not necessarily controlling although they may be helpful indicators of the parties' intentions. . . .").

Quake had been awarded the contract for the project. Jones then asked Quake to provide the license numbers of the subcontractors Quake intended to use on the project. Quake notified Jones that the subcontractors would not allow Quake to use their license numbers until Quake submitted a signed subcontract agreement to them. Jones informed Quake that Quake would shortly receive a written contract for the project prepared by Jones. To induce Quake to enter into agreements with its subcontractors and to induce the subcontractors to provide Quake and Jones with their license numbers, Jones sent Quake the following letter of intent dated April 18, 1985:

> "We have elected to award the contract for the subject project to your firm as we discussed on April 15, 1985. A contract agreement outlining the detailed terms and conditions is being prepared and will be available for your signature shortly.
>
> Your scope of work as the general contractor includes the complete installation of expanded lunchroom, restroom and locker facilities for American Airlines employees as well as an expansion of AmericanAirlines existing Automotive Maintenance Shop. The project is located on the lower level of 'K' Concourse. A sixty (60) calendar day period shall be allowed for the construction of the locker room, lunchroom and restroom area beginning the week of April 22, 1985. The entire project shall be complete by August 15, 1985.
>
> Subject to negotiated modifications for exterior hollow metal doors and interior ceramic floor tile material as discussed, this notice of award authorizes the work set forth in the following documents at a lump sum price of $1,060,568.00.
>
> a) Jones Brothers Invitation to Bid dated March 19, 1985.
> b) Specifications as listed in the Invitation to Bid.
> c) Drawings as listed in the Invitation to Bid.
> d) Bid Addendum # 1 dated March 29, 1985.
>
> Quake Construction Inc. shall provide evidence of liability insurance in the amount of $5,000,000 umbrella coverage and 100% performance and payment bond to Jones Brothers Construction Corporation before commencement of the work. The contract shall include MBE, WBE and EEO goals as established by your bid proposal. Accomplishment of the City of Chicago's residency goals as cited in the Invitation to Bid is also required. As agreed, certificates of commitment from those MBE firms designated on your proposal modification submitted April 13, 1985, shall be provided to Jones Brothers Construction Corporation.
>
> Jones Brothers Construction Corporation reserves the right to cancel this letter of intent if the parties cannot agree on a fully executed subcontract agreement."

Jones and Quake thereafter discussed and orally agreed to certain changes in the written form contract. Handwritten delineations were made to the form contract by Jones and Quake to reflect these changes. Jones advised Quake it would prepare and send the written contract to Quake for Quake's signature. No such formal written contract, however, was entered into by the parties.

At a preconstruction meeting on April 25, 1985, Jones told Quake, Quake's subcontractors, and governmental officials present that Quake was the general contractor for the project. On that same date, immediately after the meeting, American informed Quake that Quake's involvement with the project was terminated. Jones confirmed Quake's termination by a letter dated April 25, 1985. The damages Quake allegedly suffered included the money it spent in procuring the contract and preparing to perform under the contract, and its loss of anticipated profit from the contract.

The main issue is whether the letter of intent from Jones to Quake is an enforceable contract such that a cause of action may be brought by Quake. This court has previously set forth the principles of law concerning the enforceability of letters of intent:

> "The fact that parties contemplate that a formal agreement will eventually be executed does not necessarily render prior agreements mere negotiations, where it is clear that the ultimate contract will be substantially based upon the same terms as the previous document. [Citation.] If the parties * * * intended that the * * * document be contractually binding, that intention would not be defeated by the mere recitation in the writing that a more formal agreement was yet to be drawn. However, parties may specifically provide that negotiations are not binding until a formal agreement is in fact executed. [Citation.] If the parties construe the execution of a formal agreement as a condition precedent, then no contract arises unless and until that formal agreement is executed." Chicago Investment Corp. v. Dolins (1985), 107 Ill.2d 120, 126–27, 89 Ill.Dec. 869, 481 N.E.2d 712.

The Chicago court merely reiterated the rule established over 85 years ago:

> "'Where the parties make the reduction of the agreement to writing, and its signature by them, a condition precedent to its completion, it will not be a contract until that is done. And this is true although all the terms of the contract have been agreed upon. But where the parties have assented to all the terms of the contract, the mere reference to a future contract in writing will not negative the existence of a present contract.'" (Baltimore & Ohio Southwestern R.R. Co. v. People ex rel. Allen (1902), 195 Ill. 423, 428, 63 N.E. 262, quoting 7 Am. & Eng. Enc. L. 140 (2d ed. 1898).)

Thus, although letters of intent may be enforceable, such letters are not necessarily enforceable unless the parties intend them to be contractually binding.

A circuit court must initially determine, as a question of law, whether the language of a purported contract is ambiguous as to the parties' intent. If no ambiguity exists in the writing, the parties' intent must be derived by the circuit court, as a matter of law, solely from the writing itself. If the terms of an alleged contract are ambiguous or capable of more than one interpretation, however, parol evidence is admissible to ascertain the parties' intent. If the language of an alleged contract is ambiguous regarding the parties' intent, the interpretation of the language is a question of fact which a circuit court cannot properly determine on a motion to dismiss.

In determining whether the parties intended to reduce their agreement to writing, the following factors may be considered: whether the type of agreement involved is one usually put into writing, whether the agreement contains many or few details, whether the agreement involves a large or small amount of money, whether the agreement requires a formal writing for the full expression of the covenants, and whether the negotiations indicated that a formal written document was contemplated at the completion of the negotiations. Other factors which may be considered are: "where in the negotiating process that process is abandoned, the reasons it is abandoned, the extent of the assurances previously given by the party which now disclaims any contract, and the other party's reliance upon the anticipated completed transaction." A/S Apothekernes Laboratorium for Specialpraeparater v. I.M.C. Chemical Group, Inc. (N.D. Ill. 1988), 678 F. Supp. 193, 196, aff'd (7th Cir. 1989), 873 F.2d 155.

. . .

The circuit court in the case at bar dismissed Quake's complaint, relying principally on the following sentence in the letter: "Jones Brothers Construction Corporation reserves the right to cancel this letter of intent if the parties cannot agree on a fully executed subcontract agreement" (hereinafter referred to as the cancellation clause). The parties agreed during oral arguments that the subcontract agreement referred to in the cancellation clause concerned an agreement between Jones and Quake. Jones was the general contractor for the entire expansion project. Jones hired Quake as a subcontractor to handle only the work on the employee facilities and automotive shop. Quake, in turn, hired subcontractors to perform this work. The circuit court determined, based on the cancellation clause, that the parties agreed not to be bound until they entered into a formal written contract. Consequently, the circuit court held that the letter was not an enforceable contract and accordingly dismissed the complaint.

The appellate court, however, found the letter ambiguous.

. . .

We agree with the appellate court majority's analysis and its conclusion that the letter was ambiguous. Consequently, we affirm the decision of the appellate court. The letter of intent included detailed terms of the parties' agreement. The letter stated that Jones awarded the contract for the project to Quake. The letter stated further "this notice of award authorizes the work." Moreover, the letter indicated the work was to commence approximately 4 to 11 days after the letter was written. This short period of time reveals the parties' intent to be bound by the letter so the work could begin on schedule. We also agree with the appellate court that the cancellation clause exhibited the parties' intent to be bound by the letter because no need would exist to provide for the cancellation of the letter unless the letter had some binding effect. The cancellation clause also implied the parties' intention to be bound by the letter at least until they entered into the formal contract. We agree with the appellate court that all of these factors evinced the parties' intent to be bound by the letter.

On the other hand, the letter referred several times to the execution of a formal contract by the parties, thus indicating the parties' intent not to be bound by the letter. The cancellation clause could be interpreted to mean that the parties did not intend to be bound until they entered into a formal agreement. Therefore, the appellate court correctly concluded that the letter was ambiguous regarding the parties' intent to be bound by it.

Defendants contend the letter of intent did not contain all of the terms necessary for the formation of a construction contract. Defendants assert construction contracts typically include terms regarding payment, damages and termination. Defendants argue the detail in the contract is usually extensive if the value and complexity of the construction project are great. Defendants also note the letter stated the contract would include the detailed terms and conditions of the parties' agreement. The letter indicated the contract would include the MBE, WBE and EEO (Minority Business Enterprise, Women's Business Enterprise, and Equal Employment Opportunity, respectively) goals established by Quake's bid proposal. Defendants point out the letter stated certain terms of the agreement still had to be negotiated. Without the formal contract, defendants assert, the parties could not have continued toward the completion of the project because the letter excluded many terms of the agreement which would have been included in the contract. Defendants thus argue the absence in the letter of all the terms of the agreement reveals the parties' intent not to be bound by the letter.

The appellate court stated the number and extent of the terms in the letter can indicate the parties' intent to be bound by the letter. The final contract only need be substantially based on the terms in the letter as long as the parties intended the letter to be binding. Many of the details regarding the project were included in the letter. The letter adopted by reference the contents of certain documents which included even further details concerning the project. We agree Jones accepted the MBE, WBE and EEO goals established by Quake. The letter merely indicated that those goals would be reiterated in the contract. We acknowledge that the absence of certain terms in the letter indicates the parties' intent not to be bound by the letter. This only confirms our holding that the letter is ambiguous as to the parties' intent.

. . .

Defendants contend even if the letter contained all of the essential terms of a contract, the cancellation clause negated any inference that the parties intended to be bound by the letter. The clause, according to defendants, clearly established the parties' intent not to be so bound. Defendants argue the letter only sets forth the provisions which would be included in the contract if one is ever executed. Defendants point out both the circuit court and the appellate court dissent found the cancellation clause unambiguously declared the parties' intent not to be bound until the parties entered into a formal contract.

We do not find defendants' argument persuasive. The appellate court stated that, in addition to the detailed terms of the parties' agreement, the letter also contained a sentence in which Jones said it awarded the contract for the project to Quake. Moreover, the letter stated "this notice of award *authorizes* the work." (Emphasis added.) Furthermore, the appellate court pointed out, the letter was dated April 18, while at the same time the letter indicated that Quake was to begin work the week of April 22 and complete the work by August 15. We agree with the appellate court's conclusion that a "reasonable inference from these facts is that the parties intended that work on the Project would begin prior to execution of a formal contract and would be governed by the terms of the 'Letter of Intent.'" All of these factors indicate the negotiations were more than merely preliminary and the parties intended the letter to be binding. The factors muddle whatever otherwise "clear" intent may be derived from the cancellation clause.

. . .

Defendants allege that the appellate court's decision puts the continued viability of letters of intent at risk. Defendants contend if we uphold the appellate court's decision finding the cancellation clause ambiguous, negotiating parties will have difficulty finding limiting language which a court would unquestionably consider unambiguous. We disagree. Courts have found letters of intent unambiguous in several cases referred to in this opinion. Thus, the existence or absence of particular language or words will not ensure that a letter of intent is unambiguous. Our decision here follows the settled law in Illinois concerning letters of intent: The intent of the parties is controlling.

Neither we nor the appellate court have decided whether in fact a contract exists, that is, whether the parties intended to be bound by the letter. We merely hold that the parties' intent, based on the letter alone, is ambiguous. Therefore, upon remand, the circuit court must allow the parties to present other evidence of their intent. The trier of fact should then determine, based on the evidence and the letter, whether the parties intended to be bound by the letter.

. . .

[The court then upheld the appellate court's reversal of the circuit court's dismissal of counts II and III, and affirmed the appellate court's decision as to count IV, which plaintiff waived on appeal.]

For the foregoing reasons, we affirm the decision of the appellate court.

Affirmed.

Justice STAMOS, specially concurring:

Because dismissal is unwarranted unless clearly no set of facts can be proved under the pleadings that will entitle a plaintiff to recover, I agree with the majority that the circuit court should not have dismissed counts I through III of Quake's complaint. I also agree with the majority that Quake has waived the issue of dismissing count IV. Thus, I concur in the judgment.

However, even though the Jones letter of intent is just ambiguous enough for Quake's complaint to survive a motion to dismiss, I consider that any interpretation of the letter's language as potentially establishing an underlying construction contract is far less plausible than the majority implies. It would be unfortunate if the court's affirmance and remand were construed as encouraging, on the basis of the letter's barely ambiguous text, any ultimate factual finding of intent to be bound to an underlying contract. Moreover, the misuse of letters of intent by parties seemingly wishing to have their contractual cake and eat it too, or wishing merely to fudge the contract issue, ought to evoke judicial disapproval. Therefore, I write separately.

. . .

I am especially troubled by the majority's apparent view that, in regard to a construction contract, the letter's cancellation clause equally bespeaks an intent to be bound and an intent not to be bound. The parties are said to have had "no need to provide for its cancellation" if they did not intend to be bound by the letter, and the clause itself is said to imply that the parties could be bound by the letter if no "fully executed subcontract agreement" resulted. This view of the cancellation clause seems to turn it on its head and to pervert any legitimate office of letters of intent.

Instead of weighing as heavily for as against a construction contract, in my judgment the cancellation clause powerfully militates against any finding of such contract. The very language of the clause treats such a contract ("a fully executed subcontract agreement") as future possibility rather than present reality. Yet the majority would allow transmuting this prospective bargain into current obligation, by confusing a hoped-for construction contract with a cancellable preliminary expression of intent. Much as word is a shadow of deed, or wish may be father to thought, a letter of intent may lead to a contract, but it is not necessarily the contract itself.

The cancellation clause refers expressly to cancelling the letter, not to cancelling the construction contract that the letter anticipates. A construction contract certainly would bind the parties to that contract's terms, but upon acceptance by Quake the letter here would much more plausibly be viewed as, at most, only binding the parties to efforts at achieving a construction contract on the terms outlined.

. . .

Hence, the letter itself, as distinguished from the anticipated construction contract, may be regarded as a contract in its own right: a contract to engage in negotiations. If so, it was this contract, not the anticipated construction contract, that might be cancelled by Jones pursuant to the cancellation clause.

Indeed, the notion of cancelling a construction contract not yet entered into lacks meaning.

. . .

If letters of intent are to be used, their drafters would be well advised to avoid ambiguity on the point of whether the issuers are bound. As ever, obscurantist language can produce desired practical effects in the short term, but can well lead eventually to litigation and undesired contractual obligations. Extreme examples exist. Some counsel and clients may opt for ambiguity on grounds of expediency and may account for the probability of resultant litigation costs in the clients' overall business decisionmaking, but many others could benefit from more precision. In turn, counsel for recipients of such letters should remain alert to the likelihood that the instruments lack contractual force.

It is, of course, quite possible for litigation to ensue despite the utmost care in drafting. On occasion, pursuing even a slight opportunity for a favorable judicial construction will seem preferable to acquiescing in the opposing party's well-founded view of a letter's effect. However, more clarity than was displayed in this case should certainly reduce the number of such lawsuits.

Understanding the Case:

1. *Why American Wanted Out:* Beginning in the late 1960s, O'Hare International Airport in Chicago, Illinois, experienced rapid growth, doubling the amount of passengers passing through from 20 million in 1965 to 40 million in 1976. To deal with the increase in traffic and crowded terminals, in 1983, Chicago announced a $2 billion O'Hare Development Plan. Part of this plan included American Airlines' announcement of a $100 million expansion project of its own, including the addition of eleven aircraft gates and a 70 percent increase in daily flights. However, American Airlines later decided that it would be too costly to build an international terminal. Instead, American Airlines decided to operate its international flights out of its existing terminal. This case shows American Airlines's effort to get out of the contract with Quake to expand its operations at the international terminal.

2. *Incorporation of Terms from Bidding Documents:* The letter of intent referred to many terms that were incorporated from Jones's "Invitation to Bid." An invitation to bid is an invitation to contractors to submit their proposals for completing a specific project, or a specific aspect of a project. As in *Quake*, the invitation to bid typically includes specifications for the work to be performed. Specifications are detailed descriptions of the work to be performed, often with the material and workmanship standards to be met. They allow a contractor to know exactly what it is bidding on. In *Quake*, the Invitation to Bid also included drawings. Those drawings likely depicted a diagrammatic representation of the expansion project to be performed. If the parties in *Quake* were bound by the letter of intent, they would also be bound by the terms set out in the invitation to bid (along with the addendum), the specifications, and the diagram.

That is because the letter of intent incorporated those documents by reference. **Incorporating documents by reference** into a contract means the separate documents referred to in the contract are a part of the contract as if they had been fully set out in the contract.

3. *Incorporation of MBE, WBE, and EEO Goals from Quake's Proposal:* The letter of intent also said that the final definitive contract would set out MBE, WBE, and EEO goals. These abbreviations stand for minority-owned business enterprise, women-owned business enterprise, and equal employment opportunity. It is fairly common for construction contracts with the government, or construction contracts in which the government provides financial or other support (such as occurred in this case), to set out minimum diversity goals such as these for the subcontractors who will be performing the services. These goals ensure that historically disadvantaged groups are adequately represented in the mix of subcontractors performing the work. In this case, unlike the specifications, these goals were not set out in the Invitation to Bid or its related documents. However, they were set out in Quake's bid. Thus, if the parties were bound by the letter of intent, those goals would be incorporated by reference from Quake's bid, as if those goals had been fully set out in the letter of intent.

Comprehension and Thought Questions:

1. What test does the court use to determine whether Jones (on behalf of American Airlines) was bound by letter of intent?

2. According to the court, where must a court look first to determine the parties' intent to be bound? Why?

3. What provisions of the letter of intent support the letter of intent being a contract?

4. What provisions of the letter of intent support the letter *not* being a contract?

5. Did the court ultimately find that the parties were bound by the letter of intent?

6. What "middle ground" approach would concurring Justice Stamos take in responding to the question whether the parties were bound to the underlying subcontract through the letter of intent? Do you think this middle ground approach is sensible?

7. After this case, how can contracting parties ensure that they are not bound by their letter of intent where they do not intend to be bound?

Hypothetical Variations:

1. What if the letter of intent's termination clause provided in its entirety as follows: "This Letter of Intent is not binding on the parties"?

2. What if Quake had performed other airport upgrades for American Airlines before the upgrades contemplated in the case, and the sole writing

reflecting the terms of those contracts was a letter of intent similar to the one in this case?

3. What if Quake started construction and Jones and American Airlines, who were aware of that work from the start, waited three weeks to inform Quake that the contract was cancelled?

4. Implied Duty to Negotiate in Good Faith

Where it is unclear from the face of a term sheet whether the parties intend to be bound, some courts imply a **duty to negotiate in good faith**.[3] This implied duty does not require the parties to consummate the underlying transaction, but instead imposes on them a duty to negotiate the remaining terms in good faith.

In his concurrence in *Quake,* Justice Stamos regarded the letter of intent as possibly supporting such an implied duty. That would have avoided having to find either that the parties were not bound at all, or that they were bound by the underlying subcontract. It was this obligation that was terminable by Jones, Justice Stamos argued, and not the underlying subcontract.

Where a court determines that the implied duty exists, that duty imposes a framework on the parties for how they must deal with one another as they negotiate. Specifically, the implied duty precludes a party from "renouncing the deal, abandoning the negotiations, or insisting on conditions that do not conform to the preliminary agreement."[4] This duty does not, however, commit the parties to concluding the transaction if they cannot agree on the open terms. But it does require them to *try* to conclude the transaction, by requiring them to act in good faith to negotiate open terms.

To see this doctrine in action, recall the simulated transaction described in Section A. In that simulated transaction, Manufacturer proposed to acquire Supplier. The parties then prepared a term sheet, that set out all of the important terms on which the parties agreed. Recall that term sheet had stated in Section 6 that it was not binding, and that neither party would be bound unless and until they signed and delivered a definitive asset purchase agreement. Imagine that Section 6 of the term sheet had instead provided as follows:

> 6. Definitive Documents: The transaction described in this term sheet will be reflected in a definitive asset purchase agreement and other related documents. Those documents will also reflect other terms and conditions on which the parties agree and which are customary for transactions of the type this term sheet contemplates.

---

3. *See, e.g.,* Fairbrook Leasing, Inc. v. Mesaba Aviation, Inc., 519 F.3d 421, 426 (8th Cir. 2008).

4. Teachers Ins. & Annuity Ass'n of Am. v. Tribune Co., 670 F. Supp. 491, 498 (S.D.N.Y. 1987).

This language does not clearly indicate whether the parties intend to be bound by the term sheet. On one hand, the document is called a term sheet—a name reserved for preliminary agreements that are usually not binding. This provision even mentions additional terms that need to be negotiated by the parties, which argues against a present intend to be bound. Together, these facts suggest that the term sheet does not manifest the parties' intent to be bound to consummate the asset purchase.

On the other hand, the parties have set out in other parts of the term sheet the essential terms of the asset sale, and have signed the term sheet at the bottom, demonstrating their commitment to the transaction. They also have not disclaimed an intent to be bound. Consequently, the term sheet is ambiguous as to its binding effect.

Now assume that Supplier inserts the purchase price of $15 million in the definitive asset purchase agreement, rather than the $12 million that was included in the term sheet. Suppose Supplier replaced this term because Supplier's President decided to seek more money for Supplier, and not because any change in facts justified demanding more money. In this example, if the parties could not agree on final definitive documents, Manufacturer might sue Supplier arguing that (1) the parties had an implied duty to negotiate the terms of sale in good faith and (2) Supplier breached that duty by demanding more money than set out in the term sheet. Assuming the court found that the parties had an implied duty to negotiate in good faith, it likely would find a breach of that duty by Supplier. That is because Supplier insisted on a term that directly conflicts with a term agreed on in the term sheet without any justification for doing so.

In contrast, assume the final asset purchase agreement includes the $1 million hold-back. Recall that this term was not included in the term sheet because the parties agreed to it only after Manufacturer discovered during due diligence that Supplier may owe Nuts and Bolts Inc. $1 million in connection with pending litigation. In this case, if Supplier were to sue Manufacturer for breach of the implied duty to negotiate in good faith by changing the terms of the deal, a court would likely not find a breach. That is because circumstances occurring after the parties negotiated the term sheet warranted the change, and Supplier agreed to the change.

You will want to reflect on whether courts *should* imply a duty on the parties on which they themselves have not agreed. After all, as an implied duty, this would not be a provision parties have expressly agreed on. Rather, courts imply it from the parties' manifestations and from courts' expectations for how commercial parties should act. As you reflect on this doctrine, keep in mind that courts cannot rewrite the terms of a contract. So, if parties want to preclude a court from finding an implied duty or any other enforceable duty from their term sheet, they can simply state that their term sheet is not binding and disclaim the existence of a duty to negotiate terms in good faith. Assuming their conduct is consistent with this intent, a court would undoubtedly find no implied duty.

PRACTICE PROBLEM 10-2

Refer back to Practice Problem 10-1. Assume that you advise your client Jasmine Chen to have Natgo prepare a term sheet reflecting Jasmine's proposed terms of employment. The following is the term sheet Natgo prepared and that both parties signed. *(handwritten: circled "signed" with X mark)*

EMPLOYMENT AGREEMENT TERM SHEET

The purpose of this term sheet is to set out the terms of Jasmine Chen's ("Employee") employment by Natgo Food Source Inc. (the "Company").

1. <u>Title</u>: Employee will be employed as Chief Financial Officer.
2. <u>Duties</u>: Employee will perform those duties customary for someone performing the function of Chief Financial Officer. Employee will report to the President and perform additional duties assigned by the President.
3. <u>Salary</u>: Employee will be paid an initial annual salary of $250,000. For each additional year during which Employee is employed by the Company, Employee's salary will increase by 3% from Employee's annual salary of the prior year.
4. <u>Benefits</u>: Employee will be eligible to receive all benefits available to the Company's other officers, as specified in the Company's Employee Handbook.
5. <u>Start Date and Term</u>: The term of Employee's employment will start on November 1, 2019, and last for two years. The term will automatically renew for additional one-year periods unless either party delivers notice to the other of its intent to terminate Employee's employment delivered at least 30 days before the end of that year.
6. <u>Non-compete</u>: Employee will not compete with the Company in any business in which the Company engages at any time during the Employee's employment term, and in any region in which the Company operates during Employee's employment term, for a period of two years after Employee's employment with the Company terminates.
7. <u>Other Documents</u>: The terms of Employee's employment will be fully documented in a formal agreement to be signed by both of the parties.

(handwritten left margin: "yeah, not ambiguous")

(handwritten bottom left: "no \"not binding\" provision")

(handwritten: "implied informal, not still binding agreement")

Natgo Food Source Inc.

//Bryce Williams//
Bryce Williams, President
Date: October 1, 2019

//Jasmine Chen//
Date: October 2, 2019

After both parties signed this term sheet, and while they were negotiating the full employment agreement, Jasmine received a call from a Fortunate 500 company called SoftGear Inc. expressing an interest in hiring Jasmine as its CFO. SoftGear indicated that it would pay Jasmine somewhere in the ballpark of $350,000 per year. Jasmine contacts you and asks you if she can ditch efforts to finalize an employment agreement with Natgo and instead negotiate terms of employment with SoftGear Inc. In your answer, make sure you explain to Jasmine whether she has any potential legal liability if she does terminate those negotiations.

5. Moral Obligation

Even where parties are not legally bound by a term sheet, they often feel morally committed to consummate the transaction on the terms reflected in the term sheet. As such, where a party tries to negotiate for a better term than is reflected on the term sheet, that party is often seen as re-trading the terms of the proposed contract, raising questions about that party's integrity at the start of the contractual relationship. This type of re-trading can also negatively impact a party's reputation, if word gets out about this behavior. For these reasons, parties often do not try to negotiate for better terms than what they have agreed on in a term sheet, absent changed circumstances or changed assumptions upon uncovering new facts during due diligence. While term sheets do not mention this moral obligation—and often expressly state that the parties can discontinue or withdraw from negotiations at any time before they enter into a definitive agreement—this moral obligation exists as a result of our society's expectations for the behavior of others, and not because of something written in a term sheet. In addition, the fact that the opposing party may feel morally obligated to consummate the transaction based on the negotiated term sheet terms also is a reason that parties often prepare a term sheet that covers the most material terms of a significant transaction, even if the term sheet is not legally binding.

C. DUE DILIGENCE

1. What Is Due Diligence?

As you may recall from the sample pre-bargain process described in Section A above, due diligence is another pre-bargain step in which parties usually engage. You may recall from that sample process that during due diligence, Manufacturer discovered a lawsuit against Supplier for which Supplier might be liable up to $1 million. That discovery caused Manufacturer to renegotiate how and when it paid the purchase price.

Due diligence takes place in many transactions—not only sale of asset transactions. At its core, **due diligence** is a process of investigation a party undertakes before it enters into a transaction. It undertakes that investigation to learn more about the benefits and risks of a potential transaction. The party can then use that information to determine whether to enter into the transaction and, if so, on what terms.

For example, suppose a company planning to lease real estate from the owner discovers during due diligence that the owner actually co-owns that real estate. Upon discovering that, the lessee might decide to not pursue the transaction. Alternatively, it could decide to lease the property, but insist that as a condition of its duty to lease, the other owner consent to the lease as well. In that way, the information discovered in due diligence revealed a risk to the lessee, and enabled the lessee to bargain for a contractual term to protect itself.

While both parties to a potential transaction can perform a due diligence inquiry, the nature and extent of due diligence depends on the parties and the transaction. For example, if Mom and Pop Shop Inc. is interested in borrowing $1 million from Big Bank N.A., then clearly the bulk of the due diligence investigation will be by the bank. After all, the bank will want to learn about Mom and Pop Shop to make sure the Shop generates enough money to repay the loan according to the repayment schedule and other terms the parties are contemplating (and perhaps have set out in a term sheet). And Big Bank would also want to investigate what property Mom and Pop Shop owns or has other rights to, as the Bank will likely want to take a security interest in that property. With a security interest in that property, if Mom and Pop Shop ends up not being able to repay the loan according to the loan agreement, Big Bank will at least be able to realize on that property and sell it, using the sale proceeds to repay the loan.

On the other hand, Mom and Pop Shop will have very little due diligence to do on Big Bank. That is because once Big Bank provides the loan to Mom and Pop Shop per the loan agreement, Big Bank will have performed the essence of its obligations under the contract. In other words, Mom and Pop Shop will not face any real risk of the Bank not performing, as the Bank will have already performed. So Mom and Pop Shop will not have much risk exposure to Big Bank, though they may still want to investigate Big Bank's approach to relationships with borrowers, to ensure it maintains a healthy, positive relationship with its borrowers. The situation would be different, however, if Mom and Pop Shop contemplated borrowing additional funds from Big Bank in the future under the loan agreement. In that instance, Mom and Pop Shop would also want to ensure that Big Bank has adequate assets, and possibly FDIC insurance, to be able to provide that funding.

In the context of a sale of assets, a buyer performs a much more extensive due diligence investigation than the seller. That is because the buyer will want to learn all about the assets it is buying and potential liabilities it is assuming. The seller, on the other hand, only needs to make sure the buyer has or will have the money it promises to pay for those assets.

Where a party plans to request information and documents from the other party as part of its due diligence investigation, that party sends the other party a due diligence request list. This request list lists out all of the information and documents the party is requesting from the other.

2. Sample Due Diligence Request List

The following is an excerpt of a sample due diligence request list that a buyer of assets might send to the seller. These excerpted sections request information about the company's legal existence, litigation matters, and its contracts. A complete checklist would likely also request information about the company's ownership, finances, property (including real property and intellectual property), personnel and employee policies and benefits, tax matters, and insurance, among others. Such a complete request list would also run many more pages.

Again, remember that the extent of the requests on a due diligence request list varies by the type of transaction. So, a request list sent by a party who is buying one piece of machinery will be much shorter and narrower in scope than a request list sent by a party who is buying an entire business.

As you look over this excerpted request list, think about why a buyer would want to receive the information or review the documents included on the list. Specifically, think about how knowing the information requested might help the buyer better understand the risks it is taking by buying the assets from the seller, and possibly how to protect itself from those risks.

> Please provide copies of all documents, and summary descriptions of all agreements or arrangements, organized according to the following outline.
>
> 1. Organization and Standing.
>   a. A copy of the Company's Articles of Incorporation, including all amendments to it.
>   b. A copy of the current Bylaws.
>   c. A copy of the complete corporate minute books, including minutes of the meetings of the board of directors, any committees (whether of the board or otherwise) and shareholders, for the last five years to date.
>   d. Certificate of Good Standing or Existence (where available) issued by the appropriate governmental authority in the state of the Company's incorporation and in each state in which the Company is qualified to transact business as a foreign corporation.
>   e. Certificates of Authority of Qualification issued by each jurisdiction in which the Company is authorized to do business as a foreign corporation.
>   f. A list of all states and jurisdictions in which the Company is qualified to do business as a foreign corporation.
>   g. A list of all states and jurisdictions in which the Company owns or leases real estate, has employees, or stores inventory.

    h.   A list of all current and former subsidiaries of the Company.

    i.   A list of all related parties of the Company and the nature of business conducted with each for the three most recent years.

    . . .

9.   Litigation and Customer Credit.

    a.   A list of litigation and claims pending or threatened against the Company (including labor grievances).

    b.   A current accounts receivable list.

    c.   A current analysis of uncollectable accounts.

    d.   A copy of the Company's current credit policy and terms.

    e.   Copies of the Company's current pricing policy and terms of sale.

    f.   A current accounts payable list.

    . . .

11. Contracts.

    a.   Copies of all leases, installment purchase agreements, or other contracts with respect to any real or personal property to which the Company is a party (unless already disclosed under other portions of this due diligence request list).

    b.   Copies of all joint venture, distributive, sales, advertising, agency, manufacturer's representative, franchise, license, or similar contracts or commitments to which the Company is a party.

    c.   Copies of all contracts or agreements for the purchase of any single commodity, material, or piece of equipment for an aggregate purchase price exceeding $10,000 to which the Company is a party.

    d.   Copies of all contracts or agreements to which the Company is a party, which, by their terms, do not terminate or are not terminable without penalty within one year after the date of your response.

    e.   Copies of all loan agreements, security agreements, mortgages, indentures, promissory notes, conditional sales agreements, or other similar agreements or arrangements to which the Company is a party.

    f.   Copies of all written, and a description of all oral, consulting, or employment contracts to which the Company is a party.

    g.   Copies of all contracts out of the ordinary and usual course of business to which the Company is a party.

    h.   Copies of all contracts concerning the purchase or sale of securities of the Company.

    i.   Copies of all contracts that may result in a material loss to the Company, including all contracts that may result in a loss exceeding $10,000.

    j.   Copies of all contracts of guaranty of indemnification to which the Company is a party.

    k.   Copies of all contracts purporting to limit the freedom of the Company to compete in any line of business in any geographical area.[5]

---

5. Illinois Forms Legal and Business, April 2016 Update, Business Enterprises: Ch. 31A: Buying and Selling a Business, 9A Ill. Forms Legal & Bus. § 31A:21.

PRACTICE PROBLEM 10-3

Recall from the simulation presented earlier in the chapter that Manufacturer is looking to buy all of Supplier's assets. In connection with that transaction, Manufacturer's counsel has delivered to Supplier and to you, Supplier's counsel, a due diligence request list that includes the above-requested information.

1. Marie Shaw, Supplier's President, calls you to ask you why Manufacturer needs a list of litigation and claims pending or threatened against Supplier. How would you respond? *risk*

2. Shaw also asks you why Manufacturer needs to see copies of Supplier's contracts limiting its freedom to compete. How would you respond? *would ↓* *value of assets*

3. Role of Lawyers in Due Diligence

Many people make up a party's due diligence team, from the company's businesspeople to its financial analysts and accountants. That is because due diligence involves not just legal information and documents but accounting, financial, and business information.

Lawyers are an integral part of this process. For the party requesting information, lawyers (either in-house or at a law firm) usually draft the due diligence request list and send it to the other side's lawyer. They also typically manage the information and documents received, to make sure all requested information and documents are received. They then review the legal information and legal documents provided. For example, lawyers usually review the contracts provided by the other party in due diligence to ensure those contracts do not contain any provision that would prevent the other party from entering the transaction with your client. It is important to note that lawyers are providing advice with respect to a legal assessment of the documents and are not providing financial or valuation advice or opinions regarding the transaction (such as whether the deal is a "good" one). Instead, the lawyer's job is to figure out what is important to the client with respect to the transaction (such as which assets that are being purchased are most valuable) and to determine whether there are any legal issues associated with obtaining the assets (such as another party, like a bank, having a security interest or mortgage on those assets).

A lawyer who represents a party providing information also has a job to do during due diligence. That person (again, the lawyer might either be in-house or at a law firm) usually helps her client determine what information and documents are responsive to the requests on the due diligence request list. That lawyer also helps the client organize that information and those documents to ensure that they are responsive to the other party's request, and helps the client manage the other party's access to that information and those documents to protect the confidentiality of any confidential information being provided.

This may include, for example, making sure that the other party has signed an appropriate confidentiality agreement. There may also be information that, while requested from the other party, should not be disclosed. For example, an attorney would not want to disclose any information, such as attorney work product regarding ongoing litigation, that could destroy the client's ability to assert that such work product is protected under the attorney-client privilege.

4. Reasons to Cooperate with Other Party's Due Diligence Investigation

There are several reasons why a party cooperates with the other party's due diligence request. First, remember that in a business transaction, the parties are usually choosing to explore a potential transaction with one another. In other words, they both want to explore and, if all goes well, consummate, the transaction. As such, the parties have a built-in incentive to want to cooperate with the other party to provide all of the information and documents it wishes to see as part of its due diligence investigation.

Also, each party cooperates with the other party's due diligence requests to set a tone of cooperation. By setting a tone of cooperation at the early due diligence phase, the parties are maximizing the chances that their transaction will come to fruition, if the economics support the transaction. In other words, by setting a tone of cooperation, the parties can avoid killing a potential transaction that is otherwise economically justified due to uncooperativeness.

Moreover, a party's failure to disclose information could subject that party to liability. You will study the source of this liability in Chapter 20, when you study misrepresentations. For the purposes of this discussion, suffice it to say that lying about, concealing, or failing to disclose information that the other party requests or that is important might subject that party to a claim for misrepresentation.

Finally, parties cooperate because sometimes they are contractually bound to do so. That is, sometimes parties include in their term sheet or formal agreement a provision obligating them to cooperate with the other party's due diligence investigation. As mentioned above, where this term is included in a term sheet, it is usually one of the few provisions that is binding. However, in most cases, the parties cooperate with the other party not merely to comply with this legal duty, but for the reasons mentioned above.

D. CONFIDENTIALITY AGREEMENTS

As discussed above, sometimes parties include binding provisions in their term sheets that obligate them to maintain the confidentiality of information and documents provided by the other party in due diligence. However, in some transactions, the parties might not even be able to explore the essential terms of a potential transaction without sharing confidential information. For example, a buyer might want to see the financial statements of a privately owned company before preliminarily agreeing to a purchase price in a term sheet. Where this occurs, the parties will usually enter into a confidentiality agreement at the outset, before they even explore the essential terms of the transaction.

Moreover, in many transactions, parties do not prepare a term sheet. Instead, they proceed to documenting the transaction after initial discussions reveal an interest in pursuing a transaction. There, too, parties might enter into a type of contract known as a confidentiality agreement (or non-disclosure agreement) at the outset, to ensure that any information provided to the other side as part of the due diligence process, or as part of contract negotiations, is kept confidential.

In the confidentiality agreement, much like in a confidentiality provision of a term sheet, the party receiving confidential information agrees to retain the confidentiality of that information. The agreement also spells out what amounts to confidential information.

The following is an excerpt from a form confidentiality agreement for the sale of a business. Here, the business being sold is the "Company" and the business entity interested in buying the business is "you."

---

2. You have expressed interest in joining us in the possible acquisition (the "Transaction") of the Company. In this connection, you have requested certain information concerning the business, operations, finances, properties and affairs of the Company. As a condition to furnishing you with this information which has not previously been made available to the public, you agree that this information and any other information which we or the Company or any of the Company's representatives or agents furnish to you or your representatives (as subsequently defined) or which you or your representatives obtain through this access (collectively, the "Evaluation Material") will be treated and kept confidential.

3. You agree that the Evaluation Material will not be used by you, your directors, officers, employees, attorneys, accountants or other agents and advisors, including their respective employees and agents (collectively "your representatives") in any way detrimental to us or the Company and that all Evaluation Material will be kept confidential, and treated as belonging to us, by your representatives and shall not, except as subsequently provided, without our prior written consent, be disclosed by you or your representatives, in any manner whatsoever, in whole or in part and shall not be used by you or your representatives other than for the purpose of evaluating the Transaction. You further agree to transmit Evaluation Material only to your representatives who need to know this information for the purpose of evaluating the Transaction and who shall: (a) be advised by you of this Agreement; and (b) agree to be bound by the provisions of this Agreement.

As you can see, this excerpt describes what amounts to confidential information and then defines that information as "Evaluation Material." It then creates a duty on the buyer to maintain the confidentiality of that evaluation material. In so doing, it also explains how the buyer must treat that information internally. This is a precaution the seller requires the buyer to take in order to limit who internally at the buyer may access the evaluation material and how they may use such information. That limit will help the seller protect the confidentiality of its information.

PRACTICE PROBLEM 10-4

Jack Blane, the President of Manufacturer, would like to find a new supplier to supply Manufacturer with the electrical components used in its cranes. Blane has identified Crane Circuits Inc., a Bermuda corporation, as a potential new supplier. Before contacting Crane Circuits to find out whether they are interested and able to manufacture electrical components needed in Manufacturer's cranes according to Manufacturer's detailed (and confidential) specifications, Blane calls you and asks you the following:

1. Is there any legal information he should request from Crane Circuits in connection with this potential transaction?

2. Is there any reason to prepare a confidentiality agreement for this potential transaction? If so, who should draft that agreement? *Yes. Mfr; Crane specifications*

Now that you have studied pre-contract processes, read through and answer the questions that follow the Simulation Problem for Chapter 10, which is located in Appendix A.

CHAPTER 11

Contract Negotiation and Drafting

The prior chapter introduced you to the steps parties usually take before they form a contract, in furtherance of contract formation. As that chapter explained, often parties agree on important terms in a term sheet before they enter into a contract for the related transaction. One or both parties often also undertake a process called due diligence to obtain information relevant to the transaction.

For purposes of this chapter, we assume the parties agreed on the important terms in the term sheet and nothing too worrisome turned up during due diligence that derailed the transaction. Alternatively, in many transactions, parties do not prepare a term sheet or do not perform a due diligence review. In either case, the next step in the process of contract formation is for the parties to negotiate the terms of the proposed contract, assuming it is not a non-negotiable "form" contract. Once that occurs, a written memorialization of the agreed-upon terms is prepared. It is that written memorialization that parties refer to as the contract, even though it is the substantive promises contained in that written memorialization that are, technically speaking, the contract, once the contract formation requirements have been satisfied.

This chapter describes those next stages of contract formation. First, Section B discusses contract negotiation. Next, Section C discusses contract drafting. Those discussions not only explain what occurs at each of those stages, but they also explain the role of the client and the role of the lawyer in each. They also explain common ethical pitfalls lawyers face in each stage.

While this portion of the book, as with Chapter 10, focuses on lawyered transactions, Section D briefly addresses the lawyer's role in preparing and reviewing a contract that is a nonnegotiable "form."

But before we begin those discussions, Section A will once again walk you through a simulated contract negotiation and drafting scenario. The simulation is intended to give you a narrative of how the negotiation and drafting processes occur in the typical lawyered transaction.

A. SAMPLE CONTRACT NEGOTIATION AND DRAFTING PROCESS

If you recall from Chapter 10, U.S. Crane Co., a large U.S.-based company that manufactures and sells industrial cranes (called "Manufacturer"), is proposing to buy Crane Supply Inc.'s business. Crane Supply Inc. (called "Supplier") is a company that supplies U.S. Crane Co. with certain components Manufacturer uses to manufacture its cranes.

The parties agreed on a $13 million purchase price. However, they also agreed that Manufacturer will "hold back" $1 million of this purchase price. That holdback amount will be used to satisfy any amount Manufacturer might owe to Nuts and Bolts Inc. as a result of Nuts and Bolts Inc.'s pending lawsuit against Supplier. If the full holdback amount is not needed to satisfy this liability, then any remaining portion of the holdback amount not paid to Nuts and Bolts Inc. will be paid to Supplier once that lawsuit is resolved.

Jack Blane, the President of Manufacturer, asks Mildred Monk, a lawyer who works at Buyer's Counsel LP, the law firm that represents Manufacturer, to prepare the first draft of the asset purchase agreement. Blane knows that Buyer's Counsel LP will prepare the first draft because Manufacturer is the one paying money in the transaction. As such, Manufacturer is the party who needs more protection under the contract—protections to assure Manufacturer gets what it is expecting under the contract for that money: Supplier's assets.

Monk first reviews the final term sheet. She then asks Blane if he has any other agreements or understandings with anyone at Supplier as to the proposed terms of the transaction. Monk asks this question because she knows the term sheet does not need to—and in fact might not—contain all of the terms on which the parties have agreed thus far. Yet she wants to make sure the first draft reflects all of the terms the parties have agreed on. Blane assures Monk that the term sheet contains all of the terms the parties have agreed on thus far.

Next, Monk locates many precedents—that is, other contracts that she can use to help her draft the contract between Manufacturer and Supplier. Monk asks her colleagues for copies of asset purchase agreements they have worked on. Monk is careful to only use precedents from similar types of transactions (asset purchase transactions) that were drafted from the perspective of the buyer of assets, as otherwise those precedents would contain many terms that are either not relevant for the transaction between Manufacturer and Supplier, or that possibly unduly favor Supplier. Monk also looks at the American Bar Association's "model" asset purchase agreement. That model agreement will help her identify the types of terms she might need to address as she drafts.

As she drafts, Monk is mindful that the term sheet only describes in basic detail the core business terms of the transaction. However, the term sheet does not include details as to those terms. The term sheet also does not list in detail all of the terms she will need to include in the asset purchase agreement to protect her client's interests, such as Supplier's representations and warranties or conditions to closing. Despite this, she makes an initial attempt at drafting those other provisions based on what she knows about the parties and the transaction, as well as the terms customarily included in these agreements. As she drafts these provisions, Monk must identify ways in which Manufacturer might not realize the benefits it expects from the transaction and try to contractually protect her client from those risks. Yet she also needs to draft a fair contract. That is because if this transaction does not pan out, Manufacturer still intends to buy crane components from Supplier.

When she is finished drafting, Monk asks lawyers at her firm with expertise in relevant areas of the law to review her draft. That includes a tax lawyer, because she wants to make sure the transaction is structured in a way that minimizes the tax impact on Manufacturer. Those lawyers send Monk their comments. Monk then revises her draft to reflect those comments.

After incorporating those comments, Monk sends a draft of the agreement to Blane. She includes with the draft a list of questions for Blane. Blane and Monk then talk on the phone about those questions. After that call, Monk revises the document to reflect her discussion with Blane.

Finally, Monk sends the first draft of the contract to Sam Vishnu, an attorney at Seller Counsel LP, the law firm representing Supplier in the transaction. In doing so, Monk is careful to indicate at the top of every page that the contract is a "Draft" along with the draft's date to signal that the document is not final or ready for signature, and that delivery of the draft does not manifest her client's assent. Including the date of the draft will help her distinguish this draft from future drafts, if there are any.

Vishnu shares a copy of the agreement with Marie Shaw, Supplier's President. Vishnu then reviews the draft and sends a list of questions and comments he has on the draft to Shaw. He and Shaw agree that there are five significant business points that the businesspeople should discuss before sending a detailed markup of comments back to Monk. So, Shaw calls Blane and the two discuss those five business points. Fortunately, they are able to resolve them. Shaw and Blane then inform Monk and Vishnu what they agreed to.

Vishnu then sends his remaining comments to the draft to Monk. Many of Vishnu's comments are to request qualifiers to the representations and warranties, though he makes other requested changes too. The parties then schedule a time for everyone—the businesspeople and the lawyers—to discuss those comments on the phone.

Overall, the phone call goes well. In many instances, Shaw or Vishnu raises a concern with the language in the draft, explaining how it imposes too much risk on Supplier. The parties then discuss the concern and agree to modify the language to address it while still protecting Manufacturer. For example, Vishnu objects that the draft obligates Supplier to not sell any property before the transaction closes. Vishnu objects to this language because it would preclude Supplier from selling crane components to its customers, which is central to the operation of its business. Monk, on the other hand, argues that without this protection, Supplier could sell all of its assets, leaving nothing left for Manufacturer to buy. As a compromise, the parties agree that while Supplier will promise to not sell its assets, the contract will permit it to continue making sales of inventory in its ordinary course of business, consistent with past practices. Through this compromise position, both parties' interests are protected as much as possible.

Following the call, Monk circulates a revised draft of the agreement, still marked at the top as a "draft" along with the date of the new draft. He also circulates a marked (or "redlined") version that highlights the changes from the first draft he circulated. At this point, neither Vishnu nor Shaw has any remaining comments. Monk then circulates a final, "clean" copy of the asset purchase agreement, with the "Draft" language at the top removed and replaced with "Execution Copy."

Blane next calls a meeting of Manufacturer's board of directors, to occur two weeks later. At that meeting, Manufacturer's board discusses and approves the purchase of Supplier's assets on the terms set out in the draft asset purchase agreement. The board also authorizes Blane to sign the agreement and to cause Manufacturer to perform that agreement. Similarly, Shaw calls a meeting of Supplier's board of directors. Supplier's board, after reviewing and discussing the agreement, also approves it and authorizes Shaw to sign it. Supplier's board also submits the proposed transaction to Supplier's shareholders, who must also approve the transaction. Supplier's shareholders approve the transaction.

The next day, Blane and Shaw both sign the asset purchase agreement on their respective signature lines. They then deliver a copy of their signatures to the other side, manifesting their assent on behalf of their respective companies.

B. NEGOTIATING THE CONTRACT

1. Client's Role

The client plays an active role in negotiating the terms of a proposed contract. That is because it is the client who must decide when and how its business goals will be furthered by a contract.[1]

Whether a client's business goals are furthered by a contract largely depends on what the terms of the contract are. For example, in the above

---

1. *See* Model Rules of Prof'l Conduct r 1.2(a) (2002) ("Subject to paragraphs (c) and (d), a lawyer shall abide by a client's decisions concerning the objectives of representation and, as required by Rule 1.4, shall consult with the client as to the means by which they are to be pursued.").

scenario, Manufacturer's board must have decided that it would create value for Manufacturer to buy Supplier's assets for $13 million. However, if Supplier's board of directors was not willing to sell Supplier's assets for anything less than $16 million, Manufacturer's board of directors might have decided that the transaction would not be beneficial to Manufacturer. In that case, Manufacturer would not have bought Supplier's assets, and would have continued to buy crane components from Supplier.

As was discussed in Chapter 1, sometimes clients are focused less on the terms of a particular contract and more on establishing a relationship with their contractual counterparty. This is known as the relational role of contracting, and reflects the fact that sometimes contracts serve to largely lay a foundation for an ongoing relationship. Clients are most concerned with building relationships in transactions that are expected to last for some time, or to serve as a gateway to future contracts. In contrast, the relational role of contracting is less prominent in the types of transactions that are "one-off" transactions, such as the purchase of a business.

2. Lawyer's Role

While lawyers do not set the ultimate objectives to be achieved by a client in a contractual relationship, they help their clients negotiate transactions in a way that ensures their clients achieve their business objectives. They do that by using contract structure and terms, along with other tools.

For example, in the above scenario, Monk, Manufacturer's lawyer, may have advised Manufacturer to negotiate the transaction with Supplier as an asset purchase, to protect Manufacturer from Supplier's liabilities. In a purchase of assets, a buyer only buys the agreed-upon assets and only assumes agreed-upon liabilities. Thus, through an asset purchase structure, a buyer does not become bound by a seller's unknown liabilities.[2] Because they perform this transaction design function, lawyers are sometimes referred to as transaction engineers.

Lawyers perform the transaction engineering function not only for the overall transaction structure, but also for the design of specific contractual terms. For example, in the above scenario, it was likely Monk who suggested that Manufacturer hold back $1 million of the purchase price to satisfy any liability by Supplier owed to Nuts and Bolts Inc. Through this design choice, Manufacturer avoids having to recoup from Supplier any amount Manufacturer has to pay Nuts and Bolts to resolve Nuts and Bolts' lawsuit against Supplier.

---

2. There is an exception to this, under a doctrine known as successor liability. The concept of successor liability is beyond the scope of contract law, though you may learn about it in a Business Associations or Mergers and Acquisitions course.

Second, lawyers help their clients limit the downside risks from the transaction. Doing that, in turn, helps ensure that the client realizes the expected benefits from that transaction.

For example, in the above scenario, Monk would surely see risks with the proposed transaction: What if Supplier does not actually own the assets it is selling to Manufacturer? What if Supplier's equipment or machinery is in bad condition? What if, before closing, Supplier stops maintaining its equipment or machinery?

Instead of simply identifying risks such as these, a good transactional lawyer will also help protect the client from those risks. In this example, Monk could protect Manufacturer from these risks by negotiating for protective terms in the asset purchase agreement that would give Manufacturer a remedy if any of these assumptions is undermined. For example, Manufacturer could require that Supplier represent and warrant that (1) Supplier owns all its assets free of liens and (2) Supplier's assets are in good condition. If either of these representations and warranties proves to not be true because, for example, an important machine Supplier uses to make crane components is not functional, then Manufacturer could pursue a remedy for misrepresentation or breach of warranty. Similarly, Monk could have asked Supplier to make pre-closing covenants that would obligate Supplier to maintain the equipment and machinery in good condition. That way, if, during the pre-closing period, Supplier failed to maintain any equipment or machinery in good condition, Manufacturer would have a remedy for breach of covenant.[3]

Where a lawyer negotiates contract terms on behalf of the client, the lawyer has an ethical duty to deal honestly with others involved in the transaction.[4] In our simulated transaction, that means Monk should not state that his clients always receive a representation and warranty from a selling company such as Supplier that its assets are in "good condition" without regard to any wear and tear that might have affected their condition where that is not actually the case. (In fact, it is quite customary for a seller's representation and warranty about the condition of its assets to explicitly exclude "ordinary wear and tear," which simply recognizes the reality that assets deteriorate as they are used.)

Moreover, a transactional lawyer needs to be mindful of the fact that it is *the client* who makes decisions about the objectives of the representation—not the lawyer.[5] Accordingly, where a lawyer negotiates contract terms without the client present, where a client has not given the lawyer authority to agree

---

3. Recall from Chapter 3, a party often makes the truth of the other party's representations and warranties, as well as the other party's compliance with covenants, a condition to closing. As such, in addition to having these remedies for misrepresentation/breach of warranty and/or breach of covenant, Manufacturer could walk from the transaction, meaning not close because either condition would not be satisfied.

4. *See* Model Rules of Prof'l Conduct r 4.1 (2002).

5. *See* Model Rules of Prof'l Conduct r 1.2 (2002).

to those terms, the lawyer must let the counterparty know that those terms are subject to review and approval by the client. Without that, the lawyer risks not only committing malpractice, but also being subject to discipline under the rules of professional conduct.

The following case explores the limits of an attorney's authority in a transaction. It raises the concern of an attorney making business decisions (instead of merely advising) and potentially binding a client to a contract. While the attorney in this case ultimately was found to not have bound the client to a contract, consider carefully the dissent's arguments, and how either a differently comprised court or a slightly altered fact might have led to a different outcome.

Schafer v. Barrier Island Station, Inc.
United States Court of Appeals, 4th Circuit
946 F.2d 1075 (1991)

NIEMEYER, Circuit Judge:

Having purchased three condominiums on the Outer Banks of North Carolina, the plaintiffs demanded that Barrier Island Station, Inc. repurchase the condominiums pursuant to a repurchase agreement that had allegedly been agreed to. Barrier Island refused, contending that a repurchase agreement was never consummated, and this litigation resulted. At trial, the plaintiffs' proof of the agreement consisted of two different versions of the repurchase agreement, one signed by plaintiffs and the other by Barrier Island, and a letter from Barrier Island's attorney which reported that Barrier Island had agreed to the version signed by plaintiffs. The jury found that a written contract existed and entered judgment against Barrier Island in an approximate amount of $825,000, and Barrier Island appealed. Because we conclude that no contract for the repurchase of the condominiums was ever signed by Barrier Island or its authorized representative and that therefore the statute of frauds was not satisfied, we reverse.

I

John V. Schafer, Jr., and his wife Mary, Thomas Nale, III, and his wife Ann, and Gene Mentzer and his wife Ruth (Mary, Ann and Ruth are sisters) signed contracts with Barrier Island on July 28, 1984, to purchase three condominiums in a development known as Barrier Island Station in the Village of Duck, North Carolina. In each case, the contracts of sale were subject to the condition: "Repurchase agreement to be executed prior to closing, terms and conditions must be acceptable to buyer." At the same time that the plaintiffs signed the contracts of sale, they signed the repurchase agreements which provided that in specified circumstances Barrier Island would buy back the condominiums. Barrier Island executed the contracts of sale but held the repurchase contracts.

Barrier Island Station is a development of four buildings, consisting of "whole ownership" and time-sharing units. Whole ownership units are those which are not subject to time-sharing arrangements. The first two buildings were developed by Barrier Island for whole ownership units. Later, however, for economic reasons, Barrier Island decided to convert those buildings to include time-sharing units and likewise to market buildings three and four as time-sharing units. Any conversion in buildings one and two, however, required the majority consent of the owners.

For these reasons, Barrier Island added language to the repurchase contracts before signing them that made the repurchase obligation of Barrier Island contingent on the successful conversion of buildings one and two to time-sharing units. The added language, which proved offensive to the plaintiffs, read: "Majority vote of all owners in building one and two must be obtained in favor of co-ownership and/or interval ownership prior to repurchase." This added language was unacceptable to plaintiffs and became the basis of the difference between the parties.

Over the next months, several exchanges between the parties took place relating to their positions on the added language. Plaintiffs' attorney, Starkey Sharp, sent a letter dated August 23, 1984, to Barrier Island's attorney, Crouse Gray, stating:

> I can understand the desire that your client might have to avoid entering a repurchase agreement if the project did not develop so that time-sharing sales could be accomplished. However, this is not my clients' understanding and they did not intend to limit the repurchase agreement in such a fashion.

When Barrier Island saw this letter, it advised its attorney Gray that the condition must be included or "we have *no deal*!,", and Gray passed this communication on to Sharp. Putting the impasse on hold, Sharp replied in a letter to Gray dated September 10, 1984:

> I spoke with my clients concerning the position that you expressed. They have advised me that in communication with the sales personnel at Barrier Island Station they have been advised of a proposed meeting early this month. They will wait until that meeting occurs before we determine whether or not there is a matter of controversy between us.

Barrier Island principals testified that they heard nothing further of the matter and that they never agreed orally or otherwise to deleting the language offensive to plaintiffs. In response to the letter, however, Barrier Island's attorney Gray responded by letter dated September 13, 1984, in which he advised Sharp:

> I have been advised that the principals of Barrier Island Station, Inc. have already talked with the sales agent who called your clients to advise that Barrier Island Station, Inc. would agree to abide by the original repurchase agreements as they were drafted prior to the handwritten addenda.

No further correspondence took place with respect to the repurchase contracts before closing, and no repurchase contracts were signed in a form agreeable to both parties. At the closing on November 30, 1984, over two months after the last correspondence relating to the repurchase contracts, the sales for the purchase of the three condominiums closed. No repurchase agreements were presented, demanded or executed. Some time after closing, however, the parties exchanged further drafts purportedly to obtain "clean copies" of a repurchase agreement. But, despite a protracted dialogue, they never reached agreement.

On March 21, 1988, over three years after the closing, plaintiffs demanded that Barrier Island repurchase the three condominiums in accordance with the form of repurchase agreement originally signed by them on July 28, 1984, as affirmed by the letter of attorney Gray dated September 13, 1984. Barrier Island refused, taking the position that an agreement had never been reached.

From the judgment entered pursuant to a jury verdict in favor of the plaintiffs, Barrier Island has appealed.

II

[The court first addressed whether the repurchase contracts satisfied North Carolina's statute of frauds. The court held that the letter from Barrier Island's attorney Gray dated September 13, 1984 to Sharp did not satisfy the statute of frauds.]

If the letter were somehow construed to evidence an agreement, plaintiffs still would need to leap the hurdle of proving that Gray was authorized to resolve the issue for Barrier Island. They do not rely on express authority given by Barrier Island to Gray to agree to a resolution of the dispute over the added language. They rely instead on Gray's implied authority as an attorney and his apparent authority arising from the manner in which he was permitted to represent Barrier Island in this transaction and in the past.

It is undisputed that Gray was retained by Barrier Island as its attorney in the transactions with plaintiffs. The attorney-client relationship, by custom, however, does not imply that an attorney has authority to act as principal and resolve matters of substance. Thus, when a client retains an attorney to represent the client in litigation, the implied authority of the attorney is limited to conducting procedures and taking necessary steps to prosecute or defend the client in the litigation. Substantive decisions of whether to bring suit, to dismiss suit, or to settle are not by implication ones that the attorney is authorized to make. Similarly, when a client retains an attorney to represent the client in a transaction, the attorney has implied authority to negotiate the terms of an agreement or operative papers to their final form. But custom of the relationship does not imply an authority for the attorney to execute the documents on behalf of the client. This becomes particularly evident when the form of a contract is one which calls for the signature of the principals.

The absence of implied authority does not preclude a claim that Gray acted with the apparent authority of Barrier Island. While implied authority arises by custom from establishment of the attorney-client relationship, apparent authority arises from manifestations of the principal to third persons about the authority of the attorney. The Restatement (Second) of Agency well summarizes the distinction:

> Apparent authority results from a manifestation by a person that another is his agent, the manifestation being made to a third person and not, as when authority is created, to the agent. It is entirely distinct from authority, either express or implied.... If it exists, the third person has the same rights with reference to the principal as where the agent is authorized.

Restatement (Second) of Agency § 8 comment a (1958). To establish apparent authority, the plaintiffs must demonstrate that Barrier Island, by its conduct or statements, clothed Gray with the authority on which plaintiffs relied.

In this case the plaintiffs argue that the record shows that Gray was clothed with this authority by Barrier Island and that they therefore were justified in relying on Gray's letter of September 13 as an agreement on the only open issue of the repurchase contract. Because of the emphasis which plaintiffs place on the evidence on which they rely, we quote at length from their summary of the testimony which they claim justifies a finding of apparent authority:

> Gray has done virtually all of the legal work of the defendant [Barrier Island] except for time shares. He set up the defendant corporation. He has done the bulk of Shaver and Lancaster's [principals of Barrier Island] legal work since 1980. He has represented defendant in litigation matters and in negotiations with other attorneys. He is authorized to negotiate and "finalize terms" for defendant. Defendant admits, regarding this case, he was attorney for defendant "insofar as the sale of the property was concerned." He regularly represented defendant in real estate transactions. At the time of the transaction, and for some time before, Gray's office was in the building owned by Shaver and Lancaster's affiliated corporation and occupied by them, defendant and their other businesses. It was customary practice in Dare County for lawyers to handle negotiations after one side was represented. Gray acknowledged defendant authorized him to act as its spokesman in the negotiations regarding the offensive language.
>
> Gray also acted as spokesman for the defendant in all post-contract dealings between the parties. Lancaster testified that it was not characteristic of Gray to speak without authority; that he considered him to be careful and cautious; that he carried out his wishes and instructions; that if he had not, he would have gotten rid of him; and that was why Gray was still their lawyer.

Brief of Appellees at 5–6.

None of these facts, however, points to conduct, statements or other manifestations directed by Barrier Island to plaintiffs that Gray had more authority than was implied from the customary attorney-client relationship. On no prior occasion had he ever signed any contract on behalf of Barrier Island and

Barrier Island had never manifested an authorization that he do so. As plaintiffs alleged, he was authorized to negotiate and "finalize terms" for Barrier Island. His practice was to develop a final form of contract for signature by Barrier Island. Similarly, every draft circulated in the transactions with plaintiffs, whether initiated by plaintiffs or by Barrier Island, revealed that Barrier Island would sign through its principals and not through its attorney.

. . .

In summary . . . there is no evidence that Gray had implied or apparent authority to sign any binding instrument on behalf of Barrier Island to consummate a repurchase agreement. If he were simply communicating a conversation which he had heard which expressed a willingness to agree, then he no doubt had authority to send the letter. But Barrier Island vigorously denied that it ever authorized Gray to consummate any agreement or that it ever agreed in substance to eliminate the offending language. We find nothing in the record which indicates that the principals of Barrier Island manifested a different intent.

For the reasons stated, therefore, we reverse the judgment of the district court.

REVERSED.

WIDENER, Circuit Judge, dissenting:

I respectfully dissent.

The majority reverses a jury's determination that Barrier Island Station, through its attorney, agreed to enter into a repurchase agreement without an additional handwritten modification it had earlier requested. I believe, however, that there was ample evidence to support that determination.

. . .

A reasonable inference to be drawn from this evidence [referring to testimony by Gray that he could not imagine having written the letter to plaintiffs without having talked to Lancaster or Shaver, other testimony showing that Barrier Island had agreed to delete the modification, and evidence that Barrier Island had, after the date of Gray's letter, signed other repurchase agreements without the handwritten modification], is that Barrier Island was more interested in the sale of the units, than in its late added handwritten timeshare condition, and would therefore agree to be bound by a repurchase agreement without it. In any event, I suggest that the majority errs when it holds by necessary implication that such an inference was an impermissible one for the jury to have made.

Apart from what I believe to be the majority's erroneous factual inferences, I believe that reversing this jury's verdict is not well advised for another reason. In so doing, the majority has permitted Barrier Island to conduct its affairs through its attorney, and then avoid the consequences of that conduct when not to its advantage. I suggest that there would be no issue of Gray's authority if he were simply Barrier Island's agent, an incongruous result to say the least. The majority permits Barrier Island to blow hot and cold at the same time.

I would affirm.

Understanding the Case:

1. *Time-Shares:* In a time-share, multiple people have a right to use the property, and each person is allotted a period of time to use the property. In contrast, in "whole ownership," a property is sold to one person and that person controls the use and other rights to enjoy that property. In *Schafer,* the court stated that Barrier Island wanted to convert the plaintiffs' building to a time-share building "for economic reasons." That undoubtedly meant that Barrier Island would make more money by using those condos as time-shares than selling them outright to individual buyers.

2. *Multiple Drafts:* It is customary for attorneys (and clients) to trade drafts of agreements with proposed changes before a final execution version is agreed to and signed. Attorneys customarily, and it is considered courteous to, include a "clean" version of their draft as well as a "marked" or "redlined" version. The clean version is a version that incorporates all of an attorney's proposed changes without highlighting them, while a "marked" or "redlined" version highlights for the other party the changes that have been made since some prior version (typically the last version circulated by the other party). It is not clear whether the additional contractual language that Barrier Island proposed adding was set forth in a "marked" version of the agreement, but it is obvious from the parties' history of disagreement regarding the proposed language that the plaintiffs were advised of Barrier Island's proposal.

Comprehension and Thought Questions:

1. Why do you suppose the plaintiffs wanted Barrier Island to repurchase their condos?

2. Did plaintiffs and Barrier Island enter into a contract for the plaintiffs' initial purchase of the condos at issue in the case?

3. Did plaintiffs and Barrier Island enter into a contract providing for Barrier Island's repurchase of those condos?

4. What is the general rule regarding an agent's authority to bind a principal to a contract? How does that apply to an attorney such as Gray?

5. Did Gray bind Barrier Island to the version of the repurchase contract that plaintiffs signed?

6. Do you agree with the majority that Gray did not have authority to bind his client to the repurchase agreement, or do you agree with the dissent, which would have allowed the jury to find that Gray had authority?

Hypothetical Variations:

1. What if Gray had worked as an in-house lawyer for Barrier Island?

2. What if Gray had signed the same repurchase agreement that the plaintiffs had signed?

3. What if Shaver and Lancaster, Barrier Island's principals, had told Gray that he could agree to the plaintiffs' version of the repurchase agreement and so, on that basis, he signed it?

4. What if Gray had signed similar repurchase agreements on behalf of Barrier Island on prior occasions and Shaver and Lancaster knew about those instances and never objected?

PRACTICE PROBLEM 11-1

Your longtime friend Vivian Lang recently finished her medical internship in pediatric oncology and was offered a job to work at Pediatric Oncology Group Inc. (POGI), one of only two pediatric oncology medical groups in the state of Indiana. Vivian has asked you to review the draft employment agreement POGI sent her.

The draft employment agreement specifies that Vivian will be hired as a full-time pediatric oncologist for POGI, and that she will be paid $250,000 per year, with an annual increase of 5 percent of the prior year's salary. The draft also includes a non-compete covenant in which Vivian agrees that upon her departure from POGI for any reason, she will not compete with POGI anywhere in Indiana for five years. Of course, this might mean that if Vivian leaves POGI for any reason, she may have to move to a different state for five years, find a job there, and become licensed to practice medicine in that state.

After reviewing the draft employment agreement, you inform Vivian that the non-compete is likely not enforceable under Indiana contract law. Not only would the non-compete deprive Indiana residents of their choice in pediatric oncologists and deprive Vivian of a way to make a living, but it would do so for an unreasonably long time. Vivian asks you to contact POGI and try to negotiate the non-compete so it would either allow her to practice pediatric oncology at the other clinic in Indiana if she were to leave POGI, or to limit her non-compete to no more than one year.

You call POGI and speak with POGI's President, Charley Bell. You explain to Charley your concerns with Vivian's employment agreement. Charley says he understands those concerns, and asks if Vivian would be willing to limit the time of the non-compete to 18 months. You respond that she would. You then hang up, satisfied that you have addressed one of your key concerns under Vivian's employment agreement.

1. Did you have authority to agree to a non-compete period of 18 months on behalf of Vivian?

2. Have you acted in accordance with your professional responsibility as a lawyer in this situation?

3. Suppose when you called POGI, the President informed you that POGI was not going to modify the non-compete in Vivian's employment agreement, as every POGI employment agreement had the same non-compete clause. What do you do next?

C. DRAFTING THE CONTRACT

1. Lawyer's Role

This material, as with the material above on contract negotiation, is based on the authors' experiences as transactional attorneys.[6]

To begin, oftentimes, a lawyer drafts a contract after she has learned the key terms the businesspeople negotiated. In other words, she drafts the contract even before she negotiates its terms. Thus, a lawyer's role as draftsperson is integrally tied to her role as negotiator. That occurred in the simulated scenario in Section A, where Monk, Manufacturer's lawyer, drafted the asset purchase agreement even before engaging in negotiations with Supplier or Supplier's lawyer.

Recall that in that simulated scenario, Monk prepared the first draft of the asset purchase agreement. In lawyered transactions, one party's lawyer will prepare the first draft of the contract. Custom often dictates which side's counsel prepares the first draft. In most cases, where one party's primary obligation is to pay money—like a buyer's purchase of assets, or a lender's making of a loan—then that party's lawyer usually prepares the first draft of the contract. That is because that is the party who needs the bulk of the protections that a contract provides. For example, in a transaction for the sale of assets, it is the buyer who will face risks if the seller does not actually own the assets, or the assets are in bad condition. And in a loan transaction, it is the lender who will face risks if it lends money to a borrower who does not have enough money to repay the loan, or who makes risky business decisions leading to its bankruptcy.

However, in some lawyered transactions, there is no custom for who prepares the first draft, and one party is not the presumed drafter based on the risks it faces as compared to other party. This commonly occurs in partnerships, where all parties to the contract will have some degree of obligation and

---

6. The drafting process is also well described by Professor Tina Stark in her book *Drafting Contracts: How and Why Lawyers Do What They Do* (2d ed. 2014).

rights, and will be at risk from the actions of the other partners. Where that happens, and if you have any say in the matter, you should volunteer to draft. That is because there are benefits to preparing the first draft of the contract. Importantly, by preparing the first draft, a lawyer can "engineer" many of the contractual terms to benefit his or her client. That then forces the other party and its counsel to have to negotiate for specific changes to the draft.

Drafting involves much more than merely transcribing the businesspeople's agreement. For one, businesspeople often do not specify how to implement the terms of their agreement in "contract speak." In other words, while they might agree that one party will sell its assets to a buyer, they do not know that doing so requires the use of a covenant by the seller to reflect the seller's promise. It is up to the lawyer to draft those terms in a way that is clear, has legal effect, and achieves the client's goal.

Additionally, businesspeople do not usually negotiate the details of their respective legal obligation. Thus, it is up to the drafter to add details to the written contract so that the parties know how to perform, and a court can determine when a party has breached if a dispute arises.

Finally, businesspeople often do not always anticipate what events or circumstances could undermine the benefits they expect under the contract. Thus, it is the lawyer's job, through negotiation and drafting, to ensure the client receives the benefit of the agreed-upon terms by anticipating what could undermine the benefits to the client and protecting the client from those risks using tools such as contract terms. Lawyers also draft in a way to preserve flexibility in case future opportunities arise that are attractive to the client and that the client might want to pursue without breaching the contract.

a. Learning about a transaction

Wonderful news—your client is entering into a partnership and has volunteered you to prepare the first draft of the partnership agreement. Your initial reaction would undoubtedly be: Where do I start?

While the drafting process varies by client and transaction, the following is a typical drafting process:

First, a lawyer gathers all of the information he or she can about the transaction. That means obtaining a copy of the term sheet, if there is one, and any other written exchanges among the parties that contain terms. Often the lawyer will have to meet with her client to gather the full picture of the transaction.

Moreover, in many transactions, the lawyer must understand the client's operations and the other side's operations to ensure that the client's interests are adequately protected. For example, imagine that you represent the seller of a grocery store. Your client also operates the adjoining restaurant, which it is not selling. Some questions you would need to discuss with your client to understand the transaction would include: Are there any shared assets between the restaurant and the market? If so, are those being sold? If not, are they being leased to the buyer? Do any employees work for both the grocery store and the restaurant? If so, will that continue after the sale? If so, how will the parties divide up those employees' time and compensation? And if there is one landlord for the entire premises, how will the parties divide up the lease obligations? There are other questions, too. However, the point is that you often need to really dig into your client's business, as well as the counterparty's business and intentions, to understand the transaction.

Once the lawyer has learned about the transaction, the next task is typically to find precedents for purposes of preparing the first draft of the contract. "Precedents" in this context refers to other contracts that the lawyer can use to help her draft.

Often lawyers or law firms create "form" databanks from which lawyers can pull a form contract for a particular type of transaction. Even without such a databank, lawyers frequently ask fellow lawyers who worked on similar transactions for precedents. In finding precedents, a lawyer is wise to look for precedents drafted from the perspective of the party who was in the same position as her client is. If not, the lawyer might unintentionally engineer the contract in a way that is too generous to the other side.

The client is another source of precedents where the client has previously entered into a similar contract. Where that occurs, the client will likely find comfort in already having been bound by similar obligations before, and will likely want the lawyer to adhere to the terms in the precedent contract to the extent possible. Sometimes even the counterparty is the same as in the prior transaction. Where that occurs, good luck implementing any non-deal-specific changes to the precedent contract! This commonly happens in the commercial lending context, where the same lender lends to the same borrower, or to an affiliate of the borrower, at the end of the term of the prior loan. While the lender's lawyer will surely change the loan amount and interest rate to reflect the terms of the new loan, many of the other provisions of the loan agreement will remain unchanged from the prior loan agreement.

No matter what precedents a lawyer uses in drafting, the lawyer must exercise judgment and not blindly follow the precedents she is drafting from. For example, suppose you represent the buyer of assets and are drafting the asset purchase agreement using one a colleague prepared for a different transaction (and perhaps one drafted by the colleague when representing a *seller*). The precedent asset purchase agreement includes a provision that reads as follows:

> At closing, the Buyer shall assume all of the Seller's liabilities and obligations, whether known or unknown, actual or contingent, existing or arising in the future.

The term sheet you have been given states that your client is buying all of the seller's assets, but is only assuming specific contractual obligations. If you did not modify this provision of the precedent in your client's asset purchase agreement, what would result? In a nutshell, you would have failed to reflect the agreed-upon terms, and would have bound your client to assume *all* of the seller's obligations. This could potentially cost your client a LOT of money. While in most instances your client would have caught your mistake, you cannot risk the chance that the client will not. Even if your client catches the mistake before the document is sent to the seller and its counsel, you will likely not be seeing much work from that client again, or the partner who asked you to work on this deal. This is why understanding the structure of written contracts, discussed in Chapter 3, is so important. A transactional lawyer needs to understand the function of each part of a contract and how these parts work together to protect the client.

Finally, as a lawyer drafts, he or she must ensure that the contract terms are enforceable against the counterparty. After all, one of the main reasons parties enter into a contract is to obtain certainty about the counterparty's future performance, and to receive a remedy if the counterparty fails to perform an obligation. Ensuring enforceability means not only ensuring that the counterparty's obligations would be enforced as a matter of contract law in the relevant jurisdiction, but also reflects any mandatory aspects of other applicable law. If a drafter is not competent in a particular area of law that is relevant to a contract, the lawyer either needs to study up to become competent, or have another lawyer who is competent in that area assist with the contract.

For example, in New York, not only must a person who sells real estate do so in writing through a deed transferring ownership of the real estate (which deed is a contract), but the transferor's signature must be acknowledged or attested by one witness before delivery.[7] Moreover, that deed must include a legal description of the property being transferred and must be recorded in the county where the property being transferred is located.[8] If a deed does not satisfy these requirements, it is void against a person who subsequently in good faith purchases that same real estate for consideration.[9] Thus, a lawyer who works on a transaction in which real property in New York is being sold must either ensure that these requirements are met, or have another lawyer who is well versed in New York real property law assist with this aspect of the transaction.

This discussion is obviously a very cursory overview of the drafting process. If your law school offers a course on contract drafting, you can explore this process in more detail in that class.

---

7. N.Y. Real Prop. Law § 243 (1909).
8. *Id.* at § 291.
9. *Id.*

b. Reviewing a contract

Suppose that either custom dictates that the other side prepares the first draft of a contract, or that the parties have agreed that the counterparty's counsel will prepare the first draft. What is your role as the recipient of such a draft?

In this situation, your role is similar to your role as the draftsperson. That is, you must ensure that the draft reflects the parties' agreed-upon terms; that it otherwise contains terms that are customary for that transaction and, if relevant, that are similar to a prior transaction between the same parties; that the contract is fair and does not unduly shift risk to your client; that the contract preserves flexibility needed by your client; and that the contract is enforceable against the counterparty. Thus, the reviewing lawyer performs virtually all of the same tasks as the drafting lawyer, including becoming informed of the parties and the transaction and finding precedents. However, since the reviewing lawyer is confronted with a first draft, she must help her client negotiate for desired changes. In that way, the reviewing lawyer's negotiation task is even more challenging, as she has to justify requested changes in the face of the other side's initial contract design choices.

PRACTICE PROBLEM 11-2

Refer back to Practice Problem 11-1. Assume that three months after entering into an employment agreement with POGI, your client Vivian Lang informs you that her brother has been diagnosed with cancer. She would like to be there to support her brother through his treatment. So she would like to reduce her workload to 80 percent of full-time hours. She realizes this will lead to a decrease in salary—she is fine with that, though she wants to be able to ratchet back up to full time after her brother's treatment is finished.

Vivian asks you to contact POGI's General Counsel, Trey Wood, to discuss Vivian's request. You agree to call Trey. You inform Vivian that on that call, you plan to volunteer to draft the amendment.

1. What arguments can you put forth to try to persuade Trey that you should prepare the first draft of the amendment?

2. Assuming you successfully convince Trey to let you prepare the first draft, what are some resources you can use to help you prepare that draft?

c. Avoiding ambiguity

One of the most common drafting pitfalls is that the lawyer will unintentionally draft a provision in an ambiguous way. Language is **ambiguous** where it is reasonably capable of more than one meaning. One consequence of an ambiguity is that the obligated party may not know how to perform the contract. If, in fact, the parties understand the ambiguous term differently from one another, that could lead to the disappointment of expectations, where one party performs in a way the other party did not understand was called for by the contract. Ambiguity could also give a party fodder to avoid undesirable obligations in the future. In other words, where a party realizes a transaction is not delivering the benefits it desires, it might read the drafted contract with a scrutinizing eye and think about what arguments it can make to avoid obligations. Ambiguity in those obligations can create ammunition for a party to avoid its obligations. For these reasons, as a drafter, it is good to root out all ambiguity in a contract, so that the contract reflects the parties' shared understanding as to their respective rights and duties.

There are many techniques that a lawyer can use to avoid ambiguity. For one, the lawyer should familiarize herself with common ambiguities and how to root them out. For example, suppose a contract provides that a party must deliver notice **by** December 31. Here, the term "by" is ambiguous. That is because it is not clear if the party must deliver notice **before** December 31, or if the party can also deliver notice **on** December 31. The fix is to replace the word "by" with either "before" or "on or before," depending on whether the parties' intent is to allow delivery of a notice on December 31.

As another example, imagine that a contract requires a seller of its business to list in a schedule "each of the seller's material permits and contracts." Here, there is an ambiguity due to the structure of the sentence—does the word "material" qualify only permits, or also contracts? One way to resolve this ambiguity is to add the word "material" before the word "contracts" so that it is clear that the word "material" qualifies both permits and contracts. But without this or another fix, a dispute could arise later if the buyer realizes that the seller did not list all of its material contracts, but the seller did not think such disclosure was required.

Finally, a lawyer may unknowingly draft contract language with a latent ambiguity—that is, an ambiguity that is not apparent on the face of a contract. For example, imagine that a contract between a homeowner and painter provided as follows:

"Painter will paint one complete coat of paint on the inside walls of the House."

Here, the use of the term "one complete coat of paint" in a house-painting contract may generally be understood by homeowners to include a coat of primer paint. Based on this language, the homeowner may subjectively understand and intend the primer paint coat to be included, and may also reasonably believe that the painter intends this as well. The painter, on the other hand, may subjectively understand this language to not require a coat of primer paint. The painter may be reasonable in this belief if this language customarily does not include a coat of primer.

Unfortunately, this difference in the parties' understandings of this phrase might emerge when the painter starts to perform. That is when the homeowner would see that no primer paint is being applied.

Lawyers try to anticipate potential latent ambiguities like this from emerging during performance. They do that by ensuring that the written contract reflects the client's intention. If that understanding does not comport with the counterparty's understanding, the parties can then negotiate to see if they can work out that difference. That way, lawyers can help the client avoid expensive litigation during performance by ensuring that the contract is unambiguous at the outset.

In this example, the drafter could cure the ambiguity in one of many ways. One approach is to simply use different language, such as "one complete coat of primer paint and one complete coat of paint" instead of "one complete coat of paint." Alternatively, the contract could create a defined term, "Complete Coat," and define that term to mean "one complete coat of primer paint and one complete coat of paint." This would be especially useful if the contract uses this term more than once in the contract.

One final, general technique that lawyers sometimes use to root out ambiguity is to review, or ask a litigator on her team to review a draft as if the lawyer represented the counterparty wanting to avoid the contract, or specific obligations in the contract. With that mindset, a lawyer is placed in the counterparty's shoes, and sees what "outs" that party might have as a result of ambiguous language.

Thus, ideally in drafting, the lawyer helps the client have its subjective intentions expressed as clearly as possible in the written contract. By doing so, the lawyer helps identify potential future disagreements and forces the parties to resolve it prior to contract formation. This, in turn, helps the parties avoid future disputes over the meaning of the contract.

Where, despite a lawyer's drafting efforts, an ambiguous provision remains, or one party opportunistically uses an ambiguity to avoid undesired contractual obligations, the matter could lead to litigation. Where it does, a court will have to resolve the ambiguity for the parties. Chapter 13 explains the rules of interpretation and how courts resolve ambiguities. The key point here, though, is that a lawyer can help her client avoid litigation by drafting clearly and avoiding ambiguity.

Nevertheless, keep in mind that it is impossible to draft a perfectly "clear" contract. Even if you wanted to, it would be extremely expensive and time-intensive to make sure that each word in a contract had only one generally understood meaning or to provide perfect clarifications with respect to each word. For example, a simple contract for someone to mow your lawn on a weekly basis could become a document hundreds of pages long in the hands of attorneys, which would not make sense given the low value of the lawn service.

d. Drafting purposefully vague terms

While a drafter will want to avoid ambiguity, that does not mean every term in a contract must be spelled out with certainty. In fact, there are benefits to drafting using vague terms such as reasonable and material. Here, the word **vague** means open-ended or indefinite. While a vague word or phrase cannot be pinned down with certainty, an ambiguous word or phrase is one that has a definite number of mutually exclusive meanings.

Uncertainty through vagueness is a tactic lawyers uses to preserve flexibility for the future. For example, a tenant and landlord may disagree regarding whether landlord's consent should be required if tenant elects to assign the lease to an equally creditworthy third party. To solve the issue, the parties may agree the landlord has a consent right, but that such consent may not be "unreasonably withheld." Obviously, it may be unclear today under what circumstances in the future it would be unreasonable for the landlord to withhold its consent. On the other hand, the parties can likely live with that uncertainty because a dispute about that term may never arise, and each party preserves some degree of flexibility if it does. Plus, the transaction costs may be too high to justify spending too much time negotiating the specifics of this term.

e. Drafting terms to be determined in the future

Sometimes, parties enter into a contract but intend to agree on some aspect of performance in the future. As you will learn in Chapter 13, there is a risk that a court will not enforce such an indefinite agreement, as courts generally do not enforce agreements to agree. Fortunately, there is a drafting solution. It is to draft either a formula or a process for determining that term in the future, thereby removing the parties' total discretion to agree—or not agree—on the term in the future.

For example, suppose a landlord and tenant want to defer to the end of the lease term the amount of rent the tenant will pay when it renews the lease. Here, rather than simply having the parties agree to agree on the amount of rent at the time of renewal (which, as an agreement to agree, may not be enforced), the parties could agree up front on a formula to determine the renewal lease amount, which factors into increases to property values in the area, possibly using recent rental values in the area. Or the parties could identify an appraiser to fix the new rental amount based on then-current rental values in the area, possibly within specified limits.

Below is an example of a lease provision providing for a rent renewal formula. A different section of the lease would have defined the term "Renewal Period" to mean the second ten-year period of the lease, and "Base Rent" to mean the rental amount the tenant agreed to pay the landlord under the first ten years of the lease.

> Beginning at the start of the Renewal Period and for each month during the Renewal Period, Tenant shall pay Landlord rent equal to the then Fair Market Value of the Premises. For this purpose, "Fair Market Value" means the rental amount paid to lease equivalent space at a warehouse located in the same zip code as the Premises, as determined by Local Appraisers LLC or its successor. The parties agree that in no event will rent during the Renewal Period fall below the rent paid by the Tenant during the original term of the Lease. Tenant shall pay the costs of having Local Appraisers LLC appraise the Premises to determine Fair Market Value at the start of the Renewal Period.

Whatever approach the parties choose to such a term, the point is that there is a way to draft a provision to provide flexibility to the party in search of flexibility, and enough certainty to the party seeking certainty that a court will enforce the contract.

PRACTICE PROBLEM 11-3

You represent a company that sells and installs hardwood flooring and other similar flooring. Your client has agreed to sell all of its assets to a company that is in the business of selling and installing carpeting. The purchase price is $2 million, plus an additional payment of 5 percent of all of the profits generated in the business after closing. This latter portion of the purchase price is referred to as an "earnout," as the seller must essentially "earn" the additional 5 percent of profits based on the performance of the business after closing. What questions do you have for your client with respect to this earnout provision? How will this affect how you draft the contract? Explain why.

f. Ethical pitfalls

Sometimes a lawyer accidentally omits from the written contract a term the parties agreed on, or fails to delete a term that the parties agreed to remove. Where either situation happens, when one of the parties realizes the mistake, usually the other party acknowledges that the writing does not reflect the actual terms that were agreed on. The parties then will reform the writing so that it accurately reflects the agreed-upon terms.

However, where this happens, a client might want to seize on the drafting mistake to get a better deal than what was actually agreed upon. For example, assume you represent a seller of a parcel of land. The seller and buyer agreed that the purchase price would be $20,000 for the land. However, the buyer's lawyer accidentally drafted the purchase price as $22,000. You did not notice this mistake at the time the contract was drafted. However, your client noticed it at closing. Can your client demand that the buyer pay the extra $2,000?

The short answer is no. The document clearly contains a typographical mistake. Moreover, as a lawyer, you have an ethical obligation to act honestly.[10] If you help your client try to seize on this drafting mistake to earn an additional $2,000, this would be dishonest and would violate your ethical obligation as a lawyer. Moreover, as Chapter 13 explains, where a written contract contains a mistake in terms, courts have the power to equitably reform the contracts in a way to actually reflect the agreed-upon terms. So if this dispute ended up in litigation (and assuming the seller convinced the court that the parties had actually agreed on a $20,000 purchase price), the court would enforce the contract at that price. And again, you could be subject to discipline for having engaged in dishonest conduct.

Other ethical pitfalls arise during the drafting processes, too. When they do come up, keep in mind that as a lawyer, you are a professional with a duty to act honestly. These duties should help guide you through the thicket where a client or counterparty engages in conduct that seems unethical or dishonest.

PRACTICE PROBLEM 11-4

Assume your client Zee Jones owns a condominium complex. Zee decides to sell the condo complex to Alegra Guiseppe for $2 million. The parties agree that in addition to the $2 million purchase price, Alegra will pay Zee $250,000 on the first anniversary of the closing of the sale of the condo complex if rental income from the condo complex does not decrease during that first year following the change in ownership. Thus, Zee could potentially receive $2,250,000 from this sale.

Bobby Graham, Alegra's lawyer, drafts the real estate purchase agreement and sends the draft to you and Zee. The following is the language included in the draft on purchase price. Keep in mind that the term "Buyer" has already been defined as Alegra and "Seller" has already been defined as Zee.

> The purchase price is $2,250,000 payable as follows:
>
> (1) Buyer shall pay $2,000,000 of the purchase price to Seller at the Closing.
> (2) Buyer shall pay $250,000 to Seller on the first anniversary of the Closing.

Upon seeing the draft, Zee immediately calls you. He asks you to leave the purchase price provision as is, and not to make any comments to it.

1. Does the purchase price provision reflect the parties' agreement? If it does not, how is the draft inconsistent with the terms the parties agreed upon?

---

10. *See* Model Rules of Prof'l Conduct r 4.1 (2002).

2. Assuming the provision does not reflect the parties' agreement, do you have an ethical obligation to raise the mistake with Bobby?

3. What will happen if you and Zee do not notice this mistake until the first anniversary of the sale of the condo complex? If rental income drops during that first year, can your client insist that Alegra pay the additional $250,000?

4. Suppose Alegra is Canadian and her lawyer, Bobby Graham, is only licensed in Canada. Zee lives in the United States and you are licensed in the United States. Moreover, the condo complex is located in the United States. Does this change in facts create any potential ambiguities in the above contract provision? As you consider this question, remember that the currency in Canada is the Canadian Dollar, which is often denoted with a $.

2. Client's Role

If you are the contract draftsperson, once you have prepared the first draft of a contract, you will usually send it to your client for review. Your client will then review the draft and provide you with comments. It is commonplace for the lawyer to identify specific areas where she wants client input when sending the draft to the client. That way, the client knows where to focus her attention. Moreover, it is often a good idea to explain to the client where the draft addresses any terms the client identified as particularly important, to make sure the lawyer has accurately captured the client's intent.

If the other party's counsel is drafting the contract, then your client will still review the draft when it is delivered to you and your client. However, your client will review the draft with a more critical eye given that it was drafted from the other party's perspective. Again, you support this review by flagging significant terms for your client, and identifying any terms that seem overly protective of the other side, impractical for your client to perform, or not customary.

Regardless of who drafts the first draft, your client will need to ensure that it can perform the promises contained in the agreement. If not, your client will be taking a risk that it will breach the contract despite making every effort to perform. To prevent that from occurring, as discussed in Chapter 3, it is better to have your client only make promises to do and not do things within its control.

For example, suppose Manufacturer needs to obtain a $9 million loan before it can pay the $13 million purchase price to Supplier for its assets. The contract could, in theory, obligate Manufacturer to get this $9 million loan. But that would be risky, as Manufacturer can't control whether a lender would be willing to make a loan to it in this amount. However, Manufacturer could make a promise to *request* a loan for $9 million. Drafted this way, now Manufacturer can control its performance. Of course, if Manufacturer requests a loan yet cannot find a lender to make this loan, it still will not want to buy Supplier's assets. Manufacturer can be protected in this instance by including a condition to closing that it must have obtained this loan. That way, if it cannot get a loan for $9 million despite requesting one, it still will not have a duty to buy Supplier's assets.

Similarly, your client must review the representations and warranties to ensure that they are true. If not, they will need to be changed so that they are true to avoid having your client become liable for a misrepresentation or breach of warranty. There are many ways to qualify a representation and warranty to prevent your client from making a misrepresentation or breaching a warranty. As Chapter 3 discussed, one common way is to qualify the representations and warranties by a list of any exceptions to the representations and warranties (i.e., instances where the representation or warranty is not true) in disclosure schedules. Where this is done, your client will need to prepare those schedules, listing the information to be disclosed on those schedules. Often the lawyer helps her client perform this task, to make sure the information listed is responsive and complete, yet does not reveal confidential or sensitive information. These schedules, then, are attached to, and become a part of, the contract.

Below is a representation and warranty as to the condition of an asset. As you will see, part of this representation calls for disclosure on a disclosure schedule. In the example below, the content of the Disclosure Schedule is set out after the representation and warranty. In reality, the Disclosure Schedule would go at the back of the contract, after the parties' signature pages.

Seller Representation and Warranties

3.3 <u>Condition of Crane</u>. The Seller owns the Crane, and, except as provided on <u>Schedule 3.3</u>, the Crane is in good condition, ordinary wear and tear excepted.

<u>Schedule 3.3</u>
1. The slewing unit is in need of servicing so that it rotates 360 degrees.
2. The hook on the Crane is slightly rusted.

PRACTICE PROBLEM 11-5

Refer back to Practice Problem 11-4. Imagine that Bobby Graham, Alegra's lawyer, has drafted the following representation and warranty in the purchase agreement for the sale of your client Zee's condo complex:

3.7 Seller represents and warrants to Buyer that there are not currently, and have never been, any hazardous chemicals used or stored on the Premises.

After seeing the draft agreement, Zee calls you to inform you that he in fact does store hazardous chemicals at the Premises. Specifically, he stores hazardous chemicals at the Premises that are used to clean common areas at the Premises as well as chemicals that are used to perform regular maintenance on the Premises' sewage system.

How do you suggest addressing Zee's concern?

D. LAWYERS AND "FORM" CONTRACTS

Many transactions are not "lawyered," meaning that one or both the parties are not represented by counsel in the specific transaction. For example, when you buy a television from Best Buy, neither you nor Best Buy has a lawyer present to negotiate the terms of the purchase contract. Recall that these "form" contracts were discussed in Chapter 6. Because this portion of the textbook focuses on lawyered transactions, it will only briefly mention some insights into the lawyer's role with these "form" contracts.

First, as you may know from experience, it is virtually impossible to have changes made to form contracts. If you have not experienced this, try negotiating with Amazon its terms and conditions!

Second, because these contracts are not negotiated, there is not much role for the lawyer to play where the client enters one of these "form" contracts. However, sometimes a business client who is seeing a form supplied by the other side for the first time asks its lawyer to review that form contract. Here, your role is not to modify the contract to protect your client's objectives. Instead, your task is to help the client understand the contract and what risks the client faces in entering the contract. Armed with that knowledge, the client might be able to explore ways to mitigate those risks outside of the contract. For example, if a form supply contract requires a buyer to pay in full for the goods supplied within 30 days, the buyer might establish a credit line with a bank in case it does not have enough cash flow from its operations to pay amounts under the contract when owed.

Finally, clients will periodically ask their lawyer to review and update their "form" contracts. Often the purpose of this review is to ensure that the form contract complies with law, reflects customary terms as well as best practices, and, to the extent possible, preempts any inconsistent terms supplied by the other party if there is a "battle of the forms."[11] If the lawyer sees any shortcomings in the form in any of these respects, she proposes changes to the "form" contract to her client. Usually making a change to a "form" contract requires several layers of internal approval. Thus, a lawyer must be prepared to defend

---

11. Recall that Chapter 5 discussed the battle of the forms.

each of her proposed changes, as those changes might lead to changed internal processes and practices.

Now that you have studied contract drafting, read through and answer the questions that follow the Simulation Problem for Chapter 11, which is located in Appendix A.

CONTRACT TERMS AND PERFORMANCE

This part presumes that the contracting parties have satisfied the elements of contract formation. It discusses the next stage in a contract's existence—the interpretation and performance of that contract. First, Chapter 12 discusses processes clients often employ to ensure that they satisfy their contractual obligations. That chapter also explains the implied duties with which contracting parties must comply. Finally, it explains how parties can modify their obligations to ensure that they do not commit a breach. Chapter 13 then reveals some concerns with contract performance tied to a contracting party's understanding of the contract terms. In particular, it explains the concerns raised where contract language is ambiguous, as well as how the parties can (and if the matter is litigated, a court will) resolve such an ambiguity. Next, Chapter 14 discusses implied terms, but for contracts governed by UCC Article 2. Finally, Chapter 15 explains the parol evidence rule, and how that rule limits what evidence a party can introduce at trial to prove (or disprove) a written contract's terms.

The following diagram shows where the topics covered in Part IV fit into the larger scheme of this course.

PART IV—OVERVIEW DIAGRAM

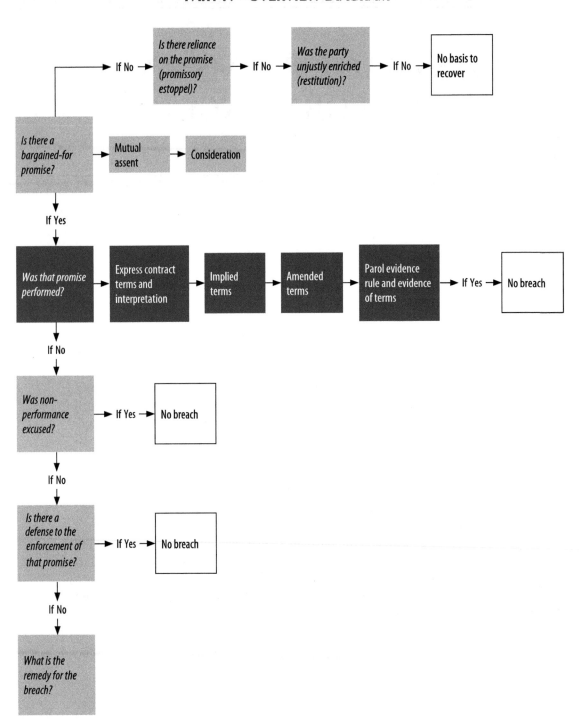

CHAPTER 12

Performing and Modifying the Contract

Once the parties have formed a contract, they need to perform their respective obligations under that contract. That means each party must perform its obligation in accordance with the contract in the manner and at the times promised in the contract. The failure to do so, without a justification for not performing, constitutes a **breach**. A breach, in turn, allows the other party to receive a remedy. In addition, in certain circumstances, a significant breach may excuse the other party from performing its remaining obligations under the contract. You will study the circumstances where the other party's breach will excuse a party from performing its obligations under a contract in Chapter 16.

It is important to note that nonperformance of *any* unexcused contractual duty is a breach—it does not have to be a significant breach or an important duty. Accordingly, it is important for clients and their attorneys to understand each party's performance obligations under a contract.

Attorneys help clients during the contract performance stage in many ways. From helping clients understand and comply with their obligations to helping clients monitor the opposing party's contractual compliance, attorneys are often deeply involved during the performance period. The attorney's role in contract performance is discussed in Section A. Section A also discusses the terms of the contract and how to determine when a client's performance obligation is due.

A party's contractual duties are not confined to the terms expressed in the written contract. Some contractual duties are actually implied by law. Some of those implied terms exist by virtue of statutes. Other implied duties exist by virtue of the common law. Section B discusses those implied duties. Chapter 14 discusses implied terms for contracts governed by Article 2 of the UCC.

As the parties perform, circumstances may arise that require a change to the contract terms. Moreover, sometimes a party decides it does not care if the other party performs a specific obligation in the manner specified in the contract. Attorneys are often involved in these processes as well. That is, they help their clients amend contracts. They also help their clients avoid unintentionally taking actions that amount to amendments. The law relating to amendments is discussed in Section C.

After reviewing the materials in this chapter, you should understand that the attorney's job is not nearly done once the contract has been formed. Later chapters will address the obvious situation that demands attorney assistance: namely, when a client has decided to sue or when a client has been sued for a breach of contract. This chapter focuses on avoiding a breach in the first place, by ensuring contract performance.

A. PERFORMING EXPRESS PROVISIONS

1. Performing the Promises; Identifying and Charting the Promises

A contract sets out the set of promises each party makes in a contract. If you recall from Chapter 3, those promises are reflected in a contract through **covenants**. Each party must then perform those covenants (i.e., promises) in the manner and at the time(s) specified in the contract. That means that if a supplier has promised to deliver 30 widgets free of liens no later than May 7 under the contract, then the supplier must deliver exactly 30 widgets free of liens no later than May 7. Any failure to do so—such as by delivering 27 widgets, or delivering any widgets subject to a lien, or delivering any widgets later than May 7—will constitute a breach, unless for some reason that supplier's obligation has been excused.

In simple contracts, parties may not need or seek an attorney's advice regarding how to understand or perform their covenants in the contract. For example, a painter who contracted to paint a homeowner's bedroom presumably would not need to have an attorney explain what the painter needed to do under the contract. The painter would have spoken with the homeowner, determined what needed to be done (what type and color of paint, how many coats, and so on), and promised to perform in exchange for payment. Once the contract was signed, the painter would understand the homeowner's requirements or, if not, could discuss with the homeowner any open questions or issues.

On the other hand, more complex contracts or contracts involving unfamiliar or irregular transactions may necessitate more attorney involvement during the post-signing period. For example, most business owners do not have extensive experience buying and selling companies or with purchase agreements that address the purchase of a business. These purchase agreements can be quite extensive, often running well over 50 or even 100 pages long. The seller often has dozens of obligations to fulfill under the purchase agreement, including the delivery of title transfer documents, required third party consents, and documents showing corporate authority to enter into the transaction. In those instances, it would be nearly impossible for a layperson to be able to understand and keep track of all of the seller's obligations.

The attorney fills this void in a few ways. Attorneys use checklists that detail all of the contractual (and noncontractual) tasks that need to be performed for complicated transactions. In sale transactions, these checklists often are shared with the other party's counsel to make sure that everyone "is on the same page" with respect to what needs to be done in order to have a successful closing. These checklists are updated on a regular basis and shared with the client where appropriate. An excerpt from a simple checklist used to purchase equipment is below.

CLOSING DATE: JULY 15, 2016

Item/Action	Responsible Party	Status
Purchase Agreement	Buyer's counsel/ Seller's counsel	Final; needs to be signed
Bill of Sale (to transfer the equipment)	Buyer's counsel	Draft to be circulated by Buyer to Seller on 6/30/16
Buyer's Payment of Purchase Price	Buyer	Need wire instructions from Seller
Consent of Seller's lender (required for transfer of the equipment under Seller's loan agreement)	Seller	Seller has contacted lender on 6/25/16; consent form has not been signed and returned yet
Evidence of governmental permit transfer (required to be delivered within 30 days of closing)	Seller	Application for permit transfer to be filed on closing date; application has been filled out but needs to be signed by Seller

By detailing out each of the contractual requirements, the attorney is able to simplify the performance process for her client. In addition, the attorney provides a valuable service to the client by managing the performance process and even performing some of those tasks on behalf of the client. For instance, in the above example, the Seller's counsel would likely be the one to follow up with the lender to try to obtain the lender's consent.

These checklists also can include items required for the transaction that are not mentioned in the contract. This is another area where an attorney can use her "business sense" to make sure that the client is thinking of all the tasks that need to be done for a transaction. For example, the Seller may want to conduct its own lien searches to make sure there is no lien against the Seller's assets, which might prevent the Seller from successfully transferring those assets free of liens. It generally makes sense to include those types of due diligence tasks, which are often not specified in the contract, in the checklist as well so that they are not forgotten.

Attorneys can also help the client keep track of the due dates for obligations. Again, with more complex transactions, clients may be overwhelmed or not focused on all of the different delivery dates for covenants. Attorneys often help by sending reminders to clients. Of course, this requires the attorneys themselves to keep track of the required timing for each covenant. Many attorneys use an integrated calendar that incorporates the different deadlines for obligations under significant client contracts. It is often useful to have a calendar send you multiple reminders, such as a week or two before the due date and again a day or two before, so that you are sure to follow up with the client as to its performance of those obligations. Other attorneys provide separate checklists to their clients of all their promised tasks with due dates specified on them. You typically will want to discuss with your clients whether they would like you to engage in this sort of performance management process.

While the above scenario contemplates a one-time transaction, parties have ongoing obligations in term contracts as well. For example, in a loan transaction, the lender may require the borrower to perform many obligations until the loan is repaid, which could be many years in the future. Many of those obligations would require the borrower to take certain actions, and refrain from taking other actions, designed to ensure that the borrower remains creditworthy while the loan is outstanding. Such a covenant may look something like this:

> SECTION 3.14 So long as any indebtedness remains outstanding under the Promissory Note executed by Borrower for the benefit of Lender, Borrower agrees that it will not (i) incur any other indebtedness, except for indebtedness to purchase equipment not to exceed $1,000,000, or (ii) sell any of its assets other than inventory in the ordinary course of business.

You may recall from Chapters 3 and 11 that lawyers help their clients negotiate these types of covenants. Thus, the Borrower's lawyer likely helped the client negotiate for the exception in subparagraph (i) that allows the Borrower to incur indebtedness up to $1 million to purchase equipment. Similarly, the lawyer likely helped the client negotiate the "ordinary course" exception to the covenant against sales of assets. By understanding and addressing the client's needs during the negotiation process, an attorney helps a client later, in the performance stage. That is because the attorney has made sure the client can perform its obligations, and does not commit a breach through its ordinary and anticipated operations.

During the contract performance stage, the lawyer would then help her client understand and actually perform those negotiated contract terms. That would mean, in this example, ensuring that the Borrower understands what types of debt it cannot incur under the loan agreement, as well as which assets it cannot sell under the agreement.

2. Satisfying Conditions

As you know, contracts do not only contain covenants. Virtually all contracts also contain conditions. As you may recall from Chapter 3, conditions are events or circumstances whose occurrence is uncertain but that need to occur before a party's performance obligation is due. If any condition to an obligation is not satisfied, then the party's obligation subject to that condition is not due. In other words, that party need not perform the obligation that was subject to that condition, and that failure will not amount to a breach.

To see how this works, imagine that a buyer of a house includes the following condition to its performance obligation in its house purchase contract:

> Buyer's obligation to purchase the Premises is expressly conditioned upon the Seller's delivery at least five business days prior to the Closing Date of an environmental report, from an environmental consulting company reasonably acceptable to Buyer, demonstrating the absence of radon or other harmful pollutants on the Premises.

Here, the buyer's obligations to buy the house and pay the purchase price are conditioned on the seller providing a clean inspection report. That means if either the inspection shows there is radon, or the seller is unable to procure such an inspection, then the buyer's obligation to buy the house never becomes due. This outcome follows from the fact that this term was stated as a "condition."

You might think that the consequence of the buyer not receiving an acceptable environmental report is fairly drastic—that is, it excuses the buyer from having to buy the house. That is true: the consequence of the non-satisfaction of a condition can be drastic. However, that is why parties include them: to not have to perform a specific obligation if the act or circumstance they find important to their performance does not occur beforehand.

Given that such an outcome is drastic, courts tend to disfavor conditions. That means if language is ambiguous (meaning, does not clearly state whether an act or circumstance is a condition), they will not interpret that act or circumstance as a condition. Instead, they will interpret it as a covenant.

In the above example, if the language were ambiguous, a court might not find that the buyer's receipt of the clean environmental report was a condition to the buyer's duty to buy the house. Rather, they would merely find that the seller agreed through a covenant to deliver that report. Interpreted in that way, if the seller does not deliver the clean environmental report, then the consequence is merely to give the buyer a claim against the seller for breach. However, the buyer would not be excused from buying the house. For this reason, parties must be extremely clear where an act or circumstance is intended to function as a condition to a party's duty.

For these reasons, and because of the significant consequence where a condition is not satisfied (i.e., a party's duty is not due), transactional attorneys pay close attention to conditions. They also ensure that where a client does not intend to perform an obligation without certain circumstances existing or events occurring, they clearly and unambiguously draft that protection as a condition.

It is important to note that conditions are party-specific. In other words, only a party for whose benefit a condition exists is excused from performing an obligation if the condition to that obligation is not satisfied. The other party's performance, however, is not excused by the non-satisfaction of that condition.

Thus, in our example, while the buyer's promise to buy the house would be excused if the inspection condition were not satisfied, the seller's duty to sell the house would not be excused. That is because the seller's performance was not conditioned on receiving such a report. However, the contract might contain a separate condition for the seller making the seller's duty to sell the house conditioned on the buyer's willingness to close. As such, this second condition would excuse the seller from performing under the contract if the buyer refused to close as well.

As you will learn in Section B of this chapter, each party has an implied duty of good faith and fair dealing. While Section B will explore that implied duty, in the context of this discussion of conditions, the existence of the implied duty requires that the party who is protected by a condition actually attempt to cause that condition to be satisfied. If that party fails to attempt to cause that condition to be satisfied, and if the matter were to proceed to litigation, a court might judicially excuse that condition because that party failed to act in good faith.

The implied duty also impacts any contractual party not protected by a condition. Because of the implied duty, that party has a duty to cooperate in making sure that condition is satisfied. Any failure by such a party to cooperate could constitute a breach, for which the opposing party might receive damages.

To see how this plays out, assume that in the above scenario, the buyer does not attempt to retain an environmental consulting company to deliver an environmental report. The buyer might engage in this conduct if it decides it does not want to buy the house. In that situation, if the seller were to sue to enforce the contract, a court might excuse the buyer's condition of getting an environmental report, meaning that buyer could not use that condition as a reason to walk from transaction. That is because such condition was not satisfied due to the buyer's own bad faith conduct.

On the other hand, if the buyer does not get the environmental report because the seller does not cooperate by, for example, not letting the buyer's environmental consulting company on its premises, then a court would not excuse that condition. That is because the condition existed to protect the buyer, not the seller. Excusing the condition would only injure the buyer. However, if the transaction did not close because of the seller's lack of cooperation, the buyer could sue the seller for breach of the implied duty, due to the seller's bad faith conduct and potentially recover monetary damages.

For all of these reasons, you need to carefully consider which condition should "belong" to each party. If it is important to a party that a particular event occur before that party's contractual obligation is due, you will want to make that party's promises in the contract subject to those conditions. Moreover, both parties need to work toward having conditions satisfied.

Keep in mind that the party for whose benefit a condition exists can waive that condition's satisfaction. Waiver is discussed in more detail in Chapter 16 as an excuse to justify one's nonperformance under the contract. For purposes of this discussion, a waiver of a condition permits a party, through words or conduct, to manifest an intent to not insist on the satisfaction of the waived condition under a contract. Where a party waives the benefit of a condition, that party's obligation is no longer conditional. In other words, that party has to perform his promises in the contract as if the condition did not exist (because he waived his rights to insist on satisfaction of that condition), and his failure to perform is no longer excused based upon that condition not being satisfied.

As you will see in the next case, courts require strict satisfaction of express condition, as a means to give effect to the bargain the parties struck. Yet sometimes, adhering to those agreed-upon terms seems unfair to a court. In the case of express conditions, that occurs where a party will suffer **substantial forfeiture** due to operation of the condition. This can arise in the case of lease renewals, where the tenant has made major improvements to the lease, yet fails to deliver the lease renewal notice on time. Strict adherence to the contract would prevent the lessee from renewing its lease where it does not deliver the renewal notice in accordance with the agreement. However, courts sometimes excuse that condition where the lessee would suffer substantial forfeiture by respecting and enforcing that condition. In making these decisions, courts commonly balance (1) the reasons for the condition, including the risks the counterparty sought to be protected from by that condition, as well as the extent to which that protection will be lost if the condition is excused, against (2) the extent of the party's forfeiture if that condition is not excused.

Thus, for example, if a tenant invested $100,000 in improvements to property, yet failed to deliver six months' notice to the landlord, which notice was a condition to renewing the lease for another five-year period, a court might excuse the condition due to substantial forfeiture if the landlord did not need the full six months to find a replacement tenant, and in fact did not look for a replacement tenant before receiving the tenant's renewal notice. If, however, the landlord needed those six months to find a replacement tenant, and in fact had found a replacement tenant, a court would likely not be as willing to excuse the condition, even though the current tenant would suffer a significant forfeiture.[1]

As you read the following case, consider why courts require strict satisfaction of conditions. You should also think about the other arguments the court considers for when to excuse an express condition, and whether you agree with the court as to whether those apply in this case.

Oppenheimer & Co. v. Oppenheim
Court of Appeals of New York
86 N.Y.2d 685 (1995)

CIPARICK, J.

The parties entered into a letter agreement setting forth certain conditions precedent to the formation and existence of a sublease between them. The agreement provided that there would be no sublease between the parties "unless and until" plaintiff delivered to defendant the prime landlord's written consent to certain "tenant work" on or before a specified deadline. If this condition did not occur, the sublease was to be deemed "null and void." Plaintiff provided only oral notice on the specified date. The issue presented is whether the doctrine of substantial performance applies to the facts of this case. We conclude it does not for the reasons that follow.

I.

In 1986, plaintiff Oppenheimer & Co. moved to the World Financial Center in Manhattan, a building constructed by Olympia & York Company (O & Y). At the time of its move, plaintiff had three years remaining on its existing lease for the 33rd floor of the building known as One New York Plaza. As an incentive to induce plaintiff's move, O & Y agreed to make the rental payments due under plaintiff's rental agreement in the event plaintiff was unable to sublease its prior space in One New York Plaza.

In December 1986, the parties to this action entered into a conditional letter agreement to sublease the 33rd floor. Defendant already leased space on the 29th floor of One New York Plaza and was seeking to expand its operations. The proposed sublease between the parties was attached to the letter agreement. The letter agreement provided that the proposed sublease would be executed only upon the satisfaction of certain conditions. Pursuant to paragraph

---

1. For a case along these lines, see J.N.A. Realty Corp. v. Cross Chelsea Bay Inc., 42 N.Y.2d 392 (Ct. App. NY 1977).

1(a) of the agreement, plaintiff was required to obtain "the Prime Landlord's written notice of confirmation, substantially to the effect that [defendant] is a subtenant of the Premises reasonably acceptable to Prime Landlord." If such written notice of confirmation were not obtained "on or before December 30, 1986, then this letter agreement and the Sublease . . . shall be deemed null and void and of no further force and effect and neither party shall have any rights against nor obligations to the other."

Assuming satisfaction of the condition set forth in paragraph 1(a), defendant was required to submit to plaintiff, on or before January 2, 1987, its plans for "tenant work" involving construction of a telephone communication linkage system between the 29th and 33rd floors. Paragraph 4(c) of the letter agreement then obligated plaintiff to obtain the prime landlord's "written consent" to the proposed "tenant work" and deliver such consent to defendant on or before January 30, 1987. Furthermore, if defendant had not received the prime landlord's written consent by the agreed date, both the agreement and the sublease were to be deemed "null and void and of no further force and effect," and neither party was to have "any rights against nor obligations to the other." Paragraph 4(d) additionally provided that, notwithstanding satisfaction of the condition set forth in paragraph 1(a), the parties "agree not to execute and exchange the Sublease unless and until . . . the conditions set forth in paragraph (c) above are timely satisfied."

The parties extended the letter agreement's deadlines in writing and plaintiff timely satisfied the first condition set forth in paragraph 1(a) pursuant to the modified deadline. However, plaintiff never delivered the prime landlord's written consent to the proposed tenant work on or before the modified final deadline of February 25, 1987. Rather, plaintiff's attorney telephoned defendant's attorney on February 25 and informed defendant that the prime landlord's consent had been secured. On February 26, defendant, through its attorney, informed plaintiff's attorney that the letter agreement and sublease were invalid for failure to timely deliver the prime landlord's written consent and that it would not agree to an extension of the deadline. The document embodying the prime landlord's written consent was eventually received by plaintiff on March 20, 1987, 23 days after expiration of paragraph 4(c)'s modified final deadline.

Plaintiff commenced this action for breach of contract, asserting that defendant waived and/or was estopped by virtue of its conduct from insisting on physical delivery of the prime landlord's written consent by the February 25 deadline. Plaintiff further alleged in its complaint that it had substantially performed the conditions set forth in the letter agreement.

At the outset of trial, the court issued an order in limine barring any reference to substantial performance of the terms of the letter agreement. Nonetheless, during the course of trial, the court permitted the jury to consider the theory of substantial performance, and additionally charged the jury concerning substantial performance. Special interrogatories were submitted. The jury found that defendant had properly complied with the terms of the letter agreement, and answered in the negative the questions whether defendant failed to perform its obligations under the letter agreement concerning submission of plans for tenant work, whether defendant by its conduct waived the February 25 deadline for delivery by plaintiff of the landlord's written consent to tenant work, and whether defendant by its conduct was equitably estopped from requiring plaintiff's strict adherence to the February 25 deadline. Nonetheless, the jury answered in the affirmative the question, "Did plaintiff substantially perform the conditions set forth in the Letter Agreement?," and awarded plaintiff damages of $ 1.2 million.

Defendant moved for judgment notwithstanding the verdict. Supreme Court granted the motion, ruling as a matter of law that "the doctrine of substantial performance has no application to this dispute, where the Letter Agreement is free of all ambiguity in setting the deadline that plaintiff concededly did not honor." The Appellate Division reversed the judgment on the law and facts, and reinstated the jury verdict. The Court concluded that the question of substantial compliance was properly submitted to the jury and that the verdict should be reinstated because plaintiff's failure to deliver the prime landlord's written consent was inconsequential.

This Court granted defendant's motion for leave to appeal and we now reverse.

II.

Defendant argues that no sublease or contractual relationship ever arose here because plaintiff failed to satisfy the condition set forth in paragraph 4(c) of the letter agreement. Defendant contends that the doctrine of substantial performance is not applicable to excuse plaintiff's failure to deliver the prime landlord's written consent to defendant on or before the date specified in the letter agreement and that the Appellate Division erred in holding to the contrary. Before addressing defendant's arguments and the decision of the court below, an understanding of certain relevant principles is helpful.

A condition precedent is "an act or event, other than a lapse of time, which, unless the condition is excused, must occur before a duty to perform a promise in the agreement arises" (Calamari and Perillo, Contracts § 11-2, at 438 [3d ed]). Most conditions precedent describe acts or events which must occur before a party is obliged to perform a promise made pursuant to an existing contract, a situation to be distinguished conceptually from a condition precedent to the formation or existence of the contract itself. In the latter situation, no contract arises "unless and until the condition occurs" (Calamari and Perillo, Contracts § 11-5, at 440 [3d ed]).

Conditions can be express or implied. Express conditions are those agreed to and imposed by the parties themselves. Implied or constructive conditions

are those "imposed by law to do justice" (Calamari and Perillo, Contracts §
11-8, at 444 [3d ed]). Express conditions must be literally performed, whereas
constructive conditions, which ordinarily arise from language of promise, are
subject to the precept that substantial compliance is sufficient. The importance
of the distinction has been explained by Professor Williston:

> "Since an express condition . . . depends for its validity on the manifested inten-
> tion of the parties, it has the same sanctity as the promise itself. Though the
> court may regret the harshness of such a condition, as it may regret the harsh-
> ness of a promise, it must, nevertheless, generally enforce the will of the parties
> unless to do so will violate public policy. Where, however, the law itself has
> imposed the condition, in absence of or irrespective of the manifested intention
> of the parties, it can deal with its creation as it pleases, shaping the boundaries
> of the constructive condition in such a way as to do justice and avoid hardship".
> (5 Williston, Contracts § 669, at 154 [3d ed].)

In determining whether a particular agreement makes an event a condition
courts will interpret doubtful language as embodying a promise or constructive
condition rather than an express condition. This interpretive preference is especially strong when a finding of express condition would increase the risk of
forfeiture by the obligee.

Interpretation as a means of reducing the risk of forfeiture cannot be employed if "the occurrence of the event as a condition is expressed in unmistakable language" (Restatement [Second] of Contracts § 229, comment *a*, at
185; *see,* § 227, comment *b* [where language is clear, "(t)he policy favoring
freedom of contract requires that, within broad limits, the agreement of the
parties should be honored even though forfeiture results"]). Nonetheless, the
nonoccurrence of the condition may yet be excused by waiver, breach or forfeiture. The Restatement posits that "[t]o the extent that the non-occurrence
of a condition would cause disproportionate forfeiture, a court may excuse the
non-occurrence of that condition unless its occurrence was a material part of
the agreed exchange" (Restatement [Second] of Contracts § 229).

Turning to the case at bar, it is undisputed that the critical language of
paragraph 4(c) of the letter agreement unambiguously establishes an express
condition precedent rather than a promise, as the parties employed the unmistakable language of condition ("if," "unless and until"). There is no doubt
of the parties' intent and no occasion for interpreting the terms of the letter
agreement other than as written.

Furthermore, plaintiff has never argued, and does not now contend, that
the nonoccurrence of the condition set forth in paragraph 4 (c) should be excused on the ground of forfeiture. Rather, plaintiff's primary argument from
the inception of this litigation has been that defendant waived or was equitably
estopped from invoking paragraph 4 (c). Plaintiff argued secondarily that it
substantially complied with the express condition of delivery of written notice

on or before February 25th in that it gave defendant oral notice of consent on the 25th.

Contrary to the decision of the Court below, we perceive no justifiable basis for applying the doctrine of substantial performance to the facts of this case. The flexible concept of substantial compliance "stands in sharp contrast to the requirement of strict compliance that protects a party that has taken the precaution of making its duty expressly conditional" (2 Farnsworth, Contracts § 8.12, at 415 [2d ed 1990]). If the parties "have made an event a condition of their agreement, there is no mitigating standard of materiality or substantiality applicable to the non-occurrence of that event" (Restatement [Second] of Contracts § 237, comment *d*, at 220). Substantial performance in this context is not sufficient, "and if relief is to be had under the contract, it must be through excuse of the non-occurrence of the condition to avoid forfeiture" (*id.*).

Here, it is undisputed that plaintiff has not suffered a forfeiture or conferred a benefit upon defendant. Plaintiff alludes to a $ 1 million licensing fee it allegedly paid to the prime landlord for the purpose of securing the latter's consent to the subleasing of the premises. At no point, however, does plaintiff claim that this sum was forfeited or that it was expended for the purpose of accomplishing the sublease with defendant. It is further undisputed that O & Y, as an inducement to effect plaintiff's move to the World Financial Center, promised to indemnify plaintiff for damages resulting from failure to sublease the 33rd floor of One New York Plaza. Consequently, because the critical concern of forfeiture or unjust enrichment is simply not present in this case, we are not presented with an occasion to consider whether the doctrine of substantial performance is applicable, that is, whether the courts should intervene to excuse the nonoccurrence of a condition precedent to the formation of a contract.

The essence of the Appellate Division's holding is that the substantial performance doctrine is universally applicable to all categories of breach of contract, including the nonoccurrence of an express condition precedent. However, as discussed, substantial performance is ordinarily not applicable to excuse the nonoccurrence of an express condition precedent.

. . .

Plaintiff's reliance on the well-known case of *Jacob & Youngs v Kent* (230 NY 239) is misplaced. There, a contractor built a summer residence and the buyer refused to pay the remaining balance of the contract price on the ground that the contractor used a different type of pipe than was specified in the contract. The buyer sought to enforce the contract as written. This would have involved the demolition of large parts of the structure at great expense and loss to the seller. This Court, in an opinion by then-Judge Cardozo, ruled for the contractor on the ground that "an omission, both trivial and innocent, will sometimes be atoned for by allowance of the resulting damage, and will not always be the breach of a condition to be followed by a forfeiture" (230 NY, at

241). But Judge Cardozo was careful to note that the situation would be different in the case of an express condition:

> "This is not to say that the parties are not free by apt and certain words to effectuate a purpose that performance of every term shall be a condition of recovery. That question is not here. This is merely to say that the law will be slow to impute the purpose, in the silence of the parties, where the significance of the default is grievously out of proportion to the oppression of the forfeiture" (*id.*, at 243-244).

The quoted language contradicts the Appellate Division's proposition that the substantial performance doctrine applies universally, including when the language of the agreement leaves no doubt that an express condition precedent was intended.

. . .

III.

In sum, the letter agreement provides in the clearest language that the parties did not intend to form a contract "unless and until" defendant received written notice of the prime landlord's consent on or before February 25, 1987. Defendant would lease the 33rd floor from plaintiff only on the condition that the landlord consent in writing to a telephone communication linkage system between the 29th and 33rd floors and to defendant's plans for construction effectuating that linkage. This matter was sufficiently important to defendant that it would not enter into the sublease "unless and until" the condition was satisfied. Inasmuch as we are not dealing here with a situation where plaintiff stands to suffer some forfeiture or undue hardship, we perceive no justification for engaging in a "materiality-of-the-nonoccurrence" analysis. To do so would simply frustrate the clearly expressed intention of the parties. Freedom of contract prevails in an arm's length transaction between sophisticated parties such as these, and in the absence of countervailing public policy concerns there is no reason to relieve them of the consequences of their bargain. If they are dissatisfied with the consequences of their agreement, "the time to say so [was] at the bargaining table" (*Maxton, supra,* at 382).

Finally, the issue of substantial performance was not for the jury to resolve in this case. A determination whether there has been substantial performance is to be answered, "if the inferences are certain, by the judges of the law" (*Jacob & Youngs v Kent,* 230 NY 239, 243, *supra*).

Accordingly, the order of the Appellate Division should be reversed, with costs, and the complaint dismissed.

Understanding the Case:

1. *Conditions in Checklist:* As discussed above, attorneys typically ensure that their clients satisfy all conditions necessary to make the opposing party's

contractual obligations binding. Working backwards, this means that the attorney should prepare a checklist of all of the tasks (and related timing) that will ensure that the other party's obligation to perform becomes due, and, in turn, her client receives the desired performance. Often, these tasks are listed in a section called "Conditions" in the contract, but typically, an attorney will closely review the agreement to make sure there are no "hidden" conditions that may allow the opposing party not to perform. The corollary of this responsibility is to make sure the attorney knows what conditions are important to his client so that these important "outs" are reflected in the contract.

Comprehension and Thought Questions:

1. What is a condition?
2. How did the court know that the requirement of the landlord's consent was a condition as opposed to another performance obligation of the plaintiff?
3. What is the doctrine of substantial performance and why was it not relevant in this case? When does that doctrine apply?
4. What is the doctrine of forfeiture and why was it not applicable in this case?
5. Why do you think there is more judicial flexibility in finding grounds to ignore the non-satisfaction of an implied condition as opposed to an express condition?

Hypothetical Variations:

1. What if on February 26 the defendant's attorney asked the plaintiff's attorney for a copy of the sublease signed by her client?
2. What if the plaintiff had spent $100,000 in refurbishing the leased space to defendant's specifications?
3. What if the plaintiff had spent $100,000 in refurbishing the leased space to comply with state and local building codes?

PRACTICE PROBLEM 12-1

Five years ago, Zoe Wood graduated from Washington University with a degree in accounting. Since then, she has been working at a large accounting firm in Springfield. Recently, Zoe decided she would rather "go it alone" and work at her own accounting firm. After making this decision, Zoe learned that Rick Davies, a well-known accountant in Springfield, had decided to retire. Zoe contacted Rick and asked him if he would be willing to sell Zoe his accounting practice. That would mean selling to Zoe all of his office equipment and supplies as well as his client list. Rick would also notify his clients that Zoe was taking over his practice and recommend that clients stick with his firm after Zoe takes over. Rick agreed to sell Zoe his practice for a payment at closing of $50,000. Zoe would also pay Rick an earnout in the amount of 5 percent of the profits of the accounting firm for each of the two years after closing. Rick would agree not to compete with the practice in Springfield for three years after closing, to ensure Zoe would benefit from the accounting practice's goodwill. These terms were agreeable to Zoe as well.

Zoe has now reached out to you to ask you to represent her on this transaction. However, before you begin to draft the purchase agreement, Zoe has asked you to explain to her whether the contract can protect Zoe from the risks that (1) Rick might not provide quality accounting services to clients before closing, (2) Rick might not bill clients for his work, and (3) Rick might turn away prospective new clients. As you advise Zoe, also consider other likely risks Zoe faces in this transaction in the "gap period" before closing and what types of terms you would suggest including in the contract to protect her from those risks.

3. Smart Contract Performance

As you may recall from Chapter 6, "smart" contracts have evolved to permit automated entry into contracts. This is accomplished through the use of algorithms, often using blockchain technology, that determine when parties should enter into a contract and the terms of that contract. Although automating entry into contracts is important, what many people view as most innovative about smart contracts is that their performance is automated. That means, in turn, that smart contracts cannot be breached, as they contain self-executing codes that ensure the parties perform. A recent law review article provides a good summary of the enforcement issues arising in the smart contract context. As you review the excerpt, consider whether smart contracts should be considered "contracts" at all if the legal regime does not have a role with respect to enforcement. After all, recall that a contract is typically defined as a promise that is legally enforceable.

> Consider a simple insurance contract under which Abby promises farmer Bob, in return for a monthly payment, a lump sum in the event the temperature exceeds 100 degrees for more than five straight days during the term of the agreement. In a traditional contracting arrangement, the parties would likely reduce that agreement to a writing, signed to memorialize mutual intent. If the temperature exceeded the threshold for six straight days and Abby failed to pay, Bob could file suit for breach and present the contract as evidence. To implement a smart contract with the same terms, Abby and Bob would translate the provisions into software code. Each would make available sufficient funds to fulfill his or her side of the agreement. An agreed mechanism would be specified to determine performance, such as the daily high temperature for the area, as published on Weather.com. Abby and Bob would then each digitally sign the agreement with

their private cryptographic key. One of them would send it as a transaction onto a blockchain, where it would be validated through the consensus process and recorded on the distributed ledger. Bob's payments would automatically be deducted each month and credited to Abby's account. Meanwhile, the smart contract would check the high temperature on Weather.com each day and store a record as needed on the blockchain. If the temperature exceeded 100 degrees for six days, the lump sum payment would be transferred from Abby's account to Bob's, and the smart contract would terminate.

The critical distinction between smart contracts and other forms of electronic agreements is enforcement. Once the computers determine that the requisite state has been achieved, they automatically perform data-oriented or computable contracts. Humans can interrupt that execution at any point. But with a smart contract, complete execution of the agreement, including any transfer of value, occurs without any such opportunity to interrupt. Accordingly, juridical forums are powerless to stop the execution of smart contracts—there is no room to bring an action for breach when breach is impossible. The computers in the blockchain network ensure performance, rather than any appendage of the state. And, because blockchains run on a distributed network of independent nodes, with no central control point, a litigant seeking to enjoin performance of a smart contract has no one to sue.

The blockchain's distributed trust facilitates smart contracts between unknown or untrusted counterparties. This radical decentralization is what potentially makes smart contracting a substitute for the state-based legal system, rather than an additional step before reaching that system. For example, a financial trading program that automatically buys certain stocks when prices match a predefined algorithm, could be described as a smart contract. If a dispute arises, however, the parties to that self-executing transaction will still turn to the courts, which will apply traditional legal doctrines to evaluate the agreement, ascertain breach, and impose a remedy if appropriate. With smart contracts, the transaction is irreversibly encoded on a distributed blockchain. A judicial decision holding a smart contract unenforceable cannot undo the results of its fully executed agreement.

Smart contracts are possible with Bitcoin because its protocols include a scripting language that can incorporate limited programmable logic into transactions. The vast majority of transactions on the Bitcoin blockchain are simple transfers of Bitcoins between accounts. Additionally, when computers on the Bitcoin network process those transfers, they can perform other functions. This allows for more complicated arrangements, like delaying payment until a specified number of parties provide confirmation.

. . .

Even though blockchain transactions are irrevocable, there are ways to build in more flexibility. There is no technical means, short of undermining the integrity of the entire system, to unwind a transfer. It is, however, possible to incorporate logic into a smart contract that permits exceptions or conditions. Enforcement could theoretically be structured to permit arbitration. Such flexibility, however, must be coded into the smart contract at the outset, which takes away from the decentralization and efficiency that make smart contracts attractive to begin with.

Sometimes a smart contract refers to facts in the world, for example, when a contract pays out if a stock exceeds a certain price on a certain date. The Bitcoin blockchain knows nothing about stock prices; it must collect that information through an external data feed. In the language of smart contracts, systems that interpret such external feeds and verify contractual performance are called "oracles." Unlike the blockchain itself, oracles are not fully decentralized. The contracting parties must, to some degree, trust the operator of the oracle and the authenticity of its data feed.

Using these capabilities, a wide variety of industries could employ smart contracts. Beyond simple financial arrangements, smart contracts could facilitate complex instruments like wills or crowdfunding systems, both of which disburse funds only if certain contingencies trigger a payout. Another category is smart property, for which the rights associated with objects attach to the objects themselves. Networked door locks on a shared car system such as Zipcar could automatically open, but only for the individual that paid the access fee. Or, a lessor could shut off a delinquent lessee's access to a leased car, and give access to the bank, but only until full payment of the principal. More broadly, over twenty-five billion devices comprising the Internet of Things, from light switches to crop moisture monitors, are expected to connect to the internet by 2020. Smart contracts would allow these devices to operate autonomously, share resources, and exchange data without central management.

Some blockchain advocates go further. They envision smart contracts as the foundation of a new kind of economic entity, the distributed autonomous organization (DAO). If a corporation is simply a nexus of contracts, why not encode those agreements into digital self-enforcing agreements? A DAO could have stock ownership, corporate governance rules, payroll arrangements, and virtually all of the economic trappings of a modern corporation, all running automatically in a completely distributed manner.

. . .

As is so often the case, though, this technology's adoption is preceding full consideration of its legal implications. Smart contracts are not just an interesting computer science innovation, because they tread on one of the most fundamental territories of the common law: the domain of contract.[2]

Comprehension and Thought Questions:

1. After reviewing the above excerpt, in what sense do you think smart contracts are actual "contracts" from a legal perspective? In particular, are parties to a smart contract even making promises, in light of how smart contracts are enforced?

---

2. Kevin Werbach and Nicolas Cornell, *Contracts Ex Machina*, 67 Duke L.J. 313, 331-38 (2017).

2. Do smart contracts serve the same contract law policies that were discussed in Chapter 1? Are there any policies that they undercut?

3. Give the limited court role in smart contract enforcement, should smart contracts be interpreted or regulated using a different body of law or enforcement mechanism? Can you think of any that might be appropriate?

B. POST-FORMATION: IMPLIED TERMS

As discussed above, attorneys often help clients understand the scope of the client's obligations under a contract. While most of those obligations are expressly set out in the contract, the law implies some duties and other terms as well. Moreover, while some implied terms arise by statute, others have been developed through common law.

Different implied terms serve different purposes of contract law. Some implied terms are gap-filling. Those gap-filling terms are often thought to reflect the terms similarly situated parties would impose on themselves. By having those terms exist by default, the parties do not need to negotiate or document them, decreasing transaction costs and, thereby, facilitating commerce. Article 2 of the UCC contains a litany of such gap-filling implied terms. You will study those implied terms in Chapter 14.

Other implied terms are designed to preclude post-formation opportunistic behavior of parties. The implied duty of good faith and fair dealing is of that ilk. In particular, the **implied duty of good faith and fair dealing** is an equitable principle that governs contracting parties' contractual conduct, to ensure that they act within community standards of decency, fairness, and reasonableness.

While the concept of good faith has always been a component of our legal system, it only became a stand-alone legal duty in the United States in the early nineteenth century. However, since then, it has figured prominently in contract law. In fact, but for a few states that have rejected it, the implied duty of good faith and fair dealing exists in all contracts.

The following is the Restatement's description of the implied duty.

> **Restatement (Second) of Contracts § 205**
> Every contract imposes upon each party a duty of good faith and fair dealing in its performance and its enforcement.

The duty is typically characterized as a doctrine used to ensure that parties actually work toward achieving their shared purpose under the contract, so that each party receives the benefits it reasonably expected under the contract. Characterized in that way, the implied duty acts as a gap-filling term. Under the duty, each party is expected to behave in a way to further the other party's contractual purpose and justified expectations, all notwithstanding that the expressed provisions of the contract fail to specify this.

As you consider the justification for the doctrine, keep in mind that no contract can be perfectly complete or exact. Judges realize this. They also realize that these shortcomings can lead to parties taking advantage of one another. In other words, one party may be inclined to avoid her contractual obligations by relying on a contract's inability to identify and remedy every instance of opportunistic behavior. Judges consequently use the implied duty of good faith and fair dealing to police such unfair behavior.

As with most gap-fillers, parties can modify the implied duty. Thus, they can identify specific conduct that is permissible and that would otherwise run afoul of the implied duty. However, parties cannot contract around the doctrine entirely by specifying that the implied duty does not apply at all.

For example, suppose a loan agreement contained the following provision:

> The Borrower may not sell any of its property, plants, or equipment without the Lender's consent, **which consent the Lender can withhold or delay in its absolute discretion**.

In this instance, without the language in bold, under the implied duty, the Lender would have to have a reason not to consent to the Borrower's request to sell any property, plant, or equipment. Thus, if the Borrower asked the Lender if it could sell a fairly insignificant piece of equipment and the Lender did not approve because it wanted to force the Borrower to commit a default under the loan agreement, it might be seen as breaching its implied duty. On the other hand, with the added language in bold, the parties have contracted around the implied duty. Thus, here, the Lender could withhold its consent for any reason or no reason, and would likely not breach the implied duty.

Somewhat oddly, the implied duty is often described by reference to conduct that amounts to bad faith rather than conduct that amounts to good faith. Presented in this way, compliance with the implied duty is inferred from the absence of "bad faith" conduct.

It is important to note that the duty does not apply until there is a contract. Although the standard of good faith is similar to the standard used with respect to the duty to negotiate in good faith, the latter duty only applies in the context leading up to contract formation and only in very limited situations. The implied duty, by contrast, applies to all contracts in all situations.

As you review the following case, pay close to attention to the test the court uses to determine whether a party has breached the implied duty of good faith and fair dealing and whether that test is objective or subjective.

Seidenberg v. Summit Bank
Superior Court of New Jersey, Appellate Division
348 N.J. Super. 243 (2002)

Clarkson S. FISHER, Jr., J.S.C. (temporarily assigned).

After settling all their disputes concerning the express terms of their commercial transaction, plaintiffs filed a second amended complaint alleging a breach of the implied covenant of good faith and fair dealing. The Law Division dismissed the action, finding that plaintiffs failed to state a claim upon which relief may be granted. Because we conclude the assessment of the validity of the claim was both erroneous and premature, we reverse.

. . .

II

Plaintiffs Richard Seidenberg and Eric Raymond formed two Pennsylvania corporations—Corporate Dynamics and Philadelphia Benefits Corporation—in 1971 and 1985, respectively. These entities marketed, provided consultation services and sold health insurance benefit plans to employers. Plaintiffs were the sole shareholders of the two entities.

In 1997, plaintiffs sold their stock in Corporate Dynamics and Philadelphia Benefits Corporation (hereafter collectively referred to as "the brokerage firms") to defendant Summit Bank ("Summit") in exchange for 445,000 shares of the common stock of Bancorp Corporation, Summit's parent corporation; in addition, plaintiffs agreed to place 49,500 shares of Bancorp Corporation into escrow until December 12, 2001 as security for any existing but unknown or undisclosed liabilities. As part of the transaction, plaintiffs retained their positions as executives of the brokerage firms and also were to be placed in charge of the daily operations of any other employee benefits insurance business which might be acquired by Summit.

. . .

In the second amended complaint, plaintiffs contend, among other things, that Summit (a) failed to allow for the creation of a close working relationship between the entities, (b) failed to create an effective cross-selling structure to generate leads, (c) failed to introduce the brokerage firms to vendors doing business with Summit as a way of increasing their potential customer base, (d) failed to develop existing relationships (referred to in the pleadings as "low hanging fruit") which could easily be picked and turned into clients for the brokerage firms, (e) failed to provide plaintiffs with information necessary to provide full advice concerning health and other employee benefits, thereby precluding plaintiffs from quoting coverage to Summit, (f) unreasonably delayed a direct mail campaign, (g) thwarted an agreed-upon joint marketing campaign, and (h) failed to advise of Summit's pursuit of the acquisition of another entity which plaintiffs claim would fall within their ambit and right to operate.

Plaintiffs claimed that Summit's lack of performance in these areas impacted their reasonable expectations of compensation and future involvement. For example, plaintiffs' salaries were reduced in exchange for a bonus to which they would be entitled based on the growth of the brokerage firms. They claim this was agreeable due to the anticipation of a substantial bonus upon the growth of the business. Accordingly, the allegations contained in the second amended complaint, briefly outlined above, are linked to plaintiffs' compensation. In addition, plaintiffs claim there was an expectation of continued employment since their employment agreements contained a minimum term of five years and provided also that, in the absence of termination by Summit, employment would continue until each reached the age of 70.

Plaintiffs assert that these allegations give rise to an inference of bad faith. They claim that these circumstances demonstrate that Summit "never had any intention to perform to begin with," and that Summit "from the start, . . . never [was] committed to developing the business with [plaintiffs], but rather simply wanted to acquire the business and seek out their own broker to run it or grow it." In December 1999, Summit terminated plaintiffs from their positions, triggering this lawsuit.

   . . .

IV

We start with the premise that in New Jersey the covenant of good faith and fair dealing is contained in all contracts and mandates that "neither party shall do anything which will have the effect of destroying or injuring the right of the other party to receive the fruits of the contract." *Sons of Thunder v. Borden, Inc.,* 148 N.J. 396, 420, 690 A.2d 575 (1997). While this general statement represents the guiding principle in such matters, determining whether the present action may be maintained requires closer examination.

The implied covenant of good faith and fair dealing has evolved to the point where it permits the adjustment of the obligations of contracting parties in a number of different ways. Some cases have focused on a plaintiff's inadequate bargaining power or financial vulnerability in order to avoid an inequitable result otherwise permitted by a contract's express terms. Other decisions have revolved around the expectations of the parties, generating a need to contrast those expectations with the absence of any express terms. And still others have emphasized the defendant's bad faith or outright dishonesty. Yet, as the implied covenant of good faith and fair dealing continues to develop, and in light of the covenant's essential factors as discerned from the existing case law, we cannot say, in examining the unadorned record in this case, that an actionable claim cannot be found in plaintiffs' allegations.

   . . .

C

The guiding principle in the application of the implied covenant of good faith and fair dealing emanates from the fundamental notion that a party to a contract may not unreasonably frustrate its purpose:

> [W]here a party alleges frustration of its expectation or fundamental purpose in entering the contract, the question of what interest will be protected by the implied duty answers itself; the plaintiff's interest is internal to the understanding of the parties and good faith requires the defendant not exercise such discretion as it may have under the literal terms of the contract to thwart plaintiff's expectation or purpose.
>
> [*Emerson Radio Corp. v. Orion Sales Inc.*, 80 F. Supp.2d 307, 314 (D.N.J. 2000), *rev'd in part on other grounds*, 253 F.3d 159 (3d Cir. 2001), cited with approval in *Wilson v. Amerada Hess Corporation*, 168 N.J. 236, 250, 773 A.2d 1121 (2001).]

. . .

[T]he application of the implied covenant of good faith and fair dealing has addressed three distinct type of situations: (1) when the contract does not provide a term necessary to fulfill the parties' expectations, (2) when bad faith served as a pretext for the exercise of a contractual right to terminate, and (3) when the contract expressly provides a party with discretion regarding its performance. This third aspect, fully examined in *Wilson*, can take at least two different forms:

> [A] contract . . . would be breached by a failure to perform in good faith if a party uses its discretion for a reason outside the contemplated range—a reason beyond the risks assumed by the party claiming the breach [or the contract would be breached] if the discretion-exercising party ... unilaterally use[s] that authority in a way that intentionally subjects the other party to a risk beyond the normal business risks that the parties could have contemplated at the time of contract formation.
>
> [168 N.J. at 246, 773 A.2d 1121, quoting with approval Burton, "Breach of Contract and the Common Law Duty to Perform in Good Faith," 94 Harv. L. Rev. 369, 386 (1980).]

Here, plaintiffs appear to urge an application of both the second and third facets of the implied covenant. The Law Division judge's decision to dismiss the second amended complaint constituted a mistaken understanding of the covenant in these areas.

. . .

[T]he court below was required to determine only whether the second amended complaint sufficiently outlined a cause of action consistent with any of these categories. In this case, the second amended complaint alleges circumstances which, if proven, might support a claim based upon Summit's termination of their relationship. To some extent, plaintiffs alleged there was an expectation—despite the express contractual right of Summit to terminate—that the relationship would last until they reached retirement age. This contention would, on its face, fall within that type of implied covenant claim prohibiting a party from terminating a contractual relationship in bad faith notwithstanding the expressed right to do so.

The second amended complaint also alleges that Summit used insufficient energy in discretionary areas. That is, plaintiffs allege that Summit failed to pursue or create leads, frustrated or delayed marketing efforts, and deprived plaintiffs of information which might improve their benefits under the contract, thus sufficiently alleging a cause of action under the discretionary tranche of the multi-faceted implied covenant of good faith and fair dealing.

D

The last element of a maintainable cause of action based upon the implied covenant of good faith and fair dealing is bad faith or ill motive. Courts have described this element in various ways. Most importantly, our Supreme Court has recently emphasized the level of bad faith and improper motive which will be required in a party's exercise of the discretion permitted by the contract:

> [A] party exercising its right to use discretion in setting price under a contract breaches the duty of good faith and fair dealing if that party exercises its discretionary authority arbitrarily, unreasonably, or capriciously, with the objective of preventing the other party from receiving its reasonably expected fruits under the contract.
>
>   . . . In that setting, an allegation of bad faith or unfair dealing should not be permitted to be advanced in the abstract and absent improper motive. Without bad motive or intention, discretionary decisions that happen to result in economic disadvantage to the other party are of no legal significance.

[*Wilson,* 168 N.J. at 251, 773 A.2d 1121 (citations omitted).]

While *Wilson*'s description of good faith relates to price setting, we fail to see why it would not be similarly applied in examining the type of performance (or lack thereof) as alleged by plaintiffs.

Before finding a breach of the implied covenant, care must be taken that the bad faith element is fully realized. Recognizing a concern for an overly ambitious application of the implied covenant, the Court in *Wilson*—in defining the level of bad faith required in such matters—charted a careful course between implying a promise to avoid an apparent unjust result and requiring parties to adhere to the bargain they freely and voluntarily made. Referencing one federal court of appeal's holdings that the covenant is not intended to supplant the prohibition on judicial rewriting of contracts or provide undue protection to contracting parties who can protect themselves,[3] the *Wilson* decision represents an increased emphasis on the importance of this factor:

> [A]n allegation of bad faith or unfair dealing should not be permitted to be advanced in the abstract and absent improper motive.
>
> Because the implied covenant of good faith and fair dealing applies to the parties' performance under the contract notwithstanding [a] provision in the contract permitting [the exercise of discretion in setting prices] . . . the issue is whether . . . [the defendant] acted in bad faith or violated any commercially reasonable standard thereby depriving plaintiffs of their right to make a reasonable profit.

[168 N.J. at 251, 253, 773 A.2d 1121.]

Providing a more precise definition of bad faith in the context of this, or any other similar case, is unrealistic. We recognize that expressions such as "bad faith," "improper motive," and other similar words and phrases used to describe this requisite state of mind provide little guidance. While the particular defining words chosen will inherently be of "little assistance to the trial judge who must distinguish bad faith from mere sharp commercial practice," *Emerson Radio*, 80 F. Supp. 2d at 311, it is best to entrust the drawing of such a line to trial judges and juries with the admonition that an unduly expansive version of bad faith, as Judge Greenberg cautioned in *Northview Motors, Inc. v. Chrysler Motors Corp.*, 227 F.3d 78, 92 (3d Cir. 2000), "could become an all-embracing statement of the parties' obligations under contract law, imposing unintended obligations upon parties and destroying the mutual benefits created by legally binding agreements." 227 F.3d at 92. In the final analysis, bad faith must be judged not only in light of the proofs regarding the defendant's state of mind but also in the context from which the claim arose. The Court in *Wilson* coupled the element of bad faith with a requirement that the plaintiff demonstrate a violation of "any commercially reasonable standard." *Wilson*, 168 N.J. at 253, 773 A.2d 1121. Accordingly, this element may be determined, at least in part, by the nature of the parties' undertaking and the standards applicable to the business or industry in which they have engaged. Ultimately, however, the presence of bad faith is to be found in the eye of the beholder or, more to the point, in the eye of the trier of fact. Any attempt to provide greater definition is to expect some "delusive exactness" which, as Justice Holmes said, is "a source of fallacy throughout the law." *Truax v. Corrigan*, 257 U.S. 312, 342, 42 S. Ct. 124, 133, 66 L. Ed. 254, 267 (1921) (dissenting opinion).

---

3. [1] "Contract law does not require parties to behave altruistically toward each other; it does not proceed on the philosophy that I am my brother's keeper." *Original Great Am. Chocolate Chip Cookie Co. v. River Valley Cookies, Ltd.*, 970 F.2d 273, 280 (7th Cir. 1992) (quoted with approval in *Wilson*, 168 N.J. at 251-52, 773 A.2d 1121). *See also, Kham & Nate's Shoes No. 2, Inc. v. First Bank of Whiting*, 908 F.2d 1351, 1357 (7th Cir. 1990) (the covenant of good faith and fair dealing "does not imply a general duty of 'kindness' in performance").

Even though the order of dismissal was not based upon some insufficiency in regard to its allegations of bad faith, we lastly pause, in providing guidance for future proceedings in this case, to observe that the second amended complaint was adequate in this regard, alleging that plaintiffs "suffered as a result of . . . Summit's bad faith" and that Summit's actions were "wanton and willful and without privilege or right." Whether plaintiffs' proofs will meet the bad faith standard defined in *Wilson*, or even survive summary judgment, remains to be seen. This question, however, certainly cannot be resolved until the parties are at least given a full and fair opportunity for further investigation and discovery.

V

. . .

The order of dismissal is reversed and the matter remanded for further proceedings in conformity herewith. We do not retain jurisdiction.

Understanding the Case:

1. *Employment Agreements:*   The plaintiffs' employment agreements contained the following language regarding working together for future brokerage business:

> Summit and [plaintiffs] shall work together to formulate joint marketing programs which will give [the brokerage firms] access to the market resources of Summit to the extent permitted by applicable laws, regulations and administrative policies and guidelines, including but not limited to those relating to customer privacy, issued by Federal or state regulatory authorities or agencies or self-regulatory organizations or financial industry trade groups.

2. *Why Plaintiffs Worked for Defendants:*   It is not unusual for the buyer of a business to retain the business's original owners as employees or independent contractors to continue operations. The original owners may have special knowledge or relationships that are important for the continued success of the business. Accordingly, a buyer may want to have consulting contracts or employment contracts to ensure that the original owners help transition the business to the buyer.[4]

---

4. Both in a business purchase agreement and in an employment or consulting agreement, the buyer will typically want the seller, as well as the owners of the seller, if the seller is an entity like a corporation, to agree to a non-compete for some period of time following the closing date. As you may recall from Chapter 1, these restrictive covenants may require the sellers not to compete with the acquired business or solicit customers or employees of the acquired business, and to keep confidential all proprietary information of the acquired business. It should be obvious why the buyer would want these restrictive covenants included in the transaction agreements. The buyer has paid the seller to acquire the business on the assumption that the business will remain with the buyer for the future and does not want the seller to start a competing business to which it might lose business after closing.

Comprehension and Thought Questions:

1. What is the implied duty of good faith and fair dealing?

2. Why did the plaintiffs believe they were entitled to relief for a breach of the implied duty?

3. According to the court, what are the elements of a claim for breach of the implied duty?

4. What alleged facts show breach of the implied duty in this case?

5. Why did the court overturn the lower court's dismissal of the claim for breach of implied duty? What will happen following the reversal of the lower court's decision?

6. What are the advantages and disadvantages of a court relying on the implied duty to award relief to a party?

Hypothetical Variations:

1. What if the contract did not reference a five-year employment period and instead included a clause that provided: "The employee understands and agrees that his or her employment may be terminated at any time without liability"? *[handwritten: makes less of a commitment than a 0.9. agreement]*

2. What if the defendants had asserted that they fired the plaintiffs because the plaintiffs failed to perform their assigned duties properly? *[handwritten: not arbitrary, unreasonably (capricious)]*

3. What if the defendants had not intentionally failed to commit resources to help the brokerage companies, but rather simply did not have the financial resources to commit?

PRACTICE PROBLEM 12-2

Recall from Practice Problem 12-1 that Rick Davies agreed to sell Zoe Wood his accounting practice for a payment at closing of $50,000. Under the terms of their agreement, Zoe would also pay Rick an earnout in the amount of 5 percent of the profits of the accounting firm for each of the two years after closing. Moreover, Rick would not compete with the transferred accounting practice in Springfield for three years after closing, to ensure Zoe would benefit from the accounting practice's goodwill.

Assume you prepared a first draft of the purchase agreement reflecting these terms. You drafted the relevant terms on the earnout and non-compete as follows (which have been excerpted from different parts of the draft). Note that you defined the term "Business" as "the accounting business previously operated by Davies and transferred to Wood under this Agreement."

> 2.4. **Earnout**: In addition to the Closing Payment, Wood shall pay Davies an earnout equal to 5% of the Profits generated in the Business in each of

> the two years following Closing. For purposes of this section, "Profits" means the net income generated by the Business, after deduction of all expenses (fixed and non-fixed) incurred in the Business.
>
> 8.1. **Non-Compete**. Beginning on the Closing Date and for a period of three years after the Closing Date, Woods shall not provide accounting services that compete with the Business in Springfield.

After she reviews the first draft, Zoe calls you to ask you some questions about the draft. Specifically, she wants to know the following:

1. Under the proposed draft, what would happen to the earnout if Zoe decides she does not like working alone and wants to return to a larger accounting firm at the end of her first year? Or, what if she is injured and has to take an extended leave of absence from work?

2. Under the proposed draft, could Rick open an accounting firm that competes with the practice he is selling to Zoe if he does not personally provide accounting services at that firm? If so, could he then provide to the accountants the list of clients from his practice that he is selling to Zoe?

In light of the fact that you are still in the drafting stage of this transaction, what changes (if any) do you suggest to the above language to respond to these concerns?

C. MODIFYING THE CONTRACT

Imagine that you previously advised a borrower in connection with the formation of a loan transaction. Your client now asks you whether it is permitted to sell its old equipment under its loan agreement so that it may buy new equipment. The following is an excerpt from your client's loan agreement:

> SECTION 3.14 So long as any indebtedness remains outstanding under the Promissory Note executed by Borrower for the benefit of Lender, Borrower agrees that it will not (i) incur any other indebtedness, or (ii) sell any of its assets.

Under the provisions of the loan agreement, you would have to advise your client that all sales of assets are prohibited, which means that your client would be breaching its obligations under the loan agreement if it sold its old equipment. If your client nevertheless decided to take that action because it was important for its business, your client could face many adverse consequences as a result. One is that the loan agreement might allow the lender to "accelerate" the loan.

Where a lender accelerates a loan, that means the lender declares the entire loan amount to be immediately due, rather than having it repaid over time. Moreover, the loan agreement might provide that the loan balance starts to accrue interest at a "default rate" that is higher than the ordinary interest rate. If the lender is "secured" by your client's assets, the lender could then realize on those assets by selling them and then using the proceeds from those sales to pay the amounts your client owes to the lender. Your client would undoubtedly be obligated to pay for all of the lender's costs in taking these actions, per the loan agreement. Plus, the lender may be excused from its ongoing obligations under the contract, such as to continue to provide credit to your client.

To avoid this situation, the parties could amend the loan agreement to reflect that your client is permitted to take such an action without breaching the contract, particularly if it is contemplated that your client is likely going to sell equipment again in the future. If it is just a one-time exception, your client may instead seek a one-time waiver of this covenant.

The following is a sample amendment provision relating to a loan agreement:

This First Amendment to Loan Agreement ("<u>First Amendment</u>") is made on June 21, 2019 ("<u>First Amendment Effective Date</u>"), between State Bank, an Ohio banking corporation ("<u>Bank</u>"), and Ordinary Corporation ("<u>Borrower</u>").

RECITALS
1. Borrower and Bank are parties to a Loan Agreement dated April 14, 2018 ("<u>Loan Agreement</u>"). Capitalized terms used but not defined in this First Amendment have the meanings given to them in the Loan Agreement.
2. The parties intend to modify the Loan Agreement in the manner set out in this First Amendment.

AGREEMENT
Bank and Borrower agree as follows:
1. **Amendments to Loan Documents.** The Loan Agreement is amended as of the First Amendment Effective Date as follows:
   (a) **Indebtedness**. Section 3.14 of the Loan Agreement is amended to read in its entirety as follows:
      (i) SECTION 3.14 So long as any indebtedness remains outstanding under the Promissory Note executed by Borrower for the benefit of Lender, Borrower agrees that it will not (i) incur any other indebtedness, except for indebtedness to purchase equipment not to exceed $1,000,000, or (ii) sell any of its assets other than inventory in the ordinary course of business

---

Many written contracts contain clauses requiring amendments to be signed by both parties in a writing identified as an amendment. The following is common contract language used for this purpose:

> The parties may only modify this Agreement by a written agreement that
> identifies itself as an amendment to this Agreement.

Assuming the parties signed the above amendment, it would satisfy these requirements. That is because it identifies itself as an amendment both in the preamble and in the recitals.

Parties commonly include this term, and it is considered best practice, to ensure that there is some formality to the amendment process. Such a clause makes it less likely that a party unintentionally manifests its agreement to an amendment informally, where none is intended. However, courts often permit parties to introduce evidence of oral modifications despite the presence of such clauses. In those circumstances, the court presumes that the parties waived application of this clause in that instance. However, the presence of such a clause often deters the parties from even claiming that they amended the contract without an amendment meeting the formality requirements specified in the above clause. Moreover, such a clause clearly places the burden on the party desiring to show amendment to prove the existence of an amendment despite the fact that the formalities required by the contract for an amendment were not met.

The other issue that occasionally arises with amendments is the question of whether the amended obligation is supported by consideration. That is because an amendment is itself a contract. Thus, a party would need to give something in exchange for the other party's increase in its obligation in an amendment for that increase to be supported by consideration, to avoid the preexisting duty rule discussed in Chapter 7.

This doctrinal requirement for new consideration to support an amended obligation is believed by some to be an attempt to police opportunistic behavior. In other words, once a contract has been entered into, the parties begin to rely on each other's promise. One party may at that time be in a position to extract additional benefits or promises from the other party even without promising to do more than what was originally promised. Accordingly, the older requirement for additional consideration for amendments may have been a judicial attempt to prevent parties from acting opportunistically. Eventually, this rule was criticized and seen as overbroad and ineffective at policing such behavior, as discussed in the following case.

Angel v. Murray
Supreme Court of Rhode Island
113 R.I. 482 (1974)

Opinion by: ROBERTS, C. J.

This is a civil action brought by Alfred L. Angel and others against John E. Murray, Jr., Director of Finance of the City of Newport, the city of Newport, and James L. Maher, alleging that Maher had illegally been paid the sum of $ 20,000 by the Director of Finance and praying that the defendant Maher be ordered to repay the city such sum. The case was heard by a justice of the Superior Court, sitting without a jury, who entered a judgment ordering Maher to repay the sum of $20,000 to the city of Newport. Maher is now before this court prosecuting an appeal.

The record discloses that Maher has provided the city of Newport with a refuse-collection service under a series of five-year contracts beginning in 1946. On March 12, 1964, Maher and the city entered into another such contract for a period of five years commencing on July 1, 1964, and terminating on June 30, 1969. The contract provided, among other things, that Maher would receive $137,000 per year in return for collecting and removing all combustible and noncombustible waste materials generated within the city.

In June of 1967 Maher requested an additional $10,000 per year from the city council because there had been a substantial increase in the cost of collection due to an unexpected and unanticipated increase of 400 new dwelling units. Maher's testimony, which is uncontradicted, indicates the 1964 contract had been predicated on the fact that since 1946 there had been an average increase of 20 to 25 new dwelling units per year. After a public meeting of the city council where Maher explained in detail the reasons for his request and was questioned by members of the city council, the city council agreed to pay him an additional $10,000 for the year ending on June 30, 1968. Maher made a similar request again in June of 1968 for the same reasons, and the city council again agreed to pay an additional $10,000 for the year ending on June 30, 1969.

The trial justice found that each such $10,000 payment was made in violation of law. His decision, as we understand it, is premised on two independent grounds. First, he found that the additional payments were unlawful because they had not been recommended in writing to the city council by the city manager. Second, he found that Maher was not entitled to extra compensation because the original contract already required him to collect all refuse generated within the city and, therefore, included the 400 additional units. The trial justice further found that these 400 additional units were within the contemplation of the parties when they entered into the contract. It appears that he based this portion of the decision upon the rule that Maher had a preexisting duty to collect the refuse generated by the 400 additional units, and thus there was no consideration for the two additional payments.

    . . .

II.

Having found that the city council had the power to modify the 1964 contract without the written recommendation of the city manager, we are still confronted with the question of whether the additional payments were illegal because they were not supported by consideration.

A

As previously stated, the city council made two $10,000 payments. The first was made in June of 1967 for the year beginning on July 1, 1967, and ending on June 30, 1968. Thus, by the time this action was commenced in October of 1968, the modification was completely executed. That is, the money had been paid by the city council, and Maher had collected all of the refuse. Since consideration is only a test of the enforceability of executory promises, the presence or absence of consideration for the first payment is unimportant because the city council's agreement to make the first payment was fully executed at the time of the commencement of this action. However, since both payments were made under similar circumstances, our decision regarding the second payment is fully applicable to the first payment.

B

It is generally held that a modification of a contract is itself a contract, which *RULE* is unenforceable unless supported by consideration. In *Rose v. Daniels*, 8 R.I. 381 (1866), this court held that an agreement by a debtor with a creditor to discharge a debt for a sum of money less than the amount due is unenforceable because it was not supported by consideration.

Rose is a perfect example of the preexisting duty rule. Under this rule an agreement modifying a contract is not supported by consideration if one of the parties to the agreement does or promises to do something that he is legally obligated to do or refrains or promises to refrain from doing something he is not legally privileged to do. In *Rose* there was no consideration for the new agreement because the debtor was already legally obligated to repay the full amount of the debt.

. . .

The primary purpose of the preexisting duty rule is to prevent what has been referred to as the "hold-up game." A classic example of the "hold-up game" is found in *Alaska Packers' Ass'n v. Domenico*, 117 F. 99 (9th Cir. 1902). There 21 seamen entered into a written contract with Domenico to sail from San Francisco to Pyramid Harbor, Alaska. They were to work as sailors and fishermen out of Pyramid Harbor during the fishing season of 1900. The contract specified that each man would be paid $ 50 plus two cents for each red salmon he caught. Subsequent to their arrival at Pyramid Harbor, the men stopped work and demanded an additional $50. They threatened to return to San Francisco if Domenico did not agree to their demand. Since it was impossible for Domenico to find other men, he agreed to pay the men an additional $50. After they returned to San Francisco, Domenico refused to pay the men an additional $50. The court found that the subsequent agreement to pay the men an additional $50 was not supported by consideration because the men had a preexisting duty to work on the ship under the original contract, and thus the subsequent agreement was unenforceable.

"hold up game"

does not apply to this fact pattern

Another example of the "hold-up game" is found in the area of construction contracts. Frequently, a contractor will refuse to complete work under an unprofitable contract unless he is awarded additional compensation. The courts have generally held that a subsequent agreement to award additional compensation is unenforceable if the contractor is only performing work which would have been required of him under the original contract.

These examples clearly illustrate that the courts will not enforce an agreement that has been procured by coercion or duress and will hold the parties to their original contract regardless of whether it is profitable or unprofitable. However, the courts have been reluctant to apply the pre-existing duty rule when a party to a contract encounters unanticipated difficulties and the other party, not influenced by coercion or duress, voluntarily agrees to pay additional compensation for work already required to be performed under the contract. For example, the courts have found that the original contract was rescinded . . . abandoned . . . or waived. . . .

Although the preexisting duty rule has served a useful purpose insofar as it deters parties from using coercion and duress to obtain additional compensation, it has been widely criticized as a general rule of law. With regard to the preexisting duty rule, one legal scholar has stated: "There has been a growing doubt as to the soundness of this doctrine as a matter of social policy. In certain classes of cases, this doubt has influenced courts to refuse to apply the rule, or to ignore it, in their actual decisions. Like other legal rules, this rule is in process of growth and change, the process being more active here than in most instances. The result of this is that a court should no longer accept this rule as fully established. It should never use it as the major premise of a decision, at least without giving careful thought to the circumstances of the particular case, to the moral deserts of the parties, and to the social feelings and interests that are involved. It is certain that the rule, stated in general and all-inclusive terms, is no longer so well-settled that a court must apply it though the heavens fall." 1A Corbin, *supra*, § 171.

modern take on preexisting duty rule

The modern trend appears to recognize the necessity that courts should enforce agreements modifying contracts when unexpected or unanticipated difficulties arise during the course of the performance of a contract, even though there is no consideration for the modification, as long as the parties agree voluntarily. Under the Uniform Commercial Code, § 2-209(1), which has been adopted by 49 states, "[an] agreement modifying a contract [for the sale of goods] needs no consideration to be binding." *See* G. L. 1956 (1969 Reenactment) § 6A-2-209(1). Although at first blush this section appears to validate modifications obtained by coercion and duress, the comments to this section indicate that a modification under this section must meet the test of good faith imposed by the Code, and a modification obtained by extortion without a legitimate commercial reason is unenforceable.

The modern trend away from a rigid application of the preexisting duty rule is reflected by § 89D(a) of the American Law Institute's Restatement Second of the Law of Contracts, which provides: "A promise modifying a duty under a contract not fully performed on either side is binding (a) if the modification is fair and equitable in view of circumstances not anticipated by the parties when the contract was made."

We believe that § 89D(a) is the proper rule of law and find it applicable to the facts of this case. It not only prohibits modifications obtained by coercion, duress, or extortion but also fulfills society's expectation that agreements entered into voluntarily will be enforced by the courts. Section 89D(a), of course, does not compel a modification of an unprofitable or unfair contract; it only enforces a modification if the parties voluntarily agree and if (1) the promise modifying the original contract was made before the contract was fully performed on either side, (2) the underlying circumstances which prompted the modification were unanticipated by the parties, and (3) the modification is fair and equitable.

The evidence, which is uncontradicted, reveals that in June of 1968 Maher requested the city council to pay him an additional $ 10,000 for the year beginning on July 1, 1968, and ending on June 30, 1969. This request was made at a public meeting of the city council, where Maher explained in detail his reasons for making the request. Thereafter, the city council voted to authorize the Mayor to sign an amendment to the 1954 contract which provided that Maher would receive an additional $ 10,000 per year for the duration of the contract. Under such circumstances we have no doubt that the city voluntarily agreed to modify the 1964 contract.

Having determined the voluntariness of this agreement, we turn our attention to the three criteria delineated above. First, the modification was made in June of 1968 at a time when the five-year contract which was made in 1964 had not been fully performed by either party. Second, although the 1964 contract provided that Maher collect all refuse generated within the city, it appears this contract was premised on Maher's past experience that the number of refuse-generating units would increase at a rate of 20 to 25 per year. Furthermore, the evidence is uncontradicted that the 1967-1968 increase of 400 units "went beyond any previous expectation." Clearly, the circumstances which prompted the city council to modify the 1964 contract were unanticipated. Third, although the evidence does not indicate what proportion of the total this increase comprised, the evidence does indicate that it was a "substantial" increase. In light of this, we cannot say that the council's agreement to pay Maher the $ 10,000 increase was not fair and equitable in the circumstances.

The judgment appealed from is reversed, and the cause is remanded to the Superior Court for entry of judgment for the defendants.

Comprehension and Thought Questions:

1. What is the preexisting duty rule? How does it relate to contract modifications?

2. Why do many courts require consideration for the enforcement of contract modifications?

3. Why does the Rhode Island Supreme Court think that the consideration requirement is not an effective rule for determining enforceability of contract modifications?

4. Why was the doctrine relating to contract modifications not applicable to the first $10,000 payment made in 1967?

5. What is the modern rule for enforceability of contract modifications, as discussed in this case?

Hypothetical Variations:

1. What if Maher had threatened not to perform his contractual obligations unless the City Council agreed to pay an additional $10,000 per year?

2. What if Maher was the only available company providing refuse collection service in the area?

3. What if there had been no additional increase in dwelling units?

PRACTICE PROBLEM 12-3

Imagine that your client wants to paint her business name on the walls in her office building. After requesting the landlord's consent to do this, as required by the lease, the landlord denies your client's request. But the landlord agrees instead to provide some additional signage for your client's business near the street. Your client agrees, and both parties sign a short document that reads as follows:

> Landlord and Tenant hereby agree that the Lease executed on October 1, 2017 between the parties is now hereby amended to provide that the Landlord will erect, at Landlord's cost and subject to Tenant's reasonable satisfaction, two additional street signs advertising Tenant's business.

Your client wants to know if this amendment is enforceable. Explain your answer. Was there anything else your client could have done to increase her chances of having this amendment enforced?

CHAPTER 13

Judicial Interpretation of Contract Terms

This chapter addresses the situation where your client and the other party disagree about the contract's terms. Inevitably, one party's expectations will be disappointed, as she may have anticipated a different performance by the counterparty than what she received. As a result, the disappointed party may sue the counterparty for breach. This chapter explains how courts resolve these situations. Learning how a court resolves such disputes also helps the transactional attorney, as the attorney can then better forecast interpretation problems, and resolve them on the front end, when advising a client in negotiating and drafting a contract.

First, in Section A, this chapter explains what happens where the parties to a contract understand contract language differently. In particular, it explores the potential implications for the contract parties where there is a mutual misunderstanding with respect to the parties' contract-formation manifestations as well as courts' general approach to resolving a mutual misunderstanding. Section B then explores the interpretive conventions courts use to determine what contractual terms mean, including how to resolve ambiguous terms. Finally, Section C addresses how courts address the unique problem of contracts with indefinite terms, such as missing terms and intentionally omitted terms.

A. EFFECT OF MUTUAL MISUNDERSTANDING AND AMBIGUITY

Sometimes parties think that they have mutually assented to a bargain only to find out later, as one party performs, that they actually have different understandings about an essential term of the bargain, or about the meaning of a party's manifestation. Where this occurs, it is said that the parties have a mutual misunderstanding. They have a **mutual misunderstanding** because an essential contract term within a purported manifestation of assent is **ambiguous**, or is reasonably susceptible to more than one mutually exclusive meaning.

To see how an ambiguity might arise and affect the existence or terms of the parties' bargain, assume Miranda Foote, the landlord of East Side Office Complex, agrees with Dale Villanova that Dale will rent shared office space in Suite 22 for $1,200 a month. While Dale has seen Miranda's "standard" lease, Dale has not yet seen a tailored version with his name, the specific space he will lease, or his monthly rental amount filled in. And given how busy Miranda is, she and Dale will not have an opportunity to exchange signed copies of the lease until the first day of Dale's lease term. Thus, Dale shows up on the first day of his lease term at Suite 22 in East Side Office Complex to meet Miranda, get his office key, and exchange signed leases. However, Miranda is not there. Dale calls her only to find out that Miranda is waiting for Dale at Suite 22 at *West Side* Office Complex. In other words, Miranda and Dale had a misunderstanding about the office complex in which Dale was going to lease office space—obviously a central term in the lease. In this scenario, Dale would undoubtedly ask himself—does he have a lease for Suite 22 in East Side Office Complex? What about in West Side Office Complex?

Where the mutual misunderstanding is of an essential term or relates to the meaning of the parties' manifestations of assent, and before the parties have performed, that disagreement might actually preclude a finding of mutual assent.

Where the ambiguity goes to an essential term, often the first step upon discovering this fact is for the parties to resolve their difference. That often means either calling the contract off or renegotiating the terms of the contract.

So, for example, once Miranda and Dale discover that they were talking about different buildings, they might decide to call off the lease if Dale does not want to lease office space at West Side Office Complex and Miranda does not have any space available at East Side Office Complex. Or, Miranda and Dale might negotiate terms of a new lease, either for different space at East Side Office Complex or for space at West Side Office Complex.

If the parties cannot resolve their mutual misunderstanding, one party might sue the other seeking to have a court enforce the contract using its meaning. In that case, where the misunderstood term is essential to the bargain, whether a court will find the existence of a contract, and, if so, whose term prevails, often can turn on whether either party knew or had reason to know the other party's meaning of the manifestation or essential term. Specifically, under the framework set out in Sections 20 and 201 of the Restatement, where a court finds that one party either knew or had reason to know of the other party's meaning, then it may find that there was a contract on the term attached by the "innocent" party—that is, the party who did not know or have reason to know of the other party's term. The rationale for this rule is that the party "in the know" could have prevented the misunderstanding from happening. As such, it is only fair to utilize the other party's meaning.

In contrast, where both parties either know or have reason to know of the other's meaning, or neither party knows or has reason to know of the other's meaning, courts may find that there is no mutual assent. In this scenario, there simply is no "innocent" party whose meaning prevails over a party who is more "at fault."

This framework is shown in the following table:

	Party B knows or has reason to know of Party A's meaning	Party B does NOT know or have reason to know of Party A's meaning
Party A knows or has reason to know of Party B's meaning	Potentially no mutual assent (or, if defined enough for mutual assent, neither party's meaning prevails)	Bargain—Party B's meaning prevails
Party A does NOT know or have reason to know of Party B's meaning	Bargain—Party A's meaning prevails	Potentially no mutual assent (or, if defined enough for mutual assent, neither party's meaning prevails)

The word *"know"* denotes actual knowledge of a party, or what that person consciously believes to be true. The expression *"have reason to know"* denotes the knowledge an ordinary person would have by inferring facts from the information that person has. The person need not have to infer a fact with complete certainty to have reason to know that fact. If the person's inference of the fact is strong enough that he would act on it, then the person has reason to know that fact. Note that a person does not have a duty to investigate a fact under this "reason to know" standard.

Courts use various interpretive tools to determine what a party had reason to know. Under one rule of interpretation commonly employed by courts, a person has reason to know the other party's meaning of a term where the term has a "plain meaning." Other common rules of interpretation are discussed in Section B. The following "classic" case demonstrates a mutual misunderstanding due to an ambiguous essential term. As you review the decision, consider whether you believe the court appropriately determined if a mutual misunderstanding existed due to an ambiguity and if its ultimate conclusion serves the contract law policies discussed in Chapter 1.

Raffles v. Wichelhaus and Another

Court of Exchequer
159 Eng. Rep. 375 (1864)

To a declaration for not accepting Surat cotton which the defendant bought of the plaintiff "to arrive ex ' Peerless' from Bombay," the defendant pleaded that he meant a ship called the "Peerless" which sailed from Bombay, in October, and the plaintiff was not ready to deliver any cotton which arrived by that ship, but only cotton which arrived by another ship called the "Peerless," which sailed from Bombay in December. Held, on demurrer, that the plea was a good answer.

. . .

Breach: that the defendants refused to accept the said goods or pay the plaintiff for them.

Plea. That the said ship mentioned in the said agreement was meant and intended by the defendants to be the ship called the "Peerless," which sailed from Bombay, to wit, in October; and that the plaintiff was not ready and willing and did not offer to deliver to the defendants any bales of cotton which arrived by the last mentioned ship, but instead thereof was only ready and willing and offered to deliver to the defendants 125 bales of Surat cotton which arrived by another and different ship, which was also called the "Peerless," and which sailed from Bombay, to wit, in December.

Demurrer, and joinder therein.

Milward, in support of the demurrer. The contract was for the sale of a number of bales of cotton of a particular description, which the plaintiff was ready to deliver. It is immaterial by what ship the cotton was to arrive, so that it was a ship called the "Peerless." The words "to arrive ex 'Peerless,'" only mean that if the vessel is lost on the voyage, the contract is to be at an end. [Pollock, C. B. It would be a question for the jury whether both parties meant the same ship called the "Peerless."] That would be so if the contract was for the sale of a ship called the "Peerless"; but it is for the sale of cotton on board a ship of that name. [Pollock, C. B. The defendant only bought that cotton which was to arrive by a particular ship. It may as well be said, that if there is a contract for the purchase of certain goods in warehouse A., that is satisfied by the delivery of goods of the same description in warehouse B.] In that case there would be goods in both warehouses; here it does not appear that the plaintiff had any goods on board the other "Peerless." [Martin, B. It is imposing on the defendant a contract different from that which he entered into. Pollock, C. B. It is like a contract for the purchase of wine coming from a particular estate in France or Spain, where there are two estates of that name.] The defendant has no right to contradict by parol evidence a written contract good upon the face of it. He does not impute misrepresentation or fraud, but only says that he fancied the ship was a different one. Intention is of

parol evidence rule?

no avail, unless stated at the time of the contract. [Pollock, C. B. One vessel sailed in October and the other in December.] The time of sailing is no part of the contract.

Mellish (Cohen with him), in support of the plea. There is nothing on the face of the contract to shew that any particular ship called the "Peerless" was meant; but the moment it appears that two ships called the "Peerless" were about to sail from Bombay there is a latent ambiguity, and parol evidence may be given for the purpose of shewing that the defendant meant one "Peerless," and the plaintiff another. That being so, there was no consenus ad idem, and therefore no binding contract. He was then stopped by the Court.

dissent

Per Curiam. (a) There must be judgment for the defendants. Judgment for the defendants.

Understanding the Case:

1. *Parol Evidence Rule:* You will learn about the parol evidence rule in Chapter 15, but for now you should understand that it is a rule that excludes evidence of prior agreements that contradict the terms of the written contract. In this instance, parol evidence (that is, evidence of the parties' intent prior to the date of the contract) was permitted to be introduced notwithstanding the parol evidence rule because the contract itself was unclear. In other words, the court could not determine what "Peerless" meant, so it had to admit other evidence to help the court ascertain what the parties intended. That parol evidence apparently suggested that each party intended a different ship, which means that the parties had a mutual misunderstanding.

Comprehension and Thought Questions:

1. Why would a party care which Peerless actually delivered the cotton? Why is that relevant to the question of mutual misunderstanding (and contract formation)?

2. Do you think the court would have reached the same conclusion if it had applied the framework of Restatement §§ 20 & 201?

3. As a transactional attorney, what lessons do you learn from the outcome of this case and the doctrine of mutual misunderstanding? *be specific*

Hypothetical Variations:

1. Do you think the outcome would have been different if the defendant had known there were two ships named "Peerless" but failed to specify which one was meant in the contract? Why or why not?

yes, still a potential misunderstanding

2. How might the outcome have been different if the dispute had been about whether Surat cotton included cotton grown just outside of the city limits of Surat? *not an essential term*

Where parties have a mutual misunderstanding as to an ancillary term, it is rare for a court to find the absence of mutual assent on that basis. That is because courts often hold that it would be a worse injustice to not enforce the contract at all than to impose an ancillary term on the parties to which they did not agree. Thus, in that scenario, courts will first typically try to determine whether either party knew or had reason to know of the other party's meaning of that disputed term and, if so, give effect to the "innocent" party's meaning. However, if nobody's meaning prevails under this framework, a court will usually impose its own meaning on the parties regardless of whether there has been performance.

To see how this plays out, assume that instead of misunderstanding which premises was to be leased, Miranda and Dale attach different meanings to the lease term "common areas." The lease employs this term by imposing an obligation on Miranda to maintain all of the common areas in good condition. Dale believes this term includes the work stations in Suite 22, as those spaces are common—meaning shared—among the lawyers in Suite 22. Miranda, on the other hand, interprets this term to mean the areas of the property that are accessible to the public. Here, regardless of whether Miranda or Dale knew or had reason to know of the other's meaning, the lack of agreement on this term's meaning would not undermine the existence of mutual assent. That is because Miranda's obligation to maintain the common areas, while important, is not the essence of the contract. Stated another way, the contract is not for Miranda's maintenance services—it is for the lease of shared office space. Surely it is important to Dale that the common areas be maintained. But just because a term is important does not mean it forms the essence of the contract.

So how do Miranda and Dale resolve their mutual misunderstanding of this ancillary term? Again, the first option is for Miranda and Dale to agree what the term "common areas" means. If Miranda is willing to maintain the work stations in Suite 22, then Dale and she have amicably resolved this misunderstanding. If, on the other hand, Miranda and Dale cannot resolve this difference on their own and Dale really cared about this term, Dale may need to sue Miranda in court to have a court enforce this term. An attorney may become involved at this point to help assist the parties resolve the dispute, or, failing that, to commence litigation after advising its client on the potential risks and costs. In court, Dale's attorney would need to persuade the court as to why Dale's meaning should prevail, either because Miranda knew or had reason to know what Dale thought the term meant, including perhaps because the term "common areas" has a plain meaning. Failing that, the court would likely impose a term on the parties utilizing some of the interpretive conventions discussed in Section B below.[1]

As a threshold matter, a court often is faced with the issue of whether the contested contractual terms is ambiguous in the first place. The following case illustrates how a court determines whether contract language is ambiguous. As you read this case, consider what evidence is admissible to show the existence of an ambiguous term, as well as the potential effect of an ambiguous ancillary term on the contract as a whole.

Sault Ste. Marie Tribe of Chippewa Indians v. Granholm
U.S. Court of Appeals for the Sixth Circuit
475 F.3d 805 (2007)

CLAY, Circuit Judge.

Plaintiff Hannahville Indian Community ("Plaintiff Hannahville") appeals the district court's grant of a Motion to Enforce Stipulation and Consent Judgment in favor of the Governor of the State of Michigan ("Defendant") pursuant to Fed. R. Civ. P. 7 and 54. For the reasons set forth below, we REVERSE the district court's decision and REMAND to the district court to resolve ambiguous terms in the Stipulation and Consent Judgment with the aid of extrinsic evidence.

BACKGROUND

I. Factual History

On October 17, 1988, the Indian Gaming Regulatory Act ("IGRA"), 25 U.S.C. § 2701 *et seq.*, was signed into law. The purpose of the IGRA was to "provide a statutory basis for the operation of gaming by Indian tribes as a means of promoting tribal economic development, self-sufficiency, and strong tribal governments." 25 U.S.C. § 2702(1). Almost immediately after the passage of the Act, Plaintiffs Hannahville, Sault Ste. Marie Tribe of Chippewa Indians, the Grand Traverse Band of Ottawa and Chippewa Indians, the Keweena Bay Indian Community, the Bay Mills Indian Community, the Lac Vieux Desert Band of Lake Superior Chippewa Indians, and the Saginaw Chippewa Tribe of Indians (collectively "the Tribes") began engaging in negotiations with Defendant to enter into an agreement that would govern the operation of class III games ("slot machines") on the Tribes' native lands. Disagreements about the scope of the IGRA led to a breakdown in these negotiations and subsequently to a suit filed in the district court by the Tribes alleging that Defendant refused to

---

1. Of course, this example presumes that the relevant state does not impose a duty on the landlord to maintain those common areas, and leaves such term to the parties' contract.

negotiate gaming compacts as was required by the IGRA. On August 20, 1993, the parties reached an agreement with respect to that claim, which was memorialized in a Stipulation and incorporated into a Consent Judgment.

The Stipulation and Consent Judgment set forth guidelines as to how the Tribes would operate their Michigan casinos. The district court retained jurisdiction to enforce the Consent Judgment. One of the terms of the Consent Judgment was that the Tribes agreed to "make semi-annual payments to any local unit of state government in the immediate vicinity of each tribal casino in the aggregate amount equal to two percent (2%) of the net win at each casino derived from all class III electronic games of chance." The term "net win" was defined in the Stipulation. Specifically it stated: "'[n]et win' is defined as the total amount wagered on each electronic game of chance, minus the total amount paid to players for winning wagers at said machines."

Plaintiff Hannahville owns and operates the Island Resort and Casino ("the Island Casino") in Harris, Michigan. Around 1998, the Island Casino began producing and distributing promotional tokens to customers, which were good for a free play on the promotional slot machines. The tokens, called QuickSilver tokens, were given out to customers completely free of charge. Such "comps" are standard at casinos and are often used for marketing and promotional purposes. The QuickSilver tokens could only be used while playing the QuickSilver slot machines. The QuickSilver machines accepted only those tokens, and the tokens themselves could not be redeemed for real money. The QuickSilver machines did, however, pay out in real money: One "credit" on a QuickSilver machine was denoted as a quarter, and the machines paid quarters to patrons when they won.

While the tokens were not redeemable for cash, there was some discrepancy with respect to how they were valued. In its Daily Revenue Report, which was an internal record kept to keep track of the casinos profits and losses, Plaintiff Hannahville valued QuickSilver tokens at twenty-five cents. Further, the Island Casino advertised their distribution of comps, and afforded them a dollar value in those ads, though there is some discrepancy as to whether those ads were referring to QuickSilver tokens or some other promotional wager program at the casino.

At the time Plaintiffs and Defendant entered into the Consent Judgment, the Island Casino had no promotional wagering programs in place, and accordingly, the Consent Judgment made no mention of how the casino should calculate net win with respect to promotional wagers. According to the Stipulation and Consent Judgment, the Island Casino is required to pay 2% of its net win to Defendant. A dispute arose over how to value the promotional tokens when calculating net win. Defendant argued that they should be valued at twenty-five cents, but Plaintiff Hannahville decided that the tokens should be valued as a zero cent wager. However, because the QuickSilver machines paid out in quarters, the money won by patrons on these machines was reflected in the net win calculus. The effect was that the QuickSilver machines consistently showed no money being wagered, but money being paid out. Thus, Plaintiff Hannahville's practice of assigning the tokens a zero cent value resulted in these machines necessarily producing a net loss. Because net wins are calculated across the entire floor of a casino and not on a machine by machine basis, this method of calculation lowered the Island Casino's overall profits and, accordingly, it lowered the amount Plaintiff Hannahville was required to pay Defendant.

. . .

III. Analysis

A. The district court committed reversible error by concluding that no latent ambiguity existed without first considering extrinsic evidence

"Consent decrees and judgments are binding contracts." *Engler*, 146 F.3d at 372. According to Michigan law, "[t]he cardinal rule in the interpretation of contracts is to ascertain the intention of the parties. To this rule all others are subordinate." *McIntosh v. Groomes*, 227 Mich. 215, 198 N.W. 954, 955 (1924). Our obligation in construing this Consent Judgment is to effectuate the intent of the parties, and extrinsic evidence is admissible only to the extent that it is necessary in order for us to do so. Where a contract is unambiguous on its face, extrinsic evidence is inadmissible because no outside evidence can better evince the intent of the parties than the writing itself. Only where a contract contains ambiguous terms will consideration of outside evidence be necessary. Thus, the admissibility of extrinsic evidence is contingent upon "some finding of contractual ambiguity." *City of Grosse Pointe Park v. Mich. Mun. Liab. & Prop. Pool*, 473 Mich. 188, 702 N.W.2d 106, 113 (Mich. 2005).

Ambiguity can come in two forms: Patent ambiguities and latent ambiguities. "Patent ambiguities are those that clearly appear on the face of a document, arising from the language itself." *Black's Law Dictionary* 80 (7th ed. 1999). Therefore, a patent ambiguity will be readily apparent without the aid of extrinsic evidence to detect it. A latent ambiguity, on the other hand, is one that "does not readily appear in the language of a document, but instead arises from a collateral matter when the document's terms are applied or executed." *Black's Law Dictionary* 80 (7th ed. 1999). A latent ambiguity will often arise when a term is being used within a technical or specialized field. In *J.C. Wyckoff & Assoc., Inc. v. Standard Fire Ins. Co.*, we noted that "technical terms and words of art are given their technical meaning when used in transaction within their technical field." 936 F.2d 1474, 1495 (6th Cir. 1991) (quoting Restatement (Second) of Contracts § 202(3)(b) (1981)). Thus, a word may have a meaning that is different from its ordinary meaning within a particular field and the ambiguity will only be revealed when that word is applied in context. Where both parties define a term according to its technical definition, extrinsic evidence is necessary to ascertain the actual intent of the parties.

According to Michigan law, the burden is on the party alleging the ambiguity to present an interpretation of the contract that is equally as plausible as the common sense interpretation. The party alleging the ambiguity must carry this burden because a court "cannot create an ambiguity where none exists." *Upjohn Co. v. New Hampshire Ins. Co.*, 438 Mich. 197, 476 N.W.2d 392, 397 (Mich. 1991). If the alleging party presents evidence to prove a latent ambiguity it must be considered by the court. "[T]he detection of a latent ambiguity requires a consideration of factors outside the instrument itself" and therefore "extrinsic evidence is obviously admissible to prove the existence of the ambiguity, as well as to resolve any ambiguity proven to exist." *McCarty v. Mercury Metalcraft Co.*, 372 Mich. 567, 127 N.W.2d 340, 343 (1964). In other words, the allegation of a latent ambiguity gives a court cause to consider extrinsic evidence at least once: The court must consider the extrinsic evidence to determine if there exists an ambiguity and then, if an ambiguity does exist, the court must consider extrinsic evidence to resolve that ambiguity.

. . .

In the present case, we conclude that a latent ambiguity did exist with respect to the meaning of "wager" as the term is used in the gaming industry and that extrinsic evidence is necessary to resolve it. It is beyond dispute that the district court did not consider extrinsic evidence to determine whether a latent ambiguity existed. However, this does not end our inquiry. We must determine whether a review of the extrinsic evidence would have revealed an ambiguity in order to decide whether the district court committed reversible error.

Plaintiff Hannahville attempted to introduce several pieces of extrinsic evidence: 1) the Gaming Compact between Plaintiff Hannahville and Defendant; 2) information on Plaintiff Hannahville's Nevada-approved online accounting slot information system (known as "OASIS"); 3) information on the standards for Plaintiff Hannahville's financial statements completed in compliance with Generally Accepted Accounting Principles ("GAAP"); 4) information on the standards of Plaintiff Hannahville's annual audit completed in compliance with the American Institute of Certified Public Accountants ("AICPA") Audit and Accounting Guide for Casinos ("the AICPA Guide"); 5) standards of the Nevada Gaming Commission with respect to wagering, promotional play, and reporting profits; and 6) standards of the National Indian Gaming Commission with respect to wagering, promotional play, and reporting profits. Plaintiff Hannahville alleges that these materials are relevant to illustrate that within the gaming industry it is possible, and indeed common, to contemplate a "wager" that has no monetary value.

A review of this evidence reveals a latent ambiguity with respect to the meaning of the term "wager" and whether the Consent Judgment permitted Plaintiff to use a zero cent wager. Specifically, we base our conclusion on two

pieces of evidence: the AICPA Guide, with which Plaintiff Hannahville is feder-
ally required to comply, 25 C.F.R. § 571.12, and the standards of the Nevada
Gaming Commission, which provides the basis for Plaintiff Hannahville's accounting practices. The AICPA Guide explicitly states in relevant part:

> 2.03 Promotional allowances (complementaries, or comps) represent goods and
> services, which would be accounted for as revenue *if sold*, that a casino gives to
> customers as an inducement to gamble at that establishment.

And:

> 2.04 . . . .The retail amount of promotional allowances should not be included in
> gross revenues and charged to operating expenses because that would overstate
> both revenues and expenses.

While these passages do not explicitly refer to "wagers," the term "promotional
allowances" refers to "comps," which is undisputedly what QuickSilver tokens
are considered. According to this language, casinos are advised not to include
the value of comps in their overall revenue computations unless the comps are
sold. Further, a document from the Nevada Gaming Commission states:

> 463.0161 1. "Gross revenue" means the total of all: . . .
> 2. The term does not include: . . .
> g) Cash provided by the licensee to a patron and subsequently won by the
> licensee for which the licensee can demonstrate that it or its affiliate has not
> been reimbursed.

Again, while the term "wager" is not found in this language, the passage excludes from the definition of "gross revenue" all cash given free of charge to
a patron by the casino that is then used by the patron for gambling in the
casino. This passage is describing comps. In other words, the Nevada Gaming
Commission, like the AICPA Guide, urges casinos to exclude comps from the
computation of gross revenue. We are persuaded that Plaintiff Hannahville's extrinsic evidence indicates that within the gaming industry the term "wager" has
a technical meaning that may be able to contemplate a zero cent promotional
wager. This industry specific definition creates a latent ambiguity that may only
be resolved with the aid of extrinsic evidence. Thus, the district court erred in
refusing to consider such evidence.

  . . .

B. The district court committed reversible error by concluding that Quick-Silver tokens had a cash value of twenty-five cents without first considering extrinsic evidence offered by Plaintiff Hannahville

  . . .

While we hold that Plaintiff Hannahville's extrinsic evidence is relevant
and therefore admissible, we decline to make a determination with respect to
the question of what value to assign the tokens. The admissibility of extrinsic

evidence is a question of law and is properly within our province to determine. However, the amount of weight to accord extrinsic evidence is a question of fact and must be determined by a trier of fact. We therefore remand this case to the district court and instruct that extrinsic evidence shall be considered to determine whether QuickSilver tokens should be assigned any value, and if so, what the appropriate value is.

CONCLUSION

For the foregoing reasons, we REVERSE and REMAND to the district court for further proceedings consistent with this opinion.

Understanding the Case:

1. *Consent Decree as Contract: Sault Ste. Marie Tribe of Chippewa Indians* involved the interpretation of a consent judgment. It may be confusing, however, as to why a court would use contract law principles to interpret the meaning of a judicial decree. A consent judgment is, as its name suggests, a judgment to which the parties to the action consent and typically involves promises or agreements of the parties. Although it is a "judgment" of the court, its voluntary nature suggests that it is contract-like and should be interpreted accordingly.

2. *Interpretation and Opportunistic Behavior:* It is often unclear from court opinions or party filings as to whether the parties actually understood a particular term differently or if one of the parties was, after the fact, attempting to take advantage of a supposed latent ambiguity in the contract. You should not, therefore, assume that each party is necessarily proceeding in "good faith" or innocently with respect to its stated claims. For example, a party may attempt to cover up its (or one of its agent's or employee's) mistake or oversight with respect to how to handle a particular issue. By arguing that there is an ambiguity, a party can seek to correct its initial error or at least force the other party to "share the pain" and perhaps settle the lawsuit.

Comprehension and Thought Questions:

1. The term "wager" seems to have a plain meaning. Why is there an issue regarding whether extrinsic evidence can be admitted with respect to an unambiguous term? *technical industry term suggests diff. meaning more appropriate*

2. What evidence would this court admit to suggest a latent ambiguity exists as opposed to a patent ambiguity? *lang. itself not unclear = need to see how others used that lang.*

3. Why is it relevant to the court that the gaming industry uses comps? In what sense is the promotional token at issue a comp?

technical industry term/idea that employees may have diff understanding of "wager"?

Hypothetical Variations:

1. Suppose that, upon remand, the district court determines that the term "wager" is ambiguous, and that the parties each ascribed a different meaning to the term without knowing or having reason to know of the other's understanding. What would be the court's solution? *no assent = renegotiate? or dirt curves*

2. Suppose that the parties had disputed the meaning of the word "purchase" in the contract. Do you think that the court would have permitted extrinsic evidence to be introduced to suggest that the term "purchase" constituted a latent ambiguity? *no – not a technical, industry term = patent ambiguity at most*

PRACTICE PROBLEM 13-1

After Dale tours Suite 22 of the East Side Office Complex, he is convinced that this is the right work space for him. After Dale indicates to Miranda that he wants to lease the third and only remaining work station in Suite 22, Miranda sends Dale a draft of the lease. The following is an excerpt of the provisions in the lease on rent and the deposit: *→ together or separately?*

Section 4. Rent. Tenant and each other tenant who occupies Suite 22 shall pay Landlord $1,200 each month during the Term ("Rent"), to be paid in advance no later than the fifth day of each month during the Term.

Section 5. Deposit. In addition to Rent, Tenant shall pay Landlord a deposit of $1,200 no later than the second business day after the date of this Agreement. Landlord shall return this deposit to Tenant no later than 60 days after the end of the Term, reduced by

1. any amount which Landlord reasonably determines is necessary to return the Premises to the condition it was in at the start of the Term, excluding ordinary wear and tear,
2. any amount of Rent remaining unpaid, and
3. any portion of Rent to be payable by Tenant during the remaining Term, if Landlord terminates this Agreement before the end of the Term under Section 5.

If the deposit is reduced under Section 5(3), such reduction is in addition to any other rights and remedies Landlord has upon an early termination of this Agreement.

would mean the deposit is four months' rent, which is pretty outrageous

---

After reviewing this lease (without consulting you, his attorney), Dale signs and sends it back to Miranda, who also signs. Miranda then sends Dale a fully signed copy. Dale immediately sends Miranda the $1,200 deposit.

On the first day of October, Dale starts working in Suite 22. And, on the first day of November, Dale sends Miranda $400. Dale calculated that amount by dividing the monthly rent amount—$1,200—by three, because three lawyers share Suite 22. However, Dale promptly receives a notice from Miranda notifying him of a deficiency in his rent. Specifically, according to Miranda's letter, Dale still owes Miranda $800 for the month's rent. Dale is surprised, as he understood rent to be $1,200 per month in the aggregate, shared among the three occupants of Suite 22. Dale did not think he had to individually pay $1,200 a month. When Dale calls Miranda to discuss the matter, Miranda insists that each tenant in Suite 22 has an obligation to pay $1,200 in rent each month.

Despite trying, Dale and Miranda cannot reconcile this difference. Dale is now worried that Miranda is going to sue him and force him to pay the deficiency Miranda says he owes and possibly also force him to vacate Suite 22. Dale calls you for advice. Specifically, he wants to know if Miranda were to sue him, would he have a good argument that he never had a contract with her? *no? maybe*

B. JUDICIAL INTERPRETATION OF CONTRACTUAL TERMS

When parties submit their disagreement regarding the meaning of a term to litigation, a court has to decide how to resolve that disagreement. Consistent with much of the objective approach throughout contract law, the general convention in interpretation is that clear contractual terms will be enforced as written. As mentioned earlier in this chapter, under this "plain meaning" convention, words used in a contract are interpreted and understood based on their plain and ordinary meaning. This means that courts attempt to determine whether a plain meaning would be evident to someone examining the contract without employing technical or specialized constructions. When interpreting the plain meaning of a contract's provisions, some courts will not consider extrinsic evidence of surrounding circumstances that challenge the (apparently) clear and unambiguous meaning of the language. Even where judges admit their reluctance to impose their own understandings of what the plain meaning of a term is (for fear of substituting their own judgment for that of the parties), they often refrain from looking beyond the text of the contract to determine whether an ambiguity exists. Accordingly, if the meaning is clear after interpreting the language based on its ordinary and plain meaning, then summary judgment is often appropriate and granted to the applicable party. Other courts, as in *Sault Ste. Marie Tribe of Chippewa Indians* above, will first permit extrinsic evidence regarding whether a latent ambiguity exists before excluding evidence that contradicts the plain meaning of a term.

Under this interpretive convention, the plain meaning of a term will generally prevail even if one of the parties understood the term to mean something different than its conventional definition. That is because, as with mutual assent, contracting parties are held accountable for the objective meaning of their expressed intentions, not their hidden subjective intentions. Each party is deemed to have reason to know of such objective intentions, and thus is bound by them.

Consider the following famous formulation of contractual term interpretation:

> A contract has, strictly speaking, nothing to do with the personal, or individual, intent of the parties. A contract is an obligation attached by the mere force of law to certain acts of the parties, usually words, which ordinarily accompany and represent a known intent. If, however, it were proved by twenty bishops that either party, when he used the words, intended something else than the usual meaning which the law imposes upon them, he would still be held, unless there were some mutual mistake, or something else of the sort. Of course, if it appear by other words, or acts, of the parties, that they attribute a peculiar meaning to such words as they use in the contract, that meaning will prevail, but only by virtue of the other words, and not because of their unexpressed intent.
>
> Now, in the case at bar, whatever was the understanding in fact of the banks, and of the brokers, too, for that matter, of the legal effect of this practice between them, it is of not the slightest consequence, unless it took form in some acts or words, which, being reasonably interpreted, would have such meaning to ordinary men. Of course, it will be likely that, if they both do understand their acts in the same way, usual men would have done so, too. Yet the question always remains for the court to interpret the reasonable meaning to the acts of the parties, by word or deed, and no characterization of its effect by either party thereafter, however truthful, is material. The rights and obligations depend upon the law alone.[2]

On the other hand, if both parties attach an unconventional meaning to a term, then a court will give effect to that meaning.[3] This rule allows the parties to specify in the contract their specific meaning of a term or phrase, so long as the other party does not object. By doing so, a lawyer turns her client's *subjective* understanding into an *objective* understanding by clarifying and including the subjective interpretation of the term in the contract. That meaning, then, will prevail over the conventional understanding of the term.

Under another interpretive convention, when determining the intentions of the parties, courts typically consider the entire contract and attempt to utilize and give effect to each word in the contract. In so doing, courts attempt to interpret the contract so that no parts of the contract are unnecessary.

Courts also try to interpret contracts using common sense, which means avoiding interpretations that result in absurd results (which can often result if effect is given to each word of the contract, some of which could be completely contradictory). Moreover, considerations of reasonableness and fairness are

---

2. Hotchkiss v. Nat'l City Bank of New York, 200 F. 287, 293-94 (S.D.N.Y. 1911).
3. Restatement (Second) of Contracts § 201 (1981).

relevant, particularly where the alternative construction would be one that is atypical. In addition, courts can make reasonable inferences regarding the intentions of the parties based on their express agreements in the contract.

The following section of the Restatement captures the interpretive conventions discussed above, along with several others. As you review this section, consider the reason for each of the convention and how it helps a court resolve an ambiguous or other contested term.

> **Restatement § 202. Rules in Aid of Interpretation**
>
> (1) Words and other conduct are interpreted in the light of all the circumstances, and if the principal purpose of the parties is ascertainable it is given great weight.
>
> (2) A writing is interpreted as a whole, and all writings that are part of the same transaction are interpreted together.
>
> (3) Unless a different intention is manifested,
>
>   (a) where language has a generally prevailing meaning, it is interpreted in accordance with that meaning;
>
>   (b) technical terms and words of art are given their technical meaning when used in a transaction within their technical field.
>
> (4) Where an agreement involves repeated occasions for performance by either party with knowledge of the nature of the performance and opportunity for objection to it by the other, any course of performance accepted or acquiesced in without objection is given great weight in the interpretation of the agreement.
>
> (5) Wherever reasonable, the manifestations of intention of the parties to a promise or agreement are interpreted as consistent with each other and with any relevant course of performance, course of dealing, or usage of trade.

The Restatement also states that "an interpretation which gives a reasonable, lawful, and effective meaning to all the terms is preferred to an interpretation which leaves a part unreasonable, unlawful, or of no effect." Moreover, specific and exact terms are given priority over general terms in interpretation, specifically negotiated terms are given priority over standardized terms, and express terms are given priority over course of performance, course of dealings, and trade usage.[4]

Over time, other interpretation conventions have developed to resolve information or power disparities between the parties. Accordingly, courts can employ conventions designed to reflect the circumstances surrounding the contract's negotiation and execution. For example, some courts will employ the interpretive convention of *contra proferentem*, which provides that a latent ambiguity should be construed against the drafting party. In other words, the non-drafting party's understanding of the term should be given precedence over the drafting party's understanding.

Section 5 in this list mentions course of performance, course of dealings, and usage of trade. Course of performance generally refers to a party's performance of the specific contract being interpreted. Course of dealings refers to the dealings between the same parties to the contract, but on prior transactions, which might shed light on their intent for the contract being interpreted.

---

4. Restatement (Second) of Contracts § 203.

Usage of trade, often called custom, refers to an industry-wide practice that everyone involved in that industry is aware of and expects will be observed. As you read the following case, consider which of these types of evidence the parties introduce to convince the court that their meaning should prevail, and which the court finds persuasive.

Frigaliment Importing Co. v. B. N. S. International Sales Corp.
United States District Court for the Southern District of New York
190 F. Supp. 116 (1960)

Opinion by FRIENDLY.

The issue is, what is chicken? Plaintiff says 'chicken' means a young chicken, suitable for broiling and frying. Defendant says 'chicken' means any bird of that genus that meets contract specifications on weight and quality, including what it calls 'stewing chicken' and plaintiff pejoratively terms 'fowl'. Dictionaries give both meanings, as well as some others not relevant here. To support its, plaintiff sends a number of volleys over the net; defendant essays to return them and adds a few serves of its own. Assuming that both parties were acting in good faith, the case nicely illustrates Holmes' remark 'that the making of a contract depends not on the agreement of two minds in one intention, but on the agreement of two sets of external signs—not on the parties' having meant the same thing but on their having said the same thing.' The Path of the Law, in Collected Legal Papers, p. 178. I have concluded that plaintiff has not sustained its burden of persuasion that the contract used 'chicken' in the narrower sense.

The action is for breach of the warranty that goods sold shall correspond to the description, New York Personal Property Law, McKinney's Consol. Laws, c. 41, § 95. Two contracts are in suit. In the first, dated May 2, 1957, defendant, a New York sales corporation, confirmed the sale to plaintiff, a Swiss corporation, of

'US Fresh Frozen Chicken, Grade A, Government Inspected, Eviscerated 2 1/2-3 lbs. and 1 1/2-2 lbs. each all chicken individually wrapped in cryovac, packed in secured fiber cartons or wooden boxes, suitable for export

75,000 lbs. 2 1/2-3 lbs....	@$ 33.00
25,000 lbs. 1 1/2-2 lbs....	@$ 36.50
per 100 lbs. FAS New York	

scheduled May 10, 1957 pursuant to instructions from Penson & Co., New York.'[5]

---

5. [1] The Court notes the contract provision whereby any disputes are to be settled by arbitration by the New York Produce Exchange; it treats the parties' failure to avail themselves of this remedy as an agreement eliminating that clause of the contract.

The second contract, also dated May 2, 1957, was identical save that only 50,000 lbs. of the heavier 'chicken' were called for, the price of the smaller birds was $ 37 per 100 lbs., and shipment was scheduled for May 30. The initial shipment under the first contract was short but the balance was shipped on May 17. When the initial shipment arrived in Switzerland, plaintiff found, on May 28, that the 2 1/2-3 lbs. birds were not young chicken suitable for broiling and frying but stewing chicken or 'fowl'; indeed, many of the cartons and bags plainly so indicated. Protests ensued. Nevertheless, shipment under the second contract was made on May 29, the 2 1/2-3 lbs. birds again being stewing chicken. Defendant stopped the transportation of these at Rotterdam.

This action followed. Plaintiff says that, notwithstanding that its acceptance was in Switzerland, New York law controls under the principle of *Rubin v. Irving Trust Co.*, 1953, 305 N.Y. 288, 305, 113 N.E.2d 424, 431; defendant does not dispute this, and relies on New York decisions. I shall follow the apparent agreement of the parties as to the applicable law.

Since the word 'chicken' standing alone is ambiguous, I turn first to see whether the contract itself offers any aid to its interpretation. Plaintiff says the 1 1/2-2 lbs. birds necessarily had to be young chicken since the older birds do not come in that size, hence the 2 1/2-3 lbs. birds must likewise be young. This is unpersuasive—a contract for 'apples' of two different sizes could be filled with different kinds of apples even though only one species came in both sizes. Defendant notes that the contract called not simply for chicken but for 'US Fresh Frozen Chicken, Grade A, Government Inspected.' It says the contract thereby incorporated by reference the Department of Agriculture's regulations, which favor its interpretation; I shall return to this after reviewing plaintiff's other contentions.

The first hinges on an exchange of cablegrams which preceded execution of the formal contracts. The negotiations leading up to the contracts were conducted in New York between defendant's secretary, Ernest R. Bauer, and a Mr. Stovicek, who was in New York for the Czechoslovak government at the World Trade Fair. A few days after meeting Bauer at the fair, Stovicek telephoned and inquired whether defendant would be interested in exporting poultry to Switzerland. Bauer then met with Stovicek, who showed him a cable from plaintiff dated April 26, 1957, announcing that they 'are buyer' of 25,000 lbs. of chicken 2 1/2-3 lbs. weight, Cryovac packed, grade A Government inspected, at a price up to 33 cents per pound, for shipment on May 10, to be confirmed by the following morning, and were interested in further offerings. After testing the market for price, Bauer accepted, and Stovicek sent a confirmation that evening. Plaintiff stresses that, although these and subsequent cables between plaintiff and defendant, which laid the basis for the additional quantities under the first and for all of the second contract, were predominantly in German, they used the English word 'chicken'; it claims this was done because it understood 'chicken' meant young chicken whereas the German word, 'Huhn,' included both 'Brathuhn' (broilers) and 'Suppenhuhn' (stewing chicken), and that defendant, whose officers were thoroughly conversant with German, should have realized this. Whatever force this argument might otherwise have is largely drained away by Bauer's testimony that he asked Stovicek what kind of chickens were wanted, received the answer 'any kind of chickens,' and then, in German, asked whether the cable meant 'Huhn' and received an affirmative response. Plaintiff attacks this as contrary to what Bauer testified on his deposition in March, 1959, and also on the ground that Stovicek had no authority to interpret the meaning of the cable. The first contention would be persuasive if sustained by the record, since Bauer was free at the trial from the threat of contradiction by Stovicek as he was not at the time of the deposition; however, review of the deposition does not convince me of the claimed inconsistency. As to the second contention, it may well be that Stovicek lacked authority to commit plaintiff for prices or delivery dates other than those specified in the cable; but plaintiff cannot at the same time rely on its cable to Stovicek as its dictionary to the meaning of the contract and repudiate the interpretation given the dictionary by the man in whose hands it was put. Plaintiff's reliance on the fact that the contract forms contain the words 'through the intermediary of: ', with the blank not filled, as negating agency, is wholly unpersuasive; the purpose of this clause was to permit filling in the name of an intermediary to whom a commission would be payable, not to blot out what had been the fact.

Plaintiff's next contention is that there was a definite trade usage that 'chicken' meant 'young chicken.' Defendant showed that it was only beginning in the poultry trade in 1957, thereby bringing itself within the principle that 'when one of the parties is not a member of the trade or other circle, his acceptance of the standard must be made to appear' by proving either that he had actual knowledge of the usage or that the usage is 'so generally known in the community that his actual individual knowledge of it may be inferred.' 9 Wigmore, Evidence (3d ed. § 1940) 2464. Here there was no proof of actual knowledge of the alleged usage; indeed, it is quite plain that defendant's belief was to the contrary. In order to meet the alternative requirement, the law of New York demands a showing that 'the usage is of so long continuance, so well established, so notorious, so universal and so reasonable in itself, as that the presumption is violent that the parties contracted with reference to it, and made it a part of their agreement.' *Walls v. Bailey*, 1872, 49 N.Y. 464, 472-473.

Plaintiff endeavored to establish such a usage by the testimony of three witnesses and certain other evidence. Strasser, resident buyer in New York for a large chain of Swiss cooperatives, testified that 'on chicken I would definitely understand a broiler.' However, the force of this testimony was considerably weakened by the fact that in his own transactions the witness, a careful businessman, protected himself by using 'broiler' when that was what he wanted and 'fowl' when he wished older birds. Indeed, there are some indications, dating back to a remark of Lord Mansfield, *Edie v. East India Co.*, 2 Burr. 1216, 1222 (1761), that no credit should be given 'witnesses to usage, who could not adduce instances in verification.' 7 Wigmore, Evidence (3d ed. 1940), § 1954. While Wigmore thinks this goes too far, a witness' consistent failure to rely on the alleged usage deprives his opinion testimony of much of its effect. Niesielowski, an officer of one of the companies that had furnished the stewing chicken to defendant, testified that 'chicken' meant 'the male species of the poultry industry. That could be a broiler, a fryer or a roaster', but not a stewing chicken; however, he also testified that upon receiving defendant's inquiry for 'chickens', he asked whether the desire was for 'fowl or frying chickens' and, in fact, supplied fowl, although taking the precaution of asking defendant, a day or two after plaintiff's acceptance of the contracts in suit, to change its confirmation of its order from 'chickens,' as defendant had originally prepared it, to 'stewing chickens.' Dates, an employee of Urner-Barry Company, which publishes a daily market report on the poultry trade, gave it as his view that the trade meaning of 'chicken' was 'broilers and fryers.' In addition to this opinion testimony, plaintiff relied on the fact that the Urner-Barry service, the Journal of Commerce, and Weinberg Bros. & Co. of Chicago, a large supplier of poultry, published quotations in a manner which, in one way or another, distinguish between 'chicken,' comprising broilers, fryers and certain other categories, and 'fowl,' which, Bauer acknowledged, included stewing chickens. This material would be impressive if there were nothing to the contrary. However, there was, as will now be seen.

Defendant's witness Weininger, who operates a chicken eviscerating plant in New Jersey, testified 'Chicken is everything except a goose, a duck, and a turkey. Everything is a chicken, but then you have to say, you have to specify which category you want or that you are talking about.' Its witness Fox said that in the trade 'chicken' would encompass all the various classifications. Sadina, who conducts a food inspection service, testified that he would consider any bird coming within the classes of 'chicken' in the Department of Agriculture's regulations to be a chicken. The specifications approved by the General Services Administration include fowl as well as broilers and fryers under the classification 'chickens.' Statistics of the Institute of American Poultry Industries use the phrases 'Young chickens' and 'Mature chickens,' under the general heading 'Total chickens.' and the Department of Agriculture's daily and weekly price reports avoid use of the word 'chicken' without specification.

Defendant advances several other points which it claims affirmatively support its construction. Primary among these is the regulation of the Department of Agriculture, 7 C.F.R. § 70.300-70.370, entitled, 'Grading and Inspection of Poultry and Edible Products Thereof.' and in particular 70.301 which recited:

Chickens. The following are the various classes of chickens:

(a) Broiler or fryer . . .
(b) Roaster . . .
(c) Capon . . .
(d) Stag . . .
(e) Hen or stewing chicken or fowl . . .
(f) Cock or old rooster . . .

Defendant argues, as previously noted, that the contract incorporated these regulations by reference. Plaintiff answers that the contract provision related simply to grade and Government inspection and did not incorporate the Government definition of 'chicken,' and also that the definition in the Regulations is ignored in the trade. However, the latter contention was contradicted by Weininger and Sadina; and there is force in defendant's argument that the contract made the regulations a dictionary, particularly since the reference to Government grading was already in plaintiff's initial cable to Stovicek.

Defendant makes a further argument based on the impossibility of its obtaining broilers and fryers at the 33 cents price offered by plaintiff for the 2 1/2-3 lbs. birds. There is no substantial dispute that, in late April, 1957, the price for 2 1/2-3 lbs. broilers was between 35 and 37 cents per pound, and that when defendant entered into the contracts, it was well aware of this and intended to fill them by supplying fowl in these weights. It claims that plaintiff must likewise have known the market since plaintiff had reserved shipping space on April 23, three days before plaintiff's cable to Stovicek, or, at least, that Stovicek was chargeable with such knowledge. It is scarcely an answer to say, as plaintiff does in its brief, that the 33 cents price offered by the 2 1/2-3 lbs. 'chickens' was closer to the prevailing 35 cents price for broilers than to the 30 cents at which defendant procured fowl. Plaintiff must have expected defendant to make some profit—certainly it could not have expected defendant deliberately to incur a loss.

Finally, defendant relies on conduct by the plaintiff after the first shipment had been received. On May 28 plaintiff sent two cables complaining that the larger birds in the first shipment constituted 'fowl.' Defendant answered with a cable refusing to recognize plaintiff's objection and announcing 'We have today ready for shipment 50,000 lbs. chicken 2 1/2-3 lbs. 25,000 lbs. broilers 1 1/2-2 lbs.,' these being the goods procured for shipment under the second contract, and asked immediate answer 'whether we are to ship this merchandise to you and whether you will accept the merchandise.' After several other cable exchanges, plaintiff replied on May 29 'Confirm again that merchandise is to be shipped since resold by us if not enough pursuant to contract chickens are shipped the missing quantity is to be shipped within ten days stop we resold to our customers pursuant to your contract chickens grade A you have to deliver us said merchandise we again state that we shall make you fully responsible for all resulting costs.'[6] Defendant argues that if plaintiff was sincere in thinking it was entitled to young chickens, plaintiff would not have allowed the shipment under the second contract to go forward, since the distinction between broilers and chickens drawn in defendant's cablegram must have made it clear that the larger birds would not be broilers. However, plaintiff answers that the cables show plaintiff was insisting on delivery of young chickens and that defendant

---

6. [2] These cables were in German; 'chicken', 'broilers' and, on some occasions, 'fowl,' were in English.

shipped old ones at its peril. Defendant's point would be highly relevant on another disputed issue—whether if liability were established, the measure of damages should be the difference in market value of broilers and stewing chicken in New York or the larger difference in Europe, but I cannot give it weight on the issue of interpretation. Defendant points out also that plaintiff proceeded to deliver some of the larger birds in Europe, describing them as 'poulets'; defendant argues that it was only when plaintiff's customers complained about this that plaintiff developed the idea that 'chicken' meant 'young chicken.' There is little force in this in view of plaintiff's immediate and consistent protests.

When all the evidence is reviewed, it is clear that defendant believed it could comply with the contracts by delivering stewing chicken in the 2 1/2-3 lbs. size. Defendant's subjective intent would not be significant if this did not coincide with an objective meaning of 'chicken.' Here it did coincide with one of the dictionary meanings, with the definition in the Department of Agriculture Regulations to which the contract made at least oblique reference, with at least some usage in the trade, with the realities of the market, and with what plaintiff's spokesman had said. Plaintiff asserts it to be equally plain that plaintiff's own subjective intent was to obtain broilers and fryers; the only evidence against this is the material as to market prices and this may not have been sufficiently brought home. In any event it is unnecessary to determine that issue. For plaintiff has the burden of showing that 'chicken' was used in the narrower rather than in the broader sense, and this it has not sustained.

This opinion constitutes the Court's findings of fact and conclusions of law. Judgment shall be entered dismissing the complaint with costs.

Understanding the Case:

1. *Burden of Proof and Planning:* One way to understand *Frigaliment* is by examining which party was bearing the burden of proof with respect to the contested term. In the case, the plaintiff bore the burden of demonstrating that an ambiguous term was used in a "narrower rather than in the broader sense." That is because the plaintiff was suing the defendant for breach of contract. It therefore had the burden to prove its case. From a planning perspective, this procedural requirement may be desirable since it forces a party, before entering into a contract, to clarify in the contract whether any term is being used in an unusual or narrower sense than otherwise might be expected before it can recover for breach of such term. Business cases are often decided with this "forward-looking" perspective. In other words, there may be unfortunate results for businesspeople caught unaware by an ambiguity (injustice from a backward-looking perspective), but businesspeople going forward will now understand that they need to plan better in order to avoid such an unfortunate result. The decision accordingly provides benefits going forward, even if there may be costs to the present parties to the suit.

Comprehension and Thought Questions:

1. What contractual promise is plaintiff alleging that defendant breached?
2. How does the court know that the term "chicken" is ambiguous?
3. Why were each of the following relevant to the interpretation of the disputed term: (i) the discussions between Bauer and Stovicek, (ii) Strasser's testimony, (iii) the Department of Agriculture regulations, (iv) current market prices for chicken, and (v) the May 28 and May 29 communications?
4. How could the parties have avoided this dispute when drafting the contract?

Hypothetical Variations:

1. Would the case have been decided differently if the negotiation communications between the parties had used the German word "huhn" instead of the English word "chicken"? *less no ambiguity*
2. What if the shipments made from the defendant to the plaintiff prior to the disputed shipments had always included only young chickens?
3. What if, prior to contract formation, the defendants had orally asked the plaintiffs why they wanted to order chickens, and the plaintiffs indicated that they needed them for frying and broiling?

PRACTICE PROBLEM 13-2

Raj Vijay is a real estate broker who works at Columbia Realty Company in Springfield, Columbia. As a real estate broker, Raj helps clients sell and buy homes.

Raj recently talked with Pat and Sam Brighton about listing their home for sale. During that conversation, Raj explained that the Brightons would have to pay Columbia Realty Company a 3 percent commission of the proceeds from the sale of their home, net of all selling costs. The Brightons would also have to pay the buyer's real estate agent a 3 percent commission on the sale proceeds, again, net of all selling costs.

The Brightons agreed to these terms. However, they also informed Raj that they had already tried selling their home on their own through a FSBO, or For Sale By Owner, for two months. They identified several potential buyers during the FSBO. If any of the potential buyers they identified during the FSBO actually bought their house, the Brightons thought it was only fair that they only have to pay Columbia Realty Company a 1 percent commission. Raj agreed to this. He then sent a letter to the Brightons to confirm the parties' agreement on this topic. The following is the relevant language Raj included in the letter:

The Brightons agree to pay a commission to Columbia Realty Company and any buyer's real estate agent in the amount of 6% of the proceeds from the sale of the Brighton's home. If, however, the buyer is someone who the Brightons have identified as being interested in buying their home, then the Brightons only have to pay a commission of 4% of the sales proceeds.

Assume you are the Brightons' friend, and that they have asked you to review the letter. Has Raj properly reflected the parties' intent in this letter? Do you see any terms that are potentially ambiguous? If so, what risks does that present? Finally, consider how you would redraft this provision to eliminate the ambiguities.

C. MISSING TERMS

Sometimes parties agree at the time of contracting that they will agree on a term at a later time. They then begin performing, only to find out later that they cannot agree on that term.

For example, suppose a landlord leases a warehouse to a tenant for ten years. The tenant manufactures crane components at the warehouse. The parties agree in the lease agreement that the tenant will have an option to extend the lease by another ten years at the end of the first ten-year term. The tenant insists on including this provision in the lease agreement because the tenant does not want to have to remove its manufacturing equipment from the warehouse at the end of only ten years if its manufacturing operation is successful.

However, assume also that the parties did not agree on the rental amount under the second ten-year period as the parties did not know what the rental market would look like in ten years. Therefore, they agreed in the lease agreement that if the tenant exercises the option to renew the lease for another ten years, the parties would agree at that time on a new rental amount.

Suppose now that it is nearly the end of the first ten years of the lease and tenant exercised its renewal option. However, landlord and tenant could not agree on a new rental amount. What happens in that situation? Alternatively, what if the landlord and the tenant did not even address in the lease agreement what the new rental amount would be under the second ten-year period if the tenant renews the lease? What happens in that situation?

In both situations, if the matter were to rise to the level of a litigated dispute, a court could take one of two approaches. One approach is for the court to not enforce the contract with an essential term that the parties have either unintentionally left open or decidedly agreed to agree on in the future on the basis that there was not mutual assent to the essential terms of the contract (where the renewal period provision is viewed as a separate contract). The court may label the parties' agreement instead as an **agreement to agree**, which is not enforceable as a contract. From a doctrinal standpoint, if the parties have not manifested commitment in some way to particular essential terms, mutual assent to a bargain presumably cannot exist.

Courts also typically rationalize this approach on the theory that if the parties could not agree on an essential term themselves, the court will not impose a term on the parties. This rationalization applies even though the parties' conduct manifests an intention to form a contract. However, sometimes courts are willing to supply an omitted term, or supply a term where the parties could not agree on that term. Those courts rationalize this approach on the basis that it gives effect to the parties' intent to be bound. Yet ultimately it is the court, and not the parties, supplying the terms of the contract. These terms may also be affected or influenced by the court's understanding of the implied duty of good faith and fair dealing.

As you read the following case, ask yourself how the court decided whether terms were missing and why that issue was important. Also ask yourself what consequences might result from the court's approach to ascertaining indefiniteness or missing terms, and what policies are supported (and potentially undermined) by the court's holding.

B. Lewis Productions, Inc. v. Angelou
United States District Court for the Southern District of New York
2005 U.S. Dist. LEXIS 9032 (2005)

OPINION & ORDER

Michael B. MUKASEY, U.S.D.J.

Plaintiff B. Lewis Productions, Inc. (BLP) sues defendant Maya Angelou for breach of contract and breach of the duty of good faith and fair dealing. BLP also sues defendant Hallmark Cards, Inc. for tortious interference with BLP's alleged contract with Angelou. As an alternative to its breach of contract claim against Angelou, BLP asserts a quantum meruit claim for services BLP performed in Angelou's interest for which BLP was not compensated. Jurisdiction is based on diversity of citizenship. Defendants Angelou and Hallmark move for summary judgment. For the reasons set forth below, both motions are denied.

I.

. . .

B. Factual History

. . .

Butch Lewis is the president and sole owner of plaintiff corporation B. Lewis Productions, Inc. BLP's business consists primarily of promoting boxing and other sports and entertainment events. Defendant Maya Angelou, a resident of North Carolina, is a renowned poet. Defendant Hallmark Cards, Incorporated, a Missouri corporation, manufactures greeting cards and related products. In this action, BLP claims that Angelou breached an agreement in which she granted BLP the exclusive right to exploit her original literary works for publication in greeting cards and similar products. Angelou claims that no enforceable contract existed. BLP claims also that Hallmark tortiously interfered with its contract with Angelou.

Lewis and Angelou became acquainted in early 1994 when, at Lewis's request, Angelou visited Mike Tyson at an Indiana prison. At that meeting, Angelou and Lewis discussed how she might reach a broader base of readers by publishing her works in greeting cards. Several months after this initial meeting, Lewis met with Angelou at her North Carolina home to discuss a potential collaboration between Angelou and BLP to market Angelou's works to greeting card companies. In November 1994, Lewis and Angelou signed a "letter agreement" that established what the letter called a "Joint Venture" to publish Angelou's writings in greeting cards and other media forms. The letter agreement, dated November 22, 1994 and signed by both parties, reads as follows:

> This letter agreement made between B. LEWIS PRODUCTIONS, INC. (BLP) with offices at 250 West 57th Street, New York, N.Y. 10019 and MAYA ANGELOU (ANGELOU) whose address is 2720 Reynolda Road, Suite # 1, Winston-Salem, NC 27106, sets forth the understandings of the parties with reference to the following:
>
> 1. The parties will enter into a Joint Venture (Venture), wherein ANGELOU will exclusively contribute original literary works (Property) to the Venture and BLP will seek to exploit the rights for publishing of said Property in all media forms including, but not limited to greeting cards, stationery and calendars, etc.
> 2. BLP will contribute all the capital necessary to fund the operation of the Venture.
> 3. ANGELOU will contribute, on an exclusive basis, original literary works to the Venture after consultations with and mutual agreement of Butch Lewis, who will be the managing partner of the Venture.
> 4. The Venture shall own the copyrights to all of ANGELOU's contributions to the Venture.
>> (a) If any of the subject copyrights do not produce any income for a consecutive five (5) year period as a result of the exploitation referred to [in] paragraph 1 herein then the ownership of these copyrights shall revert to Angelou exclusively.
> 5. The name of the Venture shall be mutually agreed upon.
> 6. Gross Revenue shall be distributed and applied in the following order:
>> (a) Return of BLP's capital contribution.
>> (b) Reimbursement of any and all expenses of the Venture.
>> (c) Balance (net profits) to be shared equally between BLP and ANGELOU.
>> (d) ANGELOU shall have the right at any time, upon reasonable notice, to inspect all records including but not limited to the financial records of the Venture.

> This Agreement shall be binding upon the parties until a more formal detailed agreement is signed.

In late 1994,[7] BLP began to market Angelou's work to Hallmark and several other greeting card companies. Lewis began to negotiate a license agreement with Hallmark on Angelou's behalf. When Hallmark asked Lewis for confirmation that he was indeed authorized to act on Angelou's behalf, on June 19, 1996, Lewis sent Hallmark a letter signed by Angelou that stated:

> This will confirm that BUTCH LEWIS PRODUCTIONS, INC. (BLP) has the exclusive right to represent DR. MAYA ANGELOU for the exploitation of her work product in the area of greeting cards, stationery, calendars, etc. as per the contract executed by BLP and Dr. Angelou dated November 22, 1994 which is still in full force and effect.

BLP declined to send Hallmark the November 22, 1994 agreement itself because Lewis wanted to keep its terms confidential.

In March 1997, after extended negotiations, Hallmark sent BLP a license agreement for the use of Angelou's future exclusive works which would have paid her and BLP 9% of gross revenues from sales of licensed products, with a $ 50,000 advance payment and a guaranteed minimum $100,000 in royalties. Angelou's greeting cards would be administered through Hallmark's Ethnic Business Center.

Also in March 1997, Lewis and Angelou encountered one another at an event in Las Vegas, where Angelou saw Lewis, who is black, punctuate a conversation with white people by grabbing his crotch. After she witnessed Lewis's behavior, Angelou "burned up his ears." She claims that she told him that the "venture" between them was off, and that she no longer wanted to work with him. Lewis denies that Angelou made any such comment at the time.

However, when Lewis forwarded the Hallmark license agreement to Angelou, she did not sign it, and later told her literary agent Helen Brann to "start putting a little cold water on the prospect of this deal with Hallmark." After meeting with Lewis and his associate Joy Farrell, Brann sent a letter to Lewis on May 5, 1997, informing him "that it is not going to work out now for Dr. Maya Angelou to make any deal with Hallmark Cards." In her letter, Brann cited Angelou's commitment to Random House as the publisher of all of Angelou's "major work" as a reason for not proceeding with Hallmark. Brann noted that "neither Dr. Angelou nor I like to say never, and I suppose that sometime in the future we might all figure out a way, in cooperation with Random House

---

7. [1] Lewis began promoting Angelou's work to Hallmark even before the November 22, 1994 Agreement was signed. Lewis and his associate Joy Farrell met with Hallmark executives on November 11, 1994 to discuss a line of greeting cards featuring Angelou's work. (Angelou 56.1 Statement P14)

and Hallmark and us, to launch some kind of greeting card program, but this year is definitely not the year to contemplate such a move."

Lewis claims that at a later meeting in 1997, Angelou told him that she would sign the licensing agreement with Hallmark "after the New Year," and that in February 1998, she told him she was planning to sign the agreement "as soon as she [got] everything off her table." However Angelou did not sign the Hallmark licensing agreement,[8] and according to Lewis's associate Farrell, when Farrell left BLP in mid-1998, in her opinion the deal was "dead," and the project was over. Additionally, because Hallmark did not hear from Lewis after it sent him the licensing agreement in 1997, Hallmark executives eventually concluded that the collaboration between BLP and Angelou was "dead."

Hallmark wrote Angelou's agent Brann in March 1998 to inquire whether Angelou was still interested in pursuing a program of greeting cards, stating that its "discussions with Mr. Lewis ended in early 1997 when he could not deliver a program." Brann responded that Angelou was not interested in entering into an agreement with Hallmark at that time. However, in June 1999, Angelou's close friend Amelia Parker, who was acquainted with an executive at Hallmark,[9] convinced Angelou to have lunch with Hallmark executives at the company's St. Louis headquarters when Angelou was in town for an unrelated speaking engagement. Angelou was encouraged by this meeting and decided to try to arrange a licensing deal with Hallmark.

Simultaneously, Angelou sought to assure that her ties to Lewis were severed. On June 16, 1999 Angelou's North Carolina counsel sent a letter to BLP stating that "any business relationship that you may have had or contemplated pursuant to a letter dated November 22, 1994 from you to Dr. Angelou, has been terminated." Lewis claims that he never received this letter, and that as far as he was concerned, the November 1994 letter agreement was still in force in 1999. According to Lewis, he contacted Angelou in 1999 about the Hallmark licensing agreement and she put him off again; at this point Lewis stopped trying to communicate with Angelou about Hallmark, and instead kept abreast of her views on the matter by communicating with her close friend Bob Brown, who did not tell Lewis that the "venture" had been terminated. Lewis learned that Hallmark and Angelou had reached an agreement without his assistance when he saw a press release about the deal in November 2000.

On June 28, 2000, after more than a year of negotiations and discussions, Hallmark and Angelou signed a licensing agreement which featured a sliding royalty scale based on net revenues, guaranteed Angelou a minimum payment of $ 2 million, and gave her a $ 1 million advance. This agreement allowed

---

8. [2] Angelou declined also to sign a more formal version of the November 22, 1994 letter agreement between her and BLP that Lewis forwarded to her in 1997.

9. [3] Parker and Marquetta Glass, a Hallmark executive, were acquaintances and had corresponded in May, 1999 about exploring a "partnership" between Hallmark and Angelou.

Hallmark to use Angelou's previously published work as well as future works she would create for the project; additionally, the marketing of Angelou's products would not be restricted to ethnic consumers.

II.

. . .

The court finds that there is at least an issue of fact as to whether the Agreement was sufficiently definite to constitute a contract, with the result that it gave rise to good-faith obligations of performance by both BLP and Angelou.

A. Definiteness and Essential Terms

"In order for an agreement to be enforced, it must be sufficiently 'definite and explicit so [that the parties'] intention may be ascertained to a reasonable degree of certainty.'" *Best Brands Beverage, Inc. v. Falstaff Brewing Corp.*, 842 F.2d 578, 587 (2d Cir. 1987) (quoting *Candid Prods., Inc. v. Int'l Skating Union*, 530 F. Supp. 1330, 1333 (S.D.N.Y. 1982)) (alteration in original); *see also* 1 Corbin on Contracts § 4.1 ("A court cannot enforce a contract unless it can determine what it is. It is not enough that the parties think that they have made a contract. They must have expressed their intentions in a manner that is capable of being understood. It is not even enough that they have actually agreed, if their expressions, when interpreted in the light of accompanying factors and circumstances, are not such that the court can determine what the terms of the agreement are.").

Moreover, an agreement cannot be enforced if it lacks essential terms, and if the court is unable to supply such missing terms in a reasonable fashion that is consistent with the parties' intent. See Restatement (Second) of Contracts § 204 (1981) ("When the parties to a bargain sufficiently defined to be a contract have not agreed with respect to a term which is essential to a determination of their rights and duties, a term which is reasonable in the circumstances is supplied by the court.").

A court may not "rewrite the contract and impose liabilities not bargained for." *A/S Atlantica v. Moran Towing & Transp. Co.*, 498 F.2d 158, 161 (2d Cir. 1974) (internal quotation marks omitted). However, New York and North Carolina courts are reluctant to strike down contracts for indefiniteness. *See Gonzalez v. Don King Prods.*, 17 F. Supp. 2d 313, 314-15 (S.D.N.Y. 1998) (holding that refusing to enforce a contract as indefinite and meaningless "'is at best a last resort'"); *Goodyear v. Goodyear*, 257 N.C. 374, 379, 126 S.E.2d 113, 117 (1962) ("Where . . . the parties have attempted to put in writing an agreement fixing the rights and duties owing to each other, courts will not deny relief because of vagueness and uncertainty in the language used, if the intent of the parties can be ascertained."). Courts are cautioned not to turn the requirements of definiteness and essential terms into a fetish, because at some point virtually every agreement can be said to have a degree of indefiniteness, and if the doctrine is applied with a heavy hand it may defeat the reasonable expectations of the parties in entering into a contract. While there must be a manifestation of mutual assent to essential terms, parties also should be held to their promises and courts should not be pedantic or meticulous in interpreting contract expressions.

Cobble Hill Nursing Home, Inc. v. Henry & Warren Corp., 74 N.Y.2d 475, 483, 548 N.E.2d 203, 548 N.Y.S.2d 920, 923 (1989) (internal quotation marks omitted).

A term is essential if "it seriously affects the rights and obligations of the parties and there is a significant evidentiary dispute as to its content." *Ginsberg Machine Co. v. J. & H. Label Processing Corp.*, 341 F.2d 825, 828 (2d Cir. 1965). Terms that may be considered essential in any agreement include the price to be paid, the work to be done, and the time of performance. *See* 1 Williston on Contracts § 4.18. When a court encounters indefinite terms, but finds that the parties did intend to form a contract, as the court found in its first decision in this case, the court then must attempt to "attach a sufficiently definite meaning to [the] bargain." 1 Williston § 4.18. A court should be especially willing to do so if the plaintiff has fully or partly performed under the agreement "since the performance may either remove the uncertainty or militate in favor of recovery even if the uncertainty continues." *Id.* (citing Restatement (Second) of Contracts § 34)); *see also* 1 Corbin § 4.1 ("The fact that one [party], with the knowledge and approval of the other, has begun performance is nearly always evidence that [the parties] regard the contract as consummated and intend to be bound thereby.").

Of course, the court may not make a contract for the parties, *see* 1 Corbin § 4.1. However, because the parties in this case did intend a contract, the court is obligated to fill any gaps their Agreement contains, if it reasonably is able to do so. Voiding an agreement for lack of essential terms "is a step that courts should take only in rare and extreme circumstances." *Shann v. Dunk*, 84 F.3d 73, 81 (2d Cir. 1996).

Angelou claims that the Agreement in this case is unenforceable because it lacks multiple essential terms. She notes that the Agreement does not specify or describe: what "original literary works" she would be contributing to the project; whether these literary works would be new or chosen from her previously published works; the quantity of works Angelou was to produce; when she was to contribute these works; the duration of the Agreement; or the extent of BLP's substantive or financial obligations under the Agreement. Further, Angelou argues that the Agreement's designation of BLP's right to exploit Angelou's work in "all media forms" is overbroad and does not express the parties' intent, because this provision would have affected Angelou's agreement with her literary publisher Random House. As explained below, these allegedly indefinite or missing terms are capable of reasonable interpretation.

1. Price

The general rule is that price is "an essential ingredient" of every contract, and that a compensation clause is enforceable only if payment can be determined from the agreement without any "further expression by the parties." *Van Diepen v. Baeza*, No. 96 Cv. 8731, 1998 U.S. Dist. LEXIS 5763, at *21-*22 (S.D.N.Y. Feb. 26, 1998) (internal quotation marks omitted). Angelou notes that the Agreement does not state how much capital, if any, BLP was obligated to contribute to the project, and argues that this constitutes a failure to specify the essential term of price. The Agreement does state, however, that BLP will contribute "all the capital necessary." The Agreement further specifies how gross revenue generated by the "Venture" was to be distributed: BLP's capital is returned, any of the Venture's expenses are reimbursed, and any net profits are shared equally between BLP and Angelou. There is at least a material question of fact as to whether this payment and distribution scheme was sufficiently definite. BLP was obligated under the Agreement to contribute "all" capital—an arrangement with a meaning that arguably is capable of enforcement. Moreover, the capital necessary to a "Venture" of the sort at issue here would be modest, if indeed any capital expenditures would have been necessary. Even expense items were likely to be limited to funds required to produce greeting card mock-ups, postage, and perhaps some travel.

If Angelou had signed the Hallmark license agreement that Lewis had negotiated on her behalf, and if revenue had been generated from Angelou's line of greeting cards, the Agreement between BLP and Angelou would have provided clear guidelines for distribution of that revenue. A compensation clause need not specify dollar figures to be definite.

BLP's part performance too shows that the parties had a meeting of the minds on the financial aspects of the Agreement. *See* Restatement (Second) of Contracts § 34; 1 Corbin § 4.1. BLP paid all initial expenses as Lewis began to negotiate licensing deals with various greeting card companies, and Angelou raised no objection during that time.

The price terms of the Agreement are capable of reasonable interpretation, and therefore arguably are sufficiently definite for enforcement.

2. Duration

Angelou claims also that the Agreement's lack of a duration term renders it too vague for enforcement. Indeed, in his deposition, Lewis admitted that "there was no time set" on the Agreement. The parties dispute whether the Agreement's copyright provision contains an implicit duration term. However, the court need not decide this issue because the Agreement's lack of a duration term is not material.

Under both New York and North Carolina law, a duration clause is not necessary in a contract for services. If such a contract makes no provision for duration, the contract is presumed to be terminable at will. If the Agreement between Angelou and BLP is viewed not as a joint venture but as a simple bilateral contract, BLP was contracting for Angelou's services as a writer and Angelou was contracting for BLP's services as a marketer of her work; under this view, the Agreement is a contract for services that need not contain a provision for duration, and may be terminated at will.[10]

3. Subject Matter

Angelou argues that the Agreement insufficiently defined the works she would supply to the project and the form in which her works would be exploited. The Agreement provides that Angelou will "exclusively contribute original literary works (Property) to the Venture and BLP will seek to exploit the rights for publishing of said Property in all media forms including, but not limited to greeting cards, stationery and calendars, etc." The Agreement adds that Angelou will contribute, "on an exclusive basis, original literary works to the Venture after consultations with and mutual agreement of Butch Lewis, who will be the managing partner of the Venture."

BLP claims that the Agreement's subject matter was sufficiently definite because the Agreement stated that the details of the work would be mutually agreed upon, and could not be finalized until a licensing agreement with a specific greeting card company had been reached. Angelou claims that this admission confirms her argument that the Agreement was merely an "agreement to agree," and not a binding Agreement in and of itself. However, this court has already held that the Agreement was more than simply an "agreement to agree"—the parties intended a binding contract here. *BLP Prods.*, 2003 U.S. Dist. LEXIS 12655, at *28. The parties understood that they were agreeing to work together to publish Angelou's writings in greeting cards, and potentially in related media forms such as calendars and stationery. The details of the arrangement would become final as individual projects were undertaken. When the Agreement was signed, there was a meeting of the minds as to its subject matter, and given the expressed intent of the parties, the court reasonably would be able to supply missing details, if necessary. Any omitted details are not material.

Again, BLP partially performed under the Agreement when it procured from Hallmark at least a draft that proposed the licensing of Angelou's writings for use in greeting cards and related products. Although Angelou did not enter into this deal, neither did she question the propriety of BLP's discussions with Hallmark, or suggest that her obligations under the Agreement were too indefinite to

---

10. [5] Again, because Angelou has not moved for summary judgment on the issue of termination, the court expresses no opinion on the issue of whether the Agreement here was terminated, and if it was, what repercussions such termination would have on BLP's claim against Angelou.

validate those discussions. BLP's part performance thus helps to resolve uncertainty about the Agreement's subject matter—if there was any such uncertainty to begin with. *See* 1 Corbin § 4.1 ("The argument that a particular agreement is too indefinite to constitute a contract frequently is an afterthought excuse for attacking an agreement that failed for reasons other than the indefiniteness."). Although defined in broad strokes, the Agreement's subject matter was not so indefinite as to constitute "rare and extreme" circumstances justifying invalidation of a binding contract intended by both parties. *Shann*, 84 F.3d at 81.

. . .

For the reasons set forth above, both motions for summary judgment are denied.

Understanding the Case:

1. *Implied Duty of Good Faith and Fair Dealing:*   In an omitted part of the opinion, BLP argued that each party's duty of good faith and fair dealing would help supply any missing terms relating to the parties' obligations under the agreement. The court agreed:

> [T]he profit-sharing arrangement between the parties here meant that Angelou and BLP had nothing to gain from the Agreement if either failed to perform or gave minimal effort. Therefore we must assume that each party arguably had an obligation to make "reasonable efforts" in furtherance of the Agreement in order to vindicate the "business efficacy" that both parties must have contemplated when they entered the Agreement.[11]

In support, the court cited facts indicating that the parties intended for their arrangement to be binding as well as the contract's repeated references to the "exclusive" nature of the relationship. Accordingly, Angelou's failure to contribute works to the project suggested that she was failing to make the required "reasonable efforts" and therefore breaching her implied duty of good faith and fair dealing.

2. *Settlement Agreement as Contract:*   The parties ultimately settled this lawsuit by entering into a settlement agreement, but that was not the end of their disputes. Lewis Production ultimately filed a subsequent lawsuit alleging that Angelou breached the settlement agreement by failing to pay the required "30.5% of all net funds paid to Dr. Angelou as royalties," specifically with respect to $800,000 paid to Angelou by Hallmark prior to the date of the settlement agreement. The court found that the $800,000 payment was not a royalty and, in any event, the settlement agreement only required payment to Lewis with respect to royalties received by Angelou after the date of the settlement agreement.

---

11. B. Lewis Prods. v. Angelou, 2005 U.S. Dist. LEXIS 9032, at *30-31 (S.D.N.Y. 2005).

Comprehension and Thought Questions:

1. What is the test the court uses to determine whether to enforce a contract despite missing terms?

2. What terms are alleged to be missing from this contract? What evidence does the court use to determine whether terms are actually missing?

3. What terms did the court conclude were missing? Why is it relevant whether missing terms are material?

4. Did the court supply any missing terms?

5. What are the risks and problems associated with courts imposing additional (and unnegotiated) terms on the parties to the contract?

Hypothetical Variations:

1. What if the written agreement had included the phrase "This letter agreement is an expression of the parties' preliminary intentions"?

2. What if the parties had exchanged e-mails at the time of execution of the letter agreement that acknowledged the need to negotiate final pricing or contract duration?

3. What if the written contract between BLP and Angelou had included a provision that provided "Notwithstanding anything in this letter agreement to the contrary, BLP acknowledges and agrees that Angelou is not required to contribute any products to the Venture"?

As you read the above case, you might have been asking yourself why parties would ever either leave a term open, or agree to agree on a term in the future. The answer is that this often happens where parties are not represented by counsel, or counsel has not effectively contemplated every situation that might come to pass. Again, because contracts govern future relationships, it is impossible to foresee every eventuality that might come to pass in the future. Thus, it is impossible to specify every term that might be relevant to that relationship.

Now that you have studied term disputes, read through and answer the questions that follow the Simulation Problem for Chapter 13, which is located in Appendix A.

CHAPTER 14

Implied Terms Under the UCC

This chapter examines the approach of Article 2 of the UCC with respect to implied duties, other implied terms, and missing terms. As you may recall from Chapter 2 of this textbook, one of the goals of the UCC is to supply default contract terms that make it easier to conduct commerce, in this instance, with respect to the sale of goods under Article 2. By anticipating what commercial parties typically want in their transactions, the UCC's terms can meet the needs of most parties while giving parties flexibility to tailor their particular contracts as appropriate.

This chapter begins in Section A by examining the implied duty of good faith and fair dealing. You may recall from chapter 12 that such an implied duty exists in all contracts. This chapter briefly describes the existence of the implied duty in the context of contracts governed by Article 2 of the UCC. Next, Section B reviews the main warranties implied under Article 2. As you will undoubtedly realize in reading that section, those implied warranties provide much greater protection to buyers of goods than exist in other types of contracts without such implied warranties. Then Section C surveys other terms that are implied in contracts governed by the UCC where the parties' contract does not provide for one of those terms.

A. IMPLIED DUTY OF GOOD FAITH

Like the common law, the UCC implies a mandatory obligation of good faith on each party to a contract that cannot be disclaimed or waived by contract. "Good faith" is defined in UCC 1-201(b)(20) as "honesty in fact and the observance of reasonable commercial standards of fair dealing." As for the first part of this definition, honesty is generally understood as subjective honesty, including that a party cannot conceal or misrepresent facts to the other party. As for the second part of this definition, the "observance of reasonable commercial standards of fair dealing" is generally understood to mean that a party must act objectively reasonably given the standards of that party's trade.

As under the common law, a court will not typically use the implied duty to rewrite a contract to impose additional obligations that were not included in the contract. On the other hand, the UCC's implied duty of good faith attempts to police problematic or opportunistic behavior such as extracting additional benefits once the contract has been formed, arbitrary exercises of power, or preventing the other party from performing.

Because we discussed the implied duty of good faith and fair dealing in Chapter 12, we will not repeat that discussion here. But keep in mind that the discussion of the implied duty of good faith discussion in Chapter 12 would be equally relevant here. In fact, the "observance of reasonable commercial standards of fair dealing" has perhaps even more relevance to sale-of-good contracts than other types of contracts, given that with the "standardization" (to an extent) of sale-of-good contracts, standards are more likely to develop around what amounts to commercially reasonable behavior than with other, less regularized contracts.

B. IMPLIED WARRANTIES

Recall from Chapter 3 that parties can include express warranties with respect to the title, performance, or condition of the service or product being purchased. Article 2 of the UCC provides that certain warranties are automatically included (or implied) in sale-of-goods contracts. These warranties pertain to certain fundamental issues concerning the goods being purchased, such as seller's title and the condition of the goods. In general, these implied warranties address certain assumptions that most buyers would make when purchasing a good: namely, that the good is owned (and capable of being sold by) the seller, and that the good is in good condition and fit for the purpose for which it was sold. These warranties provide a backdrop against which the parties can negotiate. In other words, the parties do not need to negotiate a contract that includes express warranties regarding title because the statute already imposes them by default, but they can modify those express warranties as necessary. For example, where goods are knowingly being transferred subject to a lien that the buyer is comfortable assuming, the implied warranty would need to be modified in the written sales contract to eliminate the warranty about the absence of liens.

The following are two important implied warranties from Article 2.

§ 2-312. Warranty of Title and Against Infringement; Buyer's Obligation Against Infringement.

(1) Subject to subsection (2) there is in a contract for sale a warranty by the seller that

(a) the title conveyed shall be good, and its transfer rightful; and

(b) the goods shall be delivered free from any security interest or other lien or encumbrance of which the buyer at the time of contracting has no knowledge.

(2) A warranty under subsection (1) will be excluded or modified only by specific language or by circumstances which give the buyer reason to know that the person selling does not claim title in himself or that he is purporting to sell only such right or title as he or a third person may have.

(3) Unless otherwise agreed a seller who is a merchant regularly dealing in goods of the kind warrants that the goods shall be delivered free of the rightful claim of any third person by way of infringement or the like but a buyer who furnishes specifications to the seller must hold the seller harmless against any such claim which arises out of compliance with the specifications.

§ 2-314. Implied Warranty: Merchantability; Usage of Trade.

(1) Unless excluded or modified (Section 2-316), a warranty that the goods shall be merchantable is implied in a contract for their sale if the seller is a merchant with respect to goods of that kind. Under this section the serving for value of food or drink to be consumed either on the premises or elsewhere is a sale.

(2) Goods to be merchantable must be at least such as

(a) pass without objection in the trade under the contract description; and

(b) in the case of fungible goods, are of fair average quality within the description; and

(c) are fit for the ordinary purposes for which such goods are used; and

(d) run, within the variations permitted by the agreement, of even kind, quality and quantity within each unit and among all units involved; and

(e) are adequately contained, packaged, and labeled as the agreement may require; and

(f) conform to the promise or affirmations of fact made on the container or label if any.

(3) Unless excluded or modified (Section 2-316) other implied warranties may arise from course of dealing or usage of trade.

To see how these warranties apply, imagine that a tractor manufacturer enters into contracts from time to time with its suppliers for different components of the tractor, such as engine parts. Such contracts might be in the form of a simple purchase order that only specifies price, quantity, and delivery requirements. Nevertheless, even without including additional terms, each supplier would be making a warranty that the engine parts were owned free and clear of liens by the supplier and that the engine parts were of sufficient quality to be sold and purchased, including being fit for the ordinary purpose for which the part was purchased. Accordingly, if the engine part ordered was a fuel filter, then it would need to be of sufficient quality to perform the ordinary purpose of a fuel filter, which is to remove undesirable materials from the fuel. If it did not do so, then the seller would have breached the implied warranty of merchantability. Because they are implied, all of these terms would be included in the sale contracts without negotiation or any written expression of them.

In some instances, a purchaser may be particularly dependent on the seller with respect to the goods being purchased, and the seller may know that the good is being used for a particular purpose (as opposed to an ordinary purpose). The following is the implied warranty that protects buyers in that circumstance:

§ 2-315. Implied Warranty: Fitness for Particular Purpose.

Where the seller at the time of contracting has reason to know any particular purpose for which the goods are required and that the buyer is relying on the seller's skill or judgment to select or furnish suitable goods, there is unless excluded or modified under the next section an implied warranty that the goods shall be fit for such purpose.

PRACTICE PROBLEM 14-1

A rental car company in a rural county negotiates with a parts supplier for the purchase of additional suspension springs to its fleet of cars to address the additional "twisting and jarring" on the dirt roads in that area. The springs subsequently fail to prevent damage to cars arising from the bumpiness of the roads. In addition, one of the rental car company's customers is stranded on the road because the suspension spring broke on one of the bumpiest roads in the county. The parties' contract was silent about warranties.

Can the customer recover against the rental car company for breach of UCC § 2-314 or § 2-315? Can the rental car company recover against the parts supplier for breach of UCC § 2-314 or § 2-315?

While the above warranties exist by default, a seller may disclaim these implied warranties by including particular and explicit language in the contract to that effect. In other words, a seller can specifically inform the buyer that an implied warranty does not apply. Absent such a disclaimer, the warranty will apply to the sale, and the buyer will have a remedy if the seller breaches that warranty. Again, these rights arise even in the absence of express contractual provisions concerning the particular issues.

The following are some of the UCC provisions concerning disclaimers or modification of implied warranties. It is important for transactional attorneys to understand which warranties can be modified or even disclaimed as well as the proper manner in which to do so, to make sure where a modification or disclaimer is intended, it is done properly.

§ 2-316. Exclusion or Modification of Warranties.

(1) Words or conduct relevant to the creation of an express warranty and words or conduct tending to negate or limit warranty shall be construed

wherever reasonable as consistent with each other; but subject to the provisions of this Article on parol or extrinsic evidence (Section 2-202) negation or limitation is inoperative to the extent that such construction is unreasonable.

(2) Subject to subsection (3), to exclude or modify the implied warranty of merchantability or any part of it the language must mention merchantability and in case of a writing must be conspicuous, and to exclude or modify any implied warranty of fitness the exclusion must be by a writing and conspicuous. Language to exclude all implied warranties of fitness is sufficient if it states, for example, that "There are no warranties which extend beyond the description on the face hereof."

(3) Notwithstanding subsection (2)

(a) unless the circumstances indicate otherwise, all implied warranties are excluded by expressions like "as is", "with all faults" or other language which in common understanding calls the buyer's attention to the exclusion of warranties and makes plain that there is no implied warranty; and

(b) when the buyer before entering into the contract has examined the goods or the sample or model as fully as he desired or has refused to examine the goods there is no implied warranty with regard to defects which an examination ought in the circumstances to have revealed to him; and

(c) an implied warranty can also be excluded or modified by course of dealing or course of performance or usage of trade.

(d) Remedies for breach of warranty can be limited in accordance with the provisions of this Article on liquidation or limitation of damages and on contractual modification of remedy (Sections 2-718 and 2-719).

As suggested above, it is important for an attorney advising a client to pay attention to any language that might disclaim or modify an implied warranty. Sellers often want to have "as-is" sales contracts, thereby potentially negating all implied warranties, while buyers want their contracts to include not only express warranties but also implied warranties (by not having them disclaimed or modified). As seen in the language of § 2-316 above, there are various requirements for disclaimers that need to be met, and attorneys need to be careful to make sure their client is giving or receiving the desired implied warranty.

PRACTICE PROBLEM 14-2

Imagine that you represent the parts company that supplied the suspension springs in Practice Problem 14-1, and the rental car company sues the parts company for breaches of various implied warranties. The relevant purchase order provided that "all purchase orders are subject to the terms posted on the company's website." The terms, which are posted via hyperlink and appear in ten-point font, provide "No warranty, express or implied, is made with respect to the parts' fitness for a particular purpose." Explain to your client your opinion regarding the client's potential exposure under § 2-314 and § 2-315 in light of the terms posted on the company's website.

C. OTHER IMPLIED (MISSING) TERMS UNDER THE UCC

As you might recall from Chapter 5, a contract may be formed under UCC § 2-204 even where one or more terms are missing or left open so long as the parties intended to form a contract and an appropriate remedy can be awarded. However, the parties still need to know what those missing terms are. In other words, if the parties did not include a price term but intended to form a contract, what is the price? The UCC's solution is to provide a number of provisions that supply terms when they are missing from a contract. Merchants and buyers can therefore rely on the enforcement of their contracts even when their contracts are missing material terms. As you review these sections, consider the differences between the UCC and common law with respect to open or missing material terms.

§ 2-305. Open Price Term.

(1) The parties if they so intend can conclude a contract for sale even though the price is not settled. In such a case the price is a reasonable price at the time for delivery if

(a) nothing is said as to price; or

(b) the price is left to be agreed by the parties and they fail to agree; or

(c) the price is to be fixed in terms of some agreed market or other standard as set or recorded by a third person or agency and it is not so set or recorded.

(2) A price to be fixed by the seller or by the buyer means a price for him to fix in good faith.

(3) When a price left to be fixed otherwise than by agreement of the parties fails to be fixed through fault of one party the other may at his option treat the contract as cancelled or himself fix a reasonable price.

(4) Where, however, the parties intend not to be bound unless the price be fixed or agreed and it is not fixed or agreed there is no contract. In such a case the buyer must return any goods already received or if unable so to do must pay their reasonable value at the time of delivery and the seller must return any portion of the price paid on account.

§ 2-308. Absence of Specified Place for Delivery.

Unless otherwise agreed

(a) the place for delivery of goods is the seller's place of business or if he has none his residence; but

(b) in a contract for sale of identified goods which to the knowledge of the parties at the time of contracting are in some other place, that place is the place for their delivery; and

(c) documents of title may be delivered through customary banking channels.

§ 2-309. Absence of Specific Time Provisions; Notice of Termination.

(1) The time for shipment or delivery or any other action under a contract if not provided in this Article or agreed upon shall be a reasonable time.

(2) Where the contract provides for successive performances but is indefinite in duration it is valid for a reasonable time but unless otherwise agreed may be terminated at any time by either party.

(3) Termination of a contract by one party except on the happening of an agreed event requires that reasonable notification be received by the other party and an agreement dispensing with notification is invalid if its operation would be unconscionable.

As you might expect, the disputes involving these sections of the UCC typically involve what a "reasonable" price or time for delivery is. Courts have latitude in determining what is reasonable. For example, when determining what price to impose, a court may look at the intentions of the parties, such as if there were oral discussions regarding how to set the price, or to the fair market value at the time of delivery (how much the good could have been purchased for at the market rate, assuming the good was obtainable in the market). If there are different markets, the court will have to choose which market price to use. Courts may also look to past contracts or transactions by the parties as indicative of what is reasonable to impose in a particular instance.

Recall that the UCC is intended to make it easier for businesses to engage in transactions. That explains why it supports finding an enforceable contract despite missing terms. It then supplies reasonable terms commercial parties would expect to govern. In addition, by providing those terms as reasonable rules, sophisticated and repeat-player businesses can expressly contract around those default rules in their contracts when those rules are not desired. For example, if a party does not want to rely on a "reasonable" price or the "seller's place of business" as the default term, the party can clarify its desires through its contracts.

PRACTICE PROBLEM 14-3

A West Virginia coal company has agreed to ship 10,000 tons of coal to a Wyoming company pursuant to a contract that does not specify price, date of delivery, or place of delivery. The contract was signed by the presidents of both companies. The general manager of the West Virginia plant, however, had earlier conversations with the Wyoming company's purchasing manager regarding delivery of the coal to the Wyoming company's facility in Wyoming. Wyoming produces almost four times as much coal on an annual basis than does West Virginia, so coal is cheaper to purchase in Wyoming. If the parties cannot agree on the price, date of delivery, or place of delivery, how would a court likely determine those terms of the contract? For purposes of this question, assume that both West Virginia and Wyoming have adopted the provisions of the UCC discussed in this chapter.

CHAPTER 15

The Parol Evidence Rule

Part of identifying the terms of a contract involves identifying what evidence a party can introduce in court to prove those terms. After all, if a party cannot introduce evidence into court to prove what that party understood to be the contract terms, it does not matter, at least for purposes of getting a contract law remedy, whether the parties actually agreed on those terms. This chapter addresses a rule—the parol evidence rule—that has important implications for what evidence a party can introduce to prove contractual terms.

In general, the parol evidence rule is an exclusionary rule that prevents the introduction in court of evidence of prior or contemporaneous additional or different agreements if a written agreement meeting the rule's requirements exists. The purpose of the parol evidence rule is to permit parties to rely conclusively on written contracts as evidence of their agreement without worrying about the court admitting evidence of additional or contradictory promises that the parties may have made to one another before or at the time of signing the written contract. Essentially, it would undermine the utility of written contracts if one of the parties could introduce evidence that the parties had previously or contemporaneously made different or additional promises, even though the written contract was intended to be final and complete in nature. Section A first discusses the application of the parol evidence rule. It explores (1) when the parol evidence rule applies and (2) the types of evidence it excludes.

Importantly, the parol evidence rule does not exclude evidence except to prove a conflicting and possibly additional term of a contract. Importantly, it does not exclude evidence introduced to interpret the contract. Section B explores the purposes for which evidence is not precluded by the parol evidence rule.

Note at the outset that while the parol evidence rule is often described as a rule of evidence, it also is a substantive rule of law. The consequence of this is that while a party generally waives an objection to the introduction of evidence if it does not object at trial, a party cannot waive an objection to the introduction of evidence that violates the parol evidence rule. In other words, no matter at what stage in litigation a dispute occurs, if a court determines that evidence violates the parol evidence rule, the court will exclude that evidence from the fact-finder's consideration as to the terms of the contract.

A. PAROL EVIDENCE RULE REQUIREMENTS AND OPERATION

1. Is the Written Contract Final?

As highlighted above, the parol evidence rule excludes evidence of parties' oral or written agreements exchanged before or simultaneously with their entry into a written contract to contradict the terms of the written contract. It will only do so, however, if the parties intended the written contract to be their *final* expression with respect to the term or terms in question.

For example, suppose a homeowner and painter both sign the painter's standard form painting agreement. That agreement addresses, among other things, the number of coats of paint the painter will apply to the house. It states that "Painter shall apply one full coat of paint to the house." What if the homeowner claims that the painter agreed to put three coats of paint on the house in an e-mail exchange that predated the date on which the written contract was signed? Here, if the signed paint agreement was intended by the parties to be a final expression of the parties' agreement on the painter's duty to paint and the number of coats of paint, then the painter would argue that the parol evidence rule should exclude the earlier e-mails as evidence because the written contract addresses the issue and was intended to provide the parties' final agreement with respect to that term. And that final expression obligates the painter to only apply one coat, not three.

Accordingly, before parties can rely on their written contract as the final word and receive the protection of the parol evidence rule, we first ask whether the written contract is the final expression with respect to the term in question. The court has to determine the answer to this question as a matter of law. Many courts decide the answer to this question simply by looking at the face of the written contract. If it appears to be final from its face—based on, for example, a clause that states that it is intended to be the parties' final expression of their agreement, and the fact that it contains their signatures—then the court will conclude it is their final expression. It will then not permit the introduction of any evidence that contradicts the terms in that final expression.

Some courts are less willing to decide whether a writing is intended to be final based on the face of the written agreement. Those courts, reflecting a more modern perspective, do not find writings conclusive of the parties' intent if other evidence exists to disprove that intent. Thus, if, in the example above, the painter stated in his e-mail to the homeowner that despite the painter's form agreement saying the painter would only paint one coat of paint, the painter will paint three coats of paint, under the modern perspective, a court might permit introduction of that e-mail. That is because, while on its face, the form agreement appears to be final, the e-mail shows that in fact it was not intended to be final. Of course, permitting introduction of the e-mail in some respects undermines the parol evidence rule, as it again introduces uncertainty as to the terms of the agreement despite a written agreement that appears final. Yet modern courts are sometimes willing to introduce that uncertainty to ensure that the parties' actual intent is enforced.

2. Is the Written Contract Partially or Fully Integrated?

The preceding discussion contemplates that the parties have reflected some of the terms in a final writing, but not all. A writing that reflects some of the terms of the parties' agreement but not all is referred to as a **partial integration**. It is partial because it only reflects some of the terms of the agreement, not all. If, however, the writing reflects all of the terms of the parties' agreement, it is referred to as a **full integration**. Where a writing fully integrates the terms of an agreement, under the parol evidence rule, in addition to not being able to introduce evidence of prior or contemporaneous oral or written agreements that contradict the written terms, a party *also* cannot supplement the terms. In other words, a party cannot introduce evidence of prior or contemporaneously agreed on additional terms that relate to the same subject matter as the written contract. Again, that is because the final writing is seen as complete. As such, it is viewed as most reliable as to the transaction it covers, and precludes evidence of prior or contemporaneous oral or written agreements as to additional terms.

For example, imagine a written contract between MedEquip Co., a medical equipment leasing company, and Medical Associates Inc., a corporation owned by doctors providing medical services. In the written contract, Medical Associates agrees to lease certain x-ray equipment from MedEquip, and Medical Associates agrees to pay for any repairs to the x-ray equipment that are needed during the term of the lease, regardless of how the damage was caused. Assume that the Chief Executive Officer (CEO) of MedEquip had promised in an earlier e-mail that MedEquip would provide patient benches free of charge to use while the doctors at Medical Associates were using the x-ray machine. The written contract did not address patient benches. Should evidence of the e-mail be excluded? The answer would be yes if the written agreement was intended to be completely integrated.

As with the question on whether a written agreement is final, whether a written agreement is a complete integration is a question of law for a court. One widely accepted approach to this question is known as the "four-corners" test, which refers to a court only examining the "four corners" of the written contract to determine whether a contract is completely integrated. In other words, the court examines the written contract to determine whether the parties intended for the written contract to be their complete and exclusive agreement as to the subject matter it covers. If the written contract appears to be a final and complete expression of the parties' agreement, then, under this test, the parol evidence rule would exclude any evidence of prior or contemporaneous agreements of the parties with respect to additional terms. Since the parties reduced their final agreement to a writing, then any omitted terms are viewed as intentionally omitted, and to permit one party to introduce evidence of such omitted terms would undermine the purpose of the parol evidence rule.[1]

Note, however, that the four-corners test would not preclude evidence of an entirely separate, wholly independent contract between parties that would not be expected to be contained in the written agreement. Thus, for example, if MedEquip had also agreed to sell a car used by its CEO to Medical Associates for $5,000, a court would likely not exclude evidence of that separate agreement under the parol evidence rule, as it relates to an entirely independent subject matter (i.e., it has nothing to do with x-ray equipment or its use).

More modern courts are more likely to permit a party to introduce evidence that shows that the parties in fact did not intend a writing to fully integrate their agreement as to the subject matter of the contract. They are also more likely to find that additional terms are of such a nature that they would not necessarily be expected in the written contract. That is especially the case where there is separate consideration for a promise a party is seeking to prove outside of a written agreement, even where that separate promise relates to the same subject matter of the agreement.

An illustration of the more modern approach is reflected in the Restatement:

Restatement (Second) of Contracts § 216

(1) Evidence of a consistent additional term is admissible to supplement an integrated agreement unless the court finds that the agreement was completely integrated.

(2) An agreement is not completely integrated if the writing omits a consistent additional agreed term which is

(a) agreed to for separate consideration, or

(b) such a term as in the circumstances might naturally be omitted from the writing.

Continuing with our above example, suppose that MedEquip also promised in an e-mail, sent a few days before the written contract was signed, to provide patient benches for use during x-raying for a rental fee of $10 per month per bench, and that MedEquip subsequently failed to provide those benches. If Medical Associates sues for breach, can it introduce evidence of that e-mail?

---

1. For an example of a court applying this classic approach to exclude evidence of a warranty where the court viewed a written agreement as complete on its face, *see* Thompson v. Libby, 34 Minn. 374 (1885).

Here, under the four-corners approach, the parol evidence rule might exclude evidence of this "omitted" term since the executed written contract appears to be the final expression of the parties regarding the general subject of leasing x-ray equipment. The more modern approach would instead more openly consider the question of whether this additional term is of the type that might reasonably be expected to be excluded from the executed written agreement. It might find that this term would be expected to be separate, especially because it provides for separate consideration.

Parties typically include in the general/miscellaneous section of their written contract a provision called an integration clause or merger clause. They include this type of provision in an attempt to show their intent to the court that the writing is both (1) final and (2) a complete integration. The following is a sample integration clause:

> This Agreement reflects the final, exclusive agreement between the parties on the matters contained in this Agreement. All earlier and contemporaneous negotiations and agreements between the parties on the matters contained in this Agreement are expressly merged into and superseded by this Agreement.

PRACTICE PROBLEM 15-1

1. Suppose that the written contract between MedEquip and Medical Associates had provided that "The parties have no other agreements or understandings other than as set forth in this agreement." On that basis, do you think Medical Associates would likely be able to introduce into evidence the e-mail regarding patient benches? *not w/ "four corners" approach*

2. Suppose the written contract had provided "The parties have no other agreements or understandings with respect to the x-ray machines that are the subject matter of this agreement." On that basis, do you think Medical Associates would likely be able to introduce into evidence the e-mail regarding patient benches? *yes - in terms of other subject matter*

3. Is the Evidence Subject to Exclusion Under the Parol Evidence Rule?

Even if the written agreement is deemed to be a full integration, the parol evidence rule does not exclude all evidence of other or different agreements between the parties. It only precludes evidence of *prior* or *contemporaneous* oral or written agreements that contradict the final written contract or that supplement the written agreement if it is a full integration.

For example, imagine in the written contract between MedEquip Co. and Medical Associates Inc., Medical Associates agrees to lease certain x-ray equipment from MedEquip, and Medical Associates agrees to pay for any repairs to the x-ray equipment needed during the term of the lease, regardless of how the damage was caused. MedEquip subsequently repairs two defective x-ray machines for Medical Associates, and Medical Associates refuses to pay. In the subsequent lawsuit instituted by MedEquip for breach of contract, Medical Associates seeks to introduce the following evidence:

(1) e-mails between the parties exchanged one day after the date on which the written contract was executed indicating that MedEquip would provide a one-time credit of $1,000 to Medical Associates with respect to a defect,

(2) testimony by James Illing, the CEO of Medical Associates, that, prior to the execution of the current written contract, the president of MedEquip orally promised James that MedEquip would make all necessary repairs to any defective machines, free of charge, and

(3) testimony from industry experts that it is customary for leasing companies to repair all defective equipment free of charge.

Assume MedEquip seeks to exclude all of the above evidence under the parol evidence rule. In this example, the first question is to determine whether the written contract is final as well as a full integration. Assume that it is. Thus, we must next address what the purpose of the evidence is, and whether it should be excluded under the parol evidence rule. The following table illustrates this analysis.

DETERMINING WHETHER THE PAROL EVIDENCE RULES APPLIES

Evidence to be introduced	Should the evidence be excluded under the parol evidence rule because it is evidence of a prior or contemporaneous agreement that contradicts or supplements the integrated term of the contract?
E-mails relating to a one-time credit provided by MedEquip	No, because it is not evidence relating to a *prior* or *contemporaneous* agreement between the parties. The court may still choose to discount or exclude the evidence, but its decision would not be based on the applicability of the parol evidence rule.
Testimony regarding oral promises made before the current agreement was executed	Yes, because it is evidence relating to a prior oral agreement between the parties on the subject matter of the contract and it contradicts the contract term as to Medical Associates' duty to pay for repairs.
Testimony regarding industry practice regarding payment of repairs	No, because it is not evidence of a prior or contemporaneous agreement between the parties. The court may still choose to discount or exclude the evidence, but it would not be based on the applicability of the parol evidence rule.

The following case synthesizes the above material on the parol evidence rule. Specifically, it shows how a court determines whether an agreement is independent versus one that would be expected to be incorporated in the integrated writing, what effect a court gives to a merger clause, and how the parol evidence rule operates to exclude evidence.

Theatrical Services & Supplies, Inc. v. GAM Products, Inc.

Supreme Court of New York, Suffolk County

34 Misc.3d 1224(A) (2012)

Elizabeth H. EMERSON, J.

. . .

The plaintiff is a domestic corporation in the business of selling theatrical supplies. Its principal place of business is in Hauppauge, New York. The defendant, GAM Products, Inc. ("GAM"), is a manufacturer and distributor of specialty lighting products, including those used in the television, theater, and motion-picture industries. Its principal place of business is in Los Angeles, California. In 2007, the parties entered into negotiations that would lead to the plaintiff's becoming a distributor of GAM's products on the East Coast. It is undisputed that the parties executed a written distributor agreement dated September 1, 2007, which gave the plaintiff a non-exclusive right to sell GAM's products.

The written agreement, which provides that it is governed by the laws of the State of California, contains the following merger clause:

> All understandings and agreements between the parties are contained in this agreement which supersedes and terminates all other agreements between the parties.

The plaintiff contends that, in addition to the aforementioned written agreement, the parties entered into an oral master-distributor agreement, as evidenced by e-mails dated May 24 and June 7, 2007. According to the plaintiff, the written agreement gave it the right to sell GAM's products to retail end-users, while the purported oral agreement gave it the right to sell GAM's products to small distributors on the East Coast who could not meet GAM's minimum purchase requirements and to whom GAM would not otherwise sell or distribute products. The plaintiff contends that, during the negotiations leading up to the oral agreement, it relied on representations made by GAM that it would not compete with the plaintiff for sales orders under $75 as well as other small purchases, that GAM would direct orders from small east-coast distributors and dealers (i.e., those with sales of less than approximately $10,000 per year) to the plaintiff, and that GAM would dedicate staff and resources to facilitate the plaintiff's transition to a wholesale master distributor.

In anticipation of becoming a master distributor, and as required by the terms of the parties' written agreement, the plaintiff ordered $30,000 worth of

GAM merchandise, which it was subsequently unable to sell. The plaintiff contends that GAM fraudulently induced it to enter into the oral master-distributor agreement and that GAM breached both the oral and written agreements by selling its products to small dealers and distributors without regard to the minimum order requirements, by not requiring east-coast dealers and distributors to place their orders through the plaintiff, and by failing to provide sales support and training. The complaint contains causes of action for breach of contract, breach of the covenant of good faith and fair dealing, and fraud in the inducement. . . .

New York, like California, applies the parol evidence rule to exclude evidence of any prior oral or written agreements and any contemporaneous oral agreements that contradict, vary, add to, or subtract from the terms of an agreement when, as here, the agreement has been reduced to an integrated writing. An integrated agreement is one that represents the entire understanding of the parties to the transaction. When an agreement contains a merger clause, it requires full application of the parol evidence rule in order to bar the introduction of extrinsic evidence to vary or contradict the terms of the writing. A merger clause accomplishes this objective by establishing the parties' intent that the agreement be considered a completely integrated writing. The parties' written agreement in this case clearly contains a merger clause, precluding any extrinsic proof to add to or vary its terms.

The plaintiff contends, without citing any authority therefor, that the parol evidence rule does not apply when, as here, there are two separate agreements. The plaintiff is correct that the parol evidence rule has no application to an oral contract separate from, and independent of, the written contract, even when the collateral contract was made contemporaneously with the written contract. However, before evidence of an alleged parol collateral contract is admissible, three conditions must exist: (1) the agreement must be collateral in form, (2) it must not contradict express or implied provisions of the written contract, and (3) it must be an agreement that the parties would not ordinarily be expected to embody in the writing.

Cases in which an agreement is found to be wholly independent and collateral are relatively rare and distinguishable from this case. In *Nationwide Mut. Ins. Co. v Timon*, 9 A.D.2d 1018 (App. Div. 1959), the collateral agreement was embodied in a letter agreement that was not inconsistent with the written agreement and that covered a subject matter not incorporated in the written agreement. In *J.W. Mays, Inc. v Hertz Corp.*, 15 A.D.2d 105 (1961), the parol evidence was not offered to vary or contradict the terms of the written agreement or to show any express agreement or promise at all, but merely to establish a material element of an independent gratuitous bailment. The subject of the bailment (i.e., the storage of merchandise) was not expressly the subject of the written agreement.

Here, the oral agreement covers the same subject matter as the written agreement, i.e., the plaintiff's sale and distribution of GAM's products, and would ordinarily be expected to be embodied in the writing. Additionally, the oral agreement contradicts the written agreement, which clearly gave the plaintiff a non-exclusive distributorship, by giving the plaintiff an exclusive distributorship over the entire eastern seaboard. Since the purported oral master-distributor agreement fails to meet the criteria enunciated by the Court of Appeals in *Mitchill v. Lath, supra,* the first cause of action is dismissed insofar as it alleges a breach thereof.

Liberally construing the complaint, accepting the alleged facts as true, and according the plaintiff the benefit of every possible favorable inference, the court finds that it is legally sufficient to state a cause of action for breach of the parties' written agreement. The plaintiff alleges that the defendant failed to provide training sessions, conduct annual visits, and assign sales representatives, as required by the written agreement, and that it was damaged thereby. Accordingly, the court declines to dismiss the first cause of action insofar as it alleges a breach of the written agreement.

Implicit in all contracts is a covenant of good faith and fair dealing in the course of contract performance. This covenant is breached when a party to a contract acts in a manner that, although not expressly forbidden by any contractual provision, would deprive the other party of the right to receive the benefits under their agreement. To state a claim for breach of the applied covenant of good faith and fair dealing, the plaintiff must show that the defendant sought to prevent performance of the contract or to withhold its benefits from the plaintiff.

Liberally construing the complaint, accepting the alleged facts as true, and according the plaintiff the benefit of every possible favorable inference, the court finds that it is legally sufficient to state a cause of action for breach of the implied covenant of good faith and fair dealing. The plaintiff alleges that, in 2009, GAM changed its policies by accepting minimum purchase orders under $75 and by revoking all minimums for purchases made directly from GAM. The plaintiff contends that, by allowing small purchases to be made directly from GAM without penalty, GAM competed with the plaintiff for east-coast sales, thereby depriving the plaintiff of the benefits of their agreement. Accordingly, the court declines to dismiss the second cause of action.

The third cause of action, which alleges that GAM fraudulently induced the plaintiff to enter into the oral master-distributor agreement, is dismissed since evidence of that agreement is barred by the parol evidence rule.

. . .

Understanding the Case:

1. *Merger Clause and Multiple Agreements:*   Although it is often found in the "boilerplate" section of a contract, a merger clause can be pivotal in establishing the parties' intentions, particularly with respect to the application of the parol evidence rule. It can be confusing for courts where, as here, there are multiple agreements on similar or related subjects. For example, consider a sale transaction in which the purchase agreement contains a merger clause claiming to encompass the entire understanding of the parties with respect to "all transactions related to the sale." However, in purchase transactions, there are often many "transaction documents," including a promissory note and bill of sale. Lawyers must be careful to draft the merger clause in a way that would not preclude the introduction into evidence of one of these related transaction documents.

Comprehension and Thought Questions:

1. What test did the court use to determine whether to permit introduction into evidence of GAM's oral agreement?

2. Applying that test, did the court permit plaintiff to introduce that oral agreement into evidence?

3. How did the merger clause affect the court's analysis?

4. How should a court determine whether a merger clause that purports to be the "final agreement of the parties with respect to the subject matter of the agreement" covers an ancillary term?

5. Since the merger clause was effective, why was the plaintiff successful in not having its claim for breach of contract dismissed?

Hypothetical Variations:

1. What if the written contract had provided that "Theatrical Services & Supplies, Inc. is not relying on any representations, warranties, covenants, or other promises of GAM Products, Inc. other than those expressly set forth in this Agreement"?

2. What if the contract did not contain a merger clause?

3. What if plaintiff sought to introduce evidence showing that GAM had previously promised by e-mail that the lights were of good quality?

B. EVIDENCE NOT PRECLUDED BY THE PAROL EVIDENCE RULE

1. Using Parol Evidence to Identify and Explain Ambiguity

As discussed above, even if the parties intend the written contract to be final and complete with respect to a particular subject matter, it does not mean that the parol evidence rule will exclude all evidence. It only excludes evidence of prior and contemporaneous agreements that is being used to *contradict* the terms of a final written contract, and excludes evidence of prior or contemporaneous agreements that is being used to *supplement* the terms of a final written contract that is a full integration. Thus, extrinsic evidence is permissible for other purposes, including to interpret the contract, to show the existence of amendments and waivers, and to prove breach and an available defense.

What if the evidence is sought to be introduced to explain what the terms of the written contract mean where a party is arguing in favor of a special or uncommon meaning to the terms? As discussed in Chapter 13, if the term appears to be unambiguous, courts are often reluctant to admit parol evidence. That is because they do not want a party to undermine the parol evidence rule by arguing for the interpretation of a term that in fact conflicts with the terms actually used.

That might occur where, in our above example, the homeowner seeks to introduce evidence showing that the phrase "one coat of paint" actually was intended to mean "three coats of paint." In that case, the homeowner would be arguing that it is not seeking to contradict the contract—it is merely seeking to explain the contract by arguing for an uncommon meaning of "one coat of paint." Of course, if a court allowed the introduction of such evidence on the premise that it is merely seeking to understand the parties' agreement, that could indirectly undermine the certainty associated with written agreements.

To take another example, imagine in the medical equipment leasing example above that MedEquip had explained in e-mails prior to the date of execution of the written contract that "repairs" only referred to "damage caused by use as opposed to design flaws"? Should Medical Associates be allowed to introduce the e-mails as evidence to help explain what the term "repairs" means in the written contract, or would such evidence contradict the terms of the written contract in violation of the parol evidence rule? This is a tricky issue, as the plain meaning of the word "repair" would not match the meaning of the word suggested by the e-mails. Should the court rely on the plain meaning (and refer only to the written instrument itself), or should extrinsic evidence be permitted to explain the specific meaning of a term (even if the term appears to be unambiguous)? Stated more generally, what evidence should a court consider to determine whether a term is ambiguous where a party argues for an uncommon or special meaning of terms in light of the parol evidence rule?

The cases below show two different approaches to this thorny issue. As you will see, the first case was decided by the California Supreme Court, while the second case was decided by the Court of Appeals for the 9th Circuit following the precedent set by the California Supreme Court in the first case presented. As you review these opinions, consider whether the California Supreme Court's approach effectively serves the policy concerns of contract law discussed in Chapter 1, or if you share the 9th Circuit's concerns.

Pacific Gas & Electric Co. v. G. W. Thomas Drayage & Rigging Co.
Supreme Court of California
69 Cal. 2d 33 (1968)

TRAYNOR, C. J.

Defendant appeals from a judgment for plaintiff in an action for damages for injury to property under an indemnity clause of a contract.

In 1960 defendant entered into a contract with plaintiff to furnish the labor and equipment necessary to remove and replace the upper metal cover of plaintiff's steam turbine. Defendant agreed to perform the work "at [its] own risk and expense" and to "indemnify" plaintiff "against all loss, damage, expense and liability resulting from . . . injury to property, arising out of or in any way connected with the performance of this contract."Defendant also agreed to procure not less than $50,000 insurance to cover liability for injury to property. Plaintiff was to be an additional named insured, but the policy was to contain a cross-liability clause extending the coverage to plaintiff's property.

During the work the cover fell and injured the exposed rotor of the turbine. Plaintiff brought this action to recover $25,144.51, the amount it subsequently spent on repairs. During the trial it dismissed a count based on negligence and thereafter secured judgment on the theory that the indemnity provision covered injury to all property regardless of ownership.

Defendant offered to prove by admissions of plaintiff's agents, by defendant's conduct under similar contracts entered into with plaintiff, and by other proof that in the indemnity clause the parties meant to cover injury to property of third parties only and not to plaintiff's property.[2] Although the trial court observed that the language used was "the classic language for a third party indemnity provision" and that "one could very easily conclude that . . . its whole intendment is to indemnify third parties," it nevertheless held that the "plain language" of the agreement also required defendant to indemnify plaintiff for injuries to plaintiff's property. Having determined that the contract had a plain meaning, the court refused to admit any extrinsic evidence that would contradict its interpretation.

When the court interprets a contract on this basis, it determines the meaning of the instrument in accordance with the ". . . extrinsic evidence of the judge's own linguistic education and experience." (3 Corbin on Contracts (1960 ed.) [1964 Supp. § 579, p. 225, fn. 56].) The exclusion of testimony that might contradict the linguistic background of the judge reflects a judicial belief in the

---

2. [1] Although this offer of proof might ordinarily be regarded as too general to provide a ground for appeal, since the court repeatedly ruled that it would not admit extrinsic evidence to interpret the contract and sustained objections to all questions seeking to elicit such evidence, no formal offer of proof was required.

possibility of perfect verbal expression. This belief is a remnant of a primitive faith in the inherent potency and inherent meaning of words.[3]

The test of admissibility of extrinsic evidence to explain the meaning of a written instrument is not whether it appears to the court to be plain and unambiguous on its face, but whether the offered evidence is relevant to prove a meaning to which the language of the instrument is reasonably susceptible.

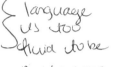

A rule that would limit the determination of the meaning of a written instrument to its four-corners merely because it seems to the court to be clear and unambiguous, would either deny the relevance of the intention of the parties or presuppose a degree of verbal precision and stability our language has not attained.

Some courts have expressed the opinion that contractual obligations are created by the mere use of certain words, whether or not there was any intention to incur such obligations.[4] Under this view, contractual obligations flow, not from the intention of the parties but from the fact that they used certain magic words. Evidence of the parties' intention therefore becomes irrelevant.

In this state, however, the intention of the parties as expressed in the contract is the source of contractual rights and duties.[5] A court must ascertain and give effect to this intention by determining what the parties meant by the words they used. Accordingly, the exclusion of relevant, extrinsic, evidence to explain the meaning of a written instrument could be justified only if it were feasible to determine the meaning the parties gave to the words from the instrument alone.

If words had absolute and constant referents, it might be possible to discover contractual intention in the words themselves and in the manner in which they were arranged. Words, however, do not have absolute and constant referents. "A word is a symbol of thought but has no arbitrary and fixed meaning like a symbol of algebra or chemistry, . . ." (*Pearson v. State Social Welfare Board* (1960) 54 Cal. 2d 184, 195 [5 Cal. Rptr. 553, 353 P.2d 33].) The meaning of particular words or groups of words varies with the ". . . verbal context and surrounding circumstances and purposes in view of the linguistic education and experience of their users and their hearers or readers (not excluding judges). . . .

---

3. [3] "'Rerum enim vocabula immutabilia sunt, homines mutabilia,'" (Words are unchangeable, men changeable) from Dig. XXXIII, 10, 7, § 2, de sup. leg. as quoted in 9 Wigmore on Evidence, op. cit. supra, § 2461, p. 187.

4. [4] "A contract has, strictly speaking, nothing to do with the personal, or individual, intent of the parties. A contract is an obligation attached by the mere force of law to certain acts of the parties, usually words, which ordinarily accompany and represent a known intent." (*Hotchkiss v. National City Bank of New York* (S.D.N.Y. 1911) 200 F. 287, 293. See also 4 Williston on Contracts (3d ed. 1961) § 612, pp. 577-578, § 613, p. 583).

5. [5] "A contract must be so interpreted as to give effect to the mutual intention of the parties as it existed at the time of contracting, so far as the same is ascertainable and lawful." (Civ. Code, § 1636; see also Code Civ. Proc., § 1859; *Universal Sales Corp. v. California Press Mfg. Co.* (1942) 20 Cal. 2d 751, 760 [128 P.2d 665]).

judges are human

A word has no meaning apart from these factors; much less does it have an objective meaning, one true meaning." (Corbin, *The Interpretation of Words and the Parol Evidence Rule* (1965) 50 Cornell L.Q. 161, 187). Accordingly, the meaning of a writing ". . . can only be found by interpretation in the light of all the circumstances that reveal the sense in which the writer used the words. The exclusion of parol evidence regarding such circumstances merely because the words do not appear ambiguous to the reader can easily lead to the attribution to a written instrument of a meaning that was never intended. [Citations omitted]." (*Universal Sales Corp. v. California Press Mfg. Co.*, (1942) 20 Cal. 2d 751, 776 (concurring opinion)).

Although extrinsic evidence is not admissible to add to, detract from, or vary the terms of a written contract, these terms must first be determined before it can be decided whether or not extrinsic evidence is being offered for a prohibited purpose. The fact that the terms of an instrument appear clear to a judge does not preclude the possibility that the parties chose the language of the instrument to express different terms. That possibility is not limited to contracts whose terms have acquired a particular meaning by trade usage,[6] but exists whenever the parties' understanding of the words used may have differed from the judge's understanding.

Accordingly, rational interpretation requires at least a preliminary consideration of all credible evidence offered to prove the intention of the parties.[7] Such evidence includes testimony as to the "circumstances surrounding the making of the agreement . . . including the object, nature and subject matter of the writing . . ." so that the court can "place itself in the same situation in which the parties found themselves at the time of contracting." *Universal Sales Corp. v. California Press Mfg. Co., supra,* 20 Cal. 2d 751, 761. If the court decides, after considering this evidence, that the language of a contract, in the light of

all places where OA may find ambiguity in language that seems clear on its face

---

6. [6] Extrinsic evidence of trade usage or custom has been admitted to show that the term "United Kingdom" in a motion picture distribution contract included Ireland (*Ermolieff v. R.K.O. Radio Pictures, Inc.* (1942) 19 Cal. 2d 543, 549-552 [122 P.2d 3]); that the word "ton" in a lease meant a long ton or 2,240 pounds and not the statutory ton of 2,000 pounds (*Higgins v. California Petroleum etc. Co.* (1898) 120 Cal. 629, 630-632 [52 P. 1080]); that the word "stubble" in a lease included not only stumps left in the ground but everything "left on the ground after the harvest time" (*Callahan v. Stanley* (1881) 57 Cal. 476, 477-479); that the term "north" in a contract dividing mining claims indicated a boundary line running along the "magnetic and not the true meridian" (*Jenny Lind Co. v. Bower* (1858) 11 Cal. 194, 197-199) and that a form contract for purchase and sale was actually an agency contract. (*Body-Steffner Co. v. Flotill Products* (1944) 63 Cal. App. 2d 555, 558-562 [147 P.2d 84]). See also Code Civ. Proc., § 1861; Annot., 89 A.L.R. 1228; Note (1942) 30 Cal. L. Rev. 679.)

7. [7] When objection is made to any particular item of evidence offered to prove the intention of the parties, the trial court may not yet be in a position to determine whether in the light of all of the offered evidence, the item objected to will turn out to be admissible as tending to prove a meaning of which the language of the instrument is reasonably susceptible or inadmissible as tending to prove a meaning of which the language is not reasonably susceptible. In such case the court may admit the evidence conditionally by either reserving its ruling on the objection or by admitting the evidence subject to a motion to strike. (See Evid. Code, § 403.)

all the circumstances, "is fairly susceptible of either one of the two interpretations contended for . . ." *Balfour v. Fresno C. & I. Co.* (1895) 109 Cal. 221, 225 [41 P. 876], extrinsic evidence relevant to prove either of such meanings is admissible.[8]

In the present case the court erroneously refused to consider extrinsic evidence offered to show that the indemnity clause in the contract was not intended to cover injuries to plaintiff's property. Although that evidence was not necessary to show that the indemnity clause was reasonably susceptible of the meaning contended for by defendant, it was nevertheless relevant and admissible on that issue. Moreover, since that clause was reasonably susceptible of that meaning, the offered evidence was also admissible to prove that the clause had that meaning and did not cover injuries to plaintiff's property.[9] Accordingly, the judgment must be reversed.

. . .

Understanding the Case:

1. *Indemnity Clause:* An indemnity clause sets out a party's duty to indemnify—which means, essentially, to reimburse to make whole—the other for certain losses the other party incurs. While technically speaking, indemnification speaks to making a party whole for losses it incurs *to a third party*, parties often use the term even where it relates to making a party whole for its own losses. In this case, the interpretive question centered around whether

---

8. [8] Extrinsic evidence has often been admitted in such cases on the stated ground that the contract was ambiguous (e.g., *Universal Sales Corp. v. California Press Mfg. Co., supra*, 20 Cal. 2d 751, 761). This statement of the rule is harmless if it is kept in mind that the ambiguity may be exposed by extrinsic evidence that reveals more than one possible meaning.

9. [9] The court's exclusion of extrinsic evidence in this case would be error even under a rule that excluded such evidence when the instrument appeared to the court to be clear and unambiguous on its face. The controversy centers on the meaning of the word "indemnify" and the phrase "all loss, damage, expense and liability." The trial court's recognition of the language as typical of a third party indemnity clause and the double sense in which the word "indemnify" is used in statutes and defined in dictionaries demonstrate the existence of an ambiguity. (Compare Civ. Code, § 2772, "Indemnity is a contract by which one engages to save another from a legal consequence of the conduct of one of the parties, or of some other person," with Civ. Code, § 2527, "Insurance is a contract whereby one undertakes to indemnify another against loss, damage, or liability, arising from an unknown or contingent event." Black's Law Dictionary (4th ed. 1951) defines "indemnity" as "[a] collateral contract or assurance, by which one person engages to secure another against an anticipated loss or to prevent him from being damnified by the legal consequences of an act or forbearance on the part of one of the parties or of some third person." Stroud's Judicial Dictionary (2d ed. 1903) defines it as a "Contract . . . to indemnify against a liability. . . ." One of the definitions given to "indemnify" by Webster's Third New International Dict. (1961 ed.) is "to exempt from incurred liabilities.")

Plaintiff's assertion that the use of the word "all" to modify "loss, damage, expense and liability" dictates an all inclusive interpretation is not persuasive. If the word "indemnify" encompasses only third-party claims, the word "all" simply refers to all such claims. The use of the words "loss,"

the indemnity clause only required the defendant to indemnify the plaintiff for any amount the plaintiff owed to third parties for losses suffered, or whether it also required the defendant to indemnify the plaintiff for the plaintiff's own property losses.

Comprehension and Thought Questions:

1. Why did the plain meaning of "indemnify" not preclude introduction of parol evidence?

2. The court indicates that words "do not have absolute and constant referents." Do you think the court is right? If the court is right, can a party ever preclude the introduction of parol evidence with a written contract?

3. The court also found that "the exclusion of relevant, extrinsic, evidence to explain the meaning of a written instrument could be justified only if it were feasible to determine the meaning the parties gave to the words from the instrument alone." How, in the court's view, could the parties have avoided this dispute?

4. What problems do you see with the court's approach to the parol evidence rule, keeping in mind that the rule seeks to determine the intention of the parties at the time of contract formation?

Hypothetical Variations:

1. What if the indemnity clause stated that the defendant indemnifies plaintiff "against all loss, damage, expense and liability *to third parties* resulting from . . . injury to property, arising out of or in any way connected with the performance of this contract"?

"damage," and "expense" in addition to the word "liability" is likewise inconclusive. These words do not imply an agreement to reimburse for injury to an indemnitee's property since they are commonly inserted in third-party indemnity clauses, to enable an indemnitee who settles a claim to recover from his indemnitor without proving his liability. (*Carpenter Paper Co. v. Kellogg* (1952) 114 Cal. App. 2d 640, 651 [251 P.2d 40]. Civ. Code, § 2778, provides: "1. Upon an indemnity against liability . . . the person indemnified is entitled to recover upon becoming liable; 2. Upon an indemnity against claims, or demands, or damages, or costs . . . the person indemnified is not entitled to recover without payment thereof; . . .")

The provision that defendant perform the work "at his own risk and expense" and the provisions relating to insurance are equally inconclusive. By agreeing to work at its own risk defendant may have released plaintiff from liability for any injuries to defendant's property arising out of the contract's performance, but this provision did not necessarily make defendant an insurer against injuries to plaintiff's property. Defendant's agreement to procure liability insurance to cover damages to plaintiff's property does not indicate whether the insurance was to cover all injuries or only injuries caused by defendant's negligence.

2. What if the court followed the classic approach and was unwilling to permit extrinsic evidence to prove the meaning of contract language that is clear and unambiguous on its face?

Trident Center v. Connecticut General Life Insurance Co.
United States Court of Appeals, 9th Circuit
847 F.2d 564 (1988)

KOZINSKI, Circuit Judge:

. . .

The facts are rather simple. Sometime in 1983 Security First Life Insurance Company and the law firms of Mitchell, Silberberg & Knupp and Manatt, Phelps, Rothenberg & Tunney formed a limited partnership for the purpose of constructing an office building complex on Olympic Boulevard in West Los Angeles. The partnership, Trident Center, the plaintiff herein, sought and obtained financing for the project from defendant, Connecticut General Life Insurance Company. The loan documents provide for a loan of $ 56,500,000 at 12 1/4 percent interest for a term of 15 years, secured by a deed of trust on the project. The promissory note provides that "maker shall not have the right to prepay the principal amount hereof in whole or in part" for the first 12 years. Note at 6. In years 13-15, the loan may be prepaid, subject to a sliding prepayment fee. The note also provides that in case of a default during years 1-12, Connecticut General has the option of accelerating the note and adding a 10 percent prepayment fee.

Everything was copacetic for a few years until interest rates began to drop. The 12 1/4 percent rate that had seemed reasonable in 1983 compared unfavorably with 1987 market rates and Trident started looking for ways of refinancing the loan to take advantage of the lower rates. Connecticut General was unwilling to oblige, insisting that the loan could not be prepaid for the first 12 years of its life, that is, until January 1996.

Trident then brought suit in state court seeking a declaration that it was entitled to prepay the loan now, subject only to a 10 percent prepayment fee. Connecticut General promptly removed to federal court and brought a motion to dismiss, claiming that the loan documents clearly and unambiguously precluded prepayment during the first 12 years. The district court agreed and dismissed Trident's complaint. The court also "*sua sponte,* sanction[ed] the plaintiff for the filing of a frivolous lawsuit." Order of Dismissal, No. CV 87-2712 JMI (Kx), at 3 (C.D. Cal. June 8, 1987). Trident appeals both aspects of the district court's ruling.

. . .

B. Extrinsic Evidence

Trident argues in the alternative that, even if the language of the contract appears to be unambiguous, the deal the parties actually struck is in fact quite different. It wishes to offer extrinsic evidence that the parties had agreed Trident could prepay at any time within the first 12 years by tendering the full amount plus a 10 percent prepayment fee. As discussed above, this is an interpretation to which the contract, as written, is not reasonably susceptible. Under traditional contract principles, extrinsic evidence is inadmissible to interpret, vary or add to the terms of an unambiguous integrated written instrument.

Trident points out, however, that California does not follow the traditional rule. Two decades ago the California Supreme Court in *Pacific Gas & Electric Co. v. G. W. Thomas Drayage & Rigging Co.*, 69 Cal. 2d 33, 442 P.2d 641, 69 Cal. Rptr. 561 (1968), turned its back on the notion that a contract can ever have a plain meaning discernible by a court without resort to extrinsic evidence. The court reasoned that contractual obligations flow not from the words of the contract, but from the intention of the parties. "Accordingly," the court stated, "the exclusion of relevant, extrinsic, evidence to explain the meaning of a written instrument could be justified only if it were feasible to determine the meaning the parties gave to the words from the instrument alone." *Id.* at 38.

. . .

Under *Pacific Gas,* it matters not how clearly a contract is written, nor how completely it is integrated, nor how carefully it is negotiated, nor how squarely it addresses the issue before the court: the contract cannot be rendered impervious to attack by parol evidence. If one side is willing to claim that the parties intended one thing but the agreement provides for another, the court must consider extrinsic evidence of possible ambiguity. If that evidence raises the specter of ambiguity where there was none before, the contract language is displaced and the intention of the parties must be divined from self-serving testimony offered by partisan witnesses whose recollection is hazy from passage of time and colored by their conflicting interests. We question whether this approach is more likely to divulge the original intention of the parties than reliance on the seemingly clear words they agreed upon at the time.

Pacific Gas casts a long shadow of uncertainty over all transactions negotiated and executed under the law of California. As this case illustrates, even when the transaction is very sizeable, even if it involves only sophisticated parties, even if it was negotiated with the aid of counsel, even if it results in contract language that is devoid of ambiguity, costly and protracted litigation cannot be avoided if one party has a strong enough motive for challenging the contract. While this rule creates much business for lawyers and an occasional windfall to some clients, it leads only to frustration and delay for most litigants and clogs already overburdened courts.

It also chips away at the foundation of our legal system. By giving credence to the idea that words are inadequate to express concepts, *Pacific Gas* undermines the basic principle that language provides a meaningful constraint on public and private conduct. If we are unwilling to say that parties, dealing face to face, can come up with language that binds them, how can we send anyone to jail for violating statutes consisting of mere words lacking "absolute and constant referents"? How can courts ever enforce decrees, not written in language understandable to all, but encoded in a dialect reflecting only the "linguistic background of the judge"? Can lower courts ever be faulted for failing to carry out the mandate of higher courts when "perfect verbal expression" is impossible? Are all attempts to develop the law in a reasoned and principled fashion doomed to failure as "remnant[s] of a primitive faith in the inherent potency and inherent meaning of words"?

Be that as it may. While we have our doubts about the wisdom of *Pacific Gas*, we have no difficulty understanding its meaning, even without extrinsic evidence to guide us. As we read the rule in California, we must reverse and remand to the district court in order to give plaintiff an opportunity to present extrinsic evidence as to the intention of the parties in drafting the contract. It may not be a wise rule we are applying, but it is a rule that binds us.

. . .

Understanding the Case:

1. *Kozinski Strikes Again:* In addition to his criticisms of the rule from *Pacific Gas & Electric* in *Trident*, Judge Kozinski also wrote another famous opinion applying the "plain meaning" rule to a Virginia contract and rejecting the admission of extrinsic evidence under the parol evidence rule:

> The answer to the question presented in this appeal is, yes, Virginia, there is a parol evidence rule. . . . Notwithstanding the importance of its function, the parol evidence rule has been severely eroded in many jurisdictions during the past few decades. Often, this erosion has been so complete as to render the parol evidence rule essentially meaningless in ensuring the binding power of the written word. For example, in *Pacific Gas & Electric* the California Supreme Court, without expressly abolishing the parol evidence rule, cut the life out of it by permitting the introduction of extrinsic evidence to demonstrate the existence of an ambiguity even when the language of a contract is perfectly clear. Thus, even in a case such as this, where the contract was negotiated and drafted with the aid of counsel, and where the parties are sophisticated businesses engaged in a multi-million dollar real estate venture, the contract's plain language may be challenged as not manifesting the deal that was actually made. Were we to apply California law to this case, we would no doubt be required to affirm the denial of Wilson Arlington's motion for summary judgment. But this isn't California; it's Virginia.[10]

2. *Prepayment:* Loan agreements often permit the borrower to prepay the loan. Prepaying a loan means paying all outstanding principal (i.e., the amount borrowed and not yet repaid), coupled with all outstanding interest. While you might think a lender would want a borrower to prepay a

---

10. Wilson Arlington Co. v. Prudential Ins. Co. of Am., 912 F.2d 366, 367-70 (9th Cir. 1990).

loan, so that the lender does not have to continue to take on the risk that the borrower will not repay the loan, it also means that the lender will no longer be able to collect interest on the outstanding loan. For that reason, lenders sometimes preclude prepayment, though more commonly, they simply impose a prepayment penalty to compensate them for some aspect of lost interest.

Comprehension and Thought Questions:

1. The court explains why the prepayment clause is unambiguous. Do you find these arguments convincing?

2. If the prepayment clause is unambiguous, why did the court determine that extrinsic evidence was admissible to interpret that clause?

3. Why does the court find this outcome to be problematic?

4. Which approach to the parol evidence rule do you believe better serves the purpose of a written contract and contract law—that reflected in *Pacific Gas & Electric*, or the approach favored by the 9th Circuit in *Trident*?

5. Do you think courts are well equipped to make decisions, as a matter of law, regarding whether the terms of a contract are ambiguous?

Hypothetical Variations:

1. What if Trident sought to introduce evidence to show that after the parties entered into the loan agreement, Connecticut General agreed that Trident could prepay the loan and pay a 10 percent prepayment fee?

2. What if Trident did not seek a declaration that it was entitled to prepay the loan, but instead decided to commit a default under the agreement as a way to trigger the prepayment of the loan?

2. Other Permitted Uses of Parol Evidence

In addition to not precluding evidence of a contract's meaning, the parol evidence does not preclude evidence to establish a defense. The following Restatement section captures other exclusions from the parol evidence rule:

> Restatement (Second) of Contracts § 214
> Agreements and negotiations prior to or contemporaneous with the adoption of a writing are admissible in evidence to establish
> (a) that the writing is or is not an integrated agreement;
> (b) that the integrated agreement, if any, is completely or partially integrated;
> (c) the meaning of the writing, whether or not integrated;

(d) illegality, fraud, duress, mistake, lack of consideration, or other invalidating cause;

(e) ground for granting or denying rescission, reformation, specific performance, or other remedy.

While this section of the Restatement expressly states that a party may introduce evidence to prove fraud, in fact some courts exclude some such evidence on the basis that it violates the parol evidence rule. The issue often arises in the context of a contract with a merger or integration clause, where the court has to determine whether a merger or integration clause preclude the affected party from proving the oral statement that serves as the basis for a misrepresentation or fraud claim. For example, imagine that in deciding whether to enter into a contract with MedEquip, Medical Associates wants to make sure the x-ray equipment is new. Suppose in response to this question, the CEO of MedEquip informs the CEO of Medical Associates that all x-ray equipment to be leased is no more than three years old. On this basis, the CEO of Medical Associates signs the equipment lease agreement, which contains a merger clause. That clause states that neither party is relying on any oral or written representations or warranties made by the other party except those contained in the equipment lease agreement, and the equipment lease agreement is silent about the age of the x-ray equipment.

What happens if, when Medical Associates gets the x-ray equipment, it is all old equipment?

Here, under the parol evidence rule, Medical Associates would be precluded from admitting MedEquip CEO's oral statement about the age of the x-ray equipment because it would contradict the term in the contract stating there are no oral representations or warranties. On the other hand, that statement would provide evidence of fraud (discussed in more detail in Chapter 20), because it was a false statement made to induce Medical Associates to enter into the contract, Medical Associates entered into the contract on the basis of that statement, and Medical Associates was justified to assent on the basis of that statement because it did not know that the statement was false.

Some courts would permit the introduction into evidence of the oral statement on the basis that the parol evidence rule should not preclude evidence of fraud. Other courts would permit such evidence unless the contract clearly and specifically disclaimed a party's reliance on such a representation or warranty. The next case, *Italian Cowboy*, shows a common approach courts take to this issue. This case also distinguishes the effect of such a merger clause from a clause through which a party disclaims its reliance on representations and warranties, effectively undermining one of the elements of a fraud claim.

Italian Cowboy Partners, Ltd. v. Prudential Insurance Company of America
Supreme Court of Texas
341 S.W.3d 323 (2011)

Justice GREEN delivered the opinion of the Court in which Chief Justice Jefferson, Justice Wainwright, Justice Medina, Justice Johnson, and Justice Lehrmann joined.

[In this case, Italian Cowboy (owned by the Secchis) entered into a contract with Prudential with respect to a lease for a location for the Secchis' new restaurant, Italian Cowboy. During lease negotiations, Fran Powell, the manager of Prizm, Prudential's property management company, made representations regarding the fact that the property was "problem free," that no problems had been experienced by the prior tenant, and as to the property's suitability as a site for a restaurant. The Secchis subsequently learned that the director was aware of persistent and severe odor problems that plagued the prior tenant, and these same odor problems were experienced by Italian Cowboy. Italian Cowboy then sued Prudential and Prizm, asserting claims for fraud, negligent misrepresentation, breach of the implied warranty of suitability, and constructive eviction, and also sought rescission of the lease. The court in this instance had to determine whether the presence of a merger clause eliminated Italian Cowboy's ability to recover or rescind the contract for fraud.]

We recognized decades ago that agreeing to a merger clause does not waive the right to sue for fraud should a party later discover that the representations it relied upon before signing the contract were fraudulent. The principal issue in this case is whether disclaimer-of-representations language within a lease contract amounts to a standard merger clause, or also disclaims reliance on representations, thus negating an element of the petitioner's claim for fraudulent inducement of that contract. We conclude that the contract language in this case does not disclaim reliance or bar a claim based on fraudulent inducement. Accordingly, we reverse the take-nothing judgment of the court of appeals and remand the case to that court for further proceedings consistent with this opinion.

. . .

II. Disclaimer of Reliance and Fraudulent Inducement

We turn first to whether the lease contract effectively disclaims reliance on representations made by Prudential, negating an element of Italian Cowboy's fraud claim. We conclude that it does not. First, a plain reading of the contract language at issue indicates that the parties' intent was merely to include the substance of a standard merger clause, which does not disclaim reliance. Moreover, even if the parties had intended to disclaim reliance, the contract provisions do not do so by clear and unequivocal language. For these reasons, we hold as a matter of law that the language contained in the lease agreement at issue does not negate the reliance element of Italian Cowboy's fraud claim.

A contract is subject to avoidance on the ground of fraudulent inducement. For more than fifty years, it has been "the rule that a written contract [even] containing a merger clause can [nevertheless] be avoided for antecedent fraud or fraud in its inducement and that the parol evidence rule does not stand in the way of proof of such fraud." *Dallas Farm Mach. Co. v. Reaves,* 158 Tex. 1, 307 S.W.2d 233, 239 (1957). In *Reaves,* we quoted approvingly the "sound public policy" supporting the rule on merger clauses:

> The same public policy that in general sanctions the avoidance of a promise obtained by deceit strikes down all attempts to circumvent that policy by means of contractual devices. In the realm of fact it is entirely possible for a party knowingly to agree that no representations have been made to him, while at the same time believing and relying upon representations which in fact have been made and in fact are false but for which he would not have made the agreement. To deny this possibility is to ignore the frequent instances in everyday experience where parties accept, often without critical examination, and act upon agreements containing somewhere within their four corners exculpatory clauses in one form or another, but where they do so, nevertheless, in reliance upon the honesty of supposed friends, the plausible and disarming statements of salesmen, or the customary course of business. To refuse relief would result in opening the door to a multitude of frauds and in thwarting the general policy of the law.

307 S.W.2d at 239 (quoting *Bates,* 31 N.E.2d at 558).

Decades later, we recognized an exception to this rule in *Schlumberger Technology Corp. v. Swanson,* 959 S.W.2d 171 (Tex. 1997), and held that when sophisticated parties represented by counsel disclaim reliance on representations about a specific matter in dispute, such a disclaimer may be binding, conclusively negating the element of reliance in a suit for fraudulent inducement. In other words, fraudulent inducement is almost always grounds to set aside a contract despite a merger clause, but in certain circumstances, it may be possible for a contract's terms to preclude a claim for fraudulent inducement by a clear and specific disclaimer-of-reliance clause. We stated that we had a clear desire to protect parties from unintentionally waiving a claim for fraud, but also identified "a competing concern—the ability of parties to fully and finally resolve disputes between them." We held that "[p]arties should be able to bargain for and execute a release barring all further dispute," and to that end, "parties may disclaim reliance on representations, [a]nd such a disclaimer, where the parties' intent is clear and specific, should be effective to negate a fraudulent inducement claim." *Id.; see also* TEX. CIV. PRAC. & REM. CODE § 154.002 ("It is the policy of this state to encourage the peaceable resolution of disputes

. . . and the early settlement of pending litigation through voluntary settlement procedures.") . . .

Here, the parties dispute whether a disclaimer of reliance exists, or whether the lease provisions simply amount to a merger clause, which would not disclaim reliance. The question of whether an adequate disclaimer of reliance exists is a matter of law.

. . .

Prudential focuses our attention on section 14.18 of the lease contract (*"Representations"*), suggesting that Italian Cowboy's fraud claim is barred by its agreement that Prudential did not make any representations outside the agreement, i.e., that Italian Cowboy impliedly agreed not to rely on any external representations by agreeing that no external representations were made. Standard merger clauses, however, often contain language indicating that no representations were made other than those contained in the contract, without speaking to reliance at all. Such language achieves the purpose of ensuring that the contract at issue invalidates or supersedes any previous agreements, as well as negating the apparent authority of an agent to later modify the contract's terms. . .

We conclude that the only reasonable interpretation of the contract language at issue here is that the parties to this lease intended nothing more than the provisions of a standard merger clause, and did not intend to include a disclaimer of reliance on representations. Therefore, we need not consider any extraneous evidence of the parties' intent to ascertain the true meaning of the instrument.

Pure merger clauses, without an expressed clear and unequivocal intent to disclaim reliance or waive claims for fraudulent inducement, have never had the effect of precluding claims for fraudulent inducement.

. . .

Here, the only plain reading of the contract language in sections 14.18 and 14.21 is that the parties intended to include a well-recognized merger clause. Nothing in that language suggests that the parties intended to disclaim reliance. Prudential and the dissent would have us hold that parties no longer have to disclose known defects if they include a general merger clause in the lease agreement. This is outside a well-settled body of law on the proper legal effect of merger clauses and represents unsound policy.

We have repeatedly held that to disclaim reliance, parties must use clear and unequivocal language. This elevated requirement of precise language helps ensure that parties to a contract—even sophisticated parties represented by able attorneys—understand that the contract's terms disclaim reliance, such that the contract may be binding even if it was induced by fraud. Here, the contract language was not clear or unequivocal about disclaiming reliance. For instance, the term "rely" does not appear in any form, either in terms of relying on the other party's representations, or in relying solely on one's own judgment. This provision stands in stark contrast to provisions we have previously held were clear and unequivocal:

Schlumberger	*Forest Oil*	*Italian Cowboy*
[E]ach of us . . . expressly warrants and represents . . . that no promise or agreement which is not herein expressed has been made to him or her in executing this release, and that none of us is *relying* upon any statement or representation of any agent of the parties being released hereby. Each of us is *relying* on his or her own judgment. . . .	[We] expressly represent and warrant . . . that no promise or agreement which is not herein expressed has been made to them in executing the releases contained in this Agreement, and that they are not *relying* upon any statement or representation of any of the parties being released hereby. [We] are *relying* upon [our] own judgment. . . .	Tenant acknowledges that neither Landlord nor Landlord's agents, employees or contractors have made any representations or promises . . . except as expressly set forth herein.

We decline to extend our holdings in *Schlumberger* and *Forest Oil*—each of which included clear and unequivocal language expressly disclaiming reliance on representations, and representing reliance on one's own judgment—to the generic merger language contained in the contract at issue in this case. As a matter of law, the lease agreement at issue does not disclaim reliance, and thus does not defeat Italian Cowboy's claim for fraudulent inducement.

Justice HECHT, joined by Justice Willett and Justice Guzman, dissenting.

Francesco and Jane Secchi owned and operated two successful Dallas-area restaurants. Italian Cowboy was to be the third. To find just the right location, they secured a broker, conducted demographic studies, examined restaurant reports by the Texas Alcoholic Beverage Commission, and viewed many potential sites. They learned that a restaurant was closing in the Keystone Park Shopping Center, an area they liked. They had eaten at other restaurants in the shopping center, and they found out those restaurants were operating profitably. They met with the landlord's agent, and for five months, assisted by their attorney, they negotiated a lease. In the meantime, they inspected the property repeatedly, sometimes with the agent present and sometimes by themselves. The lease went through seven drafts. The Secchis had been in the restaurant business twenty-five years. This was not their first rodeo.

On October 18, 2000, Francesco Secchi signed a lease on behalf of the tenant, Italian Cowboy Partners, Ltd. Not quite nine months later, on July 12, 2001, the Secchis sued the landlord, Prudential Insurance Co., and its agent, Prizm Partners.

The lease stated:	The petition stated:
Tenant acknowledges that neither Landlord nor Landlord's agents, employees or contractors have made any representations or promises with respect to the Site, the Shopping Center or this lease except as expressly set forth herein.	Italian Cowboy Partners and the Secchis reasonably and detrimentally relied on the representations of Prudential and Prizm that the Premises were suitable for use as a restaurant and were a prime restaurant site.

Each statement is a statement of *fact*, like "the sun is shining" or "the sky is blue". In the lease, Italian Cowboy stated that Prudential and Prizm *did not make* representations other than those contained in the lease. In the petition, Italian Cowboy stated that Prudential and Prizm *did make* representations, representations that were not contained in the lease. Both statements cannot be true. Either representations not contained in the lease were made, or they were not made.

The Secchis knew full well whether the statement in the lease was true when they made it. They were Italian Cowboy's only representatives. They do not claim to have been mistaken—that representations made by Prudential and Prizm were supposed to have been included in the lease but were inadvertently omitted by mistake. They do not claim to have been tricked—that important provisions were surreptitiously removed from the lease before Francesco signed it. The Secchis do not contend that after studying seven drafts of the lease with their lawyer, they just forgot to include representations that Prudential and Prizm had made about the suitability of the site for use as a restaurant. They do not plead that they were only rubes duped into stating something that was not true. The lease stated the facts as the Secchis knew them to be: representations not included in the lease were not made. . .

Understanding the Case:

1. *Contract Terms:* The relevant clauses of the contract in *Italian Cowboy* were as follows:

> 14.18 *Representations.* Tenant acknowledges that neither Landlord nor Landlord's agents, employees or contractors have made any representations or promises with respect to the Site, the Shopping Center or this Lease except as expressly set forth herein.
>
> 14.21 *Entire Agreement.* This lease constitutes the entire agreement between the parties hereto with respect to the subject matter hereof, and no subsequent amendment or agreement shall be binding upon either party unless it is signed by each party. . . .

2. *State Variations:* State law can vary widely with respect to the effect of an integration clause. Hopefully this case illustrates how important it is for a transactional attorney to understand whether and how a contract can be

utilized to prevent claims with respect to misrepresentations. These same considerations, though, arise in other instances, such as whether a contract can limit the amount or types of damages recoverable, limit the nature of the claims that can be asserted against a party, or reduce the statute of limitations with respect to bringing a claim for a breach. You will explore limits on these types of clauses in later chapters of this book on remedies. The important point to note here, though, is that in each instance, you as a transactional attorney will need to familiarize yourself with the limits of contracting for your state.

Comprehension and Thought Questions:

1. What test did the court use to determine whether to exclude evidence of Powell's false statements made outside of the contract?

2. How did the court apply that test in this case?

3. Why did Sections 14.18 and 14.21 of the contract not preclude the Secchis and Italian Cowboy from introducing evidence of Powell's false statements made outside of the contract? What language could have prevented such evidence from being introduced?

4. With whom do you agree—the majority, who did not interpret the integration clause as preventing the Secchis and Italian Cowboy from relying on Powell's extra-contractual statements, or the dissent, who would have interpreted the integration clause as preventing the Secchis from even introducing such extra-contractual statements?

5. Do you think the outcome of a case such as this one should turn on whether the contract clause disclaims reliance on extra-contractual representations? Does your answer to this question depend on whether the clause is negotiated?

Hypothetical Variations:

1. What if the contract had provided that the Secchis "were not relying on any statements or representations" made by Powell or anyone else on behalf of Prizm or Prudential, though this language had not been negotiated?

2. What if the Secchis had informed Powell prior to execution of the lease that they "were not relying on any statements" made by Powell and that they were relying exclusively on the written statements in the contract?

Now that you have studied the parol evidence rule, read through and answer the questions that follow the Simulation Problem for Chapter 15, which is located in Appendix A.

JUSTIFICATION NOT TO PERFORM

P art V presumes that the parties have properly created a contract and that one party has failed to perform one of its obligations under that contract. In that situation, typically the aggrieved party will sue the nonperforming party for breach. However, the nonperforming party might have an excuse for not having performed. Those excuses are discussed in Chapter 16, and generally involve either the other party's nonperformance or declared future nonperformance or events occurring outside of the parties' control that undermine their assumptions in entering into the contract. If the nonperforming party has one of these excuses, then it has not committed a breach.

Alternatively, a nonperforming party might argue that even though it is not excused from performing an obligation, either the entire contract or the nonperformed obligation is not enforceable. There are many reasons why a contract or contract term is not enforceable against a party—the contract might not follow necessary formalities required by the Statute of Frauds (Chapter 17), that party might lack capacity to contract (Chapter 18), the other party might have misled that party or placed unfair pressure on that party to enter into the contract (Chapters 19 and 20), or the terms may be unfair (Chapter 21).

The following diagram shows where the topics covered in Part V fit into the larger scheme of this course.

PART V—OVERVIEW DIAGRAM

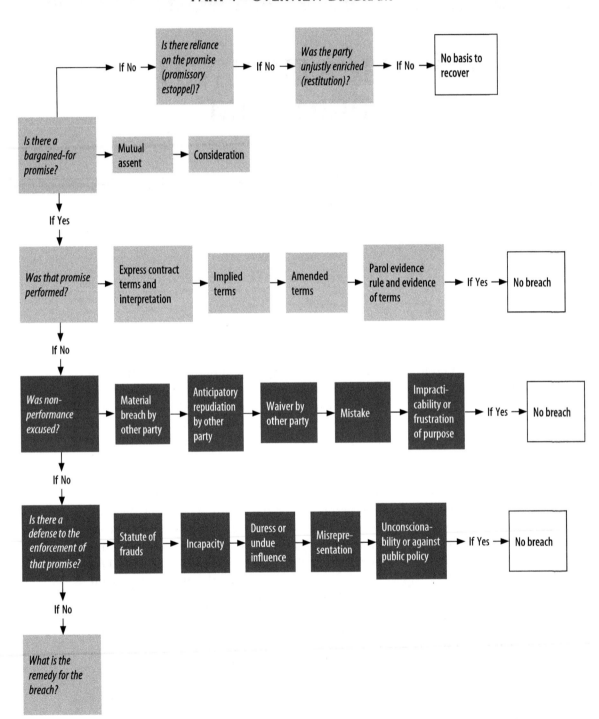

CHAPTER 16

Excuses to Performance

This chapter discusses what are commonly referred to as "excuses" to performance. In other words, this chapter presumes that parties validly formed a contract. It also presumes that the contract is enforceable against the parties. However, there are instances where, either because of extra-contractual events or the other party's behavior, a party can be excused from performing its obligations under the contract. Recall that nonperformance of a duty under a contract is a breach only if the performance is in fact due. Thus, if your client's performance is excused under one of the excuses discussed in this chapter, your client would not have breached the contract by not performing. Of course, the other party to a contract might also use one of these excuses in defense to your client's allegation of breach.

In this chapter we first discuss the other party's material breach in Section A and the other party's anticipatory repudiation of its obligations in Section B. In Section C, we discuss when a party is excused due to the other party waiving contractual rights. Section D discusses where a mistake of one or both of the parties excuses the mistaken from having to perform under the contract. In Section E, we discuss supervening events (meaning occurring after contract formation) and when those events give rise to an excuse due to impracticability or frustration of purpose. Finally, Section F explains how parties can provide for their own excuse due to a supervening event using a force majeure clause.

Keep in mind that a party's duty to perform might be excused due to the express language of the contract. In particular, recall that a party's obligation might not be due because a condition to that party's obligation has not occurred yet. Conditions were discussed in Chapter 12 rather than here, as that excuse relates to the terms of the contract as opposed to an excuse that exists solely by operation of law. In addition, a party's obligation might not be due because the parties amended the time period for performance through a contract modification. Again, modifications were discussed in Chapter 12 rather than here, as that excuse relates to the express terms of the contract rather than being based solely on operation of law.

A. MATERIAL BREACH/FAILURE

A party will have a cause of action for breach if the other party failed to perform any of its obligations under a contract and that failure was not justified. Any breach may entitle the affected party to receive a remedy.

A material breach may also excuse a party's performance under the contract. For example, if Bill sues Jane for Jane's nonperformance under the contract, Jane may be able to avoid liability for breach if she can demonstrate that Bill materially breached the contract first. If Jane is ultimately justified in not performing, her material failure to perform under the contract can, in turn, excuse Bill from performing his remaining obligations. That is because, again, a party is excused from performing where the other materially fails to perform its obligations under a contract.

In this instance, the party arguing material breach is not seeking to recover damages, but instead is trying to defend herself from an allegation that she breached. For example, imagine that you have contracted with a painter to paint the interior of your house, but it will be necessary for you to remove all of the paintings and furniture that are in front of the walls in your house so that the painter can paint. Assume you fail to remove the paintings and furniture, thereby preventing the painter from painting. There are two different scenarios that might arise as a result: the painter might sue you for breaching the contract, or you might sue the painter for failing to paint your house. The excuse of material breach is relevant in the latter situation, where you sue the painter for breach. In that situation, the painter will seek to excuse her failure to paint your house because of your failure to remove the paintings and furniture, by alleging that the failure constitutes a material breach.

You might argue that you did not remove the paintings and furniture because your house was being fumigated for roaches, and you were not allowed to enter your house the several days before painting day. If so, then while you also failed to perform, that failure to perform might itself be excused and not give rise to damages under the contract if the house painter chose to sue you. You would likely argue that you were excused under the doctrine of impracticability, which is discussed later in this chapter. The house painter, however, would still argue that even if your failure to move the paintings and furniture was justified, it still constituted a material failure to perform your end of the bargain, which would, in turn, excuse the painter from painting your walls. In other words, a party can be excused from performing due to the other party's material failure, even where the other party's material failure did not amount to a breach.

There are a few important factors to consider when understanding the concept of material failure or material breach. The first is the procedural posture where material failure is relevant. A party argues this affirmative defense where it seeks to be excused from its obligations due to the other party's material failure to perform. The materiality of a failure thus is important when one is *defending* against a claim of breach. There are different requirements when a party is seeking to *affirmatively* sue to recover based on the other party's breach. In that case, the party must demonstrate the existence of a contract, breach (regardless of whether it was material), the fact that it was injured as a result of the breach, and the fact and amount of any damages suffered. In contrast, where one is defending against a claim of breach by utilizing the defense that the other party failed to perform, the other party's failure must be material, but one is not required to demonstrate causation or damages arising from the other party's failure. This should be somewhat intuitive because in a defense situation, one is not seeking to recover damages, so one should not be required to prove the amount of damages in order to be able assert the defense.

In the home-painting example, where you are suing the painter for failing to perform and the painter seeks to be excused, the painter is not required to demonstrate how much money the painter lost as a result of your failure because she is not seeking an affirmative remedy for your breach. Instead, she is attempting to avoid liability to you arising from her failure to paint the house as contractually required. Accordingly, if she can demonstrate that you materially failed to perform the contract, then she will not be liable to you. Again, that does not mean that she is entitled to recover damages from you arising from your failure to pay. She would have to assert her own affirmative claim against you for a breach of contract and otherwise satisfy the requirements for recovering damages arising from such breach in order to recover damages from you.

The defense of material failure is necessarily forward-looking in the sense that it excuses yet-unperformed contractual obligations, whereas seeking to recover damages is backward-looking in that it seeks compensation for past-due contractual obligations. As the following case demonstrates, one must always be mindful of the distinction between seeking to recover for another's breach and relying on another's material breach to excuse performance.

Melaleuca, Inc. v. Foeller
Supreme Court of Idaho
155 Idaho 920 (2013)

J. JONES, Justice.

. . .

I.

BACKGROUND

Melaleuca, Inc., an Idaho corporation, produces and markets nutritional and cosmetic goods. Rick and Natalie Foeller are former Melaleuca contractors who reside in Ontario, Canada. The Foellers entered into an Independent Marketing Executive Agreement ("IMEA") with Melaleuca in September 1999 and became "independent marketing executives." Independent marketing executives are eligible to receive commissions and bonuses for "buying" Melaleuca's products and for enrolling new independent marketing executives with Melaleuca. Melaleuca calculates the commissions it pays to its marketing executives "based on a number of factors, including the products purchased within their Melaleuca organization, the number of their personal enrollees, their status as a marketing executive, the organizational volume of their Melaleuca business, and the Leadership Points that they generate through specified activities." Melaleuca pays its marketing executives monthly, "contingent upon whether they were in good standing throughout that entire month."

To remain in good standing, a marketing executive must comply with the IMEA, which contains a non-compete clause and several provisions dealing with competition and solicitation. The IMEA's "Policy 20" provides as follows:

> Marketing Executives are independent contractors and may be active in other business ventures while they are Marketing Executives for Melaleuca. However, . . . [i]t is a violation of this policy to recruit a Melaleuca Customer or Marketing Executive to participate in another business venture. . . .

In the event of a breach, the IMEA provides for a forfeiture of commissions under Policy 20(c)(i):

> Violation of any provision of this Policy 20 constitutes a Marketing Executive's voluntary resignation and cancellation of his/her Independent Marketing Executive Agreement, effective as of the date of the violation, and the forfeiture by the Marketing Executive of all commissions or bonuses payable for and after the calendar month in which the violation occurred.

Policy 20(c)(ii) provides for a similar forfeiture, requiring a refund of any commissions paid after a breach:

> If Melaleuca pays any bonuses or commissions to the Marketing Executive after the date of violation, all bonuses and commissions for and after the calendar month in which the violation occurred shall be refunded to Melaleuca.

The Foellers received monthly commission checks from Melaleuca. They received their last check from Melaleuca in October 2008 for September 2008 commissions. The Foellers do not dispute that at some point in 2008, in violation of Policy 20, they became involved with Melaleuca's competitor, Max International, and began enrolling Melaleuca customers in Max programs while still receiving Melaleuca commissions. In November 2008, the Foellers ended their relationship with Melaleuca. After its relationship with the Foellers ended, Melaleuca learned of the Foellers' breach.

On April 29, 2009, Melaleuca filed a complaint seeking an injunction and damages.[1] Melaleuca alleged that the Foellers, "in violation of their agreement,

---

1. [3] In briefing to the trial court, Melaleuca explained that it was "entitled to choose the damages it wish[ed] to pursue . . . ." Yet, Melaleuca "was conservative," and did not pursue its right to attempt to recover for the loss of customers when the Foeller's actions "decimat[ed] its sales force and/or customer base." Instead, Melaleuca seeks "to recover only for the second way in which it was damaged by the Foeller's breach—the monthly commission payments wrongly paid to the Foellers after their breach of the IMEA, which Melaleuca had no obligation to make."

and in violation of controlling law, used confidential and proprietary business information and trade secrets in an effort" to persuade other Melaleuca independent marketing executives and customers to leave Melaleuca and join Max International.

On July 9, 2010, Melaleuca filed a motion for summary judgment arguing that under Policy 20 of the IMEA, it was entitled to a return of commissions paid out to the Foellers from the time they first violated the IMEA in June 2008. The Foellers countered that the amount requested by Melaleuca was incorrect and that Policy 20 was unenforceable. On December 1, 2010, the district court denied the motion, finding that a genuine issue of material fact remained as to what damages Melaleuca suffered as a result of the Foellers' breach of the IMEA.

On October 19, 2011, Melaleuca filed a motion for reconsideration and on October 20, 2011, the Foellers filed a motion for summary judgment. On December 21, 2011, the district court granted Melaleuca's motion and entered judgment in its favor. It ordered the Foellers to pay $23,856.71 CDN, with interest. The Foellers timely appealed.

. . .

A. *Melaleuca cannot recover money it paid to the Foellers under an "excuse" theory and must prove damages.*

The district court erred when it held that Melaleuca could recover the commissions paid to the Foellers because the Foellers' breach "simply excuse[d]" Melaleuca from paying. The court stated that because "the Foellers breached the contract, Melaleuca's performance, specifically that of payment of commissions to the Foellers, was excused." In the court's view, Melaleuca was entitled to recover those "commissions paid after Melaleuca's performance was excused because . . . . [i]f Melaleuca had learned of the breach earlier or for some other reason had not paid the commissions to the Foelleres, they would not be entitled to any repayment under Policy 20(c)(i) and would have no damages under that provision." Because the district court's decision rests on contract interpretation, this Court reviews that decision freely. Thus, at issue is whether a plaintiff may recover damages for breach of contract on the theory that its performance would have been excused had it stopped performing when the defendant breached.

A plaintiff who wishes to recover for a breach of contract bears the "burden of proving the existence of a contract and fact of its breach . . ." *Idaho Power Co. v. Cogeneration, Inc.*, 134 Idaho 738, 747, 9 P.3d 1204, 1213 (2000). Furthermore, even if the plaintiff establishes that he "has been legally wronged, he may not recover damages unless he has been economically 'injured.'" *Bergkamp v. Martin*, 114 Idaho 650, 653, 759 P.2d 941, 944 (Ct. App. 1988). Thus, "the measure of damage—as well as the fact of damage—must be proven beyond speculation." *Wing v. Hulet*, 106 Idaho 912, 919, 684 P.2d 314, 321 (Ct. App. 1984).

To avoid liability once the plaintiff meets its burden, the defendant must prove that its performance was legally excused. "If a breach of contract is material, the other party's performance is excused." *J.P. Stravens Planning Associates, Inc. v. City of Wallace*, 129 Idaho 542, 545, 928 P.2d 46, 49 (Ct. App. 1996). Thus, a party sued for damages may defend on the grounds that its performance was excused by the other party's material breach.

A plaintiff's duty to prove damages should not be conflated with a defendant's duty to prove a defense. Indeed, it would be "curious and inappropriate" to plead the breach defense as an affirmative ground for relief. For example, in *J.P. Stravens*, the plaintiff sued the defendant to recover payments allegedly due under a personal services contract, but the district court held that the defendant was excused from paying because the plaintiff had breached the contract. On appeal, the plaintiff argued that to have been excused from performance, the defendant should have been required to prove damage from the breach. Rejecting that theory, the Court of Appeals noted that the plaintiff's argument "evidences a misunderstanding of the [defendant's] position and of governing contract law." *Id.* Because the defendant "did not seek an affirmative recovery" but instead "sought only a judgment relieving [it] of any obligation to pay [the plaintiff's] claimed fees," it "had no need to prove damages." *Id.* Thus, the excuse defense is not an appropriate means of seeking relief because excuse is unconcerned with damages, and the issue of damage is integral to affirmative recovery on a breach of contract claim.

Here, relying on *J.P. Stravens*, Melaleuca argues that "because the Foellers materially breached their commitment" it "had no obligation to continue performing, and therefore no commissions were 'due and payable' at any point after the Foeller's breach in July 2008." Melaleuca contends that because it was "excused" from performing, the Foellers must repay the commissions they received after they had breached the contract. Like the plaintiff in *J.P. Stravens*, Melaleuca conflates the plaintiff's duty to prove damages with the defendant's duty to prove defenses. By claiming that the Foellers' breach excused its performance and it can therefore recover commissions without proving damages, Melaleuca "curiously and inappropriately" attempts to use a breach defense as an affirmative ground for relief. Melaleuca maintains that had it known of the Foellers' breach when the breach first occurred, it could have stopped paying commissions to the Foellers because its performance would have been excused under Policy 20. Whether this hypothetical is correct is irrelevant—Melaleuca's horse is out of the barn. Despite Melaleuca's ignorance of the Foellers' breach, when it paid commissions to the Foellers, it performed. Thus, the question of whether Policy 20 would have excused Melaleuca from liability had it chosen not to pay commissions is theoretical.

Further, there is nothing in the IMEA that would allow retroactive application of an excuse remedy. Policy 20 merely provides that "Melaleuca reserves the right to cease paying compensation." This is forward looking. Similarly,

Provision 15 of the IMEA's Terms and Conditions states that a violation of the IMEA "may result, at Melaleuca's discretion, in forfeiture of commission and bonus checks or other payments. . . ." Aside from being a clear forfeiture provision, this is forward looking.

Because an excuse theory does not apply to Melaleuca's attempt to recover commissions it paid to the Foellers, it must prove that is suffered damages as a result of the Foeller's breach.[2] Here, the district court found that "based on the evidence presented in briefs and at oral argument, the proper amount of damages sought by Melaleuca was $23,856.41 CDN." Thus, the district court simply added up the value of the commissions that Melaleuca claims were improperly paid to the Foellers, reasoning that "[t]his amount . . . is the exact amount of damages suffered by Melaleuca as it represents commissions paid to the Foellers after the breach." Therefore, in the district court's view, Melaleuca's damages are equal to the commissions paid after the Foeller's breached.

The Foellers argue that Melaleuca has not presented any evidence of its damages, so there is a genuine issue of material fact and summary judgment was inappropriate. . . .

Melaleuca's reliance on [*Schroeder v. Rose*, 108 Idaho 707, 701 P.2d 327 (Ct. App. 1985)] is misguided. In *Schroeder*, a realtor sued a seller of real property to recover a commission he claimed the seller owed him, and the seller countered that the realtor had breached his fiduciary duty to the seller, thereby forfeiting his right to collect a sales commission. Thus, the seller raised the realtor's alleged breach as a defense. The Court of Appeals held that when a defendant raises a breach as a defense, he uses the plaintiff's breach "as a shield" rather than "a sword," and does not need to "prove actual injury or intentional fraud." *Id.* at 710, 701 P.2d at 330. Instead, the defendant need only show that if a breach occurred, the breach "was substantial and represents the failure of a condition precedent to collecting a commission," not that he suffered "actual injury." *Id.* If, however, the tables had been turned and the seller had sued the realtor for breach, it "would be pertinent" if the seller had actually been harmed. *Id.*

Here, unlike the defendant in *Schroeder*, Melaleuca is not raising breach as a shield. Instead, it uses the Foellers' breach as a sword because it alleges that it is entitled to recover damages. Thus, Melaleuca does not fall under the *Schroeder* holding that a party raising breach as a defense need only show that the breach "was substantial and represents the failure of a condition precedent to collecting a commission." Instead, it is "pertinent" if Melaleuca has

---

2. [5] Melaleuca has argued on appeal that it is entitled to recover the payments it made to the Foellers under a mistake theory. However, there is absolutely no mention of a mistake theory in Melaleuca's memorandum seeking reconsideration. The memorandum repeatedly references "excuse" and "excused." Where a party fails to argue an issue to the district court in support of its position on a motion for summary judgment, we will not consider the issue on appeal. Since the issue of mistake was not raised below, we will not consider it on appeal.

been harmed and Melaleuca must therefore prove actual injury. One aspect of proving injury is demonstrating the basis of the commission payments. Since Melaleuca has failed to show that it suffered actual injury, there is a genuine issue of material fact as to damages.

. . .

V.

CONCLUSION

We vacate the judgment of the district court and remand the case for further proceedings consistent with this opinion. The Foellers are awarded their costs on appeal.

Comprehension and Thought Questions:

1. In order to recover for damages arising from a breach, what must the plaintiff contracting party show?

2. The court does not question that the Foellers materially breached the contract. Why, in the court's opinion, is that fact insufficient to permit Melaleuca to recover damages?

3. What will Melaleuca need to demonstrate to the district court on remand in order to recover based on the Foellers' breach? How does that differ from what Melaleuca demonstrated in the original proceeding?

4. What policy is served by distinguishing between affirmatively suing upon a breach and defending based on a material breach?

Hypothetical Variations:

1. What if Melaleuca had refused to pay commissions throughout 2008 and the Foellers sued Melaleuca for a breach of contract? Would Melaleuca be able to assert an excuse based on material breach?

2. What if the Foellers had started to work for a competitor in 2008 because Melaleuca had failed to pay them 10 percent of the commissions they were owed in 2007? What if Melaleuca had failed to pay the Foellers half of the commissions that they were owed in 2007 instead of just 10 percent?

As discussed above, the critical factor in whether a party will be excused from performance as a result of another party's failure to perform is whether the other party's failure is "material." In other words, a party should not be excused from performing under a contract just because the other party committed a minor transgression under the contract, particularly one that did not affect the party's ability to perform and receive all the benefits under the contract. This is obviously a fact-specific inquiry that will justify different answers in different contexts.

For example, in the home-painting example discussed earlier in this chapter, imagine that the painter does not paint your house as desired. If you sue the painter for breach of contract, the painter should perhaps be excused from her failure to perform if you refused to remove the items necessary for her to paint as required by the contract or if you refused to make the required advance deposit of half the contract price. On the other hand, perhaps the painter should not be excused if you were one day late in notifying the painter of the paint color (as you were required to do by the contract) since slight tardiness in notification is presumably irrelevant to the painter's general ability to paint the house two weeks from that date as required in the contract.

An important factor to consider with respect to whether a failure to perform is "material" is the standard of performance that should be expected from each party. In the sale of goods context, the Uniform Commercial Code typically imposes a standard of strict performance, which means that the buyer can reject the seller's goods if, in *any* respect, they do not conform to the buyer's specified requirements. This means that a buyer's failure to pay following the receipt of non-conforming goods may not give rise to a successful seller claim for a breach. If the seller brings a claim against the buyer, the buyer will be able to point to the seller's material breach based on the goods' nonconformity with the contract's requirements.

The Restatement provides a list of factors that may be helpful in determining when a particular breach is material in other types of contracts.

> § 241 Circumstances Significant in Determining Whether a Failure Is Material
> In determining whether a failure to render or to offer performance is material, the following circumstances are significant:
>   (a) the extent to which the injured party will be deprived of the benefit which he reasonably expected;
>   (b) the extent to which the injured party can be adequately compensated for the part of that benefit of which he will be deprived;
>   (c) the extent to which the party failing to perform or to offer to perform will suffer forfeiture;
>   (d) the likelihood that the party failing to perform or to offer to perform will cure his failure, taking account of all the circumstances including any reasonable assurances;
>   (e) the extent to which the behavior of the party failing to perform or to offer to perform comports with standards of good faith and fair dealing.

Under the Restatement, where a party commits a material failure under the above factors, the other party may only be temporarily excused from performing, and the failing party may be permitted to cure its failure. On the other hand, where either it is unlikely that a party will cure its material failure, or time is of the essence such that the other party cannot wait for cure, for example, because it will miss out on a chance to make alternative arrangements, then the aggrieved party is permanently excused from performing its obligations.[3]

To see how these rules work in practice, imagine that Bobby Su is a law professor who has decided to write a Contracts textbook for Big Publisher. The textbook manuscript is due on October 1. Per Bobby's book proposal, the book will contain 29 chapters. The publisher will pay Bobby a modest bonus upon delivering the manuscript, as well as small royalties upon book sales.

Now imagine that on October 1, Bobby is not done with Chapter 29. Bobby anticipates that it will be completed within one week. Here, can the publisher be excused from performing (i.e., paying Bobby) because of Bobby's failure? Using the above factors, under factor (a), the extent of Bobby's failure is fairly modest. Bobby has already completed 28 out of 29 chapters, and is only going to be delayed by one week on the last chapter. Thus, factor (a) suggests that the failure is not material. Under factor (b), it is not clear whether the publisher could be compensated for this breach in damages, as the financial consequences to the publisher of delaying receipt of the manuscript by one week are not clear. For example, does the publisher miss out on one week's worth of marketing time? If so, how do we know if that marketing would have led to more book adoptions? Thus, factor (b) could potentially argue in favor of a material failure. However, under factor (c), if the publisher were excused due to Bobby's failure, such excuse would lead to a total forfeiture by Bobby. That is because the publisher would not have to pay Bobby anything for work performed. This factor argues against Bobby's failure being material. Under factor (d), Bobby clearly is working toward finishing the last chapter up in one week's time. Thus, there is a great likelihood of cure, making it less likely that this failure is material. Under factor (e), nothing suggests that Bobby has acted with anything other than good faith. The fact that Bobby is working hard toward cure suggests good faith performance of the contract. In sum, apart from factor (b), all factors suggest that Bobby's failure is not material. Even if Bobby's failure were deemed to be material, the publisher may not be excused from performing its obligations under the contract if Bobby can in fact supply the remaining chapter within a week and the deadline was not actually that important to publishing the book on time.

1. Part Performance

Sometimes, courts will apportion parties' respective obligations under a contract to avoid a finding of material breach. They do that where there are

---

3. Restatement (Second) of Contracts § 242 (1981).

agreed equivalents under the contract that can be explicitly and separately linked. In other words, by apportioning obligations under a contract, the contract is essentially broken up into parts, where the nonperforming party is seen as performing some of the allocated parts of the contract, thereby triggering the obligation of the other party with respect to those delivered parts. By doing that, a party avoids being in material breach of the obligations it has performed.

To see how this works in practice, imagine that Stacia Seller has agreed to sell ten computers to Bernie Buyer. Each computer is an independent, stand-alone computer with a separate list price. Now assume that Stacia only delivers three computers to Bernie, informing Bernie that no more computers will be delivered. In this example, Stacia likely committed a material breach, as she only delivered a fraction of the computers she promised to deliver, and she indicated that she would not be curing. Thus, if we apply the material breach doctrine in its classic sense, Bernie would be excused from paying Stacia any amount under the contract. (Of course, he would have to make restitution of the computers already delivered to him, as he cannot retain that benefit and not pay for it.) However, a court applying the apportionment doctrine could find that Stacia performed the contract with respect to the three delivered computers, since they are independent computers with separate list prices. It would therefore not excuse Bernie from paying for those three computers. However, since Stacia materially failed to perform the other part of the contract, Bernie would be excused from paying for the remaining seven undelivered computers.

PRACTICE PROBLEM 16-1

Imagine that on October 1, Bobby only delivered 10 book chapters. Bobby promised the publisher that she would deliver the remaining 19 chapters on January 1 of the following year, but on January 1, she only delivered 5 more chapters. Thus, 13 chapters remained to be delivered. Bobby promised to deliver the remaining 13 chapters by June 1, but she only delivered 2 more chapters by then. The reason for Bobby's repeated delays is that she has overcommitted herself on other work obligations, and cannot find the time to finish her book manuscript.

1. If, on June 1, the publisher wants to terminate its relationship with Bobby and find someone else to write a Contracts textbook, would it be excused from performing?

2. Could Bobby successfully argue that the contract with the publisher should be apportioned such that the publisher should pay for the chapters she has delivered, even if she does not deliver the remaining chapters?

2. Constructive Conditions

Some courts use the concept of **constructive conditions** to analyze material failure.[4] As you recall, a condition is an event that is not certain to occur, but that must occur before a party's obligation is due. The concept of *constructive* means it is implied by law rather than expressed by the parties. Thus, a constructive condition is a condition, implied by law, that must be satisfied before a party's performance is due. Using this concept, where a party commits a material failure, then a constructive condition to the other party's performance has not been satisfied, and its performance is not due.

In *Jacobs & Youngs v. Kent*, the classic constructive condition case (described in more depth in Chapter 24), the court found that each contract contains a constructive condition that the other party has substantially performed its obligations under the contract.[5] If that constructive condition is not satisfied, then the other party's performance is not due. Thus, if a home builder substantially completes building the house, the constructive condition to the homeowner's duty to pay the builder is satisfied, meaning the homeowner has to pay the builder. On the other hand, if the builder does not substantially perform, then the constructive condition to the homeowner's duty to pay is not satisfied, and the homeowner's duty to pay the full purchase price is not due.

To determine if the builder had substantially performed, the court in *Jacobs & Youngs* looked at whether the failure could be "atoned for" through a substitute performance, whether it undermined the purpose of the contract, the excuse for the failure, and the harshness of requiring adherence to the contract instead of excusing the homeowner.[6]

The Restatement no longer uses the terminology "constructive condition." However, it includes a rule that effectively leads to the same outcome. The following is the applicable language from the Restatement:

> § 234 Order of Performances
>
> (2) Except to the extent stated in Subsection (1), where the performance of only one party under such an exchange requires a period of time, his performance is due at an earlier time than that of the other party, unless the language or the circumstances indicate the contrary.

Note that this principle only applies where one party's performance obligation takes time and the other party's obligation does not, such as the obligation to pay money. That is usually the case with construction contracts, as in *Jacobs & Youngs*, as well as other types of service contracts. There, the law implies that the party with the longer-term performance obligation must perform first, before

---

4. *See, e.g.,* National Audubon Soc'y v. Watt, 678 F.2d 299 (D.C. Cir. 1982).
5. *See* Jacobs & Youngs, Inc. v. Kent, 129 N.E. 889, 890 (N.Y. 1921).
6. *See id.*

the paying party's obligation is due. Again, its material failure to so perform excuses the paying party under the material failure doctrine discussed above.

Where, in contrast, both parties' performances can occur simultaneously, they are to perform simultaneously—or at least tender performance simultaneously. This is also captured by the Restatement.

§ 234 Order of Performances

(1) Where all or part of the performances to be exchanged under an exchange of promises can be rendered simultaneously, they are to that extent due simultaneously, unless the language or the circumstances indicate the contrary.

Under this language, in the case of a house purchase contract, a seller does not need to convey title to her home if the buyer does not show up at closing with her money—or does not indicate that she is prepared to tender her money at the closing. That is because both performances can and are expected to occur simultaneously. If the buyer does not tender her money at closing, the seller is excused from performing due to the other party's material breach.

Of course, the law will not imply a condition where the parties, through their words or conduct, have expressed a different intent, modifying these default implied terms. Hence, if the seller and buyer agreed that the seller would transfer title to the property after the buyer pays half of the purchase price, then the seller cannot withhold the transfer where the buyer does not tender the full purchase price at closing.

PRACTICE PROBLEM 16-2

Robert Leek entered into an agreement to purchase a car dealership from Tracey Pessory. Leek agreed to purchase the dealership for $100,000, $50,000 of which would be paid on the closing date (January 1, 2015) and the rest of which would be paid in three separate annual installments plus interest. The agreement required Pessory to remain with the dealership for three years as a salesperson. On June 1, 2015, Pessory left the dealership in order to open an art framing shop. Leek subsequently refused to make the remaining annual installments. Pessory filed suit in 2017 based on a breach of Leek's obligation to pay the balance of the purchase price due under the agreement. Leek seeks to excuse his failure to pay based on Pessory's alleged material breach in leaving the dealership early. Consider the following facts:

1. Leek testifies at trial that during his initial discussions concerning the purchase of the distributorship, he told Pessory that he would only consider purchasing the business if Pessory remained with the business because Pessory was very experienced in the business, knew the employees, and was an aggressive and effective salesperson.

2. Pessory testified that she was aware of the three-year obligation to remain with the dealership in the contract.

3. During the period between June 1, 2015, and the date the suit was filed, Leek's dealership realized a profit despite declining sales. Leek admits in testimony that declining sales were already occurring during the time that Pessory was working for the dealership.

4. Half of the purchase price has been paid to date.

5. Leek testified that even if business declined to the point that the dealership would be forced to lay off employees, Pessory would have been the last one to have been laid off.

6. Once informed of Pessory's desire to leave the business, Leek had offered to return the dealership to Pessory in exchange for the purchase price paid to date, but Pessory refused.

Discuss whether, based on any or all of the facts above, you believe that Pessory's failure to remain with the dealership constitutes a material breach that excuses Leek's failure to pay the balance of the purchase price.

B. ANTICIPATORY REPUDIATION

As indicated by the discussion of material breach above, one party can be excused from performing where the other party has committed a material failure to perform a contract. That doctrine requires that the failure to perform already occur. However, a party can also be excused even where the other party's obligations are not due yet, where the other party states it will not, in the future, perform. Such a statement is referred to as a repudiation of the contract or, more formally, as an **anticipatory repudiation**. As with material failure, a repudiation also excuses the non-repudiating party from performing its obligations under the contract. That party might also sue for damages.

Not every statement that suggests that a party might not perform amounts to a repudiation. To amount to a repudiation, such a statement must be clear and unequivocal that the party will not perform material obligations.

A party can also repudiate through conduct. However, such conduct, too, must be clear and unequivocal that the party will not perform. That might occur where, for example, a party takes action that renders it impossible to perform its contract. For example, assume Sarah has agreed to sell a parcel of real estate to Binoy, with closing scheduled for March 30. If Sarah sells that same real estate to Zara on March 1 and Binoy discovers that fact, then Sarah has repudiated her contract with Binoy because she has engaged in conduct making it impossible for her to perform on her contract with Binoy. At that point, Binoy can make alternate arrangements because he is excused from performing on his contract with Sarah. He can also sue Sarah for breach.

1. Retraction

Now imagine that before Sarah actually sold her real estate to Zara, she backed out of that contract, thus making it possible for her to sell to Binoy. In this case, Sarah has retracted her repudiation. A **retraction** essentially manifests that the party is still willing to perform on the earlier contract despite the subsequent repudiation. Generally, a party is free to retract a repudiation.

However, courts commonly apply two limitations to a party's ability to retract a repudiation. Under one limitation, a party may not retract a repudiation where the other party has materially changed its position in reliance on the retraction. Thus, if, before Binoy discovered that Sarah was not going to sell her property to Zara, Binoy had already entered into a contract to purchase a different parcel of real estate, Sarah would not be able to retract her repudiation. That is because Binoy materially changed his position in reliance on the repudiation.

The other limitation to a party's ability to retract a repudiation occurs where the non-repudiating party indicates that it intends to treat that repudiation as final. That might occur where, for example, the non-repudiating party sends a "I plan to sue you" letter or actually files suit. Either of those actions indicates that the party intends to treat the repudiation as final. Thus, the repudiating party cannot later retract its repudiation.

2. Reasonable Assurances

Sometimes, a party might indicate that it is unable or unwilling to perform, but the party's manifestation does not clearly and unequivocally indicate that the party is repudiating the contract. Similarly, sometimes a party fails to perform a contract, yet it is not clear whether that amounts to a material failure. In either of these situations, the party has a legitimate concern about the other party's ability to perform.

For example, imagine that you enter into a contract for a singer to perform at your wedding, which is scheduled to take place in twelve months. Payment is due in full three days prior to the wedding. You find out, one week prior to your wedding, that the singer has been hospitalized with a severe case of influenza and is suffering from, among other symptoms, laryngitis. Should you be excused from performance under the contract, or are you required to pay the singer three days prior to the wedding despite knowing that she is unlikely to be performing? In addition, since it appears that the singer will be unable to perform, should you be able to recover damages against her for not performing? Since the singer has not actually committed a breach at this point in time (since the date of the wedding is still a week away and the singer has not yet failed to render the singing performance when due), then it may appear that your options are limited, as you are not yet excused under the material failure doctrine discussed in Section A.

In this situation, where a party has **reasonable grounds for insecurity** as to the other party's performance, the party does not want to have to wait for the inevitable material failure to occur before it is excused. The law recognizes this. It thus allows a party to request **reasonable assurance**s from the other party that the other party will be able to and intends to perform. While the requesting party is waiting for that assurance, it is permitted to suspend its performance if reasonable. If that requested reasonable assurance is not forthcoming, the requesting party may be entitled to treat the failure to provide such reasonable assurance as a repudiation of the contract.

In the example above, imagine that you called and e-mailed the singer seven days before the wedding to confirm that she would be able to perform at your wedding. While you are waiting for her reply, you may suspend your performance under the contract, meaning that you can withhold your payment due three days prior to the wedding date. If she does not reply within a reasonable amount of time, you could treat her failure to do so as a repudiation of the contract. This, in turn, would excuse you from paying her under the contract and also potentially give rise to a claim against the singer for damages, such as increased costs you had to incur because you had to arrange for another performer, assuming her failure amounts to a breach.

An example of the formulation of the law surrounding anticipatory repudiation and the right to request reasonable assurances is found in UCC § 2-609 below.

§ 2-609. Right to Adequate Assurance of Performance.

(1) A contract for sale imposes an obligation on each party that the other's expectation of receiving due performance will not be impaired. When reasonable grounds for insecurity arise with respect to the performance of either party the other may in writing demand adequate assurance of due performance and until he receives such assurance may if commercially reasonable suspend any performance for which he has not already received the agreed return.

(2) Between merchants the reasonableness of grounds for insecurity and the adequacy of any assurance offered shall be determined according to commercial standards.

(3) Acceptance of any improper delivery or payment does not prejudice the aggrieved party's right to demand adequate assurance of future performance.

(4) After receipt of a justified demand failure to provide within a reasonable time not exceeding thirty days such assurance of due performance as is adequate under the circumstances of the particular case is a repudiation of the contract.

While this language comes from the UCC, courts in non-UCC cases often apply a similar doctrine in non-UCC cases.

Seeking assurances of another party's ability and intention to perform in the face of uncertainty about its performance can serve many purposes. Obviously, your client may want to feel comfortable from a planning perspective that, notwithstanding the circumstances suggesting otherwise, the party with whom your client has contracted still intends to perform. From a legal perspective, demanding such assurances also can protect your client from having to perform in the face of uncertainty about the other party's performance. Moreover, it helps ensure that your client is not the first to commit a material breach in the face of insecurity about the other party's performance. By allowing your client to specify what reasonable assurances it wishes to seek in the face of reasonable grounds for insecurity as to the other party's performance, and then to declare a repudiation when those assurances are not provided, your client can have more security that it will not be the first party to commit a material breach. This doctrine also gives rise to contractual remedies, even though the other party's performance was not yet due. By asking for the assurance, you in some sense accelerate the obligations of the other party in that his failure to provide the requested assurance constitutes a breach of his performance obligation.

Thus, going back to our example, once you discover that your wedding singer is in the hospital for influenza, you might reasonably request a note from the singer's medical care provider explaining how long he or she expects hoarseness from the laryngitis to last. If that type of note is not forthcoming, then assuming that was a reasonable assurance request, you could declare the singer as having repudiated. You could then make alternate arrangements for wedding entertainment without fear of being the first to commit a material breach.

PRACTICE PROBLEM 16-3

Hustle Financial Advisors Inc. (HFA) is a financial advising company that advises its clients on ways to protect and enhance their wealth. Mary Stokes is the President of HFA. Mary recently decided that to remain competitive, HFA needed to revamp its marketing plan and marketing literature. Mary, on behalf of HFA, retained Keith Wager, a consultant, to help with this project. Specifically, Keith was retained to rewrite HFA's marketing plan and develop a host of new marketing materials. In exchange for this work, Keith would be paid $25,000, though the contract did not specify when this amount was due. In addition, Keith would receive a $10,000 bonus after the end of the year following Keith services, if HFA's profits increased by more than 3 percent that year, on the premise that any increase in profits beyond HFA's standard annual 3 percent increase would likely be due in part to Keith's services.

The parties entered into the contract on March 1, 2019. Per the contract, the marketing plan was due no later than June 30 and the marketing literature due no later than September 30. Each deliverable under the contract was to be prepared using reasonable professional standards, and free of any copyright infringement. The contract also required Keith to maintain the confidentiality of all confidential information disclosed to him in connection with his preparation of the marketing plan and materials.

1. Assume that on June 15, Keith informed Mary that he was behind schedule, and would likely not be able to deliver the marketing plan until July 15. He thinks he might similarly be delayed by two weeks in delivering the marketing materials. Mary contacts you, HFA's outside counsel, wanting to know whether HFA can terminate Keith's consulting agreement and not pay Keith as a result of this. Alternatively, she wants to know whether HFA has any recourse as a result of Keith's failure.

2. Assume that on July 20, after Keith has delivered the marketing plan, Mary learns from Jan Smith, the President of Tuff n Stuff Inc., a food distribution company, that Keith took a full-time job as the Chief Marketing Officer of Tuff n Stuff. Mary contacts you, HFA's outside counsel, wanting to know whether HFA can terminate Keith's consulting agreement and not pay Keith as a result of this.

3. Continuing with the facts from Question 3, assume that on July 30, Keith informed Mary that he had taken the Chief Marketing Officer position with Tuff n Stuff and would not be able to complete his work for HFA. During the first two weeks of August, Mary spent 15 hours researching and conducting interviews of alternative marketing consultants. On August 15, Mary was ready to make an offer to one of those consultants when Keith called Mary to explain that he decided to step down from his position at Tuff n Stuff and resume his consulting business. Thus, he could resume with his work for HFA. Mary wants to know whether HFA must proceed to work with Keith or if it can instead retain one of the other consultants Mary interviewed without liability to Keith.

4. Assume that it is November 15, 2020, and Keith has finished performing all services under the consulting agreement with HFA. HFA is on track to exceed its profits from the prior year by 5 percent, which means, per its contract with Keith, HFA must pay Keith a $10,000 bonus at the end of that year. However, that day, Mary learns that for the past three months, Keith has been using HFA's confidential information in performing consulting work for another financial advisory company. Mary wants to know whether HFA can withhold Keith's $10,000 bonus as a result of Keith's actions.

C. WAIVING CONTRACTUAL OBLIGATIONS AND CONDITIONS

A party also may seek to excuse its non-performance of an obligation under a contract because of the other party's waiver of that obligation. Where a party

waives an obligation, that party agrees that it will not insist on full satisfaction of that obligation. By doing so, the party forgoes its rights to sue the counterparty for breach of that obligation despite variance from the contract.

A waiver in general must be voluntary, intentional, and informed. That means a party must have relevant information before granting a waiver. The waiver then must be voluntarily and intentionally granted in light of that information.

Sometimes a party waives its contractual right temporarily. That means it agrees to not insist on the counterparty's performance of an obligation for a period of time. Sometimes, a party waives a contractual right in one instance only, manifesting that it is a one-time waiver, and that the party reserves the right to insist on full satisfaction of that obligation in the future.

Parties sometimes also grant waivers as to the satisfaction of conditions. Where they grant a waiver to a condition, that means the party does not intend to insist on satisfaction of that condition before its obligation is due. Alternatively, a party might waive satisfaction of some aspect of a condition, but not the entire condition. For example, if a buyer of a car has as a condition to its duty to close (meaning, to pay for that car) that a mechanic has inspected the car and delivered a report of that inspection at least five days before closing, the buyer could either waive this condition entirely, which means it would no longer insist on receiving the inspection at all before it has a duty to buy the car, or it could waive the need to get that inspection five days before closing, instead allowing the condition to be satisfied up until closing.

Although parties sometimes grant express waivers, sometimes a party impliedly grants a waiver. That occurs where a party, through conduct, demonstrates that it does not intend to insist on an obligation's strict performance or on a condition's strict satisfaction. In this way, the concept of waiver is sometimes used by a party as an excuse to a breach of contract claim. In that context, the party against whom a breach is alleged argues that the other party waived its contractual right to the nonperforming party's performance of that obligation. Or, the aggrieved party might argue the nonperforming party waived a condition through its conduct.

Courts uphold waivers for the same reasons they enforce contracts and amendments to contracts—because they support the policy of giving effect to the parties' intent. They also often lead to reliance by the party for whose benefit an obligation or condition is being waived. On the other hand, courts are reluctant to deem conduct as an implied waiver. That is because consideration is required for each party's promise or set of promises to form a contract. The consideration requirement gives us assurance that the parties intended to engage in the conduct of forming a contract, as each side presumably considered whether the promise bargained for was worth the promise to be given in exchange. Courts are cognizant of the fact that contracts, properly formed, permit each party to rely on the other's promise and to plan accordingly for the future. Changes to a party's contractual obligations, whether through modification or waiver, must therefore be scrutinized very carefully. To the extent that contract law makes it too easy to modify or waive one's contractual rights, the utility of contracts will be reduced since the risk of a court not enforcing a party's contractual rights strictly will have been increased. This makes it more difficult for parties to rely on the initial contractual promises.

Courts are less willing to deem conduct a waiver of a condition if the condition being purportedly waived was a material part of the agreed exchange. Where it is a material part of the agreed exchange—meaning, where that condition is one of the important terms protecting a party—courts are often reluctant to find a waiver in the absence of consideration.

To see the concept of waiver, imagine that two parties enter into a contract for office-cleaning services. If the service provider provides cleaning services twice a week instead of three times a week as stated in the contract, the customer may bring a claim for breach of contract. If it is too easy for the service provider to prove that the contract was modified to twice a week or that the customer somehow waived its right to have the third cleaning each week by failing to object the first time the service provider failed to provide the third cleaning in a week, then the customer will not enjoy the intended benefits of the contract. Such decisions collectively would make it more difficult for contracting parties to rely on a contract, which is undesirable.

Waivers are particularly suspect because they are often not accompanied by any new consideration. That means the party seeking the waiver often does not offer to compensate the party waiving a contractual right. Recall from Chapter 7 that courts were initially more comfortable enforcing contractual modifications only where additional consideration was present. Over time, courts have become more comfortable with a contextual approach that examines whether the modification was reasonable based on circumstances arising after formation that were not contemplated by the parties initially and whether the parties were acting in good faith. By examining each situation carefully to detect opportunistic behavior and determine whether one party is being taken advantage of after the contract has been formed, judges can be more confident in their decisions that a proper and fair modification to the contract has occurred.

Similarly, with respect to waivers, judges want to be absolutely certain that a party has agreed to forgo its contractual rights before determining that such rights have been given up without remedy. Thus, they consider whether the circumstances that have arisen were unforeseen. Given that one of the purposes of utilizing a contract in the first place is to provide a legal remedy in the event of the other party's non-performance, it should not be easy to demonstrate that the legal right was waived with respect to that non-performance. Accordingly, judges use exacting tests to determine that waivers were made intentionally, voluntarily, informed, and with respect to the particular events or circumstances in question.

Even where waivers are found to exist, they may be construed very narrowly. For example, a court may find that a seller's intentional waiver of a late fee provision for a buyer's late payment in March under the contract does not constitute a waiver of the same late fee provision as it may apply to buyer's late payment in May. As you review the case below, consider the burden placed on the party asserting waiver and whether you believe it adequately protects contracting parties' ability to rely on contractual promises.

Vratsinas Construction Co. v. Triad Drywall, LLC

Court of Appeals of Georgia, First Division
321 Ga. App. 451 (2013)

DILLARD, Judge.

After the completion of a commercial construction project in which the project owner declared bankruptcy, Triad Drywall, LLC ("Triad"), a subcontractor, sued Vratsinas Construction Company ("VCC"), the general contractor, to recover money owed for its work on the project. VCC defended the lawsuit based upon a "pay-if-paid" provision contained in the parties' contract, which provided that Triad would not be paid unless and until VCC was first paid by the project owner. The trial court denied VCC's motions for summary judgment, directed verdict, and judgment notwithstanding the verdict, holding that the question of whether VCC waived the pay-if-paid provision presented an issue for jury resolution. The jury ultimately awarded damages to Triad, and the parties filed cross-appeals. In Case No. A12A2317, VCC argues, inter alia, that the trial court erred in submitting the issue of waiver to the jury.

Construed in the light most favorable to Triad, the facts show that VCC was the general contractor under an agreement with Thomas Enterprises/Fourth Quarter Properties (the "Owner") to build the Ashley Park shopping center (the "Project") in Newnan. In January 2007, VCC contracted with Triad to install drywall and drop ceilings, and to perform other work on the Project (the "Subcontract"). The Subcontract contained the following pay-if-paid provision:

> Notwithstanding anything contained herein to the contrary, save and except when the failure to receive payment is the result of default by [VCC] in the performance of its obligations under the Contract Documents unrelated to [Triad's] performance of the Subcontract, all payments by [VCC] to [Triad] under the Subcontract, including without limitation, progress payments, full payment or partial release of retainage, payment for change orders and final payment, are expressly and unequivocally contingent upon and subject to Owner's acceptance of all Subcontract Work and [VCC's] receipt of payment from Owner for the Subcontract Work. Subcontractor expressly acknowledges that it relies on payment under the Subcontract on the creditworthiness of Owner, and not that of Contractor. It is expressly understood that any other basis for such non-payment by Owner, including the bankruptcy or insolvency of Owner, will not excuse this

condition precedent to payment from [VCC] to [Triad]. [Triad] further agrees that Owner's acceptance of the Subcontract Work and Owner's payment to [VCC] for the Subcontract Work are express, independent conditions precedent to any obligation of [VCC] to make any payments to [Triad] and are not merely expressions of the time or manner of such payments.

It is undisputed that VCC paid Triad's first three payment applications for which the Owner paid VCC in full. But as rumors started swirling about the solvency of the Owner, Gadi Gal—a co-owner of Triad—requested a meeting with John Davenport, VCC's project manager. During that meeting (which took place in the fall of 2007), Gal—who was acutely aware of the contractual pay-if-paid provision—expressed concern about the Owner's ability to pay for the Project. According to Gal, Davenport told him not to worry about the Owner's finances and to keep working, stating that VCC would pay Triad from its "own pocket" if necessary.[7]

After this meeting, Triad continued work on the Project and submitted a fourth payment application to VCC, who paid Triad the entire outstanding balance (via two separate checks—one issued in November and one issued in February), despite not having been paid in full for that work by the Owner. VCC refused to pay subsequent payment applications, however, and by the time Triad finished work on the Project in the spring of 2008, Triad had *seven* unpaid applications totaling approximately $465,888. The Owner did not pay any monies to VCC after September 2007, despite the continuing work and ultimate completion of the Project, and VCC tendered no payment to Triad after the February 2008 check.

In March 2009, Triad filed the instant lawsuit against VCC to recover the outstanding balance owed on the remaining payment applications. VCC argued, in accordance with the pay-if-paid provision, that it was not contractually obligated to pay Triad because it had not received payment from the Owner. Triad, on the other hand, maintained that VCC waived the pay-if-paid provision through its conduct when (1) Davenport assured Triad that VCC would pay Triad from its "own pocket," and (2) VCC paid Triad's fourth payment application despite not having been paid in full by the Owner. The trial court denied VCC's motion for summary judgment after holding that the issue of whether VCC waived the pay-if-paid provision presented a genuine issue of material fact for jury resolution and, at the conclusion of Triad's case, denied VCC's motion for a directed verdict. The jury returned a verdict in favor of Triad for $465,888 plus interest and the trial court entered judgment on the verdict.

---

7. [3] At trial, Davenport agreed that he met with Gadi Gal, but denied telling Gal that VCC would pay Triad from its own pocket. In accordance with our standard of review, however, we must assume that this statement was made as represented by Gal. See *Hill Roofing Co., Inc.*, 265 Ga. App. at 822, 595 S.E.2d 638.

These cross-appeals follow the trial court's denial of VCC's motion for judgment notwithstanding the verdict.

1. IN CASE NO. A12A2317, VCC ARGUES THAT THE TRIAL COURT ERRED IN DENYING ITS MOTIONS FOR DIRECTED VERDICT AND JUDGMENT NOTWITHSTANDING THE VERDICT BECAUSE TRIAD FAILED AS A MATTER OF LAW TO PRESENT SUFFICIENT EVIDENCE TO SHOW WAIVER OF THE PAY-IF-PAID PROVISION. WE AGREE.

To begin with, we note that a party to a contract may waive a contractual right, and that any such waiver may be accomplished expressly or implicitly through the party's conduct. But the law will not infer the waiver of an important contract right unless "the waiver is *clear and unmistakable*." And because waiver is not favored under the law, the evidence relied upon to prove a waiver "must be so clearly indicative of an intent to relinquish a then known particular right or benefit as to exclude any other reasonable explanation." Indeed, all the attendant facts, taken together, must amount to an "intentional relinquishment of a known right, in order that a waiver may exist." The burden of proof lies with the party asserting waiver and, although generally a jury question, when "the facts and circumstances essential to the waiver issue are clearly established, waiver becomes a question of law."

The essential facts in the case sub judice fail to create a jury question as to the issue of waiver. The sole evidence of waiver consists of Davenport's statement to Gal that VCC would pay Triad out of its own pocket and VCC's subsequent payment of Triad's fourth payment application when it had only received a partial payment from the Owner. We do not, however, consider these facts in a vacuum, but instead are charged with examining all of the attendant facts and circumstances contextually in order to assess whether there was a clear and unmistakable intent by VCC to waive an important contract right.

And here, after the alleged waiver of the pay-if-paid provision by VCC, Triad continued working and submitted *seven* additional payment applications in accordance with the parties' practice. Importantly, VCC refused payment for each and every one of these applications. Indeed, Gadi Gal testified that during the interim period after the alleged waiver and prior to finishing the Project, he called VCC "many times" to request payment, and VCC consistently refused his requests, and that because of these refusals "he knew then that [Triad was] in trouble."

Moreover, Triad's account manager—who was responsible for billing on the Project—testified during the trial that she was never informed (nor did she understand) that any changes had been made to the pay-if-paid procedure with VCC. Thus, she continued to send out standard e-mails to VCC inquiring as to whether VCC had yet received payment from the Owner in order that Triad's outstanding payment applications could be paid. The record contains e-mail correspondence between the account manager and VCC in both June 2008 and April 2009, which reflects that she clearly anticipated and understood that Owner payment to VCC was a prerequisite to Triad's receipt of payment from VCC; and VCC repeatedly informed Triad that it had not yet received payment from the Owner.

Finally, Ziv Gal—a relative of Gadi Gal and Triad's then co-owner—testified, stating that he was aware of the pay-if-paid provision and that nothing in his dealings with VCC either during or after the Project led him to believe that the owner-pay contingency was ever changed by either party or waived by VCC. Indeed, he attended a payment meeting with VCC personnel after the completion of the Project and described them as "very forthcoming with information" and said that they "encouraged [Triad] to protect [its] rights in the [P]roject." But according to Ziv Gal, no one from VCC ever suggested at any time that anything short of strict compliance with the payment terms of the Subcontract would be followed or accepted.

Under the foregoing circumstances, the trial court erred in submitting the issue of waiver to the jury. As previously noted, when "the facts and circumstances essential to the waiver issue are clearly established, waiver becomes a question of law." The statements and conduct of both Triad and VCC during and after the Project clearly establish a lack of intent or understanding that VCC waived the important contract right contained within and enshrined by the pay-if-paid provision. We are, therefore, constrained to reverse.

. . .

Understanding the Case:

1. *Subcontracts and Contractor Risk:*   Contractors often depend on multiple subcontractors to complete a particular job. When bidding on a job, the contractor is not only assuming that the subcontractor will perform but also that the end client—the owner—will pay the contractor. Accordingly, attorneys need to carefully draft both the client contract as well as the subcontractor contracts to make sure that the contractor is not bearing too much financial or performance risk. *Vratsinas* demonstrates the use of a pay-if-paid clause to mitigate that risk for the general contractor.

2. *Written Waivers:*   Parties often include waiver requirements in their contracts, such as requiring that all waivers be in writing to be effective. Similar to written contract provisions that state that the parties may only amend the contract through a written amendment identifying itself as an amendment, these clauses are often not enforced by courts. Nevertheless, such clauses, even if not effective, may still encourage better communication between the parties regarding their expectations for performance.

Comprehension and Thought Questions:

1. What does the "pay-if-paid" provision in the contract do?

2. Why was the "pay-if-paid" provision (and its alleged waiver) relevant to Triad's ability to recover for VCC's failure to make payments under the contract?

3. According to the court, "waiver is not favored under the law." Why is this so? Do you agree with this position?

4. What facts led the court to determine that it was not clear, as a matter of law, that VCC waived the "pay-if-paid" provision?

5. Can you think of any counterarguments to suggest that there was a waiver based on those same facts? Why was the existence of such counterarguments irrelevant to the court's decision?

6. What could Triad have done differently if, at the time of performance, it had intended to rely on VCC's waiver of the "pay-if-paid" provision?

PRACTICE PROBLEM 16-4

Imagine that your client Nezar entered into a lease agreement as a tenant with the following provision:

> 1. Payment of rent is due prior to the fifth day of each month. Any late payments will constitute a breach of this contract, and without limiting any of Landlord's other remedies, will entitle Landlord to charge a 5 percent late payment fee and to terminate the contract.
>
> 2. No consent or waiver, express or implied, by Landlord to or of any breach or default by Tenant in the performance of his obligations hereunder shall be deemed or construed to be a consent or waiver to or of any other breach or default in the performance by Tenant of the same or any other obligation of Tenant hereunder. Any and all consents or waivers hereunder shall be effective only if in writing and signed by Landlord. Failure on the part of Landlord to object to any act or failure to act of Tenant or to declare Tenant in default, irrespective of how long such failure continues, shall not constitute a waiver by Landlord of his rights hereunder.

Nezar accidentally paid the first month's rent two days late. The late payment was accompanied by a letter apologizing for the tardiness of the payment and asking the Landlord to inform Nezar whether the Landlord objected to the late payment. Nezar never received any communication from the Landlord regarding the late payment and the Landlord continued to deposit Nezar's monthly rental checks.

After eleven months under the contract, the Landlord sends Nezar a letter purporting to terminate the contract immediately because his first month's payment was two days late. Nezar is exasperated and thinks that the only reason the Landlord wants to terminate the contract is because rental rates have skyrocketed and the Landlord knows he can get a better rate either by threatening termination or renting the space to someone else. Is the Landlord likely to succeed in terminating the contract? How should you advise Nezar?

As with a repudiation, a party may **retract** a waiver. By retracting a waiver, the party reinstates the original obligation or condition waived. However, for fairness reasons, courts generally do not permit a party to retract a waiver once the other party has materially changed its position in reliance on the waiver.

D. MISTAKE

You may recall from Chapter 7 that courts generally do not inquire into the adequacy of consideration. This means that parties are free to make subjective judgments about the advisability of different contracts, including the value of the promises being received and the value of the promises being given, and courts will not typically protect a party from making a poor judgment. For example, if Connor promises to tutor David for $25 per hour, and David agrees to pay, David cannot avoid the contract later by saying that he made a poor choice and that Connor's services were not really worth $25 per hour. That is because parties are not protected from mistakes in judgment. If the consequences of a transaction do not pan out as a party wished they would, that party cannot later argue that it should be excused for that reason.

On the other hand, a party may be able to avoid its obligations under a contract where it made a mistaken assumption in entering into the contract.

1. Mutual Mistake

Where both parties to a contract make such a mistake, it is referred to as a **mutual mistake**. The following is the Restatement's approach to excusing a party where there is a mutual mistake.

§ 152 When Mistake of Both Parties Makes a Contract Voidable

(1) Where a mistake of both parties at the time a contract was made as to a basic assumption on which the contract was made has a material effect on the agreed exchange of performances, the contract is voidable by the adversely affected party unless he bears the risk of the mistake under the rule stated in § 154.

(2) In determining whether the mistake has a material effect on the agreed exchange of performances, account is taken of any relief by way of reformation, restitution, or otherwise.

Thus, a party can rescind a contract under this doctrine where (1) both parties are mistaken (2) about a fact that was a basic assumption on which they made the contract, (3) that mistake has a material effect on the agreed exchange of performance, and (4) the party did not bear the risk of that mistake. Each of these elements is discussed below.

First, it is important to note what counts as a mistake for purposes of this doctrine. A mistake is typically understood as a "belief that is not in accord with the facts."[8] Because this doctrine generally speaks to mistaken assumptions about facts, it does not cover subjective value judgments, even if poor or arguably mistaken.

For example, if David agreed at the time to pay Connor $25 per hour for tutoring services because David thought that was a fair rate, then David cannot assert mistake to protect himself later and avoid liability under the contract. This would be true even if the going rate for tutoring services was $15 per hour. As a different example, if Alisson agrees to purchase a share of company stock because she believes the company will earn a certain amount of money in the coming years, but it fails to do so, her belief was not a mistake for contract law purposes.

Mistakes can also relate to legal requirements or permissions. If, for example, both parties to a real estate purchase agreement incorrectly believed that the land could be used for commercial development but this was actually prohibited by a recent zoning regulation, that would be a mistake. In this instance, a belief that the land could be used for commercial development was not in accord with the facts, as commercial development was actually prohibited.

Under the second element, the fact that a mistake is about a "basic assumption" on which the contract was made means it involves a mistake that goes to the core of the subject matter of the contract. To the extent that a person is necessary to the performance of a contract, it is a basic assumption that that person will be alive to perform. Similarly, to the extent that specific property is necessary to perform the contract, the fact that that property will not be destroyed by the time performance is to occur is a basic assumption of the parties.

For example, if parties to a real estate purchase agreement both believed that the land to be sold comprised 100 acres, but due to a surveying error, it actually comprised 250 acres, then the parties would have made a mistake. Objectively, 100 acres is not the same as 250 acres, and the parties' belief that the contract covered 100 acres would not be in accord with the facts.

In contrast, the mistake doctrine does not recognize as a basic assumption that there will continue to be demand for a good or service. That is because it is always contemplated that market demands might change. Similarly, it is not a safe basic assumption that a party will continue to have financial resources to

---

8. Restatement (Second) of Contracts § 151 (1981).

perform. Again, that is because it is always a possibility that a party's financial fortunes will turn. Thus, where the parties are "mistaken" about the existence of a market or a party's financial condition that later proves to not have been correct, that mistake will not excuse the party under the mistake doctrine.

Under the third element, the mistake also must "have a material effect on the agreed upon performances." This means that the mistake leads to such an imbalance in the consideration that it upsets the very basis for the contract. As the Restatement provides, "the resulting imbalance must be so severe that he [the party seeking to be excused] can not fairly be required to carry it out."[9]

In the real estate purchase agreement example, the ability of a party to purchase 250 acres for the price of 100 acres, coupled with forcing the selling party to sell 250 acres for the price of 100 acres, could potentially be very unfair, as it could give a windfall to the buyer, who would presumably pay far less than market value for the property. It could also be unfair to the seller, who would only recover 40 percent of the value of the property, assuming all acres were equally valuable.

On the other hand, if the resulting exchange is disadvantageous to one party, but the other party is not necessarily advantaged, then the mistake may not be sufficiently material as to constitute an excuse. For example, if the market rate for land in a particular area was the same regardless of whether or not it could be used for commercial development, then a seller would not necessarily be advantaged by the mutual mistaken belief of the parties that the seller's parcel was eligible for commercial development. The parties would have made a mistake, and the purchaser would be disadvantaged since the purchaser purchased land not useable for her intended use, but the lack of an advantage to the seller might convince a court that the mistake did not necessarily have a material effect on their agreed exchange in light of the market rate for land. Similarly, if the surveying error was the addition of 2 acres instead of 150 acres, perhaps that mutual mistake would not be sufficiently material to permit the seller to avoid the contract.

For a contract to be voidable by a party due to mutual mistake, the last requirement is that the party must not have borne the risk of the mistake. A party bears the risk of the mistake where the party is aware of the limitations of its knowledge on a particular fact, yet proceeds with the contract nonetheless. Where that occurs, the party is said to have been consciously ignorant of the fact. Thus, in our ongoing example, if the seller knew that the survey he had for his property was not current or accurate, yet he decided to move forward with the sale regardless, arguably the seller would be consciously ignorant of the fact as to acreage. As such, the seller might not be able to rescind the contract due to the mutual mistake.

---

9. *See* Restatement (Second) of Contracts § 152 n. c. (1981).

A party also bears the risk of a mistake where the contract allocates that risk to the party. Thus, if the contract provides that the seller agrees to sell his entire property to the buyer regardless of what the survey reveals to be the actual acreage, the seller would have assumed the risk that he was transferring more than 100 acres to the buyer. Thus, he could not avoid the contract due to the parties' mutual mistake about the actual acreage.

Finally, courts retain discretion to allocate the risk to a party where it is reasonable and just to do so.

Where there is a mutual mistake, the contract is voidable by the adversely affected party. However, the contract still can be enforced by the adversely affected party if she wants to enforce it. Moreover, the party who is unfairly benefited by the mistake does not have the ability avoid the contract.

In our ongoing example, that means the seller who thought she was selling 100 acres, not 250 acres, could avoid the contract if desired. However, the buyer could not.

2. Unilateral Mistake

In certain circumstances, a party's **unilateral mistake** may justify excusing her performance under a contract. The circumstances under which a party may avoid a contract due to unilateral mistake are virtually the same as with mutual mistake. However, because of the unfairness to the non-mistaken party of avoiding the contract due to the other party's unilateral mistake, there is an additional element to unilateral mistake, which often can be satisfied in one of two ways. The first way looks at the culpability of the non-mistaken party with respect to the other party's mistake to determine whether the non-mistaken party had reason to know of the other party's mistake or caused that mistaken belief. Thus, as we have seen in other contract law doctrines (such as contract interpretation), the law generally does not allow a contracting party to take advantage when she knows or has reason to know of another party's misunderstanding or, in this instance, mistake. Alternatively, a party may satisfy this additional element by showing that it would be "unconscionable" to enforce the contract in light of the party's mistake. For this purpose, the concept of unconscionability refers to the gross unfairness in the substance of the exchange—it does not mean the party must prove the elements of unconscionability discussed in Chapter 21.

The following is the Restatement's expression of the unilateral mistake doctrine:

§ 153 When Mistake of One Party Makes a Contract Voidable
Where a mistake of one party at the time a contract was made as to a basic assumption on which he made the contract has a material effect on the agreed exchange of performances that is adverse to him, the contract is voidable by him if he does not bear the risk of the mistake under the rule stated in § 154, and

(a) the effect of the mistake is such that enforcement of the contract would be unconscionable, or

(b) the other party had reason to know of the mistake or his fault caused the mistake.

Thus, assume that a buyer of real estate believes that the land he has contracted to buy could be used for commercial development, when in reality, such use would be prohibited by a recent zoning regulation. If the seller was on the zoning board where the land was located and knew that purchaser was under the mistaken impression that the land could be commercially developed, then the purchaser may be able to avoid the contract *even though* only the purchaser had the mistaken belief. That is because the seller would have reason to know of the mistake. In fact, when you study misrepresentation, in some circumstances a seller has a "duty" to disclose information about the property being purchased to the buyer. If the seller fails to disclose such required information in those circumstances, then the seller commits a misrepresentation. Thus, if, in our example, the seller had a duty to disclose to the buyer that the land could not be commercially developed, then in addition to potentially being able to avoid the contract on the basis of a mistake, the buyer could potentially avoid the contract on the basis of the seller's misrepresentation due to omission.

You will study misrepresentation in Chapter 20. But for now, keep in mind that if a party's unilateral mistake is caused by the other party's false assertions, concealments (i.e., hiding the truth of facts), or omissions where it had a duty to speak, then in addition to possibly being excused under unilateral mistake, that party might be able the avoid the contract due to misrepresentation.

The following case demonstrates a court's approach to mistake. As you read this case, think about how the court analyzed each element of the mistake doctrine. Also ask yourself whether you agree with the court's approach as to when a party bears the risk of a mistake.

Lenawee County Board of Health v. Messerly
Supreme Court of Michigan
417 Mich. 17 (1982)

RYAN, Justice.

In March of 1977, Carl and Nancy Pickles, appellees, purchased from appellants, William and Martha Messerly, a 600-square-foot tract of land upon which is located a three-unit apartment building. Shortly after the transaction was closed, the Lenawee County Board of Health condemned the property and obtained a permanent injunction which prohibits human habitation on the premises until the defective sewage system is brought into conformance with the Lenawee County sanitation code.

We are required to determine whether appellees should prevail in their attempt to avoid this land contract on the basis of mutual mistake and failure of consideration. We conclude that the parties did entertain a mutual mis-apprehension of fact, but that the circumstances of this case do not warrant rescission.

I

The facts of the case are not seriously in dispute. In 1971, the Messerlys acquired approximately one acre plus 600 square feet of land. A three-unit apartment building was situated upon the 600-square-foot portion. The trial court found that, prior to this transfer, the Messerlys' predecessor in title, Mr. Bloom, had installed a septic tank on the property without a permit and in violation of the applicable health code. The Messerlys used the building as an income investment property until 1973 when they sold it, upon land contract, to James Barnes who likewise used it primarily as an income-producing investment.

Mr. and Mrs. Barnes, with the permission of the Messerlys, sold approximately one acre of the property in 1976, and the remaining 600 square feet and building were offered for sale soon thereafter when Mr. and Mrs. Barnes defaulted on their land contract. Mr. and Mrs. Pickles evidenced an interest in the property, but were dissatisfied with the terms of the Barnes-Messerly land contract. Consequently, to accommodate the Pickleses' preference to enter into a land contract directly with the Messerlys, Mr. and Mrs. Barnes executed a quit-claim deed which conveyed their interest in the property back to the Messerlys. After inspecting the property, Mr. and Mrs. Pickles executed a new land contract with the Messerlys on March 21, 1977. It provided for a purchase price of $25,500. A clause was added to the end of the land contract form which provides:

"17. Purchaser has examined this property and agrees to accept same in its present condition. There are no other or additional written or oral understandings."

Five or six days later, when the Pickleses went to introduce themselves to the tenants, they discovered raw sewage seeping out of the ground. Tests conducted by a sanitation expert indicated the inadequacy of the sewage system. The Lenawee County Board of Health subsequently condemned the property and initiated this lawsuit in the Lenawee Circuit Court against the Messerlys as land contract vendors, and the Pickleses, as vendees, to obtain a permanent injunction proscribing human habitation of the premises until the property was brought into conformance with the Lenawee County sanitation code. The injunction was granted, and the Lenawee County Board of Health was permitted to withdraw from the lawsuit by stipulation of the parties.

When no payments were made on the land contract, the Messerlys filed a cross-complaint against the Pickleses seeking foreclosure, sale of the property, and a deficiency judgment. Mr. and Mrs. Pickles then counterclaimed for rescission against the Messerlys, and filed a third-party complaint against the

Barneses, which incorporated, by reference, the allegations of the counterclaim against the Messerlys. In count one, Mr. and Mrs. Pickles alleged failure of consideration. Count two charged Mr. and Mrs. Barnes with willful concealment and misrepresentation as a result of their failure to disclose the condition of the sanitation system. Additionally, Mr. and Mrs. Pickles sought to hold the Messerlys liable in equity for the Barneses' alleged misrepresentation. The Pickleses prayed that the land contract be rescinded.

After a bench trial, the court concluded that the Pickleses had no cause of action against either the Messerlys or the Barneses as there was no fraud or misrepresentation. This ruling was predicated on the trial judge's conclusion that none of the parties knew of Mr. Bloom's earlier transgression or of the resultant problem with the septic system until it was discovered by the Pickleses, and that the sanitation problem was not caused by any of the parties. The trial court held that the property was purchased "as is", after inspection and, accordingly, its "negative * * * value cannot be blamed upon an innocent seller". Foreclosure was ordered against the Pickleses, together with a judgment against them in the amount of $25,943.09.[10]

Mr. and Mrs. Pickles appealed from the adverse judgment. The Court of Appeals unanimously affirmed the trial court's ruling with respect to Mr. and Mrs. Barnes but, in a two-to-one decision, reversed the finding of no cause of action on the Pickleses' claims against the Messerlys. It concluded that the mutual mistake between the Messerlys and the Pickleses went to a basic, as opposed to a collateral, element of the contract, and that the parties intended to transfer income-producing rental property but, in actuality, the vendees paid $25,500 for an asset without value.

Since the mutual mistake issue was dispositive in the Court of Appeals, we find its consideration necessary to a proper determination of this case.

We granted the Messerlys' application for leave to appeal.

II

We must decide initially whether there was a mistaken belief entertained by one or both parties to the contract in dispute and, if so, the resultant legal significance.

A contractual mistake "is a belief that is not in accord with the facts". 1 Restatement Contracts, 2d, § 151, p 383. The erroneous belief of one or both of the parties must relate to a fact in existence at the time the contract is executed. That is to say, the belief which is found to be in error may not be, in substance, a prediction as to a future occurrence or non-occurrence.

---

10. [3] The parties stipulated that this amount was due on the land contract, assuming that the contract was valid and enforceable.

The Court of Appeals concluded, after a de novo review of the record, that the parties were mistaken as to the income-producing capacity of the property in question. We agree. The vendors and the vendees each believed that the property transferred could be utilized as income-generating rental property. All of the parties subsequently learned that, in fact, the property was unsuitable for any residential use.

Appellants assert that there was no mistake in the contractual sense because the defect in the sewage system did not arise until after the contract was executed. The appellees respond that the Messerlys are confusing the date of the inception of the defect with the date upon which the defect was discovered.

This is essentially a factual dispute which the trial court failed to resolve directly. Nevertheless, we are empowered to draw factual inferences from the facts found by the trial court.

An examination of the record reveals that the septic system was defective prior to the date on which the land contract was executed. The Messerlys' grantor installed a nonconforming septic system without a permit prior to the transfer of the property to the Messerlys in 1971. Moreover, virtually undisputed testimony indicates that, assuming ideal soil conditions, 2,500 square feet of property is necessary to support a sewage system adequate to serve a three-family dwelling. Likewise, 750 square feet is mandated for a one-family home. Thus, the division of the parcel and sale of one acre of the property by Mr. and Mrs. Barnes in 1976 made it impossible to remedy the already illegal septic system within the confines of the 600-square-foot parcel.[11]

Appellants do not dispute these underlying facts which give rise to an inference contrary to their contentions.

Having determined that when these parties entered into the land contract they were laboring under a mutual mistake of fact, we now direct our attention to a determination of the legal significance of that finding.

A contract may be rescinded because of a mutual misapprehension of the parties, but this remedy is granted only in the sound discretion of the court. Appellants argue that the parties' mistake relates only to the quality or value of the real estate transferred, and that such mistakes are collateral to the agreement and do not justify rescission, citing *A & M Land Development Co. v. Miller*, 354 Mich. 681, 94 N.W.2d 197 (1959).

In that case, the plaintiff was the purchaser of 91 lots of real property. It sought partial rescission of the land contract when it was frustrated in its

---

11. [10] It is crucial to distinguish between the date on which a belief relating to a particular fact or set of facts becomes erroneous due to a change in the fact, and the date on which the mistaken nature of the belief is discovered. By definition, a mistake cannot be discovered until after the contract is executed. If the parties were aware, prior to the execution of a contract, that they were in error concerning a particular fact, there would be no misapprehension in signing the contract. Thus stated, it becomes obvious that the date on which a mistaken fact manifests itself is irrelevant to the determination whether or not there was a mistake.

attempts to develop 42 of the lots because it could not obtain permits from the county health department to install septic tanks on these lots. This Court refused to allow rescission because the mistake, whether mutual or unilateral, related only to the value of the property.

> "There was here no mistake as to the form or substance of the contract between the parties, or the description of the property constituting the subject matter. The situation involved is not at all analogous to that presented in Scott v Grow, 301 Mich 226; 3 NW2d 254; 141 ALR 819 (1942). There the plaintiff sought relief by way of reformation of a deed on the ground that the instrument of conveyance had not been drawn in accordance with the intention and agreement of the parties. It was held that the bill of complaint stated a case for the granting of equitable relief by way of reformation. In the case at bar plaintiff received the property for which it contracted. The fact that it may be of less value than the purchaser expected at the time of the transaction is not a sufficient basis for the granting of equitable relief, neither fraud nor reliance on misrepresentation of material facts having been established." 354 Mich. 693-694, 94 N.W.2d 197.

Appellees contend, on the other hand, that in this case the parties were mistaken as to the very nature of the character of the consideration and claim that the pervasive and essential quality of this mistake renders rescission appropriate. They cite in support of that view *Sherwood v. Walker*, 66 Mich. 568, 33 N.W. 919 (1887), the famous "barren cow" case. In that case, the parties agreed to the sale and purchase of a cow which was thought to be barren, but which was, in reality, with calf. When the seller discovered the fertile condition of his cow, he refused to deliver her. In permitting rescission, the Court stated:

> "It seems to me, however, in the case made by this record, that the mistake or misapprehension of the parties went to the whole substance of the agreement. If the cow was a breeder, she was worth at least $750; if barren, she was worth not over $80. The parties would not have made the contract of sale except upon the understanding and belief that she was incapable of breeding, and of no use as a cow. It is true she is now the identical animal that they thought her to be when the contract was made; there is no mistake as to the identity of the creature. Yet the mistake was not of the mere quality of the animal, but went to the very nature of the thing. A barren cow is substantially a different creature than a breeding one. . . .
>
> "The court should have instructed the jury that if they found that the cow was sold, or contracted to be sold, upon the understanding of both parties that she was barren, and useless for the purpose of breeding, and that in fact she was not barren, but capable of breeding, then the defendants had a right to rescind, and to refuse to deliver, and the verdict should be in their favor." 66 Mich. 577-578, 33 N.W. 919.

As the parties suggest, the foregoing precedent arguably distinguishes mistakes affecting the essence of the consideration from those which go to its quality or value, affording relief on a per se basis for the former but not the latter.

However, the distinctions which may be drawn from *Sherwood* and *A &
M Land Development Co.* do not provide a satisfactory analysis of the nature
of a mistake sufficient to invalidate a contract. Often, a mistake relates to an
underlying factual assumption which, when discovered, directly affects value,
but simultaneously and materially affects the essence of the contractual consideration. It is disingenuous to label such a mistake collateral.

Appellant and appellee both mistakenly believed that the property which
was the subject of their land contract would generate income as rental property. The fact that it could not be used for human habitation deprived the property of its income-earning potential and rendered it less valuable. However, this
mistake, while directly and dramatically affecting the property's value, cannot
accurately be characterized as collateral because it also affects the very essence
of the consideration. . . .

We find that the inexact and confusing distinction between contractual mistakes running to value and those touching the substance of the consideration
serves only as an impediment to a clear and helpful analysis for the equitable
resolution of cases in which mistake is alleged and proven. Accordingly, the
holdings of *A & M Land Development Co.* and *Sherwood* with respect to the
material or collateral nature of a mistake are limited to the facts of those cases.

Instead, we think the better-reasoned approach is a case-by-case analysis
whereby rescission is indicated when the mistaken belief relates to a basic
assumption of the parties upon which the contract is made, and which materially affects the agreed performances of the parties. Rescission is not available,
however, to relieve a party who has assumed the risk of loss in connection with
the mistake.

All of the parties to this contract erroneously assumed that the property
transferred by the vendors to the vendees was suitable for human habitation
and could be utilized to generate rental income. The fundamental nature of
these assumptions is indicated by the fact that their invalidity changed the character of the property transferred, thereby frustrating, indeed precluding, Mr.
and Mrs. Pickles' intended use of the real estate. Although the Pickleses are
disadvantaged by enforcement of the contract, performance is advantageous
to the Messerlys, as the property at issue is less valuable absent its income-
earning potential. Nothing short of rescission can remedy the mistake. Thus,
the parties' mistake as to a basic assumption materially affects the agreed performances of the parties.

Despite the significance of the mistake made by the parties, we reverse the
Court of Appeals because we conclude that equity does not justify the remedy
sought by Mr. and Mrs. Pickles.

Rescission is an equitable remedy which is granted only in the sound discretion of the court. A court need not grant rescission in every case in which the
mutual mistake relates to a basic assumption and materially affects the agreed
performance of the parties.

In cases of mistake by two equally innocent parties, we are required, in the exercise of our equitable powers, to determine which blameless party should assume the loss resulting from the misapprehension they shared. Normally that can only be done by drawing upon our "own notions of what is reasonable and just under all the surrounding circumstances".[12]

Equity suggests that, in this case, the risk should be allocated to the purchasers. We are guided to that conclusion, in part, by the standards announced in § 154 of the Restatement of Contracts 2d, for determining when a party bears the risk of mistake. Section 154(a) suggests that the court should look first to whether the parties have agreed to the allocation of the risk between themselves. While there is no express assumption in the contract by either party of the risk of the property becoming uninhabitable, there was indeed some agreed allocation of the risk to the vendees by the incorporation of an "as is" clause into the contract which, we repeat, provided:

> "Purchaser has examined this property and agrees to accept same in its present condition. There are no other or additional written or oral understandings."

That is a persuasive indication that the parties considered that, as between them, such risk as related to the "present condition" of the property should lie with the purchaser. If the "as is" clause is to have any meaning at all, it must be interpreted to refer to those defects which were unknown at the time that the contract was executed.[13] Thus, the parties themselves assigned the risk of loss to Mr. and Mrs. Pickles.[14]

We conclude that Mr. and Mrs. Pickles are not entitled to the equitable remedy of rescission and, accordingly, reverse the decision the Court of Appeals.

WILLIAMS, C.J., and COLEMAN, FITZGERALD, KAVANAGH and LEVIN, JJ., concur.

RILEY, J., not participating.

Comprehension and Thought Questions:

1. Which fact did the Pickleses allege both parties were mistaken about?

2. How did the court determine that the mistake was about a fact that existed pre-contract-formation? Did that matter?

---

12. [14] Hathaway v. Hudson, 256 Mich. 702, 239 N.W. 859, quoting 9 C.J., p. 1161.

13. [15] An "as is" clause waives those implied warranties which accompany the sale of a new home, Tibbitts v. Openshaw, 18 Utah 2d 442, 425 P.2d 160 (1967), or the sale of goods. M.C.L. § 440.2316(3)(a); M.S.A. § 19.2316(3)(a). Since implied warranties protect against latent defects, an "as is" clause will impose upon the purchaser the assumption of the risk of latent defects, such as an inadequate sanitation system, even when there are no implied warranties.

14. [16] An "as is" clause does not preclude a purchaser from alleging fraud or misrepresentation as a basis for rescission. See 97 A.L.R.2d 849. However, Mr. and Mrs. Pickles did not appeal the trial court's finding that there was no fraud or misrepresentation, so we are bound thereby.

3. What test did the court use to determine whether the Pickleses could avoid the contract on the basis of that mistake?

4. How did the court apply that test to the facts of this case?

5. Why did the court shift the risk of the mistake to the Pickleses? Do you think the court should have allocated the risk to them on the grounds that it did?

Hypothetical Variations:

1. What if the Messerlys knew that the septic tank was defective before entering into the contract with the Pickleses? → *Unilateral mistake; diff*

2. What if the Pickleses were instead mistaken about the market for rental properties such that, after closing, they could not find anyone to rent out the apartments in the building they bought? *not relevant*

PRACTICE PROBLEM 16-5

An Ohio real estate development company decides to enter into a construction contract with a state-licensed contractor to build condominiums. The day before the contract is signed, the Ohio contractors' licensing board decides to permit any contractor that is licensed anywhere in the United States to qualify automatically as licensed in Ohio. Neither the real estate development company nor the state-licensed contractor believed the Ohio contractors licensing board would make this change. Overnight, thousands of contractors descend on Ohio and begin soliciting business, which drops the market rate for construction services. → *not a mistake*   *seems to go more to the subjective value*

1. Did the parties make a mistake? Can the real estate development company excuse nonperformance under the contract because of mutual mistake or unilateral mistake? Can the contractor? Who would want to avoid the contract due to this change? *→ development co. - b/c they are the adversely affected party*

2. Assume that in negotiating the terms of the contract, the contractor informed the real estate development company that he was (apparently incorrectly) told by the chairperson of the contractor's regulatory board that the board was extremely unlikely to permit contractors licensed in other states to qualify automatically in Ohio. Does that change your answer? *PQ?*

Contractor's fault → not development mistake   *→ mutual mistake, but still doesn't but can still happen change anything*

E. CHANGED CIRCUMSTANCES: IMPRACTICABILITY AND FRUSTRATION OF PURPOSE

The mistake doctrine discussed above potentially excuses a party from a contract due to a mistake about facts occurring *before the contract is entered into,* though the facts are revealed after the contract is formed. However, changed circumstances occurring *after the contract is entered into* can sometimes excuse a party's performance under a contract. This may seem counterintuitive, since a contract is supposed to allocate the risk between the parties with respect to their respective performances. In other words, the parties agreed that they would each be responsible to perform and strictly liable for failing to do so, so it may seem odd that there are doctrines that intervene and excuse performance based on future changed circumstances. These doctrines, however, are based on the lack of fault of the party seeking to employ the excuse and, perhaps more importantly, the contract having been entered into based on a shared assumption that the changed circumstance would never occur. Thus, as with the mistake doctrine discussed above, these doctrines also turn on the parties' basic assumptions going into the contract.

For example, parties to a supply contract might have reasonably assumed when entering into the contract that there would not be an outbreak of war that would prevent the supplier from supplying ordered goods. If there is an outbreak of war that does in fact prevent the supplier from performing, under this doctrine, the supplier might be excused, either temporarily or permanently, depending on how long the war lasts (assuming that the supplier did not start the war).

The Restatement divides this changed circumstance doctrine into three separate categories: impossibility, impracticability, and frustration of purpose. **Impossibility** refers to the literal impossibility of a party performing a contract due to a changed circumstance. That might occur, for example, where a party necessary to the contract dies. **Impracticability** refers to an uncontemplated and uncontrollable event that makes it unreasonably more difficult, dangerous, or expensive for a party to perform. **Frustration of purpose** refers to an uncontemplated and uncontrollable event that virtually eliminates the value of the other party's performance.

Again, these doctrines all contemplate a changed circumstance that occurs post-contract. However, they differ based on the *effect* of that changed circumstance on a party. Where a post-contract change occurs that does not impair either party's ability to perform, but makes that performance largely without value for one of the parties, then frustration of purpose is the relevant analytical excuse doctrine. Where a post-contract change occurs that significantly and adversely affects a party's ability to perform, then impracticability is the relevant analytical excuse doctrine. Because a changed circumstance can potentially have many effects on a party, one event might in fact give rise to an excuse under several of these defenses.

Of course, all of these doctrines presume that the party seeking to be excused did not cause the post-contract change, meaning that the change was not her fault. If a party caused the changed circumstance to occur, she cannot later be excused from the consequences of that change under these doctrines.

↑ Corona??

Moreover, as with the mistake doctrine, a party cannot avoid a contract under any of these defenses where it expressly assumed the risk of that event in the contract.

The following is the Restatement's description of these excuses:

§ 261 Discharge by Supervening Impracticability

Where, after a contract is made, a party's performance is made impracticable without his fault by the occurrence of an event the non-occurrence of which was a basic assumption on which the contract was made, his duty to render that performance is discharged, unless the language or the circumstances indicate the contrary.

§ 265 Discharge by Supervening Frustration

Where, after a contract is made, a party's principal purpose is substantially frustrated without his fault by the occurrence of an event the non-occurrence of which was a basic assumption on which the contract was made, his remaining duties to render performance are discharged, unless the language or the circumstances indicate the contrary.

These doctrines are typically thought to capture events occurring after the contract is made that arise out of either "acts of God" or acts of third parties. Thus, they could capture changes in law, assuming that the new law is not the "fault" of one of the parties. Again, if the supervening event occurs as a result of the fault of the party seeking to be excused, then it is not covered by this section. Note that if the supervening event occurs as a result of the fault of the other party not seeking the excuse, that also would not be covered by this doctrine. However, in that situation, the aggrieved party would likely have a claim for breach.

To see what situations these doctrines cover, imagine that you hired Peter Performer to sing at your wedding and signed a written contract promising to pay him $5,000 to do so. If Peter dies before the wedding, Peter (and his estate) will be excused from performing in the event you choose to sue his estate for breach. In this instance, both parties assumed that Peter would be alive on the day of the wedding and therefore would be able to sing, and his death would make it impossible for him to perform. Thus, it would excuse him and his estate from liability for breach. Similarly, imagine that you hired Peter Performer to sing at the grand opening of your new office building on May 1. If the office building burns to the ground on April 16, then you would potentially be excused from paying Peter, since both parties assumed that the building would be in existence on May 1, and Peter cannot perform at the building since it does not exist. Here, too, performance might be seen as impossible since the subject matter for the contract has been destroyed. In both of these examples, the parties' basic assumption at the time of contracting—that a person or property necessary to perform the contract would be alive or would exist, respectively—has been undermined. Moreover, in both of these circumstances, these supervening events where not the fault of the party seeking to be excused. Finally, the facts do not indicate that the contract allocated the risk of these events to the nonperforming party.

A changed circumstance might give rise only to a temporary excuse under the doctrines discussed in this section. Thus, if a changed circumstance is temporary, the excuse might only be temporary. Similarly, if a party can make alternate arrangements to mitigate the effects of a changed circumstance, that party might be excused only so long as is needed to put those alternate arrangements in place.

Thus, for example, if a hurricane shuts down a computer screen manufacturing facility in Texas for one week, that manufacturer might be excused from performing its contracts with the buyer for a week, assuming the manufacturer could resume its operations after that week. It would not, however, be permanently excused from its contracts because of the short-lived changed circumstance.

Keep in mind how the doctrines discussed in this section relate to the mistake doctrine discussed in the prior section. Both doctrines potentially excuse a party where facts and circumstances that are extrinsic to the transaction itself, but that nevertheless are important to the transaction, are different from what the party knew or was expecting. However, they differ as to *when* those facts and circumstances arose. While mistake generally relates to a mistake about facts *existing at the time or before the parties entered into the contract*, the doctrines discussed in this section generally cover circumstances that changed *post-contract*.

The following classic case exemplifies a situation in which a party is excused where the contemplated context for performance has changed. As you read the case, keep in mind that it is an old English case. Thus, its format and presentation appear different from most other cases in this book. However, you should still be able to pull the relevant information from this historic case. Consider whether you believe that the result serves the policy concerns of contract law regarding predictability and freedom of contract. What other policy concerns are implicated? Did the judge reach the right result from a policy perspective?

Krell v. Henry
United Kingdom Court of Appeal
2 KB 740 (1903)

Appeal from a decision of Darling, J. [against the plaintiff]

The plaintiff, Paul Krell, sued the defendant, C.S. Henry, for £50, the balance of a sum of £75, for which the defendant had agreed to hire a flat at 56A, Pall Mall on the days of June 26 and 27, for the purpose of viewing the processions to be held in connection with the coronation of His Majesty. The defendant denied his liability, and counterclaimed for the return of the sum of £25, which had been paid as a deposit, on the ground that, the processions not having taken place owing to the serious illness of the King, there had been a total failure of consideration for the contract entered into by him.

. . .

Vaughan WILLIAMS, L.J. read the following written judgment:

The real question in this case is the extent of the application in English law of the principle [found] in Taylor v Caldwell. That case at least makes it clear that

> "where, from the nature of the contract, it appears that the parties must from the beginning have known that it could not be fulfilled unless, when the time for the fulfilment of the contract arrived, some particular specified thing continued to exist, so that when entering into the contract they must have contemplated such continuing existence as the foundation of what was to be done; there, in the absence of any express or implied warranty that the thing shall exist, the contract is not to be construed as a positive contract, but as subject to an implied condition that the parties shall be excused in case, before breach, performance becomes impossible from the perishing of the thing without default of the contractor"

. . .

What are the facts of the present case? The contract is contained in two letters of 20 June 1902, which passed between the defendant and the plaintiff's agent, Mr Cecil Bisgood. These letters do not mention the coronation, but speak merely of the taking of Mr Krell's chambers, or, rather, of the use of them, in the daytime of 26 and 27 June 1902, for the sum of 75 pounds, 25 pounds then paid, balance 50 pounds to be paid on the 24th. But the affidavits, which by agreement between the parties are to be taken as stating the facts of the case, show that the plaintiff exhibited on his premises, third floor, 56A, Pall Mall, an announcement to the effect that windows to view the royal coronation processions were to be let, and that the defendant was induced by that announcement to apply to the housekeeper on the premises, who said that the owner was willing to let the suite of rooms for the purpose of seeing the royal procession for both days, but not nights, of 26 and 27 June. In my judgment, the use of the rooms was let and taken for the purpose of seeing the royal processions. It was not a demise of the rooms or even an agreement to let and take the rooms. It was a licence to use rooms for a particular purpose and none other. And in my judgment the taking place of those processions on the days proclaimed along the proclaimed route, which passed 56A, Pall Mall, was regarded by both contracting parties as the foundation of the contract. I think that it cannot reasonably be supposed to have been in the contemplation of the contracting parties, when the contract was made, that the coronation would not be held on the proclaimed days, or the processions not take place on those days along the proclaimed route; and I think that the words imposing on the defendant the obligation to accept and pay for the use of the rooms for the named days, although general and unconditional, were not used with reference to the possibility of the particular contingency which afterwards occurred.

. . .

The test seems to be, whether the event which causes the impossibility was or might have been anticipated and guarded against.

. . .

I think this appeal ought to be dismissed.

Comprehension Thoughts and Questions:

1. Why did the court determine that the occurrence of the royal procession was essential to the contract? *"foundation" of the K*

2. Why did it matter that the occurrence of the royal procession was essential to the contract? *implied assumption that it would happen - basis for K*

3. What problems do you see with a court determining that a particular event was essential to, or the "foundation of," a contract?

→ freedom of K - predictability - wasn't written in as a condition

Hypothetical Variations:

no knowledge of K - not a basic assumption of the K

1. What if the contract had been between Henry and a cab driver hired to take Henry to the flat? Do you think that would have changed the court's analysis? What if it was a contract for a limousine to transport Henry? *→ maybe knowing*

2. How do you think it would have affected the court's analysis if Krell had not known Henry's motivation for reserving the room? *dates occur*

3. Would the outcome have been different if Krell was also planning to throw himself a 40th birthday party in the room? *might still occur, not like the room*

The following is a more modern example of a court applying the frustration doctrine. As you read it, consider why the frustration doctrine applied rather than the impracticability doctrine. Also, think about what this case says about who needs to raise an affirmative defense and when.

JB Pool Management, LLC v. Four Seasons at Smithville Homeowners Association, Inc.

Superior Court of New Jersey
431 N.J. Super. 233 (2009)

SABATINO, J.A.D.

I.

The plaintiff and counterclaim-defendant in this case, JB Pool Management, LLC, ("JB Pool") is a private company that provides lifeguards and pool maintenance services to various customers in New Jersey. Defendant-counter-claimant Four Seasons at Smithville Homeowners Association, Inc. ("Four Seasons" or "the association") is a not-for-profit entity that maintains the common property of a residential community in Galloway Township. The retirement community has approximately 1,100 houses. The condominium property includes both an outdoor pool and an indoor pool for use by the association's members and their guests.

In or about 2004, JB Pool began entering into annual agreements to provide lifeguard and pool management services to Four Seasons for the indoor pool and the outdoor pool, as well as aerobics classes. Separate contracts were executed for the indoor pool and the outdoor pool. The successive contracts typically covered a full calendar year from January 1 through December 31.

As to calendar year 2008, the relevant period for this lawsuit, the parties' indoor pool contract called for JB Pool to receive an annual fee of $61,880. The contract specified that the annual fee was to be paid in monthly installments of $5,688, except for July and August when the monthly installments were reduced to $2,500.

One lifeguard was to be provided by JB Pool at all times during the hours specified by the contract. Among other things, the lifeguard was responsible for keeping the pool clean, vacuuming it, backwashing the filter, cleaning pool filter cartridges, and maintaining the pool area in a neat and orderly condition. JB Pool was further obligated to provide chemicals to treat the water in the pool, and to test the water daily. The contract also required JB Pool to maintain a $2 million liability insurance policy, naming the association as an additional insured. The indoor pool was scheduled to be open year-round, except for New Year's Day, Thanksgiving, and Christmas.

Significantly for the present dispute, the contract contained the following terms that would apply in the event of a pool closure:

DATES AND TIMES OF SERVICES:

The pool will be open during the stated dates and times with the following exceptions:

1. *Inclement weather*—[JB Pool] will determine if the weather is unsatisfactory—for pool operation based on the guidelines from the NEW JERSEY STATE SANITARY CODE:

"Outdoor bathing shall be prohibited during an electrical storm."

If the pool is determined not to be able to be opened before 4:00 p.m. on any day, the pool will be closed the entire day. If the pool must be closed at least one hour after 4 p.m. on a given day, then it will not be reopened that day. *There will be no reduction in charges as outlined in this agreement.* The Customer will be notified of each closing.

2. [JB Pool] will have *no liability for its failure to perform this Agreement, or any part thereof, where such failure is attributable to reasons beyond its control, including but not limited to inclement weather, acts of God, acts of war, labor disputes, strikes, riots, fire or other casualty, or customer requested closing. There will be no reduction in charges of the contract amount for any closing.* [Emphasis added.]

The 2008 contract further provided that it "shall be governed by the laws of the State of New Jersey." It was signed in November 2007 by JB Pool's president, Jacqueline Bartilucci, and a representative of Four Seasons.

Toward the end of January 2008, shortly after the annual contract period began, mold was discovered in the indoor pool area. The pool was closed while efforts to remediate the mold problem were undertaken, apparently at the direction of the county board of health. Although initially the parties had hoped that the mold problem could be abated quickly, the pool was not reopened until after Labor Day in September 2008. Consequently, the indoor pool was closed for over seven full months (February, March, April, May, June, July, and August) of the twelve-month contract period for 2008. The outdoor pool remained open.

For the first three full months while the pool was closed (February, March, and April), JB Pool billed Four Seasons its usual monthly fee, and Four Seasons paid those sums.[15] However, as the problem progressed, discussions took place in about April 2008 between the association's Pool Committee and Bartilucci. According to Bartilucci, and as acknowledged by the testimony of Josephine Mongiello, who was then the Pool Committee's Chairwoman, the Pool Committee requested that the lifeguards for the indoor pool continue to be paid while the indoor pool was closed.[16] As a result of those discussions, the billing arrangements changed, at least for several months.

. . .

When the 2009 annual contract for pool services was being negotiated, Bartilucci made a proposal in a December 2008 letter to the association's property manager, Allen Haller. Specifically, Bartilucci proposed that JB Pool would "forgive" the $16,376 balance of the 2008 contract for the indoor pool, which had not been charged when the pool was closed, provided that the association agree to grant JB Pool a contract extension through December 31, 2009, and also agree to refrain from exercising its right to cancel the contract during that time.[17] Evidently, Four Seasons never accepted that particular proposal. Instead, the parties entered into a 2009 contract extension that was silent concerning the previous 2008 four-month period of nonpayment. The parties entered into another contract for 2010, which again did not address the 2008 nonpayment issue. In the meantime, the parties' relationship soured.

On July 6, 2010, JB Pool gave Four Seasons written notice that it was terminating the parties' agreement. Two days later, JB Pool sent the association an

---

15. [1] Four Seasons has not sought to recoup those initial three months of payments from JB Pool.

16. [2] The record is unclear whether the lifeguards were all reassigned to the outdoor pool or to other JB Pool customers, or whether they and the other lifeguards were able to work the same number of hours at the open locations.

17. [3] In that regard, we note that the 2008 contract had provided that either party could cancel the agreement with sixty days' notice.

invoice for $16,376 relating to the four unpaid months from 2008. Four Seasons declined to pay that invoice, thereby precipitating the present litigation.

In September 2010, JB Pool filed a three-count complaint in the Law Division against Four Seasons, alleging breach of contract (count one), unjust enrichment (count two), and quantum meruit (count three). The complaint sought payment of $22,357.25, a sum which apparently included late fees.

In October 2010, Four Seasons filed an answer denying liability, along with ten enumerated separate defenses, and a counterclaim alleging that JB Pool had negligently damaged the association's indoor pool cover when it closed the pool. . . . Notably, the separate defenses did not mention the contractual doctrines of impossibility of performance nor frustration of purpose.

About a year later, Four Seasons moved for summary judgment, which JB Pool opposed. In its reply brief in support of that motion, Four Seasons asserted, for the first time in the lawsuit, that JB Pool's claims for contract damages were precluded by the doctrine of impossibility of performance. The reply brief cited Sections 237, 239, and 267 of the Restatement (Second) of Contracts (1981) (the "Second Restatement"). The brief discussed the legal principles delineating impossibility and various reported decisions applying that particular doctrine of contract avoidance. The reply brief did not mention, however, the related doctrine of frustration of purpose.

The trial court denied summary judgment and the matter proceeded to a three-day jury trial in March 2012. The jury heard testimony from Bartilucci, Mongiello, Haller, and the former President of the association's Board of Trustees, Katherine McGovern. The jury also considered numerous exhibits including the contract documents, JB Pool's invoices, and various written communications between the parties.

The trial testimony indicated that during the four-month hiatus in 2008 when the indoor pool was closed, JB Pool provided only limited services to the association, which specifically included draining the pool at the association's request. Bartilucci testified in this regard that JB Pool continued to test, backwash, and vacuum the pool while it was closed, although those activities were not acknowledged by the association's property manager, Haller. In addition, JB Pool continued to maintain the insurance coverage called for under the contract. Even so, it is undisputed that no lifeguard services were provided by JB Pool for the indoor pool while it was closed. Because JB Pool did not quantify its expenses for the limited services it performed while the pool was closed, the trial judge ultimately dismissed its claims for unjust enrichment and quantum meruit before summation.

During the midst of the trial, JB Pool's counsel objected to Four Seasons presenting any evidence or legal argument concerning the doctrine of impossibility. Emphasizing that the doctrine had not been identified in the association's pleadings as an affirmative defense, counsel argued that JB Pool had been deprived of fair notice of that theory and an opportunity to conduct discovery concerning it. The association's lawyer countered that there was no unfair surprise. He noted that the theory had been elucidated in the briefing on the summary judgment motion, also pointing out that further discovery had been conducted after the motion was denied. The trial judge reserved decision on the issue, permitting the trial to proceed in the meantime.

The judge ultimately addressed the impossibility issue during the charge conference. In essence, the judge found that JB Pool could not have been surprised by the association's contention that the mold-related shutdown of the indoor pool excused its monthly payment obligations during the closure period. However, the judge observed that the language in the model jury charge concerning the impossibility doctrine did not precisely fit the present case. The judge noted that the impossibility doctrine pertains to situations in which a supervening event makes a defendant's obligations impractical or impossible to perform. Here, perhaps recognizing that Four Seasons had the ability to pay JB Pool when the indoor pool was closed, the judge found that the impossibility doctrine was not on point. Instead, the judge observed, the related doctrine of frustration of purpose where—performance may be excused where the "main purpose" of a contract is frustrated or destroyed—was more appropriately implicated.

JB Pool's counsel objected to the court interjecting the doctrine of frustration of purpose. She repeated her contentions of unfair surprise and prejudice, and the lack of discovery on that issue. The court rejected those contentions, finding that neither party had contemplated an extended closure of the pool during the contract period. Meanwhile, the association's counsel acceded to the court providing a jury charge on frustration rather than impossibility, although he expressed "some chagrin" about having overlooked the charge in his trial preparation.

Consequently, counsel addressed frustration principles, in an impromptu fashion, in their respective summations. Counsel also addressed the association's separate claim that JB Pool had waived its right to collect on the unpaid four months of charges. The court then issued the following charge to the jury on frustration of purpose, tracking the language of the model charge and notably making a judicial finding that "the purpose of the underlying contract was that the [indoor] pool would be opened for use."

> Now, sometimes, if the main purpose of a contract is frustrated or destroyed, the plaintiff may not enforce the contract against the defendant. That is, the plaintiff may not make the defendant perform what the contract required or make the defendant pay money damages for failing to do what the contract required.
>
> The defendant claims that the main purpose of the contract in this case was frustrated or destroyed, because this pool was closed by the State due to mold infestation. The plaintiff denies this.

In order to prove a defense based on frustration of purpose, the defendant must first show, by clear and convincing evidence, that the plaintiff and the defendant implicitly agreed that their contract and their promise were conditioned on the pool being open for use.

That is a question for me to decide, and I have found that the parties did implicitly agree that the purpose of the underlying contract was that the pool would be opened for use. That formed the foundation of the contract. But, this does not end the issue.

Defendant must still persuade you, by clear and convincing evidence, that the condition was not merely one of several, but was the essence of the contract. Defendant must also show that the closing of the pool by the mold occurred, that it occurred through no fault of the defendant, and that it totally destroyed the whole purpose of the contract.

It is important to keep in mind that only those circumstances that the defendant could not reasonably be expected to have known will excuse the defendant's performance based on frustration of purpose. If the defendant ... should reasonably have been expected to be aware of the circumstances that frustrated the contract's purpose, then the defendant may not be excused from [d]efendant's obligation to perform the contract.

[Emphasis added.]

During deliberations, the jurors requested, among other things, that the court clarify the charge on frustration of purpose. The jurors also requested a written copy of the charges as a whole. The judge explained to the jurors that, given the logistics of the charge's preparation, he was unable to furnish them with a written copy of the charge, but did repeat the frustration charge orally in open court with the consent of both counsel.

After further deliberations, the jury returned a verdict the next day. By a six-to-two vote, the jurors concluded that Four Seasons had not breached its obligations and that it owed JB Pool nothing further on the 2008 contract. The jury separately and unanimously found that Four Seasons had prevailed on its counterclaim regarding the damaged pool cover, and awarded $1,535.20 in counterclaim damages.

JB Pool now appeals the final judgment, principally arguing that the trial court improperly and prejudicially charged the jury on the doctrine of frustration of purpose, despite the fact that Four Seasons had not raised the doctrine as an affirmative defense in its pleadings. JB Pool contends that by such omission, Four Seasons waived the affirmative defense. JB Pool further argues that the trial court erred in failing to enforce the language in the contract that "[t]here will be no reduction in charges of the contract amount for any closing." (Emphasis added). Finally, JB Pool contends that the counterclaim award should be vacated because the court failed to instruct the jury on the elements of negligence with respect to the proofs relating to the pool cover.

II.

A.

doctrine

The respective concepts of impossibility of performance and frustration of purpose are, in essence, doctrinal siblings within the law of contracts. Both doctrines may apply to certain situations in which a party's obligations under a contract can be excused or mitigated because of the occurrence of a supervening event. The supervening event must be one that had not been anticipated at the time the contract was created, and one that fundamentally alters the nature of the parties' ongoing relationship.

Both the impossibility and frustration doctrines are concerned with "[a]n extraordinary circumstance [that] may make performance [of a contract] so vitally different from what was reasonably to be expected as to alter the essential nature of that performance." *Second Restatement* ch. 11, intro. note at 309. The doctrines stem from the concept of an implied condition within a contract. As this court observed decades ago in *Edwards, supra,* "courts under a more modern philosophy [of contract law] may and do exercise the power to infer from the nature and substance of the contract and the surrounding circumstances that a critical and vital condition which is not expressed constituted a foundation on which the parties contracted." 20 N.J. Super. at 57, 89 A.2d 264 (emphasis added). "[T]he concept is that a contract is to be considered 'subject to the implied condition that the parties shall be excused in case, before breach, the state of things constituting the fundamental basis of the contract ceases to exist without default of either of the parties.'" *A-Leet Leasing Corp. v. Kingshead Corp.,* 150 N.J. Super. 384, 397, 375 A.2d 1208 (App. Div.) (emphasis added) (quoting *Edwards, supra,* 20 N.J. Super. at 54, 89 A.2d 264), *certif. denied,* 75 N.J. 528, 384 A.2d 508 (1977); *see also Facto v. Pantagis,* 390 N.J. Super. 227, 231, 915 A.2d 59 (App. Div. 2007) (applying similar principles of implied condition to a claim of "impracticability" of performance).

A successful defense of impossibility (or impracticability) of performance excuses a party from having to perform its contract obligations, where performance has become literally impossible, or at least inordinately more difficult, because of the occurrence of a supervening event that was not within the original contemplation of the contracting parties.

By comparison, under the related doctrine of frustration of purpose, the obligor's performance can still be carried out, but the supervening event fundamentally has changed the nature of the parties' overall bargain.

The *Second Restatement* expresses the concept of frustration of purpose in Section 265 as follows:

> Where, after a contract is made, a party's principal purpose is *substantially frustrated without his fault* by the occurrence of an event the non-occurrence of which was *a basic assumption* on which the contract was made, his remaining

duties to render performance are discharged, *unless the language or the circum-stances indicate the contrary.*
   [Emphasis added.]

So defined, frustration of purpose "deals with the problem that arises when a change in circumstances makes one party's performance worthless to the other, frustrating his purpose in making the contract." *Id.* at cmt. (a). "The frustration must be so severe that it is not fairly to be regarded as the risks that [the party invoking the doctrine] assumed under the contract." *Ibid.*

   . . .

A key facet of the frustration of purpose doctrine, as it is applied in this state, is that "relief from performance of contractual obligations on this theory will not be lightly granted[.]" *A-Leet Leasing, supra,* 150 N.J. Super. at 397, 375 A.2d 1208. The evidence satisfying the doctrine's requirements "must be clear, convincing and adequate." *Ibid.*

B.

Here, the trial judge astutely recognized that the most appropriate doctrine that might relieve Four Seasons of its contractual duties for payment to JB Pool for the four months when the indoor pool was closed is not impossibility of performance, but rather frustration of purpose. The judge correctly noted that the impossibility doctrine does not readily fit the facts of this case. Instead, the frustration of purpose doctrine, which, the judge noted, follows in the section immediately after impossibility within the model civil jury charges, is the concept that most closely relates to the association's theory here for resisting liability, in addition to its waiver defense. In this regard, the judge should be commended for his perceptiveness, as well as defense counsel for his candor to the court in acknowledging his improvident designation of the most appropriate defense as "impossibility" rather than "frustration."

The procedural problem, however, that arises here is that JB Pool's counsel was not given notice that the frustration doctrine was being invoked in this case until the charge conference, long after discovery was completed. The trial judge detected no prejudice flowing from that late notice. We respectfully disagree. Had JB Pool's trial counsel been alerted sooner that her adversary would be arguing frustration of purpose to the jury, she might well have explored the elements of that doctrine in discovery and in her trial preparation.

For example, JB Pool might have pursued discovery regarding whether any actions or inactions on the part of the association might have contributed to the mold problems that led to the pool's closure. In this regard, counsel might have deposed on that subject the governmental health officials who closed the pool, or representatives of Four Seasons, in an effort to challenge the trial court's premise that the mold problem was totally unanticipated by the association. JB Pool's attorney also might have amplified the testimony of her trial witnesses to address the intention of the parties at the time the contract was entered into, exploring whether the risk of a lengthy closure for any reason, if not mold, had been envisioned and allocated to one party or another. In that vein, JB Pool also might have undertaken to have one or more witnesses address the intended meaning of the contract's force majeure clause, as well as its specific related language that the contract charges would not be reduced for "any closing."

To be sure, we cannot ascribe significant blame to Four Seasons for this failure of notice because neither the Court Rules, as presently written, nor the present case law in our State, explicitly require the doctrine of frustration of purpose to be pleaded as an affirmative defense.

. . .

Given the unsettled state of the law, we do not believe that imposing such a pleading requirement on Four Seasons in this case after the fact would be consistent with principles of substantial justice. Instead, we hold that, in future cases, the defense of frustration of purpose, or impossibility of performance, be raised in a responsive pleading, unless exceptional circumstances excuse that oversight. Indeed, the model jury charges already treat these doctrines as affirmative defenses. Hence, the appropriate remedy in the present case is to vacate the final judgment and remand for additional discovery germane to the frustration defense and a new trial.

C.

A second and independent reason for reversal and a remand in this case stems from the trial judge's analysis of the frustration of purpose elements as applied to the parties' contract and the trial record. During the charge conference, the judge offered the following reasons for issuing a frustration charge to the jurors:

It's clear to me, and it's clear to me by clear and convincing evidence, that the— this contract was conditioned upon the pool being opened for use. *Now, when we had testimony from Plaintiff's principal, and it was observed by the Court, and I believe significant to the Court, with regard to the clause in the contract, the operative clause that is, you know, of concern, about whether or not services are rendered and payment is made, something to that effect, and I'm paraphrasing, because I don't have the contract in front of me.*

But, as explained by Plaintiff's principal, herself, out of her own mouth, was that it did reasonably seem that this—get paid, you know, whether the pool was used, was, to use her own words, this is a quote, "*rain time.*"

And, it seems, that's reasonable, what they're talking about. Not that this pool is down for seven months or four months or one year or something like that.

So, the Court is satisfied by clear and convincing evidence that the underlying purpose of this contract was conditioned upon the pool being open for use. Not, like, a couple days, it's raining and you can't—the people can't use the pool, or as the plaintiff's principal indicated, lightning is going on, you can't use the indoor pool because it, you know, is not safe.

So, that's the case, it seems to me. And, the frustration of purpose is exactly what we have here.

At least, enough to charge the jury. They have to make a decision.

[Emphasis added.]

The judge's reference to "rain time" concerns the following trial testimony of Bartilucci:

Q. Okay. Now is there a provision in P-1 that deals with the situation when the pool is closed?

A. Yes. *In our contracts, because we deal with weather issues all the time and we have staff that we have to pay, so in the contract it states that the contract, there'll be no reduction in price in the contract if the pool has to be closed through no fault of JB Pool Management. So that means that they'll pay us whether it's thundering and lightning out and we can't open the pool or, and even with an indoor pool you can't have it open during thunder and lightning storms,* so there's times that we did have to close the pool and send the staff home, and that's the standard contract.

Q. Okay. And why is that clause in your contract?

A. Well because we do pay the guards when they're not there. They get paid a certain amount for, we call it rain time. We have to still operate the pool, there's still expenses. The contracts, the yearly contract, the expenses for the year are, we break them down into these payments to make it easier for the associations to pay, but like our insurance when the pool's closed, we can't cancel our insurance, the insurance continues. *We still have expenses we have to pay so,* and that's just standard operating for us.

[Emphasis added.]

Although Bartilucci's testimony certainly provides some evidence about the intent of the parties in allocating the risks of a supervening event that might frustrate the contract's purpose, her testimony is not exhaustive or necessarily conclusive. Notably, none of the association's representatives who testified addressed the intended meaning of the contract language themselves. We also note that the language within the contract's operative paragraph is literally unconditional, declaring that "[t]here will be *no reduction* in charges of the contract amount for *any* closing." (Emphasis added).

The trial judge did not comment explicitly about those words within the contract and attempt to reconcile his analysis with them. Nor did the judge make a finding that the words of the contract provision were ambiguous, or that there was a need to consult parol evidence to determine the parties' intent. These omissions are potentially significant for, as the *Second Restatement* instructs, a party's duties to perform are not discharged under the frustration doctrine where "the [contract] language or the circumstances indicate the contrary." *Id.* at § 265.

As we have noted, the law generally prohibits "the enforcement of an implied contract or an implied provision that conflicts or is inconsistent with the parties' express contract[.]" *Kas Oriental Rugs, Inc. v. Ellman,* 394 N.J. Super. 278, 287, 926 A.2d 387 (App. Div.), *certif. denied,* 192 N.J. 74, 926 A.2d 858 (2007). On remand, the proofs concerning the mutually intended meaning of the contract's "no reduction" language should be amplified. The trial court should then reexamine its determination in light of those amplified proofs and decide whether the consideration of such extrinsic proofs are warranted to resolve any ambiguity in the contract language.

. . .

Understanding the Case:

1. *Waiver:* The court also addressed, in omitted portions of the opinion, whether JB Pool had waived its right to collect the unpaid 2008 fees (the $16,376) when it did not insist on payment of them earlier and also when the 2009 contract did not address resolution of those charges. Because it was unclear from the record whether the jury had found in Four Seasons' favor because of the waiver defense as opposed to the frustration of purpose defense, the court made it clear that on remand, Four Seasons still would be permitted to argue that JB Pool had waived its rights.

Comprehension and Thought Questions:

1. Why was impossibility not an appropriate defense in this case?

2. Do you think impracticability could have been pleaded in this case? What about mistake?

3. Why did it matter to the court whether frustration of purpose was pleaded as an affirmative defense?

4. Why did the court excuse Four Seasons for failing to plead frustration of purpose correctly and timely as an affirmative defense? Why was the court not concerned that its decision would not lead to future cases where the plaintiff is not notified timely of a frustration of purpose defense?

5. In the appellate court's opinion, what did the trial court do "wrong"?

6. Based on your review of the contract terms and the testimony reflected in the court's decision, do you think the frustration of purpose defense should be successful when the trial court reconsiders it?

Hypothetical Variations:

1. What if the contract had included a clause that provided "JB Pool shall be entitled to be paid its fees under this Contract, regardless of whether any services are rendered, in the event that the pool is closed for any reason and JB Pool is unable to perform its obligations hereunder." Do you think that clause would have defeated a frustration of purpose defense in this case?

2. What if clause 2 of the Dates and Times of Service was not included in the contract? Do you think the appeals court still would have reached the same conclusion? Would Four Seasons potentially have been permanently or temporarily excused in that situation?

3. What if the mold grew around the indoor pool because Four Seasons had improperly maintained the seal for that room?

PRACTICE PROBLEM 16-6

1. Laura hires Catherine under a one-year contract to be the accountant for her new company. Catherine, however, is recalled by the Army and is deployed overseas for the year. Is Catherine's duty to perform excused under the contract? *impracticl*

2. Harry owns an apartment complex and wants to permit his renters to use the services at a local laundromat free of charge. Harry enters into a contract with the laundromat's owner, under which Harry is to pay $5,000 per month, and the laundromat will provide dry-cleaning services to all apartment residents up to twice a month. The entire condominium complex burns to the ground due to a spreading wildfire, and Harry is unable to rebuild the apartment complex. If Harry refuses to make future payments to the laundromat's owner, is his duty to make monthly payments excused? *frustration of purpose*

3. Thomas agrees to sell athletic socks to a sports team. Before Thomas can begin manufacturing the socks in his factory, the factory is destroyed by a fire started by a lightning strike. Athletic socks meeting the contractual specifications could be purchased from other sellers. Thomas does not deliver the socks when required. Is Thomas's duty to deliver the socks excused? *not excused.*

F. SUPERVENING EVENTS AND FORCE MAJEURE CLAUSES

As you saw in *JB Pool*, rather than relying on common law conceptions of what constitutes a supervening event that excuses performance, contracting parties can "contract around" these excuse doctrines by allocating between the parties the risk of future events occurring. Thus, a contract can either expressly excuse a party from performing upon the occurrence of specified future events, or it might state that a party assumes all risks despite future changed circumstances.

One of the typical clauses that parties include in their contracts to contract around these excuse doctrines is called a **force majeure clause**. These clauses attempt to define the scope of the unanticipated events that will excuse a party's performance under a contract. Sometimes they purport to exclusively define what events will excuse a party, while other force majeure clauses simply set out nonexclusive examples of types of events will excuse a party's performance.

The following is a sample force majeure clause:

> No party to this Agreement is liable to any other party for losses due to, or if it is unable to perform its obligations under the terms of this Agreement because of, acts of God, fire, war, terrorism, floods, strikes, electrical outages, equipment or transmission failure, or other causes reasonably beyond its control.

As the following case demonstrates, including a force majeure clause will not always excuse a party. The parties may still disagree about whether a particular event qualifies as a force majeure under the force majeure clause under the contract. While reviewing the following case, consider whether the parties realistically could and should have been able to draft a better force majeure clause to address the supervening event.

Pillsbury Co. v. Wells Dairy, Inc.
Supreme Court of Iowa
752 N.W.2d 430 (2008)

WIGGINS, Justice.

. . .

I. BACKGROUND FACTS AND PROCEEDINGS

On or about January 28, 1999, Pillsbury entered into a production contract with Wells for the production of Haagen-Dazs ice cream. On March 27 there was an explosion at Wells' south ice cream manufacturing facility in Le Mars.

. . .

C. The Force-Majeure Clause

The production contract between Wells and Pillsbury contained a force-majeure clause. The language of the clause relevant to this appeal states:

FORCE MAJEURE: Neither party will be liable for delays or suspension of performance (other than the obligation to pay for services and goods sold and delivered) caused by acts of God or governmental authority, strikes, accidents, explosions, floods, fires or the total loss of manufacturing facilities or any other cause that is beyond the reasonable control of that party ("Force Majeure") so long as that party has used its best efforts to perform despite such Force Majeure.

D. Analysis

The district court found that the force-majeure clause is ambiguous because it is reasonably susceptible to more than one interpretation. It concluded the placement of the phrase "that is beyond the reasonable control of that party" creates the ambiguity. The district court held one reasonable interpretation of the force-majeure clause is that this phrase modifies "acts of God or governmental authority, strikes, accidents, explosions, floods, fires or the total loss of manufacturing facilities or any other cause." Under this interpretation, the explosion and fire at the south ice cream manufacturing facility would not excuse Wells' nonperformance under the contract if the explosion and fire were not beyond the reasonable control of Wells.

The district court found another reasonable interpretation of the force-majeure clause is that this phrase only applies to "any other cause." Under this interpretation, the explosion and fire at the south ice cream manufacturing facility excuse Wells' performance under the contract even if the explosion and fire were within the reasonable control of Wells.

The determination of whether the language of a contract is ambiguous is ordinarily one of law for the court. We understand how the district court came to the conclusion that the placement of the phrase "that is beyond the reasonable control of that party," can make the force-majeure clause reasonably susceptible to two meanings, if the district court examined the force-majeure clause out of context with the entire agreement. However, when a court is required to make a determination of whether a clause is ambiguous, the words and phrases of sentences cannot be read in isolation. The determination of whether "an agreement is ambiguous must be reached through a process of synthesis in which words, phrases, and sentences are assigned a meaning in accordance with the apparent purpose of the agreement as a whole." *Metro Office Parks Co. v. Control Data Corp.*, 295 Minn. 348, 205 N.W.2d 121, 124 (Minn. 1973).

Applying these principals to the force-majeure clause, we disagree with the district court and find the force-majeure clause is not ambiguous. "Force majeure" is "an event that can be neither anticipated nor controlled." *Black's Law Dictionary* 657 (7th ed. 1999). A "force-majeure clause" is a clause "allocating the risk if performance becomes impossible or impracticable as a result of an event or effect that the parties could not have anticipated or controlled." *Id.* A force-majeure clause is not intended to shield a party from the normal risks associated with an agreement.

Wells claims the parties to the contract did not intend the force-majeure clause to have its common meaning; thus, Wells is relieved from performing even if a strike, accident, explosion, flood, fire or the total loss of the manufacturing facilities was caused by an event within its control. Had the parties meant to change the common meaning of the force-majeure clause, the parties should have had a discussion or negotiations regarding the definition of a force-majeure event. The record is clear that when the parties entered into the 1999 production contract they did not negotiate what would constitute a force-majeure event. The only discussion between the parties involved what would be the obligations of the parties if a force-majeure event occurred. Therefore, in light of the lack of discussion between the parties concerning the meaning of the force majeure clause, Wells' claim that the common-law meaning of the force majeure clause, Wells' claim that the common-law meaning of the force majeure clause does not apply is an unreasonable interpretation of the contract.

In addition, Wells' interpretation of the force-majeure clause is not reasonable in light of the purpose of the contract. The purpose of the contract was for Wells to provide Pillsbury with a specific amount of product in a defined period of time. When the contract is read in its entirety, the obligations of each party are described in detail. There is nothing in the language used by the parties, which describes each party's various obligations, that indicates a party's negligence would excuse nonperformance of a specific obligation. Moreover, an agreement excusing a party's performance due to that party's negligence defeats the purpose of having an agreement requiring specific performance within a specified period of time.

Wells' interpretation of the force majeure clause is inconsistent with the absence of any discussions between the parties indicating the common understanding of a force-majeure clause was not intended by the parties and with the purpose of a production contract that requires specific performance to be completed in a specified period. Therefore, the contract is not reasonably susceptible to more than one interpretation.

Accordingly, as a matter of law we find the phrase "that is beyond the reasonable control of that party" modifies all the events enumerated by the parties in the force-majeure clause. Consequently, we find that Wells is not entitled to summary judgment based on the force-majeure clause, and we reverse the district court's ruling on this issue.

. . .

VI. DISPOSITION

. . . REVERSED AND CASE REMANDED.

Understanding the Case:

1. *Force Majeure Clause and Contract Interpretation:* As discussed in Chapters 12 and 13, contracts are typically enforced "as written" and utilizing the plain meaning of terms. This court was forced to refer to the policies underlying force majeure clauses because the grammar made the scope of a particular provision ambiguous. If the clause had been drafted more clearly

with respect to that scope, it would have been easier for the court to interpret it (without regard to the underlying policies of force majeure clauses). This is why, again, it is important for you to understand why it is important for an attorney to draft clearly and precisely.

Comprehension and Thought Questions:

1. An explosion at a manufacturing facility would seem to qualify as being covered by the term "explosions" mentioned in the force majeure clause and therefore excuse Wells's performance under the contract. Why does the court disagree with that interpretation?

2. In the court's opinion, what purpose is served by force majeure clauses?

3. What contract interpretation principles does the court use to interpret the force majeure clause?

4. How would you have drafted the contract to clarify what events qualified as a force majeure (you can pick which interpretation you want to have implemented)?

5. What will the district court have to determine upon remand with respect to the explosion?

Hypothetical Variations:

1. What do you think the result would have been if the last part of the force majeure clause had ended after "facilities"? Why?

2. What if there had been a storm that took out Pillsbury's power for two weeks?

3. What if the parties' contract had not included the force majeure clause?

Now that you have studied excuses to performance, read through and answer the questions that follow the Simulation Problem for Chapter 16, which is located in Appendix A.

CHAPTER 17

Introduction to Defenses to Enforcement and the Statute of Frauds

In Chapter 16, we discussed various legal doctrines that may excuse a party's performance under a contract. Over the next five chapters, we move on to defenses that preclude enforcement of contracts that otherwise satisfy the formation requirements. These defenses generally are based on contracting circumstances, party characteristics, or behaviors that undermine the assumptions that underlie the enforceability of contracts. In other words, these defenses arise where a supervening public policy overrides the policies served by enforcing a contract—the policies of predictability and reliance, freedom of contract, and efficiency.

For example, assume that Barbara and Tony enter into a contract under which Tony agrees to kill Barbara's boss for $10,000. Here, the parties have created a bargained-for contract in which the parties have mutually assented to an exchange of Barbara's promise to pay Tony $10,000 in exchange for Tony's promise to kill Barbara's boss. Assume also that Tony kills Barbara's boss, but Barbara (foolishly) decides to not pay Tony the promised $10,000.

Here, Barbara would be foolish not to pay Tony because, given Tony's profession, he might seek an extrajudicial mechanism to enforce Barbara's promise—one that may involve a threat of bodily harm or death. But imagine Tony instead decides to sue Barbara in court to enforce her promise. Would a court order Barbara to pay? Your gut is hopefully telling you that a court surely would not enforce this promise given that hiring someone to kill someone else is a crime. By enforcing Barbara's promise, a court would be supporting the commission of a criminal act. Barbara's promise is void because it violates public policy. Chapter 21 explains when the public policy defense applies and when it prevents an otherwise validly created contract from being enforced.

To take another example, assume that Andrea wants to work as a loan officer at The Great American Bank N.A. However, The Great American Bank only hires people with finance degrees or at least three years of work experience in finance to work as loan officers. Sherri does not have this experience. But, to get the job, she tells The Great American Bank that she received a degree in finance. So The Great American Bank hires Sherri, agreeing to keep Sherri on for at least two years. When The Great American Bank finds out that Sherri lied about her degree, it fires Sherri.

Here, if Sherri were to sue The Great American Bank for breach, would a court find that the bank breached? Once again, hopefully your gut is telling you that a court would not enforce this promise, as The Great American Bank was induced to employ Sherri on the basis of her fraudulent statement about her degree. Under contract law, the Bank's promise is said to have been induced by fraud and therefore unenforceable. Chapter 20 explains when the misrepresentation defense applies and when it prevents an otherwise validly created contract from being enforced.

The next several chapters are organized by category of affirmative defense. This chapter discusses the defense to enforcement tied to certain formalities that admit or document a contract—called the Statute of Frauds. Chapter 18 discusses the defense based on the status of a contracting party, called the incapacity defense, explaining in what situations a person's lack of capacity leads to the creation of voidable obligations. Chapters 19 and 20 then discuss the various defenses to enforcement tied to the wrongful conduct of one of the contracting parties leading up to contract formation. Such defenses are referred to as "inducement" defenses because the wrongful party's conduct plays an important part in inducing (causing) the other party's assent. Finally, Chapter 21 discusses the defenses of unconscionability and public policy, both of which consider to an extent the substance of the contract.

We begin this chapter by discussing how these affirmative defenses to enforcement work in practice. As with other parts of this book, this discussion contemplates how these defenses are used in litigation as well as in a transactional context.

A. HOW DEFENSES TO ENFORCEMENT WORK IN PRACTICE

As with excuses, defenses to enforcement are most relevant in litigation, in defense to an action to enforce a contract. Thus, they are typically raised by a defendant in response to the plaintiff's claim that the defendant breached a contract. A defendant will typically respond to a plaintiff's breach claim first, by challenging the plaintiff's proof that a contract even exists. For example, a defendant may offer evidence that contradicts the plaintiff's contention that mutual assent to the contract existed. Such arguments are not *affirmative defenses*, as they simply represent a defendant attempting to contest or disprove the plaintiff's claim—a claim for which a plaintiff has the burden of proof—that a contract exists. However, even if a court does find that a contract exists, a defendant often tries to show that under an affirmative defense, either the party is excused from performing (which was discussed in the prior chapter) or the contract is not enforceable. If a validly created contract is not enforceable, a court will not award a remedy to the plaintiff.

Some of the affirmative defenses to enforcement are defenses to the enforcement of the *entire contract*. In other words, a defendant raises one of these defenses seeking to avoid the entire contract. Most of the inducement defenses work in this fashion, for the plaintiff's wrongful conduct undermines the integrity of the defendant's assent. Thus, the entire contract is tainted by the plaintiff's misconduct. However, other affirmative defenses to enforcement can serve as a basis to void only specific provisions.

Because some affirmative defenses to enforcement can be used to void only specific provisions, a party might even use one of these "defenses" when suing as a plaintiff. For example, in one common situation, a customer sues a merchant for various claims, such as fraud and violation of consumer protection statutes. The defendant then argues that the plaintiff must arbitrate those claims, per the parties' contract, which contains mandatory arbitration as the applicable dispute resolution mechanism. In response, the plaintiff argues that the arbitration clause is not enforceable because it is unconscionable (but that the remainder of the contract is enforceable). If the plaintiff is successful, it can continue to pursue its claims in court rather than in arbitration.

When a court finds that a contract or provision is **void**, that means that that contract or provision has no effect, and the court will not award a remedy to a plaintiff even if the other party failed to perform the contract or provision. In contrast, when a court finds that a contract or provision is **voidable** (i.e., capable of being voided), that means that the relevant party can decide whether or not it wants the court to enforce the contract or provision. The relevant party must then elect to void the voidable contract or provision to have that provision voided. A party elects to void a voidable provision by seeking the remedy of rescission. **Rescission** means a contract or provision is effectively cancelled and the parties are returned to their statuses before the contract or provision was made.

A party can actually waive a challenge to a voidable contract or provision, such as by seeking to enforce a contract despite the availability of a defense to enforcement. However, a party cannot waive a void contract or provision. That is because a contract or provision that is void is cancelled by operation of law, without a party requesting that relief. Whether a contract or contract provision is void or voidable depends on the affirmative defense at issue. It often also turns on whether conduct violates criminal law, or whether conduct is extremely unfair.

It is up to the party seeking to challenge the enforcement of a voidable contract to raise affirmative defenses in litigation. Thus, for example, even if a plaintiff seeks to enforce an oral contract that falls under, yet does not satisfy, the Statute of Frauds, a court will not *sua sponte* find the contract unenforceable due to the lack of a signed writing. Rather, it is up to the party seeking to enforce that contract to affirmatively argue that the contract is voidable because it falls under the Statute of Frauds and the Statute's requirements were not satisfied. However, a court (and sometimes third parties) can inquire into the availability of an affirmative defense to enforcement where the defense would make a contract or contract provision void.

While affirmative defenses to enforcement are most relevant in litigation, they are also relevant to a transactional lawyer. Namely, a transactional lawyer must always be aware of these defenses so she can counsel her client to avoid engaging in conduct that would give rise to one of these defenses. So, for example, a lawyer must advise her client not to overstate the quality of property being transferred, to avoid giving the counterparty a basis to rescind the contract due to fraud, as well as to avoid potential disciplinary action herself for assisting a client engage in a fraud.

Moreover, in drafting and reviewing a contract, a transactional lawyer must ensure that the contract does not include a term that is unenforceable under the rules in this chapter. Including an unenforceable provision could undermine the benefits either the client or the counterparty seeks to obtain under the contract, leading to disappointment and potentially dispute. Moreover, a lawyer who fails to advise her client about the unenforceability of a provision in a contract may be subject to malpractice as well as discipline for failure to act competently.

A transactional lawyer can reduce the risk posed by the potential application of some of these affirmative defenses through the contract language the lawyer utilizes when drafting. For example, as you will learn, the unconscionability defense often hinges on the readability and understandability of the contract as well as the fairness of contract terms. In light of this, a transactional lawyer representing a business client in drafting a "form" contract for customers would be wise to draft that contract in what is often called "plain English" (which essentially means that it is readable and understandable to laypeople), make key provisions conspicuous, and include terms that are not overreaching.

B. DEFENSE AS TO FORM: STATUTE OF FRAUDS

Although people routinely think of contracts in terms of a written agreement, recall that a contract is simply an enforceable promise, regardless of its form. Through our exploration of mutual assent and consideration, you hopefully understand that a contract can exist even where there is not written evidence that promises were exchanged. Accordingly, if you can demonstrate that Lawrence manifested a promise to paint your house for $5,000 through a telephone conversation (and you agreed), then a contract will be deemed to have been formed and you can enforce Lawrence's promise against him.

As discussed in Chapter 9, transactional attorneys typically advise their clients to utilize written contracts for planning, reliance, and evidentiary purposes. There is an obvious danger to enforcing oral promises as contracts. To do so, one must rely on oral and eyewitness testimony regarding the existence of a promise. When there is a dispute regarding whether an oral contract was formed, the court will be forced to rely on the parties' testimony, and this testimony will necessarily be self-serving and potentially untruthful. The party seeking to avoid the contract will likely testify that the parties never manifested their assent, and the party seeking to enforce the contract will probably testify that the parties did manifest their assent. This may not be problematic if we are confident in courts' or juries' ability to determine which party is more credible or when the likelihood of litigation is low (e.g., when the value of the contract is low). For certain types of contracts, though, it may be prudent to require something more than oral testimony before recognizing the formation of a contract and the enforceability of a party's promises.

Consequently, states typically require evidence of certain types of contracts to be in writing and signed by the party whose promise is sought be enforced. Such requirements, known as Statutes of Frauds, are typically based on the first English Statute of Frauds (known as "An Act for the Prevention of Frauds and Perjuries"), which was adopted in 1677.

Note that, as suggested by their name, Statutes of Frauds arise by virtue of statutes. In fact, each state has a host of statutes that each contain what is referred to as a Statute of Frauds. For example, a state might include a Statute of Frauds in its chapter on real property, specifying the types of real property contracts that fall under that Statute of Frauds, and specifying those requirements; a Statute of Frauds in its version of Article 2 of the UCC, specifying the types of sale-of-goods contracts that fall under that Statute of Frauds, and specifying the requirements that apply to them; and many other Statutes of Frauds in other chapters of that state's statutes. Thus, Statutes of Frauds do not emerge from common law. However, as you will see later in this chapter, the common law still applies to fill in gaps in Statutes of Frauds, and to interpret those Statutes.

The following section of the Restatement generally describes the different types of contracts that typically are subject to states' Statutes of Frauds:

§ 110 Classes of Contracts Covered ✓

(1) The following classes of contracts are subject to a statute, commonly called the Statute of Frauds, forbidding enforcement unless there is a written memorandum or an applicable exception:

(a) a contract of an executor or administrator to answer for a duty of his decedent (the executor administrator provision);

(b) a contract to answer for the duty of another (the suretyship provision);

(c) a contract made upon consideration of marriage (the marriage provision);

(d) a contract for the sale of an interest in land (the land contract provision);

(e) a contract that is not to be performed within one year from the making thereof (the one-year provision).

(2) The following classes of contracts, which were traditionally subject to the Statute of Frauds, are now governed by Statute of Frauds provisions of the Uniform Commercial Code:

(a) a contract for the sale of goods for the price of $ 500 or more (Uniform Commercial Code § 2-201);

(b) a contract for the sale of securities (Uniform Commercial Code § 8-319);

(c) a contract for the sale of personal property not otherwise covered, to the extent of enforcement by way of action or defense beyond $ 5,000 in amount or value of remedy (Uniform Commercial Code § 1-206).

1. Is the Contract Subject to the Statute of Frauds?

There are two steps in determining whether the Statute of Frauds precludes enforcement of a contract. The first is whether the contract to be enforced falls under a Statute of Frauds. In other words, does the contract fall within the relevant Statute of Frauds? If a contract is not subject to the Statute of Frauds, then the Statute of Frauds does not need to be satisfied, and the failure to satisfy its requirements would not operate as an affirmative defense.

It may be fairly easy to determine whether some contracts' promises fall under a Statute of Frauds, such as a contract for the sale of goods for over $500 or a contract to guaranty the debts of another. Others, however, may be a bit more complicated. For example, it can be tricky to determine whether a contract that is not to be performed within one year is subject to the Statute of Frauds. The following is the Restatement's description of this type of Statute of Frauds:

§ 130 Contract Not to Be Performed Within a Year

(1) Where any promise in a contract cannot be fully performed within a year from the time the contract is made, all promises in the contract are within the Statute of Frauds until one party to the contract completes his performance.

(2) When one party to a contract has completed his performance, the one-year provision of the Statute does not prevent enforcement of the promises of other parties.

Under this test, would an employment contract between ABC Company and 30-year-old Cassie for the rest of Cassie's life (a "lifetime" contract) fall within the Statute of Frauds? Presumably, Cassie is going to live beyond a year and may well work for many years, so it may appear that the contract does fall within the Statute of Frauds. However, what actually happens in the future, or what is likely to happen in the future, is not usually the test. The question for these purposes is typically whether the contract *could* be completely performed within a year. The answer is yes, because Cassie could die one day after the contract is formed, and both parties could have performed all of their obligations under the contract within one year. Accordingly, the contract would not fall within the Statute of Frauds.

The analysis can become a little more complicated where the contract is for a term longer than one year (such as a three-year term) but the contract also contains provisions recognizing the ability of one party to be excused from performance under certain circumstances. For example, if Cassie's employment contract was for three years but also provided that she and ABC Company would be excused from performing in the event of her death, would the contract still be subject to the Statute of Frauds? Cassie could have died within one year of the formation of the contract, and both parties would have performed, but most states distinguish between the term of the contract and clauses that discharge or excuse a party from performance. In this instance, because the contract required services for three years, many courts would conclude that the contract is within the Statute of Frauds, even though the parties might be excused from future performance within one year of contract formation. That is because the full benefits expected by the parties under the contract would only be realized at the end of three years.

On the other hand, if the contract expressly gave Cassie the right to terminate the contract before the end of the third year—for example, by delivering 30 days' notice to ABC Company—then again, this contract might not fall under the Statute of Frauds. That is because it could be completely performed in fewer than three years simply by giving notice of intent to terminate.

2. If the Contract Is Subject to the Statute of Frauds, Have Its Requirements Been Met?

The next step in the analysis under a Statute of Frauds is to determine if its requirements are met.

Imagine that Alec agreed to lease a farm from Chet for one year. A leasehold interest is an interest in real property, so the promises to pay for, and sell, that interest may fall under the Statute of Frauds. The following is the Restatement's general description of this type of Statute of Frauds:

> § 125 Contract to Transfer, Buy, or Pay for an Interest in Land
>
>   (1) A promise to transfer to any person any interest in land is within the Statute of Frauds.
>
>   (2) A promise to buy any interest in land is within the Statute of Frauds, irrespective of the person to whom the transfer is to be made.

(3) When a transfer of an interest in land has been made, a promise to pay the price, if originally within the Statute of Frauds, ceases to be within it unless the promised price is itself in whole or in part an interest in land.

(4) Statutes in most states except from the land contract and one-year provisions of the Statute of Frauds short-term leases and contracts to lease, usually for a term not longer than one year.

For now, let's assume that that the state's Statute of Frauds does apply to the one-year lease of the farm. If the contract were not subject to the Statute of Frauds, then the additional writing requirements would not apply (unless otherwise required by a separate statute or judicial decision).

Satisfying the Statute of Frauds is a little more complicated than you might expect. The Statute of Frauds generally does not require that the entire contract be in writing or that both parties have signed a writing. Instead, the Statute typically requires that the party whose promise is sought to be enforced has to have signed something in writing that sufficiently admits the existence of the contract and describes the essential terms that have yet to be performed. Thus, the entire contract does not have to be in writing or signed. Moreover, the writing does not need to be a formal documentation of the contract or prepared with an intent to evidence the contract. The Restatement's formulation of these typical Statute of Frauds requirements are below.

§ 131 General Requisites of a Memorandum

Unless additional requirements are prescribed by the particular statute, a contract within the Statute of Frauds is enforceable if it is evidenced by any writing, signed by or on behalf of the party to be charged, which

(a) reasonably identifies the subject matter of the contract,

(b) is sufficient to indicate that a contract with respect thereto has been made between the parties or offered by the signer to the other party, and

(c) states with reasonable certainty the essential terms of the unperformed promises in the contract.

In the example of the one-year lease of a farm discussed above, we have already established that the contract may be subject to the State of Frauds. We then would need to understand which of the parties is seeking to enforce the lease. If Alec is trying to enforce Chet's promise to lease the farm to Alec, then in a legal dispute, Chet could attempt to avoid enforcement by asserting that the contract is subject to the Statute of Frauds and that the facts, as alleged, do not satisfy its requirements. Assuming that the court agreed, Alec would then be required to produce written evidence signed by Chet that sufficiently admits that a lease was entered into and sets forth the essential terms of Chet's promise. Presumably, at a minimum, the writing would need to identify the land, the rent, and the term, but it is possible that a court may also identify as essential other elements of Chet's promises (which also then would need to be included in the writing signed by Chet).

Importantly, it is Chet's signature that is required, since Alec is the one trying to enforce Chet's promise. If Chet were the party attempting to enforce the contract against Alec, then Alec could potentially avoid enforcement of his promises under the Statute of Frauds unless Chet was able to introduce into evidence a writing signed by or on behalf of Alec that admitted the existence of a contract and identified the essential terms of Alec's promise.

In many transactions, attorneys will make sure that their clients are not bound until there is a written contract designed not only to reflect the parties' binding obligations but also to satisfy the Statute of Frauds. Nevertheless, technology and communication advances can present interesting questions regarding the satisfaction of the Statute of Frauds. In the following case, neither party contests that the contract is subject to the Statute of Frauds, but there is a question regarding whether a text message can satisfy the Statute's writing requirements. There also are questions regarding what that writing must provide where it does not set out all of the essential terms of the contract. As you review the case, consider whether the purpose of the Statute of Frauds is supported or undermined by the court's conclusion and whether the Statute of Frauds still serves a valuable purpose.

St. John's Holdings, LLC v. Two Electronics, LLC
Massachusetts Land Court
2016 Mass. LCR LEXIS 49

FOSTER, J.

MEMORANDUM AND ORDER DENYING DEFENDANT'S SPECIAL MOTION TO DISMISS

At least one dictionary defines a "text message" as "a short message sent electronically usually from one cell phone to another." *Merriam-Webster Dictionary*, www.merria-webster.com/dictionary/text%message (visited April 12, 2016). The question raised by defendant's Special Motion to Dismiss is whether a text message, all too familiar to most teenagers and their parents, can constitute a writing sufficient under the Statute of Frauds to create an enforceable contract for the sale of land. In its complaint, St. John's Holdings, LLC (SJH) alleges that a text message from a real estate broker for defendant Two Electronics, LLC (Two Electronics) constituted acceptance of a binding offer from SJH to buy Two Electronics' property at 2 Electronics Drive, Danvers, MA (Subject Property). After SJH filed its complaint and the court allowed SJH's ex parte motion for endorsement of a memorandum of lis pendens, Two Electronics filed a Special Motion to Dismiss pursuant to G.L. c. 184, §15, seeking dismissal of the complaint, dissolution of the lis pendens, and an award of attorney's fees and costs.

. . .

FACTS

For the purposes of the deciding the Special Motion to Dismiss, the following facts are undisputed or are inferred in SJH's favor:

1. SJH is a Massachusetts limited liability company with a principal place of business located at 301 Edgewater Place, Wakefield, MA. Frederick McDonald, Jr. (McDonald) is the manager of SJH.

2. Two Electronics is a Massachusetts limited liability company with a principal place of business located at 2 Draper Street, Woburn, MA. Matthew Piccione (Piccione) is the manager of Two Electronics. Two Electronics is the owner of the Subject Property pursuant to a deed recorded in the Essex South District Registry of Deeds (registry) in Book 27435, Page 475.

3. The Subject Property is a one-story commercial building located in an industrial park in Danvers. It is occupied by multiple office users under commercial leases.

4. Stephen Cefalo (Cefalo) is a licensed Massachusetts real estate broker with Stephen Cefalo Real Estate. Cefalo acted as the broker and authorized agent of SJH at all times relevant with respect to the Subject Property.

5. Timothy Barry (Barry) is a licensed Massachusetts real estate broker with Barry Realty Group. Barry acted as the broker and authorized agent of Two Electronics at all times relevant with respect to the Subject Property.

6. SJH first reached out to Barry in December 2015, initially expressing interest in leasing space at the Subject Property from Two Electronics.

7. In January 2016, SJH indicated that they were interested in purchasing the Subject Property. McDonald, Piccione, Cefalo, and Barry met in person to commence initial negotiations surrounding the acquisition of the Subject Property by SJH through a purchase transaction.

8. Throughout January, the parties met several times. At these meetings, McDonald outlined to Piccione the basic terms of an offer to purchase the Subject Property. Piccione requested that McDonald submit a written offer to purchase with the terms discussed. Piccione also directed McDonald and Cefalo to work through Barry as his broker for the Subject Property. Thereafter, the parties continued negotiating the terms of an offer to purchase the Subject Property.

9. On January 27, 2016, Barry received by email a written "Binding Letter of Intent" from Cefalo, on behalf of SJH, that contained a description of the terms under which SJH would buy the Subject Property, including the purchase price of $3,232,000, due diligence period, deposit, and the closing date (First LOI). The First LOI was not signed by a representative of SJH. Barry emailed the First LOI to Piccione who reviewed and made certain comments to Barry by telephone about terms he would like revised.

10. On January 29, 2016, Barry received by email a second "Binding Letter of Intent" from Cefalo on behalf of SJH (Second LOI). The Second LOI contained revisions of the essential terms in the First LOI and was also not signed by a representative of SJH. Barry emailed the Second

LOI to Piccione to review. The only difference between the First and Second Letters of Intent was that the nonrefundable deposit offered by SJH was increased from $128,000 to $168,000. Again, Piccione reviewed and made comments to Barry by telephone about certain terms in the letter. In particular, Piccione indicated to Barry that the provision that SJH would pay $200,000 of the purchase price on a date 60 months after the closing without interest was unacceptable, that the proposed due diligence period was too long, and that SJH's right to unilaterally extend the closing date for 30 days was unacceptable.

11. On February 1, 2016, Barry sent an email to Cefalo stating that Two Electronics was "ready to do this," but that Piccione had three issues regarding the offer in the Second LOI. Barry wrote:

> "The first matter is he would like to give you guys three weeks instead of 4 on the due diligence. Number two, he doesn't want to give the 30 day extension. And number three, is he would like to have a penalty applied to the deal if the $200,000 is not paid at the end of 48 months."

12. On February 2, 2016, Cefalo sent Barry as an email attachment a third written "Binding Letter of Intent" (Final LOI). The Final LOI was also not signed by a representative of SJH. The only revision contained in the Final LOI was the date on which the final $200,000 of the purchase price would be due and payable to the seller. It was reduced from 60 months post-closing to 48 months post-closing. None of the issues raised in the February 1, 2016 email from Barry to Cefalo were incorporated into the Final LOI.

13. The Final LOI set forth a method for Two Electronics to accept the offer from SJH:

> "Please indicate your agreement to the above summary of discussions by signing and returning a copy of this letter to the undersigned no later than Feb. 4, 2016. If you have any questions concerning the items to be addressed, please feel free to call."

14. Barry sent an email to Piccione with the Final LOI the same day, which Piccione received at 7:58 PM on February 2, 2016. Piccione states that he did not review the substance of the offer at that time because the document was not signed by SJH.

15. Also on February 2, 2016, Two Electronics received a signed offer to purchase the Subject Property from a third party for a purchase price of $3,080,000.

16. At 2:12 PM on February 3, 2016, Barry sent Cefalo the following text message in response to receiving the Final LOI from Cefalo the previous day:

> "Steve. It [Two Electronics] wants you [SJH] to sign first, with a check, and then he will sign. Normally, the seller signs last or second. Not trying to be

stupid or contrary, but that is the way it normally works. Can Rick [McDonald] sign today and get it to me today? Tim"

17. On February 3, 2016, McDonald executed four original copies of the Final LOI with the deposit check and gave them to Cefalo to deliver to Barry for signature by Piccione.

18. At 4:25 PM on February 3, 2016, Cefalo sent a text message to Barry stating:

"Tim, I have the signed LOI and check it is 424 [PM] where can I meet you?"

19. Later that day, Cefalo and Barry spoke by telephone and agreed that Cefalo would bring the signed Final LOI and the deposit check to Barry's office for Two Electronics' execution. After, Cefalo met with Barry in person and delivered the four originals of the executed Final LOI and the deposit check to be passed along to Piccione to sign.

20. Two Electronics accepted the third party's offer to buy the Subject Property by countersigning the written offer on February 3, 2016. Two Electronics and the third party buyer have entered into a written purchase and sale agreement with a closing date tentatively set for April 27, 2016.

21. The following day, on February 4, 2016, Cefalo sent a text message to Barry looking for an update on the executed Final LOI. Barry responded with a text message to Cefalo and stated:

"Matt [Piccione] was out of town today. He will get back to us tomorrow."

22. Two Electronics thereafter refused to execute and deliver to SJH the executed Final LOI.

DISCUSSION

SJH brought this complaint seeking to enforce its rights as a buyer of the Subject Property pursuant to a binding letter of intent to purchase it alleged it entered into with the owner and seller defendant Two Electronics. SJH submits that the letter of intent was binding based on an exchange of emails and text messages between the parties' real estate brokers that constitute an agreement on all essential terms that satisfies the Statute of Frauds. In its complaint, SJH pleads three causes of action: (1) Breach of Contract, (2) Declaratory Judgment, and (3) Specific Performance.

The ultimate dispute in this case is whether the parties merely engaged in negotiations regarding the purchase of the Subject Property, or whether their dealings, carried out through electronic communications, gave rise to a binding and enforceable contract for the purchase and sale of the real estate. The issue in this Special Motion to Dismiss is the threshold question necessary to determine if a contract was formed: whether Cefalo's email of the Final LOI and Barry's text message in response constituted a writing containing the essential elements of the agreement and a signature sufficient to bind the parties under the Statute of Frauds.

. . .

Contracts for the sale of land, whether by oral promise or written agreement, are enforceable only if they are supported by a writing that includes the agreement's essential terms and is signed by the party against whom enforcement is sought—in this case, Two Electronics. Whether a writing satisfies the Statute of Frauds is a question of law. In the Special Motion to Dismiss, Two Electronics argues that Barry's February 3rd text message cannot satisfy the Statute of Frauds. SJH argues that it does. Resolving this issue requires determining whether (a) a text message can be a writing under the Statute of Frauds, (b) whether the alleged writing contains sufficiently complete terms and an intention to be bound by those terms, (c) whether the text message is signed, and (d) whether there is an offer and acceptance.

Whether text messages qualify as a writing under the Statute of Frauds is a novel issue in the Commonwealth. In general, writings of relative informality and brevity can satisfy the statute. The writing need not be a formal contract, but the terms of the writing must be sufficiently complete and definite and the writing must reflect a present intent of the parties at the time of formation to be bound. The writing must contain directly, or by implication, all of the essential terms of the parties' agreement. "It is a court's function, therefore, to determine what provisions are essential to an agreement sought to be enforced and whether an omitted provision can be supplied by implication." *Simon v. Simon*, 35 Mass. App. Ct. 705, 709, 625 N.E.2d 564 (1994), citing Restatement (Second) of Contracts § 131, comment g (1979).

To support its position, Two Electronics directs the court to *Singer v. Adamson*, a prior Land Court decision that addressed a similar issue involving emails between real estate agents where the court decided that the emails did not meet the demands of the Statute of Frauds. *Singer v. Adamson*, 11 LCR 338, 342 (2003), *aff'd*, 65 Mass. App. Ct. 1103, 837 N.E.2d 313 (2005). In reaching its decision, the court noted that emails "by their quick and casual nature, tend to lack in many instances the cautionary and memorializing functions a traditional signed writing serves under the Statute of Frauds." *Id.* The Land Court judge further acknowledged that "[e]-mails facilitate rapid, almost instantaneous communication, but in many cases they analogize more closely to telephone calls, or at least to voice mail messages, shot back and forth between parties whose chief goal is prompt response. . . . It is far from obvious that average parties launching e-mails to each other appreciate that their quickly-composed electronic missives are contractual in nature, and will constitute, when assembled into one long 'thread' after the fact, a memorandum of a binding and enforceable agreement. In many instances, the e-mails reveal that the parties are really just 'talking' with the help of the internet, and not sitting down across a virtual table to electronically 'write up' a memorandum of any contractual significance." *Id.*

Singer was decided over a decade ago. Since then the use of electronic communications, particularly in the legal field, has advanced immensely and become commonplace. Several more recent decisions acknowledge that emails may be writings that satisfy the Statute of Frauds and create a binding contract. Moreover, the facts in *Singer* are distinguishable from this case. In *Singer*, the court found that the emails lacked specificity on many key terms including the dates of performance, deposit terms, rights to inspection, mortgage and other contingencies. The parties themselves "had no prior history of contracting, no definitive written agreement had been signed by them previously, and they did not communicate directly, even using e-mail." *Singer*, 11 LCR at 342. These are not the circumstances of the present case.

The facts in *Shattuck v. Klotzbach* are more similar to this matter. *Shattuck v. Klotzbach*, No. 011109A, 2001 Mass. Super. LEXIS 642, 2001 WL 1839720, at *3-4 (Mass. Super. Dec. 11, 2001). The court in *Shattuck* denied a seller's motion to dismiss, holding that email messages exchanged between a prospective buyer and seller satisfied the Statute of Frauds. *Id.* The plaintiff-buyer and defendant-seller had engaged in negotiations concerning the sale of property through their attorneys that were conducted in person, by telephone, and email. Several emails were exchanged addressing specific contractual provisions, including the closing date, purchase price, deposit amount, and waivers of contingencies. The court found that these emails reflected detailed attention to many of the provisions that would govern the purchase and sale, and signified a close involvement of the parties' attorneys in forming the transaction. On these facts, the court had little difficulty denying the seller's motion to dismiss.

. . .

Based on the undisputed facts and drawing inferences in SJH's favor, the Court finds that the February 3rd text message is a writing and that, read in the context of exchanges between the parties, it contains sufficient terms to state a binding contract between SJH and Two Electronics. The communications between SJH and Two Electronics before the text message evidenced a meticulous attention to provisions that would govern the agreement to purchase the Subject Property. The parties began communicating in December 2015, through their real estate brokers, initially over leasing the Subject Property. Communications between the parties and their real estate agents, including multiple telephone calls, emails, and face to face meetings, continued through January 2016. Over the course of their negotiations Cefalo, as an agent acting on behalf of SJH, sent two binding letters of intent to Barry, after which Piccione reviewed the terms and made revisions that were reiterated back to Barry. Barry systematically conveyed to Cefalo the terms that were acceptable to Two Electronics. The terms discussed included the purchase price, seller financing, the due diligence period, the closing date, and the deposit amount. These back-and-forth communications culminated in Cefalo's attaching of the Final LOI to an email to Barry on February 2nd. The Final LOI set out all essential terms for the purchase and sale of the Subject Property, and stated explicitly that it was binding. Barry sent a text message to Cefalo the following day indicating that the Final LOI was received and made no additional changes to the terms except as to the method of acceptance.

Under the Statute of Frauds, multiple writings relating to the subject matter of the agreement may be read together as long as the writings, when considered as a single instrument, contain all the material terms of the contract and are authenticated by the signature of the party to be charged. The writings may, but need not, incorporate each other by reference. Parol evidence may be introduced to show that "two or more papers were so connected in the minds of the parties that they adopted all of them as indicating their purpose." *SAR Grp. Ltd. v. E.A. Dion, Inc.*, 79 Mass. App. Ct. 1123), quoting *Tzitzon Realty Co., Inc.*, 352 Mass. at 653. The text message from Barry to Cefalo implicitly incorporated the Final LOI and the provisions mentioned therein. The text message, together with Cefalo's email of the Final LOI and the conduct of the parties throughout the course of negotiations, satisfies the writing requirement. The way in which the parties handled the transaction was sufficient for them to appreciate that the text message would memorialize the contractual offer and acceptance.

Two Electronics asserts that even if the communications between the agents constituted a writing, the text message from "Tim" was not a signature that binds Two Electronics under the Statute of Frauds. For the purposes of the Special Motion to Dismiss the parties stipulated that the real estate agents were duly authorized agents acting on behalf of their respective companies. The signature of a duly authorized agent, rather than the party to be charged, is sufficient to be binding. While the legality of a signature in a text messages has not been addressed by courts in the Commonwealth, several cases address the validity of electronic signatures.

Several courts have found the requirements for a signature to satisfy the Statute of Frauds to be relatively minimal. "A memorandum is signed in accordance with the Statute of Frauds if it is signed by the person to be charged, in his own name, or by his initials, or by his Christian name alone, or by a printed, stamped or typewritten signature, if in signing in any of these methods he intended to authenticate the paper as his act." *Irving v. Goodimate Co.*, 320 Mass. 454, 458, 70 N.E.2d 414 (1946). "Emails between the parties may create a binding contract that satisfies the Statute of Frauds, provided the emails contain all essential terms, even in the absence of a formal signature." *Slover*, 24 LCR at 5; *Feldberg*, 2012 Mass. Super. LEXIS 214, 2012 WL 3854947 at *6 (allowing certain parts of an email to satisfy the signature requirement of the Statute of Frauds). The typed name at the end of an email is indicative of a party's intent to authenticate because the sender of an email types and sends the message on his own accord and types his own name as he so chooses. Moreover, courts have relied on the Uniform Electronic Transactions Act,

G.L. c. 110G, which applies "to transactions between parties each of which has agreed to conduct transactions by electronic means." *Feldberg*, 2012 Mass. Super. LEXIS 214, 2012 WL 3854947 at *6, citing G.L. c. 110G, §5. Whether parties have agreed "is determined from the context and surrounding circumstances, including the parties' conduct." G.L. c. 110G, §5. When parties use email to conduct the negotiations it "arguably constitutes an agreement to conduct transactions by electronic means." *Feldberg*, 2012 Mass. Super. LEXIS 214, 2012 WL 3854947 at *6. An electronic signature is "an electronic . . . symbol or process attached to or logically associated with a record and executed or adopted by a person with the intent to sign the record." *Id.*, citing *May Trucking Co.*, 238 Or. App. at 35.

In the February 3rd text message from Barry to Cefalo, Barry signed his name "Tim" at the end of lengthy message requesting that SJH sign first. This form of signature is consistent with the previous emails between Barry and Cefalo, which contained typewritten signatures at the end of each message, not a formal script signature or a signature block. In the February 1st email from Barry to Cefalo, Barry signed his name "Tim." Likewise, Cefalo signed his name "Steve Cefalo" at the end of the February 2nd email to Barry in which he sent the Final LOI. A series of unsigned text messages between Cefalo and Barry followed over the next few days, which were briefer and less formal, requesting updates on the status of the executed Final LOI. These communications are evidence that each of the parties opted into electronic means to conduct their transaction. Typing their names at the end of certain messages containing material terms, but declining to do so for more informal discussions, is indicative that the parties chose to be bound by those signed communications. In the context of these exchanges between the parties, the court infers that the text message sent by Barry was intended to be authenticated by his deliberate choice to type his name at the conclusion of his text message. Unlike subsequent text messages of a more informal nature, where Barry did not choose to use a signature, the use of his signature at the end of the February 2nd text message is evidence of his intent to have the writing be legally binding.

. . .

It follows that Two Electronics has not met its burden on the Special Motion to Dismiss. SJH's claims are not frivolous or devoid of any factual support or basis in law within the meaning of G.L. c. 184, § 15(c). The Final LOI contains all the specific terms of a purchase and sale agreement. The text message from Barry to Cefalo, together with Cefalo's email of the Final LOI, read in the light most favorable to SJH as the nonmoving party, gives rise to the kind of writing which satisfies the Statute of Frauds.

. . .

Understanding the Case:

1. *Modern Writings:* One of the primary reasons courts have a difficult time determining whether a writing satisfies the Statute of Frauds is because of evolving contracting practices. One hundred years ago, it required much more effort to draft and print a written contract. The only "writings" that existed were writings that could be printed on actual paper and signed with a pen. With technological advances, parties can now send virtual, digital, and other types of intangible communications that do not involve ink and paper. Legislatures have attempted to "keep up" by enacting statutes that enable certain electronic communications to constitute signatures, such as the United States Electronic Signatures in Global and National Commerce (ESIGN) Act, and the Uniform Electronic Transactions Act (UETA). Judges, as seen in this case, also utilize earlier case law principles to address modern problems.

Thought and Comprehension Questions:

1. Why was the contract to purchase the Subject Property within the Statute of Frauds?

2. How did Barry's text message satisfy the Statute of Frauds given that it did not contain all of the terms of the letter of intent?

3. Would the parties' text messages have been relevant to the initial determination of whether a contract was formed in the first place?

4. How was the signature requirement of the Statute of Frauds satisfied through text message? Why is the Uniform Electronic Transactions Act relevant to this discussion?

5. Do you think Barry contemplated the binding nature of his text message when he put his name at the bottom?

6. Do you see any dangers associated with utilizing text messages or other informal communications with respect to satisfying the Statute of Frauds, as suggested by the *Singer* case?

Hypothetical Variations:

1. What if Barry had not included his name at the end of the February 2 text message?

2. What if Barry had also noted in his February 2 text message that Piccione was still considering the terms of the final letter of intent?

3. What if the contracting parties were not using real estate brokers but were unsophisticated, inexperienced, 20-year-olds negotiating for the sale of real property?

States are free to go beyond the scope and requirements of traditional Statutes of Frauds and require other contracts to be in writing or evidenced by a writing signed by the promissor. For example, in *Foss v. Circuit City Stores, Inc.*, which you will read in Chapter 18, the court recognizes the Maine statute that requires a minor, upon reaching the age of majority, to affirm in writing a contract previously entered into while still a minor. Maine's legislature had presumably enacted that Statute of Frauds because it determined that minors require additional protection beyond that traditionally provided by common law rules regarding disaffirmance, and, consequently, decided to require written evidence before enforcing a contract entered into by a minor.

You should also be aware that the applicability of (and inability to satisfy) the Statute of Frauds to a particular contract may not necessarily leave a party without a remedy. Alternative remedies, such as those based on reliance (discussed in Chapter 22), may be available depending on the jurisdiction. Other jurisdictions, however, may preclude alternative remedies such as those based on reliance, reflecting a judgment that the applicability of the Statute of Frauds should preclude any contract-like recovery. In other words, those jurisdictions view the purpose and efficacy of the Statute of Frauds as being undermined if parties can simply evade its requirements by pleading alternative grounds for recovery.

3. The UCC Statute of Frauds

Article 2 of the UCC has a Statute of Frauds that applies to the sale of goods for more than $500, but it relaxes a number of common law requirements. As discussed in other chapters, the UCC is designed to facilitate transactions and tends to favor the finding of contracts in the commercial setting. Relaxing the requirements of the Statute is consistent with this general approach. Section 2-201 sets forth the Statute of Frauds for the UCC.

§ 2-201. Formal Requirements; Statute of Frauds.

(1) Except as otherwise provided in this section a contract for the sale of goods for the price of $500 or more is not enforceable by way of action or defense unless there is some writing sufficient to indicate that a contract for sale has been made between the parties and signed by the party against whom enforcement is sought or by his authorized agent or broker. A writing is not insufficient because it omits or incorrectly states a term agreed upon but the contract is not enforceable under this paragraph beyond the quantity of goods shown in such writing.

(2) Between merchants if within a reasonable time a writing in confirmation of the contract and sufficient against the sender is received and the party receiving it has reason to know its contents, it satisfies the requirements of subsection (1) against such party unless written notice of objection to its contents is given within 10 days after it is received.

(3) A contract which does not satisfy the requirements of subsection (1) but which is valid in other respects is enforceable

(a) if the goods are to be specially manufactured for the buyer and are not suitable for sale to others in the ordinary course of the seller's business and the seller, before notice of repudiation is received and under circumstances which reasonably indicate that the goods are for the buyer, has made either a substantial beginning of their manufacture or commitments for their procurement; or

(b) if the party against whom enforcement is sought admits in his pleading, testimony or otherwise in court that a contract for sale was made, but the contract is not enforceable under this provision beyond the quantity of goods admitted; or

(c) with respect to goods for which payment has been made and accepted or which have been received and accepted.

Note that the basic requirements of Article 2's Statute of Frauds are substantially similar to the requirements of Statutes of Frauds that apply to non-sale-of-good transactions. Under Article 2's Statute of Frauds, the party to be charged must have signed a writing that indicates that a contract exists. Toward that end, the UCC clarifies that the writing indicating that a contract exists can omit terms or even contradict terms of the contract. Recall that the purpose of a Statute of Frauds is to prevent a party from being held to the terms of certain types of contracts based on oral testimony alone. Accordingly, the contradictory or missing terms in the writing (used to indicate that a contract existed) are irrelevant to whether the party actually entered into a contract. The writing is not being used to clarify what the terms of the contract are. Instead, it is being used to indicate that the party against whom enforcement is sought acknowledged that a contract existed. This written acknowledgment reduces the risk of fraud and makes any oral testimony somewhat more credible.

Article 2 further liberalizes the writing requirements. Section 2-201(2) actually removes the requirement for the writing to be signed by the party to be charged where the party is a "merchant," has received written confirmation of the contract from the other party, and does not object to the confirmation within ten days. This recognizes that, in the course of commerce, there will be many communications between repeat players (merchants), and that each merchant should be bound by the terms of contracts that have been tacitly agreed to, in this instance by not rejecting written confirmation of the contract received from the other party. Merchants often will not expect to exchange formal written signed agreements, and the presence of a written confirmation that has not been objected to satisfies the intention of the Statute of Frauds to prevent fraud. In other words, if you are a merchant and do not object to a written confirmation, it is unlikely that the oral testimony used against you to enforce the contract is fraudulent (at least as to the existence of a contract). It is worth remembering again that the Statute of Frauds requirements do not reduce or modify the mutual assent requirements. In other words, although silence does not typically mean assent for mutual assent purposes, silence (by not objecting to a written confirmation of contract) can in certain instances satisfy Article 2's Statute of Frauds.

Article 2 also recognizes that there are other circumstances that reduce the likelihood of oral testimony of a contract being fraudulent, in which the requirement of a signed writing by the party to be charged can be removed. For example, if the seller has begun working on an unusual good that cannot otherwise be sold to others, the seller's oral testimony regarding the existence of a contract for the buyer to purchase that good is presumably less suspect than it might otherwise be. The reason such testimony would be less suspect (thus justifying relaxing the writing requirement for the Statute of Frauds) is that it is unlikely that a seller of goods would begin incurring the expense associated with specially manufactured goods unless the seller actually believed that there was a contract with the buyer. Such specially manufactured goods could not be sold to other buyers in the marketplace, so the seller could potentially lose a lot of time and money if the goods remained unsold and, accordingly, would be unlikely to begin producing such goods unless there was a binding contract in place. In this way, § 2-201(3) addresses both the fraud concerns of the original Statute of Frauds as well as the commercial realities of the marketplace.

PRACTICE PROBLEM 17-1

[handwritten: → yes! > 1yr]

1. Brandi enters into an oral contract with her accountant Katrina for tax services, pursuant to which Katrina agrees to work for Brandi for the rest of Katrina's life. Is the contract subject to the Statute of Frauds? *[handwritten: no—she could die]*

2. Justin Beeper, a singer, and an 88-year-old fan of his enter into an oral agreement pursuant to which Beeper will be paid $499 for performing at the fan's 90th birthday party. Is the contract subject to the Statute of Frauds? *[handwritten]*

3. Vikram and Leigh enter into an oral contract for the sale of a building that Leigh owns. Vikram sends to Leigh a letter that states: "This will confirm our agreement that you will sell to me and I will buy from you the lot located at 660 Woodsmith Avenue, legally described as Lot 101 in Map 43 recorded in the Register of Deeds of Wayne County, Ohio." The letter spells out all of the material terms of the transaction. Leigh receives the letter, but she does not respond. Is the contract subject to the Statute of Frauds? Can Leigh use the Statute of Frauds as a defense to Vikram's enforcement of the contract against her? Can Vikram use the Statute of Frauds as a defense to Leigh's enforcement of the contract against him?

4. Detroit Urban Farming, Inc. enters into an oral contract with Atwater Brewery for the sale of 10,000 bushels of hops at $3.00 per bushel. Atwater's General Manager sends Detroit Urban Farming's President a note as follows: "This will confirm our agreement that you will sell 10,000 bushels of hops

[handwritten: merchant rule 2-201(2)]

at $2.00 per bushel." The President does not respond and decides that she does not want to do business with someone who cannot be trusted. If Detroit Urban Farming is sued by Atwater Brewery for breach of contract, will Atwater be able to utilize the Statute of Frauds as a defense?

Now that you have studied defenses to enforcement, read through and answer the questions that follow the Simulation Problem for Chapter 17, which is located in Appendix A.

CHAPTER 18

Incapacity

One of the reasons to enforce contractual promises is that we believe individuals are capable of acting in their best interests, including by making promises governing and constraining their future behavior. The policy concerns of contract law identified in Chapter 1, including predictability, efficiency, and reliance, are only served well if the individuals entering into contracts are actually in a position to act in their best interest. Presumably, where Leigh agrees to pay Maximo $20,000 to redesign her office, Leigh knows what is in her best interest and that she values the redesign of her office by Maximo more than she values the $20,000 she is willing to exchange for Maximo's services. Contract law therefore respects and enforces Leigh's promise as a contract.

On the other hand, if an individual is unable to act in his best interest, then enforcing his contractual promises against him would not enhance his welfare and would actually be inefficient. Along the same lines, it may not be reasonable from a societal perspective to enforce contractual promises against someone unable to protect himself. In such instances, it is unreasonable, or at least undesirable, to permit a third party to rely on such a person's promise, sometimes even if the third party is unaware of the promissor's incapacity. Accordingly, contract law provides for defenses to enforcement of promises where the presumption about a contracting party's ability to act in his best interest is undermined.

It is important to note that these capacity defenses do not attack the contract formation requirements themselves. These defenses exist and are independent of the presence of mutual assent and consideration. In many cases, the party employing a capacity defense admits that the *prima facie* case of contract has been made. In other words, the party utilizing the capacity defense admits that the parties made manifestations of assent to a bargain and that the promises exchanged induced one another. However, the promissor seeks to avoid the enforcement of her contractual promises based on her lack of capacity.

In the example above, if Leigh were to seek to avoid enforcement of her promise to pay Maximo, Leigh may concede that she manifested her intent to be bound. She may also concede that, objectively, her promise was made to induce Maximo's promise to redo Leigh's office (and vice versa). Leigh's counsel nevertheless may point to an appropriate capacity defense as a reason that her contractual promise should be unenforceable. In that situation, such a capacity defense would provide a reason for not enforcing Leigh's promise despite the satisfaction of the elements for contract formation.

Of course, the party utilizing the capacity defense may also separately defend against enforcement of the promise by attempting to demonstrate a lack of mutual assent or consideration. Thus, for example, Leigh's counsel *may also* argue that it was unreasonable for Maximo to believe Leigh intended to be bound based on her words or conduct. However, such argument is separate from the lack of capacity defense.

These capacity defenses may be statutory or based on common law. Statutory capacity defenses reflect legislative judgment that certain classes of individuals or individuals with certain characteristics should be able avoid enforcement of their otherwise valid contractual promises. Common law, of course, reflects evolving judicial opinions regarding the same issues. In many instances, these defenses are personal to a particular party, meaning that the other party cannot point to another's lack of capacity in an attempt to avoid enforcement of the contract. For example, if Leigh lacks capacity to contract (as recognized by one of the doctrines discussed in this chapter), then Maximo cannot point to Leigh's incapacity to avoid his obligations under their contract.

Section A discusses the infancy defense, which is based on a contracting party's age, while Section B explores the incompetence defense based on a contracting party's mental state. As you review these capacity defenses, you should consider whether the legislature or courts have made appropriate judgments regarding the ability of certain individuals to contract. You should also consider whether these rules provide useful and practical guidance for contracting parties engaging in contracting as well as judges attempting to ascertain capacity.

A. INFANCY

The **infancy** defense generally permits minors to avoid enforcement of their contractual promises based on their age. The general rule is that minors only incur voidable contractual duties, which means that the contract is legally permissible, but the other party to the contract will be unable to enforce the minor's contractual promise against him if the minor chooses to utilize the infancy defense. Notably, the contract is not void as a result of the minor's infancy, but is voidable, which means that the minor can elect to utilize the defense to avoid enforcement of the contract. If the minor chooses not to do so, the contract otherwise will be valid, and the minor will be able to enforce the contract against the other party to the contract. For example, if Carla is a minor and enters into a contract with David, David may not be able to enforce the contract against Carla if Carla breaches, assuming that Carla asserts the defense of infancy. On the other hand, the contract will continue to be binding on David, and Carla may enforce the contract against David if David breaches.

The age of majority in each state is the age at which a child becomes legally responsible for his actions. In most states, it is 18 years old. At the age of majority, a person is no longer bound by the decision, or subject to the oversight or control, of his parents.[1] These actions include entering into contracts.

The infancy doctrine is premised on the idea that minors may be unable to make reasonable judgments in their best interest and are vulnerable to being taken advantage of by adults. This bright-line rule (either you are an adult or not based on your age) assumes that all minors are similarly situated and that minors will not seek to take advantage of adults by entering into contracts knowing that they can avoid enforcement if it suits them later. Over time, courts have recognized that unfortunate results and undesirable social behavior may arise if minors' promises are not enforceable in all instances, and exceptions to the infancy doctrine have arisen, although some of the exceptions are not strictly based in contract law. For example, some states find a contract is not voidable by a minor when the minor misrepresented her age when entering into the contract. Some states also permit enforcement of employment contracts with adolescents over a certain age. Each of these exceptions to the bright-line test of an absolute age cutoff is intended to address, in some way, situations where the normal policy concerns underlying the infancy defense are not as strong or are outweighed by contract law policies.

1. Disaffirmance

One common issue that arises in infancy cases is the effect of the minor turning the age of majority while the contract still is in effect. Is the minor automatically bound by the contract upon turning the age of majority? For example, you could interpret the minor's enjoyment of the benefits of a contract after turning the age of majority as suggesting the minor (now an adult) is ratifying and otherwise manifesting assent to the terms of the contract. Courts often are faced with the question of whether the minor should have to explicitly affirm the contract in order to be bound, or conversely, should have to explicitly **disaffirm** the contract in order *not* to be bound. Most states typically require the minor

---

1. A child can become emancipated even before reaching the age of majority, where the child is beyond the care, custody, and control of his parents and no longer needs adult support.

to disaffirm the contract within a reasonable amount of time after achieving the age of majority. If the minor does not disaffirm the contract within that time frame, then the minor will be bound in all respects under the contract, including with respect to services or benefits already received while a minor. On the other hand, if the minor disaffirms, the minor may be responsible for returning the goods already provided (or paying the fair value of the goods or services provided) but otherwise would be excused from performing under the contract. Some jurisdictions, however, permit the minors to "keep" the benefits already provided without paying for them.

In the following case, Maine has adopted a more exacting standard for enforcing contracts against contracting minors who achieve the age of majority. As you review the following case, consider the policy concerns that underlie Maine's infancy doctrine as well as the facts and circumstances the court utilizes to determine whether the minor did in fact affirm the contract upon reaching the age of majority.

Foss v. Circuit City Stores, Inc.
United States District Court, District of Maine
477 F. Supp. 2d 230 (2007)

ORDER ON MOTION TO COMPEL ARBITRATION AND
TO STAY THE PROCEEDINGS

SINGAL, Chief Judge.

Before the Court are Defendant Circuit City Stores, Inc.'s Motions to Compel Arbitration and to Stay the Proceedings. Plaintiff Andrew Foss ("Foss") objects to Defendant's Motion on the grounds of infancy and unconscionability of the agreement to arbitrate. For the reasons stated below, Defendant's Motions to Compel Arbitration and to Stay the Proceedings are DENIED.

I. BACKGROUND

Circuit City Stores, Inc. ("Circuit City") is a national retailer of name brand consumer electronics, entertainment software and related goods. Headquartered in Richmond, Virginia, Circuit City operates over six hundred stores in forty-seven states, including a store in South Portland, Maine. Since September of 2003, Circuit City has maintained an online application system. As an individual progresses through the application, he or she is required to provide information and consent to various agreements. The initial screen provides: "Before beginning the employment application, we will ask for your Social Security Number, contact information, consent to arbitration, and consent to perform a background check." At numerous times throughout the application, applicants are provided with opportunities to withdraw their application and exit the system.

After consenting to proceed electronically, the applicant is presented with Circuit City's Dispute Resolution Agreement ("the Agreement"). The Agreement provides in pertinent part:

> [B]oth Circuit City and I agree to settle any and all previously unasserted claims, disputes or controversies arising out of or relating to my application or candidacy for employment, employment and/or cessation of employment with Circuit City, exclusively by final and binding arbitration before a neutral Arbitrator. By way of example only, such claims include claims under federal, state and local statutory or common law, such as the Age Discrimination in Employment Act, Title VII of the Civil Rights Act of 1964, as amended, including the amendments of the Civil Rights Act of 1991, the Americans with Disabilities Act, the Family Medical Leave Act, the law of contract and law of tort. I understand that if I do file a lawsuit regarding a dispute arising out of or relating to my application or candidacy for employment, employment or cessation for employment, Circuit City may use this Agreement in support of its request to the court to dismiss the lawsuit and require me instead to use arbitration.

The applicant is then required to consent to the Agreement. When an applicant is less than eighteen years of age, the applicant is directed to obtain parental consent to the Agreement. Without parental consent, a person under eighteen is exited from the system. Throughout the application process, the applicant is given numerous opportunities to review and print a copy of the Agreement. Notably, an applicant must read and consent to the Agreement in order to be considered for employment.

On October 7, 2004, Foss applied for a non-management position with the Circuit City store in South Portland, Maine via the online application system. Foss was born on February 4, 1987 and thus was under eighteen at the time he applied for employment with Circuit City. As a result, when Foss reached the Agreement, he was directed to obtain a parent's consent. Foss's employment application reflects that the name "Sharon Foss" was entered and that this person consented to the Agreement. Sharon Foss is Andrew Foss's mother. Sharon Foss, however, has declared: "I never signed the Circuit City Dispute Resolution Agreement or gave my consent to Andrew to enter into the Agreement." Esten Foss, Andrew Foss's father, likewise maintains that he never signed or consented to the Agreement. Furthermore, through an affidavit, Foss states that neither parent signed or consented to the Agreement. On October 14, 2004, before Foss was actually hired by Circuit City, he was presented with and signed a hard copy of the Agreement. Notably, Circuit City did not require a parent's signature on this hard copy.

Foss began working for Circuit City in South Portland in October of 2004. Foss turned eighteen on February 4, 2005. In October 2005, Foss was transferred to the Circuit City in Keene, New Hampshire. While employed at the Keene Circuit City, Foss alleges that his supervisor created a hostile work environment. In December 2005, Foss provided two weeks' notice that he was going to terminate the employment. He was asked to stay for another week and was promised a transfer to the store in South Portland. Foss maintains that as a result of informing management of the hostile environment, including calling the Human Resources Department of Circuit City, he was terminated on December 15, 2005. The reason provided to Foss for the termination was "improperly punching in." Foss alleges that this reason was a pretext and claims retaliation motivated his termination.

Foss filed this lawsuit on September 15, 2006 claiming a hostile work environment and retaliation in violation of Title VII of the Civil Rights Act of 1964, 42 U.S.C. § 2000e, et. seq., and the Civil Rights Act of 1991, 42 U.S.C. § 1981(a). Circuit City has moved to compel arbitration and to stay the proceedings pursuant to sections 2 and 4 of the Federal Arbitration Act ("FAA"). 9 U.S.C. §§ 2 & 4 (2006).

II. DISCUSSION

A. The Federal Arbitration Act

The FAA embodies a "liberal federal policy favoring arbitration agreements." *Gilmer v. Interstate/Johnson Lane Corp.*, 500 U.S. 20, 25, 111 S. Ct. 1647, 114 L. Ed. 2d 26 (1991). Congress passed the FAA "to reverse the longstanding judicial hostility to arbitration agreements" and "to place arbitration agreements upon the same footing as other contracts." *Gilmer*, 500 U.S. at 24. Thus, section 2 of the FAA guarantees that:

> A written provision in any maritime transaction or a contract evidencing a transaction involving commerce to settle by arbitration a controversy thereafter arising out of such contract or transaction . . . shall be valid, irrevocable, and enforceable, save upon such grounds as exist at law or in equity for the revocation of any contract.

9 U.S.C. § 2. In addition, section 4 provides a mechanism to compel arbitration by a party aggrieved by another party's refusal to arbitrate. Section 4 directs that "upon being satisfied that the making of the agreement for arbitration or the failure to comply therewith is not in issue, the court shall make an order directing the parties to proceed to arbitration in accordance with the terms of the agreement." *Id.* Section 3 allows a court to stay the proceedings until the arbitration is complete.

Circuit City petitions the Court to compel arbitration pursuant to section 4 on the ground that the parties have agreed to arbitrate "any and all previously unasserted claims, disputes or controversies arising out of or relating to my application or candidacy for employment, employment and/or cessation of employment with Circuit City." Foss resists the motion to compel arbitration for two reasons. First, Foss asserts that because he was under eighteen when he signed the Agreement and he never ratified the Agreement in writing, no valid contract was ever formed. Second, Foss claims that even if there is a binding contract, the Agreement is unconscionable and therefore unenforceable. Because the Court finds the issue of infancy determinative, it does not reach the claim of unconscionability.

   . . .

C. Whether a Contract Was Ever Validly Formed

In determining whether a valid contract exists at all in a motion to compel arbitration, "state law, whether of legislative or judicial origin, is applicable if that law arose to govern issues concerning the validity, revocability, and enforceability of contracts generally." *Perry v. Thomas*, 482 U.S. 483, 492 n.9, 107 S. Ct. 2520, 96 L. Ed. 2d 426 (1987). The Court thus looks to Maine law to determine whether the contract to arbitrate exists.

The general law in Maine regarding the validity of a minor's contracts is clear: "No action shall be maintained on any contract made by a minor, unless he, or some person lawfully authorized, ratified it in writing after he arrived at the age of 18 years, except for necessaries or real estate of which he has received the title and retains the benefit." 33 M.R.S.A § 52. Since at least 1832, Maine has recognized the "infancy doctrine" and the need to protect minors. As the Law Court stated in 1947: "These disabilities of the minor are really privileges which the law gives him, and which he may exercise for his own benefit. The object is to secure him in his youthful years from injuring himself by his own improvident acts." *Reed Bros., Inc. v. Giberson*, 143 Me. 4, 54 A.2d 535, 537 (Me. 1947). These same cases contain a warning to those who endeavor to contract with an infant: "Any person dealing with one who has not reached his majority, must do so at his peril." *Id.*

Circuit City acknowledges that Foss was less than eighteen years of age when he signed the agreement. Nonetheless, Circuit City maintains that the Agreement is valid because Foss ratified the contract after turning eighteen and Circuit City obtained the consent of Foss's parents.

Ratification of a contract by a minor in Maine stands in contrast to ratification under the common law. Whereas under the common law and in some states, a minor can ratify a contract by actions or by a failure to disaffirm, Maine requires the ratification to be in writing. To be effective, ratification "should be voluntary, not obtained by circumvention, not under ignorance of the fact that he was entitled to claim the privilege." *Reed Bros., Inc.*, 54 A.2d at 538. In *Reed Bros., Inc.*, the Law Court declined to find ratification of a promissory note where an infant had joined in a mortgage, in which he acknowledged that the mortgage was subject to the promissory note. The Law Court stated that "[t]he ratification required by the statute must be something more than a recognition of the existence of the debt and the amount due thereon. It must be a deliberate written ratification." *Id.* The ratification must also evidence a decision by the infant to be bound by the contract.

Although Circuit City offers several forms of ratification, the Court finds each offer to be is insufficient. First, Circuit City maintains that Foss ratified the Agreement "[b]y completing and submitting daily time cards, upon which Circuit City relied and upon which Foss was paid. . . ." Mere completion and submission of a time card, is, at most, an acknowledgement of the time actually worked; it does not evidence intent by the infant to be bound by an independent agreement to arbitrate. If a mortgage that contained an acknowledgement of the promissory note in *Reed Bros., Inc.*, did not ratify the promissory note, the completion and submission of a time card cannot function to ratify an independent contract. In this situation, the Court is unable to state that punching and turning in a time card is a deliberate, voluntary and knowing written ratification of a separate agreement, which states "I agree to settle any and all previously unasserted claims . . . exclusively by final and binding arbitration."

Second, Circuit City claims that by continuing to work after turning eighteen, "Foss expressly consented to the Agreement." In Maine, action is insufficient for ratification absent a "deliberate written ratification." *See Lamkin & Foster v. Ledoux*, 101 Me. 581, 64 A. 1048, 1049 (Me. 1906) ("The defendant's conduct after coming of age may have shown a sufficient ratification at common law, but there was no ratification in writing, and hence the statute bars the action.").

Finally, Circuit City claims that Foss ratified the contract by filing this lawsuit, "as the Agreement was an integral part of Foss's employment arrangement upon which he is now suing." This proposition misconstrues the nature of the lawsuit. Foss is suing on statutory grounds independent of the Agreement, not upon any provision or action under the contract. Furthermore, other courts have found in similar cases that the filing of a lawsuit for sexual harassment is repudiation of the contract, not ratification.

Circuit City maintains that the Agreement is nonetheless enforceable because Circuit City obtained parental consent. As indicated previously, because Foss was under eighteen at the time he completed the online application for employment, he was required by the online application system to obtain parental consent. The name "Sharon Foss" appears in the application as having consented. In affidavits attached to Plaintiff's Opposition to Compel Arbitration, both Andrew Foss and Sharon Foss state that parental consent was not obtained or given to the Agreement. Furthermore, there is no claim that parental consent was provided when Foss signed the hard copy of the agreement on October 14.

The only conclusion the Court is left with is that Foss entered his mother's name without obtaining her consent. This misrepresentation, however, will not act as an estoppel to prevent Foss from asserting his infancy. This immature and false representation is exactly why the law acts to protect the infant. As the Law Court stated in 1923: "It is simply the result of the improvidence of infancy which the law has always in mind." *Whitman v. Allen*, 123 Me. 1, 121 A. 160, 163 (Me. 1923).

III. CONCLUSION

The Court finds that without written ratification, the Agreement never came into existence between Foss and Circuit City. Therefore, there is no agreement to arbitrate the dispute, and the Motions to Compel Arbitration and Stay the Proceedings are DENIED.

Understanding the Case:

1. *Parents and Guardians:* Parents historically have had the authority to enter into contracts on behalf of their minor children, which is why the issue of parental consent was relevant in the *Foss* case. Court-appointed legal guardians, whether appointed on behalf of a minor child or an incompetent adult (discussed in the next section), also typically have the authority to contract on behalf of a minor or incompetent adult. The scope of this authority has sometimes been questioned based on the inability of the minor child or incompetent adult to revoke or contest this authority, as the principal would be able to in the normal principal-agent relationship (as discussed in Chapter 9). Disaffirmance upon reaching the age of majority is one defense that a minor has with respect to a contract entered into on his behalf by a parent.

2. *Arbitration Advantage:* As you have seen throughout the book, many companies include arbitration clauses in their contracts, particularly when contracting with employees or customers. As discussed in Chapter 6, arbitration can provide many advantages to a contracting party that potentially may face many lawsuits. Arbitration proceedings are typically confidential, which means that a company that chooses to "act badly" may be able to continue doing so and simply address any complaints through arbitration. Parties can also specify in detail the rules that will be used for the arbitration process (which is much more limited with respect to conventional courts), such as the rules of evidence, the amount of discovery permitted, and the number of arbitrators. It also can limit the number of appeals permitted. There is significant literature criticizing the historical business relationship between the agencies and companies providing arbitrators and large companies, as well as empirical research suggesting business-favorable results in arbitration, which may suggest a conflict of interest on the part of the arbitration firms.

3. *Arbitration Decisions:* The decisions of arbitrators typically are enforceable in any court of competent jurisdiction. This means that, although a court will not consider or decide the contractual issues subject to arbitration, it will enforce the arbitrator's decision.

Comprehension and Thought Questions:

1. What is the rule in Maine regarding whether minors who achieve the age of majority are bound by contracts entered into while they are below the age of majority?

2. What acts of Foss does Circuit City point to that suggest Foss should be bound by the contract? Why is the court unconvinced of these arguments?

3. Do you think the Maine infancy doctrine is overly protective of minors? Is it a desirable policy? What downside do you see to such a doctrine?

Hypothetical Variations:

1. What do you think the result would have been if, above the time clock where Foss punched in, there was a sign that said "By punching in, you (the employee) agree and reaffirm all the terms and conditions of your employment contract with Circuit City"?

2. What if Foss's mom had OK'd Foss's signing of the arbitration agreement on her behalf?

3. What if upon turning 18, Circuit City required Foss to sign a ratification of the Agreement as a condition to his receiving accrued compensation?

2. Necessaries

The ratification doctrine discussed above is based on the actions of the minor upon achieving the age of majority. Courts and legislatures have also recognized that, in order to incentivize parties to provide vital goods and services to minors, people should be compensated to the extent that they provide "necessary" goods or services to minors that the minors are unable to secure through their parents. The fear is that if minors' contracts are always unenforceable, minors will be unable to obtain important goods and services because the providers of such goods and services will be unwilling to provide them (knowing that they may not be compensated for doing so). Importantly, these contracts generally are only enforceable if the minor's parents are unable or unwilling to secure the goods or services for the minors. Put another way, we assess whether a minor is in need of something based on the minor's particular situation at the time the contract was entered into, not whether the goods or services contracted for are a necessity for all minors. This limits the scope of the exception and can put a person in the unenviable position of attempting to ascertain what might or might not constitute a necessary for the particular minor with whom the person is contracting.

Although contracts for necessaries may be enforceable against the minor, the measure of damages is not based on what the minor actually promised. Instead the measure of damages is typically based on an assessment of the fair value or benefit of the services or goods provided. For example, a contract with a minor to render medical services may be enforceable, but the minor may only be required to pay for the value of the services rendered, as opposed to the contractually stated amount to be charged for the medical services. Thus, this duty to pay arises not out of the existence of a contract, but out of the unjust enrichment of the minor. Unjust enrichment will be discussed in Chapter 23.

A promise to pay for lifesaving medical services may be a clear example of a promise that should be enforceable based on the necessity of such services, but it can be difficult to ascertain whether other important, though not necessarily vital, goods or services are provided. For example, courts are sometimes faced with the question of whether legal services are "necessaries," and the answer in those instances may turn on whether the legal services relate to protecting important or vital interests of the child, such as prosecuting a civil action to recover amounts for injury suffered by the child or protecting the child's welfare or security.

PRACTICE PROBLEM 18-1

1. Rafael, a 16-year-old, decides to run away from home because he felt as though his parents were "smothering him" and treating him like a baby. He immediately enters into a lease agreement for an apartment with a landlord. In the agreement, Rafael represents that he is 18 years old, which is the age of majority in the state.

    a. If Rafael refuses to pay the first month's rent and the landlord subsequently sues him, will Rafael be able to employ the defense of incapacity?

    b. What if Rafael does not refuse to pay rent until the first month after he turns 18?

    c. What if Rafael does not refuse to pay rent until the sixth month after he turns 18?

    d. Would your answer to any of the questions above change if Rafael had not misrepresented his age?

2. Zachary's mother entered into a contract on Zachary's behalf with an attorney to provide legal services. The legal services were to assert a claim for inheritance against the father's estate (the mother and father were not married). Under the contingency fee arrangement, the attorney would be entitled to receive one-third of any recovery. The mother agreed to this arrangement after explaining that she could not afford to pay the attorney's hourly rate. After the attorney prevailed on behalf of Zachary, which took years and occurred after Zachary became an adult, Zachary sought to disaffirm the contract. Do you think he will succeed, or will the attorney be able to recover? If the attorney

wins, how much will he likely be paid? Would your answers to the above change if the legal services provided had been to assist Zachary in seeking asylum (successfully) in the country?

3. Brooke Swords's parents enter into a modeling contract for her when she is ten years old. The modeling contract permits the photographer to utilize the pictures of Brooke for any purposes. When she turns the age of majority, Brooke decides that she does not want the pictures to be published anymore and seeks to disaffirm the contract. The state in which the contract was made enacted a statute that makes it a crime (and also provides for a private right of action) to use a living person's name, portrait, or picture without consent, "which may include parental consent on behalf of a minor." Will Brooke be able to disaffirm the contract?

B. INCOMPETENCE

Contracting individuals may also suffer from cognitive diseases or defects that undermine the presumption that individuals are well positioned to act in their own interests. As this presumption is undermined, other policies, such as fairness, began to conflict with contract law policies of predictability and freedom of contract. Contract law purports to protect a party's reliance on, and expectations regarding, another party's contractual promise, but fairness suggests that we do not want individuals bound to contracts when they are unable to protect themselves.

Consequently, as with minors, contract law recognizes that in certain instances, individuals may be unable to act in their own best interests due to mental disease or defect and may be taken advantage of by others. For example, if Sheena does not realize, because she is delusional, that she is making a contractual promise to Leo to build his house, it seems improper for contract law nevertheless to permit enforcement of that promise against her. It may be unfair to Leo to excuse Sheena's performance, but this excuse may be justified when weighing the fairness of who is best situated to "suffer" or bear the loss.

As in most instances when a defense has been employed, the question is not whether someone will suffer a loss, but instead which person should be forced to bear the loss. Contract law suggests that, as between an incompetent person and a competent person, the loss arising from the incompetent person's nonperformance should be borne by the competent person. However, if the defense is too easy to prove, the concern arises that people will be unable to rely on contracts for fear of the other party avoiding them by asserting that defense. On the other hand, if the defense is too difficult to prove, the concern will be that too many incompetent individuals will be bound by contracts they did not or would not have desired had they been competent.

Assessing **incompetence** can be a lot more difficult than simply setting an age of majority, as in the case of the infancy defense. There may be a number of factors contributing to someone's mental incapacity, including mental illness, brain damage, psychological conditions, and congenital mental defects. As you have studied or will study in criminal law, there are many different potential tests when assessing someone's competence. The Restatement addresses mental incompetence in two different ways, as described below.

Restatement (Second) Contracts § 15

(1) A person incurs only voidable contractual duties by entering into a transaction if by reason of mental illness or defect

(a) he is unable to understand in a reasonable manner the nature and consequences of the transaction, or

(b) he is unable to act in a reasonable manner in relation to the transaction and the other party has reason to know of his condition.

(2) Where the contract is made on fair terms and the other party is without knowledge of the mental illness or defect, the power of avoidance under Subsection (1) terminates to the extent that the contract has been so performed in whole or in part or the circumstances have so changed that avoidance would be unjust. In such a case a court may grant relief as justice requires.

Section (1)(a) addresses what is the most commonly accepted test to assess whether someone is sufficiently competent to enter a contract. It is commonly referred to as the cognition test, as it turns on the mental cognition of the person seeking to use the defense. Under that test, the party pleading the defense must demonstrate that the party suffered from a mental disease or defect that precluded him from *understanding* the transaction in a reasonable manner. Accordingly, the party must first demonstrate that there was a mental disease or defect. A party will often introduce medical testimony to prove this element. The medical field's opinion of what constitutes a mental disease or defect has changed over time and can be contested in court. The party also must demonstrate that the disease or defect precluded her reasonable understanding of what was transpiring in the transaction.

For example, if Paul was suffering from a mental defect at the time he signed a contract, he could later argue that the contract is voidable by him because of that defect. Even if the counterparty argued that Paul knew he was signing a piece of paper, that evidence would not undermine Paul's defense if his mental defect prevented him from understanding that he was entering into a contract.

Section 1(b), in contrast, examines whether a person is unable to *act* reasonably with respect to a transaction and the other party has knowledge of such inability. This test, commonly referred to as the volition test, requires a closer assessment of the behavior actually engaged in to determine whether it was reasonable and whether the other party had knowledge of that condition.

An examination of what constitutes a "reasonable" act in terms of a party's choices is necessarily controversial. For example, how is a court supposed to know whether a choice was reasonable but reflected poor subjective judge-ment, or instead reflected the party's inability to choose reasonably? Recall that a person's personal or subjective preferences generally will be respected in determining whether parties' exchange was supported by consideration.

Similarly, it may be difficult for a court to be confident in its hindsight as-sessment that a decision, when made, resulted from a party's inability to act in a reasonable manner with respect to the transaction. The decision may have been reasonable at the time but appear unreasonable based on changed circum-stances later. In one famous case, *Ortelere*,[2] a teacher that suffered a nervous breakdown subsequently revoked her retirement benefit election to instead elect one that provided a larger lifetime benefit but no death benefit. Since she died a few months later, this election appeared to the court to support (togeth-er with other medical testimony) that she was unable to act reasonably with respect to the transaction. That would, however, only be the case if she in fact knew (which no one could know with certainty, despite her other medical con-ditions) that she was going to die soon. The option she chose was one that was available to others, and presumably their decisions were binding with respect to choosing that option. The decision in some sense begged the question of whether all people who chose that option were acting unreasonably in making their retirement benefit choice.

The other problem with proving that the mental disease or defect prevented the individual from acting reasonably with respect to the transaction is proof. That is because under the volition test, the evidence that the person was unable to act reasonably will typically be the fact that the person acted unreasonably, which is unhelpful if we are truly trying to ascertain whether someone can control his or her inclination to act unreasonably. For example, the evidence utilized in *Ortelere* was the fact that the teacher chose an unreasonable benefit plan choice. But people make unreasonable choices all the time, and unreason-able or even irrational acts are not always suggestive of a lack of control over one's decisions or an inability to act reasonably or rationally.

It is questionable, too, whether a party's knowledge of the other's incompe-tence should be relevant when determining whether to enforce an incompetent person's contractual promise. It is unclear why "fault" (knowing that someone has a mental condition) should be a requirement for the incompetent defen-dant to prove. Again, if one balances the interests, one could conclude that society should protect those with mental conditions that preclude reasonable understanding or behavior, regardless of whether the other party knows of the defendant's condition.

In the following case, consider the interplay between legislation and com-mon law and whether you believe the legislature created an appropriate and workable standard for assessing incapacity due to mental incompetence. As

---

2. Ortelere v. Teachers' Retirement Bd., 25 N.Y.2d 196 (1969).

you read this, see if you can identify which aspect of the capacity defense Ms. Brunson's guardian was arguing: the cognition test or the volition test. In addition, pay attention to the precedent the court cites to, and whether that precedent set out a cognition test or volition test.

In re Doar (Brunson)
Supreme Court of New York, Queens County
900 N.Y.S.2d 593 (2009)

Charles J. THOMAS, J.

In March 2008 the New York City Commissioner of Social Services submitted a petition pursuant to Mental Hygiene Law article 81 for the appointment of a guardian for Hermina Brunson. Dimas Salaberios was appointed temporary guardian for Ms. Brunson.

At the time of the hearing which was commenced on February 28, 2009, and continued on various dates until May 8, 2009, Ms. Brunson's home had been in foreclosure. The foreclosure action has been stayed pending the conclusion of the guardianship proceeding.

As part of the guardianship proceeding petitioner seeks to establish that Ms. Brunson was incapacitated from the year 2000 forward and that she lacked the capacity (1) to execute the deed transferring the property to her brother Joseph, and (2) to enter into mortgage agreements with Financial Freedom Senior Funding Corp. (hereinafter Financial Freedom) signed in December 2001 and June 2003. The temporary guardian seeks to vacate the mortgages because of Ms. Brunson's incapacity and claims that the proceeds were used solely for the benefit of Ms. Brunson's brother, Joseph Brunson. He also alleged that Ms. Brunson signed the mortgage agreement under physical and emotional duress from her brother.

Financial Freedom, which has appeared in this action with regard to the issues involving the mortgage, claims that Ms. Brunson had sufficient capacity to enter into the mortgage agreements on December 28, 2001 and June 20, 2003 and that even if she did not, the proceeds of the mortgage were used for her benefit. That being the case, Financial Freedom claims it is entitled to repayment of the monies expended from the mortgage proceeds.

It is agreed between the parties that Ms. Brunson purchased a one-family home in 1974 and held the property individually in fee simple until October 12, 2001. At that time, Ms. Brunson signed a deed transferring her property to herself and her brother Joseph Brunson as joint tenants with the right of survivorship. It is also agreed that two reverse mortgages were executed by both Ms. Brunson and her brother Joseph Brunson—the first on December 30, 2001 for $300,000; the second on June 20, 2003 for $375,000. The second mortgage paid off and satisfied the first mortgage leaving only the June 20, 2003 mortgage outstanding.

At the hearing, Dr. Arthur Pierre Lewis testified that he treated Ms. Brunson from December 2000, when she was transferred from Elmhurst Hospital to Creedmore Psychiatric Hospital, until 2006. As her treating physician, Dr. Pierre Lewis diagnosed Ms. Brunson's condition as chronic schizophrenia paranoid type. Dr. Pierre Lewis testified that he saw Ms. Brunson on a monthly basis and that Ms. Brunson was also treated by Dr. Penny, a psychologist, on a biweekly basis.

At the end of 2001, Ms. Brunson began suffering from a cognitive impairment that included a loss of memory and inability to function. She complained of hearing voices and suffered from delusions, including the delusion that her neighbor, who had recently been released from prison, was trying to take her home away from her. She also claimed that she no longer had the deed to the house.

At approximately the same time, Ms. Brunson also expressed anxiety and great fear of her brother, Joseph. Ms. Brunson claimed, among other things, that her brother was not feeding her. On several occasions Dr. Pierre Lewis witnessed the interaction between Ms. Brunson and her brother Joseph Brunson. Dr. Pierre Lewis felt that based on his expertise as a psychiatrist and on the interaction between the two siblings on these occasions, Joseph Brunson was mistreating Ms. Brunson. His findings resulted in his referring the matter to Adult Protective Services which, after reviewing the complaint, took no further action and closed the case.

Based upon the testimony of Dolly Cook, Ms. Brunson's sister, and Dr. Pierre Lewis, the court finds that Ms. Brunson suffers from a mental illness which, from the time of her hospitalization in the year 2000, rendered her incapable of handling her financial affairs and from understanding the nature of the reverse mortgages entered into in 2001 and 2003 and their long-term implications. Her psychosis and delusions, which seem to center around the loss of her home, made it unlikely that she could have distinguished that which was real from that which was delusional.

Prior to the enactment of Mental Hygiene Law article 81, the rights of the parties to a contractual agreement where one of the parties was incapacitated was set forth by the Court of Appeals, in *Ortelere v Teachers' Retirement Bd.* (25 N.Y.2d 196, 303 N.Y.S.2d 362, 250 N.E.2d 460 [1969]).

> "The avoidance of duties under an agreement entered into by those who have done so by reason of mental illness, but who have understanding, depends on balancing competing policy considerations. There must be stability in contractual relations and protection of the expectations of parties who bargain in good faith. On the other hand, it is also desirable to protect persons who may understand the nature of the transaction but who, due to mental illness, cannot control their conduct. Hence, there should be relief only if the other party knew or was put on notice as to the contractor's mental illness" (205).

In 1992 when the legislature enacted article 81 of the Mental Hygiene Law, the requirement of knowledge of one party's incapacity by the other was not included in the statute. Section 81.29 (d) of the Mental Hygiene Law provides as follows:

"(d) If the court determines that the person is incapacitated and appoints a guardian, the court may modify, amend, or revoke any previously executed . . . contract, conveyance, or disposition during lifetime or to take effect upon death, made by the incapacitated person prior to the appointment of the guardian if the court finds that the previously executed . . . contract, conveyance, or disposition . . ., was made while the person was incapacitated."

Nevertheless, the Appellate Division continued to require that a mortgagee have knowledge of the mortgagor's incapacity before the contract which is otherwise voidable could be voided. In order to void a contract which is voidable because of incapacity, the mortgagor must establish that the mortgagee had knowledge of the "incapacity and were . . . not bona fide mortgagees for value." (*See Weisberg v DeMeo*, 254 A.D.2d 351, 678 N.Y.S.2d 661 [1998].)

In 1996, Congress authorized the National Housing Act which created reverse mortgages aimed at providing the elderly access to the equity in their home. When it did so, the Department of Housing and Urban Development stressed its concern about the intricacies of a reverse mortgage and the need to insure that elderly individuals not risk their hard earned equity by entering into a reverse mortgage unless they fully understood the terms and significance of the mortgages to which they are agreeing. The very nature of the intended recipients of these mortgages renders such transactions suspect and thus a greater obligation is appropriately placed on the mortgagee than in an otherwise arm's length transaction. Hence, the burden of knowledge which had been placed on the proponent seeking to void the contract due to the lack of capacity of a party by the *Ortelere* court must be shifted to the mortgagee when dealing with a reverse mortgage. In such cases it is sufficient if the mortgagee knew or could have known by the reasonable fulfilment of its statutory obligations. To rule otherwise would render the protections meaningless.

Congress' concern is reiterated and codified in 24 CFR 206.41, the regulations that accompany the National Housing Act. To that end, the statute requires both counseling of the prospective mortgagors as well as the execution and submission of a certificate attesting that the counseling requirement had been either satisfied or waived. The statute requires that an attorney or certified counselor discuss and advise the prospective mortgagors of their rights and responsibilities under a Department of Housing and Urban Development guaranteed reverse mortgage. This certification was not meant to be perfunctory or a mere rubber stamp for the banking and mortgage industry. It was intended to secure that the rights of elderly homeowners were protected. The mortgagee is entrusted with the responsibility of conducting an inquiry of the applicant's understanding of the mortgage agreement.

The purpose of the counseling is twofold. First, to insure that no one enters into a mortgage contract without a full understanding of his or her rights under the mortgage. Second, that a reviewing court can ascertain that the intent of the legislation has been accomplished and that the statutory requirements have been fulfilled. Here the court is not satisfied as to either.

Freedom Fidelity, which was unable to produce the individual who filled out the certificate of counseling, was unable to substantiate the details of what Ms. Brunson had been told. While the certificate, indicating that a Rosa Colarte certified that the homeowners had received counseling, was submitted into evidence, there was no evidence as to the qualifications of Ms. Colarte or the counseling itself. The certificate states that the counseling was not face-to-face but over the phone and that the total time was 45 minutes. The information on the certificate does not inform the court whether Ms. Colarte actually spoke to Ms. Brunson and, if so, what portion of the conversation was with Ms. Brunson as opposed to Joseph Brunson, who clearly dominated his sister's actions. The court cannot ascertain what information Ms. Brunson was given by Ms. Colarte and whether she had or asked questions and, if so, what they were and whether her questions were answered.

There is no evidence that Ms. Brunson understood the terms of the mortgage or the counseling certificate that she signed on June 20, 2003. Under the circumstances of this case, any responsible counselor would have unearthed Ms. Brunson's mental illness and her delusions regarding her house and determined that Hermina Brunson lacked the capacity to enter into the mortgage, or, at the very least, that further counseling was needed. While the certificate of counseling is an indication that information was given to the homeowners it is not dispositive of the issue of the mortgagor's knowledge and understanding of the implications of a reverse mortgage or that the requirements under the National Housing Act have been satisfied. That determination rests ultimately with the court.

Under these circumstances, the court finds that Hermina Brunson was incapable of understanding the agreements that she signed on April 21, 2003 and that Financial Freedom is charged with the responsibility to determine, and was in a position to know of her incapacity. Therefore, the court finds the mortgages on June 20, 2003 void.

The court, however, recognizes that Ms. Brunson used a portion of the funds to benefit and protect her ownership rights in the property and to such extent Financial Freedom should be compensated.

Accordingly, the guardian is directed to reimburse Financial Freedom for monies paid out at the closing, including taxes, water charges and the New York City Department of Social Services liens.

Understanding the Case:

1. *Reverse Mortgages:* In a reverse mortgage, just as in any other mortgage loan, a homeowner (often an elderly person) agrees to borrow money from a bank, and that loan is secured by a mortgage on the home. What is different is that, instead of borrowing a lump sum and paying it back over time with interest, in a reverse mortgage the borrower receives funds from the bank and is not required to pay interest. In this way, the homeowner can "tap" the equity in his home and use the funds tax-free to pay bills and so on, much like an annuity. Interest, however, is accruing on the borrowed/received funds, and the entire loan must be repaid when the homeowner dies or sells the home. These mortgages can be very complicated and are inadvisable for individuals in many situations. For example, lenders may be able to "call" the loan (accelerate the loan and declare the entire amount due immediately) if the homeowner vacates the home for a certain period of time due to a medical condition. This is obviously undesirable and would not be possible under a conventional home mortgage structure. Reverse mortgages have also been marketed aggressively through infomercials and have over time obtained a poor reputation. Concerns over the practices of lenders engaged in reverse mortgages have led to heavier regulation of the industry, as discussed in the case.

Comprehension and Thought Questions:

1. What is the test for incapacity under New York law? How is it different from the Restatement's formulation? Does that test focus on the cognition (ability to understand the transaction in a reasonable manner) or volition (ability to act reasonably) of the person alleging lack of capacity?

2. Why is the National Housing Act relevant to the determination of incapacity in this instance? Why do you think the relevant law and regulations were adopted with respect to reverse mortgages?

3. What evidence was introduced to prove Ms. Brunson lacked capacity under that test?

4. Why was the counselor's determination of mental capacity not determinative?

5. Do you think the New York test is sufficiently protective of those who lack capacity? Is it overprotective?

Hypothetical Questions:

1. What if the counselor had met face-to-face with Ms. Brunson? Would it matter if the brother had been present at the face-to-face counseling session?

2. What if Ms. Brunson had not been diagnosed or treated by a doctor for her condition?

PRACTICE PROBLEM 18-2

1. A 55-year-old attorney suffers from an anxiety disorder (among other conditions) and subsequently decides to retire. The attorney decides to cash in a life insurance policy and purchase a houseboat by promising to make partial payments of the purchase price over five years. The attorney dies in a boating accident three years later. The attorney's heirs seek to rescind his agreement to purchase the boat (and recoup the payments already made) because of his incapacity. At trial, his psychologist testifies that, at the time the decision was made, the attorney suffered from mentally debilitating conditions that prevented him from making "rational decisions," but would appear otherwise competent to others.

   a. Would the defense of incapacity be available here under New York law from *In re Doar*? Under the Restatement?

   b. Would your answer change under (a) above if the boat seller was aware of the attorney's condition at the time of his purchase?

CHAPTER 19

Duress and Undue Influence

Several defenses to enforcement arise because of defects in the process leading up to contract formation. These defects stem from behavior by a party that is viewed as wrongful given our social norms. In each case, the wrongful conduct must induce the counterparty to assent for the counterparty to be able to rescind the contract on the basis of that wrongful conduct. For that reason, these defenses are called **inducement defenses**. As you will see, this inducement requirement is captured through a "causation" element in each of these defenses.

The defenses of **duress** and **undue influence** discussed in this chapter both involve pressure one party places on the other in inducing it to enter into a contract. To begin, there is some amount of pressure involved in nearly all contracting decisions. For example, when the salesperson at the Gap tells you that you are holding the last pair of jeans in your size, you feel pressure to make the decision as to whether to buy those jeans knowing you hold the last pair and if you set them down, might lose out on the jeans to another customer.

On the other hand, there is some amount of free will involved in all contracting decisions. For example, if the Gap salesperson holds a gun to your head and tells you if you do not buy that last pair of jeans, she will shoot you, you still have a decision to make: Should you buy the jeans or get shot?

The purpose of the duress and undue influence doctrines is to demarcate those instances where a person is improperly pressured to enter into a contract, to the point where we say that their contracting decision is largely the result of that pressure and not the contracting person's own independent judgment.

The following diagram shows the gradual nature of pressure versus free will. The goal of the duress and undue influence doctrines is to indicate where pressure becomes improper, undermining a party's exercise of free will in making a contracting decision.

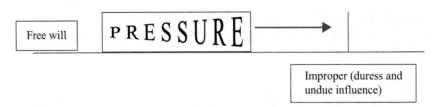

While both duress and undue influence deal with improper pressure, the doctrines differ in the manner and extent to which that pressure is exerted. Section A explains duress, while Section B will explore undue influence.

A. DURESS

Since early common law, a contract has been unenforceable as a result of duress where a party entered into the contract under physical imprisonment or physical compulsion. Usually contracts made through this type of pressure are void. Thus, if Moby locks Nathan in his car and tells Nathan that he cannot get out until Nathan agrees to sell his car to Moby for $20, and Nathan agrees to sell his car to Moby as a result, such agreement would be void.

A contract is also unenforceable based on the defense of duress where a party makes an *improper threat*, where the person who is threatened has *no reasonable alternative but to agree*. Such a threat can be of personal injury or of damage to or destruction of property. The threat may be expressed or implied from the party's conduct. In these instances, generally the contract is voidable, such that the threatened party must choose to rescind the contract if she wishes not to be bound. Thus, if Moby tells Nathan that if Nathan does not sell him Nathan's car for $20, Moby will scrape Nathan's car, and Nathan agrees to sell Moby his car for $20 because of that threat, the contract may be voidable by Nathan.

Some courts also recognize **economic duress**, also known as business compulsion. In these cases, the threat is not to damage or destroy property, but instead to take action that adversely affects the business's ability to operate.[1]

The following is a listing from the Restatement of other types of "improper threats":

§176 When a Threat Is Improper
    (1) A threat is improper if
        (a) what is threatened is a crime or a tort, or the threat itself would be a crime or a tort if it resulted in obtaining property,

---

1. Not every state recognizes the economic duress defense. *See, e.g.*, Finstad v. Ranson-Sargent Water Users, Inc., 849 N.W.2d 165, 170 (N.D. 2014) (holding that North Dakota law does not recognize economic duress).

(b) what is threatened is a criminal prosecution,

(c) what is threatened is the use of civil process and the threat is made in bad faith, or

(d) the threat is a breach of the duty of good faith and fair dealing under a contract with the recipient.

Where the wrongful conduct is a threat, the aggrieved party must also have no reasonable alternative but to agree.[2] Whether a party has a reasonable alternative depends on the particular facts of the situation. For example, where a person threatens to commence civil litigation against another knowing he has no good faith basis for that claim, as a way to induce that party to assent to a contract, the aggrieved party might have a reasonable alternative: defending himself in that litigation. Thus, such a threat may not amount to duress. However, if the aggrieved party's exigencies do not allow him to defend himself in that litigation, then defending himself in litigation would not be a reasonable alternative and the party might be able to rescind due to duress.

Similarly, where a party makes a threat to breach a contract in bad faith, the aggrieved party's reasonable alternative may be to sue that threatening party, and to obtain any promised property or services that the party is withholding from another source. However, if the aggrieved party needs the goods or services promised by the threatening party to perform on another contract, and its failure to perform could lead to significant financial losses, then it would not have reasonable alternatives.

The duress defense may even be relevant to a fee arrangement agreed on as part of the attorney-client relationship. For example, in *Traystman*,[3] a client was presented with a promissory note for $26,973 in legal fees after the trial for which the lawyer had been retained had already begun. The attorney told the client that if the client did not sign the note, then the attorney would withdraw from the case and the client would have to find another attorney or proceed *pro se*. The client requested that another attorney review the note but was urged to sign it right away and have the other attorney look it over later. The client felt as if he had no choice and ultimately signed the note. After trial, the client challenged the enforceability of that note. The trial court found that because the attorney threatened to drop the case if the client did not sign the note, the note was signed under duress and, therefore, was unenforceable.

Finally, remember that a party who seeks to avoid a contract on the basis of an inducement defense must prove *causation*. That means the party seeking to rescind a contract under one of these defenses must prove that the misconduct substantially contributed to that party's assent. For this purpose, the analysis looks subjectively at the party's rationale for assent, and not at what a reasonable person would do in a similar situation.

---

2. Restatement (Second) of Contracts § 175.
3. Traystman, Coric & Keramidas v. Daigle, 855 A.2d 996 (Conn. App. Ct. 2004).

The following case demonstrates how the duress doctrine applies in a modern situation.

Gilkerson v. Nebraska Colocation Centers L.L.C.
United States District Court, District of Nebraska
2016 WL 3079705 (2016)

John M. GERRARD, United States District Judge

The plaintiff, Timothy Gilkerson, is suing his former employer, Nebraska Colocation Centers, L.L.C. (NCC), for allegedly breaching Gilkerson's employment contract. NCC contends the contract was validly rescinded by the parties, but Gilkerson claims the rescission is void due to duress. This matter is before the Court on the defendant's motion for summary judgment. The defendant's motion will reluctantly be granted.

BACKGROUND

Gilkerson was hired in 2011 to be NCC's Vice President and General Manager. Gilkerson and NCC agreed to a 10-year employment contract, paying Gilkerson an annual base salary of $84,000, quarterly sales bonuses, and a retirement bonus upon the expiration of Gilkerson's employment period. Gilkerson was responsible for developing NCC's information technology infrastructure. The parties disagree about the extent to which Gilkerson was expected to help with NCC's sales, and his commissions under the employment contract were based on the company's sales, not his.

The employment contract provided that if NCC terminated Gilkerson's employment without cause before the 10-year term expired, Gilkerson would receive his remaining salary for the balance of the term in a lump sum, another 5 years' bonuses, and his full retirement bonus. But if Gilkerson were to be terminated with cause, he would receive only his unpaid compensation for services already performed. As relevant, "cause" for termination could include Gilkerson's "willful misconduct" in carrying out his duties; or "persistent failure to perform the duties and responsibilities of his employment hereunder; which failure is not remedied by him within 30 days after [his] receipt of written notice from [NCC] of such failure."

NCC was evidently unhappy about Gilkerson's performance helping with sales, and NCC's president, Jerry Appel, talked with Gilkerson about how he wanted Gilkerson to "[c]lose more deals." Gilkerson's performance review was generally average to positive, except for "[u]nsatisfactory" ratings in "[a]chieves sales goals" and "[f]ulfills the terms of his contract." The review indicated that Gilkerson's "lack of sales is irrefutable and of great concern[,]" and detailed Gilkerson's alleged failings in sales. Gilkerson signed the review on February 5, 2013, acknowledging its receipt. Gilkerson's comments on the review express his disagreement regarding sales goals, generally explaining that his experience was not in sales and that "except in the startup phase when everyone needed to pitch in and wear many hats[,]" he had understood that sales would be the responsibility of a dedicated sales team.

Appel announced the hiring of a new "Vice President—Sales and Marketing" on July 8, 2013. On the same day, Appel told Gilkerson that Gilkerson's office was to be given to the new hire, and that Gilkerson's job title had been changed to "Director: Field Engineering and Channel Services." Gilkerson was also informed that Appel was "developing a new compensation program for [his] new position. It [would] retain [his] salary at the current level, provide incentives for channel and carrier sales, and bonuses for field engineering and product development." Then, on July 15, 2013, Appel met with Gilkerson and presented Gilkerson with a document captioned "Mutual Rescission," which would rescind Gilkerson's employment contract. Gilkerson was also presented with a "term sheet" setting forth proposed terms of Gilkerson's continued employment.

Although Gilkerson contends he was given different term sheets at different times, it is clear that the term sheet he ultimately signed provided Gilkerson with the same base salary as the employment contract, a higher commission rate, and an additional bonus contingent upon certain goals. But it limited calculation of commission to Gilkerson's "customers" as defined by the term sheet, and did not include the retirement bonus. And the term sheet did not prohibit Gilkerson's termination.

Gilkerson did not immediately agree to the rescission and term sheet. He met with Appel again on July 17, 2013. Both meetings were recorded. During the meetings, Appel was sharply critical of Gilkerson's performance. Appel clearly presented Gilkerson with a choice between agreeing to the rescission and term sheet, or being fired for cause. For instance, when Gilkerson asked Appel whether his employment contract "means nothing," Appel replied,

> No. In their opinion you didn't live up to what your obligations were in this contract, which is to be—make this thing successful, make this thing work. . . . I'm going to tell you, you go ahead and go—If you're going to go to your lawyer, go to your lawyer, but you'll go to your lawyer without a job.

Appel warned Gilkerson that money was available for litigation, and that NCC could "outlast" Gilkerson. But Appel tried to persuade Gilkerson to accept the rescission and term sheet and continue working for NCC, asserting that he still believed Gilkerson could be successful and earn as much as he would have earned under the employment contract. Appel also pointed out that it "would be tough" for Gilkerson to be unemployed, in part because Gilkerson had health problems and couldn't afford to lose his insurance. Appel told Gilkerson, "If I were in your shoes and if I'm thinking clearly, I'm saying, Wait a second. What's my alternative? 30 days from now I'm without a job. That's my alternative. Do I want that?" Appel agreed that he was "basically saying" that if Gilkerson did not sign the rescission, Gilkerson would be fired.

Gilkerson was able to briefly consult with counsel after the first meeting with Appel. But Gilkerson ultimately signed the rescission and term sheet on July 18, 2013. NCC fired Gilkerson on January 8, 2014. Gilkerson sued NCC in state court, alleging breach of contract and violation of the Nebraska Wage Payment and Collection Act, Neb. Rev. Stat. § 48-1228 et seq. After some procedural confusion that is no longer relevant, NCC eventually removed the case to this Court. Now before the Court is NCC's motion for summary judgment.

Gilkerson's Wage Payment and Collection Act Claim is, so far as the Court can tell, premised on NCC's alleged failure to pay Gilkerson compensation that would have been due under the employment contract. In other words, both of Gilkerson's claims rest on the validity of the employment contract and effect of the rescission, and need not be addressed separately.

DISCUSSION

The primary issue presented in this case is whether the parties' rescission of Gilkerson's employment agreement is voidable as the product of duress. Duress is coercion that is wrongful as a matter of law. Lawful coercion becomes impermissible when employed to support a bad-faith demand: one that the party asserting it knows (or should know) to be unjustified.

To constitute duress, there must be an application of such pressure or constraint that compels a person to go against that person's will and takes away that person's free agency, destroying the power of refusing to comply with the unjust demands of another. But, "[t]o be voidable because of duress, an agreement must not only be obtained by means of pressure brought to bear, but the agreement itself must be unjust, unconscionable, or illegal." *Waste Connections*, 809 N.W.2d at 745. The essence of duress is the surrender to unlawful or unconscionable demands; it cannot be predicated upon demands which are lawful, or the threat to do that which the demanding party has the right to do.

The Court is aware that generally, at common law, those requirements may be disjunctive: that is, duress might be found where either (1) a threat is so shocking that a court will not inquire into the fairness of the resulting exchange, or (2) the impropriety consists of the threat in combination with resulting unfairness. But that does not reflect Nebraska law, as promulgated by the Nebraska Supreme Court in *Carpenter Paper* and expressly reaffirmed in *Omaha Steaks, Lustgarten, Bock, Kosmicki*, and *Waste Connections*.

So, in *Omaha Steaks*, the Nebraska Supreme Court affirmed the dismissal on demurrer of the defendant's counterclaim for duress, because "the agreement, supposedly the result of pressure, must be either illegal, unjust, or unconscionable," and the defendant's answer had "in no way allege[d] that the amended agreement produced a contract the terms of which were either illegal, unjust, or unconscionable. Having failed to allege an essential element of the defense of economic duress or business coercion, the answer was subject to demurrer." 307 N.W.2d at 793. . . .

By contrast, in *McCubbin v. Buss*, the Nebraska Supreme Court found clear and convincing evidence of a voidable transaction where the plaintiff was compelled to cancel a stock purchase contract under threat of losing his job. *McCubbin v. Buss*, 144 N.W.2d 175, 178 (Neb. 1966). The transaction was unjust because "the consideration for the discharge of the stock-purchase contract was inadequate." *Id.* at 179. In *Edwards*, this Court found that an agreement to repay a debt was voidable where an employee had been threatened with termination unless he signed it, because the agreement forced the employee "to repay a debt he did not owe due to [the employer's] fraud[,]" "had no relationship to his job performance," and was invalid due to fraudulent concealment. *Edwards*, 45 F. Supp. 2d at 750. And in *Waste Connections*, the Nebraska Supreme Court affirmed the district court's finding that an agreement increasing the price the defendant charged the plaintiff for services was voidable because of duress, because the new rate was a 41 percent increase from a rate set only a month earlier, the new rate was not charged to any other customers, and there was no economic justification for charging the plaintiff more. *Waste Connections*, 809 N.W.2d at 745-46.

In short, under Nebraska law, whether a contract is voidable as the product of duress depends not only on the coercion employed to produce the agreement, but whether the agreement "is itself unjust, unconscionable, or illegal." *Kosmicki*, 652 N.W.2d at 893. And there is nothing in this case to suggest that the agreement reached here—the rescission, and the term sheet that served as consideration for the rescission—was unjust, unconscionable, or illegal. In essence, Gilkerson accepted a reassignment: his title and employment responsibilities were changed, he received the same base salary but a different bonus structure, and he became an employee at will. Had the revised terms of his employment been given to a newly-hired employee, they would certainly be seen as fair, or even generous. While Gilkerson might have seen it (reasonably) as a demotion, and the terms may have been less advantageous to him than the terms of his previous employment contract, they were not unjust, unconscionable, or illegal.

And Gilkerson really does not argue otherwise. The focus of his brief is arguing that the pressure brought to bear upon him to sign the rescission and term sheet was coercive. And with that, the Court does not disagree—there is, at least, a genuine issue of material fact as to whether the threat of termination would support a claim of duress. The parties have not presented the Court with much from which it could evaluate Gilkerson's job performance, which means that NCC, as the party moving for summary judgment, has not demonstrated that the threat to terminate Gilkerson's employment "for cause" under the employment contract was made in good faith. A factfinder could conclude that

NCC had no sound basis to make that threat, and therefore that the threat was unlawfully coercive. But as explained above, under Nebraska law, that is not enough to void the subsequent rescission. NCC is entitled to summary judgment.

IT IS ORDERED:

1. The defendant's motion for summary judgment is granted.
2. The plaintiff's complaint is dismissed.
3. A separate judgment will be entered.

Understanding the Case:

1. *Subsequent History:* On appeal, a three-judge panel of the Eighth Circuit Court of Appeals reversed the trial court's holding. While the Eighth Circuit upheld the trial court's statement of law on duress, it found that when viewing the facts most favorable to Gilkerson (as the court does in ruling on a motion for summary judgment), the Rescission Agreement and term sheet were "unjust and thus voidable as a product of duress given the alleged pressure brought to bear on him [Gilkerson] to sign the Mutual Rescission and Term Sheet. We specifically take issue with the Term Sheet's provision that made Gilkerson an at-will employee, and indeed NCC ultimately fired him a mere six months later. There was no 'economic justification' for requiring Gilkerson to accept an at-will employment agreement, other than it allowed NCC to avoid the provisions of the Contract that were most favorable to Gilkerson." Consequently, the Eighth Circuit remanded the case for a trial on the merits. *See Gilkerson v. Nebraska Colocation Centers, LLC,* 859 F.3d 1115 (2017). It appears that the parties settled the dispute in February 2018, thus avoiding a trial on the merits.

2. *The "Rescission Agreement and Term Sheet" as Contract:* Gilkerson entered into his original employment agreement with NCC in 2011. However, on July 18, 2013, Gilkerson signed a Rescission Agreement and term sheet. Together, those documents set out (1) NCC's and Gilkerson's agreement to rescind the 2011 employment agreement and (2) NCC's and Gilkerson's agreement to the new terms of Gilkerson's employment. While the document setting out Gilkerson's new terms of employment was labeled "term sheet," the court treated that document (together with the Rescission Agreement) as a contract. Remember from Chapter 10 that parties can be bound by a term sheet if that is their manifested intent. That must have been the situation in this case, though the court did not analyze whether the parties intended to be bound to the term sheet in the above opinion.

3. *Novation:* Where a contract is replaced by a new contract, such as in this case, that is referred to as a **novation**. The new contract essentially replaces the old contract such that a party cannot sue to enforce any rights under the original contract. In this case, the Rescission Agreement and term sheet

together novated the terms of Gilkerson's employment. Thus, unless they were voidable by Gilkerson, Gilkerson was not able to sue NCC for terminating Gilkerson's employment before the end of his ten-year term, as NCC no longer had an obligation to employ Gilkerson for ten years.

Comprehension and Thought Questions:

1. Why did Gilkerson want to rescind the Rescission Agreement and term sheet?

2. What test did the court apply to determine if Gilkerson could rescind the Rescission Agreement and term sheet due to duress? Should it matter whether Gilkerson was an at-will employee or an employee with a term agreement?

3. Did the court find that NCC's coercive conduct satisfied the test for duress? Was it economic duress?

4. Do you agree with the trial court that the terms of the Rescission Agreement and term sheet were not unjust to Gilkerson?

5. Do you believe there is good policy to support Nebraska's requirement that to be induced by duress, a party must prove that the contract made as a result of coercive conduct was "unjust, unconscionable, or illegal"?

6. What would the outcome of the case likely have been using the Restatement's test for duress, which requires that a party prove that (1) a wrongful threat, (2) induces a party to assent, (3) in circumstances where the party had no reasonable alternative?

7. What could Gilkerson have done to protect himself in this situation at the time he was asked to assent to the Rescission Agreement and term sheet?

Hypothetical Variations:

1. What if it was clear to NCC that Gilkerson's poor performance did not give them "cause" to terminate Gilkerson under his employment agreement, but they still used that argument to justify getting Gilkerson to sign the Rescission Agreement and term sheet?

2. What if Gilkerson had been employed at will?

3. What if under the Rescission Agreement and term sheet, Gilkerson was to be paid half of the salary he was to be paid under his original employment agreement, but the other terms in the term sheet were the same as in the case?

PRACTICE PROBLEM 19-1

PharmaX is a pharmacy located in the small town of Humidville, Texas. Vera Harlowe, a Humidville native, started PharmaX with her husband, Jerry, in 1980. While Vera's husband passed away in 2005, Vera has remained very active in running PharmaX's business.

PharmaX is located right next door to the Humidville Medical Complex, which is the only large medical complex within 30 miles of Humidville. As such, most of PharmaX's business comprises filling prescriptions for patients of doctors at the Humidville Medical Complex, as well as selling food and sundry items to people visiting the Humidville Medical Complex. PharmaX usually makes around $400,000 a year in profit.

Commercial Retail Space Inc. ("CommerRs") owns and operates the building in which PharmaX is located. CommerRS is a large property investment and management company. It has historically invested its assets in medical-related properties, such as medical facilities and pharmacies. That is why CommerRS originally bought the property on which PharmaX is located.

PharmaX has three years left on the term of its lease with CommerRS.

For various reasons, CommerRS recently decided to shift its investment strategy away from small towns and toward more urban locations. Thus, CommerRS decided to sell the property on which PharmaX operates. On September 1, Radiology Associates agreed to buy that property from CommerRS for $2 million. Radiology Associates plans to tear down PharmaX's building and replace it with one that can accommodate large radiology equipment.

The sale is conditioned on a number of things happening, including PharmaX's agreeing to terminate its lease with CommerRS. That is because under the lease agreement between CommerRS and PharmaX, CommerRS has no right to terminate the lease due to a sale of the property on which PharmaX is located. Thus, CommerRS needs PharmaX's consent to terminate that lease to avoid breaching the lease.

When Vera was first approached by Yolanda Gregory, the Vice President of CommerRS's acquisitions group, about terminating the lease, Vera said that she would not agree to a lease termination, as this was one of the only suitable locations in Humidville for PharmaX, given that it depends on its proximity to the Humidville Medical Complex for business. In response, Yolanda offered to have CommerRS pay PharmaX $50,000, which represents one year's rent, if PharmaX agreed to terminate the lease. Still, Vera would not agree. As a last resort, Yolanda explained that if Vera did not agree to terminate the lease with CommerRS, CommerRS would sue PharmaX for breach of the lease agreement, as PharmaX always paid its rent on the fifth of each month, while the lease agreement said that PharmaX had to pay rent no later than the fourth of each month. CommerRS had never raised a concern with late payments before. Yolanda said that assuming CommerRS won that suit, PharmaX would have to vacate its premises and would recover no money from CommerRS. She also said that Vera had one day to decide whether she would terminate the lease or be sued. Yolanda stressed that given CommerRS's size and resources, there was simply no way PharmaX would win in court, as CommerRS could financially outlast PharmaX in any litigation.

Faced with this choice and a short time to make a decision, Vera agreed to terminate PharmaX's lease with CommerRS in exchange for $50,000. However, after the fact, she decided to meet with you, her lawyer, to evaluate if she made the right choice.

Given all of the above facts, does PharmaX likely have any basis to rescind its contract with CommerRS to terminate the lease?

B. UNDUE INFLUENCE

1. Components of Undue Influence

As with duress, undue influence involves improper pressure placed on a contracting party that causes that party to assent. However, unlike with duress, there need not be a single wrongful act by a contracting party to induce that assent. Instead, **undue influence** involves a stronger party using its position of strength to exert unfair pressure on a susceptible party, which causes that susceptible party to assent. That unfair pressure may result from many different party actions and circumstances.

The following case addresses undue influence, including some of the typical "hallmarks" of excessive pressure and undue susceptibility.

Odorizzi v. Bloomfield School District
Court of Appeal of California, Second Appellate District, Division Two
26 Cal. App. 2d 123 (1966)

FLEMING, Justice.

Appeal from a judgment dismissing plaintiff's amended complaint on demurrer.

Plaintiff Donald Odorizzi was employed during 1964 as an elementary school teacher by defendant Bloomfield School District and was under contract with the district to continue to teach school the following year as a permanent employee. On June 10 he was arrested on criminal charges of homosexual activity, and on June 11 he signed and delivered to his superiors his written resignation as a teacher, a resignation which the district accepted on June 13. In July the criminal charges against Odorizzi were dismissed under Penal Code, section 995, and in September he sought to resume his employment with the district. On the district's refusal to reinstate him he filed suit for declaratory and other relief.

Odorizzi's amended complaint asserts his resignation was invalid because obtained through duress, fraud, mistake, and undue influence and given at a time when he lacked capacity to make a valid contract. Specifically, Odorizzi declares he was under such severe mental and emotional strain at the time he signed his resignation, having just completed the process of arrest, questioning by the police, booking, and release on bail, and having gone for 40 hours without sleep, that he was incapable of rational thought or action. While he was in this condition and unable to think clearly, the superintendent of the district and the principal of his school came to his apartment. They said they were trying to help him and had his best interests at heart, that he should take their advice and immediately resign his position with the district, that there was no time to consult an attorney, that if he did not resign immediately the district would suspend and dismiss him from his position and publicize the proceedings, his "aforedescribed arrest" and cause him "to suffer extreme embarrassment and humiliation"; but that if he resigned at once the incident would not be publicized and would not jeopardize his chances of securing employment as a teacher elsewhere. Odorizzi pleads that because of his faith and confidence in their representations they were able to substitute their will and judgment in place of his own and thus obtain his signature to his purported resignation. A demurrer to his amended complaint was sustained without leave to amend.

. . .

Undue influence, in the sense we are concerned with here, is a shorthand legal phrase used to describe persuasion which tends to be coercive in nature, persuasion which overcomes the will without convincing the judgment. The hallmark of such persuasion is high pressure, a pressure which works on mental, moral, or emotional weakness to such an extent that it approaches the boundaries of coercion. In this sense, undue influence has been called overpersuasion. Misrepresentations of law or fact are not essential to the charge, for a person's will may be overborne without misrepresentation. By statutory definition undue influence includes "taking an unfair advantage of another's weakness of mind, or . . . taking a grossly oppressive and unfair advantage of another's necessities or distress." (Civ. Code, § 1575.) While most reported cases of undue influence involve persons who bear a confidential relationship to one another, a confidential or authoritative relationship between the parties need not be present when the undue influence involves unfair advantage taken of another's weakness or distress.

. . .

In essence undue influence involves the use of excessive pressure to persuade one vulnerable to such pressure, pressure applied by a dominant subject to a servient object. In combination, the elements of undue susceptibility in the servient person and excessive pressure by the dominating person make the latter's influence undue, for it results in the apparent will of the servient person being in fact the will of the dominant person.

Undue susceptibility may consist of total weakness of mind which leaves a person entirely without understanding; or, a lesser weakness which destroys the capacity of a person to make a contract even though he is not totally incapacitated; or, the first element in our equation, a still lesser weakness which provides sufficient grounds to rescind a contract for undue influence Such lesser weakness need not be longlasting nor wholly incapacitating, but may be merely a lack of full vigor due to age, physical condition, emotional anguish, or a combination of such factors. The reported cases have usually involved elderly, sick, senile persons alleged to have executed wills or deeds under pressure. In some of its aspects this lesser weakness could perhaps be called weakness of spirit. But whatever name we give it, this first element of undue influence resolves itself into a lessened capacity of the object to make a free contract.

In the present case plaintiff has pleaded that such weakness at the time he signed his resignation prevented him from freely and competently applying his judgment to the problem before him. Plaintiff declares he was under severe mental and emotional strain at the time because he had just completed the process of arrest, questioning, booking, and release on bail and had been without sleep for forty hours. It is possible that exhaustion and emotional turmoil may wholly incapacitate a person from exercising his judgment. As an abstract question of pleading, plaintiff has pleaded that possibility and sufficient allegations to state a case for rescission.

Undue influence in its second aspect involves an application of excessive strength by a dominant subject against a servient object. Judicial consideration of this second element in undue influence has been relatively rare, for there are few cases denying persons who persuade but do not misrepresent the benefit of their bargain. Yet logically, the same legal consequences should apply to the results of excessive strength as to the results of undue weakness. Whether from weakness on one side, or strength on the other, or a combination of the two, undue influence occurs whenever there results "that kind of influence or supremacy of one mind over another by which that other is prevented from acting according to his own wish or judgment, and whereby the will of the person is overborne and he is induced to do or forbear to do an act which he would not do, or would do, if left to act freely." (*Webb* v. *Saunders,* 79 Cal. App. 2d 863, 871 [181 P.2d 43].) Undue influence involves a type of mismatch which our statute calls unfair advantage. (Civ. Code, § 1575.) Whether a person of subnormal capacities has been subjected to ordinary force or a person of normal capacities subjected to extraordinary force, the match is equally out of balance. If will has been overcome against judgment, consent may be rescinded.

The difficulty, of course, lies in determining when the forces of persuasion have overflowed their normal banks and become oppressive flood waters. There are second thoughts to every bargain, and hindsight is still better than foresight.

. . .

However, overpersuasion is generally accompanied by certain characteristics which tend to create a pattern. The pattern usually involves several of the following elements: (1) discussion of the transaction at an unusual or inappropriate time, (2) consummation of the transaction in an unusual place, (3) insistent demand that the business be finished at once, (4) extreme emphasis on untoward consequences of delay, (5) the use of multiple persuaders by the dominant side against a single servient party, (6) absence of third-party advisers to the servient party, (7) statements that there is no time to consult financial advisers or attorneys. If a number of these elements are simultaneously present, the persuasion may be characterized as excessive.

. . .

[I]f a day or two after Odorizzi's release on bail the superintendent of the school district had called him into his office during business hours and directed his attention to those provisions of the Education Code compelling his leave of absence and authorizing his suspension on the filing of written charges, had told him that the district contemplated filing written charges against him, had pointed out the alternative of resignation available to him, had informed him he was free to consult counsel or any adviser he wished and to consider the matter overnight and return with his decision the next day, it is extremely unlikely that any complaint about the use of excessive pressure could ever have been made against the school district.

But, according to the allegations of the complaint, this is not the way it happened, and if it had happened that way, plaintiff would never have resigned. Rather, the representatives of the school board undertook to achieve their objective by overpersuasion and imposition to secure plaintiff's signature but not his consent to his resignation through a high-pressure carrot-and-stick technique—under which they assured plaintiff they were trying to assist him, he should rely on their advice, there wasn't time to consult an attorney, if he didn't resign at once the school district would suspend and dismiss him from his position and publicize the proceedings, but if he did resign the incident wouldn't jeopardize his chances of securing a teaching post elsewhere.

. . .

The judgment is reversed.

Comprehension and Thought Questions:

1. In an omitted section of the opinion, the court determined that duress was not available as a defense. Why do you think duress was not present?

2. What factors does the court give to assist it in determining whether undue influence is present? Which of those factors were present?

3. Following the reversal of the judgment, what would the lower court be required to do with respect to the defense of undue influence?

4. What are the downsides with recognizing a defense like undue influence? What are the policy rationales for this defense?

Hypothetical Variations:

1. What if Odorizzi actually had been well rested when he signed his resignation?

2. What if Odorizzi's counsel had been with him at the time Odorizzi had been asked to sign his resignation?

3. What if this case had been brought in 2019?

The following case demonstrates a more modern application of undue influence. As you read the decision, consider whether you believe the approach in *Odorizzi* or *Beckner* is more appropriate in determining whether undue influence exists.

Friendly Ice Cream Corp. v. Beckner
Supreme Court of Virginia
268 Va. 23 (2004)

Elizabeth B. LACY, Justice.

In this appeal we review the chancellor's decree rescinding an amendment to a lease because the lease amendment was the result of undue influence.

FACTS

Beatrice Beckner and her husband entered into a commercial lease with Friendly Ice Cream Corporation (Friendly) allowing Friendly to build and operate a retail store on property owned by the Beckners. The lease commenced in 1976 with an original term of 15 years. Friendly could exercise five renewal options of five years each. If all five options were exercised, the lease would terminate in 2016. In addition to a monthly base rent, the lease required an annual payment of two percent of the store's annual gross sales exceeding $275,000 (percentage rent). FriendCo Restaurants, Inc. (FriendCo) operated the retail ice cream store through a sublease with Friendly. In 2001, the lease generated a base rent of $1,105.00 per month and a percentage rent of $7,984.68, for a total income of approximately $21,200.00.

In December 2001, Friendly and FriendCo decided to close the retail store. Fourteen years remained on the lease if the renewal option were fully exercised. Riggs Bank, N.A. (Riggs), among others, expressed an interest in acquiring Friendly's interest in the lease. Riggs planned to demolish the existing retail building and build a bank building on the property. Riggs was willing to pay Friendly approximately $800,000 for terminating the sublease and assigning the lease to Riggs if the lease were amended to relieve Riggs from payment of the percentage rent.

On December 26, 2001, Sandra L. Hughes, Vice-President and Deputy General Counsel for FriendCo, wrote to the Beckners seeking their consent to the assignment of the lease to Riggs, to the proposed redevelopment of the property, and to an agreement that the percentage rent requirement would not apply to Riggs' use of the property as a bank. On January 3, 2002, in response to a telephone call from Mrs. Beckner, Hughes went to Mrs. Beckner's home and discussed the provisions of a proposed amendment to the lease that would meet Riggs' conditions for the lease assignment. At that meeting Mrs. Beckner, then widowed and 80 years old, told Hughes that her lawyer was Norman Hammer.

Hughes contacted Hammer and, at Hammer's request, sent him a letter dated January 25, 2002, setting out the history of payments made on the percentage rent, offering to increase the base rate by $5,000 a year, and proposing an amendment to the lease eliminating the percentage rent. Hammer replied on February 20, stating that he had no counter offer and that he wanted to confer with Mrs. Beckner's son, Robert O. Beckner.

In a February 27 telephone call to Hughes, Mrs. Beckner stated that Hammer was no longer her attorney and that she wanted to meet with Hughes to discuss the amendment to the lease. Hughes went to Mrs. Beckner's home and discussed the terms of the proposed amendment to the lease, including the offer to increase the annual base rent by $5,000. Mrs. Beckner replied that she wanted the base rate increased by $8,940 a year, from $1,105 per month to $1,850 per month. Hughes agreed to submit Mrs. Beckner's proposal to Friendly.

On February 28, Hammer sent a facsimile to Hughes instructing Hughes not to contact Mrs. Beckner directly and terming the "present offer" unacceptable. Hughes replied by facsimile on March 1, telling Hammer that she had met with Mrs. Beckner at Mrs. Beckner's request; that Mrs. Beckner stated that Hammer no longer represented Mrs. Beckner; that Hughes was a principal of FriendCo, the subtenant; and that "principals may talk to one another at any time, without going through lawyers if they so choose."

Hammer met with Mrs. Beckner on March 7, 2002 to discuss the amendment to the lease and his representation of her. Also present at the meeting were Robert Beckner, Clyde R. Christopherson—a lawyer who had also represented Mrs. Beckner, and Leroy Jackson, Mrs. Beckner's long-time friend and insurance agent. Mrs. Beckner agreed that Hammer should negotiate with Friendly on her behalf regarding the proposed amended lease. Christopherson drafted a letter reflecting this decision and, after reviewing the letter with Mrs. Beckner on March 8, sent the letter to Hughes' superior, David J. Norman.

Mrs. Beckner telephoned Hughes on Friday, March 8, reiterated her desire to deal directly with Hughes, and asked if Friendly had responded to the increase in base rent that Mrs. Beckner had requested. Hughes told Mrs. Beckner that Friendly had agreed to the increase. Although Mrs. Beckner wanted to sign the amendment to the lease immediately, Hughes could not meet with her until Monday, March 11. Hughes sent Mrs. Beckner a copy of the amendment to the lease along with a copy of Christopherson's March 8 letter and the facsimile exchanges between Hammer and Hughes on February 28 and March 1.

On March 11, Hughes arrived at Mrs. Beckner's home, reviewed the amendment to the lease with her, and then, at Mrs. Beckner's direction, went with her to the bank where a bank employee with whom Mrs. Beckner had dealt in the past notarized her signature on the documents. Hughes then presented Mrs. Beckner with a letter Hughes had drafted for Mrs. Beckner's signature stating that Mrs. Beckner wanted to deal directly with Hughes. Mrs. Beckner signed the letter.

Shortly thereafter, Robert Beckner informed Hughes and Norman that he was concerned about his mother's actions. After receiving copies of the documents Mrs. Beckner had signed, Christopherson wrote Norman indicating Christopherson considered the documents to be invalid and that the documents should be resubmitted to Mrs. Beckner for further consideration.

PROCEEDING

On March 22, 2002, Mrs. Beckner filed a bill of complaint against Friendly and FriendCo seeking rescission of the amendment to the lease on four grounds: fraud, gross inadequacy of consideration, unjust enrichment, and undue influence, Counts I through IV, respectively. The fraud count was dismissed by agreed order prior to trial and Mrs. Beckner abandoned the unjust enrichment count at trial. Friendly and FriendCo (collectively "Friendly's") filed a motion for summary judgment asserting that Mrs. Beckner was not entitled to rescission because she had acquiesced to the terms of the amended lease when she cashed checks she received pursuant to the terms of the amended lease. The chancellor denied this motion as not appropriate for summary judgment.

Following an *ore tenus* hearing, the chancellor entered a decree in favor of Mrs. Beckner on Counts II and IV. The chancellor found that the amendment to the lease was the product of undue influence because Mrs. Beckner produced clear and convincing evidence that she suffered from great weakness of mind, Hughes had a confidential relationship with her consisting of a formal and informal relationship regarding business matters, and the consideration for the amendment to the lease was grossly inadequate and occurred in suspicious circumstances. The chancellor rescinded the amendment to the lease and required Mrs. Beckner to pay $5,888.23, the amount she received under the amended lease exceeding that which she would have received prior to the amendment. We awarded Friendly's an appeal.

COUNT IV—UNDUE INFLUENCE

On appeal, Friendly's raises five assignments of error. We first consider the three assignments of error that challenge the chancellor's action rescinding the lease amendment based on its finding of undue influence.

A court of equity will not set aside a contract because it is "rash, improvident or [a] hard bargain" but equity will act if the circumstances raise the inference that the contract was the result of imposition, deception, or undue influence. To set aside a deed or contract on the basis of undue influence requires a showing that the free agency of the contracting party has been destroyed.

Because undue influence is a species of fraud, the person seeking to set aside the contract must prove undue influence by clear and convincing evidence.

Direct proof of undue influence is often difficult to produce. In the seminal case of *Fishburne v. Ferguson*, 84 Va. 87, 111, 4 S.E. 575, 582 (1887), however, this Court identified two situations which we considered sufficient to show that a contracting party's free agency was destroyed, and, once established, shift the burden of production to the proponent of the contract. The first involved the mental state of the contracting party and the amount of consideration:

> [W]here . . . great weakness of mind concurs with gross inadequacy of consideration, or circumstances of suspicion, the transaction will be presumed to have been brought about by undue influence.

Id. Thus, if the party seeking rescission of the deed or contract produces clear and convincing evidence of great weakness of mind and grossly inadequate consideration or suspicious circumstances, he has established a prima facie case of undue influence and, absent sufficient rebuttal evidence, is entitled to rescission of the document.

The second instance *Fishburne* identified arises when a confidential relationship exists between the grantor and proponent of the instrument:

> [W]here one person stands in a relation of special confidence towards another, so as to acquire an habitual influence over him, he cannot accept from such person a personal benefit without exposing himself to the risk, in a degree proportioned to the nature of their connection, of having it set aside as unduly obtained.

84 Va. at 112–13, 4 S.E. at 582. Here, equity considers the benefit to the person in the relation of special confidence presumptively invalid and, once that relationship and benefit is established, the burden of going forward with evidence that the transaction was fair rests on the proponent of the transaction.

Initially, we note that in this case the trial court stated that Mrs. Beckner had established "the three elements of [the undue influence] presumption." We assume this refers to the statement in *Martin v. Phillips*, 235 Va. 523, 528, 369 S.E.2d 397, 400 (1988), that the presumption of undue influence arises if weakness of mind, grossly inadequate consideration or suspicious circumstances, and a fiduciary or confidential relationship are established by clear and convincing evidence. As we have discussed, the presumption of undue influence arises and the burden of going forward with the evidence shifts when weakness of mind and grossly inadequate consideration or suspicious circumstances are shown or when a confidential relationship is established. To the extent *Martin* requires all three elements to be shown before the presumption of undue influence can be invoked, it is overruled. Nevertheless, under the principles established in *Fishburne* and subsequent cases, the chancellor's findings in this case, if supported by the record, entitled Mrs. Beckner to the presumption of undue influence under either situation—a confidential relationship or weakness of mind and grossly inadequate consideration or suspicious circumstances.

We now review the chancellor's findings, applying established principles of appellate review. We must accept the chancellor's findings of fact unless they are plainly wrong or without evidence to support them.

A. Confidential Relationship

We begin our review by considering whether the evidence supports the finding that Hughes had a confidential relationship with Mrs. Beckner regarding matters of business. The chancellor did not identify any evidence upon which he based his finding. Mrs. Beckner argues, however, that the requisite confidential relationship existed because Hughes took "actions expressly designed to . . . ingratiate[] herself with Mrs. Beckner to the exclusion of Mrs. Beckner's attorneys" and "acted virtually as counsel to Mrs. Beckner, while adverse to her interests" by giving Mrs. Beckner legal advice in explaining sections of the lease and proposed amendment.

We have described a confidential relationship as a relationship that is

> "not confined to any specific association of the parties; it is one wherein a party is bound to act for the benefit of another, and can take no advantage to himself. It appears when the circumstances make it certain the parties do not deal on equal terms, but, on the one side, there is an overmastering influence, or, on the other, weakness, dependence, or trust, justifiably reposed; in both an unfair advantage is possible."

Trust alone, however, is not sufficient. We trust most men with whom we deal. There must be something reciprocal in the relationship before the rule can be invoked. Before liability can be fastened upon one there must have been something in the course of dealings for which he was in part responsible that induced another to lean upon him, and from which it can be inferred that the ordinary right to contract had been surrendered. If this were not true a reputation for fair dealing would be a liability and an unsavory one an asset.

We have also held that a confidential relationship exists between a parent and child when accompanied by an attorney-client or principal-agent relationship, or between family members when the family member provides financial advice or handles the finances of another family member.

Mrs. Beckner does not suggest that an attorney-client or any other fiduciary relationship existed between herself and Hughes; rather Mrs. Beckner suggests that the confidential relationship arose from Hughes' "legal advice" on the terms of the lease and amendment and from Hughes' attempt to "exclude all others" including Hammer and Christopherson. Finally, Mrs. Beckner argues that the evidence shows that she "liked and trusted" Hughes and did not think Hughes "would attempt to cheat her." These conclusions are neither sufficient to establish a confidential relationship nor are they supported by the evidence.

The record demonstrates that the relationship between Mrs. Beckner and Hughes had the hallmarks of a business relationship, not those of a confidential relationship. There was no history of financial interaction of any kind between Hughes and Mrs. Beckner. The relationship was of short duration, consisting of approximately eight contacts beginning on December 26, 2001 and ending on March 11, 2002, six of which Mrs. Beckner initiated. When Mrs. Beckner initially told Hughes that Hammer was representing her, Hughes contacted Hammer and sent him a copy of the proposed amendment to the lease.

Mrs. Beckner testified that she knew Hughes was "with Friendly's," that the percentage rent under the lease was going down every year, that some Friendly's stores were closing in the area, and that she would not receive any percentage rent if the store on her property closed. The record is clear that during the course of this three-month relationship, Mrs. Beckner did not allow Hughes to make decisions for her regarding the second amendment to the lease. In fact, Mrs. Beckner negotiated a monthly base rent higher than the rate Hughes proposed. Mrs. Beckner received a copy of the proposed amendment to the lease in advance of signing it and she chose the bank and bank employee who notarized her signatures on the amendment to the lease.

Hughes testified that she considered Mrs. Beckner to be her landlord and that negotiations regarding the second amendment to the lease involved "[d]ealing with the other side."

The relationship Hughes and Mrs. Beckner described did not involve any requirement that Hughes act on Mrs. Beckner's behalf, nor did either party presume that Hughes should or would do so. Although Mrs. Beckner may have liked and trusted Hughes, such trust alone is insufficient to establish a confidential relationship. The record at most reflects a commercial relationship in which the parties trusted each other.

Mrs. Beckner failed to carry her burden of proof to show she and Hughes had a confidential relationship, formal or informal, regarding matters of business. Thus, she was not entitled to the presumption of undue influence and would not be entitled to judgment in her favor on this basis.

B. Mental Status and Consideration

The chancellor also found that Mrs. Beckner was entitled to a presumption of undue influence because she suffered from "great weakness of mind," and that the consideration she received was grossly inadequate and the transaction occurred under suspicious circumstances. Again, although the chancellor did not identify the evidence upon which he based these findings, Mrs. Beckner points to a number of factors which she asserts support the chancellor's findings.

Beginning with the adequacy of the consideration, Mrs. Beckner first claims that under the original or amended lease, the base rent was "significantly below prevailing market rates." Mrs. Beckner claimed that the rental value of the property "had risen dramatically" and, according to her expert witness, the current fair market rental value would be between approximately $5,000 and $8,000 a month. However, Mrs. Beckner's expert did not consider the impact the outstanding lease would have on the fair market rental value of the property. The chancellor, while refusing to strike the testimony of this expert, considered it "weightless." We agree with the chancellor that evidence of current fair market rental value without consideration of the existence of the lease or its conditions is not probative of whether the consideration for the amendment to the lease is grossly inadequate.

Next, Mrs. Beckner argues that the consideration was grossly inadequate because the increase in base rent contained in the amendment did not significantly increase the annual amount she received compared to the aggregate amount of base and percentage rent she received under the lease before the amendment. The base rent in the amended lease produced only $80 a month more than she received in 2001 from the combined base and percentage rents, thereby making the consideration received grossly inadequate, according to Mrs. Beckner.

We disagree. The increase in the base rate was in an amount Mrs. Beckner specifically requested. Over the likely lifetime of the amended lease, Mrs. Beckner would receive $310,800 in base rent, $125,160 more than she would have received in base rent without the amendment. The record also shows that the percentage rent in 2001 declined from the prior year. There is no evidence in the record that the value of percentage rent would remain at 2001 levels or would increase. Although Mrs. Beckner labels as speculative the suggestion that Friendly's would or could close the retail store, thereby discontinuing the obligation to pay percentage rent, the uncontradicted evidence was that Friendly's had decided to close the store and that Mrs. Beckner was aware of that decision. Mrs. Beckner testified that she understood that, if the store closed, she would no longer receive any percentage rent. Thus, the increase in base rent was not grossly inadequate in light of the additional income it would produce and the uncertainty of the amount or continuation of revenue from the percentage rent.

Mrs. Beckner next argues that the possibility that she might own a bank building valued at $800,000 at the end of the lease period should not be included as part of the consideration because it also was speculative. Here again the uncontradicted evidence was that, if the lease was amended, Riggs planned to build such a building. This potential asset was a known part of the business transaction and, in the absence of fraud, may be considered as part of the benefit Mrs. Beckner received from agreeing to the lease amendment.

Finally, Mrs. Beckner asserts that the appropriate comparison of "value exchanged" is to compare the additional $80 per month Mrs. Beckner would receive under the amendment with the $800,000 Friendly's would receive for the assignment of the lease to Riggs. This disparity, she maintains, shows that the consideration she received was grossly inadequate. The amount Friendly's would receive from Riggs to assign the lease is irrelevant to the adequacy of the consideration Mrs. Beckner received. Mrs. Beckner could not recover any amount from Riggs because she could not assign the lease to Riggs. The lease had, at a minimum, four years remaining, with the potential to extend, if the tenant so desired, to fourteen years, and contained no provisions for termination by the landlord other than for nonpayment of rent or insolvency of the tenant. Therefore, the value of Mrs. Beckner's consideration must be measured not simply in the amount of increase in base rent but also in light of the rights that she possessed regarding the property and her options at the time of the amendment.

Consideration is grossly inadequate when the "'inequality [is] so strong, gross and manifest that it must be impossible to state it to a [person] of common sense without producing an exclamation at the inequality of it . . . .'" Jackson, 193 Va. at 741, 71 S.E.2d at 185 (quoting *Gwynne v. Heaton*, 1 Bro. Ch. 1, 9, 28 Eng. Rep. 949 (1778)). That others could have bargained for a higher base rent or secured more favorable terms for the execution of the lease amendment does not affect the determination of grossly inadequate consideration. In this case, by executing the amendment to the lease, Mrs. Beckner received an annual increase of $8,940 in base rent regardless of whether the lease was assigned to another party and whether any business was operating on the property. She also acquired the possibility of owning the new bank building at the end of the lease. This record does not support a finding that the consideration Mrs. Beckner received was grossly inadequate.

Mrs. Beckner also asserts the chancellor was justified in finding that the transaction occurred under suspicious circumstances because Hughes did not further investigate whether Mrs. Beckner was represented by counsel following Christopherson's March 8 letter and because Hughes drafted a letter for Mrs. Beckner's signature stating that Mrs. Beckner wanted to deal with Hughes directly. As noted above, the record clearly shows that Mrs. Beckner herself initiated all but two of the contacts with Hughes. Mrs. Beckner's active participation in the negotiations regarding the lease amendment belies the existence of circumstances that would give rise to a level of suspicion sufficient to support the presumption of undue influence and rescission of the amendment.

We need not address the chancellor's finding that Mrs. Beckner suffered from great weakness of mind because even assuming that the finding is supported by the record, weakness of mind alone will not entitle Mrs. Beckner to rescission.

Because the record is insufficient to support the chancellor's findings that Mrs. Beckner had a confidential relationship with Hughes and that the consideration she received was grossly inadequate or the transaction occurred under suspicious circumstances, Mrs. Beckner was not entitled to a presumption of undue influence. Therefore, the chancellor erred in rendering judgment in favor of Mrs. Beckner on Count IV, Undue Influence.

. . .

Accordingly, for the reasons stated, we will reverse the trial court's decree rescinding the amendment to the lease and requiring repayment of funds by Mrs. Beckner.[4]

Reversed and final judgment.

Understanding the Case:

1. *Assignment:* In this case, Friendly's sought to assign the lease with Beckner to Riggs. An assignment of a contract occurs where a party assigns its rights under that contract to a third party. The word "rights" refers to the benefit of the other party's performance. Thus, by Friendly's assigning its rights under the lease to Riggs, Riggs would get the benefit of Beckners' promises relating to use of the leased property, meaning Riggs would get to use the leased property. Friendly's would also delegate its duties under the lease, such as Friendly's obligation to pay Mrs. Beckner rent, to Riggs. Riggs, in turn, would assume those obligations, meaning it would agree to perform those obligations instead of Friendly's. By default, in most contracts, a party may assign its rights and delegate its duties without getting the counterparty's approval. In this instance, even if the assignment was not required by the terms of the lease, Riggs (among other things) needed Mrs. Beckner's approval to modify the rent term, as Friendly's had been paying a portion of rent based off its sales, which would not make sense as a rent formula for a bank. Friendly's also presumably wanted to be released from its obligations under the agreement, for which it may still have been secondarily liable notwithstanding its assignment and delegation to Riggs. Chapter 29 will discuss in more detail the concepts of assignment and delegation.

2. *Confidential Relationships and Undue Influence:* At early common law, undue influence was often available as a defense only where a confidential relationship existed between contracting parties. More modern contract law does not require that a confidential relationship exists.[5] Nevertheless, the holding in *Beckner* reflects the continued relevance of a confidential relationship to an undue influence defense.

Comprehension and Thought Questions:

1. According to the court, what are the two situations where a party can make out a *prima facie* case of undue influence?

2. Why was there not a confidential relationship between Mrs. Beckner and Friendly's justifying the court in shifting the burden to Friendly's to prove the contract was fair?

---

4. [2] In light of this determination, we need not address the remaining assignments of error.

5. *See, e.g.,* Restatement (Second) of Contracts § 177 (1981) (not mentioning the existence of a confidential relationship in the undue influence defense).

3. What facts showed that the consideration Mrs. Beckner received under the contract was not grossly inadequate? Why is the adequacy of consideration relevant to this defense given that it is supposed to be based on an improper bargaining process?

4. While the court did not analyze it, do you think Mrs. Beckner was unduly susceptible and needed protection from Friendly's under the undue influence defense?

5. How does the court's test for undue influence differ from the *Odorizzi* test set out above?

6. Which test for undue influence do you think better protects a party in need of protection from a stronger party—the test in *Beckner* or in *Odorizzi*?

7. Which test provides a clearer, more predicable legal standard—*Beckner* or *Odorizzi*?

8. If Mrs. Beckner had been your client, would you have had any concerns when you discovered that your client was demanding that the contractual counterparty negotiate directly with her instead of you? If so, what would you have done to address your concerns?

Hypothetical Variations:

1. What if the court had used the test for undue influence set out in *Odorizzi*?

2. What if Mrs. Beckner never retained an attorney to represent her in her interactions with Friendly's and Friendly's demanded that Mrs. Beckner sign the assignment document immediately after agreeing on the new rental amount in the amendment?

3. What if Riggs only agreed to pay Mrs. Beckner the same base rent that Friendly's was obligated to pay under the lease?

Even where a party can demonstrate that undue influence existed, he may be unable to utilize the defense if the party subsequently ratified the contract or otherwise enjoyed the benefits of it. In *Gengaro v. City of New Haven,*[6] an employee (Gengaro) agreed to resign pursuant to a confidential settlement agreement following allegations of sexual harassment and inappropriate sexual behavior by Gengaro. Under the settlement agreement, Gengaro would receive a lump-sum payment as well as limited other benefits. He had three weeks to consider and sign the agreement, along with an additional week to rescind his agreement. Around ten months after he signed the agreement, Gengaro sued the City of New Haven seeking to rescind the contract.

The court found that even if Gengaro could make out a case for undue influence, his actions of accepting the benefits of the settlement agreement for months after signing it constituted a ratification of that agreement. That is

---

6. 984 A.2d 1133 (Conn. App. Ct. 2009).

because those acts showed that Gengaro intended to be bound by the agreement a reasonable time after the circumstance making it voidable (the alleged undue influence) passed. Thus, Gengaro's behavior showed that he ratified the settlement agreement, precluding him as a matter of law from voiding it.

The inability of Gengaro and Mrs. Beckner to void their respective contracts on the basis of undue influence should give you a sense for the limited success parties often have in proving that a contract is unenforceable due to undue influence. Once again, these defenses do not always fail—in some circumstances, such as in the *Odorizzi* case discussed above, the undue influence defense potentially permits a party to void a contract. But, as with duress, courts are fairly chary when granting a remedy of rescission under this defense.

2. Other Protections from Undue Influence

Federal regulation and state law protect consumers from some of the pressures seen in the above cases. For the most part, those laws give consumers a certain number of days to cancel a purchase contract, to counter the potential high-pressure sales tactics used to sell them those items. For example, the Federal Trade Commission regulations give consumers three days to cancel contracts of sale made at their homes for a price of $25 or more.[7] The Federal Truth in Lending Act similarly requires lenders to give borrowers a three-day "cooling-off" period to cancel their mortgage loan contracts.

State statutory protections generally fit within the consumer protection statutes discussed in Chapter 4. But the specific provisions within those statutes that are most relevant to an undue influence defense are, as with the federal protections discussed above, the ones that give consumers a "cooling off" period to cancel the contract. Many states have statutes that largely mirror the federal statutes discussed above. Some, however, provide for additional protections. Ohio, for example, gives a consumer a number of days to cancel an entertainment contract where the consumer has to pay for those services before enjoying them.[8] The statute then sets out how to calculate the number of days based on when the contract is signed in relation to timing for services.[9]

3. "Contracting Around" Undue Influence

While parties cannot "contract around" the undue influence defense, they do sometimes include provisions in their contracts intended to demonstrate the

---

7. 16 C.F.R. Part 429, Trade Regulation Rule Concerning Cooling-Off Period for Sales Made at Homes or at Certain Other Locations.

8. *See* Ohio Rev. Code Ann. § 1345.43.

9. *See id.*

absence of some of the facts considered in undue influence cases. For example, businesses often include a provision like the following in their contracts:

> The Employee acknowledges that the Employee is not relying upon the advice of the Company or the Company's counsel and has been advised, and has been provided sufficient time, to engage independent counsel to assist the Employee in evaluating this Agreement.

In this provision, the Employee is acknowledging a set of facts that, if true, would make an undue influence case against the Company less likely to be successful. That is, the Employee acknowledges that she has had adequate time to engage independent counsel to advise her on this transaction. Even if the Employee decided to not retain independent counsel, she could have. Moreover, this acknowledgment shows that the Employee had time to consider the agreement herself. Both of these facts would make it hard for the Employee to later establish undue influence. On the other hand, a court might see this acknowledgment as self-serving by the Company, especially if the Company drafted it. As such, a court might still inquire into whether these acknowledged facts were true if the Employee raised an undue influence defense.

PRACTICE PROBLEM 19-2

Review the facts in Practice Problem 19-1. Would PharmaX have a good argument to rescind its agreement with CommerRS to terminate the lease due to undue influence?

CHAPTER 20

Misrepresentation

This chapter addresses contract defenses based on different types of misstatements or misrepresentations. These are process-based defenses that suggest that one party's assent to the contract was improperly obtained due to a misstatement by the other party. Given that the "fault" associated with such misstatements necessarily resides with the party that made them, the innocent party may be able to avoid enforcement of the contract.

First, Section A discusses the misrepresentation defense in general, laying out what constitutes a misrepresentation as well as how a party satisfies the other elements of a misrepresentation claim. Then, Section B discusses application of those concepts in the case of a promise a party does not intend to keep, referred to as promissory fraud. Section C discusses application of those concepts where a party's misrepresentation is not about an underlying fact, but about either the existence or terms of a contract, referred to as fraud in the execution.

A. MISREPRESENTATION

Imagine you are deciding whether to lease an apartment at Campus Apartments or an apartment at a different complex. One of the factors you are considering is which apartment complex provides good sound barriers between apartments, as you intend to study in your apartment. So you will only rent an apartment that will be quiet enough to allow you to study.

The landlord of Campus Apartments, Tom Cook, is anxious to have you lease an apartment at Campus Apartments. To induce you to lease that apartment, Tom lies and tells you that each apartment has soundproofing between the walls and in the ceiling of each apartment, to provide tenants with a quiet place to live. Tom tells you this after you tour Campus Apartments and tell him about your need for a quiet apartment. Because of Tom's statement (which you obviously could not confirm during your tour), you decide to rent an apartment at Campus Apartments. Upon moving in, you discover that you can hear the conversations of your neighbor tenants through the walls. Moreover, you can hear every footstep of the tenants above you.

Do you have any basis to avoid your contract with Campus Apartments? The answer is probably yes. The misrepresentation defense would likely protect you from Tom's false statement.

More specifically, a party may rescind a contract due to a misrepresentation where

1. the other party makes a statement not in accordance with the facts,
2. either that false fact is stated fraudulently or it is material (i.e., important),
3. that fact induces the first party to assent, and
4. the "wronged" party is justified in relying on the false statement of fact.

Continuing with the above example, Tom's statement to you was not in accordance with the facts—that is, while Tom said that the apartment had sound-proofed walls and a soundproofed ceiling, it did not. Tom made that statement to you knowing that it was not true, which makes it fraudulent (more on that below); even if he had not intentionally lied, the misstated fact regarding sound-proofing might still have qualified as material (more on that below as well). Tom's false statement induced you to assent to the lease, since you only wanted to lease an apartment if it was quiet. Moreover, you likely did not know or have any reason to know that the apartment you wished to lease did not have soundproofing, assuming that you did not hear the neighbors during your tour. Therefore, you would likely have a basis to rescind your lease due to Tom's misrepresentation.

While this example shows how the misrepresentation defense applies in general, each of the above elements requires more explanation and, in some cases, expansion, to give you a more complete picture of this defense. Each element will be discussed in turn.

1. Statement Not in Accordance with the Facts

This element typically refers to a party who makes a positive statement, also called an assertion, about a past or current circumstance or event that is not true. This is the type of misrepresentation Tom made in the above example when he stated a present fact about soundproofing in the apartment that was not true.

However, a party can also make a misrepresentation by concealing the truth of a fact. This commonly occurs where a seller of real estate physically places items to obstruct a buyer's view of defects in the property being purchased. There, while the party is not making an assertion, the fact that he is hiding the property's actual condition is deemed to be an assertion that the defect he is hiding does not exist—an assertion that obviously is not true.

An *omission* of a fact can also amount to a misrepresentation. While in general a party to a contract does not have a "duty to speak"—meaning, a duty to disclose a fact she knows without which she commits a misrepresentation— sometimes a party makes a misrepresentation due to such a failure. That occurs, though, only in a few limited situations where the law imposes such a "duty to speak." In general, that includes where the party has disclosed information to the counterparty and later discovers that the information is not true.[1] In that case, the party has a duty to speak to correct the previously disclosed information that was incorrect. A party also has a duty to speak where it has a fiduciary or other similar duty that obligates the party to protect the best interest of the other party in a contract. And a party has a duty to speak where doing so is necessary to correct a mistake of the other party, and the failure to speak would not comport with good faith and fair dealing. This last category often occurs where a seller has information about property it is selling that materially affects that property's value, where the buyer does not have access to that information, and the seller fails to disclose that information to the buyer. In that case, courts often find that the seller should have disclosed that information to the buyer in order to act in good faith and with fair dealing, and its failure to do so amounts to a misrepresentation.

Finally, because a misrepresentation is a false statement of *fact*, it generally does not include statements of opinion. That is because statements of opinion are statements not of fact, but of *personal beliefs*. For example, if Tom the landlord tells you that Campus Apartments are fairly quiet, Tom has given an opinion rather than made a statement of fact.

However, in some limited circumstances, a party can commit a misrepresentation through an opinion. First, that can occur where a party gives an opinion about facts that are inconsistent with the facts known to that person, where the underlying facts are not known to the party receiving the opinion. This might occur, for example, where a seller states that a house being sold is in great condition. Such a statement of opinion might amount to a misrepresentation where the seller knows there are structural problems with the foundation and termite damage to the walls that the buyer would not be able to discover through a customary inspection. In that case, the facts as the seller knows them are inconsistent with the seller's opinion that the house is in great condition. Assuming the buyer does not know or have reason to know, such as through

---

1. Under the Restatement (Second) of Contracts § 161, a party has a duty to speak where a party makes an innocent misrepresentation but does not learn the truth until later—the party has to disclose the truth to prevent the prior assertion from being fraudulently made. And a party has a duty to speak to prevent a prior misrepresentation from being material, where the party learns of the other party's special circumstances that make reliance likely.

an inspection, that the house contains those defects, the buyer might be able to rescind this contract on the basis of misrepresentation. Still, courts do allow some amount of "sales puffery," which often weighs against a court finding that a statement of opinion constitutes a misrepresentation.

A party can also commit a misrepresentation through opinion where a party gives an opinion to a person in a relationship of trust and confidence; where the person giving the opinion has special skills or judgment with respect to the subject of the opinion; or where the person receiving the opinion is particularly susceptible to a misrepresentation. In these cases, a party can avail itself of the misrepresentation defense even if the person giving the opinion is not opining about facts but merely expressing his judgment.

Syester v. Banta[2] provides an example of a party committing misrepresentation through opinions. In that case, Ms. Syester, a 70ish-year-old widow, visited the Des Moines Arthur Murray Dance Studio. She later was sold a package of dance lessons by the studio, which sold dance lessons by the hour. Before Ms. Syester completed all of the hours under her initial contract, Ms. Syester was sold additional hours. For example, on one occasion, she bought 1,200 additional hours of instruction for $6,000, when she had already bought 2,022 hours and had used only 261 of those hours. For her alleged dance proficiency, Ms. Syester was awarded numerous dance awards, though Ms. Syester's instructor testified at trial that it would take a total of 200-400 hours of instruction to teach Ms. Syester to dance in the manner she was dancing at her peak performance.

The Dance Studio trained its instructors extensively in sales techniques to get customers to buy lessons. For example, in a document titled "Eight Good Rules for Interviewing," which was given to instructors, instructors were told to tell customers "Did you know that the three most important points on this D.A. are: rhythm, natural ability and animation? You've been graded Excellent in all three."

At one point, Ms. Syester's instructor, Mr. Carey, was fired by the Dance Studio. After this, Ms. Syester quit the studio and sued its owners. In response, the dance studio hired Mr. Carey back and instructed him to use his leverage to get Ms. Syester to drop her lawsuit against the studio. Mr. Carey convinced Ms. Syester to drop her suit and return to the studio, telling her "she still had the ability to be a professional, excellent dancer" and that "she did not need an attorney; after all Mrs. Theiss [one of the owners] and myself were her only friends." Consequently, Ms. Syester signed a release in which she agreed to drop her suit and release all claims against the dance studio in exchange for the return of approximately $6,000.

Ms. Syester eventually renewed her lawsuit against the dance studio, arguing that the dance studio committed fraud against her. She sought damages,

---

2. 133 N.W.2d 666 (Iowa 1965).

including punitive damages, as a result of their fraud. She also argued that the release she had signed in dropping her prior suit was unenforceable due to misrepresentation.

On appeal, the Iowa Supreme Court found that the dance company had engaged in fraud, and that the fraud both induced her to enter into dance contracts and to release her prior lawsuit against the dance studio. In particular, the Iowa Supreme Court deferred to the jury's finding that the dance studio's statements were of fact and not opinion, even though the main actionable misrepresentations related to opinions about Ms. Syester's dancing capabilities. The Court then held that the dance studio had made misrepresentations. In particular, the dance studio instructor's opinions about Ms. Syester's dancing abilities that were inconsistent with the facts—the instructor said that Ms. Syester was capable of being a professional dancer when he knew that that was not possible given her age and agility. Moreover, Ms. Syester reasonably relied on the instructor's opinions given his special skills and judgments about dance proficiency. And Ms. Syester was vulnerable given her age and seeming gullibility. Thus, Ms. Syester was able to rescind her release under the contract law defense of misrepresentation, and recover damages (including punitive damages) under the tort of fraud due to the dance studio's conduct in relation to the dance contracts.

PRACTICE PROBLEM 20-1

Christine Chan, an experienced newspaper editor in Florida, was in the market to buy a house. On March 1, Christine toured a beautiful, fully renovated Queen Anne house that she fell in love with. The price of the house, located at 123 E. Adams Place, was listed as $450,000.

The seller of the house, an experienced house flipper named Keith Stiles, was present during Christine's tour. Throughout the tour, Keith answered Christine's questions about the various improvements he had made to the house in the nine months he had owned it. At one point, Christine asked about the neighborhood. Specifically, Christine wanted to know if it was safe and quiet. Keith responded that the neighborhood was safe. He also said it was quiet and the neighbors seemed really nice.

In reality, a drug dealer lived in the house across the street. The neighbors were all aware of this because there were always people coming and going from that house at all hours of the day and night, none of whom stayed for more than ten minutes. While the police had investigated the house for drug connections several times, they never caught anyone engaged in illegal activities.

Because Keith was a house flipper, he did not live at 123 E. Adams Place. He did notice some suspicious activity across the street with so many people coming and going, but he decided to keep his nose down and finish up with renovating the house.

At the end of the tour, Christine expressed how much she liked the house. Keith responded by telling her that if Christine did not make an offer fast, she would likely lose out, as there were bound to be other people interested in buying the house. Worried that she might lose out on the house, Christine offered to buy it at full list price. Christine used Florida's standard house purchase agreement for her offer. She attached to that form a copy of the "Disclosure Schedule" that Keith had provided Christine and every other person who toured the house. That Disclosure Schedule did not call for any information about the neighborhood. There was a space at the end that called for the disclosure of any other "problems or defects" with the property being sold. Keith had marked "none" in response to that question.

Keith accepted Christine's offer.

After closing and upon moving into the house, Christine discovered the fact that the house across the street was used for drug deals. Concerned that she has moved into an unsafe neighborhood, she has come to you, her lawyer, for advice. Specifically, she wants to know whether Keith made any misrepresentation to her that might potentially serve as a basis to rescind the contract. For purpose of this question, focus only on whether a misrepresentation was made, and not the other elements of a potential misrepresentation claim.

2. Fraudulent or Material

The next requirement is that the misrepresentation has to be stated fraudulently, or the misrepresented fact has to be material. A person misstates a fact fraudulently where she states a fact she knows to not be true with the intent to induce assent. This was the type of misrepresentation Tom made in inducing you to sign a lease for an apartment at Campus Apartments, for Tom stated a fact he knew was not true (that the apartment walls were soundproofed) to induce you to assent. However, a party can even make a fraudulent misrepresentation recklessly, where she does not know the truth of the fact she asserts and does not have any regard for whether or not the fact is true, yet she makes it to induce assent. For example, if Tom is a new apartment manager and does not know whether apartments are soundproofed, he could still commit a fraudulent misrepresentation by telling you that the apartments walls are soundproofed. That is because he would make that statement to you with utter disregard for the truth of his statement, to induce you to assent.

As will be explained in further detail below, where a party makes a fraudulent misrepresentation, the aggrieved party can either choose to rescind the contract or choose to sue the party for the tort of fraud.

An aggrieved party may even rescind a contract where the other party commits an innocent misrepresentation or a negligent misrepresentation. A party makes an innocent misrepresentation where she states a false fact, the truth of which she does not know or have reason to know.

Where a misrepresentation is made other than fraudulently, in general, the counterparty may only rescind where the misrepresentation is *material*. Under this "material" element, a counterparty may rescind when a party makes a misrepresentation about a fact that either the party knows is important to the specific counterparty, such that it would be likely to induce that counterparty's assent, or about a fact that would be important to a reasonable counterparty, such that it would be likely to induce that counterparty's assent.

For example, imagine Brooke Wesley buys real estate and, in the course of that purchase transaction, is assured that the property has never had termite damage. Brooke's customary inspection did not reveal any termite damage, as such damage was hidden behind the walls. Her inspector did assure her, however, that there were no live termites.

Assume that in fact the property has termite damage, but that the prior owner either did not know that or did not disclose it to Brooke. When Brooke sells the property, she represents that the property has not had any termite damage. On that basis, the buyers buy Brooke's property. Shortly thereafter, they discover that there is extensive termite damage to the property. They therefore sue to rescind the contract with Brooke.

Here, Brooke has committed a misrepresentation, as she has made a statement not in accordance with the facts. However, she did not make that statement intentionally, as she did not know that the house had prior termite damage. She also likely did not make that statement recklessly, as she is probably reasonable to think she has a basis to make this assertion given the representations made to her when she bought the house and the inspection that indicated no termites. Even so, the buyers would have a basis to rescind that contract, assuming either that Brooke knows the absence of termite damage is important to her buyers (which the facts do not suggest), or that such information is likely to induce a reasonable person to assent.[3]

You may question why a party should be able to rescind a contract where a counterparty commits an innocent misrepresentation. After all, it was not the "fault" of the misrepresenting party in the same way as a fraudulent misrepresentation is. However, keep in mind that contract law is not fault-based. As such, doctrines do not necessarily turn on whether a party is at fault for certain contractual behavior. Moreover, contract law doctrines often reflect a balance between predictability and other contract law policies favoring enforcement, on the one hand, and fairness on the other. In the context of innocent misrepresentations, courts view it as unfair for an innocent party to have to live with a contract that that party entered into on the basis of an innocent misrepresentation where that misrepresentation is about an important fact. Instead, on balance, they view it as fairer to impose the risk on the party committing the misrepresentation.

---

3. This case is loosely based on Hill v. Jones, 151 Ariz. 81 (1986).

PRACTICE PROBLEM 20-2

Refer back to the facts in Practice Problem 20-1. Advise Christine on whether any of the arguable misrepresentations made to her were fraudulent or material. ~~yes & yes~~

3. Inducement

The misrepresentation must also induce the other party to assent to the contract. Courts usually interpret this causation element to mean that the misrepresentation must have substantially contributed to the aggrieved party's assent. In other words, a misrepresentation need not be the sole or even primary factor causing a party to assent, so long as it was among the mix of information considered when the party assented.

In the ongoing example, it was clear that Tom's statement about soundproofed walls was important to you in assenting to the lease. However, it is likely that other factors were even more important to you, including the location of the apartment and the rent. Nevertheless, Tom's misrepresentation was among the information you considered in deciding to assent. Thus, the inducement element would likely be satisfied.

4. Justifiable Reliance

The aggrieved party also has to be justified in relying on the false statement of fact. A party is only justified in relying on a false statement where the party does not know or have reason to know of the truth of the fact. Thus, if a party knows that a statement of fact the other party makes is not true, it cannot justifiably rely on that false statement, and it cannot use the misrepresentation defense. Moreover, a party cannot rely on the truth of a false statement where that party, if acting reasonably, would know the truth of a fact. This typically occurs where a party is on notice of either the falsity of a statement made by the counterparty, or of an undisclosed defect in the subject matter of the contract, and has a reasonable opportunity to investigate, but fails to do so.[4]

In our ongoing example, you were justified in relying on Tom's statement because there was no way for you to verify the soundproofing of apartments given that this type of barrier is placed inside the walls and ceiling. On the other hand, if you heard neighbors during your tour of Campus Apartments, you likely would not be justified in relying on Tom's statement, as you would have

---

4. *See, e.g.*, Lehman v. Keller, 677 S.E.2d 415 (Ga. Ct. App. 2009). Some courts require that a party act negligently before they find that the party was not justified, while other courts, and the Restatement, only find a party not justified where its failure to discover the truth fails to rise to the level of good faith and fair dealing. Restatement (Second) of Contracts § 172 (1981).

known, or at least had reason to know, that either the apartments were not soundproofed, or that such soundproofing did not effectively block out neighbor noises.

Importantly, recall from Chapter 15 that parties can to an extent contract around this element by including a clause in their agreement disclaiming reliance on all representations and warranties except those set out in the written agreement. Where parties include such a provision, then as you saw in *Italian Cowboy*, each party is potentially precluded from making a claim for misrepresentation for a statement made outside the contract, as making such a claim would necessarily require that party to demonstrate reliance that had been disclaimed. However, effectively disclaiming such reliance must be done through clear and specific language to that effect. Moreover, many courts do not enforce such "no reliance" clauses where the relevant misrepresentation was fraudulent.

PRACTICE PROBLEM 20-3

Refer back to the facts in Practice Problem 20-1. Advise Christine whether she could likely satisfy the inducement and justifiable reliance elements for any of her misrepresentation claims against Keith.

Keep three important points in mind as you synthesize this material on misrepresentations.

First, fraudulent misrepresentation is also a tort. As a tort, it allows a party to recover common law damages similar to damages for breach of contract. In addition, with egregious claims, a party can recover punitive damages. In contrast, where a party argues the contract law defense of fraudulent misrepresentation, the only available remedy is rescission of contract. However, a party cannot choose to pursue both a tort fraud claim and argue the contract law fraud defense—it must pick one of these paths. Which path a party chooses depends on what remedy the party seeks. If the party wants to avoid the contract, then it must argue the contract law misrepresentation defense. If the party wants to obtain damages, including possibly punitive damages, but remain a party to a contract, then it must allege the tort of fraud. Where a pleading is not clear which type of fraud claim a party is making, a court will usually decide that by looking at which remedy the party seeks.

Second, as you saw in Chapter 3, written contracts often contain sections titled "Representations and Warranties." That section lists numerous statements of fact. By including those statements of fact in the written contract as "representations," the party for whose benefit those statements are being made can rescind the contract under the misrepresentation defense if any of those statements proves to be untrue, assuming the other elements of misrepresentation are satisfied. By including those statements of fact as warranties, the party for whose benefit those statements are being made can sue the counterparty for breach of warranty if any of those statements proves to be untrue.

However, a party cannot both sue to rescind the contract due to the misrepresentation *and* sue for damages due to breach of warranty. Rather, the aggrieved party must select which remedy it desires and then pursue the right type of claim based on the remedy it seeks. Moreover, if a party cannot satisfy any of the elements of misrepresentation, such as the reliance element or the fraudulent/materiality element, then it would only be able to pursue the breach of warranty claim, as breach of warranty claims rest solely on the falsity of an assertion, regardless of the intent of the maker of the assertion or the recipient's reliance on that assertion.[5]

Third, as will be discussed in more detail in Chapter 25, parties can agree in their contract to limit the consequences due to a misrepresentation. Such a limit might include, for example, limiting the legal consequences from a misrepresentation to monetary damages rather than rescission, and/or imposing a cap on damages for misrepresentation. Such a provision could also limit the time period that a party has to pursue such a remedy. The following is sample language limiting the remedy for misrepresentation:

> The Seller's liability for any misrepresentation of fact or breach of warranty contained within the Agreement is capped at 4% of the Purchase Price (the "Cap"), except to the extent such claim arises out of fraud, in which case the Cap does not apply. Any such liability must be pursued under the indemnification provisions of this Agreement, which is the exclusive remedy for any misrepresentation claim against the Seller, and bars a rescission claim.[6]

This provision affects a potential misrepresentation claim against the Seller in a number of ways. First, it provides that if the Seller commits a misrepresentation, the Buyer's sole remedy is to receive indemnification from the Seller. That means that the Buyer must seek to be paid its damages arising out of the misrepresentation under the contract's indemnification provisions. The Buyer cannot seek to rescind the contract on the basis of that misrepresentation. This provision also caps the Seller's liability for any such misrepresentation claim at 4 percent of the Purchase Price paid by the Buyer under the Agreement. Through these features, this provision allocates more risk of factual errors to the Buyer than does the common law.

---

5. Courts in some states do not allow a party to sue for breach of warranty where it did not in fact rely on the misrepresented fact, because it knew the truth of the fact. And in other states, courts allow a party to recover where a party knows the truth behind a misrepresented fact, but only if the party expressly reserves its right to sue.

6. This clause is loosely based on one discussion in Abry Partners V, L.P. v. F&W Acquisition LLC, 891 A.2d 1032 (Del. Ch. 2006).

While courts often uphold provisions through which a party limits the consequences of its misrepresentations, they do so only if such provision is reasonable. While what is reasonable depends on the facts and circumstances, some courts have found that it is not reasonable to apply these limitations to fraudulent misrepresentations. As one court has stated, "[t]he public policy against fraud is a strong and venerable one that is largely founded on the societal consensus that lying is wrong."[7]

The following two cases demonstrate how the misrepresentation defense works in practice. The first case demonstrates a situation involving an innocent though material misrepresentation, while the second involves a misrepresentation through omission. As you read these cases, see if you can identify how each of the above elements was satisfied.

Cousineau v. Walker
Supreme Court of Alaska
613 P.2d 608 (1980)

BOOCHEVER, Justice.

The question in this case is whether the appellants are entitled to rescission of a land sale contract because of false statements made by the sellers. The superior court concluded that the buyers did not rely on any misrepresentations made by the sellers, that the misrepresentations were not material to the transaction, and that reliance by the buyers was not justified. Restitution of money paid under the contract was denied. We reverse and remand the case to the superior court to determine the amount of damages owed the appellants.

In 1975, Devon Walker and his wife purchased 9.1 acres of land in Eagle River, Alaska, known as Lot 1, Cross Estates. They paid $140,000.00 for it. A little over a year later, in October, 1976, they signed a multiple listing agreement with Pat Davis, an Anchorage realtor. The listing stated that the property had 580 feet of highway frontage on the Old Glenn Highway and that "ENGINEER REPORT SAYS OVER 1 MILLION IN GRAVEL ON PROP." The asking price was $245,000.00.

When the multiple listing expired, Walker signed a new agreement to retain Davis as an exclusive agent. In the broker's contract, the property was again described as having 580 feet of highway frontage, but the gravel content was listed as "minimum 80,000 cubic yds of gravel." The agreement also stated that 2.6 acres on the front of the parcel had been proposed for B-3 zoning (a commercial use), and the asking price was raised to $470,000.00.

An appraisal was prepared to determine the property's value as of December 31, 1976. Walker specifically instructed the appraiser not to include the

---

7. *See id.* at 1035.

value of gravel in the appraisal. . . . Under the heading, "Assumptions and Limiting Conditions," the report stated the appraisal "does not take into account any gravel . . . ." But later in the report the ground was described as "all good gravel base . . . covered with birch and spruce trees." The report did not mention the highway footage of the lot.

Wayne Cousineau, a contractor who was also in the gravel extraction business, became aware of the property when he saw the multiple listing. He consulted Camille Davis, another Anchorage realtor, to see if the property was available. In January, Cousineau and Camille Davis visited the property and discussed gravel extraction with Walker, although according to Walker's testimony commercial extraction was not considered. About this time Cousineau offered Walker $360,000.00 for the property. Cousineau tendered a proposed sales agreement which stated that all gravel rights would be granted to the purchaser at closing.

Sometime after his first offer, Cousineau attempted to determine the lot's road frontage. The property was covered with snow, and he found only one boundary marker. At trial the appraiser testified he could not find any markers. Cousineau testified that he went to the borough office to determine if any regulations prevented gravel extraction.

Despite Walker's reference to an "Engineer Report" allegedly showing "over 1 million in gravel," Walker admitted at trial that he had never seen a copy of the report. According to Walker's agent, Pat Davis, Camille Davis was told that if either she or Cousineau wanted the report they would have to pay for it themselves. It was undisputed that Cousineau never obtained the report.

In February, 1977, the parties agreed on a purchase price of $385,000.00 and signed an earnest money agreement. The sale was contingent upon approval of the zoning change of the front portion of the lot to commercial use. The amount of highway frontage was not included in the agreement. Paragraph 4(e) of the agreement conditionally granted gravel rights to Cousineau. According to the agreement, Cousineau would be entitled to remove only so much gravel as was necessary to establish a construction grade on the commercial portion of the property. To remove additional gravel, Cousineau would be required to pay releases on those portions of ground where gravel was removed. . . .

Soon after the earnest money agreement was signed, the front portion of the property was rezoned and a month later the parties closed the sale.

There is no reference to the amount of highway frontage in the final purchase agreement. An addendum to a third deed of trust incorporates essentially the same language as the earnest money agreement with regard to the release of gravel rights.

After closing, Cousineau and his partners began developing the commercial portion of the property. They bought a gravel scale for $12,000.00 and used two of Cousineau's trucks and a loader. The partners contracted with South Construction to remove the gravel. According to Cousineau's testimony, he first learned of discrepancies in the real estate listing which described the lot when a neighbor threatened to sue Cousineau because he was removing gravel from the neighbor's adjacent lot. A recent survey shows that there is 415 feet of highway frontage on the property not 580 feet, as advertised.

At the same time Cousineau discovered the shortage in highway frontage, South Construction ran out of gravel. They had removed 6,000 cubic yards. To determine if there was any more gravel on the property, a South Construction employee bulldozed a trench about fifty feet long and twenty feet deep. There was no gravel. A soils report prepared in 1978 confirmed that there were no gravel deposits on the property.

After December, 1977, Cousineau and his partners stopped making monthly payments. At that time they had paid a total of $99,000.00 for the property, including a down payment and monthly installments. In March, 1978, they informed Walker of their intention to rescind the contract. A deed of trust foreclosure sale was held in the fall of 1978, and Walker reacquired the property. At a bench trial in December, Cousineau and his partners were denied rescission and restitution. . . .

I. RESCISSION OF THE CONTRACT

Numerous cases hold and the Restatement provides that an innocent misrepresentation may be the basis for rescinding a contract. There is no question, as the trial judge's findings of fact state, that the statements made by Walker and his real estate agent in the multiple listing were false.[8] Three questions must be resolved, however, to determine whether Cousineau is entitled to rescission and restitution of the amount paid for the property on the basis of the misrepresentations. First, it must be determined whether Cousineau in fact relied on the statements. Second, it must be determined whether the statements were material to the transaction that is, objectively, whether a reasonable person would have considered the statements important in deciding whether to purchase the property. Finally, assuming that Cousineau relied on the statements and that they were material, it must be determined whether his reliance was justified.

A. Reliance on the False Statements

. . . [I]n his findings of fact, the trial judge stated, "The plaintiffs did not rely on any misinformation or misrepresentations of defendants." Because this case was

---

8. [1] The statements made regarding highway frontage and gravel content in the two listing agreements cannot be characterized as "puffing." They were positive statements "susceptible of exact knowledge" at the time they were made. Although not applicable to real property sales, it is revealing that under the Uniform Commercial Code, where it is frequently necessary to distinguish "sales talk" from those statements which create express warranties, such definite statements as those made in the listing agreements would most probably be construed as creating an express warranty.

decided by a judge without a jury, our standard of review of factual findings is the "clearly erroneous" standard. When a finding leaves the court with the definite and firm conviction on the entire record that a mistake has been made, it is clearly erroneous. In our opinion, the trial judge's finding that Cousineau and his partners did not rely on the statements made by Walker is clearly erroneous.

. . . [T]he uncontroverted facts are that Wayne Cousineau was in the gravel extraction business. He first became aware of the property through a multiple listing that said "1 MILLION IN GRAVEL." The subsequent listing stated that there were 80,000 cubic yards of gravel. Even if Walker might have taken the position that the sale was based on the appraisal, rather than the listings, the appraisal does not disclaim the earlier statements regarding the amount of highway frontage and the existence of gravel. In fact, the appraisal might well reaffirm a buyer's belief that gravel existed, since it stated there was a good gravel base. All the documents prepared regarding the sale from the first offer through the final deed of trust make provisions for the transfer of gravel rights. Cousineau's first act upon acquiring the property was to contract with South Construction for gravel removal, and to purchase gravel scales for $12,000.00. We conclude that the court erred in finding that Cousineau did not rely on Walker's statement that there was gravel on the property.

We are also convinced that the trial court's finding that Cousineau did not rely on Walker's statement regarding the amount of highway frontage was clearly erroneous. The Cousineaus were experienced and knowledgeable in real estate matters. In determining whether to purchase the property, they would certainly have considered the amount of highway frontage to be of importance. Despite Walker's insistence that Cousineau knew the location of the boundary markers, neither Cousineau nor the appraiser ever found them. It is improbable that Cousineau would have started removing gravel from a neighbor's property had he known the correct location of his boundary line.

B. Materiality of the Statements

Materiality is a mixed question of law and fact. A material fact is one "to which a reasonable man might be expected to attach importance in making his choice of action." W. Prosser, Law of Torts § 108, at 719 (4th ed. 1971). It is a fact which could reasonably be expected to influence someone's judgment or conduct concerning a transaction. Under § 306 of the tentative draft of the Restatement (Second) of Contracts, a misrepresentation may be grounds for voiding a contract if it is either fraudulent or material. The reason behind the rule requiring proof of materiality is to encourage stability in contractual relations. The rule prevents parties who later become disappointed at the outcome of their bargain from capitalizing on any insignificant discrepancy to void the contract.

We conclude as a matter of law that the statements regarding highway frontage and gravel content were material. A reasonable person would be likely to consider the existence of gravel deposits an important consideration in developing a piece of property. Even if not valuable for commercial extraction, a gravel base would save the cost of obtaining suitable fill from other sources. Walker's real estate agent testified that the statements regarding gravel were placed in the listings because gravel would be among the property's "best points" and a "selling point." It seems obvious that the sellers themselves thought a buyer would consider gravel content important.

The buyers received less than three-fourths of the highway frontage described in the listings. Certainly the amount of highway frontage on a commercial tract would be considered important. . . .

C. Justifiable Reliance

The trial judge concluded as a matter of law that the plaintiffs "were not entitled to rely on the alleged misrepresentation."

The bulk of the appellee's brief is devoted to the argument that Cousineau's unquestioning reliance on Walker and his real estate agent was imprudent and unreasonable. Cousineau failed to obtain and review the engineer's report. He failed to obtain a survey or examine the plat available at the recorder's office. He failed to make calculations that would have revealed the true frontage of the lot. Although the property was covered with snow, the plaintiffs, according to Walker, had ample time to inspect it. The plaintiffs were experienced businessmen who frequently bought and sold real estate. Discrepancies existed in the various property descriptions which should have alerted Cousineau and his partners to potential problems. In short, the appellees urge that the doctrine of caveat emptor precludes recovery.

In fashioning an appropriate rule for land sale contracts, we note initially that, in the area of commercial and consumer goods, the doctrine of caveat emptor has been nearly abolished by the Uniform Commercial Code and imposition of strict products liability. In real property transactions, the doctrine is also rapidly receding. Alaska has passed the Uniform Land Sales Practices Act, AS 34.55.004-.046, which imposes numerous restrictions on vendors of subdivided property. Criminal penalties may be imposed for violations. . . . Many states now imply warranties of merchantability in new home sales. Wyoming has recently extended this warranty beyond the initial purchaser to subsequent buyers.

There is a split of authority regarding a buyer's duty to investigate a vendor's fraudulent statements, but the prevailing trend is toward placing a minimal duty on a buyer. Recently, a Florida appellate court reversed longstanding precedent which held that a buyer must use due diligence to protect his interest, regardless of fraud, if the means for acquiring knowledge concerning the transaction were open and available. In the context of a building sale the court concluded: "A person guilty of fraudulent misrepresentation should not be permitted to hide behind the doctrine of caveat emptor." Upledger v. Vilanor, Inc., 369 So.2d 427, 430 (Fla. App.), cert. denied, 378 So.2d 350 (Fla. 1979).

The Supreme Court of Maine has also recently reversed a line of its prior cases, concluding that a defense based upon lack of due care should not be allowed in land sales contracts where a reckless or knowing misrepresentation has been made. This is also the prevailing view in California, Idaho, Kansas, Massachusetts, and Oregon. On the other hand, some jurisdictions have reaffirmed the doctrine of caveat emptor, but as noted in Williston on Contracts, "The growing trend and tendency of the courts will continue to move toward the doctrine that negligence in trusting in a misrepresentation will not excuse positive willful fraud or deprive the defrauded person of his remedy." W. Jaeger, Williston on Contracts § 1515B at 487 (3d ed. 1970).

There is also authority for not applying the doctrine of caveat emptor even though the misrepresentation is innocent. . . .

The recent draft of the Restatement of Contracts allows rescission for an innocent material misrepresentation unless a buyer's fault was so negligent as to amount to "a failure to act in good faith and in accordance with reasonable standards of fair dealing." Restatement (Second) of Contracts § 314, Comment b (Tent. Draft. no. 11, 1976). . . .

A buyer of land, relying on an innocent misrepresentation, is barred from recovery only if the buyer's acts in failing to discover defects were wholly irrational, preposterous, or in bad faith.

Although Cousineau's actions may well have exhibited poor judgment for an experienced businessman, they were not so unreasonable or preposterous in view of Walker's description of the property that recovery should be denied. Consequently, we reverse the judgment of the superior court.

II. RESTITUTION

Walker received a total of $99,000.00 from Cousineau and his partners, but the appellants are not entitled to restitution of this amount. Cousineau apparently caused extensive damage to one building on the property, and he removed 6,000 cubic yards of gravel. Walker should be allowed some recoupment for these items, plus an amount for the fair rental value of the property less reasonable costs of rental.

It is necessary to remand this case to the trial court to determine the correct amount of damages.

REVERSED and REMANDED.

Comprehension and Thought Questions:

1. What misrepresentations did Cousineau allege were the basis for him to rescind the contract?

2. What test did the court use to determine whether Cousineau could in fact rescind on the basis of those misrepresentations?

3. How did the court apply that test in this case?

4. Why do you think the trial court determined that Cousineau was not justified to rely on that misrepresentation?

5. Why did *caveat emptor* not preclude Cousineau's recovery?

6. Should a party be able to rescind a contract due to the other party's innocent misrepresentation?

Hypothetical Variations:

1. What if Cousineau had seen the Engineering Report *before* deciding to buy the property?

2. What if Cousineau had seen the Engineering Report *after* deciding to buy the property but before closing?

3. What if Cousineau had seen the Engineering Report after closing?

4. What if Cousineau had seen the survey markers that showed where the actual boundaries of the property were, but he purchased the property nonetheless?

Stambovsky v. Ackley
New York Supreme Court, Appellate Division
169 A.D.2d 254 (1991)

RUBIN, J.

Plaintiff, to his horror, discovered that the house he had recently contracted to purchase was widely reputed to be possessed by poltergeists, reportedly seen by defendant seller and members of her family on numerous occasions over the last nine years. Plaintiff promptly commenced this action seeking rescission of the contract of sale. Supreme Court reluctantly dismissed the complaint, holding that plaintiff has no remedy at law in this jurisdiction.

The unusual facts of this case, as disclosed by the record, clearly warrant a grant of equitable relief to the buyer who, as a resident of New York City, cannot be expected to have any familiarity with the folklore of the Village of Nyack. Not being a "local", plaintiff could not readily learn that the home he had contracted to purchase is haunted. Whether the source of the spectral apparitions seen by defendant seller are parapsychic or psychogenic, having reported their presence in both a national publication (Readers' Digest) and the local press (in 1977 and 1982, respectively), defendant is estopped to deny their existence and, as a matter of law, the house is haunted. More to the point, however, no divination is required to conclude that it is defendant's promotional efforts in publicizing her close encounters with these spirits which fostered the home's reputation in the community. In 1989, the house was included in a five-home walking tour of Nyack and described in a November 27th newspaper article as "a riverfront Victorian (with ghost)." The impact of the reputation thus created goes to the very essence of the bargain between the parties, greatly impairing both the value of the property and its potential for resale. The extent of this impairment may be presumed for the purpose of reviewing the disposition of this motion to dismiss the cause of action for rescission and represents merely an issue of fact for resolution at trial.

While I agree with Supreme Court that the real estate broker, as agent for the seller, is under no duty to disclose to a potential buyer the phantasmal reputation of the premises and that, in his pursuit of a legal remedy for fraudulent misrepresentation against the seller, plaintiff hasn't a ghost of a chance, I am nevertheless moved by the spirit of equity to allow the buyer to seek rescission of the contract of sale and recovery of his down payment. New York law fails to recognize any remedy for damages incurred as a result of the seller's mere silence, applying instead the strict rule of caveat emptor. Therefore, the theoretical basis for granting relief, even under the extraordinary facts of this case, is elusive if not ephemeral.

> "Pity me not but lend thy serious hearing to what I shall unfold" (William Shakespeare, Hamlet, Act I, Scene V [Ghost]).

From the perspective of a person in the position of plaintiff herein, a very practical problem arises with respect to the discovery of a paranormal phenomenon: "Who you gonna' call?" as a title song to the movie "Ghostbusters" asks. Applying the strict rule of caveat emptor to a contract involving a house possessed by poltergeists conjures up visions of a psychic or medium routinely accompanying the structural engineer and Terminix man on an inspection of every home subject to a contract of sale. It portends that the prudent attorney will establish an escrow account lest the subject of the transaction come back to haunt him and his client—or pray that his malpractice insurance coverage extends to supernatural disasters. In the interest of avoiding such untenable consequences, the notion that a haunting is a condition which can and should be ascertained upon reasonable inspection of the premises is a hobgoblin which should be exorcised from the body of legal precedent and laid quietly to rest.

It has been suggested by a leading authority that the ancient rule which holds that mere nondisclosure does not constitute actionable misrepresentation "finds proper application in cases where the fact undisclosed is patent, or the plaintiff has equal opportunities for obtaining information which he may be expected to utilize, or the defendant has no reason to think that he is acting under any misapprehension" (Prosser, Torts § 106, at 696 [4th ed 1971]). However, with respect to transactions in real estate, New York adheres to the doctrine of caveat emptor and imposes no duty upon the vendor to disclose any information concerning the premises unless there is a confidential or fiduciary relationship between the parties or some conduct on the part of the seller which constitutes "active concealment". Normally, some affirmative misrepresentation is required to impose upon the seller a duty to communicate undisclosed conditions affecting the premises.

Caveat emptor is not so all-encompassing a doctrine of common law as to render every act of nondisclosure immune from redress, whether legal or equitable. "In regard to the necessity of giving information which has not been asked, the rule differs somewhat at law and in equity, and while the law courts would permit no recovery of damages against a vendor, because of mere concealment of facts under certain circumstances, yet if the vendee refused to complete the contract because of the concealment of a material fact on the part of the other, equity would refuse to compel him so to do, because equity only compels the specific performance of a contract which is fair and open, and in regard to which all material matters known to each have been communicated to the other" (*Rothmiller v Stein*, 143 NY 581, 591-592 [emphasis added]). Even as a principle of law, long before exceptions were embodied in statute law (see, e.g., UCC 2-312, 2-313, 2-314, 2-315; 3-417 [2] [e]), the doctrine was held inapplicable to contagion among animals, adulteration of food, and insolvency of a maker of a promissory note and of a tenant substituted for another under a lease. Common law is not moribund. *Ex facto jus oritur* (law arises out of facts). Where fairness and common sense dictate that an exception should be created, the evolution of the law should not be stifled by rigid application of a legal maxim.

The doctrine of caveat emptor requires that a buyer act prudently to assess the fitness and value of his purchase and operates to bar the purchaser who fails to exercise due care from seeking the equitable remedy of rescission. For the purposes of the instant motion to dismiss the action pursuant to CPLR 3211 (a) (7), plaintiff is entitled to every favorable inference which may reasonably be drawn from the pleadings, specifically, in this instance, that he met his obligation to conduct an inspection of the premises and a search of available public records with respect to title. It should be apparent, however, that the most meticulous inspection and the search would not reveal the presence of poltergeists at the premises or unearth the property's ghoulish reputation in the community. Therefore, there is no sound policy reason to deny plaintiff relief for failing to discover a state of affairs which the most prudent purchaser would not be expected to even contemplate.

The case law in this jurisdiction dealing with the duty of a vendor of real property to disclose information to the buyer is distinguishable from the matter under review. The most salient distinction is that existing cases invariably deal with the physical condition of the premises, defects in title, liens against the property, expenses or income and other factors affecting its operation. No case has been brought to this court's attention in which the property value was impaired as the result of the reputation created by information disseminated to the public by the seller (or, for that matter, as a result of possession by poltergeists).

Where a condition which has been created by the seller materially impairs the value of the contract and is peculiarly within the knowledge of the seller or unlikely to be discovered by a prudent purchaser exercising due care with respect to the subject transaction, nondisclosure constitutes a basis for rescission as a matter of equity. Any other outcome places upon the buyer not merely the obligation to exercise care in his purchase but rather to be omniscient with respect to any fact which may affect the bargain. No practical purpose is served by imposing such a burden upon a purchaser. To the contrary, it encourages predatory business practice and offends the principle that equity will suffer no wrong to be without a remedy.

Defendant's contention that the contract of sale, particularly the merger or "as is" clause, bars recovery of the buyer's deposit is unavailing. Even an express disclaimer will not be given effect where the facts are peculiarly within the knowledge of the party invoking it. Moreover, a fair reading of the merger clause reveals that it expressly disclaims only representations made with respect to the physical condition of the premises and merely makes general reference to representations concerning "any other matter or things affecting or relating to the aforesaid premises". As broad as this language may be, a reasonable interpretation is that its effect is limited to tangible or physical matters and does not extend to paranormal phenomena. Finally, if the language of the contract is to be construed as broadly as defendant urges to encompass the presence of poltergeists in the house, it cannot be said that she has delivered the premises "vacant" in accordance with her obligation under the provisions of the contract rider.

To the extent New York law may be said to require something more than "mere concealment" to apply even the equitable remedy of rescission, the case of *Junius Constr. Corp. v Cohen* (257 N.Y. 393), while not precisely on point, provides some guidance. In that case, the seller disclosed that an official map indicated two as yet unopened streets which were planned for construction at the edges of the parcel. What was not disclosed was that the same map indicated a third street which, if opened, would divide the plot in half. The court held that, while the seller was under no duty to mention the planned streets at all, having undertaken to disclose two of them, he was obliged to reveal the third.

In the case at bar, defendant seller deliberately fostered the public belief that her home was possessed. Having undertaken to inform the public-at-large, to whom she has no legal relationship, about the supernatural occurrences on her property, she may be said to owe no less a duty to her contract vendee. . . . Where, as here, the seller not only takes unfair advantage of the buyer's ignorance but has created and perpetuated a condition about which he is unlikely to even inquire, enforcement of the contract (in whole or in part) is offensive to the court's sense of equity. Application of the remedy of rescission, within the bounds of the narrow exception to the doctrine of caveat emptor set forth herein, is entirely appropriate to relieve the unwitting purchaser from the consequences of a most unnatural bargain.

Accordingly, the judgment of the Supreme Court, New York County (Edward H. Lehner, J.), entered April 9, 1990, which dismissed the complaint pursuant to CPLR 3211 (a) (7), should be modified, on the law and the facts, and in the exercise of discretion, and the first cause of action seeking rescission of the contract reinstated, without costs.

SMITH, J.

(Dissenting). I would affirm the dismissal of the complaint by the motion court.

. . .

"It is settled law in New York State that the seller of real property is under no duty to speak when the parties deal at arm's length. The mere silence of the seller, without some act or conduct which deceived the purchaser, does not amount to a concealment that is actionable as a fraud. The buyer has the duty to satisfy himself as to the quality of his bargain pursuant to the doctrine of caveat emptor, which in New York State still applies to real estate transactions." (*London v Courduff*, 141 AD2d 803, 804 [1988], *lv dismissed* 73 NY2d 809 [1988].)

The parties herein were represented by counsel and dealt at arm's length. This is evidenced by the contract of sale which, inter alia, contained various riders and a specific provision that all prior understandings and agreements between the parties were merged into the contract, that the contract completely expressed their full agreement and that neither had relied upon any statement by anyone else not set forth in the contract. There is no allegation that defendants, by some specific act, other than the failure to speak, deceived the plaintiff. Nevertheless, a cause of action may be sufficiently stated where there is a confidential or fiduciary relationship creating a duty to disclose and there was a failure to disclose a material fact, calculated to induce a false belief. However, plaintiff herein has not alleged and there is no basis for concluding that a confidential or fiduciary relationship existed between these parties to an arm's length transaction such as to give rise to a duty to disclose. In addition, there is no allegation that defendants thwarted plaintiff's efforts to fulfill his responsibilities fixed by the doctrine of caveat emptor.

Finally, if the doctrine of caveat emptor is to be discarded, it should be for a reason more substantive than a poltergeist. The existence of a poltergeist is no more binding upon the defendants than it is upon this court.

Based upon the foregoing, the motion court properly dismissed the complaint.

Comprehension and Thought Questions:

1. What "fact" was the basis for the buyer's misrepresentation claim?

2. How did the seller make a misrepresentation about that fact? Was it an assertion? A concealment? An omission?

3. What test did the court use to determine whether the buyer could rescind the purchase contract?

4. How did the court apply that test in this case?

5. Why wasn't the buyer precluded from rescinding on the basis of *caveat emptor*?

6. Why didn't the merger clause preclude the buyer from rescinding due to the misrepresentation?

7. What does the dissent disagree with—the majority's test or its application of that test to the facts of this case?

Hypothetical Variations:

1. What if the seller had not publicly advertised her house as haunted, but she nonetheless believed that her house was haunted?

2. What if the seller did not disclose to the buyer that her house was haunted because she did not actually believe that her house was haunted?

3. What if the buyer learned about the house's reputation as haunted before closing?

Keep in mind that the misrepresentation defense is an "inducement" defense. That means it is only available where a misrepresentation induces a party to assent. Nevertheless, some courts apply it where a misrepresentation induces a party not to assent to the contract, but to perform an essential obligation under a contract.

For example, imagine that Brooke Wesley represents to a buyer that her house is free of termites on January 1. As of January 1, that statement is true. That assertion of fact induces the buyer to enter into the contract to buy Brooke's house. But imagine that, as with most purchase contracts, closing is to occur after that date, such as on March 1. As you studied in Chapter 3, there is usually a gap period in purchase contracts to give the buyer time to line up financing and inspect the property being purchased. In virtually all of those contracts, a party is deemed to repeat the same representations at closing; many contracts require a party to do so explicitly. Here, that would mean Brooke would repeat her representation that her house is free of termites as of March 1, the day of closing. Now imagine that during that two-month gap period, Brooke's house is attacked by termites. If a court only allowed a party to rescind a contract where the misrepresentation induced the party to assent, then the court would not allow the buyer to rescind this contract even though this representation is not true at closing. Instead, the buyer would be limited to the remedy of suing Brooke for breach of warranty.

If, on the other hand, a court allowed a party to rescind a contract on the basis of a misrepresentation that induced a party to perform essential obligations, then such a court might allow the buyer to rescind this contract with Brooke. That is because the buyer would be induced to close and buy Brooke's house on the basis of her misrepresentation made at closing about the absence of termites.

In any event, assuming the buyer had protected herself by including a condition to closing in her contract that requires the seller's representations and warranties to be true as of closing, the buyer would not need to purchase the house at closing. That is because the condition would not be satisfied. Of course, if the buyer only discovers the misrepresentation after closing, then she cannot turn back time and not close. Instead, she would likely seek a remedy due to the misrepresentation.

B. PROMISSORY FRAUD

There are several, specific applications of the misrepresentation doctrine discussed above. One occurs in the context where a party makes a promise it does not intend to keep in order to induce the other party's assent. Where a party makes such a promise to induce the other to enter into the contract, the promisor is said to have committed **promissory fraud**. Thus, similar to a misrepresentation claim, discussed above, the elements are that (1) the promisor makes a promise (2) that the promisor did not intend to keep (3) to induce the promisee to assent, (4) the promisee is in fact induced by that promise to assent, and (5) the promisee is justified in so relying. Here, the misrepresentation is about the promisor's state of mind—by making the promise, the promisor is viewed as intending to perform its promise, while the fact that the promisor actually intends to not keep that promise shows the misrepresentation.

C. FRAUD IN THE EXECUTION

Another specific application of the misrepresentation doctrine occurs where a party makes a misrepresentation about the existence or terms of a contract. In particular, a party may avoid an entire contract, or a specific provision, where the counterparty misrepresents the existence or terms of the contract. This type of misrepresentation is called **fraud in the execution** because the misrepresentation goes not to the surrounding facts that a party considers in assenting, but instead to the existence or terms of the contract itself. Thus, under fraud in the execution, a party signs either a document that it does not know is a contract, or a contract with terms it did not know were included or excluded—in either case, as a result of the other party's fraudulent misrepresentation.

For example, imagine Blah Corp. wants to buy Funtastic Corp. for $2 million. Mr. Blah, the President and sole owner of Blah Corp., negotiates a purchase contract with Mrs. Funtastic, the President and sole owner of Funtastic Corp. During their conversation, Mr. Blah and Mrs. Funtastic agree that $100,000 of the purchase price will be paid as a deposit within ten days of signing the purchase contract, $900,000 will be paid at closing of this transaction, and $1 million will be paid through an earnout from the new combined company's profits.

What if, on the eve of signing the purchase contract, after both parties have seen and approved of the contract, Mr. Blah instructs his attorney to change the timing for payment of the purchase price so that the entire $2 million purchase price is paid through the earnout? He would want to do this to delay Blah Corp.'s payment obligation for as long as possible. If Mr. Blah did not discuss or mention this change to Mrs. Funtastic, and simply presented the purchase contract to Mrs. Funtastic to sign, then he has likely committed a fraud in the execution. That is because he has intentionally changed the written terms with an intent to induce Mrs. Funtastic to assent.

If Mrs. Funtastic were to raise this defense in court, Mr. Blah would surely argue that Mrs. Funtastic has a duty to read the contract. However, at some point a party's fraudulent conduct overrides a party's duty to read— that occurs where a party, acting reasonably, nevertheless is defrauded as to the existence or terms of a contract. Here, Mrs. Funtastic was likely acting reasonably by not rereading the terms of the contract immediately before she signed, since she had read the full terms the day before, and had no reason to think they were changed. Thus, the fraud would override her duty to read.

Where the fraud goes to an essential term in a contract, a court will typically void the entire contract. However, where the fraud goes to a nonessential term, a court will usually only void the specific provision executed due to fraud. Alternatively, a court can equitably reform the language to reinstate the terms the parties agreed on. Thus, in our ongoing example, Mrs. Funtastic might request a court to reinstate the purchase price terms that were actually agreed on.

Where the fraud in the execution goes to the very existence of the contract, the aggrieved party's remedy is to have the court declare that no contract exists. That is because the party did not manifest assent to what it signed. That would occur where, for example, Mr. Blah asks Mrs. Funtastic to sign a confidentiality agreement to keep the parties' discussions about the sale of Funtastic Corp. confidential, while Mr. Blah slips into the packet to be signed a contract by which Funtastic Corp. agrees to sell all of its assets to Blah Corp. for $2 million. Here, while Mrs. Funtastic signed, and ordinarily signing a contract manifests assent, in this context, the assent was intended to be to the Confidentiality Agreement and not the purchase agreement. Mrs. Funtastic's signature landed on the purchase agreement only because Mr. Blah hid its pages within the Confidentiality Agreement, thereby amounting to fraud in the execution. In this circumstance, a court would find that Mrs. Funtastic did not assent to the purchase agreement.

The following case exemplifies fraud in the execution in an increasingly common situation.

Ramos v. Westlake Services LLC
Court of Appeals, First District, Division 2, California
242 Cal. App. 4th 674 (2015)

MILLER, J.

Defendant Westlake Services LLC appeals from the trial court order denying its motion to compel arbitration as to plaintiff Alfredo Ramos. We affirm.

FACTUAL AND PROCEDURAL BACKGROUND

A. Ramos's Underlying Complaint

Alfredo Ramos, and coplaintiffs who are not parties to this appeal,[9] sued Defendant Westlake Services LLC (Westlake) for causes of actions arising out of their purchase of used automobiles. In the operative first amended complaint filed July 30, 2013, Ramos alleged that he "purchased an automobile from Pena's Motors. Upon arrival, he was greeted by one of this dealership's employees, who spoke with him in his native tongue (i.e., Spanish). Negotiations for this transaction were conducted primarily in Spanish. Pena's Motors and its employees had authority to sell and make representations on behalf of Westlake with respect to the sale of its GAP contracts covering automobiles. Defendant eventually charged Ramos money for a GAP contract to cover the vehicle he purchased. A copy of the GAP contract ('Guaranteed Auto Protection—GAP Waiver' form) was not provided to him in Spanish."

As alleged by Ramos, a "GAP" contract is an "optional insurance policy contract that is sold to or purchased by a consumer in conjunction with his or her purchase and financing of an automobile. In exchange for the payment of a premium by the consumer and/or purchaser of the automobile, the 'GAP' insurance policy contract, which identifies the respective rights and liabilities of the parties to the contract, is purportedly intended to pay the difference between the actual cash value of the financed automobile and the then-current outstanding balance on the loan for the automobile should the financed automobile be destroyed or 'totaled' in an accident."

Ramos asserted three causes of action based on Westlake's failure to provide a translation of the GAP contract: (1) violation of the Consumers Legal Remedies Act (CLRA), Civil Code section 1750, et seq.; (2) violation of section

---

9. [1] Coplaintiffs were Lorena Castillo and Jesus Vasquez. Only Ramos is party to this appeal.

1632[10]; and (3) violation of the unfair competition law (UCL), Business and Professions Code section 17200, et seq.

B. Westlake Moves to Compel Arbitration

On November 14, 2013, Westlake moved to compel arbitration of Ramos's and his coplaintiffs' claims, relying on the arbitration provisions contained in the underlying sales contracts they each had signed. In support of the motion, Westlake provided the declaration of John Schwartz, the manager of dealer compliance and first payment collection for Westlake, and one of its custodians of records. Pertinent for our purposes is exhibit 3 to Schwartz's declaration, which Schwartz identified as a copy of the "Conditional Sale Contract and Security Agreement that Alfredo Ramos entered into when he purchased his 2005 Ford Expedition from Pena's Motors in July 2011." According to Schwartz, Ramos's contract was later assigned to Westlake.

The Conditional Sale Contract and Security Agreement attached to Schwartz's declaration is in English (English Contract). It is signed by Ramos and a representative from Pena's Motors. Page 6 of the contract has a section heading highlighted in bold that states "Please Read Carefully! Notice of Arbitration." This section of the contract contains the arbitration agreement that is the basis of defendant's motion; it purports to cover "any claim or dispute in contract, tort, statute or otherwise between you and us or our employees . . . that arises out of or relates to your credit application, this Contract or any related transaction or relationship." The arbitration agreement ends by stating: "CAUTION: It is important that you read this *Arbitration Agreement thoroughly before you sign this Contract. By signing it, you are saying that you have read and understand this Arbitration Agreement, and have received a copy of it. If you do not understand something in this Arbitration Agreement, do not sign this Contract; instead ask your lawyer. You or we may reject this Arbitration Agreement by sending to the other a rejection notice by certified mail or by messenger service within 10 days after signing this Contract."

---

10. [3] Section 1632 provides in relevant part that "[a]ny person engaged in a trade or business who negotiates primarily in Spanish" in certain transactions, including auto sales, "shall deliver to the other party to the contract or agreement and prior to the execution thereof, a translation of the contract or agreement in the language in which the contract or agreement was negotiated, that includes a translation of every term and condition in that contract or agreement." (§ 1632, subd. (b).) Notwithstanding the translation provided, the "terms of the contract or agreement that is executed in the English language shall determine the rights and obligations of the parties," but the translation "shall be admissible in evidence only to show that no contract was entered into because of a substantial difference in the material terms and conditions of the contract and the translation." (§ 1632, subd. (j).) If a translation is not provided, "the person aggrieved may rescind the contract or agreement." (§ 1632, subd. (k).)

C. Ramos's Opposition to the Motion to Compel Arbitration

In support of his opposition to the motion to compel, Ramos submitted his own declaration, which had been prepared with the assistance of an interpreter. Each English paragraph in Ramos's declaration is followed by a Spanish translation of the text.

Ramos's declaration is the only evidence in the record of what happened in connection with his purchase of the used automobile, and we quote it verbatim, omitting only the paragraph numbers. "On July 2, 2011, I purchased an automobile from Pena's Motors in Brentwood. Upon arrival, I was greeted by one of the dealership's employees, who spoke with me in my native language, Spanish. . . . Negotiations for this transaction were conducted primarily in Spanish. . . . During the negotiations for the transaction and the signing of the paperwork, arbitration and alternative dispute resolution never came up. . . . Although the dealer provided me with a Spanish translation of a conditional sale contract, the Spanish copy of the contract was different than the English copy of the contract which I was told to sign. The Spanish version of the sales contract does not have the 'Arbitration' clause. Further, I do not recall ever receiving a Spanish translation of the actual GAP contract or of any forms pertaining to GAP coverage. . . . For the first time, I learned from my attorney that I had 'agreed' to arbitrate all claims against Defendant. I was surprised and had I known about these I would not have agreed to it."

. . . It is also undisputed that the Spanish version of the contract offered by Ramos (Ramos Translation) has no arbitration clause. The Ramos Translation contains Ramos's typewritten name and address, his signature on a number of pages, and terms of the car purchase (for example, the price, vehicle identification number, and the like).

Ramos argued in his opposition to the motion to compel arbitration that there was no agreement to arbitrate between him and Westlake. The contract was negotiated primarily in Spanish and an accurate translation that included the arbitration provision was never provided. Ramos, citing *Rosenthal v. Great Western Financial Securities Corp.* (1996) 14 Cal. 4th 394, 58 Cal. Rptr. 2d 875, 926 P.2d 1061 (*Rosenthal*), argued that there was fraud in the execution of the arbitration agreement and thus mutual assent was lacking because the parties never discussed arbitration, and he had never seen the arbitration clause because it was "hidden in the English version of the [underlying sales contract]." Ramos also argued that Westlake's failure to provide an accurate Spanish translation resulted in a violation of section 1632 and, as a result, the entire contract was "unenforceable and void, including the arbitration clause"; and that the arbitration agreement was procedurally and substantively unconscionable and should not be enforced.

. . .

In sum, while Ramos offered a Spanish translation of the underlying sales contract that made no reference to arbitration, Westlake produced in reply a Spanish translation of the underlying sales contract that included an arbitration agreement. This was the evidence presented to the trial court.

. . .

DISCUSSION

A. Trial Court's Admission of the Ramos Translation

[The court first addresses Westlake's challenge to the admissibility of the Ramos Translation. It holds that the trial court did not abuse its discretion in admitting the Ramos Translation and finding, as a factual matter, that the Ramos Translation was the Spanish translation Ramos received at the time of the transaction.]

B. Whether an Arbitration Agreement Exists

On appeal, Westlake argues the trial court erred by finding that Westlake had not demonstrated the existence of an agreement to arbitrate. Westlake contends that because there is no dispute that Ramos signed the English Contract containing the arbitration agreement, the only remedy available to Ramos for a violation of section 1632 is to rescind the entire English Contract, not to excise the arbitration provision. We conclude substantial evidence supports the trial court's conclusion that Westlake failed to prove the existence of an agreement to arbitrate. However, we reach this conclusion through application of contract formation principles and not section 1632 and therefore need not address Westlake's arguments regarding the proper remedy under that statute.

1. Relevant Law

Code of Civil Procedure section 1281.2 provides that "[o]n petition of a party to an arbitration agreement alleging the existence of a written agreement to arbitrate ... the court shall order the petitioner and respondent to arbitrate the controversy if it determines that an agreement to arbitrate the controversy exists...." Arbitration is a matter of contract.

Thus, when presented with a motion to compel arbitration, the court's first task is to determine whether the parties have entered into an agreement to arbitrate their claims. (*Avery, supra*, 218 Cal. App. 4th at p. 59, 159 Cal. Rptr. 3d 444.) Courts "apply general California contract law to determine whether the parties formed a valid agreement to arbitrate their dispute." (*Id.* at p. 60, 159 Cal. Rptr. 3d 444.) "General contract law principles include that '[t]he basic goal of contract interpretation is to give effect to the parties' mutual intent at the time of contract[.]'" (*Mitri v. Arnel Management Co.* (2007) 157 Cal. App. 4th 1164, 1170, 69 Cal. Rptr. 3d 223.) "Contract law also requires the parties agree to the same thing in the same sense." (*Avery, supra*, 218 Cal. App. 4th at p. 60, 159 Cal. Rptr. 3d 444.) "The petitioner [seeking arbitration] bears the burden of proving the existence of a valid arbitration agreement by a preponderance of the evidence, while a party opposing the petition bears the burden of proving by a preponderance of the evidence any fact necessary to its defense. The trial court sits as the trier of fact, weighing all the affidavits, declarations, and other documentary evidence, and any oral testimony the court may receive at its discretion, to reach a final determination. [Citation.]" (*Ruiz v. Moss Bros. Auto Group, Inc.* (2014) 232 Cal.App.4th 836, 842, 181 Cal. Rptr.3d 781.)

. . .

2. Discussion

It is undisputed that Ramos signed the English Contract and that this contract contains an arbitration agreement. Ramos, however, argues that he was not aware that he was entering into an arbitration agreement because "[t]he words 'arbitration' or 'alternative dispute resolution' never came up during Plaintiff's discussions with the dealership, and Plaintiff never saw the arbitration clause because it was hidden in the English version of the RISC." Although there is no evidence to contradict these facts, typically these arguments would not be dispositive and a person would be bound by the arbitration agreement he or she had signed. "'No law requires that parties dealing at arm's length have a duty to explain to each other the terms of a written contract[.]'" (*Brookwood v. Bank of America* (1996) 45 Cal. App. 4th 1667, 1674, 53 Cal. Rptr. 2d 515.) Further, "'one who accepts or signs an instrument, which on its face is a contract, is deemed to assent to all its terms, and cannot escape liability on the ground that he has not read it. If he cannot read, he should have it read or explained to him.'" (*Randas v. YMCA of Metropolitan Los Angeles* (1993) 17 Cal. App. 4th 158, 163, 21 Cal. Rptr. 2d 245 (*Randas*), quoting 1 Witkin, Summary of Cal. Law (9th ed. 1987) § 120, p. 145.)

The circumstances of this case, however, are not typical. Spanish, not English, is Ramos's primary language. When Ramos went to Pena's Motors, he was greeted in Spanish and the negotiations for the purchase of the automobile were conducted primarily in Spanish. Pena's Motors then provided Ramos with what purported to be a translation of the English language contract he was about to sign. In his declaration, which was prepared with the assistance of a Spanish translator, Ramos contended that he was not aware that the English contract he signed on July 2, 2011, contained an arbitration provision until he spoke with his attorney much later. All of these facts give rise to a reasonable inference that Ramos has a limited ability to understand English. The contract he ultimately signed, however, was in English.

Under the general contract principles just discussed, the fact that Ramos signed a contract in a language he may not have completely understood would not bar enforcement of the arbitration agreement. If Ramos did not speak or understand English sufficiently to comprehend the English Contract, he should have had it read or explained to him. Here, however, Ramos is not attempting to avoid the arbitration agreement because of his limited understanding of the English language. Rather, he is relying on the fact that Pena's Motors provided him with what purported to be a Spanish translation of the English Contract he was being asked to sign, a Spanish translation which did not contain the arbitration agreement.

The trial court made a factual finding that the Ramos Translation was a "true and correct copy of the one [Ramos] was given" and that "the Spanish language translation of the RISC provided to Ramos at the time of the auto purchase transaction did not include an arbitration provision." As a result of its factual findings, the trial court concluded, "by operation of . . . section 1632," that Westlake "failed to establish the existence of an arbitration provision." We agree with the trial court's ruling denying the motion to compel arbitration but affirm on a different ground raised by Ramos, but not explicitly addressed by the trial court: there was no mutual assent because the arbitration agreement was hidden in the English Contract and not included in the Ramos Translation. This is a claim of fraud in the execution (otherwise known as fraud in the inception) of the arbitration agreement.[11] We conclude that Westlake failed to establish an agreement to arbitrate because it did not demonstrate the existence of mutual assent.

A contract is void for fraud in the execution where "the fraud goes to the inception or execution of the agreement, so that the promisor is deceived as

---

11. [10] We treat Ramos's fraud in the execution argument as a challenge to the formation of the arbitration agreement specifically, and not to the English Contract as a whole. The arbitration agreement is, in effect, its own contract contained within the English Contract. In the English Contract, the arbitration provision is described as an arbitration "agreement," and it expressly states that "[t]his Arbitration Agreement survives any termination, payoff or transfer of this Contract." The arbitration agreement also has its own severability clause as well as a provision allowing either party to specifically reject it by "sending to the other a rejection notice by certified mail or by messenger service within 10 days after signing this Contract."

Treating the arbitration agreement as distinct from the contract as a whole finds support in case law. For example, in Prima Paint Corp. v. Flood & Conklin Mfg. Co. (1967) 388 U.S. 395, 87 S.Ct. 1801, 18 L.Ed.2d 1270, the United States Supreme Court addressed whether a "a claim of fraud in the inducement of the entire contract is to be resolved by the federal court, or whether the matter is to be referred to the arbitrators." (Id. at p. 402, 87 S.Ct. 1801.) The Supreme Court held that, "if the claim is fraud in the inducement of the arbitration clause itself—an issue which goes to the 'making' of the agreement to arbitrate—the federal court may proceed to adjudicate it. But the [Federal Arbitration Act] does not permit the federal court to consider claims of fraud in the inducement of the contract generally." (Id. at pp. 403–404, 87 S.Ct. 1801.) Further, in Mt. Holyoke Homes, L.P. v. Jeffer Mangels Butler & Mitchell, LLP (2013) 219 Cal. App. 4th 1299, 162 Cal. Rptr. 3d 597, the court rejected a claim of fraud in the execution of an arbitration provision contained in a legal services agreement, holding that the defendants' failure to explain the existence of the arbitration agreement did not "invalidate the arbitration contract." (Id. at p. 1309, 162 Cal. Rptr. 3d 597.) Mt. Holyoke Homes provides an example of a court examining whether the arbitration agreement itself was secured through fraud in the execution.

to the nature of his act, and actually does not know what he is signing, or does not intend to enter into a contract at all." (*Rosenthal v. Great Western Fin. Securities Corp.* (1996) 14 Cal. 4th 394, 415, 58 Cal. Rptr. 2d 875, 926 P.2d 1061 (Rosenthal).) In this instance, "'mutual assent is lacking, and [the contract] is void. In such a case it may be disregarded without the necessity of rescission.'" (*Id.*) In a fraud in the execution case, "California law . . . requires that the plaintiff, in failing to acquaint himself or herself with the contents of a written agreement before signing it, not have acted in an objectively unreasonable manner. One party's misrepresentations as to the nature or character of the writing do not negate the other party's apparent manifestation of assent, if the second party had 'reasonable opportunity to know of the character or essential terms of the proposed contract.'" (*Id.* at p. 423, 58 Cal. Rptr. 2d 875, 926 P.2d 1061). Thus, a "party's unreasonable reliance on the other's misrepresentations, resulting in a failure to read a written agreement before signing it, is an insufficient basis, under the doctrine of fraud in the execution, for permitting that party to avoid an arbitration agreement contained in the contract." (*Id.*)

. . .

In the instant case, however, the sole factual issue raised by the parties involved the question of which Spanish translation Ramos received. As discussed above, the trial court resolved this factual dispute in favor of Ramos. Beyond this, Ramos's declaration is uncontradicted as Westlake failed to offer any declarations by a witness to the underlying automobile transaction. The only declarations offered by Westlake were authored by John Schwartz, a custodian of records for Westlake with no firsthand knowledge of what occurred when Ramos bought a used automobile from Pena's Motors. Accordingly, there are no disputed facts that need to be resolved.

Under *Rosenthal*, the issue is whether, on these facts, Ramos's reliance on the Ramos Translation was reasonable. We hold that it was. By providing Ramos with a document that purported to be the Spanish translation of the English Contract it was asking him to sign, Pena's Motors implicitly represented to Ramos that it was, in fact, accurate. Ramos was entitled to rely on this representation. The Ramos Translation was not just inaccurate. Rather, it completely omitted the arbitration agreement that Westlake now seeks to enforce. By providing Ramos a translation that did not even reference arbitration, let alone translate the terms of the arbitration agreement, Pena's Motors "deprived [Ramos] of a reasonable opportunity to learn the character and essential terms of the [arbitration agreement he] signed." (*Rosenthal, supra,* 14 Cal. 4th at p. 428, 58 Cal. Rptr. 2d 875, 926 P.2d 1061.)

Because the fraud in the execution in this case only extends to the arbitration agreement, our holding below does not affect the validity or enforceability of the English Contract as a whole or any rights Ramos may have under it.

Our holding that Ramos's reliance on the Ramos Translation was reasonable is supported by the existence of section 1632. As we detailed above, section 1632 requires merchants to provide translations of certain contracts (including retail installment contracts for automobiles) when those contracts are negotiated primarily in a foreign language. The Legislature enacted the statute to "increase consumer information and protections for the state's sizeable and growing Spanish-speaking population." (§ 1632, subd. (a)(1).) The very purpose behind this provision is to ensure that non-English speaking customers receive accurate information regarding the terms and conditions of the contracts they are being asked to sign. Given this, it would be anomalous to hold that Pena's Motors was required to provide Ramos a translation of the English Contract, but that under all of the facts of this case Ramos was not entitled to rely on the accuracy of that translation.

Ramos reasonably relied on a Spanish translation of the English Contract that Pena's Motors provided him and that did not include the arbitration agreement. Accordingly, mutual assent as to the arbitration agreement is lacking, it is void, and the trial court correctly denied Westlake's motion to compel arbitration. Because of our holding, we need not address the parties' arguments regarding the scope of section 1632's remedies or the trial court's finding that the arbitration agreement was unenforceable due to unconscionability.

DISPOSITION

The judgment of the trial court is affirmed.

Understanding the Case:

1. *Another Assigned Contract:* As in other cases we have seen, this case involves a contract that was assigned. Specifically, while Ramos entered into the Conditional Sales Contract and Security Agreement with Pena's Motors, the used car dealer, Pena's Motors then assigned its rights under that contract to Westlake Services LLC. That is why Westlake is the defendant seeking to compel arbitration.

2. *Declarations and Facts:* To assist the trial court's determination of what occurred when Ramos bought his vehicle from Pena's Motors for purposes of deciding Westlake's motion to compel arbitration, the parties each submitted declarations. A declaration is a person's sworn statement of fact. Thus, in Ramos's declaration, he declared (among other things) that when he bought his car, he was given a Spanish translation of Pena's Motors' Conditional Sales Contract and Security Agreement that did not include an arbitration provision. And in his declarations, John Schwartz, Westlake's manager of dealer compliance and payment collection as well as a custodian of records, attached a fully executed copy of the Conditional Sales Contract and Security Agreement. He also attached a copy of the Spanish version of Ramos's Conditional Sale Contract and Security Agreement that Pena's Motors provided to Westlake when

Westlake purchased Ramos's contract. That version contained an arbitration clause. In other words, the parties' sworn statements present conflicting facts. It is not at all unusual for this to occur. Where this does occur, it is up to the trial court—the court that hears the evidence—to decide whose evidence to believe. In this case, the trial court believed the Spanish translation that Ramos introduced was the version presented to him when he bought his car, because (1) Ramos attested to the fact that he was given the version without an arbitration clause; (2) the version he presented included his signature and initials in various places, while the version presented by Westlake did not; and (3) Schwartz was not present for any part of the transaction, he only attested to what version was given to him by Pena's Motors, not what version was given to Ramos. Moreover, Westlake did not provide declarations from anyone at Pena's Motors about which version was given to Ramos. Unless facts are clearly erroneous, a court on appeal will not disturb a lower court's findings of fact, and the court in this instance did not do so.

3. *A Contract Within a Contract:* The court treated the arbitration clause in the Conditional Sales Contract and Security Agreement as if it were an entirely separate contract. It did so because precedent (*Prima Paint*) supported taking this approach. Moreover, the court found that the arbitration clause was intended to be a "stand-alone" clause since a party could reject only that clause while being bound by the remainder of the contract. And the clause contained its own severability clause, showing that it had its own independent approach to interpretation. Treating the arbitration clause as if it were a separate contract allowed the court to find that the parties had not mutually assented to the arbitration clause, while not undermining mutual assent as to the rest of the contract. However, the same outcome would have followed had the court allowed Ramos to void the arbitration clause instead of finding the absence of assent to that clause.

4. *Void Versus No Mutual Assent:* The *Ramos* trial court held that the arbitration clause was void, either because it violated Section 1632 of the California Civil Code or because it was unconscionable. In comparison, the California Court of Appeals did not find that the arbitration clause was void. Instead, it found that the parties did not mutually assent to that provision. While there may not be a significant difference between a provision being void and a provision not being binding because it was not assented to, in some situations there could be a difference. That is because if a party's challenge rests on the absence of mutual assent, then the statute of limitations, the concept of ratification, and other limitations may not be relevant, although they could limit a party's ability to use a defense to enforcement.

Comprehension and Thought Questions:

1. What was the main purpose of the contract between Alfredo Ramos and Pena's Motors?

2. Why did Pena's Motors supply Ramos with a Spanish translation of that contract?

3. How accurately did the Spanish translation reflect the English version of the contract that Ramos signed? How do you know that?

4. On what theory did the trial court allow Ramos to avoid that contract and what test did the court use to determine that?

5. Recall from Chapter 4 that parties have a "duty to read" their contracts. Why was Ramos not bound by the English version of the contract under that duty?

6. Why did the appellate court instead analyze whether Ramos had assented to the contract?

7. What was the appellate court's basis for holding that Ramos had not assented?

8. Do you agree that Pena's Motors' conduct undermined Ramos's assent?

Hypothetical Variations:

1. Explain how you think the court would have ruled if the contract had included the following provision:

this would only probably work for small mistakes of translation

> By signing below, the Purchaser [defined as Ramos] agrees that he has read and understands this Agreement. Moreover, he acknowledges that even if he has been given a Spanish translation of this Agreement, only this English version will be binding. Moreover, the Purchaser may not rely on any terms from that Spanish translation in making any claims or raising any defenses against Pena's Motors.

2. What if Pena's Motors had not supplied Ramos with a Spanish translation of the English contract before Ramos signed, though Ramos could not read or understand English?

3. What if Ramos could read and understand English in addition to Spanish, though Pena's Motors still supplied Ramos with a Spanish translation that excluded the arbitration clause?

4. What if Ramos had wanted to return the car and get his money back, and argued that there was not mutual assent to the entire Conditional Sales Contract and Security Agreement?

PRACTICE PROBLEM 20-4

Refer back to the facts from Practice Problem 20-1.

Assume that when Christine gave Keith the offer, Keith accepted the offer by signing on his signature line at the bottom of the page, right below Christine's signature. But before signing, Keith handwrote on page three (of eight) that the sale excluded all kitchen appliances and window coverings. Without that notation, the sale would have included those items, together valued at approximately $20,000. Keith then sent a copy of the contract to Christine, who did not even notice the handwritten addition on page three.

At the same time that Christine discovered that the house across the street was used for drug dealing, she also noticed that all kitchen appliances and window coverings were missing. It was then that she reread the agreement and saw Keith's hand-notation about excluding the kitchen appliances and window coverings.

Christine asks you whether she has any basis to rescind the contract as a result of Keith's handwritten change on the agreement. Alternatively, she asks whether she has a right to avoid being bound by Keith's hand-written notation.

→ not fraud, just basic rules of offer acceptance

"last shot" rule

CHAPTER 21

Unconscionability and Public Policy

The inducement defenses, which were discussed in the previous chapters, all hinged on a specific defect in the process of contract formation. For example, with duress, a party exerted a wrongful threat on the other to induce the other party to assent; and with misrepresentation, a party misrepresented the facts relating to the subject of the contract, thereby inducing the other party to assent. However, those defenses generally did not factor in the substance of the bargain struck as a result of the defective contract formation process.[1] The defenses explored in this chapter, in contrast, consider problems with the substance of the contractual terms. First, Section A explores unconscionability, which considers weaknesses in the parties, the contracting process, and the appearance of contractual terms, in addition to the fairness of contract terms. Then, Section B discusses the public policy defense, which considers when other policies outweigh contract law policies and thus justify not enforcing a contract or contract term. As that discussion explains, that defense looks solely to the terms of the contract, and not to any defects in the contracting process or weakness in contracting parties. As we explore each of these defenses, consider whether the doctrines strike the right balance both for contract law and competing public policy purposes.

---

1. Recall in *Friendly's*, though, that one of the court's tests for undue influence considered whether the consideration was grossly inadequate.

A. UNCONSCIONABILITY

Like the inducement defenses, **unconscionability** can involve unfair conduct by a party leading up to the formation of a contract. However, this doctrine also considers the ability of a party to understand contract terms (for example, considering the contracting party's education and intellect as well as the conspicuousness and understandability of contract terms), the voluntariness with which the party acts in entering into the contract (for example, by looking at the contracting party's need for the contracted-for item and availability of other providers), and the fairness of the transaction terms. For this reason, unconscionability often acts as a "safety valve" for problematic behavior or processes that do not satisfy one of the other defenses might make a contract or contract term unconscionable.

More specifically, to be unconscionable, most jurisdictions require that a contract be both *procedurally* as well as *substantively* unconscionable. However, these two elements can be present in varying degrees. Thus, with *more* evidence of procedural unconscionability, a court may require *less* evidence of substantive unconscionability, and vice versa.

To be procedurally unconscionable, a contract must essentially give a party no meaningful choice but to agree. This often happens with adhesion contracts. Adhesion contracts are contracts that a party must simply accept (or adhere to). In other words, they are form contracts supplied by the stronger party to the weaker party that the weaker party cannot negotiate.

More generally, a contract may be procedurally unconscionable where there is a gross disparity in bargaining power. In addition, procedural unconscionability is said to involve unfair surprise of the aggrieved party. This surprise happens often in the way the contract, or a specific contract term, is presented. For example, if a term is buried in fine print, or written in legal jargon such that the counterparty cannot understand it, then the counterparty is surprised to later learn of either the inclusion or meaning of that term. This is even more problematic where the weaker party lacked education or sophistication and therefore did not understand the language of the contract.

Procedural unconscionability may also follow from a party's misrepresentations. Where that occurs, then the misrepresentation doctrine may serve as a stronger basis to rescind the contract. If, however, it is not entirely clear if a party's conduct satisfies the misrepresentation defense (for example, because it is not clear if the counterparty had a duty of disclosure where the misrepresentation results from an omission), then the aggrieved party may also argue that the contract is voidable due to unconscionability.

Procedural unconscionability may also occur due to a party's vulnerability, mental illness, or other capacity defects. Thus, a contract may be procedurally unconscionable where a party has a mental illness or defect, yet that illness or defect does not satisfy the capacity defense. The case for procedural unconscionability is even greater where the stronger party seeks to take advantage of the weaker party. In that way, this defense can apply in similar situations to the undue influence defense, though again, procedural unconscionability can exist without this type of defect.

As you can see from these factors, whether a contract is procedurally unconscionable is very fact-specific, turning on the parties, the circumstances, their manner of dealing with one another, and the appearance of the contract terms. Procedural unconscionability sometimes exists where facts potentially giving rise to a defense such as lack of capacity, misrepresentation, or undue influence exist, yet a party does not want to rely entirely on one of these other defenses.

For a contract, or a contract term, to be substantively unconscionable, courts usually look at whether a term is unfair or unreasonably favorable to one side. Courts often look to see if there is a large disparity in the consideration given by the parties—while parity in consideration is not necessary, a great disparity in consideration does suggest substantively unfair terms. Moreover, courts often look to see whether a stronger party is protected more than is necessary given the risks it faces. That is sometimes suggested where one party is protected from the exact same risks that the other party faces, yet the other party is not so protected. You will see one example of this type of alleged substantive unconscionability in the *Taylor* case, below.

To see an example of substantive unconscionability, imagine that on January 1, 2018, Payday Lender lends Hussein Wood $100 because Hussein has to pay for his family's food and lodging. Per the loan agreement, Hussein is to repay this principal with interest to the lender in biweekly installments of $40.16 over the course of 26 payments. At the end of the loan term, Hussein has to pay an additional $50.34. This means that at the end of the loan term, Hussein will have paid $999.71 in finance charges on a $100 loan. This equates to an interest rate of approximately 1,147 percent.

In this example, even if charging such a high interest rate is not illegal, a court might find that the loan terms are substantively unconscionable. It could find this if the court finds that the interest rate is higher than is reasonably necessary to protect Payday Lender from the risk of a payment default, and that this interest rate is unfair.[2]

Because substantive unconscionability considers the fairness of terms, like the public policy defense discussed in Section C, it protects parties from socially undesirable contract terms. However, it is generally easier to prove that a term is unfair under substantive unconscionability than it is to prove that a term violates public policy.

---

2. For an actual case with similar facts, *see* State of New Mexico, ex rel King v. B&B Investment Group, Inc., 329 P.3d 658 (Sup. Ct. N.M. 2014).

Either an entire contract can be unconscionable, or a specific term can be unconscionable. An entire contract is unconscionable where the unconscionability either imbues the entire contract or affects essential terms. In that case, an aggrieved party may rescind the entire contract. In contrast, where the unconscionability only affects a specific term, and that term is not an essential term, the aggrieved party may void only the unconscionable term.

Moreover, a court may enforce a contract in a way to avoid an unconscionable result apart from merely voiding the unconscionable term. For example, if a court decides that a contract or term is unconscionable, it may deny a party specific performance. Or it may limit or decide to not award monetary damages.

Thus, in the above example, the court might strike the unconscionable term on interest rate. Then, the court might supply a gap filler for a reasonable interest rate.

Finally, while the unconscionability defense turns on the specific factual context, courts generally decide whether a contract is unconscionable as a matter of law.

Keep in mind that often there are federal and state statutes that protect consumers from similar conduct for which the unconscionability defense applies. Chapter 4 discussed some of those those statutory protections, and that discussion will not be repeated here. However, for purposes of this chapter, note that the remedy under those statutes often consists of civil penalties and injunctive orders to prevent the party from continuing to engage in the unlawful conduct. Those statutes generally do not provide a right to rescind an unfair contract. For that remedy, the aggrieved party must resort to a contract law defense, such as unconscionability.

The following case shows how the doctrine of unconscionability can be used to challenge the enforceability of a contract provision. This case once again involves a challenge to an arbitration agreement, which is the subject of the greatest number of challenges under the unconscionability doctrine.

East Ford, Inc. v. Taylor
Supreme Court of Mississippi
826 So. 2d 709 (2002)

SMITH, P.J., for the Court.

East Ford, Inc. appeals to this Court from an adverse ruling in favor of James E. Taylor, Jr., by the Hinds County Circuit Court. Taylor filed suit in the Hinds County Circuit Court against East Ford, Inc. on March 15, 2000, alleging that it had sold him a used truck, which was represented to him as new. Taylor signed an "Offer to Purchase or Lease Vehicle" on the date of the sale which contained an arbitration clause. After Taylor filed suit, East Ford filed a Motion to Compel Arbitration. The circuit court ultimately found the arbitration agreement to be unconscionable. This Court subsequently granted permission for this interlocutory appeal.

This Court writes to express to the bench and bar that we adhere to federal policy favoring arbitration and that arbitration agreements are not per se inherently unconscionable.

However, where as here, an arbitration agreement is found to be unconscionable pursuant to general state law principles, then it may be invalidated without offending the Federal Arbitration Act.

We find that the circuit court was correct in holding the arbitration clause unconscionable in this case, and we therefore affirm and remand to the circuit court for a full trial on the merits.

FACTS

Relying on the salesman's statement that the truck was "new" and had never been titled, on May 10, 1999, James E. Taylor, Jr. purchased a 1998 Ford F-150 pickup truck from East Ford, Inc. for $22,051.77. Taylor completed the transaction by signing several forms, including an "Offer to Purchase or Lease Vehicle." That agreement provided in pertinent part as follows:

> B. ARBITRATION AGREEMENT: With only the exceptions described below, the parties acknowledge, understand and agree that: (1) any controversy, claim, action or inaction arising out of, or relating to, the transaction evidenced by the OFFER together with any resulting written agreements including, but not being limited to, any finance, lease, insurance and/or vehicle service agreements (the OFFER and all resulting agreements are hereinafter collectively referred to as the "AGREEMENTS"), or any breach thereof, together with any repair or service to the vehicle performed or provided by [East Ford, Inc.], shall be settled by arbitration administered by the American Arbitration Association in accordance with its Commercial Arbitration Rules; and (2) judgment of the award rendered by the arbitrator(s) may be entered in any court of competent jurisdiction; and (3) the arbitration proceeding shall be conducted in Jackson, Mississippi; and (4) the arbitrator(s) will have no authority to award punitive damages and may not in any event, make any ruling, finding, or award that does not conform to the terms and conditions of the AGREEMENTS; and (5) the AGREEMENTS evidence a transaction involving interstate commerce; and (6) the Federal Arbitration Act, 9 U.S.C. § 1 et seq. (1947, as amended) shall govern the interpretation and enforcement of this Arbitration Agreement; and (7) the only claims which may arise among the parties which are not subject to this Arbitration Agreement are: (a) claims by [East Ford, Inc.] (including its agents, successors and assigns) that one or more events of default as identified in the AGREEMENTS has occurred on the part of OFFEROR(S) (such claims include, but are not limited to, OFFEROR(S) failure to make payments in compliance with the AGREEMENTS)—the parties agree that all such claims may be pursued in any court of competent jurisdiction; and (b) claims subject to the Arbitration Agreement; and (8) the parties' respective rights and obligations

under this Arbitration Agreement will survive the breach, sale, assignment, cancellation, termination, revocation, expiration, novation and/or modification of any or all the AGREEMENTS.

After buying the truck, Taylor discovered that it was not in fact new, but rather that it had been previously titled to another person. When confronted by Taylor, East Ford's representative initially denied that the truck was sold as new, but when presented with a bill of sale which reflected the truck was sold as new, East Ford merely issued an amended bill of sale which reflected the truck was sold as used. Taylor's expert provided an affidavit in which he stated that the difference in cost between a new truck and the used one is $6,676.77.

Taylor subsequently filed suit against East Ford in the Hinds County Circuit Court alleging common law fraud, breach of contract and breach of express warranty. East Ford filed a Motion to Compel Arbitration asserting that Taylor was required to arbitrate the dispute. In response to East Ford's motion, Taylor filed several affidavits, including his own.

In his affidavit, Taylor states that he signed the Offer to Purchase or Lease Vehicle without being advised of the arbitration agreement. He asserts that he has had no legal training and that he did not wilfully agree to arbitration. He further alleges that the agreement was not discussed with him. An affidavit provided by the salesman, Bryan Childress, confirms not only that he did not discuss the arbitration agreement with Taylor, but also that Childress had no knowledge that an arbitration agreement was part of the transaction between East Ford and Taylor. Childress's affidavit further states that he had never discussed an arbitration agreement with any of the customers to whom he has sold vehicles, nor had he ever been given any information regarding such an agreement by East Ford.

The circuit court found the arbitration clause to be unconscionable and, therefore, denied East Ford's Motion to Compel Arbitration. East Ford then filed a Petition for Interlocutory Appeal with this Court, which we subsequently granted.

STANDARD OF REVIEW

The grant or denial of a motion to compel arbitration is reviewed de novo. In determining the validity of a motion to compel arbitration under the Federal Arbitration Act, courts generally conduct a two-pronged inquiry. The first prong has two considerations: (1) whether there is a valid arbitration agreement and (2) whether the parties' dispute is within the scope of the arbitration agreement.

In the present case, the outcome of the first prong is not disputed. Under the second prong, the United States Supreme Court has stated the question is "whether legal constraints external to the parties' agreement foreclosed arbitration of those claims." *Mitsubishi Motors Corp. v. Soler Chrysler-Plymouth,*

Inc., 473 U.S. 614, 626, 105 S.Ct. 3346, 87 L.Ed.2d 444 (1985). Under the second prong, applicable contract defenses available under state contract law such as fraud, duress, and unconscionability may be asserted to invalidate the arbitration agreement without offending the Federal Arbitration Act.

ANALYSIS

I. WHETHER THE ARBITRATION CLAUSE IS UNCONSCIONABLE.

The Federal Arbitration Act provides that arbitration agreements "shall be valid, irrevocable, and enforceable, save upon such grounds as exist at law or in equity for the revocation of any contract." 9 U.S.C. § 2. The Act establishes a "'federal policy favoring arbitration,' . . . requiring that 'we rigorously enforce agreements to arbitrate.'" *Shearson/Am. Exp., Inc. v. McMahon*, 482 U.S. 220, 226, 107 S.Ct. 2332, 2337, 96 L.Ed.2d 185 (1987). "Absent a well-founded claim that an arbitration agreement resulted from the sort of fraud or excessive economic power that 'would provide grounds for the revocation of any contract,' the Arbitration Act 'provides no basis for disfavoring agreements to arbitrate statutory claims by skewing the otherwise hospitable inquiry into arbitrability.'" *Id.* "[Q]uestions of arbitrability must be addressed with a healthy regard for the federal policy favoring arbitration . . . The Arbitration Act establishes that, as a matter of federal law, any doubts concerning the scope of arbitrable issues should be resolved in favor of arbitration, whether the problem at hand is the construction of the contract language itself or an allegation of waiver, delay, or a like defense to arbitrability." *Moses H. Cone Mem'l Hosp. v. Mercury Constr. Corp.*, 460 U.S. 1, 24-25, 103 S.Ct. 927, 74 L.Ed.2d 765 (1983). This Court has adopted this preference for arbitration.

It has been recognized that in order to determine whether legal constraints exist which would preclude arbitration, "courts generally . . . should apply ordinary state-law principles that govern the formation of contracts." *Bank One, N.A. v. Coates*, 125 F. Supp. 2d 819, 827 (S.D. Miss. 2001) (quoting *Webb v. Investacorp, Inc.*, 89 F.3d 252, 257 (5th Cir. 1996)). However, "[c]ourts may not . . . invalidate arbitration agreements under state laws applicable only to arbitration provisions." *Doctor's Assocs., Inc. v. Casarotto*, 517 U.S. at 687, 116 S.Ct. at 1655 (quoting *Allied-Bruce Terminix Cos. v. Dobson*, 513 U.S. 265, 281, 115 S.Ct., 834, 843, 130 L.Ed.2d 753 (1995)). In other words, the usual defenses to a contract such as fraud, unconscionability, duress, and lack of consideration may be applied to invalidate an arbitration agreement, so long as the law under which the provision is invalidated is not applicable only to arbitration provisions. It was under this prong that the trial court found the arbitration agreement to be unconscionable.

The courts have recognized "two types of unconscionability, procedural and substantive." *Pridgen v. Green Tree Fin. Servicing Corp.*, 88 F. Supp. 2d 655 (S.D. Miss. 2000) (quoting *York v. Georgia-Pac. Corp.*, 585 F. Supp. 1265, 1278

(N.D. Miss. 1984)). Procedural unconscionability may be proved by showing "a lack of knowledge, lack of voluntariness, inconspicuous print, the use of complex legalistic language, disparity in sophistication or bargaining power of the parties and/or a lack of opportunity to study the contract and inquire about the contract terms." *Id.*

Substantive unconscionability may be proven by showing the terms of the arbitration agreement to be oppressive. Substantively unconscionable clauses have been held to include waiver of choice of forum and waiver of certain remedies. In the present case, Taylor argues that the provision is both procedurally and substantively unconscionable. First Taylor argues that the arbitration provision is procedurally unconscionable because although he signed the provision, he did not read it because the salesman did not tell him that he should. Taylor alleges that at the time he signed the contract, he did not know what arbitration was or that he was agreeing to submit to it. Taylor further argues that the location and the typeset of the terms of the agreement render it unconscionable. East Ford argues that none of these factors render the agreement procedurally unconscionable.

Taylor further argues that the arbitration provision is substantively unconscionable because, under the terms of the agreement, only he is required to arbitrate while East Ford retains the right to pursue most, if not all, of its claims against Taylor in a court of law. Furthermore, Taylor points out, that his remedy is limited to actual damages because the arbitration provision prevents an award of punitive damages no matter how egregious the conduct on the part of East Ford might be. East Ford argues that the foregoing reasons are insufficient to find the arbitration clause substantively unconscionable.

In the case below, the circuit court found the arbitration clause to be both procedurally and substantively unconscionable. The circuit court found in relevant part:

> In the present case, it is clear that an arbitration agreement between Plaintiff and Defendant existed. It is not so clear as to whether the arbitration agreement is enforceable. By reviewing the Offer to Purchase or Lease Vehicle agreement, it is noticeable that certain words are in boldface, large letters which stand out conspicuously to the reader. Defendant states in the Motion to Compel Arbitration that the arbitration agreement appears in bold type. Yet, the Court could not discern any bold printing. The arbitration clause is not in boldface and it appears less than one third the size of many other terms in the document. As a matter of fact, every detail that is inserted onto the agreement concerning the vehicle Plaintiff purchases is in boldface print. However, the arbitration clause along with the additional terms and status and compensation clause are all in very fine print and regular typing font.
>
> Defendant also states that the arbitration clause is outlined and separated from the remainder of the Offer to Purchase or Lease Vehicle Agreement. From

the Courts [sic] examination of the document, the arbitration clause is enclosed in a box setting along with additional terms and status of and compensation clause. The box setting format is used in other parts of the agreement as well. The arbitration clause also does not have any underlining nor any other effect which would alert the reader of the importance of its terms.

Furthermore, the arbitration clause is clearly one-sided. The agreement is a standard, preprinted form unilaterally drafted by East Ford, Inc. The administers of the arbitration agreement, the American Arbitration Association, do not have any authority to award punitive damages. The arbitration clause also states that the only claims which may arise among the parties which are not subject to this arbitration agreement are claims by East Ford, Inc. and those subject to Lemon Law Rights. Even if the consumer proceeds to file a grievance under the Lemon Law, the consumer must first seek resolution before the Dispute Settlement Board. Thus, East Ford is unilaterally allowed to rescind the entire agreement. The only instance where the consumer is allowed to rescind the arbitration agreement is in the purchase of a lemon. East Ford, Inc. has an unfair advantage. Therefore, the arbitration clause in the Offer to Purchase or Lease Vehicle agreement will not be enforced because it is unconscionable both procedurally and substantively.

In *Entergy Miss., Inc. v. Burdette Gin Co.*, 726 So. 2d 1202 (Miss. 1998), this Court examined unconscionability.

Unconscionability has been defined as "an absence of meaningful choice on the part of one of the parties, together with contract terms which are unreasonably favorable to the other party." To show that a provision is conscionable, the party seeking to uphold the provision must show that the provision bears some reasonable relationship to the risks and needs of the business.

We went on to discuss procedural unconscionability:

The indicators of procedural unconscionability generally fall into two areas: (1) lack of knowledge, and (2) lack of voluntariness. A lack of knowledge is demonstrated by a lack of understanding of the contract terms arising from inconspicuous print or the use of complex, legalistic language, disparity in sophistication of parties, and lack of opportunity to study the contract and inquire about contract terms. A lack of voluntariness is demonstrated in contracts of adhesion when there is a great imbalance in the parties' relative bargaining power, the stronger party's terms are unnegotiable, and the weaker party is prevented by market factors, timing or other pressures from being able to contract with another party on more favorable terms or to refrain from contracting at all.

Entergy Miss., Inc., 726 So.2d at 1207.

We further found in relevant part:

Procedural unconscionability "is most strongly shown in contracts of adhesion presented to a party on a 'take it or leave it basis.'" *York*, 585 F. Supp. at 1278 (quoting *Holyfield*, 476 F. Supp. at 108).

Entergy Miss., Inc., 726 So.2d at 1207-08.

A contract of adhesion has been described as one that is "drafted unilaterally by the dominant party and then presented on a 'take-it-or-leave-it' basis to the weaker party who has no real opportunity to bargain about its terms. Such contracts are usually prepared in printed form, and frequently at least some of their provisions are in extremely small print." *Bank of Indiana, Nat'l Ass'n v. Holyfield*, 476 F. Supp. 104, 108 (S.D. Miss. 1979) (quoting Restatement 2d, Conflicts, § 203, Comment b). As the Fifth Circuit has held, "[c]ontracts in which one party has minimal bargaining power, also referred to as contracts of adhesion, *are not automatically void.*" *See Hughes Training, Inc. v. Cook*, 254 F.3d 588, 593 (5th Cir. 2001) (emphasis added) (citing *Dillard v. Merrill Lynch, Pierce, Fenner & Smith, Inc.*, 961 F.2d 1148, 1154 (5th Cir. 1992)). Similarly, arbitration agreements are not inherently unconscionable. The fact that an arbitration agreement is included in a contract of adhesion renders the agreement procedurally unconscionable only where the stronger party's terms are unnegotiable and "the weaker party is prevented by market factors, timing or other pressures from being able to contract with another party on more favorable terms or to refrain from contracting at all." *Entergy Miss., Inc.*, 726 So.2d at 1207 (quoting *Bank of Indiana, Nat'l Ass'n v. Holyfield*, 476 F. Supp. at 109-10). While *Burdette* concluded that an indemnity clause within a contract of adhesion is presumptively unconscionable, the same is not true for arbitration clauses. *Burdette* involved an agreement to indemnify, which essentially allows a party to contract away or escape liability. Arbitration agreements merely submit the question of liability to another forum—generally speaking, they do not waive liability. Furthermore, Congress has expressed no federal interest in enforcing indemnification agreements as it has in guaranteeing the enforcement of valid arbitration agreements. As noted, "questions of arbitrability must be addressed with a healthy regard for the federal policy favoring arbitration," with any doubt concerning the scope of the agreement resolved in favor of arbitration. *Bank One*, 125 F. Supp. 2d at 827 (quoting *Moses H. Cone Mem'l Hosp. v. Mercury Constr. Co.*, 460 U.S. at 24-25, 103 S.Ct. 927).

As previously stated, the circuit court found in the present case that the arbitration provision appears less than one-third the size of many other terms in the document, appears in very fine print and regular type font. The circuit court further observed that all of the details concerning the vehicle Taylor purchased are in boldface print, while the arbitration provision is not. Additionally, the arbitration provision is preprinted on the document. Taking all of the foregoing into consideration, we find the arbitration clause in this case is procedurally unconscionable.

Although raised by Taylor below, the circuit court did not address Taylor's lack of consideration argument. Because we find that the arbitration clause in this case is procedurally unconscionable, we find it unnecessary to address Taylor's lack of consideration argument, as well as his arguments regarding substantive unconscionability.

CONCLUSION

Federal law favors arbitration as is evident from the existence of the Federal Arbitration Act. In disputes in commercial settings we have held that "[a]rticles of agreement to arbitrate, and awards thereon are to be liberally construed so as to encourage the settlement of disputes and the prevention of litigation, and every reasonable presumption will be indulged in favor of the validity of arbitration proceedings." *IP Timberlands Operating Co. v. Denmiss Corp.*, 726 So.2d 96, 108 (Miss. 1998) (quoting *United Steelworkers v. Am. Mfg. Co.*, 363 U.S. 564, 567, 80 S.Ct. 1343, 4 L.Ed.2d 1403 (1960)). However, where an arbitration agreement is found to be unconscionable pursuant to general state law principles, as is the case here, then the arbitration provision may be invalidated without offending the Federal Arbitration Act. Therefore, we affirm the judgment of the circuit court and remand this case for a full trial on the merits.

AFFIRMED AND REMANDED.

McRAE, P.J., dissenting.

I dissent to the majority's announcing that it favors pre-disposition arbitration and adhesion contracts. It is difficult to knowingly and intelligently waive a trial by jury and an arbitration clause in pre-disposition arbitration because the consumer does not actually know what is involved in giving up their rights. For the majority to say that "[a]rbitration agreements merely submit the question of liability to another forum" is disingenuous because arbitration does not allow for the following by a court of law or review, generally punitive damages or discovery, subpoena of witnesses out of state or in state, or some form of damages. It is merely a cost or expense matter.

While I agree that in some commercial settings arbitration should be allowed as illustrated in *IP Timberlands Operating Co. v. Denmiss Corp.*, 726 So.2d 96, 103 (Miss. 1998), arbitration clauses in most consumer contracts involve overreaching, unconscionability, and precluding small business and individuals from pursuing a remedy when wronged via trial by jury which is guaranteed by our Constitution.

Under the Federal Arbitration Act, automobile dealers were being required to arbitrate any disputes with automobile manufacturers until Congress had to step in and pass a law that released dealers from the strictures of arbitration. By the same token, individuals and small businesses should be afforded the same rights.

Article 3, Section 24 of the Mississippi Constitution of 1890 provides that for every injury there shall be a remedy:

> All courts shall be open; and every person for an injury done him in his lands, goods, person, or reputation, shall have remedy by due course of law, and right and justice shall be administered without sale, denial, or delay.

Article 3, Section 25 of the Mississippi Constitution of 1890 provides that the courts shall be open to all people:

> No person shall be debarred from prosecuting or defending any civil cause for or against him or herself, before any tribunal in the state, by him or herself, or counsel, or both.

Finally Article 3, Section 31 provides:

> The right of trial by jury shall remain inviolate, but the legislature may, by enactment, provide that in all civil suits tried in the circuit and chancery court, nine or more jurors may agree on the verdict and return it as the verdict of the jury.

The arbitration clause in the present case clearly forecloses Taylor's constitutional right to a jury trial, as well as his constitutional right to have a judicial remedy for any wrong which he may have suffered at the hands of East Ford. In addition, the clause waives Taylor's right to collect punitive damages against East Ford. This Court has held, "[c]lauses limiting liability are given rigid scrutiny by the courts, and will not be enforced unless the limitation is fairly and honestly negotiated and understandingly entered into." *Farragut v. Massey*, 612 So.2d 325, 330 (Miss. 1992) (quoting 17 Am. Jur. 2d Contracts § 297, at 298 n. 74 (1991)). In the present case, it is clear that the arbitration clause was anything but fairly and honestly negotiated and that Taylor did not understandingly enter into the arbitration clause which severely limits his legal rights. Furthermore, the salesperson did not know or understand the arbitration clause.

   . . .

In the case at bar, the arbitration provision waives Taylor's constitutional right to a jury trial, his right to collect punitive damages from East Ford, and effectively forecloses his right to access to the courts of Mississippi guaranteed by the Constitution of the State of Mississippi, while at the same time preserving East Ford's right to pursue legal action against Taylor in the courts of Mississippi in most of the situations. As such, the arbitration clause lacks mutuality of obligation because it is so one-sided and unreasonably favorable to East Ford, which drafted the provision, that it is unconscionable and oppressive. "Courts, while zealous to uphold legal contracts, should not sacrifice the spirit to the letter nor should they be slow to aid the confiding and innocent." *United States Fid. & Guar. Co. v. Ferguson*, 698 So.2d 77, 80 (Miss. 1997) (quoting *Andrew Jackson Life Ins. Co. v. Williams*, 566 So.2d 1172, 1188-89 (Miss. 1990)).

Accordingly, I dissent as to the majority's reasoning but concur in the affirmance of the circuit court's order denying arbitration and in the remand of this case for a full trial on merits.

Understanding the Case:

1. *Lemon Laws:* According to the arbitration agreement, the only instance where Taylor would not need to arbitrate his dispute with East Ford was

where he asserted his lemon law rights. Lemon laws generally protect a customer in his purchase of a car that has substantial defects. Where the car cannot be repaired after a reasonable number of attempts, lemon laws give the consumer the right to rescind the contract. That means the consumer returns his car and gets his money back. However, lemon laws only apply where a car is covered by the manufacturers' warranty. In this case, it is not clear if Taylor's car was still covered under the manufacturer's warranty. Moreover, East Ford would only be liable under the lemon law if they were a franchised dealer of Ford. You can find Mississippi's lemon laws at Miss. Stat. Ann. § 63-17-151 *et seq.*

Comprehension and Thought Questions:

1. Why did Taylor sue East Ford under their contract?
2. Did Taylor's claims fall within the Offer to Purchase or Lease Vehicle agreement's arbitration agreement? If so, how did the court know?
3. Why did East Ford likely want Taylor to arbitrate his claims?
4. What legal test did the court use to determine whether the arbitration agreement was unconscionable?
5. How did the court apply that test in this case?
6. In what respect did the dissent disagree with the majority? Whose argument do you find more compelling—that of the majority or that of the dissent?

Hypothetical Variations:

1. What if the arbitration agreement had been mutual and required East Ford to arbitrate any claims against Taylor?
2. What if Taylor had placed his initials in a small box next to the arbitration agreement?
3. What if Bryan Childress, the East Ford salesman who sold Taylor his car, had explained to Taylor that the Offer to Purchase or Lease Vehicle agreement was going to contain an arbitration clause?
4. What if Taylor had been a lawyer?

PRACTICE PROBLEM 21-1

Pam Lee is a horse riding instructor. Pam became an instructor after high school, realizing that going to college would only rack up expenses she could not afford to pay. Plus, a college education would not help her advance her equestrian skills.

Pam does not make much money as a horse riding instructor. Her income is largely dependent on the demand for her lessons at the barn where she works.

Thus, in good-weather months, Pam can make as much as $4,000 a month. In cold-weather months, Pam makes an average of $2,000 a month, which is not enough for her to pay her bills.

Because of her irregular income, Pam has to borrow money during cold-weather months to be able to pay her bills. She then repays those loans as soon as the good weather, and her clients, return.

Most recently, on February 1, desperate for cash to pay her rent and food costs, Pam received a $1,500 loan from PayDay Lender Inc. (PLI). As PLI told Pam, the loan would contain a bullet payment at the end of one year, meaning that the entire $1,500 would be due on February 1 of the following year.

While there was one other payday lender where she lived who might make this loan to Pam, on February 1, that lender was not making new loans.

In processing Pam's loan, PLI presented Pam with a loan agreement that was five pages long. The entire agreement was in eight-point font and had half-inch margins. Words filled up most of each page. While Pam said to Verne Crock, the loan officer at PLI, that she wanted to read the agreement when it was handed to her, Verne informed Pam that there was a line behind her and if Pam wanted the $1,500, she had to read and sign quickly. Pam skimmed the agreement and then signed on the last page, indicating that she agreed to its terms.

As she skimmed, Pam saw that she would owe interest of $125 per month on the loan. While Pam did not calculate that out (since she was rushed), it amounted to an annual interest rate of 100 percent. Pam did not notice that if she did not pay any interest when it was due, she would owe interest at $250 per month until she paid off the entire loan. Again, while Pam did not calculate that out, it amounted to an annual interest rate of 200 percent. The agreement also provided that if Pam did not pay any interest when due, the loan would accelerate, and she would owe the entire $1,500 immediately. While she saw this term, Pam did not understand what it meant.

Unfortunately for Pam, it was an unseasonably cold spring. Thus, Pam missed her first three interest payment dates. While Pam received several letters from PLI demanding that she pay the loan, Pam ignored them, as she did not have any money to pay PLI.

By June 1, Pam had started to make some money by giving riding lessons. She then sought to repay all accrued interest on the loan from PLI. Thus, she showed up at PLI with a check for $450, representing three months of interest. Verne responded by informing Pam that she had one week to pay the entire $1,500 loan plus accrued interest of $750 or PLI would send Pam to collection. Frightened that she will be forced into bankruptcy, Pam contacts you to represent her on this matter. Specifically, Pam wants to know whether there is any basis for her to avoid her contract with PLI or, at a minimum, to avoid the default interest provision of the loan agreement.

B. DEFENSE DUE TO DEFECTS IN TERMS (PUBLIC POLICY)

The public policy defense is another defense that is tied to the substantive contract terms. It is available based on the existence and relevance of other recognized public policy interests that supersede the policies or interests associated with the enforceability of a contract. It essentially involves a balancing of contract law policies along with competing policies that support not enforcing a contract or contract term.

For example, it obviously is in a state's interest not to enforce contracts to perform illegal acts, such as a contract in which one individual promises to murder a third party in exchange for another individual's promise to pay. In that instance, the public policy in favor of not having people murdered outweighs the interest of individuals (in this instance, criminals) being able to rely upon the enforceability of another's contractual promises and the predictability, reliance, and efficiency policies served by such enforceability.

When weighing these competing policies, a court may consider the relative harm to contract law policies caused by not enforcing the particular contract relative to the benefits of serving the public policy of not enforcing the contract. In the example above, a court may determine that, although the predictability of enforcing contracts may be undermined by not enforcing the contract to murder someone, it is unlikely that people will utilize or rely on contracts less as a result of such a decision. Most people, after all, are not engaged in contract promises with respect to illegal activity and accordingly, will be unlikely to perceive contracts as being unreliable simply because such promises are not enforceable as contracts. On the other hand, people may perceive the government as not serving the general public's interest and instead tacitly approving the ability to engage in illegal (and harmful) activity if the contract to murder someone is enforceable and damages can be recovered for breaching that contract.

There are many sources of "public policies" that can potentially compete with contract law's policies. Legislatures, for example, may pass legislation that forbids or restricts the enforceability of certain types of contracts. Many states have usury statutes that preclude the enforcement of any promise to pay interest above a certain rate. Some statutes may even punish individuals with civil or criminal penalties for charging an illegal interest rate in a contract. Such statutes reflect the legislature's determination that certain types of contractual promises are detrimental to the public, regardless of whether the public otherwise would desire to enter into such contracts. These determinations are often linked to a concern that certain segments of the population may be unable to protect themselves from troubling contractual terms. If they are in fact unable to protect themselves, then the government can step in to fill the gap by refusing to enforce certain types of promises. Consumer protection laws have developed in many areas to protect consumers from some of those harmful provisions (as well as to require the inclusion of certain implied terms or protections for the consumer).

Where competing public policy concerns are not as compelling, the legislature may develop exceptions to permit such contracts. Michigan, for example, criminalizes charging an interest rate above 25 percent simple interest, but there is a general exception for loans made by traditional lenders (banks, credit unions, and other finance entities) to a business entity. This exception presumably reflects the legislature's judgment that businesses do not need the same protections from the usury statute as individuals and that the policies underlying the usury statute would not otherwise be served by applying the usury statute to transactions between lenders and businesses. In each instance, the legislation may provide courts with guidance on how and when to enforce the contracts at issue.

Public policy as a contract defense becomes a more complicated issue where the legislature has not acted explicitly to approve or disapprove the enforceability of certain types of contracts or provisions. For example, the legislature may forbid or regulate certain types of conduct but not expressly prohibit contracts relating to such conduct. In those instances, it is left to the courts to develop common law recognition of public policy exceptions to the general rule of contract enforceability. The question obviously is how courts should determine what public policy is and how to weigh the competing interests of that public policy against contract law policies. Often in conducting this analysis, courts look at the purpose for the statutory protection. If it serves an important health, safety, or other objective of the state, the court might view enforcing a contract that provides for a party performing an act in violation of that statute to violate public policy. If, on the other hand, the law largely serves a revenue-raising function, it might still enforce the contract despite noncompliance with state law.

For example, some states have statutes that requires car mechanics to become licensed in that state before providing car maintenance and repair services. There is usually a fee associated with granting that license. Now assume that Jane contracts with auto mechanic Vada to have her car repaired in a state where such licensure is required, but Vada had not obtained her license as required by law. Here, if Jane did not pay Vada for her services, could Vada enforce Jane's obligation to pay? If the purpose of this law is to protect the safety of the public, it would likely not enforce Jane's obligation, as doing so could undermine public safety by inducing Vada to engage in an illegal act. If, however, the law merely serves an administrative and/or revenue-raising purpose, then the court might enforce the contract notwithstanding that it induced Vada to violate law. There may, however, be sanctions against Vada for violating the law.

The following is the Restatement's approach to the public policy defense.

§ 178 When a Term Is Unenforceable on Grounds of Public Policy

(1) A promise or other term of an agreement is unenforceable on grounds of public policy if legislation provides that it is unenforceable or the interest in its enforcement is clearly outweighed in the circumstances by a public policy against the enforcement of such terms.

(2) In weighing the interest in the enforcement of a term, account is taken of
> (a) the parties' justified expectations,
> (b) any forfeiture that would result if enforcement were denied, and
> (c) any special public interest in the enforcement of the particular term.

(3) In weighing a public policy against enforcement of a term, account is taken of
> (a) the strength of that policy as manifested by legislation or judicial decisions,
> (b) the likelihood that a refusal to enforce the term will further that policy,
> (c) the seriousness of any misconduct involved and the extent to which it was deliberate, and
> (d) the directness of the connection between that misconduct and the term.

As you can see, under the Restatement, where public policy is derived from sources other than direct legislation that speaks to the enforceability of contracts, a balancing test is performed. Under that test, where contract law policies in favor of enforcement are "clearly outweighed" by a competing public policy, then the contract or contract term is not enforceable. Where, in contrast, such a competing public policy does not clearly outweigh the interest in enforcing that contract or term, then the court will enforce the contract or term.

The Restatement also describes a number of situations where courts commonly find that the interest in enforcement is clearly outweighed by competing public policy interests. Chapter 20 on misrepresentations already explained one of those situations: where a contract provision unreasonably exempts a party from the consequences of his or her misrepresentation. The following is another important situation:

§ 195 Term Exempting from Liability for Harm Caused Intentionally, Recklessly or Negligently

(1) A term exempting a party from tort liability for harm caused intentionally or recklessly is unenforceable on grounds of public policy.

(2) A term exempting a party from tort liability for harm caused negligently is unenforceable on grounds of public policy if
> (a) the term exempts an employer from liability to an employee for injury in the course of his employment;
> (b) the term exempts one charged with a duty of public service from liability to one to whom that duty is owed for compensation for breach of that duty, or
> (c) the other party is similarly a member of a class protected against the class to which the first party belongs.

(3) A term exempting a seller of a product from his special tort liability for physical harm to a user or consumer is unenforceable on grounds of public

policy unless the term is fairly bargained for and is consistent with the policy underlying that liability.

Once a court determines that public policy concerns clearly outweigh contract law policies, the court retains discretion to fashion a solution: it may choose to void the entire contract, it may strike the void provision and enforce the remaining portions of the contract that are enforceable, or it may revise the contract's terms to make them enforceable.

As discussed briefly in *Duffner* in Chapter 1, non-compete agreements often raise public policy concerns that justify limiting or refusing their enforcement. Some states expressly restrict non-compete agreements through statute, while others rely on the common law to do so.

In the case of non-competes, they raise public policy concerns relating to the restriction of competition and employment, which conflict with the contract law policies of enforcement of freely bargained-for contract terms. Indeed, there are a number of reasons often given in support of the need for non-competes. For example, an employer may only be willing to train and share confidential information with an employee if the employer knows that the employee will not disclose or otherwise use that information to compete with the business for some period of time after the termination of employment. The employer is relying on the employment agreement to provide security and predictability with respect to protecting the business's confidential information and customer/supplier relationships.[3] On the other hand, if the employee provides a valuable service (such as medical services), it may be undesirable to permit employers to restrict their employees' ability to provide services to certain geographic areas. In addition, if non-compete agreements are enforceable, then individuals may be unable to earn a living because of their inability to relocate, particularly if the geographic scope of the non-compete agreement is broad and those individuals lack other skills to gain employment. Public policy might suggest refusing to enforce non-compete agreements based on these competing interests and factors.

As discussed above, courts in different states utilize different approaches to the problem of an overbroad or undesirable non-compete agreement. Some courts refuse to enforce any portion of the non-compete agreement, while others (utilizing the "blue pencil" rule) change the contract to be as enforceable to the greatest extent possible by removing or revising any offensive terms. As the following case shows, public policy concerns can arise with respect to enforcing both the choice-of-law provision in the contract as well as the non-compete provisions in the contract. As you review the case, see if you can identify the competing interests with respect to the non-compete and consider the tests utilized to weigh these competing interests.

---

3. As suggested by the *Duffner* case, the context in which the non-compete covenant was entered into, such as where a seller agrees not to compete with the purchased business, is also important to courts when considering public policy defenses.

Industrial Techs. v. Paumi

Superior Court of Connecticut, Judicial District of Fairfield, At Bridgeport
1997 Conn. Super. LEXIS 1499 (1997)

Memorandum of Decision on Motion for a Temporary Injunction
STEVENS, J.

STATEMENT OF THE CASE

This is an action instituted by the plaintiff, Industrial Technologies, Inc., seeking injunctive relief to enforce noncompete and nondisclosure provisions contained within an employment agreement signed by the defendant, Joseph Paumi. Pending before the court is the plaintiff's application for a temporary injunction.

. . .

The primary facts concerning the parties' relationship and the employment agreement are not in dispute. Except for one brief interruption, from 1974 to 1996, the defendant was employed by a company called Intec Corporation (Intec). Intec started its business in 1971 and has continually maintained its headquarters in Connecticut. Intec's business involved the designing and selling of camera and laser inspection devices used by companies during the manufacturing process to identify product defects or nonconformities. Over the years, the defendant has held numerous positions with Intec. In 1974, he started with Intec as an engineer. By 1992, the defendant was Intec's Director of Marketing, in charge of the company's entire marketing and sales activities. In 1994, the defendant became the general manager of Intec.

In 1992, a company named Aerodyne Products Corporation (Aerodyne) purchased Intec. Aerodyne maintained its principal office in Massachusetts. After Aerodyne purchased Intec, it required all Intec managerial employees, including the defendant, to execute new employment agreements. The defendant received the employment agreement in 1992, but did not sign the agreement until May 5, 1994. This employment agreement contains the noncompete and nondisclosure provisions at issue in this case. In 1994, Aerodyne moved its headquarters to Connecticut, and changed its name to Industrial Technology, Inc., the plaintiff in this case.

In August 1996, the defendant resigned from Intec. His last day of employment was on or about August 17, 1996. Soon after his resignation, the defendant began to work for a company called Mayan Automation (Mayan). Mayan is the Intec's exclusive supplier of an inspection camera that Intec uses for one of its primary product lines. Mayan also has started selling this same inspection camera, with different application features, in the same markets as Intec. Hence, Mayan is a competitor of Intec, and thus, the plaintiff. From these facts, there is no dispute that the defendant's employment with Mayan violates the noncompete provision of his employment agreement with the plaintiff. The crux of the parties' dispute is whether the noncompete provision is enforceable, and if so, to what extent.

DISCUSSION

I

The first issue presented is whether Connecticut law or Massachusetts law governs the employment agreement, and thus, the determination of the enforceability of the noncompete provision. The employment agreement provides under paragraph 6.2 that the agreement "shall be governed in accordance with the laws of the Commonwealth of Massachusetts." The parties agree that the courts of Connecticut and Massachusetts have adopted the rules on conflict of laws set forth in the Restatement of the Law, and under these rules, substantial weight and deference is required to be given to the parties' choice of law.

Yet, despite the weight and deference that is afforded to the parties' choice of law, the Restatement further provides that the parties' choice of Massachusetts law will be disregarded if either: 1) Massachusetts has no substantial relationship to the parties or transaction and there is no other reasonable basis for the parties' choice; or 2) the application of Massachusetts law would be contrary to a fundamental policy of Connecticut and Connecticut has a materially greater interest in the matter than Massachusetts.

[The court applies the first test and determines that the parties' choice of Massachusetts law was not without a reasonable basis.]

The second test under the Restatement is whether the parties' choice of Massachusetts law should be rejected because application of Massachusetts law would be contrary to a fundamental policy of the State of Connecticut. Defendant emphasizes that under Connecticut law, noncompete provisions are restraints of trade that will only be enforced if they are reasonable. The Massachusetts policy on this issue is essentially the same—noncompete provisions are valid only to the extent that they are reasonable. As noted by the parties, the only pertinent difference between Connecticut and Massachusetts law with regard to the enforcement of a noncompete provision is the extent to which the courts are permitted to "blue pencil" a facially unenforceable noncompete provision so that it may be enforced. This different use of the so called "blue pencil" rule is explained by the Connecticut Supreme Court in *Beit v. Beit*, 135 Conn. 195 63 A.2d 161 (1948).

. . .

The defendant insists that this difference between the laws of Connecticut and Massachusetts is a sufficient reason to reject application of Massachusetts law. However, as described in *Beit*, these different views regarding the application of the "blue pencil" doctrine are matters involving different rules of contract interpretation or construction, rather than different principals of fundamental public policy. Indeed, the *policies* of Connecticut and Massachusetts are essentially the same—noncompete provisions are not enforceable if they are unreasonable and are only enforceable to the extent they are reasonable.

Concededly, the Massachusetts "blue pencil" rule sanctions greater court involvement to make otherwise objectionable noncompete provisions reasonable and enforceable. Such a rule, however, does not foster the enforcement of noncompete provisions that violate Connecticut public policy. The defendant cannot seriously contend that a noncompete provision restructured and construed to be reasonable under Massachusetts law would be viewed as being "unreasonable" under Connecticut law. Thus, the true essence of the defendant's argument is not that the use of Massachusetts law would violate a fundamental public policy of Connecticut, but that such use may result in a more limited, entirely reasonable enforcement of the parties' noncompete provision as compared to a complete invalidation of the provision. In this regard, the defendant's position conflicts with the comments of the Restatement: "The forum will not refrain from applying the chosen law merely because this would lead to a different result than would be obtained under the local law of the state of the otherwise applicable law. 1 Restatement (Second), *supra*, 187, comment g.

. . .

Hence, Connecticut, as Massachusetts, uses a rule of construction to transform an unreasonable noncompete provision into a reasonable provision. The defendant has not cited to, and the court has not found, a Connecticut public policy that would be violated by a Connecticut court enforcing a noncompete provision made reasonable by the court wielding the broad "blue pencil" rule utilized by Massachusetts law.

In summary, under the provisions of the Restatement, the parties' choice of law will be accepted and Massachusetts law will be applied to govern the validity and enforcement of the parties' agreement.

II

As previously indicated, under Massachusetts law, a noncompete provision is enforceable if it is reasonable. The reasonableness of a particular agreement is governed by the facts of each case and requires an evaluation of all the pertinent circumstances. The general factors considered in evaluating the reasonableness of a noncompete provision include whether the agreement is: necessary to protect the legitimate business interests of the employer; reasonably limited in time and space and subject matter; and, consistent with the public interest.

A

First, the court rejects defendant's blanket argument that the parties' agreement is completely unenforceable because it in no way protects Intec's (the defendant's employer) good will, but instead, only restrains ordinary competition. See *All Stainless, Inc. v. Colby, supra*, 308 N.E.2d 484 (restraint must protect employer's good will and not merely be a restraint on ordinary competition). The court credits plaintiff's evidence that its competitive advantage in the industry is in part based on its specialized knowledge and ability to apply and adopt available systems to the unique or specific needs of its customers. Its customer lists and actual customer leads are proprietary and not generally known. Moreover, the defendant worked with Intec for over twenty years during which time he became general manager and acquired responsibility for the company's marketing and sales operation in this country and abroad. He certainly must have acquired information about these issues which was unique to his status with the company. As explained below, while the Court agrees that aspects of the non-competition agreement are so broad that they do not reasonably protect plaintiff's legitimate business interests, the Court wholly rejects defendant's argument that Intec does not have any good will or confidential information to protect.

. . .

B

The defendant further argues that the precise provisions of the parties' non-compete provision are so broad that enforcement of the provision in its entirety would offend public policy. The court agrees.

First, the scope of the noncompete provision is very broad because it is not governed by the business activities of the defendant's employer, Intec, but by the business activities of Intec's parent or umbrella company, the plaintiff. The plaintiff's business concerns are obviously more extensive than Intec's activities. The business interests which the plaintiff is most interested in protecting, however, are those which the defendant has the greatest liability to exploit—which are those based on the defendant's years of employment with Intec. Although the evidence did not establish whether Intec is a division of the plaintiff or a separate subsidiary, the record is clear that the defendant was an employee of Intec only. Thus, Intec was the actual entity which provided the consideration to support the employment agreement. This is not to say that the defendant had insignificant contacts with the plaintiff and its other affiliated companies or that the plaintiff has no interest in the noncompete provision. The point here is that the scope of the provision covers business activities so far beyond the defendant's actual employment activities with Intec that the restraint is not entirely consistent with the protection of the good will which the defendant reasonably threatens.

The very broad scope of the noncompete provision is also evidenced by the fact that the provision is not limited to plaintiff's actual or potential competitors. Under the provision, the defendant is precluded from working with a competitor, as well as for anyone who is or ever has been a "client, customer, consultant, collaborator or supplier" of the plaintiff. The defendant is also precluded from being employed by any enterprise involved with any product, process or service that the plaintiff has either engaged in or even "had under consideration" during his period of employment. Contrary to the plaintiff's characterization, the provision does not "merely restrain the defendant from working for a creditor." It precludes him from working with any employer whose business overlaps with the plaintiff's actual or contemplated business activities, irrespective of any competition between the new employer and the plaintiff.

C

Additionally, the parties' noncompete provision does not contain any geographic limitation. The plaintiff contends that because of its "worldwide" operation, any geographic limitation would be insufficient to protect its business interests and good will around the world. The problem with this contention is that while plaintiff has operations in various parts of the world, it does not have operations in every part of the world. Plaintiff's business is about equally divided among the areas of Asia, Europe and the Western Hemisphere. These areas certainly do not constitute the entire world. Moreover, the evidence does not indicate that the plaintiff actually does business in every country in these areas.

A noncompete provision that has worldwide application has been held not to be a per se violation of public policy. Nonetheless, because of the breadth of such a provision, the other terms of the provision must be very narrowly drawn and clearly defined in order to insure that the overall provision is reasonable.

In the present case, the excessive scope of the noncompete provision; the absence of any geographic limits; and, the one year enforcement period, all combine to make the terms of the noncompete provision unreasonable. The plaintiff has not cited any case, and the court has not located any case, enforcing a noncompete provision with such extensive and expansive characteristics.

> . . .

D

As discussed earlier, Massachusetts courts have exercised rather broad discretion to reconstruct objectionable noncompete provisions to make the restrictions reasonable and the provisions enforceable. When restructuring the limits of a covenant not to compete, the Massachusetts courts often focus on the geographic and time limitations of the agreements. A geographic restraint that is very broad may be valid if imposed for a short time and a narrow geographic restraint may be valid for a longer time. These considerations lead the court to conclude that enforcement of the noncompete provision can only be considered reasonable and enforceable if the scope of the agreement, the geographic limits, and the enforcement period are reduced.

Therefore, the court holds that, under Massachusetts law, the parties' non-compete provision is reasonable, and thus, enforceable, providing its scope is limited as follows: The geographic area of the agreement is limited to the plaintiff's presently existing markets in Asia, Europe and the Western Hemisphere. The enforcement of the noncompete provision shall be limited to ninety days, from the date of the defendant's resignation. Additionally, the language of the covenant precluding the defendant from working with individuals who are only consultants, collaborators or suppliers of the plaintiff shall be deemed unenforceable as being beyond the reasonable scope of the plaintiff's legitimate business interests.

. . .

Comprehension and Thought Questions:

1. How do Massachusetts and Connecticut law differ on how they treat non-compete provisions?

2. Why was that difference relevant to the case?

3. What is the test for enforceability of non-compete provisions under Massachusetts law?

4. Why was the non-compete provision in this case not deemed to be enforceable? What were the competing factors or interests the court had to consider?

5. What solution did the court fashion with respect to the unenforceable non-compete provision?

6. Do you think the Massachusetts or Connecticut solution for unenforceable non-compete provisions is preferable? What are the risks or downsides of each solution?

Hypothetical Variations:

1. What if Paumi had been paid one year's salary as severance upon termination?

2. What if the employer was the purchaser of the employee's business and asked the employee to sign a five-year non-compete provision in connection with the sale with the same geographic limitations. Do you think that such a provision is more or less likely to be enforceable than the non-compete provision in the case? Why?

3. What if the court had decided to follow Connecticut law?

PRACTICE PROBLEM 21-2

Why might the following contracts be unenforceable for public policy reasons? What are the competing interests?

1. A poor but healthy individual wants to contract to sell one of her kidneys to a person in need of a transplant for $25,000. What if the healthy individual were wealthy?

2. Isaiah promises to pay Gerard $10,000 if the Chicago Cubs win the World Series, and Gerard promises to pay Isaiah $10,000 if they do not.

3. A married couple want to contract to pay Kathryn $100,000 to act as a surrogate for their baby.

4. A father contracts to pay his son $100,000 if the son refrains from getting married for ten years.

5. A married couple enter into a separation agreement under which the father agrees to assume responsibility for raising the children in exchange for the mother's promise of child support and giving up custody of the children.

Now that you have studied unconscionability and public policy defenses, read through and answer the questions that follow the Simulation Problem for Chapter 21, which is located in Appendix A.

ALTERNATIVE THEORIES OF RECOVERY

Up until now, this textbook has focused on contracts created through bargains. Part VI presumes that no enforceable contract exists but a party is still seeking relief in court for some action it took in reliance on a promise (though not a promise enforceable as a bargained-for contract) or for some benefit it conferred on another (again, not pursuant to a bargained-for contract). In either circumstance, a court might allow a party to recover where equity calls for such a recovery. Because this part presumes there is no contract, the term "parties" does not refer to parties to a contract but rather to parties to litigation.

Chapter 22 begins by examining the equitable doctrine of promissory estoppel, which allows a party to recover for a broken promise on which it reasonably relied. Chapter 23 then turns to the equitable doctrine of restitution, which allows a party to recover for a benefit it conferred on another in situations where it would be unfair for the recipient to retain that benefit without paying for it.

The below diagram shows where the topics covered in Part VI fit into the larger scheme of this course.

PART VI—OVERVIEW DIAGRAM

Is there reliance on the promise (promissory estoppel)? → If No → Was the party unjustly enriched (restitution)? → If No → No basis to recover

If No ↑

Is there a bargained-for promise? → Mutual assent → Consideration

If Yes ↓

Was that promise performed? → Express contract terms and interpretation → Implied terms → Amended terms → Parol evidence rule and evidence of terms → If Yes → No breach

If No ↓

Was non-performance excused? → Material breach by other party → Anticipatory repudiation by other party → Waiver by other party → Mistake → Impracticability or frustration of purpose → If Yes → No breach

If No ↓

Is there a defense to the enforcement of that promise? → Statute of frauds → Incapacity → Duress or undue influence → Misrepresentation → Unconscionability or against public policy → If Yes → No breach

If No ↓

What is the remedy for the breach?

CHAPTER 22

Promissory Estoppel

This chapter addresses **promissory estoppel**, an alternative theory that may permit recovery for a broken promise even in the absence of an enforceable contract based upon a traditional bargained-for exchange. Importantly, this theory of recovery is employed in litigation to recover damages and is not used as a planning device as are bargain-based contracts.

Promissory estoppel, like restitution (discussed in Chapter 23), is largely based on equitable considerations. That means courts examine whether it would be inequitable (or unfair) for a party not to recover damages, even though the party could not demonstrate that the requirements for a bargained-for contract were satisfied. In the case of promissory estoppel, courts consider many factors when deciding whether to intervene, including the aggrieved party's reliance on the other's promise, the nature of the damages suffered, the foreseeability of the damages, whether the damages were avoidable, and the effect of awarding damages in any given case on future parties and situations.

To see how this doctrine works, imagine that Andy wanted to secure Brenda's enforceable promise to sell him Brenda's car for $5,000. To achieve this, Andy would presumably enter into a bargained-for contract where Andy would promise to pay Brenda $5,000 and Brenda would promise to sell him Brenda's car. This exchange of promises, if it satisfied the requirements of mutual assent and consideration, would constitute an enforceable contract that Andy could rely on for legal redress in the event that Brenda failed to deliver the car when promised. Chapters 10-11 walked you through how parties use the backdrop of an enforceable bargained-for contract to conduct their business negotiations, due diligence, drafting, and execution of contracts. All of these actions are taken in anticipation of the existence of an enforceable contract, which again allows the parties to plan for the future and rely on the promises of others.

Sometimes, however, a party may seek to recover damages even though the parties did not enter into a bargained-for exchange. This decision to attempt to recover, as discussed above, will necessarily be taken after the parties have interacted in a manner that did not satisfy the requirements for forming a contract. In other words, the parties did not use (or failed to use correctly) the planning device of a bargained-for contract, but nevertheless, one of the parties feels aggrieved and believes it is entitled to a recovery that may closely resemble the recovery to which it would be entitled had there been an enforceable contract.

For instance, in the example above, imagine that Brenda said to Andy, "I know you have wanted to buy my car for a long time and that you need a car to travel out of state next weekend for a business trip. I promise I will sell it to you on Thursday for $5,000 so that you are able to get there in time." Andy says nothing, but on Wednesday borrows $5,000 from the bank. In the meantime, Brenda has sold the car to another person and calls on Thursday to let Andy know this before Andy attempts to meet her. Andy incurred attorney's fees of $500 and bank fees of $250 in order to obtain the loan. Because of Brenda's failure to perform, Andy is forced to rent a car for $125 per day for three days to be able to make his trip out of state.

In the traditional bargained-for contract analysis, a contract probably was not formed from the parties' interaction, which would mean that Andy could not recover for any damages suffered from Brenda's failure to perform. Let's examine why this is so. Brenda made a promise (the promise to sell on Thursday for $5,000), but there was no return promise from Andy. Since there was no return promise, there probably was no mutual assent. A court might interpret Andy's silence as assent, but as we saw in Chapter 4, courts are typically reluctant to interpret silence as indicating assent absent prior agreement or conduct by the parties that indicates that silence is a reasonable method to indicate assent. Andy likely also did not manifest assent by beginning to perform, as he did not begin to perform the requested return act, which was paying Brenda $5,0000. While Andy was *preparing to* perform, by getting a loan, that act is not what Brenda was bargaining for—she wanted the money.

Consideration also may be missing because Brenda's promise was not made to induce any return promise from Andy, and Andy does not make a promise that induces Brenda's promise. You could argue that Brenda's promise was made to induce Andy's return promise to pay, but since he never makes this promise, consideration would be lacking.

Viewed another way, Brenda's statement could be construed as an offer: an offer to sell on Thursday that Andy can accept by a return promise (accepting by return promise) or by showing up on Thursday with $5,000 (accepting by performance). This offer presumably was revoked when Brenda informed Andy that the car had been sold to someone else. Andy never made a return promise or rendered performance, so that offer was never accepted. Without a finding of mutual assent, a court will have a difficult time finding that the parties entered into a binding contract. It also would be difficult to argue that the parties had an option contract that required Brenda to keep the offer open until Thursday, because Brenda never purported to keep the offer as firm. Moreover, there was no consideration for any such "option."

Once Brenda revokes, the parties are no longer in the planning stage and contemplating an enforceable contract. Instead, one of the parties (Andy) may feel aggrieved notwithstanding the parties' failure to enter into a binding contract. Andy expended funds in advance of the anticipated sale (bank fees and attorney fees) and also ended up expending funds following Brenda's failure to deliver the car as promised. If Andy ends up purchasing a comparable car, he also may end up spending more for the car than the sale price offered by Brenda. Andy may want to recover some or all of these damages from Brenda even though the parties had not satisfied the technical requirements for contract formation.

Andy now is forced to develop a theory of recovery that does not rely on the existence of a bargained-for contract. Here, Andy would likely argue that Brenda's promise is enforceable under promissory estoppel. Note that while the above example demonstrates a basis to recover on a promise absent a bargained-for exchange, the parties contemplated creating (and perhaps even tried to create) a binding contract through a bargain. However, promissory estoppel is often argued to apply even where no bargained-for contract is contemplated, such as with promises to make gifts. Thus, it would also potentially apply had Brenda promised to give Andy her car as a gift and it was foreseeable that Andy would rely upon that promise.

PRACTICE PROBLEM 22-1

1. In the situation between Andy and Brenda, what factors suggest that damages should be awarded to Andy?

2. Is there any downside to a court awarding damages to Andy? What factors suggest that awarding damages will be inappropriate?

3. If a court does decide to award damages to Andy, which damages should be awarded and on what basis?

Section A of this chapter discusses the theory of promissory estoppel and how it evolved. Section B then walks you through the elements of the doctrine of promissory estoppel. Section C discusses how promissory estoppel is utilized in litigation, particularly when there may be other claims available, such as breach of bargained-for contract. Finally, Section D discusses the unique issue of whether the Statute of Frauds defense is available when the aggrieved party is asserting a claim based on promissory estoppel, where the promise sought to be enforced would otherwise fall under the Statute of Frauds if it were being enforced as a bargained-for contract.

A. THEORY OF PROMISSORY ESTOPPEL

Promissory estoppel, as mentioned above, is a theory of recovery that can be employed to recover damages in the absence of a bargained-for contract. Promissory estoppel evolved out of a recognition by courts that certain promises, based on the type of promise, reliance, and damages suffered, should be enforceable against the promissor even where the promissor did not receive a promise or performance in return. If a party *reasonably relied* on another's promise, then a court may feel compelled to award damages even where the promise was not made as part of a bargained-for contract. Promissory estoppel is a doctrine used to remedy "wrongful" (unfulfilled) promises that harm others without their consent (such as via contract), reflecting where the promissor should be required to provide a remedy for the harms suffered in reliance on the broken promises.

Promissory estoppel is related to, though distinguishable from, equitable estoppel. **Equitable estoppel** is a long-standing defense that can be employed at trial to preclude a party from taking advantage of its own misrepresentation of facts. For example, imagine that you called your credit card company to find out when your payment for next month was due to avoid a late fee, and the representative told you that it was due by the fifth of next month. In reliance on that statement, you dutifully send payment in to the company, which is received on the fourth of the month. The credit card agreement, however, actually states that payment is due on the first of each month, and the credit card company includes a late fee on your next bill.

If you refuse to pay the late fee, the credit card company may be estopped, or prevented, from asserting that the late fee was actually due on the first of each month under the doctrine of equitable estoppel. The credit card company made a factual statement (that the due date was the fifth) that you reasonably relied on (by not making payment until the fourth of the month), and the credit card company should not be permitted to take an inconsistent position for purposes of recovering against you for your failure to pay by the first of the month (as was actually required under the written contract). A court so holding might look at whether the credit card company should have foreseen your reliance on the statement and whether your reliance was reasonable. These factors help indicate whether it is fair to prevent the credit card company from recovering damages to which it otherwise would be entitled. In this instance, a court might find it very easy to find that the company should have foreseen that you would not pay until after the first (since the representative told you that you did not have to) and that your reliance (paying after the first but before the fifth) was reasonable.

Importantly, though, equitable estoppel was only available to parties in litigation to defend themselves by pointing to incorrect factual statements by the plaintiff that led the defendant to take particular actions that, in the absence of such incorrect factual statements, otherwise would suggest recovery. Equitable estoppel did not permit the defendant *affirmatively* to recover from the plaintiff for any damages suffered by the defendant because of the plaintiff's misstatement of fact. The following case explains the origins of and rationale for promissory estoppel, and explains how it evolved to allow a party to affirmatively recover to avoid injustice.

Olson v. Synergistic Technologies Business Systems
Supreme Court of Minnesota
628 N.W.2d 142 (2001)

Heard, considered, and decided by the court en banc.
ANDERSON, Paul H., Justice.

. . .

Promissory estoppel's origins lie in the early equity decisions of England's Chancery courts, which were the first courts to grant relief to plaintiffs who "had incurred detriment on the faith of the defendant's promise." J.B. Ames, *The History of Assumpsit*, 2 Harv. L. Rev. 1, 14 (1888). The Chancery court's power to validate and enforce promises predicated on good-faith reliance was based on that court's imperial authority to decide matters pursuant to the principles of "Conscience, Good Faith, Honesty, and Equity." General Writ, 1349, 18 Edw. 3 (Eng.); 1 Spencer W. Symons, *Pomeroy's Equity Jurisprudence* § 35, at 40 (5th ed. 1941). A hallmark of the Chancery court's early decisions was the desire to compensate a plaintiff for harm suffered as a result of the plaintiff's good-faith reliance on a defendant's otherwise unenforceable promise. Cases enforcing promises unsupported by consideration on the basis of good-faith reliance have appeared throughout English jurisprudence ever since.

As the power and influence of the Chancery courts grew, the common-law courts "advised pleaders to pay more attention to actions on the case," which were personal actions within the jurisdiction of the common-law courts. Ames, *supra* at 14. The common-law courts then sanctioned the action of assumpsit to provide relief to plaintiffs pleading actions on the case, and dependence on the Chancery courts to enforce promises predicated on reliance declined but did not disappear. The relief provided by the common-law courts under the writ of assumpsit was based on the plaintiff's consideration in the form of action or forbearance in reliance on the promise, *i.e.*, detrimental reliance as a form of consideration. In contrast, the Chancery courts provided equitable relief based solely on the plaintiff's good-faith reliance. Thus, the English Chancery and common-law courts sanctioned their own distinct forms of a reliance-based cause of action.[1]

---

1. [5] Here, the special concurrence misses the point of the majority's analysis. Our analysis recognizes the marked distinctions between the historical grounds for a cause of action based

American courts adopted the Chancery court's equitable cause of action based on good-faith reliance to enforce promises unsupported by consideration— not as a consideration substitute, but rather as a doctrine based on reliance that the courts could use to prevent injustice. Eventually, the American courts characterized this line of cases as "promissory estoppel," and identified the key elements of the doctrine of promissory estoppel as (1) a promise, (2) the promisee's right to rely on the promise and the promisor's duty to prevent reliance, and (3) harm suffered in reliance on the promise. Over time, the doctrine of promissory estoppel evolved, and courts began to focus on the promisee's right to rely rather than the promisor's duty to prevent reliance. As the doctrine developed, many courts adopted the Restatement of Contracts § 90 (1932) (setting out the elements of promissory estoppel), but in Minnesota, we limited relief available under Restatement of Contracts § 90 to the extent necessary to prevent injustice. For jurisdictions adopting the Restatement of Contracts § 90, the equitable remedy was not a mechanical calculation, but rather it was determined ad hoc on a case by case basis. In contrast, when a plaintiff pleaded a common-law cause of action based on detrimental reliance as a consideration substitute, the legal remedy consisted of compensating the plaintiff for the full value of the promise.

In Minnesota, we have consistently recognized and applied the equitable aspects of promissory estoppel. As early as 1858, we recognized a theory of relief based on harm suffered as a result of relying on a promise. *Emmet & Keifer v. Rotary Mill Co.*, 2 Minn. 286 (Gil. 248) (1858). In *Emmet*, we stated that "had the plaintiffs relied upon a promise made by the defendants to pay for the lumber furnished they should have so pleaded," but we did not discuss whether the nature of such a cause of action is legal or equitable. Later, in *Tice v. Russell,* we enforced a purchaser's promise to waive his legal rights as to the time of redemption with respect to a foreclosure sale. 43 Minn. 66, 69, 44 N.W. 886, 887 (1890). Our decision allowed the debtor to redeem her house within a reasonable time after the foreclosure instead of within the time allowed by the statute of limitations.

Our first case to apply the label of promissory estoppel to a cause of action as a potential basis for relief was *Horan v. Keane In re Stack's Estate*, 164 Minn. 57, 204 N.W. 546 (1925). In *Horan*, the issue was enforcement of a charitable subscription unsupported by consideration. While we did not base our decision in *Horan* on promissory estoppel, we did recognize that other courts were beginning to apply this doctrine to enforce charitable subscriptions

---

on equitable good-faith reliance and the distinct cause of action based on the common-law principle of detrimental reliance in the form of action or forbearance. The Chancery Court's cause of action based on good-faith reliance evolved into what we now label promissory estoppel, and the common-law courts' cause of action based on detrimental reliance in the form of action or forbearance evolved into a form of consideration.

unsupported by consideration. In addition, in *Constructors* we reaffirmed the equitable character of promissory estoppel when we stated that "promissory estoppel is not a substitute for acceptance, consideration, or mutuality, but a doctrine based on reliance which courts may use in a proper case to prevent injustice." 291 Minn. at 120, 190 N.W.2d at 75.

More recently in *Ruud v. Great Plains Supply, Inc.*, we stated that promissory estoppel is a creature of equity. 526 N.W.2d 369, 372 (Minn. 1995). In *Ruud*, we relied heavily on our earlier cases and stated that the "application of promissory estoppel requires the analysis of three elements: (1) Was there a clear and definite promise? (2) Did the promisor intend to induce reliance, and did such reliance occur? (3) Must the promise be enforced to prevent injustice?" *Id.* We relied on this definition again in our recent decision in *Martens v. Minn. Mining & Mfg. Co.*, 616 N.W.2d 732, 746 (Minn. 2000).

This historical review of our case law and the doctrine of promissory estoppel leads us to the conclusion that in Minnesota the elements of promissory estoppel evolved from the equitable cause of action unique to England's Chancery courts based on good-faith reliance. This equitable cause of action based on good-faith reliance forms the roots of our modern doctrine of promissory estoppel.[2]

. . .

Comprehension and Thought Questions:

1. Why did courts develop a theory of promissory estoppel?

2. According to the court, why is promissory estoppel an equitable theory as opposed to a theory of law?

3. How is a reliance-based theory for enforceable promises different from a bargained-for exchange theory for enforceable promises?

Promissory estoppel expanded equitable relief to include promises that were not fulfilled. Just as significant, promissory estoppel could be used as an affirmative theory of recovery instead of only as a defense like equitable estoppel. If the party had in fact made a particular type of promise, the party was estopped from denying responsibility for the damages suffered following the party's failure to perform the promise. Accordingly, even in the absence of mutual promises that satisfy the bargained-for exchange requirement for enforceable contracts, plaintiffs now can seek to recover for damages that arise from broken promises under the theory of promissory estoppel.

---

2. [8] Our recognition of the equitable grounding of promissory estoppel is consistent with the case law from other states that also recognizes the equitable nature of promissory estoppel. *Holmes*, supra §§ 8.11-8.12.

B. ELEMENTS OF PROMISSORY ESTOPPEL

1. Promise

This Section examines the customary requirements for recovery under promissory estoppel. As you study these requirements, consider how they relate to remedies designed for contract as opposed to tort law issues.

The first requirement that must be satisfied for recovery under promissory estoppel is the existence of a promise. This may seem easy to satisfy, as we could just look for words of commitment. Recall, however, that for purposes of finding a bargained-for exchange contract, we look to a number of factors to determine whether a sufficient manifestation of commitment has been made. For example, if Claire says to David "I will build your house for $150,000," and David accepts, we may have the formation of a bargained-for exchange contract. Claire has made a manifestation by speaking to David, and it may be reasonable for David to believe that Claire is inviting David's acceptance based on the language she used. On the other hand, the absence of a number of material terms may preclude a finding of mutual assent necessary for the finding of an enforceable contract. The parties have not discussed how big of a house, the specifications, the timing, or many other important factors relevant to such a significant business transaction. Consequently, a court might find that the parties did not make the requisite showing of mutual assent, as it might not be reasonable for David (or Claire, depending on who is seeking to enforce the "contract") to believe that the other party is manifesting assent when so many material terms are missing. So, the promises made above may be insufficient for mutual assent purposes.

Such promises, however, may be sufficient for purposes of awarding damages under a theory of promissory estoppel. Recall that promissory estoppel seeks to compensate for damages suffered when another has made a promise and the promisee reasonably relied on that promise. In this instance, we are necessarily looking for promises that could justify reliance, not promises that can justify the finding of a bargained-for contract. Consequently, the promise may not necessarily have to be as "fully baked" as one might expect for the formation of a traditional contract. Instead, courts typically look for manifestations that clearly and definitively indicate commitment.

In the home-building example above, we discussed how there were many details missing from the promises exchanged that consequently might preclude a finding of mutual assent. For promissory estoppel purposes, however, Claire may have manifested a sufficient present intent to commit based on the language used by using the words "will build" and reference to a particular price. Would it be reasonable for David to rely on this manifestation and incur expenses in reliance on it, such as obtaining a bank loan, employing an architect, and ceasing negotiations with other builders? Again, the reference point is whether the statement is sufficiently "promissory" for purposes of reliance, not whether the parties had manifested their assent to a commercial bargain. As with the investigation into a finding of mutual assent, courts will examine the facts and circumstances surrounding the manifestation to determine whether a party had made a sufficient "promise" for promissory estoppel purposes. Remember that the promise potentially enforceable under promissory estoppel need not be made to induce an exchange. Thus, even if Claire promised her nephew David that she would help him build a house and David relies on that promise, a court may enforce Claire's promise.

The Restatement does not distinguish between promises for contract purposes and promises for promissory estoppel purposes (i.e., there are not two different definitions of "promise" in the Restatement). Nevertheless, as you will see in the *Hoffman v. Red Owl Stores* case explored later in the chapter, courts appear to use different requirements for a promise depending on the theory of recovery. Why do you think there is a different standard for a "promise" for a contract theory of recovery as opposed to promissory estoppel? Are there any problems with using different standards?

PRACTICE PROBLEM 22-2

Which of the following exchanges satisfy a finding of mutual assent for a contract? Which of the following satisfy a finding of a promise for promissory estoppel purposes?

1. Evangeline asks Francisco to build a tree house for her kids for $500. Francisco says that he will, assuming he can find time to do it on Tuesday. Francisco fails to build the house because he is occupied with his other full-time job.

2. Greta offers to provide "tax services" to Horatio for $1,000 each year. Horatio agrees and fires his current accountant. Greta purports to perform the contract by sending e-mails to Horatio that contain monthly updates regarding new tax law developments. Horatio, realizing that Greta is not going to help him prepare his return, is forced to hire another accounting firm for $5,000 and also incurs $10,000 in late filing fees from the IRS.

3. Ira is concerned that his employer will treat him differently if his wife accepts an offer of employment from a competitor of his employer. His employer tells him that he does not need to be concerned and that his wife's employment would have no bearing on his continued employment with the company. Once the employer finds out that Ira's wife is actually performing services for a competitor, the employer reduces Ira's duties and limits his interaction with clients. The employer subsequently terminates Ira's employment.

2. Reasonable Reliance

Assuming that there is a sufficient promise, the next element that most courts will examine is whether the promisee "reasonably relied" on the promise. This examination gets at whether justice requires enforcement, for justice may not call for enforcement of a promise upon which someone did not actually rely. This element also helps define the damages that should be available to the promisee. By looking to whether the promisee actually suffered damages by relying on the promise, a court can determine whether it is appropriate to award damages.

Recall the car sale situation above, where Andy engaged in the following actions following Brenda's promise to sell him her car for $5,000: (1) borrowing $5,000 from the bank, and (2) hiring an attorney and incurring attorney's fees to assist with the loan. A court may conclude that Andy would not have engaged in these actions had Brenda not made the promise, which means that Andy did in fact *rely* on her promise. Note that Andy's subsequent car rental (because of Brenda's failure to perform) is not an action taken by Andy in reliance on Brenda's promise because, at the point in time when Andy rented the car, he knew that she had broken her promise, so he could not actually rely on it any longer. The car rental, however, may be evidence of some of the harm suffered by Andy because of Brenda's failure to fulfill her promise.

The court also has to assess the reasonableness of the promisee's reliance on the promise.

In the ongoing example, a court would have to determine whether it would be reasonable for Andy to borrow $5,000 from the bank and hire an attorney to assist with the transaction after Brenda made her promise. In other words, are the actions that Andy took reasonable in light of what was promised? The bank loan was for the car sale promised by Brenda, and it seems reasonable for a buyer to try to obtain financing for a large purchase so that the buyer can consummate the transaction. It also seems reasonable for a buyer to obtain attorney assistance in a loan transaction to make sure the loan is completed as desired and with the agreed-upon terms.

Imagine, however, that Andy found out about Brenda's sale of the car to another purchaser before Andy obtained the bank loan or hired an attorney. In that instance, a court might not find those acts to be reasonable since Andy was aware that Brenda already sold the car. In light of his awareness of this fact, it is no longer reasonable for him to rely on her promise and to incur such obligations and expenses. It may also be unreasonable for Andy to take actions that are out of proportion to the promise. For example, it may be unreasonable for Andy, prior to purchasing the car, to enter into a $100,000 contract with a body shop to restore the car to its original condition. Given the value of the transaction ($5,000) relative to the body shop contract ($100,000), it may not be reasonable for Andy to enter into the body shop contract before title to the car has actually passed to him given the lack of a conventional contract between Brenda and Andy regarding the sale of the car.

PRACTICE PROBLEM 22-3

How does the promisee rely in each of the following scenarios? Is the promisee's reliance "reasonable"?

1. Evangeline asks Francisco to build a tree house for her kids for $500 on Saturday. Francisco says that he will unless he informs Evangeline on Tuesday that he will not have time to build the tree house. On Monday, Evangeline spends $5,000 on furnishings for the tree house. On Tuesday, Francisco informs Evangeline that he will not have time to build the tree house. What if Evangeline had incurred such expenses on Wednesday after not hearing anything from Francisco on Tuesday? *no K - promissory estoppel*

2. Greta offers to provide "tax services" to Horatio for $1,000 each year. Horatio agrees and fires his current accountant. Greta purports to perform the contract by sending e-mails to Horatio that contain monthly updates regarding new tax law developments. Horatio is forced to hire a new accountant (his old one would not provide services to him any longer) for $2,000, which was more than he had paid to his prior accountant. *K (terms definite enough) OR promissory estoppel*

3. Ira is concerned that his employer will treat him differently if his wife accepts an offer of employment from a competitor of his employer. His employer tells him that he does not need to be concerned and that his wife's employment would have no bearing on his continued employment with the company. Once the employer finds out that Ira's wife is actually performing services for a competitor, the employer reduces Ira's duties and limits his interaction with clients. The employer subsequently terminates Ira's employment. *no K - promissory estoppel b/c no consideration*

3. Foreseeable Reliance

Another factor courts typically consider in determining whether a promisee should be entitled to recover under a theory of promissory estoppel is how foreseeable the promisee's reliance was. In some sense, this factor helps assess how much fault should be ascribed to the promissor based on whether the promissor should have anticipated the promisee's reliance.

In our ongoing car sale example, if Brenda was aware that Andy needed the car for the weekend and that he had wanted to purchase the car for some time, her knowledge means that she could probably anticipate that Andy would take steps in reliance on her promise to sell the car, such as obtaining a car loan and forgoing a car rental. On the other hand, consider how the situation would have been different if, after Brenda had made her promise to sell the car to Andy for $5,000, Andy had entered into a contract to sell the car (after he purchased it from Brenda) to Doug for $10,000. Is Andy's reliance (entering into the contract to sell the car) foreseeable to Brenda? It appears that she anticipated his use of the car for traveling and was aware that he had wanted to purchase the car for a long time. This suggests that perhaps it was not foreseeable to Brenda that Andy would enter into a contract to sell the car immediately after purchasing it from her. On the other hand, one could question whether Brenda knew why Andy had wanted to purchase the car for such a long time. If she knew he wanted it because he was a car dealer or otherwise engaged in the business of buying and selling used cars, then perhaps his contract with Doug is foreseeable. This, of course, is not suggested by the facts above.

Foreseeability is somewhat related to the reasonableness requirement, as it is likely that it is more difficult for the promissor to anticipate unreasonable reliance by the promissee. They are, however, not the same, in part because they focus on different actors. Reasonableness examines the actions of the promissee in light of what the promissee knows or has reason to know about the promise (e.g., has it been revoked?) and whether the actions taken in reliance on the promise are out of proportion to what was promised (e.g., is the reliance in proportion to what was promised?). Foreseeability, on the other hand, examines how blameworthy the promissor is based on whether the promissor could have anticipated the promissee's reliance on the promissor's promise. There can be some overlap, of course. For example, if Andy entered into the $100,000 body shop contract, a court could conclude that Andy's reliance in so doing was unreasonable *and* that Brenda could not have reasonably foreseen that Andy would enter into such a contract.

PRACTICE PROBLEM 22-4

Is the promissee's reliance "foreseeable" in each of the following scenarios?

1. Evangeline asks Francisco to build a tree house for her kids for $500 on Saturday. Francisco says that he will unless he informs Evangeline on Tuesday that he will not have time to do it. On Monday, Evangeline spends $25,000 on furnishings for the tree house. On Tuesday, Francisco informs Evangeline that he will not have time to build the tree house. What if Evangeline had incurred such expenses on Wednesday after not hearing anything from Francisco on Tuesday?

2. Greta offers to provide "tax services" to Horatio for $1,000 each year. Horatio agrees and fires his current accountant. His current accountant then

sues Horatio for age discrimination, and Horatio loses the lawsuit and is forced to pay damages to the accountant.

3. Ira is concerned that his employer will treat him differently if his wife accepts an offer of employment from a competitor of his employer. His employer tells him that he does not need to be concerned and that his wife's employment would have no bearing on his continued employment with the company. His wife accepts employment. Once the employer finds out that Ira's wife is actually performing services for a competitor, the employer reduces Ira's duties and limits his interaction with clients. The employer subsequently terminates Ira's employment.

4. Damages and Limitations on Recovery

As discussed above, the modern concept of promissory estoppel is based on a flexible tort-like theory where the promissee has suffered damages based on another's broken promise. Originally, however, promissory estoppel was seen as a substitute for consideration, meaning that the enforceable promise was equated to that in a bargained-for contract. Understanding which "version" of promissory estoppel is employed is most important for assessing the type and amount of damages for which the promissor should be liable. In Chapter 24, we will see that the typical measure of damages for a breach of contract is **expectation damages**, meaning that the promissee should be put in the position that she would have been in had the promise been fulfilled. If the same measure is used for promissory estoppel purposes, it would mean awarding contract-like damages. If, on the other hand, the measure of damages is based on remedying the amount of losses actually caused by the broken promise, this could mean awarding damages only for those losses suffered in reliance on, and as a result of the non-fulfillment of, the promise. These different measures of losses, as you will you explore in more depth in Chapter 24, often lead to different damage calculations.

For example, the Restatement suggests that enforcement of a promise under a theory of promissory estoppel can be "limited as justice requires." As with the reasonableness and foreseeability factors, this allows courts to fashion a remedy that is appropriate given the facts and circumstances of the situation and not necessarily provide the remedy otherwise suggested by bargain-based contract law. Instead, this limitation suggests that the promissee may only be put back into her original position, not the position that she would have been in had the promise been fulfilled.

For example, if Brenda fails to sell her car to Andy for $5,000 as promised, then Andy may not be able to subsequently sell the car to a third party that indicated his interest in purchasing the car for $10,000 (although he did not enter into a contract with Andy). If promissory estoppel is conceived of as a perfect substitute for consideration, then one measure of damages might be the profit that was lost because Andy could not sell the car to the third party, or $5,000 ($10,000–$5,000, representing or expectation damages), plus the other losses incurred due to Brenda's failure to perform (the car rental fees). On the other hand, if promissory estoppel is attempting to remedy reliance-based losses, as opposed to exchange-based losses, then the measure of damages might be limited to those directly caused by Andy relying on Brenda's promise (the attorney and bank fees).

Note that, in the example above, it is unclear whether Andy should be entitled to recover for the rental fees incurred under a promissory estoppel theory. If we are putting Andy back into his original place without the promise, he still would have had to pay someone for transportation. On the other hand, if Andy would have been able to obtain cheaper rental fees if he had booked the rental earlier, such as on the date when Brenda made her promise, then perhaps promissory estoppel would suggest a recovery for the difference between the higher rental rate and the rate that otherwise could have been secured.

What about the $5,000 borrowed? The $5,000 does not necessarily represent damages, other than any interest charged by the bank prior to repayment, because Andy can repay that amount to the bank and not have any further obligations to the bank. Moreover, any gas that Andy has bought for the rental car also does not count as compensable expenses because presumably Andy would have had to pay for gas even if Brenda had performed and sold the car to Andy. On the other hand, there potentially could be damages if the car rental charges more for gas or if the rental car company requires a more expensive grade of gasoline than Brenda's car.

PRACTICE PROBLEM 22-5

Assuming that a court decided that promissory estoppel suggested an award of damages, what should the measure of damages be?

1. Evangeline asks Francisco to build a tree house for her kids for $500 on Saturday. Francisco says that he will unless he informs Evangeline on Tuesday that he will not have time to build the tree house. On Monday, Evangeline spends $5,000 on furnishings for the tree house. On Tuesday, Francisco informs Evangeline that he will not have time to build the tree house. Other tree-house builders are available for comparable rates, but Francisco has special expertise in the type of tree house Evangeline would like for her kids.

2. Greta offers to provide "tax services" to Horatio for $1,000 each year. Horatio agrees and fires his current accountant. His current accountant then

sues Horatio for age discrimination, and Horatio loses the lawsuit and is forced to pay $30,000 in damages to the accountant.

3. Ira is concerned that his employer will treat him differently if his wife accepts an offer of employment from a competitor of his employer. His employer tells him that he does not need to be concerned and that his wife's employment would have no bearing on his continued employment with the company. His wife accepts the employment. Once the employer finds out that Ira's wife is actually performing services for a competitor, the employer reduces Ira's duties and limits his interaction with clients. The employer subsequently terminates Ira's employment.

5. Avoiding Injustice

If you recall from *Olson*, discussed above, promissory estoppel is based on a long-standing equitable tradition to provide a remedy for good faith reliance on a promise. Given its roots in equity, it is unsurprising that courts considering awarding damages under promissory estoppel examine whether, in the words of the Restatement, "injustice can be avoided only by enforcement of the promise."[3] This is where courts can weigh considerations of fairness and determine whether it is appropriate to provide some measure of relief in the wake of a broken promise. Hopefully, it is obvious that there are no bright-line tests that will help determine whether "injustice" will exist unless the promise is enforced. Courts look to some combination of the other factors described above concerning the clarity of the promise and the reasonableness and foreseeability of reliance to determine blameworthiness and who should bear the loss.

In the car sale example we have used in this chapter, a court might look to the definiteness of Brenda's promise to sell the car, Brenda's knowledge of why Andy wanted the car, her knowledge that he had wanted to purchase the car for a long time, the nature and extent of Andy's "customary" buyer actions in securing financing, and the car rental fees suffered by Andy once Brenda broke her promise to determine that it would be unjust to permit Brenda to break her promise without compensating Andy. On the other hand, if Andy could have purchased the same model car for the same price from another seller, then a court might decide that there is not really any injustice in permitting Brenda to break her promise without compensating Andy for his losses.

Now that you have reviewed the doctrinal requirements of promissory estoppel, consider how they were analyzed in perhaps the most famous modern promissory estoppel case, *Hoffman v. Red Owl Stores*. As you review the case, be sure to pay attention to how promissory estoppel differs from traditional contractual claims not only in terms of the doctrinal elements but also the remedy available.

---

3. Restatement (First) of Contracts § 90 (1932).

Hoffman v. Red Owl Stores, Inc.
Supreme Court of Wisconsin
26 Wis. 2d 683 (1965)

Action by Joseph Hoffman (hereinafter "Hoffman") and wife, plaintiffs, against defendants Red Owl Stores, Inc. (hereinafter "Red Owl") and Edward Lukowitz.

The complaint alleged that Lukowitz, as agent for Red Owl, represented to and agreed with plaintiffs that Red Owl would build a store building in Chilton and stock it with merchandise for Hoffman to operate in return for which plaintiffs were to put up and invest a total sum of $18,000; that in reliance upon the above-mentioned agreement and representations plaintiffs sold their bakery building and business and their grocery store and business; also in reliance on the agreement and representations Hoffman purchased the building site in Chilton and rented a residence for himself and his family in Chilton; plaintiffs' actions in reliance on the representations and agreement disrupted their personal and business life; plaintiffs lost substantial amounts of income and expended large sums of money as expenses. Plaintiffs demanded recovery of damages for the breach of defendants' representations and agreements.

The action was tried to a court and jury. The facts hereinafter stated are taken from the evidence adduced at the trial. Where there was a conflict in the evidence the version favorable to plaintiffs has been accepted since the verdict rendered was in favor of plaintiffs.

Hoffman assisted by his wife operated a bakery at Wautoma from 1956 until sale of the building late in 1961. The building was owned in joint tenancy by him and his wife. Red Owl is a Minnesota corporation having its home office at Hopkins, Minnesota. It owns and operates a number of grocery supermarket stores and also extends franchises to agency stores which are owned by individuals, partnerships, and corporations. Lukowitz resides at Green Bay and since September, 1960, has been divisional manager for Red Owl in a territory comprising Upper Michigan and most of Wisconsin in charge of 84 stores. Prior to September, 1960, he was district manager having charge of approximately 20 stores.

In November, 1959, Hoffman was desirous of expanding his operations by establishing a grocery store and contacted a Red Owl representative by the name of Jansen, now deceased. Numerous conversations were had in 1960 with the idea of establishing a Red Owl franchise store in Wautoma. In September, 1960, Lukowitz succeeded Jansen as Red Owl's representative in the negotiations. Hoffman mentioned that $18,000 was all the capital he had available to invest and he was repeatedly assured that this would be sufficient to set him up in business as a Red Owl store. About Christmastime, 1960, Hoffman thought it would be a good idea if he bought a small grocery store in Wautoma and operated it in order that he gain experience in the grocery business prior to operating a Red Owl store in some larger community. On February 6, 1961, on the advice of Lukowitz and Sykes, who had succeeded Lukowitz as Red Owl's district manager, Hoffman bought the inventory and fixtures of a small grocery store in Wautoma and leased the building in which it was operated.

After three months of operating this Wautoma store, the Red Owl representatives came in and took inventory and checked the operations and found the store was operating at a profit. Lukowitz advised Hoffman to sell the store to his manager, and assured him that Red Owl would find a larger store for him elsewhere. Acting on this advice and assurance, Hoffman sold the fixtures and inventory to his manager on June 6, 1961. Hoffman was reluctant to sell at that time because it meant losing the summer tourist business, but he sold on the assurance that he would be operating in a new location by fall and that he must sell this store if he wanted a bigger one. Before selling, Hoffman told the Red Owl representatives that he had $18,000 for "getting set up in business" and they assured him that there would be no problems in establishing him in a bigger operation. The makeup of the $18,000 was not discussed; it was understood plaintiff's father-in-law would furnish part of it. By June, 1961, the towns for the new grocery store had been narrowed down to two, Kewaunee and Chilton. In Kewaunee, Red Owl had an option on a building site. In Chilton, Red Owl had nothing under option, but it did select a site to which plaintiff obtained an option at Red Owl's suggestion. The option stipulated a purchase price of $6,000 with $1,000 to be paid on election to purchase and the balance to be paid within thirty days. On Lukowitz's assurance that everything was all set plaintiff paid $1,000 down on the lot on September 15th.

On September 27, 1961, plaintiff met at Chilton with Lukowitz and Mr. Reymund and Mr. Carlson from the home office who prepared a projected financial statement. Part of the funds plaintiffs were to supply as their investment in the venture were to be obtained by sale of their Wautoma bakery building.

On the basis of this meeting Lukowitz assured Hoffman: ". . . [E]verything is ready to go. Get your money together and we are set." Shortly after this meeting Lukowitz told plaintiffs that they would have to sell their bakery business and bakery building, and that their retaining this property was the only "hitch" in the entire plan. On November 6, 1961, plaintiffs sold their bakery building for $10,000. Hoffman was to retain the bakery equipment as he contemplated using it to operate a bakery in connection with his Red Owl store. After sale of the bakery Hoffman obtained employment on the night shift at an Appleton bakery.

The record contains different exhibits which were prepared in September and October, some of which were projections of the fiscal operation of the business and others were proposed building and floor plans. Red Owl was to procure some third party to buy the Chilton lot from Hoffman, construct the building, and then lease it to Hoffman. No final plans were ever made, nor were bids let or a construction contract entered. Some time prior to November

20, 1961, certain of the terms of the lease under which the building was to be rented by Hoffman were understood between him and Lukowitz. The lease was to be for ten years with a rental approximating $550 a month calculated on the basis of 1 percent per month on the building cost, plus 6 percent of the land cost divided on a monthly basis. At the end of the ten-year term he was to have an option to renew the lease for an additional ten-year period or to buy the property at cost on an instalment basis. There was no discussion as to what the instalments would be or with respect to repairs and maintenance.

On November 22d or 23d, Lukowitz and plaintiffs met in Minneapolis with Red Owl's credit manager to confer on Hoffman's financial standing and on financing the agency. Another projected financial statement was there drawn up entitled, "Proposed Financing For An Agency Store." This showed Hoffman contributing $24,100 of cash capital of which only $4,600 was to be cash possessed by plaintiffs. Eight thousand was to be procured as a loan from a Chilton bank secured by a mortgage on the bakery fixtures, $7,500 was to be obtained on a 5 percent loan from the father-in-law, and $4,000 was to be obtained by sale of the lot to the lessor at a profit.

A week or two after the Minneapolis meeting Lukowitz showed Hoffman a telegram from the home office to the effect that if plaintiff could get another $2,000 for promotional purposes the deal could go through for $26,000. Hoffman stated he would have to find out if he could get another $2,000. He met with his father-in-law, who agreed to put $13,000 into the business provided he could come into the business as a partner. Lukowitz told Hoffman the partnership arrangement "sounds fine" and that Hoffman should not go into the partnership arrangement with the "front office." On January 16, 1962, the Red Owl credit manager teletyped Lukowitz that the father-in-law would have to sign an agreement that the $13,000 was either a gift or a loan subordinate to all general creditors and that he would prepare the agreement. On January 31, 1962, Lukowitz teletyped the home office that the father-in-law would sign one or other of the agreements. However, Hoffman testified that it was not until the final meeting some time between January 26 and February 2, 1962, that he was told that his father-in-law was expected to sign an agreement that the $13,000 he was advancing was to be an out-right gift. No mention was then made by the Red Owl representatives of the alternative of the father-in-law signing a subordination agreement. At this meeting the Red Owl agents presented Hoffman with the following projected financial statement:

Hoffman interpreted the above statement to require of plaintiffs a total of $34,000 cash made up of $13,000 gift from his father-in-law, $2,000 on mortgage, $8,000 on Chilton bank loan, $5,000 in cash from plaintiff, and $6,000 on the resale of the Chilton lot. Red Owl claims $18,000 is the total of the unborrowed or unencumbered cash, that is, $13,000 from the father-in-law and $5,000 cash from Hoffman himself. Hoffman informed Red Owl he could not go along with this proposal, and particularly objected to the requirement that his

"Capital required in operation:		
"Cash	$ 5,000.00	
"Merchandise	20,000.00	
"Bakery	18,000.00	
"Fixtures	17,500.00	
"Promotional Funds	1,500.00	
"TOTAL:		$62,000.00
"Source of funds:		
"Red Owl 7-day terms	$5,000.00	
"Red Owl Fixture contract		
(Term 5 years)	14,000.00	
"Bank loans (Term 9 years)		
Union State Bank of Chilton	8,000.00	
"(Secured by Bakery Equipment)		
"Other loans (Term No-pay)		
No interest	13,000.00	
"Father-in-law		
"(Secured by None)		
"(Secured by Mortgage on		
"Wautoma Bakery Bldg.)	2,000.00	
"Resale of land	6,000.00	
"Equity Capital: $5,000.00 — Cash		
"Amount owner has 17,500.00 — Bakery Equip.		
"to invest:	22,500.00	
"TOTAL:		$70,500.00"

father-in-law sign an agreement that his $13,000 advancement was an absolute gift. This terminated the negotiations between the parties.

The case was submitted to the jury on a special verdict with the first two questions answered by the court. This verdict, as returned by the jury, was as follows:

> "*Question No. 1:* Did the Red Owl Stores, Inc., and Joseph Hoffmann on or about mid-May of 1961 initiate negotiations looking to the establishment of Joseph Hoffmann as a franchise operator of a Red Owl Store in Chilton? *Answer:* Yes. (Answered by the Court.)
>
> "*Question No. 2:* Did the parties mutually agree on all of the details of the proposal so as to reach a final agreement thereon? *Answer:* No. (Answered by the Court.)
>
> "*Question No. 3:* Did the Red Owl Stores, Inc., in the course of said negotiations, make representations to Joseph Hoffmann that if he fulfilled certain conditions that they would establish him as a franchise operator of a Red Owl Store in Chilton? *Answer:* Yes.
>
> "*Question No. 4:* If you have answered Question No. 3 'Yes,' then answer this question: Did Joseph Hoffmann rely on said representations and was he induced to act thereon? *Answer:* Yes.
>
> "*Question No. 5:* If you have answered Question No. 4 'Yes,' then answer this question: Ought Joseph Hoffmann, in the exercise of ordinary care, to have relied on said representations? *Answer:* Yes.
>
> "*Question No. 6:* If you have answered Question No. 3 'Yes' then answer this question: Did Joseph Hoffmann fulfill all the conditions he was required to fulfill by the terms of the negotiations between the parties up to January 26, 1962? *Answer:* Yes.
>
> "*Question No. 7:* What sum of money will reasonably compensate the plaintiffs for such damages as they sustained by reason of:
>
> "(a) The sale of the Wautoma store fixtures and inventory?
> "*Answer:* $16,735.
> "(b) The sale of the bakery building?
> "*Answer:* $2,000.
>
> . . .
>
> "(d) Expenses of moving his family to Neenah?
> "*Answer:* $140.
> "(e) House rental in Chilton?
> "*Answer:* $125."

Plaintiffs moved for judgment on the verdict while defendants moved to change the answers to Questions 3, 4, 5, and 6 from "Yes" to "No," and in the alternative for relief from the answers to the subdivisions of Question 7 or a new trial. On March 31, 1964, the circuit court entered the following order:

"It Is Ordered in accordance with said decision on motions after verdict hereby incorporated herein by reference:

"1. That the answer of the jury to Question No. 7 (a) be and the same is hereby vacated and set aside and that a new trial be had on the sole issue of the damages for loss, if any, on the sale of the Wautoma store, fixtures and inventory.

"2. That all other portions of the verdict of the jury be and hereby are approved and confirmed and all after-verdict motions of the parties inconsistent with this order are hereby denied."

Defendants have appealed from this order and plaintiffs have cross-appealed from paragraph 1, thereof.

Opinion by: CURRIE

The instant appeal and cross appeal present these questions:

. . .

(2) Do the facts in this case make out a cause of action for promissory estoppel?

(3) Are the jury's findings with respect to damages sustained by the evidence?

. . .

APPLICABILITY OF DOCTRINE TO FACTS OF THIS CASE.

The record here discloses a number of promises and assurances given to Hoffman by Lukowitz in behalf of Red Owl upon which plaintiffs relied and acted upon to their detriment.

Foremost were the promises that for the sum of $18,000 Red Owl would establish Hoffman in a store. After Hoffman had sold his grocery store and paid the $1,000 on the Chilton lot, the $18,000 figure was changed to $24,100. Then in November, 1961, Hoffman was assured that if the $24,100 figure were increased by $2,000 the deal would go through. Hoffman was induced to sell his grocery store fixtures and inventory in June, 1961, on the promise that he would be in his new store by fall. In November, plaintiffs sold their bakery building on the urging of defendants and on the assurance that this was the last step necessary to have the deal with Red Owl go through.

We determine that there was ample evidence to sustain the answers of the jury to the questions of the verdict with respect to the promissory representations made by Red Owl, Hoffman's reliance thereon in the exercise of ordinary care, and his fulfilment of the conditions required of him by the terms of the negotiations had with Red Owl.

There remains for consideration the question of law raised by defendants that agreement was never reached on essential factors necessary to establish a contract between Hoffman and Red Owl. Among these were the size, cost, design, and layout of the store building; and the terms of the lease with respect to rent, maintenance, renewal, and purchase options. This poses the question of whether the promise necessary to sustain a cause of action for promissory estoppel must embrace all essential details of a proposed transaction between promisor and promisee so as to be the equivalent of an offer that would result in a binding contract between the parties if the promisee were to accept the same.

Originally the doctrine of promissory estoppel was invoked as a substitute for consideration rendering a gratuitous promise enforceable as a contract. In other words, the acts of reliance by the promisee to his detriment provided a substitute for consideration. If promissory estoppel were to be limited to only those situations where the promise giving rise to the cause of action must be so definite with respect to all details that a contract would result were the promise supported by consideration, then the defendants' instant promises to Hoffman would not meet this test. However, sec. 90 of Restatement, 1 Contracts, does not impose the requirement that the promise giving rise to the cause of action must be so comprehensive in scope as to meet the requirements of an offer that would ripen into a contract if accepted by the promisee. Rather the conditions imposed are:

(1)   Was the promise one which the promisor should reasonably expect to induce action or forbearance of a definite and substantial character on the part of the promisee?

(2)   Did the promise induce such action or forbearance?

(3)   Can injustice be avoided only by enforcement of the promise?[4]

We deem it would be a mistake to regard an action grounded on promissory estoppel as the equivalent of a breach-of-contract action. As Dean Boyer points out, it is desirable that fluidity in the application of the concept be maintained. While the first two of the above listed three requirements of promissory estoppel present issues of fact which ordinarily will be resolved by a jury, the third requirement, that the remedy can only be invoked where necessary to avoid injustice, is one that involves a policy decision by the court. Such a policy decision necessarily embraces an element of discretion.

We conclude that injustice would result here if plaintiffs were not granted some relief because of the failure of defendants to keep their promises which induced plaintiffs to act to their detriment.

DAMAGES.

Defendants attack all the items of damages awarded by the jury.

The bakery building at Wautoma was sold at defendants' instigation in order that Hoffman might have the net proceeds available as part of the cash capital

---

4. [2] See Benjamin F. Boyer, *Promissory Estoppel: Requirements and Limitations of the Doctrine*, 98 U. Penn. L. Rev. 459, 460 (1950). "Enforcement" of the promise embraces an award of damages for breach as well as decreeing specific performance.

he was to invest in the Chilton store venture. The evidence clearly establishes that it was sold at a loss of $2,000. Defendants contend that half of this loss was sustained by Mrs. Hoffman because title stood in joint tenancy. They point out that no dealings took place between her and defendants as all negotiations were had with her husband. Ordinarily only the promisee and not third persons are entitled to enforce the remedy of promissory estoppel against the promisor. However, if the promisor actually foresees, or has reason to foresee, action by a third person in reliance on the promise, it may be quite unjust to refuse to perform the promise. Here not only did defendants foresee that it would be necessary for Mrs. Hoffman to sell her joint interest in the bakery building, but defendants actually requested that this be done. We approve the jury's award of $2,000 damages for the loss incurred by both plaintiffs in this sale.

. . .

We also determine it was reasonable for Hoffman to have paid $125 for one month's rent of a home in Chilton after defendants assured him everything would be set when plaintiff sold the bakery building. This was a proper item of damage.

Plaintiffs never moved to Chilton because defendants suggested that Hoffman get some experience by working in a Red Owl store in the Fox River Valley. Plaintiffs, therefore, moved to Neenah instead of Chilton. After moving, Hoffman worked at night in an Appleton bakery but held himself available for work in a Red Owl store. The $140 moving expense would not have been incurred if plaintiffs had not sold their bakery building in Wautoma in reliance upon defendants' promises. We consider the $140 moving expense to be a proper item of damage.

We turn now to the damage item with respect to which the trial court granted a new trial, i.e., that arising from the sale of the Wautoma grocery-store fixtures and inventory for which the jury awarded $16,735. The trial court ruled that Hoffman could not recover for any loss of future profits for the summer months following the sale on June 6, 1961, but that damages would be limited to the difference between the sales price received and the fair market value of the assets sold, giving consideration to any goodwill attaching thereto by reason of the transfer of a going business. There was no direct evidence presented as to what this fair market value was on June 6, 1961. The evidence did disclose that Hoffman paid $9,000 for the inventory, added $1,500 to it and sold it for $10,000 or a loss of $500. His 1961 federal income-tax return showed that the grocery equipment had been purchased for $7,000 and sold for $7,955.96. Plaintiffs introduced evidence of the buyer that during the first eleven weeks of operation of the grocery store his gross sales were $44,000 and his profit was $6,000 or roughly 15 percent. On cross-examination he admitted that this was gross and not net profit. Plaintiffs contend that in a breach-of-contract action damages may include loss of profits. However, this is not a breach-of-contract action.

The only relevancy of evidence relating to profits would be with respect to proving the element of goodwill in establishing the fair market value of the grocery inventory and fixtures sold. Therefore, evidence of profits would be admissible to afford a foundation for expert opinion as to fair market value.

Where damages are awarded in promissory estoppel instead of specifically enforcing the promisor's promise, they should be only such as in the opinion of the court are necessary to prevent injustice. Mechanical or rule-of-thumb approaches to the damage problem should be avoided. In discussing remedies to be applied by courts in promissory estoppel we quote the following views of writers on the subject:

> "Enforcement of a promise does not necessarily mean Specific Performance. It does not necessarily mean Damages for breach. Moreover the amount allowed as Damages may be determined by the plaintiff's expenditures or change of position in reliance as well as by the value to him of the promised performance. Restitution is also an 'enforcing' remedy, although it is often said to be based upon some kind of a rescission. In determining what justice requires, the court must remember all of its powers, derived from equity, law merchant, and other sources, as well as the common law. Its decree should be molded accordingly."
> 1A Corbin, Contracts, p. 221, sec. 200.

. . .

At the time Hoffman bought the equipment and inventory of the small grocery store at Wautoma he did so in order to gain experience in the grocery-store business. At that time discussion had already been had with Red Owl representatives that Wautoma might be too small for a Red Owl operation and that a larger city might be more desirable. Thus Hoffman made this purchase more or less as a temporary experiment. Justice does not require that the damages awarded him, because of selling these assets at the behest of defendants, should exceed any actual loss sustained measured by the difference between the sales price and the fair market value.

Since the evidence does not sustain the large award of damages arising from the sale of the Wautoma grocery business, the trial court properly ordered a new trial on this issue.

By the Court. —Order affirmed. Because of the cross appeal, plaintiffs shall be limited to taxing but two thirds of their costs.

Understanding the Case:

1. *Financial Structure:* The breakdown in negotiations between the parties was based on the characterization of the $13,000 that Hoffman received from his father-in-law. Red Owl wanted the $13,000 to be a gift, while Hoffman understood the $13,000 to be a debt obligation to be a loan. Red Owl presumably wanted to make sure that the store would be successful and did not want the store to be overburdened by indebtedness.

Comprehension and Thought Questions:

1. Why was Hoffman unable to recover under a traditional bargain contract theory?

2. What promise or promises were allegedly made to Hoffman that justified recovery under promissory estoppel?

3. How did Hoffman rely? Was it reasonable and foreseeable? Was it of a definite and substantial character?

4. What damages did Hoffman suffer in reliance?

5. How did the court determine that injustice could only be avoided by enforcement of the promise? Do you agree?

6. Why was Hoffman unable to recover for the lost profits from prematurely selling the Wautoma store?

7. Do you think that promissory estoppel is an appropriate theory for recovery? Do you think it seems more like a tort theory or a contract theory?

8. *Hoffman* was expected to be the progenitor of many successful promissory estoppel recoveries, but in practice, claims based on promissory estoppel are rarely successful. Why do you think that is so?

Hypothetical Variations:

1. What if Hoffman had sold the Wautoma store prior to negotiations with Red Owl?

2. What if Red Owl's representatives had assured Hoffman that he would receive a store "provided that parties entered into a mutually satisfactory definitive agreement"?

PRACTICE PROBLEM 22-6

Tracey Vector, a married woman, obtained a loan from A-One Mortgage Corporation on April 20, 2010. The loan was evidenced by a note secured by a deed of trust on Vector's residence. Vector borrowed $400,000 at an initial rate of 7 percent. After two years, the rate became adjustable. The term of the loan was 30 years.

In January 2008, Vector could no longer afford the monthly payments on the loan. On March 26, 2008, A-One Mortgage recorded a "Notice of Default and Election to Sell Under Deed of Trust." Shortly thereafter, Vector filed for bankruptcy protection under chapter 7 of the Bankruptcy Code, imposing an automatic stay on the foreclosure proceedings. Vector contacted A-One Mortgage and was told that, once her loan was out of bankruptcy, the bank "would work with her on a mortgage reinstatement and loan modification." She was asked to submit documents to A-One Mortgage for its consideration.

Vector intended to convert her chapter 7 bankruptcy case to a chapter 13 case and to rely on the financial resources of her husband "to save her home" under chapter 13. In general, chapter 7, entitled "Liquidation," permits a debtor to discharge unpaid debts, but a debtor who discharges an unpaid home loan cannot keep the home; chapter 13, entitled "Adjustment of Debts of an Individual with Regular Income," allows a homeowner in default to reinstate the original loan payments, pay the arrearages over time, avoid foreclosure, and retain the home.

A-One Mortgage filed a motion in the bankruptcy court to lift the stay so it could proceed with a nonjudicial foreclosure. On or about November 12, 2008, Vector's bankruptcy attorney received a letter from A-One Mortgage's counsel. The letter requested that Vector's attorney agree in writing to allow A-One Mortgage to contact Vector directly to "explore Loss Mitigation possibilities." Thereafter, Vector contacted A-One Mortgage's counsel and was told they could not speak to her before the motion to lift the bankruptcy stay had been granted.

In reliance on A-One Mortgage's promise to work with her to reinstate and modify the loan, Vector did not oppose the motion to lift the bankruptcy stay and decided not to seek bankruptcy relief under chapter 13. On December 4, 2012, the bankruptcy court lifted the stay. On December 9, 2012, although neither A-One Mortgage nor A-One Mortgage's counsel had contacted Vector to discuss the reinstatement and modification of the loan, A-One Mortgage scheduled Vector's home for public auction on January 9, 2013.

On January 9, 2013, Vector's home was sold at a trustee's sale to A-One Mortgage. On February 11, 2013, A-One Mortgage served Vector with a three-day notice to vacate the premises and, a month later, filed an unlawful detainer action against her and her husband. Vector and her husband vacated the premises during the eviction proceedings. Vector thinks that A-One Mortgage never intended to work with Vector to reinstate and modify the loan. The bank so promised only to convince Vector to forgo further bankruptcy proceedings, thereby permitting the bank to lift the automatic stay and foreclose on the property.

Vector comes to you and indicates that she would like to sue A-One for breaking its promise. Do you think she can recover? Consider all of the different elements for both contract and promissory estoppel.

C. PLEADING ALTERNATIVE THEORIES

You may be wondering at this point whether a party has to choose a particular theory of recovery (bargained-for contract or promissory estoppel) when asserting a claim for a breach of another party's promise. Under state law, parties may plead multiple theories of recovery in their initial complaint. Accordingly, after describing the facts of the situation in the complaint, parties often will assert claims under a breach of contract theory as well as a promissory estoppel theory. It is important for parties to include the necessary facts to support each theory in case a court determines that one of the theories of recovery is not available. Excerpts from a simplified complaint, based on the car sale example used throughout this chapter, is below.

General Allegations

A. On Tuesday, June 1, 2018, Brenda and Andy had a telephone conversation.

B. During that telephone conversation, Brenda said the following to Andy: "I know you have wanted to buy my car for a long time and that you need a car to travel out of state next weekend for a business trip. I promise I will sell it to you on Thursday for $5,000 so that you are able to get there in time."

C. Brenda only owned one car, a 2008 Honda Accord, and Andy and Brenda had had previous conversations about Andy's purchase of that vehicle.

D. On Wednesday, June 2, 2018, Andy borrowed $5,000 in funds from Huntington Bank.

D. The loan with Huntington Bank had a term of five years and an interest rate of 8% per annum.

E. Huntington Bank charged Andy $250 as a loan initiation fee.

F. Andy hired Fatima Alourney to review the loan agreements, and Fatima charged Andy $500 for doing so.

G. On Thursday, June 4, 2018, Brenda had another telephone conversation.

H. During that telephone conversation, Brenda informed Andy that she had sold the car to another person.

I. During that telephone conversation, Andy informed Brenda that he had already secured a loan and was prepared to purchase the car.

J. On Friday, June 5, 2018, Andy rented a Toyota Camry from Alamo Rental Company for three days at a cost of $75 per day. Andy was required to return the car with a full tank of gas.

K. On Monday, June 8, 2018, Andy purchased a 2009 Honda Accord for $7,500 from a Honda dealership.

L. Andy secured the $7,500 by modifying his loan with Huntington Bank for the larger amount but increasing the interest rate to 10% for the entire loan.

Count I—Breach of Contract

A. Andy incorporates by reference the preceding paragraphs as if fully stated and set forth herein.

B.   Andy and Brenda entered into a contract on June 1, 2018 for Brenda to sell her 2008 Honda Accord to Andy, under which Andy would pay $5,000 on June 3, 2018.

C.   Andy secured $5,000 in order to be able to pay the purchase price on June 3, 2013.

D.   Brenda breached the contract by refusing to sell her 2008 Honda Accord as agreed to by the parties.

E.   Andy has suffered damages of at least $4,650 as a direct and proximate result of Brenda's breach.

Wherefore, Andy respectfully requests that this Court enter judgment against Brenda in the amount of $4,650, along with attorney fees and other such relief as is just and equitable.

Count II—Promissory Estoppel

A.   Andy incorporates by reference the preceding paragraphs as if fully stated and set forth herein except for any references to the existence of a contract.

B.   This count is presented by way of alternative pleading in the event that the Court finds that no contract existed between Andy and Brenda.

C.   On June 1, 2018, Brenda promised to sell her 2008 Honda Accord to Andy for $5,000 on June 3, 2018.

D.   Brenda's promise to sell Andy her 2008 Honda Accord services was clear, definite, and unequivocal and was specifically made to induce Andy to secure and pay $5,000 for the car.

D.   In reliance on the promise, and to Andy's substantial detriment, Andy secured a $5,000 loan and incurred attorney fees, bank fees, and other expenses.

E.   Brenda refused to fulfill her promise to sell her 2008 Honda Accord to Andy.

F.   To avoid injustice, this Court must enforce Brenda's promise to sell her 2008 Honda Accord to Andy.

G.   At the time Brenda made the promise to sell her 2008 Honda Accord to Andy and induced Andy's actions, Brenda could reasonably foresee that Andy would rely upon Brenda's promise and that Brenda's failure to perform pursuant to the promise to pay Andy would cause Andy to suffer damages.

E.   As a direct and proximate result of Brenda's failure to perform her promise, Andy has suffered damages of at least $4,650.

Wherefore, Andy respectfully requests that this Court enter judgment against Brenda in the amount of $4,650, along with attorneys' fees and other such relief as is just and equitable.

PRACTICE PROBLEM 22-7

1. Do you think Andy's complaint with respect to a breach of contract would survive Brenda's motion to dismiss for failure to state a claim?

2. Do you think Andy's complaint with respect to promissory estoppel would survive Brenda's motion to dismiss for failure to state a claim?

3. What damages do you think are properly included in Andy's breach of contract claim? What about his promissory estoppel claim?

4. How do you think Andy arrived at $4,650 as the amount of damages?

D. APPLICABILITY OF THE STATUTE OF FRAUDS IN PROMISSORY ESTOPPEL CASES

One issue that can emerge in promissory estoppel cases is whether recovery can be made notwithstanding the Statute of Frauds. As you recall from Chapter 17, the Statute of Frauds precludes enforcement of certain types of contractual promises unless there is a writing indicating the existence of the contract signed by the party to be charged with performance. If promissory estoppel acts merely as a substitute for consideration, meaning that a contract is deemed to be have been formed based on the promise made (assuming the requirements of promissory estoppel are satisfied), then the Statute of Frauds may preclude enforcement of that promise. In other words, even though there is an enforceable contract (based on the existence of mutual assent and promissory estoppel as a consideration substitute), the contract will nevertheless be unenforceable against the promissor unless the promissor executed a writing that admitted the existence of the contract. On the other hand, if promissory estoppel is an independent equitable theory for relief separate and distinct from contract, then the Statute of Frauds may also be equitably dispensed with, thereby permitting relief under promissory estoppel even in the absence of a writing signed by the promissor.

One factor in determining the answer to this question is whether the purpose of the Statute of Frauds would be undermined by not applying the Statute of Frauds in situations involving promissory estoppel. The Statute of Frauds, as discussed in Chapter 17, is designed to prevent fraudulent oral testimony from establishing the existence of a contract with respect to certain "important" types of contracts. If the Statute of Frauds can be avoided simply by pleading promissory estoppel as the theory of relief instead of breach of contract, then plaintiffs may nevertheless be able to establish the existence of a "contract" through potentially fraudulent testimony. On the other hand, if promissory estoppel does not permit relief because of the applicability of the Statute of Frauds, then the plaintiff may unfairly suffer a loss notwithstanding the relative blameworthiness of the promisor. In the following case, the court considers these arguments. As you read it, consider whether you are convinced that the court came to the right policy conclusion when assessing the Statute of Frauds' applicability with respect to a claim for relief under promissory estoppel.

Kolkman v. Roth
Supreme Court of Iowa
656 N.W.2d 148 (2003)

CADY, Justice.

In this appeal, we must determine if the promissory estoppel exception to the statute of frauds applies to an action for breach of an oral lease in excess of one year. The district court determined the exception applied and entered judgment for the appellee following a jury trial. The court of appeals affirmed the judgment of the district court. On further review, we affirm the decision of the court of appeals and the judgment of the district court.

I. BACKGROUND FACTS AND PROCEEDINGS.

Corrine Roth inherited 800 acres of farmland located in Des Moines County from her father following his death in December 1995. At the time, Dean Kolkman farmed the land pursuant to an oral crop-share lease. The lease term was year-to-year, with profits shared on a fifty-fifty basis between Kolkman and Roth's father. Roth also worked for her father on the farm over the years until approximately two years prior to his death. She was primarily involved in her father's livestock operation. Kolkman was also involved in the livestock operation, especially during the two years prior to the time Roth inherited the farm. During these two years, Kolkman ran the cattle operation under an arrangement similar to the grain operation.

In the spring of 1996, Roth asked Kolkman if he would continue to farm the ground and raise the cattle as he did for her father. Roth and Kolkman agreed that Kolkman would continue in the farming operation. They also agreed Kolkman and his wife would reside in one of the houses on the farm rent-free. Unfortunately, this agreement, and any additional terms, was not reduced to writing.

Kolkman and his wife moved to the farm in June 1996, and Kolkman successfully operated the farm, without incident, until 1999. During this time, Kolkman raised cattle, cultivated and harvested crops, and improved and cared for the land by fixing buildings and removing debris and manure. The farm was generally run down at the time it was inherited by Roth, and Kolkman improved its condition by performing work not typically done by a tenant farmer.

In 1999 Roth sought to charge Kolkman rent for the farmhouse in which he was residing in the amount of $550 a month. Roth also proposed a written farm lease between them that would terminate in 2000. Kolkman refused to execute the written proposals, and Roth sought to terminate the tenancy.

Kolkman responded by filing an action against Roth for breach of contract. He claimed the 1996 oral agreement with Roth included a term permitting him to live in the house rent free and remain the tenant on a fifty-fifty basis until he "retired or couldn't work any more." Kolkman further claimed he relied on this promise in several ways, including selling his former residence and moving to the farm, purchasing various farm equipment, and improving the land by making repairs and removing debris.

Roth denied any term regarding the length of their lease, and sought summary judgment. She claimed the statute of frauds prevented Kolkman from establishing an oral contract between the parties. The district court denied summary judgment and the case proceeded to trial. At trial, the district court, after finding Kolkman established the elements of promissory estoppel, determined the statute of frauds did not bar oral evidence of a lease. The jury then found the parties entered into a contract, supported by consideration, based on the terms asserted by Kolkman. It found Roth breached this contract and awarded Kolkman damages of $154,429.

Roth appealed and Kolkman cross-appealed. We transferred the case to the court of appeals. The court of appeals affirmed the judgment of the district court and Roth sought further review. The single issue presented on further review is whether the doctrine of promissory estoppel can be used to remove a claim based on an oral contract to lease land in excess of one year from the domain of the statute of frauds.

. . .

III. STATUTE OF FRAUDS.

Under our statute of frauds, evidence of certain types of contracts is inadmissible, unless it is "in writing and signed by the party" sought to be charged. Iowa Code § 622.32 (1999). One type of contract included within the statute is a contract creating or transferring an interest in real estate other than leases for a term less than one year. The statute "does not void such oral contracts," but "makes oral proof of them incompetent." *Pollmann v. Belle Plaine Livestock Auction, Inc.*, 567 N.W.2d 405, 407 (Iowa 1997).

. . .

Promissory estoppel developed as a doctrine in the law in response to the strict traditional requirements for the formation of a contract, especially the requirement that all enforceable contracts be supported by consideration. Thus, the theory behind promissory estoppel was to make parties "liable for their promises despite [the] absence of" consideration required under contract law. *Schoff v. Combined Ins. Co. of Am.*, 604 N.W.2d 43, 48 (Iowa 1999). For this reason, we have viewed the effect of promissory estoppel to imply a contract in law based on detrimental reliance. However, other principles of contract law can conflict with the doctrine of promissory estoppel, such as the requirement of a writing for some types of contracts under the statute of frauds, and *Miller v. Lawlor*, 66 N.W.2d 267 (Iowa 1954) opened the door to expand the promissory estoppel doctrine beyond its role as a substitute for consideration. Thus, promissory estoppel is not only a substitute for consideration, but is also recognized as an exception to the statute of frauds even in cases where the promise may be supported by consideration. Like part performance, it focuses on reliance.

. . .

Finally, Roth claims that such unbridled use of the promissory estoppel exception will essentially swallow the statute of frauds rule when applied to real estate leases because a tenant will always be able to claim the existence of an oral lease in excess of one year. Roth claims this result is incongruous to the purposes behind the statute of frauds and the specific statutory exclusion for leases with a term less than one year. She argues our legislature would not have excluded oral leases for a term less than one year from the category of real estate cases covered under the statute of frauds, and then establish an exception to avoid the statute of frauds for leases in excess of one year.

We recognize other courts have been cautious to use promissory estoppel to overcome the statute of frauds. The argument advanced by Roth that the promissory estoppel doctrine essentially engulfs the statute of frauds is also commonly used by courts in those states that have been slow to apply promissory estoppel as an exception to the statute of frauds. Nevertheless, we find the argument insufficient to alter what we find to be our longstanding use of promissory estoppel as an exception to the statute of frauds.

The doctrine of promissory estoppel does not eviscerate the statute of frauds, but only applies to circumvent the statute when necessary to prevent an injustice. It requires the party asserting it as a means to avoid the statute of frauds to prove:

(1) a clear and definite promise; (2) the promise was made with the promissor's clear understanding that the promisee was seeking assurance upon which the promisee could rely and without which he would not act; (3) the promisee acted to his or her substantial detriment in reasonable reliance on the promise; and (4) injustice can be avoided only by enforcement of the promise.

We require strict proof of all the elements. This includes strict proof of a promise that justifies reliance by the promisee. It also requires strict proof that the reliance inflicted injustice that requires enforcement of the promise.[5] Clearly, much more than mere nonperformance of a promise must be shown

---

5. [4] Restatement (Second) of Contracts section 139 (1981) enumerates the significant circumstances to consider in determining whether injustice can be avoided only by enforcing the promise. These circumstances are:

(a) the availability and adequacy of other remedies, particularly cancellation and restitution;

to obtain the benefits of promissory estoppel. Thus, the strict standards we follow in applying promissory estoppel as a means to avoid the statute of frauds ameliorate the concerns presented by Roth and prevent the statute of frauds from being used to create an unjust result. Additionally, we observe that the majority of courts take a similar approach in applying the doctrine of promissory estoppel to the statute of frauds.

We also observe those jurisdictions that limit the use of promissory estoppel often point out the anomaly created by utilizing promissory estoppel to remove an oral promise from the statute of frauds when the very promise relied upon under promissory estoppel is the same promise declared unenforceable under the statute of frauds. Yet, even these jurisdictions seem to acknowledge that compelling circumstances have been encountered to justify the occasional use of promissory estoppel to avoid the statute of frauds. Thus, it is not really the use of the doctrine of promissory estoppel that is objectionable, and properly limited, promissory estoppel does serve the needed function of preventing the same fraud sought to be avoided by the statute of frauds itself. There is simply no strong reason to restrict the doctrine itself from any particular type of a contract included in the statute of frauds, as long as the doctrine is carefully applied.

Lastly, we perceive no inconsistency between permitting the promissory estoppel exception to the statute of frauds to be used in cases involving leases in excess of one year under a statutory scheme such as ours that excludes leases less than one year from the domain of the statute of frauds. To the contrary, it would be inconsistent to include certain types of leases within the real estate category of cases covered by the statute of frauds, then refuse to apply a broad exception for real estate cases, established to prevent fraudulent use of the statute of frauds, to such leases.

. . .

We conclude the promissory estoppel doctrine is available as an exception to the statute of frauds for leases claimed to be in excess of one year. We otherwise affirm the decision of the court of appeals and the judgment of the district court.

(b) the definite and substantial character of the action or forbearance in relation to the remedy sought;

(c) the extent to which the action or forbearance corroborates evidence of the making and terms of the promise, or the making and terms are otherwise established by clear and convincing evidence

(d) the reasonableness of the action or forbearance; and

(e) the extent to which the action or forbearance was foreseeable by the promisor.

We adopted these circumstances in *Warder & Lee Elevator, Inc. v. Britten*, 274 N.W.2d 339, 343 (Iowa 1979) (adopting the tentative draft language of Restatement (Second) of Contracts section 217A, later renumbered as section 139).

Comprehension and Thought Questions:

1. What promise was the plaintiff attempting to enforce?

2. How were each of the elements of promissory estoppel satisfied in this case?

3. Why did the plaintiff have to rely on a theory of promissory estoppel instead of a bargained-for contract?

4. How does the court respond to the argument that permitting recovery under a theory of promissory estoppel does not undermine the purpose of the Statute of Frauds? Are you convinced?

5. The court suggested that other states have been slow to recognize a promissory estoppel exception to the Statute of Frauds. How should transactional attorneys respond to this uncertainty when advising clients?

Hypothetical Variations:

1. Imagine that Kolkman was denying the existence of an oral lease and refused to pay for the time during which he occupied the farm. Is the Statute of Frauds available as a defense to Roth? What exceptions might be applicable?

2. What if, in the original facts of the case, Kolkman had orally promised Roth that the family could occupy the farm until Kolkman decided differently. Would recovery under promissory estoppel be available? Is the Statute of Frauds relevant in this situation?

CHAPTER 23

Alternative Theories of Recovery Absent a Bargain or Reliance

This chapter continues our exploration of alternative theories of recovery in the absence of a bargained-for contract. As we discussed in the previous chapter, promissory estoppel provides for relief even where the promise was not made in a bargained-for exchange. That theory recognizes that the reliance by a promissee on a promise may provide sufficient grounds to justify awarding a remedy even where the promissor did not bargain for the promisee's reliance. Accordingly, a bargain or reliance may provide justification for enforcing a promise.

Even in the absence of explicit bargaining *or* reliance, it still may be desirable to enforce certain promises. Further, there sometimes may be good reasons for requiring a party to compensate another for benefits received even in the absence of a promise, let alone a bargain or reliance. For example, if you buy a friend a cup of coffee, consider whether he should be obligated to compensate you for it. What if he promised to pay you for it after you had already delivered it to him? Imagine that instead of buying your friend a cup of coffee, you save his life by pushing him out of the way of oncoming traffic, and you suffer permanent injuries. If he subsequently promises to pay you a salary for the rest of your life, should that promise be enforceable? If he did not make a promise, should he nevertheless be forced to compensate you for saving his life?

This chapter discusses the situation of unbargained-for benefits and whether the recipient of such benefits should be forced to compensate the party providing the benefits. First, in Section A, it discusses a party's right to recover on a promise made for benefits conferred; second, in Section B, it discusses a party's right to recover for benefits conferred where no promise is made to pay for those benefits; and third, in Section C, it addresses policy considerations involved in providing for such noncontractual recoveries.

It is important to note at the outset that none of these situations involve bargaining or reliance on an express promise, and sometimes they do not even involve a promise at all. In particular, these situations do not involve the utility of contracts as a planning or forward-looking device. Thus, it may appear that the recipient of such benefits may be entitled to retain such benefits without paying for them from a contract law perspective. Yet, as you will see in this chapter, in some circumstances, courts determine that justice requires that the beneficiary of a received benefit pay for that benefit. Such an argument is even more compelling in the context where the beneficiary promises to pay for the benefit previously conferred, thereby showing that the benefit provided was valuable and valued by him. Thus, as explored in this chapter, there are possible remedies even in these "unplanned" situations. The remedies provided in these situations are completely different than with a bargained-for contract, given that they emerge out of a noncontractual cause of action. Accordingly, this chapter may not seem appropriate for a Contracts casebook since the claims are not necessarily contract-based. In many litigation situations, however, these claims are pleaded alongside contract-based claims, and it is important for you to have familiarity with them and understand the interplay and overlap between these claims and their remedies as well as those relevant in contract.

A. PROMISES IN RECOGNITION OF A PAST MATERIAL BENEFIT

You learned in Chapter 7 that to satisfy consideration, each promise must induce the other's promise to render a future performance, or actual performance. If a party has already rendered a performance, then that performance cannot be used to induce another's promise.

For example, let us suppose that after a snowfall, your neighbor voluntarily and without informing you shoveled your driveway, which took her a half hour. You are happy with this outcome and promise to pay her $25 for doing so. Because she had already rendered the performance, your promise cannot be understood to have induced her to render her performance. From a bargained-for consideration perspective, this may be the end of the story. A court may not enforce your promise to pay as a contract because of the absence of valid consideration.

Courts have recognized, however, that certain situations may arise where negotiations are unlikely or impractical and the benefits received are significant enough to justify relief. These situations inevitably depend on whether it would be unjust for the promissor not to pay for the benefits received under its promise. The Restatement formulates this rule as follows:

§ 86 Promise for Benefit Received

(1) A promise made in recognition of a benefit previously received by the promisor from the promisee is binding to the extent necessary to prevent injustice.

(2) A promise is not binding under Subsection (1)

(a) if the promisee conferred the benefit as a gift or for other reasons the promisor has not been unjustly enriched; or

(b) to the extent that its value is disproportionate to the benefit.

The rule set out in this section of the Restatement is often referred to as the "material benefit rule." That is because, as shown by this Restatement language, a court enforces a subsequent promise to pay for a benefit conferred only where justice requires it. Often, that is the case where the benefit provided was "material," meaning of significance to the beneficiary.

In the snow-shoveling example above, a promise (to pay $25) was made to the person that shoveled the snow. It is not clear, though, that this promise needs to be enforced to prevent injustice. Perhaps the low value of the transaction suggests that the promise is not enough to justify a conclusion that there would be "injustice" if the promise to pay was not enforced. Also, a lack of compensation for rendering a half hour's worth of services may not strike a fact-finder as particularly unjust. Under Restatement § 86(2)(a), a promise is deemed not to be binding if the benefit was conferred as a gift. Presumably, your neighbor provided the benefit not to be compensated but to be neighborly, which suggests that the service was provided as a gift. On the other hand, if the neighbor's business was snow removal, then perhaps the neighbor was indeed seeking compensation, even though no words were exchanged prior to the service being rendered.

Historically, the material benefit rule was used to enforce promises that had been made as part of a bargained-for contract, where the enforcement of that contract was suspended by application of some aspect of positive law. In other words, it was used to support enforcement of a bargained-for contract where there originally had been consideration, yet due to operation of some aspect of contract law, a claim for breach of that promise was precluded.

Thus, for example, imagine a situation where a person promises to pay $1,000 in exchange for the sale of the car. Assume that the buyer does not pay that $1,000 when due, and the seller does not sue the buyer to collect on it until he really needs the money seven years later. If the applicable statute of limitations for breach of contract is six years, then the seller might be precluded by operation of the statute of limitations from recovering on that broken promise. However, imagine that the buyer renews his promise to pay that $1,000 in year seven. In that case, courts would traditionally use the material benefit rule to enforce the initial promise. That is because the initial promise had been part of a bargained-for contract. The subsequent promise was merely an expression of an intent to remain bound by the original promise, despite the legal doctrine rendering that initial promise voidable. In this way, the doctrine merely supports enforcement of an initial enforceable bargain.[1]

More recently, courts do not limit the material benefit rule to those situations where there had been a bargained-for contract that became voidable due to operation of law. The following discussion reviews the typical elements of a modern claim for unjust enrichment due to benefits conferred where a promise is subsequently made to pay for those benefits.

1. The Benefit Conferred

Courts have struggled to determine an appropriate or consistent test for whether a promise for a benefit previously conferred should be enforceable. The significance of the benefit as well as whether the recipient of the benefit promised to pay for the benefits conferred are often looked to as important factors to determine whether the subsequent promise to pay should be enforced.

One famous case involved a promise to subsequently pay a third party caregiver for the expenses he incurred in providing necessary medical care.[2] In that situation, a parent made a promise to the caregiver to pay him for the expenses he incurred in taking care of the parent's adult son. The benefits received by the adult son were material, meaning not insignificant. Nevertheless, the court did not enforce the parent's promise to pay because the child was an adult. Therefore, the medical services did not benefit the parent as they would have with a minor child. Because a minor child is under the care and guardianship of his parents, a parent would benefit from having necessary medical services rendered to his child. The benefit is more clear in that instance because the parent would normally be responsible for securing those medical care for the minor child, even without the parent's knowledge or consent. In that situation, the parent's promise would have suggested adequate recognition of the benefit conferred *on the parent* and indicated that it would be unjust for the promise for payment for valuable medical services not to have been enforced.

As you can see from the Restatement language set out above, it retains the requirement under the material benefit rule that the promisor himself or herself must have received the benefits conferred.

---

1. Courts apply this doctrine to promises rendered voidable due to lack of capacity, mistake, misrepresentation, duress or undue influence. *See* Restatement (Second) of Contracts §86 cmt b.
2. Mills v. Wyman, 20 Mass. (3 Pick.) 207 (1825).

This may seem like an unsatisfactory distinction; after all, whether a parent benefits from medical services rendered to his child does not seem to turn on whether the child is an adult. On the other hand, examining whether the promissor has personally been unjustly enriched may help provide a useful limit on the overenforcement of promises rendered in gratitude after the fact.

2. Ascertaining Injustice

As in other equitable tests, a court retains the discretion to decide when a promise made in recognition of a past benefit needs to be enforced to "prevent injustice." The Restatement attempts to restrain enforcement of all promises made after receipt of a benefit based on the motivation of the party rendering the initial benefit. There is presumably less injustice if the party providing the benefit was motivated to provide a gift as opposed to having an expectation of compensation.

On the other hand, courts do not generally inquire into the motivation of the promisor in providing its promise. Despite this, courts and commentators often describe the material benefit rule as arising out of a "moral obligation." That is because they characterize the promisor's intent in making his promise as one arising out of a moral obligation, due to benefits received. But again, courts generally do not inquire into the promisor's underlying motivation for providing his promise. In other words, while the promisor's intent in making a promise for benefits received might be presumed to be moral, such a moral intent is not required to enforce a promise for benefits conferred.

In deciding whether justice requires enforcement of a promise for benefits conferred, courts also look at the context for the promise. For example, if bargaining before the benefits were received was impossible due to the urgency of when the benefits were needed, a court may be more willing to enforce a promise provided after the fact despite the absence of bargaining. Similarly, if a party has some time to reflect on whether to make a promise for benefits conferred before making its promise, a court may be more likely to enforce that promise.

The fact that a person makes a promise for a benefit conferred also tends to show that the benefit is valuable to the beneficiary. It even places a specific value on that benefit, obviating the court's need to make that calculation. Finally, the fact that the beneficiary made the promise might provide some evidence that the benefit, at least from the beneficiary's perspective, was not understood to have been provided gratuitously. In this way, the fact that a beneficiary made a promise for benefits conferred permits a recovery on a promise in circumstances where, had there not been a promise, the beneficiary might not have had to pay for those benefits under restitution. Keep this in mind as you study restitution absent a promise in Section B.

For example, imagine you and a co-worker are in a workplace when a large beam falls and is headed directly for your co-worker. You likely will be unable to bargain with your co-worker as to whether he would like you to save his life and what he will promise you if you save his life (and instead suffer a serious injury yourself). Accordingly, if you decide to act without bargaining and save your co-worker, the co-worker's subsequent promise to compensate you for injuries suffered and career opportunities is the kind of promise a court potentially will enforce under the material benefit rule despite the lack of a bargain. The fact that time did not permit bargaining as well as a court's confidence that the promissor likely would have been happy to have made the promise ahead of time (if such bargaining had been possible) suggest that enforcing the promise is necessary to prevent injustice.[3]

In other cases, the injustice arising from not enforcing a particular promise may be based on the relationship between the parties as opposed to the ability of the parties to negotiate and bargain ahead of time. That is so because often with family, benefits conferred are intended to be, and understood to be, gratuitously provided. As such, injustice cannot be avoided by requiring the beneficiary pay for such gratuitous benefits, even where the beneficiary promises to pay for them. However, the following case demonstrates that the existence of a family relationship does not necessarily preclude enforcement of a promise for a benefit conferred. As you read this case, consider why the nature of the relationship between the promissor and promissee is deemed relevant to the court in terms of the enforceability of a subsequent promise to pay for services.

McMurry v. Magnusson
Court of Appeals of Missouri, Eastern District, Division Two
849 S.W.2d 619 (1993)

CRANDALL, Presiding Judge.

Plaintiff, Freda McMurry, appeals from the judgment in her favor, entered pursuant to a jury verdict, against defendant, Charles Magnusson, in a personal injury action which arose as a result of an automobile accident. Plaintiff also appeals from a judgment in favor of defendant, Cecil Lindsay, in the same trial. We affirm in part and reverse and remand in part.

The evidence, viewed in the light most favorable to the plaintiff, established that on November 5, 1988, plaintiff, a sixty-two-year-old widow, was a passenger in an automobile driven by Magnusson. Magnusson ran into the rear of a vehicle driven by defendant, Cecil Lindsay, who stopped to avoid hitting a camper shell lying in his lane of traffic. The camper shell had blown off of a truck owned and operated by defendant, Richard Crandall.

---

3. For a case with similar facts, *see* Webb v. McGowin, 168 So. 196 (Ala. Ct. App. 1935).

As a result of the collision between Magnusson's and Lindsay's vehicles, plaintiff suffered back injuries for which she was hospitalized. Following hospitalization, plaintiff, who lived in St. Louis, moved into her sister's home in St. James, Missouri. Her sister cared for her for approximately four months.

After trial, the jury returned a verdict in favor of plaintiff and against defendant-Magnusson and assessed damages in the amount of $25,000.00. The jury also found against plaintiff and in favor of defendants, Lindsay and Crandall. Plaintiff later dismissed her cause of action against defendant-Crandall.

In her first point, plaintiff contends that the trial court erred in giving a withdrawal instruction regarding the evidence of damages she incurred for the home health care provided by her sister. Plaintiff argues that the reasonable value of her sister's services was an appropriate element of recoverable damages which the jury should have considered in reaching its verdict.

After plaintiff was released from the hospital she was unable to walk without help and to care for herself. She was also on medication for back pain. She left her own home in St. Louis and went to stay at her sister's home in St. James, Missouri. Her sister cared for her from November 10, 1988 to March 24, 1989. During that time, her sister provided for all her personal and medical needs. Plaintiff testified that she agreed to pay her sister for the services her sister rendered:

> *[Plaintiff's Counsel]:* Have you promised to pay her for [services]?
>
> *[Plaintiff]:* I told her I would.
>
> *[Plaintiff's Counsel]:* And have you come up with a figure for what that service is worth?
>
> *[Plaintiff]:* Well, I told her that that [sic] I thought she deserved as much as a home health nurse would get.
>
> *[Plaintiff's Counsel]:* Is that the home health nurse that came in to see you?
>
> *[Plaintiff]:* Yes, that came in and visited me for fifteen minutes. I thought that she deserved as much for all day as the other one did for fifteen minutes, so I told her I would give her seventy-five dollars a day.

Later, plaintiff testified during cross-examination as follows:

> *[Defense Counsel]:* Well, let me ask you about this seventy-five dollar charge that you have arranged with your sister. This is what you promised to pay her, correct?
>
> *[Plaintiff]:* I thought that was fair.
>
> *[Defense Counsel]:* Before moving in did your sister ask you to pay her any money?
>
> *[Plaintiff]:* No, not really.
>
> *[Defense Counsel]:* She invited you to move in with her because she's your sister, correct?
>
> *[Plaintiff]:* Mainly.

As of the time of trial, plaintiff had not paid her sister for services rendered.

At the close of the evidence the trial court submitted the following withdrawal instruction, patterned on MAI 34.02 [1978 Revision], to the jury: Instruction No. 7

> The evidence of damages for plaintiff's home care from her sister is withdrawn from the case and you are not to consider such evidence in arriving at your verdict.

In overruling plaintiff's objection to the instruction, the court reasoned that "the services the sister rendered were gratuitous and . . . not an element of damages that can be submitted to the jury. . . ."

. . .

Where valuable service is rendered by one person for another and such is accepted by the person for whom such service is performed, the law will presume an implied promise to pay. When no family relationship exists, the law presumes an intent to charge for services rendered. The defense of a family relationship is an affirmative defense and defendant has the burden of proof. The existence of a family relationship, once it is established, gives rise to a presumption that services rendered were intended to be gratuitous. The burden in such cases rests upon plaintiff to rebut such a presumption by evidence tending to show that the parties intended and understood that the services were to be paid for by the recipient thereof.

Here, the initial question is whether the relationship between plaintiff and her sister, as a matter of law, gave rise to a presumption of gratuitous services. If so, in the absence of evidence to the contrary, the jury was properly precluded from considering the cost of home care as an element of plaintiff's damages.

Whether a family relationship existed is a factual issue. The term "family" is one of great flexibility and is capable of many different meanings according to the context in which it is used. In the context of a zoning ordinance, the definition of family may be based on the biological or legal relationships among the household members. The determination of whether a relationship is sufficient to give rise to the presumption that services rendered and accepted were gratuitous, however, does not turn on whether the parties are related by blood or affinity, except where the relationship is that of parent and child. For purposes of raising the presumption that services were rendered gratuitously, a family is defined as "a collective body of persons under one head and one domestic government, who have reciprocal, natural, or moral duties to support and care for each other." *Boyher v. Gearhart's Estate*, 367 S.W.2d 1, 5 (Mo. App. 1980).

In the case before us, the evidence was that plaintiff and her sister were adults who had lived apart for years. Each sister lived some distance from the other, in her own home. Plaintiff moved in with her sister, arguably not for the purpose of establishing a family relationship but for the purpose of receiving the care she needed and was unable to provide for herself. It was a matter for the jury to determine from all the circumstances whether a family relationship existed between plaintiff and her sister, and thus whether the services rendered by her sister were gratuitous in nature.

In the absence of a family relationship, the law will presume an implied promise on plaintiff's part to pay for her sister's services. In addition, there was evidence that plaintiff made a promise to pay. Assuming that the sister's services were not rendered gratuitously, the promise to pay, even if made after the fact, may give rise to an express contract.

Whether there was an implied or express contract or whether the services were rendered as a gift from sister to sister was a question of fact. The jury should have been able to consider whether the expenses plaintiff claimed for her sister's services constituted a proper element of damages. The trial court erred in giving the withdrawal instruction to the jury. Plaintiff's first point is granted.

. . .

Understanding the Case:

1. *A Sister's Lawsuit:* This case illustrates that the existence of a contract or enforceable promise is relevant not only to lawsuits premised on a recovery under that contract. In this instance, the sister who rendered medical care was not seeking to enforce the injured sister's promise (or implied promise) to pay for the services rendered. Indeed, the sister could have brought a separate lawsuit if her injured sister in fact refused to pay for the services rendered. Instead, the injured sister was seeking to recover damages from the parties causing the accident that injured her, and the injured sister wanted the amount she owed her sister to be included in the calculation of damages. The court determined that the test of recovery would be based on whether she in fact owed her sister for the value of services rendered, and whether she owed her sister for such services turned on whether she had made an enforceable promise to pay for such services. Sometimes, it is the value of the contract (if it exists) that is important to the case, not whether anyone actually will be or is seeking to recover under that contract.

Comprehension and Thought Questions:

1. Why was the existence of a "family relationship" relevant to whether the plaintiff could recover for the value of services rendered by her sister?

2. Could the plaintiff have recovered for the value of her sister's services if the plaintiff had not promised to pay for them? Why or why not?

3. Why do you think the family/non-family distinction is useful in the context of examining promises to pay for services rendered?

4. What other relationship factors do you think a jury should consider when determining whether a subsequent promise to pay for services rendered should be enforceable?

Hypothetical Variations:

1. What if the plaintiff had not promised to pay her sister for the in-home services provided?

2. What if the plaintiff had signed a written agreement with her sister promising to pay for in-home services if her sister permitted her to move in and take care of her?

3. What if the sisters lived in the same city and were 22 and 23 years old, respectively, at the time of the accident and services being rendered?

4. What if the sisters were not actual sisters but instead sisters-in-law?

B. RECOVERY IN THE ABSENCE OF A PROMISE

Contract law, by definition, relies on a promise having been made either expressly or by conduct. Even in the preceding section, granting a remedy for one who voluntarily provided benefits turned on a promise that acknowledged the benefit and, for one reason or another, was not made by the promissor before the benefits were rendered. Nevertheless, contract or contract-like remedies may be available even in the absence of an express promise.

As discussed in Chapter 4, the conduct of parties might create an implied-in-fact contract, such as where you acknowledge or encourage another's performance by nodding your head or waving someone on to continue in the current course of conduct, particularly where you have previously compensated the person for having performed this conduct in the past. Consider, for example, if you had previously paid someone to mow your lawn, and the person subsequently shows up to mow your lawn. If you make eye contact with that person and point to the lawn (perhaps because you are on the telephone), a court might find that an implied-in-fact contract was made. This implied contract would be no different from any other bargained-for contract. The "implication" that the contract was made is based on the situation and conduct of the parties, meaning that the parties manifested an intent to create a contract but did not necessarily manifest those intentions through express words. The terms of the contract, such as the price paid for mowing the lawn and which lawn to mow, can be implied based on prior dealings, and the manifestation of assent can be implied by the parties' behavior (bringing the lawn mower to the person's lawn and the other person nodding in response).

Somewhat confusingly, contract-like remedies may even be available where the parties did not make a promise at all, whether by express statement or conduct and whether before or after the other party performed or otherwise provided a benefit. In these situations, a remedy based on an implied-in-law contract is sometimes available where a promise was not made but perhaps *should have* been made in light of the circumstances. In these instances, the remedy is predicated on an implied contract, but not one that is implied-in-fact based on the conduct of the parties. Instead, the implied contract is *implied-in-law*, meaning that a promise to pay for the benefit conferred is deemed to have been made by operation of law, regardless of the acts or intentions of the parties to manifest assent to a bargain or otherwise to promise to pay for those benefits. This means that a remedy can be fashioned or created by the court based on that implied contract.

The remedy is distinctly not contractual because is not based on satisfaction of the legal requirements for formation of a contract. Instead, the court is being asked to provide a recovery that fixes the unfair result that otherwise would arise because of the lack of available legal remedies. In most instances, the plaintiff is seeking recovery for the value of the benefit conferred on the defendant, even though the defendant did not promise to pay for it. This recovery is not premised on a bargain having been made between the parties or reliance on another's promise, but instead is based on the inequitable results as they stand in light of the absence of a contract or other means of legal recovery. In other words, the plaintiff is asserting that it would be unfair for the defendant not to pay for what the defendant received from the plaintiff.

Courts have developed various tests to determine the availability of recovery, but generally they require an examination of the benefit conferred by the plaintiff, of the defendant's knowledge that the benefit was being conferred, and of whether it would be unfair for the defendant to retain the benefits without compensation.

Accordingly, plaintiffs often plead multiple theories of recovery that are related in some way to contract. A plaintiff may make a claim for recovery under (1) an express contract or implied-in-fact contract based on bargain and manifestations made by the parties, (2) promissory estoppel based on the plaintiff's reliance on the defendant's promise, (3) a subsequent promise made by the defendant after the plaintiff had provided a benefit through performance, and (4) a quasi-contract or implied-in-law contract (sometimes referred to as **unjust enrichment** or **restitution**), because it would be inequitable for the defendant to receive the benefits of plaintiff's performance without some form of compensation even though the defendant never promised to pay for that performance. Although quasi-contracts are often lumped in with contract claims, the requirements for recovery are different and often the remedies provided are different as well.

The case below examines the test commonly used for whether and when recovery on an implied-in-law contract is available. This case also shows how parties often confuse implied-in-fact and implied-in-law contracts. Although unjust enrichment for benefits conferred is rooted in equitable concerns, you should pay close attention to the court's categorization of the legal or equitable nature of a claim for unjust enrichment and the impact of this categorization on the court's remedy.

Commerce Partnership 8098 Ltd. Partnership v. Equity Contracting Co.
Court of Appeal of Florida, Fourth District
695 So. 2d 383 (1997)

EN BANC

GROSS, Judge.

Equity Contracting Company, Inc. ("Equity") filed a one-count complaint against Commerce Partnership 8908 Limited Partnership ("Commerce"). The count was set forth under the heading "Quantum Meruit." The complaint contained the following allegations:

> Commerce was the owner of an office building. Commerce contracted with a general contractor, World Properties, Inc., to perform improvements on its property. Equity was the stucco and surfacing subcontractor for the job, having contracted with the general contractor to perform the work. Because it inspected the job on a weekly basis, Commerce was aware of Equity's work. Equity completely performed its subcontract and the reasonable value of its work was $17,100. Commerce failed to pay the general contractor the full amounts due for the job. The general contractor did not pay Equity. Commerce was unjustly enriched because it had accepted Equity's services without paying any entity for them.

In its answer, Commerce asserted that it had paid the general contractor in full.

At the non-jury trial, Equity presented its direct case in under 30 minutes. Equity's president testified that his company had contracted with the general contractor to stucco Commerce's property for $17,100. He indicated that at the start of the job he expected payment only from the general contractor and not from Commerce. Both the general contractor and a representative from Commerce inspected the work as it progressed. After the work was completed, Commerce gave Equity a punch list of remedial work. When Equity's president asked for at least partial payment from Commerce, the latter's representative indicated that "he couldn't do it." Having received no payment, Equity did not complete the punch list. Equity brought suit against the general contractor, who later declared bankruptcy. Equity adduced no evidence regarding Commerce's payments to the general contractor under the construction contract or to any other party for work covered by the contract.

After Equity rested, Commerce moved for an involuntary dismissal, arguing that the evidence did not establish a contract implied in fact. Commerce's attorney contended that the term "quantum meruit" was synonymous with a contract implied in fact. The trial court denied the motion. During closing argument, Equity asserted that it had established a claim for quantum meruit, which it interpreted to mean unjust enrichment. Arguing that a quasi contract claim had first been injected into the case during closing argument, Commerce's attorney obtained permission to reopen his case. By this point in the trial, there was no agreement as to the cause of action at issue or the requirements of proof. The trial judge observed, "we are in equity and I have some difficulty with wondering what the issues are and who is going to prove what."

Commerce's witness testified that the contract price it had negotiated with the general contractor for the improvements was $256,894. He identified three payments totalling $223,065.04 that Commerce made to the general contractor—$173,088.07 in progress payments, $24,976.97 in response to application for payment number 8, and $25,000 in final settlement of the general contractor's lawsuit against Commerce. Commerce also sought to introduce evidence that it had paid $64,097 directly to three subcontractors who had performed work on the building, who were not paid by the general contractor, and who had perfected mechanics' liens. The trial court sustained Equity's objection to this testimony on the ground of relevance.

Relying on *Zaleznik v. Gulf Coast Roofing Co., Inc.*, 576 So. 2d 776 (Fla. 2d DCA 1991), the trial court entered judgment in favor of Equity for $17,100.

CONTRACT IMPLIED IN FACT AND QUASI CONTRACT

This case is a paradigm for the confusion that often surrounds the litigation of implied contracts.

A contract implied in fact is one form of an enforceable contract; it is based on a tacit promise, one that is inferred in whole or in part from the parties' conduct, not solely from their words. Where an agreement is arrived at by words, oral or written, the contract is said to be "express." A contract implied in fact is not put into promissory words with sufficient clarity, so a fact finder must examine and interpret the parties' conduct to give definition to their unspoken agreement. It is to this process of defining an enforceable agreement that Florida courts have referred when they have indicated that contracts implied in fact "rest upon the assent of the parties." *Policastro v. Myers*, 420 So. 2d 324, 326 (Fla. 4th DCA 1982); *Tipper v. Great Lakes Chemical Co.*, 281 So. 2d 10, 13 (Fla. 1973). The supreme court described the mechanics of this process in *Bromer v. Florida Power & Light Co.*, 45 So. 2d 658, 660 (Fla. 1950):

> [A] court should determine and give to the alleged implied contract "the effect which the parties, as fair and reasonable men, presumably would have agreed upon if, having in mind the possibility of the situation which has arisen, they had contracted expressly thereto." 12 Am. Jur. 766.

Common examples of contracts implied in fact are where a person performs services at another's request, or "where services are rendered by one person for another without his expressed request, but with his knowledge, and under circumstances" fairly raising the presumption that the parties understood and intended that compensation was to be paid. *Lewis v. Meginniss*, 30 Fla. 419, 12 So. 19, 21 (Fla. 1892); *Tipper*, 281 So. 2d at 13. In these circumstances, the law implies the promise to pay a reasonable amount for the services.

A contract implied in law, or quasi contract, is not based upon the finding, by a process of implication from the facts, of an agreement between the parties. A contract implied in law is a legal fiction, an obligation created by the law without regard to the parties' expression of assent by their words or conduct. The fiction was adopted to provide a remedy where one party was unjustly enriched, where that party received a benefit under circumstances that made it unjust to retain it without giving compensation.

The elements of a cause of action for a quasi contract are that: (1) the plaintiff has conferred a benefit on the defendant; (2) the defendant has knowledge of the benefit; (3) the defendant has accepted or retained the benefit conferred and (4) the circumstances are such that it would be inequitable for the defendant to retain the benefit without paying fair value for it. Because the basis for recovery does not turn on the finding of an enforceable agreement, there may be recovery under a contract implied in law even where the parties had no dealings at all with each other. This is unlike a contract implied in fact which must arise from the interaction of the parties or their agents.

To describe the cause of action encompassed by a contract implied in law, Florida courts have synonymously used a number of different terms—"quasi contract," "unjust enrichment," "restitution," "constructive contract," and "quantum meruit." This profusion of terminology has its roots in legal history. Concerned about the confusion between contracts implied in law and fact, two legal scholars sought to "extirpate the term 'contract implied in law' from legal usage and to substitute for it the term 'quasi contract'." 1 *Corbin on Contracts* § 1.20. As Corbin explains, although the term "quasi contract" took hold, "the older term successfully resisted extirpation to the further confusion of law students and lawyers." *Id.*

The term "quantum meruit" derives from common law forms of pleading. The action of assumpsit was available for the "recovery of damages for the breach or non-performance of a simple contract . . . or upon a contract implied by law from the acts or conduct of the parties." *Hazen v. Cobb*, 96 Fla. 151, 117 So. 853, 857 (Fla. 1928). There were two divisions of assumpsit, general, upon the common counts, and special. In general assumpsit, on the common counts, only an implied contract could be the basis of the action. The common counts were "abbreviated and stereotyped statements" that the defendant was indebted to the plaintiff for a variety of commonly recurring reasons, such as goods sold and delivered or work and labor done. 1 *Corbin on Contracts* § 1.18.

The count asking judgment for work done was quantum meruit; for goods sold the count was quantum valebant. The common counts were used to enforce contracts implied *both* in law and in fact. Because so many quasi contract actions were brought in the common counts, and because courts and lawyers were not careful to draw the distinction, the term "quantum meruit" is often used synonymously with the term "quasi contract."

At trial in this case, Commerce's attorney understood "quantum meruit" to mean a contract implied in fact. Equity and the trial court were proceeding under a theory of quasi contract. This confusion over "quantum meruit" is understandable, since there are cases to support both positions.

. . .

The blurring of the distinction between contract implied in fact and quasi contract has been exacerbated by the potential for both theories to apply to the same factual setting. For example, a common form of contract implied in fact is where one party has performed services at the request of another without discussion of compensation. These circumstances justify the inference of a promise to pay a reasonable amount for the service. The enforceability of this obligation turns on the implied promise, not on whether the defendant has received something of value. A contract implied in fact can be enforced even where a defendant has received nothing of value.

However, where there is no enforceable express or implied in fact contract but where the defendant has received something of value, or has otherwise benefitted from the service supplied, recovery under a quasi contractual theory may be appropriate. When properly raised in the pleadings, this overlapping of theories may require a fact finder to view the facts as they might apply to both.

Contrary to Commerce's belief at trial, Equity was asserting a quasi contract claim against it, not a contract implied in fact.

A SUBCONTRACTOR'S QUASI CONTRACT ACTION AGAINST AN OWNER

In *Maloney v. Therm Alum Industries, Corp.*, 636 So. 2d 767 (Fla. 4ᵗʰ DCA), *rev. denied*, 645 So. 2d 456 (Fla. 1994), this court considered the availability of a quasi contract theory to a construction subcontractor seeking recovery against an owner of property, where there had been no dealings between the owner and the subcontractor. Pursuant to a contract with the general contractor, the subcontractor in *Maloney* furnished glass walls, windows and doors for the construction of an office building. The subcontractor was not paid in full for its work. The general contractor and subcontractor submitted their claims against each other to arbitration. In the circuit court action, the subcontractor sought to recover damages against the owner on a quasi contract theory. Relying on two out-of-state cases, this court held that a subcontractor could maintain a quasi contract action against an owner, provided that it pled and proved two elements to establish that the enrichment of the owner was unjust—that the subcontractor had exhausted all remedies against the general contractor and still remained unpaid and that the owner had not given consideration to any person for the improvements furnished by the subcontractor. We quoted the following passage from *Paschall's Inc. v. Dozier*, 219 Tenn. 45, 407 S.W.2d 150, 155 (1966):

> The most significant requirement for a recovery on quasi contract is that the enrichment to the defendant be unjust. Consequently, if the landowner has given any consideration to any person for the improvements, it would not be unjust for him to retain the benefit without paying the furnisher. Also, we think that before recovery can be had against the landowner on an unjust enrichment theory, the furnisher of the materials and labor must have exhausted his remedies against the person with whom he had contracted, and still has not received the reasonable value of his services.

636 So. 2d at 770. *Maloney* reversed the judgment for the contractor based upon quasi contract because the status of the subcontractor's arbitration claim with the general contractor was not established at trial. Under these circumstances, we held that it was "premature and therefore improper to permit the subcontractor to pursue" a quasi contract claim against the owner. *Id.* at 769.

. . .

There is language in *Maloney* which can be read to suggest that we imposed a third limitation on the ability of a subcontractor to maintain a quasi contract claim against an owner. *Maloney* quotes two paragraphs from *Construction and Design Law* § 8.8C.1(1989), which include the following sentence:

> First, the subcontractor may not recover an equitable remedy if he has failed his legal remedies, such as a statutory mechanic's lien.

636 So. 2d at 770. We expressly recede from this statement in *Maloney* because it is without support in Florida law.

Florida's construction lien statute does not purport to be the exclusive remedy for a lienor, such as a subcontractor, against an owner. Section 713.30, Florida Statutes (1995), provides that the construction lien part of Chapter 713 "shall be cumulative to other existing remedies." The plain language of the statute does not supersede any remedies available to a party seeking payment.

. . .

Drawn from *Paschall's, Inc.* and *Tum-a-Lum Lumber v. Patrick*, 95 Ore. App. 719, 770 P.2d 964 (1989), the two requirements that *Maloney* imposes on a subcontractor's quasi contract action against an owner—exhaustion of remedies against the contractor and the owner's receipt of the benefit conferred without paying consideration to anyone—limit the cause of action to those situations where the enrichment of the owner is truly unjust when compared to the uncompensated subcontractor. The contractor with whom the subcontractor is in privity is always the pocket of first resort. Moreover, the owner can be liable only where it received a windfall benefit, something for nothing.

By our reliance on *Paschall's, Inc.* and *Tum-a-Lum*, we intended in *Maloney* to align ourselves with that line of cases which allow a subcontractor's recovery in quasi contract against an owner, even where the subcontractor has failed to perfect its construction lien.

. . .

REVERSAL IS REQUIRED UNDER THE FACTS OF THIS CASE

In this case, Equity did not prove at trial that Commerce had not made payment to any party for the benefits conferred on the property by Equity. This was not an affirmative defense, but an essential element of a quasi contract claim by a subcontractor against an owner. Had Commerce moved for an involuntary dismissal on this ground, the motion should have been granted. Contrary to the trial court's evidentiary ruling, Commerce's attempt to prove that it had paid $64,097 directly to subcontractors for work on the building was relevant to issues in this case. What Commerce expended on this project was central to Equity's cause of action. Commerce contended that these payments were for work covered under the construction contract for which the subcontractors had not been paid by the general contractor. If the $64,097 is added to the $256,894 that Commerce paid to the general contractor, then the total amount Commerce spent on the project exceeded the contract price for the improvements. As we have observed, where an owner has given consideration for the subcontractor's work by paying out the contract price for the work, an unpaid subcontractor's claim that the owner has been unjustly enriched must fail.

The trial court's reliance on *Zaleznik* was misplaced. In that case it was undisputed that the owner received over $70,000 in construction work for which it paid no one. What Commerce paid out on this project was not fully litigated below, so whether its "enrichment" was "unjust" is an open question.

The judgment appealed is reversed, and the cause is remanded to the trial court to take additional evidence from the parties on whether Commerce made payment to or on behalf of its general contractor covering the benefits Equity conferred on the subject property. Equity shall have the burden of proving its claim of a contract implied in law that Commerce has failed to make such payment by the greater weight of the evidence. If the court shall determine that Commerce has not paid anyone for the benefits conferred by Equity, then it shall enter judgment for Equity; correspondingly, if the court shall determine that Equity has failed to prove that Commerce made such payment, then the court shall enter judgment for Commerce.

Comprehension and Thought Questions:

1. What was the nature of Commerce's confusion regarding the claim being made by Equity?

2. What is the test for recovery under an implied-in-law contract?

3. Why is Commerce's payment to the general contractor relevant to the availability of Equity's recovery under an implied-in-law theory?

4. Why was the lien statute potentially relevant to whether a recovery was available for an implied-in-law theory? Why did the court believe it was irrelevant in this instance?

5. What are the risks involved when a court is attempting to ascertain whether a quasi-contractual remedy is available?

Hypothetical Variations:

1. What if, upon remand, it is determined that Commerce paid the general contractor the entire agreed-upon contract price; will Equity be able to recover under its implied-in-law contract theory?

2. What if the relevant lien statute provided that "This lien statute is the exclusive remedy for subcontractors against owners."

3. What if Commerce and Equity had a valid written contract regarding Commerce's payment obligations? Could Equity bring a claim for recovery under a quasi-contract theory?

C. POLICY CONCERNS

As discussed earlier in this chapter, remedies are often sought after benefits have been conferred even in the absence of a bargain or foreseeable reliance. In these instances, the court is often being asked not to protect a party's ability to plan or to protect the utility of contracts for commercial transaction, but instead to fashion a remedy based on inequitable results. Importantly, these inequitable results do not necessarily arise from any wrongdoing on the part of the recipient of the benefits. If they did, there potentially would be a recovery in tort. Quasi-contracts and promises in recognition of a previous benefit conferred necessarily implicate a particularly gray area where outcomes are unpredictable and where multiple policy concerns may need to be considered. In the following case, consider the balancing of interests that the court has to undertake in order to determine whether an award based upon unjust enrichment should be available and, in so doing, whether the difficulty in such a task suggests anything about the utility of such remedies.

McBride v. Boughton

Court of Appeal of California, First Appellate District, Division Two

123 Cal. App. 4th 379 (2004)

RUVOLO, J.

This case calls upon us to decide, as a matter of first impression in this state, whether an unmarried man who has expended funds to support a child, in reliance on the mother's representation that he is the child's father, may sue the mother on an unjust enrichment theory for the return of the funds after discovering that the child is not his biological offspring. As a matter of public policy, we conclude that such a suit cannot be maintained. Accordingly, we affirm the trial court's judgment dismissing this case after sustaining the defendants' demurrer.

I. FACTS AND PROCEDURAL BACKGROUND

Appellant Richard McBride was romantically involved with respondent Garianne Dashiell, then known as Garianne Boughton. At some time during 1996, presumably in the fall, McBride moved to Chile. In December 1996, however, Boughton contacted him in Chile and informed him that she was pregnant with a child that she represented was his. Based on this representation, McBride returned to the United States and took a teaching job in order to support Boughton and the child.

The child, a girl, was apparently born on or about May 26, 1997. During the month of May 1997, McBride and Boughton orally agreed that McBride would support Boughton for a year so that she could stay home and take care of the child. In June 1998, when the child was about a year old, Boughton began working again, and McBride resigned his job in order to become the child's full-time caregiver. It is not entirely clear from the complaint, but McBride and Boughton apparently lived together in the Los Angeles area during this time.

In December 1998, Boughton moved out of McBride's house, and told him, as alleged in the complaint, "that she would soon stop paying the bills, and that he would have to return to work." The child was not yet ready to adapt to day care, however, so McBride continued to act as her full-time caregiver for about another five or six months.

In May 1999, when the child was about two years old, McBride went back to work, taking a position as a flight attendant. In June 1999, McBride and Boughton agreed orally that McBride would have custody of the child 10 days each month. Nevertheless, in September 1999, Boughton told McBride that she was moving to San Francisco, evidently with the child, and that he would be able to see the child only two weekends a month. In October 1999, McBride filed a paternity proceeding seeking custody of the child, who was by then almost two and one-half years old.

In connection with the paternity proceeding, genetic tests were done, and the testing service reported that McBride was "excluded as the biological father of the child. . . ." McBride learned the results of the genetic tests in December 1999. Evidently, he then abandoned his efforts to seek custody of the child.

. . .

II. DISCUSSION

. . .

B.

McBride's second amended complaint includes two causes of action. The first is captioned as one for unjust enrichment. After incorporating the factual allegations summarized above, this cause of action avers that respondents were unjustly enriched by McBride's having paid for the care and support of Boughton and the child, because respondents "were legally responsible for the monies paid out by [McBride], and would have had to incur those expenses if [McBride] had not done so." The premise of this claim is that McBride's expenditures for the support of the child unjustly enriched respondents, as the child's biological parents, because McBride was not the child's biological father.

. . .

C.

In sustaining respondents' general demurrer, the trial court relied on *Nagy v. Nagy*, (1989) 210 Cal. App. 3d 1262. In *Nagy*, the plaintiff's estranged wife revealed during a deposition in their dissolution proceeding that the couple's child was not the plaintiff's biological offspring. The court held that the former husband's action against his former wife for fraud and intentional infliction of emotional distress was barred because, among other reasons, it would be contrary to public policy to allow a putative father to recover damages "for developing a close relationship with a child misrepresented to be his." (*Id.* at p. 1269.) The *Nagy* court placed the plaintiff's claims in the same category as "'betrayal, brutal words, and heartless disregard of the feelings of others, [which] are beyond any effective legal remedy and any practical administration of law.'" (*Ibid.*)

Prior to the decision in *Nagy*, this division reached a similar result in *Richard P. v. Superior Court* (1988) 202 Cal. App. 3d 1089 [249 Cal. Rptr. 246] (*Richard P.*). In *Richard P.*, the plaintiff was a married man, Gerald, who had separated from his wife. After the separation, the wife's lover, Richard, established that he was the biological father of the couple's children. Gerald then sued Richard, alleging that Richard had previously misrepresented to him that the children were biologically Gerald's, and had thereby induced Gerald to support them and develop a relationship with them. We held that Gerald's tort claims seeking damages for fraud and intentional infliction of emotional distress, on the basis of misrepresentations as to paternity, were barred by public policy, reasoning that "the innocent children here may suffer significant harm from having their family involved in litigation such as this[,] and . . . this is exactly the type of lawsuit which, if allowed to proceed, might result in more social damage than will occur if the courts decline to intervene." (*Id.* at p. 1094.)

Richard P. is not dispositive of the present case, however. As McBride's brief in the present case correctly points out, in a footnote in *Richard P.*, we expressly declined to "foreclose the possibility that a man in [McBride]'s position might be able to recover actual out of pocket costs incurred in supporting another man's child[] on an equitable theory for reimbursement, such as unjust enrichment." (*Richard P., supra*, 202 Cal. App. 3d at p. 1096, fn. 3.) We expressly noted that the issue was not before us, and that we were not required to decide it.

. . .

Under the law of restitution, "[a]n individual is required to make restitution if he or she is unjustly enriched at the expense of another. A person is enriched if the person receives a benefit at another's expense." (*First Nationwide Savings v. Perry* (1992) 11 Cal. App. 4th 1657, 1662 [15 Cal. Rptr. 2d 173] (*First Nationwide*).) However, "[t]he fact that one person benefits another is not, by itself, sufficient to require restitution. The person receiving the benefit is required to make restitution only if the circumstances are such that, as between the two individuals, it is *unjust* for the person to retain it." (*Id.* at p. 1663, italics in original).

In keeping with the doctrine's focus on the *unjust* nature of the enrichment, "[i]t is well settled that restitution will be denied where application of the doctrine would involve a violation or frustration of the law or opposition to public policy." (*Lauriedale, supra*, 7 Cal. App. 4th at p. 1449.) Thus, "[d]etermining whether it is unjust for a person to retain a benefit may involve policy considerations. For example, if a person receives a benefit because of another's mistake, policy may dictate that the person making the mistake assume the risk of the error." (*First Nationwide Savings v. Perry, supra*, 11 Cal. App. 4th at p. 1663.) Moreover, a person otherwise entitled to restitution may lose that entitlement if "restitution would seriously impair the protection intended to be afforded by common law or by statute to persons in the position of the transferee or of the beneficiary, or to other persons." (Rest., Restitution, § 62, p. 241.)

Applying these principles to the present case, we conclude that two of the most fundamental public policies of this state—the enforcement of parents' obligations to support their children, and the protection of children's interest in the stability of their family relationships—preclude us from requiring Boughton to make restitution to McBride based on his claim of unjust enrichment. Under circumstances such as those presented here, if we granted the former putative father the right to restitution from the child's biological parents, who retain responsibility for its support, we would give priority to the former putative father's desire to be made financially whole, to the potential detriment of the child's ongoing needs.

More importantly, at least from the child's perspective, by *declining* to recognize an unjust enrichment claim, we create a *dis*incentive for an unmarried man to form a parental bond with a child if the bond is likely to be severed upon the child's proving to be another man's genetic offspring. The potential emotional and psychic costs to the child of such a rupture are far more significant than any financial injury a grown man might suffer from mistakenly supporting another man's child for a temporary period.

. . .

Moreover, our holding—that it is not unjust enrichment for a mother to retain child support she has received—serves an important public policy by sending the message to unmarried putative fathers that they should verify their paternity at an early stage if there is any doubt about the matter. Significantly, the Legislature has sent the same message to married men by providing a statutory incentive for them to resolve promptly any doubts they may have as to the paternity of their wives' children. Under the applicable statutory scheme, if a married man fails to request paternity testing within two years of the birth of a child to his wife, and he is neither infertile nor impotent, he will be conclusively presumed to be the child's father, with all the concomitant responsibilities as well as rights.

In addition, we note that determining whether Boughton was *unjustly* enriched would involve inquiring into the very subjects which *Nagy, supra,* 210 Cal. App. 3d 1262, and *Richard P., supra,* 202 Cal. App. 3d 1089, held public policy requires courts to avoid. Issues of this type would include, but not be limited to: (1) the extent to which McBride's expenditures exclusively benefited the child, rather than Boughton personally, and if so, the effect of that fact on the equities of McBride's restitution claim against Boughton and Dashiell; (2) if restitution is owed, whether its amount should be reduced by the value of any benefit, emotional or financial, that McBride received from his relationship with the child; and (3) how, if at all, the equities of McBride's restitution claim may be affected by his decision to end his relationship with the child rather than pursuing any rights he may have had under Family Code section 7611, subdivision (d).

Because of the lurking presence of issues such as these, we concur with the *Richard P.* court's concern that the "innocent child here may suffer significant harm from having [her] family involved in litigation . . . which, if allowed to proceed, might result in more social damage than will occur if the courts decline to intervene." (*Richard P., supra,* 202 Cal. App. 3d at p. 1094.) We recognize that *Richard P.* declined to consider whether this rationale would extend to a suit seeking only restitution for support paid rather than emotional distress damages, because the issue was not presented in that case. Having now considered it, in a case in which it is squarely presented, we have concluded that the type of harm to the child about which *Richard P.* expressed concern is as likely to be realized here as it was in that case.

In short, for much the same public policy reasons on which *Nagy* and *Richard P.* relied in declining to authorize a tort claim for the loss of a purported father's relationship with a child, we likewise decline to authorize a restitution remedy for support payments based on facts such as those pleaded in this case. Accordingly, we conclude that the trial court properly sustained respondents' demurrer to McBride's cause of action alleging unjust enrichment.

. . .

III. Disposition

The judgment of dismissal is affirmed.

Comprehension and Thought Questions:

1. What facts supported McBride's cause of action alleging a quasi-contract?

2. Why was McBride's claim based on quasi-contract and not an express contract or promissory estoppel?

3. Why did the court sustain the demurrer instead of allowing the matter to proceed to trial to determine whether the mother and biological father had in fact been unjustly enriched?

4. What public policy considerations did the court believe were relevant to determining whether recovery under a quasi-contract theory was available to McBride?

Hypothetical Variations:

1. If McBride and Dashiell had entered into a written contract regarding the payment of child support in exchange for visitation rights, and after discovering that the child was not his, McBride wanted to bring a claim for unjust enrichment, should he be permitted to do so?

2. What if McBride and Dashiell had entered into a written contract regarding the payment of child support in exchange for visitation rights concerning a child that was not McBride's? If Dashiell refuses to extend the visitation rights to McBride as required under the contract, should McBridge be permitted to bring a breach of contract claim? What about an unjust enrichment claim?

Now that you have studied alternate theories of recovery, read through and answer the questions that follow the Simulation Problem for Chapter 23, which is located in Appendix A.

REMEDIES FOR BREACH

Part VII presumes that the parties have created an enforceable contract, that one party has failed to perform an obligation under that contract, and that that failure is not excused. Where that occurs, the nonperforming party has committed a breach, and the aggrieved party is entitled to a remedy. This part explains the remedies that are potentially available to the aggrieved party as a result of that breach—either court-awarded monetary damages, specific performance, or a remedy agreed on in the contract. First, Chapter 24 explains these different types of remedies. It then discusses the remedy of damages and how to calculate a party's damages. Chapter 25 then explains the limits that courts impose on an aggrieved party's damage recovery. Chapter 26 discusses other potential remedies a party might obtain other than common law damages—specific performance or a remedy specified by the parties in the contract. Chapter 27 explains the types of damages courts disallow, while Chapter 28 discusses specific rules on damages applicable to sale-of-goods contracts governed by UCC Article 2.

The following diagram shows where the topics covered in Part VII fit into the larger scheme of this course.

PART VII—OVERVIEW DIAGRAM

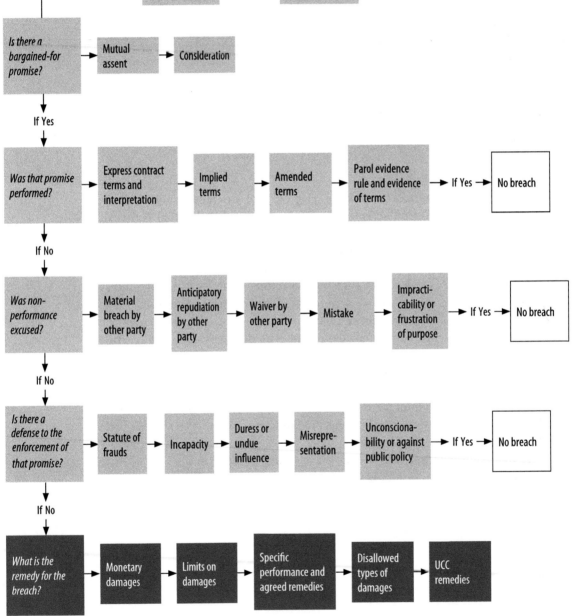

CHAPTER 24

Remedies Generally; Damages

The prior chapters explained how to determine when a party makes an enforceable contract. This chapter explains *why* that determination matters. Specifically, if a party breaches an enforceable contract, then a court will enforce that contract by providing a remedy for that breach to the other party. This chapter discusses what remedy or remedies the party on the receiving end of a breach—referred to as an aggrieved party—might receive due to the other party's breach.

Keep in mind that most contracts are performed and do not give rise to breach. Moreover, even where a party does breach, that breach might not lead to litigation. That is the case for several reasons. For one, the parties might address the breach on their own, such as through modifying the contract terms. For example, if a borrower does not pay principal and interest on a loan when those amounts are due, the lender might agree to modify the repayment terms to give the borrower more time to pay, even if not required to do so under the contract (the lender may also charge additional fees for doing so, of course). That modification might be the most effective way for the lender to get repaid. It might also help advance the lender's reputation as a reasonable commercial party with whom other borrowers want to do business.

Additionally, sometimes an aggrieved party decides it is not worth the hassle to sue the breaching counterparty. That would be especially likely if the breaching party does not have resources from which the aggrieved party could collect a judgment, if the breach is not significant, or if the parties expect to have a long-term relationship. As suggested above, sometimes an aggrieved party decides there will be a negative reputational impact from suing a breaching counterparty. Lawyers commonly worry about this concern in deciding whether to sue a nonpaying client.

Finally, sometimes parties include indemnification clauses in their contracts. In an **indemnification clause**, parties specify types of losses for which one party will reimburse the other party. Such indemnifiable losses might be those arising from misrepresentations or breaches of warranties or covenants by the other party in the contract, or such losses might arise due to losses incurred as a result of liability to a third party. Either way, the indemnification clause is a way for the contracting parties to privately agree in what circumstance one party will owe money to another, what types of losses are covered, and the timing and other processes for such payments. In that way, they set out a private arrangement for compensation due to breach.

Note that indemnification clauses are not the same as liquidated damage clauses, which you will study in Chapter 26. In a liquidated damage clause, parties agree *up front* on the amount of damages one party will owe to the other upon breach. In contrast, in an indemnification clause, one party agrees to essentially reimburse the other for *actual losses* it incurs, so long as those losses fit within the scope of the indemnification clause.

In short, a court-awarded remedy only comes into play where an aggrieved party sues a counterparty for breach, and a court finds in that lawsuit that the counterparty in fact breached an enforceable obligation.

Remedies in some sense complete the circle of understanding contract law. Once you have formed a contract and are attempting to enforce its promises, it is necessary to understand the consequences of not complying with the contract. One must obviously understand what it means to have created an enforceable contract that has been breached to fully understand the context for remedies. On the other hand, without understanding what it means for an aggrieved party to have a remedy for the other party's breach, and what that remedy might be, there is no context for discussing whether a party has made an enforceable promise. The interrelatedness of each aspect of contract law, and their convergence around the question of whether a promise is enforceable and supplies a remedy for breach is the reason that some professors disagree about whether damages should be taught at the beginning of a Contracts course or at the end.

Whether you start or end your education in Contract law with this chapter, the key point is that a party will seek to enforce a promise where it desires a remedy for breach. And a court will award a remedy where a promise has been breached. Even where there are no actual injuries from the breach, a court can award an aggrieved party nominal damages due to the counterparty's breach.[1]

This chapter begins in Section A with an explanation of the purposes of contract law remedies. It is important to understand the purposes for remedies, as the purposes dictate what remedies are available. As you will see in that discussion, there is no single purpose for remedies. However, there is enough convergence around the general goals of contract law remedies that courts are constrained in what remedies they can and do award.

Next, Section B explains why monetary damages are the remedy usually awarded to an aggrieved party. That discussion then leads into Sections C through E, which discuss specific measures of monetary damages. First, Section

---

1. Restatement (Second) of Contracts § 346 (1981).

C discusses the expectation-based measure of damages, where an aggrieved party is awarded the benefits it was promised—and thus expected—under the contract. Next, Section D discusses the reliance-based measure of damages, which generally compensates an aggrieved party for its costs in relying on the other party's breached promise. Section E then discusses the restitution-based measure of damages, which reflects the value of benefits conferred on a party under a contract.

Parties to sophisticated transactions do not want to have to wait until there is a breach to find out if a court will enforce a contract by awarding a remedy due to the other party's breach. To address this concern, often parties in sophisticated contracts require that the counterparty's lawyer give a legal opinion as to the enforceability of the contract. These legal opinions, referred to as remedies opinions, are discussed in Section F.

We make three final points before launching into the first part of this chapter.

First, even where an aggrieved party has suffered losses due to a breach and has a valid claim for monetary damages against the breaching party, oftentimes the aggrieved party may not be fully compensated for all of its losses. That is true for a number of reasons, including the fact that several doctrines limit the damages that a party may recover, while some types of damages are generally disallowed. Those limits and disallowances are discussed in Chapters 25 and 27, respectively.

Second, damages are not the only potential remedy for a breach. In some circumstances, instead of awarding damages, a court will order a party to perform its breached promise or promises. Chapter 26 discusses this remedy, known as specific performance. Moreover, sometimes parties agree in a contract on the amount of damages a party must pay if it breaches. Those types of clauses are referred to as liquidated damage clauses because the parties liquidate (that is, put into monetary terms) the amount by which they expect they will be damaged if the other side breaches. Chapter 26 also explores liquidated damage clauses, including the limits courts place on enforcing such clauses.

Finally, while this chapter focuses on enforcement of promises by a court, parties can agree to resolve disputes through an alternative dispute resolution forum. For example, it is typical for merchants to include mandatory arbitration provisions in their contracts with consumers. Thus, if the consumer wishes to sue the merchant for a breach of warranty, it must make its claim in the manner and before the arbitrator specified in the contract instead of before a court.

A. PURPOSE OF REMEDIES

Contract law remedies—at least monetary damages—largely seek to compensate the aggrieved party for the nonperforming party's breach. They are not necessarily designed to punish the breaching party for its breach.

The broad goal of compensating an aggrieved party does not, however, explain *how* to compensate an aggrieved party. For example, should the aggrieved party be put in the same position it would have been in had the breaching party performed? Should the aggrieved party be put in the same position it was in before the parties entered into the contract? Or should the aggrieved party be compensated in a different way?

In a famous 1936 article, Lon Fuller and William Perdue identified three compensable interests that are protected by contract law remedies: the expectation interest, the reliance interest, and the restitutionary interest. This analytical framework has been widely used to explain contract law damages that protect those interests. The following is an excerpt from this famous article.

> It is convenient to distinguish three principal purposes which may be pursued in awarding contract damages. These purposes, and the situations in which they become appropriate, may be stated briefly as follows:
>
> First, the plaintiff has in reliance on the promise of the defendant conferred some value on the defendant. The defendant fails to perform his promise. The court may force the defendant to disgorge the value he received from the plaintiff. The object here may be termed the prevention of gain by the defaulting promisor at the expense of the promisee; more briefly, the prevention of unjust enrichment. The interest protected may be called the restitution interest. For our present purposes it is quite immaterial how the suit in such a case be classified, whether as contractual or quasi-contractual, whether as a suit to enforce the contract or as a suit based upon a rescission of the contract. These questions relate to the superstructure of the law, not to the basic policies with which we are concerned.
>
> Secondly, the plaintiff has in reliance on the promise of the defendant changed his position. For example, the buyer under a contract for the sale of land has incurred expense in the investigation of the seller's title, or has neglected the opportunity to enter into other contracts. We may award damages to the plaintiff for the purpose of undoing the harm which his reliance on the defendant's promise has caused him. Our object is to put him in as good a position as he was in before the promise was made. The interest protected in this case may be called the reliance interest.
>
> Thirdly, without insisting on reliance by the promisee or enrichment of the promisor, we may seek to give the promisee the value of the expectancy which the promise created. We may in a suit for specific performance actually compel the defendant to render the promised performance to the plaintiff, or, in a suit for damages, we may make the defendant pay the money value of this performance. Here our object is to put the plaintiff in as good a position as he would have occupied had the defendant performed his promise. The interest protected in this case we may call the expectation interest.
>
> . . .
>
> It is obvious that the three "interests" we have distinguished do not present equal claims to judicial intervention. It may be assumed that ordinary standards

of justice would regard the need for judicial intervention as decreasing in the order in which we have listed the three interests. The "restitution interest," involving a combination of unjust impoverishment with unjust gain, presents the strongest case for relief. If, following Aristotle, we regard the purpose of justice as the maintenance of an equilibrium of goods among members of society, the restitution interest presents twice as strong a claim to judicial intervention as the reliance interest, since if A not only causes B to lose one unit but appropriates that unit to himself, the resulting discrepancy between A and B is not one unit but two.

On the other hand, the promisee who has actually relied on the promise, even though he may not thereby have enriched the promisor, certainly presents a more pressing case for relief than the promisee who merely demands satisfaction for his disappointment in not getting what was promised him. In passing from compensation for change of position to compensation for loss of expectancy we pass, to use Aristotle's terms again, from the realm of corrective justice to that of distributive justice. The law no longer seeks merely to heal a disturbed status quo, but to bring into being a new situation. It ceases to act defensively or restoratively, and assumes a more active role. With the transition, the justification for legal relief loses its self-evident quality. It is as a matter of fact no easy thing to explain why the normal rule of contract recovery should be that which measures damages by the value of the promised performance. Since this "normal rule" throws its shadow across our whole subject it will be necessary to examine the possible reasons for its existence.

Lon Fuller & William Perdue, *The Reliance Interest in Contract Damages*, 46 Yale L.J. 52, 53-57 (1936).

The following cake-shaped diagram attempts to depict Fuller and Perdue's prioritization of compensable interests protect in contract law, with the base of the cake representing the most essential interest to be protected (restitutionary interest), and decreasing interests going up each added layer of the cake.

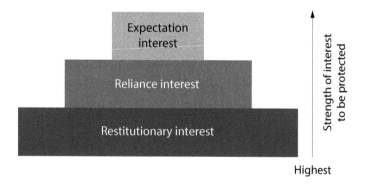

You can see Fuller and Perdue's framework in the Restatement's description of the overall goals of damages:

Restatement (Second) of Contracts § 344

Judicial remedies under the rules stated in this Restatement serve to protect one or more of the following interests of a promisee:

(a) his "expectation interest," which is his interest in having the benefit of his bargain by being put in as good a position as he would have been in had the contract been performed,

(b) his "reliance interest," which is his interest in being reimbursed for loss caused by reliance on the contract by being put in as good a position as he would have been in had the contract not been made, or

(c) his "restitution interest," which is his interest in having restored to him any benefit that he has conferred on the other party.

There is a wealth of academic commentary challenging Perdue and Fuller's classification of the purpose of remedies, or at least its relevance to today's remedies decisions.[2] In one particularly potent challenge, Professor Richard Craswell argues that Perdue and Fuller's classifications do not tell a court *when* to protect which interest.

According to Craswell, the important starting point in an analysis of remedies is to ask what policy is to be served by remedies. Is it to maximize damages to minimize the chances of breach? To approximate the remedy the parties would have agreed on had they agreed on the remedy (without knowing which side of the breach they would be on)? In other words, according to Craswell, the remedy flows not from the interest to be protected, but instead from the goal sought to be achieved in the particular situation.

The following passage captures the essence of Craswell's critique:

Whatever Fuller may have intended, though, those three remedial "interests" receive most of the attention today. For example, the Restatement (Second) of Contracts begins its sections on remedies by announcing that all remedies "serve to protect one or more of the following interests of a promisee," followed by definitions of Fuller and Perdue's three interests. Almost every casebook begins its materials on remedies in the same way—either directly, by excerpting or paraphrasing Fuller and Perdue or the second Restatement; or indirectly by way of the opinion in Sullivan v O'Connor, which itself uses Fuller and Perdue's classification. In academic scholarship, many law-and-economics analyses begin with these same three remedies, as do any number of non-economic writings.

It is this use of Fuller and Perdue's three "interests" that I wish to criticize here. . . .

I . . . argue that the very classification employed by Fuller and Perdue—their famous distinction between the restitution, reliance, and expectation interests—is not a useful starting point for normative analysis. To most modern scholars (as to Fuller and Perdue), remedies can be defended only by reference to some

---

2. *See, e.g.,* Richard Craswell, *Against Fuller and Perdue,* 67 U. Chi. L. Rev. 99 (2000); Michael B. Kelly, *The Phantom Reliance Interest in Contract Damages,* 1992 Wis. L. Rev. 1755 (1992); David W. Barnes, *The Net Expectation Interest in Contract Damages,* 48 Emory L.J. 1137 (1999).

purpose or policy they might serve. We might adopt broader or narrower remedies in order to create efficient incentives, for example, or to achieve certain distributional goals, or to affirm an important symbolic message. Under any of these approaches, the analysis starts with the particular goal to be achieved— efficiency, distribution, or what have you—and proceeds on that basis to decide what remedy ought to be awarded. Under these approaches, then, there is no reason to think that the remedy that best serves the chosen substantive goal will necessarily coincide with one of Fuller and Perdue's three "interests." Moreover, even when one of these approaches does happen to coincide (in its recommended remedy) with one of those three "interests," that coincidence will appear only at the conclusion of the analysis: the particular "interest" that is selected will not have played any role in the analysis leading up to that conclusion. There thus is no reason to begin our analysis with Fuller and Perdue's three "interests," or to treat those "interests" as key concepts of any sort.

Richard Craswell, *Against Fuller and Perdue*, 67 U. Chi. L. Rev. 99, 105-07 (2000).

Craswell thus challenges Fuller and Perdue's framework that says contract law remedies should protect the restitutionary interest, reliance interest, and expectancy interest. Instead, Craswell argues that these interests may be protected by contract law remedies, but only incidentally, as courts should and do award remedies to advance certain policies.

According to Craswell, one policy goal courts seek to achieve through contract law remedies is to create economic efficiency. For example, "the threat of a larger remedy might deter a promisor from deliberately breaking her promise, while a reduction in the remedy might reduce that incentive."[3] However, achieving economic efficiency does not necessary always require the award of expectation damages.

Another goal Craswell identifies is the goal of retribution against the breaching party.[4] While contract law damages are not punitive, they can serve as an expression of our society's disapproval of conduct. In that way, the wrongfulness of a party's action could lead to a scaling of the damages amount.

Thus, Craswell does not merely challenge Fuller and Perdue's framework— he also offers up his own theory behind contract law remedies, and what considerations courts take into account in deciding which remedy is appropriate.

Comprehension and Thought Questions:

1. Do you find Fuller and Perdue's framework, in which they identify the restitutionary, reliance, and expectation interests, to be a useful framework for purposes of understanding damages? Why or why not?

---

3. Richard Craswell, *Against Fuller and Perdue*, 67 U. Chi. L. Rev. 99, 108 (2000).
4. *See id.* at 115.

2. Which interest(s) would you want protected if your client agreed to pay you $2,000 to review a contract for him and you completed the review, but then your client failed to pay you for this work (through no fault of yours)?

3. Which interest(s) would you want protected if your client, after hiring you to perform contract review work that led you to reject other work and before you performed the work, changed his mind and asked you to refrain from the review (again, through no fault of yours)?

4. Do you think there needs to be a single widely accepted framework to guide courts and litigants in deciding which remedy to award and when?

While the above discussion is useful in exploring the purposes for and policies behind remedies, practical realities often dictate which remedy a court awards. Namely, in litigation, the party who sues for breach has the burden to prove that the requested remedy fairly and adequately compensates that party for the other party's breach. Where a party might not have adequate evidence to establish one remedy, that party can argue for an alternative remedy or remedies. So, for example, if a party sues the contractual counterparty for breach and requests the remedy of specific performance, that party would have to convince the court why specific performance was appropriate and satisfy any tests that courts in that jurisdiction apply in deciding to award specific performance. In case that party cannot do so, the party might, in the alternative, request expectation damages. The party would then have to convince the court that expectation damages are appropriate and satisfy the court's legal tests for deciding whether to award the requested damages, as well as how much to award.

Courts commonly state that expectation damages, reliance damages, and restitutionary damages are mutually exclusive alternatives. As such, a court will award only one of them. But the reality is that sometimes such measures of damages do not compensate a party for the same injury. In those instances, courts do not necessarily treat these measures of damages as mutually exclusive and permit a party to recover a damage award that protects more than one of these interests.

B. MONETARY DAMAGES

By and large, the most common remedy awarded to an aggrieved party due to the other party's breach of contract is damages. **Damages** refers to an amount of money an aggrieved party recovers from the breaching party to compensate it for the breaching party's breach.

There are historic, practical, and economic reasons for courts to award damages instead of other remedies, such as specific performance.

Historically, as early as Roman times, courts awarded monetary damages for breaches of some promises. Eventually, European courts awarded monetary damages due to failed promises. While there were several types of writs (which are akin to causes of action) that served as the foundation for common law breach, each carried a remedy of damages due to a violation of the applicable writ.

Eventually, these writs merged into the English action of assumpsit, which is the immediate predecessor to a breach of contract claim in the United States. An action of assumpsit, too, carried with it a claim for damages for breach. Thus, the origins of our legal system have seen monetary damages as the primary legal remedy for a breach of contract law. Of course, the same remains true today, even though in some instances, other remedies (such as specific performance) are awarded.

Damages are awarded for breach of contract claims for practical reasons, too. It is usually easier for a court to oversee an order of one party to pay the other money than it is for a court to oversee a party's performance, especially where that performance will take place over time or will otherwise be difficult to oversee. For example, if a general contractor breached a construction contract with an owner before it had prepared detailed specifications for the work (perhaps because the primary engineer who was going to prepare those specifications left the company), it might be difficult for the court to oversee an order requiring the contractor to finish performing the construction contract. That is because many details for the work have yet to be worked out, there remains much work to supervise, and, potentially, the contractor no longer has the expertise needed to perform on its contract.

Courts also favor monetary damages because it allows for efficient breaches. Under the notion of **efficient breach**, a party should breach a contract if doing so will put that party in a better position by breaching, so long as she can put the aggrieved party in the same position as if the breaching party had fully performed.

For example, assume Jacob agreed to sell his car to Nathan for $3,000, with closing to occur the following week, to give Nathan time to get a loan. Before closing, Jill comes along and offers to buy Jacob's car for $4,000. Jill is willing to pay more for the car because she has an affinity for the color of Jacob's car, and she knows Jacob takes great care of his cars. If Jacob sells his car to Jill for $4,000, he will breach his contract with Nathan. However, Jacob will receive an extra $1,000 by doing so. If Jacob can fully compensate Nathan for the extra costs Nathan will have to incur in finding and buying an equivalent car from someone else for less than $1,000, then this is an efficient breach. That is because Jill will get the car she wants, Nathan will be put in the same position he would have been in had he bought Jacob's car once Jacob pays him for any additional costs he incurs in finding and buying an equivalent car, and Jacob will make more money by selling his car to Jill (after factoring in the amount he has to pay Nathan to make Nathan whole).

In this way, overall social welfare can be gained by allowing a party to breach a contract and instead provide her goods or services to a higher-paying third party. The remedy of specific performance could undermine a party's ability to efficiently breach a contract by forcing that party to stick with the less efficient original contract.

While the notion of efficient breach might seem to justify damages as a remedy for breach, the reality is that, as you will learn in subsequent chapters, an aggrieved party is usually not made whole through damages. That is in part due to limits on the amount of damages courts award (discussed in Chapter 25) as well as the fact that some damages are not recoverable (discussed in Chapter 27). Together, these limitations can lead to an aggrieved party being undercompensated for the other party's breach, in contravention of the efficient breach assumption that the aggrieved party will be placed in the same position as if the other party had not breached.

Moreover, there is nothing to suggest that it is better for social welfare for a party to breach and pay damages as compared to simply having the third party find another supplier, or having the breaching party pay the aggrieved party an amount of money in order to be released from the parties' contract. Thus, skeptics argue that the notion of efficient breach is a fallacy and does not support the award of damages as a remedy for breach.[5]

Despite the limits on monetary damages mentioned above, courts commonly award an aggrieved party monetary damages for breach. The typical measure of such damages is to protect a party's expectation interest. The following section explains in more detail the rationale for awarding expectation damages, and also discusses how to calculate expectation damages.

C. EXPECTATION DAMAGES

1. Purpose of Expectation Damages

As mentioned in Section A above, the goal of expectation damages is to give the aggrieved party the benefit it was expecting under the contract. But *why* should the law award a party expectation damages? After all, giving an aggrieved party the benefit of a bargain is not simply compensatory—instead, it is redistributing property from one party (the breaching party) to the other (the aggrieved party), to put the aggrieved party in a better position than it was in at the start of the contract.

In their 1936 article discussed above, Professors Fuller and Perdue give two primary justifications for the award of expectation damages: first is the need to facilitate reliance on business agreements, and second is the need to cure and undo the harm caused by a party's reliance on a promise.[6] The award of

---

5. For a good critique of the efficient breach concept, see Ian R. Macneil, *Efficient Breach of Contract: Circles in the Sky*, 68 Va. L. Rev. 947 (1982).

6. *See* Lon Fuller & William Perdue, *The Reliance Interest in Contract Damages*, 46 Yale L.J. 52, 61 (1936).

expectation damages cures and undoes the harm caused by a party's reliance because that party will have given up opportunities to enter in other transactions. Protecting a party's expectation interest obviates the need for that party to prove that it actually lost such other opportunities through reliance. In this way, the doctrine supports economic activity by protecting a party from forgone opportunities.

Expectation damages also facilitate reliance on business agreements. As Fuller and Perdue have put it,

> [w]hen business agreements are not only made but are also acted on, the division of labor is facilitated, goods find their way to the places where they are most needed, and economic activity is generally stimulated. These advantages would be threatened by any rule which limited legal protection to the reliance interest. Such a rule would in practice tend to discourage reliance. The difficulties in proving reliance and subjecting it to pecuniary measurement are such that the business man knowing, or sensing, that these obstacles stood in the way of judicial relief would hesitate to rely on a promise in any case where the legal sanction was of significance to him. To encourage reliance we must therefore dispense with its proof. For this reason it has been found wise to make recovery on a promise independent of reliance, both in the sense that in some cases the promise is enforced though not relied on (as in the bilateral business agreement) and in the sense that recovery is not limited to the detriment incurred in reliance.[7]

Again, Professor Craswell criticizes Fuller and Perdue for failing to start their analysis of remedies with the policies sought to be achieved. According to Craswell,

> expectation damages may give promisors just the right incentive to choose between performing and breaking a contract (the 'efficient breach' effect), at least when subsequent renegotiation between the parties is unlikely. Expectation damages may also provide the right incentive to take precautions against any contingencies that would leave the promisor unable to perform. And if the promisee is risk-averse while the promisor is risk-neutral or risk-preferring, expectation damages can also provide the best allocation of risk between the two parties.[8]

However, Craswell argues that other economic factors might argue against expectation damages in a particular situation.

> For example, if both parties are risk-averse, the optimal allocation of risk will usually be achieved by a remedy that is somewhat less than the full expectation measure (although it will not necessarily equal the reliance measure). Similarly, the incentives to research the relevant contingencies prior to signing a contract may also be optimized by a remedy that is below the expectation measure— though for this effect, too, the optimal remedy could be either above or below the reliance measure. In other cases, if there is a significant probability that a

---

7. *Id.* at 61-62.
8. Richard Craswell, *Against Fuller and Perdue*, 67 U. Chi. L. Rev. 99, 109 (2000).

breach of contract will not be detected or will not be brought to trial, the optimal remedy could exceed the expectation measure.[9]

Applying Craswell's critique to the above example, if Jacob were risk-averse, then the potential that he would have to pay less than Nathan's full expectation damages would be adequate to deter Jacob's breach, and any additional damages might discourage Jacob's optimal breaching. Thus, the fact that Jacob might have to pay full expectation damages to Nathan might deter Jacob from accepting Jill's offer to buy his car for $4,000, even though at that level, it might be optimal for Jacob to sell to Jill instead. Moreover, the fact that Nathan might not receive full expectation damages might push him to perform more due diligence on Jacob's trustworthiness and possibly seek other potential sellers if Jacob were to breach.

Craswell also argues that expectation damages protect the property interest of a party in a contract.[10] That is because once parties have entered a contract, they each in effect have a property right to the benefits the other has promised under that contract. When one party breaches, that deprives the aggrieved party of its property right to the promised benefits. Thus, expectation damages fulfill the non-breaching party's property rights.

Regardless of the rationales for expectation damages you support, courts often award expectation damages. Thus, it is important to know how to calculate them.

Comprehension and Thought Questions:

1. Do you agree with Fuller and Perdue's justification for expectation damages? Why or why not?

2. Do you agree with Craswell's multifactor approach to expectation damages? Why or why not?

2. How to Calculate Expectation Damages

This subsection explains how to calculate expectation damages.

The Restatement states the general rule for calculating expectation damages as follows:

§ 347 Measure of Damages in General

Subject to the limitations stated in §§ 350–53, the injured party has a right to damages based on his expectation interest as measured by

(a) the loss in the value to him of the other party's performance caused by its failure or deficiency, plus

(b) any other loss, including incidental or consequential loss, caused by the breach, less

(c) any cost or other loss that he has avoided by not having to perform.

---

9. *Id.* at 109–10.
10. *Id.* at 122.

This general rule can be restated as a formula as follows:

Expectation Damages = loss in value + other losses − costs and losses avoided

Let us break down this formula into components and explain each one.

Loss in value represents the actual loss to the aggrieved party from the breaching party's defective or failed performance.

Where a party commits a breach that is so substantial that it justifies the aggrieved party in no longer performing—referred to in the Restatement as a total breach[11]—the aggrieved party's loss in value represents the benefits the party expected but did not receive under a contract. So, for example, if a homeowner contracts with a housecleaner to clean the homeowner's house for $100 and the housecleaner does not clean the house, that would be a total breach of the contract, thereby excusing the homeowner from performing. Here, the homeowner's loss in value is $100—the value of those services.

If it is the homeowner instead who breaches and fails to pay the housecleaner after services are rendered, the housecleaner's loss in value is the full $100 per the contract.

As another example, if a buyer contracts to buy a bike for $100 and the seller backs out in total breach of the contract, the buyer's net loss in value is the difference between $100 and the value of the bike. If the bike was actually worth $120, then the buyer has a net loss of $20. If the bike is only worth $100, then the buyer has not suffered any net loss. Of course, one of the challenges here is to determine what the bike's value actually is. The *Crabby's* case, discussed below, addresses that issue.

If it is the seller who backs out of buying the bike, the buyer gets the difference between $100 and the value of the bike (if any).

In the case of **partial breach**—meaning, a breach that is not so substantial as to permanently excuse the other party from performing the contract—the aggrieved party's loss is the difference in value between what the aggrieved party expected and what she received under the contract. Thus, if the housecleaner in the above example showed up but only cleaned half of the house in partial breach of the contract, the homeowner would be entitled to $50 in damages from the cleaner, as that represents the difference in value between what the homeowner was expecting (a clean house worth $100) and a half-clean house (presumably worth $50). If the homeowner breached and only paid the cleaner $50, the cleaner would be entitled to the remaining $50 as its loss in value.

---

11. Recall the discussion in Chapter 16 of where the other party's breach excuses a party from performing its obligations under a contract. As we discussed in that chapter, the Restatement uses the term "total breach" to refer to the type of breach that permanently excuses the aggrieved party from performing. Some courts instead use the term "material breach." Regardless of this difference, the important point is that this discussion is intended to describe the situation where the other party's breach permanently excuses the aggrieved party from performing.

Considering the other example, if the seller of the bike did not back out but instead delivered a bike in bad condition in breach of a warranty in the contract, then the buyer's loss in value, which the seller would have to pay, would be the difference between the purchase price ($100) and the value of the bike as delivered. On the other hand, if the buyer committed a partial breach by only paying part of the purchase price, then the seller's loss would be the remaining portion of the purchase price, which the buyer would have to pay.

Other losses refer to what are often described as incidental or consequential damages. Those damages indirectly result from a breach. They include, for example, other costs an aggrieved party incurs to avoid losses caused by a breach (called mitigation, which is discussed in Chapter 25), as well as injury to people and damage to property that resulted from the breach. One of the most significant components of "other losses" is lost profits from other business relations. Thus, for example, if the seller of the bike breached by failing to deliver the bike to the buyer, and as a result, the buyer lost out on $40 he would have earned as a bike courier delivering packages, then those $40 in lost profits are potentially recoverable by the buyer as other losses. Keep in mind that there are limits on the buyer's ability to recover those lost profits. Those limits are discussed in the next chapter.

Costs and losses avoided *decrease* an aggrieved party's recovery. Recall that an aggrieved party is excused from performing remaining obligations where a breaching party commits a total breach of a contract. Where that occurs, the aggrieved party benefits from not having to perform, and that party's damage recovery is reduced by that cost savings. An aggrieved party's damage recovery is also reduced by losses the aggrieved party avoided by mitigating its losses. An aggrieved party's recovery is also reduced by losses the party *could have* avoided had it taken reasonable steps to mitigate its losses, even if the party failed to take those steps. Using the example from above, the homeowner presumably could have contracted with someone else to clean the house, perhaps for the same contract price of $100 (suggesting that the damages suffered from the breach were close to zero). Again, Chapter 25 discusses the concept of mitigation.

To see how to calculate expectation damages under this entire formula, imagine that Bob Owner leases an apartment to Tia Tenant for $2,500 a month. The parties agree to a lease term of two years. After the first year, Tenant finds a location she likes better and notifies Owner that she is vacating the premises at the end of the 15th month of the lease. As a result of that early vacancy, Owner advertises the open apartment, spending $100 for that advertising. Owner finds someone else to rent the same premises for the last three months of the lease at a monthly rent of $2,000.

If no provision of the lease or law excused Tenant from performing, Tenant's termination of the lease before the end of the two-year term is a breach. Assuming Tenant refuses to pay Owner the remaining amount on the lease, Owner might sue Tenant for damages arising out of that breach.

In this situation, Owner lost his expectancy for nine months on the lease. Thus, his *loss in value* was $22,500 (Tenant's rent of $2,500 × 9 months). On the other hand, by finding a new tenant to mitigate his losses, Owner *avoided losing* $6,000 of that (the new rent of $2,000 × 3 months). Thus, Owner's actual net loss was $16,500 ($22,500 – $6,000).

In addition, Owner incurred $100 in advertising costs to find a new tenant as a result of Tenant's breach, which represents *other costs*. Therefore, Owner is entitled to $16,600 ($16,500 + $100) in damages. This amount will largely put Owner in the same position Owner would have been in had Tenant performed. Of course, this amount would not make Owner whole for any reputational loss he might suffer as a result of having a vacant apartment for six months. Parties are frequently not compensated for such unquantifiable losses stemming from breach.

If Owner saved money due to Tenant's breach, such as by not having to pay for utilities, those would further reduce Owner's recovery, as they would have been *other losses avoided*.

Remember this formula works regardless of which party breaches. Thus, for example, suppose Owner wrongfully evicted Tenant nine months early. As a result, Tenant had to find a new equivalent apartment to lease and ended up having to pay $3,000 a month. Ignoring for the moment any landlord-tenant laws that would protect Tenant in this situation, what would Tenant's damages be? Here, Tenant would not have suffered any loss in value, as she still had an apartment to live in. However, she had to pay an additional $4,500 ($500 × 9 months) for that benefit. So, Owner would owe Tenant $4,500. And, of course, if Tenant incurred any search costs to find the new apartment, those, too, would be recoverable by Tenant.

The following two cases exemplify how a court calculates expectation damages in the case of both a breached sales contract (*Crabby's*) and a breached service contract (*Lukaszewski*). As you read these cases, consider whether the courts' calculation of damages comport with the above formula.

Crabby's, Inc. v. Hamilton
Missouri Court of Appeals, Southern District
244 S.W.3d 209 (2008)

GARY W. LYNCH, Chief Judge.

Buyers under a contract for sale of real estate appeal the trial court's judgment awarding Seller damages due to Buyers' breach of that contract. We affirm.

. . .

FACTUAL AND PROCEDURAL BACKGROUND

Fred and Carolyn Billingsly are the shareholders of a Missouri corporation called Crabby's, Inc. ("Seller"), which owned and operated Crabby's restaurant in Joplin, Missouri, for several years. In 2003, Seller listed the restaurant and accompanying real property with Dee Kassab of Pro 100 Realty. The original listing price was $ 325,000, and Seller rejected an initial purchase offer for $ 275,000. James Hamilton, through his real estate agent Kent Eastman of Pro 100 Realty, then offered to purchase the property for $ 290,000, and this offer was accepted on May 17, 2003. Hamilton thereafter assigned his interest in the contract to Paragon Ventures, L.L.C. ("Paragon"), a business that Hamilton and Richard Worley set up to operate a restaurant. Hamilton also remained as an individual buyer on the contract. Hamilton and Paragon are hereinafter referred to collectively as "Buyers."

The contract contained the following financing contingency provision:

> This contract is contingent on Buyer's [sic] ability to obtain a conventional loan or loans in the amount of $ 232,000, payable over a period of not less than 15 years and bearing interest at a rate of not more than 5.5% per annum. Seller shall not be obligated to pay any of the expenses incidental to the obtaining of such loan or loans. Buyer shall use reasonable diligence in seeking to obtain such loan or loans, and if Buyer does not furnish seller with a copy of an effective written loan commitment within 30 days from the Effective Date, then this Contract shall automatically terminate and the Earnest Money shall be returned to Buyer.

Buyers never furnished Seller with a copy of an effective written loan commitment within 30 days of the effective date of the contract.

After entering into the contract on May 17, 2003, Buyers made arrangements for financing at the Bank of Joplin. Buyers applied for and were approved by the bank for a loan in the amount of $ 340,000.00. . . . Buyers did not apply for a loan with any other financial institution.

On June 10, 2003, Buyers' real estate agent was furnished a title insurance commitment from Jasper County Title showing sales tax liens attached to the property.

The contract originally specified a June 30, 2003 closing date. Following an inspection of the property, certain repairs were made, and an appraisal was performed as a requirement of the financing by Bank of Joplin. As a result of some appraisal requirements, the parties, on a date not disclosed by the record, entered into an agreement extending the closing date to July 14, 2003. Following this extension, the parties discussed other additional repairs and this led to an agreement whereby Buyers would receive a credit of $ 1,373.54 against the purchase price in lieu of additional repairs being made.

By a second extension agreement dated July 18, 2003, the closing date was again extended, this time to August 1, 2003. On that same date, the parties also entered into an agreement that allowed Buyers to take possession of the property prior to closing so that they could start cleaning it. Also around this same time period, Buyers made application for appropriate licenses to operate a restaurant on the property and had the utilities for the property transferred into Buyers' name.

Nothing in any of the subsequent agreements entered into between the parties altered any of the terms of the financing contingency contained in the original contract.

Immediately prior to July 30, 2003, all documentation was in place at the title company and ready for closing on August 1, 2003. Financing was in place from the Bank of Joplin. All parties were ready to close. The tax liens, mentioned in the title commitment provided to Buyers, were satisfied on the morning of August 1, as contemplated by the July 18 extension agreement between the parties, and Sellers obtained a certificate of "No Sales Tax Due" from the state. U.S. Bank (Seller's lender) had agreed to accept $ 266,000.00 to apply on Sellers' indebtedness and release its lien on the property. According to the closing statement prepared by the realtor, after payment of mortgages, real estate taxes, and liens, Seller was to receive a cash balance of $ 1,757.72 when the transaction closed.

On July 30, 2003, Buyers sent a letter to the realtor and Seller stating their intention not to close the transaction. In this letter, Buyers claimed "items, which we consider fixtures, have been taken from the premises." This missing property consisted of two used televisions, a couple of mirrors, a set of stereo speakers, and a computerized cash register. These items were not part of the list of personal property that was to be transferred in the sale, which was itemized and attached to the contract. This letter also specified the existence of the tax liens as an additional reason for Buyers' refusal to close the transaction as scheduled. Buyers made no mention of any inability to obtain satisfactory financing. Buyers failed to appear for closing as scheduled on August 1, 2003.

On August 5, 2003, Paragon offered to buy a building at 520 Main Street in Joplin, Missouri, for the purpose of establishing a restaurant. This offer was accepted by those sellers on August 6, 2003 and closed September 22, 2003. The purchase price for that property was $ 170,000.00.

After Buyers refused to close the sale with Seller on August 1, 2003, Seller's realtor continuously tried to sell the property. However, no offers were received until May of 2004, when J and A Cafe of Kansas, L.L.C., offered to purchase the property for $ 235,000.00. Sellers accepted this offer, and the transaction closed on July 15, 2004. Seller thereafter filed suit against Buyers for breach of contract. As part of its damages, Seller claimed the difference in sales price between Buyers' $ 290,000 contract price which should have closed on August 1, 2003, and the $ 235,000 price actually obtained when the property subsequently sold eleven and one-half months later on July 15, 2004. Seller also claimed real estate and personal property taxes, utilities, and mortgage interest accruing during that period as damages.

The trial court entered judgment in favor of Seller and against Buyers in the total amount of $ 95,547.30. Buyers timely appeal this judgment.

Additional facts will hereinafter be disclosed as needed to appropriately discuss Buyers' points relied on.

DISCUSSION

Buyers Waived the Financing Contingency

Buyers' first point claims that the trial court erred in finding they breached the contract, "because the contract terminated pursuant to its own financing contingency provision when [Buyers] could not obtain financing." Buyers initially argue that as a matter of law they could not have breached the contract by refusing to close on August 1, 2003, because by its explicit terms the contract automatically terminated when Buyers did not "furnish Seller with a copy of an effective written loan commitment," as required by the financing contingency provision in the contract. Buyers alternatively argue that if the trial court's judgment rests on an implicit finding that the contract had not automatically terminated under the financing contingency provision, then the trial court erred in interpreting the term 'reasonable diligence' and finding that the defendants had not used such diligence in finding a loan. Seller counters Buyers' point, contending that Buyers, by their conduct after entering into the contract, waived the financing contingency provisions in the contract.

A provision in a real estate contract that makes the contract contingent upon the buyer's obtaining financing is a condition. Because such conditions are meant to protect the buyer, they are a condition of the buyer's duty, but not a condition of the seller's duty under the contract. [I]n a real estate contract containing a contingency clause, upon the nonoccurrence of the condition (i.e., the buyers obtaining financing), the buyer is ipso facto excused from performance. However, the buyer can elect to waive the contingency and proceed with the contract under the rule that a party may waive any condition of a contract in that party's favor.

Parties to an agreement may by their oral agreement or their conduct waive the provisions of a contract between them. This doctrine applies equally to provisions requiring written communications.

Waiver of rights under a contract has been defined as follows:

> "Waiver" has been defined as an intentional relinquishment of a known right, on the question of which intention of the party charged with waiver is controlling and, if not shown by express declarations but implied by conduct, there must be a clear, unequivocal, and decisive act of party showing such purpose, and so consistent with intention to waive that no other reasonable explanation is possible.

The contract in the instant case defines its Effective Date as "the date and time of final acceptance on the signature page." Seller finally accepted the contract by signing the signature page on May 17, 2003. Thus, the effective date of the contract was May 17, 2003. The financing contingency in paragraph five of the contract provided: "if Buyer does not furnish Seller with a copy of an effective written loan commitment within 30 days from the Effective Date, then this Contract shall automatically terminate and the Earnest Money shall be returned to Buyer." This thirty-day time period expired on June 16, 2003.

The evidence is undisputed that Buyers did not furnish Seller with a copy of an effective written loan commitment within this time period. Therefore, by its explicit terms, the contract "automatically terminated" on June 16, 2003. Yet, Buyers' actions after that date were inconsistent with such a termination.

On July 17, 2003, a month after the contract supposedly automatically terminated, Buyers executed a written amendment to the contract extending the closing date from July 14, 2003 to August 1, 2003. This amendment additionally provided for the assignment of the contract to Paragon as a buyer in addition to Hamilton and for a $ 1,373.54 credit against the purchase price in exchange for Buyers releasing Seller from any obligation to perform any further repairs to the property. Finally this amendment provided: "**IT IS UNDERSTOOD BY ALL PARTIES THAT ALL OTHER TERMS AND CONDITIONS OF THE CONTRACT REMAIN UNCHANGED.**" Buyers entered into this amendment with the intention of closing the contract on August 1, 2003.

Also on July 17, 2003, Buyers executed an "Agreement for Possession Prior to Closing—Contract Rider," which granted them the right to take possession of the property as a tenant on July 21, 2003. This agreement provided that "this Rider shall become a part of the Contract" and "[p]ossession is for the sole purpose of cleaning only." To effectuate their possession, Buyers accepted a key to the property from Seller. During this time period, Buyers had the utilities to the property switched over and put in their name. Also during this time, and as late as July 25, 2003, Buyers were in the process of securing appropriate licenses to operate their restaurant on the property after closing.

Nothing in either the amendment or the agreement for possession purported to modify or extend any of the provisions of the financing contingency in the contract. Thus, by the specific provision of the amendment, in bold and all capital letters, the financing contingency "**REMAINED UNCHANGED.**" Furthermore, Buyers' real estate agent, Kent Eastman, testified that if the parties had extended the financing contingency, it should have been accomplished through a written amendment to the contract. Because the time period for Buyers to "furnish Seller with a copy of an effective written loan commitment" contained in the financing contingency had already expired as of July 17, 2003, and the amendment and agreement for possession signed by Buyers on that date did not otherwise extend that time period, the only reasonable explanation possible for and consistent with Buyers' signatures on these documents is their waiver of this contract requirement and the resulting automatic termination of the contract.

Nevertheless, Buyers argue that, regardless of their waiver of the automatic termination provision in the financing contingency, their inability to obtain financing on the terms otherwise set forth in the financing contingency relieved them of their obligations under the contract. However, Seller counters that Buyers' conduct evidenced a clear and unequivocal intention to waive all of the financing terms in the financing contingency.

Initially, there is no evidence in the record that Buyers ever made any application for a loan "in the amount of $ 232,000, payable over a period of not less than 15 years and bearing interest at a rate of not more than 5.5% per annum," as provided in the financing contingency. Chris Crouch, the loan officer at Bank of Joplin testified that Buyers applied for a loan in the amount of $ 340,000.00. Other than this one application, Buyers did not apply for any other loans. Failing to seek a loan on the terms set forth in the financing contingency evidences Buyers' failure to use reasonable diligence to obtain such financing as required by the contingency. We need not address that issue, however, because such action, coupled with Buyers' conduct on July 17, 2003, and thereafter, also evidences Buyers' waiver of the entire financing contingency. . . .

Thus, on July 17, 2003, Buyers: (1) had never applied for financing on the exact terms set forth in the financing contingency; (2) had secured and been approved for financing on terms that were acceptable to them even in the absence of a written loan commitment; (3) executed an amendment to the contract extending the closing date of the contract without any extension of the financing contingency and without providing a written loan commitment within the time period called for by the financing contingency; (4) executed an agreement to take possession of the property prior to closing; (5) accepted and used a key to effectuate that possession, and, thereafter (6) proceeded to have the utilities to the property transferred to them and to secure appropriate licensing to operate a restaurant on the property. . . .

All of these actions by Buyers are clear, unequivocal, and decisive acts showing Buyers' intentional relinquishment of the benefit of the entire financing contingency, and are so consistent with the intention to waive that contingency that no other reasonable explanation is possible. . . . Point I is denied.

The Trial Court's Determination of Fair Market Value is Supported by Substantial Evidence

The Buyers' second point claims that the trial court's judgment is not supported by substantial evidence of the fair market value of the property as of the date the contract was breached by the Buyers—August 1, 2003—in that Seller did not offer any direct evidence of the fair market value of the property on that date. Buyers contend that the actual sale price of $ 235,000.00 received by Seller on July 15, 2004, is not substantial evidence of the fair market value of the property on August 1, 2003 for two reasons: first, being eleven and one-half months after the relevant date, it is too remote in time; and, second, it was the product of a distress sale in that the Seller was compelled to sell the property in that transaction. We disagree with both contentions.

A seller's measure of damages for a buyer's breach of a contract for the sale of land with a structure on it is the difference between the purchase price and the fair market value of the property on the date of breach. That is, the measure of damages is the difference between the contract price and the fair market value of the property on the date the sale should have been completed. An essential element of the seller's case is proof of market value, and if he does resell within a reasonable time after the breach, the price obtained is some evidence of market value. Conflicts in the evidence concerning real estate values are for resolution by the fact finder. It is sufficient if the value set by the fact finder is "within the range" of the evidence.

While Buyers acknowledge that the sale price received by a seller from a subsequent sale of the property is substantial evidence to support a trial court's determination of the fair market value of a property as of the date of the breach if the subsequent sale occurs within a reasonable time after the date of the breach, they claim that a sale eleven and one-half months after the breach, as occurred in this case, is not within a reasonable period of time as a matter of law. Buyers cite no Missouri cases supporting their contention. They cite only *Chris v. Epstein* for the proposition that a resale of realty that occurred an entire year after the contract breach was not only not representative of fair market value a year earlier, but irrelevant.

Seller points us to *Hawkins v. Foster* where we held that the price obtained in a subsequent sale which occurred a little over eleven and one-half months after the date of the buyer's breach of a real estate contract supported an award of damages in favor of the seller based upon the fair market value of the property. Buyers have failed to distinguish how the time period approved by us in Hawkins materially differs from the essentially same time period in the instant case. Thus, Buyers have not convinced us that we should depart from our holding in Hawkins. Based upon that holding, the subsequent sale by Seller in the case at bar on July 15, 2004, occurred within a reasonable time after the date of Buyers' breach of the contract, such that it provided substantial evidence to support the trial court's determination of the fair market value of the property on the date of Buyer's breach of the contract.

Buyers next contend that the subsequent sale price received by Seller is not substantial evidence of the fair market value of the property as of the date of the breach because the subsequent sale was a distress sale in that Seller was "compelled" to sell the property. Buyers claim that because fair market value is defined as "the price which property will bring when it is offered for sale by an owner who is willing but under no compulsion to sell and is bought by a buyer who is willing or desires to purchase but is not compelled to do so[,]", and because Seller was compelled to sell the property, then the sale price could not, by definition, reflect the fair market value of the property. The flaw in Buyers' argument is that the evidence they cite in support of their claim does not exist.

Buyers direct us to the testimony of Carolyn Billingsly, one of Seller's owners, to support their contention. Buyers' trial counsel asked Billingsly: "And so, you were compelled to sell it, I mean, you wanted to sell it bad; true?" She responded: "We did." Counsel's question was a compound question—"you were compelled to sell it" and "you wanted to sell it bad." The wording of her response—"We did"—corresponded to the latter question and not the former. If she had been responding to the first question, her answer would have been in the form "We were." Thus, while Billingsly's testimony supports that Seller wanted badly to sell the property at the time of the subsequent sale, it does not support that Seller was compelled to do so.

Buyers fail to cite to any authority for the proposition that a sale in which the seller is highly motivated or badly wants to sell, as opposed to being compelled to sell, eliminates that sale from being considered as a fair market value sale of the property. Their reliance on *Carter* is misplaced. In *Carter*, the sale was made pursuant to a plan of liquidation which had to be completed within a one-year period under a provision of the tax code, and, in addition, the property was under the threat of condemnation which would have compelled a forced sale. While Seller here was financially motivated to sell and was highly desirous of selling the property at the time of the subsequent sale, it was not compelled to sell as was the seller in Carter. Point II is denied.

DECISION

The trial court's judgment is affirmed.

Understanding the Case:

1. *Assignment of Rights Under Contract:* While Hamilton was the original buyer of the real estate, he "assigned his interest in the contract to Paragon Ventures, L.L.C. ("Paragon"), a business that Hamilton and Richard Worley set up to operate a restaurant." As you will learn in Chapter 29, what this means is that Paragon, as an assignee of Hamilton's rights, could enforce Crabby's obligations under the contract. By default, the law permits such an assignment of rights unless a contract precludes it. Here, presumably, the contract did not preclude this assignment.

2. *Delegation of Duties Under Contract:* Hamilton also delegated his duties under the contract to Paragon. As Chapter 29 discusses, that means that Paragon was obligated to pay for the real estate, once the buyer's conditions in the contract were satisfied (or, as happened in the case, were waived). By default, a party may delegate his duties under a contract unless either the contract precludes it or the duties are of a type that are personal in nature. Typically, by default a party may not delegate a duty to pay money. That is because a party could avoid its responsibility to pay money by delegating that duty to a third party who does not have enough assets to pay amounts owed. Here, while the court did not discuss it, presumably the contract permitted Hamilton to delegate his duties to Paragon.

3. *Hamilton Remains Bound:* The court noted that Hamilton also remained as an individual buyer on the contract. Thus, despite the fact that Paragon became bound to perform Hamilton's obligations under the contract, Hamilton also remained bound to perform those obligations. Hamilton likely remained obligated because, as will be discussed in Chapter 29, a party who delegates duties to a third party remains obligated for those duties unless the non-delegating party agrees to release the delegating party from his obligation. In the context of this case, that means that to release Hamilton from his obligations as buyer, Crabby's would have had to agree to that release. Presumably, Crabby's declined to release Hamilton because Paragon was so new of an entity and probably did not have a lot of assets with which to pay the purchase price.

Comprehension & Thought Questions:

1. Why did Paragon (the buyer) not want to buy Crabby's (the seller's) real estate?

2. What was Paragon's main argument as to why it did not have an obligation to buy that real estate?

3. Why did the contract not automatically terminate when Paragon did not furnish a copy of the bank's loan commitment?

4. Why was Paragon not excused from buying the property when it did not obtain a loan in the amount specified in the contract?

5. What formula did the court use to calculate Crabby's damages due to Paragon's breach?

6. Why did the court admit (and not exclude) evidence of the actual sales price for the property given that it sold 11½ months later?

7. Did the court's calculation of damages make Crabby's whole for the damages it suffered as a result of Paragon's breach? As you think about this, remember that in general, a party must pay its own costs of litigation.

8. Paragon argued that the actual sales price was not evidence of the value of the real estate on the date of breach because it was a distress sale. Can you identify facts from the case not discussed by the court that argue in favor of this not being a distress sale?

Hypothetical Variations:

1. What if Paragon continually tried to get a loan "in the amount of $232,000, payable over a period of not less than 15 years and bearing interest at a rate of not more than 5.5 percent per annum," per the contract, but could not find a loan on those terms at a rate of less than 5.75 percent, and for that reason, decided to not buy the property? *not breach; failure of condition*

2. What if in the period between Paragon's breach and Crabby's sale of its real estate, there had been a collapse in the real estate market in the United

States akin to what happened in 2007 and 2008 during the housing crisis. Do you think that that would have affected the court's calculation of damages? Should it?

3. What if Crabby's breached instead of Paragon because there had been another buyer willing to pay $310,000 for the property? How would the court likely have calculated damages? Do you think damages are the appropriate remedy in this situation?

4. What if Crabby's breached instead of Paragon because it decided it wanted to stay at the premises and, thus, decided to not sell the real estate? How would the court likely have calculated damages? Do you think damages are the appropriate remedy in this situation?

Handicapped Children's Education Board of Sheboygan County v. Lukaszewski
Supreme Court of Wisconsin
332 N.W.2d 774 (1983)

CALLOW, Justice.

This review arises out of an unpublished decision of the court of appeals which affirmed in part and reversed in part a judgment of the Ozaukee county circuit court, Judge Warren A. Grady.

In January of 1978 the Handicapped Children's Education Board (the Board) hired Elaine Lukaszewski to serve as a speech and language therapist for the spring term. Lukaszewski was assigned to the Lightfoot School in Sheboygan Falls which was approximately 45 miles from her home in Mequon. Rather than move, she commuted to work each day. During the 1978 spring term, the Board offered Lukaszewski a contract to continue in her present position at Lightfoot School for the 1978–79 school year. The contract called for an annual salary of $10,760. Lukaszewski accepted.

In August of 1978, prior to the beginning of the school year, Lukaszewski was offered a position by the Wee Care Day Care Center which was located not far from her home in Mequon. The job paid an annual salary of $13,000. After deciding to accept this offer, Lukaszewski notified Thomas Morrelle, the Board's director of special education, that she intended to resign from her position at the Lightfoot School. Morrelle told her to submit a letter of resignation for consideration by the Board. She did so, and the matter was discussed at a meeting of the Board on August 21, 1978. The Board refused to release Lukaszewski from her contract. On August 24, 1978, the Board's attorney sent a letter to Lukaszewski directing her to return to work. The attorney sent a second letter to the Wee Care Day Care Center stating that the Board would take legal action if the Center interfered with Lukaszewski's performance of her contractual obligations at the Lightfoot School. A copy of this letter was sent to the Department of Public Instruction.

Lukaszewski left the Wee Care Day Care Center and returned to Lightfoot School for the 1978 fall term. She resented the actions of the Board, however, and retained misgivings about her job. On September 8, 1978, she discussed her feelings with Morrelle. After this meeting Lukaszewski felt quite upset about the situation. She called her doctor to make an appointment for that afternoon and subsequently left the school.

Dr. Ashok Chatterjee examined Lukaszewski and found her blood pressure to be high. Lukaszewski asked Dr. Chatterjee to write a letter explaining his medical findings and the advice he had given her. In a letter dated September 11, 1978, Dr. Chatterjee indicated that Lukaszewski had a hypertension problem dating back to 1976. He reported that on the day he examined Lukaszewski she appeared agitated, nervous, and had blood pressure readings up to 180/100. It was his opinion that, although she took hypotensive drugs, her medical condition would not improve unless the situation which caused the problem was removed. He further opined that it would be dangerous for her to drive long distances in her agitated state.

Lukaszewski did not return to work after leaving on September 8, 1978. She submitted a letter of resignation dated September 13, 1978, in which she wrote:

> "I enclose a copy of the doctor's statement concerning my health. On the basis of it, I must resign. I am unwilling to jeopardize my health and I am also unwilling to become involved in an accident. For these reasons, I tender my resignation."

A short time later Lukaszewski reapplied for and obtained employment at the Wee Care Day Care Center.

After Lukaszewski left, the Board immediately began looking for a replacement. Only one qualified person applied for the position. Although this applicant had less of an educational background than Lukaszewski, she had more teaching experience. Under the salary schedule agreed upon by the Board and the teachers' union, this applicant would have to be paid $1,026.64 more per year than Lukaszewski. Having no alternative, the Board hired the applicant at the higher salary.

In December of 1978 the Board initiated an action against Lukaszewski for breach of contract. The Board alleged that, as a result of the breach, it suffered damage in the amount of the additional compensation it was required to pay Lukaszewski's replacement for the 1978–79 school year ($1,026.64). A trial was held before the court. The trial court ruled that Lukaszewski had breached her contract and awarded the Board $1,249.14 in damages ($1,026.64 for breach of contract and $222.50 for costs).

Lukaszewski appealed. The court of appeals affirmed the circuit court's determination that Lukaszewski breached her contract. However, the appellate court reversed the circuit court's damage award, reasoning that, although the Board had to pay more for Lukaszewski's replacement, by its own standards it obtained a proportionately more valuable teacher. Therefore, the court of appeals held that the Board suffered no damage from the breach. We granted the Board's petition for review.

There are two issues presented on this review: (1) whether Lukaszewski breached her employment contract with the Board; and (2) if she did breach her contract, whether the Board suffered recoverable damages therefrom.

I.

It is undisputed that Lukaszewski resigned before her contract with the Board expired. The only question is whether her resignation was somehow justified. Lukaszewski argues that, because she resigned for health reasons, the trial court erred in finding a breach of contract. According to Lukaszewski, the uncontroverted evidence at trial established that her employment with the Board endangered her health. Therefore, her failure to fulfill her obligation under the employment contract was excused. . . .

In order to excuse Lukaszewski's nonperformance, the trial court would had to have made a factual finding that she resigned for health reasons. The oral decision and supplemental written decision of the trial court indicate that it found otherwise. . . .

We conclude that the trial court's findings of fact are not against the great weight and clear preponderance of the evidence and, therefore, must be upheld. Accordingly, we affirm that portion of the court of appeals' decision which affirmed the circuit court's determination that Lukaszewski breached her employment contract.

II.

This court has long held that an employer may recover damages from an employee who has failed to perform an employment contract. Damages in breach of contract cases are ordinarily measured by the expectations of the parties. The nonbreaching party is entitled to full compensation for the loss of his or her bargain—that is, losses necessarily flowing from the breach which are proven to a reasonable certainty and were within contemplation of the parties when the contract was made. Thus damages for breach of an employment contract include the cost of obtaining other services equivalent to that promised but not performed, plus any foreseeable consequential damages.

In the instant case it is undisputed that, as a result of the breach, the Board hired a replacement at a salary exceeding what it had agreed to pay Lukaszewski. There is no question that this additional cost ($1,026.64) necessarily flowed from the breach and was within the contemplation of the parties when the contract was made. Lukaszewski argues and the court of appeals held, however, that the Board was not damaged by this expense. The amount a teacher is paid is determined by a salary schedule agreed upon by the teachers' union and the Board. The more education and experience a teacher has the greater her salary will be. Presumably, then, the amount of compensation a teacher receives reflects her value to the Board. Lukaszewski argues that the Board suffered no net loss because, while it had to pay more for the replacement, it received the services of a proportionately more valuable teacher. Accordingly, she maintains that the Board is not entitled to damages because an award would place it in a better position than if the contract had been performed.

We disagree. Lukaszewski and the court of appeals improperly focus on the objective value of the services the Board received rather than that for which it had bargained. Damages for breach of contract are measured by the expectations of the parties. The Board expected to receive the services of a speech therapist with Lukaszewski's education and experience at the salary agreed upon. It neither expected nor wanted a more experienced therapist who had to be paid an additional $1,026.64 per year. Lukaszewski's breach forced the Board to hire the replacement and, in turn, to pay a higher salary. Therefore, the Board lost the benefit of its bargain. Any additional value the Board may have received from the replacement's greater experience was imposed upon it and thus cannot be characterized as a benefit. We conclude that the Board suffered damages for the loss of its bargain in the amount of additional compensation it was required to pay Lukaszewski's replacement.

This is not to say that an employer who is injured by an employee's breach of contract is free to hire the most qualified and expensive replacement and then recover the difference between the salary paid and the contract salary. An injured party must take all reasonable steps to mitigate damages. Therefore, the employer must attempt to obtain equivalent services at the lowest possible cost. In the instant case the Board acted reasonably in hiring Lukaszewski's replacement even though she commanded a higher salary. Upon Lukaszewski's breach, the Board immediately took steps to locate a replacement. Only one qualified person applied for the position. Having no alternative, the Board hired this applicant. Thus the Board properly mitigated its damages by hiring the least expensive, qualified replacement available.

We hold that the Board is entitled to have the benefit of its bargain restored. Therefore, we reverse that portion of the court of appeals' decision which reversed the trial court's damage award.

The decision of the court of appeals is affirmed in part and reversed in part.

DAY, Justice (dissenting).

I dissent. The majority opinion correctly states, "The only question is whether her resignation is somehow justified." I would hold that it was.

Elaine Lukaszewski left her employment with the school board. She suffered from high blood pressure and had been treated for several years by her physician for the condition. She claimed her hypertension increased due to stress caused when the Board refused to cancel her teaching contract. Stress can cause a precipitous rise in blood pressure. High blood pressure can bring on damage to other organs of the body.

. . .

It seems clear from the trial judge's comments that if he had found her physical condition had been caused by the Board's "harassment," he would have let her out of the contract. This is the only logical conclusion from the statement by the trial judge that, "The Court finds that the defendant's medical excuse was a result of the stress condition she had created by an attempted repudiation of her contract, and was not the product of any unsubstantiated, so-called, harassment [sic] by the plaintiff's board."

In either instance, whether "caused" by the Board or "self induced" because of her gnawing feeling of being unfairly treated, the objective symptoms would be the same.

Either, in my opinion, should justify termination of the contract where the physical symptoms are medically certifiable as they admittedly are here. . . .

If the trial court had found that she quit merely for the better job and *not* because of her health problems brought on by the high blood pressure, this would be an entirely different case. However, that is *not* what the trial court found in my opinion. The trial court found her medical problems were self induced and concluded they were therefore unworthy of consideration.

I would reverse the court of appeals decision that held she breached her contract.

Because I would hold that on this record there was no breach, I would not reach the damage question.

Understanding the Case:

1. *Who Is the Plaintiff?:* Wisconsin statutes have historically required that when public school districts hire teachers to fill vacant positions, the school board must contract directly with the teacher.[12] However, where the need arises, Wisconsin county boards, instead of the school boards, occasionally employ schoolteachers. This circumstance was present during the 1970s after the Wisconsin legislature granted Handicapped Children Education Boards advisory and policy-making functions associated with special education programs and services in some counties.[13] As a result of this legislative power, many county Handicapped Education Boards had authority to establish their own schools and hire teachers for the schools within their respective counties.[14]

---

12. Wis. Stat. § 118.21 (2015-16) ("The school board shall contract in writing with qualified teachers. . . .").

13. 77 Op. Att'y Gen. 196, 196 (1988). (county personnel and procurement ordinances, and other similar ordinances that regulate administration of county government generally, apply to the operation of such county special education programs and services).

14. *See id.* at 196-97.

One county board that used its authority to operate a handicapped school was the Handicapped Children's Education Board of Sheboygan County, which operated the Lightfoot School in Sheboygan Falls Wisconsin.[15]

2. *Employment for Term Versus At-Will:* Most employees are employed at-will. That means the employer or employee can terminate the employee's employment at any time with or without cause or notice, and such termination does not amount to a breach. However, some employment relationships are for a term, such as in *Lukaszewski.* In that situation, unless the contract otherwise provides or there is a contract law excuse, a termination of the employee's employment by either the employer or the employee before the end of the term is a breach. Keep in mind that even where employment is at-will, there are some instances where an employer's termination of that employee amounts to a breach, such as where the employer terminates an employee's employment with the purpose of depriving the employee of accrued benefits.[16]

Comprehension and Thought Questions:

1. What duty did Lukaszewski breach in her contract with the board?

2. On what basis did Lukaszewski argue that she was excused from performing her duties under her contract with the board?

3. Did the court excuse Lukaszewski from performing her duties under that contract? Do you think she should have been excused?

4. What did the board do to mitigate the damages it suffered as a result of Lukaszewski's breach?

5. Why was the board entitled to the extra cost it incurred in hiring a replacement teacher, as the board received a more experienced teacher?

6. Would any measure of damages have allowed the board to recover the extra compensation Lukaszewski received by switching employment to the Wee Care Day Care Center? Should the board be able to recover that extra compensation?

7. On what basis did the dissent disagree with the majority? Which opinion do you find more persuasive on that point—the majority or dissent?

Hypothetical Variations:

1. What if the board had been unable to hire a replacement teacher for the year and, as a result, had to send several children to other daycares, leading to losses of $10,000?

[handwritten:] ↳ consequential damage

---

15. *See* Handicapped Children's Educ. Bd. of Sheboygan Cty. v. Lukaszewski, 332 N.W.2d 774, 775 (Wis. 1983).

16. Restatement of Employment Law § 2.07 (2006).

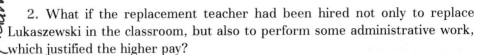

2. What if the replacement teacher had been hired not only to replace Lukaszewski in the classroom, but also to perform some administrative work, which justified the higher pay?

3. What if Lukaszewski was employed at-will instead of for a term?

4. What if it had been the board who had breached, by firing Lukaszewski six months into her one-year term. As a result, Lukaszewski switched her employment to the Wee Care Day Care Center. What would Lukaszewski's damages have been?

PRACTICE PROBLEM 24-1

Bob Jones is a general contractor hired to install a new indoor adventure park for Racing Adventures Inc. The adventure park will include indoor rides, go-kart racing on an indoor track, and an arcade. The parties signed a written document setting out the terms of their contract. Under those terms, Jones will install Racing Adventures' rides, go-kart racing track, and arcade within the next year. The total price for this work is $100,000 (of which $20,000 is Jones's profit, and the remainder of which covered Jones's labor and materials costs). The parties agreed that Racing Adventures will pay half of the contract amount when the work is half done, and the rest when the work is completed.

Six months into the contract, Jones (along with his employees) installed the go-kart racing track and arcade, which was roughly half of the work. At that time, Jones submitted an invoice to Racing Adventures for $50,000. As of that time, Jones had additionally incurred $2,000 materials that had not yet been incorporated into the project and which were not covered by the first $50,000 invoice. However, before Racing Adventures paid Jones the invoiced amount, and before Jones installed the indoor rides, Racing Adventures' President resigned and a new President took over. The new President decided to abandon the indoor adventure park. Thus, the President notified Jones to immediately stop work.

After Racing Adventures notified Jones to stop work (which termination was not permitted by the contract), Jones immediately redirected his employees to another project. Jones had to spend an additional $3,000 in licensing and bonding fees to become qualified to work on the new project. Of the $2,000 worth of materials already purchased and not included in the initial invoice sent to Racing Adventures, Jones was able to use $1,000 of those on the other job.

1. If Jones were to submit a final invoice to Racing Adventures for everything Racing Adventures owed Jones, determined using the expectation damages calculation, what amount would Jones seek and why? As you consider this question, break down each component of such an award and explain why Racing Adventures would likely have to pay that amount.

2. If you were Jones's lawyer and Jones asked you to draft a cover letter to send to Racing Adventures with the final invoice, what would you have Jones say in that letter? What would be the tone of that letter?

While *Crabby's* and *Lukaszewski* exemplify the typical way in which expectation damages are calculated, there are some circumstances that call for different calculation techniques.

One instance involves a contractor who substantially completes the construction of a building but then breaches. In that circumstance, a court can, as an alternative to the loss-in-value measure of damages, order the contractor to pay **cost-to-complete damages.**[17] It might award such a measure of damages where typical loss-in-value damages would not be fair or just. However, a court might not award cost-to-complete damages where they would be grossly disproportionate to the loss in value.

The famous *Jacobs & Youngs* case exemplifies the circumstance where a court might decline to order the contractor to pay cost-to-complete damages—or in that case, the amount to be offset from the amount owed to the contractor where the contractor breached. In that case, a contractor had promised to build a home for a homeowner according to specifications. One of the specifications stated that "[a]ll wrought-iron pipe must be well galvanized, lap welded pipe of the grade known as 'standard pipe' of Reading manufacture."[18] After the contractor finished the home, the homeowner learned that the contractor had not used pipe manufactured by Reading. Instead, he had used pipe equivalent to Reading pipe in quality, appearance, market value, and cost. Because the contractor had not followed the contract's specifications (and likely because the owner was frustrated by the contractor's delays), the homeowner refused to pay the remaining $3,483 he owed to the contractor. The contractor sued to recover this final payment.

The Court of Appeals of New York held that the divergence from the contract was insignificant in relation to the entire project. As the court stated, "[t]he courts never say that one who makes a contract fills the measure of his duty by less than full performance. They do say, however, that an omission, both trivial and innocent, will sometimes be atoned for by allowance of the resulting damage, and will not always be the breach of a condition to be followed by a forfeiture."[19] In other words, while a party who fails to perform the contract according to its term breaches, an innocent, trivial breach will be accounted for not by excusing the paying party from its payment obligation, consistent with the material in Chapter 16 on material breach, but by addressing the breach in the measure of damages. In doing so, the court calculated the homeowner's damages to be offset from the remaining amounts owed to the contractor not using cost to complete, which would have been substantial, but instead the loss in value in the house due to the installation of the non-Reading pipe. Because the installed pipe was equivalent to Reading

---

17. *See, e.g.*, Spence v. Ham, 57 N.E. 412, 413 (N.Y. 1900).
18. Jacobs & Youngs, Inc. v. Kent, 129 N.E. 889, 890 (N.Y. 1921).
19. *Id.*

pipe, there was no difference in value and no damages to offset from amounts owing to the contractor.

Consistent with *Jacobs & Youngs*, the Restatement permits cost-to-complete damages in the case of defective construction. However, it provides that such cost-to-complete measure is only to be used where the loss in value to the aggrieved party cannot be calculated with reasonable certainty, and only where the cost to complete "is not clearly disproportionate to the probable loss in value to him [the aggrieved party]."[20]

PRACTICE PROBLEM 24-2

Review the facts from Practice Problem 24-1. For purposes of this question, assume that Racing Adventures did not terminate the contract early, and that Jones finished his work under the contract. However, Jones only made the go-kart track 17 feet wide, in contravention of the contract specifications, which required the track to be at least 18 feet wide. When Racing Adventures demanded that Jones widen the track per the specifications, Jones responded that the extra foot of width would not impact the functioning of the go-kart track. Racing Adventures, on the other hand, thought it would deter some younger drivers, who would not want to make as much contact with other go-karts and who would thus prefer a wider track. Thus, Racing Adventures hired another contractor to widen the track. Because the asphalt from the track had already been poured and sealed, the safety guard rails installed, and the necessary buffer zone around the track measured out exactly, it cost Racing Adventures $50,000 to widen the track the extra foot. Once the work was complete, Racing Adventures sent an invoice to your client Jones for this work.

1. Advise Jones, your client, why you think Racing Adventures believes it is entitled to $50,000 from Jones. In other words, what measure of damages is Racing Adventures using in seeking to recover this additional expense?

2. If Racing Adventures were to sue Jones and prove that Jones breached the contract, which alternative damages calculation would you argue for in court and what arguments would you make in support of that measure of damages?

D.   RELIANCE DAMAGES

If you recall the discussion of the justifications for expectation damages in Section A, Professors Fuller and Perdue saw expectation damages as a way to

---

20. Restatement (Second) of Contracts § 348 (1981).

compensate an aggrieved party for all losses resulting from the other party's breach, including future lost opportunities. In contrast, reliance damages for breach of contract only cover costs incurred by a party in actual reliance on the other party's promises in that contract. Thus, reliance damages cover a party's costs incurred in *preparing to perform* under a contract and in *performing* that contract. Moreover, a party can recover "indirect" reliance damages, which cover costs incurred in preparing to perform collateral—meaning other related—contracts. Reliance damages do not, however, compensate an aggrieved party for opportunities it lost on account of having relied on the other party's promise. Thus, a party cannot collect profits it lost from its business as a result of the counterparty's breach.

If reliance damages do not include lost profits and therefore are typically less than expectation damages, why would a party ever seek to recover reliance damages instead of expectation damages? There are two situations where a party commonly seeks reliance damages instead of expectation damages: the first relates to legal limits on the recovery of damages, and the second relates to unprofitable contracts.

As you will study in further detail in Chapter 25, a party can only recover damages that are *reasonably foreseeable* as a probable result of a breach, evaluated at the time of contracting. In addition, a party can only recover damages that are calculable with reasonable certainty. These limits often prevent a party from recovering full expectation damages. So, for example, if a party cannot prove with reasonable certainty what profits it lost due to a counterparty's breach of contract, it cannot recover those lost profits even though, in theory, those lost profits are recoverable as expectation damages.

These limits are generally not barriers to a party's recovery of reliance damages, however. That is because it is fairly easy to foresee which preparation and performance actions a party actually took in reliance on a promise. It is also easier to calculate out-of-pocket costs with reasonable certainty by looking at a party's actual expenditures.

The second situation where a party might seek reliance damages instead of expectation damages is where the party enters a contract in which it will lose money. While not common, sometimes a party enters an unprofitable contract to establish a rapport with a counterparty, in the hopes of laying a foundation for future profitable contracts. Or a party might enter an unprofitable contract where it makes incorrect financial assumptions or a calculation error, yet that error does not excuse the party from performing. Either way, if the party who will lose money on the contract sues the counterparty for breach and wins, it would not be able to recover its own lost profits on that contract, as it had none. In that situation, it might be better for that party to instead seek to recover its reliance damages, as those would at least include the party's costs incurred to perform as well as its costs in preparing to perform.

Here, though, any recovery would be reduced by the aggrieved party's expected loss on the contract. That is because courts generally do not permit reliance damages to exceed expectation damages. The burden is on the breaching party to prove what loss the aggrieved party would have incurred under the contract. But that recovery might still exceed what the aggrieved party would receive as expectation damages.

Keep in mind that this discussion addresses reliance damages that are recoverable for breach of a bargained-for contract. It does not refer to reliance damages under promissory estoppel. While this material is undoubtedly useful in calculating damages for a breached promise under promissory estoppel, the focus here is on the reliance damage remedy for breach of a bargained-for contract.

The following case exemplifies how and why a court might award a party reliance damages instead of expectation damages for breach of contract. As you read this case, ask yourself why the court awarded reliance damages instead of expectation damages, and what damages the employee missed out on as a result of not receiving expectation damages.

Reimer v. Badger Wholesale Co.
Court of Appeals of Wisconsin
433 N.W.2d 592 (1988)

SCOTT, Chief Judge.

Badger Wholesale Company, Inc. (Badger), appeals from a judgment awarding its former employee, Dennis Reimer, $16,500 on a breach of contract claim. Badger argues that Reimer was an employee-at-will and therefore could not bring a breach of contract claim after his termination. In the alternative, Badger argues that the measure of damages was incorrect. It also appeals an order which denied its motion for a new trial.

We conclude that the contractual breach was unrelated to the term or duration of employment; therefore, a breach of contract claim will lie. Further, we conclude that the measure of damages was correct; however, credible evidence, in the light most favorable to Reimer, only supports a judgment of $16,245.81. We therefore modify the judgment to reflect this amount. The order denying the motion for a new trial is affirmed.

FACTS

We state the facts in the light most favorable to the jury verdict. Reimer worked in Missouri as a wholesale foods salesperson. Following a death in the family in Wisconsin, Reimer considered moving back to the area if he received an offer of suitable employment.

Over the course of several meetings between Badger representatives and Reimer, an agreement evolved whereby Reimer would receive a minimum wage base salary plus commission. He also was offered an exclusive territory in the Neenah-Menasha area and an opportunity to expand Badger's business into the Oshkosh area. Badger representatives further told Reimer that he would have a ninety-day trial period to make $10,000 in sales. Based on Reimer's experience, he was told that he could expect to earn between $20,000 and $25,000 a year.

After accepting Badger's offer, Reimer quit his previous employment where he earned $350 per week without commission. He and his family incurred moving expenses of slightly over $2000.

After beginning work for Badger, Reimer discovered that other sales representatives already handled twenty-six accounts in the Neenah-Menasha area. When he pressed Badger about opening up territory near Oshkosh, it established a minimum number of sales, under which it would not make deliveries, forcing Reimer to deliver goods himself.

Badger terminated Reimer after seventeen and a half working days for lack of sales. Reimer had made thirteen sales in his brief employ, considered by an expert witness to be very good for a salesperson in new territory.

Reimer brought suit against Badger, alleging breach of contract, misrepresentation, promissory estoppel and wrongful dismissal. The last two causes of action were dismissed on Badger's motion for summary judgment. Prior to submission of the case to the jury, Reimer elected to proceed on the contract theory.

A special verdict was submitted which asked: (1) if there was a contract; (2) if it had been breached; and (3) if so, what were appropriate damages. The first question was answered by the court in the affirmative. The jury found a breach and awarded $16,500 in damages. Badger appealed.

BREACH OF CONTRACT

Badger argues that Reimer was an employee-at-will under *Brockmeyer v. Dun & Bradstreet*. Therefore, it reasons that Reimer could be discharged for any reason or no reason at all without Badger incurring liability. Reimer responds by pointing out that the breaches involved went beyond the premature termination of his employment. Rather, Reimer argues that the backbone of his claim was the failure of Badger to provide him with an exclusive territory in Neenah-Menasha or a reasonable opportunity to expand the Oshkosh area.

First, we note that in dismissing Reimer's wrongful discharge claim the trial court made a finding that this was an employment-at-will situation. This fact does not, however, relieve Badger of its responsibility for any and all promises made to Reimer as a prospective employee.

The language of *Yanta* cannot be read as broadly as Badger suggests. "[A]n employer may discharge [an at-will employee] for any reason *without incurring liability therefor*". In other words, the at-will doctrine protects the employer from liability *for the termination*. Here, breaches were committed by Badger prior to Reimer's termination; the termination was merely one of the results brought about by the previous breaches.

Reimer alleged and proved that Badger's failure to provide him with the promised exclusive territory and opportunity for expansion prevented him from doing his job to the expectations of himself and others. As a result, he was terminated for these "poor sales." Because Reimer's claim was not dependent on his status as an at-will employee or otherwise, this was a legitimate breach of contract case.

DAMAGES

The jury awarded $16,500 to Reimer as damages on the breach of contract claim. A summary of damages prepared by Reimer as an exhibit broke down damages as follows:

Loss of income while employed at Badger (Difference between salary at Badger and previous salary in Missouri)	$ 1,188.00
Loss of income following termination until time of trial (Based on salary in Missouri)	12,950.00
Moving expenses	2,107.81
Incidental and consequential damage	5,000.00
TOTAL	$21,245.81

We take note that the damages award approximated Reimer's summary with the exception of the incidental and consequential damages.

Badger argues that the damages should be limited to what Reimer would have earned at Badger had he stayed there for the term of his employment—ninety days. It relies on *Wassenaar v. Panos*, which states:

> According to black-letter law, when an employee is wrongfully discharged, damages are the salary the employee would have received during the unexpired term of the contract plus the expenses of securing other employment reduced by the income which he or she has earned, will earn, or could with reasonable diligence earn, during the unexpired term.

The fallacy in Badger's argument is that, as previously noted, this is not a wrongful discharge case but a breach of contract action. Remedies for breach of contract protect three interests: the expectation interest, the reliance interest, and the restitution interest. We consider the damages proven by Reimer to be based upon his reliance interest.

Remedies for injury to a reliance interest are defined as being reimbursed for loss caused by reliance on the contract by being put in as good a position as he would have been in had the contract not been made. Had the contract between Reimer and Badger not been made, he would not have had moving expenses and would still be employed in Missouri. These reliance damages are particularly appropriate where proof of the expectation interest, i.e., profit, is uncertain. Reimer's profit would have been difficult to determine because of his short sales history with Badger.

Badger also disputes the calculation of damages in that it is based on the time period between Reimer's termination and the date of trial. Our review of the record reveals no attempt by Badger to prove that Reimer failed to mitigate his damages with respect to seeking or obtaining employment prior to trial. If the damages here reflected Reimer's expectation interest, there would be a concern about the length of time for which damages would be awarded, particularly since this was an at-will employment situation. However, Reimer chose to present his reliance interest as the measure of damages. As a result, the relevant inquiry, as contained in the Restatement cited earlier, is what sum of money would put Reimer in the position he would have been had the contract not been made.

Badger, at trial and on appeal, chose to argue only that damages should be limited to ninety days of salary at Badger's rate. The failure to argue the alternative measure of damages proposed by Reimer and present a mitigation-based defense left the jury, like us, in an evidentiary vacuum. In the absence of a proposal for a different cutoff date for damages, we cannot say that using the date of trial created an improper measure of damages.

MOTION FOR NEW TRIAL

Badger moved for a new trial on the bases that the verdict was contrary to the law of damages in Wisconsin and that the damages were excessive. We have already dealt with the first ground alleged and concluded that the measure of damages was appropriate.

If there is any credible evidence which, under any reasonable view, supports the jury's damage figure, we will not disturb the finding unless the award shocks judicial conscience, especially where the verdict has the trial court's approval. We initially express our opinion that the amount of the jury verdict, $16,500, does not shock judicial conscience. Therefore, we turn to the question of whether credible evidence supports this amount.

After examining the record, we cannot find support for an award which exceeds $16,245.81. The only evidence on damages was presented by Reimer. In addition to lost wages of $14,138 and moving expenses of $2107.81, Reimer made a claim of $5000 for incidental and consequential damages. No proof of this figure was received other than Reimer's statement when referring to his "summary of damages" exhibit that he was claiming this amount. Mere conclusions of a witness that he has been damaged to a certain extent without stating the facts on which the estimate is made is too uncertain. We therefore reduce the award from $16,500 to $16,245.81 and affirm the judgment as modified.

JUDGMENT MODIFIED AND, AS MODIFIED, AFFIRMED; ORDER AFFIRMED.

Understanding the Case:

1. *Badger's Sales Model:* Badger is a wholesale grocery distributing company that started as a family grocer in Green Bay, Wisconsin, over 100 years ago.[21] Badger started with two locations in Green Bay, but in 1950, greatly expanded by buying a major Wisconsin distributor, Valley Distributing. Badger's sales model was to assign to its outside salespeople specific territories and customers.[22] Badger compensated those salespeople by paying them a base salary in addition to a commission on any new sales that they generated.[23] As a result of this structure, earning commissions was a critical part of salespepeople's livelihoods. In fact, an employer's future promise of a key territory can often induce a salesperson to leave one company, or even relocate, to join another.[24] Note that outside salespeople are not required to be paid overtime wages under Section 13(a)(1) of the Fair Labor Standards Act.[25]

Comprehension and Thought Questions:

1. How did Badger breach its contract with Reimer given that Reimer was employed at-will?
2. Why did Reimer not seek expectation damages?
3. What test did Badger argue the court should use to calculate Reimer's damages?
4. Why did the court reject that test?
5. What test did the court use to calculate Reimer's reliance damages?
6. What amounts did the court allow Reimer to recover using that test?
7. Why did the court allow Reimer to recover the difference between his salary at Badger and his salary at his prior employer in Missouri *after Badger terminated Reimer's employment*?
8. Why did the court not allow Reimer to collect the $5,000 consequential damages he had requested?

---

21. Badger Wholesale Foods, *About Us,* http://www.badgerwholesalefoods.com (last visited Sept. 23, 2018).

22. *See* Reimer v. Badger Wholesale Co., Inc., 433 N.W.2d 593, 593 (Wis. Ct. App. 1988).

23. *Id.*

24. Manesh K. Rath, *Left Standing at the Altar: How Relocation Affects the Employment Relationship,* 37 S. Tex. L. Rev. 813, 844 (1996).

25. 29 C.F.R. § 541.500 ("The term 'employee employed in the capacity of outside salesman' in section 13(a)(1) of the Act shall mean any employee whose primary duty is making sales within the meaning of section 3(k) of the Act, or obtaining orders or contracts for services or for the use of facilities for which a consideration will be paid by the client or customer; and who is customarily and regularly engaged away from the employer's place or places of business in performing such primary duty").

Hypothetical Variations:

1. What if Badger terminated Reimer after 90 days of employment because Reimer had only produced $7,000 in sales during that period?

2. What if Badger had given Reimer an exclusive territory in Neenah-Menasha but Badger terminated Reimer after only 17 days on the job due to Badger's sudden economic woes?

3. What if Reimer would have earned $1,000 less at his old job than he did at Badger during the time he was employed at Badger?

E. RESTITUTIONARY DAMAGES

Recall that in Chapter 23 you studied restitution as an alternative theory of recovery where a contract does not exist. This discussion, in contrast, focuses on the situation where there is a contract, the claim is for breach of contract, and the aggrieved party seeks a remedy to protect its restitutionary interest. Such a remedy would require the counterparty to restore in-kind what was delivered under the contract, or to otherwise pay for the fair value of benefits conferred.[26]

Where a party seeks a restitutionary recovery under a contract, some courts test to see if the elements of restitution are satisfied. By running through the elements for restitution, those courts imply that they are not actually enforcing the contract. Instead, they appear to view restitution as the relevant claim. On the other hand, other courts do not run through the test for restitution where a party seeks to recover under a contract and merely use restitution as a measure of damages.

Where courts do run through the elements for restitution, the existence of the contract satisfies most of those elements. For example, the fact that one party agreed to pay for benefits under a contract shows that (1) the provided services or property were viewed as benefits, (2) those benefits were not rendered gratuitously, and (3) the benefits were not officiously conferred, all supporting the need for a remedy to avoid injustice.

While the contract price is not conclusive of the value of the benefit conferred, it is some evidence of that fact. Thus, courts often look at the contract price in deciding how much a party should pay for the value of the benefit conferred. But again, courts are not tied to the contract price when deciding on a remedy for restitution. And in fact, a court would exclude any element of profit in looking to the contract price to determine the value of benefit conferred, as profits represent a gain beyond the value of benefits conferred.

---

26. Restatement (Second) of Contracts § 344(c) (1981).

However, a restitutionary recovery has some nuanced applications where there is an underlying contract. First, a party may only sue for a restitutionary recovery where the counterparty has committed a total breach or repudiated the contract, thereby excusing the aggrieved party from performing its remaining obligations under the contract. A party may not recover a restitutionary remedy where the counterparty has merely committed a partial breach. In the case of a partial breach, the aggrieved party must instead sue the breaching or repudiating party on the contract that it negotiated.

Another limitation applies where a party has fully performed its obligations under a contract and the only obligation the counterparty has failed to perform is the payment of a liquidated sum of money. In that instance, a court will not allow the performing party to use the restitutionary measure of damages to recover more than the contract price. That is because to allow this would create an incentive for a party to negotiate a low contract price and then, if the counterparty fails to timely pay, sue for a restitutionary recovery instead of the contract price. It also imposes a burden on the court to value benefits conferred where parties have already valued that performance.

You should also note that even a breaching party may be entitled to restitution where its breach excused the aggrieved party from performing. A court will award such a remedy where it would be unjust for the aggrieved party to keep benefits conferred by the breaching party without making restitution for them.

Finally, where a party seeks a remedy to protect its restitutionary interest, the remedy is often described as one for quantum meruit. The term **quantum meruit** literally means "as much as is deserved." It specifically refers to the fair value of services and materials provided to a party that benefited that party. However, as you saw in Chapter 23, this term is used not only to express a restitutionary recovery where there is a contract, but also where there is not a contract, as the party's claim for recovery.

You will see the "quantum meruit" term used in the following case. This case exemplifies why a party might seek such a remedy instead of expectation damages, as well as how a court calculates such damages. This case also demonstrates some of the above limits on a restitutionary recovery for a breach of contract.

Coon v. Schoeneman
Court of Civil Appeals of Texas, Dallas
476 S.W.2d 439 (1973)

GUITTARD, Justice.

This suit was brought by the builder of eleven houses against the owner of the lots upon which they were built to recover a share of the profits from their sale, and in the alternative for the reasonable value of his services as builder. At the trial plaintiff abandoned his claim for profits and sought to recover the value of his services. The trial court excluded evidence of the value of his services and sustained defendant's motion for instructed verdict. Plaintiff appeals, contending that the trial court erred in refusing to permit proof of the elements of Quantum meruit and in refusing to submit issues on Quantum meruit.

The question is whether proof of an express contract for compensation as a share of profits excludes recovery for value of services, where there is evidence that defendant's breach of the contract prevented plaintiff from completing it. We hold that plaintiff could elect to recover the value of his services and was entitled to go to the jury on his alternative plea.

The question turns on the distinction between damages and restitution as remedies for breach of contract. Damages is the amount which would put plaintiff in as good position as if the contract had been performed by both parties. It gives him the benefit of his bargain, including any profit he would have made, and is determined by the contract price, less any amount saved by his being excused from further performance. Restitution is the amount which would put plaintiff in as good a position as he would have been in if no contract had been made. It restores to plaintiff the value of what he parted with in performing the contract. When defendant has committed a breach of contract which is serious enough to excuse plaintiff from performing further, plaintiff is entitled to elect between these remedies. He may pursue both remedies in the same suit by alternative pleadings and make his election at the trial. The remedy of restitution, which is normally pursued by an action in Quantum meruit for reasonable value of services rendered, is not under these circumstances an action upon an implied or quasi-contract, as in a case where there is no express contract and plaintiff sues for reasonable value of services accepted by defendant. It is rather an alternative remedy for breach of an express contract. The measure of such restitution is the value of plaintiff's services on the market rather than the benefit to defendant.

An important limitation on the right of a plaintiff to elect between the remedies of damages and restitution is that when plaintiff's performance of the whole or a separable part of the contract entitles him to compensation in an agreed amount or at an agreed rate, he is limited to the compensation specified in the contract. This rule is stated in Restatement, Contracts §§ 350, 351 (1932) as follows:

> 'The remedy of restitution in money is not available to one who has fully performed his part of a contract, if the only part of the agreed exchange for such performance that has not been rendered by the defendant is a sum of money constituting a liquidated debt; but full performance does not make restitution unavailable if any part of the consideration due from the defendant in return is something other than a liquidated debt.'

> Restitution is not available as a remedy with respect to any performance by the plaintiff for which a definite part of the consideration was apportioned in the contract as its equivalent in exchange, if

> (a) the consideration so apportioned has been rendered in full, or
> (b) it is a liquidated sum of money.'

This limitation is reasonable because if plaintiff has obligated himself to perform services for a certain amount, and he has already earned that amount, it is just to measure his compensation by the amount he agreed to take for such services. The authorities relied on by defendant fall into this category. They hold that upon performance of an express contract for the rendition of services for a certain price, the contract fixes the measure of compensation and precludes recovery in Quantum meruit for the value of services rendered. On the other hand, in cases where plaintiff's complete performance has been prevented by defendant's breach, Texas authorities support the first rule above stated, that plaintiff may elect either to recover his damages under the contract or treat the contract as rescinded and recover the reasonable value of his work in Quantum meruit.

Application of these principles to the present case brings us to the conclusion that plaintiff's evidence raised issues for the jury as to breach by defendant preventing his further performance and the reasonable value of his services. The only evidence is the testimony of plaintiff Harold Coon. He testified that defendant Frank Schoeneman had told him he had certain lots in Irving and Arlington and that he needed somebody to build houses on them. Schoeneman proposed that Coon build the houses, Schoeneman would finance them, they would get a third person to sell them, and they would split the profits three ways. Coon agreed and started building. After he had built seven houses in Irving, including six 'model homes,' and had started four in Arlington, Schoeneman told him the rest of the Irving lots had been sold and proposed that Coon proceed with the project in Arlington on a different deal, which was that Coon would pay him $350 a house, Schoeneman would furnish the lots, and Coon would get all the profit. Coon agreed, with the understanding that he would have five houses under construction or ready for sale continuously and that no lots should be sold to other builders in the immediate area. Schoeneman agreed to these conditions. When Coon had finished four houses on the Arlington lots and was ready to start a fifth, he discovered that Schoeneman had sold the rest of the lots and other contractors were preparing to build on lots next to the houses Coon had built. Coon built no more houses on Schoeneman's lots. Schoeneman said he would send Coon his part of the profits from the houses that were built, but he sold the houses and never gave Coon any of the proceeds. Coon never received anything for his work.

Defendant objected to plaintiff's testimony concerning the value of his services on the ground that the proof established an express agreement to share profits and plaintiff was limited to recovery of such profits. The objection was sustained, and plaintiff gave his testimony concerning the value of his services in the form of a bill of exceptions. At the close of plaintiff's direct testimony the trial court sustained defendant's motion to instruct a verdict in his favor on the ground that plaintiff had shown only that there was a verbal agreement to share profits, but had not shown that there were any profits.

Since the trial court instructed a verdict for defendant, we must view the evidence in the light most favorable to plaintiff. Viewing Coon's testimony in that light, we conclude that a jury would have been justified in finding that Schoeneman breached the contract by selling off the Arlington lots contrary to his agreement that he would allow Coon to keep five houses ready for sale or under construction and would not sell lots to other contractors in the immediate area. Coon was thus prevented by Schoeneman's breach from building any more houses. Though the oral contract, as described by Coon, is not definite as to how many houses Coon was entitled to build, it did give him the right to build at least five and to be free from competition by other builders on Schoeneman's lots in the immediate area. On Schoeneman's breach of that agreement, Coon was entitled under the above authorities either to sue for his damages under the contract, including his share of profits on the houses he had built and the profits he would have made on other houses, or to treat the contract as rescinded and recover the reasonable value of his services.

We have considered whether the contract was divisible and the consideration apportionable, so that on completion and sale of each house plaintiff became entitled to compensation in a liquidated amount for his share of the profit and should be limited to that amount. Probably the contract is not divisible, since six of the houses in Irving were 'model homes,' which presumably were not expected to be sold at as much profit as others to be built. The mere fact that there is a contract rate of payment per unit of performance does not make the contract divisible, since the parties may not have been willing to contract separately for each unit. However, we conclude that the divisibility of the contract does not matter, since even if the profits were apportionable to each house, the amount was not liquidated. It depended on the sale price and the various factors making up the cost. Consequently, under the rule stated in either § 350 or § 351 of the Restatement, plaintiff was not limited to the contract measure of compensation.

The case is analogous to one in which the agreed exchange for services is something other than a determinable amount of money, such as property or an interest in the business. In that case even a plaintiff who has fully performed may recover the reasonable value of his services rather than the value of what was promised to him. This rule seems to be based on the idea that since plaintiff cannot obtain his specific Quid pro quo under the contract, and proof of its value may be difficult, he should not be limited to recovery of damages but should be able to recover the reasonable value of his services by way of restitution. Likewise, in this case, since defendant repudiated the contract and prevented plaintiff from continuing performance, plaintiff is entitled to elect his remedy of restitution, and should not be required to assume the burden of establishing the profit on the sale of each of eleven houses in order to recover compensation for his services.

One of the problems here is that both of the oral contracts described by plaintiff provided for compensation in terms of profit, and, therefore, contractual compensation was contingent on the existence of profits, which were not proved. Thus defendant contends that plaintiff failed to prove that he was entitled to any compensation at all. The question is whether the contingent character of the contractual compensation renders unavailable the alternative remedy of restitution, so that plaintiff is without remedy for defendant's breach unless he can prove that profits were realized in the past, or would have been realized in the future if the contract had been fully performed.

In our opinion the contingent nature of the contractual compensation does not affect the plaintiff's right to restitution upon defendant's material breach of the contract. Proof that no profits were made on the houses sold would not establish that no profits would have been realized if defendant had complied with the contract. Presumably, greater profits were anticipated from sale of subsequent houses than from the 'model homes.' Moreover, defendant's principal breach was his sale of adjacent lots to competing builders. Such a breach may in itself have prevented any profit on the four houses in Arlington or may have reduced the amount of profit, but proof would be difficult. The party who has wrongfully prevented the other party from completing the contract should not benefit from his own wrong. Consequently, we hold that even though the contractual compensation was contingent on profits, the same rule of restitution applies as in other cases where defendant's breach has prevented further performance by plaintiff. Plaintiff should have his election to treat the contract as rescinded and recover the reasonable value of his services.

. . .

Reversed and remanded.

Understanding the Case:

1. *Background on Construction Projects:* The single largest contributor to the United States' gross domestic product is the construction industry. Construction projects are typically multiparty transactions that are documented in multiple contracts in which the parties set out a complex set of rights and obligations. Not surprisingly, major construction projects can generate litigation between contracting parties stemming from breaches of those bargained-for rights and obligations. Common owner claims are that a contractor provided defective work not in accordance with the plans and specifications or that the contractor failed to substantially complete the project within the time required in the contract. The typical contractor's counterclaim is that the owner changed the contract's scope of work by his or her actions, as occurred in *Coon*. In this case, Frank Schoeneman was a prominent developer in the Dallas, Texas area. As early as the 1950s, he developed multiple real estate projects, including Eltroy Heights, Arlington Estates, Schoeneman Manor, and

Briarwood and BuenaVista additions, representing approximately 1,200 lots in the Dallas area. While constructing a series of houses in Arlington, Texas, Schoeneman proposed to Coon, a building contractor, that if Coon would construct the houses, Shoeneman would finance them, and a third person would sell them.

2. *One or Two Contracts:* In some places, the court's opinion describes multiple contracts, suggesting that there were separate contracts for the Irving and Arlington lots. However, in other places, the court's opinion refers to the "contract" and implies that the parties' relationship was reflected in a single contract. Ultimately, it does not matter whether the terms of the parties' bargain for the Irving lots and the Arlington lots amounted to a single set of exchanged promises (i.e., one contract) or two sets of exchanged promises (i.e., two contracts), as Schoeneman breached his duties under both, whether delivered as one contract or two.

3. *Alternative Pleadings:* In his complaint, Coon specified alternative remedies. Thus, in one part of his complaint, Coon sought expectation damages due to Schoeneman's breach of contract. However, in a separate part of his complaint, Coon alternatively sought restitutionary damages. As the court mentioned (and as discussed in Chapter 22), such alternative pleadings are permitted. Coon just had to pick which remedy he sought at trial. By proceeding in this way, Coon could conduct pretrial discovery and then decide which remedy to pursue.

4. *Model Homes:* The court mentions that six of the seven houses Coon built in Irving were "model homes." A model home is a home a builder builds to let prospective buyers see potential floor designs for houses the builder can build for them in the area. Often model homes also display finishing and fixture choices, allowing the prospective buyer to see and choose those features they want in their homes. However, model homes typically sell for less than non-model homes given that they receive a lot of foot traffic while they are used as models, resulting in wear and tear. They also sell for less because they are often located in high-traffic areas to ensure visibility to potential buyers. Moreover, a buyer cannot select its desired furnishings and fixtures when buying a former model home, which makes that home less valuable. Thus, the Irving model homes might not have even generated a profit when sold.

Comprehension and Thought Questions:

1. What promise or promises did Coon allege that Schoeneman breached?

2. Why was it relevant whether the contract was divisible? Why did the court conclude that the contract was not divisible?

3. Why did Coon seek restitution instead of expectation damages?

4. According to the court, what limits a party's ability to recover restitutionary damages where the aggrieved party sues for breach of contract?

5. Did any of those limitations prevent Coon from recovering restitutionary damages in this case?

6. Should a party be able to recover restitutionary damages where expectation damages cannot be calculated with reasonable certainty? Why or why not?

Hypothetical Variations:

1. What if the contract between Coon and Schoeneman provided that Coon was to be compensated $300,000 for the construction of each house instead of a share of profits from their sale?

2. Using the same facts as in Hypothetical Variation Question 1, what if Coon actually incurred $350,000 in constructing each of the houses?

3. What if Schoeneman allowed Coon to finish building all of the houses on the two lots, but then breached his contract with Coon by not paying Coon the profit share to which Coon was entitled? What remedy would a court likely award Coon in that situation?

PRACTICE PROBLEM 24-3

Winny Xiao is a home decorator with exquisite taste. On October 1, the famous actress Sheba Davis hired Winny to decorate Sheba's Florida palace. Per the contract, Winny was required to decorate the house in an extravagant Middle Eastern style. However, Winny had considerable discretion in specific design choices. Winny agreed to complete this work no later than December 31. The price for this work was $300,000. Sheba agreed to pay $100,000 of this amount up front, an additional $100,000 once the house was fully painted, and the remaining $100,000 once the house was fully furnished.

While Winny figured it would cost around $325,000 to decorate Sheba's palace, she decided to only charge $300,000 because she wanted to impress Sheba so that Sheba would hire Winny to decorate Sheba's five other houses. Plus, Winny was hoping Sheba would put in a good word for Winny with other actors, expanding Winny's network of prospective clients.

Winny got to work right away. On October 2, Winny hired an architect to draw Sheba's house. That way, Winny could use the drawing to determine the exact dimensions for each room, so she could use that to determine quantity of supplies and furniture needed. This work cost Winny $10,000.

Next, with the architect's drawing in hand, on October 10, Winny hired a painter to paint the internal rooms of Sheba's palace with rich colors. Winny paid $20,000 up front for this work. Winny also commissioned an artist to paint a fresco on the atrium ceiling of Sheba's palace. The painter said he charged by the hour ($400 per hour). He could not estimate how long the work would take until he familiarized himself with the texture and shape of the ceiling and had a clearer idea of what Sheba wanted. But knowing the work would take at least 125 hours, the artist required a $50,000 up-front nonrefundable deposit. Finally, Winny went furniture shopping and found an exquisite dining room set and living room set for the close-out price of $60,000. Because she bought them at a closeout, the two sets could not be returned.

The painter showed up at the house on October 12 and began to paint the walls in Sheba's palace. Sheba did not object to this work. By October 15, the painter was halfway done.

Winny showed up at Sheba's palace on October 15 to check on the painter, receive delivery of the new dining room and living room sets and to let the fresco artist in. However, when she showed up at Sheba's house, Sheba was livid. She thought the dining room and living room sets were tacky and the fresco artist tired and unoriginal. Sheba told Winny to stop all work and to leave the house at once. She also declared that she was not going to pay Winny anything more for her work.

Assuming Sheba breached the contract, if Winny were to sue Sheba for breach:

1. What would Winny recover (if anything) if she were to receive expectation damages?

2. What would Winny recover (if anything) if she were to receive reliance damages?

3. What would Winny recover (if anything) if she were to receive restitutionary damages?

F. REMEDIES OPINIONS

In some transactions, a lawyer is required to deliver a legal opinion to the other side about the enforceability of a contract or a set of contracts. That opinion is called a **remedies opinion** because in it, the lawyer opines on whether a court would award a remedy to the counterparty if the contract were breached by the lawyer's client.

Legal opinions are a common staple in financing transactions, where the borrower's counsel is required to deliver the legal opinion to the lender. In those transactions, the borrower's counsel opines on the enforceability of the loan agreement and other related contracts, such as security agreements and guarantees. However, legal opinions can be required in other transactions too.

The following is sample language for a remedies opinion being delivered by a borrower's counsel to the lender:

It is the opinion of our firm that the Loan Agreement and other Transaction Documents are enforceable against the Borrower in accordance with their terms, except as enforceability may be limited by

(a) applicable bankruptcy or insolvency laws or other similar laws affecting the rights or remedies of creditors generally, or
(b) general principles of equity.

We have omitted other language that is typically included in this type of legal opinion, such as the state's laws under which the opinion is given. The lender will require that the law firm give this opinion under the law that governs the loan agreement and other related contracts.[27] Obviously, the law firm that represents the borrower will only give this opinion if it has a lawyer licensed in that state who can confirm the accuracy of this opinion. If not, the borrower will have to hire a lawyer who is licensed in the state of the governing law to give this legal opinion, even if that lawyer does not have any other connection to this transaction.

A lender requests this opinion because it provides the lender with extra security that a court will provide a remedy should the borrower breach any provision in the contract. The security comes from the need for the borrower's lawyer to complete enough research to satisfy the lawyer of the enforceability of the loan agreement and other related contracts. After all, a lawyer may be liable to the lender if he or she is negligent in rendering this opinion.[28] Needless to say, if the lawyer believes any provision of any of those contracts would not be enforced for any reason, the lawyer needs to except out that provision in its legal opinion to avoid incurring liability. Doing so identifies an area of risk for the lender, which the lender can potentially address through a change in the contract terms. On the other hand, it is fairly uncommon for the lender to first learn of a potentially unenforceable contract provision through a remedies opinion. That is because, if you recall from Chapter 11, it is usually the lender's counsel who drafts the loan agreement. As such, that lawyer would likely already be aware of any potentially unenforceable provisions.

Notice that this opinion has two standard exceptions. The first refers to bankruptcy and related laws. Lawyers typically exclude bankruptcy laws from the scope of their legal opinions because bankruptcy courts have discretion to discharge contractual obligations and a lawyer accordingly cannot determine in advance what will happen with a contractual obligation in bankruptcy.

---

27. *See, e.g.*, In re Chrysler LLC, et al., No. 09-50002, 2009 WL 1360863 (Bankr. S.D.N.Y. May 4, 2009).

28. *See* Greyhound Leasing & Fin. Corp. v. Norwest Bank, 854 F.2d 1122 (8th Cir. 1988) (the attorney in this case was not held to be negligent because of the plaintiffs' contributory negligence).

The second standard exception refers to principles of equity. Lawyers usually except those principles from the scope of their legal opinion because equitable principles give courts discretion to award or deny remedies based on notions of fairness. Thus, a lender's conduct or fairness of terms could lead a court to deny the lender a remedy.

You may be wondering how the lender exacts this legal opinion from the borrower's counsel. After all, the lawyer is not a party to the loan agreement or other related contracts. The answer comes through the use of conditions. In the case of a loan, for example, the loan agreement will contain a condition to the lender's obligation to lend money to the borrower that the lender must have received a legal opinion from the borrower's counsel as to the enforceability of the loan agreement and other transaction documents.[29] Thus, the lawyer must deliver the legal opinion if it wants to assist its client in getting the loan.

PRACTICE PROBLEM 24-4

You represent Guidesmith Inc., an early-stage company headquartered in Springfield, Columbia. Guidesmith has developed software that provides users with an interactive educational guide for geographic points of interest as they travel anywhere in the United States. Because it is still in an early stage, Guidesmith does not have a lot of money. So, to expand sales of its software, Guidesmith needs a loan.

Springfield Local Bank N.A. is willing to provide a loan to Guidesmith in the amount of $2 million to finance this expansion. The Bank's lawyer recently sent you the first draft of the loan agreement. That draft included the following provision:

> If Borrower defaults in paying either interest or principal on the loan when due, the interest rate on the loan will automatically increase by an additional 4 percent, even if and after the default, the Borrower cures its default.

The interest rate on the loan is a current market rate of 5 percent.

The draft loan agreement also contains a condition to closing that you must have delivered a legal opinion as to the enforceability of the loan agreement. It provides that it is governed by Tennessee law.

After conducting research, you discover a Columbia case that holds as follows:

> Default charges on loans are subject to the reasonableness test. A default provision providing for an unreasonable increase in the contract interest rate is

---

29. *See, e.g.,* In re Chrysler LLC, et al., No. 09-50002, 2009 WL 1360863 (Bankr. S.D.N.Y. May 4, 2009).

unenforceable as a penalty. Columbia cases have invalidated enhanced default rates if their size suggests a punitive intent.

1. Would you deliver the requested legal opinion based on the content of the loan agreement? Why or why not?

2. If you would not be willing to deliver a legal opinion, how would you go about addressing your concerns?

CHAPTER 25

Limits on Damages

As you know from Chapter 24, when courts enforce contracts, they generally award the remedy of damages. However, contract law imposes several limits on damages. Those limits often prevent an aggrieved party from being fully compensated for the party's actual losses. However, these limits, too, serve important policy objectives. In general, those limits are that damages must be (1) foreseeable at the time of contracting, (2) calculable with reasonable certainty at the time of breach, and (3) caused by the breach. Each of these limits is discussed below, with foreseeability in Section B, calculability with reasonable certainty in Section C, causation in Section D, and other limits in Section E. The *Florafax* case in Section F shows each of these limits in action.

A party's recovery of damages may also be limited by that party's own behavior. In particular, under the doctrine of mitigation, a party generally may not recover damages that it could have avoided using reasonable efforts. Mitigation is discussed in Section G.

However, before we look at mandatory contract law limits on damages, first we explore how parties can privately agree among themselves to limit damages. That topic is explored in Section A below.

A. AGREED LIMITS ON DAMAGES

Often, contracting parties agree to limit the damages for which they are potentially liable. Those limits might either cap the amount of damages a party might owe, set a floor below which a party is not liable (sometimes referred to as a "basket" or "deductible"), or limit a party's liability for certain types of damages. In this way, parties can to some extent control their liability exposure, enabling them to have better visibility into the financial impact of a breach. Moreover, a cap on a party's liability allows that party to assure that it does not owe more money as damages than it generates by entering into the contract.

Such caps are commonly incorporated into the indemnification clauses in significant purchase transactions. Recall from Chapter 24 that indemnification clauses set out one party's duty to reimburse the other for certain losses the other party incurs, whether as a result of a breach of contract or otherwise. In those transactions, the parties often agree that the seller is only liable to indemnify the buyer for misrepresentations/breaches of warranties or covenants up to an agreed-upon cap. That cap is typically a percent of the purchase price. Here is an example of an indemnification clause that caps the seller's liability for losses arising out of misrepresentations/breaches of warranty:

> The Seller's liability in respect of any misrepresentation or breach of warranty under this Agreement will not exceed an amount equal to 15% of the Purchase Price (the "Cap") except to the extent that such claim arises out of fraud, in which case, the Cap does not apply.

In this example, while the Seller is liable for the Buyer's losses arising out of a Seller misrepresentation/breach of warranty, under this language, the Seller's maximum liability for such claims is 15 percent of the purchase price for the assets. This exception does not apply, however, where the Seller commits fraud. In that case, due to the higher level of culpability and risk that a party who is held not liable for the results of its fraud might have an incentive to commit fraud, that type of conduct is not subject to this cap. In fact, even without this language, some courts would not enforce the clause where it would **exculpate** (meaning hold a party not financially liable for) its own fraudulent, willful, or negligent acts. As one New York court has stated, such a clause is not enforceable where "the misconduct for which it would grant immunity smacks of intentional wrongdoing."[1]

Parties sometimes also create baskets—or minimum amounts—below which a party is not liable. In the context of an indemnification clause in a purchase agreement, those provisions commonly set out the seller's agreement to reimburse the buyer for its losses arising due to a misrepresentation/breach of warranty or breach of covenant so long as the aggregate amount of the buyer's losses exceeds a minimal amount. The contract would also then need to address whether, once that floor is reached, the seller is liable for *all* Buyer losses, starting from the first dollar, or only for losses exceeding that floor. Parties include these baskets to avoid the hassle of having one party owe the other small amounts of money for breaches.

The following is a sample indemnification clause with a liability floor.

---

1. Kalisch-Jarcho, Inc. v. City of New York, 448 N.E.2d 413, 416 (N.Y. 1983).

> The Buyer is not entitled to receive any amount from the Seller for losses incurred by the Buyer arising out of the Seller's misrepresentation or breach of warranty (each, a "Claim") unless
>
> (i)   the Buyer's losses from that Claim individually exceed $10,000, though if the Buyer's losses for that Claim exceed $10,000, the Seller shall pay the Buyer all of Buyer's damages arising out of that Claim, including the first $10,000 of damages, and
>
> (ii) the aggregate of the Buyer's losses for all Claims in the aggregate exceed $50,000, though once the Buyer's losses for all Claims in the aggregate exceed $50,000, the Seller shall pay the Buyer all of the Buyer's damages arising out of all Claims, including the first $50,000 in damages.

Subsection (i) provides that the Seller does not owe money to the Buyer for a single claim that generates less than $10,000 in Buyer losses. So, if the Seller makes a misrepresentation/breaches a warranty (for example, it represents and warrants that its assets are in good condition when an essential machine is not working), but the resulting loss to the Buyer is only $9,000, then the Seller would not owe the Buyer any money for that claim under this subsection.

Moreover, even if that misrepresentation/breach of warranty leads to $10,000 in Buyer losses, under subsection (ii), the Buyer cannot recover from the Seller unless the Seller made other misrepresentations and breaches of warranty that, together with the new claim, generated Buyer losses of at least $50,000. Once that amount is reached, the Buyer can recover for *all* losses from the Seller for each claim that generated $10,000 or more in Buyer losses. Thus, if, for example, the Seller had also made a misrepresentation and breached a warranty about the absence of pending litigation against the Seller, and that led to Buyer losses of $45,000, then the Buyer would be able to recover $45,000 on that claim because all claims in the aggregate now exceed $50,000 under subsection (ii) and that claim alone led to losses of at least $10,000 under subsection (i). Note that the parties could have agreed to a different structure where the first $50,000 of Buyer's losses were not recoverable at all (even once the $50,000 threshold was met), in which case the basket would serve as a deductible that the Buyer would have to pay or suffer.

While these "caps" and "baskets" might seem complicated, the important point is that parties can privately agree on caps and minimum thresholds for when a party is liable to the other.

Contracts can also limit or exclude a party's liability for certain types of damages. These clauses are found in many types of contracts, and do not appear only in those with indemnification clauses. One of the frequent exclusions is a party's liability for consequential damages. The following is YouTube's limitation of liability for consequential damages:

> 10. Limitation of Liability
>
> TO THE FULLEST EXTENT PERMITTED BY LAW, IN NO EVENT SHALL YOUTUBE, ITS OFFICERS, DIRECTORS, EMPLOYEES, OR AGENTS, BE LIABLE TO YOU FOR ANY DIRECT, INDIRECT, INCIDENTAL, SPECIAL, PUNITIVE, LOSSES OR EXPENSES OR CONSEQUENTIAL DAMAGES WHATSOEVER RESULTING FROM ANY (I) ERRORS, MISTAKES, OR INACCURACIES OF CONTENT, (II) PERSONAL INJURY OR PROPERTY DAMAGE, OF ANY NATURE WHATSOEVER, RESULTING FROM YOUR ACCESS TO AND USE OF OUR SERVICES, (III) ANY UNAUTHORIZED ACCESS TO OR USE OF OUR SECURE SERVERS AND/OR ANY AND ALL PERSONAL INFORMATION AND/OR FINANCIAL INFORMATION STORED THEREIN, (IV) ANY INTERRUPTION OR CESSATION OF TRANSMISSION TO OR FROM OUR SERVICES, (IV) ANY BUGS, VIRUSES, TROJAN HORSES, OR THE LIKE, WHICH MAY BE TRANSMITTED TO OR THROUGH OUR SERVICES BY ANY THIRD PARTY, AND/OR (V) ANY ERRORS OR OMISSIONS IN ANY CONTENT OR FOR ANY LOSS OR DAMAGE OF ANY KIND INCURRED AS A RESULT OF YOUR USE OF ANY CONTENT POSTED, EMAILED, TRANSMITTED, OR OTHERWISE MADE AVAILABLE VIA THE SERVICES, WHETHER BASED ON WARRANTY, CONTRACT, TORT, OR ANY OTHER LEGAL THEORY, AND WHETHER OR NOT THE COMPANY IS ADVISED OF THE POSSIBILITY OF SUCH DAMAGES.
>
> WE UNDERSTAND THAT, IN SOME JURISDICTIONS, WARRANTIES, DISCLAIMERS AND CONDITIONS MAY APPLY THAT CANNOT BE LEGALLY EXCLUDED, IF THAT IS TRUE IN YOUR JURISDICTION, THEN TO THE EXTENT PERMITTED BY LAW, YOUTUBE LIMITS ITS LIABILITY FOR ANY CLAIMS UNDER THOSE WARRANTIES OR CONDITIONS TO EITHER SUPPLYING YOU THE SERVICES AGAIN (OR THE COST OF SUPPLYING YOU THE SERVICES AGAIN).
>
> YOU SPECIFICALLY ACKNOWLEDGE THAT YOUTUBE SHALL NOT BE LIABLE FOR CONTENT OR THE DEFAMATORY, OFFENSIVE, OR ILLEGAL CONDUCT OF ANY THIRD PARTY AND THAT THE RISK OF HARM OR DAMAGE FROM THE FOREGOING RESTS ENTIRELY WITH YOU.[2]

Merchants often include these liability limitations in their contracts with consumers. These limits give the merchant more certainty about potential damages it might owe if it breaches the contract by removing the uncertainty associated with consequential damages. Actually, YouTube also disclaims liability for direct damages in the above waiver, undoubtedly because it provides its services to customers for "free."

On the other hand, such limits might prevent the counterparty from receiving full expectation damages. Where that happens and the counterparty breaches, the aggrieved party might seek specific performance instead, on the theory that it does not have an adequate remedy at law given the limitation on the other party's liability.

---

2. YouTube Inc., https://www.youtube.com/static?template=terms&gl=AU (last visited Sept. 23, 2018).

Note that contractual provisions that limit a party's liability are not typically subjected to the high level of scrutiny to which liquidated damages clauses are subject, as you will study in Chapter 26. But they may be challenged under other contract law doctrines you have studied, such as the defenses of unconscionability. Moreover, some states have statutes that place limits on these types of limitations on damages,[3] while some courts interpret these types of limitation clauses narrowly.[4]

PRACTICE PROBLEM 25-1

Sheila Brooks and Jerome Zell have entered a contract for the sale of Sheila's hairstyling business, called "Pump It Up," to Jerome. Under the contract, Sheila agreed to transfer all her assets used in Pump It Up to Jerome, including her valuable customer list so Jerome could try to retain those people as customers. In exchange, Jerome agreed to pay Sheila $30,000.

In addition to a non-compete covenant, the asset purchase agreement also included the following non-disparagement clause:

> Brooks agrees that for a period of one year, she will not defame, slander, or otherwise criticize or make negative statements about Zell to Brooks's customers, suppliers, or others with whom Brooks dealt as hair salon owner.

The asset purchase agreement also contained the following limitation of liability:

> Brooks's liability for any misrepresentation, breach of warranty or breach of covenant under this Agreement will not exceed an amount equal to 15% of the Purchase Price (the "Cap").

The transaction closed on October 31. However, during the first week of November, Jerome discovered that most of Sheila's customers cancelled their regular appointments. When he asked one customer who did not cancel why so many customers had cancelled, that customer informed Jerome that Sheila had been telling all of her customers that Zell did not know how to cut hair. Sheila had also been recommending that her customers have their hair cut by one of Sheila's friends.

1. Has Sheila breached her agreement with Jerome? If so, how?

2. Assume Sheila has breached and Jerome could prove that his actual damages were $15,000. What damages would the court likely award Jerome and why?

---

3. *See, e.g.,* Fla. Stat. Ann. § 558.0035 (2018).

4. *See* Blake D. Morant, *Contracts Limiting Liability: A Paradox with Tacit Solutions,* 69 Tul. L Rev. 715 (1994).

B. FORESEEABILITY

Imagine that you hired Doug Bowser, a professional dog walker, to take your dog Duncan for a walk on October 5 from 4:00 to 6:00 P.M. You hired Doug to walk your dog then because you are hosting a work function at your house and know that if your crazy dog Duncan is at the party, he will surely embarrass you with his drooling and barking. You are also worried that he will bite someone at the party. Then, not only might you not be promoted, but you might be fired, or even sued for a tort. You do not know Doug at all and do not communicate these concerns to him.

At 3:45 on October 5, Doug calls you to tell you he is sick and cannot come to walk Duncan at 4:00, as promised. You are distraught, as you do not want Duncan at the party, but cannot find anyone else to walk your dog during the party on such short notice.

The party indeed turns out to be a fiasco. Duncan jumps on everyone and bites a hole through your boss's one-of-a-kind Italian silk shirt. One week after the party, your boss says he has lost confidence in you and demotes you to a position with less responsibility, where you earn $10,000 less per year.

If you were to sue Doug for breach of contract, would he be liable for this $10,000 loss?

The answer to this question largely depends on whether those damages were reasonably foreseeable by Doug as a probable result of breach by him at the time of contracting. The following is the Restatement's description of this limitation:

> **§ 351 Unforeseeability and Related Limitations on Damages**
>
> (1) Damages are not recoverable for loss that the party in breach did not have reason to foresee as a probable result of the breach when the contract was made.
>
> (2) Loss may be foreseeable as a probable result of a breach because it follows from the breach
>
> > (a) in the ordinary course of events, or
> >
> > (b) as a result of special circumstances, beyond the ordinary course of events, that the party in breach had reason to know.
>
> (3) A court may limit damages for foreseeable loss by excluding recovery for loss of profits, by allowing recovery only for loss incurred in reliance, or otherwise if it concludes that in the circumstances justice so requires in order to avoid disproportionate compensation.

A party does not need to foresee the damages that would result from its breach with absolute certainty. Again, the standard is that the party foresee such damages as a *probable* result of breach. Moreover, a party needs to foresee more than the fact that some loss will result from its breach; the party must foresee *that type of loss*. Finally, under the Restatement, the injured party need not also foresee the loss; only the breaching party must foresee it. Note that some courts describe the test in a way that suggests both parties must have foreseen such damage as a probable result of breach. Yet despite stating the test in this way, courts tend to only analyze whether the damage was foreseeable to the breaching party. That is likely because the aggrieved party does not challenge the fact that it foresaw the damage; in fact, by seeking such damage recovery, the aggrieved party concedes that such damage was foreseeable to it.

The reason for this limitation is that if a party cannot foresee a type of damage that might result from its breach, it cannot factor that damage in when deciding (1) whether to enter the contract or (2) what consideration to provide or require from the counterparty when negotiating the terms of the contract. Moreover, people might be unduly discouraged from contracting if they might be held liable for damages they cannot foresee at the time of contracting.

Applying this foreseeability test to the above facts, Doug would likely not be liable for your lost salary. Here, Doug had no idea that that would be the consequence of his failing to walk Duncan on October 5. Not only did you not communicate to him the possible consequences if he did not show, but it is not a typical consequence that flows from a breach of a dog-walking contract. At worst, usually an unwalked dog has extra energy and chews up shoes or furniture.

The following case is a classic case on the foreseeability doctrine. As you review the decision, consider what factors make or should make different types of damages arising from a breach foreseeable. Are any of those factors within the control of the contracting parties, and if so, how might that affect contract negotiations and contract drafting?

Hadley v. Baxendale
Exchequer Court
156 Eng. Rep. 145 (1854)

At the trial before Crompton, J., at the last Gloucester Assizes, it appeared that the plaintiffs carried on an extensive business as millers at Gloucester; and that, on the 11th of May, their mill was stopped by a breakage of the crank shaft by which the mill was worked. The steam-engine was manufactured by Messrs. Joyce & Co., the engineers, at Greenwich, and it became necessary to send the shaft as a pattern for a new one to Greenwich. The fracture was discovered on the 12th, and on the 13th the plaintiffs sent one of their servants to the office of the defendants, who are the wellknown carriers trading under the name of Pickford & Co., for the purpose of having the shaft carried to Greenwich. The plaintiffs' servant told the clerk that the mill was stopped, and that the shaft must be sent immediately; and in answer to the inquiry when the shaft would be taken, the answer was, that if it was sent up by twelve o'clock any day, it would be delivered at Greenwich on the following day. On the following day the shaft was taken by the defendants, before noon, for the purpose of being conveyed to Greenwich, and the sum of 2l. 4s. was paid for its carriage for the whole distance; at the same time the defendants' clerk was told that a special entry, if required, should be made to hasten its delivery. The delivery of the shaft at Greenwich was delayed by some neglect; and the consequence was, that the plaintiffs did not receive the new shaft for several days after they would otherwise have done, and the working of their mill was thereby delayed, and they thereby lost the profits they would otherwise have received. On the part of the defendants, it was objected that these damages were too remote, and that the defendants were not liable with respect to them. The learned Judge left the case generally to the jury, who found a verdict with damages beyond the amount paid into Court. Whateley, in last Michaelmas Term, obtained a rule nisi for a new trial, on the ground of misdirection.

The judgment of the Court was now delivered by

ALDERSON, B. We think that there ought to be a new trial in this case; but, in so doing, we deem it to be expedient and necessary to state explicitly the rule which the Judge, at the next trial, ought, in our opinion, to direct the jury to be governed by when they estimate the damages. It is, indeed, of the last importance that we should do this; for, if the jury are left without any definite rule to guide them, it will, in such cases as these, manifestly lead to the greatest injustice. The Courts have done this on several occasions; and, in Blake v. Midland Railway Company (18 Q. B. 93), the Court granted a new trial on this very ground, that the rule had not been definitely laid down to the jury by the learned Judge at Nisi Prius.

. . .

Now we think the proper rule in such a case as the present is this:—Where two parties have made a contract which one of them has broken, the damages which the other party ought to receive in respect of such breach of contract should be such as may fairly and reasonably be considered either arising naturally, i.e., according to the usual course of things, from such breach of contract itself, or such as may reasonably be supposed to have been in the contemplation of both parties, at the time they made the contract, as the probable result of the breach of it. Now, if the special circumstances under which the contract was actually made were communicated by the plaintiffs to the defendants, and thus known to both parties, the damages resulting from the breach of such a contract, which they would reasonably contemplate, would be the amount of injury which would ordinarily follow from a breach of contract under these special circumstances so known and communicated. But, on the other hand, if these special circumstances were wholly unknown to the party breaking the contract, he, at the most, could only be supposed to have had in his contemplation the amount of injury which would arise generally, and in the great multitude of cases not affected by any special circumstances, from such a breach of contract. For, had the special circumstances been known, the parties might have specially provided for the breach of contract by special terms as to the damages in that case; and of this advantage it would be very unjust to deprive them. Now the above principles are those by which we think the jury ought to be guided in estimating the damages arising out of any breach of contract. It is said, that other cases such as breaches of contract in the non-payment of money, or in the not making a good title to land, are to be treated as exceptions from this, and as governed by a conventional rule. But as, in such cases, both parties must be supposed to be cognisant of that well-known rule, these cases may, we think, be more properly classed under the rule above enunciated as to cases under known special circumstances, because there both parties may reasonably be presumed to contemplate the estimation of the amount of damages according to the conventional rule. Now, in the present case, if we are to apply the principles above laid down, we find that the only circumstances here communicated by the plaintiffs to the defendants at the time the contract was made, were, that the article to be carried was the broken shaft of a mill, and that the plaintiffs were the millers of that mill. But how do these circumstances shew reasonably that the profits of the mill must be stopped by an unreasonable delay in the delivery of the broken shaft by the carrier to the third person? Suppose the plaintiffs had another shaft in their possession put up or putting up at the time, and that they only wished to send back the broken shaft to the engineer who made it; it is clear that this would be quite consistent with the above circumstances, and yet the unreasonable delay in the delivery would have no effect upon the intermediate profits of the mill. Or, again, suppose that, at the time of the delivery to the carrier, the machinery of the mill had been in other respects defective, then, also, the same results would follow. Here it is true that the shaft was actually sent back to serve as a model for a new one, and that the want of a new one was the only cause of the stoppage of the mill, and that the loss of profits really arose from not sending down the new shaft in proper time, and that this arose from the delay in delivering the broken one to serve as a model. But it is obvious that, in the great multitude of cases of millers sending off broken shafts to third persons by a carrier under ordinary circumstances, such consequences would not, in all probability, have occurred; and these special circumstances were here never communicated by the plaintiffs to the defendants. It follows, therefore, that the loss of profits here cannot reasonably be considered such a consequence of the breach of contract as could have been fairly and reasonably contemplated by both the parties when they made this contract. For such loss would neither have flowed naturally from the breach of this contract in the great multitude of such cases occurring under ordinary circumstances, nor were the special circumstances, which, perhaps, would have made it a reasonable and natural consequence of such breach of contract, communicated to or known by the defendants. The Judge ought, therefore, to have told the jury, that, upon the facts then before them, they ought not to take the loss of profits into consideration at all in estimating the damages. There must therefore be a new trial in this case.

Understanding the Case:

1. *Context for Case:* In a discussion of this case in the book *Contracts Stories*, Professor Richard Danzig notes the important contextual history for this case. Specifically, this case took place during the Industrial Revolution, when England was transitioning toward becoming a modernized economy. That historical context explains why the shaft was handcrafted, and why there was a significant delay in delivery when the shaft had to be sent by canal instead of rail, as initially planned. Moreover, the law did not yet recognize the limited liability of a business—in other words, owners were personally liable for the debts of their businesses. That explains why the business owners (the Hadleys and Baxendale), and not their respective businesses, were named parties to the lawsuit. And finally, at the time the case was decided, Parliament was in the process of passing a law that allowed a common carrier to limit its liability for loss and injury by printed notice. While that bill had not yet passed at the time *Hadley* was decided, the court might have seen the writing on the wall, and imposed a judge-made limit on damages. For more insights into this interesting case, you may want to read Professor Danzig's article in *Contract Stories*.

Comprehension and Thought Questions:

1. How did Baxendale, the owner of Pickford & Sons, breach the contract with the Hadleys?

2. What damages did the Hadleys seek to recover from that breach?

3. What test did the court use to determine whether the Hadleys were entitled to receive those damages?

4. Did the court find that the Hadleys were entitled to their claimed damages under that test?

Hypothetical Variations:

1. What if when the Hadleys's employee delivered the broken shaft to Pickford & Sons, that employee said "Please rush the delivery of this shaft—we don't have a backup!"?

2. Continuing with the facts from Hypothetical Variation 1, what if the cause for the delay in delivering the shaft to the manufacturer in Greenwich was that the railroad leading to Greenwich (which was the fastest way to transport the shaft to Greenwich) was impassable for one week?

3. What if the Hadleys informed Pickford & Sons of the lack of a back-up shaft while Pickford & Sons' courier was en route to Greenwich with the broken shaft? Would it matter whether Pickford & Sons could communicate with their courier?

Keep in mind that the foreseeability test applies regardless of the type of damages a party seeks. However, it typically only limits "indirect" damages—and specifically lost profits from other transactions—rather than direct damages. That is because the latter types of damages arise "naturally" following a breach.

Contracting parties can to an extent control the risk that a court will not award lost profits because they are not foreseeable. One common way they do this is by including statements in the recitals of the contract explaining special circumstances that exist at the time of contracting. By doing this, the parties make their special circumstances explicit to one another and to a court, which makes losses resulting from those special circumstances foreseeable. Courts can also allow a party to admit extrinsic evidence of special circumstances known to the other party at trial, in making a case for the other party to be liable for indirect damages. This type of evidence would not violate the parol evidence rule, as such evidence would not be used to contradict or supplement the terms of the parties' bargain. But as a matter of planning, it is better to include express recitals in the contract than to rely on the admissibility and credibility of extrinsic evidence to prove foreseeability.

C. REASONABLE CERTAINTY

In addition to needing to be foreseeable, damages must be *reasonably certain*. More specifically, a party can only recover damages for losses that she *proves* with reasonable certainty. If a party's evidence at trial does not prove her losses with reasonable certainty, she cannot recover those losses.

If a party's evidence only proves part of her losses with reasonable certainty, she can recover the losses she proves with reasonable certainty. In other words, this test might limit some, but not all, of a party's damages.

Under this test, damages do not need to be calculated with absolute mathematical precision. The test only requires "reasonable" certainty. Thus, under this flexible standard, a court might find evidence of the approximate amount of losses sufficient to satisfy the test. That is especially so where the counterparty engaged in misconduct and such misconduct is the reason the aggrieved party does not have better evidence of its losses.

On the other hand, a party cannot speculate as to her losses. In other words, proving losses requires more than mere guesswork or unfounded estimation.

In contrast to the foreseeability test, which is evaluated from the perspective of the time of contracting, this test is assessed from the perspective of *the time of trial*. That is because the test depends on the adequacy of a party's evidence at trial in proving losses.

Like the test on foreseeability, this test most often limits a party's recovery of indirect damages, especially lost profits from secondary transactions. That is because it is often hard to prove with reasonable certainty what profits a party would have earned from its related operations had the other party not breached. This is especially the case where an aggrieved party's lost profits are from potential future transactions, and the aggrieved party does not have a history of profits from those transactions yet.

For example, suppose Dr. Shari Cohn, an orthopedic doctor, contracts to buy an innovative piece of diagnostic medical equipment from Medical Equipment Inc. Because this piece of equipment is new, there is no track record as to its effect on a medical practice. Suppose Dr. Cohn agreed to buy this piece of equipment for $500,000. Her expectation is that this piece of equipment will make her more efficient in her diagnostic screening, increasing the number of patients she can see (and treat). It will also help her diagnose problems sooner, also increasing the amount of procedures she performs. She believes that both increases will more than make up for the $500,000 cost of the equipment.

Now assume that Medical Equipment fails to deliver the equipment to Dr. Cohn per the contract. If Dr. Cohn sues Medical Equipment, can she recover the profits she lost from not being able to provide services to more patients, and not being able to perform procedures on those patients who would have been diagnosed using the new equipment? The problem with such a recovery is that there is no way Dr. Cohn can calculate her lost profits with reasonable certainty. Since this is a new machine that she has not used in practice—and presumably other doctors have not used in practice for any length of time, given that it is new—she does not know how much more efficient she would have been, or how many more patients she would have been able to diagnose. Thus, she would simply be guessing in calculating her lost profits, which makes those lost profits speculative.

In comparison, it is easier to prove with reasonable certainty how much a party expended in reliance on a promise, or how much a party unjustly enriched a counterparty. For that reason, where a party cannot prove its lost profits with reasonable certainty, it might instead seek an alternative measure of damages that might yield a greater award. Sometimes that occurs by seeking reliance damages or restitutionary damages. Alternatively, a party might seek specific performance or injunctive relief where it cannot prove its damages with reasonable certainty.

Still, parties can, and often do, meet this test in proving lost profits. Types of evidence that parties often introduce to prove such lost profits with reasonable certainty, where such evidence exists and is probative of lost profits, include the aggrieved person's history of performance or subsequent performance, performance at peer companies, expert valuations, and market and financial data.

PRACTICE PROBLEM 25-2

On May 1 of this year, Bright Light Inc., a lighting company that manufactures and sells high-end lighting fixtures throughout the northeast, hired Marcía Luna as its Vice President of Sales. Before hiring Marcía, Bright Light did not have a Vice President of Sales. However, the recent growth in orders—from

$1 million worth of orders the prior two years to $2 million in orders for the current year *so far*—convinced the Chief Executive Officer, Greta Goodman, that Bright Light needed to hire someone to lead the sales team. Greta hoped that with a Vice President of Sales overseeing sales efforts, Bright Light could be more targeted and efficient with its sales force, growing sales even further.

Per the parties' contract, Marcía's employment term is two years, though as is standard, Bright Light retains the discretion to terminate Marcía's employment early for "cause." Under the agreement, Marcía receives an annual salary of $150,000. In addition, Marcía has a right to receive a commission equal to 2 percent of all sales that she directly participates in.

Right away, Marcía conflicted with Greta. While Marcía wanted to expand Bright Light's sales efforts into other regions, Greta wanted to deepen Bright Light's sales efforts in the northeast. Moreover, Greta disapproved of Marcía's casual, hands-off management style. On September 1, Greta informed Marcía that her employment was terminated. There is no question that that termination was without "cause" under the employment agreement.

Marcía has now retained you to help her in connection with her lawsuit against Bright Light. Before she sues Bright Light, Marcía would like to understand her rights and remedies. For this purpose, assume that you have already explained to Marcía that Bright Light breached its contract with Marcía by terminating her employment early and that, as a result, Marcía likely can receive a remedy of damages. Marcía now wants you to explain to her what remedy she will likely receive at trial. In particular, she wants to know if she can likely receive damages to compensate her for the commissions she lost, as she was expecting that to be the major component of her compensation.

D. CAUSATION

In addition to being foreseeable and reasonably certain, damages must be *caused* by a breach. In other words, a party is not liable for damages it did not cause, even if those damages were foreseeable as a probable result of breach, and even if those damages can be proven with reasonable certainty.

To see how causation applies, suppose Dr. Cohn contracted to buy a standard piece of medical equipment from Medical Equipment Inc. for $500,000. That piece of equipment would replace Dr. Cohn's old (but still functional) version of the same piece of equipment. Studies and experience in other medical offices show that this new model works ten times faster than the prior model, which would allow Dr. Cohn to see three more patients per day. Once again, Medical Equipment fails to deliver this piece of equipment to Dr. Cohn per the contract, breaching that contract. However, at that same time, Dr. Cohn commits medical malpractice, which becomes publicly known through local news media. Dr. Cohn's patient portfolio decreases by 75 percent. Should Medical

Equipment be liable to pay for all of Dr. Cohn's losses due to the 75 percent decline in her patient portfolio? You undoubtedly realize that Medical Equipment's breach did not *cause* all of Dr. Cohn's lost profits. Instead, the bulk of the decrease was caused by her own malpractice. As such, Medical Equipment would not be liable for most of those losses even though Dr. Cohn could likely prove the amount of her losses with reasonable certainty. And the loss of profits from lost patients would be foreseeable by Medical Equipment as a probable result of its breach at the time of contracting.

There is some doctrinal confusion on the role of causation in the remedies analysis. That is because courts sometimes do not specify causation as a separate requirement of damages; rather, they tuck the causation requirement in with either the foreseeability test or the reasonable certainty test. Thus, it is not always clear whether causation is a separate stand-alone requirement, or if it is part of the foreseeability and certainty tests.

Professor Daniel O'Gorman has recently written an article laying out a principled way to look at causation in contract remedies.[5] According to O'Gorman, the type of causation described above is **cause-in-fact**—the general causation requirement—and is analyzed separately from foreseeability and certainty. As he describes it, "[t]he general causation requirement involves whether the defendant's breach caused the *particular type of loss* for which recovery is sought."[6]

However, O'Gorman argues that the foreseeability and certainty tests also evaluate causation. The certainty test focuses on causation for the *amount of loss*. Thus, in the above example, that test would require there to be reasonable certainty as to the amount of damages *caused by Medical Equipment's breach*. And "[t]he foreseeability requirement is similar to tort law's proximate cause requirement, in the sense that it tends to preclude liability for a loss when there were multiple factors that contributed to the loss, making the loss that occurred an unlikely consequence of the breach."[7]

Keep these expert insights in mind as you read cases on limitations on damages, such as *Florafax*. That way, you will not be surprised when you see one court describe causation as a stand-alone limit on damages, and another court tuck causation into one of the other limits described in this chapter.

E. OTHER LIMITS

Even where losses are foreseeable, are calculable with reasonable certainty, and are caused by a breach, a court is not obliged to award them. Specifically, a court can always limit the award of damages in the interest of justice.

---

5. Daniel O'Gorman, *Contracts, Causation, and Clarity*, 78 U. Pitt. L. Rev. 273 (2017).
6. *Id.* at 282-83.
7. *Id.* at 306-07.

One example where courts sometimes limit damages in furtherance of justice is where the loss suffered by an aggrieved party is extremely disproportionate to the contract price. Courts in this situation can limit the aggrieved party's recovery on the theory that the contract price did not cover the risk of such losses occurring.

Courts also sometimes limit damages where the dealings between parties were informal, without a written contract, and included no formal attempt by the parties to allocate risk between them. In this situation, too, courts occasionally limit a party's recovery. This typically occurs in noncommercial contracts, such as those between family members. In that instance, either the parties might not intend to impose the risk of loss on one of the parties, or the court might conclude that it would be unjust to impose the full risk on one of the parties.

Keep in mind that these other limits are only applied in the most extreme of circumstances. In other words, just because we have described them in this book does not mean you should argue that they apply in all cases. Thus, as you begin to develop your legal knowledge and skills, you will want to start practicing the skill of making important judgments about which arguments to make given the facts.

F. LIMITS IN ACTION

The following case demonstrates a modern-day application of many of the limits on damages discussed in this chapter.

Florafax International, Inc. v. GTE Market Resources, Inc.
Supreme Court of Oklahoma
933 P.2d 282 (1997)

LAVENDER, Justice.

We consider the appropriateness of a jury award of lost profits over a two year time period in favor of appellee/counter-appellant, Florafax International, Inc. against appellant/counter-appellee, GTE Market Resources, Inc., for breaching a contract requiring GTE to provide telecommunication and/or telemarketing services for Florafax. The profits were those Florafax claimed it stood to make from a collateral contract it had with a third party, but allegedly lost when the collateral contract was canceled purportedly because GTE breached its contract with Florafax. The Court of Civil Appeals reversed the lost profit award-remanding with instructions for a determination of lost profits incurred during a sixty (60) day period, a time frame chosen on the basis the collateral contract contained a clause allowing either party to it to terminate the collateral contract on sixty (60) days notice. Both parties sought certiorari, Florafax claiming error by the Court of Civil Appeals in limiting lost profits to a sixty (60) day period and GTE attacking the propriety of any lost profit award.

We previously granted both parties' petitions for certiorari and now hold the Court of Civil Appeals erred in limiting lost profits as it did. Instead, we hold the award of lost profits was consistent with our substantive law and was supported by competent evidence. Therefore, we vacate the Court of Civil Appeals' Memorandum Opinion to the extent it disturbed the jury's verdict and trial court's judgment as to the award of lost profits. Instead, we affirm that part of the judgment awarding lost profits based on the jury's verdict.

. . .

II. FACTS.

Florafax is generally a flowers-by-wire company acting as a clearinghouse to allow the placement and receipt of orders between florists throughout the United States and internationally. Basically the system works as follows: retail florists become members of the Florafax network (apparently, thousands of retail florists join Florafax's wire service). Florafax maintains a list of the members and circulates a directory to them. The members are then able to send and receive orders among each other throughout the system. In other words, a consumer orders flowers at a retail florist at a certain location (e.g. Oklahoma City) to be delivered to someone in another location (e.g. Los Angeles). Florafax assists the transactions by collecting money from the florist taking the order from the customer and guarantying payment to the florist delivering the flowers. It processes the credit card activity on the transactions and charges a fee or fees for this service. Florafax also maintains a computer network whereby member florists can send and receive orders by computer—if they have such technology—without using the telephone. It also has a division that advertises floral products by the use of brochures, and other sales and promotional materials, allowing consumers to place a telephone order for floral products directly without going through a florist in their hometowns.

Evidence at trial showed at the time the agreements giving rise to this dispute were entered that Florafax was one of the largest floral wire services of its kind in the nation, and, in fact, certain evidence placed it third world-wide behind Florists' Transworld Delivery Association (FTD) and a company known as Teleflora. Evidence also showed Florafax had been headquartered in Tulsa, Oklahoma since, at least, 1979.

In addition to the above activities, Florafax solicits agreements with third party clients such as supermarket chains, American Express and other entities that advertise the sale of floral products by various methods (e.g. television, radio, newspapers, billing circulars, mass mailings to consumers) which allow a consumer to order floral arrangements via the use of a 1-800 telephone call, with Florafax agreeing to handle the actual inbound and outbound communication aspects of the transactions. In other words, when a consumer responds to an advertisement, it is not the advertiser that answers the telephone call to take the order, or that makes a telephone call or computer communication to a retail florist for fulfillment, but it is Florafax who handles these activities. Such orders would, of course, be fulfilled, if possible, by retail florist members taken from the Florafax directory maintained by it and, again, Florafax would handle the mechanics of processing the transactions, e.g. credit card processing. The advertiser would pay Florafax a certain fee or fees for its services.

One client that signed up for an arrangement like that described immediately above was Bellerose Floral, Inc., d/b/a Flora Plenty, a leading marketer of floral products advertising sales through use of the telephone number 1-800-FLOWERS. Florafax and Bellerose entered a contract in early October 1989 whereby Florafax and/or its designee would accept direct consumer orders (i.e. inbound calls and orders) placed via the 1-800-FLOWERS number and, of course, it also agreed to handle the outbound placement of orders either by telephone or computer transmission. The Florafax/Bellerose contract provided Florafax would be paid certain fee(s) per order. As we read the contract its initial term was for one year, to be automatically renewed from month to month thereafter, but that either party, with or without cause, could terminate the agreement upon sixty (60) days written notice.

GTE, on the other hand, was a company providing telecommunication and/or telemarketing services for other businesses. It provided for other businesses a call answering center where telemarketing sales representatives (TSRs) physically answered telephones when orders from promotional activities came in from consumers and took care of transmitting the orders by telephone or computer for fulfillment. For certain management and business-related reasons Florafax subcontracted out much of the telecommunication and telemarketing services of its business.

In mid-October 1989, about two weeks after Florafax signed its agreement with Bellerose, the Florafax/GTE contract was entered. In essence, it provided GTE would via a call answering center (apparently located in the Dallas, Texas area) handle much, if not all, of the activities connected with taking incoming orders and placing outgoing calls or computer transmissions directed to it by Florafax associated with the purchase and fulfillment of floral orders throughout the United States and internationally. The agreement required Florafax to pay GTE certain fees for this service depending on the type of order.

The Florafax/GTE contract generally ran for a term of three years from the effective date. [T]he parties anticipated Florafax would begin directing calls to GTE for floral orders—a date anticipated to be in early December 1989. It also contained certain provisions that in essence might result in termination after a two year period based upon application of a price/fee renegotiation clause. In answer to one of the questions submitted via a special verdict form, the jury determined the Florafax/GTE contract could be terminated after two years based on this clause.

The contract further contained a clause concerning lost profits providing in pertinent part:

20. *Termination*

a. *Termination for cause* Any non-defaulting party shall have the right to terminate this agreement at any date not less than forty-five (45) days after an event of default occurs and so long as it continues. In the event GTE [ ] ceases to perform its duties hereunder after a notice of termination is given or otherwise, Florafax may suffer tremendous damage to its business. GTE [ ] agrees to pay Florafax consequential damages and lost profits on the business lost.

The contract also specifically noted GTE would be providing services not only for Florafax, but for others.

In addition to the above express contractual provisions, evidence was presented that officials with GTE knew prior to signing the contract that GTE would be providing its services not only directly for Florafax, but that Florafax had been soliciting business from entities such as Bellerose, business that was anticipated to be at least partially directed through GTE's call answering center. In fact, competent evidence exists in this record showing GTE specifically knew when it signed the contract with Florafax that Bellerose was considering turning over a portion of its inbound and outbound business to Florafax, and that Bellerose received somewhere between 100,000–200,000 orders annually. Evidence was also presented that showed GTE, prior to contract execution, considered it a positive aspect of entering the agreement that Florafax was constantly marketing and promoting its business by the addition of outside clients and that this addition of clients would lead to revenue increases. Evidence also existed that Bellerose was Florafax's largest customer and that it had been an ongoing business for at least sixteen (16) years prior to the date of trial.

Evidence was also submitted showing that before GTE entered the contract, its director of finance and administration did a financial analysis of the Florafax/GTE contract and determined GTE would make little or no money from it. His immediate supervisor (the general manager of GTE) was informed of the analysis. GTE, however, made the decision to enter the contract, apparently because it needed new customers and/or in the hope this financial analysis was wrong.

Although from December 1989 through Valentine's Day in February 1990 certain problems surfaced in regard to the adequacy of GTE's performance, at some point after Valentine's Day the problems appeared to worsen. At some time after Valentine's Day and leading up to Mother's Day in May 1990, the latter holiday being described as the largest floral holiday of the year, the adequacy of GTE's performance became subject to serious question. What appears from the evidence to be the most glaring breach on GTE's part was a failure during the week leading up to Mother's Day to provide sufficient TSRs to answer calls anticipated to be directed to it by Florafax, including calls from Bellerose. Without adequate TSRs to take the calls, floral product orders would obviously be lost and Florafax income lost in the process.

Coupled with this evidence of a failure to adequately staff for anticipated calls, there was also evidence that during the term of the contract GTE's project manager for the Florafax account admitted to Florafax's off-site manager stationed at the GTE facility to look out for Florafax's interests there, that GTE no longer wanted the Florafax account—in essence, because GTE was not making money under the contract's pricing scheme. This same Florafax employee was also told by the same GTE project manager and another employee of GTE that GTE would not provide sufficient numbers of TSRs for the Florafax project essentially for the same reason, i.e. GTE was not making money on the project under the pricing terms in the contract. Evidence also showed that as early as April 1990 GTE was requesting from Florafax a change in the pricing terms of the contract, but that such change was never finally agreed to by Florafax. In effect then, there was both direct and circumstantial evidence tending to show that GTE intentionally failed to adequately perform its duties and obligations under its agreement with Florafax to provide telecommunication/telemarketing services in an effort to coerce Florafax into agreeing to a price renegotiation adjustment not required under the terms of the contract. Although other evidence from GTE disputed the evidence of Florafax that GTE intentionally failed to provide sufficient staffing for Florafax at its call answering center, as noted in I. STANDARD OF REVIEW, as an appellate court we are in no position to weigh the evidence in such regard—that responsibility belonged to the jury.

In addition, evidence was presented that GTE's failure to perform caused Bellerose to terminate its agreement with Florafax and Bellerose ceased its relationship with Florafax apparently some time in July 1990, directing no more calls from its 1-800-FLOWERS number through GTE after that time. The President of Bellerose essentially testified that he anticipated his agreement with Florafax to be a long-term relationship if things worked out and, although his testimony was not absolute in such regard, that he pulled out of his relationship with Florafax because of the poor performance of GTE. In such latter regard, although the President of Bellerose acknowledged that he was also upset with Florafax, primarily because it did not manage the situation with GTE in such a way to insure adequate performance, we believe a reasonable conclusion from his testimony was that, the inadequate performance of GTE was the direct cause of Bellerose's decision to terminate the Florafax/Bellerose contract and that had GTE adequately performed, the relationship between Florafax and Bellerose would have been a long-term one, rather than being canceled in July 1990. Clearly, the evidence does not show any other major factor connected with Bellerose's termination of its relationship with Florafax other than the insufficient performance by GTE of duties and obligations it was required to perform under its contract with Florafax. In fact, the President of Bellerose testified that the most important issues leading to Bellerose's decision to terminate its relationship with Florafax were the performance issues—i.e. performance that was directly the responsibility of GTE under the Florafax/GTE agreement.

As a result of GTE's breach, in addition to losing Bellerose as a client, Florafax incurred costs primarily associated with taking steps necessary to set up its own call answering center in Tulsa to perform the duties GTE was supposed to handle so that it would not lose other clients or business relationships as it had lost Bellerose. Florafax finally left the GTE facility at the end of September 1990.

In addition to seeking damages attributable to costs associated with performing the services GTE was supposed to perform, Florafax sought lost profits it claimed would have been realized from the Florafax/Bellerose contract. In support of and in opposition to the lost profit claim the parties presented conflicting economic projections through expert witnesses (Florafax through an economist, GTE through a Certified Public Accountant) as to how much profit, if any, Florafax would have made from the Bellerose contract over varying lengths of time. Although the two experts differed on certain aspects of their formulations (e.g. sale close ratios and percentage increase, if any, of Bellerose business) the projections were basically grounded on the pricing terms of the Florafax/GTE contract and projections of the number of Bellerose orders. A starting point for the latter projections had as their basis the number of calls actually received by GTE from Bellerose customers during the five to seven month period Bellerose calls and orders were actually being handled at the GTE facility.

. . .

The jury determined GTE breached its contract with Florafax and, in addition to other damages, awarded Florafax $750,000.00 in lost profits that would have been earned under the Florafax/Bellerose contract over a two year period of time. Other damages awarded to Florafax included a little over $820,000.00, the majority of which reflected costs and expenses associated with setting up and/or expanding a call center in Tulsa, Oklahoma to perform those functions GTE was supposed to perform under the Florafax/GTE contract. On appeal, GTE, although not admitting liability—i.e. that it breached its contract with Florafax—does not contest the jury determination that it did breach the contract. We now turn to the lost profit damage issues to be reviewed.

III. LOST PROFITS FROM A COLLATERAL CONTRACT MAY BE RECOVERED AS A PROPER ELEMENT OF DAMAGE FOR BREACH OF CONTRACT.

GTE raises two basic arguments on the propriety of the recovery of lost profits. These are: 1) lost profit damages cannot include profits from third-party collateral contracts or, if they are recoverable, Florafax failed to prove entitlement to them because it failed to show the prospect of profits from the Florafax/Bellerose contract or, conversely, the loss of such profits upon GTE's breach, were in the contemplation of GTE and Florafax at the time they entered the

Florafax/GTE contract; and, 2) if lost profits from the Florafax/Bellerose contract are recoverable they must be limited to a sixty (60) day period, because profits beyond this time must be deemed too remote, speculative or uncertain, and Florafax could not be said to be reasonably assured of any profits from its relationship with Bellerose for any longer period, given the Florafax/Bellerose contract clause allowing either Florafax or Bellerose the right to terminate that contract upon sixty (60) days notice. In our view, each argument is without merit.

III(A). COLLATERAL CONTRACTS AND LOST PROFITS.

GTE asserts Oklahoma jurisprudence has not squarely addressed the question of whether a party suing for breach of contract may recover lost profits arising from a collateral contract. Although this Court may not have used the exact phrase "lost profits from third-party collateral contracts" a review of Oklahoma law makes clear if such damages are properly proved they are recoverable. Thus, GTE's apparent view that lost profits from a collateral contract are never recoverable for breach of contract because as a matter of law they are inherently too remote, speculative and/or unforeseeable, is mistaken.

The time-honored general rules on recovery of damages for breach of contract are found in *Hadley v. Baxendale,* 9 Ex. 341, 156 Eng. Rep. 145 (1854)—rules this Court has generally followed. They are: 1) where no special circumstances distinguish the contract involved from the great mass of contracts of the same kind, the damages recoverable are those as would naturally and generally result from the breach according to the usual course of things, and 2) where there are special circumstances in the contract, damages which result in consequence of the special circumstances are recoverable, if, and only if, the special circumstances were communicated to or known by both parties to the contract at the time they entered the contract. The lost profits involved here fall under the second branch of the *Hadley v. Baxendale* formulation.

Generally speaking, this Court has long espoused the view that loss of future or anticipated profit—i.e. loss of expected monetary gain—is recoverable in a breach of contract action: 1) if the loss is within the contemplation of the parties at the time the contract was made, 2) if the loss flows directly or proximately from the breach—i.e. if the loss can be said to have been caused by the breach—and 3) if the loss is capable of reasonably accurate measurement or estimate. An award in the form of a loss of profits, in fact, is generally considered a common measure of damages for breach of contract, it frequently represents fulfillment of the non-breaching party's expectation interest, and it often closely approximates the goal of placing the innocent party in the same position as if the contract had been fully performed.

Our cases also recognize that where there is sufficient evidence presented on the issue of the recovery of special damages—including lost profits—what

was or was not in the contemplation of the parties at the time of contracting is a question of fact to be determined by the trier of fact. Liability for
lost profits arises where the loss of anticipated profits upon breach can reasonably be said to be in the contemplation of the parties at the time of
contracting.

    . . .

Here, there is clearly sufficient competent evidence to show GTE had within
its contemplation at the time of contracting the potential for profits from a
Florafax association with Bellerose. As we noted in section II. FACTS above,
GTE knew it would be providing services not only directly for Florafax, but for
others on behalf of Florafax. It knew Florafax was soliciting other entities to
use the services of a call answering center like GTE's and, in fact, GTE looked
upon Florafax's solicitation of these other entities as a positive aspect of a
contractual relationship with Florafax because of the potential for increased
revenue.

Trial evidence also showed the Florafax/Bellerose contract was entered
two weeks prior to the Florafax/GTE agreement and that GTE officials knew
either before or contemporaneously with signing the latter contract that
Bellerose was considering turning over a portion of its inbound and outbound
business via its 1-800-FLOWERS network to Florafax-business GTE also knew
consisted of 100,000–200,000 orders annually. Further, as already noted,
a clause in the Florafax/GTE contract itself expressly reflects the parties'
contemplation of the recovery of lost profits by Florafax should GTE cease
to perform its duties and obligations during the term of the contract—and,
as also noted, evidence exists in this record that GTE intentionally failed
to perform during part of the term of the contract, a failure on its part we
conclude would support a determination the lost profit clause of the Florafax/
GTE contract was implicated.

In our view then, contrary to the arguments of GTE, lost profits from a collateral contractual relationship may be recovered in a breach of contract action
if such damages can be said to have been within the contemplation of the parties at the time of contracting. Here, there is evidence in the record—if believed
by the jury—that plainly would support a finding special circumstances were
communicated to or known by GTE at the time of contracting, so that a reasonable conclusion would be that the prospect of profits and, conversely, their loss
upon breach, were in the contemplation of the parties at the time of contracting and would be suffered by Florafax should GTE cease to adequately perform
under the Florafax/GTE agreement. Therefore, GTE's apparent positions—that
profits to be derived from a collateral contract are never recoverable or, even
if otherwise recoverable, they are not so here because the prospect of such
profits or damages from their loss cannot be said to have been in GTE's contemplation at the time of contracting—are without merit and provide no reason
to disturb the award of lost profits by the jury.

III(B). THE SIXTY (60) DAY TERMINATION CLAUSE IN THE FLORAFAX/BELLEROSE CONTRACT DOES NOT PRECLUDE THE RECOVERY OF LOST PROFITS BEYOND THE SIXTY (60) DAY PERIOD.

GTE, in addition to arguing no lost profits are proper, alternatively asserts that if their recovery is appropriate, they must be limited to a period of sixty (60) days because of the termination notice clause of the Florafax/Bellerose contract which allowed either party to that agreement to terminate that contract, with or without cause, upon sixty (60) days written notice. For this position prime reliance is placed on *Osborn v. Commanche Cattle Industries, Inc.*, 545 P.2d 827 (Okla. Ct. Civ. App. 1975), an opinion of the Oklahoma Court of Civil Appeals. Although we believe the rule of law laid down in *Osborn* is sound, the rule is not controlling here.

Osborn involved a situation where plaintiff had contracted with a feedlot to perform certain cleaning functions, stockpiling and disposal of manure and some other duties. The contract was for a term of three years, but contained a clause allowing either party to terminate the agreement by giving the other thirty (30) days advance notice. The feedlot was sold and the new owner, without knowing of the previous owner's contract with plaintiff, hired someone else to perform the duties plaintiff was to perform. Plaintiff, not knowing of the feedlot's sale, began to purchase equipment necessary to perform his duties under the contract. No formal notice was ever given to plaintiff by the feedlot that its contract with him was terminated. The breach in *Osborn* was a failure to give plaintiff thirty (30) days advance notice of the contract's termination. Plaintiff sued the previous owner to recover the profits he would have made over the three year life of the contract, plus certain other damages. The trial court allowed the lost profit issue to go to the jury with instructions allowing their recovery for the entire three year period, over defendant's objection only nominal damages were appropriate because either party to the contract had the right to terminate it upon thirty (30) days notice.

The *Osborn* court found error in submitting the lost profit issue to the jury for a longer period than the thirty (30) day notice time frame based on the following rule of law: no party to a contract may recover more in damages for a breach of the contract than might have been gained by full performance. Such rule of law is essentially codified at 23 O.S.1991, § 96, which provides, with certain exceptions not applicable here, "no person can recover a greater amount in damages for the breach of an obligation, than he could have gained by the full performance thereof on both sides. . . ." The rule applied in *Osborn* because full or complete performance under the contract could have been supplied by defendant simply giving the agreed-to notice and, therefore, plaintiff's expectation interest could have been no greater than the prospect of profit over the length of the notice period. In that plaintiff was never assured of performance by the breaching party beyond the length of the notice period his prospect of net gain, likewise, could never extend beyond this period of time. Plaintiff could not recover more than thirty (30) days lost profits because he could not recover more in profits than he might have made from full performance. In other words, in *Osborn* it was absolutely certain plaintiff could not establish lost profits for any greater period of time because the defendant had an absolute right to terminate the contract upon giving the agreed notice and exercise of this right would have provided full performance on the defendant's part.

The situation here is quite different. First off, we must note that Florafax does not rely on any violation of the sixty (60) day notice provision by Bellerose to support its lost profit claim. It contends, instead, that it was the breach of GTE that caused Bellerose to terminate its relationship with Florafax when it did and its relationship with Bellerose would have continued as a long-term relationship generating profits to Florafax well into the future, had it not been for GTE's breach.

Secondly, GTE had no right to terminate either the Florafax/GTE or Florafax/Bellerose contracts upon any short specified notice provision. That right belonged only to Florafax and Bellerose, and only in relation to the latter contract. Thus, full performance could not have been supplied by the simple expediency of GTE giving sixty (60) days notice to Florafax that it was terminating their agreement. Instead, the Florafax/GTE contract, according to the unchallenged finding of the jury, had a minimum term of two years based on the effect of the price renegotiation provisions of the contract, i.e. Florafax was guaranteed performance by GTE for a full two years.

Thus, the rule of *Osborn* that a non-breaching party may not receive more in damages than he might or could have gained from full performance is inapplicable because this record contains competent evidence Florafax could have made profits from the Florafax/Bellerose contract for a period longer than the sixty (60) day notice period had GTE fully performed under the Florafax/GTE contract. In fact, competent evidence exists supporting the view it is probable some additional profits would have been made from the Bellerose relationship for a longer period of time. Further, application of the *Osborn* rule here would improperly allow GTE to benefit from a cancellation right it had no ability to exercise. Accordingly, the rule of *Osborn* does not preclude Florafax's recovery of lost profit damages associated with the loss of the Bellerose relationship in excess of a sixty (60) day period.

III(C). COMPETENT EVIDENCE EXISTS TO SUPPORT THE AWARD OF LOST PROFIT DAMAGES TO A REASONABLE CERTAINTY.

Even though the rule of *Osborn* is inapplicable, GTE's arguments as to the termination notice clause of the collateral contract do, however, implicate the legal principle that before lost profit damages are recoverable it must be adequately shown such profits were reasonably certain to have been made by the non-breaching party absent breach. We believe the answer to the reasonable certainty question is not one subject to decision as a matter of law under this record, but was one of fact to be decided by the trier of fact—here the jury.

In order for damages to be recoverable for breach of contract they must be clearly ascertainable, in both their nature and origin, and it must be made to appear they are the natural and proximate consequence of the breach and not speculative and contingent. It is not necessary, however, for the recovery of lost profits shown to have been caused by a breach of contract, that the profits be established with absolute certainty and barring any possibility of failure, but it is only required that it be established with reasonable certainty that profits would have been made had the contract not been breached. In essence, what a plaintiff must show for the recovery of lost profits is sufficient certainty that reasonable minds might believe from a preponderance of the evidence that such damages were actually suffered. This requirement of proof applies to the fact of lost profits, the causation of lost profits and the amount of lost profits.

The above rules, at least in part, are essentially reflected in Oklahoma's statutory law found at 23 O.S.1991, § 21, which provides:

> For the breach of an obligation arising from contract, the measure of damages . . . is the amount which will compensate the party aggrieved for all the detriment proximately caused thereby, or which, in the ordinary course of things, would be likely to result therefrom. No damages can be recovered for a breach of contract, which are not clearly ascertainable in both their nature and origin.

Once it is made to clearly appear that loss of business profits has been suffered by virtue of the breach, it is proper to let the jury decide what the loss is from the best evidence the nature of the case admits. When a breach of a contractual obligation with resulting damages has been established, although the amount of damages may not be based on mere speculation, conjecture and surmise alone, the mere uncertainty as to the exact amount of damages will not preclude the right of recovery. It is sufficient if the evidence shows the extent of damage by just and reasonable inference. We believe sufficient evidence was presented so that Florafax carried its burden to prove the fact, cause and amount of its lost profit damages with the requisite degree of reasonable certainty.

The fact of lost profit damage beyond merely a sixty (60) day period is shown by the testimony of Bellerose's President. Although not absolute, his testimony was, in essence, he considered the relationship with Florafax a long-term one had things worked out and that the most important issues to him in making the decision to terminate were issues concerning performance. This testimony showed the relationship in all probability would have continued long after it was terminated had GTE adequately performed. Although it is true—given the existence of the sixty (60) day notice provision—Bellerose might have terminated the Florafax/Bellerose contract at some point in time even had GTE performed, the state of this record does not require a conclusion Bellerose would have exercised its right of termination for some other reason.

We are also of the view that the fact of damage is partially shown by the projections for profits of both the damage experts presented by the parties. Although they differed in their ultimate conclusions as to the extent or amount of lost profits, both presented estimates that Florafax could have made profits from the Florafax/Bellerose relationship had it survived.

Causation is also shown by sufficient competent evidence, evidence that partially overlaps with that of the fact of damage in this case. There is enough evidence to support a reasonable determination that Bellerose's decision to cancel or terminate its relationship with Florafax was the direct result of GTE's failure to render adequate performance and, that GTE's breach of the Florafax/GTE contract caused the cancellation. Therefore, there is sufficient evidence in this record upon which reasonable minds might rely that profits from the Florafax/Bellerose relationship would have actually been made by Florafax beyond a sixty (60) day period and that GTE's breach of its contract with Florafax caused the loss of Bellerose as a client.

As to the exact extent or amount of damages, the record contains sufficient evidence to take the matter out of the realm of mere speculation, conjecture or surmise. A track record existed which showed the calls coming to GTE from Bellerose during the five to seven months Bellerose business was actually being routed to GTE. There was also evidence that although the business relationship between Florafax and Bellerose was relatively new, Bellerose had been in business for a number of years, and it had experienced 100,000–200,000 orders annually. Such evidence clearly was appropriate to consider on the issue of the extent of lost profits. Although this case is not exactly like our cases dealing with the destruction of an established business by a breach of contract, it is sufficiently close to be analogized to the established business situation, where we have allowed the recovery of lost profits.

Evidence also existed which showed that Bellerose, after terminating its relationship with Florafax, experienced a substantial increase in its sales volume in 1991. In other words, there was not only evidence tending to show a certain volume of orders prior to the breach, but evidence tending to show that level of sales would have in all probability increased substantially during part of the term of the Florafax/GTE contract had Bellerose continued its relationship with Florafax. This post-breach evidence is proper to be considered at arriving at a reasonable estimate of the loss caused by a breach of contract because all facts which would reasonably tend to make certain the amount of injury inflicted are admissible. Although the jury apparently did not totally credit the testimony or documentation presented by either Florafax's or GTE's experts as to their projections of profits lost, the $750,000.00 awarded for the two year period was within the range of the estimates of the two experts. Accordingly, not only was the fact and causation of lost profit damages adequately shown to a reasonable certainty, but the amount of lost profit damages awarded was sufficiently shown through competent evidence contained in this record to take the matter out of the realm of mere speculation, conjecture and surmise.

IV. CONCLUSION.

The award of the jury of lost profit damages associated with the Florafax/ Bellerose contract was an appropriate remedy for GTE's breach of its contract with Florafax. It was consistent with our substantive law as to the recovery of lost profits for a breach of contract and was supported by competent evidence.

Comprehension and Thought Questions:

1. What losses did Florafax seek to recover from GTE as a result of GTE's breach? *Consequential?!*

2. What test did the court use to determine whether Florafax's lost profits from its contract with Bellerose were reasonably foreseeable?

3. What did the court conclude when applying that test to the facts?

4. What test did the court use to determine whether Florafax's lost profits from its contract with Bellerose were reasonably certain?

5. What did the court conclude when applying that test to the facts?

6. Did GTE's breach "cause" those lost profits? How did the court determine this?

7. Did the damages award put Florafax in the same position it would have been in had GTE not breached? As you think about this question, consider whether Florafax might have suffered other losses that it did not seek to recover.

Hypothetical Variations:

1. What if GTE only learned about Florafax's contract with Bellerose one week *after* GTE had entered its contract with Florafax?

2. What if Bellerose had been a new start-up floral business and only had six months of operations before GTE breached its contract with Florafax?

3. What if the GTE-Florafax contract did not contain a clause expressly making GTE liable for consequential damages in the event of its breach?

4. What if the contract between GTE and Florafax disclaimed GTE's liability for all consequential damages?

Normally would apply, but GTE is in bad faith = court won't apply it here

---

PRACTICE PROBLEM 25-3

Three years ago, Ravi King decided to follow his dream of starting and managing his own restaurant. Specifically, his idea was to start a build-your-own-burrito business—a restaurant idea that was innovative and one-of-a-kind in downtown Springfield. He opened Burrito Builder in Unit C of 1000 Oak Street, which was one of the only available locations for rent in the heart of downtown Springfield. By locating his restaurant there, King was able to tap into the business lunchtime crowd. Per Burrito Builder's lease with Commercial Properties Inc., the landlord of this space, the lease term was four years, with an option to renew the lease for an additional four years. Burrito Builder paid $4,000 per month for this space.

In the first year of its operation, Burrito Builder lost $15,000. While Burrito Builder had a great location and great food, it took time to build up a loyal customer base. Indeed, it its second year of operation, Burrito Builder sold an average of $2,000 worth of burritos a month, for a total of $24,000 in annual sales. While this level of sales was modest, King figured it reflected a positive financial trend for his restaurant.

Halfway through Burrito Builder's third year of operations, Burrito Builder was already averaging $5,000 in sales a month, for a total of $30,000 so far that year. It was then that King received a notice in the mail from Ralph Schneider, the leasing manager at Commercial Properties, notifying King that Commercial Properties was terminating its lease with Burrito Builder because of the long lines of customers who showed up for lunch every day, creating a pedestrian bottleneck in front of 1000 Oak Street.

King was surprised, as the lease said nothing about Commercial Properties having the right to terminate the lease early due to long lines or any other similar circumstance. Plus, Burrito Builder's customers were always orderly when lining up for the restaurant, and King never received any complaints about the lines.

While King tried to convince Schneider to reconsider, Schneider refused.

So, King had to promptly close Burrito Builder. Three months later, he reopened his restaurant at the only suitable location nearby, which was at 2011 W. Elm Street, ten blocks away. The lunchtime foot traffic at that location was not nearly as good. As a result, Burrito Builder only received half the number of customers that it had received each month at 1000 Oak Street. Thus, in the second half of Burrito Builder's third year of operation, Burrito Builder only generated an average of $2,500 in sales per month, for a total of $15,000 in sales during those six months.

Burrito Builder is now in its fourth year of operation and King has decided to seek legal advice on whether Burrito Builder has any legal claims against Commercial Properties.

Assume you have already determined that Commercial Properties breached the lease agreement with Burrito Builder when it terminated the lease early. What damages would Burrito Builder likely be able to obtain from Commercial Properties for that breach? In your answer, make sure you identify any potential limitations to Burrito Builder and evaluate the likelihood that those limitations will actually limit Burrito Builder's recovery.

G. MITIGATION

Mitigation is another doctrine that limits a party's recovery of damages. Under **mitigation**, an aggrieved party must attempt to avoid losses resulting from the counterparty's breach. A failure of the aggrieved party to avoid losses that are avoidable using reasonable efforts will prevent that party from recovering damages for the losses it could have avoided had it used reasonable efforts.

Under this doctrine, when a party discovers that the other party has committed a total breach, or that the other party has anticipatorily repudiated a contract (meaning that the other party's performance is not forthcoming), the aggrieved party usually cannot continue to perform, as doing so will just rack up additional losses for which the breaching party might be liable. Moreover, the aggrieved party typically will need to make substitute arrangements to avoid losses. That often means for a seller of goods or services, finding the next highest paying buyer, or for an employer, finding the least expensive reasonably equivalent employee.

Under this doctrine, a party gets credit for mitigating even if it is unsuccessful in avoiding losses. Thus, for example, if an employer improperly terminates an employee's employment at the end of the sixth month of a one-year employment term, the employee must use reasonable efforts to find equivalent substitute employment to limit his losses. If, however, the employee cannot find such an equivalent substitute position for the remainder of his year employment term despite using reasonable efforts, he can still recover for his losses due to the employer's breach.

A party need only act reasonably in mitigating its damages. Thus, a party need not go to all lengths to avoid losses. Namely, a party generally does not need to incur additional, unreasonable expense or risk or expose itself to undue harm or humiliation in order to avoid losses.

In the context of litigation, the party seeking damages has the burden to prove that damages were caused by the breaching party's breach, to prove that they were reasonably foreseeable as a probable result of breach, and to prove its damages to reasonable certainty. The burden of proof is then on the breaching party to show that the aggrieved party should not recover all of its claimed losses because they were avoidable. The breaching party then must show by how much the aggrieved party's losses should be reduced due to its failure to adequately mitigate its damages.

The following case is a classic case demonstrating the concept of mitigation.

Rockingham County v. Luten Bridge Co.
U.S. Court of Appeals, 4th Circuit
35 F.2d 301 (1929)

PARKER, Circuit Judge.

This was an action at law instituted in the court below by the Luten Bridge Company, as plaintiff, to recover of Rockingham county, North Carolina, an amount alleged to be due under a contract for the construction of a bridge. The county admits the execution and breach of the contract, but contends that notice of cancellation was given the bridge company before the erection of the bridge was commenced, and that it is liable only for the damages which the company would have sustained, if it had abandoned construction at that time[.]

. . .

On January 7, 1924, the board of commissioners of Rockingham county voted to award to plaintiff a contract for the construction of the bridge in controversy. Three of the five commissioners favored the awarding of the contract and two opposed it. [A member of the board who voted in favor of the construction resigned and was replaced by a new member opposed to the project. The County rescinded the contract issuing a unanimous resolution on February 21.]

At the time of the passage of the first resolution, very little work toward the construction of the bridge had been done, it being estimated that the total cost of labor done and material on the ground was around $1,900; but, notwithstanding the repudiation of the contract by the county, the bridge company continued with the work of construction.

On November 24, 1924, plaintiff instituted this action against Rockingham county, and against Pruitt, Pratt, McCollum, Martin, and Barber, as constituting its board of commissioners. Complaint was filed, setting forth the execution of the contract and the doing of work by plaintiff thereunder, and alleging that for work done up until November 3, 1924, the county was indebted in the sum of $ 18,301.07.

. . .

As the county now admits the execution and validity of the contract, and the breach on its part, the ultimate question in the case is one as to the measure of plaintiff's recovery, and the exceptions must be considered with this in mind.

. . .

Coming, then, to the third question—i.e., as to the measure of plaintiff's recovery—we do not think that, after the county had given notice, while the contract was still executory, that it did not desire the bridge built and would not pay for it, plaintiff could proceed to build it and recover the contract price. It is true that the county had no right to rescind the contract, and the notice given plaintiff amounted to a breach on its part; but, after plaintiff had received notice of the breach, it was its duty to do nothing to increase the damages flowing therefrom. If A enters into a binding contract to build a house for B, B, of course, has no right to rescind the contract without A's consent. But if, before the house is built, he decides that he does not want it, and notifies A to that effect, A has no right to proceed with the building and thus pile up damages. His remedy is to treat the contract as broken when he receives the notice, and sue for the recovery of such damages, as he may have sustained from the breach, including any profit which he would have realized upon performance, as well as any other losses which may have resulted to him. In the case at bar, the county decided not to build the road of which the bridge was to be a part, and did not build it. The bridge, built in the midst of the forest, is of no value to the county because of this change of circumstances. When, therefore, the county gave notice to the plaintiff that it would not proceed with the project, plaintiff should have desisted from further work. It had no right thus to pile up damages by proceeding with the erection of a useless bridge.

The contrary view was expressed by Lord Cockburn in *Frost v. Knight*, L. R. 7 Ex. 111, but, as pointed out by Prof. Williston (Williston on Contracts, vol. 3, p. 2347), it is not in harmony with the decisions in this country. The American rule and the reasons supporting it are well stated by Prof. Williston as follows:

> "There is a line of cases running back to 1845 which holds that, after an absolute repudiation or refusal to perform by one party to a contract, the other party cannot continue to perform and recover damages based on full performance. This rule is only a particular application of the general rule of damages that a plaintiff cannot hold a defendant liable for damages which need not have been incurred; or, as it is often stated, the plaintiff must, so far as he can without loss to himself, mitigate the damages caused by the defendant's wrongful act. The application of this rule to the matter in question is obvious. If a man engages to have work done, and afterwards repudiates his contract before the work has been begun or when it had been only partially done, it is inflicting damage on the defendant without benefit to the plaintiff to allow the latter to insist on proceeding with the contract. The work may be useless to the defendant, and yet he would be forced to pay the full contract price. On the other hand, the plaintiff is interested only in the profit he will make out of the contract. If he receives this it is equally advantageous for him to use his time otherwise."

. . .

The measure of plaintiff's damage, upon its appearing that notice was duly given not to build the bridge, is an amount sufficient to compensate plaintiff for labor and materials expended and expense incurred in the part performance of the contract, prior to its repudiation, plus the profit which would have been realized if it had been carried out in accordance with its terms.

The judgment below will accordingly be reversed, and the case remanded for a new trial.

Reversed.

Comprehension and Thought Questions:

1. What damages did Luten seek to recover?

2. What test did the court use to determine if Luten could recover damages for losses it incurred from continuing to construct the bridge even after it received notice from the county that it did not want the bridge built?

3. In applying that test, could Luten recover those damages?

Hypothetical Variations:

1. What if Luten had stopped construction of the bridge when it first received notice from the county? What remedy would Luten have likely received in that circumstance?

2. What if Luten had unused building materials at the time it received the county's notice to stop construction, which it kept and did not try to sell? Could Luten likely recover for the cost of those unsold building materials?

People often say that a party has a "duty" to mitigate its losses resulting from a breach of contract. However, that is not technically correct. The term "duty" refers to a legal obligation, created by a promise which, if not performed, amounts to breach. However, there is no legal duty for a party to mitigate its damages. Moreover, a party's failure to mitigate its losses does not constitute a breach. Rather, as you saw in *Luten*, the consequence of a party's failure to mitigate its damages is the reduction in that party's recovery equal to the losses it could have avoided.

As a final note, in the same article discussed in Section D above, Professor Daniel O'Gorman argues that mitigation is yet another test for causation.[8] He argues that it evaluates whether an affected party's conduct (i.e., not avoiding losses) contributed to its losses. If so, the party cannot recover for those losses, as its own behavior caused them to some degree. Again, this doctrinal observation might be useful to you as you try to grasp the various limits on damages.

The following case is a modern example of an application of the mitigation doctrine.

Fischer v. Heymann
Supreme Court of Indiana
12 N.E.3d 867 (2014)

RUSH, Justice.

This is the second appeal in protracted litigation over the breach of a real-estate sales contract. The first appeal established that Buyers breached the contract when they unreasonably demanded that Seller fix a minor electrical problem as a condition of purchase. In this second appeal, we granted transfer to consider whether the trial court acted within its discretion in calculating Seller's damages. Both parties appealed the trial court's findings regarding Seller's efforts to mitigate her damages. Seller argues that her efforts were reasonable and justify a full award. Buyers argue Seller failed to mitigate her damages in two ways: 1) by failing to respond to their demand for electrical repairs and thus preserve the contract, and 2) by failing to accept a substitute

---

8. *See* Daniel O'Gorman, *Contracts, Causation, and Clarity*, 78 U. Pitt. L. Rev. 273, 305 (2017).

offer to purchase the property after the agreement fell through. The trial court disagreed with Buyers' first argument but agreed with the second, and reduced Seller's damages accordingly. We hold the trial court was within its discretion to reach this conclusion, and therefore affirm the award of damages and attorney fees.

FACTS AND PROCEDURAL HISTORY

On February 4, 2006, Defendants Michael and Noel Heymann agreed to buy a condominium from Plaintiff Gayle Fischer for $315,000. Both parties signed a purchase agreement ("Agreement"), and the Heymanns paid $5,000 in earnest money. The Agreement authorized the Heymanns to terminate if Fischer refused to fix any "major defect" discovered upon inspection, but did not permit them to terminate if Fischer refused to perform "routine maintenance" or make "minor repair[s]." On February 10, 2006, the Heymanns demanded Fischer fix an electrical problem after an inspection report revealed electricity was not flowing to three power outlets. The Heymanns thought this was a "major defect" under the Agreement and conditioned their purchase on Fischer's timely response. Fischer failed to timely respond to their demand—even though she eventually fixed the problem for $117 on February 20—and the Heymanns tendered a mutual release. Fischer refused to sign the release and later sued for specific performance, or damages in the alternative, on May 9, 2006—two days before the original date of closing.

The trial court rejected Fischer's claim after the initial bench trial on the merits. The court found the Heymanns reasonably believed the electrical problem was severe, which justified their termination of the Agreement. But a divided panel of the Court of Appeals disagreed. The panel held that the Heymanns' demand itself breached the Agreement because the demand stemmed from an objectively unreasonable belief that the electrical problem was a "major defect." *Fischer v. Heymann*, 943 N.E.2d 896, 902–03 (Ind. Ct. App. 2011), trans. denied ("*Fischer I*"). The Court of Appeals thus reversed and remanded for the trial court to determine damages.

On remand, Fischer sought $306,616.73 in total damages, attorney fees, and court costs. Broken down, her damages request accounted for (1) the difference between the Heymanns' purchase price of $315,000 and the 2011 sale price of $180,000; (2) $12,333.89 in closing costs; (3) $139,075.54 for the cost of maintaining the condo from 2006, when the Heymann deal fell through, until 2011 when she sold the property; (4) $11,222.50 in attorney fees; and (5) $8,984.80 in court costs. As the litigation continued on Fischer's second appeal, she argued those fees and costs have increased to $12,268.24 and $9,834.80, respectively.

The trial court entered its findings and conclusions after hearing extensive testimony. It concluded Fischer failed to mitigate her damages because she could have accepted an offer to sell the condo in 2007 for $240,000, instead of waiting to sell it in 2011 for only $180,000. Had she sold in 2007, she could have avoided all carrying costs and maintenance expenses she incurred between 2007 and 2011. As a result, the trial court concluded she was only entitled to $93,972.18—the difference between the original $315,000 selling price and the $240,000 offer, plus all carrying costs, expenses, and attorney fees that accrued from the moment of breach until Fischer rejected the $240,000 offer.

Fischer brought this interlocutory appeal, arguing she reasonably mitigated her damages and the trial court erred in calculating damages. The Heymanns cross-appealed, arguing Fischer could have avoided all damages except the $117 repair bill if she had responded to their demand to fix the electrical problem, thus preserving the Agreement. A divided panel of the Court of Appeals agreed with the Heymanns and awarded only $117 in damages. *Fischer v. Heymann*, 994 N.E.2d 1151, 1160–62 (Ind. Ct. App. 2013) (*"Fischer II"*). Judge Bradford dissented. He concluded that requiring Fischer to respond to the Heymanns to mitigate damages undermined a non-breaching party's right to immediately terminate the contract upon breach. We granted transfer, which vacated the Court of Appeals' decision. Ind. Appellate Rule 58(A). Further facts will be provided as needed.

DISCUSSION AND DECISION

Neither party disputes that Fischer had a duty to exercise reasonable diligence to mitigate her damages once the Heymanns breached the Agreement. In view of Fischer I, this duty began on February 10, 2006, when the Heymanns demanded that Fischer fix a minor electrical problem as a condition of their purchase. After the deal fell through in 2006, Fischer attempted to mitigate her damages by selling the condo. But in the ensuing months, the housing market entered one of its worst downturns in recent memory. She received many offers, ranging as high as $240,000 to as low as $150,000. Eventually, in November 2011, over five years after the Heymanns breached the Agreement, Fischer sold the condo to a third party for $180,000. Here, both parties take issue with the trial court's damage award. The Heymanns argue, and the Court of Appeals held, that Fischer could have mitigated nearly all of her damages had she responded to the Heymanns' demand to fix the electrical problem. Fischer, conversely, argues she is entitled to the full $306,616.73 sum she requested before the trial court, plus fees and costs incurred after the damages hearing, because her refusal to sell the condo for $240,000 in 2007 was reasonable. But because neither party has shown clear error, we affirm the trial court's findings and conclusions.

I. Fischer's Duty to Mitigate Damages.

Fischer had a right to damages for the "loss actually suffered as a result of the breach" once the Heymanns breached the Agreement, but not "to be placed in a better position than [she] would have been if the contract had not been broken." *Roche Diagnostics Operations, Inc. v. Marsh Supermarkets, LLC*, 987 N.E.2d 72, 89 (Ind. Ct. App. 2013) (citations omitted), trans. denied. She also had a duty to mitigate her damages. "[T]he duty to mitigate damages is a common law duty independent of the contract terms" that requires "a non-breaching party [to] make a reasonable effort to act in such a manner as to decrease the damages caused by the breach." *Geller v. Kinney*, 980 N.E.2d 390, 399 (Ind. Ct. App. 2012); *Salem Cmty. Sch. Corp. v. Richman*, 406 N.E.2d 269, 275 (Ind. Ct. App. 1980). Still, "the burden of proving that the non-breaching party has failed to use reasonable diligence to mitigate damages" lies with the party in breach—here, the Heymanns. And since assessing Fischer's diligence is a question of fact, we defer to the trial court's discretion and reverse only if there are no facts to support its conclusion either directly or by inference.

A. The Record Does Not Compel a Finding That Fischer Unreasonably Rejected the Heymanns' Demand.

The Heymanns argue the trial court should have found that Fischer's only reasonable option to mitigate her damages was to respond to the Heymanns' demand. The trial court found that "[t]he [Heymanns] gave [Fischer] more than a reasonable amount of time to agree to fix the identified electrical problems," and "had [Fischer] remained in contact with [the Heymanns] and informed [them] that she would be making changes prior to closing, [the Heymanns] would have proceeded to closing, and [Fischer] would not have been damaged." The Heymanns argue these findings compel the conclusion that Fischer should have mitigated her damages by responding to their demand.

But the Heymanns overlook that the trial court qualified its findings about Fischer's delayed response. Immediately after it stated these findings, the trial court referenced *Fischer I*: "However, as determined by the Court of Appeals, [the Heymanns] . . . breached the Purchase Agreement" because their request to void the contract was not based on "an objectively reasonable belief" concerning the magnitude of the electrical problem. Thus, the trial court relied on *Fischer I* to avoid finding that Fischer needed to yield to the very demand that put the Heymanns in breach to mitigate her damages. We hold the trial court acted within its discretion when it considered the implications of the Heymanns' demand in light of *Fischer I*'s holding—namely that the demand was a breach, and Fischer acted reasonably by not surrendering to the breach.

Fischer, like all non-breaching parties, had three options for recourse after the Heymanns repudiated the contract. First, she could "treat the contract as rescinded and recover in quantum meruit as far as [she had] performed." *Twin Lakes*, 568 N.E.2d at 1080. Second, she could "keep the contract alive for the benefit of [all] parties, remaining at all times ready, willing, and able to perform [her] part of the contract; then, at the time fixed for performance, . . . sue and recover according to the terms of the contract." *Id.* Or third, she could "treat the breach or repudiation as putting an end to the contract for all purposes of performance and sue at once to recover the damages due from the wrongful refusal to carry out the contract according to its terms." *Id.* Regardless of which option she chose, she had an obligation to reasonably "decrease the damages caused by the breach." *See Richman*, 406 N.E.2d at 275. "In rare instances the appropriate course [for mitigating damages] may be to complete performance instead of stopping," Restatement (Second) of Contracts, § 350 cmt. g (1981)—but in every case, "[t]he over-arching requirement is merely one of reasonableness." 11 Joseph M. Perillo, Corbin on Contracts § 57.11 (Rev. ed. 2005).

Here, there was evidence that Fischer acted reasonably by continuing to perform under the Agreement (option two), but without yielding to the precise terms of the Heymanns' breach—and so the trial court was not required to find otherwise. She did not immediately terminate the Agreement but remained "ready, willing, and able" to sell the condo to the Heymanns. And she did not bring suit until two days before the original date of closing. Fischer even repaired the electrical problem by having an electrician push the reset button on three outlets and change a light bulb—albeit a few days later than the Heymanns had demanded. None of her actions strayed from the terms freely negotiated by the parties.

Under these circumstances, we agree with Judge Bradford that Fischer did not need to "surrender to the very demand which generated [the] breach" to mitigate her damages. *Fischer II*, 994 N.E.2d at 1164 (Bradford, J., dissenting). Just as breaching parties may not take advantage of their breach to relieve them of their contractual duties, neither may they take advantage of their breach to require non-breaching parties to perform beyond their contractual duties. And just as non-breaching parties may not place themselves in a better position because of the breach, neither may breaching parties.

Holding otherwise would require sellers like Fischer to choose between surrendering to the terms of a breach or forfeiting damages whenever a buyer breaches an agreement by conditioning purchase on strict compliance with an unreasonable demand. This predicament would let buyers demand minor repairs with impunity and undermine sellers' ability to enforce the "major defects" clause of countless real-estate contracts. To the contrary, if the contract terms permit, sellers may refuse to replace the bathroom mirror, produce the warranty for household appliances, or—as in Fischer's case—timely repair an electrical problem by pushing the reset button on three outlets and replacing a light bulb.

Thus, while continued performance may have been necessary for Fischer to mitigate her damages, the evidence does not compel the finding that she had to surrender to the terms of the Heymanns' breach to do so. Rather, the trial court relied on the Court of Appeals' holding in Fischer I that the Heymanns breached by making an unreasonable demand, which did not impose upon Fischer a duty to respond. Fischer did not deviate from her contractual duties under the Agreement and remained "ready, willing, and able to perform," *Twin Lakes*, 568 N.E.2d at 1080, under the original contract terms—just not under the additional terms the Heymanns demanded. We therefore affirm the trial court's refusal to find that Fischer's only reasonable option to mitigate her damages was to respond to the Heymanns' demand.

B. The Trial Court Did Not Err in Finding That Fischer Should Have Mitigated Her Damages by Selling the Condo for $240,000.

The trial court did, however, conclude Fischer fell short of exercising reasonable diligence in mitigating her damages when she listed the condo at an "unreasonably high [price] from at least the beginning of 2007 to early 2011," and rejected a third-party offer to purchase the condo for $240,000 in February 2007 by making an "unreasonably high" counter-offer of $286,000. Again, a party's reasonableness in mitigating damages is a question of fact. As long as the trial court does not "appl[y] the wrong legal standard," *Berkel & Co. Contractors, Inc.*, 814 N.E.2d at 658, it has discretion to determine whether parties have reasonably mitigated their damages in calculating a final damage award, and we will not disturb the final award if the evidence supports it.

Here, though the parties disputed the evidence, the trial court acted within its discretion in finding that Fischer's asking price was unreasonably high from 2007 to 2011. By the time Fischer finally sold the condo in November 2011, it had languished on the market for eight years. Two real-estate agents testified they had never seen a property on the market for that length of time, and Fischer's own agent admitted she had never before listed a property for eight years. Multiple witnesses also testified that the listing price was unreasonably high, and inconsistent with the condo's 2011 appraisal value. Admittedly, it was difficult for Fischer to anticipate how far the value of her condo would fall in an extremely depressed housing market, and several witnesses acknowledged the difficult economic climate. But weighing Fischer's conduct in light of those factors was the trial court's prerogative. We only determine whether the record supports the findings, "either directly or by inference," *Berkel & Co. Contractors, Inc.*, 814 N.E.2d at 658. Here, it does.

The record also supports the trial court's finding that Fischer could have sold the condo for $240,000 in 2007. On February 13, 2007, a third party, Joe Johnson, offered to purchase the condo for $240,000—the highest offer Fischer ever received after the Agreement with the Heymanns fell through. Fischer responded on February 16, 2007, by making a counter-offer of $286,000, which Johnson rejected. The trial court heard testimony that Fischer "overstated" the asking price by "[a] substantial amount," and made an unreasonable counter-offer, particularly for a unit in "an original non-updated condition." Fischer argues Johnson's ability to actually close on the offer was speculative, but this is an invitation to reweigh the evidence, which the standard of review forbids.

We affirm the trial court's conclusion that Fischer may receive only $75,000 in compensatory damages—the difference between the Heymann deal ($315,000) and the Johnson offer ($240,000). We also affirm its conclusion that Fischer is entitled to only $15,109.68 in carrying costs and maintenance fees she incurred as consequential damages from the time the Heymanns breached the Agreement until the date Fischer made her unreasonable counter-offer to Johnson. The trial court therefore acted within its discretion when it awarded $90,109.68 for damages resulting from the Heymanns' breach.

II. Attorney Fees.

The trial court found Fischer was entitled to reasonable attorney fees based on a provision in the Agreement granting "reasonable attorney fees" to the "prevailing party" in any litigation involving the Agreement. But the trial court only awarded fees and costs incurred prior to February 16, 2007 in the amount of $3,862.50. Fischer argues this was an abuse of discretion because even if she had sold the condo to Johnson, the litigation would not have ceased in 2007, and attorney fees would have continued to accrue well beyond the amount the trial court awarded. Fischer thus seeks a total of $12,268.24 in attorney fees and $9,834.80 in court costs.

We will enforce a contract allowing for recovery of attorney fees, but "[t]he amount recoverable for an award of attorney fees is left to the sound discretion of the trial court." *Dempsey v. Carter*, 797 N.E.2d 268, 275 (Ind. Ct. App. 2003). "When determining the amount of a reasonable attorney fee, 'the court may consider such factors as the hourly rate, the result achieved . . . and the difficulty of the issues.'" *Heiligenstein v. Matney*, 691 N.E.2d 1297, 1304 (Ind. Ct. App. 1998) (emphasis added) (quoting *Dougherty v. Leavell*, 582 N.E.2d 442, 443 (Ind. Ct. App. 1991)). Here the trial court considered the ultimate "result achieved" by Fischer's attorney, and limited the award for fees based on Fischer's failure to mitigate. This was within the trial court's discretion, and we thus affirm the trial court's award of $3,862.50 in attorney fees and costs.

CONCLUSION

The record supports the trial court's findings and conclusions on Fischer's duty to mitigate. The trial court acted within its discretion by finding that Fischer could have mitigated her damages by selling the condo in 2007 instead of waiting until 2011, and in refusing to find that her duty to mitigate required yielding to the Heymanns' breach. The trial court also acted within its broad discretion in determining reasonable attorney fees and costs based on the results that Fischer achieved in this litigation. We therefore affirm the trial court's award of $93,972.18.

DICKSON, C.J., and DAVID and MASSA, JJ., concur.

RUCKER, J., concurs in result.

Understanding the Case:

1. *How Many Fischers Are There?:* This case had two decisions that were appealed. The first one—*Fischer I*—addressed whether or not the Heymanns breached the contract. While the trial court found that they had not, on remand, the appellate court found that they had by terminating the contract due to minor electrical problems with the condo. The above case—*Fischer II*—addressed the remedy for that breach.

Comprehension and Thought Questions:

1. The court says that Fischer had "a duty to exercise reasonable diligence to mitigate her damages." What does the court mean by this?

2. Did Fischer act reasonably when she refused to make the minor and inexpensive electrical fixes the Heymanns demanded? Why or why not?

3. Did Fischer act reasonably when she declined the 2007 offer of $240,000? Why or why not?

4. What should the Heymanns have done differently if they wanted to save the deal yet have the electrical problems fixed?

5. What should Fischer have done differently to either save her deal with the Heymanns or maximize her damage recovery?

Hypothetical Variations:

1. What if the electrical problem was the result of faulty wiring that ran throughout the condo and posed a risk of a fire? *buyers would have had an "out"*

2. What if the offer Fischer ultimately accepted was made and accepted by her in 2008?

3. What if after the Heymanns breached, Fischer spent $40,000 to improve the condo and then sold the condo one year later for $180,000? What would her damages likely be?

PRACTICE PROBLEM 25-4

Refer back to the facts from Practice Problem 25-3. Assume that you recently discovered that after Ralph Schneider, the leasing manager at Commercial Properties, notified Ravi King that the lease with Burrito Builder was terminated, King immediately identified a new location for his restaurant one block away from its prior location at 1000 Oak Street. The new location, 1100 Oak Street, was leasing for $4,000 a month, which was the same as the rent Burrito Builders had been paying at 1000 Oak Street. However, King would need to invest $3,000 at the outset to retrofit that location to accommodate his burrito bar business. King did not have that amount of money available, and did not want to take out a loan, as he did not trust banks to keep his personal information confidential. He also did not want to put in the time and effort to do that construction work. So he kept looking for an alternate location. Finally, three months later, King reopened Burrito Builders at 2011 W. Elm Street, which was ten blocks away. The rent at the new location was $5,000 a month. Again, Burrito Builder only generated on average $2,500 per month from sales, half of the level of sales it had generated in the prior location.

Consider whether you should change your advice to King as to what damages Burrito Builder is likely able to obtain from Commercial Properties in light of these new facts.

CHAPTER 26

Specific Performance and Agreed Remedies

Recall from Chapter 24 that courts generally award monetary damages to an aggrieved party where the other party breaches. Usually that means that an aggrieved party is entitled to receive expectation damages, meaning money to compensate it for the benefits it was promised and did not receive under the contract. Of course, a monetary damage award may be limited due to application of the doctrines discussed in Chapter 25.

In some circumstances, a party will request a court to order the breaching party to perform its breached promise or promises. This remedy is known as specific performance and is often thought to be the best way to protect a party's expectation interest, as the aggrieved party receives the very benefit of its bargain rather than a monetary damages substitute. However, courts are often reluctant to specifically enforce a contract. Section A explains why this is so and discusses the factors courts often consider in deciding whether to award specific performance.

Sometimes parties agree in a contract on the remedy a party will receive due to the other party's breach. For example, parties might set out an amount of damages a party must pay if it breaches. Those types of clauses are referred to as liquidated damage clauses because the parties liquidate (that is, put into monetary terms) the amount by which they expect they will be damaged if the other side breaches. Section B explores liquidated damage clauses, focusing on the limits courts place on enforcing such clauses.

A. SPECIFIC PERFORMANCE

Specific performance refers to a court order requiring a party to actually perform its promised obligations under a contract. Thus, it amounts to the ultimate expectation remedy, because it ensures an aggrieved party gets the benefit for which it bargained.

There are a number of reasons why courts generally award damages rather than specific performance. For one, an order to perform takes away the free will of the breaching party. In our society, we are generally opposed to forcing people to take a particular action.

Moreover, there may be challenges for a court in overseeing a party's performance, especially where a breaching party is being ordered to perform an extended obligation or where the terms of the promise are not laid out in detail. In either case, if the party fails to perform, or fails to perform to the level required in the contract, the aggrieved party will need to again seek judicial assistance. This, in turn, requires more time and judicial resources. Moreover, if the terms of the promise a party has been ordered to perform are not clearly laid out, it is hard for a court to know whether a party has in fact performed as promised.

Ordering a breaching party to specifically perform a promised obligation also runs counter to the notion of efficient breach. Under that theory, if the party's breach would create more value overall,[1] even after factoring in damages to the aggrieved party, then the law should not preclude such an efficient breach. Of course, you may recall counterarguments to this point, one of which is that an aggrieved party is often undercompensated when it receives damages, due to the many limits placed on damages. Thus, while more value might be created by a party breaching, an aggrieved party is often not made whole following that breach where it receives monetary damages.

Finally, historically, courts of equity were the only courts that could provide equitable relief such as specific performance. Courts at law could not. However, a party could not file its claim or seek a remedy in a court of equity unless a court at law could not provide relief for breach. While today, for the most part, we do not have separate courts of law and equity, the preference for damages remains. Thus, our courts generally award damages, and only if damages are not adequate will the court award equitable relief such as specific performance. However, the strength of this hierarchy has also weakened, in part because of the UCC, which "takes a more liberal attitude" toward specific performance.[2]

These historical, social, and practical explanations for why courts are hesitant to award specific performance have led to the rule that courts may only award specific performance in their discretion where justice requires, and only where damages are an inadequate remedy. As the Restatement provides,

---

1. Recall that sometimes a party breaches to opportunistically obtain more advantages under the existing contract.

2. U.C.C. § 2–716 cmt. 1 (1977).

Specific performance or an injunction will not be ordered if damages would be adequate to protect the expectation interest of the injured party.[3]

The Restatement also enumerates circumstances affecting a court's decision whether damages would be an adequate remedy.

§ 360 Factors Affecting Adequacy of Damages

In determining whether the remedy in damages would be adequate, the following circumstances are significant:

(a) the difficulty of proving damages with reasonable certainty,

(b) the difficulty of procuring a suitable substitute performance by means of money awarded as damages, and

(c) the likelihood that an award of damages could not be collected.

Thus, if damages cannot be calculated with reasonable certainty, or if a breaching party is judgment-proof because it is insolvent, then a party could use that fact to argue for specific performance. Similarly, if the subject of the contract is unique such that the aggrieved party could not use its damage recovery to buy a suitable substitute, then the aggrieved party could use that fact to support its request for specific performance. This is commonly the case with land sales contracts and contracts for other one-of-a-kind pieces of property such as artwork.

Even if a damages remedy would not be adequate, a court still may not order specific performance if the terms of the promise to be enforced are not certain enough to serve as the basis for a court order. Typically, the certainty required for an order of specific performance is greater than the certainty needed to form a contract. That is because in the case of specific performance, a court needs to be able to determine whether a party is performing its precise obligations in the contract, and not merely calculate damages to a reasonable degree of certainty.

Note that specific performance is awarded where a party has failed to perform a contractual obligation and the court orders that party to perform. Where, in contrast, an aggrieved party seeks an order *preventing* a counterparty from taking certain action, such as breaching a contract, the court awards an **injunction**. So, for example, if an employee starts to compete with his former employer in breach of the non-compete covenant included in his employment agreement with his former employer, the employer would seek an injunction against the employee. A court might award injunctive relief in this scenario because this type of breach could create incalculable damages for the employer. If awarded, the injunction would enjoin the employee from competing, per the non-compete covenant.

Given the discretionary nature of specific performance and injunctive relief, both of which provide equitable relief to further the interests of justice, either

---

3. Restatement (Second) of Contracts § 359(1).

may be awarded in whole or in part. In other words, a court may decide to order a party to specifically perform part of its promised obligation but not all breached obligations. In that case, the aggrieved party would likely seek an alternative remedy for the breached obligations not remedied by specific performance. Or a court might enjoin a party from engaging in some breaching conduct but not all, if damages can compensate the aggrieved party for some aspects of the counterparty's breach.

Moreover, given the discretionary nature of equitable relief, a court will only award it where justice requires such a remedy. Thus, a court can use its discretion to not award equitable relief where a party comes to the court with "unclean hands,"[4] or does not deal fairly with the counterparty, such as by acting dishonestly or unfairly even if the conduct falls short of a legal defense. Nor will a court award equitable relief where doing so would create a substantial hardship for the breaching party or a third party. The following is the Restatement's description of these limits on equitable relief:

> § 364 Effect of Unfairness
> (1) Specific performance or an injunction will be refused if such relief would be unfair because
>> (a) the contract was induced by mistake or by unfair practices,
>> (b) the relief would cause unreasonable hardship or loss to the party in breach or to third persons, or
>> (c) the exchange is grossly inadequate or the terms of the contract are otherwise unfair.
>
> (2) Specific performance or an injunction will be granted in spite of a term of the agreement if denial of such relief would be unfair because it would cause unreasonable hardship or loss to the party seeking relief or to third persons.

In addition, a court will only grant equitable relief where, in its discretion, the benefits of doing so clearly outweigh the costs on the court in supervising the court order. This, too, is captured by the Restatement:

> § 366 Effect of Difficulty in Enforcement or Supervision
> A promise will not be specifically enforced if the character and magnitude of the performance would impose on the court burdens in enforcement or supervision that are disproportionate to the advantages to be gained from enforcement and to the harm to be suffered from its denial.

Here, it usually takes fewer judicial resources to supervise performance of a promise that has been well defined, does not require much discretion by the breaching party or cooperation with the aggrieved party, and is performable over a short time period, such as at a single closing. Still, courts sometimes do oversee orders to specifically perform obligations that require discretion or cooperation to perform or that are performable over time, especially where

---

4. Restatement (Second) of Contracts § 357 cmt. c (1981).

there would be a hardship on the aggrieved party in not receiving what was promised, and the terms of the promise are clear.[5]

Sometimes parties specify in their contract that one of the parties is entitled to equitable relief if the counterparty breaches a specified obligation. This type of provision is commonly included in confidentiality and non-compete covenants in employment agreements. The following is an example of such a provision:

> I acknowledge and agree that irreparable injury to the Company may result in the event I breach any covenant contained in this Agreement and that the remedy at law for the breach of any such covenant will be inadequate. Therefore, if I engage in any act that breaches any provision of this Agreement, I agree that the Company is entitled to, in addition to any other remedies and damages as may be available to it by law or under this Agreement, injunctive relief to enforce the provisions of this Agreement.

Despite such a provision, courts do not defer to the parties as to whether damages are adequate and, consequently, whether the court will award equitable relief. However, courts do afford them some evidentiary weight as to the facts acknowledged. As such, they can increase the chances of a court awarding equitable relief.

The following case demonstrates a current example of how a court responds to a party's request for specific performance. As you read this case, consider the court's justification for why the test it uses to determine whether to award specific performance differs from the tests discussed above.

Ash Park, LLC v. Alexander & Bishop, Ltd.
Supreme Court of Wisconsin
324 Wis.2d 703 (2010)

ANN WALSH BRADLEY, J.

. . . In 2007, Ash Park was the owner of a vacant parcel of real estate that was subject to a mortgage. On April 6, Alexander & Bishop made an offer to purchase the parcel of real estate with the plan of developing it into a multi-tenant retail shopping center.

Ash Park submitted a counter-offer, which incorporated by reference most of the terms of Alexander & Bishop's offer to purchase. It set the purchase price at $6.3 million, with the closing date to take place on or before December 14, 2007. The counter-offer was accepted by Alexander & Bishop and is the contract that forms the basis of this lawsuit.

---

5. *See, e.g.,* Eastern Rolling Mill Co. v. Michlovitz, 145 A. 378 (Md. 1929).

The parties' contract included a leasing contingency that gave Alexander & Bishop the option to terminate the contract if it was unable to secure an anchor tenant:

> This Offer is contingent upon Buyer negotiating a lease with Buyer's principal tenant . . . with terms and conditions acceptable to Buyer . . . on or before July 20, 2007. If Buyer is unable to negotiate such lease by said date, this Offer may be terminated at the option of Buyer and all earnest money shall be returned to Buyer. . . .

Upon timely notice, Alexander & Bishop also had the right to extend the lease contingency period:

> [T]he Buyer shall have the right to extend the lease contingency period for two (2) additional periods of two (2) calendar months, i.e. to September 20, 2007 and November 20, 2007, provided Buyer (1) provides written notice to Seller of its intent to exercise such extension prior to the expiration of the lease contingency period and (2) pays to Seller, with its notice of exercise, a non-refundable extension fee . . . of $25,000 for each extension period. The non-refundable extension fee shall be non-refundable but applicable to the purchase price at closing.

The contract specified that all contingencies would be waived if not invoked by July 20, 2007.

The contract also included a default clause, which enumerated remedies in the event of a breach. Among other remedies, the contract explicitly provided for specific performance as a remedy for "material failure to perform any obligations under this Offer":

> Seller and Buyer each have the legal duty to use good faith and due diligence in completing the terms and conditions of this Offer. A material failure to perform any obligation under this Offer is a default which may subject the defaulting party to liability for damages or other legal remedies.

If Buyer defaults, Seller may:

> (1) sue for specific performance and request the earnest money as partial payment of the purchase price; or
> (2) terminate the Offer and have the option to [pursue liquidated or actual damages.]

If Seller defaults, Buyer may:

> (1) sue for specific performance; or
> (2) terminate the Offer and request the return of the earnest money, sue for actual damages, or both.
> In addition, the Parties may seek any other remedies available in law or equity.
> The Parties understand that the availability of any judicial remedy will depend upon the circumstances of the situation and the discretion of the courts. . . .

Alexander & Bishop had not secured an anchor tenant by July 20, 2007, and it exercised its option to terminate the contract. However, on August 1, the parties signed an "Agreement to Reinstate Vacant Land Offer to Purchase," which stated that "the parties desire to reinstate the Offer on its original terms, except as specifically set forth herein[.]" It provided that upon the execution of the agreement by both parties "and the deposit by the Buyer [of] the Extension Fee with the Escrow Agent, the Offer shall be fully reinstated in accordance with its terms[.]"

The reinstatement agreement did not alter the extension dates, the closing date, or the terms of the lease contingency. Thus, until the next extension deadline, Alexander & Bishop retained two options: (1) extend the lease contingency for an additional period of two months, or (2) terminate the contract. Alexander & Bishop did not exercise either one of these options. As a result, the contract became binding on September 20.

On October 9, however, Alexander & Bishop informed Ash Park that its prospective anchor tenant was not interested in immediately leasing the property. The parties discussed amending their agreement, but their negotiations were unsuccessful.

Ash Park prepared for the December 14 closing, but the closing did not take place. Shortly thereafter, Ash Park filed a complaint for breach of contract, demanding "judgment from and against the Defendant for specific performance or damages at law, at the election of [Ash Park], in accordance with the terms of the parties' Purchase and Sale Contract."[6]

In response to Ash Park's motion for summary judgment, Alexander & Bishop asserted that there was no breach of contract because the contract had not been reinstated.[7] It acknowledged that specific performance was an available remedy that "rests in the discretion of the court," but it contended that specific performance "only comes into play when damages that could be had at law are an inadequate remedy.". . .

Further, Alexander & Bishop contended that Ash Park had elected the remedy of liquidated damages consisting of $50,000 in earnest money and that such a remedy was adequate. It contended that "[i]t would be inconsistent [for Ash Park] to retain the earnest money and sue for specific performance." Alexander & Bishop did not argue that specific performance was impossible because it could not pay the purchase price.

---

6. [3] Ash Park also demanded damages arising subsequent to the breach, including "holding costs, taxes, interest, maintenance, commissions, insurance, penalties and opportunity costs, together with statutory costs and disbursements of this action."

7. [4] Specifically, Alexander & Bishop argued that because it had failed to deposit the $25,000 called for in the reinstatement agreement, the contract had not been reinstated. In addition, it asserted that Ash Park had failed to provide merchantable title and failed to disclose material adverse conditions of the property.

After arguments, the circuit court determined that the contract had been reinstated and that Alexander & Bishop had breached the contract. The court granted summary judgment in favor of Ash Park and ordered the parties to specifically perform the contract. It reasoned that the property was unique, that specific performance was the preferred remedy under Wisconsin law, and that under the terms of the contract the parties had bargained for this remedy. . . .

On appeal, the court of appeals concluded that the circuit court did not erroneously exercise its discretion by ordering specific performance and interest. . . .

Alexander & Bishop now contends that the circuit court erroneously exercised its discretion by ordering specific performance here. . . .

The decision to grant or deny the equitable remedy of specific performance is within the discretion of the circuit court. . . . A reviewing court will affirm the circuit court's exercise of discretion unless it was erroneous. The circuit court erroneously exercises its discretion if it makes an error of law or neglects to base its decision upon the facts of the record.

Whether we should alter Wisconsin jurisprudence presents a question of law. We decide questions of law independently of the determinations rendered by the circuit court and the court of appeals.

We begin by setting forth the several remedies available to a seller of real estate upon the buyer's breach. Then we determine whether the circuit court erroneously exercised its discretion by awarding specific performance. Next, we discuss Alexander & Bishop's proposals for altering the analytical framework governing the remedies available to a seller of real estate. . . .

III. REMEDIES

When a buyer breaches a contract, several different remedies may be available to the seller. The seller may seek actual damages, often measured as the difference between the contract price and the value of the property.[8] The seller may select liquidated damages—typically, retention of earnest money. Finally, the seller may seek specific performance of the contract.

Actual damages and liquidated damages are considered damages at law—a legal remedy. By contrast, specific performance is an equitable remedy that seeks to award performance of the contract as specifically agreed. The purpose of specific performance is to order the breaching party to do that which it agreed to do in the contract.

---

8. [13] The seller may sell the property to a third-party buyer and seek a money judgment for the deficiency against the breaching buyer. Alternatively, the seller may choose to keep the property and seek the difference between the contract price and the fair market value of the property. When a seller seeks damages for breach of contract, the injured party has a duty to use reasonable means to mitigate damages.

Here, the parties' contract provided specific performance as one of several remedies Ash Park could seek in the event of Alexander & Bishop's breach.[9] When a contract specifies remedies available for breach of contract, the intention of the parties generally governs. Additionally, under Wisconsin common law, specific performance is a remedy available to a seller of real estate.

The availability of specific performance as a remedy does not mean that the court will automatically grant specific performance upon a seller's request. Rather, as an equitable remedy, an award of specific performance is discretionary. The fairness of ordering specific performance depends on the facts and equities of the individual case before the circuit court and will vary from case to case.

Before ordering specific performance, the court must be satisfied that the claim is fair, just, reasonable, and not the product of an unconscionable or oppressive bargain. Further, impossibility of performance is a defense to specific performance: "[W]here it would be impossible for a party to perform the contract, specific performance will not be granted." *Anderson*, 155 Wis.2d at 512, 455 N.W.2d 885.

IV. CIRCUIT COURT'S EXERCISE OF DISCRETION

Alexander & Bishop contends that the circuit court erroneously exercised its discretion by failing to "hold an evidentiary hearing to determine whether specific performance was appropriate," either because the seller might be able to sell the property to someone else, or because the buyer could demonstrate that it was unable to close. In essence, this argument charges the circuit court with two discrete errors. First, Alexander & Bishop asserts that the circuit court erred by not requiring Ash Park to demonstrate that it had no adequate remedy at law. Second, it asserts that the circuit court erred by failing to determine whether performance of the contract was "impossible." We address each argument in turn.

A

In some contexts, specific performance is unavailable where legal damages are adequate to remedy the breach.

In the context of contracts for land, however, Wisconsin law does not require a seller to demonstrate the inadequacy of a remedy at law as a prerequisite to an award of specific performance. Wisconsin statutes provide that "specific performance of contract or covenant" is an available remedy for "any person having an interest in real property . . . unless the use of a remedy is denied in a specific situation." Wis. Stat. § 840.03(1)(f).

---

9. [14] The contract listed actual damages, retention of the earnest money, specific performance, and "any other remedies available in law or equity" as remedies available to the seller.

Further, Wisconsin courts have not restricted a seller's remedy of specific performance to cases in which a remedy at law is inadequate. In *Heins*, the seller of a parcel of land sought specific performance, and this court determined that specific performance was an available remedy. Similarly, in *Taft v. Reddy*, 191 Wis. 144, 150, 210 N.W. 364 (1926), this court concluded that "the [land contract] vendor's right to specific performance is established beyond question[.]" None of these cases requires the seller to demonstrate that a legal remedy would be inadequate.

Alexander & Bishop cites *Henrikson v. Henrikson*, 143 Wis. 314, 127 N.W. 962 (1910), for the proposition that specific performance is unavailable as a remedy when the buyer breaches a contract to purchase land and there is an adequate remedy at law. *Henrikson* does not support Alexander & Bishop's argument. In that case, there was no valid and enforceable contract to transfer land. Rather, the agreement at issue was an oral contract that did not satisfy the statute of frauds. *Id.* at 317, 127 N.W. 962. *Henrikson* does not address the remedies available to a seller when the buyer breaches an enforceable contract for the sale of land.

Wisconsin law is consistent with the general rule across jurisdictions. Courts have traditionally awarded specific performance of a contract for the sale of land without a prerequisite that the non-breaching party demonstrate that legal damages would be inadequate.

Although Ash Park does contend that damages at law would be an inadequate remedy, we need not decide this factual question here. We conclude that the circuit court did not erroneously exercise its discretion by ordering specific performance without requiring Ash Park to demonstrate that a remedy at law would be inadequate.

B

We turn to Alexander & Bishop's second argument that performance of the contract would be impossible. Wisconsin law recognizes impossibility as a defense to specific performance. "The defense of impossibility rests on the common-sense principle that a court of equity will not order an impossible act." Yorio, *supra*, § 5.5 at 112.

In its arguments to this court, Alexander & Bishop asserts that it is "impossible" for it to perform the contract: "[T]he anchor tenant never committed which made it impossible for Alexander & Bishop to get financing and close on the deal."

However, Alexander & Bishop never asserted impossibility in the circuit court as a defense to specific performance. . . .

As a result, the circuit court has not made any factual findings about whether performance would be impossible, and there is no finding of fact for this court to review. . . .

V. PROPOSED CHANGES TO WISCONSIN LAW

Having determined that the circuit court did not erroneously exercise its discretion under current Wisconsin law, we examine next Alexander & Bishop's various proposals for changing the law. Alexander & Bishop has urged us to "tweak" current law in one of three ways.

Alexander & Bishop's first proposal asks us to harmonize the law of remedies available to a seller of real estate with the remedies available to a seller of goods by declaring that specific performance may not be ordered when there is an adequate remedy at law. This proposal would preclude a circuit court from ordering specific performance in the first instance unless the court determined that money damages were inadequate.

Alexander & Bishop's second and third proposals would permit the court to order specific performance even without concluding that money damages were inadequate. However, these proposals would alter the administration or enforcement of the remedy of specific performance once ordered. Alexander & Bishop encourages us to adopt a rule requiring a mandatory judicial sale and money judgment for any deficiency once specific performance has been ordered and the buyer cannot or will not pay. In the alternative, it asks us to hold that a seller who is awarded interest in addition to specific performance has a duty to mitigate its damages by attempting to resell the property.

All three proposals would affect the viability and meaningfulness of specific performance as a remedy for sellers of real estate under Wisconsin law. We address each proposal in turn.

A

Alexander & Bishop asserts that we should harmonize the remedies for a buyer's breach of a real estate contract with the remedies available for a buyer's breach of a contract for goods.[10] Typically, specific performance will not be decreed as a seller's remedy for breach of a contract to sell personal property unless a remedy at law is inadequate.

In support, it offers the Uniform Land Transactions Act, which was drafted in 1975. The uniform act does not recognize the remedy of specific performance for a seller of real estate and does not permit a seller to bring an action for the price under most circumstances.

In the 35 years since it was drafted, no state has adopted the Uniform Land Transactions Act. Furthermore, the uniform act was withdrawn by the National Conference on Uniform State Laws in 1990. We are not persuaded that we

---

10. [21] The Uniform Commercial Code, which covers the sale of goods, does not permit specific performance as a seller's remedy when legal damages would be an adequate remedy. Wis. Stat. § 402.716; see also Welch v. Chippewa Sales Co., 252 Wis. 166, 168, 31 N.W.2d 170 (1948).

should alter our longstanding practices by adopting an act that has since been withdrawn by the National Conference on Uniform State Laws.

We conclude that granting or denying specific performance as a remedy is best left to the sound discretion of the circuit court on a case-by-case basis. In exercising its discretion, a circuit court may consider whether a remedy at law would be adequate to remedy a buyer's breach. If the court determines that legal damages are perfectly adequate, the court may in its discretion choose to award damages at law rather than specific performance. Yet, because this decision is best made on the facts and equities of each individual case, we decline to adopt the rule proposed by Alexander & Bishop.

B

[The court then rejects Alexander & Bishop's other two proposals.]

. . .

In sum, we conclude that the circuit court did not erroneously exercise its discretion when it ordered specific performance of this contract. The contract provides that specific performance is an available remedy, and neither the contract nor Wisconsin law requires Ash Park to demonstrate that a legal remedy would be inadequate as a precondition to relief. Further, although impossibility is a defense to specific performance, Alexander & Bishop failed to present evidence that performance would be impossible in the proceedings before the circuit court.

. . .

The decision of the court of appeals is affirmed, and the cause remanded to the circuit court.

Comprehension and Thought Questions:

1. How and when did Alexander & Bishops breach the contract with Ash Park?

2. Why was Ash Park entitled to both retain the deposit and seek specific performance?

3. What test did the court use to determine whether to grant specific performance?

4. Is the court's test applicable to all types of contracts or only contracts for the sale of real estate? If different, why do you suppose the test is different?

5. How did the court apply that test in this case?

6. How did Alexander & Bishops want the test changed?

7. Why did the court decline to change the test in the manner requested by Alexander & Bishops?

Hypothetical Variations:

1. What if the parties' contract had been silent about a remedy upon breach?

2. What if Alexander & Bishops had argued in their answer that it was impossible for them to perform because they could not locate an anchor tenant?

3. What if this transaction had been for the sale of 100 computers instead of the sale of real estate?

4. What if Alexander & Bishops had not been able to locate an anchor tenant because Ash Park had not cooperated with Alexander & Bishop's efforts to market the location to prospective anchor tenants?

PRACTICE PROBLEM 26-1

Beatrice Williams is a firefighter who faithfully served in the Columbia Fire Department for three decades. While Williams has always been a dedicated, heroic firefighter, she did something in March 2017 that gained her national fame—she risked her own life to save 22 people stuck in a building that was engulfed in flames. As a result of her bravery, Williams received a Medal of Valor, a badge awarded for performance above and beyond the call of duty at extreme personal risk.

Viewing the medal as a culmination of her career, Williams decided to retire at the end of 2017. At that time, Vicki Short at SeaPress Publishers approached Williams about having Williams write her memoir about her time in the Columbia Fire Department. Her experience was viewed as special not merely because of her longevity on the job and heroics, but because she was one of the longest serving African-American women firefighters. Vicki was confident there would be a huge market for Williams's book if she was willing to write it.

After giving it some thought, Williams decided she would write the book. So she reached back out to Vicki to indicate her agreement to write a book to be published by SeaPress.

Vicki, in turn, sent Williams SeaPress's form Publication Agreement. The Agreement set out Williams's agreement to write the book, with a deadline of July 31, 2019, for the final manuscript of the book. It also specified that Williams would receive a 5 percent royalty on each copy of her book sold. SeaPress additionally agreed to "publish and market the Book at its own expense."

After reviewing the form, Williams signed it and returned it to Vicki. Vicki also signed the agreement on behalf of SeaPress.

It is now August of 2019, and Williams has yet to deliver her book manuscript to Vicki. While Vicki has sent many gentle reminders to Williams, Williams has not sent the draft manuscript. From her conversation with Williams, Vicki believes that Williams is delayed in writing the book due to her involvement in many volunteer activities and projects. In other words, Williams simply has not made time to write the book.

Vicki contacts you, SeaPress's outside counsel, for advice. Specifically, she wants your help with the following:

1. What are some possible solutions SeaPress can use to get Williams to finish writing the book?

2. If SeaPress decides to pursue its rights in court, could SeaPress request a remedy of specific performance? If so, would a court likely award such a remedy?

B. AGREED REMEDIES: LIQUIDATED DAMAGES

While, as discussed above, sometimes parties agree on the availability of equitable relief, other times they agree to an amount of damages. In particular, parties set out in their contract the measure of damages that one party will pay to the other upon certain instances of breach. Those agreed-to damages are referred to as **liquidated damages**. They are "liquidated" because the parties have quantified the amount of damage one party will suffer as a result of the other party's breach, or as a result of some other undesirable circumstance.

The following is a sample liquidated damages clause from an employment agreement.

> The parties agree that no exact measure of damage to the Company can be made in the event of the Employee's premature termination of the Employee's employment without Good Reason. In the event of such termination, the Employee will pay the Company $10,000 as liquidated damages. This sum is fixed as an attempted reasonable estimate of probable loss, and not as a penalty.[11]

You may be wondering why a party would ever agree up front how much it would pay should it breach. The answer is that this type of clause gives the parties more certainty in planning. Knowing how much a party must pay upon breach allows that party to more intelligently know the price of breaching. Moreover, parties include these types of provisions in contracts where it would

---

11. This is based on Basic Legal Transactions § 21:11, Enforceability and operable terms of the agreement—Terms to be included—Items generally encompassed in an employment agreement—Enforcement terms.

be difficult to quantify, or to prove, actual damages, as either of these limitations could undermine a party's ability to receive damages, as discussed in Chapter 25.

In the employment agreement example set out above, the employer (defined as the "Company" in the above clause) would have included this liquidated damages clause because it would likely be hard to calculate to the required degree of certainty how much the employer would be injured if the employee terminated his employment early. In that situation, it could be difficult to calculate forgone opportunities due to the employee's departure.

Similarly, owners of construction projects often include liquidated damages clauses in contracts with their contractors and subcontractors. In those contracts, liquidated damages usually come in the form of a "late fee" for each day that the project is delivered past an agreed-upon due date.[12] In that setting, it is difficult to quantify the damages the project owner will suffer due to a delay. Thus, those liquidated damages set out in advance of breach the parties' expectations for what those damages would be.

Note that parties do not need to label an amount as liquidated damages for it to constitute liquidated damages. They might either use a different label depending on the circumstances (such as termination fee, break-up fee, or late fee), or not use a label at all.[13] However, if the contract specifies an amount that one party owes to the other as a result of its breach or other undesirable circumstance, then the provision is a liquidated damages provision, regardless of what it is called.

It is important to determine if a provision is a liquidated damages provision because if it is, a court will generally only enforce such a provision if it is not intended to be a penalty for breach. More specifically, in general, a court will only enforce a liquidated damages clause if (1) actual damages cannot be ascertained with reasonable certainty, assessed at the time of contracting, and (2) the liquidated damage amount reasonably approximates actual damages that would be suffered by the aggrieved party, assessed at the time of contracting. Moreover, in some states, a court will only enforce a liquidated damages clause if (3) it reasonably approximates actual damages, measured at the time of breach.[14]

Courts do not enforce punitive liquidated damages clauses because they violate the purpose of contractual remedies, which is to compensate a party for breach. Contract damages are not intended to punish a party for breach given that contract law is not a fault-based system. Moreover, it is thought

---

12. *See, e.g.,* Hungerford Constr. Co. v. Florida Citrus Exposition, Inc., 410 F.2d 1229 (5th Cir. 1969), *cert. denied,* 396 U.S. 928 (1969).

13. *See, e.g.,* Garrett v. Coast & S. Fed. Sav. & Loan Ass'n, 511 P.2d 1197, 1199 (Cal. 1973) (using the term "late charges").

14. *See, e.g.,* Wheeling Clinic v. Van Pelt, 453 S.E.2d 603, 609 (W. Va. 1994).

that punishment would deter efficient breaches. Thus, if a liquidated damages clause was intended to punish a party for breach, a court will not enforce that clause.

Finally, just because a contract includes a liquidated damages clause does not mean that liquidated damages are an exclusive remedy.[15] In other words, parties can specify a liquidated damages amount due to one party's breach or other undesirable conduct, and also allow the aggrieved party to sue the breaching party for common law damages. However, often where parties agree to a liquidated damages clause, they intend for those liquidated damages to be an exclusive remedy. After all, why would a party agree to pay a specified amount upon breach while also allowing the aggrieved party to sue it for additional common law damages? Where the parties desire that outcome, the contract needs to specify that liquidated damages are an exclusive remedy. While a court might interpret a liquidated damages clause as being an exclusive remedy based on all the facts, it is best to manifest that intent through explicit language in the contract. The following is an example of such language:

> The liquidated damages specified in this contract are an exclusive remedy for the Employee's early termination of this Agreement, and preclude any claim at law or in equity for the Employee's early termination of this Agreement.

The following case demonstrates a typical challenge to a liquidated damages clause as an unenforceable penalty.

Pima Savings and Loan Ass'n v. Rampello
Court of Appeals of Arizona
812 P.2d 1115 (1991)

HOWARD, Presiding Judge.

This is an appeal from the granting of a partial summary judgment in favor of Pima Savings and Loan Association (Pima). Pima sued the Rampellos for breach of contract and for violation of A.R.S. § 12–671 (insufficient funds checks) which arose out of the Rampellos' contract with Pima to purchase 65 condominium units located in Bullhead City, Arizona. The facts leading up to this suit are as follows.

I.

On April 15, 1988, the Rampellos contracted to buy the Roadhaven Condominiums from Pima for $4.7 million with a $290,000 cash downpayment

---

15. *See, e.g.,* Sutton Madison, Inc. v. 27 East 65th Street Owners Corp., 779 N.Y.S.2d 461 (N.Y. App. Div. 2004).

and the balance to be financed by purchase money loaned by Pima. John Rampello gave a $165,000 check as part of the down payment.

The contract provided for liquidated damages as follows:

> If the closing does not occur due to default of buyer, the parties agree that Pima shall be paid the sum of two hundred ninety thousand dollars ($290,000.00) as liquidated damages, which sum the parties agree is a reasonable sum considering all of the circumstances existing on the date of this agreement. . . .

The contract also gave the Rampellos through April 24, 1988, to review and inspect the condition of the real estate and the condition of its title, and made the sale contingent upon the Rampellos' approval by the end of April 24. If they did not give written notice of disapproval within the period, the contract provided that the Rampellos would be deemed to have approved.

John Rampello conducted his inspection of the premises one or two days prior to April 24, 1988. On April 29, he sent a $125,000 check for the balance of the down payment. On May 20, 1988, well after the time set forth in the agreement, Rampello sent a letter rescinding the contract which Pima received on May 25, 1988. After it received the Rampellos' letter, Pima approved Rampello's loan. The checks that Pima had received from the Rampellos were returned due to insufficient funds and Pima demanded that they pay, as liquidated damages, the sum of $290,000 as set forth in the contract. This suit followed the Rampellos' refusal to pay.

Pima's motion for summary judgment was supported by the testimony of one its employees, Michael Foor, who had negotiated the agreement on Pima's behalf and who was responsible for calculating the liquidated damages that were set forth in the agreement. He testified as to the various factors he took into consideration in arriving at the figure of $290,000. Those factors which were considered difficult to estimate were: any loss of the opportunity to sell the property while it was in escrow, the effect of a failed sale on the market value of the property, the depreciation of the property until it is sold and the effect of such depreciation on market values, and potential hazards of ownership not fully covered by insurance. He also considered one or two factors which may not have been compensable damages; however, he did not assign any dollar value or percentage to any of the factors.

There was also evidence that one year before the Rampello agreement, Pima entered into an agreement with another buyer, New Age Investment (NAI), which provided for liquidated damages in the sum of $25,000. An affidavit presented by Pima stated that Pima's damages were $77,573.87, not including financing discounts, Pima's in-house administrative costs, and anticipated ongoing warranty expenses. Furthermore, the evidence was that, at the time of the motion for summary judgment, all but three of the units had been sold. Pima moved for summary judgment on its claim for liquidated damages, which was granted by the trial court.

The main issue in this case is whether the provision for liquidated damages constituted an unenforceable penalty. The Rampellos also contend that the previous contract with NAI raised an issue as to the reasonableness of the liquidated damage provision and that there was evidence that they rescinded the contract, thus precluding summary judgment in Pima's favor.

II.

The traditional role of liquidated damages provisions is to serve as an economical alternative to the costly and lengthy litigation involved in a conventional breach of contract action, and efforts by the contracting parties to avoid litigation and to equitably resolve potential conflicts through the mechanism of liquidated damages should be encouraged. However, the parties to a contract are not free to provide a penalty for its breach. The central objective behind the system of contract remedies is compensatory, not punitive. Punishment of a promisor for having broken his promise has no justification on either economic or other ground and a term providing such a penalty is unenforceable on the grounds of public policy.

Whether a stipulation is for liquidated damages or a penalty is a question of law for the court.

The test for whether a contract fixes a penalty or liquidated damages is whether payment is for a fixed amount or varies with the nature and extent of the breach, which means that an agreement made in advance of a breach is a penalty unless both of two conditions are met. First, the amount fixed in the contract must be a reasonable forecast of just compensation for the harm that is caused by any breach. Second, the harm that is caused by any breach must be one that is incapable or very difficult of accurate estimation.

The difficulties of proof of loss are to be determined at the time the contract is made and not at the time of the breach. Furthermore, the amount fixed is reasonable to the extent that it approximates the loss anticipated at the time of the making of the contract, even though it may not approximate the actual loss. However, the amount retained upon a contract's breach will be considered a penalty if it is unreasonable.

The Maine court stated in a case similar to ours:

> A case of liquidated damages, when the liquidated damage amount is not unreasonable on its face, is not converted as a matter of course to one of ordinary breach of contract by the seller's fortuitous resale of the contract real estate subsequent to the buyer's breach. Sellers are inescapably bound by the liquidated damage provisions in such contracts. Buyers should be bound as well unless the plaintiff proves that the circumstances are so extraordinary that the sellers' retention of the liquidated damage amount would truly shock the conscience of the court.

Leeber v. Deltona Corp., 546 A.2d at 456.

The liquidated damage amount of $290,000 in this case is little more than six percent of the total contract price and was reasonable on its face. We note that real property is not a liquid asset easily converted into cash. Who knew how long it would take to dispose of it and what it would sell for in the market-place? That Pima was subsequently able to resell the real estate through their own efforts and in doing so reduce its actual losses flowing from the Rampellos' breach does not make the retention of the downpayment so extraordinary or unfair as to shock the conscience of this court.

The Rampellos do not contend that the percentage is unreasonable but argue that certain factors which were considered by Pima in arriving at the amount of liquidated damages were not compensable. The record does not show what weight these factors were given. In any event, the question is whether the stip-ulated amount was, when all the facts are considered, reasonable at the time of the contract and not whether it was reasonable with the benefit of hindsight. We believe that it was. Further, the second prong of the test was also met. At the time of the contract it was difficult to estimate the damages accurately because it was unknown when the property would be resold.

III.

The Rampellos argue that the NAI contract entered into approximately one year prior to the Rampello contract and providing for only $25,000 liquidated damages, creates a question of fact as to the reasonableness of the amount. We do not agree. The undisputed evidence was that the NAI contract was a "sweetheart deal" fostered by in-house personnel at Pima who believed there was no chance that the escrow would not close. In any event, since the question of whether the provision here is a penalty or not is a question of law for the court, the NAI contract creates no question of fact.

IV.

The agreement gave the Rampellos nine days from the date of execution to con-duct an inspection of the property and notice their disapproval. The provision in question stated:

> 8.00 *Due Diligence*. BUYER shall have through April 24, 1988 to review and inspect the condition of the REAL ESTATE and the condition of its title and all other matters related to the REAL ESTATE or its title.
>
> The sale contemplated herein is subject to and contingent upon BUYER's approval *within such period*, of the above, which approval may not be unrea-sonably withheld. If BUYER does not give PIMA written notice of disapproval within such period (which notice must be actually received by PIMA *within such period* to be effective, notwithstanding the general notice provisions hereof), BUYER shall be deemed to have approved all such matters.

. . .

(Emphasis added.)

The Rampellos contend that the above provision gave them a reasonable time after April 24, 1988, to give written notice of disapproval and that whether their notice of disapproval mailed on May 20 and received May 25, 1988, was reasonable was a question of fact for the trier of fact, thus precluding summary judgment. We do not agree. When the language of the contract provides an option to terminate "on or before" a specified time or date or "within" a specified period of time, the option cannot be exercised after the time period or date has gone by. The contract provision here provides for the exercise of the option to terminate "within" a specified period of time and the Rampellos' failure to do so is fatal.

Pima has asked for and is entitled to its attorney's fees on appeal, which will be granted upon its compliance with Ariz. R. Civ. App. P. 21(c), 17B A.R.S.

Affirmed.

Understanding the Case:

1. *Due Diligence Out:* Section 8 of the contract between Pima and the Rampellos gave the Rampellos what is called a "due diligence out." Under a due diligence out, a party specifies in the contract that it must be satisfied with its due diligence review of the property being purchased as a condition to closing. If the party is not to satisfied with anything discovered during that review, that condition is not met, and the party can "walk" from the transaction. Due diligence outs are fairly uncommon in purchase transactions, as they give a party a right to walk from the transaction for essentially any reason during the due diligence out period. That is why where they are included, parties often negotiate specific limits on the out, such as a short time frame for the condition as well as notice requirements.

2. *Deposit as Liquidated Damages:* In this case, as is often the case in purchase agreements, the parties specified that the liquidated damage amount was the amount of the buyer's deposit for the property. Those amounts are often the same for practical reasons—it is easier for a seller to simply keep a deposit already in its possession as liquidated damages than to have to collect additional sums as liquidated damages from the buyer.

3. *Size of Liquidated Damages:* In the case, the liquidated damage amount was roughly equal to 6 percent of the contract price. In evaluating the reasonableness of a liquidated damage clause, courts often compare the proportionate size of the liquidated damage amount to those in similar contracts.[16] While not conclusive of reasonableness, the fact that many commercial parties

---

16. *See, e.g.,* Hooper v. Breneman, 417 So. 2d 315, 317-18 (Fla. Dist. Ct. App. 1982).

include similarly sized liquidated damage clauses often supports a conclusion of reasonableness.

Comprehension and Thought Questions:

1. What test did the court use to determine if the liquidated damage clause was enforceable versus an unenforceable penalty?
2. How did the court apply that test in this case?
3. Why was the fact that Pima had included a liquidated damages amount of $25,000 in a similar contract with NAI not conclusive evidence that the $290,000 liquidated damages amount in this case was unreasonable?
4. Was the fact that Pima had sold all but three units in the apartment building by the time Pima moved for summary judgment relevant to the court in analyzing whether the $290,000 liquidated damages amount was unreasonable? Should that fact be relevant?

Hypothetical Variations:

1. What if Pima's actual damages from NAI's breach of its purchase agreement with Pima were $30,000?
2. What if the Rampellos' checks had not bounced so that Pima kept the down payment to satisfy the Rompellos' duty to pay liquidated damages, where the Rampellos believed (as in the case) that they did not owe liquidated damages?

PRACTICE PROBLEM 26-2

Refer back to the facts from Practice Problem 26-1.

For purposes of this question, assume that the Publication Agreement also included the following provision:

> If Author [defined as Williams] fails to deliver a final manuscript for the Book to SeaPress by July 31, 2019, then SeaPress has a right to offset from the royalty payable to Author under this Agreement an amount equal to $1,000 for each day that the final manuscript is late. If Author fails to deliver the final manuscript for the Book to SeaPress by July 31, 2020, then SeaPress may terminate this Agreement and recover from Author $1 million, to compensate SeaPress for lost profits.

The $1,000 daily offset for a late-delivered manuscript is standard and is included in each SeaPress Publication Agreement. The termination fee is standard in SeaPress's Publication Agreement too, though the amount of that fee varies in each agreement. Vicki had calculated this amount at $1 million by looking at SeaPress's profits for memoirs published within the prior year regardless of the celebrity status of the authors. She did not, however, try to project actual sales or profits of Williams's book.

Once again, it is now August 2019, and Williams has yet to deliver her book manuscript to Vicki. While Vicki has sent many gentle reminders to Williams, Williams has not sent the draft manuscript.

Vicki contacts you, SeaPress's outside counsel, for advice. Specifically, she wants your help with the following:

1. If Williams finishes the manuscript after July 31, 2019, but before July 31, 2020, do you foresee any concerns with SeaPress applying the $1,000 per day offset? What if Williams were to challenge that offset in court?

2. If Williams does not finish the manuscript by July 1, 2010, do you foresee any concerns with SeaPress recovering $1 million from Williams due to her breach?

Now that you have studied remedies from a variety of angles, read through and answer the questions that follow the Simulation Problem for Chapters 24-26, which is located in Appendix A.

CHAPTER 27

Disallowed Damages

The past few chapters have introduced the different types of contract reme-dies that are available to an aggrieved party, including the remedy of money damages, as well as how to calculate the proper amount of such damages. We also examined certain limitations on damages, including the requirement for damages to be foreseeable, reasonably calculable at the time of breach, and caused by the other party's breach. This chapter, by contrast, explores specific types of damages that are typically disallowed under contract law. Section A discusses punitive damages, Section B addresses attorneys' fees, and Section C explores damages for emotional distress. Consider in each section why the rules disallowing such damages exist and whether and how such rules conflict with other contract policy concerns.

A. PUNITIVE DAMAGES

Contract law is a no-fault system. In other words, a party who breaches is not viewed as a bad actor or subject to a specified penalty simply because the party breached. Instead, if a party breaches, regardless of its reason, the other party is entitled to a remedy to compensate it for that breach. In other words, there is strict liability for a contractual breach, without regard to the reasons for the party's breach.

Because breach is not fault-based, remedies do not seek to punish a breach-ing party—instead, they are designed to compensate the injured party. That means courts generally do not award punitive damages for breach of contract, as the purpose of punitive damages is to punish a party for bad behavior—again, a goal not advanced by contract law.

The absence of punitive damages in contract law also reflects the view of contracts as facilitating the goal of economic efficiency. Thus, as was discussed in Chapter 24 in the context of a discussion of efficient breach, if it makes economic sense for a party to breach a contract (even considering a remedy it will likely owe), then contract law remedies should not prevent that outcome. In other words, it would be undesirable for penalty damages to discourage an efficient breach.

There are a few exceptions to the no-punitive-damages rule, however. For one, courts award punitive damages for the breach of certain types of contracts, such as a promise to marry. And in most jurisdictions, courts award punitive damages for breach of an insurance contract where an insurance company fails in bad faith to resolve a claim brought by a third party against the insured. This type of claim is referred to as a **third-party claim** because it covers the insured's liability to a third party. An example of such a third-party claim exists where a person is injured in an auto accident and seeks to recover from the insured's insurance company. The following explains one court's rationale for awarding punitive damages in this circumstance:

> The special nature of an insurance contract has been recognized by courts and legislatures for many years. A whole body of case and statutory law has been developed to regulate the relationship between insurer and insured. An insurance policy is not obtained for commercial advantage; it is obtained as protection against calamity. In securing the reasonable expectations of the insured under the insurance policy there is usually an unequal bargaining position between the insured and the insurance company. When the loss insured against occurs the insured expects to have the protection provided by his insurance. Often the insured is in an especially vulnerable economic position when such a casualty loss occurs. The whole purpose of insurance is defeated if an insurance company can refuse or fail, without jurisdiction, to pay a valid claim. We have determined that it is reasonable to conclude that there is a legal duty implied in an insurance contract that the insurance company must act in good faith in dealing with its insured on a claim, and a violation of that duty of good faith is a tort.

Noble v. National American Life Insurance Co., 624 P.2d 866, 867-68 (Ariz. 1981).

As the *Noble* court held, an insurance company is liable for acting in bad faith where it has no reasonable basis to deny a claim, and the insurance company's conduct in that instance constitutes a tort. It is this tort quality of the breach that subjects the insurance company to punitive damages.

Courts do not award punitive damages as frequently for breaches of first-party insurance claims. A first-party claim is a claim that is brought by an insured as a result of the insurance company's denial of the insured's claims resulting from losses *suffered by the insured*. An example of a first-party claim is flood damage to the insured's house, or theft of the insured's car. While courts generally do not award punitive damages for first-party claims, some do for the same reasons mentioned by the *Noble* court.

Courts award punitive damages for other tortious breaches of contracts, too. As Restatement § 355 provides, "Punitive damages are not recoverable for a breach of contract unless the conduct constituting the breach is also a tort for which punitive damages are recoverable." Most commonly, this occurs where a party engages in the tort of fraud. However, some courts even award punitive damages where a party's breach was willful or fraudulent, even if not all the elements of a tort are satisfied.

For example, in *Ainsworth v. Franklin County Cheese Corp.*,[1] Franklin County Cheese Corp. (FCCC) hired Ainsworth to manage FCCC's cheese manufacturing plant in Enosburg, Vermont. The parties entered into a written employment agreement that provided for successive one-year terms that automatically renewed unless one party gave the other at least 30 days' notice of its wish to terminate.[2] Under the contract, if Ainsworth was terminated without "cause," he was entitled to a severance payment upon his termination. However, if Ainsworth's employment was terminated for "cause," then he was not entitled to any severance benefits.

Eventually FCCC terminated Ainsworth's employment, stating it was for "cause" due to Ainsworth's failure to follow directions and the company's operations manual. Consequently, FCCC did not pay Ainsworth any severance benefits. Ainsworth sued, arguing that there was no evidence supporting FCCC's claim of "cause." The jury sided with Ainsworth, finding that the company had given a false pretext for Ainsworth's firing. As a result, it found that Ainsworth was entitled to receive the severance benefits. The jury also awarded Ainsworth punitive damages. On appeal, the Vermont Supreme Court upheld that award even though FCCC's conduct had not constituted a tort. According to the court, "punitive damages are appropriate in contract actions 'in certain extraordinary cases where the breach has the character of a willful and wanton or fraudulent tort.'"[3]

Comprehension and Thought Questions:

1. Should punitive damages be awarded for non-tortious breaches? Why or why not? What goals would be served by awarding such damages?

2. Should punitive damages be awarded even for insurance companies' denial of first-party claims in insurance contracts? Why or why not? What goals would be served by awarding such damages?

---

1. 592 A.2d 871 (Vt. 1991).
2. This type of automatic renewal provision is referred to as an evergreen provision.
3. Ainsworth v. Franklin County Cheese Corp., 592 A.2d at 874 (citation and emphasis omitted).

B. ATTORNEYS' FEES

The general rule in the United States is that each party pays for its own litigation costs. That means the party who prevails in litigation still must pay for its own attorneys, court costs, and other costs in resolving a dispute. This is true not only for contract cases but for other types of cases too.

There are some statutory exceptions to this rule. In particular, some statutes either require or at least permit the court to award attorneys' fees to the prevailing party in a contract action. For example, California Code of Civil Procedure § 1780 *requires* a court to award attorneys' fees and other costs to any prevailing *plaintiff* consumer in litigation who suffers damage as a result of any number of fraudulent or deceptive commercial practices, such as advertising goods or services with an intent to not sell them as advertised. That same section also *permits* a court to award attorneys' fees to a prevailing *defendant* where the court finds the plaintiff's prosecution of its claim was not made in good faith.

In addition, parties can agree between themselves that the losing party in litigation will pay the prevailing party's attorneys' fees and other litigation costs. Such provisions are typically enforced so long as attorneys' fees are reasonable.[4] These provisions ensure that the prevailing party is compensated for any out-of-pocket costs that would not otherwise be recoverable. For example, without such a provision, a successful defendant would still have suffered a loss—the amount of any attorneys' fees and other litigation costs. Below is a one-sided fee-shifting provision from a residential mortgage. A mortgage is an agreement through which a party—the mortgagor—grants a lien on real property to secure its debt owed to the lender, called the mortgagee in this document.

> Mortgagor shall be liable to Mortgagee for all legal costs, including but not limited to reasonable attorney fees and costs and charges of any sale in any action to enforce any of its rights hereunder whether or not such action proceeds to judgment.[5]

As suggested above, loan agreements and other related loan documents, like a mortgage, often include these attorney fee-shifting clauses because the lender does not want to relinquish any portion of its expected loan income by having to pay to enforce the loan agreement against a defaulting borrower. For example, if a lender negotiates to receive interest at a rate of 5 percent per annum, it certainly does not want to effectively reduce that to 3 percent per annum, or

---

4. *See, e.g.,* Cal. Civil Code § 1717 (West 2009).
5. *See* Wilborn v. Bank One Corp., 906 N.E.2d 396 (Ohio Sup. Ct. 2009). The Ohio Supreme Court upheld this provision in *Wilborn*.

even less, after taking into account litigation costs in enforcing the borrower's obligation to repay the loan.

The fact that a party must pay its own litigation costs can deter litigation, especially where a party's expected recovery in litigation is less than its anticipated attorneys' fees. This is commonly the case in consumer transactions, where a merchant's breach might only mean a loss of $10, or even $100, to the consumer, yet lead to several thousands of dollars in litigation costs if the consumer were to enforce the contract. For this reason, often no single consumer has the financial capacity or interest to sue individually.

This limitation explains California's mandatory fee-shifting provision discussed above, which is available to consumers who sue for certain fraudulent and deceptive commercial practices. It also explains why consumers often act by class action—as a class, they can recover a significant enough sum from a merchant to justify litigation-related costs. Of course, many people see these class actions as only benefiting the lawyers who represent the consumer class, as they are often the only ones who individually have a significant recovery. The consumers, by contrast, often end up receiving only a fraction of the total recovery.

Merchants increasingly avoid class actions by including mandatory arbitration clauses in their consumer contracts. As Chapter 6 explained, those clauses not only require consumers to enforce contracts in arbitration, but often also preclude consumers from acting as a class in those arbitration proceedings. With this ability to act as a class removed, once again, there may not be adequate financial incentives in place for consumers to enforce contracts.

C. DAMAGES FOR EMOTIONAL DISTRESS

By and large, contract law does not award a party damages to compensate for emotional distress. That is because such damages are typically not foreseeable as a probable result of breach at the time the parties entered into the contract. Instead, contracts are seen as tools to facilitate economic exchange, where a person's emotions are largely not relevant. Similarly, damages for emotional distress are usually difficult to quantify with reasonable certainty, since they are not pecuniary in nature. Such difficulty can, in turn, make it hard for a party to price the risks associated with a contract, and thereby discourage contract formation.

However, courts occasionally do allow a party to recover damages for emotional distress for breach of contract. One situation where courts sometimes allow a party to recover damages for emotional distress occurs where the other party's breach gives rise to bodily harm.[6] That might occur, for example, where a homeowner is seriously injured due to defects in a builder's construction of

---

6. Restatement (Second) of Contracts § 353 (1981).

the home. While such claims might more properly sound in tort, courts often do not require a party to separately plead the elements of tort, and instead allow a party to recover these damages as part of its contract remedy.[7]

The second situation where courts sometimes allow a party to recover damages for emotional distress occurs with contracts where emotional distress is likely to occur due to breach.[8] That happens with contracts that are often described as "personal" in nature, where performance is closely related with a person's emotions. For example, one court awarded damages for emotional distress to a widow for a breach of a contract to bury her dead husband, where the funeral home did not adequately seal the casket from water and the wife had to reintern her husband.[9] Another court awarded a professional entertainer damages for emotional distress where her plastic surgeon, who was hired to improve her face, ended up disfiguring her face.[10] However, apart from these exceptional situations, courts have been reluctant to award damages for emotional distress.

Comprehension and Thought Questions:

1. Will a party who is seriously emotionally injured by the counterparty's breach of contract be made "whole" as a result of a damages award where the party does not receive damages for his or her emotional injury?

2. Should courts be more willing to award a party damages for emotional injury? Why or why not?

Now that you have studied disallowed damages, read through and answer the questions that follow the Simulation Problem for Chapter 27, which is located in Appendix A.

---

7. *See* Restatement (Second) of Contracts § 353 cmt. a (1981).
8. Restatement (Second) of Contracts § 353 (1981).
9. Lamm v. Shingleton, 55 S.E.2d 810 (N.C. 1949).
10. Sullivan v. O'Connor, 296 N.E. 2d 183 (Mass. 1973).

CHAPTER 28

UCC Remedies

As with mutual assent, Article 2 of the UCC also has some specialized rules on remedies for breach of a contract governed by Article 2. As you will see, Article 2's remedy provisions are similar to the common law rules on remedies discussed in the prior chapters. However, these rules have been tailored to reflect modern commercial practices. They also reflect the fact that goods are usually fungible and can be procured from other sources.

The UCC divides up its provisions on remedies between remedies available to a seller where a buyer of goods breaches, and those available to a buyer where a seller of goods breaches. We will do the same. Thus, Section A discusses remedies available to sellers, and Section B discusses remedies available to buyers.

A. SELLER REMEDIES

A buyer may breach a contract for the sale of goods in many ways. A buyer may wrongfully reject goods that conform to the contract (referred to as "conforming goods"), it may accept conforming goods and then wrongfully revoke its acceptance, or it may fail to pay for conforming goods per the contract.

A seller's remedies depend in part on whether a buyer has accepted delivered goods. If a buyer accepts goods and then breaches by failing to pay, the seller has a right to recover the full contract price for those goods.

If a buyer has *not* accepted conforming goods, then the seller's recovery depends on whether or not the seller sells the relevant goods to another buyer. If the seller sells those goods to another buyer in good faith in a "commercially reasonable manner," then under UCC § 2–706, the seller "may" recover the difference between the contract price and the resale price.[1]

---

1. As with the common law, if the seller recovers more on the resale than the price promised in the contract with the breaching buyer, the buyer does not get to share in those profits. *See* U.C.C. § 2–706(6) (2011).

If, on the other hand, the seller does not sell those goods to another buyer, then under § 2–708, the seller recovers damages measured by the difference between the contract price and the fair market value of those goods. Here, "fair market value" is substituted for the resale price because there is no resale price to use for purposes of calculating damages.

You will note that both of these measures of damages largely reflect the calculation of expectation damages under the common law. Recall that under the common law, where one party breaches a contract, damages are generally calculated based on the difference between the contract price and the market price on the date of breach. We saw that measure of damages in *Crabby's, Inc. v. Hamilton* in Chapter 24. There, where the buyer failed to buy the seller's property per their sales contract, the seller recovered the difference between the contract price of the property and its fair market value on the date of breach. In addition, the seller recovered consequential damages, which included its costs in maintaining the property for resale following the buyer's breach.

So, too, where a buyer of goods breaches, a seller can recover the difference between the contract price and fair market value of goods on the date of breach. However, recognizing that there may be a readily available substitute buyer for goods, the UCC substitutes "fair market value" with actual sales price, where a substitute sale occurs in a commercially reasonable manner. In essence, the sales price to that substitute buyer reflects fair market value.

One might question what happens where a seller resells goods and recovers more than the goods' fair market value. In that situation, can the seller recover damages calculated using fair market value of the goods instead of the resale price? In other words, and using the following diagram, can the seller recover *more* than its actual losses (shown as "A" on this diagram) by measuring its damages by the difference between the contract price and the fair market value for those goods on the date of breach (shown by "B" on this diagram)?

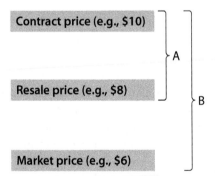

This question is raised because § 2–706 is discretionary in that it indicates that a seller *may* recover the difference between the contract price and its sales price where the seller sells the goods to a substitute buyer, suggesting that the seller does not *have to* use this measure of damages where it resells the goods.

Professors White and Summers, two prominent contract law scholars, have argued that allowing a seller to calculate its damages using fair market value on the date of breach where it has made a substitute sale in compliance with § 2–706 would undermine the purpose of contract law damages, of compensating a party for actual damages.[2] Courts generally seem to hold consistent with this view.[3]

The UCC does recognize that damages calculated under either measure mentioned above might not make a seller whole due to a buyer's breach. That might happen, for example, where a seller is a "lost volume seller." That term refers to a seller that is sufficiently large that it can supply as many goods as are demanded. For example, Apple is a lost volume seller of iPhones, for it can supply as many phones as are demanded. Sellers like Apple have no trouble finding alternative buyers for goods that a buyer fails to buy; however, the seller still will have lost profits from a buyer's failure to accept, or a buyer's subsequent rejection of, conforming goods. In that circumstance, under § 2–708(2), the seller can instead recover the profits it failed to receive on the contract with the buyer.

A seller can also recover profits it failed to receive on a contract with a buyer where the buyer breaches while a seller is in the process of manufacturing goods for the buyer. In that case, it might not be commercially reasonable for the seller to complete manufacturing those goods for resale, especially if they are specialty items for which there is not a market.

Regardless of what measure is used to calculate direct damages, as with the common law calculation of damages, a seller may also recover consequential damages. Such damages might include, for example, costs the seller incurred to hold goods for resale, or to care for goods after the buyer's breach. In addition, as with the common law calculation of damages, a seller's recovery will be reduced by any costs it saved in not having to perform under the breached contract.

Finally, in addition to monetary damages, where a buyer breaches by failing to pay for goods or repudiates a contract, a seller can withhold delivery of goods. It can even stop goods in transit to the buyer.

PRACTICE PROBLEM 28-1

Specialty Chairs Co. makes custom chairs for commercial needs. Its specialty is conference room chairs and ergonomic work chairs, all custom-made for height, width, weight, and lumbar support specifications. A purchaser can

---

2. White & Summers, 1 Uniform Commercial Code (3d ed. 1988).
3. *See, e.g.,* Tesoro Petroleum Corp. v. Holborn Oil Co., 547 N.Y.S.2d 1012 (N.Y. App. Div. 1989).

also choose the material and design for ordered chairs from a list of approved materials and designs provided by Specialty Chairs.

On June 1, Taylor Law Offices L.P., a small boutique law firm, ordered 20 chairs from Specialty Chairs. Of those, 12 were to be conference room chairs, customized in terms of material and design to match Taylor Law Offices' conference room table. However, they were otherwise standard as to height, width, weight, and lumbar support. The remaining 8 chairs were to be office chairs, custom-made for each attorney and staff member of Taylor Law Offices based on that person's specific needs and preferences.

In placing this order, the office manager of Taylor Law Offices, Beth Shavano, used Specialty Chairs' order form. The order form contained virtually no terms except for the chair specifications. Specialty Chairs' confirmation of this order set out the estimated delivery date of October 1 and total price of $5,800—with a price of $350 for each custom-made office chair and $250 for each conference room chair. This would generate a profit to Specialty Chairs of $100 per chair, as the custom chairs cost it $250 to make and the conference room chairs cost it $150 to make.

On August 1, Taylor Law Offices agreed to be acquired by The Noble Law Firm, a large law firm with an office in Springfield, Columbia. The plan was for all of the attorneys at Taylor Law Offices to move to The Noble Law Firm's office in Springfield as of September 1.

Given these developments, and after conversations with The Noble Law Firm's office manager, on August 10, Shavano called Arturo Gomez, the Vice-President of Sales at Specialty Chairs, to inform him that Taylor Law Offices had to cancel its chair order. Shavano apologized, but said her law firm no longer needed the chairs.

As of that time, Specialty Chairs had already made the 12 conference room chairs. And it had completed 4 of the 8 custom-made office chairs. It had not yet started to manufacture the remaining 4 custom-made office chairs.

Upon learning this information, Gomez immediately began to market the chairs that Taylor Law Offices had ordered but was now refusing to buy. After advertising the chairs through customary marketing channels, Specialty Chairs was able to sell the 12 conference room chairs for $225 each. Because the customized office chairs that were completed were specifically made for each person, Specialty Chairs had to severely discount those chairs, selling them for $150 each.

Assume you represent Specialty Chairs and that you already determined that Taylor Law Offices repudiated its contract for the chairs. Gomez asks you what damages Specialty Chairs could likely collect from Taylor Law Offices if Specialty Chairs were to pursue its claim against Taylor Law Offices:

1. What remedy can Specialty Chairs likely recover for the 4 custom office chairs Taylor Law Offices ordered that Specialty Chairs has not yet manufactured?

2. What remedy can Specialty Chairs likely recover for the 4 custom office chairs Taylor Law Offices ordered that Specialty Chairs has already manufactured?

3. Can Specialty Chairs recover damages for the 12 conference room chairs that it sold to a different buyer? If so, how much can it recover for those?

4. Would your answer to Question 3 change if Specialty Chairs sold those chairs for $250 each as it had a long backlog of orders for similar "standard" conference room chairs?

B. BUYER REMEDIES

A seller might breach a contract for the sale of goods in several ways. First, the seller may fail to deliver some or all of the promised goods on the agreed-upon timetable. This is referred to as a problem with "tender" of the contracted-for goods. Second, a seller may deliver goods that do not conform to the contract. An example of such a nonconforming sale occurs where a seller delivers goods that fail to satisfy an express or implied warranty as to the quality of those goods.

Where a seller fails to deliver promised goods, or a buyer rightfully rejects (or revokes acceptance of) goods because they do not conform to the contract, the buyer is left without the goods it was promised under the contract. In those situations, under § 2–711, the buyer may cancel the contract. Moreover, the buyer may recover the purchase price it paid for those undelivered or rejected nonconforming goods.

In addition, a buyer may recover either

(1)   any losses it suffers by having to "cover" its losses by obtaining replacement goods elsewhere, referred to as "cover" damages (§ 2–712), or

(2)   the loss in value it suffered by not receiving the promised goods, referred to as "market damages," where a buyer does not buy replacement goods (§ 2–713).

Where a buyer chooses to buy replacement goods per paragraph (1), it *may* recover "cover" damages—meaning the difference in cost between the contract price and the cost of those replacement goods—but only where the buyer in good faith makes a reasonable substitute purchase and without unreasonable delay. That means that this measure of damages will not be available if a buyer buys superior or significantly different goods.

As in the case of seller's damages, here, too, the UCC looks to measure damages by using the actual price of substitute goods instead of the fair market value of the goods on the date of breach where a buyer buys substitute goods. Such measure is used because goods are largely fungible. Thus, the cost of replacement goods is an effective measure of fair market value of those nondelivered goods, so long as they are bought within a reasonable time from breach.

On the other hand, buying substitute goods is within the discretion of a buyer. Where a buyer does not buy substitute goods, it instead measures its damages under § 2–713, which is paraphrased in paragraph (2) above. Under that section, the buyer's damages are the difference between the contract price and the fair market value of the promised goods on the date the buyer learned of the breach. This section of the UCC also explains how to determine which market price to use. In general, the relevant market location is that at which the goods are to be tendered under the contract, though if the goods have already been tendered, the relevant market is the place of arrival.

Similar to the discussion above under seller's remedies, there is some question how §§ 2–712 and 2–713 work together. In particular, the UCC is not clear whether a buyer can buy substitute goods but, because "cover" damages are discretionary, opt to recover market damages under § 2–713 instead where they are greater. Here, again, if the purpose of damages is to put the aggrieved party in the same position it would have been in had the other party not breached, a party should not be able to obtain damages in excess of its actual damages. That would mean that a party who buys substitute goods should not recover market damages simply because they are greater.

Conversely, if a buyer retains nonconforming goods, the buyer cannot recover "cover" damages or "market" damages because it has chosen to retain the nonconforming goods instead of buying substitute goods or losing the entire value of undelivered (or rejected) goods. In that situation, under § 2–714, the buyer may recover "the loss resulting in the ordinary course of events from the seller's breach as determined in any manner which is reasonable." While this language is quite vague, paragraph (2) of § 2–714 specifically addresses damages for breach of warranty for nonconforming goods, recognizing that this is the most common claim where nonconforming goods are retained. That paragraph specifies that such breach-of-warranty damages are equal to "the difference at the time and place of acceptance between the value of the goods accepted and the value they would have had if they had been as warranted. . . ."[4] However, this is not the only measure of damages for breach of warranty. Specifically, this section recognizes that "special circumstances [might] show proximate damages of a different amount."[5]

As was the case with a buyer breach, and consistent with the common law calculation of damages, where a seller breaches, under § 2–715, a buyer may also recover consequential damages. Such consequential damages might include costs incurred by a buyer to store, safe-keep, or transport nonconforming goods back to the seller. In addition, consistent with the common law calculation of damages, a buyer's recovery will be reduced by any costs it saved in not having to perform under the breached contract.

---

4. U.C.C. § 2–714(2) (1977).

5. *Id.*

In alternative to a damages remedy, a buyer may instead seek to specifically enforce a contract for the sale of goods. Under § 2–716, specific performance is available "where the goods are unique or in other proper circumstances."

PRACTICE PROBLEM 28-2

Refer back to the facts from Practice Problem 28-1. Assume that The Noble Law Firm's office manager decided that The Noble Law Firm still needed the chairs Shavano had ordered. Therefore, Shavano did not cancel Taylor Law Offices' chair order with Specialty Chairs.

However, on August 15, Specialty Chairs received an order for 1,000 office chairs from Office To The Max Inc., a large office equipment and supply store. Office To The Max demanded that the chairs be finished by January 1. To finish the chairs by then, Specialty Chairs had to dedicate all of its personnel and manufacturing capacity to the manufacture of those chairs, which meant that it had to delay the manufacture of chairs under all other existing orders (a move Specialty Chairs decided was worthwhile given the size of Office To The Max's current and potential future orders).

On August 17, Arturo Gomez, the Vice-President of Sales at Specialty Chairs, contacted all customers with pending orders and explained the situation and that delivery of their chairs would be delayed for at least six months. While many customers were fine with a delay, Taylor Law Offices was not. As Shavano told Gomez on that call, Taylor Law Offices had already committed to delivering its old office chairs to a local charity on October 1. Therefore, it needed its chairs by then. Gomez apologized, and noted that at least Taylor Law Offices would receive the completed 12 conference room chairs and 4 custom-made office chairs by October 1.

Shavano responded by canceling Taylor Law Offices' order for the 4 remaining custom office chairs that had not yet been manufactured. She then sought another company to manufacture those chairs. Because this order was of such a small number of chairs, manufacturers were unwilling to give any good deals. The lowest quote was from Magic Seat Inc., which quoted $500 per chair. Without other options, Shavano placed an order with Magic Seat for the remaining 4 customized office chairs.

Again, assume you represent Specialty Chairs. Assume also that you have concluded that Specialty Chairs repudiated its duty to manufacture the 4 remaining custom chairs for Taylor Law Offices. Gomez has come to you for advice on the following in connection with a potential lawsuit by Taylor Law Offices against Specialty Chairs for that repudiation:

1. Will Specialty Chairs likely be liable to Taylor Law Offices for the extra costs Taylor Law Offices incurs in buying the 4 customized chairs ordered from Magic Seat?

2. What if Taylor Law Offices decides to keep its current chairs instead of donating them to charity? Would Specialty Chairs still owe damages to Taylor Law Offices for the nondelivery of those 4 chairs? If so, how much?

3. What if it turns out that the 4 customized office chairs Specialty Chairs delivers to Taylor Law Offices do not conform to specifications, as they have the lumbar support in the wrong spot, making them uncomfortable for the people for whom they were customized. What remedy might Taylor Law Offices demand due to this breach?

PART VIII

THIRD PARTIES

P art VIII discusses how third parties affect, and are affected by, contracts. Namely, Chapter 29 explores when a person who is not a party to a contract, referred to as a third party, can enforce a contract against a contractual party. It also explains how a contractual party assigns its rights and delegates its duties under a contract to a third party and analyzes the enforceability of contractual provisions that try to limit that power. Finally, Chapter 29 explains where a third party might be liable for tortious interference with contract where it interferes with a contracting party's existing contractual relationship.

CHAPTER 29

Rights, Duties, and Liabilities of Third Parties

In general, a contract only sets out rights and obligations of the parties to a contract. In other words, a contract generally does not affect people who are not parties to the contract—referred to as **third parties**.

However, sometimes contracts do affect rights and duties of third parties. That occurs where a third party is a beneficiary of the parties' conduct under the contract. Section A below discusses how a third party becomes a third-party beneficiary under a contract.

Moreover, a contracting party might voluntarily assign its rights under a contract to a third party. And a third party might voluntarily assume a contracting parties' duties. In fact, you have read a number of cases in this book in which a party assigned its rights and delegated its duties under a contract to a third party, who then became bound to perform the assigning party's obligations and received the benefits of the counterparty's performance. Section B discusses these concepts of assignment of rights and delegation of duties by a contracting party to a third party.

A contract can even create tort liability for a third party. That occurs where the third party intentionally interferes with a party's performance of a contract, known as tortious interference with a contract. We discuss this tort in Section C. We cover this tort in our contracts textbook because it is integrally related to contract creation and performance, similar to how fraud can create tort liability. Put simply, one cannot fully understand the law of contracts, or how to advise a client in contracting, without understanding this tort.

A. THIRD-PARTY BENEFICIARY

Contracts inevitably affect third parties. For example, suppose you lease a desirable apartment. If there were multiple other potential tenants interested in that same apartment, they would clearly be disappointed by your lease of that space. Similarly, if you represent a client in selling its business where multiple bidders are seeking to buy that business, the losing bidders will surely be disappointed, as they will not have the opportunity to expand their business in the way they had hoped.

Sometimes third parties are disappointed by others' contracting behavior—but third parties often are pleased that others have entered into a contract. For example, your family is bound to be proud when you enter into a contract for employment as an attorney. And many Whole Foods customers were undoubtedly pleased when Whole Foods merged with Amazon, making Whole Foods' products available for online order and delivery through Amazon's platform.

While third parties were disappointed by some contracts and pleased with others, in none of the examples above did those third parties incur any right to enforce the contracts or incur any obligations under these contracts. For example, even though your family will be pleased when you receive an employment contract, they will have no right to enforce the contract against your employer if your employer terminates your employment in breach of the contract. Only you, the contracting party, will have the right to enforce that contract against the counterparty.

However, in some circumstances, a third party does have the right to enforce a contract against a contracting party. That occurs where one or more parties to a contract makes a promise to perform in favor of a third party, *and the parties to the contract intend for that third party to directly benefit from that promise.* The parties' intent is determined by looking at all of the facts and circumstances. Thus, while such an intention might be apparent from the face of the contract, it might also be implied by the circumstances.

For example, assume María Gomez bought a life insurance policy, which is a contract. In it, she named her daughter Rocío as the beneficiary. That means when María dies, all of the proceeds from the insurance policy will be paid to Rocío. In this case, while Rocío is not a party to the contract, the insurance policy is designed to benefit Rocío. Thus, Rocío is an intended third-party beneficiary. Therefore, if the insurance company does not pay out the proceeds to Rocío per the insurance policy, Rocío can sue the insurance company for breach.

When ascertaining the parties' intent regarding whether there are third party beneficiaries, courts may give weight to a clause in the contract that disclaims the parties' intent for any third party to benefit from the contract.

Others, however, will not, particularly where it otherwise was clear based on the purpose of the contract (such as in the life insurance policy example above) that the contract was intended, at least in part, to benefit a third party. The following is an example of such a disclaimer:

> The provisions of this Agreement are solely for the benefit of the parties to this Agreement and are not intended to confer upon any person except the parties to this Agreement any rights or remedies under this Agreement. There are no third party beneficiaries of this Agreement and this Agreement does not provide any third person with any remedy, claim, liability, reimbursement, claim or other right in excess of those existing without reference to this Agreement.

A person also may be a third-party beneficiary where a new promisor promises to pay a debt of the original debtor to satisfy the original debtor's debt to that third party. In this case, the third party can enforce the new promisor's promise in favor of that third party. That is the case even if the original debtor's debt to the third party is discharged due to bankruptcy or is otherwise unenforceable.

To see how this works, suppose that on January 1, Billy borrows $10,000 from Big Bank N.A. The entire principal amount is due on December 31 of that same year. As of December 25, Billy does not have the money. Katelyn, Billy's aunt, decides to help out and promises Billy that she will pay Big Bank $10,000 on December 31. If on December 31 neither Billy nor Aunt Katelyn pays the $10,000, Big Bank can sue to enforce that promise not just against Billy, but also against Aunt Katelyn. Here, while Big Bank does not have a contract with Aunt Katelyn, it is a third-party beneficiary of Aunt Katelyn's promise to Billy to satisfy Billy's contractual obligation. As such, Big Bank can sue to enforce Aunt Katelyn's promise. That is true even if Billy's promise to pay Big Bank is discharged in bankruptcy.

The above examples involve an **intended third-party beneficiary**. In each of these cases, where the contracting parties intend for a third party to benefit from a contracting party's performance, that third party can sue to enforce that performance.

However, a third party might instead be an **unintended, or incidental, beneficiary of a contract**. That occurs where a person has a direct economic interest in a contract, but is not intended to be a beneficiary. While an incidental beneficiary benefits from a party's performance under a contract, that party does *not* have standing to sue for any breach in performance. For that reason, a third-party beneficiary will often try to argue that it was an intended beneficiary, while the promisor will argue that the third party was an incidental beneficiary. The following case shows one court's approach to this type of question.

The James Family Charitable Foundation v. State Street Bank & Trust Co.

Appeals Court of Massachusetts, Suffolk
80 Mass. App. Ct. 720 (2011)

WOLOHOJIAN, J.

Hamilton James (James), a client of State Street Bank and Trust Company (State Street), wished to make a charitable gift of mutual fund shares to The James Family Charitable Foundation (foundation). The shares were in the custody of State Street pursuant to a custodianship agreement (agreement) between James and State Street that, among other things, required State Street to transfer assets when instructed to do so by James. James, through his investment agent, instructed State Street to transfer the shares to the foundation's broker in order to effectuate his charitable gift. State Street failed to initiate the transaction properly, thus delaying the transfer to the foundation. The foundation alleges that it consequently was unable to sell the shares until after their value had significantly declined.

The foundation seeks to maintain a breach of contract claim against State Street even though the foundation was not a party to the agreement. The foundation argues that it has standing because it is an intended beneficiary of the custodianship agreement and, as such, is entitled to maintain a claim for breach of the agreement against the promisor (State Street). The judge below disagreed and allowed State Street's motion for summary judgment. We now reverse.

Background. In April, 2002, James and State Street entered into the agreement whereby State Street agreed, for a monthly fee, to serve as custodian of certain of James's assets. We find State Street's summary of its obligations under the agreement helpful for these purposes and accordingly set it out here:

> "One of State Street's contractual obligations was to receive James'[s] assets into custody *and transfer them out upon receipt of authorized instructions.* Other obligations of State Street under the Custodianship Agreement includ[ed] acting on Mr. James'[s] investment instructions; collecting the proceeds of sales, maturities, and other dispositions; collecting income, dividends and other proceeds of investments; responding to shareholder actions; responding to information requests from securities issuers; providing account statements and value appraisals; deducting the investment manager's fees; issuing 1099 Forms; making authorized wire transfers; and voting proxies." (Emphasis added.)

Because the agreement contained no termination date, and had no fixed term, State Street's obligations were to continue until one party or the other gave notice of termination.

The agreement itself did not specify which assets were to be placed in State Street's custody. Rather, the agreement provided that State Street would "hold all property turned over to it from time to time" by James. Similarly, the agreement did not contain any specific instructions from James. Instead, the agreement provided that State Street would carry out instructions as they were received in the future from James or his authorized investment agent.

From time to time between 2002 and 2007, James instructed State Street to transfer shares of stock to the foundation's account. State Street acted on each of those instructions in a timely and effective manner, except as described below.

By the beginning of February, 2007, James had more than 800,000 shares of Vanguard Emerging Markets Stock Index Fund (VEIEX) in State Street's custody, and he decided to make a charitable gift of these shares to the foundation. Accordingly, on February 13, 2007, James instructed State Street to transfer all of the VEIEX shares in its custody "FOR CREDIT TO THE JAMES FAMILY CHARITABLE FOUNDATION ACCOUNT # [xxxxx]." This instruction was made in writing on a State Street form intended to be used for this purpose. In response to State Street's request on the form for an explanation for the transfer, the following appeared: "GIFT TO JAMES FAMILY CHARITABLE FOUNDATION."

State Street acted on these instructions immediately by correctly completing a letter of instructions. However, instead of sending the letter of instructions to Vanguard as it should have done, State Street mistakenly sent the letter to the foundation's broker. Despite multiple inquiries from James's agent over the next several days as to the status of the transfer, State Street did not discover its error until February 22, 2007. On that day, it sent a second letter of instructions, this time properly directed to Vanguard. For reasons not pertinent here, the shares did not reach the foundation's account until March 1, 2007.

The foundation contends that, had State Street carried out its obligations under the agreement when it received James's instructions on February 13, 2007, the foundation would have been able to sell the shares while the price was above twenty-five dollars.[1] The foundation further contends that State Street's breach of its obligations under the agreement caused the foundation to have to sell the shares at a lower price, resulting in a loss of over $1.6 million to the foundation.[2]

2. Discussion. The sole issue on appeal is whether the foundation has standing to sue for breach of contract as a third-party beneficiary of the agreement between James and State Street. In 1982, our courts adopted the intended beneficiary theory of standing from the Restatement (Second) of Contracts §§ 302–315 (1981). Although we have had occasion to discuss the doctrine in the thirty years since its adoption, those occasions have been infrequent and

---

1. [5] VEIEX shares traded from February 15, 2007, through February 23, 2007, at above twenty-five dollars per share. The foundation contends that it would have sold the shares during that period because James had instructed that the shares were to be sold by the foundation upon receipt.

2. [6] Similarly, the foundation contends that it was required to sell at the lower price, rather than to hold the shares until the price rose, because of James's instruction to sell upon receipt.

have not involved facts such as presented here. We accordingly begin by survey-ing the doctrine generally.

The Restatement (Second) of Contracts recognizes the right of an intended beneficiary of a contract to sue for its enforcement or breach: "A promise in a contract creates a duty in the promisor to any intended beneficiary to perform the promise, and the intended beneficiary may enforce the duty." Restatement (Second) of Contracts § 304. This statement is a modern articulation of a principle we have long recognized in Massachusetts, namely that "when one person, for a valuable consideration, engages with another, by simple contract, to do some act for the benefit of a third, the latter, who would enjoy the benefit of the act, may maintain an action for the breach of such engagement." *Brewer v. Dyer*, 61 Mass. 337, 7 Cush. 337, 340 (1851), quoted with approval in *Rae v. Air-Speed, Inc., supra* at 195, 435 N.E.2d 628.

In contrast to an intended beneficiary, an incidental beneficiary obtains no right to enforce the contract. To determine whether a beneficiary is intended, rather than merely incidental, we look to the intent of the parties. As set out in the Restatement:

> "(1) Unless otherwise agreed between promisor and promisee, a beneficiary of a promise is an intended beneficiary if recognition of a right to performance in the beneficiary is appropriate to effectuate the intention of the parties and either
>
> > "(a) the performance of the promise will satisfy an obligation of the promisee to pay money to the beneficiary; or
> >
> > "(b) the circumstances indicate that the promisee intends to give the beneficiary the benefit of the promised performance."

Restatement (Second) of Contracts § 302. There is no dispute that James (the promisee) intended to give the foundation the benefit of the promised perfor-mance (the transfer of the shares). Subsection (b) is thus clearly satisfied. The issue, therefore, is whether giving the foundation a right to performance under the contract is "appropriate to effectuate the intention of the parties."

"We look at the language and circumstances of the contract for indicia of intention" for purposes of determining whether a particular person is an intended beneficiary. *Anderson v. Fox Hill Village Homeowners Corp.*, 424 Mass. 365, 366, 676 N.E.2d 821 (1997). The intent of the contracting par-ties must be "clear and definite." *Lakew v. Massachusetts Bay Transp. Authy.*, 65 Mass. App. Ct. 794, 798, 844 N.E.2d 263 (2006), quoting from *Anderson v. Fox Hill Village Homeowners Corp., supra* at 366–367, 676 N.E.2d 821. That said, there is no requirement that the intended beneficiary be identified by name in the contract or even that the intended beneficiary be identified at the time the contract is entered into. "The fact that a beneficiary cannot be identified when the contract is made may have a bearing on the question whether the promisee intended to make a gift to him or otherwise to confer on him a right to the promised performance, and thus may determine whether he is an intended beneficiary or an incidental beneficiary. It may also bear on the

question whether the right created is revocable or not. But there is no requirement of identification prior to the time for enforcement of the right." *Id.* § 308
comment. a (citations omitted).

One need not be a beneficiary of every provision of the contract in order
to be an intended beneficiary with enforceable rights; it is enough to be the
intended beneficiary of the promise one is seeking to enforce.

With these general principles in mind, we turn to their application to the
facts of this case, keeping in mind that summary judgment is the context in
which we do so. "If a contract . . . is unambiguous, its interpretation is a question of law that is appropriate for a judge to decide on summary judgment. . . .
Where, however, the contract . . . has terms that are ambiguous, uncertain, or
equivocal in meaning, the intent of the parties" may depend on disputed facts
requiring a trial. *Seaco Ins. Co. v. Barbosa*, 435 Mass. 772, 779, 761 N.E.2d
946 (2002). Neither party has argued that the contract is ambiguous, and our
own review convinces us that the language of the agreement, as supplemented
by the subsequent transfer instructions from James, is unambiguous and that,
as a result, we may determine whether the foundation was an intended beneficiary as a matter of law.

The agreement established an ongoing arrangement between James (as
promisee) and State Street (as promisor) whereby, among other things, State
Street agreed to transfer assets in accordance with instructions from James
in the future. State Street obligated itself to carry out future instructions from
James, even though the details were not known at the time the agreement was
entered into and would not be known until the instructions were received. Once
James gave such instructions, they supplemented the agreement and identified State Street's obligations with respect to the particular asset to be transferred. In other words, once received, the instructions formed an integrated
whole with the agreement. We look, therefore, to the two documents together
to determine whether the foundation was an intended beneficiary under the
agreement with respect to the instructions given by James in February, 2007.

As we have set out above, the foundation need not be an intended beneficiary of every undertaking in the agreement. It need only be an intended
beneficiary of the promise it is seeking to enforce. In this case, that promise is
contained in the instructions from James to State Street to transfer the VEIEX
shares to the foundation. Those instructions clearly and definitely identified the
foundation as the recipient of the transfer and also stated that the purpose of
the transfer was to make a charitable gift to the foundation. There is no doubt
that James "intend[ed] to give the [foundation] the benefit of the promised
performance." Restatement (Second) of Contracts § 302(1)(b). It makes no
difference that the foundation was not identified as an intended beneficiary at
the time the agreement was entered into. The nature of the arrangement was
that State Street agreed to carry out future instructions as they were received,
on terms that would not be given until the future, and for the benefit of those

who would only later be identified. Although we would reach the same result had this been the first time James instructed State Street to make a transfer for the benefit of the foundation, the case is all the stronger when we consider that he had given such instructions several times before. The foundation was not unknown to State Street as an intended beneficiary of James's instructions pursuant to the agreement.

We conclude that the foundation has standing to pursue a breach of contract claim against State Street. Our holding here is limited to standing; we expressly note that we do not address whether State Street breached the agreement and, if so, whether the breach caused the foundation any loss. Those issues remain to be resolved on remand.

The portion of the judgment awarding summary judgment to State Street on the plaintiff's breach of contract claim is reversed, and the case is remanded to the Superior Court for further proceedings. The judgment is otherwise affirmed.

So ordered.

Understanding the Case:

1. *Mutual Fund Shares:* A mutual fund is a company that invests in stocks of hundreds of different companies. Individuals buy shares in mutual funds instead of directly in the companies in which mutual funds invest because it is often seen as too risky to directly invest in a handful of specific companies' shares. Plus, mutual funds hire professional managers to decide in which companies to invest—a task many ordinary investors either do not wish to perform or are not skilled to perform. By investing in a mutual fund, an ordinary investor is less prone to small changes in the stock market affecting a particular industry or company, as mutual funds, with hundreds of different investments, are diversified. In this case, James owned more than 800,000 shares of Vanguard Emerging Markets Stock Index Fund (VEIEX). However, investing in mutual funds is not without risk. In fact, as you can see from the case, the value of the shares in VEIEX dropped in the period between when James delivered his instruction to State Street (February 13) and the day the shares were actually transferred to the foundation (March 1). When State Street eventually transferred the shares and the foundation sold them, the shares in the aggregate were allegedly worth at least $1.6 million less than they would have been had State Street transferred them on February 13, when they received James's transfer instruction.

2. *Custodian Arrangement:* In the case, State Street was the custodian for James's VEIEX shares. A custodian is someone who safe-keeps property of others. The duties of the custodian depend on the property being maintained and the contract between the custodian and the counterparty. In this case, in its contract with James, State Street promised to not only safekeep his shares, but also to "*transfer them out upon receipt of authorized instructions.*"

Comprehension and Thought Questions:

1. How did State Street allegedly breach the custodian agreement with James?

2. Why did the James Family Charitable Foundation sue State Street instead of James to enforce that contract?

3. What was the test the court used to determine whether the James Family Charitable Foundation was an intended third-party beneficiary of the custodian agreement rather than an incidental beneficiary? Why does that determination matter?

4. In applying that test, did the court find that the James Family Charitable Foundation was an intended beneficiary or an incidental beneficiary?

5. Did it matter to the court in applying that test that the James Family Charitable Foundation was not identified as a beneficiary in the custodian agreement?

Hypothetical Variations:

1. What if on February 13, James had instructed State Street to sell his VEIEX shares, and once he received the proceeds from that sale, James was going to use those proceeds to make a charitable contribution to the James Family Charitable Foundation, but that State Street, in breach of its obligation to James, only sold them on March 1? For purposes of this question, assume State Street *did* know that this was James's plan.

2. What if on February 13, James had instructed State Street to sell his VEIEX shares, and once he received the proceeds from that sale, James was going to use those proceeds to make a charitable contribution to the James Family Charitable Foundation, but State Street, in breach of its obligation to James, only sold them on March 1? For purposes of this question, assume State Street did *not* know that this was James's plan.

3. Suppose that State Street continued to hold James's VEIEX shares and, during that time, the shares dropped in value by $2. Appreciating that those shares would one day be transferred to it, the James Family Charitable Foundation sued State Street for breach of the custodian agreement with James. What result?

PRACTICE PROBLEM 29-1

The City University hired Gema Construction to build a new student residence hall on campus. Gema Construction is a general contractor. As such, it manages and oversees construction projects such as the construction of the new residence hall. Its duties include hiring subcontractors to perform specific aspects of the work and coordinating all work to ensure the project is completed on time and in accordance with specifications and applicable building codes. The contract between Gema and The City University requires Gema to obtain a performance bond in the amount of half of the contract price. This bond ensures that if Gema does not pay any of its subcontractors, those subcontractors can recover payment on the bond.

In managing construction of the new residence hall, Gema hired Ace Plumbing to perform the plumbing work. After Ace was done with its work but before it was paid by Gema, Ace learned that Gema had been sued by a prior project owner and that Gema would likely have to file for bankruptcy protection due to expected damages from that lawsuit.

Ace promptly submitted its invoice to Gema for $50,000, but indeed, Gema failed to pay that invoice.

Ace has come to you, its legal counsel, for advice. Specifically, Ace wants to know the following:

1. Can Ace likely recover under Gema's performance bond if it cannot recover its full contract price from Gema?

2. Can Ace likely recover from The City University as a third-party beneficiary if it cannot recover its full contract price from Gema or under the performance bond? Is there another potential basis for Ace to recover from The City University?

3. Can Ace potentially recover from any of the students who will be living in the residence hall as third-party beneficiaries if it cannot recover its full contract price from Gema?

B. ASSIGNMENT OF RIGHTS AND DELEGATION OF DUTIES

Recall that a party has a right where a counterparty has a contractual duty to perform. In general, by default, a party is free to **assign** its rights under a contract to a third party, so long as doing so does not materially change the other party's duty. Thus, where a party assigns its right (which makes that party an assignor) under a contract, the person to whom those rights are assigned—the assignee—not only gets the benefit of the other, non-assigning party's performance, but it can also sue that party for breach.

To see how this rule works, suppose Sue Chin sells her used Honda Pilot sports utility vehicle to Beau Daniels on January 1 for $15,000. In negotiating the terms of sale, Beau informed Sue that Beau did not have the entire $15,000 available. However, he said that he could pay $5,000 of that up front and could pay the remaining $10,000 in monthly installments over the next 36 months, with interest. After performing due diligence in which she reviewed Beau's credit history and a copy of Beau's recent paycheck stub, Sue agreed to these terms of sale. The terms of the loan are set out in a promissory note.

On August 1 of the same year, Sue matriculates in law school and quickly realizes that she needs some extra money for living expenses. Her law school does not permit her to work during her first year, so Sue's options are limited. Sue decides to "cash in" on the promissory note. Specifically, Sue assigns her right to receive monthly payments from Beau to Bernie Banker. Of course, Bernie is not willing to pay Sue the entire principal amount and interest that Beau has left to pay under the promissory note, as there is a chance Beau will stop paying over the course of the note's term (since Bernie is being asked to pay for all amounts owed up front instead of over time, as provided in the note). Thus, Bernie discounts the expected payment, and pays Sue 90 percent of the amount that Beau owes on the note.

In this example, Sue has assigned her right to receive payments under the note to Bernie. Thus, she is the assignor, or the person who has assigned a right. It is now Bernie, the assignee, to whom future payments on the note must be paid.

Thus, by assigning Sue's rights under Beau's note to Bernie, Bernie becomes entitled to the benefit of Beau's performance—the obligation to make payments under the note. If Beau stops paying on the note, Bernie, as the assignee, can sue Beau to enforce his obligation. This again reflects the fact that someone who has a contractual right to another's performance can sue that party to enforce that right.

Here, Sue can assign her right to be paid under the note because doing so does not materially change Beau's obligation. While the assignment means that Beau has to pay a different person (Bernie instead of Sue), it does not increase or otherwise change how much he has to pay or when he has to pay under the note.

Where a party assigns a right to a third party, the assignor's right is extinguished. Thus, in this example, once Sue assigns her rights under the note to Bernie, Sue can no longer enforce the note against Beau.

You might wonder *why*, by default, rights are generally freely assignable. To answer that question, consider why Sue assigned her right under the note to Bernie. She did so because she preferred to receive an up-front cash payment rather than wait for Beau to pay under the note. This is consistent with the policy of free assignability of contract rights: it allows parties to allocate resources in a way that is most meaningful to them. It is also consistent with our notion of property, and a person's ability to deal with her property (here, a contract right) as she sees fit. Here, Sue valued an up-front payment of 90 percent of the amounts due under the note more than Beau's promise to repay all of the money over time. Similarly, Bernie valued Beau's promise to pay the full amount of the promissory note over time more than the up-front cash payment he made to Sue. Thus, both are better off by allowing the assignment.

At this point you might be wondering whether Beau can transfer his duty to pay under the note to a third party. For example, he might want to transfer his duty to pay to his brother, who has no money. By doing so, Beau could effectively be released from the note, placing his brother (without any money) in his shoes as the obligor under the note. And his brother would not pay because he does not have any money with which to pay the note.

Where a party transfers a duty under a contract, that is referred to as a **delegation**. In other words, here, Beau would be looking to delegate his duty to pay money under the note to his brother.

While in general, by default, a party can delegate duties under a contract, some duties cannot be delegated. In particular, duties that are personal in nature by default cannot be delegated. Stated differently, where a party has a "substantial interest" in having the specific counterparty perform a duty under the contract, then by default, that duty is not delegable. Thus, if Steven Spielberg agreed with DreamWorks Studios to direct a new movie on aliens, he could not delegate his duties under that contract to you. That is because Spielberg's duty to perform is unique to him, and DreamWorks would have a substantial interest in having Spielberg (and not you!) perform.

A duty to pay money also by default cannot be delegated, as it is personal to the obligor based on the strength of her credit. Thus, in our ongoing example, unless the promissory note specified to the contrary, Beau would not be able to delegate his duty to pay money under the note to his brother.

Even where a party can delegate a duty, the **obligee**—i.e., the new person who the obligor wants to perform her duty—must agree to assume the delegated duty. In addition, and very importantly, unless the counterparty agrees, the original obligor remains secondarily liable. Thus, suppose Industrial Cleaners Inc. agrees to perform weekly cleaning services for City Law School in exchange for weekly payments of $500. Now suppose Industrial Cleaners decides to focus on cleaning industrial facilities and wants to delegate its cleaning duties under its contract with City Law School to Sammy's Cleaning Co. Industrial Cleaners would be able to make that delegation, as those services are not personal or unique to Industrial Cleaners Inc. Here, Sammy's Cleaning Co. would have to agree to assume those duties in order to be obligated to perform them. Moreover, unless City Law School agrees otherwise, Industrial Cleaners would remain secondarily liable under the contract. Thus, if Sammy's Cleaning Co. does not perform as promised, City Law School could sue Industrial Cleaners and Sammy's Cleaning Co. for damages.

Keep in mind that the above rules are default rules. In other words, while rights are generally assignable, parties often purport to limit a counterparty's ability to assign its rights under the contract through appropriate contractual language. Moreover, parties can remove a party's ability to delegate duties that are otherwise delegable through relevant contractual language. They often do so using the following language:

> Neither party may assign its rights or delegate its duties under this Agreement. Any assignment or delegation in contravention of this provision is void.

Sometimes, parties to an agreement contemplate at the outset that one of the parties will assign its rights or delegate its duties, or both. This often happens where one party to a contract is a company within a larger corporate group, and the corporate group is contemplating a corporate restructuring. In that case, an affiliated member of the same corporate group will become obligated on the contract instead of the original obligor. In that circumstance, the contract will typically permit that assignment and delegation. The following is sample language capturing this permission:

> Neither party may assign its rights or delegate its duties under this Agreement, except that ABC Co. may assign its rights and delegate its duties under this Agreement to XYZ Co. Upon any such delegation of duties by ABC Co. to XYZ Co., ABC Co. will be released from all of its obligations under this Agreement. Any assignment or delegation in contravention of this provision is void.

This provision expressly authorizes ABC Co. to assign its rights and delegate its duties to XYZ Co. In addition, it contracts around the default rule of having a delegating obligor remain secondarily liable by expressly releasing ABC Co. from any obligations upon such delegation.

Some courts are reluctant to allow contracting parties to remove a party's power to assign rights under a contract given the policy reasons in favor of assignment discussed above. Thus, they often interpret ambiguous non-assignment language in a contract as only precluding delegation of duties, but not precluding assignment of rights. The following case demonstrates another way a court might limit application of a non-assignment clause.

In re Wehr Constructors, Inc. v. Assurance Company of America
Supreme Court of Kentucky
384 S.W.3d 680 (2012)

Opinion of the Court by Justice VENTERS.

Pursuant to CR 76.37(1), this Court granted the certification request of the United States District Court for the Western District of Kentucky to answer the following question of Kentucky law:

> Whether an anti-assignment clause in an insurance policy that requires an insured to obtain the insurer's prior written consent before assigning a claim under the policy is enforceable or applicable when the claimed loss occurs before the assignment, or whether such a clause would, under those circumstances, be void as against public policy.

For the reasons stated below, we conclude that under Kentucky law, a clause in an insurance policy that requires the insured to obtain the insurer's prior written consent before assigning a claim for an insured loss under the policy is not enforceable or applicable to the assignment of a claim under the policy where the covered loss occurs before the assignment, and that such a clause would, under those circumstances, be void as against public policy.

I. FACTUAL AND PROCEDURAL BACKGROUND

Murray Calloway County Hospital Corp. (Hospital) planned to build an addition onto its facilities. It purchased from Assurance Company of America (Assurance) a "builder's risk" insurance policy. The builder's risk policy included this provision:

> **F. Transfer of Your Rights and Duties Under This Policy** Your rights and duties under this policy may not be transferred without [Assurance's] written consent except in the case of death of an individual named insured.

The Hospital contracted with Wehr Constructors, Inc. (Wehr) for the installation of concrete subsurfaces and vinyl floors as part of a project to expand the hospital. After installation, a portion of the floors and subsurface done by Wehr was damaged. The Hospital claimed a loss exceeding $75,000.00 and sought recompense under the builders risk policy, but Assurance denied the claim.

As a result of a dispute over its contract with the Hospital, Wehr filed suit against the Hospital in state court to recover money alleged to be due from the Hospital. Eventually, Wehr and the Hospital settled the claim. As part of that settlement, the Hospital agreed to, and did, assign to Wehr any claim or rights the Hospital had against Assurance arising out of the builder's risk insurance policy. More specifically, the assignment states as follows:

> [The Hospital] hereby transfers and assigns to [Wehr], free and [clear] of any claims, liens and encumbrances, all of [the Hospital's] right, title and interest, legal or equitable, in any and all claims and causes of action for insurance coverage and insurance proceeds which [the Hospital] had, or may have had, under a Builders [sic] Risk Insurance policy No. EC43657395, believed to have been issued by Zurich Insurance Company, Inc.,[3] and which arose out of certain damage to the floor and subfloor that occurred at a construction project known as Murray Calloway County Hospital, located in Murray, Kentucky.

It is undisputed that this assignment occurred after the damage to the floors had occurred. Therefore, if the loss was in fact covered under the builders risk policy, Assurance was at the time of the assignment already liable for payment under the contract.

Wehr, as the Hospital's assignee, brought suit in federal court against Assurance seeking to recover payment due under the builder's risk policy for the damaged floor claim. After filing an answer to the complaint, Assurance moved for judgment on the pleadings, invoking the anti-assignment provision of

---

3. [2] Assurance Company of America is a subsidiary of Zurich American Insurance Company.

the policy quoted above. Assurance argued that because it had not consented to the assignment of the Hospital's claim to Wehr, the assignment was unenforceable against Assurance. In opposition to the motion Wehr argued that since the loss for which the Hospital sought coverage had already occurred at the time of the assignment and the basis for the insurer's potential liability was fixed, the Hospital's right to the proceeds under the policy was a chose in action that was freely assignable and, as such, the assignment did not require the insurer's consent, and that pursuant to the rule applicable in the vast majority of states, such an anti-assignment clause is unenforceable.

II. MAJORITY AND MINORITY RULES

There are two primary views concerning the issue we address, one of which is overwhelmingly endorsed as the legally sound position upon general considerations of contract law, principles relating to the assignment of debt, restraints on the alienability of personal property, and public policy. The resolution of the District Court's question depends upon whether we adopt the majority rule, which favors Wehr, or the minority rule, which favors Assurance. Both sides agree that no Kentucky appellate court has spoken to the issue. We therefore begin our discussion with a synopsis of the majority and minority rules.

A. The Majority Rule

In summary, the majority rule holds that an anti-assignment clause such as the one we examine is unenforceable once an insured occurrence takes place because at that point the insured is entitled to recovery under the policy; that right is a chose in action; a chose in action is a form of personal property; the anti-assignment provision amounts to a restraint upon the alienation of this property right; and, a restraint upon the alienation of property is in opposition to public policy. As further noted below, other public policy considerations likewise weigh against the enforcement of an anti-assignment clause once a loss has occurred.

We begin by noting that Couch on Insurance identifies the majority rule relating to anti-assignment clauses such as the one we review as follows:

> Although there is some authority to the contrary, the great majority of courts adhere to the rule that general stipulations in policies prohibiting assignments of the policy, except with the consent of the insurer, apply only to assignments before loss, and do not prevent an assignment after loss[.]

3 Couch on Ins. § 35:8 (footnotes omitted).

Thus, the rationale, for the majority view is that an anti-assignment clause ordinarily only prohibits the assignment of the policy itself, but does not apply to assignment of a claim arising under the policy. The purpose of an anti-assignment clause is to protect the insurer from unforeseen exposure and increased liability that may ensue if the policy was assigned to an entity that the insurer would prefer not to insure; or, would have insured only at a higher premium. However, after an insured loss that gives rise to the insurer's liability, the insurer's risk cannot be increased by a change in the identity of the party to whom payment is to be made. An assignment of the policy, or rights under the policy, before the loss is incurred transfers the insurer's contractual relationship to a party with whom it never intended to contract, but an assignment after loss is simply the transfer of the right to a claim for money. The entity asserting the claim under those circumstances has no effect upon the insurer's duty under the policy.

A cogent explanation for the majority rule is found in *Conrad Brothers v. John Deere Ins. Co.*, 640 N.W.2d 231, 237–38 (Iowa 2001), which describes the rationale for this view as follows:

> [O]nce the loss has triggered the liability provisions of the insurance policy, an assignment is no longer regarded as a transfer of the actual policy. Instead, it is a transfer of a chose in action under the policy. At this point, the insurer-insured relationship is more analogous to that of a debtor and creditor, with the policy serving as evidence of the amount of debt owed. Moreover, if we permitted an insurer to avoid its contractual obligations by prohibiting all post-loss assignments, we could be granting the insurer a windfall. (Internal citations omitted).

The public policy invoked to avoid the effect of an anti-assignment clause after a loss has occurred is that enforcement of the provision unduly "restricts the relation of debtor and creditor by restricting or rendering, subject to the control of the insurer, an absolute right in the nature of a chose in action." 3 Couch on Ins. § 35:9. Thus, under the majority rule, once a loss occurs and the insurer's liability becomes fixed, the insured may assign its rights under the policy regardless of an anti-assignment clause.

In *Antal's Restaurant, Inc. v. Lumbermen's Mut. Casualty Co.*, 680 A.2d 1386 (D.C. 1996), the District of Columbia Court of Appeals considered a post-loss assignment by the property owners to the restaurant owners following a fire at the business, a situation substantially analogous to this case. The insurance company sought to enforce an anti-assignment agreement identical to the one we review. In explaining the difference between the enforceability of a pre-loss assignment and a post-loss assignment, the Court stated as follows:

> The reason for the distinction is that, whereas before loss the insurer might be unwilling to underwrite a risk for a person of questionable "integrity and prudence," after loss "the delectus personae [is] no longer . . . material" since "the insurer becomes absolutely a debtor to the assured for the amount of the actual loss. . . ." *Ocean Accident & Guar. Corp. [v. Southwestern Bell Tel. Co.]*, 100 F.2d [441] at 445-46 [(8th Cir. 1939)]. The assignment at that point is "of a chose in action the right to compel [the insurer's] payment of insurance proceeds in accord with that interest . . . recognized in the policy and defined in the contract."

Id. at 1388.

. . .

In summary, the courts that have considered this issue have overwhelmingly concluded that once an insured occurrence has transpired, the insured's claim then ripens into a chose in action,[4] a type of personal property, which, pursuant to fundamental principles of debtor-creditor relationships, may not, ordinarily, be restrained from alienability.

B. The Minority Rule

The minority rule, on the other hand, holds that the unambiguous language of an anti-assignment clause, like the one present in this case, should be enforced as written. It is of course a fundamental tenet of this jurisdiction that the unambiguous language of a contract will be enforced as written and that the courts will not re-write the contract in contradiction of its plain meaning. "A fundamental rule of contract law holds that, absent fraud in the inducement, a written agreement duly executed by the party to be held, who had an opportunity to read it, will be enforced according to its terms." *Conseco Finance Servicing Corp. v. Wilder*, 47 S.W.3d 335, 341 (Ky. App. 2001). "Where the terms of an insurance policy are clear and unambiguous, the policy will be enforced as written." *Kemper Nat. Ins. Companies v. Heaven Hill Distilleries, Inc.*, 82 S.W.3d 869, 873 (Ky. 2002).

Assurance contends that the legislature has made clear that our normal rule of enforcing contracts as written should apply in this case, thereby compelling adoption of the minority rule, by its enactment of KRS 304.14-250(1), which provides that "[a] policy may be assignable or not assignable, as provided by its terms"; however, this statute manifestly does not apply to the issue we review. The statute, rather, obviously provides that a provision prohibiting the assignment of an insurance policy is not assignable if the policy terms so provide. That, however, is far different from a provision prohibiting the assignment of a ripened claim after an insured occurrence has occurred under the policy thereby resulting in a chose in action belonging to the insured. Other courts which have considered this identical provision have identified and applied this distinction. Because the distinction is manifest, we follow these decisions and hold that KRS 304.14-250(1) is not, as Assurance argues, applicable to the issue we review.

The low esteem for the minority rule may be well-illustrated by the observation that the only cases Assurance cites us to applying the rule are cases applying Texas law.

---

4. [7] *Black's* defines and discusses the term "chose in action" as follows: chose in action. (17c) 1. A proprietary right in personam, such as a debt owed by another person, a share in a joint-stock company, or a claim for damages in tort. . . . 2. The right to bring an action to recover a debt, money, or thing. 3. Personal property that one person owns but another person possesses, the owner being able to regain possession through a lawsuit.—Also termed *thing in action*. BLACK'S LAW DICTIONARY (9th ed. 2009).

In upholding non-assignment clauses post-loss, the Texas courts apply a framework familiar to our courts as described above; that is, they apply the plain meaning of the contractual provision as written:

> Generally, a contract of insurance is subject to the same rules of construction as other contracts. If the insurance contract is worded so that it can be given a certain definite meaning or interpretation, then it is not ambiguous, and the court will construe the contract as a matter of law. Moreover, where there is no ambiguity, it is the court's duty to give words their plain meaning. The non-assignment clause, contained in the General Provisions portion of the contract, is unambiguous and provides:
>
> Your rights and duties under this policy may not be assigned without our written consent.
>
> Non-assignment clauses have been consistently enforced by Texas courts, , and by the Fifth Circuit applying Texas law. In addition, the prohibition against the assignment of rights by a named insured to an insurance contract has been upheld by this court.

Gerdes, 880 S.W.2d at 217–218 (Tex. App.-Fort Worth 1994).

Thus, adoption of the minority rule would require us to simply apply the term as it is written according to our well-established principles of contract interpretation; however, this would also require us to at the same time conclude that the public policy considerations identified in our discussion of the majority rule do not compel a deviation from our usual rules of contract construction.

III. THE MAJORITY RULE BETTER SERVES THE PUBLIC INTEREST

We begin this section of our discussion by again noting that " 'in the absence of ambiguity a written instrument will be enforced strictly according to its terms,' and a court will interpret the contract's terms by assigning language its ordinary meaning and without resort to extrinsic evidence." *Frear v. P.T.A. Industries, Inc.*, 103 S.W.3d 99, 106 (Ky. 2003) (citations omitted). "A contract is ambiguous if a reasonable person would find it susceptible to different or inconsistent interpretations." *Hazard Coal Corp. v. Knight*, 325 S.W.3d 290, 298 (Ky. 2010).

Here, the language of the contract provision is not ambiguous. The provision is captioned "F. Transfer of Your Rights and Duties Under This Policy." The provision itself straight-forwardly directs that "Your rights and duties under this policy may not be transferred without [Assurance's] written consent except in the case of death of an individual named insured." Thus, the contractual language itself plainly and obviously prohibits the Hospital from assigning its rights under the policy to anyone at anytime absent Assurance's consent, except in the case of the death of the insured. Accordingly, our preference for enforcing a contract pursuant to its plain language would strongly favor the minority position; particularly, as here, where the parties are of equal bargaining power. In this vein, if the Hospital, as an entity of strong bargaining power,[5] was opposed to the provision as written, it could have bargained to have the clause apply only to pre-occurrence assignments or shopped elsewhere for its insurance. Accordingly, there is substantial merit to Assurance's position.

Nevertheless, as necessity may require, contractual provisions may be held to be unenforceable as against public policy. Further, we have fully considered that the public policy of the Commonwealth is normally expressed through the acts of the legislature, and not through decisions issued by the courts.

However, as discussed above, we reject Assurance's argument that KRS 304.14-250(1) expresses the public policy of the legislature in regard to the enforceability of a non-assignment clause post-loss. Nor do we find from any other source a specific expression of the legislature's intent in this area. Accordingly, in our review we are not constrained by a specific public policy preference expressed by the legislature, and so may undertake for ourselves to define the public policy in this particular area of the law.

Based upon the authorities cited above in our discussion of the majority rule, we believe that the relevant public policy interests are best served by our adoption of the majority rule that a non-assignment clause in an insurance policy, while certainly enforceable prior to an occurrence of a covered loss, is not enforceable for assignments made after the occurrence. This conclusion is fully consistent with our prior holdings adverse to contractual provisions tending to restrain the alienability of choses in action, which, as explained above, is the principal underpinning of the majority rule.

"[A] chose in action more properly includes the right both of the thing itself and of the right of action as annexed to it. . . . Choses in action are personal property[.]" *Button v. Drake*, 302 Ky. 517, 195 S.W.2d 66, 69 (Ky. 1946).

"The common-law rule against restraint on alienation was designed to prevent the taking from the owner of the power to alienate property." *Three Rivers Rock Co. v. Reed Crushed Stone Co.*, 530 S.W.2d 202, 205 (Ky. 1975). Thus, clearly, restraints on alienation are not viewed favorably, as public policy in Kentucky supports "the right of a person to be free and uninhibited in the disposition of his property[.]" *Id.*

Further, "It is the settled law . . . that an assignee of a chose in action may maintain suit thereon in his own name, since by the assignment he becomes vested with title and is entitled to the proceeds of the assigned chose [.]" *Fields' Adm'r v. Perry County State Bank*, 214 Ky. 24, 282 S.W. 555 (1926); *Louisa Nat. Bank v. Paintsville Nat. Bank*, 260 Ky. 327, 85 S.W.2d 668 (1935).

---

5. [8] As distinguished from an individual member of the general public, who will normally have considerably less bargaining power than the insurance company from whom he purchases his policy, and thus will generally be compelled to accept the company's standardized adhesion contract.

The contractual provision we review, therefore, is fundamentally in opposition to our Commonwealth's long-standing rules relating to restraints upon the alienability of choses in action. Further, Assurance has presented no persuasive reason for us to deviate from the settled proposition that restraints on alienation of property, including personal property, are to be stringently disfavored. We therefore, resolve the request of the United States District Court for the Western District of Kentucky, by adopting the majority rule. An anti-assignment clause in an insurance policy that requires an insured to obtain the insurer's prior written consent before assigning the claim under the policy is not enforceable or applicable when the claimed loss occurs before the assignment; such a clause would, under those circumstances, be void as against public policy.

It is also worth noting that the majority rule also facilitates our important public policy of encouraging settlements by the parties to a lawsuit by facilitating settlement agreements, as well-illustrated by what occurred in this case.

IV. CONCLUSION

For the reasons stated, we conclude that under Kentucky law, an anti-assignment clause in an insurance policy that requires an insured to obtain the insurer's prior written consent before assigning the claim under the policy is not enforceable or applicable when the claimed loss occurs before the assignment; such a clause would, under those circumstances, be void as against public policy.

The law is hereby certified to the United States District Court for the Western District of Kentucky.

MINTON, C.J., ABRAMSON, CUNNINGHAM, NOBLE and SCOTT, JJ., concur. NOBLE, J., also concurs, by separate opinion. SCHRODER, J., not sitting.

NOBLE, J., concurring:

In addition to the policy rationale in the Opinion of the Court, I believe this case can be resolved as a pure legal question. The limiting language in the policy, "Your rights and duties under this policy may not be transferred without [Assurance's] written consent except in the case of death of an individual named insured," does not state whether the limitation applies before or after an occurrence. This creates a latent ambiguity in answering the raised question of when the clause applies, and thus this Court must construe the term. I would interpret this latent ambiguity to mean that it does not apply after a claim is made, thereby giving substantive support to the Court's policy decision.

Understanding the Case:

1. *Insurance:* Insurance policies are contracts in which an insurer agrees to pay the insured for any loss incurred by the insured arising out of covered events in exchange for the payment of a premium. Such covered events might include, for example, fire, flood, or accident. Insurers calculate the amount of the premium by considering the probability of a covered event occurring and the likely size of the loss. It also writes many insurance policies for similar risks. In that way, the insurer effectively spreads the risk of loss among all of the insureds, as all pay premiums, whereas only a few will actually have a loss due to a covered event that the insurer will have to pay.

2. *Diagram of Transaction:* Where a transaction involves multiple parties, it is often helpful to diagram out the transaction. Such a diagram clarifies the relationships among the parties. When diagrammed out, the transaction in this case looks like this:

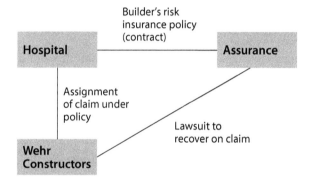

3. *Certified Question:* This case involved a certified question from the United States District Court for the Western District of Kentucky to the Kentucky Supreme Court. Thus, the dispute itself was being resolved by the District Court for the Western District of Kentucky. However, the district court sought guidance on an open question of Kentucky law from the Kentucky Supreme Court. Many courts have similar state procedures, which allow a federal court or highest appellate court in another jurisdiction to pose such a certified question to a state supreme court where there is no controlling legal precedent on that issue, and that issue is determinative of the outcome of the case. *See, e.g.,* Kentucky Rules of Civil Procedure CR 76.37.

Comprehension and Thought Questions:

1. Why did the Hospital assign its insurance claim against Assurance to Wehr Constructors? In other words, why wasn't the Hospital pursuing that claim itself?

2. Did the court interpret the builder's risk insurance policy as precluding the assignment of post-loss claims made under the policy? What rule of interpretation supported the court's interpretation?

3. Whose analysis of contract interpretation do you find more persuasive: that of the majority or that of the concurrence?

4. Why did the court hold that the non-assignment clause was unenforceable as to post-loss claims? What policies did the court give to support this holding?

5. Do you agree with the majority of courts (and this court), or the minority of courts who enforce such non-assignment clauses even for post-loss claims?

Hypothetical Variations:

1. What if the builder's risk insurance policy expressly provided that not only was the policy not assignable, but neither was any claim made under the policy?

2. What if the Hospital had assigned its rights under the builder's risk insurance policy to County Hospital, which was a different hospital building an expansion, before any loss had occurred?

3. Continuing with the same facts from Question 2, what if County Hospital made a $10,000 claim under the assigned builder's risk insurance policy, which Assurance paid, but subsequently, when County Hospital made a $75,000 claim, Assurance denied it on the basis of the non-assignment clause?

PRACTICE PROBLEM 29-2

Refer back to Practice Problem 29-1. For purposes of this question, assume Ace Plumbing (along with Gema's other subcontractors) was listed as a beneficiary under Gema's performance bond. As a beneficiary, if Gema did not pay Ace in accordance with their contract, Ace could recover any unpaid amounts under that contract from the issuer of the bond.

When it became apparent that Gema was not going to pay Ace Plumbing as a result of the lawsuit filed against Gema, The City University indicated that it would be willing to pay Ace the $50,000 that Ace had invoiced Gema if Ace assigned its rights under the performance bond to The City University. However, The City University said it wanted to make sure the bond was indeed assignable to it before agreeing to this arrangement.

The following is the provision in the construction bond on assignability:

> No party to this bond, including any beneficiary, may assign its rights under this bond.

As Ace's counsel, advise your client whether it can assign its rights under the bond to The City University and if such an assignment would effectively transfer to The City University Ace's right to be paid $50,000 by the bond issuer.

C. TORTIOUS INTERFERENCE WITH CONTRACT

As you recall from Section A, only an intended third-party beneficiary can sue to enforce a contract. However, there are consequences to a party being an incidental third-party beneficiary. Namely, where a third party is neither an intended nor incidental third-party beneficiary to a contract, it is said that the third party is a **stranger to a contract**. While a stranger to a contract cannot enforce a contract, it can create contractual liability for itself. That is, a stranger to a contract can tortiously interfere with a contract. A stranger **tortiously interferes with a contract** where that person intentionally and improperly interferes with a party's existing contractual or business relationship, causing that party economic harm. Such tortious interference might take the form of the stranger improperly causing a contractual party to breach the contract, or it might take the form of the stranger improperly causing a party to not enter into a contract that it is considering.[6]

One common situation where tortious interference arises is where a prospective employer induces an employee to leave his or her current employer. Where the prospective employer causes the employee to breach her current employment contract in this departure, either through inducing her to leave before the end of her term or inducing her to improperly take her current employer's confidential information with her, such action by the prospective employer may amount to tortious interference.

Again, only a stranger to a contract, and not a third-party beneficiary, can commit this tort. The fact that only a stranger to a contract can commit tortious interference often means that courts must address whether a person is a stranger to a contract or a third-party beneficiary. Section A above explains how courts determine whether a party is an *intended* third-party beneficiary. However, some courts find that even unintended third-party beneficiaries cannot commit tortious interference.

One case that exemplifies how a court addresses who can commit tortious interference is *Howerton v. Harbin Clinic*.[7] In that case, Mindy Howerton was employed by the Floyd Medical Center (FMC) as a surgical technician. In that position, she assisted doctors during their medical procedures.

Howerton was assigned to a surgical team working with doctors having first-shift surgeries. Kenneth C. Sands, M.D., a doctor at Harbin Clinic LLC, conducted first-shift surgeries and was assisted by Howerton's surgical team.

---

6. Where the stranger improperly causes a party to not enter into a contractual relationship, that technically is referred to as tortious interference with *prospective* contractual relations. However, the elements of the two torts are essentially the same.

7. 776 S.E.2d 288 (Ga. Ct. App. 2015).

The parties' relationship can be depicted by diagram as follows:

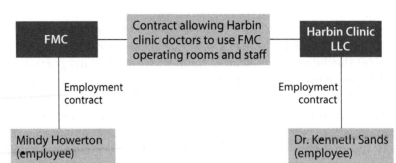

From 2008 to 2011, during surgery, Sands "engag[ed] in unprofessional conduct of a sexual nature" with Howerton.[8] For example, "Sands ask[ed] Howerton about her sex life . . . Sands groped Howerton's breasts while reaching for an instrument during surgery on at least one occasion; . . . and asked Howerton to his home to have a glass of wine and relax, explaining that his wife and children were out of town."[9] One of the culminating incidents occurred in December 2010 when Sands indicated that he wanted to have an affair with Howerton.

In 2011, Howerton began discussing with her superiors switching to second shift, motivated in part to avoid working with Sands. In asking for the switch, Howerton informed the assistant director of FMC about Sands's inappropriate conduct. Howerton was told not to worry, that she would be switched to the second shift. However, before Howerton could be transferred to second shift, Sands had a telephonic confrontation with Howerton's husband, Scott. On that call, Scott told Sands that his wife had been wearing a wire and could prove that Sands had been making inappropriate sexual advances on his wife. Sands told Scott on that call that Howerton was fired. Sands also told Howerton's superiors the following day about the fact that Howerton had been wearing a wire in violation of the Health Insurance Portability and Accountability Act of 1996 (HIPAA). Howerton was then informed that she did not have the skill set to be transferred to the second shift. Instead, she was assigned to an entirely separate position with reduced hours and income.

Unable to afford her house and car with her reduced salary, Howerton left FMC's employment. She then sued FMC, Sands, and Sands's employer, the Harbin Clinic. Among other claims, Howerton argued that Sands and Harbin Clinic had tortiously interfered with her contract with FMC. The question whether Sands and his employer, the Harbin Clinic, could be liable for

---

8. *Id.* at 291.
9. *Id.*

tortious interference depended on whether they were third-party beneficiaries of Howerton's contract with FMC or strangers. For only if they were strangers could they be liable for tortious interference. The trial court dismissed these claims, holding that Sands was a third-party beneficiary of Howerton's contract with FMC. The Court of Appeals of Georgia reversed. That court stated the law on this issue as follows:

> To prevail on her tortious interference claim against Sands, Howerton must prove that she had a valid employment contract with FMC; that Sands acted wrongfully and without privilege when he reported to Howerton's superiors that she was recording conversations in the operating room; that Sands acted deliberately and maliciously; that as a result of Sands's conduct, Howerton's employment with FMC was adversely affected; and that consequently Howerton suffered damages.
>
> "To establish that a defendant acted without privilege, the plaintiff must show that the defendant was a stranger to the contract" with which he allegedly interfered; one who is not a stranger to a contract cannot be held liable for tortiously interfering with that agreement. In this case, the trial court found that Sands was not a stranger to Howerton's employment contract because he was an unintended third-party beneficiary of that contract. This holding was in error.
>
> The rule that a third-party beneficiary of a contract is not a stranger thereto evolved from the law providing that an intended third-party beneficiary may sue to enforce a contract even though he is not a party to the agreement. "In order for a third party to have standing to enforce a contract, it must clearly appear from the contract that it was intended for his or her benefit." *Boller v. Robert W. Woodruff Arts Ctr.*, 311 Ga. App. 693, 698(3), 716 S.E.2d 713 (2011). To have standing to sue on a contract, "[t]he third-party beneficiary need not be specifically named [therein]; the dispositive issue is whether the [contracting] parties' intention to benefit the third party is shown on the face of the contract." *Dillon v. Reid*, 312 Ga. App. 34, 40(4), 717 S.E.2d 542 (2011). Thus, the mere fact that an individual would receive some incidental benefit from performance of a contract is insufficient to make them an intended third-party beneficiary of the agreement.
>
> In the context of a tortious interference claim, the category of third-party beneficiaries excluded from the so-called "'stranger doctrine' has been expanded to cover those who benefit from the contract of others, without regard to whether the beneficiary was intended by the contracting parties to be a third-party beneficiary." *Atlanta Market Ctr. Mgmt.*, 269 Ga. at 609(2), 503 S.E.2d 278. To be an unintended third-party beneficiary, an individual or entity must have a legitimate and direct economic interest in the contract at issue. Thus, where a particular project or transaction involves "'a comprehensive interwoven set of contracts,'" each of the parties to any individual contract involved in the transaction is a third party-beneficiary of the other contracts necessary to complete the project. *Atlanta Market Ctr. Mgmt.*, 269 Ga. at 609(2), 503 S.E.2d 278, quoting *Jefferson–Pilot Communications Co. v. Phoenix City Broadcasting of Atlanta*, 205 Ga. App. 57, 60(1), 421 S.E.2d 295 (1992). Notably, however, one does not

become an unintended third-party beneficiary of a contract simply because he might receive some incidental benefit from performance of that agreement.[10]

Applying this law to the facts, the court held that Sands was not an unintended third-party beneficiary of Howerton's contract with FMC.[11] That is because Sands did not prove that he had a direct economic interest in Howerton's contract with FMC—the contract with which Howerton alleged Sands had tortiously interfered. While Sands benefited from having Howerton work for FMC, such relationship was not part of a single interwoven framework involving Harbin Clinic's contract with FMC and Sands's contract with Harbin Clinic. Rather, each was a stand-alone contract that existed separate and apart from the other. Moreover, in FMC's contract with Harbin Clinic, FMC was merely required to staff operating rooms with qualified personnel. Thus, FMC had control over whom to employ. In other words, Harbin Clinic had no particular interest in Howerton's employment agreement with FMC. Consequently, Sands was a stranger to Howerton's employment contract with FMC, and was not immune from Howerton's tortious interference claim.

Moreover, the court found that Howerton had adequately alleged facts supporting the other elements of a tortious interference claim against Sands. Namely, Howerton had alleged that Sands acted deliberately and maliciously in reporting her HIPAA violation to undermine her job prospects and her sexual harassment allegations given that at the time, he did not even know whether she had violated HIPAA. Howerton also argued that this conduct adversely affected her employment with FMC, ultimately leading to a reduction in her hours and loss in salary.

The appellate court therefore reversed the trial court's grant of Sands's motion for summary judgment on this claim.

Understanding the Case:

1. *HIPAA:* The Health Insurance Portability and Accountability Act of 1996 is a federal law that requires health plans and health care providers to take measures to protect the privacy of patient medical records and patient health information. In this case, Sands argued that he reported Howerton to her superiors because, if Howerton had recorded discussions during operations, that would violate the HIPPA privacy rights of the patient. However, Howerton argued in response that her husband had never said that Howerton had recorded operating room discussions. The appellate court agreed with the trial court that there was enough evidence on this question of fact to submit it to a jury.

---

10. *Id.* at 294-95.
11. The court also concluded that Sands was not an intended third-party beneficiary of Howerton's contract with FMC.

2. *Other Allegations:* In addition to her tortious interference claim, Howerton alleged claims against Sands for intentional infliction of emotional distress, assault, and battery as well as a claim against Harbin Clinic for the negligent hiring, retention, and supervision of Sands. The trial court granted Harbin Clinic's and Sand's motions for summary judgment on all of Howerton's claims except on her claims against Sands for assault and battery. As you know from the case discussed above, the Georgia Court of Appeals reversed the trial court's order as to the tortious interference claim. That court also reversed the trial court's grant of summary judgment on Howerton's claim against Sands for intentional infliction of emotional distress given the outrageousness of Sands's conduct. However, the appellate court affirmed the other grants of summary judgment.

Comprehension and Thought Questions:

1. What test did the court use to determine whether Sands and Harbin Clinic were third-party beneficiaries under Howerton's employment contract with FMC?

2. How did the court apply that test in the case?

3. Why does it matter whether Sands and the Harbin Clinic were third-party beneficiaries under that employment contract?

4. What are the elements of a tortious interference claim?

5. What facts did Howerton allege to establish each of those elements?

6. Do you agree that even an unintended third-party beneficiary should not be sued for tortious interference? What policy or policies does such a rule serve?

Hypothetical Variations:

1. What if Harbin Clinic's contract with FMC had specified the technicians who were permitted to work with Harbin Clinic's doctors, and Howerton's name was on that list?

2. What if Sands had been justified in thinking that Howerton's conduct violated HIPAA?

3. What if Harbin Clinic's contract with FMC specified that any doctor of FMC had authority to terminate any of FMC's technicians for "cause"?

Appendix A: Simulation Problems

Simulation Problem Chapter 1

Victor Tally is a licensed real estate broker. From 2005 to 2015, Victor worked as a real estate broker in Springfield, Columbia (a fictitious city and state located in the United States). In that position, Victor helped clients buy and sell properties ranging from warehouses to apartment buildings.

Unfortunately for Victor, since 2007, the market for buying and selling real estate has slowed down. To adapt to this change, in 2015, Victor decided to become a real estate manager instead of a broker. He named his real estate management business TallyMan, and Victor formed a Columbia corporation for this business, which he named TallyMan Services Inc.

TallyMan manages the properties of its clients. For example, TallyMan performs routine maintenance as well as oversees non-routine service work needed at the properties it manages. TallyMan also finds tenants for the properties it manages, negotiates and collects rents from those tenants, and otherwise performs the owners' obligations and exercise the owners' rights under those leases. Finally, TallyMan ensures that the ownership and use of its clients' buildings comply with applicable law. While TallyMan performs real estate brokerage services for its clients as well, that is only a small part of TallyMan's business.

Since Victor started TallyMan in 2015, TallyMan has become quite successful. In fact, Victor recently decided that he needed to hire a senior-level employee to help him oversee new and existing clients, and the performance of obligations under TallyMan's contracts with its clients.

Victor asks you to represent TallyMan in its hiring of this senior-level employee. As TallyMan's lawyer, Victor asks you the following questions in preparing for TallyMan's hiring of this employee:

1. Should TallyMan enter into a contract with the new senior-level employee? Why or why not?
2. If TallyMan does enter into a contract with the new employee, what terms should TallyMan include in that contract to protect its interests? For example, should that contract address the length of the employee's employment? The employee's compensation? Other terms? If so, how will those terms benefit TallyMan?
3. Victor wants to ensure that the new employee does not take TallyMan's clients, its standard, customized "form" contracts, or other confidential information when the employee leaves TallyMan. So Victor wants to include a non-compete covenant that would preclude this employee from performing any real estate services, including as a real estate broker, real estate manager, real estate investor, or otherwise, at any time after that employee leaves TallyMan's employment. Below is Columbia's law on the enforceability of non-competes. Do you have any concerns with including this provision in the employment agreement?

> A covenant by an employee not to compete with his or her employer during the term of the employment, or after the termination of that employment, within a specified territory and during a specified time is lawful and enforceable only if the restrictions imposed are reasonably necessary for the protection of the employer. Any covenant, described in this section, imposing an unreasonable restraint is illegal, void and unenforceable even as to any part of the covenant or performance that would be a reasonable restraint.[1]

Simulation Problem Chapter 2

After interviewing ten potential employees, Victor decides to hire Springfield resident Agatha Tran on behalf of TallyMan. Agatha's official title is Investment Property Manager. In that role, Agatha will focus her efforts on finding tenants for TallyMan's clients who own investment properties and negotiating the lease terms with those prospective tenants.

Victor asks you, TallyMan's lawyer, to draft TallyMan's employment agreement with Agatha. Given the concerns you previously raised with the enforceability of a non-compete covenant, Victor asks you to draft that contract to be governed by Delaware law, as he has heard that Delaware law would likely uphold the non-compete.

1. Can you draft the employment agreement between TallyMan and Agatha to be governed by Delaware law? Should you? Why or why not? (For purposes of this question, do not actually draft the agreement.)

---

1. This provision is based on Wisconsin's non-compete law at Wis. Stat. § 103.465.

2. If you do include such a choice-of-law provision in the employment agreement, would a court in Columbia likely uphold that choice?

Simulation Problem Chapter 3

With your assistance, TallyMan entered into a contract with Agatha to work for TallyMan as its Investment Property Manager (though Victor remains the sole owner of TallyMan). Agatha has now worked in that role for six months.

A new client, WindyLakes Properties Inc., contacts Victor on August 30 about having TallyMan manage WindyLakes' two new apartment buildings in Columbia. Because WindyLakes owns dozens of rental properties in other states, it has its own "standard" property management agreement. On September 1, María Gomez, WindyLakes' President, e-mails Victor that "standard" agreement, which reads as follows (with some provisions not relevant to your client's questions redacted):

Real Property Management Agreement

This Real Property Management Agreement (this "**Agreement**") is dated as of September 30, 2019, by and between WindyLakes Properties Inc., a New York corporation ("**Company**"), and TallyMan Services Inc., a Columbia corporation ("**Manager**").

ARTICLE 1. APPOINTMENT; TERM

1.1 **Appointment/Acceptance.** Effective as of 9 a.m. on the date of this Agreement, Company appoints Manager, and Manager accepts appointment, on the terms and conditions provided in this Agreement, as nonexclusive managing and leasing agent for all of Company's properties located in Columbia (the "**Properties**" and each, individually, a "**Property**").

1.2 **Term.** Subject to early termination as provided in Article 4, the initial term of this Agreement (the "**Initial Term**") is a period of one year from the date of this Agreement. The term of this Agreement will automatically be extended for additional one-year periods (each, an "**Additional Term**," and all Additional Terms, together with the Initial Term, the "**Term**") unless terminated in writing by either Company or Manager at least 30 days before the expiration of the then applicable Term.

ARTICLE 2. MANAGER'S DUTIES

2.1 **Property Management.** Company grants to Manager full power and authority to exercise all functions and perform all duties in connection with the operation and management of the Properties, subject to the right retained by Company to supervise the activities of Manager pursuant to this Agreement. The power and authority of Manager includes

(a) Using good faith efforts to lease vacant space in the Properties and renew existing leases with tenants in accordance with the current rental schedule from time to time submitted by Manager and approved by Company or, in the absence of such current rental schedule approved by Company, at rents reasonably determined by Manager taking into consideration market factors then prevailing, and on such other terms and conditions as Manager in its sole discretion determines.

(b) Collecting all monthly rentals and other charges due from tenants, users of parking spaces and from users or lessees of other facilities in the Properties.

(c) Causing the buildings, appurtenances and grounds on the Properties to be maintained according to customary industry standards.

(d) Making contracts for water, electricity, gas, fuel, oil, telephone, pest control, trash removal, insurance and other necessary services as Manager deems necessary or desirable, in Manager's good faith judgment; and placing purchase orders for such equipment, tools, appliances, materials and supplies as are necessary or desirable, in Manager's good faith judgment, to properly maintain the Properties.

(e) Taking such action as may be necessary or desirable, in Manager's good faith judgment, to comply with any orders or requirements affecting the Properties issued by federal, state, county or municipal authority having jurisdiction over the Properties.

(f) Maintaining all risk casualty insurance, and public liability insurance for the Properties in such amounts as Manager deems appropriate.

2.2 **Agency.** All action taken by Manager pursuant to the provisions of this Agreement will be done as agent of Company and obligations or expenses incurred hereunder will be for the account, on behalf and at the expense of Company, but any such actions may be taken or made either in Company's name or Manager's name.

2.3 **Bank Account.** Manager shall establish and maintain, in a manner to indicate the custodial nature thereof, with a bank, whose deposits are insured by the Federal Deposit Insurance Corporation, a separate bank account as agent of Company for the deposit of rentals and collections from the Properties, which shall not be commingled by Manager with funds from other projects or other funds of Manager. Manager has authority to draw thereon (a) for any payments to be made by Manager pursuant to the terms of this Agreement, (b) to discharge any liabilities or obligations incurred pursuant to this Agreement, and (c) for the payment of the Management Fee and Leasing Fee and the various expense reimbursements due Manager under this Agreement.

2.4 **Records.** Manager shall maintain, or cause to be maintained, books of account of all receipts and disbursements from the management of the

Properties. Manager shall provide monthly statements to Company containing occupancy information and collection and disbursement reports. Manager shall allow Company's accountant or other representatives to review the books and records of the Properties during reasonable business hours. Manager also shall provide Company with an annual report for the Properties containing information about occupancy and receipts and disbursements for the immediately preceding calendar year.

ARTICLE 3. COMPENSATION OF MANAGER

3.1 **Management Fee.** Company shall pay to Manager, as base compensation for Manager's duties and obligations under this Agreement, a management fee (the "**Management Fee**") equal to five percent (5%) of the Effective Gross Revenues. The Management Fee is payable quarterly, within 30 days after the end of each fiscal quarter, based upon the Effective Gross Revenues generated during that fiscal quarter. For purposes of this Agreement, "**Effective Gross Revenues**" means all payments actually collected from tenants and occupants of the Properties, excluding (a) security and deposits (unless and until such deposits have been applied to the payment of current or past due rent) and (b) payments received from tenants in reimbursement of expenses of repairing damage caused by tenants.

3.2 **Leasing Fee.** Company shall pay to Manager a leasing fee (the "**Leasing Fee**") in the amount of (a) 6% of the Base Rental Revenues to be received from new leases and (b) 4% of the Base Rental Revenues from expansion of existing leases and from renewals of existing leases. Company shall pay the Leasing Fee within 60 days from the execution of each lease or lease renewal. For purposes of this Agreement, "**Base Rental Revenues**" means the amount of rental revenues that are fixed or otherwise determinable at the time the related lease is executed.

3.3 **Reimbursement of Expenses.** Within 60 days of a request by Manager, Company shall reimburse Manager for all reasonable and necessary expenses incurred or monies advanced by Manager in connection with the management and operation of the Properties as provided in this Agreement.

ARTICLE 4. TERMINATION

4.1 **Default.** Either party may terminate this Agreement before the end of the Term in the event of a default by the other party if such default is not cured within ten days after the other party receives written notice of that default. Additionally, Company may immediately terminate this Agreement at any time upon written notice to Manager in the event of Manager's fraud, gross malfeasance, gross negligence or willful misconduct. Any such termination is without regard to the terminating party's rights and the other party's duties set out in the Agreement.

4.2 Termination Payments. Upon termination of this Agreement, Company and Manager shall immediately account to each other with respect to all matters outstanding and all sums owing each other as of the effective date of termination.

. . .

IN WITNESS WHEREOF, the parties have executed this Agreement as of the date first written above.

WindyLakes Properties Inc.

By: _____

María Gomez, President

TallyMan Services Inc.

By: _____

Victor Tally, President

Victor has a number of questions on WindyLakes' agreement that he wants to ask you. Specifically, he wants to know the following:

1. What is the term of this agreement? In other words, for how long will TallyMan have to perform the services provided for in the agreement?
2. Might WindyLakes appoint another property manager in Columbia during the term of the Agreement? If so, is this a concern for TallyMan? If it is, do you have any suggestions for how to address TallyMan's concerns?
3. What duty does TallyMan have in negotiating rents for new leases it enters into on behalf of WindyLakes? Or, alternatively, can it just set whatever rent it deems fair?
4. What is the difference between the Management Fee and Leasing Fee?
5. What happens if, at the end of a year, WindyLakes does not pay TallyMan those fees as required by the Agreement?

Simulation Problem Chapter 4

After you answer Victor's questions about WindyLakes' "standard" property management agreement from Chapter 3's Simulation Problem, you and Victor identify the main concerns for TallyMan under that agreement. Then, on September 3, two days after receiving the "standard" agreement from María Gomez, Victor sends María an e-mail listing the changes TallyMan must see to WindyLakes' agreement before agreeing to be bound. Those changes are to

(1) extend the initial term to two years, given how much time and resources it will take TallyMan to get up to speed in performing its obligations under the agreement, (2) make TallyMan WindyLakes' exclusive property manager in Columbia during the term of the Agreement, and (3) require WindyLakes to pay TallyMan the Management Fee on a monthly basis instead of on a quarterly basis, as well as to pay the Management Fee within ten days from the end of each month.

Victor's e-mail concludes by saying "If WindyLakes agrees to these changes, we are prepared to move forward to conclude this contract."

María is out of the office from September 2 through September 5. She sees Victor's e-mail on Monday, September 8. She sends an e-mail back to Victor that day. Her e-mail reads as follows:

> Dear Victor,
>
> I understand TallyMan's concerns behind the requested changes. WindyLakes can agree to extend the initial term to two years and make TallyMan WindyLakes' exclusive property manager in Columbia during the term. WindyLakes can also agree to pay TallyMan the Management Fee monthly instead of quarterly. However, for administrative purposes, WindyLakes cannot pay TallyMan that fee within 10 days of the end of each month. However, WindyLakes can agree to pay TallyMan within 15 days of the end of each month. I assume this is acceptable to you.
>
> Best,
> María.

After receiving this e-mail, Victor sets up internal systems to ensure that TallyMan is prepared to perform all obligations under its contract with WindyLakes. Victor also hires an additional employee on behalf of TallyMan to negotiate new leases at the Properties.

On September 20, Victor e-mails María asking for a list of WindyLakes' current tenants and utility providers so that TallyMan can be ready to perform on September 30. Victor does not hear back from María by September 25, so he resends his e-mail to María. Victor does not hear back from María by September 30, the day on which TallyMan is supposed to start performing under the management service agreement. In desperation, Victor calls María several times on September 30. He finally reaches María. On that call, María explains that since she had not heard back from Victor right away, she assumed TallyMan did not intend to enter into the contract with WindyLakes. As a result, WindyLakes retained another property management firm to manage the Properties.

Victor then calls you, TallyMan's lawyer, for advice. Specifically, he wants your advice as to whether TallyMan and WindyLakes entered into a contract for property management services for the Properties.

Simulation Problem Chapter 6

Victor has become extremely busy in managing TallyMan's clients' properties. In fact, he is so busy, Victor has decided it is time to invest in a computer program called PropSoft—sold by a company after whom this software was named—to help Victor become more efficient at work.

PropSoft is specialized property management software that helps property managers like TallyMan track tenant lease terms and renewals, issue lease renewal notices, track lease payments and deposits, log expenses incurred in performing property management services for clients, and submit invoices for reimbursement of those expenses. The program costs $5,000, which includes the software, a two-hour training session, as well as a one-year service package that allows the user to call PropSoft to ask questions and have PropSoft troubleshoot. After the first year, a user has to pay PropSoft $500 a year to obtain these troubleshooting services.

On October 1, Victor submitted an online order for PropSoft. Right before he placed his order, a dialogue box appeared saying "By clicking 'Submit,' you agree to PropSoft's Terms of Service." Victor could not complete his order without clicking "Submit," so he did. However, Victor did not read PropSoft's Terms of Service, which were only available through a link on PropSoft's home page—a link Victor had not clicked on when he was on the home page. He also did not consider navigating back to the home page to read those Terms of Service before placing his order, as he would have to restart the process of placing his order if he did.

If Victor had read those Terms of Service, Victor would have seen the following provision:

> 21. No Right of Return. At any time before downloading any software purchased from PropSoft, Customer has the right to return that software for a full refund of Customer's purchase price. Customer has no right to return any software purchased from PropSoft after Customer has downloaded any software purchased from PropSoft. If there are any defects in any software purchased from PropSoft, Customer's sole remedy is to have PropSoft fix that defect.

Immediately after placing his order, Victor received a link to schedule a time to have a PropSoft technician out to perform the two-hour training for PropSoft. Victor took the first appointment available, which was on October 30.

Victor did not install the PropSoft software before his scheduled appointment on October 30, as he did not want to do anything wrong in the download. During the scheduled appointment, the PropSoft technician installed PropSoft on all of TallyMan's computers, remarking as he did that he regularly downloads PropSoft for customers. The technician clicked on the dialogue box that appeared right before PropSoft was about to be downloaded asking the user to consent to the Terms of Service. Those Terms of Service were the same Terms of Service included on PropSoft's website. The technician also performed the two-hour training for Victor and Agatha at that time.

Unfortunately, TallyMan's problems with PropSoft began shortly after the install. First, none of the deadlines Victor had placed on TallyMan's existing management software merged into PropSoft as Victor had been told would happen. Further, PropSoft began deleting deadlines that had been placed on TallyMan's existing management software. Without those deadlines, TallyMan could not send out the notices, reimbursement requests, or perform the other tasks that it was contractually obligated to perform under management service contracts with clients.

After many hours on the phone with PropSoft's help desk, Victor discovered that PropSoft was not compatible with TallyMan's computer hardware. Moreover, TallyMan's existing property management software was not compatible with PropSoft, which is why there had been so many problems transferring all of the deadlines from TallyMan's existing software into PropSoft. Victor therefore was told that he had to buy a new computer system for TallyMan's offices and then key in each of the dates from TallyMan's existing contracts into PropSoft.

Victor does not want TallyMan to have to buy a whole new computer system. He also does not want to dedicate personnel time to reinserting all deadlines into PropSoft. So Victor informs one of the help desk technicians that he would like to return PropSoft and get a refund. The technician responds that it is too late; that since TallyMan already installed PropSoft, it could not return the software.

Upset, Victor has come to you, TallyMan's lawyer, for advice. Specifically, Victor wants to know if there is indeed a contract between TallyMan and PropSoft, and if that contract precludes him from returning the PropSoft software.

Simulation Problem Chapter 8

Tenants R US Inc. (TRUSI) is a real estate company that owns residential apartment buildings. TRUSI is considering buying an apartment building called the Blackbird Building, which is located in Springfield, Columbia. It currently has an option to buy the Blackbird Building from the owner, Real Estate Ventures Inc., for $5 million, which matched TRUSI's appraiser's determination of the property's current fair market value.

That option agreement provides as follows:

This Option Agreement, dated as of October 15, 2019, is between Tenants R US Inc., a Delaware corporation ("Buyer"), and Real Estate Ventures Inc., a Delaware corporation ("Owner").
Background:

1. Owner owns the apartment building known as the Blackbird Building located at 747 W. Addison Avenue in Springfield Columbia (the "Premises").

2. Owner would like to sell to Buyer, and Buyer is considering buying, the Premises on the terms offered by Owner and set out in the Purchase Agreement attached as <u>Exhibit 1</u> (the "Purchase Offer").

Now, therefore, the parties agree as follows:

In consideration for $200, which Buyer has paid to Owner, Owner agrees to keep the Purchase Offer open until the sooner to occur of (1) November 15, 2019 and (2) the date on which Buyer accepts the Purchase Offer.

This Agreement is governed by the laws of Texas.

Real Estate Ventures Inc.

//ss//

By: Felicia San, President

Tenants R US Inc.

//ss//

By: Ben Voght, President

While the contract specifies that TRUSI has paid $200 for this option, TRUSI never actually paid this amount.

Before it exercises its option, TRUSI would like to hire a property management company to manage that property for it. After conducting interviews, Ben Voght, the President of TRUSI, decides to hire TallyMan to provide property management services if TRUSI does exercise its option and buy the Blackbird Building.

While Victor is happy that TallyMan was selected as TRUSI's property management company, his enthusiasm waned after he learned that Real Estate Ventures is negotiating the sale of the Blackbird Building to another real estate company.

Wanting more certainty about the possibility that TRUSI will buy the Blackbird Building and that TallyMan will be the manager of that property, Victor contacts you. He wants to know the following:

1. Does TRUSI have a binding option contract to buy the Blackbird Building? *yes*
   If so, what does that bind Real Estate Ventures to do? *Sell if accepted*
2. If TRUSI does have a binding option contract with Real Estate Ventures, can TallyMan enter into a property management services agreement with TRUSI even before TRUSI exercises its option? Should it?

Simulation Problem Chapter 9   *yes*

TallyMan's business continues to thrive. However, Victor has realized that TallyMan's business ebbs and flows with the market for residential apartments. As such, his business slows down significantly in the summer and picks up again in the fall. As a consequence of this, TallyMan's income fluctuates up and down at various times during the year, making it challenging to pay TallyMan's bills and to pay Victor a stable salary.

To address this concern, in March, Victor decides to investigate having TallyMan partner with a property management company that manages nonresidential properties. Since the nonresidential commercial property lease market does not fluctuate as much throughout the year, partnering with a firm that manages those types of properties would allow TallyMan to earn more stable income throughout the year.

Victor broaches the idea of partnering with Jane Goode, who is the sole owner and President of Stargazer Properties Inc. Stargazer manages commercial buildings in Springfield other than apartment buildings, such as commercial storage facilities and manufacturing facilities.

Jane is interested in having Stargazer partner with TallyMan. Both agree that if the partnership comes to fruition, Victor (on behalf of TallyMan) would manage the residential lease operations and Jane (on behalf of Stargazer) would manage the nonresidential lease operations. TallyMan and Stargazer would equally share all profits.

While Jane is enthusiastic about this opportunity, she is concerned about the costs the parties will have to incur to draw up the necessary documents to implement this arrangement. Victor assures Jane that TallyMan's lawyer (you!) can draw up the necessary documents on behalf of TallyMan and Stargazer.

Victor calls you and relays his conversation with Jane. He asks you the following:

1. Can you represent both TallyMan and Stargazer in preparing the necessary contracts to document this partnership? If so, should you?

Jane ends up asking her aunt who is a lawyer, Zeva Woods, to represent Stargazer in putting this partnership structure in place. All parties agree that you (TallyMan's lawyer) will draft the partnership agreement.

You eventually prepare and send to Zeva the first draft of the partnership agreement. In your first draft, you list the partners as TallyMan and Stargazer. One of Zeva's comments is that the parties to the contract should be Jane and Victor.

2. Is Zeva correct on this issue? More specifically, are the correct parties to the contract TallyMan and Stargazer or Jane and Victor? Explain the basis for your answer.

By May 31, the parties have exchanged several drafts of the partnership agreement. While Victor and Jane have agreed on most important terms, they are still negotiating voting and other control rights.

That day, you send what you hope is a final draft of the partnership agreement to Jane and Zeva. You call Zeva that afternoon to make sure she and Jane saw the revised draft and are OK with its terms. You find out then that Jane is on vacation and unreachable for the following two weeks. When you inform Victor of this fact, he panics, as TallyMan is about to hit its summer months, and Victor is not confident that it will have enough income to pay its bills. Victor asks if there is any way the partnership agreement can be finalized before Jane returns.

You suggest that perhaps Delilah Singh, Stargazer's Vice President of Operations, could finalize and sign the partnership agreement on behalf of Stargazer. From your review of Stargazer's Bylaws, you see that Delilah's duties as Vice President of Operations are to "perform the duties of President when the President is unavailable." The President's duties in the Bylaws are to "act as the chief operating officer of the corporation, with general responsibility for the management and control of the operations of the corporation. The President shall have the power to affix the signature of the corporation to all contracts that have been authorized by the Board of Directors."

3. Based on this, can Delilah finalize the terms and sign the partnership agreement? If Delilah can finalize and sign the agreement, what actions must be taken for her to do so? Even if Delilah can finalize the terms and sign, should she, or should the parties wait until Jane returns?

Simulation Problem Chapter 10

When Jane returns from her vacation in June, she and Victor continue to negotiate the terms of the proposed partnership agreement discussed in the Simulation Problem for Chapter 9. However, they cannot work out their difference about management. Namely, Jane wants the right to be able to approve all management services that the partnership provides, while Victor, knowing that Jane is regularly difficult to reach, does not want to have to slow down the pace of business as he awaits Jane's approval.

Eventually, Jane decides to call off the partnership and makes Victor an offer to have Stargazer buy TallyMan.[11] In other words, all of TallyMan's business (including contractual relationships) would be taken over by Stargazer, and Victor would no longer work at the business. Stargazer would pay Victor $2 million, plus 10 percent of TallyMan's profits for three years after the sale. Jane says that for tax reasons, this transaction would have to close by September 30. Jane adds that after closing, Victor would not be able to compete with Stargazer in the same business in which TallyMan is engaged for a period of time, to allow Stargazer time to develop its name and reputation as a manager of commercial residential properties, and to benefit from the existing contractual relationships Stargazer is buying from TallyMan.

Victor is interested in exploring this transaction, as it will allow him to receive a lucrative payout while also allowing him to go back to his professional roots as a real estate broker. Victor also finds the proposed terms agreeable, though he clarifies that the sale will exclude all computers and hardware TallyMan uses, as those computers and hardware are Victor's personal property and not the property of TallyMan.

Thrilled that Victor is interested, Jane sends Victor a document that both describes the key terms of the transaction and lists the documents and information that Stargazer would like to receive in due diligence. Victor then sends the document to you for review.

June 30, 2019
Victor Tally
President
TallyMan Services Inc.
Dear Victor

I am thrilled that you are interested in selling TallyMan Services Inc., a Columbia corporation (the "Company") to Stargazer Properties Inc., a Columbia corporation (the "Buyer"). As we discussed, the purchase price will be $2 million, plus 10% of profits from the Buyer's residential property management business for three years after the sale. The transaction will close on August 31, or any other date we agree on, but no later than September 30 of this year. You will not compete with the Buyer in the business in which the Company is currently engaged for a reasonable period of time.

In connection with this transaction, and as a condition to the Buyer's duty to buy the Company, please provide copies of the indicated documents or the information requested, as appropriate, on behalf of the Company.

1. Basic Partnership Documents:
   a. Partnership agreement.
   b. Minutes of all meetings of partners.
   c. List of all states where property is owned or leased or where employees are located, indicating in which states the Company is qualified to do business.
   d. List of all partners, their ownership percentages, and any contracts or understandings by or among partners and/or the Company not reflected in the partnership agreement.
   e. List of any rights of a current Partner or other person to acquire a partnership interest.
   f. List of all subsidiaries.

2. Material Contracts:
   a. Credit agreements, including any amendments, renewal letters, notices, waivers, correspondences, etc.
   b. Other agreements evidencing outstanding loans to or guarantees by the Company.
   c. All outstanding leases for real and personal property.
   d. Material contracts with suppliers or customers.
   e. Model sales and manufacturing contracts.
   f. Agreements for loans to and any other agreements (including consulting and employment contracts) with officers, directors or employees.

g. Schedule of all insurance policies covering property of the Company and any other insurance policies such as "key person" policies, director indemnification policies or product liability policies.

h. Bonus plans, retirement plans, pension plans, deferred compensation plans, profit sharing and management incentive agreements.

i. Form of employee confidentiality invention assignment agreement.

j. Any other material contracts outstanding.

3. Manufacturing:

a. A breakdown by manufacturing site of the products manufactured, personnel employed, number of shifts and capacity, if any.

b. List of major suppliers showing total and type of purchases from each supplier during the last and current fiscal years, and indicating which are sole sources.

c. List of contract manufacturers or assemblers, if any, showing total and type of purchases from each contract manufacturer or assembler during the last and current fiscal years.

d. Material contracts with suppliers, manufacturers, etc., if any.

e. Description of all toxic chemicals used in production and manner of storage and disposition.

f. Description of any EPA or other investigation or claim.

4. Tangible Property:

a. List of real and material personal property owned by the Company.

b. Documents of title, mortgages, deeds of trust and security agreements pertaining to the properties listed in (a) above.

c. All outstanding leases for real and personal property to which the Company is either a lessor or lessee.

d. List of any security interests in personal property.

5. Litigation:

a. Information regarding any material litigation to which the Company is a party or in which it may become involved, including complaints, answers, etc.

b. Any litigation settlement documents.

c. Any decrees, orders or judgments of courts or governmental agencies.

d. Description of any warranty claims which have been made against the Company, any subsidiary, or any partnership or joint venture and the resolution of such claim.

6. Environmental:

a. Schedule of hazardous materials stored, manufactured or located at any facility of the Company either now or in the past, or that the Company ships or transports.

b. Schedule of chemicals, toxic substances or air contaminants which are regulated by OSHA present in any facility of the Company.

c. Schedule of any incidents involving the release or spill of a potentially hazardous amount.

  d. Schedule of all the facilities of the Company that discharge waste into any body of water, stream or any sanitation systems.
  e. Schedule of all permits or approvals obtained from any governmental body responsible for environmental or health regulation.
  f. Any notices of violation or requests for information that have been received or threatened at any time for alleged failure of any facility to comply with applicable air pollution laws or with any air quality permit.

If the foregoing is acceptable to you, please sign and date this letter below. The parties will then work toward concluding a formal writing reflecting the terms of this transaction.

This letter is to be governed by and construed in accordance with the laws of Columbia.

Sincerely,
//ss//

Jane Goode
President, Stargazer Properties Inc.

Agreed to and accepted this _____ day of July, 2019.
TallyMan Services Inc.

_____

Victor Tally, President

Victor does not understand the purpose for this letter, and therefore asks you the following:

1. Whether if, by signing the above letter, Victor is committing to selling TallyMan to Stargazer.
2. What Stargazer will do with all of the information and documents it obtains from TallyMan in response to this request. He also wants to know whether Stargazer has to keep the information confidential, as Victor does not want other property management companies to learn TallyMan's service pricing formula.
3. Whether you have any concerns with any of the information or documents requested from TallyMan.

To respond to Victor's third request, prepare a list for Victor of any concerns you have with information and documents included on this due diligence checklist, such as items that do not seem relevant either for this transaction or to TallyMan's organizational structure or business.

Simulation Problem Chapter 11

After you explain to Victor all of your concerns with the letter Jane Goode, the President of Stargazer Properties Inc., sent you in the Simulation Problem for

Chapter 10, Victor convinces Jane to hire a transactional lawyer to prepare the purchase agreement for Stargazer's purchase of TallyMan.

The following is an excerpt of some of the provisions from the purchase agreement drafted by Stargazer's counsel.

Asset Purchase Agreement

This **Asset Purchase Agreement**, dated as of July __, 2019, is between TallyMan Inc., a Columbia corporation (the "<u>Seller</u>"), and Stargazer Properties Inc., a Columbia corporation (the "<u>Buyer</u>"). *"Services"*

BACKGROUND:

The Seller is engaged in the business of providing property management services to owners of apartment buildings in Springfield, Columbia (the "<u>Business</u>").

The Buyer wishes to buy all of the Seller's assets used in the Business, including all of the Seller's rights under contracts with clients entered into in the Business.

The Buyer will engage in the Business after Closing and provide lease management services to the Seller's existing clients.

Accordingly, the parties agree as follows:

ARTICLE 2 PURCHASE AND SALE

2.1. Sale of Assets.

At the Closing, and subject to the provisions of this Agreement, the Seller shall sell, and the Buyer shall buy, all of the Seller's assets used in the Business (the "<u>Assets</u>"), which includes all of the following assets of the Seller used in the Business:

a. Rights under contracts with clients (the "<u>Client Contracts</u>").
b. Rights under computer software licenses (the "<u>Licenses</u>").
c. Rights under all other contracts to which the Seller is a party and that relate to the Business (the "<u>Other Contracts</u>," and together with the Client Contracts and the Licenses, the "<u>Contracts</u>").
d. Trademarks and tradenames, including the name "TallyMan" and associated goodwill.
e. Computers, printers, and other computer-related hardware. *(remove)*
f. Equipment.
g. Supplies.
h. Marketing and promotional plans and material.

did not want to sell

2.2. Purchase Price.

a. The purchase price for the Assets is the following (the "<u>Purchase Price</u>"):
   (i) $2,000,0000 (the "<u>Closing Payment</u>"), plus
   (ii) 5% of the annual profits generated by the Buyer in its business during each of the two calendar years after Closing, beginning on January

10% for 3 yrs

why not start off immediately after closing?

1, 2020 and ending on December 31, 2021 (the "Earnout," and the period for which the Earnout is payable, the "Earnout Period").

b. Subject to the provisions of this Agreement, the Buyer shall pay the Seller the Purchase Price as follows:

   (i)   The Buyer shall pay the Seller the Closing Payment by certified check at Closing; and

   (ii) The Buyer shall pay the Seller under the Earnout no later than 90 days after the end of each year during the Earnout Period for the profits generated during the immediately preceding year. The Buyer shall make all such payments by certified check.

2.3. Assumption of Liabilities. At the Closing, and subject to the provisions of this Agreement, the Buyer shall assume all of the Seller's liabilities and obligations arising under the Contracts as of Closing.

2.4. Time and Place of Closing. The Closing is to take place on August 30, 2019 at the Buyer's office at 10:00 A.M. local time, or at such other time and date as to which the parties agree, but no later than 11:59 p.m. on September 31, 2018 (the time and date of the Closing, the "Closing Date").

[handwritten margin note: cliff / date than term sheet]

2.5. Seller's Closing Deliveries. At the Closing, the Seller shall deliver the following documents to the Buyer:

a. A signed bill of sale transferring ownership of all of the physical Assets to the Buyer;

b. A signed assignment agreement in which the Seller assigns all of its rights under the Contracts to the Buyer; and

c. A non-competition agreement signed by the Seller and Victor Tally ("Tally") in which the Seller and Tally agree to not engage in any property management services for five years after Closing within 100 miles of Springfield, Columbia.

2.6. Buyer's Closing Deliveries. At the Closing, the Buyer shall deliver the following documents to the Seller:

a. The certified check referred to in Section 2.2(b)(i) above; and

b. A signed assumption agreement in which the Buyer assumes all of Seller's obligations and liabilities under the Contracts.

ARTICLE 3 SELLER REPRESENTATIONS AND WARRANTIES

The Seller represents and warrants to the Buyer that

[handwritten margin note: but its a Columbia corporation]

3.1. Organization and Authority; Enforceability. The Seller is a corporation duly incorporated, validly existing, and in good standing in Delaware, with full corporate power and authority to own its assets and operate its business in the manner presently conducted. The Seller has all necessary corporate power and authority to enter into and perform this Agreement. The Seller has duly executed and delivered this Agreement, and this Agreement constitutes a valid and binding obligation of the Seller, enforceable against the Seller in accordance with its terms.

3.2. **Ownership of Assets.** The Seller owns all of the tangible Assets free of liens.

3.3. **Assignment of Contracts; No Defaults.** The Seller has the power and legal right to assign all of its rights under the Contracts to the Buyer without needing the consent of any person except for (1) the consent of Blackbird Realties Inc. pursuant to the Property Management Agreement dated July 30, 2012 and (2) the consent of Junebug Realties Inc. pursuant to the Property Management Agreement dated January 15, 2015 (together, the "Consents"). The Seller is not in default under any Contracts, and no event has occurred that, with notice or lapse of time or both, would constitute a default under any Contract.

. . .

[handwritten annotations: can't promise a nc outside; ns control; can only promise to use its best efforts? the buyer can instead make it a condition]

ARTICLE 5 SELLER COVENANTS

5.1 **Consents.** Beginning on the date of this Agreement and ending on the Closing Date, the Seller shall obtain the Consents.

5.2. **Operation of Business.** Beginning at Closing and during the Earnout Period, the Buyer shall continue to operate the Business in the ordinary course of business consistent with past practices.

[handwritten annotation: wrong place; nd separate article for buyers covenant]

ARTICLE 7 BUYER'S CONDITIONS TO CLOSING

The Buyer's obligation to consummate the transactions that this Agreement contemplates is subject to satisfaction of each of the following conditions:

7.1. **Seller's Representations and Warranties.** The Seller's representations and warranties must have been true on the date of this Agreement and must be true on the Closing Date as if made on that date.

7.2. **Seller's Covenants.** The Seller must have performed each of its covenants to have been performed by it at or before Closing.

7.3. **Consents.** The Seller must have obtained the Consents at or before Closing.

. . .

ARTICLE 9 MISCELLANEOUS

9.1 **No Oral Amendments.** The parties may amend this Agreement only by a written agreement that identifies itself as an amendment to this Agreement.

9.2 **Integration.** This Agreement together with the Non-Compete Agreement, the Bill of Sale, the Assignment Agreement and the Assumption Agreement (together, the "**Transaction Documents**") together constitute the final and exclusive agreement of the parties as to the terms of the transaction that they contemplate. All earlier and contemporaneous negotiations and agreements between the parties on the matters contained in the Transaction Documents are expressly merged into and superseded by the Transaction Documents.

9.3 **Severability**. If any provision of this Agreement is determined to be illegal or unenforceable, the remaining provisions of this Agreement remain in full force if the essential provisions of this Agreement for each party remain legal and enforceable.

. . .

1. Identify any concerns you have with the terms reflected in this draft Asset Purchase Agreement that you should raise with Victor. As part of this task, consider whether the draft reflects the terms agreed on in the term sheet, reflected in the Simulation Problem for Chapter 10, or whether it includes any terms that you think may not be enforceable.

2. You consider contacting Stargazer's lawyer about your concerns with the non-compete before you speak with Victor. If you do, can you request changes to the non-compete even before discussing those requested changes with Victor? Should you?

3. You decide to discuss your concerns with the Asset Purchase Agreement with Victor before contacting Stargazer's lawyer. After that discussion, Victor contacts Jane and informs her that he will not agree to a non-compete period that lasts longer than two years. Jane agrees to this change. However, Stargazer's lawyer unintentionally changes the non-compete period to one year instead of two. You notice this change when you review the new draft. May you inform Stargazer's lawyer about this mistake without talking to Victor about it? Must you?

Simulation Problem Chapters 12-13

On July 31, Victor and Jane Goode, the President and owner of Stargazer Properties Inc., finalize and sign the Asset Purchase Agreement in which TallyMan agrees to sell all of its assets to Stargazer, including all of its contractual rights relating to TallyMan's business. The terms of the contract are reflected in the excerpt of the Asset Purchase Agreement set out in the Simulation Problem for Chapter 11, though the final version corrects all of the mistakes you identified in the Simulation Problem for Chapter 11. Moreover, the non-compete has been changed to only last for two years, to only apply to the Springfield, Columbia area, and to only preclude Victor from engaging in "residential property management services consistent with the Seller's past operation of the Business."

Jane informs you and Victor that Stargazer's counsel is in the process of preparing drafts of the documents to be delivered at closing.

1. Prepare a chart to help you and Victor keep track of all tasks that need to occur before closing. Indicate on that chart who is responsible for each task.

On August 10, three weeks before the scheduled closing date for the sale to Stargazer, Brett Voss, the President of ValueLive Inc., e-mails Victor about having Victor act as real estate broker for ValueLive in selling two of its residential apartment buildings. Victor would be paid a fixed fee of $150,000 plus a commission equal to 3 percent of the sales prices from these two buildings. With each building expected to sell for around $4 million, Victor expects to make $240,000 plus the $150,000 fixed fee on this transaction, for a total of $390,000.

Victor jumps at this opportunity, and signs an agreement with ValueLive on August 15 on behalf of TallyMan.

Jane learns of this contract right away, as good news travels quickly in the small Springfield real estate industry. She congratulates Victor on procuring yet another excellent contract for TallyMan, and assures Victor that after closing, Stargazer will be able to perform all of the services required of TallyMan under the contract with ValueLive.

Confused, Victor calls you, TallyMan's lawyer, for advice. Specifically, Victor wants to know the following:

2. Is TallyMan's contract with ValueLive one of the contracts that will be assigned to Stargazer under the Asset Purchase Agreement?
3. If Victor provides these services to ValueLive under the contract after closing (assuming the contract is not assigned to Stargazer), will he violate his non-compete covenant with Stargazer by performing that contract?
4. Can Victor negotiate with Jane to have Stargazer pay TallyMan an additional amount to add the contract with ValueLive to the contracts being assigned to Stargazer? If so, and if Jane agrees to this, how should the parties accomplish this?

Simulation Problem Chapter 15

Stargazer refuses to pay TallyMan any additional amounts for TallyMan's rights under the contract with ValueLive, because it views that contract as one of the contracts being assigned under the Asset Purchase Agreement.

1. If Stargazer ends up suing TallyMan to enforce what it views as TallyMan's obligation to assign its rights under that contract to Stargazer, would Victor likely be able to introduce into evidence Jane's e-mail to Victor sent at the conclusion of due diligence, in which Jane said "Now that I have reviewed all of TallyMan's client contracts, I realize TallyMan has never performed real estate brokerage services. While I am a little

disappointed, that will not interfere with our transaction."? If so, would that evidence help TallyMan's case?

2. What if, during due diligence, TallyMan had delivered to Stargazer a copy of a contract in which TallyMan had agreed to perform real estate appraisal services. Would Stargazer likely be able to introduce this contract into evidence? If so, would that evidence help Stargazer's case?

Simulation Problem Chapter 16

Part 1:

It is now August 28, three days before the scheduled closing of the sale of TallyMan's assets to Stargazer, and Victor has not yet obtained consents from Blackbird Realties Inc. and Junebug Realties Inc. for TallyMan to assign its rights under its contracts with those clients to Stargazer. If TallyMan does not obtain those consents, TallyMan will not be able to assign its rights under those contracts—contracts that have one year remaining on their term— to Stargazer. That would be a major upset to Stargazer, as Junebug and Blackbird are two of TallyMan's most important clients. In fact, Jane previously indicated that she is not sure Stargazer would buy TallyMan if these contract rights were not assigned.

Jane asks Victor what actions he has taken to obtain these consents. Victor explains that he requested these consents three times from the principals at these two companies. However, his requests have not been answered. Jane asks whether Victor offered to pay Blackbird and Junebug for their consents. Victor responds that he has not, and that he feels it is morally wrong to have to pay for these consents. Jane insists that Victor offer to pay for these consents, but Victor maintains that it just does not feel right to him to do that.

Jane eventually indicates that if these consents are not obtained by August 31, Stargazer will walk from the transaction, and not perform its obligations under the Asset Purchase Agreement.

Victor immediately calls you and asks you:

1. If Stargazer can do that—simply walk from the transaction and not pay the purchase price if TallyMan does not get consents from Blackbird and Junebug to the assignment of their respective contracts with TallyMan to Stargazer. Can TallyMan then sue Stargazer for breach?
2. If Stargazer does walk from the transaction, might Stargazer also sue TallyMan for breach?

Part 2:

Victor still has not obtained Junebug's and Blackbird's consents by August 31. Jane says that Stargazer is still willing to buy TallyMan, but will only pay $1.6 million instead of $2 million for TallyMan's assets because of TallyMan's inability to get those consents and, therefore, its inability to assign its rights under those contracts to Stargazer. Victor orally agrees to this and the transaction closes on August 31. At closing, Stargazer pays TallyMan $1.6 million by a certified check that includes the notation "full purchase price." TallyMan signs a bill of sale transferring ownership of all of its tangible assets to Stargazer. It also signs an assignment agreement assigning all of its rights under contracts to Stargazer (except its rights under the contracts with Blackbird and Junebug). The parties also orally agree that despite Victor's non-compete, he can, through TallyMan, to continue to perform TallyMan's obligations under the contracts with Blackbird and Junebug until December 31, 2020, which is the end of those contract's initial terms.

Victor spends time thinking about the transaction the week after closing, and realizes that the purchase price was reduced more than it should have been due to the non-assignment of contracts with Blackbird and Junebug. According to Victor's calculation, those two contracts should only have been valued at $200,000, not $400,000. Thus, the purchase price should have been $1.8 million. Victor calls you on September 10 and asks you if he can demand $0.2 million more.

   3. How do you advise Victor on this?

Part 3:

In October 2020, the residential leasing market takes a significant downturn. While there are many reasons for that downturn, the primary reason is a new tax law that makes it more expensive for residential property owners to lease apartments. With many of Stargazer's clients choosing to sell apartments instead of lease them, Stargazer loses about one-third of its existing clients for whom it manages residential properties. Moreover, many of its other residential property owner clients renegotiate the fees they pay Stargazer. Consequently, Stargazer no longer makes a profit on its residential property management business. Jane therefore decides in December 2020 to have Stargazer exit the residential property management business. Jane informs Victor of this pending change. In that conversation, Jane tells Victor not to expect any more payments under the Asset Purchase Agreement's earnout.

Worried, Victor calls you. He wants to know:

   4. Is Stargazer justified in not paying TallyMan any more under the earnout?
   5. If Stargazer stops paying TallyMan under the earnout, would Victor be excused from his non-compete covenant with Stargazer? (Victor is eager to resume his residential property management business, as he does not believe that the new tax law has eroded all profits in that business.)

Simulation Problem Chapter 17

Victor is upset that Stargazer has stopped paying TallyMan under the earnout. Without your assistance, in March 2021, Victor sends a letter to Jane blaming her for the loss of Stargazer's residential management business and demanding that Stargazer continue to pay Victor under the earnout, which, per the contract, is calculated by looking at all of Stargazer's profits, and not only those generated in the business purchased from TallyMan.

Jane responds by having Stargazer hire a lawyer and file a lawsuit in the Springfield district court against Victor and TallyMan for breach of their non-compete. In its complaint, filed on April 1, 2021, Stargazer alleges that Victor and TallyMan breached their non-compete by providing residential property management services to Blackbird and Junebug both during the remaining terms of those contracts as well as after those initial terms expired. (Both Blackbird and Junebug extended the terms of those contracts for another two years after the initial terms ended.)

You and Victor are a bit surprised, as you both recall Victor and Jane orally agreeing that Victor and TallyMan would not breach the non-compete if they continued to provide services to Blackbird and Junebug. Thus, you intend to move to dismiss that complaint on the basis that the parties' amended Asset Purchase Agreement permits Victor and TallyMan to engage in those activities. You anticipate, however, that Stargazer will respond to your motion by arguing that the amendment does not satisfy the Statute of Frauds and therefore is unenforceable. How will a court likely rule on your motion in light of that expected response?

Simulation Problem Chapters 18-21

In considering Victor and TallyMan's answer to Stargazer's lawsuit alleging breach of the non-compete, Victor forwards you an e-mail from Jane sent back in July 2019 in which Jane agreed that the earnout would be calculated from all of Stargazer's profits, and not merely profits generated by its residential property management services purchased from TallyMan. According to Victor's rough estimate, that breach has deprived TallyMan of at least $1.5 million. So, you help Victor and TallyMan file a counterclaim against Stargazer for breach of the Asset Purchase Agreement.

While you are in the process of responding to motions filed by Stargazer, on May 12, Victor calls you. He informs you that he has agreed with Jane that Stargazer will pay $300,000 to settle the lawsuit with Victor and TallyMan. He therefore asks you to prepare a written reflection of his and Jane's agreement.

You are surprised, as you and Victor were confident that TallyMan would recover at least $1.5 million due to Stargazer's breach of the earnout.

In response to questions from you about the nature of Victor's discussions with Jane, you discover the following:

On May 10, Jane contacted Victor and informed him that if he proceeded with his counterclaim against Stargazer, Jane would personally ensure that everyone in the residential property management industry knew that Victor was not a man of his word since he had breached his non-compete. While

Victor reminded Jane that she had agreed to modify the non-compete to allow TallyMan to provide services to Blackbird and Junebug, Jane responded that there was no written evidence of that amendment and, therefore, it was like it did not happen. Plus, she pointed out that the amendment only permitted Victor to perform services under those contracts for the remaining portion of their initial terms—not during an extended term. Jane then told Victor that he could avoid all of these consequences if he agreed to settle the lawsuit against Victor and TallyMan for $300,000.

Victor told Jane that he would like to run Jane's proposal by you. In response, Jane cautioned that Victor should not listen to your advice on the matter, as you would undoubtedly reject it because it would mean less legal fees to you. She also indicated that her offer would only remain open for one day. After that, she would assemble Stargazer's full legal team and bring them all to bear on Stargazer's lawsuit and Victor's and TallyMan's counterclaim.

Victor felt concerned, as he did not have a lot of money to pay for litigation now that Stargazer was no longer paying him under the earnout. Hence, on May 11, Victor agreed with Jane to settle TallyMan's lawsuit for $300,000.

How do you respond to Victor's request to prepare a document reflecting the settlement terms in light of these facts?

Simulation Problem Chapters 22-23

It is September 1, 2021, and the litigation against Victor and TallyMan is still pending. In light of Stargazer's failure to pay under the earnout, Victor has decided to find an alternate source of income. He decides to explore his hand at investing in residential apartments, with financial support from investors. That is, Victor plans to invite a select group of real estate investors to invest in TallyMan with him, and then have TallyMan use those investors' money to buy buildings, modernize and improve them, convert them to apartments (if they are not already converted) and then sell them to real estate investors for a profit. Victor is confident his background as a manager of residential buildings has prepared him for this work.

On September 10, Victor meets with Ivy Zlot, a well-known (and very rich) Springfield real estate investor, about possibly having Ivy invest in TallyMan. The meeting goes quite well. Ivy loves Victor's ideas about which types of buildings to target for conversion to modern apartments. She also agrees with Victor's analysis that there is an apartment shortage in Springfield. Ivy tells Victor that she would like precise numbers about current demand for apartments. But assuming that information backs up what Victor has told Ivy, she is willing to invest at least $10 million in TallyMan to start. She also says that she does not want to involve any other investors, and that she can provide all the funding TallyMan will need to succeed during its first two years of operations.

Delighted that Ivy is eager to invest and willing to meet all of TallyMan's investment needs, Victor cancels the other two meetings he had already scheduled with the other two major real estate investors in Springfield, Aviva Gutierrez and Tal Mishra. Victor, on behalf of TallyMan, also hires ABC Consulting Co. to gather precise information about rental occupancy in Springfield. In that contract, TallyMan agrees to pay ABC $50,000 for those services.

On October 5, Victor receives and then sends Ivy a copy of ABC's report. That report confirms what Victor had previously told Ivy—that Springfield has an apartment shortage. However, it reveals that the shortage is largely in Springfield's formerly industrial north side, and not in its hip east side, as Ivy had hoped. In fact, the report gives Ivy much cause for concern given that most of her recent investments have been in apartments on the east side. In the meantime, Victor (happy that the report confirmed what he told Ivy previously) begins negotiating to purchase different land plots on the north side. On October 17, Victor enters into a contract on behalf of Tallyman with NS Investments LLC to purchase a large undeveloped lot on the north side for $10 million and incurs legal fees of $125,000.

After carefully reviewing the report, Ivy informs Victor on October 20 that she has decided not to invest in TallyMan. Because of the report, Ivy also decides to scale back her investment in apartment ventures on the east side. Ivy estimates that she will save at least $15 million by seeing ABC's report and avoiding investments that would have not generated the profits she seeks.

Victor, on the other hand, finds ABC's report useful in identifying investment opportunities on the north side of Springfield. Victor tries to use the report to convince other investors to invest in TallyMan. However, Victor finds that he is shut out of that industry, all because he cancelled on his meetings with Aviva Gutierrez and Tal Mishra when he thought Ivy was going to be the exclusive investor in TallyMan.

Victor is frustrated that Ivy did not follow through with her investment, and essentially led TallyMan to forgo potential investments from Aviva Gutierrez and Tal Mishra. He also is worried about Tallyman being sued if it is not able to secure enough investment funds to help it purchase the land on the north side as agreed to in the contract with NS Investments. He is also frustrated that TallyMan spent $50,000 on a consulting report for Ivy, which Ivy used not only to justify her failure to invest in TallyMan, but also to make money from other investment decisions.

Victor comes to you for advice as to whether he has any potential bases to recover from Ivy.

Simulation Problem Chapters 24-26

It is now October 2021, and the Springfield district court allows Victor to rescind his settlement agreement with Stargazer and therefore pursue his counterclaim against Stargazer for breach of the earnout provision of the Asset Purchase Agreement.

The Springfield district court then grants Victor and TallyMan's motion for summary judgment against Stargazer, concluding that (1) Stargazer breached the earnout provision of the Asset Purchase Agreement by not paying TallyMan 10 percent of all of Stargazer's profits during the Earnout Period and (2) TallyMan and Victor did not breach the non-compete in performing the Blackbird and Junebug contracts during the initial term. However, the Springfield district court also grants Stargazer's motion for summary judgment on one issue, finding that (3) Victor and TallyMan breached the non-compete starting on January 1, 2021, which is the day after the initial terms on those contracts expired.

The court has now asked each party to submit a brief laying out what remedy it is seeking due to the other party's breach. To the extent a party seeks damages, the court requests that party to show how much it was damaged by the other party's breach.

Write up a short memo to Victor explaining what remedy or remedies Victor and TallyMan should request due to Stargazer's breach, as well as the likelihood that the court will award such damages. If you suggest that Victor and TallyMan request damages, be sure to identify how to calculate those damages, as well as identify any additional information that is needed to actually calculate those damages. Also explain to Victor what remedy Stargazer is likely to seek due to Victor and TallyMan's breach, and if Stargazer is likely to seek damages, how much it will likely request and how much a court is likely to award.

Simulation Problem Chapter 27

Victor asks you if the Springfield district court would, on request by TallyMan and Victor, order Stargazer to reimburse TallyMan and Victor for their costs, including attorneys' fees, in connection with Stargazer's lawsuit against Victor and TallyMan.

Simulation Problem Chapter 29

Assume that the Property Management Agreement between TallyMan and Blackbird Realties Inc., as well as the Property Management Agreement between TallyMan and Junebug Realties Inc., each contained the following provision:

> Neither party to this Agreement may assign any of its rights or delegate its duties under this Agreement. Any assignment and delegation made in breach of this provision is void.

1. Assume TallyMan tried to assign its rights and delegate its duties under these contracts to Stargazer, and the counterparties later refused to perform for the benefit of Stargazer. If the matter were litigated, would a court likely uphold this provision in each contract?
2. Would your answer change if the relevant language permitted TallyMan to assign its rights and delegate its duties under either contract with the prior written consent of the counterparty, but neither Blackbird nor Junebug was willing to agree to TallyMan's assignment and delegation to Stargazer?

Appendix B: Purchase Agreement

Crane Purchase Agreement

This **Crane Purchase Agreement** (including all schedules and amendments, this "**Agreement**"), dated as of August 1, 2019, is between Equipment Sellers Inc., a Delaware corporation (the "**Seller**"), and U.S. Crane Co., a Michigan corporation (the "**Buyer**").

Accordingly, the parties agree as follows:

ARTICLE 1. DEFINITIONS

1.1 **Definitions.** The terms defined in the preamble have their assigned meanings, and each of the following terms has the meaning assigned to it:

"**Closing**" means the consummation of the transactions that this Agreement contemplates.

"**Closing Date**" has the meaning assigned to it in Section 2.5.

"**Crane**" means the certain Goodwin Crane, model # SC100-FS-12-15-10, serial number 324879, together with all components thereof.

ARTICLE 2. PURCHASE AND SALE

2.1 **Sale of Crane.** At Closing, subject to the provisions of this Agreement, the Seller shall sell the Crane to the Buyer, and the Buyer shall buy the Crane from the Seller.

2.2 **Purchase Price.** Subject to the provisions of this Agreement, the Buyer shall pay the Seller $5,000,000 for the Crane at Closing by wire transfer of funds immediately available in Detroit, Michigan. The Seller shall notify the Buyer of the bank account into which the funds are to be transferred no later than two Business Days before the Closing Date.

2.3 **The Closing.** The Closing is to occur on October 1, 2019, or on another date to which the parties agree but no later than December 31, 2019 (the "**Closing Date**"). The Closing is to take place at Seller's office beginning at 9:00 a.m. central time.

2.4 **Closing Deliveries.**

a) **Seller's Deliveries.** At the Closing, the Seller shall deliver to the Buyer all of the following:

   (i) The Crane at the Seller's premises identified in Schedule 10.4.

   (ii) An executed bill of sale for the Crane in substantially the form of **Exhibit A.**

b) **Further Assurances.** Following the Closing, at the request of the Buyer, the Seller shall deliver any further instruments of transfer and take all reasonable action as may be necessary or appropriate

   (i) to vest in the Buyer good title to the Crane; and

   (ii) to transfer to the Buyer all licenses and permits necessary for the operation of the Crane.

ARTICLE 3. SELLER'S REPRESENTATIONS AND WARRANTIES

The Seller represents and warrants to the Buyer as follows:

3.1 **Corporate Organization and Existence.** The Seller is a corporation duly incorporated, validly existing, and in good standing under the laws of Delaware.

3.2 **Due Authorization.** The Seller has all requisite corporate power and authority necessary to enter into and perform its obligations under this Agreement.

3.3 **Enforceability.** This Agreement constitutes a binding obligation of the Seller, enforceable against the Seller in accordance with its terms.

3.4 **Ownership of Crane.** The Seller owns the Crane free of liens.

3.5 **Maintenance of Crane.** The Crane is in good condition, except for ordinary wear and tear.

ARTICLE 4. BUYER'S REPRESENTATIONS AND WARRANTIES.

The Buyer represents and warrants to the Seller as follows:

4.1 **Corporate Organization and Existence.** The Buyer is a corporation duly incorporated, validly existing, and in good standing under the laws of Michigan.

4.2 **Due Authorization.** The Buyer has all requisite corporate power and authority and has taken all corporate action necessary in order to execute, deliver, and perform its obligations under this Agreement.

4.3 **Enforceability.** This Agreement constitutes a binding obligation of the Seller, enforceable against the Seller in accordance with its terms.

ARTICLE 5. SELLER'S PRE-CLOSING COVENANTS

Beginning on the date of this Agreement to the Closing Date, the Seller shall perform as follows:

5.1 **Maintain Crane.** The Seller shall maintain the Crane in good condition, ordinary wear and tear excepted.

5.2 **Not Sell or Encumber Crane.** The Seller shall not sell, grant a lien on, or otherwise encumber the Crane.

ARTICLE 6. CONDITIONS TO THE SELLER'S OBLIGATIONS

The Seller is obligated to consummate the transactions that this Agreement contemplates only if each of the following conditions has been satisfied or waived on or before the Closing Date:

6.1 **Representations and Warranties.** The Buyer's representations and warranties must have been true on the date they were made and must be true as of the Closing Date with the same force and effect as though made on and as of the Closing Date.

6.2 **Covenants.** The Buyer must have performed each of the covenants to be performed by it on or before the Closing Date.

6.3 **Buyer's Closing Certificate.** The Seller must have received a certificate of the Buyer, certifying to the truth of the statements in Sections 6.1 and 6.2.

ARTICLE 7. CONDITIONS TO THE BUYER'S OBLIGATIONS.

The Buyer is obligated to consummate the transactions that this Agreement contemplates only if each of the following conditions has been satisfied or waived on or before the Closing Date:

7.1 **Representations and Warranties.** The Seller's representations and warranties must have been true on the date that they were made and must be true as of the Closing Date with the same force and effect as though made on and as of the Closing Date.

7.2 **Covenants.** The Seller must have performed each of the covenants to be performed by it on or before the Closing Date.

7.3 **Seller's Closing Certificate.** The Buyer must have received a certificate of the Seller, certifying to the truth of the statements in Sections 7.1 and 7.2.

7.4 **Consents.** All consents required for the Seller to transfer title to the Crane to the Buyer must have been received.

ARTICLE 8. POST-CLOSING COVENANTS

The parties shall perform as follows after Closing:

8.1 **Taxes.** Each party shall pay half of any state or local sales or transfer taxes payable with respect the transfer of the Crane from the Seller to the Buyer under this Agreement.

8.2 **Confidentiality.** Neither party may disclose the terms of this Agreement to any person unless required by law or court order.

ARTICLE 9. TERMINATION

9.1 **Party's Right to Terminate.**

a) **Grounds for Termination and Notice of Termination.** Either party (the "**Terminating Party**") may send a notice to the other (the "**Receiving Party**") regarding the Agreement's termination (the "**Notice of Termination**") if any condition to the Terminating Party's duty to close has not been satisfied or waived on or before the Closing Date.

b) **Effective Date of Termination.** If a Terminating Party sends a Receiving Party a notice regarding this Agreement's termination under Section 9.1(a), this Agreement terminates on the day the Receiving Party receives that notice.

c) **Consequence of Termination.** On termination of this Agreement under Section 9.1(a), neither party has any further rights or obligations under this Agreement, except for the Terminating Party's rights and the Receiving Party's obligations arising from the Receiving Party's misrepresentation, breach of warranty, or breach of covenant, if applicable.

ARTICLE 10. GENERAL PROVISIONS

10.1 **Assignment and Delegation.** Neither party may assign any right or delegate any performance under this Agreement without the other party's consent. A purported assignment or purported delegation in violation of this Section 10.1 is void.

10.2 **Successors and Assigns.** This Agreement binds and benefits the parties and their respective permitted successors and assigns.

10.3 **Governing Law.** The laws of Michigan (without giving effect to its conflicts of law principles) govern all matters arising under and relating to this Agreement, including torts.

10.4 **Notice.**

a) **Requirement of a Writing; Permitted Methods of Delivery.** Each party giving or making any notice, request, demand, or other communication in accordance with this Agreement (each, a "**Notice**") shall give the Notice in writing and use one of the following methods of delivery, each of which for purposes of this Agreement is a writing:

(i)   Personal delivery.

(ii) Registered or Certified Mail (in each case, return receipt requested and postage prepaid).

(iii) Internationally recognized overnight courier (with all fees prepaid).

(iv) Facsimile.

(v)   E-mail.

b) **Addressees and Addresses.** Any party giving a Notice shall address the Notice to the appropriate person at the receiving party (the "**Addressee**") at the address or addresses listed out on **Schedule 10.4**:

c) **Effectiveness of a Notice.** Except as provided elsewhere in this Agreement, a Notice is effective only if the party giving the Notice has complied with subsections (a) and (b) and if the Addressee has received the Notice.

10.5 **Severability.** If any provision of this Agreement is determined to be illegal or unenforceable, the remaining provisions of this Agreement remain in full force, if the essential provisions of this Agreement for each party remain legal and enforceable.

10.6 **Amendments.** The parties may amend this Agreement only by the parties' agreement that identifies itself as an amendment to this Agreement.

10.7 **Merger.** This Agreement reflects the final, exclusive agreement between the parties on the matters contained in this Agreement. All earlier and contemporaneous negotiations and agreements between the matters contained in this Agreement are expressly merged into and superseded by this Agreement.

10.8 **No Waiver.** No party's failure to insist on the other party's strict performance of any obligation, satisfaction of a condition, nor any course of conduct under this Agreement, constitutes a waiver of the other party's breach of that performance, satisfaction of that condition, or any other obligation.

To evidence the parties' agreement to this Agreement, they have executed and delivered it as of the date set forth in the Preamble.

U.S. Crane Co.

By: _____
Name:
Title:

Equipment Sellers Inc.

By: _____
Name:
Title:

Schedule 10.4
Addresses

[insert parties' addresses]

Appendix C: Employment Agreement

SUNNYSIDE DAYCARE, LLC

_____, 2019

Jeff Rison
10775 Elgin Avenue
Lancaster, PA 17601

RE: Services

Dear Jeff,

This letter agreement is intended to set forth certain understandings between you and Sunnyside Consulting, LLC (the "<u>Company</u>"). The Company agreed to retain you as an employee, subject to the terms and conditions of this letter agreement.

The Company and you agree as follows:

1. <u>Position and Duties</u>. During the term of your employment, you shall act as the Company's general manager. You shall have the power, authority, duties, and responsibilities as are reasonably necessary for the position. The Company has the authority to expand or limit your power, authority, duties and responsibilities, and to override your actions. You shall devote your best efforts and full business time and attention exclusively to the business and affairs of the Company. During the term of your employment, you shall report directly to the President.

2. <u>Compensation</u>. In consideration for the services to be provided by you to the Company pursuant to the terms of this letter agreement, the

Company shall pay you the compensation during the term of this letter agreement as set forth below.

(a) Base Salary. During the term of your employment, your initial base salary shall be $2,000 per week and any future raises thereto will constitute the "Base Salary" for purposes of this letter agreement. The Company shall pay the Base Salary in regular weekly installments in accordance with the Company's general payroll practices and will be subject to customary withholding for applicable taxes.

(b) Benefits. During the term of this letter agreement, you may participate in any employee benefit plans, in each case subject to satisfying the applicable eligibility requirements in which the Company is the plan sponsor or a participating employer, including any health and retirement benefit plans. You agree and acknowledge that the benefits provided by the Company may be modified or terminated at any time at the sole discretion of the Company.

3. Termination. You and the Company understand and agree that your employment may be terminated by either party for any reason or no reason in the discretion of such party without notice of, or liability for, such termination.

4. Restrictive Covenants. In consideration of the Company agreeing to hire you as an Employee and to agree to this letter agreement, you agree to each of the provisions of this Section 4 below.

(a) Confidential Information. You agree and acknowledge that the information, observations and data obtained, generated or created by you while employed by the Company concerning the business or affairs of the Company, including any business plans, practices and procedures, pricing information, sales figures, profit or loss figures, this letter agreement and its terms, information relating to customers, clients, suppliers, sources of supply and customer lists ("Confidential Information"), are the property of the Company. You agree that, except as required by law or court order, you shall not disclose to any unauthorized person or use for your own account or for the account of any other person (other than the Company) any Confidential Information without the prior written consent of the President of the Company.

(b) Noncompetition. You agree that during the period commencing on the date hereof until the eighteen month anniversary of the date on which your retention hereunder is terminated (the "Restricted Period"), you shall not, within or with respect to the geographical area of the State of Pennsylvania or any other state within the United States in which the Company operates (including by contracting with customers or suppliers) or could reasonably be anticipated to operate during the Restricted Period (the "Restricted Area"), directly or indirectly, compete with the business of the Company.

(c) Nonsolicitation. You agree that during the Restricted Period, you shall not, without written consent of the Company, directly or indirectly, including causing, encouraging, directing or soliciting any other person to, contact, approach or solicit for the purpose of offering employment to or hiring (whether as an employee, consultant, agent, independent contractor or otherwise) or actually hire any person who is or has been employed or retained in the operation of the Company's business by the Company during the period commencing two years prior to the date hereof and ending on the date of termination of the Restricted Period.

(d) Enforcement. If the final judgment of a court of competent jurisdiction declares that any term or provision of this Section 4 is invalid or unenforceable, the Company and you agree that the court making the determination of invalidity or unenforceability will have the power to reduce the scope, duration, or area of the term or provision, to delete specific words or phrases, or to replace any invalid or unenforceable term or provision with a term or provision that is valid and enforceable and that comes closest to expressing the intention of the invalid or unenforceable term or provision, and this letter agreement will be enforceable as so modified after the expiration of the time within which the judgment may be appealed. In the event a court of competent jurisdiction determines you breached any term of provision of this Section 4, you consent to the court extending the duration of the non-competition provisions contained in this Section 4 to compensate the Company for the time period you were in violation of such provisions

5. Miscellaneous.

(a) Indemnification. You shall indemnify and hold harmless the Company and each of its affiliates from and against any loss, liability, deficiency, damage, or expense (including reasonable legal, consultant and expert expenses and costs and any cost or expense arising from or incurred in connection with any proceeding relating to any matter described in this clause, or in enforcing the indemnity provided by this indemnity) which such party may suffer, sustain or become subject to, as a result of any breach of any representation or warranty made by you or any failure by you to perform any covenant or obligation set forth herein.

(b) Severability. Whenever possible, each provision of this letter agreement will be interpreted in such manner as to be effective and valid under applicable law, but if any provision of this letter agreement is held to be invalid, illegal or unenforceable in any respect under any applicable law or rule in any jurisdiction, such invalidity, illegality or unenforceability will not affect any other provision or any other jurisdiction, but this letter agreement will be reformed, construed and enforced in such jurisdiction as if such invalid, illegal or unenforceable provision had never been contained in this letter agreement.

(c) <u>Successors and Assigns</u>. Except as otherwise provided in this letter agreement, this letter agreement binds and benefits and is enforceable by you and the Company, and the parties' respective successors and assigns; provided that the services provided by you under this letter agreement are of a personal nature and your rights and obligations under this letter agreement shall not be assignable, assigned or delegated.

(d) <u>Governing Law</u>. All questions concerning the construction, validity and interpretation of this letter agreement and the exhibits to this letter agreement will be governed by and construed in accordance with the laws of the State of Pennsylvania, without giving effect to any choice of law or conflict of law provision or rule (whether of the State of Pennsylvania or any other jurisdiction) that would cause the application of the laws of any jurisdiction other than the State of Pennsylvania.

(e) <u>Amendment and Waiver</u>. The provisions of this letter agreement may be amended and waived only with the prior written consent of the Company and you.

(f) <u>No Strict Construction</u>. The language used in this letter agreement is to be deemed to be the language chosen by the parties to express their mutual intent and no rule of strict construction is to be applied against any party.

Please indicate your agreement to the terms of this letter agreement where indicated below.

Sincerely,

Sunnyside DayCare, LLC

By: _____
Name: _____
Its: _____

Agreed and Acknowledged:

_____

Jeff Rison
Date: _____, 2019

TABLE OF CASES

Principal cases are noted in italics.

TABLE OF SECONDARY AUTHORITIES

Books, Articles, and Other Secondary Sources

Schwarcz, Steven L. *Explaining the Value of Transactional Lawyering,* 12 Stan. J.L. Bus. & Fin. 486 (2007), 245

Stark, Tina L. *Drafting Contracts: How and Why Lawyers Do What They Do,* 2nd ed. (Aspen Publishers 2014), 308

Werback, Kevin & Cornell, Nicolas. *Contracts Ex Machina,* 67 Duke L.J. 313, 331-38 (2017), 341

White, James & Summers, Robert. *Uniform Commercial Code,* 3rd ed. (West 1988), 801

Williston, Samuel & Lord, Richard A. *Williston on Contracts a Treatise on the Law of Contracts,* 4th ed., § 7:18, (Thomson West 1993), 206

YouTube Terms of Service, https://www.youtube.com/t/terms (last visited Sept. 22, 2018), 182

Zacks, Eric. *The Moral Hazard of Contract Drafting,* 42 Fla. St. U.L. Rev. 991, 1002-03 (2015), 8

INDEX